"...This text provides the corrections undergraduate with an opportunity to look through the correctional lenses with respect given to the dynamic nature of their preconceived reality. A rare reality of most corrections-based texts."

—Howard Henderson, Sam Houston State University

"I absolutely love [the Technology and Equipment box]!! What a cool, new, and innovative feature not seen in other correctional texts. Students will love this and it's relevant with the technological advances that have occurred."

—Jessie Krienert, Illinois State University

BALANCED COVERAGE

Balance of **Theory and Application** gives students the best of both worlds as they prepare for a career in corrections or criminal justice system.

- **Applied Theory boxes** provide clear and focused application of a specific theory to a particular issue in community corrections, allowing the student to more easily connect theory to real-world application.
- **Focus Topic boxes** provide additional depth and detail into important topics to reinforce student understanding.

APPLIED THEORY 2.1

Classical Criminology, Behavioral Psychology, and Corrections

In addition to Cesare Beccaria, another noteworthy figure associated with classical criminology was Jeremy Bentham. Bentham is known for advocating that punishments should be swift, severe, and certain. Essentially, Bentham believed that a delay in the amount of time between the crime and the punishment impaired the likely deterrent value of the punishment in the future. Likewise, he held that punishments must be severe enough in consequence as to deter persons from engaging in criminal behavior. Lastly, Bentham noted that the punishment must be assured, otherwise offenders will simply become better at hiding their crimes once they know that the punishment can be avoided.

Current research actually supports some aspects of classical criminology, while refuting others. In particular, it has been found that the certainty of the punishment does indeed lower the likelihood of recidivism. Likewise, the less time between the crime and the punishment, the less likely offenders will be to reoffend in the future. However, it has not been found to be true that the severity of the punishment is successful in reducing crime. In fact, there has been substantial historical research on the death penalty that seems to indicate that gene

alty, even though

While some offe

the community,

be returned. For those, the goal of any sanction should be to reduce the likelihood that they will commit crime again. The research of Smith, Goggin, and Gendreau (2002), however, provides evidence that the prison environment may actually *increase* the likelihood of recidivism among many offenders, leading the authors to conclude that prisons could indeed be considered "schools of crime" (p. 21). Further, they found that the longer the term of imprisonment, the more likely offenders were to recidivate. Thus, the severity of the punishment does not reduce crime and, in actuality, increases the likelihood of future crime. Other studies substantiate this research.

This alone presents a valid argument against the unnecessary use of prisons, particularly when community corrections can provide effective supervision and sanctions without the reliance on prison facilities. Community corrections sanctions can be swifter in implementation, and they are much more certain in their application. For example, many offenders may be given a certain number of years in prison but will be released early, reducing the certainty (and severity) of their intended punishment. Further, the plea-bargaining system in the United States provides an opportunity for the convicted to avoid incarceration entirely, even when a prison sentence would typically be given for the crime that the offender committed. It is then clear that the use of such pleas detracts from the certainty of the sentence.

In addition, overcrowding may delay an offender's placement

FOCUS TOPIC: 1.1

Escape From Old Newgate Prison

Just a couple of years before the first shots of the American Revolution were fired, the Connecticut General Assembly decided that what the colony needed most was a good, heavy-duty gaol. In the legislators' wisdom, any new prison would have to meet certain specifications. It would have to be fairly close to Hartford, absolutely escape-proof; self-supporting (i.e., inmates would have to be "profitably employed"); and—most important of all, then as now—cheap to build and maintain.

Near "Turkey Hills," in the region of northern Simsbury (now East Granby), there were some abandoned copper mines that had been sporadically dug with disappointing results since early in the century. The legislature immediately appointed a three-member study commission to "view and explore the copper mines at Simsbury."

The study group was mighty impressed with the prison potential of a many-shafted mine that ran deep under a mountain. Only 18 miles from Hartford, the mine boasted at least one cavern, 20 feet below ground, large enough to accommodate a "lodging room" that was 16 feet square. There were also lots of connecting tunnels where prisoners could be gainfully employed by being made to pick away at the veins of copper ore located there.

Better yet, according to the report, the only access to the mine from outside came from two air shafts: one 25 feet deep and the other 70 feet deep, the latter leading to "a fine spring of water." Still better was the low cost of mine-to-gaol conversion. By October 1773, the government had obtained a lease, carpenters had built the lodging room, and workmen had fitted a heavy iron door into the 25-foot air shaft, 6 feet beneath the surface. In the same month, the Connecticut General Assembly designated the place as "a public gaol or workhouse, for the use of this Colony"; named it Newgate Prison, after London's dismal house of detention; and appointed a "master" (or "keeper") and three "overseers" to administer the gaol.

Only men (never women) who had been convicted of the most dastardly crimes known to the colony—burglary, robbery, counterfeiting or passing funny money, and horse thieving—were eligible for a one-way trip into the state's dank, dark prison without walls. Chosen for the dubious honor of being Newgate's first prisoner was one John Hinson, a 20-year-old man about whom—considering his historic, "groundbreaking" status—surprisingly little is known. Convicted for some unrecorded crime and remanded to Newgate by the Superior Court on December 22, 1773, Hinson spent exactly 18 days in the "escape-proof" gaol before departing quietly for parts unknown. Although no one saw him leave, obviously, there was some evidence that he had used the 70-foot well shaft to climb out of the mine.

As a consequence of the successful escape of Hinson and, 3 months later, three more Newgate prisoners, it was ordered that modifications be undertaken that included, in 1802, the erection of a high stone wall around the prison.

Finally, in September 1827, after almost 54 years of operation, during which well over 800 prisoners were committed to its clammy, subterranean dungeons, Newgate Prison was abandoned, and the remaining inmates were transferred to the new state prison at Wethersfield. Significantly, the last escape attempt occurred on the night before the move to Wethersfield, when a prisoner fell back into the well—and drowned—as he tried to emulate old John Hinson of sainted memory. Coming when it did, at the bitter end of the facility's long, dark history, the death was a tragic, but somehow fitting, reminder of Newgate's most enduring legend.

SOURCE: Philips, D. E. (1992). *Legendary Connecticut: Traditional Tales from the Nutmeg State*. Willimantic, Conn.: Curbstone Press. Copyright © 1992 by Joseph L. Steinberg. Reprinted by permission of Northwestern University Press.

Provides important coverage of modern topics, typically overlooked by other texts, such as:

- **Numerous categories of offenders**—including female, geriatric, mentally ill, and gang offenders—as well as the various issues associated with specialized offender typologies
- **Community corrections**, discussed in multiple chapters throughout the book
- **Prisoner Classification, Prison Subculture, and Prison Gang Influence**, as well as **Program Evaluation** and **Evidence-Based Practices**

PRACTITIONER'S PERSPECTIVE

- **Chapter opening vignettes** showcase important issues in corrections and allow students to understand the challenges that corrections practitioners face each day.
- **Corrections and the Law** features incorporate important legal issues or Supreme Court rulings associated with the topics in the chapter to show students how the field of corrections is constantly changing.
- **Updated information on the latest technology, statistics, examples, and chapter topics** includes sentencing practices, technological innovations, and offenders with special needs.
- **Prison Tour and Inmate Videos** provide an exclusive look into the daily operations of the correctional facilities at Louisiana State Penitentiary at Angola and Richwood Correctional Center.

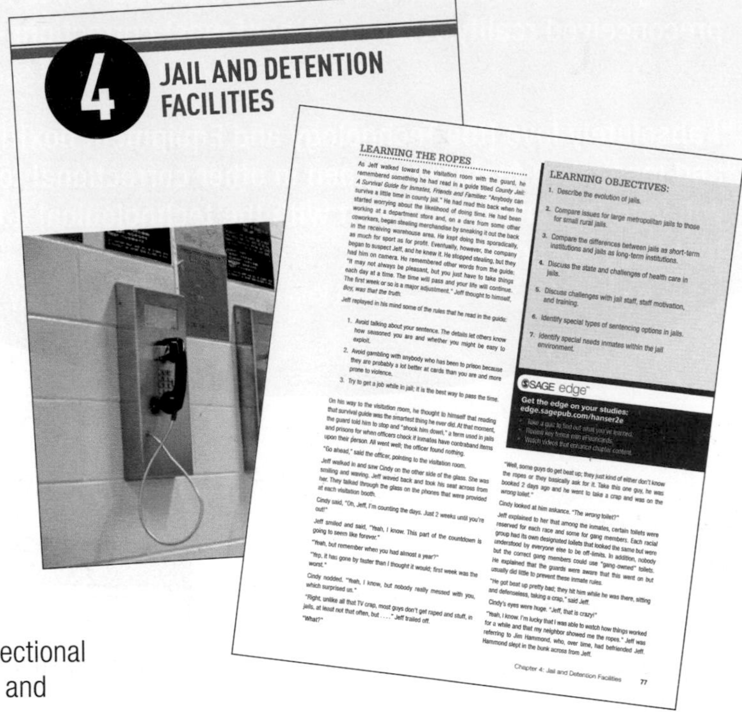

4 JAIL AND DETENTION FACILITIES

LEARNING THE ROPES

As Jeff walked toward the visitation room with the guard, he remembered something he had read in a guide titled *County Jail: A Survival Guide for Inmates, Friends and Families*: "Anybody can survive a little time in county jail." He had read this back when he started worrying about the likelihood of doing time. He had been working at a department store and, on a dare from some other coworkers, began stealing merchandise by sneaking it out the back in the receiving warehouse area. He kept doing this sporadically, as much for sport as for profit. Eventually, however, the company began to suspect Jeff, and he knew it. He stopped stealing, but they had him on camera. He remembered other words from the guide: "It may not always be pleasant, but you just have to take things each day at a time. The time will pass and your life will continue. The first week or so is a major adjustment." Jeff thought to himself, *Boy, was that the truth.*

Jeff replayed in his mind some of the rules that he read in the guide:

1. Avoid talking about your sentence. The details let others know how seasoned you are and whether you might be easy to exploit.
2. Avoid gambling with anybody who has been to prison because they are probably a lot better at cards than you are and more prone to violence.
3. Try to get a job while in jail; it is the best way to pass the time.

On his way to the visitation room, he thought to himself that reading that survival guide was the smartest thing he ever did. At that moment, the guard told him to stop and "shook him down," a term used in jails and prisons for when officers check if inmates have contraband items upon their person. All went well; the officer found nothing.

"Go ahead," said the officer, pointing to the visitation room.

Jeff walked in and saw Cindy on the other side of the glass. She was smiling and waving. Jeff waved back and took his seat across from her. They talked through the glass on the phones that were provided at each visitation booth.

Cindy said, "Oh, Jeff, I'm counting the days. Just 2 weeks until you're out!"

Jeff smiled and said, "Yeah, I know. This part of the countdown is going to seem like forever."

"Yeah, but remember when you had almost a year?"

"Yep, it has gone by faster than I thought it would; first week was the worst."

Cindy nodded. "Yeah, I know, but nobody really messed with you, which surprised us."

"Right, unlike all that TV crap, most guys don't get raped and stuff, in jails, at least not that often, but . . . ." Jeff trailed off.

"What?"

LEARNING OBJECTIVES:

1. Describe the evolution of jails.
2. Compare issues for large metropolitan jails to those for small rural jails.
3. Compare the differences between jails as short-term institutions and jails as long-term institutions.
4. Discuss the state and challenges of health care in jails.
5. Discuss challenges with jail staff, staff motivation, and training.
6. Identify special types of sentencing options in jails.
7. Identify special needs inmates within the jail environment.

SAGE edge™

Get the edge on your studies: edge.sagepub.com/hanser2e

- Take a quiz to find out what you've learned.
- Review key terms with eFlashcards.
- Watch videos that enhance chapter content.

"Well, some guys do get beat up; they just kind of either don't know the ropes or they basically ask for it. Take this one guy, he was booked 2 days ago and he went to take a crap and was on the wrong toilet."

Cindy looked at him askance. "The wrong toilet?"

Jeff explained to her that among the inmates, certain toilets were reserved for each race and some for gang members. Each racial group had its own designated toilets that looked the same but were understood by everyone else to be off-limits. In addition, nobody but the correct gang members could use "gang-owned" toilets. He explained that the guards were aware that this went on but usually did little to prevent these inmate rules.

"He got beat up pretty bad; they hit him while he was there, sitting and defenseless, taking a crap," said Jeff.

Cindy's eyes were huge. "Jeff, that is crazy!"

"Yeah, I know. I'm lucky that I was able to watch how things worked for a while and that my neighbor showed me the ropes." Jeff was referring to Jim Hammond, who, over time, had befriended Jeff. Hammond slept in the bunk across from Jeff.

Chapter 4: Jail and Detention Facilities 77

CROSS-NATIONAL PERSPECTIVE 1.1

Penal Slavery in Western Europe and East Asia

The use of penal slavery was extensive in ancient Rome, though the actual economic benefits for this type of labor were minimal. For the most part, penal slavery in Rome was restricted to those offenders who had been given a life sentence. In such cases, these offenders suffered a civil death and no longer existed in society; they were thereby permanent slaves of the state. A strong distinction was drawn between these offenders and those who did not have a life sentence. For those offenders not serving life, penal servitude was exacted. Though this was similar in most respects to penal slavery, there was a time limit after which the sentence was considered to have been served.

In many East Asian countries, penal slaves were a source of both public and private slaves. Prisoners provided the bulk of the enslaved population in Vietnam even though slavery was not an important industry in that country. In Korea, which is thought to have had one of the most advanced slave systems in East Asia, penal slavery was used but was not the primary source of slaves. In Japan around the sixth century A.D., the two primary sources of slaves were prisoners of war and the familial relatives of convicted criminals as well as the offenders themselves. However, it was the nation of China that truly used penal slavery on a widespread basis.

The enslavement of family members related to condemned offenders was, in actuality, the primary and perhaps the only source from which penal slaves in China were drawn. Due to a strong rank system whereby family honor subsumed individual identity, if a family was disgraced by the acts of a criminal, the entire family could be held accountable for the crime(s) committed. Prior to the Han Dynasty, there was a tendency to execute criminal offenders and imprison their family members, but over time Chinese royalty imprisoned all persons.

Because most if not all slaves were penal slaves in China, the common view of a slave became one of being a criminal and therefore unworthy of fair treatment. The status of criminal opened the door for mutilation, torture, and abuse, all of which were condoned by Chinese law, as was also the case in much of old Europe. However, China was unusual in one routine practice in its penal slavery policy: many penal slaves ended up becoming property of private owners. Usually given as gifts to the affluent and/or powerful, they were often acquired by unscrupulous government officials or military officers.

It would appear that many of the ancient punishments, such as flogging, and the use of different forms of the death penalty were used by cultures in the East and the West. Further, most cultures in both areas of the world refrained from using jails for anything other than holding an offender in custody until punishment could be administered. The use of prisons as a form of punishment, in and of itself, was not common in either area. However, the use of criminal offenders as cheap and exploitable labor seems to have been common to the West as well as the East. A primary distinction between East and West revolved around the strong family honor system, which, in the grand scheme of things, generated a much larger penal slave population (including women as well as men) in Imperial China. This, and the existence of slaves among private Chinese social elites, demonstrates how cultural differences can impact the means by which punishments such as penal servitude are implemented.

QUESTION 1: What are two key distinctions between penal slavery in Rome and penal slavery in Imperial China? Why did these differences exist?

QUESTION 2: For what purpose were jails used in both the Eastern and the Western parts of the world? Was there widespread use of prisons as we know them today?

SOURCE: Patterson, O. (1982). *Slavery and social death: A comparative study*. Cambridge, MA: Harvard University Press.

DESIGNED FOR STUDENT ENGAGEMENT

After reading a sample chapter, 95% of students said that this text is very readable—and is one of the better textbooks they've ever read.

- **Applied Exercises** are written assignments that ask students to dig deeper, using current and previous chapter material to continue building their base of correctional knowledge.
- **What Would You Do?** assignments provide excellent opportunities for students to think critically about the concepts, practices, and policies presented in the chapter and to make educated decisions to determine the best courses of action.
- **Technology and Equipment** boxes offer solid coverage of modern technology and equipment used in corrections and expose students to the benefits of technology such as the use of electronic surveillance systems, locking systems, and other advanced equipment.
- **Cross-National Perspectives** offer a brief examination of correctional topics as they apply to countries around the world and encourage students to consider the implications of the cross-national perspective through critical thinking questions provided at the end of the feature.

"Highly informative of life 'on the inside.'"

—JT Fountain, Student, Goodwin College

"...The cross-national components were great. That is something that you don't regularly get much detail on and the students will really enjoy learning about corrections abroad."

—Robert G. Morris, University of Texas at Dallas

> "The book is well written with the focus from a practical perspective... the book contains all the extras that could enhance the online experience"
>
> —Nancy L. Hogan, Ferris State University

SAGE edge™

SAGE edge offers a robust online environment featuring an impressive array of tools and resources for review, study, and further exploration, keeping both instructors and students on the cutting edge of teaching and learning. SAGE edge content is open access and available on demand. Learning and teaching has never been easier!

 **edge.sagepub.com/hanser2e**

TAKE A LOOK: THE CORRECTIONAL SYSTEM THROUGH AN INTERACTIVE EBOOK

Introduction to Corrections, Second Edition has multiple interactive options to get your students more involved! Links are provided in the context of the chapter coverage to relevant online resources. Study tools such as highlighting, bookmarking, note-taking, definitions, and more!

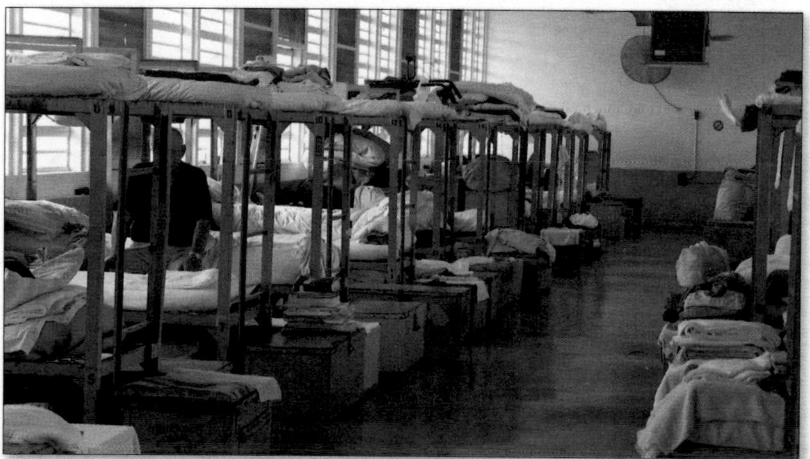

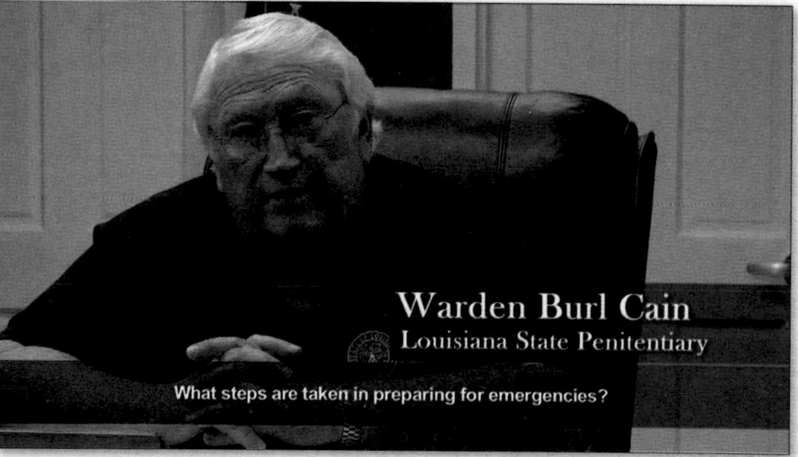
Warden Burl Cain
Louisiana State Penitentiary
What steps are taken in preparing for emergencies?

 **Video Links** to relevant episodes of PBS's *News Hour* and National Geographic's *Hard Time*

 **Audio Links** from programs like NPR

 **Web Links** to informative sites, including Federal Bureau of Prisons and Bureau of Justice Assistance

 **Journal Article Links** to SAGE Journals, such as *The Prison Journal, Crime & Delinquency,* and *Race and Justice.*

 **Prison Tour Video Links** were filmed specifically for this text. These original videos feature inmates and correctional workers from Louisiana State Penitentiary in Angola, Louisiana and Richwood Correctional Facility in Monroe, Louisiana. Various photos in the text are screenshots of the prison tour footage.

SAGE was founded in 1965 by Sara Miller McCune to support the dissemination of usable knowledge by publishing innovative and high-quality research and teaching content. Today, we publish over 900 journals, including those of more than 400 learned societies, more than 800 new books per year, and a growing range of library products including archives, data, case studies, reports, and video. SAGE remains majority-owned by our founder, and after Sara's lifetime will become owned by a charitable trust that secures our continued independence.

Los Angeles | London | New Delhi | Singapore | Washington DC

Introduction to CORRECTIONS

I dedicate this book to my wife, Gina, and our children, Tiffany, Ronnie, and Danny. I appreciate their patience and support while I spend so much time at the computer.

I dedicate this text to the Eastham UC. Through thick and thin, I could always count on you.

I dedicate this text to my brother, Sgt. Guy Hanser with the Texas Department of Criminal Justice—Institutional Division. I am proud of you and the work that you do.

Lastly but most importantly, I also dedicate this text to all the men and women who work, have worked, and will eventually work in the field of corrections, whether institutional or community-based. Your dedication to public safety and fair-minded actions under stressful circumstances are appreciated. All of us are depending on you.

Introduction to CORRECTIONS

Robert D.
HANSER
University of Louisiana at Monroe

Los Angeles | London | New Delhi
Singapore | Washington DC

Los Angeles | London | New Delhi
Singapore | Washington DC

FOR INFORMATION:

SAGE Publications, Inc.
2455 Teller Road
Thousand Oaks, California 91320
E-mail: order@sagepub.com

SAGE Publications Ltd.
1 Oliver's Yard
55 City Road
London EC1Y 1SP
United Kingdom

SAGE Publications India Pvt. Ltd.
B 1/I 1 Mohan Cooperative Industrial Area
Mathura Road, New Delhi 110 044
India

SAGE Publications Asia-Pacific Pte. Ltd.
3 Church Street
#10-04 Samsung Hub
Singapore 049483

Acquisitions Editor: Jerry Westby
Associate Editor: Jessica Miller
Editorial Assistant: Laura Kirkhuff
eLearning Editor: Nicole Mangona
Production Editor: Laura Barrett
Copy Editor: Shannon Kelly
Typesetter: C&M Digitals (P) Ltd.
Proofreader: Tricia Currie-Knight
Indexer: Wendy Allex
Cover Designer: Scott Van Atta
Marketing Manager: Amy Lammers

Printed in the United States of America

Library of Congress Cataloging-in-Publication Data

Names: Hanser, Robert D., author.

Title: Introduction to corrections / Robert D. Hanser.

Description: Second edition. | Thousand Oaks, California : SAGE, [2017] |

Includes bibliographical references and index.

Identifiers: LCCN 2015038934 | ISBN 978-1-5063-0675-9 (pbk. : alk. paper)

Subjects: LCSH: Corrections. | Corrections—United States.

Classification: LCC HV8665 .H36 2017 | DDC 364.6—dc23
LC record available at http://lccn.loc.gov/2015038934

This book is printed on acid-free paper.

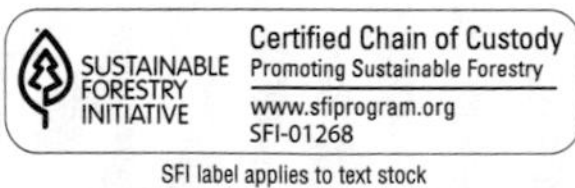

SFI label applies to text stock

16 17 18 19 20 10 9 8 7 6 5 4 3 2 1

BRIEF CONTENTS

CONTENTS

PART II: CORRECTIONAL PRACTICES

©iStockphoto.com/Bastiaan Slabbers

©Rich Pedroncelli/AP/Corbis

©iStockphoto.com/Susan Chiang

©iStockphoto.com/mediaphotos

©iStockphoto.com/C_FOR

©iStockphoto.com/C_FOR

Stockbyte/Thinkstock

REUTERS/Jim Young

CHAPTER 11: Specialized Inmate Populations 254

©iStockphoto.com/Windzepher

CHAPTER 12: Juvenile Correctional Systems 284

AP Photo/Evan Vucci

Stockbyte/Thinkstock

© Patti Sapone/Star Ledger/Corbis

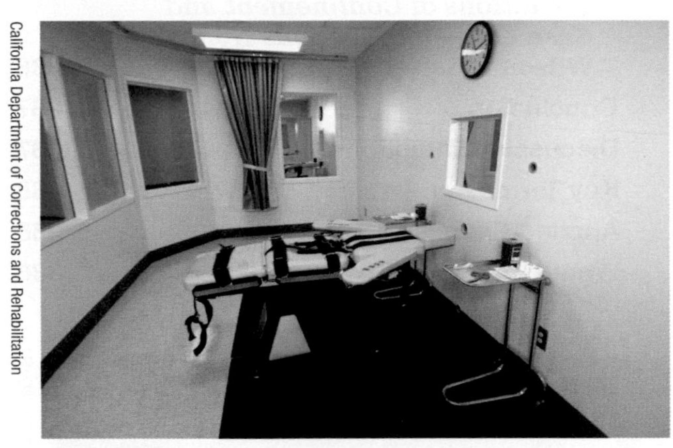
California Department of Corrections and Rehabilitation

©iStock-photo.com/mediaphotos

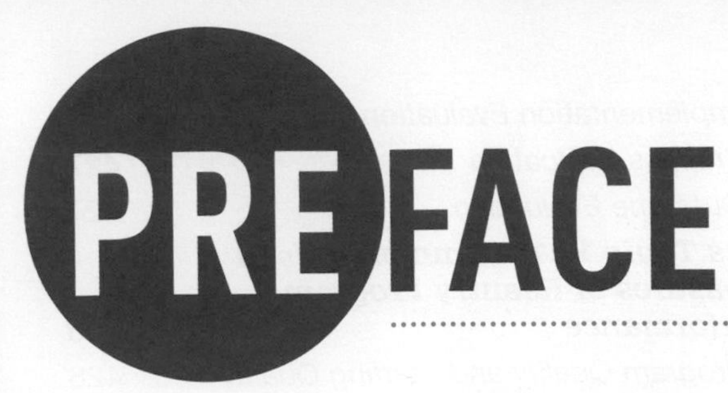

As was the first edition, this text is intended to provide the reader with a view of corrections that is both practitioner-driven and grounded in modern research and theoretical origins. Though this text does integrate research and theory within its pages, its specific strength is the practicality and realism provided in describing and explaining today's world of corrections. This single aspect of the book, along with its insightful portrayal of prison logic, exploration of subcultural issues in prison, and emphasis on persons who work within the field, both institutional and community-based, is what sets this text apart from others in the correctional textbook market. Additionally, vignettes have now been included that provide a view of correctional issues and challenges from the vantage of correctional workers and/or offenders, which helps to further portray the day-to-day reality of the correctional experience.

While this book does integrate the world of the practitioner with theoretical aspects, it is important to note that this is not a theory text. Rather, this text illustrates how the typical practitioner conducts business in the field of corrections, including both institutional and community settings. At the same time, theoretical applications are made explicit to demonstrate to the student that contemporary punishment, incarceration, and supervision schemes are grounded in theories that are often overlooked. Indeed, this text shows that theory and the practical world do not have to be disjointed and disconnected from one another. Rather, each can serve to augment the other, and, in this book, each aspect provides the student with additional facets of *how* correctional practice is implemented (reflecting the world of the practitioner) and *why* it is implemented in that manner (rooted in theoretical perspectives).

This text is intended to serve as a stand-alone text for undergraduate students in introductory courses on corrections, correctional systems, and/or correctional practices. A special effort is made to tie the readings to practical uses that the majority of our students will encounter in the world of work. This includes discussions on qualifications of specific types of officers, stressors confronted in daily correctional work, examples of tools and instruments that are used in the field, and so forth. The organization of the book follows a logical flow through the correctional system, in terms of both historical evolution and operational developments in the field. In short, this text covers the full array of topics related to nearly any aspect of corrections—on an introductory level, of course.

In addition, the role of technology has been highlighted throughout this book. Indeed, each chapter has a specific Technology and Equipment section that highlights some type of development in technology or equipment that is used within the field of corrections. These sections, along with other areas of focus throughout the text, provide the student with an idea of how the correctional industry has developed and continues to develop and adapt to the changing demands of working with the offender population. The role of technology in security processes, assessment/classification/case management, intermediate sanctions, drug testing, medical procedures, and other correctional processes is highlighted throughout this text. This again provides a practitioner focus as the student becomes familiar with the tools and equipment used by people who work in this segment of the criminal justice system. Further, this allows the student to see how corrections has evolved into a profession that uses state-of-the-art technology applications.

Finally, this text is also unique in one other critical aspect. The data, figures, tables, and various programs showcased here are predominantly drawn from federal government documents and briefings. Thus, the data and programs selected are solid and tend to be of better quality than one might typically use. Federal research by the National Institute of Corrections abounds, and the right to public domain of much of this material has allowed the author to integrate it within the pages of this text. This provides for rich data and examples that are guaranteed to aid in student learning. Further, the sources have been subjected to rigorous scrutiny and consideration, ensuring that all information is valid and up to date.

NEW TO THIS EDITION

- Throughout the text, information has been updated to include new legislation, statistics, examples, and topics, such as sentencing practices, technological innovations, and offenders with special needs.
- More coverage of gender diversity and the impact of the Prison Rape Elimination Act (PREA) upon prison system operations has been added to relevant chapters.
- The organization of the text has been strengthened by adding part titles and revising the structure of some chapters to create a clearer grouping of information that is more navigable for students.
- Learning objectives now utilize Bloom's taxonomy and have a closer connection to the key concepts in each chapter.
- Each chapter now opens with an engaging vignette that highlights an important issue in corrections and helps students see some of the challenges corrections practitioners face.
- Some chapters have been combined and streamlined, resulting in a 17-chapter text that more closely aligns with the traditional course schedule.
- The popular Cross-National Perspective feature has been moved from the end of chapter material into the main body of the text to demonstrate the close connection it has to the concepts covered in each chapter and to highlight the importance of considering corrections from a global perspective.
- Where available, recent statistics have been added to the figures and tables to provide students a contemporary snapshot of the status of corrections today.
- New engaging chapter-opening vignettes have been added to highlight important issues in corrections and allow students to understand the challenges corrections practitioners face each day.

APPROACH AND STRUCTURE OF THE TEXT

Significantly and perhaps uniquely, this text not only connects the practical world of corrections to the theoretical, but also connects treatment and security aspects in the field of corrections to show the dichotomous relationship between these two types of approaches in offender management. Further, the practical aspects of this book are reinforced with specific exercises in which students themselves apply and synthesize the various concepts found throughout the chapters. In providing this content, this text consists of 17 chapters that cover all the basic aspects of correctional systems and practices. These chapters are summarized as follows:

Chapter 1: Early History of Punishment and the Development of Prisons in the United States

This chapter serves as an introduction to and overview of the historical development of corrections in Europe and the United States. Included in this chapter is a history of the development of sanctions as well as an overview of many classic figures in the history of corrections, including Charles Montesquieu, Cesare Beccaria, William Penn, and John Howard, among others. This chapter also discusses prisons in the United States, from the earliest prison used in the original 13 colonies to modern-day maximum-security facilities; the development of prisons and prison systems at both the state and federal levels is also discussed. The Pennsylvania system, the Auburn system, southern penology, the reformatory era, and the use of the Big Houses are all covered. Different models of correctional operation are provided, as is a brief overview of modern-day prison facilities.

Chapter 2: Ideological and Theoretical Underpinnings to Sentencing and Correctional Policy

This chapter revisits the purpose of corrections as a process whereby practitioners from a variety of agencies and programs use tools, techniques, and facilities to engage in organized security and treatment functions intended to correct criminal tendencies among the offender population. It is with this purpose in mind that a variety of philosophical underpinnings are presented, including retribution, incapacitation, deterrence, rehabilitation, restorative justice, and reintegration. Discussion regarding the use of incarceration as a primary tool of punishment is provided, and community-based sanctions are given extensive coverage. The death penalty is presented as the most serious sanction available. Lastly, types of sentencing models, as well as disparities in both prison and death penalty sentences, are highlighted. In discussing the issue of disparity, the distinction between disparity and discrimination is made clear.

Chapter 3: Correctional Law and Legal Liabilities

This chapter demonstrates how there has been a constant interplay between state-level correctional systems and the federal courts recently in America. Amidst this evolution of correctional operations, the interpretation of constitutional standards has been a central feature, as has the Supreme Court's interpretation of its own role in ensuring that those standards are met. The distinctions between federal suits and state suits are clarified. Lastly, a brief overview of injunctions and other forms of court-oriented remediation is presented. These actions are what ultimately led to the sweeping changes that we have seen in the field of corrections.

Chapter 4: Jail and Detention Facilities

Jail facilities are presented as complicated facilities that are not usually appreciated for the vital role that they play within the criminal justice system. The different types of tasks, such as the holding of persons prior to their court date, providing a series of unique sentencing variations, and the incarceration of persons who are technically part of the larger prison system, are all considered. The problems and challenges for jail facilities can be quite varied, and this creates a demanding situation for jail staff and administrators. Overall, jails have been given short shrift in the world of corrections, but they will be given much more attention in times to come. Data for this chapter has been extensively updated from the time that the first edition was published.

Chapter 5: Probation

The evolution of probation is presented, from the early days of recognizance and suspended sentences through modern-day uses. This chapter also includes a variety of different types of probation administrative models. Also discussed are the qualifications of officers, supervisory strategies, and responsibilities of offenders. Presentence investigation reports and revocation and legal procedures are also included. Extensive updates in statistics and illustrative figures related to probation officer employment have been integrated within this chapter.

Chapter 6: Intermediate Sanctions

This chapter provides an overview of several types of intermediate sanctions that are used around the country. The use of community partnerships is again emphasized. Various intermediate sanctions, such as community service, the payment of fines, intensive supervision, GPS monitoring, home detention, and day reporting centers, are discussed. Together with community involvement, agency collaboration, and solid case management processes, intermediate sanctions are shown to be a key interlocking supervision mechanism that improves the overall goal of public safety.

Chapter 7: Facility Design to Meet Security and Programming Needs

This chapter demonstrates that the physical features of a prison require forethought before ground is even broken at the construction site. Issues related to the location of the prison facility, the types of custody levels and security, the function of the facility, logistical support for the facility, and institutional services (such as laundry, kitchen, and religious services) are all important considerations. Technological developments and improvements in security, including cell block and electric fence construction, are presented. Challenges associated with technological innovations in security are also highlighted in this chapter.

Chapter 8: Classification and Custody Levels

Effective classification is presented as an essential aspect of both security needs and the needs of the inmate. This chapter discusses Alexander Maconochie's impact on correctional classification processes through his mark system. It shows as well that classification processes are important for both security and treatment purposes.

Chapter 9: Prison Subculture and Prison Gang Influence

This chapter provides a glimpse of the "behind the scenes" aspects of the prison environment. The notion of a prison subculture, complete with norms and standards that are counter to those of the outside world, is presented. The effects of professionalism within the correctional officer ranks, the diversity of correctional staff, and the difference in this generation of inmates all have led to changes in the inmate subculture in modern times. Gangs have emerged as a major force in state prison systems. From this chapter, it is clear that prison gangs have networks that extend beyond the prison walls. Additional information is provided that covers the Prison Rape Elimination Act of 2003 (PREA) and how this has impacted prison subculture in today's contemporary correctional environment.

Chapter 10: Female Offenders in Correctional Systems

Female offenders, though a small proportion of the correctional population, are rapidly growing in number. The need for improved services and programming for female offenders is discussed in this chapter. Mother-child programming is presented as critical to female offender reformation. Legal issues specific to female offenders are discussed, and guiding principles to improve female offender reentry are provided. As with Chapter 9, this chapter also provides information related to the PREA and its impact on security and programming services for female offenders.

Chapter 11: Specialized Inmate Populations

In this section, we include a discussion on the supervisory strategies used for a special offender population, which includes sex offenders, substance abusers, mentally ill offenders, and mentally disabled offenders. This growing population in the community presents special concerns for community safety and supervisory strategies. This section addresses some of these concerns and provides suggestions for effective supervisory strategies. This chapter contains numerous updates in data related to offenders with special needs as well as figures and information related to surprising trends concerning HIV/AIDS in prison.

Chapter 12: Juvenile Correctional Systems

In this chapter, a very brief overview of both institutional and community-based supervision strategies used for juvenile offenders is presented. These strategies include detention, probation, residential programs, juvenile aftercare, and even adult prisons when youth are tried as adults. Legal developments in juvenile justice are discussed. Additional topics include types of abuse and neglect of youth and youth gangs. This chapter also includes a discussion of how the PREA has impacted the maintenance and operation of juvenile facilities in the United States. Additional updates on Supreme Court rulings related to juvenile corrections have also been included in this edition.

Chapter 13: Correctional Administration

This chapter provides an overview of the organizational structure of both the federal and state prison systems in the United States. Styles of management and the delegation of responsibility are discussed. The rise of women in the field of corrections is presented. Private prison management is included in this chapter, along with the conclusion that such programs can be quite successful. Lastly, emergency response issues and emergency response management are discussed.

Chapter 14: Prison Programming

This chapter provides an overview of many of the typical programs offered to inmates within the prison environment. Educational, vocational, drug treatment, medical, recreational, food service, and religious programs are all presented, but a more streamlined approach is utilized to give improved focus and clarity on the overall notion of offender programming inside institutions. Prison programming is shown to be effective in inmate management and also to produce positive benefits for offender reentry. Thus, prison education, work, and other forms of programming have public safety benefits.

Chapter 15: Parole and Reintegration

This chapter provides an overview of the evolution of parole to its modern-day usage. Additional and up-to-date data and figures are included in the discussion of parole in the United States. Early historical figures who contributed to the development of parole, such as Sir Walter Crofton and Alexander Maconochie, are noted. This chapter also includes a variety of different types of parole administrative models that include not only the qualifications of officers but also the supervisory strategies and responsibilities of offenders. The use of prerelease planning and mechanisms, along with the parole board and parole revocation, are also included. The controversial nature of parole and other early release mechanisms is discussed.

Chapter 16: The Death Penalty

This chapter provides students with an understanding of the reasons and justifications that are commonly touted for implementation of the death penalty and also presents typical criticisms that are leveled toward the use of this sanction. This chapter includes a plethora of updates in statistical information as well as tables and figures that showcase very recent findings. Further, the means by which the death penalty is implemented, and the types of offenses and offenders likely to receive the death penalty, are also presented. Disparities in the use of the death penalty are examined. A completely new Cross-National Perspectives feature has been added to this chapter.

Chapter 17: Program Evaluation, Evidence-Based Practices, and Future Trends in Corrections

This chapter illustrates the importance of evaluative research and distinguishes between process and outcome measures. This chapter has been expanded from its first edition version by including all of the features common in prior chapters (i.e., Applied Theory section, Cross-National Perspectives insert, Corrections and the Law segment, and a Technology and Equipment insert). As with the first edition, the use of the assessment-evaluative cycle in corrections is discussed. Information on evidence-based practices is presented but is showcased in a more succinct manner to better illustrate how these practices aid agencies to excel in service delivery. A variety of future trends in the correctional field are also presented during the last few pages of this chapter. Unlike the first edition, this chapter is now a fully stand-alone chapter of the text.

PEDAGOGICAL AIDS

A number of pedagogical aids have been included in each chapter of this text. Their primary goal is to facilitate student learning and to aid the student in synthesizing the learning goal and applying it to the modern world of corrections. Through these added features, specific theories are identified and linked to a particular point in the correctional setting. Also, cross-national perspectives are provided within each chapter to acquaint the student with applications that exist in other nations around the globe. In addition, this text has a number of ancillaries that accompany it, all as a means of further improving student learning. The pedagogical features and ancillaries associated with this text are listed below.

- ***Opening Vignettes***: At the very beginning of each chapter, a short story is provided that is related to the chapter's topic. Each story provides a high sense of realism in portraying issues that are encountered within the correctional environment.
- ***Improved Chapter Learning Objectives***: At the beginning of each chapter is a set of learning objectives. These objectives serve as cues for the student and also provide for easy assessment of learning for the instructor. These points are germane to the chapter and prompt the student as to the information that will be covered. They also let the student know what is critical to the text readings. Each of these learning objectives is clearly linked to headings and subheadings throughout the text.
- ***Focus Topics Boxes***: Many chapters include Focus Topic boxes that provide additional insight regarding specific points in the chapter. The topics typically help to add depth and detail to a particular subject that is considered important or interesting from a learning perspective. The inclusion of these boxes has been made with care and consideration to ensure that the material does indeed reinforce the learning objectives at the beginning of each chapter.

- ***Applied Theory Inserts***: Within most chapters, Applied Theory inserts are included. These inserts provide clear and focused application of a specific theory to a particular issue or set of issues in community corrections. This is an important feature because many textbooks fail to navigate the disconnect that seems to exist between the world of theory and the world of the practitioner. These inserts bridge the two worlds and also highlight issues specific to the chapter from a theoretical perspective.
- ***Technology and Equipment Inserts***: Also within most chapters is an insert that showcases some type of technological development in the field of corrections or some type of tool or equipment germane to work in the field. This provides the student with an additional glimpse of the practitioner's world through the examination of the working tools of the trade. This also provides the student with an awareness of the many developments that have occurred and continue to occur within the field of corrections.
- ***Corrections and the Law Inserts***: In each chapter, students will find legal inserts that explain, in detail, some type of important legal issue or Supreme Court ruling that is associated with the topic of the chapter. This again shows the student how the field of corrections is constantly changing and also provides the student with additional insight regarding the legal concerns and considerations experienced by many correctional administrators. All Corrections and the Law inserts contain current rulings.
- ***Key Terms/Key Cases***: At the end of each chapter is a list of key terms/key cases that help to augment information relevant to the chapter learning objectives. The terms and cases are in bold throughout the text and are included in the glossary.
- ***Discussion Questions***: At the end of each chapter is a list of five to seven discussion questions. These questions usually ask students about chapter content that is relevant to the learning objectives found at the beginning of each chapter. In this way, they serve the function of reinforcing specific knowledge that is applicable to the learning objectives and further clarify for the student the main points and concepts included therein.
- ***"What Would You Do?" Exercises***: At the close of each chapter, these exercises present some sort of modern-day correctional scenario that the student must address. In each case, a problem is presented to students, and they must explain what they would do to resolve the issue or solve the problem. This feature provides an opportunity for students to apply and synthesize the material from the chapter and ensures that higher-order learning of the material takes place.
- ***Applied Exercise Features***: These assignments require the student to perform some type of activity that integrates the material in the text with the hands-on world of the practitioner. In some cases, these assignments require that the student interview practitioners in the field, while in other cases students may need to utilize specific tools or instruments when addressing an issue in corrections. In each case, the student is required to demonstrate understanding of a particular aspect of the chapter readings and must also demonstrate competence in using the information, techniques, or processes that he or she has learned from the chapter. These exercises often also require the student to incorporate information from prior chapters or other exercises in the text, thereby building upon the prior base of knowledge that the student has accumulated.
- ***Cross-National Perspective Segments***: Within each chapter, these additions provide a brief examination of a related topic in corrections as it applies to a country other than the United States. In addition to a brief write-up on the subject, students are provided website information to read further on the cross-national topic, and they are also encouraged to consider the implications of the cross-national perspective through critical thinking questions at the end of the segment.
- ***Text Glossary***: A glossary of key terms is included at the end of the text. These key terms are necessary to ensure that students understand the basics of corrections. Definitions are provided in simple but thorough language.

ANCILLARIES

To enhance this text and to assist in the use of this book, a variety of different ancillaries have been created. This text is one of several by SAGE that strives to give the text its own sense of life through the use of various media and online resources that enhance the reading of the text, particularly online.

SAGE edge offers a robust online environment featuring an impressive array of tools and resources for review, study, and further exploration, keeping both instructors and students on the cutting edge of teaching and learning. SAGE edge content is open access and available on demand. Learning and teaching has never been easier!

http://edge.sagepub.com/hanser2e

SAGE edge for instructors supports teaching by making it easy to integrate quality content and create a rich learning environment for students.

- **Test banks** provide a diverse range of pre-written options as well as the opportunity to edit any question and/or insert personalized questions to effectively assess students' progress and understanding.
- Editable, chapter-specific **PowerPoint® slides** offer complete flexibility for creating a multimedia presentation for the course.
- EXCLUSIVE! Access is provided to full-text **SAGE journal articles** that have been carefully selected to support and expand on the concepts presented in each chapter to encourage students to think critically.
- **Chapter-specific discussion questions** help launch classroom interaction by prompting students to engage with the material and by reinforcing important content.
- **Video and multimedia links** includes original SAGE videos that appeal to students with different learning styles.
- **Lecture notes** summarize key concepts by chapter to ease preparation for lectures and class discussions.
- A **course cartridge** provides easy LMS integration.

SAGE edge for students provides a personalized approach to help students accomplish their coursework goals in an easy-to-use learning environment.

- Mobile-friendly **eFlashcards** strengthen understanding of key terms and concepts.
- Mobile-friendly practice **quizzes** allow for independent assessment by students of their mastery of course material.
- Carefully selected chapter-by-chapter **video and multimedia links** enhance classroom-based explorations of key topics.
- A customized online **action plan** includes tips and feedback on progress through the course and materials, which allows students to individualize their learning experience.
- **Learning objectives** reinforce the most important material.
- Lively and stimulating **chapter activities** that can be used in class to reinforce active learning. The activities apply to individual or group projects.
- EXCLUSIVE! access is provided to full-text **SAGE journal articles** that have been carefully selected to support and expand on the concepts presented in each chapter.

ACKNOWLEDGMENTS

At this time, I would like to first thank the executive editor, Jerry Westby. Jerry's continued support and faith in this project has been an inspiration and is greatly appreciated, as are those efforts and the support of Jessica Miller, who has been instrumental in assisting with the organization of the text and development of the overall product. These individuals were able to maintain a three-way dialogue between the authors, editors, and reviewers, which resulted in this text being a top-notch product, both in content and in delivery.

I would like to extend special gratitude to all of the correctional practitioners who carry out the daily tasks of our correctional system, whether institutional or community-based. These individuals deserve the highest praise as they work in a field that is demanding and undervalued—I thank you all for the contributions that you make to our society.

I would also like to thank Secretary LeBlanc of the Louisiana Department of Public Safety and Corrections; Ms. Pam Laborde, communications director for the Louisiana DPS&C; and all those who allowed me to interview and showcase various elements of that state's correctional system. In addition, Warden Burl Cain and Assistant Warden Cathy Fontenot deserve thanks and gratitude for allowing the filming and photo shoots at Louisiana State Penitentiary Angola.

In addition, I would like to thank Mr. Billy McConnell, Mr. Clay McConnell, Warden Keith Deville, and Warden Ray Hanson, as well as other personnel and staff of LaSalle Southwest Corrections. Their support for this text and willingness to be interviewed and allow filming and photo shoots at Richwood Correctional Center added a very unique, useful, and educational element to the text.

I am also grateful to the many reviewers (see below) who spent time reading the document and making a considerable number of recommendations that helped to shape the final product. Every effort was made to incorporate those ideas. Their suggestions and insights helped to improve the final product that you see here, a product that, in truth, is a reflection of all those who were involved throughout its development.

Reviewers for the second edition:

Patricia L. Donze, J.D. Ph.D., California State University, Dominguez Hills

Gabriel Kovnator, Los Angeles Mission College

David E. Olson, Ph.D., Loyola University Chicago

Joseph V. Williams, John Jay School of Criminal Justice

Jane C. Daquin, M.S., Georgia State University

Irina Zakirova, Ph.D., John Jay College of Criminal Justice

James R. Jones, Ph.D., Ashford University

Nancy L. Hogan, Ferris State University

Dr. Patrick Ibe, Albany State University

Larry E. Spencer, Alabama State University

Reviewers for the first edition:

Gaylene Armstrong, Sam Houston State University

Kelly Asmussen, Peru State College, Nebraska

Jack Atherton, Northwestern State University, Louisiana

Jeri Barnett, Virginia Western Community College

Debra Baskin, Cal State Los Angeles/Rio Hondo College

Lindsey Bergeron, Nova Southeastern University

Ashley G. Blackburn, University of North Texas

Kristie Blevins, University of North Carolina Charlotte

Michael Botts, Arkansas State University

Pauline Brennan, University of Nebraska, Omaha

Mark Brown, University of South Carolina

Brenda Chappell, University of Central Oklahoma

Roger Cunningham, Eastern Illinois University

Marie Griffin, Arizona State University

Jennifer Grimes, Indiana State University, Terre Haute

Ricky S. Gutierrez, California State University, Sacramento

Zachary Hamilton, Washington State University

Howard Henderson, Sam Houston State University

Pati Hendrickson, Tarleton State University

Carly Hilinski, Grand Valley State University, Michigan

Robert Homant, University of Detroit

Rob Huckabee, Indiana State University

Martha Hurley, The Citadel

Polly Johnson, Austin Community College

David Keys, New Mexico University

Janine Kremling, California State University, San Bernardino

Jessie Krienert, Illinois State University

Margaret Leigey, Cal State University Chico

Richard Lemke, University of West Georgia

Cathy Levey, Goodwin College, Connecticut

Robert McCabe, Old Dominion University

Danielle McDonald, Northern Kentucky University

Alfredo Montalvo, Emporia State University

Michael Montgomery, Tennessee State University

Robert Morris, University of Texas at Dallas

Robert Peetz, Midland College

O. Elmer Polk, University of Texas at Dallas

Karla Pope, Mississippi Gulf Coast Community College

Magnus Seng, Loyola University-Chicago

Diane Sjuts, Metropolitan State Community College

Quanda Stevenson, University of Alabama

Sheryl Van Horne, Widener University

Lindsey Vigesaa, Nova Southeastern University

Brenda Vose, University of North Florida

Arnold Waggoner, Rose State College

Ted Wallman, University of North Florida

ABOUT THE AUTHOR

Robert D. Hanser is a full professor and chair of the criminal justice program at the University of Louisiana at Monroe. Rob has also administered a regional training academy in northeastern Louisiana (North Delta Regional Training Academy) that provides training to correctional officers, jailers, and law enforcement throughout a 12-parish region in Louisiana. He is also the program director of the Blue Walters Substance Abuse Treatment Program at Richwood Correctional Center, a prison-based substance abuse treatment program in Louisiana, and he is the director of Offender Programming for LaSalle Corrections. Further, Rob is the director and lead facilitator for the Fourth Judicial District's Batterer Intervention Program (BIP). He serves as the board president for Freedmen Inc., a faith-based organization that provides reentry services for offenders in Louisiana. Lastly, he is the board president and CEO of a nonprofit organization that provided contract therapeutic services for the Fourth Judicial District Adult Drug Court and DWI Court in Northeast Louisiana for over a four year period. He has dual licensure as a professional counselor in Texas and Louisiana, is a certified anger resolution therapist, and has a specialty license in addictions counseling.

EARLY HISTORY OF PUNISHMENT AND THE DEVELOPMENT OF PRISONS IN THE UNITED STATES

SAGE/Jessica Miller

PRISONER NUMBER ONE AT EASTERN PENITENTIARY

In 1830, Charles Williams, prisoner number one at Eastern State Penitentiary, contemplated his situation with a sense of somber and solemn reflection. He did this undisturbed due to the excruciating silence that seemed to permeate most of his incarceration. On occasion, he could hear keys jingling, and he might hear the sound of footsteps as guards brought his food or other necessities. Sometimes he could hear the noise of construction, as the facility was not yet finished and would not be fully functional for years to come. Otherwise, there was no other sound or connection to the outside world, and silence was the most common experience throughout most of the daylight hours and the entire night.

To be sure, Charles had all of his basic needs met at Eastern. He had his own private cell that was centrally heated and had running water. He had a flushing toilet, a skylight, and a small, walled recreation yard for his own private use. In his high-pitched cell, Charles had only natural light, the Bible, and his assigned work (he was involved in basic weaving) to keep him busy throughout the day. He was not allowed interaction with the guards or other inmates, and his food was delivered to him via a slot in the door. In addition, he was to not leave his cell for anything other than recreation in his own walled yard, and even then he was required to wear a special mask that prevented communication with other guards or inmates while he entered the yard.

Charles was a farmer by trade. He had been caught and convicted of burglary after stealing a $20 watch, a $3 gold seal, and a gold key. He was sentenced to 2 years of confinement with hard labor and entered Eastern on October 23, 1829. He had served 7 months of his sentence and already he felt as if he had been incarcerated for an eternity. He reflected daily (and quite constantly) on his crime. Before his arrival, he had had no idea what Eastern State Penitentiary would be like. As it turned out, it was quite numbing to Charles's sense of mental development, and he sometimes felt as if he did not even exist. Charles remembered his first glimpse of the tall, foreboding exterior of the unfinished prison as his locked carriage approached. It was an intimidating sight, and Charles, who was only 18 at the time of his sentencing, felt remorseful. He remembered when Warden Samuel R. Wood received him and explained that he would be overseeing Charles's stay at Eastern. The warden was very direct and matter-of-fact and exhibited a mean-spirited temperament. Charles found the warden to be reflective of his entire experience while serving in prison cell number one at Eastern. He thus had determined that he did not want to spend any more of his life in such confinement.

Charles considered the fact that he still had 18 months on his sentence—an eternity for most 18-year-olds. He knew that other inmates would soon follow his stay in the expanding prison. However, he was not the least bit curious about the future of Eastern. He was indeed repentant, but not necessarily for the reasons that early Quaker advocates might have hoped when they advocated for the penitentiary. Rather than looking to divine inspiration as a source of redemption from future solitary incarceration, he simply decided that he would never again be in a position where he could be accused of, guilty of, or caught in the commission of a crime. He just wanted to go back to simple farming and leave Eastern State Penitentiary out of both sight and mind for the remainder of his years.

LEARNING OBJECTIVES:

1. Define *corrections* and the role it has in the criminal justice system.
2. Identify early historical developments and justifications in the use of punishment and corrections.
3. Discuss the influence of the Enlightenment and key persons on correctional reform.
4. Discuss the development of punishment in early American history.
5. Describe the changes to prison systems brought about by the Age of the Reformatory in America.
6. Identify the various prison systems, eras, and models that developed in the early and mid-1900s in America.
7. Explain how state and federal prisons differ and identify the Top Three in American corrections.

DEFINING CORRECTIONS: A VARIETY OF POSSIBILITIES

In this text, **corrections** will be defined as a process whereby practitioners from a variety of agencies and programs use tools, techniques, and facilities to engage in organized security and treatment functions intended to correct criminal tendencies among the offender population. This definition underscores the fact that corrections is a process that includes the day-to-day activities of the practitioners who are involved in that process. Corrections is not a collection of agencies, organizations, facilities, or physical structures; rather, the agencies and organizations consist of the practitioners under their employ and/or in their service, and the facilities or physical structures are the tools of the practitioner. The common denominator between the disparate components of the correctional system is the purpose behind the system. We now turn our attention to ancient developments in law and punishment, which, grounded in the desire to modify criminal behavior, served as the precursor to correctional systems and practices as we know them today.

The Role of Corrections in the Criminal Justice System

Generally speaking, the criminal justice system consists of five segments, three of which are more common to students and two of which are newer components, historically speaking. These segments are law enforcement, the courts, corrections, the juvenile justice system, and victim services. Of these, it is perhaps the correctional system that is least understood, least visible, and least respected among much of society. The reasons for this have to do with the functions of each of these segments of the whole system.

Unlike the police, who are tasked with apprehending offenders and preventing crime, correctional personnel often work to change (or at least keep contained) the offender population. This is often a less popular function to many in society, and when correctional staff are tasked with providing constitutional standards of care for the offender population, many in society may attribute this to "coddling" the inmate or offender.

On the other hand, the judicial or court segment is held in much more lofty regard. The work of courtroom personnel is considered more sophisticated, and jobs within this sector are more often coveted. Further, there tends to be a degree of mystique to the study and practice of law, undoubtedly enhanced by portrayals in modern-day television and the media. In this segment of the system, legal battles are played out, oral arguments are heard, evidence is presented, and deliberations are made. At the end, a sentence is given and the story concludes that all parties involved have had their day in court.

The juvenile justice system is unique from these other systems because much of it is not even criminal court but is instead civil in nature. This is because our system intends to avoid stigmatizing youthful offenders, hopes to integrate family involvement and supervision, and views youth as being more amenable to positive change. The juvenile justice system is designed to help youth and is, therefore, less punitive in theory and practice than the adult system. Again, the entire idea is that youth are at an early stage in life where their trajectory is not too far off the path; with the right implementation, we can change their life course in the future.

Victim services is, naturally, the easiest segment to sympathize with because it is tasked with aiding those who have been harmed by crime. The merits of these services should be intuitively obvious, but such programs are often underfunded in many states and struggle to help those in need. In addition to state programs, many nonprofit organizations are also dedicated to assisting victims.

After this very brief overview of each segment of the criminal justice system, we come back to the correctional system. The correctional system, despite its lesser appeal, is integral to the ability of the other systems to maintain their functions. As we will see later in this chapter, it is simply not prudent, realistic, or civilized to either banish or put to death every person who commits an offense. Indeed, such reactions would be extreme and quite problematic in today's world. Thus, we are stuck with the reality that we must do something else with those individuals who have offended. Naturally, some have committed serious crimes while others have not. Discerning what must be done with each offender based on the crime, the criminal, and the risk that might be incurred to society is the role of the correctional system. Further, it is the responsibility of this system to keep these persons from committing future crimes against society, a task that the other segments of the system seem unable to do.

Corrections: A process whereby practitioners engage in organized security and treatment functions to correct criminal tendencies among the offender population.

The correctional system is impacted by all of the other systems and, largely speaking, is at their mercy in many respects. Indeed, as police effect more arrests, more people are locked up and jails and prisons must contend with housing more inmates. When courts sentence more offenders, the same happens. A court has the luxury of engaging in plea agreements to modify the contours of a sentence, but the correctional system has few similar forms of latitude, other than letting offenders out early for good behavior—an option that many in society bemoan as the cause for high crime rates. Likewise, the juvenile system has a correctional segment that gets sufficient sympathy from the public, but state correctional facilities find themselves being given the "worst of the worst" of youthful offenders, making notions of rehabilitation more challenging than is desirable. And of course there is the victim services segment, through which the correctional system often attempts to redeem itself by ensuring that offenders are made accountable for their crimes and by generating revenue through fines, restoration programs, and compensation funds for victims. Amidst this, correctional systems engage in victim notification programs and many include victim services bureaus for those who have questions or requests of the correctional system.

This complicated system of sanctioning offenders while operating within the broader context of the criminal justice system is the result of a long and winding set of historical circumstances and social developments. In this chapter, we will explore how this story has unfolded, starting with the reality that initially the role of corrections was simply to *punish* the offender. This punishment, it was thought, would be instrumental in *changing* the behavior of the offender. These notions are just as relevant in today's world of corrections, though the means of implementation have become much more complicated. Because these early debates, ideologies, and perspectives on corrections laid the groundwork to our current system, it is the role of this chapter to give the reader an understanding of how and why they developed as they did.

THE NOTION OF PUNISHMENT AND CORRECTIONS THROUGHOUT HISTORY

As might be determined by the title of this section, there has been a long-standing connection between the concepts of punishment and correction. It is as if our criminal justice system considers these two concepts as being one in the same. However, as we will find, these two terms are not always synonymous with one another. Rather, the purpose that underlies each is probably a better guide in distinguishing one from the other, not identifying their similarities. It is the application of penalties that has the longest history, and it is with this in mind that punishment is first discussed, with additional clarification provided in defining the more modern term of *corrections*. As we will see later in this chapter and in other chapters, the distinction between *corrections* and *punishment* may be quite blurred.

Prison Tour Video Link
Punishment Reform and Living and Working Conditions

When applying punishments, it was hoped that the consequence would prevent the offender from committing future unwanted acts. Though one would consider it a good outcome if offenders are prevented from committing further crimes, this is not necessarily an act of *correction* regarding the offender's behavior. This is a very important point because it sets the very groundwork for what we consider to be corrections. Essentially, the common logic rests upon the notion that if we punish someone effectively, he or she will not do the crime again and is therefore corrected. Naturally, this is not always the final outcome of the punishment process. In fact, research has found cases where exposure to prison actually increases the likelihood of future criminal behavior (Fletcher, 1999; Golub, 1990). Likewise, some research has demonstrated higher rates of violent crime when the death penalty is applied, seemingly in reaction to or correlated with the use of the death penalty (Bowers & Pierce, 1980). This observation is referred to as the **brutalization hypothesis**, the contention of which is that the use of harsh punishments sensitizes people to violence and essentially *teaches* them to use violence rather than acting as a deterrent (Bowers & Pierce, 1980).

Early Codes of Law

Early codes of law were designed to guide human behavior and to distinguish that which was legal from that which was not. These laws often also stated the forms of punishment that would occur should a person run errant of a given edict. Because laws reflected the cultural and social norms of a given people and tended to include punishments, it could be said that the types of punishment used

Brutalization hypothesis: The contention that the use of harsh punishments sensitizes people to violence and *teaches* them to use it.

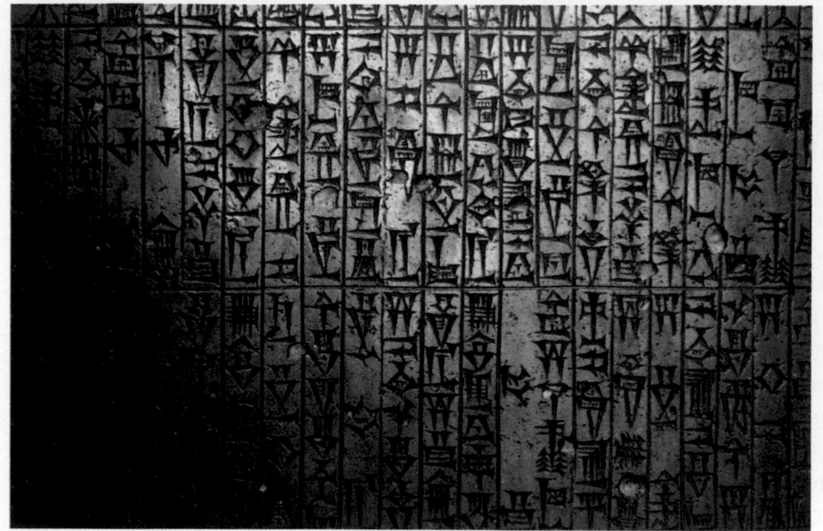

■ PHOTO 1.1 The Code of Hammurabi is one of the most ancient attempts to codify criminal acts and their corresponding punishments.

by a society might give an outside observer a glimpse of that society's true understanding of criminal behavior as well as its sense of compassion, or lack thereof.

Babylonian and Sumerian Codes

The earliest known written code of punishment was the **Code of Hammurabi**. Hammurabi (1728–1686 B.C.) was the ruler of Babylon sometime around 1700 B.C., which dates back nearly 3,800 years before our time (Roth, 2011). This code used the term ***lex talionis,*** which referred to the Babylonian law of equal retaliation (Roth, 2011). This legal basis reflected the instinctive desire for humans who have been harmed to seek revenge. While Hammurabi's Code included a number of very harsh corporal punishments, it also provided a sense of uniformity in punishments, thereby organizing the justice process in Babylon (Stohr, Walsh, & Hemmens, 2009).

Video Link
Code of Hammurabi

Roman Law and Punishment and Their Impact on Early English Punishment

Punishments in the Roman Empire were severe and tended to be terminal. Imprisonment was simply a means of holding the accused until those in power had decided the offender's fate. From what is known, it would appear that most places of confinement were simply cages. There are also recorded accounts of quarries (deep holes used for mining/excavating stone) used to hold offenders (Gramsci, 1996). One place of confinement in Rome that was well known was the Mamertine Prison, which was actually a sprawling system of underground tunnels and dungeons built under the sewer system of Rome sometime around 64 B.C. This was where the Christian apostles Paul and Peter were incarcerated (Gramsci, 1996).

Rome and other societies during this period considered convicted offenders to have the legal status of a slave, and they were treated as if they were essentially dead to society. In this "civil death," the offender's property would be excised by the government and the marriage (if any) between the offender and his or her spouse was declared void, providing the status of widow to the spouse.

Early Historical Role of Religion, Punishment, and Corrections

Perhaps the most well-known premodern historical period of punishment is the Middle Ages of Western Europe. The Middle Ages was a time of chaos in Europe during which plague, pestilence, fear, ignorance, and superstition prevailed. Throughout these dark times, the common citizenry, which consisted largely of peasants who could neither read nor write, placed their faith in religious leaders who were comparatively better educated and more literate.

While one might stand at trial for charges brought by the state, it was the **trial by ordeal** that emerged as the Church's equivalent to a legal proceeding (Johnson, Wolfe, & Jones, 2008). The trial by ordeal consisted of very dangerous and/or impossible tests used to prove the guilt or innocence of the accused. For instance, the ordeal of hot water required that the accused thrust a hand or an arm into a kettle of boiling water (Johnson et al., 2008). If after 3 days of binding the arm, the offender emerged unscathed, he or she was considered innocent. Of note was the general reason provided by the Church for its use of punishments. It would seem that the Church response to aberrant (or sinful) behavior was, at least in ideology, based on the desire to save the soul of the wayward offender. Indeed, even when persons were burned at the stake, the prevailing belief was that such burning would free their souls for redemption and ascension to Heaven. The goal, in essence, was to purify the soul as it was released from the body. This was especially true of persons who were convicted of witchcraft and who were believed to have consorted with spirits and/or were believed to be possessed by evil spirits.

Code of Hammurabi: The earliest known written code of punishment.

Lex talionis: Refers to the Babylonian law of equal retaliation.

Trial by ordeal: Very dangerous and/or impossible tests to prove the guilt or innocence of the accused.

CROSS-NATIONAL PERSPECTIVE 1.1

Penal Slavery in Western Europe and East Asia

The use of penal slavery was extensive in ancient Rome, though the actual economic benefits for this type of labor were minimal. For the most part, penal slavery in Rome was restricted to those offenders who had been given a life sentence. In such cases, these offenders suffered a civil death and no longer existed in society; they were thereby permanent slaves of the state. A strong distinction was drawn between these offenders and those who did not have a life sentence. For those offenders not serving life, penal servitude was exacted. Though this was similar in most respects to penal slavery, there was a time limit after which the sentence was considered to have been served.

In many East Asian countries, penal slaves were a source of both public and private slaves. Prisoners provided the bulk of the enslaved population in Vietnam even though slavery was not an important industry in that country. In Korea, which is thought to have had one of the most advanced slave systems in East Asia, penal slavery was used but was not the primary source of slaves. In Japan around the sixth century A.D., the two primary sources of slaves were prisoners of war and the familial relatives of convicted criminals as well as the offenders themselves. However, it was the nation of China that truly used penal slavery on a widespread basis.

The enslavement of family members related to condemned offenders was, in actuality, the primary and perhaps the only source from which penal slaves in China were drawn. Due to a strong rank system whereby family honor subsumed individual identity, if a family was disgraced by the acts of a criminal, the entire family could be held accountable for the crime(s) committed. Prior to the Han Dynasty, there was a tendency to execute criminal offenders and imprison their family members, but over time Chinese royalty imprisoned all persons.

Because most if not all slaves were penal slaves in China, the common view of a slave became one of being a criminal and therefore unworthy of fair treatment. The status of criminal opened the door for mutilation, torture, and abuse, all of which were condoned by Chinese law, as was also the case in much of old Europe. However, China was unusual in one routine practice in its penal slavery policy: many penal slaves ended up becoming property of private owners. Usually given as gifts to the affluent and/or powerful, they were often acquired by unscrupulous government officials or military officers.

It would appear that many of the ancient punishments, such as flogging, and the use of different forms of the death penalty were used by cultures in the East and the West. Further, most cultures in both areas of the world refrained from using jails for anything other than holding an offender in custody until punishment could be administered. The use of prisons as a form of punishment, in and of itself, was not common in either area. However, the use of criminal offenders as cheap and exploitable labor seems to have been common to the West as well as the East. A primary distinction between East and West revolved around the strong family honor system, which, in the grand scheme of things, generated a much larger penal slave population (including women as well as men) in Imperial China. This, and the existence of slaves among private Chinese social elites, demonstrates how cultural differences can impact the means by which punishments such as penal servitude are implemented.

QUESTION 1: What are two key distinctions between penal slavery in Rome and penal slavery in Imperial China? Why did these differences exist?

QUESTION 2: For what purpose were jails used in both the Eastern and the Western parts of the world? Was there widespread use of prisons as we know them today?

SOURCE: Patterson, O. (1982). *Slavery and social death: A comparative study.* Cambridge, MA: Harvard University Press.

Sanctuary

While the Church may have had a role in the application of punishments throughout history, it also provided some unique avenues by which the accused might avoid unwarranted punishment. One example would be the granting of sanctuary to accused offenders.

During ancient times, many nations had a city or a designated building, such as a temple or a church, where accused offenders could stay, free from attack, until such time that their innocence could be established (presuming that they were, in fact, innocent). In Europe, the use of sanctuary began during the fourth century and consisted of a place—usually a church—that the king's soldiers were forbidden to enter for purposes of taking an accused criminal into custody (Cromwell, del Carmen, & Alarid, 2002). In some cases, such as in England, **sanctuary** was provided until some form of negotiation could be arranged or until the accused was ultimately smuggled out of the area. If accused offenders confessed to their crimes while in sanctuary, they were typically allowed to leave the country with the understanding that return to England would lead to immediate punishment (Cromwell et al., 2002).

Sanctuary: A place of refuge or asylum.

This form of leniency lasted for well over a thousand years in European history and was apparently quite common in England. Eventually, sanctuary lost its appeal, and from roughly 1750 onward, countries throughout Europe began to abolish sanctuary provisions as secular courts gained power over ecclesiastical courts.

Early Secular History of Punishment and Corrections

The origin of law was one of debate during medieval times. Over time, secular rulers (often royalty and nobility) became less subservient to the Church and gained sufficient power to resist some of the controls placed upon them by the ecclesiastical courts. As such, much of the royalty, nobility, merchant class, and scholarly community advocated separation between government rule (at this time the king or queen) and the Church. Though this was an ultimately successful process, many did die as a result of their views.

It was at this time that criminal behavior became widely recognized as an offense against the state. Indeed, by 1350 A.D., the royalty (consisting of kings, queens, and the like) had established themselves as the absolute power, and they became less tolerant of external factors that undermined their own rule; this meant that the Church continued to lose authority throughout Europe. Ultimately, all forms of revenue obtained from fines went to the state (or the Crown), and the state administered all punishments. This also led to the development of crime being perceived as an act in violation of a king or queen's authority.

Public and Private Wrongs

Public wrongs are crimes against society or a social group and historically tended to include sacrilege as well as other crimes against religion, treason, witchcraft, incest, sex offenses of any sort, and even violations of hunting rules (Johnson et al., 2008). Among early societies, religious offenses were considered the most dangerous since these crimes exposed both the offender and the rest of the group to the potential anger and wrath of that culture's deity or set of deities. Witchcraft was commonly thought to entail genuine magical powers that would be used by the witch for personal revenge or personal gain; the use of such magic was considered bad for a social group because it drew evil spirits in the direction of the community.

The fear of witchcraft persisted for several hundred years, reaching its height of hysteria in the 1500s. Suspicion of witchcraft and the mass execution of suspected practitioners became commonplace during this time. Indeed, during the years between 1273 and 1660, Europe executed thousands of suspected witches, the majority of them women. The total number of persons executed due to witchcraft charges may have exceeded 100,000 (Linder, 2005).

In ancient times, resorting to private revenge was the only avenue of redress for victims who suffered a **private wrong**. These types of wrongs might have included physical injury, damage to a person's property, or theft. In such cases and in many areas of Europe, there was no official authority present; the victim was on his or her own to gain any justice that could be obtained. There was also additional incentive to retaliate against perpetrators, for if the victim was able to gain revenge this was likely to deter the perpetrator from committing future crimes against the victim. However, it is not surprising that in these cases the original perpetrator sometimes fought back against the retaliatory strike from the victim, regardless of who was wrong or right. This would then lead to a continual tit-for-tat situation that might ultimately develop into a perpetual conflict. Once social groups become more advanced, the responsibility for determining punishment shifted from the individual and/or family to society as a whole.

Retaliation Through Humiliation

During early parts of European history, retaliation also occurred through the use of humiliation. A number of punishments were utilized, some of which might even be considered corporal in nature (such as the ducking stool and the stocks and pillories), but they are included in this section because their distinctive factor lies more in their intended outcome: to humiliate and embarrass the offender (Johnson et al., 2008).

One early punishment was the gag, which was a device that constrained persons who were known to constantly scold others (usually their spouse) or were guilty of habitually and abusively finding fault with others, being unjustly critical, or lying about other persons (Silverman, 2001). An even more serious form of retaliatory punishment was the use of the bridle. The

Public wrongs: Crimes against society or a social group.

Private wrongs: Crimes against an individual that could include physical injury, damage to a person's property, or theft.

bridle was an iron cage that fit over the head and included a metal plate in the front. The plate usually had spikes, which were constructed so as to fit into the mouth of the offender; this made movement with the tongue painful and thereby reduced the likelihood that the offender would talk (Silverman, 2001).

The ducking stool was a punishment that used a chair suspended over a body of water. In most cases, the chair hung from the end of a free-moving arm. The offender was strapped into the chair, which was located near a riverbank. The chair would be swung over the river by the use of the free-moving arm and would be plunged into the water while the offender was restrained therein. In most cases, this punishment would be administered during the winter months when the water was extremely cold; this alone was a miserable experience. This was a punishment typically reserved for women—in particular, women who were known to nag others or use profane or abusive language. Women who gossiped were also given this punishment (Johnson et al., 2008).

Another common punishment in the Middle Ages was the stocks and pillories. Stocks consisted of wooden frames that were built outdoors, usually in a village or town square. A set of stocks consisted of a thick piece of lumber that had two or more holes bored into it. The holes were round and wide enough so that an offender's wrists would fit through. The board was cut into halves, and a hinge was used so that the halves could be opened and then closed. The boards would be opened, the offender would be forced to rest his or her wrists into the half-circle of the bottom half of the wooden board, and then the top half would be closed over the wrists. A lock on the side opposite the hinge kept the offender trapped, hands and wrists restrained by the board. The stock was usually constructed atop a beam or post set into the ground so that the offender would have to stand (rather than sit), sometimes for days or, in extreme cases, perhaps weeks.

The pillory was similar to the stock except the pillory consisted of a single large bored hole where the offender's neck would rest. When the pillory was shut and locked, the offender was restrained with his or her head immobilized and body stooped over. The device was specifically set atop a post at a height where most adult offenders could not fully stand up straight, adding to the discomfort of the experience. As with a set of stocks, the offender would be required to stand for several days and nights. In many cases, the offender was constrained by a combination of these devices, known as a stocks and pillory, where both the offender's head and hands were immobilized.

It was at this point that the use of branding became more commonplace. **Branding** was used to make criminal offenders, slaves, and prisoners of war easily identifiable. Offenders were usually branded on their thumb with a letter denoting their offense—for instance, the letter *M* for murder

Branding: Usually on thumb with a letter denoting the offense.

Table 1.1: Types of Punishment in Early Correctional History

Name of Punishment	Purpose	Description
Trial by ordeal	Determine guilt or innocence	Very dangerous and/or impossible tests to prove the guilt or innocence of the accused.
Gag	Humiliation	A device that constrained persons who were known to constantly scold others.
Ducking stool	Humiliation and deterrence	Punishment that used a chair suspended over a body of water.
Stocks	Humiliation	Wooden frames that were built outdoors, usually in a village or town square.
Pillory	Humiliation	Similar to the stock except the pillory consisted of a single large bored hole where the offender's neck would rest.
Branding	Humiliation and warn public	Usually on thumb with a letter denoting the offense.
Whipping	Deterrence	Lashing the body of a criminal offender in front of a public audience.
Capital punishment	Deterrence	Putting the offender to death in front of a public audience.
Banishment and transportation	Deterrence	Exile from society.
Hulk imprisonment	Retribution and incapacitation	Offenders kept in unsanitary decommissioned naval vessels.
Indentured servitude	Retribution and incapacitation	Offender subjected to virtual slavery.

© Charles Stanley Reinhart / Corbis

■ PHOTO 1.2 The ducking stool was one of many punishments used in early America for what were considered fairly minor crimes. In some cases, persons subjected to this punishment drowned to death or froze if the practice was conducted during the winter months.

© J. E. Baker Reinhart / Corbis

■ PHOTO 1.3 The stocks and pillory was an uncomfortable punishment as most offenders were forced to endure this position for several days and nights. During the night, animals, bugs, and local villagers might make the experience all the more miserable, and at all times offenders were subjected to the elements, whether extreme heat, cold, rain, or other inclement conditions.

or *T* for theft. Harkening back to the connection between crime and sin, consider that even as late as the 1700s, the use of branding for humiliation occurred with the crime of adultery. In New Hampshire, a specific statute (1701) held that offenders guilty of adultery would be made to wear a discernable letter *A* on their upper-garment clothing, usually in red, but always in some color that contrasted with the color of the clothing.

Corporal Punishment

Up until the 1700s, corporal punishment tended to be the most frequently used punishment. This punishment was often administered in a public forum to add to the deterrent effect, thereby setting an example to others of what might happen if they were caught in the commission of a similar crime. Naturally, these types of punishment also included purposes of retribution. The most widely used form of corporal punishment was whipping, which dates back to the Romans, the Greeks, and even the Egyptians as a sanction for both judicial and educational discipline. Whippings could range in the number of lashes. A sentence of 100 lashes was, for most offenders, a virtual death sentence as the whipping was quite brutal; the lashes would fall across the back and shoulders, usually drawing blood and removing pieces of flesh.

Capital Punishment

This section will be brief due to more extensive coverage of the death penalty in Chapter 16. Historically speaking, the types of death penalties imposed are many and varied. Some examples include being buried alive (used in Western civilization as well as ancient China), being boiled in oil, being thrown to wild beasts (particularly used by the Romans), being impaled by a wooden stake, being drowned, being shot to death, being beheaded (especially with the guillotine), and being hanged. More contemporary methods include the use of lethal gas or lethal injection. By far, the most frequently used form of execution is hanging, which has been used throughout numerous points in history.

Banishment

In England between 1100 and 1700 there was an overreliance on the death penalty, and during this time the criminal code was nicknamed the "Bloody Code." Though the rich and powerful may have been supportive of the harsh penalties, there was an undercurrent of discontent among numerous scholars, religious groups, and the peasant population over the capricious and continuous use of the death penalty. Thus, **banishment** proved a very useful alternative that became used with increasing regularity in lieu of the death penalty.

Banishment: Exile from society.

The 1600s and 1700s saw the implementation of banishment on a widespread scale. Over time, banishment came in two versions, depending on the country in question and the time period involved. First, banishment could be permanent or temporary. Second, banishment could mean simple exile from the country or exile to and/or enslavement in a penal colony. The development of English colonies in the Americas opened up new opportunities for banishment that could rid England of her criminal problems on a more permanent basis. This form of mercy was generally only implemented to solve a labor shortage that existed within the American colonies, with most offenders shipped to work as indentured servants under hard labor.

■ PHOTO 1.4 The hulk prison ship was usually a vessel that was old and squalid inside. Little if any lighting was provided, and women, children, and men would be imprisoned together. The conditions were filthy, and rodents commonly lived among the offenders trapped therein.

Transporting Offenders

Transportation became a nearly ideal solution to the punishment of criminal offenders because it resolved all of the drawbacks associated with other types of punishment. The costs were minimal, it was difficult (if not impossible) for offenders to return to England, and offenders could become sources of labor for the new colonies. Johnson and his coauthors (2008) note that of those offenders who were subjected to transportation, the majority were male, unskilled, from the lower classes, and had probably resorted to crime due to adverse economic conditions.

Indentured Servitude

Indentured servants in the American colonies included both free persons and offenders. Generally speaking, free persons who indentured themselves received better treatment due to the fact that they had some say in their initial agreement to working requirements prior to being transported to the colonies. Such persons came of their own accord in hope of making a better life in the New World. Most of these persons were poor and had few options in England. Though this meant that their lot was one of desperation, they were still not typically subjected to some of the more harsh treatment that offenders were subjected to when indentured into servitude.

Indentured status was essentially a form of slavery, albeit one that had a fixed term of service. During the time that persons were indentured, they were owned by their employer and could be subjected to nearly any penalty except death. It is estimated that nearly half of all persons who came to the Americas during the 1600s and 1700s were indentured servants (Johnson et al., 2008).

Hulks and Floating Prisons

When the American Revolution began in 1776, there was an abrupt halt to the transporting of convicts to those colonies. Thus, England began to look for new ideas regarding the housing of prisoners. One solution was to house offenders in hulks, which were broken-down, decommissioned war vessels of the British Royal Navy. These vessels were anchored in the River Thames. This practice started with the expectation that England would ultimately defeat the American colonies and the colonies would again be available for transportation. When it became clear that the colonies would maintain their independence, hulks were used as prisons for a more extended period. During the time when hulks were most widely used (1800s), there were over 10 such vessels that held over 5,000 offenders (Branch-Johnson, 1957).

Conditions aboard these decommissioned ships were deplorable. The smell of urine and feces, human bodies, and vermin filled the air. Overcrowding, poor ventilation, and a diet lacking appropriate nourishment left offenders in a constant state of ill health. Punishments for infractions were

advocate for improvements in the conditions of these and other facilities. Howard was impressed with many of the institutions in France and Italy. In 1777, he used those institutions as examples from which he drafted his *State of Prisons* treatise, which was presented to Parliament.

Jeremy Bentham: Hedonistic Calculus

Jeremy Bentham (1748–1832) was the leading reformer of the criminal law in England during the late 1700s and early 1800s, and his work reflected the vast changes in criminological and penological thinking that were taking place at that time. Born roughly a decade after Beccaria, Bentham was strongly influenced by Beccaria's work. In particular, Bentham was a leading advocate for the use of graduated penalties that connected the punishment with the crime. Naturally, this was consistent with Beccaria's ideas that punishments should be proportional to the crimes committed.

Video Link
Jeremy Bentham

Bentham believed that a person's behavior could be determined through scientific principles. He believed that behavior could be shaped by the outcomes that it produced. Bentham contended that the primary motivation for intelligent and rational people was to optimize the likelihood of obtaining pleasurable experiences while minimizing the likelihood of obtaining painful or unpleasant experiences. This is sometimes called the pleasure-pain principle and is referred to as **hedonistic calculus**. Bentham's views are reflected in his reforms of the criminal law in England. Bentham, like Beccaria, believed that punishment could act as a deterrent and that punishment's main purpose, therefore, should be to deter future criminal behavior.

PUNISHMENT DURING EARLY AMERICAN HISTORY: 1700s–1800s

With the exception of William Penn, the penal reformists all came from Europe and did the majority of their work on that continent. Indeed, none of these persons (Montesquieu, Voltaire, Beccaria, Howard, and Bentham) were influential until after Penn's death in 1718. In fact, Beccaria, Howard, and Bentham were not born until after William Penn had passed away, while Montesquieu and Voltaire were in their mid-to-late 20s at this time. The reason that this is important is twofold. First, it is important for students to understand the historical chronological development of correctional thought. Second, this demonstrates that while the American colonies experienced reform in the early 1700s, this reform was lost when the Great Law in Pennsylvania was overturned upon Penn's death in 1718. From the time of Penn's demise until about 1787, penal reform and new thought on corrections largely occurred in Europe, leaving America in a social and philosophical vacuum (Johnson et al., 2008).

Hedonistic calculus: A term describing how humans seem to weigh pleasure and pain outcomes when deciding to engage in criminal behavior.

Old Newgate Prison: First prison structure in America.

This digression in correctional thought continued throughout the 1700s and culminated with what is today a little-known detail in American penological history. The **Old Newgate Prison**, located in Connecticut, was the first official prison in the United States. The structure of this prison reflects the lack of concern for reforming offenders that was common during this era. Old Newgate Prison was crude in design and, in actuality, served two purposes: it was a chartered copper mine and from 1773 to 1827 it was used as a colonial prison. This prison housed inmates underground and was designed to punish the offenders while they were under hard labor. Due to the desire to strengthen security of the facility (successful escape attempts had been made), a brick-and-mortar structure was built around the entry to the mine that consisted of an exterior walled compound and observation/guard towers. Thus, this facility truly was a prison, albeit a crude one. However, it was not built for correctional purposes; *its purpose was solely punishment.*

Wikimedia Commons

■ PHOTO 1.5 Connecticut's Old Newgate Prison (pictured here) was the first official prison in the United States.

FOCUS TOPIC 1.1

Escape From Old Newgate Prison

Just a couple of years before the first shots of the American Revolution were fired, the Connecticut General Assembly decided that what the colony needed most was a good, heavy-duty gaol. In the legislators' wisdom, any new prison would have to meet certain specifications. It would have to be fairly close to Hartford; absolutely escape-proof; self-supporting (i.e., inmates would have to be "profitably employed"); and—most important of all, then as now—cheap to build and maintain.

Near "Turkey Hills," in the region of northern Simsbury (now East Granby), there were some abandoned copper mines that had been sporadically dug with disappointing results since early in the century. The legislature immediately appointed a three-member study commission to "view and explore the copper mines at Simsbury."

The study group was mighty impressed with the prison potential of a many-shafted mine that ran deep under a mountain. Only 18 miles from Hartford, the mine boasted at least one cavern, 20 feet below ground, large enough to accommodate a "lodging room" that was 16 feet square. There were also lots of connecting tunnels where prisoners could be gainfully employed by being made to pick away at the veins of copper ore located there.

Better yet, according to the report, the only access to the mine from outside came from two air shafts: one 25 feet deep and the other 70 feet deep, the latter leading to "a fine spring of water." Still better was the low cost of mine-to-gaol conversion. By October 1773, the government had obtained a lease, carpenters had built the lodging room, and workmen had fitted a heavy iron door into the 25-foot air shaft, 6 feet beneath the surface. In the same month, the Connecticut General Assembly designated the place as "a public gaol or workhouse, for the use of this Colony"; named it Newgate Prison, after London's dismal house of detention; and appointed a "master" (or "keeper") and three "overseers" to administer the gaol.

Only men (never women) who had been convicted of the most dastardly crimes known to the colony—burglary, robbery, counterfeiting or passing funny money, and horse thieving—were eligible for a one-way trip into the state's dank, dark prison without walls. Chosen for the dubious honor of being Newgate's first prisoner was one John Hinson, a 20-year-old man about whom—considering his historic, "groundbreaking" status—surprisingly little is known. Convicted for some unrecorded crime and remanded to Newgate by the Superior Court on December 22, 1773, Hinson spent exactly 18 days in the "escape-proof" gaol before departing quietly for parts unknown. Although no one saw him leave, obviously, there was some evidence that he had used the 70-foot well shaft to climb out of the mine.

As a consequence of the successful escape of Hinson and, 3 months later, three more Newgate prisoners, it was ordered that modifications be undertaken that included, in 1802, the erection of a high stone wall around the prison.

Finally, in September 1827, after almost 54 years of operation, during which well over 800 prisoners were committed to its clammy, subterranean dungeons, Newgate Prison was abandoned, and the remaining inmates were transferred to the new state prison at Wethersfield. Significantly, the last escape attempt occurred on the night before the move to Wethersfield, when a prisoner fell back into the well—and drowned—as he tried to emulate old John Hinson of sainted memory. Coming when it did, at the bitter end of the facility's long, dark history, the death was a tragic, but somehow fitting, reminder of Newgate's most enduring legend.

SOURCE: Philips, D. E. (1992). *Legendary Connecticut: Traditional tales from the nutmeg state.* Willimantic, Conn.: Curbstone Press.

Students are encouraged to read Focus Topic 1.1: Escape From Old Newgate Prison for a very interesting tale and historical account of the development and use of this prison. This prison is hardly mentioned in most texts on American corrections; this should not be the case since this was a very significant development in American penological history. Further, Old Newgate Prison demonstrates how the development of prison construction and correctional thought occurred over the span of years with many lessons that were hard learned. The history of this prison is a critical beginning juncture in American penology and also demonstrates how modifications to prison structure became increasingly important when administering a system designed to keep offenders in custody. As we will see in future chapters, the concern with secure custody plagued correctional professionals throughout subsequent eras of prison development, with custody of the offender being the primary mandate of secure facilities.

The Walnut Street Jail

While the Old Newgate Prison was in full operation in Connecticut, advocates of prison reform in Pennsylvania were gaining momentum after several decades of apparent dormancy. A little over 60 years had elapsed after William Penn's death when, in the late 1780s, an American medical doctor

I. N. Phelps Stokes. Collection of American Historical Prints

■ PHOTO 1.6 The Walnut Street Jail, pictured here, was America's first attempt to actually incarcerate inmates with the purpose of reforming them.

and political activist by the name of Benjamin Rush became influential in the push for prison reform (Carlson et al., 2008). In 1787, Rush, the Quakers, and other reformers met together in what was then the first official prison reform group, the Philadelphia Society for Alleviating the Miseries of Public Prisons (which was later named the Pennsylvania Prison Society), to consider potential changes in penal codes among the colonies (Carlson et al., 2008). This group was active in the ultimate development of the penitentiary wing within the **Walnut Street Jail**, which was established in 1790 (Carlson et al., 2008). This development was America's first attempt to actually incarcerate inmates with the purpose of reforming them. A wing of the jail was designated an official penitentiary where convicted felons were provided educational opportunities, religious services, basic medical attention, and access to productive work activity. Thus, it is perhaps accurate to say that the Walnut Street Jail was also the first attempt at correction in the United States (Carlson et al., 2008). Eventually, counties throughout Pennsylvania were encouraged to transport inmates with long sentences to the Walnut Street Jail. This is thought to be the first move toward the centralization of the prison system under the authority of the state rather than of individual counties, as jails had until this time been organized.

SAGE Journal Article Link
Walnut Street Jail

While the Walnut Street Jail marked a clear victory for prison reformers, the jail (and its corresponding penitentiary wing) eventually encountered serious problems with overcrowding, time management, and organization as well as challenges with the maintenance of the physical facilities. Over time, frequent inmate disturbances and violence led to high staff turnover, and by 1835 the Walnut Street Jail was closed. This icon of reform stayed in operation only 8 years longer than the Old Newgate Prison.

However, it is extremely important that students read the following sentence very carefully: *The Walnut Street Jail was not the first prison in America; rather, it was the first penitentiary.* The difference is that a penitentiary, by definition, is intended to have the offender seek penitence and reform, whereas a prison simply holds an offender in custody for a prolonged period of time.

The Pennsylvania System

During the 1820s, two models of prison operation emerged: the Pennsylvania and Auburn systems (Carlson et al., 2008). These two systems came into vogue as the Old Newgate Prison was closed and once it became fairly clear that the Walnut Street Jail was not a panacea for prison and/or correctional concerns. With the approved allocation of **Western State Penitentiary** and **Eastern State Penitentiary**, the beginning of the Pennsylvania system was set into motion.

Walnut Street Jail: America's first attempt to incarcerate inmates with the purpose of reforming them.

Western State Penitentiary: Part of the Pennsylvania system located outside of Pittsburgh.

Eastern State Penitentiary: Part of the Pennsylvania system located near Philadelphia.

In 1826, the doors of Western State Penitentiary were open for the reception of inmates. The penitentiary opened with solitary cells for 200 inmates, following the original ideal to have solitary confinement without labor (Stanko, Gillespie, & Crews, 2004). However, doubts arose as to whether this would truly have reformative benefits among offenders and if it would be economical. Advocates of Western State Penitentiary contended that solitary confinement would be economical because offenders would repent more quickly, resulting in a reduced need for facilities (Sellin, 1970). While construction of Eastern State Penitentiary continued, planners were careful to learn from the mistakes of Western State Penitentiary. It is because of this that Eastern State Penitentiary has drawn most of the attention when historians and prison buffs talk about the Pennsylvania system of corrections.

In 1829, Eastern State Penitentiary opened. It was designed on a separate confinement system of housing inmates, similar to Western State Penitentiary. This system allowed inmates to reside in their cells indefinitely. Aside from unforeseen emergencies, special circumstances, or medical issues, inmates spent 24 hours a day in their cells. They had interactions with only a few human beings, most of them prison staff.

Eastern State Penitentiary was sometimes referred to as the Cherry Hill facility because it had been built on the grounds of a cherry tree orchard. The original structure had 252 cells, and each was much more spacious than those of Western State Penitentiary. Cells at Eastern were 12 feet long, 7 feet wide, and 16 feet high. The conditions within Eastern were quite humane and well ahead of their time. Indeed, as Johnston (2009) notes,

https://www.flickr.com/photos/jag9889/10213099685

■ PHOTO 1.7 Western State Penitentiary, located outside of Pittsburgh, Pennsylvania, first opened with approximately 200 solitary cells for inmates in 1826.

> Each prisoner was to be provided with a cell from which they would rarely leave and each cell had to be large enough to be a workplace and have attached a small individual exercise yard. Cutting edge technology of the 1820s and 1830s was used to install conveniences unmatched in other public buildings: central heating (before the U.S. Capitol); a flush toilet in each cell (long before the White House was provided with such conveniences); shower baths (apparently the first in the country). (p. 1)

It is clear that the physical conditions of this facility were sanitary even by today's standards. Further, the conditions of day-to-day treatment were also similar to what one might find in some prisons today.

Ultimately, the Pennsylvania system of separate confinement drew substantial controversy. The long periods of solitary confinement resulted in many inmates having emotional breakdowns, and various forms of mental illness emerged due to the extreme isolation. Prison suicide attempts became commonplace within the facility, which, by religious Quaker standards, meant that those inmates would not have their souls redeemed—an obvious failure at reform, both in the material world and in the spiritual world that the Quakers believed in. Eventually, the start of the Civil War made funds less available, and the practice of individual confinement was largely abandoned. Such was the demise of the Pennsylvania system of penitentiary management.

The Auburn System

In 1816, 11 years before Old Newgate Prison closed in 1827, 19 years before the Walnut Street Jail closed in 1835, 10 years prior to the opening of Western State Penitentiary in 1826, and 13 years prior to the opening of Eastern State Penitentiary in 1829, the state of New York opened the Auburn Prison (see Table 1.2). The means that New York used to operate its prisons were different than the modes of operation in Pennsylvania. This alternative system was termed the **Auburn system** or congregate system, and under its provisions inmates were kept in solitary confinement during the evening but were permitted to work together during the day. Throughout all of their activities, inmates were expected to stay silent and were not allowed to communicate with one another by any means whatsoever. Initially, this type of operation was implemented in Auburn Prison and the prison located in Ossining, New York. (Ossining would later be known as Sing Sing Prison.) The Auburn system was a significant turning point in American penology since it redefined much of the point and purpose of a prison facility.

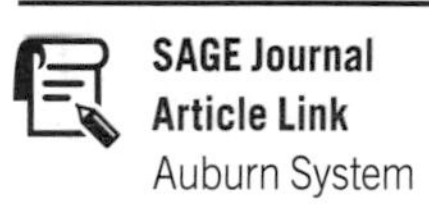
SAGE Journal Article Link
Auburn System

Auburn designs tended to have much smaller cells than the Pennsylvania system, due to the fact that inmates were allowed out of their cells on a daily basis so that they could go to work. Auburn facilities were designed as industry facilities that had some type of factory within them. The economic emphasis throughout the Auburn system was one that became popular among other states and spread throughout the nation. In 1821, Elam Lynds was made warden at Auburn, and

Auburn system: An alternative prison system located in New York.

© Philip Scalia / Alamy Stock Photo

■ PHOTO 1.8 Auburn Prison, in the state of New York, opened in 1816. Today it is still in operation but has been renamed Auburn Correctional Facility.

he was the primary organizer behind the development of the Auburn system. Warden Lynds contended that all inmates should be treated equally, and he believed that a busy and strict regimen was the best way to run a prison. Prison life included lockstep marching and very rigid discipline. It is at this time that the classic white-and-black striped uniforms appeared. All inmates were expected to work, read the Bible, and pray each day. The idea was that through hard work, religious instruction, penitence, and obedience, the inmate would change from criminal behavior to law-abiding behavior (Carlson & Garrett, 2008).

The Auburn system of prison operation initially had economic success due to several factors. First, the proceeds generated from inmate labor aided in offsetting the costs of housing the inmates. Second, the use of the congregate system allowed more productive work to take place—work that often required group effort. Third, other innovations of the Auburn system ensured its profitability. One of these was the use of inmate labor for profit through a **contract labor system**, which eventually became a mainstay feature of the Auburn system. The contract labor system utilized inmate labor through state-negotiated contracts with private manufacturers who provided the prison with raw materials so that prison labor could refine those materials (Roth, 2011). Items such as footwear, carpets, furniture, and clothing were produced through this system.

Two American Prototypes in Conflict

Both the Pennsylvania system and the Auburn system of prison construction and management had achieved attention in Europe by the late 1830s and were seen as unique models of prison management that were distinctly American in thought and innovation (Carlson et al., 2008). It was not long, however, until questions regarding the superiority of one system over the other began to emerge. Both the Pennsylvania system and the Auburn system had potential benefits and drawbacks.

Contract labor system: Utilized inmate labor through state-negotiated contracts with private manufacturers.

Ultimately, the Auburn system was the model that states adopted due to the economic advantages that were quickly realized. In addition, the political climate of the time favored an emphasis on separation, obedience, labor, and silence since sentiments toward crime and criminals were less forgiving during this era. Maintaining a daily routine of hard work was seen as the key to reform. Idleness, according to many advocates of this more stern system, provided convicts with time to teach one another how to commit future crimes. Thus, it was important to keep convicts busy so that they did not have the time or energy to dwell on the commission of criminal activity.

■ Table 1.2: Timeline for the Opening and Closure of Early American Prisons

Prison	Year Opened	Year Closed
Old Newgate Prison	1773	1827
Walnut Street Jail	1790	1835
Auburn Prison	1816	Still open. Renamed Auburn Correctional Facility.
Western State Penitentiary	1826	Closed in 2005 and reopened in 2007. Renamed State Correctional Institution at Pittsburgh.
Eastern State Penitentiary	1829	1971

CORRECTIONS AND THE LAW 1.1

Ruffin v. Commonwealth (1871)

In 1871, the Virginia State Supreme Court noted that an inmate was the "slave of the state" while serving his or her sentence. This case, known as *Ruffin v. Commonwealth* (62, Va. 790, 1871), established what has often been touted as the hands-off doctrine, whereby courts consistently left matters inside prisons to those persons tasked with their operation. Essentially, the courts (including the Supreme Court) stayed out of prison business during this period.

The reason for this approach is understandable. In the year 1871, the Civil War had come to a close just a few years prior, and it was not surprising that prior Confederate states like Virginia would consider inmates to be slaves of the state. However, this same legal principle was equally maintained in both the northern and southern regions of the United States. Much of this also had to do with the fact that issues related to state sovereignty were still a sensitive issue despite the end of the Civil War, and judges did not want to become enmeshed in legal issues that might aggravate an already tenuous situation. With this in mind, most judges refused to intervene on the grounds that their function was limited to freeing those inmates who had been illegally confined, which did not include meddling with the means by which prison administrators operated their facilities.

Thus, prisons operated in a virtual social vacuum, and wardens did not have to be concerned with public sentiments or any type of legal reprisal from inmates or their families. The legal stance of the courts all but ensured that prisons would operate in an unconstitutional manner since there was no incentive to do otherwise and since there was no punishment involved for the mistreatment of inmates. This would remain the case until the "hands-on era" arose alongside the civil rights movement, which ushered in sweeping social changes throughout the nation. The official turning point in which the hands-off doctrine began to be eclipsed came with *Holt v. Sarver* (1969).

There is one last point that should be noted. The ruling in *Ruffin v. Commonwealth* reflects a mentality regarding prisoners that harkens back to ancient Rome. As we have seen in this chapter, the Romans viewed criminals as having a "civil death" while in custody. The rights (or lack thereof) afforded in *Ruffin* are similar, the presumption being that inmates are devoid of any rights or legal standing. It would appear that the legal status of offenders had not changed much throughout the centuries, allowing atrocities and cruel behavior to go unchecked as inmates were held as the invisible slaves of society.

The Southern System of Penology: Before and After the Civil War

The climate and philosophy of southern penology has been captured on the silver screen in several classic prison movies, such as *Cool Hand Luke* and *Brubaker*. Indeed, more modern films, such as *O Brother, Where Art Thou?*, portray southern penology in a manner that is similar to its predecessors. When examining southern penology, it is important to understand the different cultural and economic characteristics of the region, particularly when comparing this type of prison system with the Pennsylvania and New York systems. From a historical, social, and cultural standpoint, students should keep in mind that the slave era took place during the early to mid-1800s (up until 1864 or so), and this impacted the manner in which corrections was handled in the South.

Prior to the Civil War, separate laws were required for slaves and free men who turned criminal. These laws were referred to as **Black Codes**, and they included harsher punishments for crimes than were given to white offenders (Browne, 2010). What is notable is that black slaves were not usually given prison sentences because this interfered with the ability of plantation owners to get labor out of the slave, a commodity desperately needed in the plantation system (Browne, 2010; Roth, 2011). Thus, during the pre–Civil War era, prisons typically had populations that included mostly white inmates with only a few free blacks (Browne, 2010).

After the Civil War, the economy was in ruin, and the social climate was chaotic throughout the southern United States. In a time when things were very uncertain, there were few resources of any sort, and ideas as to how the inmate population should be dealt with were scarce. Because there were not sufficient prison resources, the lease system continued to be implemented and expanded. It is interesting to point out that after the Civil War, over 90% of all leased inmates were in the South (McShane, 1996a, 1996b; Roth, 2011). This was largely due to the political and economic characteristics of the region as well as the termination of slavery that occurred with the South's defeat.

***Holt v. Sarver I* (1969):** Ruled that prison farms in the state of Arkansas were operated in a manner that violated the prohibition against cruel and unusual punishments.

Black Codes: Separate laws were required for slaves and free men who turned criminal.

APPLIED THEORY 1.1

The Subculture of Violence Theory and Corrections

As presented by Wolfgang and Ferracuti (1967), the *subculture of violence theory* has been used to explain violence (particularly homicide) in a number of contexts and for a variety of different social groups. In their effort to explain why some groups are more prone to violence, Wolfgang and Ferracuti utilized elements of social learning theory in their work, contending that the development of favorable attitudes and norms toward violence generally involved some type of learned behavior. According to them, the subculture of violence simply suggests that there is a very clear theme of violence in the lifestyle of subculture members. In laying out their thesis, Wolfgang and Ferracuti proposed a series of tenets or key themes to explaining violent subcultures. A select set of these tenets, and their potential application to the field of corrections, is presented below:

1. The constant state of vigilance and willingness to engage in violence demonstrates how violence permeates that culture and its sense of identity. In this case, the number of incidents where a member engages in violence and the seriousness of that violence can serve as a social barometer of the member's assimilation within the subculture. In such circumstances, the overt use of violence and the use of serious violence (especially homicide) indicate the level of commitment that a member has to that subculture. Obviously, this has very clear implications for modern-day correctional systems that contend with prison gang problems, in which members may be required to commit some act of lethal violence as a requirement for membership and/or to gain an elevated status or rank within the gang.

Wolfgang and Ferracuti (1967) also make a very interesting point to note that among members of a given subculture, one would be able to recognize quantitative differences on psychological instruments and psychometric scales between members who are more prone to violence and those who are not as committed to a belief system grounded in violence. These differences would likely include the differential perception and processing of violent stimuli (including perceived aggressive intent where there is none), levels of compassion and/or remorse for violent acts, and/or differences in cognitive problem-solving skills. This is an important point to consider because this demonstrates how mental health professionals (i.e., psychologists, social workers, and counselors) can play a critical role in the correctional process. The medical model left a lasting legacy whereby mental health interventions became part and parcel of the correctional process.

2. Nonviolence is considered a counternorm. Peaceful approaches to the resolution of conflict are not respected between and among members: For members who do not act in kind to situations that require a violent response, their acceptance by others in the subculture will decrease. In short, cowardice and weakness bring dishonor on the group and on the individual member. In cases where the requirement for violence is considered a particularly strong expectation, members who fail to meet their obligation may themselves be killed by others in the subculture. This is particularly true within some organized crime groups and is also true among some street gangs and prison gangs. Because these values are learned out on the street as they are in prison, this type of thinking is doubly reinforced. However, survival in the violent prison environment can be contingent on adhering to this precept. Thus, inmates who wish to maintain the protection of gang membership while serving time will have to be willing to engage in violence.
3. The various mechanisms of learning inherent to differential association theory and social learning theory apply to violent subcultures; violence is a learned behavior that is reinforced through shared identity and associations that favor violent acts. This tenet explains how norms and values are shaped within the group as a whole and also explain how norms may vary from group to group both in the type and in the lethality of violence as a product of differential associations and differential forms of reinforcement. This holds clear implications for correctional administrators because it is likely that unchecked violence will beget additional violence. Even more interesting is the thought that the use of violence among security staff may magnify the effects of social learning upon many inmates who are subjected to this treatment and who observe it routinely.
4. Within subcultures, the use of violence may not be perceived as wrong behavior and, as a result, is not likely to generate feelings of guilt or remorse among members. This is a very important aspect of this theory and, in actuality, tends to reflect the emotional framework of psychopaths and/or offenders diagnosed with antisocial personality disorder. These groups of offenders tend to have a greater propensity to violence than do other offenders, and,

in many cases, their autonomic nervous systems do not seem to process anxiety, fear, and even guilt or remorse as do other persons in the general population. These offenders will also tend to have psychological and personality characteristics that are quantifiable via psychometric tests, including such characteristics as levels of compassion or remorse (among others). This demonstrates again that the field of psychology provides a number of contributions for correctional systems that process offenders with offenders who are prone toward violence.

SOURCE: Wolfgang, M. E., & Ferracuti, F. (1967). *Subculture of violence: Towards an integrated theory in criminology.* London: Associated Book Publishers.

Eventually, southern states abolished the leasing system and created large prison farms that were reminiscent of the old plantations of the South (Roth, 2006). These farms operated to maximize profits and reduce the costs associated with incarceration of the inmate population. During this time, some major southern penal farms, such as Angola in Louisiana and Cummins in Arkansas, developed a sense of notoriety (Roth, 2006).

Since the majority of the law-abiding citizenry had no concern for the welfare of convicts, both of these systems proved to be lucrative and workable arrangements for businesses and state systems. With this in mind, it is perhaps accurate to say that southern penology took a step backward in correctional advancement and did so in a manner that maximized profit at the expense of long-term reform and crime reduction. Because these systems were profitable, there was no incentive to eliminate abuses.

The Chain Gang and the South

Chain gangs were a common feature within the southern penal system. This type of labor arrangement was primarily used by counties and states to build railroads and levees and to maintain county roads and state highways (Carroll, 1996). Most jurisdictions viewed this type of labor as a way to make money and also reduce overhead in housing inmates. The shackles were never removed from inmates on many chain gangs, and the men would usually sleep chained together in cages (Carroll, 1996).

In addition, the overseers of this system were poorly paid and often illiterate. This meant that, in a manner of speaking, the guard staff became dependent upon this system in which they settled for the substandard wage given as they furthered the cause of a system that exploited even them, though to a lesser extent when compared with the convict (Carroll, 1996). Given these circumstances and the limited skills of the guard staff, the use of brute force and clumsy tactics of inmate control prevailed.

The Western System of Penology

As crime rose in the Wild West, settlers responded by building crude jails in the towns that lay scattered across the desert terrain. These jails were not very secure and typically did resemble how they are often portrayed on American television (Carlson & Garrett, 2008). For the most part, they were used as holding cells, and long-term housing simply did not exist. During these years, most western states were territories that had not achieved statehood, and inmates were usually held in territorial facilities or in federal military facilities (Johnson et al., 2008).

■ PHOTO 1.9 Louisiana State Penitentiary Angola is a sprawling, farm-like state prison that was built on the grounds of a plantation in the South. This prison is now modern and sophisticated in the programming that is offered.

Arizona Leisure Vacation Guide, http://www.arizona-leisure.com/yuma-territorial-prison.html (bottom).

■ PHOTO 1.10 **Yuma prison, pictured here, is reflective of the southwestern style of penology.**

As the need for space became greater, most western states found it more economical and easy to simply contract with other states and with the federal government to take custody of their inmates (Carlson & Garrett, 2008). The western states paid a set cost each year and simply shipped their offenders elsewhere; given the social landscape at the time, this was perhaps the most viable of options that these states could choose. According to Carlson and Garrett (2008), western states paid for other states to maintain custody of their offenders. This allowed western states to avoid the costs of building and maintaining large prisons and/or plantations. As time went on, state governments in the West developed, and the region became more settled. Once this occurred, western states began to build their own prisons. These prisons were designed along the lines of the Auburn system with an emphasis on labor.

THE AGE OF THE REFORMATORY IN AMERICA

In 1870, prison reformers met in Cincinnati and ultimately established the National Prison Association (NPA). This organization was responsible for many changes in prison operations during the late 1800s, which were listed in its Declaration of Principles (Wooldredge, 1996). This declaration advocated for a philosophy of reformation rather than the mere use of punishment, progressive classification of inmates, the use of indeterminate sentences, and the cultivation of the inmate's sense of self-respect—perhaps synonymous with self-efficacy in today's manner of speaking. These innovations eventually became themes in the evolution of American corrections. This meeting and the recommendations that emanated from it were actually quite remarkable for the time period in which this occurred. It was only a handful of years after the Civil War, and the cattle drives and Old West tales had not yet become legend.

The first reformatory, **Elmira Reformatory**, was opened in July 1876 when the facility's first inmates arrived from Auburn Prison. Ironically, the site of the Elmira Reformatory had at one time been a prisoner-of-war camp for captured Confederate soldiers during the Civil War (Brockway, 1912; Wooldredge, 1996). The camp had a vile history, and thousands of southern soldiers died in the squalid, harsh, and brutal environment. However, the use of Elmira in 1876 was one of reform (thus the word *reformatory*), and this ushered in a new era in the field of penology.

The warden of Elmira Reformatory was a man by the name of Zebulon Brockway, who started his career in corrections as a prison guard in a state prison in Connecticut (Brockway, 1912). Brockway contended that imprisonment was designed to reform inmates, and he advocated for individualized plans of reform. During his term as warden, Brockway embarked on perhaps the most ambitious attempts to have the Declaration of Principles implemented within a correctional facility (Wooldredge, 1996). Judges, working within the framework of these principles and adopting an indeterminate sentencing approach, would sentence first-time offenders with modified indeterminate sentences. When serving these sentences, the reform of the offender was monitored, and, if successfully reformed, the offender was released prior to the expiration of the sentence. If the offender did not demonstrate sufficient proof of reform, he simply served the maximum term.

The Elmira Reformatory used a system of classification that had been produced due to Brockway's admiration of the work of Alexander Maconochie, a captain in the British Royal Navy who in 1837 was placed in command over the English penal colony in at Norfolk Island. While serving in this command, Maconochie proposed a system where the duration of the sentence was determined by the inmate's work habits and righteous conduct. Called a **mark system** because "marks" were provided to the convict for each day of successful toil, this system was quite well organized and thought out (Brockway, 1912).

Under this plan, convicts were given marks and were moved through phases of supervision until they finally earned full release. Because of this, Maconochie's system is considered indeterminate in nature, with convicts progressing through five specific phases of classification.

Elmira Reformatory: The first reformatory prison.

Mark system: A system where the duration of the sentence was determined by the inmate's work habits and righteous conduct.

Indeterminate sentences include a range of years that will be potentially served by the offender. The offender is released during some point in the range of years that are assigned by the sentencing judge. Both the minimum and maximum times can be modified by a number of factors, such as offender behavior and offender work ethic. The indeterminate sentence stands in contrast to the use of **determinate sentences**, which consist of fixed periods of incarceration imposed on the offender with no later flexibility in the term that is served. Brockway was a strong advocate of the indeterminate concept and believed that it was critical to turning punishment into a corrective and reformative tool. Ultimately, it was found that these institutions were actually no more successful at molding inmates into law-abiding and productive citizens than were prisons, and by 1910 the reformatory movement began to decline in use.

PRISONS IN AMERICA: 1900s TO THE END OF WORLD WAR II

Prison Farming Systems

The prison farm concept was one that began in Mississippi and then extended throughout a number of southern states. The use of this type of prison operation lasted until well after World War II. As was noted earlier, prison farms were profit driven and based on agricultural production. Even though their particular market was agricultural, much of their operation was similar in approach to industrial prisons; the key difference was simply in the product that was manufactured. Two systems in particular capture the essence of southern prison farming: Arkansas and Texas.

The Arkansas System: Worst of the Worst

The conditions within the Arkansas prison system are thought to be the worst of all those among the southern prison farm era. The Arkansas system actually only consisted of two prison plantations, the Cummins Farm, which covered approximately 16,000 acres of territory, and the Tucker Farm, which spanned about 4,500 acres of territory. Each of these facilities produced rice, cotton, vegetables, and livestock. What made this prison system so particularly terrible was the corruption, brutality, and completely inhumane means of operation that existed.

The Arkansas prison system, similar to the Mississippi prison system, placed inmates in charge of other inmates. In Arkansas, these inmates were referred to as trusties and were at the top of the inmate hierarchy. Civilian employees in the prisons in Arkansas were scarce, meaning that trusties were responsible for most of the day-to-day order on the farm. The trusties served as guards over the other inmates and carried weapons. They also controlled and operated critical services, such as food and medical services. Trusties had their own dormitory to themselves, more freedom than other inmates, and the best food, and they were free to extort other inmates for money, goods, or services. As one might expect, such extortion happened quite frequently.

The overall supervisor of this system was the superintendent, whose primary role was to ensure that the prison farm operated at a profit. This meant that the superintendent tended to provide all authority to the trusties, so long as they made the prison a profit. The control of desperate, underfed, exhausted, and often ill inmates was maintained through a process of constant punishment. Some of these punishments were nothing less than the use of torture. Punishments included whipping; the inmate's fingers, nose, ears, or genitals being pinched with pliers; and even inserting needles under the inmate's fingernails. One of the most infamous forms of torture used was the "Tucker Telephone." This device is discussed in greater detail in Technology and Equipment 1.1.

The Progressive Era

From 1900 to 1920, numerous reforms took place across the United States, and this led to some dubbing this period the Age of Reform. For prison operations, the Age of Reform reflected an era of change and attention to humane treatment of inmates. During the **Progressive Era**, a particularly influential group, known as the Progressives, cast attention on social problems throughout the nation and sought to improve the welfare of the underprivileged. The members of this group remained steadfast in the belief that understanding deviant behavior lay with social and psychological causes, and they also contended that social and psychological treatment programs were the key to offender reform. Due to this line of thought and the influence of the Progressives, the field of penology eventually included psychologists, social workers, and psychiatrists in addition to lawyers and security staff.

Indeterminate sentences: Sentences that include a range of years that will be potentially served by the offender.

Determinate sentences: Consist of fixed periods of incarceration with no later flexibility in the term that is served.

Progressive Era: A period of extraordinary urban and industrial growth and unprecedented social problems.

Glenys Gustin/iStock/Thinkstock

■ PHOTO 1.11 The Big House was typically a large stone structure with brick walls, guard towers, and checkpoints throughout the facility. The key architectural feature of Big House prisons was the use of concrete and steel. Many were several stories in height.

The Era of the "Big House"

The Big House era lasted from the early 1900s to just before the emergence of the civil rights movement.

Big House prisons were typically large stone structures with brick walls, guard towers, and checkpoints throughout the facility. The key architectural feature to Big House prisons was the use of concrete and steel. The cell blocks sometimes had up to six levels, making the entire structure large and foreboding. The interior of each cell block often was extremely hot and humid during the summer months and cold during the winter months. In addition, these structures magnified noise levels, creating echoes throughout as steel doors and keys clanged open and shut, announcements were made, and machinery operated within the facility.

The Medical Model

During the 1930s, another perspective emerged regarding inmate treatment and the likelihood for reform. The medical model developed in tandem with the rise of the behavioral sciences in the field of corrections (Carlson et al., 2008). The **medical model** can be described as correctional treatment that utilizes a type of mental health approach incorporating fields such as psychology and biology; criminality is viewed as the result of internal deficiencies that can be treated. The key to the medical model is understanding that it is rehabilitative in nature.

The medical model was officially implemented in 1929 when the U.S. Congress authorized the Federal Bureau of Prisons to open correctional institutions that would use standardized processes of classification and treatment regimens within their programming. One early proponent of the medical model and its clinical approach to rehabilitation was Sanford Bates, who was the first director of the Bureau of Prisons and had also served as a past president of the American Correctional Association (students will recall that this was originally named the National Prison Association in 1870).

At the heart of the medical model was the classification process; everything in the medical model that followed hinged on the accuracy and effectiveness of this process. The developers of the process believed that such a systematic approach would improve treatment outcomes and overall recidivism among offenders. However, as Carlson et al. (2008) note, "Although classification was one of the greatest concepts invented during this period, it became at best a management process rather than a reliable tool to aid in rehabilitation" (p. 13). This, unfortunately, emerged as the truth across the nation, and classification ultimately became a systematic process for housing and to aid institutional and community-based professionals in managing the inmate population rather than for changing the inmates' behavior.

Big House prisons: Typically large stone structures with brick walls, guard towers, and checkpoints throughout the facility.

Medical model: An approach to correctional treatment that utilizes a type of mental health approach incorporating fields such as psychology and biology.

Reintegration model: Used to identify programs that looked to the external environment for causes of crime and the means to reduce criminality.

The Reintegration Model

The **reintegration model** evolved during the last few years that the medical model was still in vogue. The term *reintegration* was used to identify programs that looked to the external environment for causes of crime and the means by which criminality could be reduced. This model was commonly used during the 1960s and 1970s as an alternative to punitive approaches that were gaining momentum. However, as crime continued to rise, strong skepticism of both the medical model and the reintegration model became commonplace. One of the sharpest and most distinctive blows to both of these models "was a rather infamous negative report produced in the early 1970s by a researcher studying rehabilitation programs across the country" (Carlson et al., 2008, p. 16). This report was the work of Robert Martinson, who had conducted a thorough analysis of research programs on behalf of the New York State Governor's Special Committee on Criminal Offenders.

Martinson (1974) examined a number of various programs that included educational and vocational assistance, mental health treatment, medical treatment, and early release. In his report, often referred to as the **Martinson Report**, he noted that "with few and isolated exceptions, the rehabilitative efforts that have been reported so far have had no appreciable effect on recidivism" (Martinson, 1974, p. 22). Martinson's work was widely disseminated and used as ammunition for persons opposed to treatment, whether individual- or community-based. Thus, skepticism of rehabilitation and/or reintegration rose to its pinnacle as practitioners cited (often in an inaccurate manner) the work of Robert Martinson.

Audio Link
Reintegration

The Crime Control Model

The **crime control model** emerged during a "get tough" era on crime. The use of longer sentences, more frequent use of the death penalty, and an increased use of intensive supervised probation all were indicative of this era's approach to crime. The use of determinate sentencing laws took the discretion from many judges so that, like it or not, sentences were awarded at a set level regardless of the circumstances associated with the charge. Increasingly, states and the federal government are realizing that the approach of the crime control era may have been a bit too ambitious, particularly since states cannot afford, in the current state of the economy, to pay the bills for the long-term incarceration that has been invoked under this approach.

Web Link
Mass Incarceration

MODERN-DAY SYSTEMS: FEDERAL AND STATE INMATE CHARACTERISTICS

The Federal Bureau of Prisons (BOP) was initially established by Congress in 1930 and has since that time become a highly centralized organization with over 33,000 employees who supervise more than 209,000 inmates. The federal system has over 100 facilities that include maximum-security prisons, supermax facilities, detention centers, prison camps, and even halfway houses. The variety of correctional services provided by this system is much greater than what most state systems provide (Federal Bureau of Prisons, 2010).

Since the War on Drugs that occurred during the 1980s, the proportion of drug offenders has remained high, constituting more than half of the BOP population (Carson, 2014). However, unlike state prisoners, most federal offenders are not violent, and their drug crimes are also not usually associated with violence. Also interesting is that roughly 12% of all federal inmates are citizens of other countries (Carson, 2014). As an indicator of the types of crimes and the types of criminals that tend to be included in the federal system, consider that 54% of federal inmates are classified as being either a low- or minimum-security risk, with the average time served for BOP inmates being around 6.5 years in length (Federal Bureau of Prisons, 2010b).

Within state correctional systems, there is quite a bit of variety, in terms of both their operation and the inmates that they house. The size of prisons within one state can have a great degree of variability. The Louisiana State Penitentiary (Angola) houses over 5,000 inmates (more than the entire state of North Dakota), while other prisons in other states may house fewer than 1,000 inmates. A wide variety of types of facilities may be included in a state system, just as with the federal system described previously. Additionally, working for one state prison system can be quite different from working for another in terms of salary, training, opportunities, and so forth.

In late 2012, national statistics indicated that more than half of all state prison inmates were violent offenders, while more than half of federal inmates were drug offenders (Carson, 2014). To make matters worse for state systems that house these difficult populations, consider that state budgets tend to not be as large as the federal budget, so funding is often an issue that keeps state systems from operating as effectively as the BOP. This also means that working conditions, salaries, and training among state prison staff tend to vary, though the American Correctional Association has been very influential in professionalizing the field of corrections throughout numerous states. All in all, state corrections tends to be the most common form of corrections, but, despite advances, these systems do not fare as well as the BOP.

It is also important to note that the majority of inmates are housed in state prison systems. Among these, most are in custody in one of the seven largest prison systems. The largest three systems each have over 100,000 inmates, including Texas (168,000 inmates), California (135,000

Martinson Report: An examination of a number of various prison treatment programs.

Crime control model: An approach to crime that increased the use of longer sentences, the death penalty, and intensive supervision probation.

TECHNOLOGY AND EQUIPMENT 1.1

The Tucker Telephone

The "Tucker Telephone" was a torture device invented in Arkansas and regularly used at the Tucker State Prison Farm (now the Tucker Unit of the Arkansas Department of Correction) in Jefferson County. It was likely used on inmates until the 1970s.

The Tucker Telephone consisted of an old-fashioned crank telephone wired in sequence with two batteries. Electrodes coming from it were attached to a prisoner's big toe and genitals. The electrical components of the phone were modified so that cranking the telephone sent an electric shock through the prisoner's body. The device was reputedly constructed in the 1960s by, depending upon the source, a former trusty in the prison, a prison superintendent, or an inmate doctor; it was administered as a form of punishment, usually in the prison hospital. In prison parlance, a "long-distance call" was a series of electric shocks in a row.

The name Tucker Prison evoked scenes of sadism and brutality prior to the prison reform initiatives put forward by Governor Winthrop Rockefeller. According to a February 20, 1967, *Newsweek* report, inmates were punished with beatings, whippings, torture with pliers, and needles put under their fingernails, in addition to the use of the Tucker Telephone. Much of the abuse was carried out by guards and the prison trusties who reported to them. The 1980 movie *Brubaker*, loosely inspired by events within the Arkansas prison system, depicts an inmate named Abraham being tortured with the Tucker Telephone.

Devices similar to the Tucker Telephone have been employed up to the present day. A Tucker Telephone was allegedly used in a Chicago violent crime unit managed by Lieutenant Jon Burge to torture suspects during the 1980s. During the Vietnam War, some American GIs reportedly converted their field phones into torture devices, and something like the Tucker Telephone was used by American interrogators to torture Iraqi prisoners at Abu Ghraib prison.

SOURCE: Lancaster, G. (2009). Tucker Telephone. Little Rock, AR: Central Arkansas Library System. Reprinted by permission of the Encyclopedia of Arkansas History and Culture.

inmates), and Florida (103,000 inmates), and all three are significantly larger than the other 47 state systems to which they can be compared (Carson, 2014). The remaining four of the largest seven systems each house between 50,000 and 55,000 inmates and include the states of Georgia, New York, Ohio, and Pennsylvania (Carson, 2014). Collectively, these four prison systems house approximately 210,000 inmates (Carson, 2014). All of the other states were reported to house less than 49,000 inmates, with most housing substantially less than this number.

The Emergence of the Top Three in Corrections

This term the *Top Three in corrections* is an apt description of the three largest state correctional systems in the United States. Texas is the largest system, California is the next largest, and Florida is third (Carson, 2014). These systems are referred to as the Top Three due to the fact that they are the largest three systems according to inmate count. We will not discuss each state individually. Rather, students should understand that the Top Three in corrections are important for a number of reasons that go beyond their mere head count.

First, these three states have large overall free-world populations as well as prison populations. This means that each of these states has a large population that is likely to be more representative of the overall U.S. population than would be the case for numerous other states. When taken in total, these three states should be considered somewhat representative of the overall U.S. population. Because they are representative, this means that research conducted from samples taken from these three states will, collectively, be likely to yield results that generalize to the rest of the United States.

Second, each of these states has had to grapple with immigration issues and the constant ingress and egress of legal and illegal persons within its borders. This is a unique characteristic that is not shared by a majority of the states. While other states may also struggle with this issue, the Top Three do so on a large-scale basis. This makes a difference because of the type of crime problems that are encountered (i.e., more drug trafficking, smuggling issues, and organized crime activity) as well as the factors that are associated with those problems (more drug use, cultural clashes, and more complicated crime problems). Third, these states all possess a truly diverse array of racial and cultural groups. The history of each of the Top Three reflects exchanges between various cultures. In all three states, the Latino population is well represented, as are the African American and Asian American populations. Other racial and cultural groups are likewise represented in each of these three states, partially due to routine immigration and also due to the unique histories of the states.

Fourth and lastly, each of these three states tends to have a fairly robust economy. The market conditions in all are active and vibrant due to their locations (all have extensive coastlines) and due to a sufficient number of urban areas within their borders. The fact that these three states tend to have more stable economies (at least throughout most of their history) impacts how well they are able to fund their correctional programs. This can make a considerable difference in the overall approach to a correctional agency's response in processing the offender population.

CONCLUSION

Corrections is a term that has origins in the need and/or desire to punish those who commit an aberrant behavior that is proscribed by society. Indeed, the terms *punishment* and *corrections* have shared common meanings throughout history. This text presents the term *corrections* as a process whereby practitioners from a variety of agencies and programs use tools, techniques, and facilities to engage in organized security and treatment functions intended to correct criminal tendencies among the offender population.

In ancient times, the ability of an aggrieved party to gain retribution for a crime required some form of retaliation. In most cases, individuals or groups only achieved retribution if they were able to personally extract it from the offender. Later, over time, rulers of various groups organized processes of achieving retribution, thereby reducing the likelihood that conflicts between individuals and groups would escalate. Regardless of the type of customs that existed in various areas of Europe, the use of physically humiliating punishments and crippling punishments was still widespread. When examining the history of punishment and corrections, it is clear that early forms of punishment were quite barbaric when compared with those today.

The rise of the Enlightenment and the writings of a variety of scholars and philosophers helped shape the use of simple punishments from barbaric cruelty to corrective mechanisms intended to reduce problematic behaviors. Further, a distinct sense of rationality was used in administering punishments, and new concepts were introduced. One of the premiere figures who advocated the use of reason was Cesare Beccaria. It was Beccaria who advocated for proportionality between the crime committed and the punishment received. Beccaria also contended that it was the certainty of punishment, not the severity, that would be more likely to deter crime. These novel concepts, as well as the contention that offenders should be treated humanely, marked the Enlightenment and the emergence of prison reform in Europe and the United States.

As prison development in America began, two competing mind-sets emerged: the Pennsylvania and Auburn systems of prison operation. Numerous dichotomies and disagreements in philosophy as to the rightful goal of prisons emerged as the Pennsylvania system and the Auburn system competed. The intent of the Pennsylvania system was strictly to reform offenders. On the other hand, the primary motive behind the Auburn system had a business-model perspective—prisons should be self-sufficient or as close to self-sufficient as possible. Ultimately, the money-making option was more compatible with the capitalist notions of the United States, and the Auburn system gave way to the penal farm, particularly in the southern United States.

The profit motive ultimately drove southern states to implement the farming prison, while the northeastern areas of the nation adopted the use of prison industries. In both cases, inmates were leased out to private businesses that could make a profit off of inmate labor. This again highlighted the impact of the Auburn system. In the South, the use of prison farms became reminiscent of the old plantation era prior to the Civil War, and, in fact, some prisons were built right on the grounds of prior plantations. The traditions in the South, along with racial discrimination and disparity and poor economic circumstances, served to replicate many of the injustices that occurred in the prior slave era, just under a different guise.

The Big House era emerged from the prison industry model, but, unlike the prison industry or the prison farming approach, inmates in the Big House were not put through grueling labor, and they were not subjected to the same level of rule setting as inmates in the past. Eventually, the Big House era, the prison industry model, and the prison farm model gave way to the state and federal systems that we now have in place. In 1930, the Federal Bureau of Prisons was established and has emerged as a premiere correctional agency. Among state prisons systems, three states (Texas, California, and Florida) are by far the largest of the state systems, with each exceeding 100,000 inmates. These three states collectively include nearly one-third of the entire state inmate population throughout the nation. Because of this, any research or other generalization made about corrections in the United States should, at least for the most part, include each of these states as an object of interest. Going further, these systems, along with four others that combined include another approximately 210,000 inmates, house most of the violent offenders throughout the United States despite the tight correctional budgets with which they must operate.

Want a better grade?

Get the tools you need to sharpen your study skills. Access practice quizzes, eFlashcards, video, and multimedia at **edge.sagepub.com/hanser2e**

SAGE edge™

DISCUSSION QUESTIONS

1. Identify *punishment* and identify *corrections*. How does each differ from the other, and why are they often confused with one another?
2. How has punishment progressed from ancient and medieval times to current practices? Are there still similarities in thought, and, if so, what are they?
3. Identify key thinkers and persons of influence who have impacted the field of corrections. For each, be sure to highlight their particular contribution(s) to the field.
4. What is the significance of Old Newgate Prison? What distinguishes this structure from the penitentiary wing added to the Walnut Street Jail? Why is Old Newgate Prison important to correctional history in the United States?
5. Explain how the classical school of criminology, behavioral psychology, and the field of corrections can be interrelated in reforming offender behavior.
6. What are some key differences between the Pennsylvania and Auburn prison systems?
7. How did different regions vary in their approaches to prison operations? Compare at least two regions.
8. What is meant by the Top Three in American corrections, and why is this important?

SAGE edge™ **Test your understanding of chapter content. Take the practice quiz.**

KEY TERMS

Auburn system, 15
Banishment, 8
Big House prisons, 22
Black Codes, 17
Branding, 7
Brutalization hypothesis, 3
Classical criminology, 11
Code of Hammurabi, 4
Contract labor system, 16
Corrections, 2
Crime control model, 23
Determinate sentences, 21
Eastern State Penitentiary, 14
Elmira Reformatory, 20
Great Law, 10
Hedonistic calculus, 12
Indeterminate sentences, 21
Lex talionis, 4
Mark system, 20
Martinson Report, 23
Medical model, 22
Old Newgate Prison, 12
Private wrongs, 6
Progressive Era, 21
Public wrongs, 6
Reintegration model, 22
Sanctuary, 5
Trial by ordeal, 4
Walnut Street Jail, 14
Western State Penitentiary, 14

SAGE edge™ **Review key terms with eFlashcards.**

KEY CASE

Holt v. Sarver I (1969), 17

APPLICATION EXERCISE 1.1

Student Debate

Many people in society believe that incarcerated offenders should be made to work as a means of paying for their crime and supporting their stay while in prison. This, in and of itself, is not a problematic notion. However, inmates must be given humane working conditions, and, as a result, there are limits to the type of work they can do and the circumstances under which it is done.

The ancient Romans essentially considered the inmate to be civilly dead and to also be a slave of the state. Though modern-day thinking by prison management does not advocate for inmates to hold such an arbitrary classification, some might say that such a classification is appropriate for offenders.

For this exercise, have half the room or forum argue for classifying offenders as slaves of the state and the other half argue against categorizing inmates in such a way.

Students should keep in mind some of the counterintuitive findings when punishment is too severe, and they should also consider the thoughts of Cesare Beccaria and other philosophers on corrections. Both teams of students should come up with at least three substantial points to argue for the side they have been assigned.

Group 1: Half of the students in the classroom (or the online forum) provide tangible and logical reasons for why inmates should be treated as slaves of the state.

Group 2: Have the other half of the room or forum argue against categorizing inmates as slaves of the state.

The instructor should regulate the debate and encourage students to find specific examples from the text and/or their own independent research.

WHAT WOULD YOU DO?

You are a judge in Old England, the year is 1798, and the Crown has given you some very explicit instructions for this week. It appears that there is no room onboard the hulks that float in the River Thames, and, due to the traitorous rebellion of the American colonies in the New World, there is nowhere to transport criminals for banishment. With this in mind, the Crown is desperate to reduce criminal acts and has recently decided that the best means to do this is by setting some very strong and severe examples to the public. Thus, you have been told that you must use one of two sentences today: provide the death penalty for anyone found guilty of any crime that is eligible for it or find those persons innocent of their charges and thereby make invalid the need for any punishment whatsoever. In other words, you must either rule innocence or give all the offenders in your court the death penalty.

This is during a time when England's criminal code has been given the nickname of the "Bloody Code" among the commoners of the British Empire. You are well aware that there is serious discontent among the peasantry in your area with this code and that the Crown has previously approached the extensive use of the gallows with trepidation; such circumstances can breed riots and, in very extreme times, rebellion. On the other hand, you know that many of the wealthy in the area are typically supportive of harsh penalties against the working poor (such penalties discourage theft of their own property). You sit at your bench, waiting to make your determination regarding three offenders who are accused of different crimes. All of the crimes for which they are accused would entail the use of the death penalty. These three offenders and their circumstances are noted as follows:

Offender 1: Mr. Drake Dravies, a brigand and a buccaneer who deflowered a 10-year-old girl against her will and attempted to kill her but was caught before doing so. *You know for a fact that this man committed this crime.*

Offender 2: Ms. Eliza Goodberry, a single spinster maid who worked in the fish market. She was found guilty of being a witch and consorting with demons. It is rumored that she gave secret birth to a demon child. *You know for a fact that this woman did not commit this crime, and you know that she is not a witch.*

Offender 3: Mr. John McGraw, a general laborer who stole food in the open market (and almost got away with it) to feed his family. Labor shortages and tough economic times have left him with few other options. *You know for a fact that this man committed this crime, and you also know that it is true that he committed this crime simply to feed his family.*

You must make a decision: either you must declare all three innocent of the crimes as charged, or you must give all three the death penalty by hanging at the gallows. There is no option to try these persons for these crimes at a later date.

What do you do?

IDEOLOGICAL AND THEORETICAL UNDERPINNINGS TO SENTENCING AND CORRECTIONAL POLICY

©iStockphoto.com/Wesley VanDinter

THE ORIGINAL GANGSTA

It was about 3:00 a.m., and Desmond's cellie, Tederick, was up on the top bunk, keeping watch. Desmond took out the shank hidden behind the toilet and worked it back and forth against his metal bunk. The noise from the continuous friction was loud enough to be heard in the cell but not so loud as to resonate throughout the entire cellblock.

Tederick continued to look out the cell onto the run below to see if the guard or anyone else was listening or aware of what was happening. All was quiet, including the cells next to theirs. The other inmates knew what was going on and minded their own business if they were awake; others slept through the noise.

Tederick asked Desmond, "So, you gonna' get him in the rec yard or in the dayroom?"

Desmond replied, "I'm going to hit him in the rec yard."

Desmond thought about the situation and how he was going to get the blade to the rec yard. The inmate that he was going to "hit," Cedric Jackson, was a member of an opposing gang who had been talking smack. Both Desmond and Cedric were members of small, local gangs in New Orleans; neither was affiliated with large gangs like the Crips or the Bloods.

Desmond had lived a life of poverty in New Orleans, and his father had died in prison. His mother did her best, working odd jobs and raising three kids as a single mom. Desmond's cousin, Nate, always had a strong influence on Desmond. Nate had a car with really fly rims, he had women, he had dope, and he had respect on the streets. But now Nate was at Angola, doing real time, and he was writing letters to Desmond to take care of some "business" for him.

Tederick looked down at Desmond and said, "I thought that you wanted to go to school and hook up with that girl?"

"Yeah, that's what I wanna do," Desmond responded.

"Then if you make this hit on Cedric to get even for Nate, you gonna be in here for a long time; maybe you should forget about ole girl and just go to school a few years from now."

Desmond thought about this. He considered how Nate had always had "stuff" when on the streets but was now stuck in Angola for at least another 15 years.

Desmond also thought about his "ole girl," Angela, and all the letters she had sent him. His mom thought well of Angela and they both had seen to it that when he got out he would be able to get settled and get a job with a nearby warehouse (his mom worked there in the administrative office). Angela would even help him get started in school.

Tederick spoke again. "You know that they are really looking at giving more good time for the drug treatment programs, don't you? The feds and the state are reducing sentences, giving more good time, and closing down prisons. . . . This is a good time to be doing time 'cause you can get out early, right?"

LEARNING OBJECTIVES:

1. Identify and discuss the philosophical underpinnings associated with correctional processes.
2. Identify and discuss different types of sanctions used in correctional operations.
3. Evaluate the outcomes of different sentencing schemes.
4. Apply criminological theories to different correctional processes.
5. Integrate philosophical underpinnings, types of sanctions, sentencing schemes, and criminological theories to develop a multifaceted understanding of corrections.

Desmond frowned. "Yeah, I guess so. What are you trying to say?"

Tederick shook his head. "Man, I am saying to hell with Nate and to hell with doing time for Nate. . . . You gotta do you, man, and get on with your life. Let Nate take care of his own business. Let Cedric run his mouth. He is getting shipped soon, anyway, and you can be out in 6 months if you play your cards right." Locking eyes with Desmond, Tederick urged, "Look man, you got a girl on the outside who cares about you, a mom who can get you a job, and you might be in school within a year, or you can sit and rot some more in here. That might be what you want, but it ain't for me, no sir!" His voice rose and he slapped his hand down on his mattress. "I am not lettin' THE MAN take my life from me, and I ain't letting all the wrong learning I got from the streets decide my life for me! You shouldn't either, homie!"

Desmond snorted. "Fine, so I let him make it; I give him a break. . . . What then; what about the gang?"

"You give me the steel and I can get rid of it. I got 3 more years, but you can be out in 6 months. Do the drug program that just accepted you and do it *for real*; then get a real life, not this hell hole. Forget the gang; right now you do not owe them. . . . It is all square business at this point. Go further with it, and you won't ever get out of it."

Desmond turned the shank over in his hands as he considered Tederick's words. He stood, looked at his cellie, and said, "You know, I ain't never had many real friends." After only a moment's hesitation, he extended the homemade blade, handle first, and dropped it onto Tederick's open palm.

Tederick smiled. "My brother, you are doing the right thing; trust me."

INTRODUCTION

This chapter focuses on the reasons for providing correctional services in today's society. In considering these reasons, it is important to understand two key aspects related to corrections. First, it is helpful to be familiar with the historical developments related to punishment and corrections. Chapter 1 provided information about how our current views on correctional practices have evolved. Understanding the history of corrections helps us to make sense of today's correctional system. This is true for legal precedent that shapes correctional policies as well as philosophical and/or political motives behind our use of correctional resources. Thus, it is the rich history of corrections that has shaped it into what we know today.

The second aspect is the need for a clear definition of the term *corrections*. As demonstrated in Chapter 1, this term can have many different meanings to many different practitioners, scholars, and researchers around the world. Nevertheless, it is important to be able to define the term in a clear and succinct manner so that one can correctly connect it with the means by which correctional practices are implemented and the reasons for implementing them. This is essential since this is what will provide clarity in purpose, which, in turn, should lead to clarity in action.

PHILOSOPHICAL UNDERPINNINGS

Within the field of corrections itself, four goals or philosophical orientations of punishment are generally recognized. These are retribution, deterrence, incapacitation, and treatment (rehabilitation). Two of these orientations focus on the offender (treatment and specific deterrence), while the others (general deterrence, retribution, and incapacitation) are thought to focus more on the crime that was committed. The intent of this section of the chapter is to present philosophical bases related to the correctional process. In doing this, it is useful to first provide a quick and general overview of the four primary philosophical bases of punishment (see Table 2.1). These bases were touched upon in Chapter 1 but are now provided in more detail and with the purpose of elucidating the true purposes and rationales behind the correctional process.

Retribution

Retribution is often referred to as the "eye for an eye" mentality, and it simply implies that offenders committing a crime should be punished in a like fashion or in a manner that is commensurate with the severity of the crime that they have committed. As discussed in Chapter 1, retribution is the justification for punishment by the concept of *lex talionis*. It is a "just desserts" model that demands that punishments match the degree of harm that criminals have inflicted on their victims (Stohr, Walsh, & Hemmens, 2009). Thus, those who commit minor crimes deserve minor sentences, and those who commit serious crimes deserve more severe punishments (Stohr et al., 2009). This model of punishment is grounded in the idea that, regardless of any secondary purpose that punishment might be intended to serve, it is right to punish offenders because justice demands it. In essence, society has an ethical duty and obligation to enforce the prescribed punishment; otherwise the sentencing process is based on lies and exceptions.

It is important that students not equate retribution with the mere practice of primitive revenge; retribution has many distinctions that set it apart from such a simplistic understanding. Retribution is constrained revenge that is tempered with proportionality and enacted by a neutral party. This neutral party is required to stay within the bounds of laws that afford offenders certain rights despite the fact that they are to be punished. As we have seen in Chapter 1, the use of this formalized method of punishment emerged out of the chaotic times where blood feuds and retaliation for private wrongs abounded. Retribution was grounded in

Retribution: Offenders committing a crime should be punished in a way that is equal to the severity of the crime they committed.

the notion that the offender (or the offender's family) must pay for the crime committed. The need to keep feuds from escalating between aggrieved families was important among the ruling class. Thus, retribution was designed to adhere to a rational process of progressive sanctions, separating it from mere retaliation.

In addition, when we hold offenders accountable for their actions, we make the statement that we (as a society) believe that offenders are free moral agents who have self-will. It is the responsibility of the offender, not society, to pay for the crime that has been committed. Once this payment (whatever the sanction might be) has been made, there is no further need for punishment. While this type of approach works well in justifying punishment of offenders who are culpable and cognizant of their crime, it is not appropriate for offenders who have mental deficiencies and/or mitigating circumstances that remove fault from them. It is in these cases where retribution loses its logical application within the punishment or correctional process.

■ PHOTO 2.1 One example of retribution would be having someone who vandalized property work to repair the damage he or she caused.

Incapacitation

Incapacitation simply deprives offenders of their liberty and removes them from society with the intent of ensuring that society cannot be further victimized by them during their term of incarceration. The widespread use of incapacitation techniques during the 1990s is purported by some experts to be the cause for the drop in crime that was witnessed after the year 2000. Though this has not been proven, the argument does seem to possess some potential validity. Regardless, it has become increasingly clear that the use of mass incarceration efforts simply cannot be afforded by most state budgets. This has led to more increased use of community corrections techniques and techniques of selective incapacitation.

Selective incapacitation is implemented by identifying inmates who are of particular concern to public safety and by providing those specific offenders with much longer sentences than would be given to other inmates. The idea is to improve the use of incapacitation through more accurate identification of those offenders who present the greatest risk to society. This then maximizes the use of prison space and likely creates the most cost-effective reduction in crime since monies are not spent housing less dangerous inmates.

Video Link
Incapacitation

Incapacitation: Deprives offenders of their liberty and removes them from society, ensuring that they cannot further victimize society for a time.

Selective incapacitation: Identifying inmates who are of particular concern to public safety and providing them with much longer sentences.

Deterrence

Deterrence is the prevention of crime by the threat of punishment (Stohr et al., 2009). Deterrence can be general or specific. **General deterrence** is intended to cause vicarious learning whereby observers see that offenders are punished for a given crime and so they are discouraged from committing a similar crime due to fear of punishment. **Specific deterrence** is simply the infliction of a punishment upon a specific offender in the hope that that particular offender will be discouraged from committing future crimes. For specific deterrence to be effective, it is necessary that a punished offender make a conscious connection between an intended criminal act and the punishment suffered as a result of similar acts committed in the past.

Stohr et al. (2009) note that the effect of punishment on future behavior also must account for the contrast effect, a notion that distinguishes between the circumstances of the possible punishment and the life experience of the person who is likely to get punished. As they explain it,

> For people with little or nothing to lose, an arrest may be perceived as little more than an inconvenient occupational hazard, an opportunity for a little rest and recreation, and a chance to renew old friendships, but for those who enjoy a loving family and the security

General deterrence: Punishing an offender in public so other observers will refrain from criminal behavior.

Specific deterrence: The infliction of a punishment upon a specific offender in the hope that he/she will be discouraged from committing future crimes.

■ PHOTO 2.2 It is hoped that placing offenders in such noxious circumstances will deter them from further criminal behavior. There is no actual empirical proof that this is the case.

of a valued career, the prospect of incarceration is a nightmarish contrast. Like so many other things in life, deterrence works least for those who need it the most. (2009, p. 10)

Thus, it appears that deterrence has as much to do with *who* is being deterred as it does with *how* deterrence is being implemented. However, research on the effectiveness of deterrence has generally been mixed, even during the mid-1990s to about 2006 (Kohen & Jolly, 2006), when the use of increased incarceration was touted to be the primary cause for lowered crime rates. It is still seemingly impossible to determine whether a deterrent effect, or simply an incapacitation effect, was being observed.

Rehabilitation

Rehabilitation implies that an offender should be provided the means to achieve a constructive level of functioning in society, with an implicit expectation that such offenders will be deterred from reoffending due to their having worthwhile stakes in legitimate society—stakes that they will not wish to lose as a consequence of criminal offending. Vocational training, educational attainment, and/or therapeutic interventions are used to improve the offender's stakes in prosocial behavior. The primary purpose of rehabilitation is solely the recovery of the offender, regardless of the crime that was committed. In other words, if it is deemed that offenders are treatable, and they are successfully treated to refrain from future criminal behavior, rehabilitation is considered a success, and concern over the severity of the past crime is not considered important. With this approach, it is feasible that offenders with lesser crimes may end up serving more time behind bars than a person with a more serious crime if it is determined that they are not amenable to rehabilitative efforts.

The rehabilitative approach is based on the notion that offenders are provided treatment rather than punishment. Punitive techniques are completely alien to the rehabilitative model; the goal is to cure the offenders of their criminal behavior, much as would be done with a medical or mental health issue. As a result, sentencing schemes under a rehabilitation orientation would be *indeterminate*, a term that will be discussed in more detail later in this chapter. Indeterminate sentences have no specific amount of time provided upon which offenders are released from custody. Rather, a minimum and maximum amount of time is awarded, and, based on offenders' treatment progress, they are released prior to the maximum duration of their sentence once rehabilitative efforts have been determined a success.

Video Link
Restorative Justice

Rehabilitation: Offenders will be deterred from reoffending due to their having worthwhile stakes in legitimate society.

Restorative justice: Interventions that focus on restoring the community and the victim with involvement from the offender.

Restorative Justice

Restorative justice is a term for interventions that focus on restoring the health of the community, repairing the harm done, meeting victims' needs, and emphasizing that the offender can and must contribute to those repairs. This definition was adapted from restorative justice advocate Thomas Quinn during his interview with the National Institute of Justice in 1998. More specifically, restorative justice considers the victims, communities, and offenders (in that order) as participants in the justice process. These participants are placed in active roles to work together to do the following: (1) empower victims in their search for closure, (2) impress upon offenders the real human impact of their behavior, and (3) promote restitution to victims and communities.

Dialogue and negotiation are central to restorative justice, and problem solving for the future is seen as more important than simply establishing blame for past behavior. Another key factor to this type of correctional processing is that the victim is included in the process. Indeed, the victim is given priority consideration, yet, at the same time, the process is correctional in nature, as offenders must face the person whom they victimized and the offenders must be accountable for the crimes that they committed against the victim.

Reintegration

Reintegration is focused on the reentry of the offender into society. The ultimate goal of reintegration programs is to connect offenders to legitimate areas of society in a manner that is gainful and productive. When used inside correctional institutions, this approach emphasizes continued contact between offenders and their families, their friends, and even the community. This approach is set against the backdrop realization that the overwhelming majority of offenders will ultimately return to society. While reintegration efforts do emphasize offender accountability, the use of reintegration processes is focused on ensuring that the offender has a maximal set of circumstances that, at least initially, diminish the need or desire to engage in crime by cultivating the connections that the offender has to legitimate society. Reintegration efforts are intended to reduce recidivism among offenders. During the past few years, there has been an upsurge in national interest in offender reentry programs, which, inherently, are all reintegrative in nature.

Thinkstock Images/Stockbyte/Thinkstock

■ PHOTO 2.3 No-contact visitation often consists of a glass partition between both parties. Each person uses the phone receiver as a means of communicating with one another.

TYPES OF SANCTIONS

It is through the use of intermediate (graduated) sanctions, various types of probation, incarceration, and the death penalty that various types of punishments (also known as sanctions) are meted out. While the public perhaps identifies prison as the final outcome for criminal offenders, the reality is that few offenders go to prison. Rather, the overwhelming majority are placed on probation or on some type of community supervision. Indeed, prisons and jails tend to hold only one-fifth to one-fourth of the entire offender population. However, chronic offenders and those who commit serious crimes tend to be given some period of incarceration.

Problems in determining the appropriate sentence for offenders are noted in the literature and have been the focus of at least one influential Supreme Court ruling. In 2005, the Court held in ***United States v. Booker*** that federal judges no longer were required to follow the sentencing guidelines that had been in effect since 1987. The Court held that federal judges now must only consider these guidelines with certain other sentencing criteria when deciding a defendant's punishment. Because of this ruling, and because of the trend toward alternative sanctions, there has been an observed trend toward more use of indeterminate sentencing (Debro, 2008). This also is consistent with much of the push for reintegrative efforts that has been observed throughout the nation.

Reintegration: Focused on the reentry of the offender into society by connecting offenders to legitimate areas of society that are gainful and productive.

***United States v. Booker*:** Determined judges no longer had to follow the sentencing guidelines that had been in place since 1987.

■ **Table 2.1: Philosophical Underpinnings in Corrections**

Philosophical Underpinning	Premise
Retribution	Implies that offenders committing a crime should be punished in a like fashion or in a manner that is commensurate with the severity of the crime.
Incapacitation	Deprives offenders of their liberty and removes them from society with the intent of ensuring that society cannot be further victimized.
Deterrence (general and specific)	General deterrence occurs when observers see that offenders are punished for a given crime and are themselves discouraged from committing crime. Specific deterrence is punishment upon a specific offender in the hope that the offender will be discouraged from committing future crimes.
Rehabilitation	Offenders will be deterred from reoffending due to their having worthwhile stakes in legitimate society.
Restorative justice	Interventions that focus on restoring the health of the community, repairing the harm done, meeting victims' needs, and emphasizing that the offender can and must contribute to those repairs.
Reintegration	Focused on the reentry of the offender into society.

CROSS-NATIONAL PERSPECTIVE 2.1

The Philosophy of Corrections in Thailand

Corrections in Thailand has historically been oriented toward the goals of retribution and deterrence, which has caused problems in providing the appropriate sentence in many cases because the mandatory minimum punishments are somewhat severe. Further, as with the United States, the desire for consistency in sentencing has been expressed, but there is a hesitance to impair discretion among the courts. Guidelines and best practices exist, but they are not compulsory. Obviously, one can see that the issues confronting Thailand's sentencing process are similar to those in the United States.

Currently, there are five primary categories of sentencing options employed by judges in Thailand: the death penalty, imprisonment, confinement, monetary fines, and forfeiture of property. These categories reflect the combined influences of the French, Italian, Indian, and Japanese penal codes. In recent decades, sentencing in Thailand has come under a great deal of scrutiny. In particular, the purposes of punishment, the use of discretion, and noted problems with disparity have impacted Thai corrections since the 1970s.

The strong emphasis on deterrence can still be seen today in the sentencing schemes that are utilized. Thai penalties are stiff, and, in response to crimes that are considered widespread or particularly problematic, the punishments get stiffer on a graduated level. Amidst this, it is not Thai policy to simply lock up offenders as a means of detaining them from further crime. Rather, the stated goal continues to be the deterrence of future crime among other persons who might consider criminal activity; this is a general deterrence philosophy.

Similar to the United States, Thailand has cracked down on drug use, with particular attention given to opium and the use of amphetamines. The typical sentence given to drug offenders (both traffickers and users) has been incarceration. The rationale for this sentence is, again, based on retribution for the crime(s) committed and general deterrence among the general public. The specific deterrence element (deterring a specific offender) is one goal as well, but it is considered secondary. As has been the case in the United States, the extensive use of incarceration in a campaign against drugs has fueled a large growth in the Thai prison population. Thus, the main challenge facing the Thai correctional system is overcrowding due to aggressive sentencing policies related to drug use.

It is important to note that the constitution of Thailand protects the human rights of inmates, including the ability to access legal assistance. Thus, it is likely that Thai prisons do provide a humane environment, regardless of how stiff the sentence may be. Interestingly, the large number of offenders who have been incarcerated has led to the development of specialized treatment programming during the past few years. The treatment regimen entails a holistic combination of medical treatment, educational services, vocational training, and religious programming. This significantly departs from the traditional emphasis on retribution and deterrence and demonstrates an awareness among Thai officials that those two philosophical approaches do not always work to reduce recidivism. Thus, the Thai Department of Corrections has assumed responsibility for providing rehabilitation programs to inmates in an effort to do more about the drug problem than just locking people up and throwing away the key.

QUESTION 1: What are some similarities that were mentioned between correctional approaches in Thailand and in the United States?

QUESTION 2: What key type of criminal activity is similar in both countries? How might this knowledge help professionals to improve treatment programs related to substance abuse and drug offending?

For a closer look at correctional treatment in Thailand, drug offense sentencing, and the response to those incarcerated in the Thai anti-drug campaign, see the following source:

SOURCE: Kuratanavej, S. (2009). *Crime prevention: Current issues in correctional treatment and effective countermeasures.*

The Continuum of Sanctions

Audio Link
Reentry Programs

The continuum of sanctions refers to a broad array of sentencing and punishment options that range from simple fines to incarceration and ultimately end with the death penalty. Between each of these visible points in the sentencing/sanctioning process (fines, incarceration, and the death penalty) is a variety of options that are used throughout the United States. The reasons for this variety of sanctions are manifold. Perhaps chief among them is the desire to calibrate the sanction in a manner that is commensurate with the type of criminal behavior.

When using the term *calibrate*, it is meant that sanctions can be selected in such a manner that allows us to, through an additive process, weight the seriousness and number of the sanction(s) that are given so that the punishment effect is as proportional to the crime as can be arranged. The desire to establish proportionality harkens back to the thinking of classical criminologists, and this should not be surprising. Classical criminologists appealed to the use of reason in applying punishments, and that is precisely what a continuum seeks to achieve as well: a reasonable, commensurate, and gradual progression of sanctions that can be consistently additive in nature so as to be logically proportional to the frequency and seriousness of the criminal behavior in question (Bosworth, 2010; Lilly, Cullen, & Ball, 2007).

In addition to the desire for proportionality, there is another reason for the use of varied sanctions, particularly intermediate sanctions: the desire to save beds in prisons. As noted earlier in this chapter, there is a push for reintegration efforts in the federal government and in many states throughout the nation. The reason for this has to do with both a shift in ideologies and, more specifically, the rising costs of imprisonment. The national and international economic crisis that began in 2008 negatively impacted numerous state budgets throughout the United States. A slow recovery is underway, but many states are still more cash-strapped than usual, making the use of alternatives in sentencing all the more appealing.

Another rationale for this continuum is associated with treatment purposes. While we have noted that rehabilitation efforts are typically not contingent on the sentence that is imposed, the fact that indeterminate sentences tend to be used with a rehabilitation orientation demonstrates the need for incentives to exist so that offenders will change their behavior. Without an indeterminate sentence, offenders might not find their efforts toward reform to have any substantive reward; thus, early release provides a strong incentive that encourages offenders to actively work toward behavior change. The use of alternative sanctions follows this same logic, where lesser sanctions can be given to those offenders who show progress in treatment, and more serious sanctions can be administered to offenders who prove to be dangerous or a nuisance to a given facility.

From this point, we move to a description of some of the more common versions of sanctions. In providing these descriptions, we will progress from the least severe to the most severe types of sanctions that are usually encountered. The list of sanctions that follows is not all-encompassing but simply is intended to provide the student with an understanding of the types used and the means by which they are categorized. We begin with sanctions that involve fines or monetary penalties and progress to the ultimate form of punishment: the death penalty.

Monetary

Most monetary sanctions come in the form of fines. Most offenders convicted of a criminal offense are assessed a fine as a punishment for committing the offense. A **fine** can be defined as a monetary penalty imposed by a judge or magistrate as a punishment for being convicted of an offense. In most cases the fine is a certain dollar amount established either by the judge or according to a set schedule dependent upon the offense committed. The logic behind the fine is that it will deter the offender from committing another offense in the future for fear of being fined again. In most jurisdictions the fines are assessed and paid in monthly payments to the receiving agency.

Probation and Intermediate Sanctions

The use of probation and other community-based sanctions accounts for all the varied types of sentencing punishments available short of a jail or prison sentence. When on probation, offenders will report to a probation officer (in most cases) on a scheduled routine that varies with the seriousness of their crime and their expected risk of recidivism. Additional community-based sanctions, tacked on to a probation sentence, further allow for the calibration of the sentence with respect to the crime that was committed and the offender who is on supervision. Intermediate sanctions are a range of sentencing options that fall between incarceration and probation and are designed to allow for the crafting of sentences that respond to the offender and/or the offense, with the intended outcome of the case being a primary consideration. The purpose of intermediate sanctions is to make available a continuum of sanctions scaled around one or more sanctioning goals. Such a continuum permits the court or corrections authority to tailor sanctions that are meaningful with respect both to their purposes and to the kinds of offenders that come before them.

Incarceration

Imprisonment is the most visible penalty to the public eye in the United States (Bosworth, 2010). Less than 30% of all offenders under supervision are in prisons or jails, but this type of sentence still draws public interest due to its ominous nature. This punishment remains the most commonly used for serious offenders. It is thought by some that imprisonment has a deterrent effect on

Fine: A monetary penalty imposed as a punishment for having committed an offense.

offenders (Bosworth, 2010). But other researchers have noted that in many respects the likelihood of recidivism increases once an offender is incarcerated. Thus, the effectiveness of incarceration to change potential criminal behavior is questionable. Because of this, it is recommended that incarceration be viewed as best suited for meeting the goals of incapacitation (and perhaps retribution) rather than rehabilitation, deterrence, or crime reduction.

Incarceration Options

Among incarceration options, the jail facility is considered the first stage of incarceration for the offender. Jail facilities come in a variety of sizes and designs, but all are generally intended to hold offenders for sentences that are short. Aside from those persons who are held for only brief periods (such as immediately after an arrest), jails tend to hold offenders who are sentenced to a year or less of incarceration. In most cases, jail facilities are the first point at which an offender is officially classified as being in the correctional component of the criminal justice system. In simple terms, a jail is a confinement facility, usually operated and controlled by county-level law enforcement, that is designed to hold persons charged with a crime who are either awaiting adjudication or serving a short sentence of 1 year or less after the point of adjudication. Similarly, the Bureau of Justice Statistics (2008) defines jails as "locally-operated correctional facilities that confine persons before or after adjudication. Inmates sentenced to jails usually have a sentence of a year or less, but jails also incarcerate persons in a wide variety of other categories." Thus, there is some degree of variance in the means by which jails are utilized, but they tend to be short-term facilities in most cases.

On the other extreme, consider the use of the supermax prison. The supermax prison is perhaps the epitome of incarceration-based sentences. There are some prison administrators who contend that supermax facilities have a general deterrent effect. However, this is unlikely because inmates in supermax facilities do not form bonds with persons in the prison or outside of the prison. Further, the disruptive inmates who will be kept in supermax facilities are least likely to care about the consequences of their actions and/or their ability to bond with other people. Deterrence as a philosophical orientation targets those inmates who would engage in antisocial behavior if not for the deterring mechanism. However, the inmates typically channeled into a supermax facility are those who have not been deterred when incarcerated in less secure environments, such as minimum-, medium-, and maximum-security facilities. Thus, these inmates are unlikely to be among those who would commit crimes were it not for the penalty of incarceration; they are impervious to the threat of incarceration and the deprivations that this sanction entails. Thus, supermax facilities act as simple holding spaces for the most incorrigible of inmates and are devoid of any deterrent and/or therapeutic value.

Because much of this text later involves coverage of the prison environment, further discussion related to specific aspects of incarceration schemes will not be provided at this time. It is sufficient to say that incarceration, while accounting for no more than 30% of the entire correctional population, tends to draw substantial public and media attention. Further, the offenders who are kept incarcerated are among those who are either repetitive or violent, or both. Therefore, the correctional process within institutions is one that deals with harder-core offenders than might be encountered among community supervision personnel.

SENTENCING MODELS

Sentencing involves a two-stage decision-making process. After the offender is convicted of a crime, the initial decision is made as to whether probation should or should not be granted. The chief probation officer or his or her designee will typically make this decision based on the presentence investigation (PSI). The presentence investigation report is a thorough file that includes a wide range of background information on the offender. This file will typically include demographic, vocational, educational, and personal information on the offender as well as records on his or her prior offending patterns and the probation department's recommendation as to the appropriate type of sentencing for the offender.

If incarceration is chosen, the second decision involves determining the length of the sentence. For many judges, deciding the length of the sentence (when they are required to do so) is not an easy task. They must consider several factors, such as the possibility for rehabilitation, the need to protect society, the need to fulfill the demand of retribution, and the implementation of deterrence strategies. The most important factor in deciding on a sanction is the seriousness of the crime. Sentencing on the basis of seriousness is one key way that courts attempt to arrive at consistent sentences. Once the seriousness of the crime has been determined, the next factor to consider is the prior record of the offender. The worse the prior record, the more likely the offender will receive a lengthy sentence. The last few issues considered in the sentencing process are mitigating and aggravating factors. **Mitigating factors** do not exonerate an offender but do make the commission of the crime more understandable and also help to reduce the level of culpability that the offender might have had. **Aggravating circumstances**, on the other hand, magnify the offensive nature of the crime and tend to result in longer sentences. Each of these factors can impact the outcome of the sentence. It is with this in mind that we turn our attention to the two types of sentencing: indeterminate and determinate sentencing.

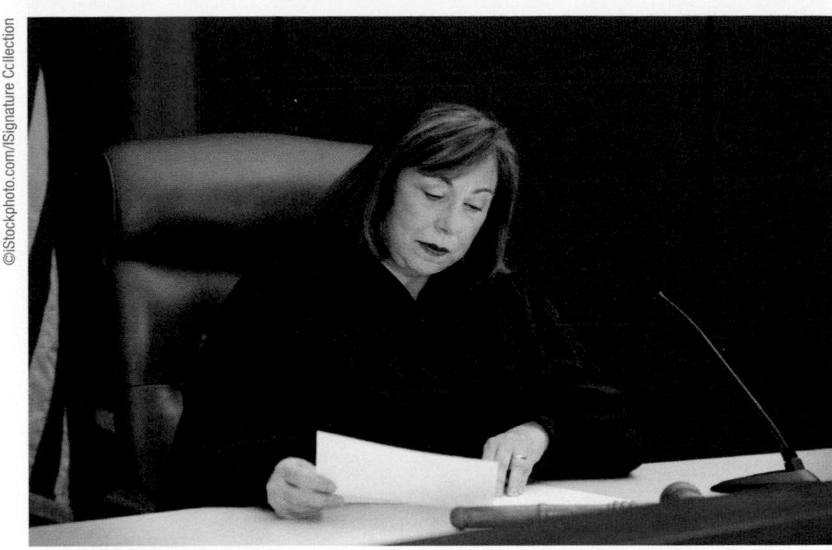

■ PHOTO 2.4 For judges, deciding the length of a sentence requires difficult calculations that take into account the possibility for rehabilitation, the need to protect society, the need to fulfill the demand of retribution, and the implementation of deterrence strategies.

Indeterminate Sentences

Indeterminate sentencing is sentencing that includes a range of years that will be potentially served by the offender. The offender is released during some point in the range of years that are assigned by the sentencing judge. Both the minimum and maximum times can be modified by a number of factors, such as offender behavior and offender work ethic. Under the most liberal of approaches using indeterminate sentences, judges will assign custody of the offender to the department of corrections, and the release of the offender is completely dependent on the agency's determination if he or she is ready to function appropriately in society. This type of sentence is typically associated with treatment-based programming and community supervision objectives. In such cases, indeterminate sentencing provides correctional officials a good deal of control over the amount of time that an offender will serve.

Penal codes with indeterminate sentencing stipulate minimum and maximum sentences that must be served in prison (2 to 9 years, 3 to 5 years, and so forth). At the time of sentencing, the judge will explain to the offender the time frame that the offender may potentially be in prison. The offender is also informed of any potential eligibility for parole once the minimum amount of time has been served. However, the actual release date is determined by the parole board, not the judge. Note that this particular sentence is different from the determinate *discretionary* sentence that will be described in the following subsection. The difference is that while the determinate discretionary sentence has a range of time to be served, the specific sentence to be served within that range is decided by the judge at the point of initial sentencing. Once this specific amount of time has been decided, there is no further modification to the sentence, regardless of the offender's progress within the institution.

Determinate Sentences

Determinate sentencing consists of fixed periods of incarceration with no later flexibility in the term that is served. This type of sentencing is grounded in notions of retribution, just desserts, and incapacitation. These types of sentences came into vogue due to disappointments with the use of rehabilitation and due to increased support for retribution. When offenders are given a determinate sentence, they are imprisoned for a specific period of time. Once that time has expired, the inmate is released from prison.

It should be pointed out that in many states inmates may be given "good time" if they maintain good behavior while in the correctional facility (Weisburd & Chayet, 1996). Generally, this entails a willingness to work in the prison, engage in educational and therapeutic programs, and participate in other prosocial activities. Good time earned is taken off the total sentence that inmates must serve, thereby allowing them to be released early from prison. While this does add some degree of variability to the total time that offenders serve in the institution, the actual sentence given to the inmates is

Mitigating factors: Circumstances that make a crime more understandable and help to reduce the level of culpability that an offender might have.

Aggravating circumstances: Magnify the offensive nature of a crime and tend to result in longer sentences.

©iStockphoto.com/PGGutenbergUKLtd

■ PHOTO 2.5 When sentencing occurs, the result can be disastrous for the defendant, who now must cope with the reality of the punishment that will be meted out.

not connected to their level of participation in treatment or to the likelihood of parole or early release (Weisburd & Chayet, 1996).

One variant of the determinate sentence is the determinate presumptive sentence. The **determinate presumptive sentence** specifies the exact length of the sentence to be served by the inmate. Judges are required to impose these sentences unless there are aggravating or mitigating circumstances, in which case they may lengthen or shorten the sentences within narrow boundaries and with written justification. This type of sentence is perhaps more realistic than a pure determinate sentencing model because it accounts for the variety of circumstances that are different from one case to another. In fact, very few criminal cases are exactly alike even when the charge is the same. The circumstances associated with each type of criminal case (e.g., theft) tend to vary, with different motivations, different outcomes, and different issues, and this may make the crime seem more or less severe in nature, especially on a human level (Carter, 1996).

To further demonstrate the potential complexity of sentencing schemes, consider also the determinate discretionary sentence. The **determinate discretionary sentence** (discussed briefly in the prior subsection) sets a stated range of time that must be served. This range of time (e.g., 3 to 5 years) is not subject to modification by judges who impose a sentence under this model (Carter, 1996). However, the judge is able to use his or her own discretion in determining the exact sentence so long as it falls within the range that has been predetermined by legislative bodies. Thus, the sentence is determinate in nature with parameters being set (in our example, a minimum of 3 years and a maximum of 5 years), but it is also discretionary since it allows the judge to select the exact time that will be served. Note that this sentence is different from the indeterminate sentence that was presented in the prior subsection. The difference is that while the indeterminate sentence often has a range of time to be served, the eventual date of release for the offender is decided by correctional officials who work with the offender and determine his or her progress toward and suitability for reintegration into society. Thus, the exact amount of time served depends on an offender's progress within the correctional treatment regimen.

Mandatory Minimum Sentences

Mandatory minimum sentences require that some minimum length of incarceration be served by offenders who commit certain specified crimes, such as drug-related crimes. In these cases, judges are extremely limited in their consideration of the offender's background or circumstances, and the use of community-based sanctions is out of the question. One type of mandatory minimum sentence is the "three strikes and you're out" law. This law requires that judges award a long-term prison sentence (in some cases life in prison) to offenders who have three felony convictions. This has resulted in the growth of prison populations around the nation and has also resulted in a graying of the prison population in the United States. As more and more inmates serve lengthy mandatory minimum sentences, the proportion of inmates who are elderly continues to climb. Since elderly inmates are more costly to house than younger inmates (due to medical care and other related costs), this has proven to be a serious drain on many state-level prison systems.

Indeed, this issue has been given considerable attention in recent years, with Texas, California, Florida, New York, and Louisiana all experiencing a rise in per-capita elderly inmates that are incarcerated. Each of the states just mentioned have either one of the largest prison populations or one of the highest rates of incarceration in the United States. In all cases, the costs that are associated with the elderly inmate are exponentially higher than those associated with the average inmate. This has led to other issues for administrators to consider, such as the possibility of early release of inmates who are expected to die, the implementation of human caregiver programs such as hospice, and

Determinate presumptive sentence: This type of sentence specifies the exact length of the sentence to be served by the inmate.

Determinate discretionary sentence: Type of sentence with a range of time to be served; the specific sentence to be served within that range is decided by the judge.

Mandatory minimum: A minimum amount of time or a minimum percentage of a sentence must be served with no good time or early release modifications.

accountability to the public. It is this accountability that places prison administrators in a dilemma since public safety is the primary concern for all custodial programs. Thus, in one generation, mandatory minimum, three strikes, habitual offender, and other enhanced sentences have created a new crisis that looms on the correctional horizon of the United States. This outcome is likely to affect sentencing patterns in the future, which, in turn, will impact the state of corrections.

Video Link
Three Strikes Legislation

Sentencing Has Become More Indeterminate in Nature

At the time that the first edition of this text was written, evolution in sentencing practices pointed to the possibility of a more indeterminate nature. While it was not clear then, and is perhaps no clearer now, whether this was the best approach from a public safety perspective, it was obvious that the 1990s had been reflective of a crime control model of criminal justice with an emphasis on mandatory minimums for sentencing and purely determinate sentencing schemes. This led to a swelling of the offender population behind bars. Many of these inmates were drug offenders rather than violent offenders, calling into question for many whether this type of mass incarceration was truly warranted.

Crime has not increased during the past few years and, in fact, has gone down. This further begs the question, is this level of mass imprisonment really necessary? It would appear that the federal government has started to ask this question of itself as well, as can be seen with recent recommendations from the United States Sentencing Commission. The United States Sentencing Commission is an independent agency in the judicial branch of government intended to establish sentencing policies and practices for the federal courts, including guidelines to be consulted regarding the appropriate form and severity of punishment for offenders convicted of federal crimes. It also advises Congress and the executive branch on effective crime policy and sentencing issues.

In 2014, the commission unanimously voted to reduce sentencing terms for drug traffickers who are already in prison. This meant that approximately 46,000 drug offenders would be eligible for early release (Greenblatt, 2014). Before any other discussion is provided, it should be pointed out that this recommendation included *drug traffickers*, not just drug users. Typically, drug traffickers are given stiffer sentences because they often are viewed as part of the cause of drug use. Given that this is a more serious charge than possession or consumption of drugs, this makes the recommendation by the commission even more noteworthy.

The commission intends for these recommendations to be indeterminate in nature, depending on the facts and circumstances of each case. Indeed, Greenblatt (2014) notes that not all offenders will be released. Rather, petitions for each will be considered on an individual basis by federal judges, reflecting the indeterminate feature to these recommendations. In addition, this process has not moved quickly; the reduction was instituted in 2014, but none of the affected offenders were released until November of 2015, which allowed an 18-month process for judges to review offender petitions before any were released.

Interestingly, the commission cited "fundamental fairness" as the primary motivation behind these sentencing changes (Greenblatt, 2014). Indeed, it has become a goal of the Department of Justice to seek leniency with nonviolent drug offenders as a means of reducing the sentencing disparities that date back to the mass incarceration of crack cocaine users in the 1980s and 1990s (Greenblatt, 2014). The Sentencing Commission, on the other hand, has gone forward with a more aggressive plan for sentence reduction that is fully retroactive, going beyond the initial efforts of the Department of Justice in reducing drug-related sentences (U.S. Sentencing Commission, 2014a).

It is important for students to understand that aside from theoretical and philosophical reasons for reducing sentencing disparities, there is a more pragmatic and mercenary reason for the commission to make such aggressive recommendations. As cited in the commission's official news release, one key priority is to reduce the inmate population in the nation's federal prisons (U.S. Sentencing Commission, 2014a). Indeed, Judge Patti Saris, the chair of the commission, noted that "this modest reduction in drug penalties is an important step toward reducing the problem of prison overcrowding at the federal level in a proportionate and fair manner" (U.S. Sentencing Commission, 2014a, p. 1). She went on to add that "reducing the federal prison population has become urgent, with that population almost three times where it was in 1991" (2014a, p. 1).

What is important to understand is that regardless of the moral, philosophical, or theoretical reasons given for many criminal justice policies, the reality is that economics always plays a strong role in how the system can and does operate. In fact, the economic circumstances of the times may not only shape sentencing processes and correctional system operations, but also are important in determining what law enforcement agencies can and will enforce. Students should understand that despite the philosophical and theoretical perspectives on punishment that may come under consideration, as discussed in Chapter 1, economics is often the "trump card" variable in determining correctional policy. This has historically been true in American corrections, as we saw when the Pennsylvania system (grounded in theories of reformation) competed with the Auburn system (grounded in terms of profit and loss). The author wants to make clear to students that in the world of the practitioner, theoretical perspectives and philosophy often take a back seat to economic pressures.

Sentencing Disparities

SAGE Journal Article Link
Sentencing Disparities

In the previous subsection, we referred to the term *disparities* and noted that the U.S. Department of Justice has made efforts to reduce these incongruous elements within sentencing policies and among the incarcerated population. The term *disparity* should be held distinct from the better-known term *discrimination*. **Disparity** refers to inconsistencies in sentencing and/or sanctions that result from the decision-making process. This typically results when the criminal justice system provides an unequal response toward one group as compared with the response given to other groups. Distinct from this is **discrimination**, which focuses on attributes of offenders when providing a given sentence. This usually results in a differential response toward a group without providing any legally legitimate reference to the reasons for that differential response. According to Neubauer (2002), the most commonly cited forms of disparity in sentencing involve geography and judicial attitudes. We now proceed with a discussion of these two types of disparity and will further explore how disparities impact corrections throughout the United States.

Geographical disparity in sentencing patterns has been tied to various areas of the United States and reflects the cultural and historical development of correctional thought in those regions. Neubauer (2002) notes that geographical differences in justice are the product of a variety of factors, such as the amount of crime, the types of crime affecting a given area, the effectiveness of police enforcement, and media attention given to criminal activity in the region. Overall, it is clear that the South imposes more harsh sentences than other areas of the nation, and the western part of the United States seems to follow suit. Interestingly, executions are concentrated in these regions as well. When one considers our discussions in Chapter 1 regarding southern penology and the development of corrections in the West, this observation may not be too surprising.

Lastly, a discussion regarding disparity in sentencing would not be complete without at least some reference to observed disparity in death penalty sentences. While this chapter will not focus on the death penalty, per se, the use of this sentence and problems regarding racial disparity in its application help to illustrate why disparity in sentencing is an important issue to the field of corrections. This also helps to illustrate a philosophical or ideological influence on the sentencing process that is at least perceived to be true by many in the public arena.

More extensive discussion regarding the death penalty and disparity in its application will be provided in Chapter 16, but the simple point to this current discussion is to highlight that disparity in sentencing may underlie other alleged reasons for sentencing outcomes that are observed. This then may undermine punishment schemes that are intended to rehabilitate and/or deter offenders. Rather, the cultural impact and/or influence from individuals of influence in the justice system may obscure and impair the intended outcome of various sentencing and punishment schemes. In regard to rehabilitation, this can create additional distrust of helping professionals from a given group that has been marginalized. From a deterrence viewpoint, these factors may only deter one group while giving the impression that criminal activity will be tolerated among other groups. It is clear that these impressions undermine the correctional process and, as a result, further complicate the process as a whole.

Disparity: Inconsistencies in sentencing and/or sanctions that result from the decision-making process.

Discrimination: A differential response toward a group without providing any legally legitimate reasons for that response.

Smarter Sentencing Act of 2014: A bill that adjusts federal mandatory sentencing guidelines in an effort to reduce the size of the U.S. prison population.

Smarter Sentencing Act: Sentence Leniency to Relieve Disparities

Increased political support in recent years to reduce many of the mandatory minimums that were enacted during the 1990s led to the **Smarter Sentencing Act of 2014**. According to GovTrack.us, the act adjusts federal mandatory sentencing guidelines for a variety of crimes in an effort to reduce the size of the current U.S. prison population and costs associated with it (2015, p. 2).This recent bill has spawned substantial discussion. While the reasons for this are many, for academic purposes, the author will point out once again that this legislation is simply a reflection of the "pendulum" of justice whereby criminal justice policy goes back and forth between harder and softer approaches to crime. As we saw in Chapter 1, different eras in modern corrections reflect an

CORRECTIONS AND THE LAW 2.1

United States v. Booker *on Determinate Sentencing*

In January 2005, the U.S. Supreme Court held in *United States v. Booker* that federal judges no longer are required to follow the sentencing guidelines in effect since 1987. Specifically, the Court held that the guidelines were unconstitutional in this particular case and, more importantly, that this could only be remedied by making the guidelines voluntary for federal judges. This was important because up until this time, the sentencing guidelines had not been officially challenged, even if judges gave sentences (due to aggravating circumstances) that went beyond them.

In the *Booker* case, a federal judge had added extra time to the offender's sentence due to additional facts that were based on a preponderance of the evidence (the standard used in a civil trial). In examining the circumstance, the Court held that federal judges now must only consider these guidelines with certain other sentencing criteria when deciding a defendant's punishment. However, the Court did note that, should a sentence beyond the guidelines be given by a judge, a separate sentencing hearing must be held before a jury, thereby placing such enhancements under the scrutiny of the defendant's peers. Because of this ruling, and because of the trend toward community supervision, alternative sanctions, and offender reintegration, it is speculated that sentencing will become more indeterminate in nature.

Debro (2008) discusses the *Booker* case and several other Supreme Court cases and notes that it is likely that American judicial practices may gradually extend more sentencing discretion to judges. In support of this notion, Debro (2008) points toward the fact that "between 2004 and 2006, 22 states enacted some form of sentencing reform. The United States Sentencing Commission also has recommended changes to federal sentencing guidelines" (p. 506). In these cases, there has been a clear intent to reduce disparities in sentencing and to increase judge-based discretion. This is a bit ironic because in the past the use of discretion was precisely what led to disparate outcomes.

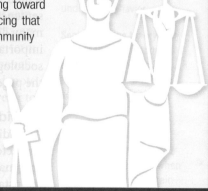

Whether this is for the better or for the worse is not completely clear, but it has historically been the case that the criminal justice system operates on a spectrum with punitive philosophies at one end and reformative philosophies on the other. The previous 10 to 15 years have been reflective of a crime control model of criminal justice that has had an emphasis on mandatory minimums for sentencing as well as purely determinate sentencing schemes. Historically speaking, the timing may begin to swing toward less restrictive prison sentencing that may lead to more use of community corrections.

SOURCE: Debro, J. (2008). The future of sentencing. In P. M. Carlson & J. S. Garrett (Eds.), *Prison and jail administration: Practice and theory* (2nd ed.) (pp. 503–510). Sudbury, MA: Jones and Bartlett.

ebb and flow between more stern approaches to criminal offending followed after a time by more humane approaches.

One of the main advocates of this legislation is Senator Ted Cruz of Texas, who in 2015 gave a speech that captures the essence of what is current and common sentiment in regard to sentencing reform in general and the Smarter Sentencing Act of 2014 specifically. According to Cruz (2005),

> The issue that brings us together today is fairness. What brings us together is justice. What brings us together is common sense. This is as diverse and bipartisan array of members of Congress as you will see on any topic and yet we are all unified in saying commonsense reforms need to be enacted to our criminal justice system. Right now today far too many young men, in particular African American young men, find their lives drawn in with the criminal justice system, find themselves subject to sentences of many decades for relatively minor non-violent drug infractions. (p. 1)

Again, what is important for students to understand is that though comments such as Cruz's plea for justice, fairness, and commonsense, there is nevertheless an ulterior purpose grounded in economics behind much of this proposed sentencing reform. For example, consider that this legislation affirms that the proposed changes are consistent with the U.S. Sentencing Commission mandate to *minimize the likelihood that the federal prison population will exceed the capacity of the federal prisons*. This legislation also directs the Justice Department to issue a report outlining the reduced expenditures and cost savings as a result of the Smarter Sentencing Act within a 6-month period of its enactment. It should be clear from these facts that the undergirding concern for the

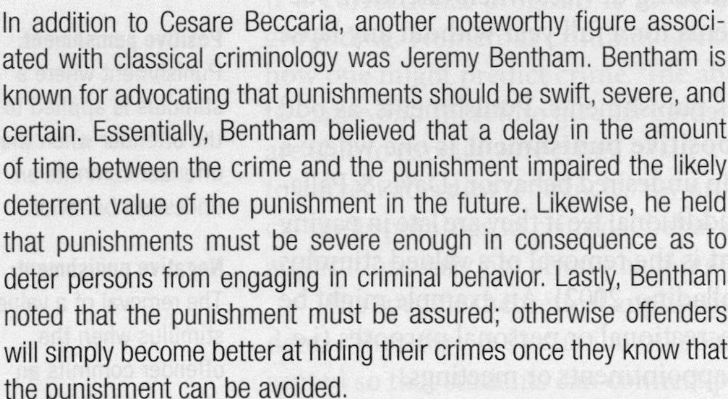

APPLIED THEORY 2.1

Classical Criminology, Behavioral Psychology, and Corrections

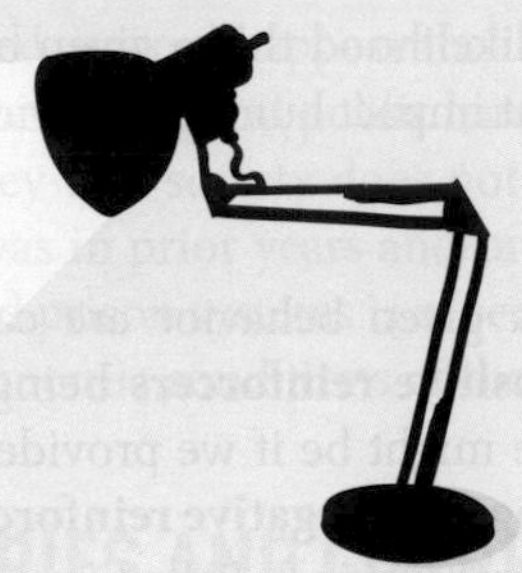

In addition to Cesare Beccaria, another noteworthy figure associated with classical criminology was Jeremy Bentham. Bentham is known for advocating that punishments should be swift, severe, and certain. Essentially, Bentham believed that a delay in the amount of time between the crime and the punishment impaired the likely deterrent value of the punishment in the future. Likewise, he held that punishments must be severe enough in consequence as to deter persons from engaging in criminal behavior. Lastly, Bentham noted that the punishment must be assured; otherwise offenders will simply become better at hiding their crimes once they know that the punishment can be avoided.

Current research actually supports some aspects of classical criminology, while refuting others. In particular, it has been found that the certainty of the punishment does indeed lower the likelihood of recidivism. Likewise, the less time between the crime and the punishment, the less likely offenders will be to reoffend in the future. However, it has not been found to be true that the severity of the punishment is successful in reducing crime. In fact, there has been substantial historical research on the death penalty that seems to indicate that general deterrence is not achieved with the death penalty, even though it is the most severe punishment that can be given.

While some offenders are simply too dangerous to be released into the community, others who are not so dangerous will ultimately be returned. For those, the goal of any sanction should be to reduce the likelihood that they will commit crime again. The research of Smith, Goggin, and Gendreau (2002), however, provides evidence that the prison environment may actually *increase* the likelihood of recidivism among many offenders, leading the authors to conclude that prisons could indeed be considered "schools of crime" (p. 21). Further, they found that the longer the term of imprisonment, the more likely offenders were to recidivate. Thus, the severity of the punishment does not reduce crime and, in actuality, increases the likelihood of future crime. Other studies substantiate this research.

This alone presents a valid argument against the unnecessary use of prisons, particularly when community corrections can provide effective supervision and sanctions without the reliance on prison facilities. Community corrections sanctions can be swifter in implementation, and they are much more certain in their application. For example, many offenders may be given a certain number of years in prison but will be released early, reducing the certainty (and severity) of their intended punishment. Further, the plea-bargaining system in the United States provides an opportunity for the convicted to avoid incarceration entirely, even when a prison sentence would typically be given for the crime that the offender committed. It is then clear that the use of such pleas detracts from the certainty of the sentence.

In addition, overcrowding may delay an offender's placement in prison, with law enforcement jail facilities holding the offender during the interim. Further, offenders are able to avoid the assumption of responsibility for their crimes when they are simply given a sentence and allowed to serve their time without being accountable to the victim and/or society. Community corrections sentencing, on the other hand, has a number of additional conditions and programs that often require the offender to make restitution, provide services, and/or pay fines to victims and/or the community (examples of these conditions will be presented in later chapters). The flexibility of this type of sanctioning provides an element of certainty that offenders will be held accountable, and these types of sanctions can be administered quite quickly.

In addition, many behavioral psychologists note that if punishment is to be effective, certain considerations must be taken into account. These considerations, summarized by Davis and Palladino (2002, pp. 262–263), are presented below:

1. The punishment should be delivered immediately after the undesirable behavior occurs. *This is similar to the "swiftness" requirement of classical criminologists.*
2. The punishment should be strong enough to make a real difference to that particular organism. *This is similar to the "severity" requirement of classical criminologists, but this point also illustrates that "severity" may be perceived differently from one person to another.*
3. The punishment should be administered after each and every undesired response. *This is similar to the "certainty" requirement of classical criminologists.*
4. The punishment must be applied uniformly with no chance of undermining or escaping the punishment. *When considering our justice system, it is clear that this consideration is undermined by the plea-bargaining process.*
5. If excessive punishment occurs and/or is not proportional to the aberrant behavior committed, the likelihood of aggressive responding increases. *In a similar vein and as noted earlier, excessive prison sentences simply increase crime, including violent crime.*
6. To ensure that positive changes are permanent, provide an alternative behavior that can gain reinforcement for the person. *In other words, the use*

of reintegrative efforts to instill positive behaviors and activities must be supplemented for those behaviors and activities that are criminal in nature.

From the presentation above, it can be seen that there is a great deal of similarity between classical criminologists and behavioral psychologists on the dynamics associated with the use of punishment. In addition, the second consideration above demonstrates the need for severity, but it illustrates a point often overlooked: Severity of a punishment is in the eye of the beholder. For instance, some offenders would prefer to simply "do flat time" in prison rather than complete the various requirements of community supervision. This is particularly true for offenders who have become habituated to prison life. In these cases, the goal should be not to acclimate offenders to prison life but instead to acclimate them to community life as responsible and productive citizens. It is for this reason that prison should be utilized only for those offenders who are simply not receptive to change and/or the assumption of responsibility for their crimes.

SOURCES: Davis, S. F., & Palladino, J. J. (2002). *Psychology* (3rd ed.). Upper Saddle River, NJ: Prentice Hall; Smith, P., Goggin, C., & Gendreau, P. (2002). *The effects of prison sentences on recidivism: General effects and individual differences.* Saint John, Canada: Centre for Criminal Justice Studies, University of New Brunswick.

the means by which such material accumulation is obtained. In other words, these authors contend that society in the United States emphasizes winning the game (of life) much more than how the game (of life) is played.

Labeling and Social Reaction

Another theoretical application that is relevant to the correctional process is **labeling theory**. This theory contends that individuals become stabilized in criminal roles when they are labeled as criminals, are stigmatized, develop criminal identities, are sent to prison, and are excluded from conventional roles (Cullen & Agnew, 2006). In essence, the label of "criminal offender" or "convict" stands in the way of the offender reintegrating back into society. Such labels impair the offender's ability to obtain employment, housing, and/or other goods or services necessary to achieve success. Tracking and labeling often result from the need to ensure public safety (as with pedophiles) and thus are simply a necessary aspect of the punishment, incapacitation, and public safety objectives of many community corrections programs. However, it may be that these functions can be achieved in a manner that aids public safety but does not prevent the offender from achieving reintegration.

Web Link
Labeling Theory

The desire to allow for an offender's past errors to be public information (due to a need to achieve public safety) without undo blockage of the offender's ability to reintegrate has been directly addressed by labeling theory scholars. One particular labeling theorist, John Braithwaite, provided a particularly insightful addition to the labeling theory literature that is specifically suited for the field of community supervision. In his work *Crime, Shame, and Reintegration*, Braithwaite (1989) holds that crime is higher when shaming is stigmatizing and criminal activity is lower when shaming effects serve a reintegrative purpose.

According to Braithwaite (1989), the negative effects of stigmatization are most pronounced among offenders who have few prosocial bonds to conventional society (such as family, religious institutions, and civic activities). This would place young males who are unmarried and unemployed at the greatest risk of being thrust further into criminality due to shaming effects. Due to their lack of resources, connections, and general social capital, these offenders find themselves further removed from effective participation in legitimate society. Over time, these offenders will find that it is much easier to join criminal subcultures where tangible reinforcements for their activities can be found. Thus, a cycle is created where a given segment of the offender population is further encouraged to repeat criminal activity simply due to the fact that other options have essentially been knifed away from them.

Labeling theory: Contends that individuals become stabilized in criminal roles when they are labeled as criminals.

Conflict Criminology

According to **conflict theory**, the concepts of inequality and power are the central issues underlying crime and its control. This theory is derived from the work of Karl Marx (Lilly et al., 2007). Conflict criminologists note that capitalism perpetuates a system that benefits the rich. In the process, the poor are denied access to economic opportunities and are therefore prevented from improving their social standing. Thus, the wide economic gap between the social classes is

Conflict theory: Maintains that concepts of inequality and power are the central issues underlying crime and its control.

increased and perpetuated with each successive generation. In a similar vein, the state—which includes the criminal law and the criminal justice system—operates to protect social arrangements that benefit those profiting from capitalism (Lilly et al., 2007). In general, the injurious acts committed by the poor and powerless are defined as crime, but the injurious acts committed by the rich and powerful are not brought within the reach of the criminal law. One can see this in sentencing practices that tend to mete out harsher terms to those groups who lack wealth and the ability to hire expensive defense attorneys but assign comparatively light sentences to those who are wealthy. Thus, critical criminologists point at the social system itself as the chief cause of America's growing prison population.

CONCLUSION

This chapter began with a review of the purpose of corrections as a process whereby practitioners from a variety of agencies and programs use tools, techniques, and facilities to engage in organized security and treatment functions intended to correct criminal tendencies among the offender population. It is with this purpose in mind that a variety of philosophical underpinnings were presented, including retribution, incapacitation, deterrence, rehabilitation, restorative justice, and reintegration. As can be seen, each of these philosophical approaches has held sway throughout the history of corrections at one time or another. However, it is clear from the definition of corrections, as provided in this text, that the ultimate and modern philosophy of corrections is one that likely includes elements of rehabilitation, restorative justice, and reintegration more than it does retribution, incapacitation, and deterrence.

Though modern corrections is considered more reintegrative in nature, the reality cannot be ignored: Prisons are not effective instruments of rehabilitation or reintegration. Research demonstrates that incarceration is not likely to lower recidivism and, in some cases, may actually increase it. Thus, other philosophical uses of prisons, such as incapacitation and deterrence, continue to proliferate among correctional agencies. However, one criminal offense is not always equal to another, and this has necessitated the need for a continuum of sanctions. This continuum provides for a number of punishments (sanctions) that have varying levels of severity. Monetary fines are perhaps the least serious of sanctions, followed by a very wide range of intermediate community-based sanctions. Community-based sanctions are given extensive coverage due to their variability in administration and their effectiveness in calibrating the punishment to the criminal offense and the criminal offender. Discussion regarding the use of incarceration as a primary tool of punishment was provided, as was an explanation of the different types of custody arrangements when using incarceration with serious offenders. Next, three types of sentencing models were presented: indeterminate, determinate, and mandatory minimum sentences. The reasons for using these types of sentences were provided, as were the pitfalls to each one. While intentions may be good, the outcomes of each of these types of sentencing schemes have not necessarily been effective in achieving the desired goal of their application. Further still, despite the use of complicated sentencing approaches and philosophical approaches to administering punishments, it is clear that sentencing disparities exist throughout America. Disparities were noted to be especially problematic in the southern and western parts of the United States, and it has been found that disparities with punishments exist with both prison sentences and the application of the death penalty. In discussion of the issue of disparity, the distinction between disparity and discrimination was made clear.

It would seem that a degree of fervor has developed regarding the sentencing schemes used in recent decades. In particular, the federal system is overcrowded with drug offenders, which has prompted the development of policies to release these offenders early from prison. To a lesser extent, this has been true in some state systems as well, where effects of the War on Drugs that have resulted in widespread racial disparities in the sentencing of African American men is promoted as the rationale for the reduction of time served. While this may seem like an altruistic concern, the reality is that these prison systems are financially broke and the use of sentence reductions can help alleviate overcrowding.

Lastly, a number of criminological theories were presented with an emphasis on their application to the field of corrections. An understanding of the theoretical bases of the criminal justice discipline in general and the correctional system in particular will aid in the correctional process. Indeed, if we are able to explain why different types of crime occur, we can then determine those factors that should be addressed to eliminate the likelihood of criminal behavior. This means that an understanding of the theoretical underpinnings to criminal behavior can improve any correctional effort. Though a diverse number of theories were presented, each provides its own vantage on how and why crime exists, and each provides a framework from which correctional agents can approach the task of providing organized security and treatment functions intended to correct criminal tendencies among the offender population and, in the process, enhance public safety.

Want a better grade?

Get the tools you need to sharpen your study skills. Access practice quizzes, eFlashcards, video, and multimedia at **edge.sagepub.com/hanser2e**

SAGE edge™

DISCUSSION QUESTIONS

1. Compare and contrast the two philosophical orientations of *incapacitation* and *deterrence*. In your opinion, which one is the better approach to correctional practice?
2. Compare and contrast the two philosophical orientations of *rehabilitation* and *retribution*. In your opinion, which one is the better approach to correctional practice?
3. Provide a topical overview of the different types of informal sanctions discussed in this chapter. Also, explain what is meant by the "continuum of sanctions" when talking about informal sanctions.
4. Compare and contrast the terms *disparity* and *discrimination*. Which one do you think is most appropriate to explaining the overwhelming proportion of minority inmates behind bars?
5. Compare and contrast indeterminate and determinate sentencing. What are the pros and cons of each?
6. What is restorative justice and how is it unique from many other perspectives on the resolution of crime?
7. According to the chapter, in what ways are classical criminology and operant conditioning similar to one another in their orientations on shaping human behavior?

SAGE edge™ **Test your understanding of chapter content. Take the practice quiz.**

KEY TERMS

Aggravating circumstances, 37
Conflict theory, 45
Determinate discretionary sentence, 38
Determinate presumptive sentence, 38
Discrimination, 40
Disparity, 40
Fine, 35
General deterrence, 31
Incapacitation, 31
Individual personality traits, 42
Labeling theory, 45
Mandatory minimum, 38
Mitigating factors, 37
Negative punishment, 43
Negative reinforcers, 43
Positive punishment, 43
Positive reinforcers, 43
Rehabilitation, 32
Reintegration, 33
Restorative justice, 32
Retribution, 30
Selective incapacitation, 31
Smarter Sentencing Act of 2014, 40
Social learning theory, 43
Specific deterrence, 31
Strain theory/institutional anomie, 43

SAGE edge™ **Review key terms with eFlashcards.**

KEY CASE

United States v. Booker (2005), 33

APPLIED EXERCISE 2.1

Match each of the following modern-day programs with its appropriate philosophical underpinning, sentencing scheme, or theoretical orientation.

Program	Ideology or Philosophy of Origin
1. You are sentenced to 10 years in prison and must serve no less than 80% of that time (8 years) without the benefit of early release or parole.	A. Restorative justice
2. Laws that select specific types of offenders and provide enhanced penalties to ensure that they are effectively removed from society (habitual offender laws, three-strikes laws, etc.).	B. General deterrence
3. Punishing an offender in public so other observers will refrain from criminal behavior.	C. Negative punishment
4. Providing the offender an opportunity to restore damages done to the victim and minimizing stigma/shame for the offender.	D. Treatment
5. Removal of visitation privileges because an offender commits the undesired criminal behavior of child abuse.	E. Indeterminate sentencing
6. Exacting a fine for undesired behavior.	F. Mandatory minimum
7. Treats crime similar to a mental health issue or along the medical model perspective.	G. Determinate sentencing
8. Providing substance abusers with certificates of graduation when completing an addiction treatment program.	H. Positive reinforcement
9. Sentencing has no flexibility in terms.	I. Positive punishment
10. Sentencing with variable terms, affected by the context of the crime and later behavior of offenders while serving their sentence.	J. Incapacitation

WHAT WOULD YOU DO?

You are the judge in a small-town court. In this town, everybody knows each other, and things are usually fairly informal. Your position and title carry a great deal of respect throughout the town, and because of this you take your role in the community very seriously. You have recently had a case appear on your docket that is very troubling. A mentally challenged man, 19 years old, is in the county jail; he bludgeoned another man to death with a ball-peen hammer, hitting the victim repeatedly across the head to the point that the deceased victim was barely recognizable. The defendant, Lenny Gratzowskowitz, was in a fit of fury during the crime and continued pounding the skull of the deceased well beyond the point of death.

The police who arrested Lenny were careful to ensure their behavior was well within ethical boundaries, and the agency ensured that legal representation was present before any questions were asked of Lenny. In fact, many of the police officers (including the chief of police) know Lenny on a semipersonal basis because of the tight-knit nature of the town. Generally, Lenny is not problematic, and he has never been known to be violent. However, throughout his history, from childhood on up, he has been subjected to ridicule and embarrassment by a handful of town residents who are of a fairly unsavory disposition.

In fact, the victim, Butch Wurstenberger, had been a childhood bully in grade school, and he had terrorized Lenny on numerous occasions. Now, as an adult, Butch was known to be an abrupt and sarcastic man, but not violent. Both Butch and Lenny had obtained jobs with a general contractor to complete construction of a Walmart supercenter that was slated for a grand opening during the upcoming year. Each had worked in the construction field: Butch had become known for his skill with foundation work and drywall setting and his experience with industrial air-conditioning and refrigeration systems; Lenny had been hired due to his routine dependability on other job sites and his willingness to work, regardless of the circumstances.

Once both arrived on the job site, Butch heckled Lenny on a few but sparing occasions. Most other members of the work crew were from out of town and were not aware of the history between Butch and Lenny. None of them had noticed any serious problems between the two men—that is, not until they reported to work one morning to find that both Butch and Lenny had arrived at the work scene early, and one of them (Butch) was dead while the other (Lenny) was bloody from the act of violence that he had committed.

Consider this situation and determine which philosophical orientation you would use when sentencing Lenny. Select only *one* of the following philosophical orientations: retribution, deterrence, incapacitation, treatment, restorative justice, or reintegration. Consider why you selected that orientation and why each of the other orientations might not be as appropriate as the one that you chose. Write this down as an essay that answers the following question:

What would you do?

PRACTICE AND APPLY WHAT YOU'VE LEARNED

► edge.sagepub.com/hanser2e

WANT A BETTER GRADE ON YOUR NEXT TEST?

Head to the study site, where you'll find:

- **eFlashcards** to strengthen your understanding of key terms
- **Practice quizzes** to test your comprehension of key concepts
- **Videos and multimedia content** to enhance your exploration of key topics

CORRECTIONAL LAW AND LEGAL LIABILITIES

©iStockphoto.com/-Oxford-

THE WRIT WRITER

"The 1960s were a time when 'rights' was a nebulous concept with many different interpretations in America, depending on who you were," Professor Schwin noted. "Back then, rights for African Americans and Caucasians were distinctly different, a woman's right to decide the fate of her own body was hotly debated, and Latinos were simply looked at as a third world source of cheap labor." The professor swept his gaze across the classroom. "And though it was not a popular topic, the rights of those who were incarcerated became an area of intense legal scrutiny."

Professor Schwin went on to note that the odd thing about prison law is that it centers on parameters of treatment that affect, paradoxically, those who have themselves broken the law. He also noted that the heroes of prison litigation are not always those who are free from blemish. Often they are criminals, which is precisely why few people sympathize with the plight of plaintiffs in prison litigation cases.

In 1960, a young Latino American man named Fred Cruz was arrested in Texas for robbery. Despite contesting his guilt, Cruz could not afford an attorney for his appeals while in the Texas Department of Corrections (TDC). Although he only had an 8th grade education, he refined his reading skills while serving time and read what law books were available to him. Over time, he became the quintessential jailhouse lawyer, and he fought and eventually won a legal battle with Texas to secure several constitutional rights for inmates not only in Texas but also throughout the United States. He became, as they call it inside the institution, a **writ writer**.

At the time of his arrest, Cruz was, by all appearances, your garden variety criminal and was sentenced to 50 years for robbery. His sentence required that he be committed to hard labor, so he would pick cotton during the hot spring and summer months in the never-ending fields of eastern Texas. But at night and when the planting and harvesting were slow, he would study law books, learning the processes to file lawsuits. He initiated numerous suits that challenged the backbreaking working conditions of TDC field labor, the brutal beatings and physical torture that occurred on prison farms, and the capricious nature of the "kangaroo courts" inside prisons that addressed disciplinary charges and processed inmate complaints. He also challenged the Texas building tender system, which allowed other inmates to act as guards and get away with abusing and exploiting other, less fortunate inmates. As punishment for his suits, Cruz was eventually sent to the Ellis Unit, which was at that time known as the Alcatraz of Texas. The Ellis Unit was headed by Warden C. L. McAdams, one of the roughest and most calloused wardens in the state.

While at the Ellis Unit, Cruz was placed in solitary confinement for long periods of time, made to live on bread and brackish water, and was sometimes beaten. His legal work was confiscated, he was restricted from writing or filing paperwork, and he was not allowed to see an attorney on numerous occasions. Even with these terrible obstacles, Cruz managed to provide assistance to other inmates within the system through means that violated institutional rules and procedures. One of these instances was discovered when an inmate was caught

LEARNING OBJECTIVES:

1. Describe the hands-off doctrine and its relevance to corrections.
2. Identify key rights inmates possess.
3. Evaluate the application of the First, Fourth, Eighth, and Fourteenth Amendments of the Constitution to corrections.
4. Discuss the shift to a more restrained, hands-on approach and the impact of the Prison Litigation Reform Act of 1995.
5. Identify and discuss legal liabilities associated with correctional staff.
6. Explain how prisons have had to change to comply with judicial orders.
7. Apply legal principles to challenges in the field of corrections.

with legal work drafted with Cruz's guidance. The work was related to the violation of rights for Islamic inmates. The prison's reaction led to an inmate uprising that included both Islamic and non-Islamic offenders and was so difficult to contain that outside involvement became necessary. This outside involvement eventually included attorneys who took interest in the issues presented and assisted Cruz in reaching the U.S. Supreme Court with the case. In *Cruz v. Beto*, the Court held that inmates must be given reasonable opportunities to exercise their religious beliefs.

A student raised his hand, and Professor Schwin nodded at him to speak.

"Was Cruz Muslim, or was he just helping them out?"

"No, Cruz was not Muslim," the professor responded. "But often, when fighting for matters of justice, we must be willing to fight for the rights of others as well as our own, even if we do not necessarily see eye-to-eye with their beliefs or lifestyle. It's a matter of principle. And it never hurts to make friends with the enemy of your enemy."

Professor Schwin then concluded by saying, "Cruz filed litigation related to a number of issues and at the behest of numerous individuals. Sometimes he was successful; other times he was not. But the key point is to understand that regardless of the times, legal principles and rights inherently secured by the Constitution are intended to extend to all of us, both large and small in social standing. It is intended that we all be equal in the eyes of the law."

INTRODUCTION

From our previous two chapters, it is clear that the field of corrections has gone through many transformations throughout the ages. But, as Chapter 2 demonstrates, some of these changes took place due to courthouse intervention into prison operations. The period when the hands-off doctrine ended marked the beginning of case law that has permanently impacted correctional operations in the United States. An understanding of this case law is critical to both the practitioner and the student. It is with this in mind that this chapter is presented, which will allow students to develop an understanding of the legal issues associated with correctional processes and practices.

During the early history of corrections in the United States, the courts were not typically involved in prison operations. This is generally because, as noted previously, inmates were seen as slaves of the state. With such a philosophy, concern for prisoners' rights seemed alien to most people at the time. As a result of the culture and the period, there was little reason for the Supreme Court to be involved with inmate issues, and, at that time, inmates would not have considered the possibility of suing the Court; such an option did not exist (Branham & Hamden, 2009).

Prison Tour Video: Laws. Many legal rulings related to prisons are in regards to the conditions of a facility. Watch two wardens describe laws and their impacts on prison.

In addition, there was a general belief that the public and even the courts should not be concerned about the goings-on inside the prisons. Since inmates were considered slaves of the state and since prisons were not intended to be pleasant places of existence, it was thought that prisons were best left in the hands of those who operated them (Branham & Hamden, 2009). There was no need to meddle, and, essentially, the "no news is good news" mentality prevailed with the public and the Court in regard to prison operations.

THE HANDS-OFF DOCTRINE

The policy of the Supreme Court and the lower courts of avoiding intervention in prison operations is generally known as the **hands-off doctrine** and was based on two primary premises. First was the premise that under the separation of powers inherent in the U.S. Constitution, the judicial branch was not justified to interfere with prisons, which were operated by the executive branch. The second premise was, simply put, that judges should leave prison administration to the prison experts. With these two premises in place, states tended to operate their prisons with impunity; they were free to do as they pleased with no fear of outside scrutiny (Branham & Hamden, 2009).

Writ writer: An inmate who becomes skilled at generating legal complaints and grievances within the prison system.

Hands-off doctrine: The policy of the courts of avoiding intervention in prison operations.

***Ex parte Hull* (1941):** Ruling that marked the beginning of the end for the hands-off doctrine.

As we have seen in the prior chapters, courts did eventually begin to intervene in prison operations during the early to mid-1900s. This was, in part, due to reform-minded persons who were active in educating the public about inmate issues. As public sentiment moved toward programs that were more rehabilitative in nature, prisons began to catch the eye of the courts more routinely. Further, the civil rights movement of the 1960s highlighted the abuses that occurred in prisons as well as the complete lack of legal protections for inmates. As civil rights issues in society took center stage, civil rights issues in prisons also drew more attention from both the public and the courts.

The Beginning of Judicial Involvement

Perhaps the clear beginning of the end for the hands-off doctrine occurred in the 1941 Supreme Court case ***Ex parte Hull.*** Prior to this case, it was common for prison officials to screen inmate mail, including legal mail. As a result, prison staff were known to misplace petitions and even deny the inmate the opportunity to mail them. In *Hull*, the Supreme Court held that no state or its officers could legally interfere with a prisoner's right to apply to a federal court for writs of habeas corpus. The term *habeas corpus* refers to a challenge of the legality of confinement and is a Latin term that means "you have the body." A writ of habeas corpus is a court order requiring that an arrested person be brought forward to determine the legality of his or her arrest. In *Hull*, the Supreme Court ruled that inmates had the right to unrestricted access to federal courts to challenge the legality of their confinement (Branham & Hamden, 2009; Stohr et al., 2009). This was important because writs of habeas corpus were the primary mechanism that inmates had to challenge unlawful incarceration. Without the ability to use this avenue of redress, inmates were powerless to make legal challenges to their confinement.

Steve Petteway

■ PHOTO 3.1 The Justices of the Supreme Court. Back row, left to right: Sonia Sotomayor, Stephen G. Breyer, Samuel A. Alito, and Elena Kagan. Front row, left to right: Clarence Thomas, Antonin Scalia, Chief Justice John G. Roberts, Anthony Kennedy, and Ruth Bader Ginsburg.

One case truly opened the door for inmate civil litigation. ***Cooper v. Pate* (1964)** validated and made clear the right of inmates to sue prison systems and prison staff. In this case, the Court ruled that state prison inmates could sue state officials in federal courts under the Civil Rights Act of 1871. This act was initially enacted to protect southern African Americans from state officials (such as judges) who were often members of the subversive group the Ku Klux Klan. This act is now codified and known as 42 U.S.C. Section 1983, or simply Section 1983 in day-to-day conversation among legal experts and/or practitioners. This act holds that

> every person who under color of law of any statute, ordinance, regulation, custom, or usage of any state or territory, subjects or causes to be subject, any citizen of the United States or other person within the jurisdiction thereof to the deprivation of any rights, privileges, or immunities secured by the Constitution and laws, shall be liable to the party injured in an action at law. (Branham & Hamden, 2009, p. 553)

Because it had been determined that the Court was responsible for protecting against misuses of power possessed by those vested with state authority, it became clear that the Court was within its purview to rule regarding any number of issues related to civil rights of the inmate. Further, it was determined that officials "clothed with the authority of state law" did include prison staff and security personnel. Therefore, state prison personnel who violated an inmate's constitutional rights while performing their duties under state law could be held liable for their actions in federal court. The clarity provided in *Cooper v. Pate* and the route of litigation opened for inmates essentially created what some have called the hands-on doctrine of correctional case law, which we now consider in the following subsection.

THE EMERGENCE OF INMATE RIGHTS

As noted earlier, much of the public concern with the rights of inmates dovetailed with the civil rights movement during the 1960s. During this time, the National Association for the Advancement of Colored People (NAACP) Legal Defense and Educational Fund and the National Prison Project of the American Civil Liberties Union (ACLU) began to advocate for the rights of inmates. At the same time, legal protections for inmates were given substantial public and political attention. In determining inmate rights, the balance between humane treatment and the need to maintain public safety remained an issue amongst the courts. Many courts used contradictory rulings to navigate the myriad complications that emerged from balancing these two overarching concerns.

The difficulty in setting this balance led to further involvement by the Supreme Court in the landmark case of ***Turner v. Safley* (1987)**. In this case, the Court ruled on a Missouri ban against

***Cooper v. Pate* (1964):** Ruling that state prison inmates could sue state officials in federal courts.

***Turner v. Safley* (1987):** A prison regulation that impinges on inmates' constitutional rights is valid if it is reasonably related to legitimate penological interests.

correspondence sent among inmates in different institutions within the state's jurisdiction (del Carmen, Ritter, & Witt, 2005). The Court upheld the ban, noting that such forms of regulations are valid if they are "reasonably related to legitimate penological interests." Further, the Court enunciated four key elements of what are known as the **rational basis test**. These four elements are as follows:

1. There must be a rational and clear connection between the regulation and the reason that is given for that regulation's existence.
2. Inmates must be given alternative means to practice a given right that has been restricted, when feasible.
3. The means by which prison staff and inmates are affected must be kept as minimal as realistically possible.
4. When less restrictive alternative means of impeding upon an inmate's rights are available, prison personnel must utilize those alternative means.

Prison Tour Video Link
Legal Research

This rational basis test has provided a good degree of clarity in resolving the conflict between inmate rights and the need for institutional and public safety. It is within these guidelines that the rights of inmates have emerged but, at the same time, been held in check sufficiently to allow correctional agencies to maintain security. Thus, inmate rights became a permanent fixture in the U.S. correctional system, but these rights were tempered with some degree of feasible pragmatism.

Rational basis test: Sets guidelines for the rights of inmates that still allow correctional agencies to maintain security.

***Johnson v. Avery* (1969):** Held that prison authorities cannot prohibit inmates from aiding other inmates in preparing legal documents.

***Bounds v. Smith* (1977):** Determined that prison systems must provide inmates with law libraries or professional legal assistance.

Access to Courts and Attorneys

In tandem with the newfound rights of inmates was a corresponding recognition that such rights were useless unless inmates were afforded access to the courts. The primary case that deals with inmate access to the courts is ***Johnson v. Avery* (1969)**. In this case, the Supreme Court held that prison authorities cannot prohibit inmates from aiding other inmates in preparing legal documents unless they also provide alternatives by which inmates may access the courts. More importantly, the Court further made it clear that, as a result, prison systems have an obligation to provide some form of documented access to the courts, to attorneys, or to some sort of legitimate legal aid (Anderson, Mangels, & Dyson, 2010).

Access to Law Libraries

The primary case that addresses the issue of law libraries is ***Bounds v. Smith* (1977)**. In this case, the Court held that even when prison policies allow jailhouse lawyers to provide assistance to inmates, prison systems must still provide inmates with either adequate law libraries or adequate legal assistance from persons trained in the law (Anderson et al., 2010). As with *Johnson v. Avery*, the opinion of the Court in *Bounds v. Smith* was far from specific in explaining what would constitute legal services and materials. However, most lower courts, in interpreting the ruling by the Supreme Court, have concluded that the requirements in *Bounds* are satisfied when states provide inmates with adequate law libraries and access to materials with some quasi-professional help (del Carmen et al., 2005).

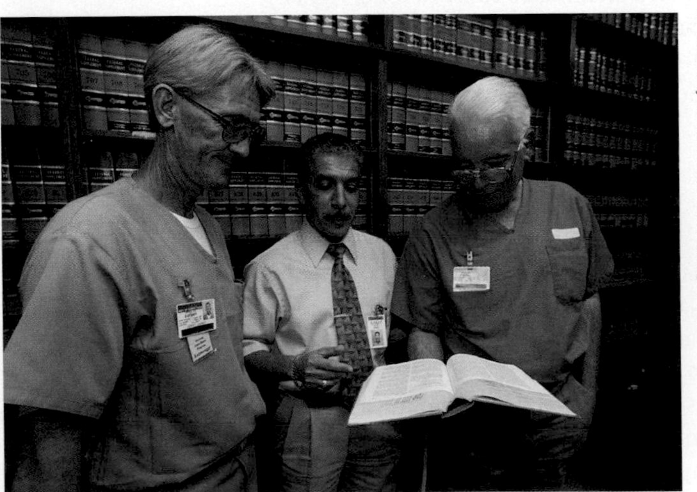
AP Photo/Daytona Beach News-Journal/Nigel Cook

■ PHOTO 3.2 Many times when inmates sue state agencies, they may use resources such as the law library.

While the specific requirements under *Bounds* are not necessarily clear, it would appear that, at a minimum, most courts currently require either an adequate law library or assistance from persons who have some sort of verifiable legal training. When determining whether the inmates of a prison have the appropriate assistance for filing court documents, courts generally consider the following four factors:

1. The number of inmates entitled to legal assistance.
2. The types of claims these inmates are entitled to bring.

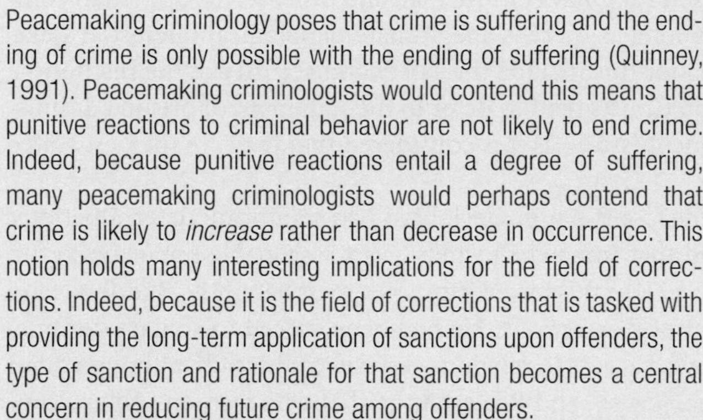

APPLIED THEORY 3.1

Peacemaking Criminology and Suffering Begets Suffering

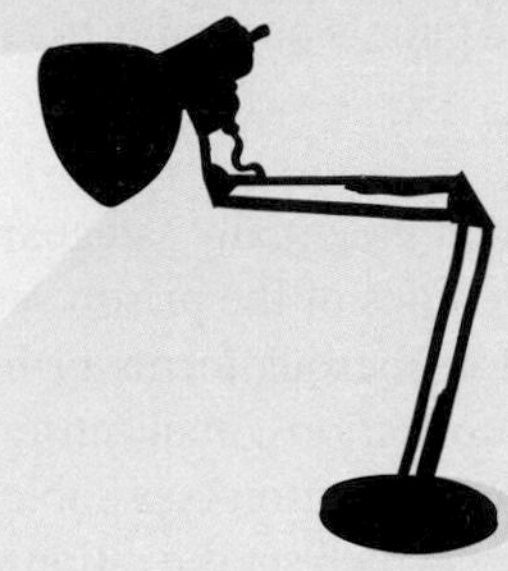

Peacemaking criminology poses that crime is suffering and the ending of crime is only possible with the ending of suffering (Quinney, 1991). Peacemaking criminologists would contend this means that punitive reactions to criminal behavior are not likely to end crime. Indeed, because punitive reactions entail a degree of suffering, many peacemaking criminologists would perhaps contend that crime is likely to *increase* rather than decrease in occurrence. This notion holds many interesting implications for the field of corrections. Indeed, because it is the field of corrections that is tasked with providing the long-term application of sanctions upon offenders, the type of sanction and rationale for that sanction becomes a central concern in reducing future crime among offenders.

As we have seen in the prior two chapters, classical criminologists such as Cesare Beccaria made note that punishments should be proportional to the crime. This is an important observation because Beccaria's contention was not just philosophical in nature; it was pragmatic as well. Beccaria had observed that when sufficiently provoked, people have strong reactions to unpleasant stimuli. Thus, whether or not an offender's punishment is deserved, those punishments that are too severe will simply elicit provocation from the offender rather than reformation. In other words, overly severe punishments are likely to make future behavior of the offender worse, not better.

Other researchers have concluded that excessive punishment will likely increase aberrant behavior, especially violent behavior (Davis & Palladino, 2002). Naturally, this can be detrimental to society. Of all the crimes, it is violent crime that we would least like to see repeated. If excessive punishment runs the risk of increasing this type of crime, then this is truly something that should be avoided.

One other interesting point that should be added, in regard to the death penalty in particular, is the brutalizing effect that may occur after the use of this most serious of sanctions. The brutalizing effect results in an increase in the number of murders due to the fact that the death penalty itself helps to reinforce the use of violence (Bowers & Pierce, 1980). Thus, it may well be that the use of this sanction further transmits the seeds of violence beyond that one offender and onward to many others in society. This may, in part, explain why many of the states in the southern and western parts of the United States tend to have higher than average crime rates; they also tend to have harsher than average prison terms and are more prone to use the death penalty.

Thus, peacemaking criminology may have some interesting insights for corrections. In order for us to lower crime, it may well be that we must seek to end the suffering and blight that breeds environments that are ripe for such behavior. In addition, it may be that correctional systems will have to moderate their use of punitive measures in a manner that emphasizes positive change rather than rigid, strict, and/or harsh techniques. As we have seen, this has, in fact, occurred within the field of corrections. As state systems have had to adopt more humane standards, the amount of suffering (particularly for suffering's sake) has been reduced among inmates. Likewise, the current emphasis on offender reentry programs is based on research that shows lower recidivism rates for those who are on community supervision when compared to those incarcerated for long periods of time. Perhaps, then, peacemaking criminology has some insights for administrators and policymakers as well as society as a whole.

3. The number of persons rendering assistance.
4. The training and credentials of those who provide legal assistance.

Although *Bounds* still remains the primary case regarding inmates' right to access to courts, another case, *Lewis v. Casey* (1996), has since narrowed the scope of this right in a manner that provides prison officials with much more leeway when establishing legal assistance that is likely to be constitutionally permissible. In *Lewis*, the Court held that any inmate who alleges a violation of *Bounds* must show that shortcomings in the prison's library or services for assistance caused an actual harm or injury that was directly attributable to the inmate's inability to pursue legitimate legal claims.

SAGE Journal Article Link
Corrections and the Constitution

CORRECTIONS AND THE CONSTITUTION

First Amendment Cases in Corrections

The First Amendment states that

> Congress shall make no law respecting an establishment of religion, or prohibiting the free exercise of religion thereof; or abridging the freedom of speech, or of the press; or

the right of the people peaceably to assemble, and to petition the government for a redress of grievances.

This amendment essentially safeguards the very right to speak, communicate, and act freely. Given the strict confines of the prison setting, it is no surprise that this amendment has been the legal basis behind numerous forms of inmate redress. Generally, case law has revolved around inmate access to publications, mail censoring processes, correspondence with family, and religious practices within the institution (see Table 3.1).

Turner v. Safley, which set the rational basis test, involved prison staff's basis for censoring different types of mail among inmates. Prison staff may censure mail and other forms of written communications and engage in oversight so long as there is a legitimate penological interest at stake. Some of the reasons that might be given for this include the safety and security of the institution, rehabilitative concerns, and prison order. Courts tend to defer to the judgment of prison administrators when considering First Amendment issues, as it is considered that they are the best suited to determine security and safety needs.

***Cruz v. Beto* (1972):** Ruling that inmates must be given reasonable opportunities to exercise their religious beliefs.

***O'Lone v. Estate of Shabazz* (1987):** Held that depriving an inmate of attending a religious service for "legitimate penological interests" was not a violation of the inmate's First Amendment rights.

***Holt v. Hobbs* (2015):** In cases of legitimate religious actions, the government must show that substantially burdening the religious exercise of an individual is "the least restrictive means of furthering that compelling governmental interest."

Religious Land Use and Institutionalized Persons Act of 2000: Prohibits the government from substantially burdening an inmate's religious exercise.

In the realm of religion in prison, the Court has made at least two significant determinations. In ***Cruz v. Beto* (1972)**, the Court ruled that inmates must be given reasonable opportunities to exercise their religious beliefs (see Table 3.1). In this case, Cruz was a member of the Buddhist faith and an inmate in the Texas Department of Corrections. He had been placed in solitary confinement and, during that time, was not allowed access to religious services for his faith although other inmates of other religions (e.g., Catholic, Jewish, and Protestant faiths) who were in solitary confinement were given such benefits. The Court held that inmates with unconventional beliefs must be afforded reasonable opportunities to exercise their religious beliefs, especially if this is afforded to inmates of other faiths (Anderson et al., 2010; Branham & Hamden, 2009).

In another case, ***O'Lone v. Estate of Shabazz* (1987)**, the Court held that the free exercise rights of a Muslim inmate were not violated when prison officials would not adjust the time of his work schedule (see Table 3.1). The reason for this ruling was that the prison system's justification for avoiding alterations in the work schedule was grounded in security and logistic concerns, which, according to the Court, were sufficient and legitimate penological interests. Since this ruling, various religious minorities among the inmate population have gained ground in securing the means for practicing their religions. As an example, lower court decisions have supported specialized dietary requirements for different religious faiths and the right to assemble for services, to contact religious leaders of the inmate's respective faith, and even to wear a beard if one's religion legitimately calls for it. Indeed, this has been upheld in ***Holt v. Hobbs* (2015)**, when the Supreme Court ruled that Muslim inmates may wear beards within institutions. A failure to allow this on the part of prison administrators is a violation of the Religious Land Use and Institutionalized Persons Act of 2000, as explained in the paragraph that follows.

The right to practice religion in prison was strengthened through the **Religious Land Use and Institutionalized Persons Act of 2000**. This act prohibits a state or local government from taking any action that substantially burdens the religious exercise of an institutionalized person unless the government demonstrates that the action constitutes the least restrictive means of furthering a compelling governmental interest. When a compelling governmental interest does exist, the government must use the least restrictive alternative to further that interest. Specifically, Section 3 contends that governments cannot impose a "substantial burden on a person residing in or confined to an institution," which of course includes inmates. The issue of religion has been under consideration for over 30 years, and it seems that just as the American cultural and religious landscape has become more diverse in society, so too has the world of corrections and correctional religious services.

Prison Tour Video: Religion in Prison. Accomodating an inmate's religion in prison presents a unique set of challenges for prison officials. Watch a warden discuss these challenges about religion in prison.

■ Table 3.1: First Amendment Prison Law Cases From the Supreme Court

First Amendment issues include inmate rights to freedom of speech and freedom of religion. Cases below are organized in chronological order.	
Court Case	**Ruling**
Fulwood v. Clemmer (1962)	The Muslim faith is a valid religion that requires prison officials to allow Muslim inmates to engage in their respective religious activities.
Gittlemacker v. Prasse (1970)	Inmates must be allowed to practice their religion, but states are not required to provide a clergy member in such cases.
Cruz v. Beto (1972)	Inmates must be given reasonable opportunities to exercise their religious beliefs.
***Procunier v. Martinez* (1974)**	Prison officials may censor inmate mail only to the extent necessary to ensure security of the institution.
Kahane v. Carlson (1975)	Jewish inmates have a right to their kosher diet as a bona fide part of their religion. If this cannot be provided, prison officials must show why such a diet cannot be provided.
Theriault v. Carlson (1977)	Bogus or fake religious sects that are not genuinely practiced with sincerity are not protected under the First Amendment.
Turner v. Safley (1987)	A prison regulation that impinges on inmates' constitutional rights is valid if it is reasonably related to legitimate penological interests.
O'Lone v. Estate of Shabazz (1987)	Prison policies that in effect prevent inmates from exercising freedom of religion are constitutional because they are reasonably related to legitimate penological interests.
Beard v. Banks (2006)	Prisons may implement policies that restrict access to magazines, publications, and photographs for inmates who are classified as higher risk to the safety and security of the institution.
Holt v. Hobbs (2015)	In cases of legitimate religious actions, the government must show that substantially burdening the religious exercise of an individual is "the least restrictive means of furthering that compelling governmental interest."

Fourth Amendment Cases in Corrections

According to the Fourth Amendment,

> the right of the people to be secure in their persons, houses, papers, and effects, against unreasonable searches and seizures, shall not be violated, and no Warrants shall issue, but upon probable cause, supported by Oath or affirmation, and particularly describing the place to be searched, and the persons or things to be seized.

***Procunier v. Martinez* (1974):** Prison officials may censor inmate mail only to the extent necessary to ensure security of the institution.

In prison settings, the Fourth Amendment has limited applicability because, for the most part, inmates do not have a legitimate expectation of privacy while serving their sentence. Indeed, the fact that they are incarcerated limits such an expectation given that prison officials must assume responsibility for their safety and security while in custody. Students should understand that inmates have no expectation of privacy when in the institution (whether in a cell or in a dorm-like setting), nor do they have such an expectation upon their person. Whenever prison staff determine appropriate, inmates are subject to search without any justification being necessary beyond a security rationale (see Table 3.2).

One area that has generated substantial litigation is that of cross-gendered searches of the person. However, when correctional staff of the opposite gender conduct a search, there is no constitutional violation. So long as the search is conducted according to policy, in a professional manner, and without sexual connotations, the inmate will have no standing for a grievance. Though this is the case, it is generally considered

■ PHOTO 3.3 Muslims attend Juma, Friday's group prayer, in a gathering room reserved for prisoner activities at a state prison in Virginia.

■ Table 3.2: Fourth Amendment Prison Law Cases From the Supreme Court

Fourth Amendment issues address unreasonable searches and seizures of persons and their things. In prisons, this tends to involve invasive searches of inmates and/or their property that inmates believe should be protected.	
Court Case	**Ruling**
Lanza v. New York (1962)	Verbal and written conversations in jail (and prison) visitation rooms do not enjoy any Fourth Amendment privacy safeguards.
United States v. Hitchcock (1972)	Searches of inmate cells and dormitories are not subject to Fourth Amendment considerations. Prison staff may conduct searches of inmate living quarters as the need arises.
Bell v. Wolfish (1979)	The use of body cavity searches of inmates after contact visits is permissible. Prison staff may search inmates' quarters in their absence. Double bunking does not deprive inmates of their liberty without due process of law.
Hudson v. Palmer (1984)	A prison cell may be searched without a warrant and without probable cause. Prison cells are not protected by the Fourth Amendment.
Albert W. Florence v. Board of Chosen Freeholders of the County of Burlington, et al. **(2012)**	Prison staff may routinely strip search minor offenders and detainees (e.g. traffic violation offenders) when they are arrested and detained within a jail or detention facility.

prudent for prison administrators to consider an inmate's privacy as much as is reasonable, especially in areas such as showers and dressing rooms. Though personal searches are not considered problematic, the use of opposite-gendered strip searches is usually prohibited by most courts. Thus, prison and jail systems with inmates of both genders will find it wise to have staff of both genders readily available as well.

Searches of the person are conducted at varying levels of intrusiveness. Some consist of the simple pat search of the outer clothing, others require strip searching of the inmate, and the most invasive form of search is the body cavity search. Policies should clearly demonstrate the need for more invasive searches and connect them to a legitimate institutional need. Thus, the more invasive the procedure, the more clear the evidence must be that a legitimate institutional interest was at stake, and the more important it is that the search be documented and justified (Branham & Hamden, 2009).

For offenders who are on probation and/or parole, the issue of searches can be a bit more complicated. In such circumstances, police officers and other external enforcement officials need to adhere to Fourth Amendment considerations when dealing with these offenders. However, community supervision staff (e.g., probation and parole officers) are not under those same restrictions, particularly if the inmate is on their own caseload. In such circumstances, police have been known to work in partnership with community supervision personnel to avoid Fourth Amendment restrictions; such partnerships exist throughout the nation and have been found to be constitutionally permissible.

Eighth Amendment Cases in Corrections

The Eighth Amendment states that "excessive bail shall not be required, nor excessive fines imposed, nor cruel and unusual punishments inflicted." This amendment is cited in most cases involving excessive use of force or other physical injuries where inmates file suit (see Table 3.3). But, in addition to such overt acts where civil rights are in question, inmates also use this amendment as the basis for a number of other issues, such as the conditions of confinement, medical care, and other minimal standards of living. In general, when determining if acts or conditions are violations under the Eighth Amendment, the courts have utilized three basic considerations:

Albert W. Florence v. Board of Chosen Freeholders of the County of Burlington, et al. **(2012):** Prison staff may strip search minor offenders and detainees within a jail or detention facility.

1. Whether the treatment shocks the general conscience of a civilized society.
2. Whether the treatment is cruel beyond necessity.
3. Whether the treatment is within the scope of legitimate penological interests.

To further aid in determining claims against prison conditions under the Eighth Amendment, federal courts have implemented a standard that takes into account various factors. This standard, which was born out of Supreme Court case law, is known as the totality of circumstances in general precedent by the Court. The totality of circumstances has been modified in prison law to consist of the **totality of the conditions**, to determine if conditions in an institution are in violation of the Eighth Amendment. In numerous cases, the Court has made a point to effect positive change in prison operations throughout the nation, and, in doing so, has laid out three principles that should be implemented when mandating change. The three principles, as articulated in *Hutto v. Finney* (1978), consist of the following:

1. Courts should consider the totality of the conditions of confinement.
2. Courts should make a point to specify each individual factor that contributed to this totality of conditions that were found to be unconstitutional, with clear orders for remediation and changes.
3. When and where possible, courts should articulate the minimal standards necessary for an institution to remedy the constitutional violation.

As noted just previously, inmates also use the Eighth Amendment as the legal basis to challenge force used against them. For instance, in *Hudson v. McMillian* (1992), the Supreme Court ruled that inmates do not need to suffer a severe physical injury in order to file an Eighth Amendment claim as long as the use of force or abusive treatment involved the "wanton and unnecessary infliction of pain," or if the force was used "maliciously or sadistically for the very purpose of causing pain." Naturally, such forms of treatment serve no legitimate penological interest and simply aggravate criminogenic mind-sets among the offender population. More recently, the case of *Brown v. Plata* (2011) serves as modern-day confirmation of the criteria set in *Hutto*. In *Brown*, it was determined that overcrowding in the California Department of Corrections and Rehabilitation (CDCR) was unconstitutional. Prior to this Supreme Court ruling, the CDCR, as a system, was designed to hold 80,000 inmates. A three-judge district court ruling required the CDCR to submit a plan to reduce the 150,000 inmates within that system by 40,000 to bring it to 110,000, which would have still been a population that was 37% above capacity for that system. The district judges noted that California had failed to obey previous orders to improve prison crowding conditions, making the reduction necessary to deal with overcrowding and very poor health care, the result of which had been at least one preventable inmate death each week, on average (Liptak, 2011). This case spurred substantial debate among the justices, particularly over concern about public safety when releasing so many inmates in such a short period of time. Nevertheless, the Court upheld the ruling of the district judges, affirming that when conditions are so bad as to be unconstitutional, states must take corrective action.

There is one other legal area that falls under Eighth Amendment consideration: the death penalty. While the death penalty has been held as constitutional since the ruling of ***Gregg v. Georgia* (1976)**, the specific means by which that penalty is administered are still subject to potential legal challenge (see Table 3.3). There is an expectation that the application of this penalty will not be arbitrary or capricious in nature. Further, as with *Hudson v. McMillian*, the imposition of the death penalty must not consist of the unnecessary infliction of pain or be malicious or sadistic in nature.

Totality of the conditions: A standard used to determine if conditions in an institution are in violation of the Eighth Amendment.

***Gregg v. Georgia* (1976):** Held that death penalty statutes that contain sufficient safeguards against arbitrary and capricious imposition are constitutional.

Fourteenth Amendment Cases in Corrections

According to the Fourteenth Amendment,

> All persons born or naturalized in the United States, and subject to the jurisdiction thereof, are citizens of the United States and of the state wherein they reside. No state shall make or enforce any law which shall abridge the privileges or immunities of citizens without due process of law, nor deny to any person within its jurisdiction the equal protection of the laws.

The primary application of the Fourteenth Amendment to prison law issues has to do with procedural due process issues and issues related to equal protection (see Table 3.4). The Fourteenth

■ Table 3.3: Eighth Amendment Prison Law Cases From the Supreme Court

Eighth Amendment issues address whether treatment of inmates entails cruel or unusual punishment.	
Court Case	**Ruling**
Estelle v. Gamble (1976)	Deliberate indifference to inmate medical needs constitutes cruel and unusual punishment and is therefore unconstitutional.
Gregg v. Georgia (1976)	Death penalty statutes that contain sufficient safeguards against arbitrary and capricious imposition are constitutional.
***Ruiz v. Estelle* (1980)**	The conditions in the prison system of Texas were found to be unconstitutional.
Rhodes v. Chapman (1981)	Double celling of inmates does not, unto itself, constitute cruel and unusual punishment.
Whitley v. Albers (1986)	The shooting of an inmate without prior verbal warning in order to suppress a prison riot does not violate that inmate's right against cruel or unusual punishment.
***Wilson v. Seiter* (1991)**	Deliberate indifference is required for liability to be attached to condition of confinement cases. This means that a culpable state of mind on the part of prison administrators must be demonstrated.
Overton v. Bazzetta (2003)	Prison staff may restrict prison visitations so long as their actions are related to legitimate penological interests.
Hill v. McDonough (2006)	Methods of implementing the death penalty are subject to suit under Section 1983 litigation.
Brown v. Plata (2011)	A court-mandated population limit is sometimes necessary to remedy violations of prisoners' Eighth Amendment constitutional rights.

Amendment often comes into play when inmates file suit regarding parole release, intraprison transfers, and disciplinary hearings. The other aspect of the Fourteenth Amendment that is relevant to prison law is equal protection. Inmates using this aspect of the amendment may file suit regarding equal protection pertaining to issues based on race, gender, or religious discrimination (Anderson et al., 2010).

The case of ***Wolff v. McDonnell* (1974)** provided guidelines for minimal due process rights that should be afforded inmates facing disciplinary proceedings (see Table 3.4). The Court held that when a prisoner faces serious disciplinary action resulting in the loss of good time or in some form of housing custody change, the procedures used should provide the following:

***Ruiz v. Estelle* (1980):** Ruled that the Texas prison system was in violation of the prohibition against cruel and unusual punishments.

***Wilson v. Seiter* (1991):** Deliberate indifference is required for liability to be attached for condition of confinement cases.

***Wolff v. McDonnell* (1974):** Inmates are entitled to due process in prison disciplinary proceedings that can result in the loss of good time credits or in punitive segregation.

1. The inmate must be given 24-hour written notice of the charges.
2. There must be a written statement by the fact finders as to the evidence relied on and reasons for the disciplinary action.
3. The inmate should be allowed to call witnesses and present documentary evidence in his or her defense so long as this does not jeopardize institutional safety and security.
4. Counsel substitute must be permitted when the inmate is illiterate or when the complexity of the issues makes it unlikely that the inmate will be able to collect and present the evidence for an adequate comprehension of the case.
5. The prison disciplinary board must be impartial.

While the above conditions must be provided, the Court has made it clear that disciplinary hearings do not rise to the standard of a true courthouse proceeding but are designed to provide some measure of protection against arbitrariness.

■ Table 3.4: Fourteenth Amendment Prison Law Cases From the Supreme Court

The Fourteenth Amendment addresses due process of law and equal protection under the law.	
Court Case	**Ruling**
Wolff v. McDonnell (1974)	Inmates are entitled to due process in prison disciplinary proceedings that can result in the loss of good time credits or in punitive segregation.
Baxter v. Palmigiano (1976)	Inmates are not entitled to counsel or cross-examination in prison disciplinary hearings. In addition, silence by inmates in a disciplinary proceeding may be used as adverse evidence against them.
***Vitek v. Jones* (1980)**	Inmates are entitled to due process in involuntary transfers from prison to a mental hospital.
Superintendent, Walpole v. Hill (1985)	Disciplinary board findings that result in loss of good time credits must be supported by a "modicum" of evidence to satisfy due process requirements.
***Kingsley v. Hendrickson* (2015)**	For claims of excessive force brought by pretrial detainees, it is only necessary to show that the force used was objectively unreasonable, not that the officer subjectively intended to injure the inmate. These protections for detainees are thus similar to those for persons who are officially convicted and incarcerated.

SOURCE: del Carmen, R. V., Ritter, S. E., & Witt, B. A. (2005). *Briefs of leading cases in corrections* (4th ed.). Anderson Publishing.

In ***Baxter v. Palmigiano* (1976)**, the distinction between prison disciplinary proceedings and genuine courtroom affairs was directly addressed (Anderson et al., 2010). The Court noted that inmates do not have the right to either retained or appointed counsel for disciplinary hearings that are not part of an actual criminal prosecution (see Table 3.4). Further, inmates are not entitled to confront and cross-examine witnesses at all times. In addition, and unlike courtroom proceedings, an inmate's decision to remain silent when faced with disciplinary proceedings can be used as adverse evidence of the inmate's guilt by disciplinary decision makers. Thus, disciplinary hearings simply require fundamental fairness and nondiscriminatory application; they are not to be confused with regular court proceedings.

Vitek v. Jones (1980): Inmates are entitled to due process in involuntary transfers from prison to a mental hospital.

Kingsley v. Hendrickson (2015): For claims of excessive force brought by pretrial detainees, it is only necessary to show that the force used was objectively unreasonable.

Baxter v. Palmigiano (1976): Determined that inmates do not have the right to counsel for disciplinary hearings that are not part of a criminal prosecution.

A RESTRAINED HANDS-ON PERSPECTIVE AND COURT DEFERENCE TO PRISONS

In changing to a more restrictive interpretation of inmate rights, two cases, ***Bell v. Wolfish* (1979)** and *Rhodes v. Chapman* (1981), served as major turning points. These cases reflect an attempt of the Court to balance institutional operations with the need to protect inmates' constitutional rights from oppressive government actions. In *Bell v. Wolfish*, the Court noted that

> maintaining institutional security and preserving internal order and discipline are essential guides that may require limitation or retractions of the retained constitutional rights of both convicted prisoners and pretrial detainees. . . . Prison officials must be free to take appropriate action to ensure safety of inmates and correctional personnel and to prevent escape or unauthorized entry. (p. 1878)

Bell v. Wolfish (1979): Determined that body cavity searches of inmates after contact visits is permissible, as are searches of inmates' quarters in their absence. Double bunking does not deprive inmates of their liberty without due process of law.

Thus, it is clear that the Court has been receptive to the challenges that face prison staff and administrators. However, in the case of *Rhodes*, the Court, in addressing the totality of conditions regarding prison facilities, noted very clearly that "the constitution does not mandate comfortable prisons," nor should prisons aspire to reach such an ideal standard of living.

From 1980 onward, the Court has taken a more balanced approach to inmate litigation. This balanced approach is known as the **one hand on, one hand off doctrine**. This doctrine contends that while incarcerated, (1) inmates do not forfeit their constitutional rights, (2) inmate rights are not as broad and encompassing as are free persons', and (3) prison officials need to maintain order, security, and discipline in their facilities.

One hand on, one hand off doctrine: More conservative rulings are being handed down from the Court, relfecting an eclipse of the hands-off doctrine.

CROSS-NATIONAL PERSPECTIVE 3.1

Human Rights in Prisons and the Story of Abu Ghraib

As can be seen throughout the previous chapters and throughout the case law in this chapter, human rights and standards of decency have been a constant concern in corrections. This is only natural since the treatment of people who are being punished can lead and has led to a number of heinous outcomes. In the past 50 years, Supreme Court cases have illustrated the need to monitor human rights issues in prisons and emphasized the fundamental concept of seeing value in the lives of human beings, regardless of their transgressions. This is particularly true for those persons in the custody of the government.

If you doubt this, consider the incidents at Abu Ghraib, which were well covered in the media. In 2004, accounts of physical, psychological, and sexual abuse in this American military prison in Iraq came to light. These acts of torture, all committed amidst the fervor of the conflict in Iraq, the antiterrorism initiative, and other factors, were committed by U.S. Army military police personnel as well as other officials. An article in the *New York Times*, released in 2005, reported testimony that indicated the following types of torture and/or techniques of degradation had taken place:

1. Urinating on detainees.
2. Jumping on a detainee's leg (a limb already wounded by gunfire) with such force that it could not thereafter heal properly.
3. Pounding detainees with collapsible metal batons.
4. Pouring phosphoric acid on detainees.
5. Sodomization of detainees with batons and other instruments.
6. Tying ropes to the detainees' legs or penises and dragging them across the floor.

In addition, many of the prison staff forced Iraqi prisoners to stand in various humiliating poses and engage in acts that were embarrassing. While engaged in these activities, numerous photos were taken of both the Iraqi prisoners and the U.S. military personnel responsible for these atrocities. These photos were ultimately disseminated throughout the mass media and were seen by millions of people in the United States and around the world. The entire affair became an international incident and led to sharp criticism of the United States and its military. Naturally, investigations were conducted into the incidents at Abu Ghraib, and this resulted in numerous military and civilian personnel being disciplined within their organizations and in criminal charges for many of them. A number of those involved were given prison sentences for their acts of abuse and torture.

Many scholars have written and spoken about the acts at Abu Ghraib in order to try to analyze the circumstances. A variety of explanations have been given as to how American military personnel could be involved in such an embarrassing and dishonorable set of events. Regardless of the reasons, it is clear that training and emphasis on ethical and professional behavior is something that is still needed among personnel. Thus, an awareness and fundamental appreciation for the human rights or civil rights of inmates is critical, even for criminal offenders or enemies of the state.

QUESTION 1: What factors do you think helped to exacerbate the likelihood of unethical behavior among military correctional personnel in Abu Ghraib?

QUESTION 2: In your opinion, if ethical and professional behavior is simply common sense, and if "everyone already knows right from wrong," why does unethical behavior continue to persist in prisons?

Over time, the Supreme Court has become even more conservative regarding inmates' rights and meddling in the affairs of prison operations. While the passage of the Prison Litigation Reform Act is seen as indication that the Court now gives deference to prison officials, rulings such as that found in *Brown v. Plata* (2011) demonstrate that the Court will become involved and rule against prison administrators when prison conditions seem to be egregious.

The Prison Litigation Reform Act of 1995

Prison Litigation Reform Act (PLRA): Limits an inmate's ability to file lawsuits and the compensation that he or she can receive.

The **Prison Litigation Reform Act (PLRA)** was initially passed through Congress with the intent of preventing the wave of frivolous lawsuits that had been filed by inmates in federal court. Essentially, the PLRA was designed to be a screening mechanism to eliminate those cases that were found to be malicious in nature, failed to state a bona fide claim that qualified for legal relief, or sought damages from agency personnel who had immunity from suit. More specifically, Carlson and Garrett (2008) note that the PLRA contains these provisions:

1. Limit inmates' ability to file lawsuits.
2. Require inmates to exhaust all available administrative remedies prior to filing suits.
3. Require the payment of full filing fees in some instances.
4. Impose harsh sanctions, including the loss of good time credit, for filing frivolous or malicious lawsuits.
5. Require that any damages awarded to inmates be used to satisfy pending restitution orders.

©iStockphoto.com/tomloel

■ PHOTO 3.4 The balanced scales are a common symbol of balanced justice in the United States. When considering the totality of the circumstances, it is the role of the court to come to reasonable rulings that are balanced, equitable, and within the bounds of the rule of law.

Further, the PLRA sets a limit on the relief that an inmate may secure from the courts, the restriction being that courts may only require of prison systems a minimum of modification so as to most expediently and in a Spartan manner address a noted deficiency. Even with this, courts must keep their requirements narrow in focus, and they must consider the potential impact that their ruling may have on overall institutional and public safety. Further, oversight from federal judges regarding prison operations was given an expiration of 2 years unless another successful hearing proves that constitutional violations continue to persist within that prison facility or system. Thus, the PLRA has provided state governments with a mechanism by which they can limit the effects of suits regarding prison conditions. This is good news for state prison systems that were, in their earlier history, under the constant scrutiny of federal courts. Figure 3.1 demonstrates the impact that the PLRA has had on the overall number of state inmates who have filed petitions in U.S. district courts.

Web Link
Prison Litigation Reform Act

It is noteworthy that the PLRA has been challenged in court but that the Supreme Court has continued to support and uphold the provisions of this act. For example, in *Booth v. Churner* (2001), the Court ruled that inmates must exhaust all of their available administrative processes for a grievance before filing suit, even if those provisions do not allow for monetary damages. This is an important point because up until this time, inmates would sometimes utilize legal remedies to simply gain monetary compensation rather than using available tools within the prison to rectify wrongs.

The PLRA and its general stance on inmate litigation are reflective of a more conservative approach with prison rulings. In fact, it appears that the Court is leaning more toward a "one hand on, one hand off" doctrine regarding intervention in prison operations. More conservative rulings are being handed down from the Court, and this reflects an eclipse of the hands-off doctrine in American corrections.

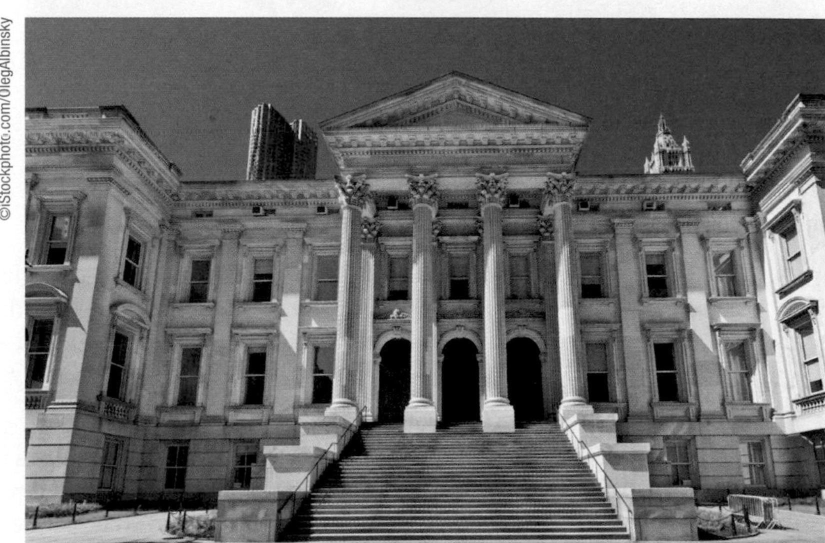

©iStockphoto.com/OlegAlbinsky

■ PHOTO 3.5 It is from the local or federal courthouse that legal suits are filed. The courthouse has the role of determining inmate rights as well as the rights of offenders on probation or parole.

STATE AND FEDERAL LEGAL LIABILITIES

Liability is a term used to note that when a person commits a wrongful action or fails to act when they had a duty to do so, they can be held legally accountable. There are many

■ **Figure 3.1: The Effect of the PLRA on Petitions Filed by State Inmates From 1990 to 2006***

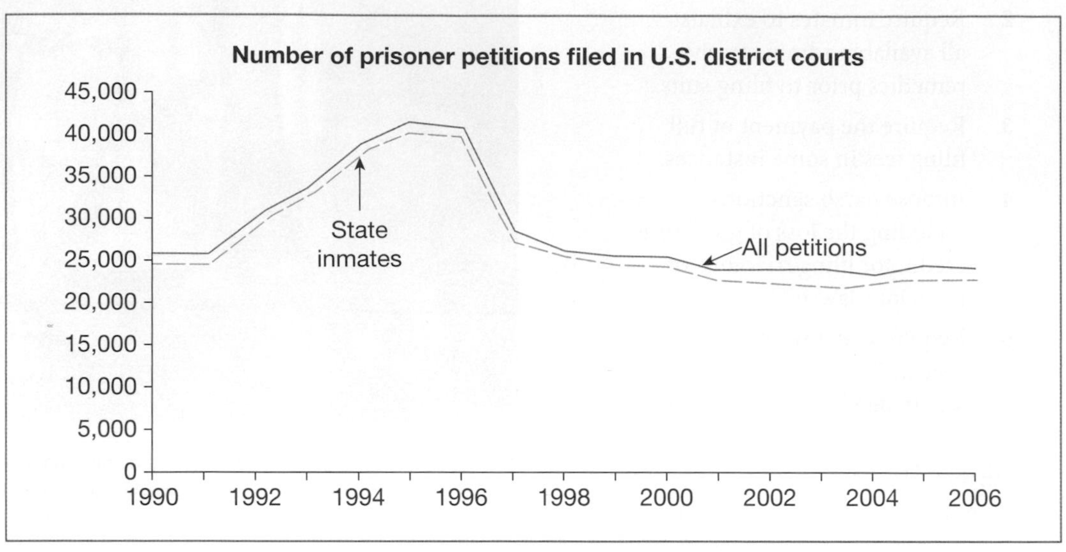

SOURCE: U.S. Department of Justice. (2009). *Civil rights complaints in U.S. district courts, 1990–2006.* Washington, DC: Author.

*Most recent data available

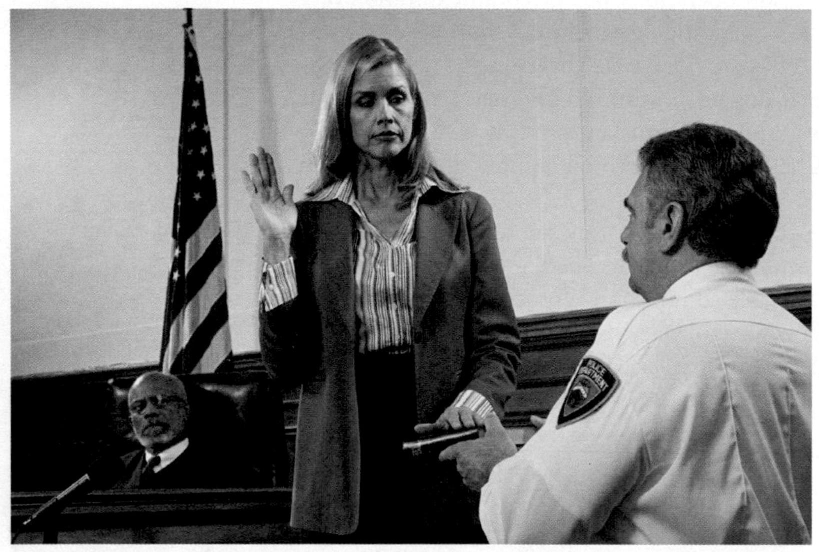

■ PHOTO 3.6 A state employee prepares to take the stand and provide testimony. In cases where employees of agencies must go to court, they are "sworn in" prior to the question-and-answer process that occurs in a court proceeding.

means by which liability may ensue. First, liability can attach at both the state and the federal levels of government. Second, liability, though most often civil, can be criminal as well. In most cases, the sources of liability are typically not restricted to community supervision officers but often serve as the bases of liability for any officer of the state. Nevertheless, just as with other practitioners who act under "color of law" (a term we will expound upon later in this chapter), community supervision officers usually incur potential liability due to their role as agents of the state (*state* being used in a general sense to cover local, state, and federal government). In addition, the types of liability may actually apply in a variety of forms and from multiple sources. For instance, civil and even criminal liability can emerge, and a correctional officer can be subject to both state and federal levels of civil liability, depending upon the circumstances. For purposes of this chapter, we will first begin with state-level forms of liability and then progress toward federal levels of liability (students should also see Table 3.5 for additional details).

State Levels of Liability

Civil liability under state law often is referred to as tort law. A **tort** is a legal injury in which the action of one person causes injury to the person or property of another as the result of a violation of one's duty that has been established by law (del Carmen, Barnhill, Bonham, Hignite, & Jermstad, 2001). Torts can be either deliberate or accidental in nature. A deliberate tort is considered intentional and refers to acts that are intended to have a certain outcome or to cause some form of harm to the aggrieved. An accidental tort would generally be one that is committed out of negligence with the intent of harm being nonexistent.

Tort: A legal injury in which a person causes injury as the result of a violation of one's duty as established by law.

CORRECTIONS AND THE LAW 3.1

Estelle v. Gamble, Farmer v. Brennan, *and the Legal Concept of Deliberate Indifference*

In ***Estelle v. Gamble*** **(1976),** it was found that deliberate indifference to an inmate's medical needs constitutes cruel and unusual punishment and is a violation of the Eighth Amendment. In this case, inmate J. W. Gamble alleged that the Texas prison system had provided him with inadequate medical care and that prison officials were "deliberately indifferent" to his medical needs. This case occurred during the time that Texas and other states were feeling the pains of federal oversight.

Estelle v. Gamble is considered important because in it the Court defined the fluid term *deliberate indifference* by stating that "deliberate indifference to serious medical needs of prisoners constitutes the unnecessary and wanton infliction of pain," which, in essence, means that prison officials go out of their way to ensure that pain will occur. Other cases since *Estelle v. Gamble* have equated deliberate indifference with having a culpable state of mind. Thus, this standard has been used widely in a number of civil cases as precedent for determining standards of care and treatment in prisons among administrators who may not be forthcoming with their activities or their failures to act in good faith.

But, as the historical development of corrections resulted in an evolutionary metamorphosis, so too did the legal developments. This was true with the concept of deliberate indifference, which between the time of *Estelle v. Gamble* and the mid-1990s had become a common term among prison law experts. In 1994, a most curious ruling came about that would take this term and significantly limit its far-reaching impact in corrections.

In ***Farmer v. Brennan*** **(1994),** it was found that a prison official is not liable under the Eighth Amendment for injury inflicted on an inmate by another inmate unless it can be determined that the prison official knew of the excessive risk of harm to that inmate and chose to disregard that harm. What is important about this case is that the Court made it clear that liability does not attach to prison officials by the reasonable person standard.

The *reasonable person standard* is a common term used by the Supreme Court when creating criteria for determinations that do not have a clear and specific answer. Often this is used in discretionary circumstances and simply means that when determining whether an action was or was not prudent, the Court considers what a reasonable and everyday person might consider appropriate. The *Farmer* case is significant because it sets a limit to the notion of deliberate indifference that was so important in the case of *Estelle v. Gamble*. In the former case, inmate Farmer was a transsexual who had been transferred from federal prison to state prison. Farmer had feminine traits and had even undergone surgical enhancements to appear as a woman. Given his appearance, it was obvious that he would face sexual assault, and ultimately he was indeed assaulted. However, the Supreme Court noted that it was not sufficient that the prison official "should have known that harm was inevitable because the risk was so obvious that a reasonable person should have noticed it." Rather, the official must have "knowingly disregarded an excessive risk of harm." This decision makes it difficult for inmates to hold prison officials liable for inmate-on-inmate altercations because it is extremely difficult to prove that officials actually *knew* that a danger existed and that they then deliberately disregarded that danger. Thus, *Farmer* breaks from the generally sympathetic attitudes of the Court that have been noted in other deliberate indifference cases, such as *Estelle v. Gamble.*

Estelle v. Gamble **(1976):** Ruled that deliberate indifference to inmate medical needs constitutes cruel and unusual punishment and is unconstitutional.

Farmer v. Brennan **(1994):** Held that a prison official is not liable injury inflicted on an inmate by another inmate unless he/she knew of the excessive risk of harm and disregarded it.

Table 3.5: Comparing State and Federal Lawsuits Against Community Supervision Officers

State Tort Cases	Federal Section 1983 Cases
Based on state law.	Based on federal law.
Plaintiff seeks money for damages.	Plaintiff seeks money for damages and/or policy change.
Usually based on decided cases.	Law was passed in 1871.
Usually tried in state court.	Usually tried in federal court.
Public officials and private persons can be sued.	Only public officials can be sued.
Basis for liability is injury to person or property of another in violation of a duty imposed by state law.	Basis for liability is violation of a constitutional right or of a right secured by federal law.
Good faith defense usually means the officer acted in the honest belief that the action taken was appropriate under the circumstances.	Good faith defense means the officer did not violate a clearly established constitutional or federal right of which a reasonable person should have been aware.

Adapted from: del Carmen, R. V., Barnhill, M. B., Bonham, G., Hignite, L., & Jermstad, T. (2001). *Civil liabilities and other legal issues for probation/parole officers and supervisors.* Washington, DC: National Institute of Corrections.

Torts

According to *Black's Law Dictionary*, an **intentional tort** is one in which the actor was judged to have possessed intent or purpose to injury, whether expressed or implied. This means that an intentional tort has numerous components, all of which must be proven by a plaintiff if the suit is to prevail. The components of an intentional tort that must be proven are as follows:

1. An act was committed by the defendant.
2. The act was deliberate and can be shown to be such due to the fact that the defendant had to have known of the potential consequences of the act.
3. The resulting harm was actually caused by the act.
4. Clear damages can be shown to have resulted from the act.

A hypothetical example might be a scenario in which Correctional Officer X conducts a search of an inmate's cell. While in the cell, the correctional officer assaults the inmate and says, "I can reach out and touch you anytime, and if you say anything about it, I will see to it that you get written up and lose your good time." The inmate is injured, has to go to the infirmary for internal injuries, and decides to disclose the source of his injuries. In this case, the correctional officer has obviously committed an intentional tort. The assault was committed by Correctional Officer X (the defendant in this case), the assault was obviously on purpose and Correctional Officer X was clearly cognizant of his actions, and clear damages in the way of physical injuries occurred as a direct result of the assault.

Intentional tort: The actor, whether expressed or implied, was judged to have possessed intent or purpose to cause an injury.

Defamation: Some form of slander or libel that damages a person's reputation.

Slander: Verbal communication intended to lower the reputation of a person where such facts would actually be damaging to a reputation.

Libel: Written communication intended to lower the reputation of a person where such facts would actually be damaging to a reputation.

Emotional distress: Refers to acts that lead to emotional distress of the client.

Malicious prosecution: Occurs when a criminal accusation is made without probable cause and for improper reasons.

Negligence: Doing what a reasonably prudent person would not do in similar circumstances or failing to do what a reasonably prudent person would do in similar circumstances.

In regard to nonphysical torts, several specific types of offenses or damages might occur. These include defamation, acts that cause harm to a person's emotional well-being, and malicious prosecution, among others. Because this area of liability is so broad, it is necessary to address many of these concepts specifically to ensure that the student has a clear understanding of each potential source of liability. Though the following discussion will not be exhaustive, it will highlight the more common areas of liability that correctional officers may face.

First, **defamation** is an invasion of a person's interest through his or her reputation. In order for this to occur, some form of slander or libel must have occurred against the aggrieved individual. Many people use the term *slander* loosely but often are unclear about its meaning, though they may not realize this. To be clear, **slander** is any oral communication provided to another party (aside from the aggrieved person) that lowers the reputation of the person discussed and where people in the community would find such facts to actually be damaging to that person's reputation. **Libel**, on the other hand, is the written version of slander.

The next category, infliction of **emotional distress**, refers to acts (either intentional or negligent) that lead to emotional distress of the client. Emotional distress can occur due to words or gestures, and of course the conduct of correctional staff. For instance, tactics used to bully or abuse an inmate would fall within this category. However, one simple incident, though not likely to be in adherence to agency policy, typically does not incur liability unless the situation can be shown to be "extreme" and "outrageous" (del Carmen et al., 2001).

The last area of nonphysical tort that will be discussed is malicious prosecution. **Malicious prosecution** occurs when a criminal accusation is made by someone who has no probable cause and who generates such actions for improper reasons. In such cases, the accused must be, as a matter of material fact, innocent of the charges that were made.

The next primary category of state tort includes acts of negligence. In the vast majority of cases, negligence suits are not successful, particularly if the officer had adhered to agency policy. Most agencies do have sufficient policy safeguards to ensure that an adequate good faith attempt at public safety is made, and, presuming that the officer follows policy, liability is not likely to be incurred. For purposes of this text, **negligence** is defined as doing what a reasonably prudent person would not have done in similar circumstances, or failing to do what a reasonably prudent person would have done in similar circumstances. The following minimal conditions are typically required to establish a case of negligence:

1. A legal duty is owed to the aggrieved person (in prisons, such a duty exists between custodial staff and inmates).
2. A breach of that duty must have occurred whether by the failure to act or by the commission of action that was not professionally sufficient to fulfill that duty.

3. The aggrieved can demonstrate that an injury did occur.
4. The person with the duty owed to the aggrieved person committed the act (or lack of action) that was the proximate cause of the injury.

Liability Under Section 1983 Federal Lawsuits

This avenue for civil redress is one of the most frequently used by persons seeking damages from the government. Though there is substantial history associated with this particular form of liability, this text will delve right into the substantive issues associated with Section 1983 liabilities. Essentially, there are two simple requirements that must exist in order for liability to be imparted to a person so charged:

1. The person charged (the defendant) acted under color of state law.
2. The person charged violated a right secured by the constitution or by federal law.

Both of these requirements need some explanation. First, the term *color of state law* must be clarified. This term simply means that the actor committed his or her behavior while under the authority of some form of government. In this case, the term *state* is meant to imply government in general, regardless of the level of the government (local, state, or federal) that is associated with the agency. Thus, local jailers, state correctional officers, and community supervision officers all act under the color of state law when they are performing their duties in the employment of their respective agencies. This liability does not, however, apply during their off-time "normal" lives. In further clarifying this concept, del Carmen et al. (2001) note that anything correctional officers do in the performance of their regular duties and during the usual hours of employment is considered as falling under the color of state law. In contrast, whatever these same people do as private citizens during their off-hours falls outside and beyond the color of state law. In closing, it should be considered that not every violation of an inmate's rights rises to be a federal or constitutional issue. Rather, the violation must be severe enough and centered on a federal or constitutionally protected right to be considered as having sufficient merit.

Forms of Immunity and Types of Defenses

One key protection for correctional staff, as agents of the state, is their potential immunity from tort suits. *Official immunity* is a term that refers to being legally shielded from suit. Official immunity is granted to those professions that must be allowed to, at least in the majority of circumstances, actively pursue their duties without undue fear or intimidation. Otherwise, law enforcement, correctional, and judicial professionals could not fulfill their duties correctly. However, official immunity comes in a number of different forms, reflecting the different levels of responsibility and liability associated with different functions in the justice system. For purposes of this text, students need only to discern between *absolute immunity* and *qualified immunity*.

Absolute immunity, meaning that the individual is not able to be subject to a lawsuit when acting in his or her professional capacity, exists for those persons who work in positions that require unimpaired decision making. Judges and prosecutors have this type of immunity since their jobs require that they make very important decisions regarding the livelihood of persons in their courts; these decisions must be made free of intimidation or potential recrimination, and therefore these court actors enjoy absolute immunity from being sued when carrying out their responsibilities (del Carmen et al., 2001). Note, however, that this does not include an immunity from criminal charges, if such was applicable. For correctional officers and community supervision officers, protection through immunity is typically referred to as qualified immunity. **Qualified immunity** requires that the community supervision officer demonstrate three key criteria were met prior to invoking this form of defense against suit. These criteria, according to del Carmen et al. (2001), are as follows:

Absolute immunity: Protection for persons who work in positions that require unimpaired decision-making functions.

Qualified immunity: Legal immunity that shields correctional officers from lawsuits, but first requires them to demonstrate the grounds for their possession of immunity

1. The community supervision officer must show that he or she was performing a discretionary act, not one that was mandatory by agency policy.
2. The correctional officer must have been acting in good faith—that is, holding the sincere belief that his or her action was correct under the circumstances.

3. The correctional officer must have acted within the scope of his or her designated authority. Thus, most correctional officers do not enjoy the same level of immunity as do their colleagues in the judicial arena since they have to demonstrate the grounds for their possession of immunity.

Beyond the initial forms of liability protection (i.e., qualified immunity and the public duty doctrine) afforded correctional officers, there are some defenses that officers can raise on their own behalf. First among these is the good faith defense. The **good faith defense** essentially buffers a correctional officer from liability in Section 1983 cases (not state tort cases) unless the officer violated some clearly established constitutional or federal statutory right that a reasonable person would have known to exist.

From the previous discussion of both state tort and Section 1983 forms of suit, it is clear that the issue of *good faith* is important. The notion that the officer acted in good faith (with the sincere belief that his or her action was appropriate) is important to establishing qualified immunity against state tort suits. The term *good faith* is the same, but its applications to both types of lawsuit (state tort and Section 1983) are different. Students are encouraged to examine Table 3.5 for further clarity in classifying each type of legal redress and its particular parameters.

Indemnification and Representation

When correctional officers are faced with lawsuits (whether state or federal), the issue of legal representation is an automatic concern. The solutions to this issue as well as that of indemnification (payment for court costs) vary greatly from state to state. As a general rule, most states are willing to provide assistance in civil cases, but this is not nearly as true when the charges are criminal in nature. While it is typical for states to cover financial costs associated with civil proceedings, many do not necessarily do this automatically, and this means that officers from time to time face such instances without any financial assistance from their place of employment—a scary thought indeed.

Most states cover an officer's act or omission to act in civil cases, provided that it is determined that the incident occurred within the scope of the officer's employment (del Carmen et al., 2001). In some cases, this may also require a good faith element where it can be reasonably shown that the officer did act in good faith within the scope of his or her duty. In most cases where good faith is established, the officer will be represented by the state's attorney general. However, the attorneys general in all states have a wide degree of discretion in agreeing to defend an officer faced with a civil suit. If the AG (as the attorney general's office may be called from time to time) does not agree to defend the officer, that individual will have to retain private counsel at his or her own expense.

Once the issue of representation is resolved, the other issue of concern tends to revolve around the payment of legal costs. Most typically, when state tort cases are involved, both the plaintiff (in this case the offender) and the defendant (the community supervision officer) would pay their own attorney's fees, and this would remain the arrangement regardless of the case outcome. Thus, even if the correctional worker is found innocent of the allegations that the offender has claimed, the worker will still likely have to pay his or her own courts costs if the case is a state tort case. To remedy these concerns, officers may, in some cases, opt to purchase their own professional liability insurance, but they will typically be required to pay the premium themselves and, in several cases, may not even have the ability to purchase such insurance since companies may not be operating in the state to underwrite the policy.

Good faith defense: The person acted in the honest belief that the action taken was appropriate under the circumstances.

Compensatory damages: Payments for the actual losses suffered by a plaintiff.

Punitive damages: Monetary awards reserved for the person harmed in a malicious or willful manner by the guilty party.

Types of Damages

Lastly, most all civil cases (particularly tort cases) seek to obtain monetary damages. The amount can vary greatly, depending on the type of injury, the type of tort that is found (i.e., gross or willful negligence), and the severity of that injury. Most often, these financial awards come in the way of **compensatory damages**, which are payments for the actual losses suffered by a plaintiff (typically the offender). In some cases, **punitive damages** may also be awarded, but these monetary awards would be reserved for an offender who was harmed in a malicious or willful manner by agency staff; these damages are often added to emphasize the seriousness of the injury and/or to serve as a warning to other parties who might observe the case's outcome. The types of award for civil rights cases under Section 1983 suits can also vary greatly and often are similar to those under tort law.

It is common for Section 1983 cases to also result in other types of remedies that go beyond financial awards. These remedies are typically geared toward agencies rather than individual officers, though both financial damages and additional awards can be made. One such nonmonetary award that is occasionally granted is the **declaratory judgment**, which is a judicial determination of the legal rights of the person bringing suit (Neubauer, 2002). An example might include a suit where an inmate sues for violation of certain due process safeguards in disciplinary proceedings. A court may award a declaratory judgment against the agency to ensure that future inmates in custody are afforded the appropriate safeguards established by prior Supreme Court case law.

■ PHOTO 3.7 Judges have the ability to issue injunctions that order correctional systems to correct a noted deficiency or set of deficiencies.

COMPLIANCE WITH JUDICIAL ORDERS

Inmates in state and federal prison have increasingly petitioned the courts for relief under a variety of statutes. Students will recall from Chapter 2 that some prison systems operated in a manner that was contrary to what progressive-minded prison advocates preferred. As such, the involvement of the courts in prison operations can be viewed as an example of how the U.S. judicial system is affected by the norms and mores of our society, which are reflected in case law and court rulings. These rulings ultimately extended into the prison world, which had, until that time, been separate and distinct from mainstream society.

Injunctions and Court-Imposed Remedies

In addition to the typical award of damages against a correctional agency or correctional staff, courts may also employ injunctions against an agency. An **injunction** is a court order that requires an agency to take some form of action(s) or to refrain from a particular action or set of actions (Neubauer, 2002). Though the PLRA has narrowed the scope of federal court interference and has limited the time frame in which judges can impose their edicts on a prison system or facility, injunctions remain an effective remedy, particularly when federal civil rights or federal statutes are violated.

If the plaintiff inmate is successful in court (which is rare, but does happen on occasion), judges may issue injunctions that order correctional systems to correct a noted deficiency or set of deficiencies. But in these cases, prison officials must be given the time and opportunity to rectify conditions that are deemed unconstitutional. For the inmate population, this is essential because inmates will likely be living in the institution for years after the ruling has been handed down. Thus, ensuring that administrators do make the required changes and that they are given the necessary tools to do so is very important to the inmate population.

Video Link
Compliance With Court Orders

In the past, injunctions or court orders have required a variety of changes of institutions. First, they have mandated the abolition of certain prison regulations and state statutes relating to discipline, censorship, and court access. Second, these orders required improvements in institutions or in the services provided, including training for correctional staff, sanitation conditions, quality of food, and other aspects previously discussed in this chapter and in prior chapters. Third, jails, prisons, and/or sections of such facilities have been ordered closed when found to house inmates under conditions determined to be in violation of Eighth Amendment requirements. Thus, injunctions have had a widespread impact upon prison systems. A fairly recent example of this would be the Supreme Court case of *Brown v. Plata* (2011). In this case, the Court upheld a previous ruling by a three-judge panel from the U.S. District Courts of the Eastern and Northern Districts of California in which California had been ordered to lower its inmate prison population to no more than 137.5% of its overall total capacity within 2 years. The Supreme Court agreed with the lower court, holding that the California Department of Corrections and Rehabilitation had violated the Eighth Amendment rights of inmates in its care. As a result, California was required to reduce its prison population within a very quick timeframe. This led to the passage of historic legislation in California, the Public Safety Realignment Act, which will be discussed in detail in later chapters.

Declaratory judgment: A judicial determination of the legal rights of the person bringing suit.

Injunction: A court order that requires an agency to take some form of action(s) or to refrain from a particular action(s).

TECHNOLOGY AND EQUIPMENT 3.1

The Use of Video Cameras in Prisons to Protect Staff From Inmate Lawsuits

Video cameras in prison are not necessarily common, but they are a very useful tool when it comes to both security and liability. One instance when cameras may be used is when corrections officers are conducting forced cell moves, which are necessary when an inmate is behaving in an unruly or dangerous manner in his or her cell and must therefore be removed from that cell. In such instances, a team of five officers will "suit up" with riot gear (padding, helmets, and a riot shield for the lead officer) and go into the cell to extract the inmate.

When conducting forced cell moves, officers are trained so that the lead officer will enter quickly, using the shield to wedge the inmate into a prone position. Other officers will work to get all four limbs (both arms and both legs) secured. Each officer will have a specific arm or leg that he or she holds and places into a restraining position. While this is happening, another officer, accompanied by a supervisor, operates a camcorder or other such videotaping device. The entire incident is filmed so that if the inmate should falsely allege that officers used excessive force, evidence to the contrary can be presented.

The inclusion of fixed video cameras can also greatly enhance security in the institution, and this will, in turn, make the institution safer for staff and inmates. The experts at VideoSurveillance.com note the following benefits of surveillance:

1. ***Improved visual coverage***—Many prisons and correctional facilities are expansive, consisting of a variety of different areas, all of which require close monitoring. While guards and officers can't be everywhere at once, security cameras can provide continuous coverage of an entire facility.
2. ***Monitor inmate activity***—The constant presence of surveillance cameras helps officers to spot suspicious inmate activity and can prevent prison incidents from getting out of hand.
3. ***Provide visual evidence***—Archived surveillance footage is an extremely valuable resource for investigations of prison incidents.
4. ***Reduce the frequency of assaults***—In prisons and correctional facilities, tension is high, and fights are inevitable. Security cameras work to deter such behavior and also help in analyzing incidents of violence.
5. ***Monitor officer behavior***—Instances where guards and correctional officers act out of line toward inmates are caught on camera. Such footage is used in investigations and can help to prevent further misconduct.
6. ***Enhanced search capabilities***—Digital surveillance technology allows video footage to be archived and stored on digital video recorders and hard drives rather than bulky cassette tapes. Searching footage is significantly easier and more efficient in digital format.

Liability for the agency is likewise minimized in many of the instances above. For instance, liability for inmate safety can be minimized if agencies can demonstrate that cameras are used to watch over the inmates so that officers can ensure they are safe from assault on the recreation yards and other high-traffic areas. In addition, inappropriate officer behavior can be severely curtailed by the ability to detect such behavior. Cameras can also be used to detect and prevent drug smuggling, especially during visitation periods when family and friends may attempt to smuggle contraband into the facility. The ability to have a video record of such instances assists in conducting investigations against persons who bring contraband into a prison.

©iStockphoto.com/martin_33/iStock

■ PHOTO 3.8 Security cameras within prisons are positioned in such a manner as to have an unobstructed view of the widest angle of vision possible.

Consent Decrees

As an alternative option to going to trial, inmate plaintiffs may have conditions remedied in a much more expedient fashion if they agree to settle with the agency in developing a suitable consent decree. Essentially, a **consent decree** is an injunction, but with the plaintiff and the agency both being involved (Carp & Stidham, 1990). This involves both parties agreeing to work out the terms of a stated settlement that is given official weight by the court. The benefits to this remedy are that time and expense are spared and the uncertainty of a trial is eliminated. This also allows for a mutually agreeable solution rather than forcing the prison system into compliance.

Consent decree: An injunction against both individual defendants and their agency.

CONCLUSION

This chapter demonstrates how during recent correctional history in America there has been a constant interplay between state-level correctional systems and the federal courts. This interplay has been marked by controversy, challenges, and conflict between state priorities regarding crime and prison operations and the need to adhere to constitutional standards. The central feature of the evolution of prison operations in the country has been the interpretation of those constitutional standards as well as the Supreme Court's interpretation of its own role in ensuring that those standards, as interpreted, are met.

The legal history of corrections in the United States reflects the norms and mores of our society in relation to crime, punishment, and prison operations. The hands-off era mirrored common public understanding regarding the incarcerated, which claimed inmates were slaves of the state and entitled to nothing in particular. Thus, the need for intervention, whether by the mainstream public or the Supreme Court, seemed to be unnecessary to all but the most ardent of reform-minded persons.

Conversely, the hands-on era of sweeping prison reform that took place during the civil rights movement reflected the sentiments of a court that was in tune with social changes occurring throughout society. The hands-on era was tumultuous for many state prison systems, and its results created larger expenses for the taxpaying public, but the ethics, integrity, and general social conscience of the corrections field were improved. It is due to these changes that the corrections field became professionalized.

Legal issues that face both administrators and line staff are important to know and understand. The distinction between federal suits and state suits is important since they have different standards that must be met. Staff must understand where their liability begins and where it ends when working in the field of corrections. Individual knowledge of the parameters associated with liability aids correctional agencies as a whole since such knowledge can act as a preventative mechanism against inmate suits being filed against correctional staff.

Lastly, a brief overview of injunctions and other forms of court-oriented remediation was presented. These actions are what ultimately led to the significant changes that we have seen in this and the preceding chapters. However, the courts have now adopted a more neutral stance in intervening in prison operations. The passage of the PLRA has been instrumental in limiting the role of the courts and reflects a growing sentiment toward a "middle ground" approach to handling inmate claims and standards in prison operations. It appears that the field of corrections has matured into a professionalized and widely recognized discipline that has adopted a new, more balanced means of operation.

DISCUSSION QUESTIONS

1. What was the hands-off doctrine, and how were prisons run during this era?
2. What was the importance of *Ex parte Hull?* How did it change corrections?
3. Give a brief overview of *Turner v. Safley.* How did this case define a variety of aspects related to correctional decision making?
4. Identify and discuss legal liabilities associated with correctional staff.
5. How would you describe the current relationship between corrections and judicial oversight? Is it now balanced, or are prisons systems still under close scrutiny?
6. Compare and contrast state tort cases and federal Section 1983 cases.
7. Discuss injunctions and consent decrees. What is the purpose of each when leveled against a correctional system?
8. Refer to Applied Theory 3.1. In what way is peacemaking criminology related to the reduction of recidivism and lower crime rates?

KEY TERMS

Absolute immunity, 67
Compensatory damages, 68
Consent decree, 70
Declaratory judgment, 69
Defamation, 66
Emotional distress, 66
Good faith defense, 68
Hands-off doctrine, 52
Injunction, 69
Intentional tort, 66
Libel, 66
Malicious prosecution, 66
Negligence, 66
One hand on, one hand off doctrine, 61
Prison Litigation Reform Act (PLRA), 62
Punitive damages, 68
Qualified immunity, 67
Rational basis test, 54
Religious Land Use and Institutionalized Persons Act of 2000, 56
Slander, 66
Tort, 64
Totality of the conditions, 59
Writ writer, 51

SAGE edge™ Review key terms with eFlashcards.

KEY CASES

Albert W. Florence v. Board of Chosen Freeholders of the County of Burlington, et al. (2012), 58
Baxter v. Palmigiano (1976), 61
Bell v. Wolfish (1979), 61
Bounds v. Smith (1977), 54
Cooper v. Pate (1964), 53
Cruz v. Beto (1972), 56
Estelle v. Gamble (1976), 65
Ex parte Hull (1941), 52
Farmer v. Brennan (1994), 65
Gregg v. Georgia (1976), 59
Holt v. Hobbs (2015), 56
Johnson v. Avery (1969), 54
Kingsley v. Hendrickson (2015), 61
O'Lone v. Estate of Shabazz (1987), 56
Procunier v. Martinez (1974), 57
Ruiz v. Estelle (1980), 60
Turner v. Safley (1987), 53
Vitek v. Jones (1980), 61
Wilson v. Seiter (1991), 60
Wolff v. McDonnell (1974), 60

APPLIED EXERCISE 3.1

For this exercise, the instructor should organize several students (perhaps up to 12 students per group) into a mock jury, with one student designated as the foreman. Students must consider the following case, which is the same case that will be introduced in the "What Would You Do?" exercise that follows (but that version of the case will have a twist not encountered in this applied exercise). Students must identify specific legal criteria to determine liability involved with Officer Jimmy Joe, Officer Hackworth, Officer Guillory, Officer Killroy, Officer Ortega, Sergeant Smith, and Nurse Hatchett. Use information from this chapter regarding personal liability issues among correctional workers as the basis in providing your response.

The defendant, Jimmy Joe, a correctional officer at the Charles C. Broderick Maximum Security Facility, has claimed that he was unable to observe any of the events that are alleged by inmate Baker. Jimmy Joe's incident report notes that he was upstairs conducting a security check of the cell block; his documentation for that day does corroborate with his story, according to date and time of the activity.

Inmate Baker alleges that Jimmy Joe watched as he was beaten in the foyer of the dayroom by Officers Hackworth, Guillory, and Killroy. Baker also insists that when he was removed from the cell block and taken to the infirmary, Ortega operated the video camera that recorded his escort. Baker contends that while Ortega was recording, he deliberately moved the angle of the camera during key times when the officers "accidentally" bumped Baker into infirmary doors and wall corners. As this was occurring, Nurse Hatchett, who Baker alleges was working in tandem with the officers, would ask the officers to have Baker moved to another room, thereby repeating the haphazard escorting process. Throughout his visit to the infirmary, Baker was handcuffed behind his back as officers Guillory and Killroy escorted him from room to room.

Baker also contends that Hatchett was deliberately rough with him when applying bandages. This process was not captured on video camera, and, as Baker contends, there are some periods where the camera appears to be pointed away from the inmate for a few seconds.

Officer Ortega claims that he has not been trained with the video camera and that this was his first time recording an escort after a use-of-force incident. An investigation of official prison records indicates that what Ortega says is true.

Sergeant John Smith had arrived on the scene with Ortega, and it was Smith who instructed Ortega to grab the camera and make his best effort to record the incident. Institutional policy precludes sergeants from using the camera when supervising infirmary escorts. According to Smith's incident report, Ortega was the only officer available at the time, and Smith had to make a quick discretionary call. He chose to not delay in responding to the situation and to aid Ortega with verbal instruction on how to operate the camera while they were on the scene and as the circumstances permitted.

When Ortega and Smith arrived on the scene with the camera, they saw Baker in cuffs and restrained on the floor by Guillory and Killroy. Hackworth had placed the cuffs and appeared to be on standby, waiting to aid in the escort once the supervisor and the camera appeared. All of these actions were consistent with institutional policy, including the restraining techniques used by Guillory and Killroy.

Baker contends that prior to the arrival of Ortega and Smith, Hackworth, Guillory, and Killroy had trapped him in a nonvisible portion of the dayroom and had repeatedly assaulted him. He also noted that Officer Jimmy Joe was near the scene the entire time and that he refused to render aid. Rather, he watched from a corner as Baker was beaten for 10 minutes by Hackworth.

Guillory, Killroy, and Hackworth contend that Baker had been acting aggressively when they tried to allow him off the cell block to go to commissary. Hackworth, noting that the cell door was closed and that the dayroom was clear of other inmates, instructed the junior officers to temporarily place Baker in the dayroom to contain the situation. Hackworth claims that his intent was to either defuse the situation or, if that did not work, escort Baker to his cell once staff in the picket (an area from which the cell doors are opened) were able to get his cell back open.

Hackworth's incident report claims that Baker began to yell and took a swing with his right arm at Guillory, whom he had a strong dislike for. When Baker did this, all three officers moved to restrain him. Baker lifts weights in the prison and has a past history of violence. Hackworth, Guillory, and Killroy all contend that Baker resisted with great force and fury and they found it difficult to restrain him. In the process, Baker received several welts and bruises from bumping into walls (while trying to get distance from the officers) and from fighting after being restrained on the concrete. He also had three chipped teeth from landing face first on the floor when placed in an arm-restraining hold. No other serious injuries were sustained.

Once the incident was over, Hackworth said to Jimmy Joe, "Quick, call a supervisor; we have an inmate down, and we need him escorted to the infirmary."

Now, as you sit on the jury, you must decide whose version of the story is true. Should any or all of these officers be found guilty of cruel and unusual punishment, as per the Eighth Amendment? Are there any areas of potential liability for the three officers in the altercation, Officer Jimmy Joe, Nurse Hatchett, Officer Ortega, Sergeant Smith, or the correctional agency? Be sure to provide specific details in regard to your response.

WHAT WOULD YOU DO?

Jimmy Joe, a corrections officer at the Charles C. Broderick Maximum Security Facility, remembers the situation all too clearly. Baker had always been a difficult inmate, and he was a tough number. While serving time at Broderick Maximum, Baker had shanked two inmates on one occasion, and he had done the same with a correctional officer on another occasion. So everyone knew that Baker was dangerous.

Even though Baker was dangerous and had been a serious problem for many of the guards working at Broderick Maximum, Jimmy Joe was not really interested in getting "revenge" on Baker. However, Officer Hackworth could not get it out of his mind. For some reason, he had a constant fixation on Baker and would often mention that no inmate should be allowed to assault an officer and live to talk about it. For a long time Jimmy Joe did not think much of Hackworth's comments—he was just another frustrated prison guard blowing off steam about the hardhead inmates on the cell block.

But one day, a hot summer day, Baker was hollering because he wanted off the cell block to go to commissary. Two officers told him no, not until they were ready to allow inmates to leave for the commissary line. On that particular day, the commissary was running late, but other inmates had told Baker that this was not true; instead he thought that the officers were lying to him as a means of "messing with his head." In fact, one inmate explained to Baker, "Man, it's like they're tryin' that guard crap again, you know, mentally punkin' you out." The inmate then added, "Ya know, they're always doing that crap with only you, all because they know you won't take it. They want you to stud up, man—what you gonna do?"

The excessive summer heat of the prison, located in the Deep South of the United States, was working on Baker, and his overall mood and demeanor had become quite sour. As the officers stood there, Baker said, "Look, you two little girls better get out of my way, and you'd better quit runnin' game on me." At this moment, Hackworth walked onto the cell block. He had arrived to assist in moving an inmate to another cell block but overheard Baker's comment and instead decided to walk over to Baker and the other two officers. Jimmy Joe was the officer in charge of the cell block and, seeing Hackworth head in that direction, kept an eye on everyone.

The dayroom was nearly empty because most of the inmates were either at work or out on the recreation yard, but a few were watching the television bolted near the ceiling. Hackworth told the officers near Baker that he would be right back. Hackworth then walked up to Jimmy Joe, who was a very new officer still on his 6-month probationary period, and said, "Look, you need to get them inmates out of that dayroom. If this gets sloppy, we don't want them hangin' around here making up crap that they think they've seen. Tell them that TV time is over and they gotta get on the rec yard." He followed this by adding, "If you ain't man enough to run them out, then let me know, and I will get their butts out of here myself."

Jimmy Joe ordered the inmates to go to the rec yard, and they went without much grumbling. They did look at Hackworth in a strange manner, almost as if they knew what was going on, and they aimed sympathetic gazes at Baker. Hackworth then told Jimmy Joe, "Look, Bub, you stay here and just man your post. If someone is about to come on the cell block, let us know."

Then "the Hack," as everyone referred to him, went back down the cell block and told the other two officers that maybe they should go ahead and let Baker approach the outer door of the cell block, just so he would be ready for the commissary call when it happened. Baker said, "Yeah, man, let me up front so I will be ready. You know it ain't even closed—y'all are just making this difficult." Hackworth walked with the two officers and Baker. As they approached the front of the cell block, the door to the dayroom was on their right. Hackworth said, "Hey Baker, look, we don't want no problems, so if you want, feel free to go into the dayroom and watch the TV until you hear the commissary call. We'll leave the door open so you can come as soon as the call is sounded."

Baker began to think that perhaps the commissary really was running late and, since he had no TV in his own cell, he liked the idea of watching one of the channels while waiting for the commissary line. He went in, sat down on a bench facing the TV, and was switching the channels when Hackworth entered with the two other officers. From his location, Jimmy Joe could barely make out their position. Hackworth then said, "Hey, Baker, next time you pick up that channel changer, you need to ask to do so—that is a prison regulation, and you just broke that regulation." Before Baker even responded, he continued. "And it looks like you are being resistant and assaultive, so I am going to have to put you on the ground."

What happened next was a blur. Hackworth and the two other officers tackled Baker and began punching him repeatedly. They made a point to do this in an area of the dayroom foyer that was not clearly visible to Jimmy Joe. Baker tried to scream, but Hackworth shoved a bandanna in his mouth, cursed at him, and continued with the pounding. Once the incident was over, the officers said to Jimmy Joe, "Quick, call a supervisor; we have an inmate down, and we need him escorted to the infirmary."

Fifteen months later, Jimmy Joe, Hackworth, the two other officers, and Baker are all together in the federal district court. Baker filed a Section 1983 lawsuit that has made it to court. A jury sits across from Jimmy Joe—a jury of real people who do not seem to give any clue as to how they feel about the case in front of them.

At the time of the incident, Hackworth and the other two officers wrote in their paperwork that the incident started because Baker had tried to assault one of the officers. Hackworth claimed that the use of force was necessary to contain the inmate and to ensure officer safety. It is now Jimmy Joe on the stand, and he is being asked whether Baker initiated the assault. In his paperwork, Jimmy Joe had indicated that he did not see or hear anything during the incident but had been doing his rounds on the cell block. If Jimmy Joe changes his testimony, he will of course end up in trouble and will be labeled a "snitch" among his coworkers. In essence, he would be better off quitting his job. If he sticks with his story, he knows that he is lying and runs the risk of the jury not believing him.

If you were Jimmy Joe, ***what would you do?***

4 JAIL AND DETENTION FACILITIES

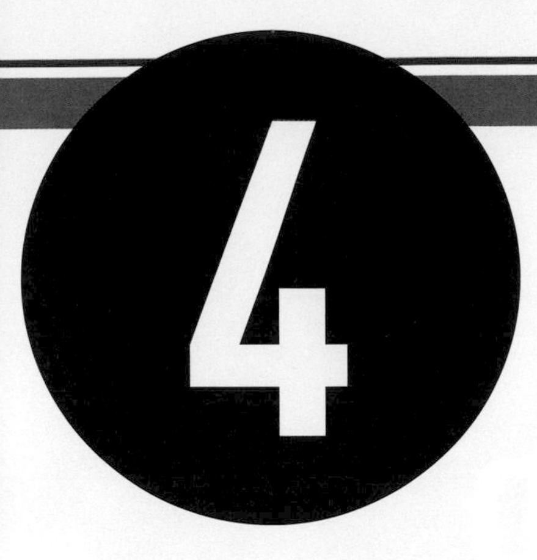

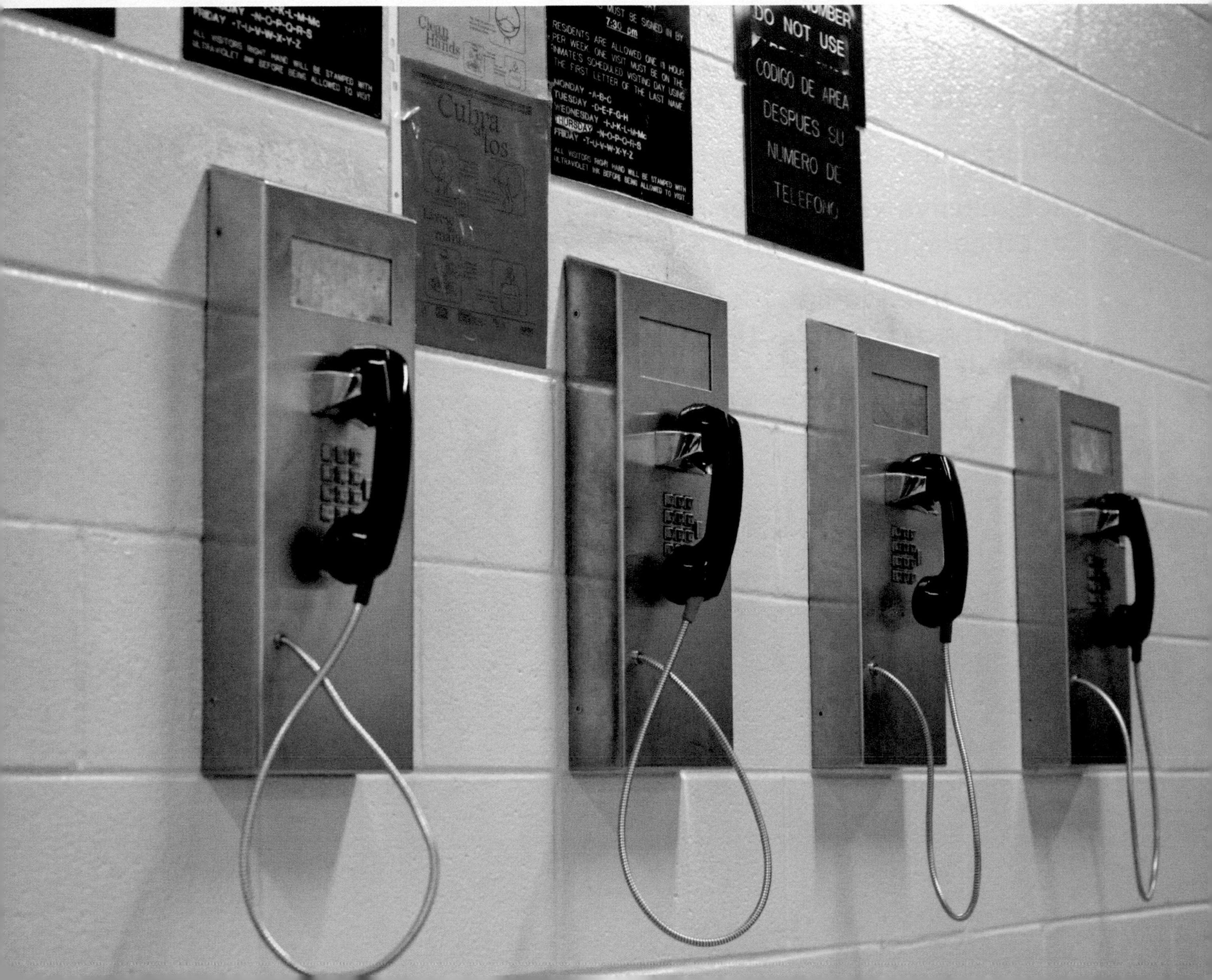

LEARNING THE ROPES

As Jeff walked toward the visitation room with the guard, he remembered something he had read in a guide titled *County Jail: A Survival Guide for Inmates, Friends and Families*: "Anybody can survive a little time in county jail." He had read this back when he started worrying about the likelihood of doing time. He had been working at a department store and, on a dare from some other coworkers, began stealing merchandise by sneaking it out the back in the receiving warehouse area. He kept doing this sporadically, as much for sport as for profit. Eventually, however, the company began to suspect Jeff, and he knew it. He stopped stealing, but they had him on camera. He remembered other words from the guide: "It may not always be pleasant, but you just have to take things each day at a time. The time will pass and your life will continue. The first week or so is a major adjustment." Jeff thought to himself, *Boy, was that the truth.*

Jeff replayed in his mind some of the rules that he read in the guide:

1. Avoid talking about your sentence. The details let others know how seasoned you are and whether you might be easy to exploit.
2. Avoid gambling with anybody who has been to prison because they are probably a lot better at cards than you are and more prone to violence.
3. Try to get a job while in jail; it is the best way to pass the time.

On his way to the visitation room, he thought to himself that reading that survival guide was the smartest thing he ever did. At that moment, the guard told him to stop and "shook him down," a term used in jails and prisons for when officers check if inmates have contraband items upon their person. All went well; the officer found nothing.

"Go ahead," said the officer, pointing to the visitation room.

Jeff walked in and saw Cindy on the other side of the glass. She was smiling and waving. Jeff waved back and took his seat across from her. They talked through the glass on the phones that were provided at each visitation booth.

Cindy said, "Oh, Jeff, I'm counting the days. Just 2 weeks until you're out!"

Jeff smiled and said, "Yeah, I know. This part of the countdown is going to seem like forever."

"Yeah, but remember when you had almost a year?"

"Yep, it has gone by faster than I thought it would; first week was the worst."

Cindy nodded. "Yeah, I know, but nobody really messed with you, which surprised us."

"Right, unlike all that TV crap, most guys don't get raped and stuff, in jails, at least not that often, but . . . ." Jeff trailed off.

"What?"

LEARNING OBJECTIVES:

1. Describe the evolution of jails.
2. Compare issues for large metropolitan jails to those for small rural jails.
3. Compare the differences between jails as short-term institutions and jails as long-term institutions.
4. Discuss the state and challenges of health care in jails.
5. Discuss challenges with jail staff, staff motivation, and training.
6. Identify special types of sentencing options in jails.
7. Identify special needs inmates within the jail environment.

SAGE edge™

Get the edge on your studies: edge.sagepub.com/hanser2e

- Take a quiz to find out what you've learned.
- Review key terms with eFlashcards.
- Watch videos that enhance chapter content.

"Well, some guys do get beat up; they just kind of either don't know the ropes or they basically ask for it. Take this one guy, he was booked 2 days ago and he went to take a crap and was on the *wrong* toilet."

Cindy looked at him askance. "The *wrong* toilet?"

Jeff explained to her that among the inmates, certain toilets were reserved for each race and some for gang members. Each racial group had its own designated toilets that looked the same but were understood by everyone else to be off-limits. In addition, nobody but the correct gang members could use "gang-owned" toilets. He explained that the guards were aware that this went on but usually did little to prevent these inmate rules.

"He got beat up pretty bad; they hit him while he was there, sitting and defenseless, taking a crap," said Jeff.

Cindy's eyes were huge. "Jeff, that is crazy!"

"Yeah, I know. I'm lucky that I was able to watch how things worked for a while and that my neighbor showed me the ropes." Jeff was referring to Jim Hammond, who, over time, had befriended Jeff. Hammond slept in the bunk across from Jeff.

Jeff paused, then said, "Cindy?"

"Yes?"

"One thing that I have learned from all of this is that you have to be observant of your surroundings and very careful when selecting friends."

The guard moved behind Jeff, glanced from him to Cindy, and declared, "Five more minutes."

"That sure did go by fast," Cindy lamented.

Jeff sighed. "Yeah, all the good moments in life do."

Robert Hanser

■ PHOTO 4.1 A jailhouse visitation room, similar to the one where Cindy visited Jeff (see chapter vignette). Visitors sit on the side where the stools can be seen while inmates sit on the other side. They talk to each other through the glass by using the phones that can be seen in this picture.

INTRODUCTION

Jails are a unique aspect of the correctional system because they fulfill many different functions. This multiplicity of functions and the rapid processing of offenders within their confines separate jails from prisons. Indeed, it is common for the population in any typical jail facility to change in composition quite quickly throughout the year, whereas a prison population will remain more stable. Jails have a very long history within the field of corrections, though their original purpose was not to correct at all. Nowadays, jails perform a number of functions that go well beyond the mere housing of inmates.

JAILS IN THE PAST

As with many aspects of the American criminal justice system, the use and operation of jail facilities owe their origin to England. During early American history, jails were informal and were used to detain persons awaiting trial. Eventually, as corrections officials came to rely less on corporal punishments, jails began to be used more frequently to house offenders (Giever, 2006). Jails eventually became a form of punishment, in and of themselves, considered suitable for minor offenders.

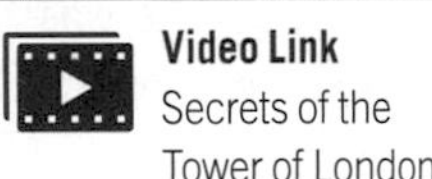

Video Link
Secrets of the Tower of London

Jails in England were referred to as **gaols** during the Middle Ages. One of the earliest examples of a gaol used for confinement purposes was the **Tower of London**, which was constructed after 1066 A.D. during the reign of King William I of England (Giever, 2006). Following this time period, various other gaols were constructed and used to house a variety of offenders. Eventually, gaols were constructed in every shire (the equivalent of a modern-day county), and each was placed under the care of the shire reeve, the early version of today's sheriff (Giever, 2006).

The first jail built in the United States was constructed in Jamestown, the first true settlement in the country. Inmates were housed in the jail as early as 1608, according to official records (Johnson, Wolfe, & Jones, 2008; Roth, 2011). Early jails had no specific architecture or design. However, most were located within close proximity of the stocks and pillory. These facilities also did not usually utilize individual cells. Rather, inmates were housed in groups, often with a mix of serious and minor offenders in each room (Carlson et al., 2008; Giever, 2006).

Gaol: A term used in England during the Middle Ages that was synonymous with today's jail.

Tower of London: One of the earliest examples of a jail used for confinement purposes.

During this time, jail inmates were required to provide their own amenities. This could be done by having family and friends provide needed items or by purchasing them from jailers (Giever, 2006). Obviously, this system led to a high level of corruption as jailers tended to exploit inmates who were in need. The practice of collecting monetary compensation from inmates for services became known as the fee system, and there is even record that some jails charged inmates for their very room and board (Giever, 2006). This system was generally successful in supplementing the jailer's meager salary, and offenders were often able to afford it since most were kept only for a short time while awaiting trial or corporal punishment (Giever, 2006). Nevertheless, some were kept in jail for exceedingly lengthy amounts of time, during which these inmates would have little recourse if family or friends were not available to provide aid. In such cases, survival was bleak and meager, with these inmates completely at the mercy of their jail caretakers.

THE MODERN JAIL

In today's justice system, jail facilities are typically the first point at which an offender is officially classified as being in the correctional component of the criminal justice system. However, this is a bit deceptive since most persons are only being detained after they have been arrested. This detainment, or detention, occurs at a local detention facility that is typically administered by the county and operated by the sheriff's office. This detention facility is typically what is thought of when we use the term *jail*. In simple terms, a **jail** is a confinement facility, usually operated and controlled by county-level law enforcement, that is designed to hold persons charged with a crime who are either awaiting adjudication or serving a short sentence of 1 year or less after the point of adjudication, similar to Jeff's experience in the chapter vignette. Similarly, the Bureau of Justice Statistics defines jails as "locally-operated correctional facilities that confine persons before or after adjudication. Inmates sentenced to jail usually have a sentence of a year or less, but jails also incarcerate persons in a wide variety of other categories" (Sabol & Minton, 2008). This is important because this means that there is quite a bit of flow in and out of a jail facility. This is the case for two reasons. First, persons who are arrested are automatically held within a jail facility, but many are released within 2 to 3 days due to the setting of bond and/or a judge releasing them on their own recognizance. Second, offenders who serve jail terms do so for 1 year or less, as longer sentences are most often reserved for persons serving true prison sentences. Thus, even among those serving a jail sentence, the turnover tends to be rapid because most sentences are only for a few months to a year.

Recent findings by Minton and Golinelli (2014) regarding jail operations and jail populations in the United States indicate the following:

1. After a peak in the number of inmates confined in county and city jails at midyear 2008 (785,533), the jail population was significantly lower by midyear 2013 (731,208).
2. At midyear 2013, the largest jail jurisdictions (172 total), meaning those with an average daily population of 1,000 or more inmates, held about 48% of the jail inmate population, despite the fact that these systems comprise a total of only 6% of all jail jurisdictions around the nation.
3. The jail incarceration rate—the confined population per 100,000 U.S. residents—declined slightly between midyear 2012 (237 persons per 100,000) and midyear 2013 (231 per 100,000). This decline continues a downward trend that began in 2007.
4. In contrast to most other jail systems, jails in the state of California have experienced an increase of about 12,000 inmates since midyear 2011.

Table 4.1 demonstrates that jail jurisdictions around the nation tend to hold lower numbers of inmates. Indeed, the number of jurisdictions that held 49 or fewer inmates grew between 2013 and 2014, with a corresponding increase in every single category of inmate total count except the category of 250–499 inmates, where a decrease of 753 total inmates was observed (Minton & Zeng, 2015). This means that there is a trend for jails to have fewer inmates per jurisdiction, which demonstrates lower per-capita growth in the total number of inmates housed. As Table 4.1 demonstrates, the largest percentage growth is in the category of jails housing 50–99 inmates, with the second largest percentage growth occurring among jails with 49 or fewer inmates.

According to data provided by the Bureau of Justice Statistics, roughly 744,600 persons are held in jails throughout a given year (Minton & Zeng, 2015). However, this number does not truly reflect how integral the jail is to the American criminal justice system as a whole. In terms of the total number of persons processed within jails throughout a year, it is estimated that anywhere from 10 million to 14 million persons enter and exit jail facilities in the United States. This figure includes persons who are briefly held in jail until their bond is secured and/or are detained temporarily for minor offenses. When compared with an overall prison population of approximately 1.4 million, it

Jail: A confinement facility, usually operated and controlled by county-level law enforcement, designed to hold persons who are awaiting adjudication or serving a short sentence of 1 year or less.

■ Table 4.1: Inmates Confined in Local Jails

Inmates confined in local jails at midyear, by size of jurisdiction, 2013–2014						
	Inmates confined at midyear[a]				Percent of all inmates	
Jurisdiction size[b]	2013	2014	Difference	Percent change	2013	2014
Total	731,208	744,592	13,384	1.8%	100%	100%
49 or fewer	23,545	25,058	1,513	6.4	3.2	3.4
50–99	38,970	42,172	3,202	8.2	5.3	5.7
100–249	95,031	96,443	1,412	1.5	13.0	13.0
250–499	102,362	101,609	–753	–0.7	14.0	13.6
500–999	123,155	128,070	4,915	4.0	16.8	17.2
1,000 or more	348,145	351,239	3,094	0.9	47.6	47.2

SOURCE: Minton, T. D., & Zeng, Z. (2015). *Jail inmates at midyear 2014—statistical tables.* Washington, DC: Bureau of Justice Statistics

Note: Detail may not sum to total because of rounding. All comparisons by jurisdiction size are not significant at the 95% confidence level. See appendix table 5 for standard errors.

[a]Number of inmates held on the last weekday in June.

[b]Standardized on the average daily population (ADP) for the 12-month period ending June 30, 2006, the first year in the current Annual Survey of Jails sample. ADP is the sum of all inmates in jail each day for a year, divided by the number of days in the year.

seems that jails process approximately 10 times the amount of inmates than do prisons throughout a given year, due in part to the transient, in-and-out nature of the jail population when compared to the more stable and long-term prison population.

Most individuals who are booked in jails remain for short periods of time that range from just a few hours to several months. The majority of infractions that entail contact with jails include misdemeanor crimes, substance abuse issues, domestic crimes, and public safety issues. In addition, it is common for persons involved in the illicit sex industry (i.e., prostitutes and their customers) and persons who fail to appear for court hearings to routinely land in jail. Thus, jails consist of a changing population of offenders who have committed a variety of legal infractions, leading to a diverse array, legally speaking. Students are encouraged to examine Figure 4.1 for additional information regarding offenders in jail facilities.

Rural Jails

Rural jails are often challenged by tight budgets and limited training for staff. The author of this text has himself visited numerous rural jails and trained their personnel. It is clear that county-level governments tasked with operating jails do so amidst a number of problems, both financial and political. Unlike most urban area jail staffs, Wallenstein and Kerle (2008) note that few jail staffs in rural areas receive official police or corrections training, and, in jurisdictions where such training *is* offered, the sheriff is hard-pressed to allow officers to attend the training due to limited numbers of security staff (Kerle, 1982).

The author of this text operated a regional training facility for years and has witnessed this problem firsthand. As a result, the regional training facility frequently has instructors travel to the jail facility itself to train persons, though this still impacts county budgets since staff members must be paid while attending the training (an additional expenditure) and they must stay late after work or arrive prior to their work shift. Thus, unless training providers with great schedule flexibility are available, training issues for rural jails are a serious concern that provides a daunting challenge to sheriff agencies and county governments.

Rural jail: Usually small jails in rural county jurisdictions that are often challenged by tight budgets and limited training for staff.

In addition, the conditions in rural jails are often substandard, and this is again exacerbated by the lack of funds that tends to be common among most such jurisdictions.

Ruddell and Mays (2007) note that rural jails face most of the same challenges of larger jails but must work with additional disadvantages related to the far-flung locations of their facilities and the small tax bases generated by rural counties. Further, many rural jails in the United States have no physician services, and less than half have regular nonemergency medical services (Ruddell & Mays, 2007). Dental services are often limited to simple tooth extractions for jail inmates. In addition, research by Applegate and Sitren (2008) found that rural jails provided less rehabilitative programming than did jails in other categories. This included fewer opportunities for work release programs and educational achievement as well as treatment programs for substance abuse and mental health interventions. Psychoeducational programming for life skills development, parenting, and/or money management were also lacking. Simply put, rural jails cannot provide the services that larger and better-funded jails can.

Because of these challenges, there is incentive to use alternatives to jail incarceration in many jurisdictions. Some proponents have advocated for placing jail operations under state-level government, to be managed by the state's correctional department (Wallenstein & Kerle, 2008). This may be one means of streamlining jail operations, but, as we will see with state prison systems, this is no panacea. In fact, many state prison systems are overcrowded, making it unlikely that states will be any better at managing jail facilities than are persons at the county level of government.

Even more interesting is that in some states there is incentive for rural departments to embrace the jail operation industry. In these cases, county facilities tend to house state-level inmates due to the fact that many states have burgeoning prison populations and there is simply no room to warehouse offenders. Because of this, the state will pay county-level jails to house state-level inmates. This can generate substantial revenue for the jail, and, as a result, sheriffs may actively solicit the state for additional inmates (Giever, 2006; Wallenstein & Kerle, 2008). This leads to a bit of an unusual situation for jails where instead of seeking to limit the inmate population, the jail administration will instead attempt to remain full to capacity as much as possible. As will be discussed in subsequent sections of this chapter, this has been the case in California, where the state prison system is under pressure to reduce its count and, as a result, relies more on its jail system to house excess inmates.

Metropolitan Jail Systems

Jails in large metropolitan areas face numerous challenges that impact their operation. First off, these facilities tend to have sizeable populations that are diverse and that present with a variety of issues. Second, there is a tendency for offenders who live rough-and-tumble lifestyles to process in

Figure 4.1: Characteristics of Jail Inmates, Midyear 2014

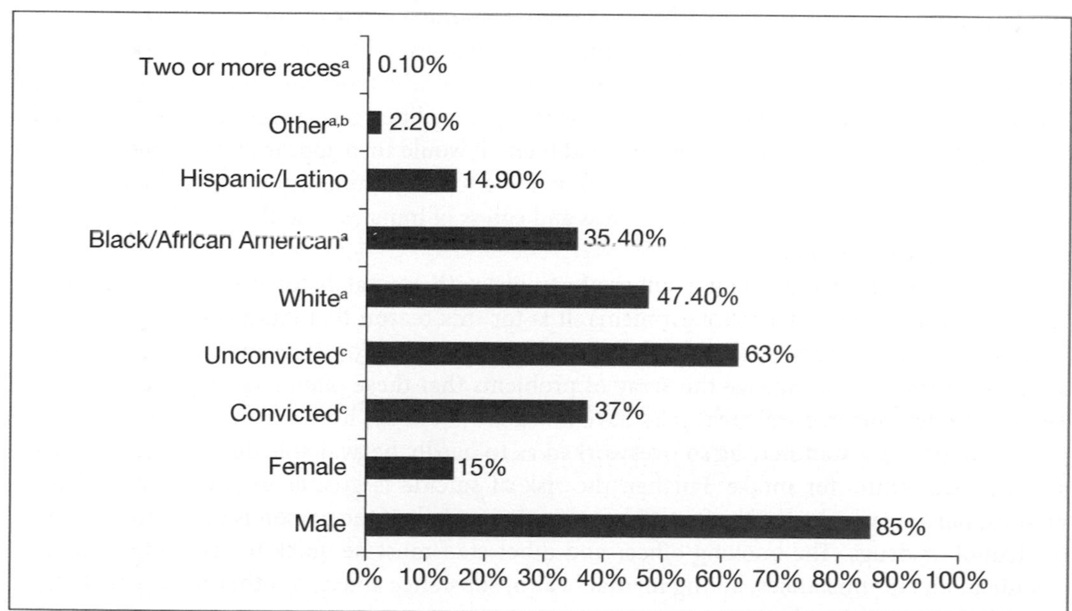

SOURCE: Minton, T. D., & Zeng, Z. (2015). *Jail inmates at midyear 2014—statistical tables.* Washington, DC: Bureau of Justice Statistics.

NOTE: Detail may not sum to total due to rounding.

[a]Excludes persons of Hispanic or Latino origin.

[b]Includes American Indians, Alaska Natives, Asians, Native Hawaiians, and other Pacific Islanders.

[c]Includes juveniles who were tried or awaiting trial as adults.

and out of the jail facility. Indeed, the average daily population data used to mark the number of persons in jail do not adequately reflect the important role of the jail to the correctional and judicial arms of the justice system.

In 2014, the midyear jail population throughout the United States was 744,600 inmates, with 11.4 million total persons being processed through jail systems during that same year (Minton & Zeng, 2015). This statistic suggests that jail facilities around the nation process roughly 15 times the number of persons than is reflected in a count taken on any given day of the year (Minton & Zeng, 2015). Further, since 2000, the jail inmate population has continued to grow by an average of 1% each year. Much of this growth has been due to an increase in the nonconvicted population, which was around 117,700 in 2014 (Minton & Zeng, 2015). This is important because, as we have seen in Chapter 3, recent Supreme Court rulings have had to address standards of confinement and treatment for persons who are detained and in a nonconvicted status (see *Kingsley v. Hendrickson* [2015] and *Albert W. Florence v. Board of Chosen Freeholders of the County of Burlington, et al.* [2012] in Chapter 3 for details).

With the exception of a handful of major jail systems (e.g., New York City; Dade County, Florida; Shelby County, Tennessee), most large jail systems operate at 90% percent capacity or more (Minton & Golinelli, 2014). Some of these systems operate with capacities over 100% of what they are intended to hold (Minton & Golinelli, 2014). Thus, jail systems in large metropolitan areas tend to have large offender populations that push the limit of what dedicated facilities can handle. In the state of California, rising jail populations have become a problem due to, as we saw in Chapter 3, the ruling of *Brown v. Plata* (2011), which has required the reduction of state prison inmates at an unprecedented rate. Many of those inmates have simply been transferred to jail systems in California, leading to a total increase of 12,000 inmates in jails throughout the state (Minton & Golinelli, 2014).

The large number of offenders in metropolitan areas, coupled with the various issues prevalent among the offender population (e.g., substance abuse, mental health issues, medical issues), requires that these facilities provide more comprehensive services. While larger jail systems may have more staff and the ability to provide more extensive services than systems located in rural regions of the United States, it seems that these services are just enough to meet the demand; more money from city tax dollars simply corresponds with the need for more extensive services. Thus, bigger jail systems often find themselves strapped for cash despite their larger revenue base in the community because of the greater needs of the offenders in these areas.

In many cases, particularly in urban jail facilities, a similar group of offenders may cycle in and out of the facility, perhaps going through intake and exit several times throughout the year. This provides a number of challenges and difficulties for jail staff who must contend with this constantly changing offender population. This also means that jail facilities have a substantial impact on the public safety of the communities that surround them. It would then appear that jail administrators have a very big responsibility, both to the jail staff and to the community at large. The jail agency, therefore, is pushed and pulled by the ingress and egress of inmates as well as the demands of and concern for the community.

Web Link
America's Largest Mental Hospital Is a Jail

Urban jails also book a large number of persons with mental disturbances, this often being comorbid with drug and alcohol problems. It is for this reason that large jail facilities tend to have mental health personnel and substance abuse specialists on staff and available 24 hours a day to diagnose and manage the array of problems that these offenders may present (Kerle, 1999). Smaller jails in rural areas may have no such staff at all, however. And even with larger jail facilities, these staff may be so overworked as to hardly be available during times not considered peak hours for intake. Further, the risk of suicide is greater in jail facilities than in prisons, particularly during the first 48 hours and especially if the person is under the influence of alcohol or drugs. The booking officer and other staff must be quick to screen for potential suicide in all circumstances, noting mental health, substance abuse, or other factors that might exacerbate its likelihood.

As noted earlier, jails may commonly house persons who cycle in and out of their confines. The reason for this is that the majority of criminal activity is committed by a small group in a community. These offenders, who are a small segment of the total offender population, commit well over half of all the crime in a local jurisdiction. While much of this crime may be petty, these repeat offenders tend to cycle in and out of jail between charges, with long-term prison terms not occurring due to the low priority of the criminal activity. Further, these offenders tend to know each other (Giever, 2006). Indeed, many are drug users who may sell, share, and/or use drugs with one another. Others may be partners in criminal activity, and, even more disturbing, some may be mutual members of a street gang. The point is that interconnections between members of the criminogenic population tend to occur due to chance meetings that happen on the streets or during their periodic contact while in jail. Thus, in many larger jurisdictions, this offender population tends to maintain contact, both in and out of jail, revolving back and forth from the community to the jail and back again.

AP Photo/Joel Page

■ PHOTO 4.2 This central area serves as an area where staff can observe the movement of inmates and also have quick access to numerous adjacent areas of the prison.

A number of these petty and small-time offenders may be homeless; this is especially true in urban areas. The homeless are particularly a problem for larger jurisdictions, where most beat cops know these individuals by name because the contact between police and the homeless is so frequent. Many homeless may have substance abuse issues, problems with trauma and anxiety, or other mental health disturbances. All of these factors are further worsened by an unstable lifestyle that consists of poor nutrition, inadequate health maintenance, and often substance abuse. Further still, communicable diseases may be more common among these individuals due to poor personal maintenance and risky lifestyle choices. This is particularly true for female offenders who may resort to prostitution to pay for either their drug habit or their basic needs. In such cases, these offenders are likely to be "regulars" for police officers in those jurisdictions and for jail staff, who will book them multiple times throughout the course of a year. It is even common among the homeless population for offenses to coincide with colder months of the year, with such persons committing petty crimes so that they may spend the winter indoors within the jail facility rather than outside on the cold streets.

Podular Direct-Supervision Jails

During the 1980s, a new kind of jail came under construction in the United States. The two key components of this jail, the **podular jail**, are rounded or "podular" architecture for living units and a "direct," as opposed to indirect, form of supervision of inmates by security staff. In short, security staff are present in the living units at all times. It was thought that this architectural design would complement the staff's ability to supervise the inmate population while negating the ability of predatory inmates to control a cell block or dormitory. Two other important facets of this type of jail are the provision of more goods and services in these units (e.g., more access to telephone privileges, visiting booths, and library facilities) and a more enriched dialogue between staff and inmates. This, in turn, enhances the staff's knowledge of individual inmates—their personalities, issues, and challenges. Such knowledge improves both security and the day-to-day operational aspects of the jail.

Though podular direct-supervision jails or prisons are not necessarily a panacea for all the challenges associated with jail operation, they are a significant improvement over more traditional jail designs. When operated effectively and when they have the most critical design components, they tend to be less costly, primarily due to the fact that fewer lawsuits occur and fewer prevail than at jail facilities using other designs (Stohr et al., 2008). This is due to the fact that the open nature of the design prevents most incidents from escalating into grounds for a lawsuit.

Innovations in Jail Operations

Other innovations in jail operations include the development of community jails and reentry programs (Stohr et al., 2008). Community jails are devised so that programming provided to offenders does not end when those offenders are released back into the community. Rather, the

Podular jail: Includes rounded architecture for living units and allows for direct supervision of inmates by security staff.

■ **Table 4.2: Confinement Status of Jail Inmates**

Persons under jail supervision, by confinement status and type of program, midyear 2000 and 2009–2014							
Confinement Status and Type of Program	Number of Persons Under Jail Supervision						
	2000	2009	2010	2011	2012	2013	2014
Total[a]	687,033	837,647	809,360	798,417	808,622	790,649	808,070
Held in jail[a]	621,149	767,434	748,728	735,601	744,524	731,208	744,592
Supervised outside of a jail facility[b]	65,884	70,213	60,632	62,816	64,098	59,441	63,478
Weekend programs[c]	14,523	11,212	9,871	11,369	10,351	10,950	9,698
Electronic monitoring	10,782	11,834	12,319	11,950	13,779	12,023	14,223
Home detention[d]	332	738	736	809	2,129	1,337	646
Day reporting	3,969	6,492	5,552	5,200	3,890	3,683	4,413
Community service	13,592	17,738	14,646	11,680	14,761	13,877	14,331
Other pretrial supervision	6,279	12,439	9,375	10,464	7,738	7,542	8,634
Other work programs[e]	8,011	5,912	4,351	7,165	7,137	5,341	7,003
Treatment programs[f]	5,714	2,082	1,799	2,449	2,164	2,002	2,100
Other	2,682	1,766	1,983	1,731	2,149	2,687	2,430

SOURCE: Minton, T. D., & Zeng, Z. (2015). *Jail inmates at midyear 2014—statistical tables.* Washington, DC: Bureau of Justice Statistics.

a. Number of inmates held on the last weekday in June 2014.
b. Number of persons under jail supervision but not confined on the last weekday in June 2014. Excludes persons supervised by a probation or parole agency.
c. Offenders serve their sentences of confinement on weekends only (i.e., Friday to Sunday).
d. Includes only persons without electronic monitoring.
e. Includes persons in work release programs, work gangs, and other alternative work programs.
f. Includes persons under drug, alcohol, mental health, and other medical treatment.

programming is a continuum that extends beyond incarceration and well into the community. This is an important concept because it addresses the fact that many jail inmates return to the jail facility, primarily because many of their needs are not met in the community. Once in the community, inmates with special needs and/or a lack of resources simply resort to criminal behavior, and the already full jail system once again must absorb the offenders into the burgeoning population. If programming occurs in both settings, regardless of whether the inmates are in or out of the facility, their needs are addressed and services are provided so that they can reintegrate into the community with greater success. This then lowers crime in the long term since recidivism is lowered.

Further, a wide range of intermediate sanctions can be used with offenders, including jail offenders (see Table 4.2). These intermediate sanctions will be covered in much more depth in Chapter 6, but for now students should know that some jails include weekend programs, electronic monitoring, home detention, day reporting, and community service, among others. This means that a stint in jail for some offenders may actually be a stint that is served partly in jail and partly in the community. This blurring of the sentence and the type of confinement serves many purposes, such as easing overcrowding and providing a means for jail offenders to keep their employment so they can afford fines and fees while they are in jail.

Jail reentry programs: Programs usually interlaced with probation and parole agencies as a means of integrating the supervisory functions of both the jail and community supervision agencies.

Jail reentry programs are somewhat similar in nature but focus more on the fact that ultimately the inmate is likely to be on some form of community supervision. Thus, jail reentry programs tend to be interlaced with probation and parole agencies as a means of integrating the supervisory functions of both the jail and the community supervision agencies. Amidst this, the continued care of the offender's specific needs is addressed (similar to community jails). One study found that effective interventions to improve reentry include everything from referral to counseling to drug treatment, depending on the needs of the offender. However, community safety must

CROSS-NATIONAL PERSPECTIVE 4.1

A Jail Facility in Canada: Central East Correctional Centre, Ontario, Canada

The Central East Correctional Centre (CECC) is a correctional/detention center in the city of Kawartha Lakes. It is operated under the jurisdiction of the Ministry of Community Safety and Correctional Services of Ontario. People convicted of crimes with custodial sentences of less than 2 years are housed in this jail, along with a large population of inmates who have been detained prior to trial. The inmates detained prior to trial have been deemed by the courts to be a flight risk or too dangerous to be at large.

The CECC is a 1,184-bed multipurpose correctional facility, consisting of six pods of 192 beds each for male accommodation (1,152) and a separate 32-bed female unit. It houses inmates in a maximum-security setting who are serving sentences of up to 2 years less a day as well as those on remand awaiting court proceedings. The CECC was built on approximately 35 hectares of land and is approximately 10 acres under roof. The institution includes areas for rehabilitation and programming and has an infirmary and separate buildings for an industrial work program. This facility, constructed in 2002, ran a cost of approximately 84 million Canadian dollars. For their money, the Ontario correctional authorities received a facility that includes the following:

1. All inmate-occupied areas are surrounded by a 16-foot fence, topped with 300 meters of razor ribbon. All doors, windows, locks, and perimeter walls are built to maximum-security standards.
2. The most advanced security technology available includes 21 different security systems. Closed-circuit television is designed to enhance sight lines for correctional officers and allows for the simultaneous viewing of several indoor and outdoor areas. The six video court suites reduce the need for offender transportation to and from court for short court appearances.
3. The design is unique in Canada and features six interconnected octagonal "pods." Each pod contains six living units, an enclosed exercise yard, and dedicated program and visiting areas. Meals and health care services are brought to the living units to reduce inmate movement throughout the facility.
4. Living units have 16 cells, each accommodating two offenders. This design features clear and unobstructed sight lines between correctional officers and inmate living areas and a small number of inmates per housing unit.
5. Core support services include a medical infirmary, a 40-bed segregation unit, a meal preparation facility, a separate inmate industries building, and administrative office space.
6. The separate female unit is inaccessible to male inmates and accommodates 32 female offenders. Also included are separate programming areas, a recreation yard, medical and segregation units, and an admissions and discharge area for female offenders.

QUESTION 1: If you had to rate your impression of this facility's security (with 1 being the lowest rating and 10 being the highest), from what you have read above, what would be your rating? Provide a brief explanation for your answer.

QUESTION 2: When considering the description of the Central East Correctional Centre in Ontario, Canada, would you consider the facility structure sufficient to address the various special issues pertaining to jails, as discussed in this chapter? Briefly explain why or why not.

SOURCES: Bondfield Construction. (2009). *Correctional and police facilities.* Retrieved from http://www.bondfield.com/correctional/centralontario.html
City of Kawartha Lakes Police Services. (2009). *Central East Correctional Centre.* Retrieved from http://www.kawarthalakespolice.com/cecc.html

remain paramount, especially if agencies hope to have support from community members in the surrounding areas. Because reentry is a complicated process that requires a team approach among many different agencies and personnel, it requires that jail staff and administrators prioritize the needs that they target and the interventions that will be applied while also considering the network of community agencies that will provide these services. In fact, Hanser (2010b) notes that this requires a collaborative process between jail security and treatment staff and members of surrounding agencies, while at the same time including members of the community in the process. Such collaborative efforts can educate the community on the process of reentry, build rapport between the community and the jail facility, and enhance the supervision of offenders since more eyes will be upon them within the community. Incidentally, this also provides the offenders with enriched support, thereby increasing the likelihood for motivated offenders to rebuild their future lives.

http://commons.wikimedia.org/wiki/file:FtMcHenrySallyPort

■ PHOTO 4.3 The sally port is used as a location where inmates can be transported into the bay area with the front gate closed behind them. This then allows for the second door or gate to open, admitting the inmates into the facility without having any point of potential escape since the outer door/gate is closed and locked.

JAILS AS SHORT-TERM INSTITUTIONS

According to Kerle (1999), **short-term jails** are facilities that hold sentenced inmates for no more than 1 year. A jail, particularly a short-term jail, is an institution where both pretrial and sentenced inmates are confined. A lockup is often a police-operated facility where individuals who have been arrested are held for 24 to 72 hours, depending on the circumstances and the jurisdiction. Once a maximum of 72 hours has elapsed, the inmate held in the lockup is transferred to the local jail, where he or she is admitted. Lockups exist in most all larger cities because they make the arrest and booking process more convenient and less complicated. Once inmates are in the lockup, other personnel transport them to the jail. Lockups are often housed at the police station itself, and they are the true "holding cell" type of facility, used for no other purpose.

Kerle (1999) notes that lockups should actually be used sparingly, if at all. Much of this has to do with the fact that most police agencies cannot sufficiently staff and operate such a facility. Also, it is during the first 24 to 48 hours that inmates are most vulnerable to mental health issues, potential medical complications, and suicide. Due to these issues, Kerle (1999) points to the International Association of Chiefs of Police (IACP), which encourages police agencies to refrain from using lockups as much as is feasible.

The Booking Area

The most important area in short-term and long-term jail facilities is where intakes occur and is usually called the booking area (Kerle, 1999). There are greater risks in the booking area than in other areas of the jail due to the fact that so many offenders and suspected offenders enter and exit the jail from this point. It is important that staff in booking areas keep very good records related to the intake of an inmate. Indeed, if the appropriate arrest or commitment papers are not possessed, then the suspected offender cannot be legally confined. Because it is the responsibility of booking officers to ensure that these records are maintained, their job as the entry point in the jail custodial process becomes even more essential (Kerle, 1999).

Audio Link
Teen Spends Years at Rikers Island Without Being Sentenced

Most all booking areas have what is commonly referred to as a sally port, which is adjacent to the booking area. The **sally port** is a secure area where vehicles can enter, with the area being closed after the transport vehicle has entered the compound. A sally port allows security staff to bring vehicles close to the admissions area in a secure fashion. In many small jails, a sally port may not exist, and, in such cases, additional care in the processing of inmates is required in order to make sure that security is provided (Kerle, 1999).

Most offenders who are arrested and brought into the booking area are under the influence of drugs or alcohol, or they may have some other factor that impairs their functioning. The stress level of those being booked is likely to be heightened, and this means that they are likely to be more problematic. Some of these individuals will present aggressive responses and may be assaultive. It is commonly observed that jail altercations occur in the booking area more often than in other areas of the jail.

Jails also book a large number of persons with mental disturbances, which often occur in tandem with drug and alcohol problems. Because of this, the booking officer must be able to identify unusual behavior; it is useful if he or she is trained through in-service processes to observe sudden shifts in mood or personality, hallucinations, intense anxiety, paranoia, delusion, and loss of memory (Wallerstein, 2014). Further, as noted above, the risk of suicide is greater in jail facilities than in prisons, particularly during the first 48 hours and especially if the person is under the influence of alcohol or drugs.

Short-term jail: A facility that holds sentenced inmates for no more than 1 year.

Sally port: Entry design that allows security staff to bring vehicles close to the admissions area in a secure fashion.

Due to the challenges associated with the booking process and the types of offenders that will be seen, it is important to have some kind of holding cell located near the booking area. Holding cells can be useful for detoxifying short-term inmates and can allow staff to book inmates without having distractions from other inmates while completing the admission process (Ruddell & Mays, 2007; Wallerstein, 2014). In short, holding cells tend to alleviate much of the chaos associated with booking. While the use of a holding cell may seem to be common sense, many smaller jails cannot afford the luxury of jail space that is not specifically used to house an inmate for a period longer than 72 hours—an indication of how cash-strapped many of these agencies tend to be (Ruddell & Mays, 2007).

Issues With Booking Female Inmates

In the past few years, a rise in the number (and proportion) of females who are housed in jails has occurred. Because female offenders, just like male offenders, may stay anywhere from a day to a year in the jail facility, it is important that staff are trained on issues related to female confinement. In this instance, it is certainly a benefit to have female employees available to assist in processing these offenders. In recent years, there has been an emphasis on recruiting women into the ranks of corrections officers, which has resulted in an increased representation of women working in jails and prisons. Nevertheless, the job of "jailer" still tends to be male dominated, and this means that in some jails, especially rural ones, female officers may not be present during one or several shifts (Morton, 2005).

Male officers who work in the booking area should be provided with additional training to ensure sensitivity to female issues. This also has advantages from a legal perspective, since male officers should use good professional discretion when processing female offenders. Given that inappropriate staff-on-inmate relations have been identified as an area of concern in recent years, it is important that male and female staff make a point to safeguard themselves from allegations.

Lastly, Kerle (1999) notes that booking forms and documents should be inclusive enough to contain questions about physical and sexual abuse, thus signifying that jail administrators recognize these issues as serious ones. This provides documentation that can be important should later allegations result in grievances or courtroom lawsuits. Aside from legal concerns, it is also useful for jail staff to develop an awareness of their own impact upon the booking process and realize how they may serve to heighten stress and generate hostility among entering inmates.

Information Technology and Integration

Unfortunately, there has been very little integration of systems between agencies and even within the police agency in regard to jail data. Often, police officers and jailers of the same agency do not engage in routine information exchange. This is not because high-quality information technology products do not exist. For instance, the SmartJAIL system, developed by CTS America, provides all the information needed to manage data and processes for jails of any size or complexity. SmartJAIL tracks and manages all aspects of an inmate's stay in a correctional facility. The system is integrated with a name index and initial arrest reports (within the records management system) to help speed up the booking process by using information already collected in these other programs. SmartJAIL is equipped to do the following:

- **Jail booking:** Tracks inmate booking, including mug shots, medical screening information, inmate property items, and all events involving the inmate.
- **Inmate visitation:** Tracks the date and time of each visit made to an inmate.
- **Inmate transportation and movement:** Tracks the movement of inmates by displaying all scheduled inmate movements, allowing time for the arrangement of transportation and scheduling.
- **Jail management configuration:** Maintains lists for use by other jail management modules, including bed and cell locations, vehicles for transport, destinations, judges, and gain-time calculations.
- **Jail log:** Enables officers to keep an electronic duty log to report activities or information to other officers.
- **Jail incidents:** Records incidents requiring use of force, disciplinary action, or institutional charges against an inmate.
- **Jail medical:** Records medical visits made by an inmate, including the initial medical screening. Historical records are maintained for easy review of an inmate's health.
- **Jail commissary:** Tracks inmate banking and purchasing at the commissary.

- **Jail search:** Provides administrators an easy, fast way to locate inmate records based on extensive search criteria.
- **Jail administrative reports:** Provides administrators easy access to dozens of the most commonly used reports in the system, including billing reports and statistical reports required by the federal government.
- **Mobile inmate tracking:** Designed for handheld devices, this module checks inmates in and out of a facility by scanning inmate ID tags and providing accurate historical tracking records.

From the above description, it is clear that automated systems exist that hold a large amount of information. Whether this information is utilized to its fullest potential is debatable. The lack of communication between agencies and even within agencies limits the use of much of the information that is stored. Over time, it is expected that jail systems will increasingly share data, both with other jail facilities and with police agencies whose officers may come into contact with jailed offenders after their release. This last application of information exchange can be particularly valuable when combating gang offenders who tend to cycle in and out from the community to the jail and back again.

JAILS AS LONG-TERM FACILITIES

Since the 1990s, an increasing number of larger jails have been required to house inmates who serve sentences that exceed the typical 1-year term. Understandably, jail facilities and the staff at those facilities have had difficulty maintaining these types of populations. Most jails are simply not designed or constructed to house inmates on a long-term basis. These facilities often lack the space for programming as well as the full recreational facilities that would be necessary for long-term populations. The use of jails for long-term inmates can be attributed to the following three broad reasons:

1. The use of longer jail sentences has resulted in the more extensive use of jails in many jurisdictions.
2. Many local and regional jurisdictions have been required to house inmates who have been sentenced to state prisons. This is because many state prisons have been so crowded that they have been unable to accept the newly sentenced offenders.
3. Some local jurisdictions have leased out beds to other jurisdictions, such as state correctional systems. These contractual agreements have created income for local sheriffs who oversee these jail facilities. This has created a situation where some sheriffs actively solicit state correctional systems for inmates to fill their beds—sometimes even soliciting systems outside of their own state, when feasible.

As crowding in state prisons became a longer-term problem, many jails began to hold sentenced inmates for anywhere from 2 to 5 years in duration (Wallenstein & Kerle, 2008). Table 4.3 contains data regarding jail facilities that house long-term inmates. Note that the states of Louisiana, Tennessee, and Kentucky utilize this approach with great frequency. Indeed, over half of all state inmates are in local jail facilities in Louisiana.

Local Jails That House State Inmates

Many of the excess jail inmates in recent years have been the legal responsibility of various state correctional facilities. However, many state correctional administrators allowed these state inmates to be held in jails to relieve prison overcrowding. Some states have had more problems with overcrowding than others. We now discuss two states that exemplify differences in overcrowding and the means by which jails provided relief to these burgeoning systems. We will focus on the prison systems of Texas and California.

In Texas, thousands of state inmates were placed into county-level jails. Much of the reason for this had to do with a significant legal development related to the Supreme Court ruling in *Ruiz v. Estelle* (1980). In this ruling (which students should recall from Chapter 3), the Texas prison system was found to be in violation of the Eighth Amendment prohibition against cruel and unusual punishments due to inadequate, unhealthy, and abusive prison practices in operation. One of the key issues in this case addressed the overcrowded facilities that existed in that system. Ultimately, this case resulted in population capacity limitations being imposed on various facilities throughout the system. This resulted in approximately 21,000 state offenders being detained in jails since the state prison system was unable to accommodate these inmates.

Later lawsuits between county jails and the state prison system resulted in the state being forced to meet its statutory obligation (see *County of Nueces, Texas v. Texas Board of Corrections*, 1989) to house inmates. If the state was unable to meet this obligation, the plaintiffs for the county jails contended that Texas would need to, at a minimum, reimburse county governments for the expense of housing such inmates. The Fifth Circuit federal court agreed, and the state was forced to pay counties a specified daily amount for each state-level inmate held within county jail facilities. This total amount ultimately added up to well over $100 million in compensation, a hefty sum by any account (Wallenstein & Kerle, 2008).

More recently, and as noted earlier in this chapter, the Supreme Court in 2011 upheld the ruling by a lower three-judge court that California must reduce its prison population to 137.5% of design capacity, which amounted to approximately 110,000 inmates being kept in a state system designed to hold about 80,000 inmates. As a result, the California State Legislature and governor enacted two laws—AB 109 and AB 117—to reduce the number of inmates housed in state prisons starting October 1, 2011 (Minton & Golinelli, 2014). These two laws are often referred to as the **Public Safety Realignment (PSR)** policy, and they are designed to reduce the prison population, in part, by placing new nonviolent, nonserious, non-sex offenders under county jurisdiction for incarceration in local jail facilities (Minton & Golinelli, 2014). Inmates released from local jails are placed under a county-directed post-release community supervision program instead of the state's parole system. In addition, California has given additional funding to the 58 counties throughout the state to deal with the increased inmate population; amidst this, each county is left to develop its own plan for custody and post-custody that best serves its needs. As can be seen in Figure 4.2, California had a low

Public Safety Realignment (PSR): A California state policy designed to reduce the number of offenders in that state's prison system to 110,000.

Table 4.3: State and Federal Inmates Held in Local Jails, End of Year, 2013

Total Population of State and Federal Inmates Held in Local Jails	
2012	83,501
2013	85,648
Percentage of State Inmate Population Housed in Local Jails (Those Having 20% or More)	
Louisiana	52.2%
Kentucky	39.1%
Mississippi	29.0%
Tennessee	27.3%
Utah	23.0%

SOURCE: Carson, A. (2014). *Prisoners, 2013*. Washington, DC: Bureau of Justice Statistics.

During the above years, approximately 5.4% of all U.S. inmates were housed in local jails.

Figure 4.2: California's Confined Jail Population, 2010 to 2013

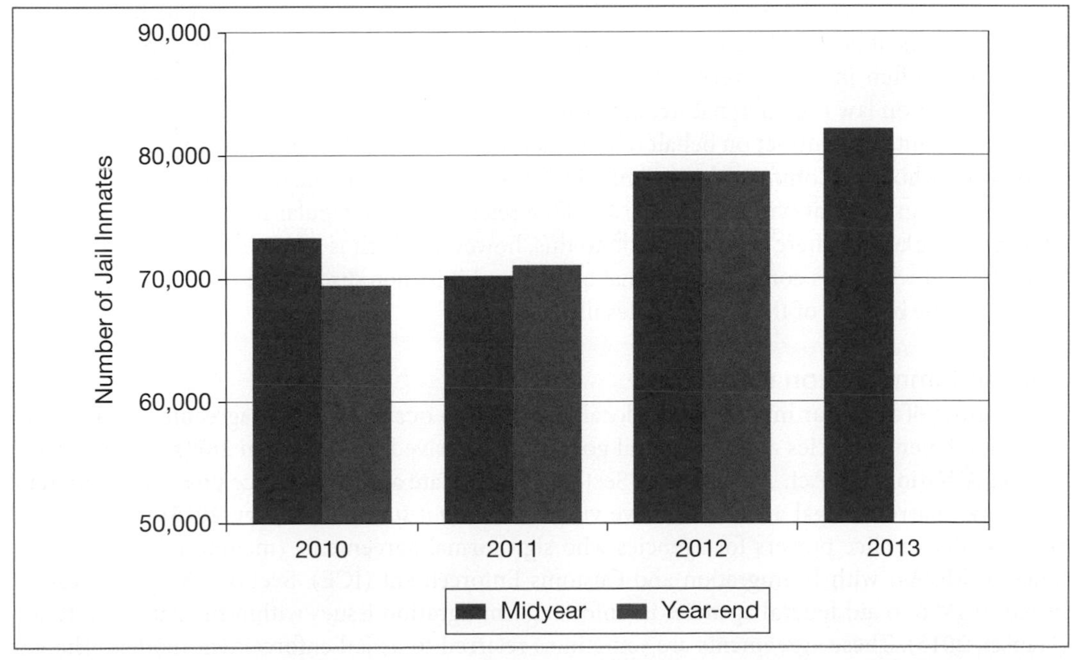

SOURCE: Minton, T. D., & Golinelli, D. (2014). *Jail inmates at midyear 2013—statistical tables*. Washington, DC: Bureau of Justice Statistics.

jail population between 2010 and 2011. However, as a result of the PSR, the California jail population increased by an estimated 7,600 inmates between year-end 2011 and midyear 2012 and by an estimated 3,500 inmates between midyear 2012 and midyear 2013 (Minton & Golinelli, 2014).

Because of this atypical influx of jail inmates from the state prison system, by 2013 it was determined that characteristics of inmates held in California jails, including inmates' race and conviction status, differed substantially from the rest of the national jail population. For example, in California jails, Hispanics accounted for 45% of the total inmate population, Caucasians represented 32%, and African Americans represented 20% (not shown). In comparison, in the rest of the country, Hispanics accounted for 11% of the national inmate population, Caucasians represented 49%, and African Americans represented 38% (Minton & Golinelli, 2014). There was also a slight difference in the inmate conviction status. At midyear 2013, 43% of inmates held in California jails were convicted, compared to 37% confined in non-California jails (Minton & Golinelli, 2014).

Jails as Overflow Facilities: For a Fee

In many states, sheriffs have begun to see the operation of jail facilities as a potential money-making endeavor. This is true in states like Louisiana, where inmates from the Department of Corrections are routinely assigned to jail facilities operated by local sheriffs for a set fee that is paid to the agency of the presiding sheriff. For rural regions, this may be a primary source of revenue and may also provide several jobs in the area that would otherwise not exist. Some critics of this type of operation note that this creates a sort of dependency on the state inmate population. On the other hand, proponents note that this type of system helps to keep costs down, eliminates the need for reduced sentences among offenders who should be kept locked up, and also disseminates revenue to areas of the state that are cash-strapped. So long as the local population does not object, it would seem that such forms of operation are win-win for both local and state government.

Some jail systems have even taken inmates from other states. For instance, the Spokane County Jail in Washington State agreed to take inmates for a fee from the District of Columbia Department of Corrections (Washington, D.C.). In another instance, Texas jails in Denton County contracted with the state of Oregon's prison system to house inmates. In this case, Denton County added stipulations that Oregon inmates would have to return to Oregon for their release and also that all accepted inmates would need to have at least 2 years remaining on their sentence.

Denton County also later set up similar contracts with the U.S. Immigration and Naturalization Service (since 2003 called U.S. Citizenship and Immigration Services) to hold federal detainees. Thus, it is clear that jail systems have been used as money-making ventures with such partnerships often involving very different regions of the nation. It is important to understand that immigration law is civil in nature, not criminal. Thus, when counties such as Denton agree to hold immigrants by contract on behalf of the federal government, they must be careful not to mix individuals who have committed no criminal offense—for example, those persons being detained only for immigration law violations, who are often referred to as irregular immigrants—with their criminal population. There is an exception to this, however, which is when agencies arrest and jail an individual who does commit a criminal offense and it is then discovered that the individual is also inside the borders of the United States illegally.

Jails and Immigration Detention

The housing of irregular immigrants in local jails has also occurred due to agreements with local law enforcement agencies and the federal government derived from Section 287(g) of the Immigration & Nationality Act. According to Section 287(g), state and local police possess an inherent authority to arrest illegal aliens who have violated *criminal statutes* (Hanser, 2015). This section also broadens police powers for agencies who sign formal agreements (memorandums of assistance or MOAs) with Immigration and Customs Enforcement (ICE). Section 287(g) was established in 1996 to aid federal agencies in enforcing immigration issues within the nation's interior (Hanser, 2015). These agreements are sometimes referred to as jail enforcement models. The jail enforcement agreements permit approved jail custodial staff to enforce immigration laws once an

Web Link
Wrongly Profiled and Deported

■ Table 4.4: Inmate Population in Jail Jurisdictions Reporting on Confined Persons Being Held for U.S. Immigration and Customs Enforcement (ICE), Midyear 2002–2014

			Confined persons held for ICE at midyear	
Year	Jurisdictions reporting on holding for ICE[a]	Inmates confined at midyear[b]	Number	Percent of all inmates
2002	2,961	626,870	12,501	2.0%
2003	2,940	637,631	13,337	2.1
2004	2,962	673,807	14,120	2.1
2005	2.824	703,084	11,919	1.7
2006	2,784	698,108	13,598	1.9
2007	2,713	683,640	15,063	2.2
2008	2,699	704,278	20,785	3.0
2009	2,643	685,500	24,278	3.5
2010	2,531	622,954	21,607	3.5
2011	2,758	672,643	22,049	3.3
2012	2,716	690,337	22,870	3.3
2013	2,685	673,707	17,241	2.6
2014	2,634	654,730	16,384	2.5

SOURCE: Minton, T. D., & Zeng, Z. (2015). *Jail inmates at midyear 2014—statistical tables.* Washington, DC: Bureau of Justice Statistics.

Note: Data are based on the reported data and were not estimated for survey item nonresponse. Comparisons were not tested due to changing coverage each year. See appendix table 9 for standard errors.

[a]Not all jurisdictions reported on holdings for ICE.

[b]Number of inmates held on the last weekday in June in jails reporting complete data or the number of inmates held for ICE.

irregular immigrant is brought in for booking. These agreements exist throughout the nation but are especially prevalent in areas of the nation where immigration issues are seen as a major concern (Hanser, 2015).

As a result of these agreements and due to the overflow experienced by ICE, the present immigration detention system is sprawling and needs more direct federal oversight and management (Immigration & Customs Enforcement, 2011). While ICE has over 32,000 detention beds at any given time, the beds are spread out over as many as 350 different facilities largely designed for penal, not civil, detention (Immigration & Customs Enforcement, 2011). ICE employees do not run most of these. The facilities are either jails operated by county authorities or detention centers operated by private contractors. Table 4.4 provides an annual tally of the number of irregular immigrants who are held by local jail jurisdictions. From this data, it can be seen that in 2013 there were 2,685 jail facilities that reported holding approximately 17,241 persons for ICE.

Jail Overcrowding and the Matrix Classification System

In many of the larger jail systems, issues related to overcrowding have led to lawsuits and legal concerns that plague jail administrators. This has prompted officials in various jurisdictions to build even more jail facilities and to add onto those that already exist. In many cases, this results in the need to generate revenue to finance this construction, which often is obtained through the use of bonds. In many cases, bonds must be passed by the voting community, and this means that in addition to everything else, the jail becomes a political issue whereby sheriff's offices attempt to get bond referendums passed for the construction of more jail space. In some instances, voters are not receptive to the needs of the sheriff's agency and fail to vote for such bonds.

Multnomah County in Oregon developed what is now known as the matrix system, which is designed to release inmates early from the jail when the facility's population exceeds the capacity of the structure. This system is designed to release the least dangerous offenders first; this is determined via a computerized scoring system. An individual booked into the jail is scored on the basis of the charges and, if applicable, failure to appear after being served a warrant. The matrix system is used to the control the population in custody without placing the community at additional risk of harm. Specifically, this system is designed to meet the following goals: (1) Remain an objective tool of assessment; (2) allow for the use of additional information related to potential danger, if it can be measured objectively; (3) have all functions fully automated; and (4) identify dangerous inmates and prevent their release.

Wallenstein and Kerle (2008) note that since Multnomah County began to use the matrix, over 10,000 inmates have been released to reduce crowding. Assessment and classification programs such as the matrix have become more and more important in many jail and prison facilities. When combined with the housing of long-term inmates, the overcrowding issue in jails becomes much more difficult in prisons, particularly since jails hold both convicted offenders and persons being detained until they see a judge.

HEALTH CARE IN JAILS

One of the largest health care systems that exists within the United States can be found in jails. Nearly every person who enters a jail receives some sort of basic medical screening and evaluation. This is necessary for risk avoidance, maintaining constitutional requirements, and institutional safety concerns. Indeed, offenders in jails often have a number of health care problems. According to a 2002 study of jail inmates conducted by the Bureau of Justice Statistics, more than a third of all jail inmates, or approximately 229,000 inmates, reported some sort of medical problem that was more serious than a cold or the flu (Maruschak, 2006). Most medical problems tend to precede the offender's placement into the jail system and include illnesses such as HIV/AIDS, hepatitis, sexually transmitted diseases, tuberculosis, heart disease and diabetes, women's issues, and disorders related to aging. And of course substance abuse issues affect many of the inmates encountered in jails.

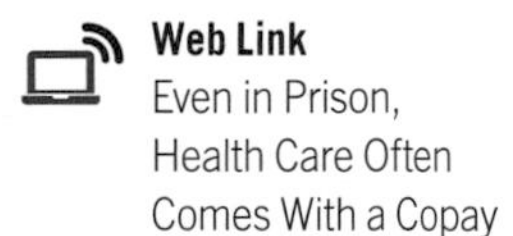

Web Link
Even in Prison, Health Care Often Comes With a Copay

As one might expect, the elderly are much more prone to certain medical problems than young inmates. Older jail inmates have been found to be more likely than younger inmates to report ever having a chronic condition or infectious disease. Indeed, jail inmates age 50 or older were twice as likely as those ages 18 to 24 to report ever having a chronic condition. In addition, jail inmates 50 years of age or older were about 3 times more likely to report having an infectious disease than younger jail inmates (Berzofsky, Maruschak, & Unangst, 2015).

Thus, when and where feasible, it is often in the best interest of the jail administrator to have nondangerous elderly offenders released as soon as possible due to their exorbitant medical costs. Naturally, this should not be done at the expense of public safety, but in those cases where elderly offenders are incarcerated for nuisance crimes and other such petty issues, it is likely that jail facilities will process these offenders out as soon as is reasonable.

Like older inmates, women in the study were also much more likely to report medical problems (53% for female inmates as opposed to 35% for male inmates). Female inmates indicated a cancer rate that was nearly 8 times that of male inmates, with the most common form of cancer for women being cervical. Indeed, for every medical problem documented in the study, female inmates reported more prevalence than male offenders, except for paralysis and tuberculosis (Stohr et al., 2008). Since female inmates tend to have more health care concerns than do male inmates, housing female inmates presents a plethora of issues regarding security procedures, specialized needs, and health care considerations.

Communicable Diseases in Jails

Blood-borne and airborne pathogens are now a serious consideration within most jail facilities (Berzofsky et al., 2015). Concerns regarding jail security and the prevention of communicable diseases are integral to most jail facilities as these diseases affect inmates, staff, and the outside community simultaneously. Communicable diseases found in jails include hepatitis A, hepatitis B, hepatitis C,

HIV/AIDS, tuberculosis, measles, and rubella (Berzofsky et al., 2015). To ensure that both staff and inmates are sufficiently protected, jails must have a written exposure plan that includes the engineering of physical facilities that help to isolate identified pathogens, work practices that control the spread of pathogens, the availability of personal protective equipment, routine staff training, the availability of appropriate vaccines, and detailed records of training provided and vaccines available (Berzofsky et al., 2015).

Further, most guidelines require that written protocols for responding to spills, occupational exposures, and other possible means of pathogen transmission be kept and disseminated among staff. In addition, confidential counseling for employees due to occupational exposure to a communicable disease must be made available. Though these procedures are becoming more commonplace, there are still some areas of operation regarding communicable diseases that need improvement in many jail systems.

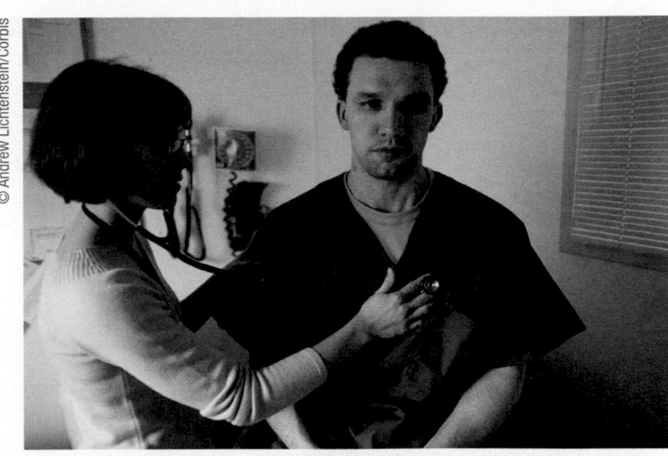

■ PHOTO 4.4 Correctional health care is an important area of service delivery in institutions. These professionals deal with a variety of issues that are complicated by the criminogenic lifestyles of most inmates who are their patients.

Data from the National Commission on Correctional Health Care (NCCHC, 2002) suggest that many jails are not adequately addressing three communicable diseases: human immunodeficiency virus/acquired immunodeficiency syndrome (HIV/AIDS), syphilis, and tuberculosis (TB). Although rudimentary HIV/AIDS education programs are becoming more widespread in jails, few jail systems have implemented comprehensive HIV/AIDS prevention programs in all of their facilities. Most jail systems provide HIV/AIDS antibody testing only when inmates ask to be tested or have signs and symptoms of HIV/AIDS. Testing is not aggressively "marketed" in most jail systems (Berzofsky et al., 2015).

Despite the availability of fairly inexpensive diagnostic and treatment modalities for STDs such as chlamydia and syphilis, testing is not thought to be automatic and/or widespread among jail systems. Research by the Centers for Disease Control and Prevention (2011) has concluded that often testing is only conducted when the presence of symptoms is observed by staff or when an inmate specifically requests the screening—and even when symptoms are observed, testing does not always occur. Even jails that report aggressive screening policies actually screen less than half (48%) of inmates (Centers for Disease Control, 2011). As a result, on average, less than one-third of jail inmates undergo laboratory testing for chlamydia or syphilis while incarcerated. Continuity of care for inmates released with chlamydia, syphilis, and other STDs is also inadequate (Centers for Disease Control, 2011).

Although more jails screen for TB than for STDs, this number should still be higher. According to the Centers for Disease Control (2006), at least three factors have contributed to the high rates of TB in detention and jail facilities. First is the disparate number of individuals who are at high risk for TB, such as substance abusers, individuals of low socioeconomic status, and individuals who are HIV positive. Second, the physical structure of many facilities enables transmission of the disease, given the close living quarters and inadequate ventilation that may exist. Third, the constant flow of persons in and out of these facilities (keep in mind this is approximately 10 to 14 million people per year), when combined with the first two factors, creates an elevated risk for contracting tuberculosis. In the United States, tuberculosis is often concentrated among disadvantaged populations, particularly immigrant populations. Immigrants in detention or in jail often come from countries with a high prevalence of TB. Due to social and legal circumstances, these individuals may not have access to testing and treatment for TB, making the jail or detention facility their first point of access to some type of medical service for the infection (Centers for Disease Control, 2006).

JAIL TRAINING STANDARDS

In many respects, jails have not been given the attention that they deserve. This is particularly true in regard to the training of staff. The National Institute of Corrections has in recent years published numerous manuals and videos and has also provided a variety of training programs for jail staff and leadership. This has been in response to the realization that jails have traditionally been

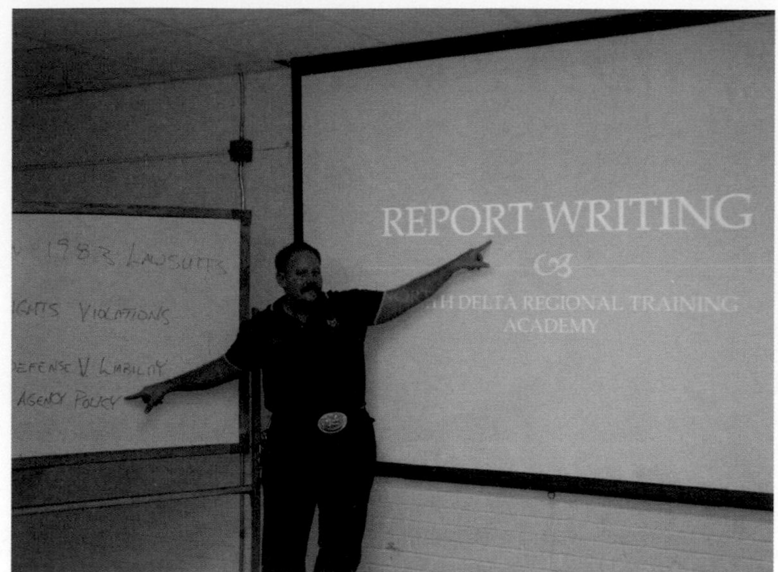

Robert Hanser

■ PHOTO 4.5 The author is a trainer at a regional academy for jailers and police officers. Hanser is seen here providing instruction at North Delta Regional Training Academy.

overlooked until the last decade. Indeed, the training of jail staff has a fairly short history, having started only 50 years ago with the Federal Bureau of Prisons (BOP). Formal training began in the BOP when federal agencies became concerned that states were not adequately training their jail staff. Thus, the BOP established a training school for sheriffs and jailers in 1948.

The type of formal training standards used varies quite considerably from state to state. Most of the short-term jails tend to use on-the-job training. This can create many problems since such training tends to be unorganized, and often there are gaps in the required knowledge that staff must have to be truly competent. Since many new staff must learn through a process of trial and error, the incidence of lawsuits tends to rise, and, even worse, the likelihood that inmate plaintiffs prevail in court against the agency also correspondingly increases. This is one of the primary reasons that many police agencies choose to refrain from operating a jail facility; the legal liability and responsibility offset the value of the convenience.

Language, Ethnic Diversity, and the Selection of Staff

Inmates processed in jail intake units reflect the cultural and linguistic diversity that exists throughout the United States. Because of this, it is important that staff have linguistic skills and that they are knowledgeable about different cultures, particularly those likely to be in the jail facility in their area. Due to this, jails need to have a diverse staff. This can even extend into the multinational realm as well as the multicultural realm. Consider, for example, that in California jails may house a substantial number of Asian offenders and Latino offenders. In some areas of the northeastern United States, the need for Jamaican, Russian, or Ukrainian staff may exist. Thus, jail administrators face the need to develop a workforce that reflects the composition of the offender population in their area.

Challenges Faced by Female Staff

Female staff face a number of challenges that are encountered with less frequency by male staff. In many jails, women are not afforded the same respect as men, both by the inmates and by their fellow officers. Much of this may have to do with the inmate subculture, the organizational culture of the agency, and other factors that impact a female officer's professional development in law enforcement. Likewise, since so many of the inmates are male, female officers find themselves a minority among both the inmates and the officers. Thus, many female officers are utilized with female inmates when and where possible to alleviate concerns over searches and maintenance security as well as medical issues common to female offenders.

Other Employee Issues

There are approximately 300,000 jail staff around the country. Typically, these staff are underpaid in relation to other law enforcement officers and/or correctional officers in state (rather than local) facilities. Many of these employees take these jobs on a temporary basis while waiting for openings in other areas of their sheriff's agency. However, often these employees have only limited education and/or skill development and do not fare as well in the competition for better positions. Therefore, they often find themselves on the jail staff for longer periods of time. Some truly do find the work rewarding, though, and/or develop a set of specialized skills within the jail that make them invaluable to the jail's operation. For these individuals, working in the jail becomes as lucrative as (and perhaps even more lucrative than) working in other positions in the agency. One example is training officers in jail settings. Over time these persons can become quite sought out among other agencies and can command a high wage for their knowledge and expertise.

For the most part, jailers in many jurisdictions do not seem to have an effective career track that is sufficiently rewarding. Turnover is very high, with many jails reporting a complete change in staff every few years. This has generated a serious concern regarding the quality of employees in many jails as well as the quality of their training. To help improve the quality of training for jailers throughout the nation, the National Institute of Corrections Jails Division has implemented programs to increase the number of trainers for jail staff to ensure that there are enough opportunities for training among employees of various agencies. While this is an admirable approach, the true long-term answer to this problem is an increase in pay and career incentives for these employees.

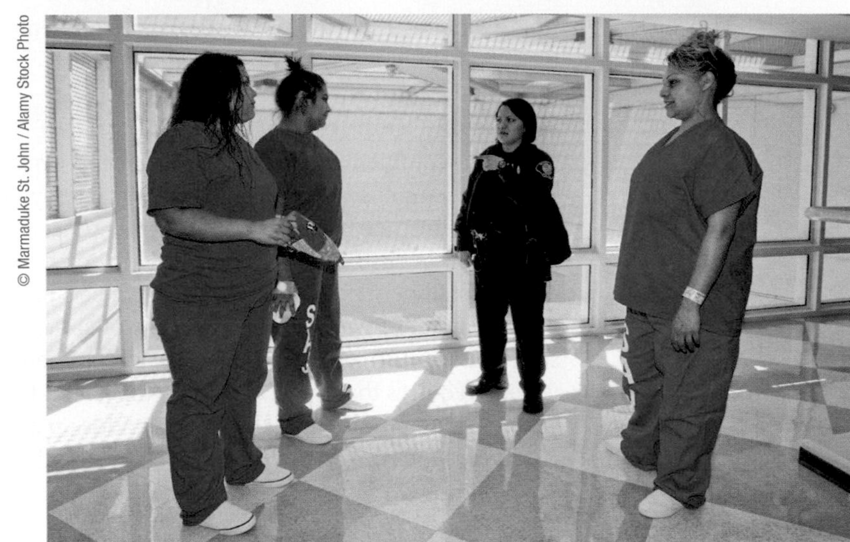

■ PHOTO 4.6 A corrections officer provides instructions to female inmates regarding a project that they will complete.

Evolving Professionalism

One of the most direct means of increasing professionalism in the jailer's career track is to utilize what Stohr et al. (2008) refer to as coequal staffing. In this type of staffing, programs provide comparable pay and benefits to those who work in the jail and those who work in routine law enforcement positions. In some jurisdictions, agencies have created two career tracks—one for law enforcement and the other for jailers—with equal pay. There is some evidence that this approach has had a phenomenal effect on the professional operation of jails (they are better staffed) and on the morale of those assigned to them (Stohr et al., 2008).

As our jails become more professionalized, the requirements for training and higher entry standards become more important. In fact, some states now require that jail officers be certified through some type of official academy training. Even in many places that require such training, however, that training still tends to fall short of the number of hours required in traditional law enforcement positions. Silverman (2001) notes that the reluctance of local jurisdictions to meet their training obligations has served as the impetus behind the American Jail Association's monthly training bulletins, which consist of video and web-based training segments. Lastly, refresher training is critical and is offered in many jurisdictions. Examples of the diverse areas in which jailers must develop expertise include the use of CPR, fire safety, aerosol pepper spray and taser proficiency, riot-control techniques, and human relations skills.

Requirements of the Peace Officer Standards and Training (POST) are used to guide agencies and training facilities in a number of states toward ensuring that jail officers have the requisite skills needed to perform their job assignment(s). Ensuring that jailers receive well-developed training that is top quality, serious, and professional improves the jail systems in the area while also providing a clear message to jailers in training: Your job is important, and we take it seriously. The result is that the jailers take their jobs seriously as well, and employee morale tends to be much higher in local agencies throughout the region.

SPECIALIZED TYPES OF JAIL SENTENCES

Extended confinement of persons who, by legal standards, are presumed innocent until proven guilty, such as with pretrial detention of the nonadjudicated offender, creates a serious custody problem for jails that prisons are not forced to contend with. The defendant who is truly innocent but is required to spend long periods of time in jail confinement will eventually develop a sense of resentment toward the criminal justice system. Further, this simply does not smack of fundamental fairness and instead creates a situation where innocent persons feel victimized, even though that is not the intent. Thus, the use of specialized jail sentences can create "middle road" forms of custody that can help to mitigate these negative effects.

Weekend Confinement

Weekend confinement is used to lessen the negative impact of short-term incarceration and to allow those in custody to maintain their employment. Jurisdictions using **weekend confinement** have implemented methods of confinement that are restricted to the weekends or other times when the person in custody is off from work. In some respects, this can be likened to serving a sentence on an installment plan, whereby other aspects of life that keep the person functional in society are not impaired, yet, at the same time, the offender is required to pay for his or her crime through a series of small stints in jail. This type of confinement typically is assigned to misdemeanants and usually requires that they check in to the jail on Friday evening and leave on Sunday at a specified time. Through these stints the offender adds up credit toward confinement until the total sentence is served. Weekend confinement is used with minimum-security facilities and with offenders who have committed minor or petty crimes.

Shock Incarceration/Split Sentences

Video Link
Without Funds to Pay Fines, Minor Incidents Can Mean Jail

For certain offenders, the mere subjection to a loss of freedom is all that is needed to get their lives in order. As a result, one mechanism used for instilling fear—the goal being to deter future criminal behavior—is shock incarceration. **Shock incarceration** is short-term incarceration followed by a specified term of community supervision in hopes of deterring the offender from recidivating. Because the brief stint of incarceration is meant to provide a sense of punitive reality to the offender, most shock incarceration programs are designed for juvenile offenders and those who have never been incarcerated before. Shock incarceration results in the offender being sentenced to incarceration for 30, 60, or 90 days in most cases and, upon completion of this time served, being resentenced by a judge to probation supervision. The idea is that this brief period of incarceration will sufficiently "shock" the offender so he or she will desist from committing further offenses. It is presumed that this short period of incarceration will have a similar deterrent effect on this type of offender as a longer one would. This method is sometimes utilized when the concern is that a longer period of incarceration might result in the hardening of the offender.

With split sentencing, offenders are sentenced to a specified term of confinement that can include up to half of their original sentence (i.e. it might be for years as opposed to only 30, 60, or 90 days), after which they finish the remainder of their sentence on probation. Unlike shock incarceration, this sentencing is all done upfront with no need for later resentencing. In some cases, this type of sentence may be utilized due to a shortage of jail beds, while in other cases it may be used for criminal offenses that are too serious to allow for a shorter period of incarceration but when, due to plea agreements, more flexibility is permissible in the amount of time that is actually to be served in jail or prison.

SPECIAL ISSUES IN JAILS

As if the various categories of offenders and their movement into and out of the facility were not enough to complicate the job of jail staff and administrators, offenders also have a host of issues with which jail systems must contend. Indeed, many jail inmates have problems with illiteracy, substance abuse, mental illness and stability, general medical conditions, communicable diseases, and suicide ideation. Because many of these issues go untreated in the community, the jail becomes the dumping ground for these offenders. Thus, jails must service a diverse offender population with specialized problems and needs. We now turn our attention to some of these specialized needs that emerge in the jail setting.

Weekend confinement: Confinement that is restricted to the weekends or other times when the person in custody is off from work.

Shock incarceration: A short period of incarceration followed by a specified term of community supervision.

Substance-Abusing Offenders in Jails

Throughout the literature it is commonly noted that substance abuse issues are rampant within the jail population. This observation is true regardless of the region of the United States and/or the time of year at which one considers this point. Simply put, substance abuse is a major problem that impacts the day-to-day operation of jails in terms of both security and programming. According to the Center on Addiction and Substance Abuse (2010), the largest increase in the percentage of substance-involved inmates was in the jail population, with nearly 85% of all jail inmates reporting

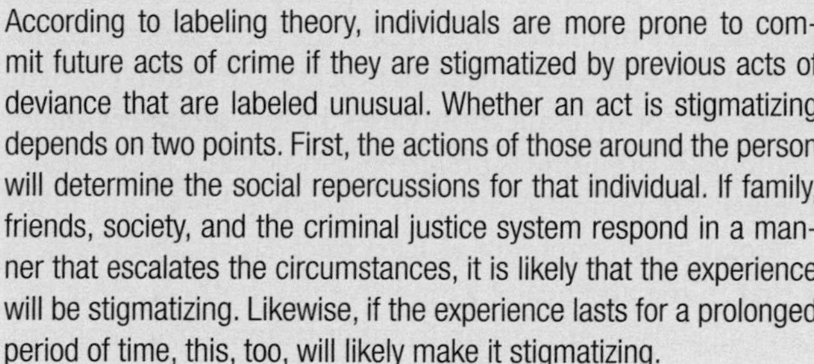

APPLIED THEORY 4.1

Labeling Theory and First-Time Jail Inmates

According to labeling theory, individuals are more prone to commit future acts of crime if they are stigmatized by previous acts of deviance that are labeled unusual. Whether an act is stigmatizing depends on two points. First, the actions of those around the person will determine the social repercussions for that individual. If family, friends, society, and the criminal justice system respond in a manner that escalates the circumstances, it is likely that the experience will be stigmatizing. Likewise, if the experience lasts for a prolonged period of time, this, too, will likely make it stigmatizing.

In many cases, a person's initial stay at a jail will be short-term. While this may not, on the face of it, seem overly serious, this can be quite problematic for a person who has never been incarcerated. The entire experience is alien, and there is a very distinct sense of the unknown. One's safety is in the hands of others, and there are few timely options of recourse if an incident occurs. However, for most persons charged with a crime, the trauma of this experience does subside once they leave the facility.

The experience does not end at this point, though. A released offender must deal with post-jail paperwork, bond payments, potential time missed at work, discussions with family, and a variety of other issues that continue to remind the person of the ordeal and also serve as additional consequences for committing an illegal act. In addition, the person now has a criminal record, which will follow him or her for life.

It is at this point that labeling can have its most damaging impact. Often, this can serve as a key point at which individuals may decide that, since things have already taken a turn for the worse, there is less harm if they continue to dabble in those activities that are questionable. This can particularly be true if these are, say, vice crimes like prostitution, small-time drug use, or drinking and driving. Further, because these persons will have criminal records, they are more vulnerable to detection should they do this behavior again. Thus, a cycle can develop where they may be more prone to engage in deviant behavior, and, because they have been detected once, they are at increased odds of getting detected again. This then results in another jail stint, and so forth. Along the way, this process is normalized by friends, family, and associates as part of this person's common behavior, and, with time, this becomes a facet of the person's everyday identity. At this point, the jail experience has resulted in the successful labeling of the individual as a criminal, and the identity ultimately becomes internalized and accepted by that individual.

substance abuse problems (p. 10). In fact, over half of all inmates reported being under the influence of drugs or alcohol at the time of their offense, while nearly one-fifth indicated that they had engaged in criminal behavior as a means of supporting their drug habit. Of those in local jails, it was found that 50.2% of those having substance abuse problems had at least one prior incarceration, while the same was true of only 27% of inmates without a drug problem. Further, drug abusers in jail had over twice the number of prior arrests than their counterparts who did not have a drug problem (Center on Addiction and Substance Abuse, 2010, p. 20). In addition, 25.2% of jail inmates were found to have both a substance abuse disorder and a mental health disorder (Center on Addiction and Substance Abuse, 2010, p. 26).

The drugs of choice for abusers and users vary and include, by prevalence of use, marijuana, cocaine or crack, hallucinogens, stimulants, and inhalants. As would be expected, those who indicated substance abuse problems were also more likely to have a criminal record. In addition, homelessness is very common among substance abusers who end up in jail. In fact, as noted above, it is not uncommon for many addicts who live on the streets to deliberately commit crimes during the winter months as a means of having a warm place to stay during the coldest periods of the year.

Treatment within the jail itself for drug abuse is somewhat unusual, unfortunately. Much of this has to do with the fact that offenders tend to move in and out of the jail facility much more quickly than in a prison facility, so there is little time between implementation of treatment and the offender's departure from the facility. Treatment programs are usually focused on jail inmates who have a substance abuse problem and have longer-term sentences, but, even in these cases, detoxification tends to be the primary approach to treatment, coupled with the support group interventions of Alcoholics Anonymous and/or Narcotics Anonymous.

Detoxification: The use of medical drugs to ease the process of overcoming the physical symptoms of dependence.

Detoxification is designed for persons dependent on narcotic drugs (e.g., heroin, opium) and is typically found in inpatient settings with programs that last for 7 to 21 days. The rationale for using detoxification as a treatment approach is grounded in two basic principles (Hanson, Venturelli, & Fleckenstein, 2011; Myers & Salt, 2000). The first is a conception of *addiction* as drug craving accompanied by physical dependence that motivates continued usage, resulting in a tolerance to the drug's effects and a syndrome of identifiable physical and psychological symptoms when the drug is abruptly withdrawn. The second is that the negative aspects of the abstinence syndrome discourage many addicts from attempting withdrawal, which makes them more likely to continue using drugs. The main objective of chemical detoxification is the elimination of physiological dependence through a medically supervised procedure.

While many detoxification programs address only the addict's physical dependence, some provide individual or group counseling in an attempt to address the psychological problems associated with drug abuse. Many detoxification programs use medical drugs to ease the process of overcoming the physical symptoms of dependence that make the detoxification process so painful. For drug offenders in jails and in prisons, the mechanism of detoxification varies by the offender's major drug of addiction. For opiate users, methadone or clonidine is preferred. For cocaine users, desipramine has been used to ease the withdrawal symptoms. Almost all narcotic addicts and many cocaine users have been in a chemical detoxification program at least once (Inciardi, Rivers, & McBride, 2008). However, studies show that in the absence of supportive psychotherapeutic services and community follow-up care, nearly all abusers are certain to suffer from relapse (Ashford, Sales, & Reid, 2002).

In all detoxification programs, inmate success depends upon following established protocols for drug administration and withdrawal. In essence, detoxification should be viewed as an initial step, after the intake process, of a comprehensive treatment process. Because jails are not typically long-term facilities, they will not usually offer much more than detoxification programs. Of course, this does not address the needs of those inmates who are kept in jails on a long-term basis, such as state prison inmates who are housed in local jails. In such cases, the services for these inmates should be on par with those for inmates who are kept long-term in prisons. While some of the larger jail systems in the United States might offer more comprehensive services, most do not. Thus, offenders who are kept on a long-term basis in a jail facility find themselves without suitable intervention services.

Mental Health Issues in Jails

Jails in this country are full of the mentally ill, and, in many cases, these offenders are homeless. Data from the Bureau of Justice Statistics indicate that roughly 64% of all jail inmates have a mental health problem (James & Glaze, 2006). This contrasts with mental health problems in prisons, where only 10.6% of inmates present with mental illnesses. Further still, for nearly every manifestation of mental illness, more jail inmates than state or federal inmates are likely to exhibit symptoms, particularly hallucinations and delusions. Jail inmates tend to have mental health problems with specific diagnoses that include mania (approximately 54%), major depression (30%), and psychotic disorders (24%), according to Stohr et al. (2008). The specific identification of a mental illness for each inmate is based on the *Diagnostic and Statistical Manual of Mental Disorders* (DSM-IV-TR). The DSM-IV-TR is a manual used by mental health clinicians that provides the specific criteria and symptoms to be considered when qualifying a person with a diagnosis and is the accepted standard among members of the American Psychiatric Association.

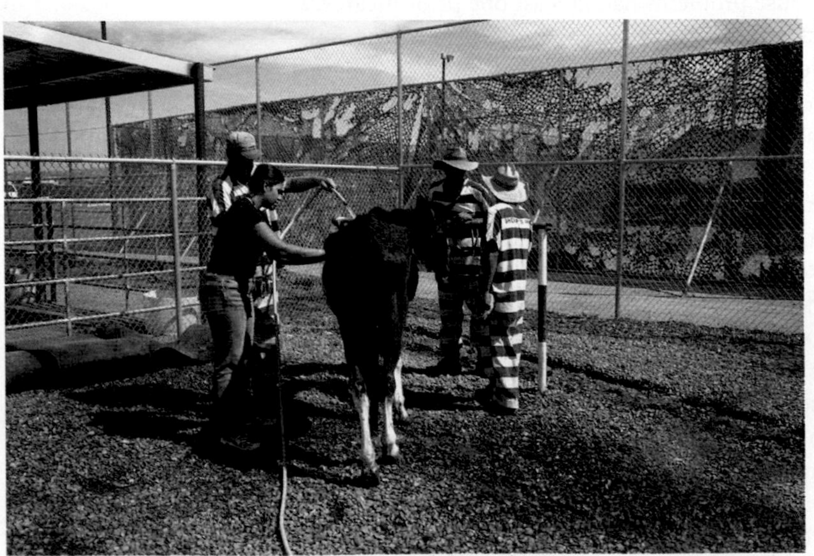
MASH/Splash News/Newscom

■ PHOTO 4.7 Some facilities have programs where inmates are given responsibility for taking care of animals owned by the facility. These types of programs provide therapeutic benefits for many offenders and are beneficial for the animals, as well.

A host of problems can be associated with mental illnesses in jail systems, including homelessness, greater criminal engagement, prior abuse, and substance use. James and Glaze (2001) found that those with a mental illness designation were almost twice as likely as other inmates to have been homeless prior to being placed in jail. In addition, inmates with mental illnesses tend to have more incidents of incarceration than do those who have no record of mental illness. Roughly three times as many jail inmates with a mental health problem have a history of physical or sexual abuse than do those without such a problem (James & Glaze, 2001; Stohr et al., 2008). Likewise, nearly 75% of inmates with a mental health issue also have a substance abuse problem. Thus, those inmates with mental health problems tend to have a multiplicity of other issues that affect them as well. Naturally, these issues affect the inmate's behavior and thus place a drain on the time and effort of jail staff.

One study in particular demonstrates how for mentally ill jail inmates there is a confluence of factors that aggravate their circumstances. McNeil, Binder, and Robinson (2005) found in their study in San Francisco County that jail inmates with mental illness were prone to have multiple issues that seemed to dovetail with their mental illness. They found that mental illness, substance abuse, and prior jail incarcerations were connected life events (Stohr et al., 2008). In addition, among those inmates who were mentally ill and/or had substance abuse or dependence issues, homelessness was a much more common phenomenon. Thus, the mentally ill inmate presents with a number of challenges for jail staff—challenges that are not easily separated from each other. While it is not clear if the mental illness itself spawned these other issues or if these issues served to increase the likelihood of mental illness, it is clear that these offenders are in need of help that extends well beyond the intended scope of most jail facilities.

Jail Suicide

When discussing jail suicide, it is important to understand that during any given year the total number of incidents fluctuates but is at or around 300 inmates (Noonan & Ginder, 2014). Thus, when we discuss jail suicide, we are usually referring to approximately 270 to 315 inmates out of 10 to 14 million individuals who are processed yearly through jails around the nation. Though this is a small number, suicide is a concern for jail administrators and is important for humanitarian reasons, if nothing else. Remaining data regarding jail suicide for this section have been drawn from a 2010 report conducted by the National Institute of Corrections and authored by Lindsey Hayes. As indicated from these data, those incarcerated in jails often enter while intoxicated, and many also have some sort of mental disability. Further, this booking may be their first experience with the incarceration process and may, therefore, be one of the lowest points in their life. In such circumstances, jail inmates are at heightened risk of suicidal ideation and attempts (Hayes, 2010; Hanser, 2002).

SAGE Journal Article Link
Suicides in Jails and Lockups

When considering the characteristics of jail suicide decedents, the overwhelming majority (93.1%) are male (Hayes, 2010, p. 12). It is interesting to note that although white inmates account for about 44% of the total jail population throughout the country, in the report they represented the majority (67%) of inmates who committed suicide, whereas African American inmates, who account for nearly the same percentage of the total jail population as whites (39%), constituted only 15% of jail suicide victims (Hayes, 2010, p. 12). Further, the majority of those who committed suicide in jail were single (42%), with only 21.4% being married (p. 12). Lastly, the overwhelming majority (90.1%) of suicide victims were in detention facilities at the time of their death (Hayes, 2010, p. 14).

Interestingly, only 38.1% of inmates who committed suicide were identified as having a history of mental illness during the intake process (Hayes, 2010, p. 17). Most of these inmates suffered from depression or psychosis. Further, Hayes found that 33.8 % of inmates who committed suicide reported a history of suicidal behavior during the intake process, which was substantially more than what had previously been reported in other federal statistics by James and Glaze (2006). This demonstrates that more detailed data collection methods can identify cases that may otherwise be overlooked (Hayes, 2010, p. 19).

When considering interventions for jail suicide risks, it is first important to note that the vast majority of inmates (over 90%) successfully complete their suicide by hanging, usually using either clothing items or bed sheets (Hayes, 2010). It is clear that suicide watches and other similar precautions are effective since only 7% of all jail suicides occur while such a watch is implemented (Hayes, 2010, p. 28). In those cases that are successful despite the watch, the issue usually has to do with the length of time between observations (e.g., every 15 minutes as opposed to continuous) of the individual with suicidal ideations. Lastly, many mental health clinicians often develop no-harm contracts with potentially suicidal inmates, seeking assurance that their clients will not engage in self-injurious behavior (Hanser & Mire, 2010). This is sometimes viewed as a buffer against liability in the event that the inmate commits suicide but it is questionable as to whether this holds any legal merit (Hanser & Mire, 2010).

It is clear that administrators understand the importance of staff training regarding jail suicide (Hanser & Mire, 2010). Research by Hayes shows that over 74% of all jail administrators provide training on at least an annual basis (2010, p. 35), with most others indicating that such training is provided biannually. Of those who did not respond positively to these inquiries, most were rural jails. Thus, it may well be that larger jail facilities with greater resources are better able to provide training and resources for staff. Other advantages of larger jails also exist. For example, younger and less experienced offenders who are apprehensive of being housed with older offenders who may victimize them can often be segregated in larger jails. In smaller jail facilities, space may not exist for such protective considerations, and inmates who are in fear of victimization and already at a low point in their life would likely be at an increased risk of suicide ideation. The ability to alleviate some of the anxiety of inmates can often reduce the likelihood for suicidal thoughts and actions.

CONCLUSION

Jail facilities are perhaps the most complicated of facilities within the field of corrections and are often not appreciated for the vital role that they play within the criminal justice system. The volume of persons processed in jail facilities, in and of itself, is sufficient to warrant a closer examination of these facilities. In addition, jails perform many different types of tasks, such as the holding of persons prior to their court date and providing a series of unique sentencing variations. They are also sometimes used for the incarceration of persons who are technically part of the larger prison system.

Jails and jail staff must attend to a variety of offenders who present with a number of issues. The range of problems and challenges can be quite varied, and this creates a demanding situation for jail staff and administrators. The variety of offender typologies, needs, and issues presents staff with problems that are not easily rectified, and, correspondingly, there is a need for staff to be well trained and well equipped. Unfortunately, jails frequently do not have sufficient funding for this. This is especially true with small rural jails where funds and expertise are limited. Overall, it appears that jails have been given short shrift in the world of corrections but that they will be given much more attention in the future.

Want a better grade?

Get the tools you need to sharpen your study skills. Access practice quizzes, eFlashcards, video, and multimedia at **edge.sagepub.com/hanser2e**

SAGE edge™

DISCUSSION QUESTIONS

1. Compare issues for large metropolitan jails to those for small rural jails.
2. Provide a discussion regarding the demographics and characteristics of the jail inmate population.
3. What are some of the challenges associated with training and motivating jail staff?
4. What are some special types of sentencing options in jails?
5. What is *booking*, and why is this area of the jail so important?
6. Discuss the dynamics of suicide within the jail facility.
7. How have communicable diseases impacted jail operations during recent years?
8. How can a first-time jail experience result in labeling a person and thereby potentially increasing his or her likelihood of continuing in a life of crime?

SAGE edge™ **Test your understanding of chapter content. Take the practice quiz.**

KEY TERMS

Detoxification, 97
Gaols, 78
Jail, 79
Jail reentry programs, 84
Podular jail, 83
Public Safety Realignment (PSR), 89
Rural jail, 80
Sally port, 86
Shock incarceration, 96
Short-term jail, 86
Tower of London, 78
Weekend confinement, 96

SAGE edge™ **Review key terms with eFlashcards.**

APPLIED EXERCISE 4.1

For this exercise, students will need to determine how they would informally address the issue of sexually transmitted diseases (STDs) and other sex-related illnesses in their institution.

You are the assistant warden of a large metropolitan jail in your city. Your jail contends with a constant ingress and egress of inmates who tend to be drawn from population groups that are traditionally high-risk for various STDs as well as HIV/AIDS. Your jail system naturally has an identification policy, and the members of your staff are trained in dealing with these types of illnesses, diseases, and viruses. Occasional in-service training is also provided to staff when and where time and resources permit.

Recently, the city of Sodom, where your jail facility is located, has experienced an outbreak of herpes that has reached epidemic proportions. In addition, your county, the county of Gomorrah, was identified last year as having the highest incidence of HIV/AIDS in the state. Thus, issues related to STDs and HIV/AIDS are taken very seriously in your jurisdiction.

Recently, in response to community concerns regarding public health, the mayor of Sodom met with the chief of police of Sodom and the sheriff of Gomorrah County to discuss the issue. It was decided that a very quick and aggressive crackdown on vice crime would be instituted in areas with high levels of prostitution, other illicit sex industry activity, and intra venous drug use. Police officers and sheriff's deputies were mobilized for this major enforcement activity. Amidst this, the mayor, police chief, and sheriff implemented plans for increased jail space in facilities throughout the city and the county; it was understood that this major enforcement effort would result in a larger number of persons jailed in the area. Thus far, resources for containing this population have been sufficient.

However, staff in the jail facilities—and your facility is the largest in the system—tend to be very stern and unsympathetic to the plight of those inmates who are being locked up for various types of criminal behavior that correlate with the spread of STDs and HIV/AIDS. While there is no specific requirement that they be particularly empathetic, the deliberate heckling of these inmates and the calloused approach that seems to predominate does not help the situation. This attitude is exacerbated by local TV and printed news media that have showcased the public health hazards, essentially dramatizing the situation to epic proportions. In fact, the media have been critical of law enforcement and the mayor's office for being a bit slow and ineffective in their response. Thus, many jail employees feel as if their agency is considered lax on this problem.

Your concern, as the assistant warden, is centered on the increased number of accidents and altercations and the general upheaval within your facility. The warden of the facility (your boss) has explained that lawsuits are likely to emerge in the near future. The city and the county both have their legal budgets stretched way beyond what allocations would typically allow. So, the warden asks you to implement some type of intervention program that will ameliorate the problems that are occurring between staff and STD-positive inmates.

The issue, it appears, has to do with the informal culture of members of the jail staff and their perceptions of the problem as well as their role in addressing that problem. It seems that by handling these offenders in a rough manner, staff are actually aggravating the long-term problem for the city and the county. While at the day-to-day level of operations the consequences of their actions do not seem to be serious, some very costly problems are likely to develop in the future. Further still, their behavior will not aid the process of trying to get these offenders to change their sexual and drug-using behaviors. It is important to the warden that something be done to change this informal culture and, if that is not possible, that some type of documentation exist to at least address this issue since the warden is quite convinced that it will be relevant in civil court in the next few months.

TO THE STUDENT: The task before you is to design some type of intervention method to address and change the behavior of staff who seem to be calloused and antagonistic toward offenders who have STDs or HIV/AIDS within your facility. This must go beyond simply making a policy statement or providing a training segment since both of these types of programs already exist in your jail system. While you may add to the policy and the training segment, explain what else you might do to address this issue, both formally and informally.

WHAT WOULD YOU DO?

Here you are again, the assistant warden of the largest jail facility in the city of Sodom, located in the county of Gomorrah. Recently, you have found that many of the offenders who have been locked up due to a crackdown on vice crime, sex industry offenses, and intravenous drug use were on some type of drug and/or alcohol at the time of their arrest. Numerous "johns" and other typically noncriminal persons have been arrested and jailed in the process of implementing the crackdown. Needless to say, many of these persons are not used to being incarcerated, and they seem to be having a difficult time with the experience. Additionally, many of these current inmates suffer from high levels of guilt and embarrassment, not to mention problems with their employer and/or spouse. While many are able to get out quickly through the bail/bonds offices in the area, many stay in the facility for several days.

An unexpected outcome is that several suicide attempts have been made by these persons. In fact, two attempts have been successful. Four other serious attempts were detected in time to prevent their completion. One of the decedents was from a very affluent family, and it is thought that the family may sue the jail facility. The sheriff has met with members of the family to attempt to mitigate some of their concerns and complaints regarding the incident, but it is not yet clear how the situation may unfold.

Your facility does have a suicide policy that requires additional supervision of inmates at risk of suicide, the use of suicide contracts, and additional services. However, the sheriff, the mayor, and the chief of police all believe that much more can be done if staff are given training on how to provide informal crisis prevention skills for new inmates, particularly those determined to be at heightened risk via jail intake protocols. The warden of the jail has talked with you and noted that she has set aside money from the budget so that you can develop and implement some type of crisis response training for jail staff. You have also been given an additional administrative staff member to help with this process.

You must first determine who is at increased risk, and then you must identify what might be done among jail staff to minimize this risk. You are given 30 days to implement this program.

What would you do?

PRACTICE AND APPLY WHAT YOU'VE LEARNED

edge.sagepub.com/hanser2e

REVIEW. PRACTICE. IMPROVE.

Head to the study site, where you'll find:

- An **online action plan** that includes tips and feedback on progress through the course and materials
- **Learning objectives** that reinforce the key concepts in each chapter

PROBATION

©Rich Pedroncelli/AP/Corbis

PROBATION OFFICER STRESS

Jillian Jackson, a consultant in organization efficiency and human resources, was recently hired to address problems with poor morale within a very large probation agency.

Recently, it had been discovered that recidivism rates in the agency's jurisdiction were higher than average, much to the dismay of the administration and the chief judge of the criminal court. Nobody really knew what to do; extensive budget cuts had been made during the past 3 years and, on top of that, the jail and prison systems were full beyond capacity most of the time. It was also clear that the types of offenders on the caseloads had issues that were often more serious and complicated than offenders in the past. And even though the number of offenders was not rising, it was not going down either.

Jillian examined the small group around her. It consisted of eight probation officers who had been brought together as a focus group to discuss workplace stress. Jillian had asked these officers for feedback and thought at first that they might be hesitant to speak out. *Boy, was I wrong,* she thought to herself.

She motioned to one of the officers, Darrel Hayes, a somewhat gruff-appearing, barrel-chested man who, though professional, spoke with a commanding presence.

Once acknowledged, Hayes said, "I can have somebody's file pulled because they are a higher-risk person and I want to focus on his supervision and service needs, and then the 16 stupid things that I shouldn't have to be dealing with at all come walking in the door. At the end of the day, I realize that the one person I really should've been spending time with didn't get any time. That frustrates me because, let's face it, those are the cases that potentially are going to blow up in your face."

Jillian responded, "Yes, Mr. Hayes, I can see how this would get pretty frustrating." Another officer, Zora Gonzales, raised her hand, and Jillian indicated for her to speak.

"I often feel intense pressure because you have such a responsibility to the community," Gonzales said. "These high-risk offenders pose such a potential threat to public safety that you feel pressure to find the right treatment for this person and to make sure that they're getting something out of it."

"So if you all were able to spend more time with the more risky offenders to ensure that they received the programming that they needed, you would feel much better about your role in maintaining public safety and be able to use some of the tools that are designed to prevent some of these recidivism problems?"

"Yeah, exactly!" said Hayes. Gonzales and four other officers nodded their heads as well.

Jillian asked, "Have you guys ever made all of this known to the chief judge and other external officials?"

LEARNING OBJECTIVES:

1. Discuss how probation impacts the jail and prison systems of a jurisdiction.
2. Describe briefly the history of probation.
3. Compare different means by which probation agencies are organized.
4. Identify the qualifications and characteristics of most probation officers.
5. List some of the reasons probation would be revoked.

SAGE edge™

Get the edge on your studies: edge.sagepub.com/hanser2e

- Take a quiz to find out what you've learned.
- Review key terms with eFlashcards.
- Watch videos that enhance chapter content.

Jason Booker replied, "Naw, I don't think any of us are really prone to talking about this stuff beyond our own group here . . . especially not to people outside of our organization. They don't understand, and they'll also probably worry even more that we don't have a handle on things."

Nodding in agreement with Booker, Susan Grundstrom added, "You know, Ms. Jackson, most probation officers' lives are kind of chaotic due to the size of our caseloads and the nature of who we have to deal with. It's hard not to reduce everything to self-preservation, routing people without getting in-depth, just to survive. On a personal level, I think most officers stay pretty closed up—like police officers. What do you do—go home and tell your husband about the child abusers and rapists you saw in the office today? It's difficult for officers not to carry their work home, and yet difficult not to be able to talk about it there."

Jillian considered Grundstrom's words. After a moment she said, "I think that we're going to have to work on the agency's idea of communication and collaboration with outside partners, and I think this is going to require many partners coming together to ensure that programs and supervision are paired up correctly, comprehensively, and consistently with these high risk-offenders. The agency staff simply can't do *everything.*"

And I think that this is going to require much more work than anyone in this administration realizes, she then thought to herself.

INTRODUCTION

Probation, as implemented by county and state jurisdictions around the nation, is the most common sanction administered in the United States. For this reason, if nothing else, attention should be given to it. However, probation is specifically important to corrections because it is, by its very nature, an option that facilitates the process of correcting offenders. In addition, probation impacts the jail and prison systems through revocation processes and by acting as a filtering device as offenders are inputted into the jail and prison systems. Since space in incarceration faculties can often be scarce, probation alleviates overcrowding problems at the front end of the criminal justice system. Thus, probation serves as an important tool for jurisdictions that operate local jails.

It is with this in mind that we will examine the use of probation and how this sanction greatly impacts the inmate flow within correctional institutions. This is particularly true within the jail setting, and it is therefore appropriate that our discussion of probation occurs just after our discussion of jail facilities and the issues that impact jail systems. Now that you, the reader, have a better understanding of jail facilities and the issues inherent to their operation, the following discussion related to probation and jail population flow should be clear.

When we speak of **probation** we are referring to its use as a control valve mechanism that mitigates the flow of inmates sent directly to the jail. However, probation is also a sentence whereby people are given a less restrictive sanction with the understanding that they will be incarcerated if they do not comply with the terms of this type of supervision within the community. We will talk later in this chapter about the common terms and conditions of probation sentences, but for now we will focus more on the history of probation and the role that it has played, systemically, in the correctional system.

Web Link History of Probation

A BRIEF HISTORY OF PROBATION

Probation is a uniquely American invention (see Focus Topic 5.1). At its inception, probation was used as an alternative to incarceration in the United States. John Augustus, a cobbler and philanthropist of Boston, is often recognized as the Father of Modern Probation. During the time that Augustus provided his innovative contribution to the field of community corrections, the temperance movement against alcohol consumption was in full swing. Augustus, aware of many of the issues associated with alcoholism, made an active effort to rehabilitate prior alcoholics who were processed through the police court in Boston.

Probation: A control valve mechanism that mitigates the flow of inmates sent directly to the jailhouse.

NYC Department of Probation

■ PHOTO 5.1 John Augustus was a volunteer of the court in the Boston area during the mid-1800s. He is regarded as the Father of Modern Probation.

While acting as a volunteer of the court, Augustus observed a man being charged for drunkenness who would have, in all likelihood, ended up in the Boston House of Correction if it were not for Augustus's intervention. Augustus placed bail for the man, personally guaranteeing the man's return to court at the prescribed time. Augustus helped the man to find a job and provided him with the guidance and support that was necessary so that the defendant was able to become a functioning and productive member within the community. When the court ordered the return of the offender three weeks later, the judge noticed a very substantial improvement in the offender's behavior. The judge was so impressed by this outcome that he granted leniency in sentencing (Augustus, 1972/1852; Barnes & Teeters, 1959). From this point in 1841 until his death in 1859, Augustus continued to bail out numerous offenders, providing voluntary supervision and guidance until they were subsequently sentenced by the court. Students should recall that corrections, as used in this text, is intended to do more than simply *punish* the offender but instead seeks to *reform* the offender. This is just as true with the use of probation as it would be with any other form of correctional sanction. While probation may act as a valve that mitigates the flow of inmates into the jailhouse, this is not and should not be its primary purpose. Rather, consistent with the earlier presented definition of corrections, probation should place primary emphasis on correcting criminal human behavior. Issues related to jail logistics and other such concerns should be

FOCUS TOPIC 5.1

Historical Developments in Probation in the United States

1841: John Augustus becomes the Father of Probation.

1869: First official probation program developed in Massachusetts (the home of probation).

1901: New York creates the first statute officially establishing adult probation services.

1925: Federal probation is authorized by Congress.

1927: Forty-nine states implement juvenile probation (all but Wyoming).

1943: Presentence investigation reports are formally created by federal probation system.

1956: Mississippi is the 50th state to formally establish adult probation.

1965: The birth of "shock probation" occurs in the state of Ohio.

1974: The American Probation and Parole Association is founded in Houston, Texas.

1979: Various risk/needs assessments are developed by the state of Wisconsin.

1983: Intensive supervised probation is born in Georgia.

1983: Electronic monitoring of offenders first starts in New Mexico.

1995: Global Positioning System technology for probation begins to be used in Florida.

secondary. This was the original intent when administering probation since Augustus was primarily concerned with the malicious treatment of offenders and the desire for revenge that could easily disrupt society.

While Augustus was aware that jail and prison conditions were barbaric in many cases, his actual goal was not necessarily to spare individuals from the misery of jail but to attempt to reform offenders. He selected his candidates with due care and caution, generally offering aid to first-time offenders. He also looked to character, demeanor, past experiences, and potential future influences when making his decisions. Thus, whether you use the word *reform, rehabilitate,* or *reintegrate,* it is clear that the initial intent of probation was to provide society with people who were more productive after sentencing than they had been prior to it. This intent stood on its own merit and purpose, regardless of jail or prison conditions that might have existed, thereby establishing the original mission of community corrections as a whole. Nevertheless, in contemporary corrections, probation often plays the role of a control valve that handles inmates that the jail facility cannot hold. We will talk about this more in the section that follows.

CONTEMPORARY PROBATION: WHEN THE JAIL IS FULL

In many cases, probation sentences are meted out at the county level of government. This is the same level of government that tends to administer jail facilities. Thus, probation is typically administered by the same courthouse that oversees the jail facility in a given jurisdiction. As a result, these two justice functions—probation and jailing—tend to work in tandem with one another. However, this is not to imply that coordination and communication between jail administrators and probation administrators is optimal; in many cases these two functions operate in a manner that is disjointed, despite the fact that the same courthouse may impact both probation and jail agencies.

While jails and probation agencies may (or may not) have a collaborative relationship, it is undeniable that the district attorney (the office that prosecutes criminals) will have a close working relationship with the local sheriff or sheriffs in the region as well as city police chiefs who collectively oversee law enforcement activities. These activities result in the flow of criminals before the courthouse and ultimately require that a judge sentence an offender to one of three likely options: community supervision (usually probation), a jail sentence (sometimes with additional community supervision requirements), or a prison sentence (if incarceration is to exceed a year in duration).

Audio Link
After Thousands of Inmates Released Early, Probation Officers Will Be Watching

Because the majority of offenders tend to commit crimes that are petty, nonserious, or nonviolent, this means that they will tend to qualify for jail or probation. Those offenders who do commit serious crimes will, naturally, be sentenced to prison and then are therefore the concern of state prison system authorities. However, the bulk of the offender population will remain at the county level, and it is in this manner that the jail population develops. In many instances, the jail facility will fill quite quickly with offenders who commit crimes, particularly in large urban areas of the nation. The use of probation becomes a critical tool to monitor and alleviate the flow of inmates into the jail.

Thus, as noted previously, one function of probation is to act as a control valve mechanism that mitigates the flow of inmates sent directly to the jailhouse. Without the use of probation sanctions, jails would simply collapse in their operation because the current jail facility structure throughout the United States could not even come close to containing the total offender population. This problem is exacerbated when state prison systems are full and jail facilities are required to keep inmates who, legally speaking, should be housed within a state prison facility. This demonstrates how the jail facility can feel pressure from inmate flow from the front end and the back end of its operational system.

Despite the tendency to use probation as a control valve mechanism for jailhouse admissions, the total number of offenders who are on probation has continued to decline since 2009. As can be seen in Table 5.1, in 2009 the total number of individuals on probation around the nation was 4,198,200, with a steady decline since then to 3,864,100 in 2014. One reason for this is that crime rates around the country are down. Additionally, such a decline also occurs when corrections departments are looking for ways to reduce their community supervision populations and provide incentives in programming to reduce overall sentences, including probation.

There is one noteworthy exception to this decline in probation rates, however: the state of California. As students may recall from Chapter 4, California passed what is known as the Public Safety Realignment (PSR) policy, which was designed to reduce the number of offenders in the state prison system to 110,000. Since this policy was implemented, entries to probation have increased nearly 15%, from an estimated 149,000 offenders in 2010 to 295,475 in 2014. Thus, one way of keeping the state's prison population from growing larger seems to be the more frequent use of probation.

Lastly, it would appear that a handful of states stand way in front in relation to the number of probationers who are supervised therein. Indeed, five states (see Table 5.2) have populations that are well above 200,000 probationers. All other states have less than 200,000 each, with only about six them having over 100,000. The state of Michigan comes in 6th in terms of the size of the probation population, with 180,583 probationers. Thus, the top five states account for approximately 1.6 million out of the nearly 4 million probationers around the country.

CHARACTERISTICS OF PROBATIONERS

When we use the term *probationers*, we are referring to those criminal offenders who have been sentenced to a period of correctional supervision in the community in lieu of incarceration (Hanser, 2010b). Among this population, the percentage of females in the adult probation

Table 5.1: U.S. Adult Residents on Probation, 2009–2014

Year	Total Number	Number per 100,000	1 in ___ Adults
2009	4,198,200	1,796	1 in 56
2010	4,055,500	1,715	1 in 58
2011	3,971,300	1,662	1 in 60
2012	3,942,800	1,633	1 in 61
2013	3,910,600	1,605	1 in 62
2014	3,864,100	1,568	1 in 64

SOURCE: Kaeble, D., Maruschak, L.M., Bonczar, T. P. (2015). Probation and Parole in the United States, 2014. Washington, DC: Bureau of Justice Statistics.

Table 5.2: Top Five State Probation Populations in 2014

State	Total Number	Number per 100,000
Georgia	471,067	6,161
Texas	388,101	1,938
California	295,475	991
Ohio	238,915	2,660
Florida	227,087	1,422

SOURCE: Kaeble, D., Maruschak, L.M., Bonczar, T. P. (2015). Probation and Parole in the United States, 2014. Washington, DC: Bureau of Justice Statistics.

■ Table 5.3: Characteristics of Adults on Probation, 2000, 2013, & 2014

Characteristic	2000	2013	2014
Sex			
Male	78%	75%	75%
Female	22	25	25
Race/Hispanic origin[a]			
White	54%	54%	54%
Black/African American	31	30	30
Hispanic/Latino	13	14	13
American Indian/Alaska Native	1	1	1
Asian/Native Hawaiian/other Pacific Islander	1	1	1
Two or more races	...	...	...
Status of supervision			
Active	76%	69%	73%
Residential/other treatment program	...	1	1
Financial conditions remaining	...	1	1
Inactive	9	6	5
Absconder	9	9	7
Supervised out of jurisdiction	3	2	2
Warrant status	...	9	6
Other	3	3	4
Type of offense			
Felony	52%	55%	56%
Misdemeanor	46	43	42
Other infractions	2	2	2
Most serious offense			
Violent	...%	19%	19%
Domestic violence	...	4	4
Sex offence	...	3	3
Other violent offense	...	12	12
Property	...	29	28
Drug	24	25	25
Public order	24	17	16
DWI/DUI	18	14	14
Other traffic offense	6	2	2
Other[b]	52	10	11

SOURCE: Kaeble, D., Maruschak, L.M., Bonczar, T. P. (2015). Probation and Parole in the United States, 2014. Washington, DC: Bureau of Justice Statistics.

Note: Detail may not sum to total due to rounding. Counts based on most recent data and may differ from previously published statistics. See *Methodology.* Characteristics based on probationers with known type of status.

... Not available.

[a]Excludes persons of Hispanic or Latino origin, unless specified.
[b]Includes violent and property offenses in 2000 because those data were not collected separately.

population increased slightly over the past decade, climbing from 22% in 2000 to 25% in 2014 (see Table 5.3). Overall, women are becoming a larger portion of inmates in the correctional system; they account for about 7.4% of the total state and federal prison population. However, women comprise a much larger segment of the probation population than the prison population. Additionally, women account for slightly more than 10% of the nation's prisoner population housed in community-based facilities, which are institutions that permit half or more of all inmates to leave the facility unaccompanied on a regular basis (Stephan, 2008, p. 4). This demonstrates that it is much more frequent for women to be given some type of community involvement or contact when sentenced for a criminal offense, even when they are serving time at a state or federal facility.

When considering race, in 2014 over half (54%) of all probationers were Caucasian, 30% were African American, and 13% were Hispanic or Latino, which is similar to the percentages in 2000. Table 5.3 shows these racial breakdowns. As we will see in later chapters, this is different from prison populations, where African Americans have a higher representation and Caucasians a lower one.

It can also be seen in Table 5.3 that the percentage of probationers supervised for a felony offense increased from 52% in 2000 to 56% in 2014. Nearly 19% of all probationers were on supervision for a violent offense, 28% were on supervision for a property offense, and 25% were on supervision for a drug offense. Another 16% were on probation for a public order offense, most of which were driving while intoxicated (DWI) or driving under the influence (DUI) charges. The remaining 11% of probationers had unclear categories due to data reporting problems.

It is important to point out that additional programming, such as involvement in substance abuse counseling, drug court supervision, or DWI classes, is required in order to complete supervision for many of the nearly 39% of probationers on supervision for drugs, DWI, or DUI offenses. This is important because this shows probation sentences are often paired with therapeutic programming rather than just acting as a release valve for jail and prison populations.

THE ADMINISTRATION OF PROBATION

Earlier in this chapter, it was noted that in many cases, probation is administered through the same jurisdiction that also oversees the jailhouse. While this is true in many cases, there are other means by which probation is administered. Indeed, the specific means by which probation operates can vary if it is not the county level of government that oversees the probation sanctioning process. Correctional systems, including community supervision components, can differ greatly from state to state. Thus, a bit more discussion on the organizational aspects of probation administration is provided since this greatly impacts the operations of probation services within a given jurisdiction.

The Probation Agency

When examining the means of operation within a probation agency, one key characteristic to consider is the degree of centralization that exists within that agency. Indeed, adult probation in one state may be administered by a single central state agency, by a variety of local agencies, or by a combination of the two. When considering local levels of administration, agencies may operate at the county or even municipal level. However, these supposedly smaller jurisdictions should not be underestimated. Consider, for example, the probation departments in New York City, where felony and misdemeanor caseloads are larger than those of many entire state systems.

Generally, probation systems can be separated into six categories, with states having more than one system in operation simultaneously (Allen & Sawhney, 2010; Hanser, 2010b). The six categories of operation are as follows:

1. **Juvenile:** Includes separate probation services for juveniles that are administered through county or municipal governments or on a statewide basis.
2. **Municipal:** Independent probation agencies that are administered through lower courts or through the municipality itself.
3. **County:** The probation agency is governed by laws and/or guidelines established by the state that empower a county to operate its own probation agency.
4. **State:** One agency administers a centralized probation system that provides services throughout the state.
5. **State combined P&P:** Probation and parole services are administered together on a statewide basis by a single agency.
6. **Federal:** Probation is administered nationally as a branch of the courts.

CROSS-NATIONAL PERSPECTIVE 5.1

The History of Probation in England

1876: Hertfordshire printer Frederic Rainer, a volunteer with the Church of England Temperance Society (CETS), writes to the society of his concern about the lack of help for those who come before the courts. He sends a donation of five shillings (25 pence) toward a fund for practical rescue work in the police courts. The CETS responds by appointing two missionaries to Southwark court with the initial aim of "reclaiming drunkards." This forms the basis of the London Police Court Mission (LPCM), whose missionaries work with magistrates to develop a system of releasing offenders on the condition that they keep in touch with the missionary and accepted guidance.

1880: Eight full-time missionaries are in place, and the mission opens homes and shelters, providing vocational training and developing residential work.

1886: The Probation of First Offenders Act allows for courts around the country to follow the London example of appointing missionaries, but very few do so.

1907: The Probation of Offenders Act gives LPCM missionaries official status as "officers of the court," later known as probation officers. The act allows courts to suspend punishment and discharge offenders if they enter into a recognizance of between one and three years, one condition of which is supervision by a person named in the "probation order."

1913: Progress seems to be occurring, as reported at the National Association of Probation Officers first annual meeting: "Of 137 prisoners, 17 had been sent for sentence as 'incorrigible rogues' and 12 others were awaiting punishment. There were only nine women. There has been a steady diminution in the number of cases ever since the new method of dealing with offenders under the Probation of Offenders Act was adopted 4 years ago. Of those who had been dealt with in that way, very few had offended again."

1918: With juvenile crime increasing during and after World War I, the Home Office concedes that probation should not be left to philanthropic or judicial bodies and that state direction is needed. The influential Molony Committee of 1927 stimulates debate about the respective roles of probation officers, local government, and philanthropic organizations. It encourages the informal involvement of probation officers in aftercare from both Borstal and reformatory schools.

1938: The Home Office assumes control of the probation service and introduces a wide range of modernizing reforms. The legal formula of "entering into a recognizance" is replaced by "consent to probation." Requirements for psychiatric treatment are also introduced, and it is made mandatory for female probationers to be supervised by women officers. The LPCM concentrates on hostels for "probation trainees" and branches out into homes for children in "moral danger," sexually abused children, and young mothers.

1948: The Criminal Justice Act incorporates punitive measures such as attendance centers and detention centers, but the stated purpose of the probation order remains intact and is reaffirmed as "advise, assist, and befriend."

1970s and 1980s: Partnerships with other agencies result in cautioning schemes, alternatives to custody, and crime reduction, while changes in sentencing result in day centers, special program conditions, the probation order as a sentence, and risk of custody and risk of reconviction assessment tools.

2000: The Criminal Justice and Court Services Act renames the probation service as the National Probation Service for England and Wales. It creates the post of director general of probation services within the Home Office and makes chief officers statutory officeholders and members of local probation boards.

2004: The government publishes *Reducing Crime, Changing Lives,* which proposes to improve the effectiveness of the criminal justice system and the correctional services in particular. The National Offender Management Service is established with the aim of reducing reoffending through more consistent and effective offender management.

2007: The probation service in England and Wales is 100 years old.

QUESTION: Discuss the commonality of early religious involvement in corrections, and explain how that affected correctional thought in England. Explain whether this religious emphasis has continued or if it appears to have diminished over time. Is this the same as or different from developments in the United States? Explain your answer.

SOURCE: Adapted from Probation Board Association of England and Wales. (2007). *Probation centenary, 1907–2007.* Retrieved February 2, 2011, from http://www.probationcentenary.org/contactus.htm

For more information about probation in the United Kingdom, visit http://www.probationcentenary.org/contactus.htm.

In many cases, the administration of probation may be determined by the seriousness of the offense. For instance, felony offenses may be supervised by state-level personnel while misdemeanor cases may be supervised by local governmental probation agencies. For instance, in Michigan, adult felony probation is administered through the state department of corrections while adult misdemeanor probation is administered through the local district courts.

Juvenile probation adds a whole new dimension of organizational considerations. Over half of all juvenile probation agencies are administered at the local level. Juvenile probation may be

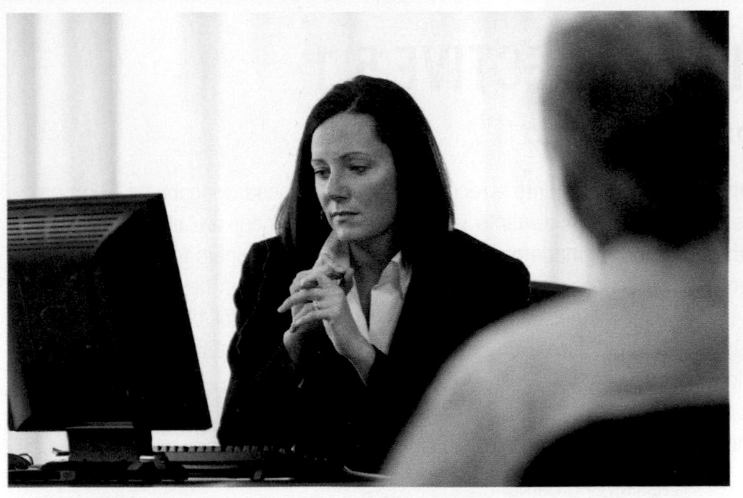

■ PHOTO 5.2 During the completion of the PSI report, the probation officer will often make several inquiries of the offender during a face-to-face interview.

provided through a separate agency or through a subdepartment of the large adult probation system. In over a dozen states, juvenile probation services are split, with the juvenile court administering services in urban jurisdictions and the state administering such services in rural areas. Lastly, some states have a statewide office of juvenile probation that is located in that state's executive branch (Allen & Sawhney, 2010; Hanser, 2010b).

The Presentence Investigation

The **presentence investigation report** is a file that includes a wide range of background information on the offender. This file will typically include demographic, vocational, educational, and personal information on the offender as well as records on his or her prior offending patterns and the probation department's recommendation as to the appropriate type of sentencing and supervision for the offender. According to the Michigan Department of Corrections, "A probation file may also consist of other reports written by counselors, psychologists, and case workers. Therefore, a large amount of personal and confidential information is maintained by the probation officer which should not be disclosed arbitrarily" (2003, p. 33). In many respects, the presentence investigation (PSI) report is the initial point of assessment, and it will often be utilized when the offender is first brought into a prison facility. In other words, the PSI report is not just used in probation sentences; it also is used when offenders are imprisoned. While writing the PSI report, a probation officer may review sentencing recommendations with the offender and even perhaps with the offender's family. Note that this is separate from any other arrangements that might be made throughout the plea-bargaining process between the offender's counsel and the prosecutor's office. In some cases, probation officers may also be required to testify in court as to their findings and recommendations.

Video Link
Presentence Investigation

The primary purpose of the PSI report is to provide the court with the necessary information from which a sentencing decision can be derived. The PSI is conducted after a defendant is found guilty of a charge (whether by pleading or by court finding) but prior to sentencing. This information in the PSI report, along with a sentencing recommendation, will aid the judge, who must ultimately fashion a sentence as well as any corollary obligations attached to that sentence.

The PSI report also tends to serve as a basic foundation for supervision and treatment planning throughout the offender's sentence, both when on probation and later if the offender is incarcerated. Quite often this document will serve as a reference point for placing the offender in a variety of programs. This can happen when the offender is on supervision or in a jail or detention facility.

Among other things, the PSI report will contain information related to the character and behavior of the offender. This means that the probation officer's impressions of the offender can greatly impact the outcome of the PSI. The PSI is typically conducted through an interview with the offender. Because the PSI report information is largely obtained from the interview process, it is naturally important that probation officers have good interviewing skills. This cannot be overstated given the fact that probation officers are in contact with persons on a routine basis where they must collect and record information. While procedures do vary from region to region, a sentencing phase will be conducted at some point during the processing of a criminal conviction. At this point, the defense counsel can have an impact on the overall process for the offender. Defense counsel will usually challenge any inaccurate, incomplete, or misleading information that ended up in the PSI report. This function of the defense counsel is actually quite critical since the PSI report will be used to classify the offender if he or she should be incarcerated and will also be used in future decisions regarding supervision issues within the community. Thus, verification of the PSI report's validity is crucial to the welfare of the defendant and keeps from creating scenarios that make an already bad situation worse.

Presentence investigation report: A thorough file that includes a wide range of background information on the offender.

From the standpoint of the probation officer, the two most important sections of the PSI report are the evaluation and the recommendation. There is typically a high degree of agreement between the probation officer's recommendations and the judge's decision when sentencing, and this means that the PSI report is very important in helping to determine the offender's fate.

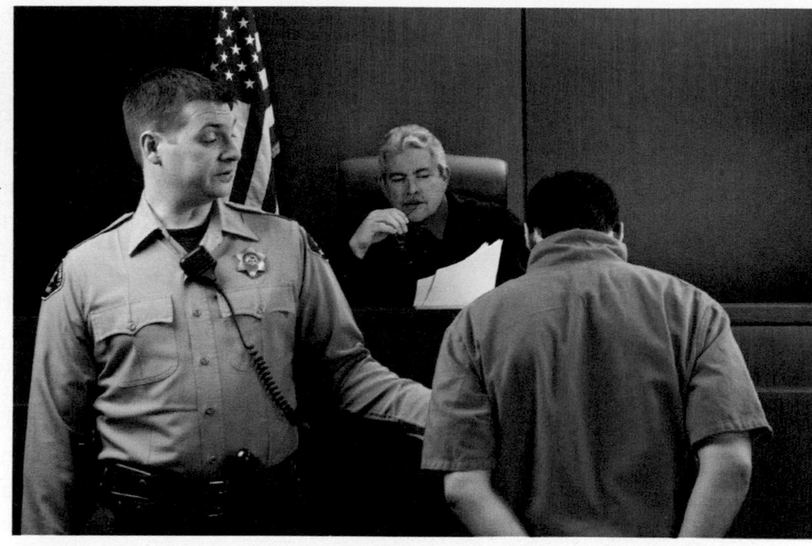

©iStockphoto.com/Deborah Cheramie

■ PHOTO 5.3 The judge of the court is the final authority on rulings related to probation sentencing and conditions. The judge will usually work closely with probation officers who deal with offenders from his or her court of jurisdiction.

Granting Probation

According to Neubauer (2007), the public perceives the judge as the principal decision maker in criminal court. But the judge often is not the primary decision maker in regard to an offender's sentencing and/or the granting of probation. This is not to say that the judge does not have ultimate authority over the court, nor does it mean to imply that judges have diminished importance when presiding over their court. Rather, Neubauer demonstrates the collaborative nature of the various courtroom actors when processing offender caseloads. Throughout this process, judges will often voluntarily defer to the judgment of other members of the court, namely prosecutors, defense attorneys, victim's rights groups, and the probation agency.

During a typical day in criminal court, judges may accept bail recommendations offered by the district attorney, plea agreements that are struck by the defense and the prosecution, and even sentences recommended by a probation officer (though there is some debate as to the actual weight given to the probation officer's recommendation, at least in some courts). The main point is that though judges do of course retain their power over the courtroom, they often share influence over the adjudication process with a variety of courtroom actors (Neubauer, 2007). This is an informal process that often takes place amongst participants who, after working together for a time, know each other in both a professional and a more informal sense (Neubauer, 2007).

There are some challenges that can emerge when judges do not allow the input of other courtroom actors. For instance, jail overcrowding may be worsened if the judge is not receptive to the input of the sheriff and/or the police chief who will administer the local county or city jail. Or probation officer caseloads can become too burdensome to ensure public safety if the judge does not consider the recommendations of the chief probation officer.

When defense attorneys and their defendants seek to have probation considered as a sentencing option, it may behoove the defense counsel to consider the specific judge who presides over the court as well as the dynamics of a given courtroom. Because of this, in larger court jurisdictions a technique of judge selection may be common (Neubauer, 2007). Through a process of implementing motions of continuances and motions for a change of judge, defense attorneys may maneuver to have their case heard by a judge who is expected to be the most receptive to the offender's plight. Though judges do strive to adhere to common guidelines in decisions and rulings, the fact of the matter is that they do tend to differ in terms of the sentences that are given, including the granting of probation and/or the conditions attached to a probation sentence (Neubauer, 2007). An understanding of these tendencies can aid the defense in achieving a more favorable outcome for the offender.

Conditions of Probation

As one can tell, the dynamics of sentencing in the courtroom can allow for some degree of leeway in the final decision-making process. Further illustrating the fluid nature of this process, consider that the setting of conditions during probation can be, at least in part, agreed upon prior to the judge's actual formal sentencing. Though the bargaining process may impact the final outcome of the probationer's sentence, the length of probation, and the conditions of that probation, the judge is always free to require additional conditions as he or she sees fit.

The conditions that may be required are quite lengthy, but some of the more commonly required ones are:

1. Refrain from associating with certain types of people (particularly those with a conviction) or frequenting certain locations known to draw criminal elements.
2. Remain sober and drug free; restrictions include using or being in possession of alcohol or drugs.
3. Obey restrictions on firearm ownership and/or possession.
4. Obey requirement to pay fines, restitution, and family support that may be due.
5. Be willing to submit to drug tests as directed by the probation officer and/or representatives of the probation agency.
6. Maintain legitimate and steady employment.
7. Refrain from obtaining employment in certain types of vocations (e.g., an embezzler would be restricted from becoming a bookkeeper, or a computer hacker would be restricted from working with automated systems).
8. Maintain a legal and legitimate residence with the requirement that the probation officer is notified of any change in residence prior to making such a change.
9. Obey the requirement that permission be requested to travel outside of the jurisdiction of the probation agency and/or to another state.
10. Refrain from engaging in further criminal activity.

Video Link
A New Probation Program in Hawaii Beats the Statistics

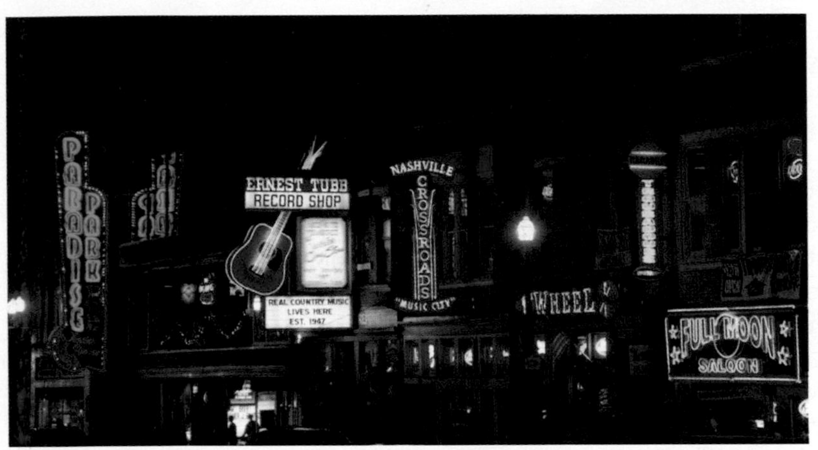

©iStockphoto.com/chapin31

■ PHOTO 5.4 **Bars, nightclubs, and other entertainment for late night party-goers are also places that are often frequented by the criminal population.**

Many of the conditions listed above may be statutorily authorized by state legislators as a means of validating their application to probation sentences. This is reflective of the fact that most legislators desire some degree of uniformity and consistency in the supervision requirements and process (del Carmen et al., 2001; Hanser, 2010b). Some states have only a few such requirements, while others have an extensive list that clearly requires judges and probationers to structure probation sentences according to a certain prescribed template of conditions. Further, and related to the use of discretionary conditions imposed by judges, some legislators may also clearly note that judges are to be given deference in assigning specialized conditions on certain types of offenders; this is especially true with sex offenders and/or substance abuse offenders (these offenders, the terms and conditions of their supervision, and their therapeutic programming will be discussed in later chapters of this text).

PROBATION OFFICERS

No chapter on the probation process would be complete without a thorough discussion of the job and function of probation personnel. As we have seen from the chapter vignette, the job of a probation officer is quite stressful and challenging and does not pay nearly as well as many other professions (see Figure 5.1 for information on annual salaries for probation officers throughout various areas of the United States). Further still, the qualifications for probation officers tend to be fairly high, at least in relation to the demands and pay that are associated with the position. This is truly an unfortunate paradox within the criminal justice arena since it is the probation officer who supervises the lion's share of offenders in the correctional system.

■ **Figure 5.1: Annual Mean Wage of Probation Officers, May 2014**

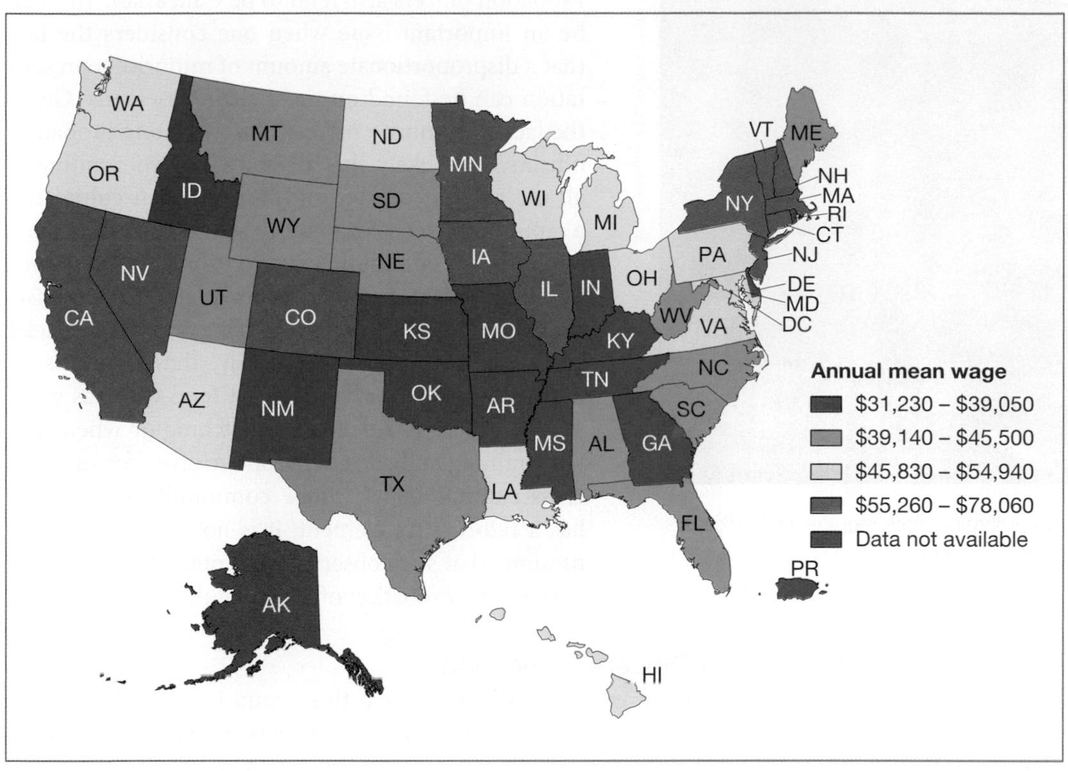

SOURCE: Bureau of Labor Statistics (2014). *Occupational employment statistics.* Washington, DC: Author.

Because of the stress involved with probation work, there is a great deal of turnover in the field. Naturally, this can have negative effects on the correctional system since personnel with expertise are hard to keep. This can impact the service delivery that agencies are able to provide, and, in some respects, is likely to affect outcomes among offenders on community supervision. Indeed, it may be likely that the prognosis for recidivism can be affected (at least in part) by the longevity of the probation officer and his or her demeanor on the job.

Thus, the content of this chapter is more than a simple introduction to work in the field of probation. This chapter also presents an aspect of the corrections field that is critical for students and other persons in society to understand: the important role played by probation personnel in the security of a community. Citizens should be grateful for these personnel since it is they, just as much as police, who are largely responsible for keeping society safe from known criminals. Interestingly, most probation agencies pay lower salaries—starting, midcareer, and managerial—than do police agencies in their same region.

Demographics of Probation Officers: Gender

One interesting aspect of probation work is the fact that a large portion of probation staff tends to be female, with exact proportions of female and male officers being dependent on the area of the United States. This is substantially different from fields such as law enforcement, where male officers tend to predominate and women tend to consist of less than 12% of the entire policing community (Federal Bureau of Investigation, 2013). This is perhaps partly due to the nature of probation as compared to law enforcement. Indeed, even among police officers, women have been found to be highly effective in defusing conflict situations and/or providing less contact-prone means of response. The National Center for Women and Policing (2003) notes that female police officers tend to be inherently more suited to facilitate cooperation and trust in stressful contact situations and that they are less prone to use excessive force. Likewise, there tend to be fewer citizen complaints against female officers. These same characteristics would seem to be well suited to probation work given the fact that probation has a reintegrative and supportive role with offenders on the officer's caseload.

© Joan Barnett Lee/ZUMA Press/Corbis

■ PHOTO 5.5 Work in the field of probation often requires that officers work together, both in the office and in the field.

Demographics of Probation Officers: Race

Probation officers also tend to be Caucasian. This can be an important issue when one considers the fact that a disproportionate amount of minority representation can be found on most client caseloads. Given the lack of minority representation among probation officers, it is likely that diversity-related training is all the more necessary and important in cultivating a rapport between community supervision personnel and those on community supervision. An abundance of literature has examined issues related to therapist-client interactions when the two are of different racial and/or ethnic groups. Generally, the prognosis in mental health research does not tend to be as good as when there is a degree of matching or when specific training and consideration are given for racial or cross-cultural issues. Since community corrections has a reformative element, it is not unreasonable to presume that such observations could also be equally true among probation officers and their probationers.

SAGE Journal Article Link
Racial Disparity in Probationers' Views About Probation

Demographics of Probation Officers: Education

Most probation officers have a college degree. This means that this group is, as a whole, a bit more educated than much of the general workforce. It may perhaps be true that this can mitigate some of the cross-cultural differences, and this also may help to lessen job dissatisfaction and stress since higher-educated persons tend to, on the whole, be motivated by more than external reward. Though this is obviously not always the case, less emphasis on money does tend to correlate with better-educated workforce members. Somewhat supporting this is the fact that several studies have found that probation work in general tends to be more enriching and challenging, requiring more of an emphasis on problem-solving skills that are likely to mesh well with high-functioning and educated persons. From this, it is clear that probation work is becoming more professionalized and has been likened to an art form since probation officers must be skilled at matching security and treatment issues with the particular offender's needs (Bureau of Labor Statistics, 2011). This, as well as the helping aspects of the profession (despite its supervisory components), is likely to appeal to educated females who seek a professional track in their lives.

Tasks and Nature of Work for Probation Officers

Probation officers supervise offenders who are placed on some form of probation and tend to spend more time monitoring the activities of these offenders than anything else. Probation officers most frequently maintain this supervision through personal contact with the offender, the offender's family, and the offender's employer. In addition to making contact with the offender through a combination of field visits and/or officer interviews, probation officers make routine contact with the offender's therapist(s), often having therapeutic reports either faxed or delivered to their office. These reports, which provide the clinician's insight as to the offender's emotional progress and/or mental health, can be very important to the probation officer's assessment of the offender's progress.

Working Conditions

The daily working conditions for probation officers can be quite safe when in the office but can be fairly dangerous when conducting field visits. Some of the offenders on a probationer's caseload may themselves be more dangerous than their arrest record or actual conviction may indicate. Further, these offenders may still (in violation of their probation) continue to maintain contact with other associates who are more prone to violence than is the probationer. In many instances, the probation officer may have to conduct fieldwork in high-crime areas.

CORRECTIONS AND THE LAW 5.1

Gagnon v. Scarpelli *(1973)*

Gagnon v. Scarpelli, 411 U.S. 778 (1973) was the second substantive ruling by the U.S. Supreme Court related to the rights of offenders who violate the terms and/or conditions of their probation or parole agreement. The prior ruling, *Morrissey v. Brewer*, 408 U.S. 471 (1972), occurred a year prior to the ruling in *Gagnon*, but was specific to parole. Because this chapter addresses the sanction of probation, emphasis is on the *Gagnon* ruling, but students should understand that *Gagnon* was based upon a similar ruling in *Morrissey* that addressed the rights of parolees who face the possibility of revocation.

The case involved Gerald Scarpelli, a man serving a probation sentence in the state of Wisconsin for armed robbery. While Scarpelli had been sentenced to 15 years of imprisonment, the judge suspended his sentence and ordered him to serve 7 years of probation instead. After the probation sentence began, Scarpelli was arrested for burglary in Illinois. Scarpelli's probation was revoked by the Wisconsin Department of Public Welfare subsequent to his confession to police that he was involved in the burglary. The confession in question was later challenged by Scarpelli as being made under duress. After the revocation proceedings, Scarpelli was incarcerated.

After serving 3 years of imprisonment, Scarpelli challenged the revocation of his probation on the basis that he should have been provided a hearing. The state of Washington, noting the legitimacy of the rationale of the revocation, contended that no such right to a hearing existed and, therefore, the revocation of Scarpelli's probation was constitutional.

The Supreme Court held, in an 8-1 decision, that a probationer's sentence can only be revoked after a preliminary revocation hearing and final revocation hearing. Justice Lewis Powell, in delivering the opinion of the Court, held that Scarpelli was indeed entitled to a hearing regarding his probation status. The Court also noted that the use of legal counsel may be required, depending on whether the offender is being tried for a new offense where information from the probation revocation proceeding may be used as evidence in later criminal proceedings.

When considering the right to a revocation proceeding, the Court determined that the probation sentence of an individual cannot be revoked without a hearing. If a probationer commits a violation of his or her probation, that probation sentence can be revoked only after a final violation hearing is held. The Court explained:

> When the view of the probationer or parolee's conduct differs in this fundamental way from the latter's own view, due process requires that the difference be resolved before revocation becomes final. Both the probationer or parolee and the State have interests in the accurate finding of fact and the informed use of discretion—the probationer or parolee to insure that his liberty is not unjustifiably taken away and the State to make certain that it is neither unnecessarily interrupting a successful effort at rehabilitation nor imprudently prejudicing the safety of the community.

In noting the need for legal counsel when a probationer is arrested and given new charges within the period of probation, the Court indicated that counsel should be provided on a case-by-case basis. Justice Powell wrote for the majority and clarified:

> The differences between a criminal trial and a revocation hearing do not dispose altogether of the argument that under a case-by-case approach there may be cases in which a lawyer would be useful but in which none would be appointed because an arguable defense would be uncovered only by a lawyer. Without denying that there is some force in this argument, we think it a sufficient answer that we deal here, not with the right of an accused to counsel in a criminal prosecution, but with the more limited due process right of one who is a probationer or parolee only because he has been convicted of a crime.

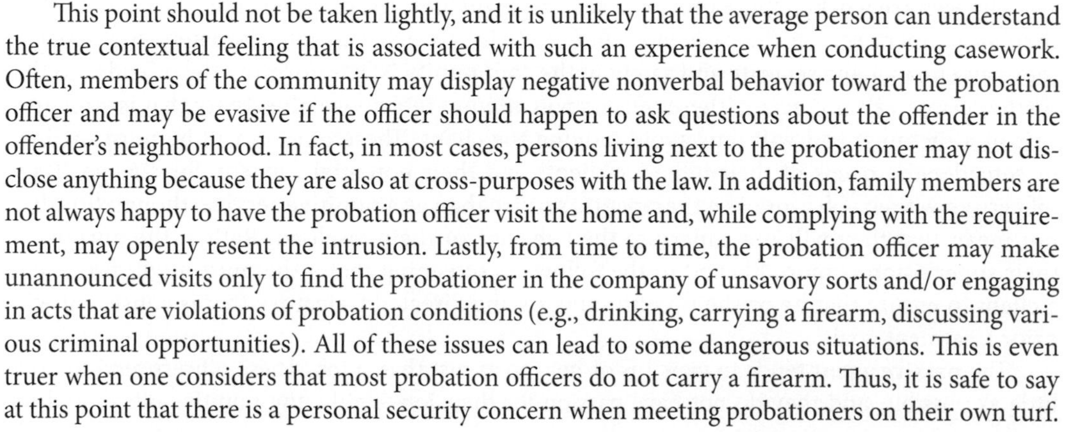

This point should not be taken lightly, and it is unlikely that the average person can understand the true contextual feeling that is associated with such an experience when conducting casework. Often, members of the community may display negative nonverbal behavior toward the probation officer and may be evasive if the officer should happen to ask questions about the offender in the offender's neighborhood. In fact, in most cases, persons living next to the probationer may not disclose anything because they are also at cross-purposes with the law. In addition, family members are not always happy to have the probation officer visit the home and, while complying with the requirement, may openly resent the intrusion. Lastly, from time to time, the probation officer may make unannounced visits only to find the probationer in the company of unsavory sorts and/or engaging in acts that are violations of probation conditions (e.g., drinking, carrying a firearm, discussing various criminal opportunities). All of these issues can lead to some dangerous situations. This is even truer when one considers that most probation officers do not carry a firearm. Thus, it is safe to say at this point that there is a personal security concern when meeting probationers on their own turf.

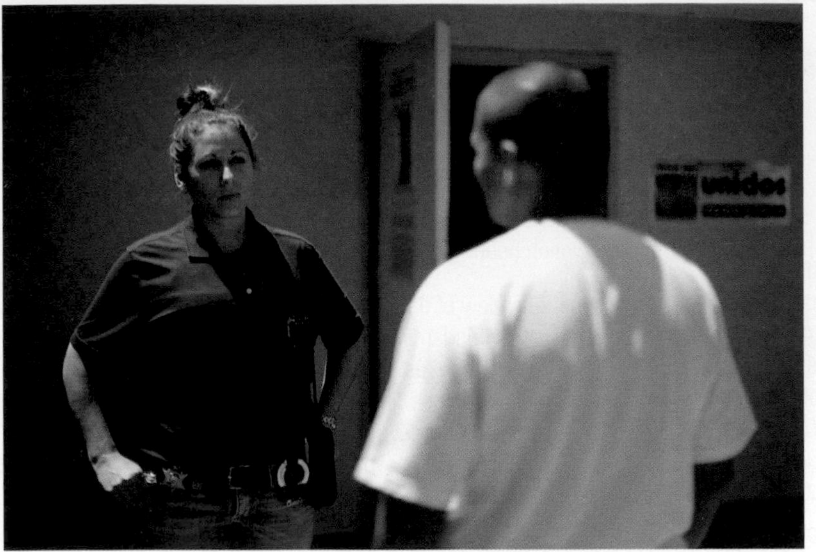

LUCY NICHOLSON/REUTERS/Newscom

■ PHOTO 5.6 Fieldwork is an important aspect of probation supervision. This requires that officers talk with the offender and others who know the offender in settings outside of the office.

Probation Officers in the Role of Law Enforcers and Brokers of Services

Probation officers tend to approach their jobs from different vantage points, much of which has to do with their own perceptions of their particular role in the community corrections process. Daniel Glaser (1964) conducted seminal research on the orientation by which community supervision officers approach their job. Though Glaser focused on parole officers, his contentions apply equally well to probation officers. Thus, Glaser's work will be utilized in this chapter to provide a general framework for probation officers and the informal roles that they play when supervising their caseloads. Basically speaking, Glaser contended that officers tend to operate at differing points along two spectrums: offender control (law enforcers) and offender assistance (brokers of services). These two spectrums work in seeming contradiction with one another, as they each tend to put officers at cross-purposes when trying to balance their job as reformer and public safety officer. This means that four basic categories emerge that describe the officer's general tendency when supervising offenders.

Paternal officers use a great degree of both control and assistance techniques (Glaser, 1964). They protect both the offender and the community by providing the offender with assistance as well as praise and blame. This type of officer can seem inconsistent at times. These officers are ambivalent to the concerns of the offender or the community; this is just a job that they do. Indeed, these officers may be perceived as being noncommittal due to taking the community's side in one case and the offender's in another. These officers tend not to have a high degree of formal training or secondary education, but they tend to be very experienced and thus are able to weather the difficulties associated with burnout within the field of probation.

Punitive officers (pure law enforcers) see themselves as needing to use threats and punishment in order to gain compliance from the offender. These officers will place the highest emphasis on control and protection of the public against offenders, and they will be suspicious of offenders on their caseload. This suspiciousness is not necessarily misplaced or unethical, however, as this is part and parcel of the supervision of offenders, but these officers may in fact never be content with the offender's behavior until they find some reason to award some form of punitive sanction. In other words, the view is that those on the caseload are doing wrong, but they are just not getting caught. Naturally, relations between this officer and those on his or her caseload are usually fairly impaired and sterile.

Paternal officer: Uses a great degree of both control and assistance techniques in supervising offenders.

Punitive officer: Sees himself or herself as needing to use threats and punishment in order to get compliance from the offender.

Welfare worker: Views the offender more as a client rather than a supervisee on his or her caseload.

Passive agent: Views his or her job dispassionately as just a job and tends to do as little as possible.

The **welfare worker** (pure broker of services) will view the offender more as a client rather than as a supervisee on the caseload. These individuals believe that, ultimately, the best way they can enhance the security and safety of the community is by reforming the offender so that further crime will not occur. These officers will attempt to achieve objectivity that is similar to that of a therapist and will thus avoid judging the client. These officers will be most inclined to consider the needs of their offender-clients and their potential capacity for change. These officers view their job more as a therapeutic service than as a punitive service, though this does not mean that they will not supervise the behavior of their caseload. Rather, the purpose of their supervision is more likened to the follow-up screening that a therapist might provide to a client to ensure that he or she is continuing on the directed trajectory that is consistent with prior treatment goals.

The **passive agent** tends to view his or her job as just that, a job. These officers tend to do as little as possible, and they do not have passion for their job. Unlike the punitive officer and the

TECHNOLOGY AND EQUIPMENT 5.1

The Use of GPS Tracking and Home Confinement

Global Positioning Systems (GPS) use a series of satellites to monitor and locate offenders. The Florida Department of Corrections first initiated this program to track probationers in real time at any point during the day or night (Champion, 2002). This system is far superior to any other program of supervision because it ensures that probation officers have near-instantaneous notification of an offender's violation of his or her community supervision. With this system, supervision officers can even tell which street the offender is on within any part of the country. Further, GPS can be programmed to detect areas of inclusion or exclusion within the limits of offender travel. This means that if an offender enters a certain area that is restricted, the supervision officer is instantly notified (Champion, 2002).

Community supervision programs utilize military-type technology to keep track of offenders. GPS devices use 24 military satellites to determine the exact location of a coordinate. By using the satellite monitoring and remote tracking, offenders can be tracked to their exact location. GPS tracking used with offenders is joined with an ankle or wrist device that sends a signal to a tracking device that houses a microtransmitter and antenna, which send a signal to the GPS. The tracking device is capable of being placed in an offender's bag, and the offender must remain within 100 feet of the receiver. After receiving the signal, a continuous report is sent to a computer that tracks the whereabouts of the offender. The GPS tracking device allows supervising officers to place location restrictions on the offenders so that certain places are off-limits. For example, sex offenders may be excluded from being within the vicinity of a schoolyard or church. If the offender enters a prohibited area, an alarm will sound. On the flip side, officers are allowed to program the offender's schedule for work and religious services and regular day-to-day whereabouts so that it can be easier to detect and verify where and when the offender does what he or she is supposed to. In some cases the system can send notification via pager or telephone that the offender is near the victim or any other excluded location. The advantage of such a program is that the offender's whereabouts are known in a more real-time manner.

There are some disadvantages to the use of GPS tracking. GPS offender tracking devices, like other satellite devices, often lose their signal during bad weather or when in an area densely populated with trees. Another frequent drawback cited is the expense. Due to the extensive nature of the parties involved, GPS tracking is very expensive, and, in this day of drastic budget cutbacks in community corrections, many agencies are not willing to provide funding for such contemporary and often unnecessary devices. Some have suggested that a way to cut back on the operational costs of GPS devices is for an agency to request the offender's whereabouts every 30 minutes or so as opposed to every minute. Others have suggested that GPS devices be reserved for the most serious offenders within the community, such as child molesters and rapists. Across the country, approximately 150,000 offenders are being supervised by electronic monitoring devices.

welfare officer, they simply do not care about the outcome of their work so long as they avoid any difficulties. These individuals are often in the job simply due to the benefits that it may provide as well as the freedom from continual supervision that this type of career affords.

In reality, it is not likely that officers would best be served using one consistent type of approach rather than using each orientation when appropriate. Thus, the community supervision process can be greatly impacted by the approach taken by the community supervision officer. Further, agencies can transmit a certain tendency toward any of these orientations through policies, procedures, informal organizational culture, or even daily memos. The tone set by the agency is likely to have an effect on the officer's morale and his or her approach to the supervision process.

Some agencies may be very clear about their expectations of community supervision officers. In this case, if the agency has a strict law-and-order flavor, the officer may be best served by utilizing the approach of a punitive officer to ensure that he or she is a good fit with agency expectations. In another agency, the emphasis might be on a combined restorative/community justice model coupled with community policing efforts designed to reintegrate the offender. In an agency such as this, the officer may find that a welfare worker approach is the best fit for that agency and that community. Thus, the culture of the community service organization will have a strong impact on the officer's orientation, and, if the officer's personal or professional views are in conflict with the organizational structure, the likelihood of effective community supervision is impaired. This is important because it is another indicator of the stress encountered among most community supervision workers.

Global Positioning System (GPS): Allows offenders to be tracked to their exact location through the use of satellite monitoring and remote tracking.

■ **Figure 5.2: Probation Officers Employed in Each State, May 2014**

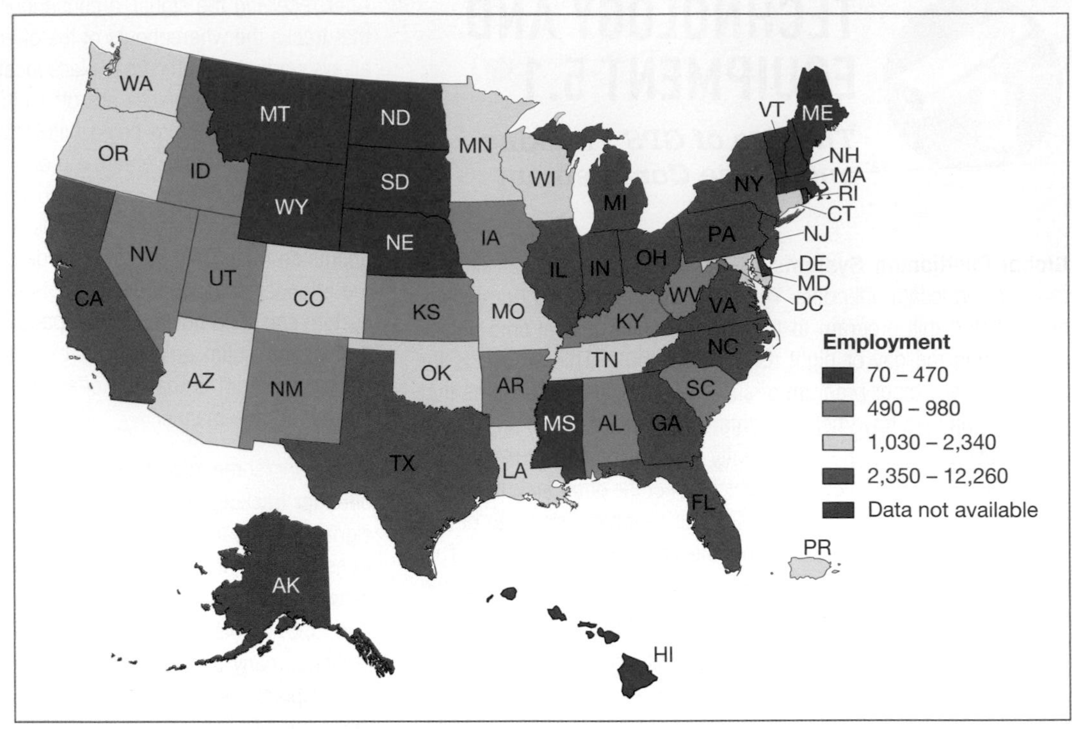

SOURCE: Bureau of Labor Statistics (2014). *Occupational employment statistics.* Washington, DC: Author.

Qualifications for Probation Officers

Some basic background qualifications for probation officers are listed in the *Occupational Outlook Handbook* (Bureau of Labor Statistics, 2012). These qualifications vary by state, but generally a bachelor's degree in criminal justice, social work, or a related field is required for initial consideration. This was not always the case in times past (some states allowed for less education when combined with experience), but it is increasingly becoming the norm in most states. Some employers may even require previous experience in corrections, casework, or a treatment-related field, or a master's degree in criminal justice, social work, psychology, or a related discipline.

SAGE Journal Article Link
What Matters Most in Probation Supervision: Staff Characteristics, Staff Skills or Program?

Entry-level probation officers should be in good physical and emotional condition. Most agencies require applicants to be at least 21 years old and, for federal employment, not older than 37 (Bureau of Labor Statistics, 2011). In many jurisdictions, persons who have been convicted of a felony may not be eligible for employment in this occupation (Bureau of Labor Statistics, 2011). Familiarity with the use of computers is typically expected given the increasing use of computer technology in probation and parole work (Bureau of Labor Statistics, 2011). Probation officers should have strong writing skills because they are required to prepare many reports. In addition, a graduate degree in a related field such as criminal justice, social work, counseling, or psychology can aid an employee in advancing into supervisory positions within the agency (Bureau of Labor Statistics, 2011).

According to the *Occupational Outlook Handbook*, applicants are usually administered a written, oral, psychological, and physical examination. Given the concern with job stress that is inherent in this field of work, it is no surprise that changes in screening mechanisms during the hiring phase have been observed (Bureau of Labor Statistics, 2011). Indeed, hiring and selection procedures may include psychological interviews and personality assessments to identify those most able to handle the stress and psychological challenges of probation and parole work (Bureau of Labor Statistics, 2011). This demonstrates that agencies are aware of the unique challenges with this type of work and wish to identify those persons hearty enough to withstand the pressures that are inherent therein. This is a wise and prudent move on the part of agencies from a liability standpoint, a public safety standpoint, and an employee-agency relations standpoint. Effective recruitment and selection at the forefront can prevent a host of problems potentially encountered by supervisors and agency leaders in the future. Students are encouraged to examine Figure 5.2 to get an idea of the number of probation officers who are employed in each state.

Caseload Management

The job of a probation officer is stressful and places numerous and diverse demands upon the professional working in such a role. The workload can be difficult to quantify since much of the time that is allocated to various functions may not always be easy to truly understand or operationalize. Nevertheless, the need to quantify expectations has resulted in an analysis of community supervision caseloads. The main considerations involved with such a formal analysis are the number of offenders and the type of offenders on one's caseload. It should be clear that if community supervision officers are stretched too thin among the various offenders being supervised, the safety of the public is compromised. Table 5.4 provides an overview of the recommended caseload for probation officers, depending on the type of offenders being supervised.

Table 5.4: Recommended Caseload Sizes When Considering Type of Offender Case

Adult Caseload Standards	
Case Type	**Cases-to-Staff Ratio**
Intensive	20:1
Moderate to high risk	50:1
Low risk	200:1
Administrative	No limit? 1,000?
Juvenile Caseload Standards	
Case Type	**Cases-to-Staff Ratio**
Intensive	15:1
Moderate to high risk	30:1
Low risk	100:1
Administrative	Not recommended

SOURCE: Burrell, B. (2006). *Caseload standards for probation and parole.* Washington, DC: National Institute of Corrections.

During the past 2 decades, the American Probation and Parole Association (APPA) has attempted to identify the ideal caseload for community supervision officers. The first official attempt to address this issue occurred in the early 1990s, when a paper issued by the APPA recommended that probation and parole agencies examine staffing needs and caseload size within their own organizations (American Probation and Parole Association, 1991; Burrell, 2006). Though this seemed to be a reasonable recommendation, it has been much harder to implement than might initially have been imagined. The quest to determine the ideal caseload size has been a tricky one that has been complicated by multiple factors that are difficult to resolve and/or include in any specific equation.

When considering prior attempts to reduce caseloads, a consensus model has slowly emerged throughout the nation (Burrell, 2006). This is the result of input from experienced and thoughtful practitioners in the field of community supervision (Burrell, 2006). Though not necessarily ideal for all agencies, these generally agreed-upon recommendations provide a baseline from which other agencies can operate, comparing and modifying their own operations against the backdrop of the consensus that has emerged. Table 5.4 provides the recommended maximum number of offenders per type of offender category. Classifying offenders on these relevant criteria is critical since it ensures that offenders are correctly matched with the level of supervision necessary to optimize their potential for completing their community supervision requirements (Burrell, 2006; Hanser, 2007).

The "evidence suggests that staff resources and services should be targeted at intensive and moderate-to high risk cases, for this is where the greatest effect will be had. Minimal contacts and services should be provided to low risk cases" (Burrell, 2006, p. 7). This reallocation of staff would shift supervision to higher-risk offenders and away from those who are low risk (Burrell, 2006). It is in this manner that community supervision caseloads can be structured to optimize overall public safety and also support the reintegrative aspects that serve as the basis of any correctional system that truly seeks to correct criminal behavior.

PROBATION REVOCATION

This discussion is intended to present the use of revocation as a sanction and a component of the probation process in circumstances where offenders are not able to complete their initially given probation sentence. Previous research demonstrates that roughly 33% of all probationers fail to complete the initial requirements of their probation (Heberman & Bonczar, 2015). However, some areas of the nation are more prone to probation revocation than others. Certain counties and/or communities may be more criminogenic in nature and will therefore tend to have more offending as well as more serious offenders processed through the local justice system. In such areas, it should not be surprising that probation departments will generate higher rates of revocation proceedings.

Preliminary hearing: Initial examination of the facts of the arrest to determine if probable cause does exist for a violation.

Hearing stage: Stage of a revocation proceeding that allows the probation agency to present evidence of the violation, which the offender is given the opportunity to refute.

Sentencing stage: When a judge determines if the offender will be incarcerated or continue his or her probation sentence under more restrictive terms.

Generally, revocation proceedings are handled in three stages. First, the **preliminary hearing** examines the facts of the arrest to determine if probable cause exists for a violation. Second, the **hearing stage** allows the probation agency to present evidence of the violation while the offender is given the opportunity to refute the evidence provided. Though the agency (or the local government) is not obligated to provide an attorney, the offender does have the right to obtain legal representation, if he or she should desire. Third, the **sentencing stage** is when a judge requires either that the offender be incarcerated or, as in many cases where the violation is minor, that the offender continue his or her probation sentence but under more restrictive terms.

Lastly, it is not uncommon for offenders to have some sort of hearing or proceeding throughout their term of probation. The longer the period of probation, the more likely this is to happen. Many offenders do eventually finish their probation terms. For those offenders who do, termination of the sentence then occurs (see Table 5.5 for additional data on completion rates and other details on probationers around the country). During 2013, 66% of the 2,131,300 probationers who exited supervision were discharged because they either completed their term of supervision or received an early discharge. These offenders are free in society without any further obligation to report to the justice system. It is at this point that their experience with community corrections ends, presuming that they lead a conviction-free life throughout the remainder of their days.

Table 5.5: Offenders Who Completed Probation and Those Who Did Not

Probationers who exited supervision, by type of exit, 2008–2013

Type of exit	2008	2009	2010	2011	2012	2013
Completion	63%	65%	65%	66%	68%	66%
Incarceration[a]	17	16	16	16	15	15
Absconder	4	3	3	2	3	3
Discharged to custody, detainer, or warrant	1	1	1	1	1	—
Other unsatisfactory[b]	10	10	11	9	9	11
Transferred to another probation agency	1	—	1	1	1	1
Death	1	1	1	1	1	1
Other[c]	4	4	4	4	4	3
Estimated number[d]	2,320,100	2,327,800	2,261,300	2,189,100	2,089,800	2,131,300

SOURCE: Herberman, E. J., & Bonczar, T. P. (2015). *Probation and parole in the United States, 2013.* Washington, DC: Bureau of Justice Statistics.

Note: Detail may not sum to total due to rounding. Percents based on most recent data and may differ from previously published statistics. Percents based on probationers with known type of exit. Reporting methods for some probation agencies changed over time. See *Methodology.*

— Less than 0.5%.

[a]Includes probationers who were incarcerated for a new offense and those who had their current probation sentence revoked (e.g., violating a condition of supervision).

[b]Includes probationers discharged from supervision who failed to meet all conditions of supervision, including some with only financial conditions remaining, some who had their probation sentence revoked but were not incarcerated because their sentence was immediately reinstated, and other types of unsatisfactory exits. Includes some early terminations and expirations of sentence.

[c]Includes, but not limited to, probationers who were discharged from supervision through a legislative mandate because they were deported or transferred to the jurisdiction of Immigration and Customs Enforcement; were transferred to another state through an interstate compact agreement; had their sentence dismissed or overturned by the court through an appeal; had their sentence administratively closed, deferred, or terminated by the court; were awaiting a hearing; and were released on bond.

[d]Counts rounded to the nearest 100. Calculated as the inverse of the exit rate times 12 months. Includes estimates for nonreporting agencies.

Court Decisions on Revocation

Essentially, there are two primary cases that established due process rights for probationers. The first was *Morrissey v. Brewer* (1972), which dealt with revocation proceedings for parolees, not probationers. However, this case was followed by another Supreme Court case, *Gagnon v. Scarpelli* (1973), which extended the rights afforded to parolees under *Morrissey* to offenders on probation as well.

The *Morrissey* court ruled that parolees facing revocation must be given due process through a prompt informal inquiry before an impartial hearing officer. The Court required that this be through a two-step hearing process. The reason for this two-step process is to first screen for the reasonableness of holding the parolee since there is often a substantial delay between the point of arrest and the revocation hearing. This delay can be costly for both the justice system and the offender if it is based on circumstances that do not actually warrant full revocation. Specifically, the Court stated that some minimal

> inquiry should be conducted at or reasonably near the place of the alleged parole violation or arrest and as promptly as convenient after arrest while information is fresh and sources are available. . . . Such an inquiry should be seen as in the nature of a "preliminary hearing" to determine whether there is probable cause or reasonable ground to believe that the arrested parolee has committed acts that would constitute a violation of parole conditions. (p. 485)

The Court also noted that this would need to be conducted by a neutral and detached party (a hearing officer), though the hearing officer did not necessarily need to be affiliated with the judiciary, and this first step did not have to be formal in nature. The hearing officer is tasked with determining whether there is sufficient probable cause to justify the continued detention of the offender.

After the initial hearing is the revocation hearing. Interestingly, the Court was quite specific on how the revocation hearings were to be conducted (del Carmen et al., 2001). During this hearing, the parolee is entitled to contest the charges and demonstrate that he or she did not violate any of the conditions of his or her parole. If it should turn out that the parolee did, in fact, violate his or her parole requirements but that this violation was necessary due to mitigating circumstances, it may turn out that the violation does not warrant full revocation. The *Morrissey* Court specified additional procedures during the revocation process, which include the following:

1. Written notice of the claimed violation of parole.
2. Disclosure to the parolee of evidence against him or her.
3. An opportunity to be heard in person and to present witnesses and documentary evidence.
4. The right to confront and cross-examine adverse witnesses.
5. A "neutral and detached" hearing body, such as a traditional parole board, members of which need not be judicial officers or lawyers.
6. A written statement by the fact finders as to the evidence relied on and reasons for revoking parole.

The *Morrissey* case is obviously an example of judicial activism, much like *Miranda v. Arizona* (1966), that has greatly impacted the field of community corrections. The Court's clear and specific guidelines set forth in *Morrissey* have created specific standards and procedures that community supervision agencies must follow. Rather than ensuring that revocation proceedings include a just hearing and means of processing, the Court laid out several pointed requirements that continue to be relevant and binding to this day.

The next pivotal case dealing with revocation proceedings and community supervision is *Gagnon v. Scarpelli* (1973). In the simplest of terms, the Court ruled that all of the requirements for parole revocation proceedings noted in *Morrissey* also applied to revocation proceedings dealing with probationers. However, this case is also important because it addressed one other key issue regarding revocation proceedings. The Court noted that offenders on community supervision do not have an absolute constitutional right to appointed counsel during revocation

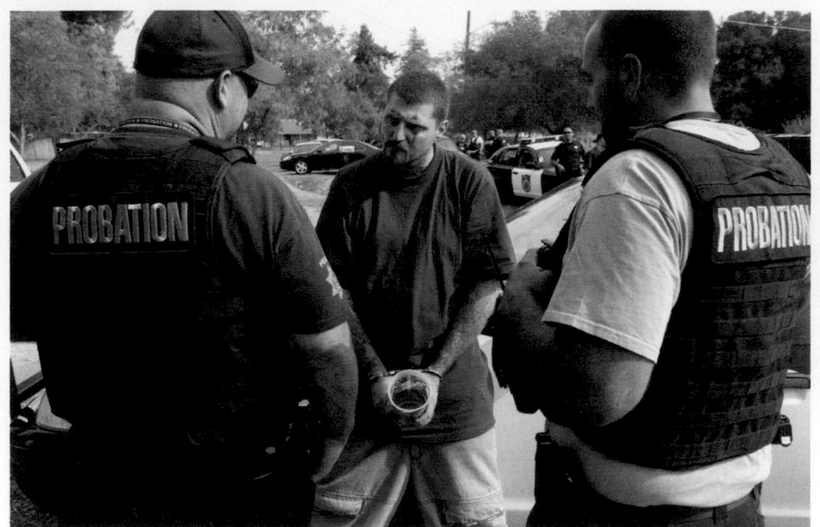

AP Photo/Rich Pedroncelli

■ PHOTO 5.7 The probation officers are taking this probationer into custody due to his continued use of drugs and alcohol while on community supervision.

proceedings. Such proceedings are not considered to be true adversarial proceedings and therefore do not require official legal representation.

Common Reasons for Revocation

There are a number of reasons that offenders may have their probation revoked. Perhaps the most frequent reason that revocation hearings are initiated is due to a probationer's failure to maintain contact with his or her probation officer (Glaze & Bonczar, 2011). Of those probationers who experience a disciplinary hearing, the most frequent reason tends to be absconding or failing to contact their probation officer (Glaze & Bonczar, 2011). Other reasons may include an arrest or conviction for a new offense, failure to pay fines/restitution, or failure to attend or complete an alcohol or drug treatment program (Glaze & Bonczar, 2011). Among probationers who have revocation hearings initiated against them, almost half are generally permitted to continue their probation sentence. For those who are allowed to continue, they will almost always have additional conditions imposed upon them, and their type of supervision will typically be more restrictive (Glaze & Bonczar, 2011).

Further complicating the picture is that some conditions of probation result in what are often called technical violations. **Technical violations** are actions that do not comply with the conditions and requirements of a probationer's sentence, as articulated by the court that acted as the sentencing authority. Technical violations are not necessarily criminal, in and of themselves, and would likely be legal behaviors if the offender were not on probation. For instance, a condition of a drug offender's probation may be that he or she stay out of bars, nightclubs, and other places of business where the selling and consumption of alcohol is a primary attraction. Another example might be if a sex offender is ordered to remain a certain distance from schools. For most citizens, going to nightclubs and/or setting foot on school grounds is not a violation of any sort, and neither of these acts is considered criminal. However, for the probationer, this can lead to the revocation of probation.

Any number of other behaviors can be technical violations. Additional examples might include the failure to attend mandated therapy, failure to report periods of unemployment, or failure to complete scheduled amounts of community service. Though these violations are substantially different from those that carry a new and separate criminal conviction, they still can lead to a revocation (Hanser, 2010b) and are important in demonstrating whether the offender is making genuine progress in the corrections process. Excessive technical violations would seem to indicate that reform is not a priority for an offender.

CONCLUSION

This chapter illustrates the importance of probation as a sanction within the correctional system. Whether one is considering community- or institution-based corrections, the use of probation affects the overall correctional system quite significantly. This is especially true when one considers the impact that probation has on the jail facility. Without probation, jail facilities would be even more overcrowded than they already tend to be. The true purpose of probation, however, is to facilitate the reformation of offenders. This has been the case since its earliest inception, when John Augustus first established this sanction in the United States. Thus, students should consider probation to have reformative value. This means that the purpose of probation is consistent with this text's definition of corrections, whereby the ultimate goal is to correct criminal tendencies among the offender population.

Technical violations: Actions that do not comply with the conditions and requirements of a probationer's sentence.

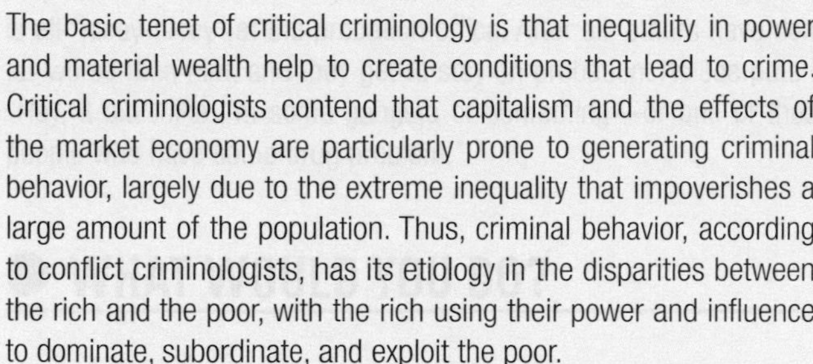

APPLIED THEORY 5.1

Critical Criminology and Probation Supervision

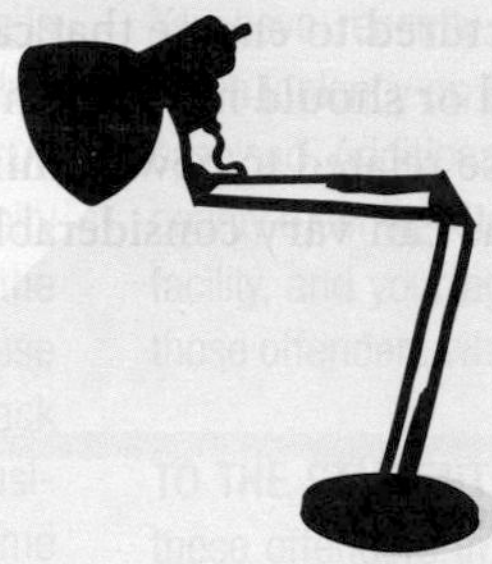

The basic tenet of critical criminology is that inequality in power and material wealth help to create conditions that lead to crime. Critical criminologists contend that capitalism and the effects of the market economy are particularly prone to generating criminal behavior, largely due to the extreme inequality that impoverishes a large amount of the population. Thus, criminal behavior, according to conflict criminologists, has its etiology in the disparities between the rich and the poor, with the rich using their power and influence to dominate, subordinate, and exploit the poor.

Though it is not necessarily the role of the community supervision officer to right the wrongs of society, it may be useful if such practitioners remain aware of the economic structures that impact society and may also impact how offenders see their plight. Most high-crime areas of the United States are impoverished, consisting of populations that have great difficulty competing in the legitimate economy. Many of these high-crime regions offer few legitimate employment opportunities, which can be a problem when offenders return to them once released on community supervision. Due to the lack of monetary resources in the community, other social services and opportunities will be likewise limited. Populations in these areas also tend to have less access to education, medical care, and other services that impact the quality of life for community members.

In such communities, there may exist a culture of poverty, with little legitimate hope of breaking out of the economically debilitating circumstances. Further, such areas may be labeled and stereotyped, which reinforces the notion that poverty-ridden communities are criminogenic and even normalizes this so that youth in such communities accept it as their lot in life. Incidentally, this portrayal is often perpetuated by rich and powerful media moguls, recording companies, and executive decision makers, all of whom fit within the upper-class and affluent society. Thus, the poor are again victimized as they are corralled into believing in and accepting a fundamentally unfair system and are, at least indirectly, taught through the media that a life of crime is perhaps their most viable option. It is due to this that police and other government agents are seen as being in league with "the man," who serves as a nefarious and obscure mastermind behind the lower class's woes. This can lead to parents teaching children to fear and/or be disrespectful to police and other agents of the criminal justice system. In many cases, the community and offender may also hold the community supervision officer to be a party to such inequalities. This can result in resentment between the probationer and the community supervision officer and can also create a chasm between the community and the agency.

Community supervision officers and correctional treatment providers cannot single-handedly repair these communities, nor can they necessarily change the subculture of resentment and mistrust that may exist in them. But they can encourage involvement in community development and stabilization projects, and they can be cognizant of the serious obstacles that face probationers and parolees who come from such communities. Agencies must work with persons in such communities who are receptive to forming multiagency partnerships, citizen volunteer groups, and the like. Above and beyond all else, agencies and agency members must emphasize a sense of respect for the community. This may help to take the sting out of the intergenerational resentment and distrust that may exist in such communities, allowing agency members to slowly change community attitudes and culture over the years that follow.

SOURCE: Cullen, F. T., & Agnew, R. (2006). *Criminological theory: Past to present* (3rd ed.). Los Angeles: Roxbury.

This chapter also highlights the importance of the presentence investigation and the report it generates for judges who sentence offenders and for later issues that may arise during an offender's sentence. The PSI report is even used in institutional settings when making early release, treatment-planning, and custody-level decisions. Due to the impact the PSI report can have on the correctional process as a whole, probation officers tend to spend a significant amount of time constructing these reports and/or referring to the information contained therein.

Probation officer qualifications and standards of training were also discussed. It is clear that the job of probation officer is not an easy one. This job requires a degree in most cases but pays little in comparison to other professions. Further, the work is stressful given the high caseloads that tend to exist for many probation officers. Qualifications and characteristics of probation officers demonstrate that this area of correctional employment may be quite different from institutional corrections and that this dimension of the correctional system has been underappreciated.

Lastly, revocation procedures were covered in detail. Leading cases related to revocation for probation and the corresponding procedures for revocation were discussed. The process of

6 INTERMEDIATE SANCTIONS

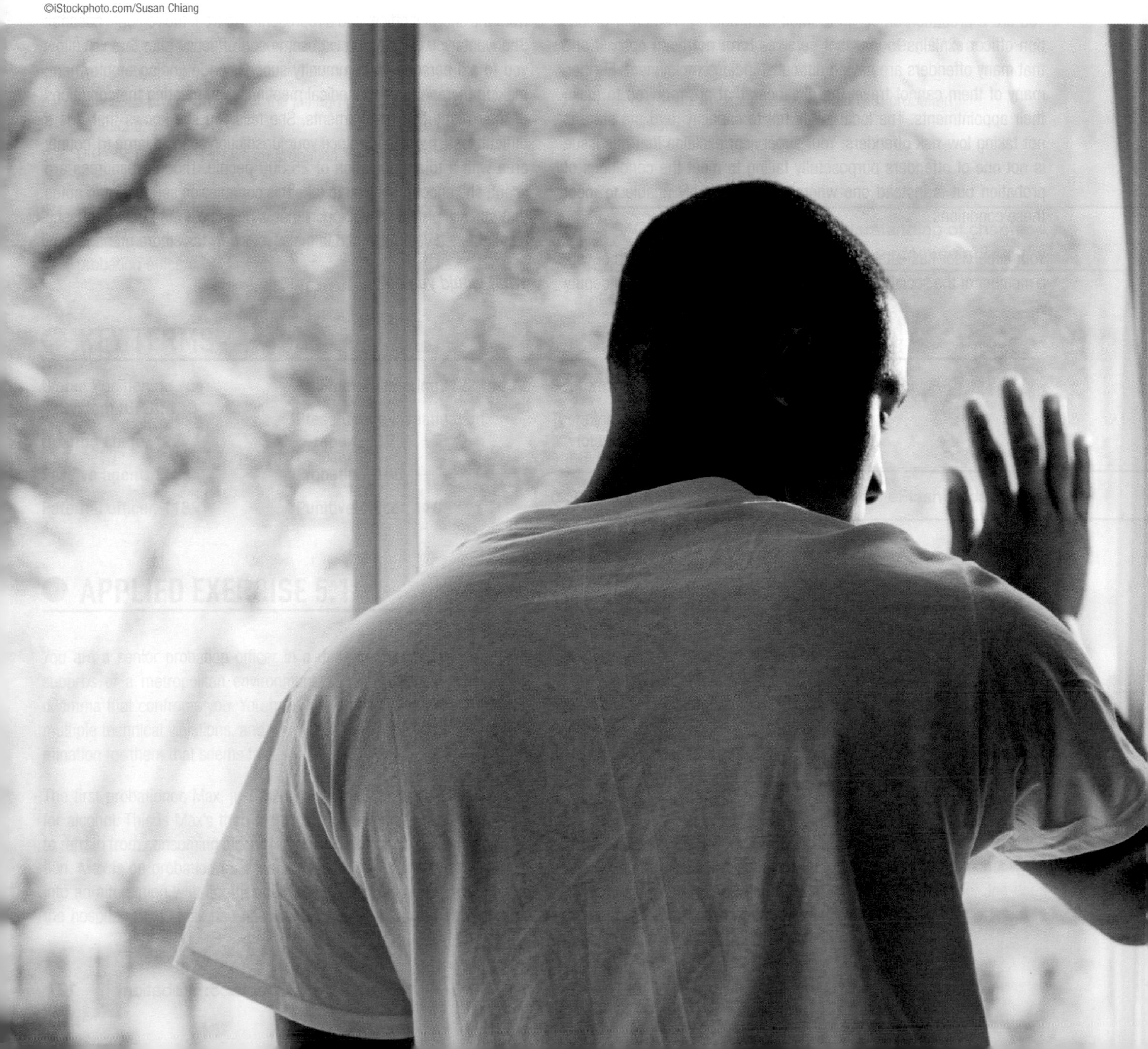

PARENTING WHILE ON PROBATION

Kevin sat on the couch. He looked down at his ankle, and, with a sigh, picked up the remote and scanned through the television channels. He thought about how he ended up on house arrest and electronic monitoring. He remembered his wife, Michelle, saying, "Kevin, honey, I'm glad that they didn't send you to prison, but really, your problems are still greatly impacting the kids and I don't know how much more of this that I can take."

Kevin had replied, "I know, I know, I know . . . but this time I am done with the dope, I promise, and no more getting people to get it for me."

Michelle scowled at him. "Kevin, that is so stupid! Of course you're done, you *have* to be done or you *will* go to prison. But I'm not just talking about the dope. In fact, if we're still worrying about *that*, then I can tell you now that we are *not* going to make it."

"Awww come on, don't be that way, I promise. . . ."

Michelle interrupted him, shoving a finger toward his chest. "Don't *even* begin making promises to me! You understand?"

Michelle was upset because just the night before she had seen their 7-year-old son, Bryan, take his watch and try to strap it around his ankle. Michelle asked Bryan what he was doing and he exclaimed, "I wanna be like Daddy!"

Michelle discouraged the behavior and asked Bryan for the watch. When Kevin got home, she commenced to explain to him that he was ruining the family. She was not at all calm when she did so, and now, unlike before, Kevin had to stay there and listen.

He remembered her saying, "And *now*, you are going to sit there on the bed and listen to *all* I have to say! No more grabbing the keys and driving off to that damned strip club and coming home drunk anymore, huh, Kevin? Welcome to the world of responsibility and . . . " she paused, a wry and sarcastic grin on her face, " . . . *welcome to house arrest*!"

Kevin sat there thinking about the situation. He was alone in the house. Michelle was at work, and Bryan was at school. Just then, there was a knock at the door. Kevin went to the door and peered through the peephole. The visitor was Greg, one of Kevin's drug buddies. Normally, Kevin would open the door and happily greet Greg.

This time, Kevin stood still by the door and made no noise. Greg knocked for what seemed like an eternity and rang the doorbell multiple times. Finally, Greg left.

Kevin exhaled. Walking away from the door, he muttered under his breath, "I ain't really got any choice. I just gotta stop or I'm gonna lose everything."

Instead of going back to the couch, he began doing some of the house work that needed to be done. He decided it was the least he could do while Michelle was at work.

LEARNING OBJECTIVES:

1. Identify the various types of intermediate sanctions and their placement within the continuum of sanctions.
2. Analyze the various means of ensuring compliance by substance abusers and sex offenders.
3. Compare the various ways intermediate sanctions are used in states around the nation.

INTRODUCTION

Currently, there is no single definition of *intermediate sanctions*, nor is there any ironclad agreement about what ought to be included within such a definition. Some researchers contend that almost anything that falls between "regular" probation and a full prison term is an intermediate sanction; others deny inclusion in this category to any sanction that involves incarceration. However, the growing popularity of residential facilities like restitution centers (see Focus Topic 6.1), work release centers, and probation detention facilities, some of which have capacities in the hundreds, makes this distinction important (Guccione, 2002).

What intermediate sanctions do have in common is the presence of features designed to enhance the desired sanctioning purpose. Regardless of whether the intent is to achieve punishment, incapacitation, rehabilitation, or specific deterrence, intermediate sanctions provide more

©iStockphoto.com/Signature Collection

■ PHOTO 6.1 In many cases, the plea-bargaining process allows for attorneys to discuss agreements on sanctions that will be given to an offender. This is a routine process in the courthouse.

options than simple probation. These sanctions also tend to vary in severity, leading to a continuum of sanctions that progresses from the most restrictive (prison) to the least restrictive (suspended sentences, deferred adjudication, and so forth). This can lead to increased surveillance and tighter controls on movement while enhancing the integration of more intense treatment to address a wider assortment of maladies or deficiencies. The use of intermediate sanctions can help to integrate supervision and treatment, offering options beyond what incarceration may usually offer.

One purpose in implementing effective and appropriate intermediate sanctions is *to make available a continuum of sanctions scaled on one or more sanctioning goals*. For example, the goal of incapacitation may be implemented through varying levels of surveillance or control of movement. Such a continuum permits the court or corrections authority to tailor sanctions that are meaningful with respect both to its purposes and to the kinds of offenders that come before it.

A current practice is to unload the complete list of sanctions on all offenders, which sets up both offenders and the program for failure. A typical offender who is supporting two children, for example, is not likely to be able to pay restitution, perform extensive community service, and participate in frequent drug counseling. Targeting specific sanctions to specific offender profiles, on the other hand, increases the chances of success for both the program and the offender. This kind of policy-directed system can also be responsive to differing and changing behavior on the part of offenders.

Currently, to combat the rising costs of incarceration, convicted offenders are being sentenced to community supervision with increasing frequency (Glaze & Palla, 2005). Despite overseeing an overwhelming number of offenders, community supervision (probation) departments have experienced budget cuts, which in turn have led to a reduction in staff and resources. Given this situation, the need for alternative means of supervision and treatment is at a premium. To this end, intermediate sanctions have become the order of the day.

TYPES OF INTERMEDIATE SANCTIONS

When it comes to finding alternatives to punishment and rehabilitation for offenders, there is no shortage of options, particularly in terms of community-based services. On a simplistic level, intermediate sanctions could be defined as alternatives to traditional incarceration that consist of sentencing options falling anywhere between a standard prison sentence and a standard probation sentence. The National Institute of Corrections (1993) has also defined *intermediate sanctions* as "a range of sanctioning options that permit the crafting of sentences to respond to the particular circumstances of the offender and the offense; and the outcomes desired in the case" (p. 18). For this text, we will use a blend of both definitions. Thus, **intermediate sanctions** are a range of sentencing options that fall between incarceration and probation, being designed to allow for the crafting of sentences that respond to the offender, the offense, or both, with the intended outcome of the case being a primary consideration. Table 6.1 provides an examination of the various intermediate sanctions and sentencing measures.

The definition of intermediate sanctions just presented provides a perspective that is highly consistent with the emphasis on reintegration found in this text. It is clear that these types of sanctions allow for a great deal of flexibility and can be adjusted to accommodate treatment and supervision considerations. These sanctions allow for consideration of the various needs, challenges, and issues associated with a particular offender and the type of offending that he or she is prone to committing. This permits the calibration of sentences so that specific details are a better fit with the type of offense committed as well as the individual variables associated with the offender. Such

Intermediate sanctions: A range of sentencing options that fall between incarceration and probation.

FOCUS TOPIC 6.1

Doing Time in the Working World

Gina Faison takes the bus every morning to the downtown Los Angeles law office where she works.

She cannot leave the building for lunch with colleagues. She cannot stop at the mall after work. Nor can she go home to her husband and three young sons at night.

Faison, a paralegal and convicted thief, is serving an unusual 3-year sentence at California's only restitution center for women.

"I don't know if I could have made it over the wall," said Faison, a 38-year-old first offender, referring to state prison.

She is one of 43 women now living at the minimum-security facility in Pico-Union, where inmates wear whatever they like, sleep two to six in a bedroom, and sip their morning coffee outside under bright blue awnings.

The program is designed to move nonviolent inmates from prison into the work force to repay their victims, said Doris Mahlum, district administrator for the state Department of Corrections.

Participants have paid $250,000 in court-ordered restitution in the last 2 years, she said.

Despite increased prosecution of white-collar criminals and the popularity of alternative sentences for nonviolent offenders, the restitution center has operated in relative obscurity since 1971.

It serves inmates from throughout California, but rarely, if ever, have all its beds been occupied at once. Several are now empty.

To qualify, inmates must be nonviolent, must have been ordered to pay restitution, and must have been sentenced to 3 years or less. They are required to get a job and turn over two-thirds of their salary to their victims and the state to defray the costs of incarceration.

The women are housed in a beige one-story structure built in 1910 as the Chase Sanatorium in a residential area on West 18th Street near Union Avenue. A 50-bed men's center is in a renovated motel in an industrial section of South La Cienega Boulevard.

Unlike the general prison population, most of the inmates are educated and have marketable job skills, said Cheryl Atterbury-Brooks, the parole officer assigned to the women's center.

"We have doctors, lawyers, nurses," she said.

A few earn more than the staff that supervises them. Program manager Ernest Green recalled a geologist convicted of fraud who was paid $30 an hour.

From the above, it is clear that intermediate sanctions accomplish numerous goals simultaneously. They allow the justice system to provide consequences for criminal offenses, collect fees and fines for victims, and also supervise the progress of the offender. Further, the offender is able to continue being a productive member of society and is also able to attend classes and meet other responsibilities of the supervision. This is a much more cost-effective approach to sanctioning and generates more benefits for both victims desiring compensation and the community as a whole.

SOURCE: "Doing their time in the working world. Restitution center is for women who stole, they pay their debts, avoid prison," by J. Guccione. *Los Angeles Times*, April 15, 2002. Copyright © 2002. Reprinted with permission.

flexibility is what provides the field of community corrections with its greatest source of leverage among the offender population, in terms of treatment and supervision.

This chapter will discuss the most commonly implemented and researched intermediate sanctions of intensive supervision, day reporting centers, day fines, home detention, electronic monitoring, shock incarceration, boot camps, community service, and various methods of compliance assurance. Due to the overcrowding problems in prison systems around the nation, it is clear that there is simply a pragmatic need for more space. As a result of the public's outcry for increased traditional sentencing of offenders and the legislative action that has responded to this demand, the use of intermediate sanctions has grown. Recent reports indicate that many parolees and probationers are supervised under some form of intermediate sanctioning, and this trend is likely to increase in the future (Mitchell, 2011; Office of Program Policy Analysis and Governmental Accountability, 2010). While we must remember that the applicability of such programming is dependent upon the potential for harm in local communities and the ability of intermediate sanctions to reduce recidivism, there is little doubt that in today's era of state-level budget cuts, many prison systems are using intermediate sanctions as alternatives to imprisonment (Mitchell, 2011). Students should refer to Table 6.2 to see the cost difference between intermediate sanctions and prison terms.

SAGE Journal Article Link
Economic Sanctions in Criminal Justice

Fines

Most offenders convicted of a criminal offense are assessed a fine as a punishment for committing the offense. A fine can be defined as a monetary penalty imposed by a judge or magistrate as a punishment for having committed an offense. In most cases, the fine is a certain dollar

■ Table 6.1: Summary Listing of Coercive Intermediate Sanction Measures and Sentencing Options

Warning measures (Notice of consequences of subsequent wrongdoing)	Admonishment/cautioning (administrative; judicial) Suspended execution or imposition of sentence
Injunctive measures (Banning legal conduct)	Travel (e.g., from jurisdiction to specific criminogenic spots) Association (e.g., with other offenders) Driving Possession of weapons Use of alcohol Professional activity (e.g., disbarment) Restitution
Economic measures	Costs Fees Forfeitures Support payments Fines (standard; day fines) Community service (individual placement; work crew)
Work-related measures	Paid employment requirements Academic (e.g., basic literacy, GED)
Education-related measures	Vocational training Life skills training Psychological/psychiatric
Physical and mental health	Chemical (e.g., methadone; psychoactive drugs)
Treatment measures	Surgical (e.g., acupuncture drug treatment)
Physical confinement measures	*Partial or intermittent confinement:* Home curfew Day treatment center Halfway house Restitution center Weekend detention facility/jail *Full/continuous confinement:* Outpatient treatment facility (e.g., drug/mental health) Full home/house arrest Mental hospital Other residential treatment facility (e.g., drug/alcohol) Boot camp Detention facility Jail Prison
Monitoring/compliance measures (May be attached to all other sanctions)	*Required of the offender:* Electronic monitoring (telephone check-in; active electronic monitoring device) Mail reporting Face-to-face reporting Urine analysis (random; routine) *Required of the monitoring agent:* Sentence compliance checks (e.g., on payment of monetary sanctions; attendance/performance at treatment, work, or educational sites) Criminal records checks Third-party checks (family, employer, surety, service/treatment provider; via mail, telephone, in person) Direct surveillance/observation (random/routine visits and possibly search; at home, work, institution, or elsewhere) Electronic monitoring (regular phone checks and/or passive monitoring device—currently used with home curfew or house arrest, but could track movement more widely as technology develops)

SOURCE: National Institute of Corrections. (1993). *The intermediate sanctions handbook: Experiences and tools for policymakers.* Washington, DC: Author.

amount established either by the judge or according to a set schedule, depending upon the offense committed (see Chapter 2). The logic behind the fine is that it will deter the offender from committing another offense in the future for fear of being fined again. In most jurisdictions, the fines are assessed and paid in monthly installments to the receiving agency. In contemporary community supervision agencies, offenders are now able to pay their fines via credit or debit cards. The feelings are mixed regarding allowing an offender to pay in this manner. Officers sometimes feel that by delaying the effect of the monetary fine, it does not allow the offender to accept personal responsibility.

As the offense seriousness increases from misdemeanor to felony, presumably the fines increase as well. This assessment of fines is totally dependent upon judicial discretion. Traditionally, there was one set fine for certain offenses regardless of the financial standing of the offenders. As time has passed, many judiciaries have begun to understand that one set fine is more punishing to the offender who happens to earn the least amount of money and a "cakewalk" to those offenders who happen to be financially blessed. Given this, there has been a push for graduated fines that are dependent upon the income of the offender at time of sentencing. In this day of drastic budget cuts and pushes for alternatives to incarceration, fines are frequently used. They allow the offender an opportunity to pay for his or her treatment and punishment as opposed to the traditional method of placing the financial burden on the state.

Community Service

Perhaps the most widely known yet least likely to be used form of intermediate sanctioning is community service (see Chapter 4). Community service is the work that one is required to perform in order to repay his or her debt to society after being found at fault for committing a criminal or deviant offense.

Community service serves a dual purpose: to rehabilitate and punish offenders. In terms of rehabilitation, community service affords the offender the opportunity to participate in something constructive, allowing him or her to build "sweat equity" in something that is beneficial to the community. Community service is punitive, too, in that the offender is forced to give up his or her own time to work off a criminal debt without being paid.

Due to the low cost of overhead in funding community service programs and the need for labor in communities, community service options will continue to be frequently utilized. One of

Table 6.2: Intermediate Sanctions Are Less Costly Than Incarceration

Intermediate Sanctions Are Less Costly Than Incarceration			
Intermediate Sanction	First Year Cost Per Offender 2008–2009	Total First Year Cost For 100 Offenders[1]	Potential Savings Per 100 Offenders[2]
Prison	$20,272	$2,027,200	–
Supervision with GPS Monitoring	$5,121	$806,954	$1,220,246
Probation and Restitution Centers	$9,492	$1,639,211	$387,989
Day Reporting	$4,191	$917,823	$1,109,377
Residential Drug Treatment	$10,539	$1,419,529	$607,671

SOURCE: Office of Program Policy Analysis and Governmental Accountability. (2010). *Intermediate sanctions for non-violent offenders could produce savings.* Tallahassee, FL: Author.

[1]The first year cost for 100 offenders is based on the actual program completion rates 2008– 2010. Offenders who do not complete the program are assumed to leave the program after 82 days and are sent to prison for the remaining 283 days of the year; the cost of prison for these offenders is included in the total first year cost estimate.

[2]The savings for 100 offenders represents the difference between the cost of prison for one year based on $55.54 per day and the total first year cost for intermediate sanctions.

Robert Hanser

■ PHOTO 6.2 Some offenders must complete community service as part of their sentence. Offenders may be given community supervision or a split sentence (which includes both jail time and community supervision). Both of these sanctions usually require the completion of some type of labor, as seen here with this offender, who is preparing to do yard work.

the most pressing problems in evaluating community service is that such opportunities vary so widely, and often offenders participate in multiple community service sites and types throughout their time under supervision. In most cases, community service is completed anywhere the offender can get the hours. For example, an offender may begin community service at the local courthouse and complete his or her hours at the homeless mission. Despite the lack of research in this area, community service is clearly an integral part of intermediate sanctioning and provides a positive avenue through which offenders and the community can learn the rehabilitative and punitive ideals.

Intensive Supervision Probation

Perhaps the most commonly known form of intermediate sanction is **intensive supervision probation (ISP)**. ISP is the extensive supervision of offenders who are deemed the greatest risk to society or are in need of the greatest amount of governmental services (e.g., drug treatment). In most cases, ISP is the option afforded to individuals who would otherwise be incarcerated for felony offenses. Early forms of ISP operated under the conservative philosophy of increasing public safety via strict offender scrutiny. Today's ISP programs are focused on a host of components.

When examining the various facets of modern-day intensive supervision, one finds that they are quite diverse. Some ISPs focus on specific offense and offender types (e.g., sex offending and younger offenders). Others differ in their level of supervision, which may range from 5 days per week to once every 2 weeks. The types of supervising officers vary from untrained community supervision officers to specialized officers who have been well schooled in the supervision of at-risk offenders. In most cases, officers are afforded a lighter than normal caseload of approximately 10 to 20 offenders. Placement into intensive supervision is dependent upon the sentencing judge, the supervision officer, the parole board, or some combination of these. In today's agencies, the decision to place an offender on intensive supervision is made based on the level of assessed offender risk of rearrest.

Electronic Monitoring

Perhaps the most widely used but least understood intermediate sanction is electronic monitoring. **Electronic monitoring** includes the use of any mechanism that is worn by the offender for the means of tracking his or her whereabouts through electronic detection. Electronic monitoring includes both active and passive monitoring systems. With both types of electronic monitoring devices, offenders are required to wear an ankle bracelet with a tracking device. The active system types are used in conjunction with the local telephone line. At random times throughout the day, the offender's home phone will ring, and the offender has a certain amount of time to answer. Once the offender answers the phone, a signal is transmitted via the tracking device, which validates that the offender is at home. With the passive system, the ankle bracelet transmits a continuous signal to a nearby transmitter, which transmits the signal to a monitoring computer. With each type, the supervising officer is sent a readout each morning of the offender's compliance.

If an offender attempts to alter the connection, most devices have alarms that will sound and send an immediate message to the monitor. It is also not uncommon for an offender to be at home, not having tampered with the ankle bracelet, and yet it appears that he or she is noncompliant. Of the two electronic monitoring types, the active system has the lower rate of false alarms. But, even though the passive system has the higher rate of false alarms, it is the fastest in determining noncompliance because it assesses the offender's whereabouts much more quickly.

Intensive supervision probation (ISP): The extensive supervision of offenders who are deemed the greatest risk to society or are in need of the greatest amount of governmental services.

Electronic monitoring: The use of any mechanism worn by the offender for the means of tracking his or her whereabouts through electronic detection.

Those in favor of electronic monitoring base their argument on the ability of the system to increase public safety due to the knowledge of the whereabouts of each offender. Simply knowing they are being personally tracked may deter offenders from committing crime. Proponents also argue that electronic monitoring provides the least punitive alternative to incarceration, as it allows for offenders to be supervised in the community. Undoubtedly, electronic monitoring is a fiscally feasible intermediate sanction in terms of saving money while diverting offenders from incarceration (see Figure 6.1). However, questions remain as to the ability of electronic monitoring to assist offenders in the desistance from criminal behavior, whether supervision officer discretion helps or hurts the outcome, and the effects of community and family involvement on electronic monitoring.

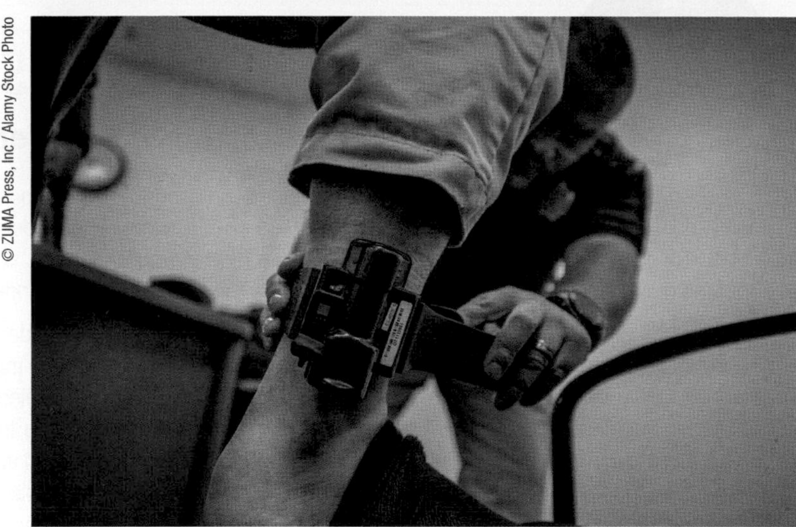

■ PHOTO 6.3 **An offender on supervision is being fitted with an ankle bracelet that will be used for tracking purposes.**

Global Positioning Systems

In this new millennium, community supervision is beginning to utilize military capabilities to keep track of offenders. A Global Positioning System (GPS) receiver uses 24 military satellites to determine the exact location of a coordinate (see Chapter 5, Technology and Equipment 5.1). As we have seen earlier in Chapter 5, GPS tracking devices allow supervision officers to detect when an offender violates one of his or her restrictions on movement due to a condition of his or her supervision.

Prison Tour Video Link
Electronic Monitoring

Despite the advances that GPS technology has provided for community corrections, there are also some disadvantages. As noted in Chapter 5, GPS tracking devices often lose their signal during bad weather or in areas densely populated with trees. Further, this equipment is expensive and can

■ **Figure 6.1: Electronic Monitoring and Supervision Costs Much Less Than Prison**

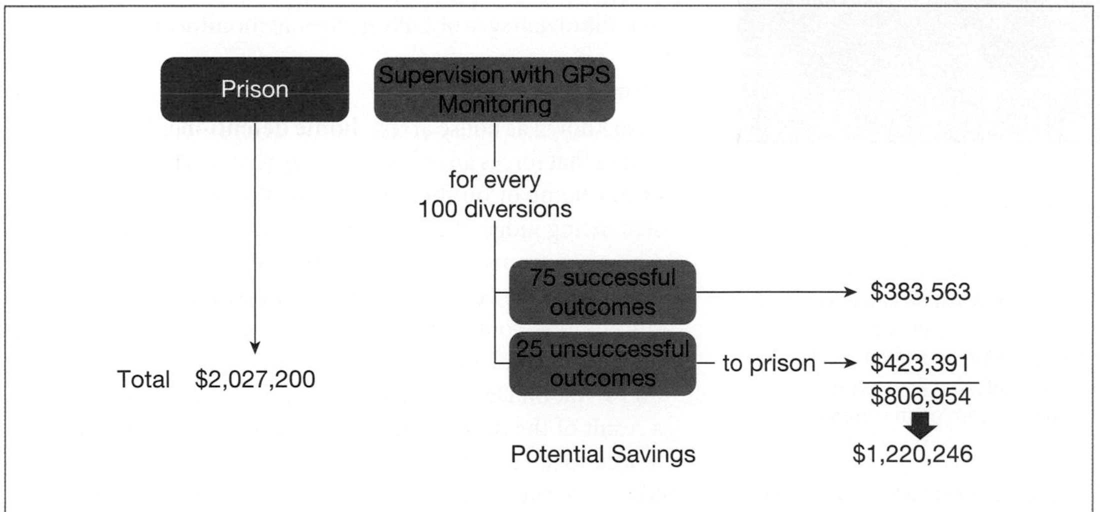

SOURCE: Office of Program Policy Analysis and Governmental Accountability. (2010). *Intermediate sanctions for non-violent offenders could produce savings.* Tallahassee, FL: Author.

NOTE: Unsuccessful exits are program outcomes that denote non-compliance with program requirements and result in termination from the program. For the purpose of estimating cost savings in this report, all offenders that unsuccessfully exit are assumed to be sent to prison.

CROSS-NATIONAL PERSPECTIVE 6.1

Electronic Monitoring in Sweden

In Sweden, approximately 13,000 people are under some type of noncustodial care, compared with only 5,000 who are sentenced to prison. Probation is the most common form of noncustodial care, but offenders may be sentenced to intensive supervision with electronic monitoring.

An offender may serve the sentence at home rather than in a correctional facility while under intensive supervision with electronic monitoring. In order to qualify, the offender must submit an application for electronic monitoring and have been sentenced to less than 2 months in prison. A local probation authority reviews the applications submitted and decides whether or not to recommend intensive supervision with electronic monitoring. Once approved, a transmitter is fastened around the offender's ankle and sends signals to a receiver attached to the telephone line in the offender's home. A computer receives these signals and compares these signals with activities planned and registered by a probation officer. The probation officer prepares a timetable, which includes the exact time an offender may leave for work and return to his or her residence. Other activities may be allowed, such as community service programs or treatment programs, but must be preplanned as well. Should the offender fail to follow the timetable set by the probation officer, an alarm is triggered, and the offender may be subject to serve the remainder of the sentence in prison.

Offenders sentenced to intensive supervision with electronic monitoring must meet certain criteria, which include a residence equipped with electricity and phone line, being employed or a student, participating in rehabilitation programs, and remaining drug and alcohol free. If employed, a portion of the offender's income goes into a fund established for crime victims. Offenders are also subject to frequent residence checks and drug tests to ensure compliance with the conditions set by their probation officer.

QUESTION: Do you believe that a similar intensive supervision with electronic monitoring program would be effective in your area? Why or why not?

SOURCE: Swedish Prison and Probation Service. (2008). *Kontakt.* Stockholm: Author.

Robert Hanser

■ PHOTO 6.4 **The equipment in this photo is used for GPS tracking. In some cases, equipment has specialized functions, such as the emission of alarms or noises that can be sounded by a community supervision officer from a distance. When an offender cannot be found physically or when he or she enters a restricted or off-limits area, an alarm can be emitted by the probation officer merely pushing a button, even from a distance of several miles. The noise can be deafening and serves as a deterrent for most offenders and as a warning to community members.**

be cost prohibitive for smaller, less affluent agencies. Because of this, only a small minority of offenders are tracked by GPS technology when compared with the entire offender population under community supervision. Nevertheless, when used in a strategic manner, this feature does provide an extra level of maintenance for those offenders where it is deemed appropriate. Table 6.3 provides a comparison of some advantages and disadvantages of GPS electronic monitoring.

Home Detention

Also known as house arrest, **home detention** is the mandated action that forces an offender to stay within the confines of his or her home or on the property until a time specified by the sentencing judge. It is the Father of Modern Science, Galileo, who provides an example of the first offender placed on home detention; after he proposed that the earth rotated around the sun, he was confined to his villa by the Roman Inquisition until his death. However, it wasn't until the late twentieth century's War on Drugs that home detention gained notoriety. As a result of the massive numbers of drug offenders being sentenced to jail or prison, officials were seeking an alternative to supervision that would allow an offender to be supervised prior to trial or just before being placed into a residential treatment facility.

Home detention: The mandated action that forces an offender to stay within the confines of his or her home for a specified time.

Many offenders sentenced to home confinement are required to complete community service and pay a host of fines, fees, and victim restitutions, while others are forced to wear electronic monitors or other detection devices to ensure that they are remaining in their residence during the specified time. In many cases, home detention is used for offenders during the pretrial phase or just

■ **Table 6.3: Advantages and Disadvantages of GPS Electronic Monitoring**

	Advantages	Disadvantages
Active GPS systems	• Seek to alleviate prison overcrowding • Immediate response capability • Data reporting in near-real time	• High daily cost • Reliance on wireless data service coverage • Labor intensive • Require immediate agency response • Greater agency liability • Tracing device size and weight
Passive GPS systems	• Small, lightweight device • Can be independent of wireless data services • Lower daily cost • Less labor intensive	• "After-the-fact" tracking data • No immediate notification of zone violations

SOURCE: *Tracking sex offenders with modern technology: Implications and practical uses with law enforcement.* (2008). Alexandria, VA: International Association for Chiefs of Police.

prior to an offender being let out of prison on a work or educational release program. If an offender leaves his or her residence without permission or against the policies set forth, the offender is seen as having technically violated the conditions of his or her supervision (Government Accounting Office, 1990). As we have seen in the Chapter 6 vignette, home detention can provide sufficient deterrence for some offenders who may contemplate returning to crime. Rather than seeing this type of sanction as being easy on the offender, it is best to view it as commensurate with the type of crime that was committed.

Video Link
Judge Marissa Alexander Released to House Arrest

Day Reporting Centers

Day reporting centers are treatment facilities to which offenders are required to report, usually on a daily basis. These facilities tend to offer a variety of services, including drug counseling, vocational assistance, life skills development, and so forth. The offenders assigned to day reporting centers are generally one of two types: those placed on early release from a period of incarceration or those on some form of heightened probation supervision. For those released early from a jail or prison term, the day reporting center represents a gradual transition into the community during which they are supervised throughout the process.

Day reporting centers: Treatment facilities to which offenders are required to report, usually on a daily basis.

The advantage of day reporting centers is that they do not require the use of bed space and therefore save counties and states a substantial portion of the cost in maintaining offenders in their custody (see Figure 6.2). Focus Topic 6.2 provides a very good example of a day reporting center, this one operated by Hampden County, Massachusetts. This example demonstrates the various facets of day reporting centers and also dovetails well with future discussions in this text regarding police and community corrections partnerships for offender treatment. The Hampden County facility is operated by that county's sheriff's department and therefore provides a strong integration of law enforcement efforts and those of community supervision agencies.

Day reporting centers are similar to residential treatment facilities except that offenders are not required to stay overnight. In some jurisdictions, the regimen of the day reporting center is designed so that offenders attend 8- to 10-hour intervention and treatment classes. This is an important element of the day reporting center since it provides added human supervision. The implementation of creative and versatile forms of human supervision serves to optimize both treatment and security characteristics of offender supervision, and day reporting centers facilitate this concept. Indeed, one staff person conducting some form of instruction class (e.g., a life skills class, a psychoeducational class on effective communication, or perhaps a parenting class) can essentially watch over several offenders at the same time. Further, the offender's time is spent in prosocial activities with little opportunity to engage in

Prison Tour Video: Day Reporting Centers. Running a day reporting center offers many opportunities and challenges for practitioners. Watch a discussion about day reporting centers and recidivism.

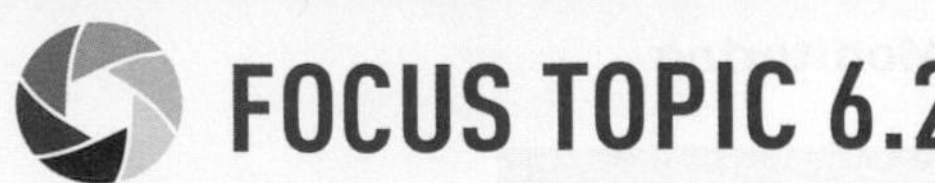

FOCUS TOPIC 6.2

An Example of a Day Reporting Center

The Hampden County Day Reporting Center: Three Years' Success in Supervising Sentenced Individuals in the Community

In Massachusetts, the county correctional system incarcerates both those in pretrial detention and those sentenced to terms of 2 1/2 years or less for crimes such as breaking and entering, larceny, driving while intoxicated, and drug possession. Thus, each county facility is both a jail for pretrial detainees and a house of correction for sentenced individuals. The sheriff of each county, an elected official, is the administrator of the jail and house of correction.

Sheriff Michael J. Ashe Jr. has been sheriff of Hampden County for over 40 years and holds a master's degree in social work. During this tenure, he has overseen the Correction Center in Springfield, Massachusetts, for more than 25 years. In October 1986, faced with worsening overcrowding, Ashe instituted what the Crime and Justice Institute refers to as the first day reporting center in the nation.

Program Description

The Hampden County day reporting center supervises inmates who are within 4 months of release and who live at home, work, and take part in positive activities in the community. Participants also are monitored randomly by "community officers." Under this system, each participant is contacted between 50 and 80 times per week.

Day reporting center participants meet with their counselors at the beginning of each week to chart out a schedule of work and attendance at positive community activities. They are responsible for following this schedule to the letter.

It is important to note that the Hampden County day reporting center is not a "house arrest" program; participants spend a good deal of time out of their homes, reentering the community. Day reporting is also not a diversion program. Sheriff Ashe was concerned that, if used as a diversion program, day reporting would just "widen the net" so that offenders who would not have otherwise gone to jail would be sentenced to day reporting.

Day reporting participants are still on sentence, in the custody of the sheriff, and have earned their way into the day reporting program by positive behavior and program participation. All have been assessed for entrance into the program based on the likelihood of their being accountable for their behavior in the community.

Program Success

It is estimated that well over 7,000 individuals have participated in the day reporting center program during the past decade, and, because of the program's close supervision, none have committed a violent crime in the community while in the program. On the Hampden County Sheriff's Department website, Sheriff Ashe provides notes on reentry and public safety, referring to a 2007 study of released inmates from the county. This study observed offender recidivism during the 12 months that followed their release. Only 12.6% of those released from day reporting were incarcerated again for a new crime, compared with 20.7% of those released from higher security institutions. This means those who were released and did not go through a program for reentry recidivated at a rate that was 64% higher than those released from the day reporting center.

This data has resulted in widespread recognition and praise for Hampden County and Sheriff Ashe and serves as the basis of a document titled *Guiding Principles of Best Correctional Policy and Practice, as Developed by the Hampden County Model, 1975–2013.*

Benefits

Advantages of the day reporting center to the department are numerous. Cell and bed spaces are saved for those who need them the most. Costs of supervising participants in the day reporting program are considerably less than 24-hour lockup. Day reporting is also the ultimate "carrot" in their institutional incentive-based program participation philosophy; inmates who behave well in jail can serve the end of their sentences at home.

Also, individuals who earn the opportunity for home and community participation at the end of their sentences have an improved chance of successful community reentry. When sentences are a continuum of earned lesser sanctions, the final step to productive and positive community living is much easier than when inmates are released from a higher-security setting. Day reporting also benefits the community because participants work, pay taxes, and perform community service.

By Richard J. McCarthy, Public Information Officer, Hampden County, MA, Sheriff's Department.

SOURCE: National Institute of Corrections. (2006). *The Hampden County day reporting center: Three years' success in supervising sentenced individuals in the community.* Washington, DC: Author.

any form of undetected criminal activity. Thus, day reporting centers enhance security processes while filling up the leisure times in an offender's day or evening with activities that are constructive and beneficial to the offender and to society; little time is left for distractions or unregulated activity.

■ **Figure 6.2: Day Reporting Centers Are Less Costly Than Prison**

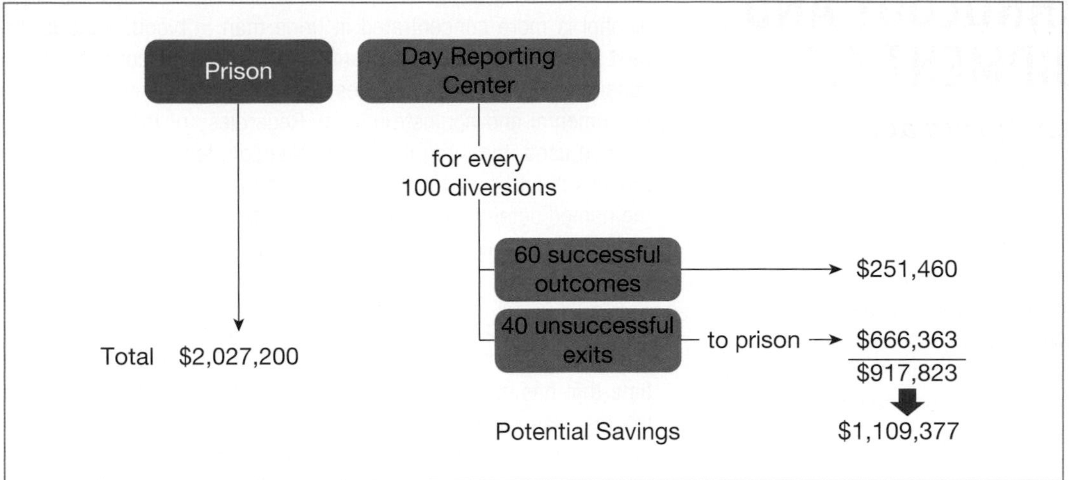

SOURCE: Office of Program Policy Analysis and Governmental Accountability. (2010). *Intermediate sanctions for non-violent offenders could produce savings.* Tallahassee, FL: Author.

NOTE: Successful completions in substance abuse treatment programs are used as a proxy for successful completions in the day reporting program. Unsuccessful exits are program outcomes that denote noncompliance with program requirements and result in termination from the program. For the purpose of estimating cost savings in this report, all offenders that unsuccessfully exit are assumed to be sent to prison.

Urine testing: Using urine samples to determine if an offender has been using drugs.

Blood testing: Using blood samples to determine if an offender has been using drugs.

METHODS OF ENSURING COMPLIANCE

Detecting Drug Use Among Offenders

The detection of offender drug use is accomplished through a number of testing procedures that use a variety of body samples. The most common samples are obtained from the offender's urine, blood, hair, sweat, or saliva. According to Robinson and Jones (2000), urine testing is the most cost-effective, reliable, and widely used drug testing procedure. Nevertheless, it is important that staff understand the drug use demographics of their own region or jurisdiction so that they can determine the most appropriate drug testing strategy to employ. This will vary according to the type of drug use that is most common in the region as well as other considerations. In general, there are five sources from which samples are drawn for drug testing. The descriptions of these sources are taken from the U.S. government document written by Robinson and Jones and published by the Office of Justice Programs. These sources are as follows:

1. **Urine testing:** Due to price and accuracy of the testing process, urinalysis is considered the most suitable method by drug courts and most criminal justice agencies for detecting the presence of illegal substances.
2. **Blood testing:** Blood tests can provide discrete information regarding the degree of an individual's impairment, but the invasiveness of the procedure and the potential danger of infection make blood testing inappropriate for drug court programs (p. 3).

Robert Hanser

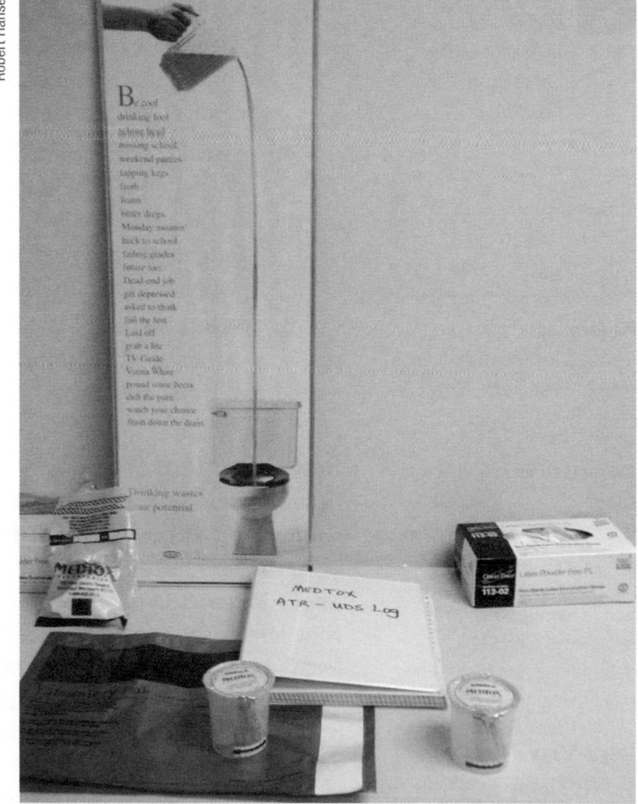

■ PHOTO 6.5 Drug testing equipment is routinely used by probation and parole officers as well as treatment specialists who work with drug courts and residential treatment programs.

TECHNOLOGY AND EQUIPMENT 6.1

Breathalyzers and Urine Tests

Breathalyzers, which are being used with considerable frequency and at a relatively minimal cost, can be particularly useful in detecting the presence and amount of alcohol that may not otherwise be detected through random urinalysis because of alcohol's relatively short life span in the human system. Breathalyzers can therefore be a very effective and relatively low-cost component of a drug court drug testing program when used in conjunction with urine testing for other substances. The test must be administered by breath alcohol technicians who are trained in the use and interpretation of breath alcohol results. Local drug court officials may wish to contact their local law enforcement agencies regarding the use of breathalyzers in their local jurisdiction for requirements such as calibration settings, interpretation of test results, and the expertise available to administer and/or provide training on breathalyzer testing.

Urine testing is also an accurate and reliable method for detecting the presence of alcohol if performed within the relatively short period following ingestion in which it can be detected. Because alcohol is more concentrated in urine than in blood, urine is the best specimen to use if one wants to determine if alcohol has been consumed. Generally, urine testing methods fall into two types: instrumental and noninstrumental. Regardless of the drug testing method used, the integrity of the collection, testing, and reporting process must be maintained to ensure that the specimen is from the named defendant, to detect adulteration, and to ensure that no contaminants have been introduced that would affect the validity of the results.

Evidence of drug use may be present in the urine in the form of the parent drug and/or metabolites. Determination of the length of time that has elapsed between the time of ingestion and the time the test was conducted depends upon the rate at which the body metabolizes and eliminates the drug, physical characteristics of the individual's metabolism, and the sensitivity of the testing procedure. The time frame also can vary depending on the duration of abuse (long-term heavy doses or infrequent use), the amount of the daily dosage, and the route of administration (oral, injected, smoked, or inhaled).

SOURCE: Office of Justice Programs Drug Court Clearinghouse. (2003). *Drug testing in a drug court environment: Common issues to address.* Washington, DC: U.S. Department of Justice.

Video Link
Parole and Probation Office Stays Busy With Drug Testing

3. **Hair testing:** The introduction of new, powerful instruments for hair analysis has increased interest in hair testing. Despite its increased popularity among agencies, caution should be used because hair analysis is subject to potential external contamination. Indeed, there are indications that hair analysis can produce tainted results, depending on the type of hair as well as the type of drug that is analyzed.
4. **Sweat testing:** Sweat samples, which are obtained from patches that can be placed on a person for a number of days, have the advantages of a longer time frame for detection and the fact that they are difficult to adulterate. They do not, however, provide a correlation regarding the degree of impairment, and they are subject to individual differences in sweat production (p. 3).
5. **Saliva testing:** Saliva samples permit a correlation with the degree of impairment and can be easily obtained. They are, however, subject to contamination from smoking or other substances (p. 3).

Hair testing: Using hair samples to determine if an offender has been using drugs.

Sweat testing: Using samples of sweat excretion to determine if an offender has been using drugs.

Saliva testing: Using samples of saliva to determine if an offender has been using drugs.

Megan's laws: Term for legislation that mandates a public notification process when sex offenders are released into the community.

Sex Offenders

Currently, every state has some type of notification process when sex offenders are released into the community. This is true whether the sex offender is on probation (having not been incarcerated) or has been released on parole (after serving a prison term). These requirements commonly fall under **Megan's laws**, which were passed as a result of the brutal rape and murder of a 7-year-old New Jersey girl named Megan Kanka. The victim's parents pushed for legislation in the state of New Jersey to mandate reporting of sex offenders who are released into the community, and in 1994 New Jersey was the first state to pass such legislation. The following year, the federal government passed similar legislative requirements. Since that time, other states have followed suit, with these laws often being informally referred to as Megan's laws out of respect for the crime victim who served as the catalyst for this reporting requirement.

The Center for Sex Offender Management (CSOM) is operated by the U.S. Department of Justice and is perhaps the leading national warehouse for training on sex offender–related issues. This organization is a federally operated program that provides a vast array of curricula that are available to the general public and are ideal for community training. The CSOM (2008) notes that in addition to the typical notification programs that exist throughout the United States, there are many occasions where public agencies (such as police, prosecutors, and community supervision agencies) are required to provide specific information pertaining to individual sex offenders. This is conducted through a variety of means, including door-to-door citizen notification, public meetings, and the distribution of written and printed notices.

Further, the CSOM notes that as more comprehensive and collaborative approaches to the management of sex offenders emerge, community members, victims, the victim's family, the offender's family, and others are invited to become partners in the sex offender management process. It is against this backdrop that we emphasize the following point made by the CSOM (2008):

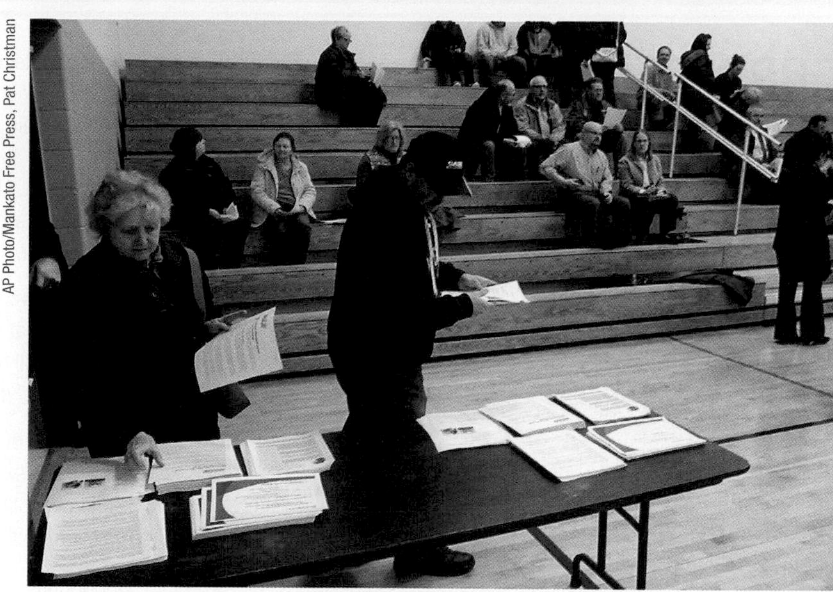
AP Photo/Mankato Free Press, Pat Christman

■ PHOTO 6.6 Some community supervision agencies provide awareness campaigns to community members. In this case, persons are being notified about sex offenders in their area as well as the process involved in supervising these offenders.

> As knowledge about the extensive occurrence of sexual assault becomes more widespread, the agencies responsible for sex offender management are beginning to recognize that community notification meetings and interactions with individual community members become opportunities to engage in sexual abuse prevention activities; to connect sexual assault victims with services; and, generally, to advance a community's ability to understand and protect itself from sexual abuse and its trauma. (p. 1)

Naturally, the ability of agencies to collaborate with community members will be specific to that region or location, as some areas are more amenable to such forms of notification and offender tracking than others. Such agency-community programs require that staff exercise sensitivity to the context and needs of individuals, families, and communities involved (CSOM, 2008). This process, while representing a very important community education component, also requires a great deal of care since victim reactions can be quite varied.

Audio Link
Megan's Law and Personal Choices

Agency-community programs generally consist of two parts. First is the notification process by which the community is made aware of the existence of a sex offender. Second is the community's involvement in ensuring that the offender is monitored by human observation, interaction, and general awareness. This provides a strong preventative component for the offender and also ensures that other potential victims are vigilant regarding the possible threat that exists within their community. These programs must also educate community members on the dynamics of sex offending and the likelihood of recidivism. For instance, in most cases, sex offenders do not recidivate; the majority of all sex offenses are actually not committed by an offender with a prior sex-offending history. This is important for community members to understand because it will increase the efficacy of reintegrative approaches while improving overall supervision of the offender.

INTERMEDIATE SANCTIONS IN DIFFERENT STATES

This section will describe a series of programs offered in a variety of states around the nation. It is interesting to see that the use and application of intermediate sanctions can vary quite considerably by the type of offender being supervised, the type of program delivery, and the particular state that is examined. The key point in showcasing these various programs is to illustrate the utility of intermediate sanctions and the flexibility associated with their implementation. This is an important

CORRECTIONS AND THE LAW 6.1

Smith v. Doe *(2003) and the Constitutionality of Sex Offender Notification Laws*

The Supreme Court has given states the green light to continue posting the names and pictures of convicted sex offenders on the Internet, and justices have rejected attempts by sex offenders to prove they are no longer dangerous.

At issue is whether such laws amount to a second punishment for those already convicted for their crimes and whether the laws violate an offender's due process rights. The Court has so far upheld the right of state legislatures to impose registries on sex offenders.

Every state has a so-called Megan's law, named after Megan Kanka, a 7-year-old New Jersey girl kidnapped, raped, and murdered by a twice-convicted sex offender who lived across the street. These laws require convicted sex offenders and certain other types of felons released from prison to register with local authorities. Such information is typically available to the public through print and Internet sources.

In ***Smith v. Doe*** (2003), the question was whether a state law violated the constitutional guarantee against punishment ex post facto, or after the fact. One man, referred to as "John Doe," was convicted of abusing his young daughter, and the other man in the case had abused a 14-year-old girl. Both men were released in 1990, before the state passed its sex offender registration law. They argued they had served their sentences and wanted to put their crimes behind them.

The Court decided the state legislature intended the law to be regulatory, not punitive in nature. Writing for a 6-3 majority, Justice Anthony Kennedy said, "Our system does not treat dissemination of truthful information in furtherance of legitimate governmental objection as punishment." He also noted, "The purpose and the principal effect of notification are to inform the public for its own safety, not to humiliate the offender."

In her dissent, Justice Ruth Bader Ginsburg disagreed. "However plain it may be that a former sex offender currently poses no threat of recidivism, he will remain subject to long-term monitoring and inescapable humiliation," she said.

Supporters of these registration laws say citizens deserve to know if convicted sex offenders are living in their neighborhoods and argue registration laws are not unfair since the convictions are already a matter of public record.

Opponents of the law call it a "government-imposed stigma" that prevents those who deserve to move on with their lives from doing so after serving their time. They say such laws represent an overly intrusive invasion of privacy since other criminal records are not subject to such readily available public scrutiny.

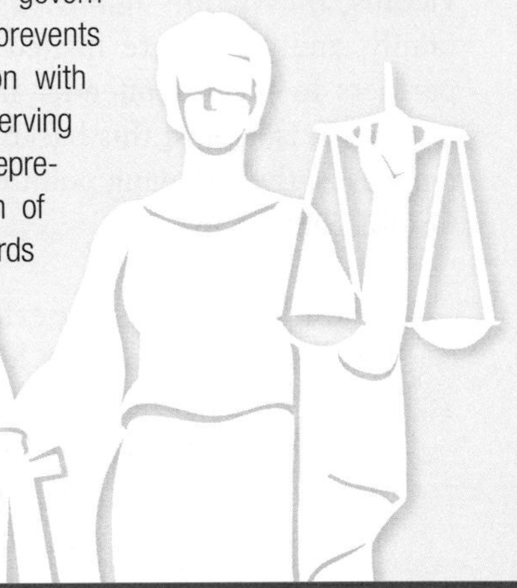

SOURCE: Adapted from Mears, B. (2003). *Supreme Court upholds sex offender registration laws.*

selling point for the increased use of intermediate sanctions since it gives agencies a set of diverse responses that address a wide array of challenges. We now turn our attention to a number of different programs from various states. The write-ups for these programs have been adapted from the public domain document titled *NIC Focus: Intermediate Sanctions,* a government publication released by the National Institute of Corrections (McGarry, 1990).

Kansas: Home Surveillance Program

The Sedgwick County Community Corrections Home Surveillance Program (HSP) provides an additional restrictive level of intensive supervision in the community for identified high-risk offenders. This house-arrest program represents the most intensive supervision currently available short of placement in the residential programs. The county's residential center provides in-house, 24-hour supervision and could be compared to a work release facility. It offers residents self-help classes during their off-work hours. Because the residential center is usually full, the HSP becomes an even more important part of the agency's range of sanctions. Clients are sentenced to the HSP by the court, if recommended by community corrections evaluators, or are placed there after their graduation from the residential center or by other case managers who have experienced difficulty with them during intensive supervision.

The daily schedule at the HSP is revealed to the offender prior to intake acceptance. All clients must agree to the HSP rules and regulations, which are explained in detail. Clients are required to keep a daily itinerary or agenda of their activities. They must sign out from their residence, stating where they are going and for what reason, and they must sign in upon their return. Each daily agenda is approved by the case manager. Offenders are also required to keep other records, such as

Alcoholics Anonymous attendance forms and, in some cases, job search forms. Every client also must submit to a minimum of one urinalysis/drug screen or breath analysis per week.

Offender contacts are preferably made at the place of residence, place of employment, or other field site. Staff conduct a minimum of four personal field contacts per week for each client, and daily contacts are attempted as time permits. Many contacts are made during the evening, usually after 10 p.m. because all clients have a 10 p.m. curfew. The HSP has two levels. Level I restricts clients to their homes with the exception of visits to their doctors or attorneys, which must be approved by the case manager. Clients who comply with Level I rules for 14 days progress to Level II, where they are allowed four 4-hour furloughs per week away from their residence, plus two 8-hour furloughs per week on their days off. All furloughs must be approved by the case manager. At the end of a 90-day period, staff review the case to decide whether the client will be placed on regular supervision. Clients not in full compliance or reasonably close to it will remain in the HSP.

Many offenders are placed in the program because they have failed to comply with the basic conditions of probation, such as reporting to their case manager and making regular payments on their court obligation. Frequent contacts in the HSP increase understanding of each client's needs and encourage clients to make their regular monthly payments. Because all HSP clients are considered high risk to some degree, staff use a two-way portable radio assigned to the sheriff's channel. The radio provides a direct link to the dispatcher, who can summon any services that may be needed in the event of a field emergency or a threat to the staff. In addition, HSP clients use a voice pager to contact the staff when necessary. The pager has proved to be an invaluable means of communication since staff members are usually in a vehicle while on duty.

The HSP seems to be effective because staff get to know clients and their habits in a very short time and frequent contacts help build rapport between clients and staff quickly. In fact, clients have requested to stay in the program when it was time for their discharge. The cost of home surveillance obviously exceeds the cost of regular field services supervision. However, it is a more economical alternative than placement in a residential program or prison. In the future, the department may expand the HSP without increasing the number of staff by adding electronic monitoring devices for higher-risk clients.

Missouri: A Control and Intervention Strategy for Technical Parole Violators

In an effort to effectively manage its offender population, the Missouri Department of Corrections has focused on a group that represents a significant number of prison commitments: technical parole violators. The department found that a large number of recommitments were offenders whose parole was revoked for technical violations rather than new convictions. Realizing that many of these violators were being returned to prison due to their inability to address alcohol and drug problems, the department, in concert with the Board of Probation and Parole, instituted a new method of dealing with them.

The program's treatment center is designed for technical parole violators whose behavior has demonstrated their need for control and intervention. This facility offers more structure than other intermediate sanctions, such as intensive supervision, house arrest, or traditional halfway house placement, because offenders are confined to the facility with no passes during their 90-day stay. Offenders are screened by local field staff in conjunction with a coordinator from the facility to determine eligibility. Offenders must be technical violators who have not been charged with new law violations.

Further, it must be demonstrated that traditional strategies have been implemented and the offender has been unresponsive to them. Finally, the violation must be serious enough to warrant revocation and commitment to the Department of Corrections. This program facility is the final stop before recommitment to prison. Because the offenders in this program have been unable to remain on supervision within the community, they are placed on a vigorous treatment schedule. This program consists of three phases dedicated to building offender responsibility through a cognitive approach in a structured, didactic, interactional, and confrontational manner. The program follows a logical progression from problem awareness to skill building to relapse prevention and follow-up. The model relies on an Alcoholics Anonymous (AA) methodology, with study and work groups that enhance the daily education and therapy classes. Counseling groups help violators apply the class material to their own needs.

APPLIED THEORY 6.1

Routine Activity Theory as Applied to Community Supervision

For the most part, the tenets of routine activity theory devised by Cohen and Felson (1979) reflect the general premise behind most intermediate sanctions. Cullen and Agnew (2006) provide a clear and effective synopsis of this theory in the following statement:

> Crime occurs when there is an intersection in time and space of a motivated offender, an attractive target, and a lack of capable guardianship. People's daily routine activities affect the likelihood they will be an attractive target and will encounter an offender in a situation where no effective guardianship is present. (p. 7)

Intermediate sanctions work to eliminate the likelihood that offenders will not have effective guardianship. In other words, an effective guardian will protect potential victims. This guardian is the use of surveillance devices and supervision programs utilized by community supervision agencies. Further, when agencies keep the community informed and when the community is encouraged to volunteer and partner with the agency, an additional layer of oversight is added to the offender's supervision.

When the offender is released into the community, members of an informed and involved community are able to modify their routines to reduce the likelihood of victimization. Further, the offender is deterred from likely recidivism due to the understanding that he or she is being supervised by a number of different persons and through a variety of potential mechanisms. Thus, heightened community vigilance and increased controls placed on the offender work to augment one another, providing an ethereal prison, of a sort, when implemented correctly.

During this process, it is hoped that the offender learns to modify his or her own activities. While under supervision, many are restricted from certain areas of the community (an alcoholic may be restricted from bars and nightclubs, a sex offender may be restricted from approaching an elementary school, and so forth, as suggested in Chapter 5). Over time, graduated sanctions are lessened as the offender demonstrates that he or she is able to maintain his or her own behavior within the constraints of prosocial behavior. It is in this way that the reinforcement of routine activities theory leads to a form of internal social learning that is operantly reinforced upon the offender whether he or she realizes it or not.

SOURCES: Cullen, F. T., & Agnew, R. (2006). *Criminological theory: Past to present* (3rd ed.). Los Angeles, CA: Roxbury; Lilly, J. R., Cullen, F. T., & Ball, R. A. (2007). *Criminological theory: Context and consequences* (4th ed.). Thousand Oaks, CA: Sage.

Phase I, which lasts 3 weeks, consists of intake, assessment, orientation, and intensive classes on the disease concept of chemical dependency. This work lays a foundation for violators to begin problem solving, using the tools furnished by AA and the 12-step recovery process. The skills violators learn through this general approach can be applied to their lives in the community, whether they have found chemicals to be a way of life or a component of an overall criminal lifestyle. Phase II makes up the next 6 weeks of the program. One topic is covered each week to bring about meaningful skill development. Topics include problem solving, understanding emotions, managing stress, assertiveness, relapse prevention, and the role of the family and others. The final 4 weeks, designated as Phase III, focus on vocational and job readiness, along with follow-up and placement planning sessions to provide the violator with a practical application of the techniques learned previously. All of these sessions are conducted by department staff, including psychologists, parole officers, and caseworkers. Custody personnel also receive training to help them adapt to the treatment approach as opposed to the traditional prison milieu.

Tennessee: GPS Tracking of Sex Offenders

In 2007, the state of Tennessee published an evaluation of its experience utilizing GPS tracking of sex offenders. This detailed report provided a multifaceted examination that produced some fairly surprising results. One of the beneficial findings was that community supervision officers were better able to establish inclusion zones, or where the offender must be located during specified time periods, such as work or home, during certain times of the day or evening. Further, GPS tracking aided in monitoring exclusion zones, or places where the offender was not permitted to enter. Thus, the use of GPS tracking aided the overall supervision quality and monitoring of the offender. However, these same types of monitoring are able to be conducted using other methods. A key distinction with GPS tracking is the fact that it allows officers to see and investigate specific patterns of activity and then follow up on frequently visited locations or suspicious areas. Further, it was held by most officers that GPS tracking seemed to deter sex offenders from engaging in other forms of deviant or criminal activity, simply due to the fact that these offenders were cognizant of the monitoring that they were under. In addition, when offenders did violate their community supervision requirements, officers were more likely to be able to determine the specific violation that occurred. Thus, the overall supervision ability was enhanced, and the ability to pinpoint specific offense behavior improved the effectiveness of officers who sought to revoke or modify community supervision parameters.

Moreover, GPS tracking helped to cultivate better partnerships between local law enforcement agencies since this tool helped to more accurately confirm or eliminate allegations of potential criminal activity. This serves as an aid to both community supervision agencies and law enforcement agencies, as accuracy in detection allows for better allocation of resources. Law enforcement officers are also provided an added benefit when attempting to resolve cases in their jurisdiction. Likewise, GPS data provide officers with information when investigating and verifying citizen claims of inappropriate offender activity. This function would likely aid in further cementing partnerships between the agency and the wider community, a primary goal noted throughout this text.

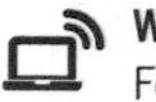

Web Link
For Some Felons, a Better Chance to Break the Reentry Cycle

However, GPS tracking has several limitations or challenges, both in implementation and in maintenance of the program. Research does indicate that lower-risk offenders who are under strict levels of supervision recidivate more frequently and have overall higher recidivism rates than similar offenders supervised at less stringent levels (Tennessee Board of Probation and Parole, 2007). Much of this recidivism is thought to be due to the negative impact on offender motivation and the contrast between increased supervision and positive, reintegrative efforts (Hanser, 2007).

In addition, evaluative research by Middle Tennessee State University (MTSU, 2007) on behalf of the Tennessee Board of Probation and Parole produced statistically significant descriptive and demographic results using subjects from both treatment and control groups. Briefly, the treatment group was administered GPS tracking while the control group was given some form of supervision that did not include GPS tracking. This allowed the evaluators to determine the impact of the GPS tracking itself since other aspects of the supervision sentence were kept roughly equal or comparable between the groups. The evaluative research by MTSU found that offenders younger than 40 years old were more likely to commit new offenses (though not necessarily sex offenses) while under GPS supervision than were offenders over 40 years old. In addition, it was found that offenders between 30 and 40 years old were statistically more likely to gain new criminal charges than were offenders in any other 10-year age category investigated. Thus, it is clear that this group is perhaps most in need of enhanced supervision. Further, offenders who had less than a high school education were more likely to commit a new offense than were those who had a background that included high school or higher levels of educational attainment.

The MTSU study clearly provides a very detailed picture of the implementation of GPS tracking. This is important because this intermediate sanction is hailed as one of the most modern and sophisticated innovations. While it certainly has its place and while it does indeed contribute to the range of supervision strategies, it has pitfalls that agencies must consider. Often, the balance between the pros and cons can be delicate when considering intermediate sanctions, and the use of GPS technology is no different.

CONCLUSION

This chapter has provided an overview of several types of intermediate sanctions that are used around the country. Specific examples have been offered to demonstrate the variety of sanctions that exist and how they are utilized. The flexibility of intermediate sanctions gives community supervision agencies a range of potential responses to offender criminal behavior. These responses fall along a continuum according to the amount of liberty that is denied the offender. These penalties vary by level of punitiveness to allow community supervision agencies to calibrate the offender's punishment with the severity of the specific offense committed and/or the offender's tendency toward recidivism. In addition, intermediate sanctions help to connect the supervision process with the treatment process. Various intermediate sanctions, such as community service and the payment of fines, create a system of restoration, while the use of flexible supervision schemes, such as electronic monitoring and GPS tracking, allows the offender to engage in employment activities.

Other programs, such as day reporting centers, ease the transition of offenders from incarceration to community membership and provide a series of constructive activities to ensure that the offender remains on task with respect to his or her reintegration process. Each of these sanctions can be used in conjunction with others to further augment the supervision process, all the while being less expensive and more productive than a prison term.

Finally, as has been the case throughout this text, the use of community partnerships is again emphasized. In this case, the community partnership aspect comes in the form of citizens monitoring the offender, who is tasked with completing various activities to fulfill his or her sentence. The use of human supervision is once more shown to be important, and intermediate sanctions are well suited to citizen involvement when ensuring offender compliance. Thus, intermediate sanctions provide an external incentive for offenders to complete their regimen within the community. These sanctions, when administered in a social vacuum, would not be expected to be effective. But when utilized against a backdrop of community involvement, agency collaboration, and solid case management processes, intermediate sanctions serve as interlocking supervision mechanisms that improve offender reintegration.

Want a better grade?

Get the tools you need to sharpen your study skills. Access practice quizzes, eFlashcards, video, and multimedia at edge.sagepub.com/hanser2e

SAGE edge™

DISCUSSION QUESTIONS

1. What is the definition of intermediate sanctions, and why are they important to corrections?
2. What are the various types of intermediate sanctions, and how do they fall within the continuum of sanctions?
3. What means do correctional staff use with substance abusers to ensure compliance?
4. What means do correctional staff use with sex offenders to ensure compliance?
5. How are Kansas, Tennessee, and Missouri taking a different approach to intermediate sanctions?
6. What are the security functions related to intermediate sanctions, and what role does treatment play?
7. How does routine activity theory apply to the use of intermediate sanctions? Explain the tenets of the theory, and provide at least one specific example of how the use of intermediate sanctions dovetails with this theory.

SAGE edge™ **Test your understanding of chapter content. Take the practice quiz.**

KEY TERMS

Blood testing, 139

Day reporting centers, 137

Electronic monitoring, 134

Hair testing, 140

Home detention, 136

Intensive supervision probation (ISP), 134

Intermediate sanctions, 130

Megan's laws, 140

Saliva testing, 140

Sweat testing, 140

Urine testing, 139

SAGE edge™ **Review key terms with eFlashcards.**

APPLIED EXERCISE 6.1

Read each of the case scenarios below, and select the type of intermediate sanction that you think is best suited for each offender. The list of possible sanctions is provided below. Once you have made your selection, write a 50- to 150-word essay for each scenario that explains why you chose a particular intermediate sanction or combination of sanctions.

Students should remember that intermediate sanctions operate on a continuum, and they will need to ensure that the sanction they choose is proportional to the offense. Similarly, students should not overpredict the likelihood of an individual committing a future crime. Total word count for this assignment is approximately 500 to 1,500 words.

Grading Rubric (This assignment is worth a maximum total of 100 points.)

1. Student provides a reasonable match between scenario and intermediate sanction(s). (Each match is worth 3 points.)
2. Student provides adequate justification for each match between scenario and intermediate sanction(s). (Each essay justification is worth 7 points.)

Applied Exercise Case Scenarios:

SCENARIO #1: A male juvenile who constantly sneaks out of the house despite his parents' attempts to prevent him. He leaves home at night to meet friends, use drugs, and commit acts of vandalism.

SCENARIO #2: A female offender who "keyed" the car of a neighbor who kept parking on the curb nearest to her own side of the street.

SCENARIO #3: A male delivery driver who is on community supervision for failing to appear in court for proceedings related to thefts in a neighborhood.

SCENARIO #4: A male gang offender who physically assaulted a man who smarted off to him.

SCENARIO #5: A female drug addict who has been busted for prostitution.

SCENARIO #6: A young male who has been committing petty acts of vandalism.

SCENARIO #7: A woman convicted of writing hot checks.

SCENARIO #8: A male teenager who made threatening prank calls to various people in the community.

SCENARIO #9: A middle-aged male who continues to drive while drunk. This is his second DWI offense. He has never been to prison.

SCENARIO #10: Several young people who were playing pranks on elderly people in the community. They egged multiple homes and caused some light property damage to porch lights and other such components of victims' homes.

Applied Exercise Intermediate Sanction Choices:

A. Intensive supervised probation/parole
B. GPS tracking and probation
C. Standard probation and restitution
D. Home detention and electronic monitoring
E. Standard probation and community service
F. Shock incarceration, probation, and community service
G. Restitution
H. Community service
I. Day reporting center and the use of ISP
J. Standard probation
K. Home detention, electronic monitoring, and ISP
L. Drug court with ISP

NOTE: Students may use any of the above options more than once to apply to the scenarios provided. Likewise, there is no requirement that students use every one of the choices presented above.

● WHAT WOULD YOU DO?

You are the executive director of a new day reporting center. You own this center and have invested a significant portion of your personal time and money into this project. You have extensive experience as a case manager but have always dreamed of running your own center. The county-level jail and the state probation/parole department have agreed to send offenders to you, and you have networked well to ensure that you are able to maintain a steady flow of clients. Further still, you recently completed a grant proposal for the Substance Abuse and Mental Health Services Administration (SAMHSA) to receive homeless drug abusers. Thus, money seems to exist to ensure that you are able to maintain your facility.

However, the state department of probation/parole and the local jail facility want to know about the different types of services that you will provide to offenders who visit your facility during the day. You are asked to provide a comprehensive outline of the different services that you plan to offer to clients.

In addition, the SAMHSA informs you that it has a number of requirements for its grant recipients and thus is asking that you explain how you will demonstrate your services are effective in the community. Though the organization does not require a statistical evaluation for the project at this time (not until after a year of funding), it does still want to know how you will ensure that your services are working.

What would you do?

7 FACILITY DESIGN TO MEET SECURITY AND PROGRAMMING NEEDS

THE CHALLENGES OF DESIGN AND SECURITY

Warden Thompson walked the long hallway that ran down the middle of the prison, nodding his head as inmates passed by on their way from breakfast, some of them giving him a friendly "Mornin', warden." Exiting the prison, he made his way to the sidewalk outside and looked up at the new camera that had been installed to observe inmate traffic. The camera was positioned so that it would be able to observe movement in an area of the external part of the building where an alcove existed.

This "nook," as this recess had been informally named by officers and inmates alike, was an area impossible to observe by security from the towers and also difficult to see by officers on the ground from a distance. In order to observe the area, one had to stand right in front of it. This was a poor design feature that was not originally part of the floor plan for the prison. Though this largely brick-and-mortar structure was over 70 years old, it was not designed with many of these types of blind spots. However, a decade ago, an addition to this wing was built, and an oversight led to an area that was not closed in, leaving a gap that was about 20 feet by 10 feet. This space was not observable by security and no cameras had been installed that covered it.

Initially, this was not such a big problem, as it was not an area from which an inmate could attempt any type of escape. It also was not an area where inmates were housed, so they did not have many opportunities to loiter there. However, the inmates began using it as a location to meet each other and potentially exchange contraband. This section of the facility was near a storage area for cleaning supplies; thus some trusty inmates passed near the nook. Trusties tend to have more mobility in prisons and, as a result, can more easily engage in trafficking and trading throughout the facility.

Later that afternoon, Thomson hosted a meeting with several regional executives who were visiting the prison. At the meeting, Thomson showed the administrations a PowerPoint presentation on how the amount of trafficked contraband in the facility had gone down in the past 6 months.

"I believe that we have identified a key weakness in our security and, as a result, our response has led to a 53% reduction in the number of incidents where contraband has been brought into our prison," Thomson stated proudly. "The cameras we installed were hidden from inmate view so we have been able to nab several inmates involved in bringing contraband inside the prison. From there, we were able to get names of outside persons who were smuggling drugs and weapons into the prison and handing them off to inmates. Outside law enforcement have brought charges against those persons."

One of the regional executives asked, "Overall, when we consider the cost of making modern additions rather than rebuilding the entire prison, and when we add these digital security features, are we being cost-effective?"

LEARNING OBJECTIVES:

1. Identify the different types of prison facility designs.
2. List examples of supermax prisons, and identify some constitutional issues that arise with supermax custody.
3. Describe the impact of compliance with the Americans with Disabilities Act on prisons.
4. Discuss the various features that improve the perimeter security of an institution.
5. Evaluate the strategies used to improve internal security.
6. Identify and discuss the importance of auxiliary programs inside the prison and their relationship to physical security.
7. Analyze technological developments in prison security.

Thomson smiled. "I knew one of you would ask that." All of the attendees chuckled. "In truth, the figures are close, but, overall, the total bill is actually a bit less than if we were to open a new facility to replace this one. Our projections show this to be true for operational costs that extend out another 10 years. After that, I am not sure. But currently, our security is tighter than ever and we are running below the costs that would be entailed if we scrapped this facility. For now, that is."

The group discussed all of the factors involved and agreed that the best course of action would be to give the warden a bit more in his budget line to improve features at the facility. Thomson also suggested some ideas that that might offset these costs but could make no guarantees. Ultimately, it was decided that it was cheaper to keep the current facility and that security could continue to be effectively maintained with the additional technological features.

Later that day, Warden Thomson drove home in his truck and thought to himself, *I have another 7 years to retirement. . . . I hope that the next warden of this facility is able to navigate the pushes and pulls of running this facility."*

INTRODUCTION

This chapter provides an overview of various physical prison facilities and their design. Students should understand that the physical design of a prison is very important to the facility's operation. The physical features of the prison serve as its most prominent aspect. In addition, the general organizational climate and operations of the prison are greatly impacted by the physical features of the facility. Historical aspects of prison design will be covered. Even more important and also more unique is the discussion on physical facilities related to prison services (kitchens, workshops, religious sections, recreational areas, etc.). This aspect of the facility can be very important in meeting programming and security requirements.

PRISON FACILITY DESIGNS THROUGHOUT HISTORY

SAGE Journal Article Link
A Social Building? Prison Architecture and Staff-Prisoner Relationships

Prison construction and development have evolved substantially in the United States. This evolution has corresponded with the needs of correctional managers throughout the ages and the availability of resources for those who provided the construction. In other words, the needs of the persons operating a prison have typically determined how the prison was designed. It is clear from Chapters 1 and 2 that prisons have come in a variety of shapes and sizes—from abandoned quarries to old decommissioned ships to huge monolithic structures, culminating in the high-tech designs of today's correctional environment. Prison construction has gone through phases in order to meet social, penal, and managerial objectives and has been affected by what a jurisdiction is willing or able to finance.

Bastille: A fortification in Paris, France, that was a symbol of tyranny and injustice for commoners and political prisoners.

Overall, there have been very few changes in the actual inmate housing unit; the basic human needs for a place to sleep, remove waste, and maintain daily hygiene tend to remain the same. Jail cells, cell blocks, dormitory spaces, and other such units tend to comprise the same basic features. Nevertheless, the form and appeal of these arrangements have changed in terms of cleanliness and/or type of building material used. In this regard, innovations in both health and security issues have advanced the living standards for inmates in the United States.

Wikimedia Commons

■ PHOTO 7.1 The Bastille (French for "little bastion") was originally built as a fortress in the late 1300s but was later used as a prison. The Bastille was a four-story stone structure that had eight closely spaced towers connected by a 15-foot-thick stone wall.

Without question, the history of prison construction has been impacted by the use of certain well-known facilities. These facilities tend to influence construction in other areas of the world, depending on the correctional era and the corresponding needs of prison administrators. We begin our discussion of these facilities by examining the French prison known as the Bastille. This prison was most famous for its eventual demise during the French Revolution in 1789.

The Bastille

The **Bastille** was a fortification built in the city of Paris and was a symbol of tyranny and injustice for both commoners and political prisoners in France. Citizens were held within its confines for an indefinite period without formal accusation or trial. During its early years, the Bastille was a prison for the upper class, mostly nobles who had been charged with treason. Political and religious prisoners were also held within its walls. By the late 1700s, however, this facility was used to house inmates of every class and profession. Ultimately, the Bastille was attacked and captured by a mob that revolted against the king of France, and it was destroyed in 1789.

Originally called the Chastel Saint-Antoine, the Bastille (French for "little bastion") was originally built as a fortress in the late 1300s. It was a four-story stone structure with eight closely spaced towers connected by a 15-foot-thick stone wall. The stone masonry of the fortress was contained within a continuous wall that surrounded Paris. The towers surrounded two enclosed courtyards, and the walls had several windows on each floor

(George, 2008). The Bastille was, in many respects, a miniature castle. This facility was the blueprint for the Western State Penitentiary of Pennsylvania, near Pittsburgh, which was built in the 1830s (George, 2008).

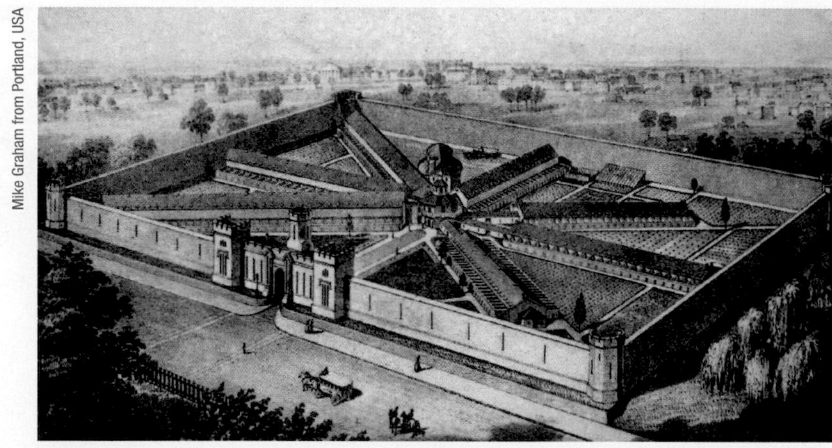

Mike Graham from Portland, USA

■ PHOTO 7.2 The first sketch of Eastern State Penitentiary is shown here. This penitentiary had many modern conveniences that did not exist in most prisons at the time.

Pennsylvania Prisons

As noted in our prior section, Western State Penitentiary, built in Pittsburgh, Pennsylvania, was based on the Bastille blueprint design. This prison was run and operated on the principle of solitary confinement, as was the norm within the Pennsylvania system of corrections. Though Eastern State Penitentiary, also built in Philadelphia, was discussed in detail in Chapter 1, this section will clarify the physical features of that facility, particularly since the Pennsylvania system was so instrumental to early American correctional development. It is important to note again that Eastern State Penitentiary was built as a design improvement to its predecessor, Western State Penitentiary.

The perimeter of Eastern State Penitentiary was rectangular, and it featured cells that were arranged along the outer walls of a cell block. The cell blocks, eight in total, were all connected to a central rotunda, and each cell block jutted out in a radial fashion similar to spokes on a wheel. Thus, cells radiated from a central hub from which the open area of each cell block could be observed.

As noted in Chapter 1, this prison had many modern conveniences that did not exist in most prisons at the time. Advents such as modern plumbing systems and outside cell configurations with lavatory fixtures and showers were, until this time, unheard of within a prison environment. The design and physical features of Eastern State Penitentiary were therefore quite novel and progressive when compared to other institutions of the era.

Auburn/Sing Sing

Prisons in the New York state system, which originated with the facilities at Auburn and Ossining, were based on a design quite different from the Pennsylvania system. Originally the Auburn/Sing Sing model utilized two back-to-back rows of multitiered cells arranged in a straight, linear plan. The typical cell was around 25 square feet, measuring about 3.5 feet wide by 7 feet long. This is obviously a very small amount of room, especially considering that in today's prisons inmates are afforded 7 to 8 feet by 10 feet of space (approximately 80 square feet). So these conditions were fairly cramped, and the design itself was unimaginative and inefficient. However, it was a simple design that was easy to construct and implement.

As time went on and as improvements in living standards brought in plumbing, electrical, and ventilation systems, the rows of cells were no longer joined in a back-to-back fashion; instead, a small corridor was built between them.

Unlike cell blocks in the Pennsylvania model, those in the Auburn/Sing Sing model did not face one another. The distance from the front of a cell to the outer building wall was usually from 7 to 10 feet,

Wikimedia Commons

■ PHOTO 7.3 This drawing shows the outside of a cell block at Sing Sing Correctional Facility. As seen here, the Auburn/Sing Sing model utilized two back-to-back rows of multitiered cells arranged in a straight, linear plan.

ASSOCIATED PRESS

■ PHOTO 7.4 The panopticon prison model was created by Jeremy Bentham in 1785. This design consists of cells that face each other across a wide circular space with an enclosed observation post at the center of the structure.

and this provided room for a long walkway along the front of the cells on the second tier and above. In most all cases, the outer walls of the building had windows that allowed sunlight and air into the facility. Inmates could not reach these windows if locked in their cells due to the distance between cell and outer wall.

Correctional officers working the cell block would either walk the first floor or along the walkways in front of the cells of the upper floors. This type of design, sometimes described as a "telephone pole" design, made it necessary for officers to conduct their security checks by passing in front of each individual cell; otherwise, they could not view the inmate(s) inside. Despite the inefficiency of this type of supervision, the telephone pole design proliferated throughout the United States during the 1900s. In fact, these features are so common that when people envision correctional facilities, it is this design that comes to mind (George, 2008).

Panopticon

This prison model was created by Jeremy Bentham in 1785. The **panopticon** was designed to allow security personnel to clearly observe all inmates without the inmates themselves being able to tell whether they were being watched. Indeed, the internal tower was constructed so that inmates could not tell if security personnel inside were watching them.

Oddly enough, this design was never adopted in England, Bentham's home nation, but was used in the United States. A handful of facilities using this architectural design were built in Virginia, Pennsylvania, and Illinois (George, 2008). Even today, the panopticon at Stateville Correctional Center in Illinois is in operation. This facility consists of cells that face each other across a wide circular space with an enclosed observation post at the center of the structure. The individual cells are arranged on the thick masonry perimeter walls, with narrow windows. The observation post consists of two stories and is accessible from the main floor. While movement on the ground level is easy enough, officers on the upper tiers of the cells must follow the curving, circumferential balcony for some distance to reach the stairs. If security staff must reach the observation post or an area near a cell block, the travel time can be quite significant.

Panopticon: Designed to allow security personnel to clearly observe all inmates without the inmates themselves being able to tell whether they are being watched.

Direct supervision design: Cells are organized on the outside of the square space, with shower facilities and recreation cells interspersed among the typical inmate living quarters.

Direct Supervision

The direct supervision type of prison design was implemented by the Federal Bureau of Prisons (BOP) due to the need to abate the conditions that contributed to a long, deadly disturbance at New York's Attica Correctional Facility in 1971. This design greatly differs from prior models. The **direct supervision design** features a large, open, central indoor recreational or day room space that can be effectively supervised by a single security person. Cells are organized on the outside of the square space, with shower facilities and recreation cells interspersed among the inmate living quarters. These types of cell blocks may consist of multiple levels of cells. Security staff on each level can walk around that level of the unit and see through the interior space to nearly any other area of the space.

Minimum-Security Prison Design (Modern)

Minimum-security prisons are, in many respects, not even prisons as envisioned by most of the public. On some occasions they are referred to as open institutions due to the low-key security that is provided at these facilities. **Minimum-security facilities** and/or open institutions are typically designed to serve the needs of farming areas or public transportation works rather than being optimized for the offender's reform. Inmates may often work on community projects, such as roadside litter cleanup or wilderness conservation. Many minimum-security facilities are small camps located in or near military bases, larger prisons (outside the security perimeter), or other government institutions to provide a convenient supply of convict labor to the institution. Minimum-security facilities include plantation-style prison farms as well as small forestry, forest fire–fighting, and road repair camps, depending on the type of labor that is needed.

Minimum-security inmates live in less secure dormitories that are regularly patrolled by correctional officers. These facilities typically have communal showers, toilets, and sinks. A minimum-security facility generally has a single fence that is watched, but not patrolled, by armed guards. In very remote and rural areas, there may be no fence at all. The level of staffing assigned tends to be much lighter than at other facilities. The facility is constructed and operated in such a manner that most inmates can access showers, television, and other amenities on their own without oversight of security staff.

Medium-Security Prison Design (Modern)

Medium-security facilities may consist of dormitories that have bunk beds with lockers for inmates to store their possessions. These facilities tend to have communal showers, toilets, and sinks. Dormitories are locked at night with one or more security officers holding watch and conducting routine patrols. Inside the dorm, supervision over the internal movements of inmates is minimal. The perimeter of these facilities, when they are not connected to another larger facility, is generally a double fence that is regularly patrolled by armed security personnel. In modern times, the external chain-link fences and other security features (e.g., cameras) may be the only clue that the grounds are, in fact, prisons for inmates.

Much of the newer prison construction during the past 4 to 5 decades has consisted of medium-security designs. Indeed, it is thought that close to one-third of all state inmates are housed within medium-security facilities. These types of prisons tend to have tighter security than do minimum-security facilities, but they are not as restricted as are maximum-security facilities. Programs for inmates, opportunities for recreation, and the ability to move throughout the grounds are much better in these institutions than in maximum-security prisons. Additionally, these types of facilities tend to implement more sophisticated technology than larger prisons.

Maximum-Security Prison Design (Modern)

Originally, when prisons were first designed, their primary and nearly only concern was security. Because of this, most all prisons were designed as maximum-security facilities. In most cases, they were surrounded by a high wall (up to 50 feet tall) that was usually made of brick-and-mortar material. Atop these stone walls could be found various forms of razor wire, and towers were built at each corner and at intervals along the walls so that security personnel could look down upon inmates inside as well as outside of the facility. These armed guards were instrumental in preventing escapes and open-yard riots.

Nowadays, **maximum-security facilities** are not likely to have stone walls but will instead use corrugated chain-link fence that is often topped with razor wire. These fences are lit by floodlights at night and may be electrified. Chain-link fences are as effective for security as stone walls, and they eliminate blind spots in security where inmates can hide. The open visibility makes it nearly impossible for inmates to approach the fence line without being detected. The perimeter is generally double fenced with chain-link and includes watchtowers that house armed security personnel. Add to this the use of cameras and sensors and the result is a fairly tightly maintained facility.

Pods

Most modern prisons are built with prefabricated sections, often referred to as **pods**. Within these pods, inmates will usually have individual cells with ding doors controlled from a secure remote control station. When out of their cells, prisoners remain in the cell block or an exterior cage. Movement out of the cell block or pod is tightly restricted, often requiring restraints and escorts by

Minimum-security facilities: Typically designed to serve the needs of farming areas or public transportation works rather than being optimized for the offender's reform. Not like typical prisons as envisioned by the public.

Medium-security facilities: Consist of dormitories that have bunk beds with lockers for inmates to store their possessions and communal showers and toilets. Dormitories are locked at night with one or more security officers holding watch.

Maximum-security facilities: These high-security facilities use corrugated chain-link fence. These fences will be lit by floodlights at night and may even be electrified and eliminate "blind spots" in security where inmates can hide.

Pods: Prefabricated sections in most modern prisons. Inmates will usually have individual cells with doors controlled from a secure remote control station.

security staff. In maximum-security facilities, inmates may be housed in one- or two-person cells operated from a remote control station. Inside these facilities, inmates may be allowed to leave their cells to complete work assignments or correctional programs. They may be also allowed in a common area in the cell block or an exercise yard.

Prison Locations

Most early prisons tended to be located in remote areas of the state, away from metropolitan areas. This was especially true when prison farms and agricultural farm-lease agreements proliferated. Given the emphasis on agriculture, it was often necessary that such prisons be in locations where there was plenty of ground space for the planting and harvesting of crops. Further, when prisons are located in remote areas of the nation, this adds a degree of security and a sense of public safety, at least in theory; the farther away offenders are from mainstream society, the less likely they can cause harm to additional victims. However, in reality this is not true since many inmates who escape do not do so on foot but instead often procure assistance with transportation and shelter from people outside of the prison walls. Thus, the location of a prison in a distant and rural area can help thwart unplanned escapes that take place on foot, but this is not foolproof against all planned escapes.

Some prison facilities may be near metropolitan areas. There are many reasons for this, such as if the prison houses inmates with serious medical needs or that require other such specialized services. Placing such facilities near hospitals or other services may make practical sense. Also, some facilities (especially minimum-security facilities) may not have as many security concerns, especially with violent crime. In other cases, it may simply be that the facility is built on whatever ground is available to the agency. Some communities may welcome a prison being located within their jurisdiction since it can mean additional jobs for the area. The reasons for a prison's particular location can be manifold, but in today's world of corrections, it is not always easy to determine the best location for a prison; the answer lies more with the point and purpose of the institution itself.

THE RISE OF THE SUPERMAX

During the 1990s, prison systems around the nation experienced problems with gang offenders and violent offenders who were serious threats to prison order. In fact, the late 1990s saw the emergence of the term *security threat groups*, which referred to the various gangs that existed in and outside of prison. Other inmates, not necessarily linked with organized groups, also proved a constant violent threat in many state systems, leading to a need for heightened security beyond maximum-security facilities.

Supermax facilities provide the highest level of prison security. These types of prisons hold the most dangerous of inmates, including inmates who have committed assaults, murders, or other serious violations in less secure facilities, and inmates known to be or accused of being prison gang members. A supermax facility can either be freestanding, where the entire facility consists of this higher security level, or it can be a specified section of a larger facility with additional security features that make it a supermax facility. Most states have at least one supermax, and the BOP has several located across the nation. The National Institute of Corrections provides a definition of supermax facilities that we will borrow for the use of this text. A **supermax facility** is a

> highly restrictive, high custody housing unit within a secure facility, or an entire secure facility, that isolates inmates from the general population and from each other due to grievous crimes, repetitive assaultive or violent institutional behavior, the threat of escape, or actual escape from high custody facility(s), or inciting or threatening to incite disturbances in a correctional institution. (Riveland, 1999, p. 5)

Supermax facility: A highly restrictive, high-custody housing unit within a secure facility, or an entire secure facility, that isolates inmates from the general population and from each other.

Alcatraz: A prison built on Alcatraz Island, California. First opened in 1934, it is considered to be the first U.S. supermax facility.

USP Marion: The Protégé of Alcatraz

Though not technically labeled a supermax facility, the penitentiary on Alcatraz Island, California, should actually be given this title. **Alcatraz** was first opened in 1934 and held a number of notorious offenders, such as Al Capone and other Mafia leaders. Though this facility was largely successful, public shift toward the medical model of correctional thought during the 1950s, along with an infamous escape, led to the ultimate closure of the facility in 1963. When Alcatraz closed, it was United States Penitentiary (USP) Marion, in rural southern Illinois, that was selected as the replacement facility to hold the challenging inmates who had called Alcatraz their home.

A special closed-custody unit was designed at **USP Marion** to house the BOP's worst inmates. While creating this addition, the BOP also created a new classification known as Level 6, which was a higher security classification than the five that the federal government typically used to classify inmates. The prison was designated as the holding place for approximately 450 inmates who were drawn from the federal system and 36 other states—these offenders being among the most notorious in the nation. Despite the enhanced security features at Marion, in 1983, during two separate incidents, two officers were stabbed to death and four others were seriously injured (Ward, 1994). Four days later, another three officers were attacked, and an inmate was killed when neutralizing the incident. In reaction, a state of emergency was declared, and USP Marion was officially placed on lockdown status.

It is important to mention that USP Marion was eventually tested within the courts for the legality of its operations. A class action suit that included several inmate rights groups charged that Marion implemented controls that constituted cruel and unusual punishment. However, after several weeks of testimony, the federal district court in southern Illinois denounced these charges, and in ***Bruscino v. Carlson* (1988)**, the Federal Circuit Court of Appeals upheld the district court's judgment (Ward, 1994). This meant that USP Marion had effectively passed the test of constitutionality. This was good news for Marion and also for many other states that had contemplated the use of a supermax security system but were hesitant due to concerns with legality (Ward, 1994). Once it was determined Marion was indeed constitutional, many states quickly set their sights on implementing similar facilities within their own prison systems.

States Utilize the Marion Model

Once word spread around the nation that the BOP had found a management strategy to control highly disruptive inmates, and once it was found that this strategy was constitutionally sound, correctional administrators from around the nation began to visit USP Marion to glean insights into its design and operation, which eventually became known as the Marion Model of prison design, at least informally. By the mid-1990s, at least 36 states had built some sort of supermax custody unit as an addition to already existing prisons or as a stand-alone facility. While the term *supermax* was commonplace, many states used different terms, such as special housing units (SHUs) or extended confinement units (ECUs). As these units proliferated throughout the state systems, new constitutional challenges emerged that sometimes had results different from those associated with USP Marion.

Video Link
Reassessing Solitary Confinement: The Human Rights, Fiscal, and Public Safety Consequences

Indeed, other supermax facilities around the nation have had problems in terms of both operations and legal criteria. Despite this, these facilities have operated effectively, for the most part. The legal issues associated with this type of supervision demonstrate how progressive sanctions can invite progressive problems for a correctional system. The challenge of containing disruptive inmates is compounded by the difficulty in adhering to civil rights requirements. The balance between these two concerns places administrators in a difficult position.

USP Florence ADMAX: "The Alcatraz of the Rockies"

In 1994, the BOP opened its first true supermax facility at Florence, Colorado. Though Marion had a section that was a supermax security facility, it was not a stand-alone structure solely dedicated to supermax operations. The facility in Florence was designed for no other purpose than to operate as a supermax and is officially referred to as the administrative maximum (ADX) facility, or **USP Florence ADMAX**. This prison originally housed over 400 inmates who were the worst of the worst in the BOP. These inmates were selected because they were either extremely violent, high escape risks, or identified gang leaders. Construction for this facility cost over $60 million, and each cell had a price tag of around $150,000, making it one of the most (if not *the* most) expensive prisons ever built and maintained. Annual maintenance for inmates is roughly $40,000 per year, with the overall cost of maintenance being around $20 million a year.

USP Florence ADMAX is located on State Highway 67, 90 miles south of Denver, 45 miles south of Colorado Springs, and 40 miles west of Pueblo. The structure's design is nearly indestructible on the inside. The cell design consists of a bed, desk, stool, and bookcase, all constructed from reinforced concrete and immovable. Each cells measures 7 feet by 12 feet and has a shower stall and reinforced plumbing within. Cell windows are designed so that all views of the outside are restricted, and inmates can only see the sky above them. In addition, cells are positioned in such a manner so that inmates cannot make eye contact with one another, so they have very little contact with other people. Food is delivered by tray through a door slot, and all visits are noncontact in

USP Marion: A special closed-custody unit designed to house the Federal Bureau of Prisons' worst inmates.

***Bruscino v. Carlson* (1988):** Ruling that the high-security practices of USP Marion were constitutional.

USP Florence ADMAX: A federal prison with a design that is nearly indestructible on the inside. Essentially, these offenders have no contact with humans.

nature. Recreation is for 1 hour a day and is completed alone. In many ways, it seems that a Pennsylvania model of operation has been implemented, but in this case the intent is to simply incarcerate and hold the inmate in place; reform is no longer a priority with these hardened inmates who have a poor prognosis due to dangerous and repetitive behavior.

This prison was much more expensive to build than others due to the enhanced security features, higher-quality locks and doors, and perimeter fencing designs. Facilities such as Florence ADMAX are expensive to maintain for two reasons. First, the advanced security features are costly to maintain, as noted above, and the additional staff security adds to the financial burden. Second, a large proportion of supermax inmates will never be released; their sentences are for very long terms, and this means that, over time, they will become more costly due to the need for geriatric medical care. Thus, the financial picture goes from bad to worse for these facilities.

As can be seen in Focus Topic 7.1, even supermax facilities are not completely secure. But given the assaultive nature of the inmates that are held within these facilities, it is easy to see that

FOCUS TOPIC 7.1

Security Breaches Can Happen, Even at USP Florence ADMAX

Recently, 46-year-old Ishmael Petty, an inmate serving time at USP Florence ADMAX, was convicted for an assault that he committed on prison staff in 2013.

According to court documents and evidence presented at trial, on September 11, 2013, Petty, who was serving a life sentence at ADX for killing his 71-year-old cell mate at the United States Penitentiary Pollock in Louisiana, attacked two BOP librarians and a case manager as they were delivering books to his cell. At ADX there is an outer door, a secure area, and then an inner door before entering the actual cell. While the BOP employees believed that Petty was in his cell, he was in fact hiding in the area between the outer and inner doors. He was wearing self-made body armor, consisting of cardboard box–like material, and had a weapon, specifically a shank. When the attack began, Petty threw hot sauce in the eyes of one BOP librarian and then attacked the other librarian. The third BOP employee, a case manager, quickly came to their aid and called for help. One of the BOP employees used their baton to try and subdue Petty. Petty ultimately took control of two batons and used them in his attack. Once the call for help was made, Petty went back into his cell.

Prior to Petty's life sentence for killing his cellmate, he was sentenced to federal prison for 420 months for an elaborate armed bank robbery in Mississippi where he was wearing a police officer's uniform.

"Defendant stands convicted of a cowardly and brutal assault on defenseless staff at ADX. The defendant, who was serving time at ADX for murdering his cellmate at another prison, ambushed and brutally assaulted two staff librarians, using his much greater size to injure the older of the two severely and permanently," said U.S. Attorney John Walsh. "Only the courageous intervention of a third staff member prevented the defendant from killing that librarian."

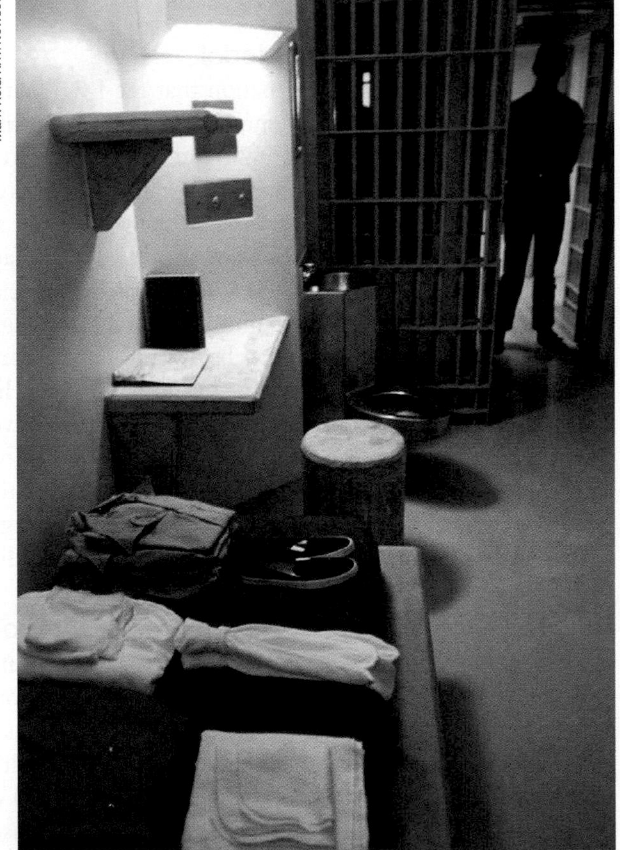

Mark Reis/KRT/Newsco

■ PHOTO 7.5 **USP Florence ADMAX has cells that consist of a bed, desk, stool, and bookcase, all constructed from reinforced concrete. Its enhanced security features made this supermax prison extremely expensive to build.**

Petty, who is currently serving a life sentence, faces not more than 20 years in prison and up to a $250,000 fine per count for each of the three counts of conviction.

SOURCE: United States Attorney's Office. (2015, July 14). *ADX inmate convicted of three counts of assault, resisting and impeding a federal employee.* Washington, DC: Federal Bureau of Investigation.

it is an important priority to ensure that these violent individuals are kept secure. The notion of rehabilitation is not a priority in supermax prisons; the seriousness of the inmates' offenses calls for more of an incapacitation approach.

Constitutional Issues With Confinement in Supermax Custody

It has been found that when kept in prolonged periods of confinement, inmates tend to exhibit mental health issues due to sensory deprivation. These issues can include states of paranoia, irrational fears, resentment, inability to control anger, depression, heightened anxiety, and forms of full mental breakdown. Suicides tend to be higher among inmates who are confined for prolonged periods of time. Many of these issues, as students may recall from Chapter 2, are similar to those of inmates confined in solitude for prolonged periods in Eastern State Penitentiary under the Pennsylvania model of prison operation. This is an important observation because it demonstrates that history does, indeed, repeat itself, and it validates the fact that extreme isolation does cause mental health problems. In modern correctional literature, the negative mental health effects of extended isolation may be referred to as **special housing unit syndrome**.

Supermax-specific case law to date is limited. The first case to capture national attention, ***Madrid v. Gomez* (1995)**, was a wide-ranging attack on operations at the Pelican Bay SHU in California. This was a supermax-type control unit facility where inmates identified as gang members; offenders with a history of violence, crime, or serious rule violations within prison; and other inmates considered major management threats were incarcerated. The Pelican Bay SHU was one of the first such facilities in modern American history explicitly planned and built as a state-level supermax facility.

In the *Madrid* case, the Ninth Circuit Court found widespread violations of the Eighth Amendment prohibition against cruel and unusual punishment. The court ordered the institution to professionalize the means by which security staff operated the prison and to improve the insufficient medical care at the facility. In addition, it was ordered that all inmates with mental illnesses be transferred to an institution more suited for their needs. In order to ensure that prison officials adhered to the orders of this injunction, the court appointed a federal monitor to the prison. Federal monitors are individuals who are assigned to inspect for deficiencies and ensure compliance of prison operations to legal requirements. It was not until 2011 that the injunction was removed, at which time it was determined that Pelican Bay SHU had sufficiently met the requirements that had been established in *Madrid*, nearly 20 years prior.

Special housing unit syndrome: The negative mental health effects of extended isolation.

***Madrid v. Gomez* (1995):** Case where the constitutionality of supermax facilities was questioned.

Americans with Disabilities Act (ADA): Requires correctional agencies to make reasonable modifications to ensure accessibility for individuals with disabilities.

ACCOMMODATIONS FOR INMATES WITH DISABILITIES

The number of inmates with disabilities in prison facilities has continued to grow throughout correctional systems nationwide. The aging inmate population, the effects of alcohol and drug abuse, and the injuries due to violence in facilities help to contribute to the challenges that inmates face (Appel, 1999). As inmate disabilities and special needs have become increasingly more important, related legal standards and requirements have also changed and become more rigorous.

Proof of this changing legal environment became most evident in 1990 when the **Americans with Disabilities Act (ADA)** was signed into action. This act created a whole set of legal obligations that largely did not exist for prison administrators prior to this time. Thus, when the ADA was first proposed, correctional administrators came together and produced over 7,000 pages of commentary and testimony of concerns and considerations about the law.

ADA Compliance

It is important that correctional agencies ensure that staff are trained on the specific issues related to the ADA and inmates. According to the U.S. Department of Justice, Civil Rights Division, Disability Rights Section (2010), the ADA requires correctional agencies to make reasonable modifications in their policies, practices, and procedures necessary to ensure accessibility for individuals with disabilities, unless making such

Prison Tour Video: ADA Compliance. With some exeptions, prisons are required to be ADA compliant. Watch two wardens discuss ADA modifications and compliance.

TECHNOLOGY AND EQUIPMENT 7.1

Dome Technology in Cell Block Design Versus Traditional Prison Construction

One innovative concept in prison design not yet used by any correctional system in the United States is dome construction. Dome structures are based on pod designs that are prefabricated, but it is the dome shape itself that holds substantial advantages for correctional agencies, in terms of both security and operational costs. The figure below provides a floor plan from Monolithic for a 1,200-bed-capacity prison that uses dome structures for cell block and dormitory living areas as well as other structures throughout the complex.

While in some ways the use of the dome configuration is reminiscent of Bentham's panopticon, the real advantage comes in the form of cost savings and additional security strength. With dome-shaped structures, the amount of heating and cooling needed is vastly reduced. This has been found to be true with numerous residential and business facilities that have utilized this technology; prisons would be no different. Also, the speed of construction is increased, and the use of sprayed concrete creates a much stronger structure than does traditional concrete; thus, these facilities are more secure and more resistant to inclement weather. Additionally, the line of sight is maximized for security personnel, adding to the interior security of the structure. This means that this design is effective in eliminating the existence of blind spots in prison security and observation—an issue that will be discussed later in this chapter. The elimination of blind spots reduces the use of redundant and overlapping assignments of security personnel and eliminates the need for extensive technological surveillance equipment. But if institutions do decide to use such equipment, the ability for it to detect institutional violations is enhanced by the open view provided by this construction design.

The diagram for this prison design features multiple two-story double-dome units that can house up to 120 inmates in single cells. The domes paired with the cells are 112 feet in diameter and 37 feet tall. Visitors enter between two 140-foot-diameter visitor's domes into the 108-foot-diameter administration and operations dome. Each visitor's dome has 11,484 square feet of open space. The Reception and Evaluation dome (110 x 37 feet) encompasses 9,500 square feet with all the modern facilities. Program Services, in a 100-foot dome, accommodates a pharmacy, an infirmary, a chaplain, a 2,500-square-foot multipurpose room, and offices. The educational facility, also in a 100-foot dome, comes complete with classrooms, library, and more. The centrally located kitchen in a 150-foot-diameter, 17,000-square-foot dome creates optimum work areas and easy access to the separate dining halls—two for inmates, one for staff—as well as private access to the storage/unloading area. Separate double gymnasiums are surrounded by locker rooms, exercise rooms, and offices in a 25,450-square-foot, 150-foot-diameter, multipurpose center. Located between the multipurpose center and dining hall a 90-foot-diameter dome houses the ample laundry and storage areas, commissary, canteen, and barber. A nondenominational chapel (60 x 25 feet) with rooms for ecclesiastical counseling provides an optional religious center.

As can be seen, this type of pod technology provides ample space and all the modern accoutrements that could be included in a state-of-the-art prison. The fact of the matter is that this design is superior to traditional prison designs. Dome prisons are structurally tougher, are less expensive to build and maintain, and eliminate the need for excessive security features since their design provides superior observation and security potential. All in all, this type of technology should be utilized by states that seek to improve their correctional system by making it both more modern and cost-effective.

SOURCE: South, D. B. (2009). *The monolithic dome as a prison?* Italy, TX: Monolithic Domes. Reprinted by permission of Monolithic Constructors, Inc.

modifications would fundamentally alter the program or service involved. There are many ways in which an agency might need to modify its normal practices to accommodate a person with a disability. Some examples include the following:

Audio Link Slate's Jurisprudence: Does ADA Apply Behind Bars?

Example 1: An agency modifies a rule that inmates or detainees are not permitted to have food in their cells except at scheduled intervals in order to accommodate an individual with diabetes who uses medication and needs access to carbohydrates or sugar to keep blood sugar at an appropriate level.

Example 2: An agency modifies its regular practice of handcuffing inmates behind their backs and instead handcuffs deaf individuals in front of their bodies in order for them to sign or write notes.

Example 3: An agency modifies its practice of confiscating medications for the period of confinement in order to permit inmates who have disabilities that require self-medication, such as cardiac conditions or epilepsy, to self-administer medications that do not have abuse potential.

Lastly, state and local government entities should conduct a self-evaluation to review their current services, policies, and practices for compliance with the ADA. When such an evaluation finds that the agency has deficiencies, the agency should develop a transition plan that identifies structural changes that need to be made. As part of that process, the ADA has encouraged entities to involve individuals with disabilities from their local communities. This process will promote access solutions that are reasonable and effective.

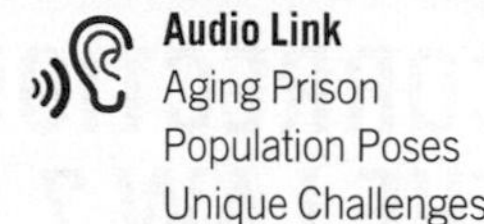

Audio Link
Aging Prison Population Poses Unique Challenges

INNOVATIVE SECURITY DESIGNS

Every correctional facility has its own challenges and needs that make it a bit different from other facilities in the respective correctional system. A variety of factors must be considered in design, such as if the site will be rural or urban, the security level needed, and the operational concerns for security and programming, which include the specific needs of inmates, the surrounding community support, the durability of materials needed, and so forth.

Prisons can vary widely in size in terms of both inmate capacity and the physical area encompassed by the prison buildings. The *National Directory of Corrections Construction*, published by the National Institute of Justice, classifies prisons into the following general types:

1. Campus style: a number of individual buildings that are not connected.
2. Ladder, telephone pole: linear cell blocks arranged in parallel configuration off a central connecting corridor.
3. Wheel, spoke, or radial: linear cell blocks that emanate from one central control area like spokes from the hub of a wheel.
4. Clusters: a number of individual buildings that are interconnected.
5. Courtyard: linear cell blocks interconnected around a central enclosed courtyard.

Perimeter security system: A collection of components or elements that, when assembled in a carefully formulated plan, achieve the objective of confinement with a high degree of confidence.

Figures 7.1 and 7.2 provide a basic illustration of each type of design and the manner in which it might be organized. There are numerous reasons that one design might be used rather than another, including the security level of the institution, the location of the prison, and/or the intended function of the facility.

■ **Figure 7.1: Various Prison Complex Designs**

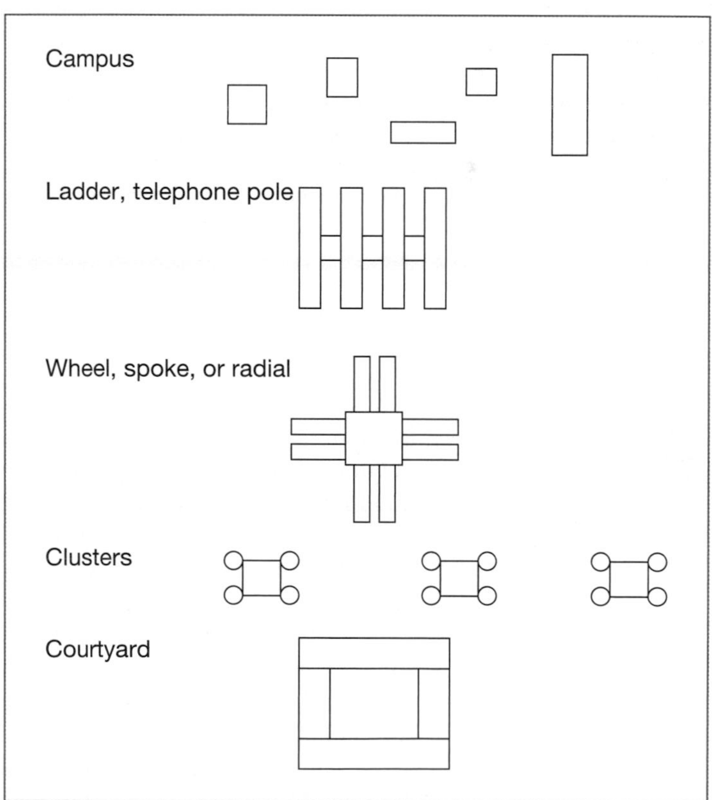

SOURCE: General Accounting Office. (1991). *Prison costs: Opportunities exist to lower the cost of building federal prisons.* Washington, DC: Author.

Perimeter Security

A prison's **perimeter security system** is, ideally, a collection of components or elements that, when assembled in a carefully formulated configuration, achieve the objective of confinement with a high degree of confidence. Anyone attempting to escape the institution by crossing the perimeter must be interdicted by responding officers before the perimeter is successfully penetrated. The perimeter system must slow the escapee down so as to ensure that this confrontation can occur. While the perimeter is capable of keeping intruders out of the facility, its primary purpose is, of course, to keep inmates contained within the facility.

Figure 7.3 (not drawn to scale) shows a cross section of a basic two-fence security perimeter. It illustrates the components of a perimeter system and their relationship to each other. The perimeter itself is delineated by a chain-link outer fence and a stone, brick, or concrete wall. The outer fence has coiled razor wire that is placed within the top Y-wedge, preventing inmates from being able to climb the fence from inside the facility. This outer fence is sometimes called an oyster fence due to the shape of the cylindrical razor wire coils that are connected to the fence. Next, an isolation zone, often about 15 to 20 feet in length, exists between the outer oyster

CORRECTIONS AND THE LAW 7.1

Protection of Inmates Known to Be in Danger

Although gang activity, drug culture, informers, rule relaxation, and the increasing rate of inmate damage suits (and the likelihood that prison officials may be held personally liable for inmates' injuries) have forced a trend toward protective custody (PC) units to safeguard certain inmates. Inmates assigned to these units are beginning to challenge the conditions of their confinement. For many inmates, the physical deprivation of PC is exacerbated by the sense that they are the objects of community contempt and by the fear of retaliation once they are released. Some prison psychiatric services personnel contend that depression, schizophrenia, and suicidal behavior may all be triggered by protective custody.

While a considerable amount of case law exists regarding both staff liability and inmate rights, very little case law exists that has dealt directly with protective custody. With respect to liability, the courts have determined that prison officials have a basic duty to take reasonable precautions to protect inmates under their care. However, in order to establish liability under the Eighth Amendment for a prison official's failure to protect an inmate, the inmate must demonstrate that the official was deliberately indifferent "to a substantial risk of serious harm" to the inmate (*Farmer v. Brennan*, 511 U.S. 825 [1994], p. 828). To demonstrate deliberate indifference, an inmate must present evidence from which a trier of fact could conclude "that the official was subjectively aware of the risk" and "disregard[ed] that risk by failing to take reasonable measures to abate it" (p. 829, 847). As noted above, the only issue before this court is whether the inmate introduces sufficient evidence to convince a trier of fact that the warden or other prison official was aware of a substantial risk of serious harm to the inmate. That awareness can be demonstrated through "inference from circumstantial evidence," and a prison official cannot "escape liability . . . by showing that, while he was aware of an obvious, substantial risk to inmate safety, he did not know that the complainant was especially likely to be assaulted by the specific prisoner who eventually committed the assault" (pp. 842–843).

Yet a 1979 Supreme Court decision upheld the idea that the courts should not interfere in matters of prison administration unless it can be shown that prison officials are making an "exaggerated response" to security problems. Legal observers believe that the decision will continue to limit the relief the courts grant to PC inmates in the future. This demonstrates that, overall, there is a lack of consensus among the courts regarding the rights of inmates in PC. The assignment of liability has become a fairly difficult task that is seldom able to be attached to the actions of prison staff.

This lack of consensus regarding the rights of inmates in PC, coupled with the high standard for liability to attach (proof of deliberate indifference being required), makes the process of obtaining protective custody status untenable. Further, Carlson and Garrett (2008) note that there is a bit of irony to the situation because while the Supreme Court has not addressed specific rights for inmates in PC, it has given extensive attention to inmates in administrative segregation. Administrative segregation is, in many cases, a status afforded to perpetrators of violence inside the prison. Thus, it appears that inmates in administrative segregation, some of whom are guilty of having victimized inmates in PC, have more due process rights that are defined than do the individuals being protected in PC.

SOURCES: Anderson, D. C. (1980). *Price of safety—"I can't go back out there."* Washington, DC: U.S. Department of Justice.

Greene v. Boyles, 2004 FED App. 0078P (6th Cir. 2004).

Web Link
Escapees May Have Eluded "Perimeter," State Police Say

fence and a 20-foot-high stone or brick wall with a thickness at the top of 16 to 24 inches. Inside the inner brick wall is a camera that is mounted atop a tall pole, allowing a bird's eye view of the inner fence and the isolation zone between the outer oyster fence and the inner fence. The lighting system is placed further inside and is usually designed so that illumination extends beyond the outer fence and includes enough coverage of the inside facility to allow detection of persons prior to their approaching this perimeter.

The system shown in Figure 7.3 is assumed to be solid brick, stone masonry, or reinforced concrete, which should discourage attempts to cut through the wall. Lighting features are also shown mounted on the top of the wall since this is typical of most stone-walled facilities. Sensor equipment is mounted on the wall and placed to detect an object or a person approaching the top of the wall or something leaning against or touching the wall. This same sensor equipment is also designed to detect persons who might scale the wall from the outside since there would be no convenient way to get over the wall and inside the yard without encountering the sensor array. Thus, this security system also serves to thwart the attempt of outside accomplices.

Figure 7.2: Typical Cell Layout and Organization

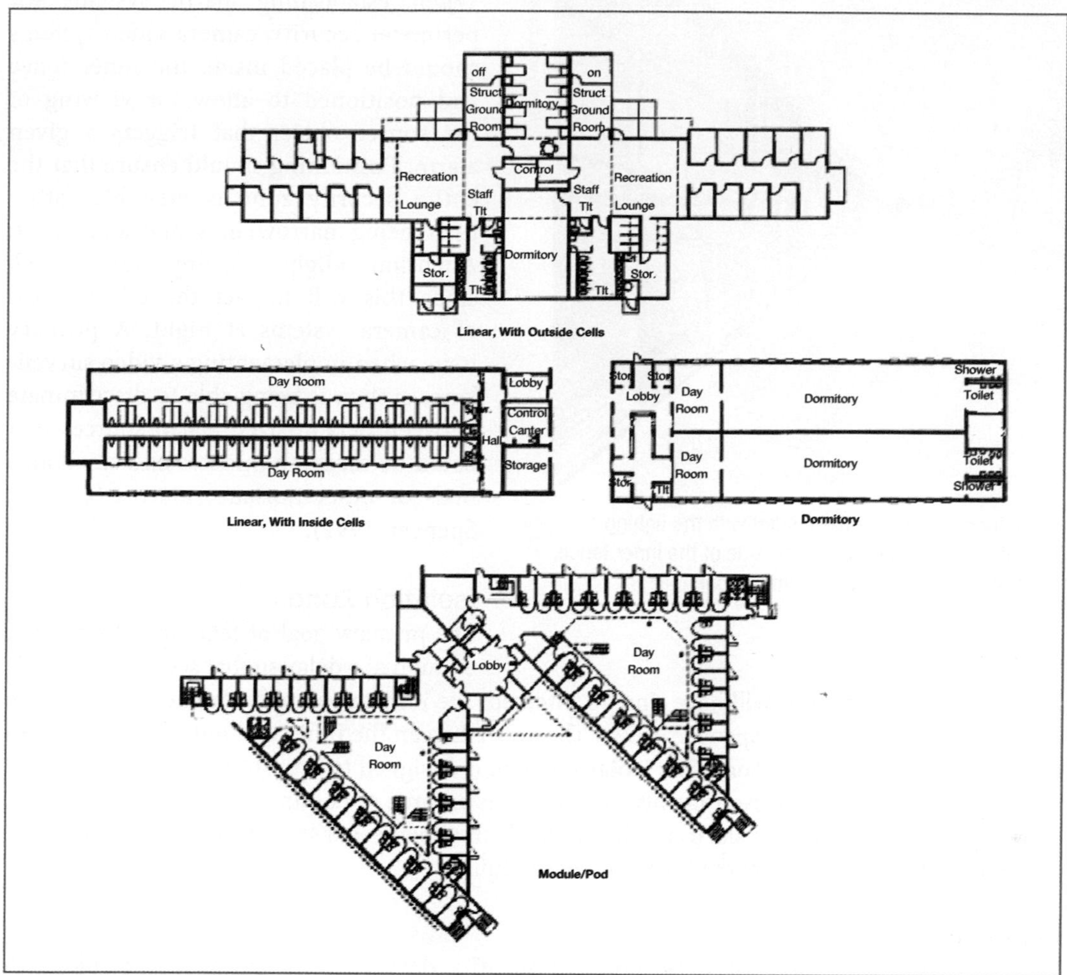

SOURCE: General Accounting Office. (1991). *Prison costs: Opportunities exist to lower the cost of building federal prisons.* Washington, DC: Author.

Figure 7.3: Fenced Perimeter of a Prison With a Stone or Concrete Wall

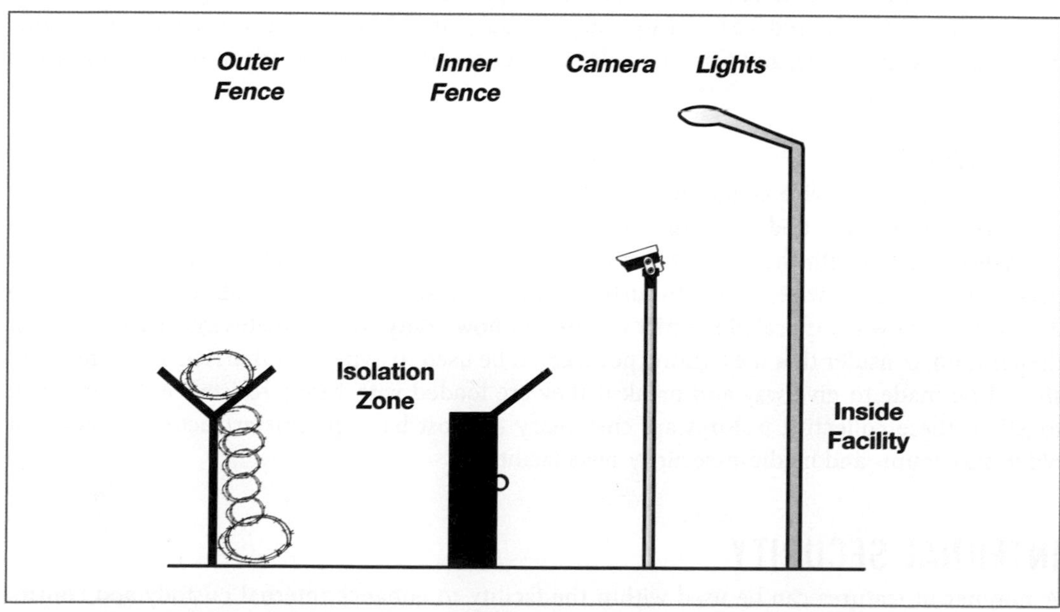

SOURCE: Crist, D., & Spencer, D. (1991). *Perimeter security for Minnesota correctional facilities.* St. Paul: Minnesota Department of Corrections.

© Mikael Karlsson / Alamy

■ PHOTO 7.6 This photo shows the inner fence (left hand side) with the lighing system towering above the fence, coils of razor wire on the outside of the inner fence, the outer fence (with additional razor wire atop), and the isolation zone that is between both fences.

Alarm Systems

When establishing alarm systems for perimeter security, camera video systems should be placed inside the inner fence and positioned to allow for viewing of the source object that triggers a given alarm. Positioning should ensure that the entire security zone is viewable rather than being narrow in scope and focus. Attention to lighting is important as well, since this will impact the effectiveness of camera systems at night. A primary issue when implementing a video surveillance system is being able to discriminate between person-sized alarm sources that could be escaping inmates and small animals or other nuisance alarms (Crist & Spencer, 1991).

Isolation Zone

The primary goal of fencing is to provide enough of a delay so that security responding to the escape attempt will have time to intercept the inmate before he or she can penetrate or clear the fence (Crist & Spencer, 1991). The area between the inner and outer fences is often referred to as the isolation zone. The **isolation zone** is designed to prevent undetected access to the outer fencing of the prison facility. It also forms an area of confinement where the inmate escapee is trapped once the alarm is triggered, which allows security staff time to respond and apprehend the inmate before the escape is successful.

Lighting

When providing lighting for these types of security designs, some problems are likely to be encountered. First, if the lighting is located atop the wall, the system will usually be about 15 feet from the sensor system and 5 or 6 feet inboard of the wall. This type of configuration produces hot spots in the lit areas that will exceed typical light-to-darkness ratios for optimal viewing. Because of this, some facilities may add light sources along the top of the wall but reduce their intensity. In addition, the lighting equipment may be directed away from the surface of the wall, just a bit, to reduce intensity and potential glare. However, the use of additional lighting fixtures is expensive, and this then adds further to the cost of the prison in terms of layout and maintenance.

Razor Wire

Three coils of razor wire create the barrier delay and are placed above the sensor, along the inner area of the wall and along the top of it. Because determined inmates may be willing to concede detection with the thought that they can clear the wall prior to the response of security personnel, the razor wire is used to further prevent most inmates from taking the chance. To demonstrate how complicated security can be and how crafty some inmates may become out of desperation, consider that the lighting poles could be used to bypass this barrier. Thus, the poles should be made to give way and break if they are loaded with heavy resistance. When taken together, these collective features are customary to most basic perimeter security systems of older maximum- and medium-security-level facilities.

INTERNAL SECURITY

Isolation zone: Designed to prevent undetected access to the outer fencing of the prison facility.

A number of features can be used within the facility to enhance internal custody and control of the inmate population. For instance, the use of touch-screen surveillance systems in control rooms can provide centralized security staff with the ability to oversee security throughout various sections of the institution. Showcased in Figures 7.4–7.7, this type of equipment can provide a sense of organization to the overall security maintenance throughout the facility and help to coordinate the use of security staff resources during times of both routine operation and crisis response.

■ Figure 7.4: Touch-Screen Control Panel

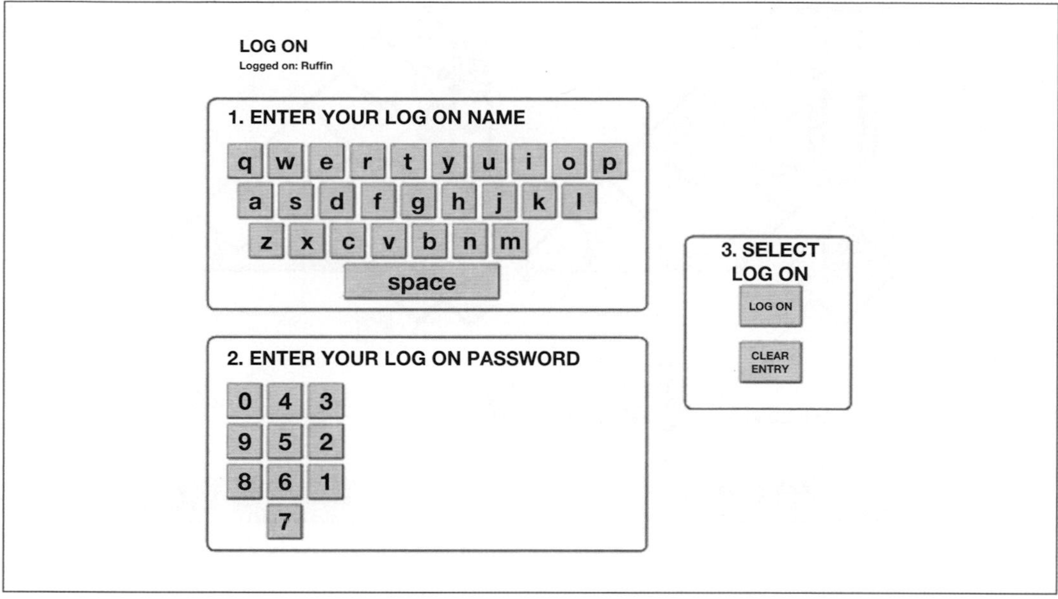

SOURCE: Reprinted by permission of Cornerstone Institutional Sales & Service, www.cisupply.com.

■ Figure 7.5: Full View of Facility

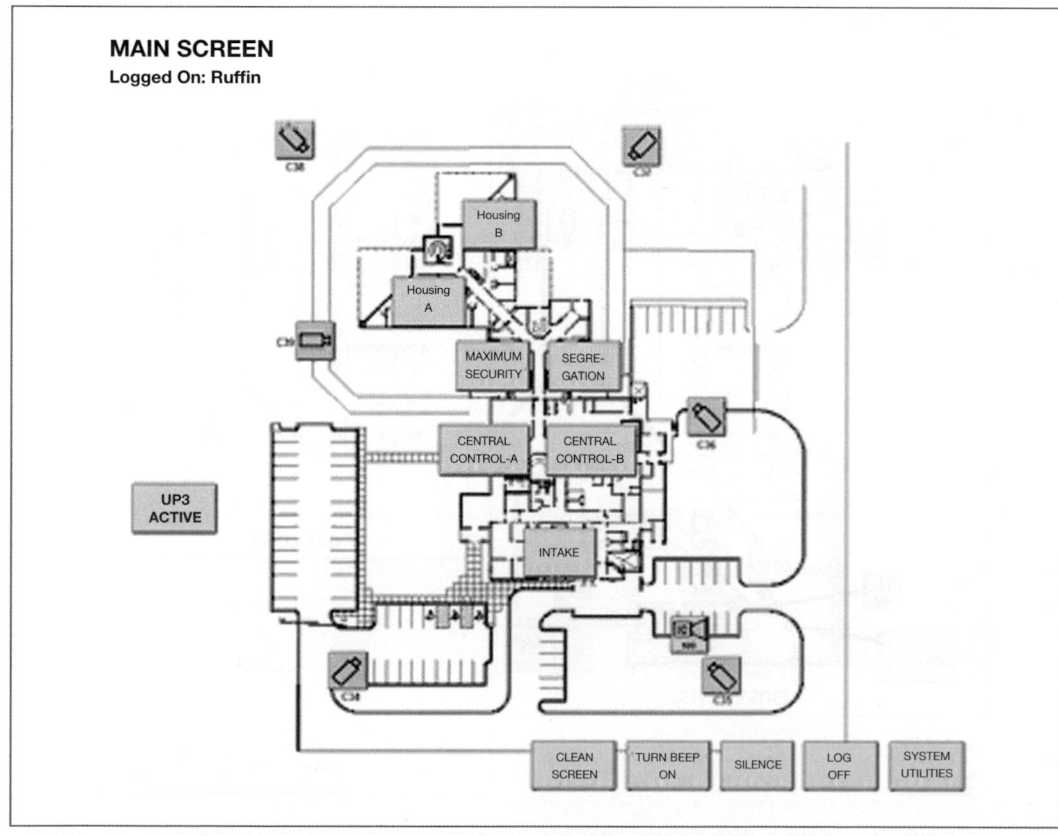

SOURCE: Reprinted by permission of Cornerstone Institutional Sales & Service, www.cisupply.com.

■ Figure 7.6: Multilevel View of Pod

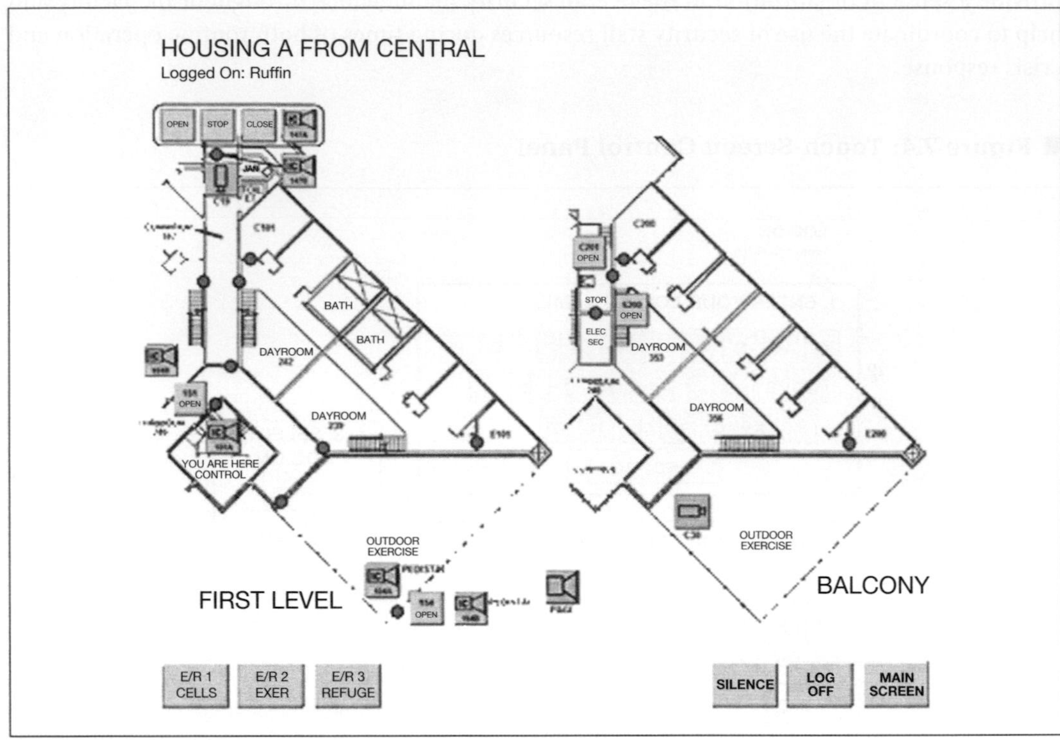

SOURCE: Reprinted by permission of Cornerstone Institutional Sales & Service, www.cisupply.com.

■ Figure 7.7: View of Segregation Pod

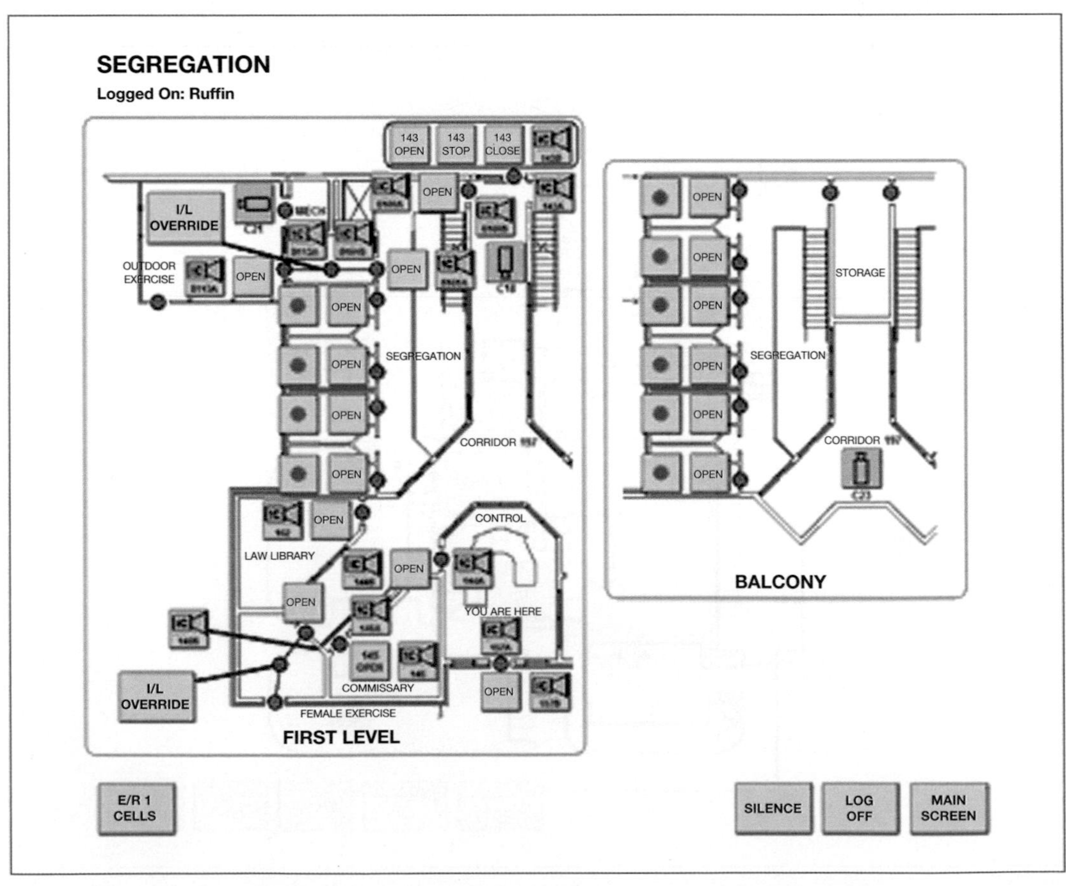

SOURCE: Reprinted by permission of Cornerstone Institutional Sales & Service, www.cisupply.com.

Redding (2004) notes that although physical design and inmate classification may be key elements of the security process, it is the security staff who are integral to maintaining custody and control of the inmate population. Regardless of how well one builds a prison and designs its attendant security features, the physical features of an institution's perimeter alone are useless without staff properly trained to be alert to their responsibilities while operating in their assigned capacities (American Correctional Association, 1998). Prison officials are responsible for the security measures that the physical design cannot control. These duties include "access control, searching of prisoners and their belongings, and movement control both inside and outside prisons and during the transportation of prisoners" (Redding, 2004).

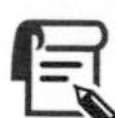

SAGE Journal Article Link
Prison Architecture and Inmate Misconduct: A Multilevel Assessment

Given that the human element is so important to internal security, it is essential that an appropriate form of organizational culture that seeks to psychologically motivate employees toward security-minded objectives be developed within an agency (Robbins, 2005). This refers to a system of shared meaning held by members of that organization. One shared meaning or belief is the need for security and an attention to detail (Robbins, 2005). This attention to detail entails the degree to which employees are expected to exhibit precision, analysis, and attention to the specific routines that occur within the agency (Robbins, 2005). Such attentiveness would provide an environmental mind-set that is conducive to security-related issues. Without such a mind-set, truly disastrous results can occur.

Consider, for instance, that inmates in a San Antonio, Texas, prison managed to steal 14 revolvers, a 12-gauge shotgun, and a rifle before they drove away in a prison van without being stopped. The security breach was due to personnel not following agency policy and security procedure. This escape led to a Christmas Eve robbery and the death of an Irving police officer (Associated Press, 2001). This example demonstrates that problems with security, particularly human compliance with security principles, can have a crucial and deadly impact on both the internal security of the prison facility and the outside community.

Avoiding Blind Spots in Correctional Facilities

Blind spots in correctional facilities can occur when the design has certain areas that are obscured from easy view of security staff and/or surveillance equipment. While the primary means of achieving internal security is the prison staff, they cannot detect all things that occur. Surveillance equipment inside the facility is often used to add a security element to areas that are less frequently patrolled and/or difficult for staff to observe in person. The use of closed-circuit television (CCTV) systems can provide good visual surveillance within a facility, but these types of systems can be costly. And, as noted in the previous subsection, this equipment is only as effective as the security personnel who use it.

Web Link
Federal Court Orders Cameras to Cover Blind Spots at North Carolina Prison

Thus, the best means of avoiding blind spots is to leave as few areas out of restricted view as possible during the design stage. In addition, staff should be aware of any areas where obstructed view occurs and physically monitor them more closely. This prevents a number of problems that go beyond just the possibility of inmate escape. The blind spot areas of a prison can allow inmates to engage in inappropriate or illicit behaviors, such as trafficking and trading of contraband, inappropriate behavior within the institution, or assaultive actions against other inmates or staff. Thus, these areas are danger zones within the prison facility and should be given maximum attention by security personnel to offset the potential breach to internal or external security.

AUXILIARY SERVICES AND PHYSICAL SECURITY

The provision of auxiliary services is very important within the world of corrections. Despite being termed *auxiliary*, these services are actually quite central to the survival of the inmate population. The ability of an institution to feed its inmates, clothe them, provide for religious services and recreational services, and provide space where job skills can be practiced requires specialized facilities. This can also create additional security needs within the institution since staff must do more than simply maintain security; they must provide security to a population that is industrious and active. Keeping watch over inmates as they perform kitchen duties or other functions in the prison provides security staff with a whole new set of responsibilities and situations besides those encountered on the cell block or in the dormitory. It is with this in mind that we turn our attention to prison kitchens. We will examine their construction and design and the need for secure kitchen facilities.

Blind spots: In correctional facilities, these occur when areas of the prison are not easily viewed by security staff and/or surveillance equipment.

Kitchen Services and Facilities

The design and development of kitchen facilities in prison environments require that equipment be able to service hundreds or thousands of individuals on a daily basis yet, at the same time, facilitate security needs of the institution. This is a difficult balance in design since any mass feeding operation is, in and of itself, a challenging process. When adding security issues to the kitchen operation process, the physical layout of the kitchen becomes very important.

In addition, the storage of cutlery equipment within the kitchen is critical. Strict monitoring of the use of culinary tools such as knives, forks, and meat saws is very important to institutional safety and security. Facilities must be designed so that the inventory of kitchen tools can be completed quickly and easily. This feature distinguishes a prison kitchen from most other types of commercial or mass-feeding kitchens.

The most common method of serving food to inmates is through a large, open, cafeteria-style room. These rooms tend to have either long tables or a series of small tables with chairs that are secured to the ground. Inmates gather at the feeding line. This line may be open so inmates can observe the persons who are serving their food or a screen may extend down several feet from the ceiling so that they do not know who prepared their tray. This feature eliminates the possibility that inmates who do not like one another will have problems regarding the food that is served on the line.

Robert Hanser

Robert Hanser

■ PHOTO 7.7 Prison kitchens and dining halls tend to be busy throughout the entire day and much of the evening. The continuous feeding process within the institution requires nearly round-the-clock work on the part of staff and inmates assigned to culinary duties. Pictured here is a jail facility kitchen (top) at Ouachita Correctional Center and a prison dining hall (bottom) at Richwood Correctional Center.

Feeding and Security

Prison kitchens can be the source for all kinds of contraband within the prison. Naturally, contraband can include any sort of kitchen tool or product: knives and cutlery, poisonous substances, or food items that can be used to make homemade alcohol, such as fruits and yeast. To maintain control over kitchen tools, an inventory is taken daily, and inmates are required to formally sign these tools out. Many kitchens use what is called a shadow board, which is usually a board with the silhouette of the item drawn on the board so that missing kitchen tools can be quickly identified.

The use of secure storage facilities for food products that can be used to manufacture alcohol is also required. Kitchen staff must be alert so that inmates are not able to sneak products out of the kitchen area. In addition to physically inspecting the inmates, staff should ensure that products have not been hidden in the kitchen, placed in the trash (so that they can be taken out of the kitchen area undetected), or hidden in items that go in and out of the dining facility. It is important to note that junior and/or inexperienced staff may not realize when certain foods can be problematic and therefore may not prevent much of the contraband that leaves from the kitchen. Because of this, they must be trained on these issues.

Food Service Facilities and Equipment

Food service facilities and equipment vary from one jail or prison to another (Johnson, 2008). Some facilities may have equipment that is not up to date and is therefore difficult for the workers to use. Most prison dining areas are set up in a cafeteria-style arrangement, as noted above, and inmates are usually fed three meals a day. It is important to note that the feeding times for inmates may not be during the hours that most people would expect. There may be some flexibility in the times that inmates are fed depending on programming requirements, work schedules, and other factors that may impact scheduling.

In addition, some areas of the prison may require that inmates be given a food tray within their cell. For instance, inmates in administrative segregation and/or solitary confinement will usually be given a plastic tray that is kept in a heated food cart or otherwise stored for portable delivery. In cases where inmates in lockdown facilities are being fed, officers in the department will usually provide the inmates with their food tray, utensils, and required liquid beverage.

Food Supplies and Storage

Video Link
Getting Prisoners Life-ready to Prevent a Return to Crime

Johnson (2008) notes that food should be of the best quality possible within budgetary constraints. This is true for multiple reasons; one of these is that providing decent food minimizes inmate discontent. Also, high-quality nutritional food keeps inmates in good health and therefore reduces the amount of health problems that might arise. This is important because lower medical costs translate to savings for prison administrators.

Food service equipment within a prison kitchen is typically similar to what one would find in any large-scale cafeteria. However, the products may have security features not found in free-world kitchens. For instance, the company Jail Equipment World markets a maximum-security convection oven. The description of this product explains that this oven prevents "the tampering of control and product settings, protect[s] ovens and essential components from vandalism and abuse, eliminate[s] hiding places for contraband and prohibit[s] the removal of parts and components for weapon fabrication" (Jail Equipment World, 2010, p. 1). These ovens carry a price tag of $5,200 to $12,000 each (Jail Equipment World, 2010, p. 1). This example demonstrates that kitchen appliances must meet functional requirements as well as security requirements and that such equipment can carry a hefty price tag.

Laundry Facilities

The need to continually wash clothes and bedding is also a routine issue in prison facilities. Prisons and jails must have reliable washers and dryers and other machinery, such as ironing equipment, that is both heavy-duty and reliable. Laundry facilities must be suitable for continual use and must also allow for adequate security over the inmate population. The constant wear-and-tear of equipment requires that it be oversized, commercially rated, and industrial in strength. Such equipment must be made to take abuse, as it is operated by inmates who, for the most part, have little incentive to adequately take care of it.

As with kitchen facilities, laundry facilities should be designed so that security staff are able to maintain effective custody and control over inmates working in them. All products must be accounted for, including items such as irons and products such as bleach and cleaning soap; these items may be traded throughout the inmate population and can be used as weapons. Laundry facilities must be designed to with the need for inventory control of tools and equipment firmly in mind.

Robert Hanser

■ PHOTO 7.8 Laundry facilities in a prison or jail must be suitable for continual use and allow for adequate security to be exercised over the inmate population.

Recreational Facilities

Though the issue of inmate recreation may be controversial, it is inevitable that prison administrators will have to attend to it. Recreation for inmates comes in many shapes and forms and can be an effective behavior management tool inside the prison. The threat of exclusion from recreation programs usually gains compliance

CROSS-NATIONAL PERSPECTIVE 7.1

Prison Programming and Design in India

As noted in this chapter, the design of a prison must accommodate numerous aspects of the facility's day-to-day operations. Among other things, facilities must be designed to accommodate a wide array of auxiliary services and/or industrial programs. The nation of India has 10 prisons, one of which is Tihar Prison. This prison has numerous industries that operate within its walls, including the following:

Weaving: This section was initially established for manufacture of cloth for staff uniforms, convict uniforms, cotton durries, and so on. It has now started manufacturing terry cloth (white), woolen carpets, convict chador, woolen chador, fine chador, double-bed chador, dosuti cloth/cloth for cotton dresses, hand loom durries, and dusters. Introduction of up-to-date technology with the installation of new power loom machines has not only augmented the production capacity of the section but also created a training ground for convicts working on these machines. Apart from meeting internal requirements of approximately 12,000 inmates, the prison has secured orders from various departments of the Government of National Capital Territory of Delhi and from the private sector. There are eight power looms and 52 hand looms in this section, and four additional power looms are being installed.

Carpentry: This is the largest section of the jail factory with a workforce of approximately 350 workers. During the last financial year, more than 30,000 excellent-quality Meranti wood desks were supplied to various schools in Delhi. This section also trains convicts in the finer works of carving and carpentry and makes furniture for sale to the general public. This is the flagship unit with the highest turnover. At present this unit is producing various types of office furniture, including office chairs and tables, visitor chairs, computer tables, center tables, sofa sets, and rocking chairs, for various private and government-run institutes. The furniture here is made from 100% teak wood.

Chemicals: Soap, phenyl manufacture, and oil expelling are the basic functions of this unit. Mustard oil of the finest quality is produced in the section. The unit was initially started for production of in-house consumption of these items, but at present the same is available for open sale to the public at much lower rates than on the market. By-products of oil from this unit, like oil cake, are also sold in the open market through open auction.

Paper: The only eco-friendly unit at the prison. The paper unit prides itself in training inmates in the art of paper-making, with products ranging from pulp to beautiful hand-made paper to various items like carry bags, fancy paper bags, file covers, file boards, envelopes, grass paper, tiger paper, leather paper, moon-rock paper, marble paper, tea paper, and cardboard paper. This unit meets the internal stationary requirements of the prison and supplies items to various government departments. Additionally, old government files and paper from various departments are recycled in this unit.

SOURCE: Tihar Prison. (2009). New Delhi: India. Retrieved from http://www.delhi.gov.in/wps/wcm/connect/lib_centraljail/Central+Jail/Home/Annual+Review+2009/Tihar+-+from+the+Eye+of+Media

from most of the inmate population, and this alone demonstrates some operational value for such programs. When the leisure time of inmates is used in the construction of arts and crafts, multipurpose activities, and participation in sports activities or physical exercise, they are less likely to be lured into other activities that are not prosocial. Recreational activities for inmates might include any of the following:

1. Intramural sports (e.g., basketball, handball, flag football, soccer)
2. Games (cards, dominoes, bingo)
3. Individual exercise (weight lifting and jogging)
4. Arts and crafts (leather working, woodworking, painting)
5. Clubs (Key Club, Jaycees, Toastmasters)

Each of the above activities will have different requirements for facility space, and some of them can be held outdoors. As with any additional prison service, effective security maintenance is key to the implementation of these programs. Naturally, some types of recreation include tools or instruments that can, if not kept under tight inventory, be trafficked among the inmate population.

For instance, leather working tools, wood-cutting saws, and other types of instruments should be subjected to very close security scrutiny.

Religious Facilities

The impact of religion and faith-based programming in prison is undeniably important. In some prisons, an actual religious gathering facility may exist, but this is rare. More typically, a general meeting room will be used, with seats and speaking equipment provided. Given that different religious orientations may be found in prisons and that states do not wish to discriminate between different religions, it is probably prudent for administrators to simply provide space for religious services on an as-needed basis.

Tool Shop Facilities

Tool shops tend to exist in many larger prisons where some type of industry is performed. Such facilities allow inmates to be productive while serving their sentence. Inmates can learn and perform repair work of appliances, lawn equipment, and even motor vehicles. Such shops produce tangible benefits for the prison and the inmate population. Nevertheless, security risks exist, as such equipment can be used to make weapons and/or effect escape attempts. Thus, the design of tool shops must accommodate security concerns and allow for the easy inventory and control of equipment and tools.

TECHNOLOGY SYSTEMS IN PRISONS

The use of technology in prisons is becoming widespread and has impacted a number of operational aspects. Surveillance equipment is essential and has undergone improvements in recent years, but other developments have been equally innovative and just as important. For instance, the physical security of the institution itself has been strengthened through improvements in building and fencing technology as well as technology related to ingress and egress from correctional institutions.

For example, in California, Colorado, Missouri, and Alabama, innovations involving lethal forms of electric fencing have been effective in deterring escape attempts (Carlson & Garrett, 2008). While these types of fences should not be seen as a full replacement of security staff, they do eliminate the need for so many staff to concentrate on perimeter security. Carlson and Garrett (2008) note that these developments

> truly do offer the opportunity to cut back on staffing in towers and external mobile patrols. California's Department of Corrections has found the installation of these fences has facilitated the deactivation of nearly all towers and has enabled administrators to redeploy staff to other important posts. (p. 417)

Thus, such technology can allow administrators to maximize the use of their employees by diverting them to areas of the prison that can benefit from more personalized and human-oriented job functions.

Prison Tour Video: Prisoner Identification. Recent innovations in technology have greatly changed how corrections officers can monitor inmates. Watch an assistant warden describe prisoner identification and tracking.

Prisoner Identification

New processes regarding inmate identification are being developed that greatly enhance institutional security and cost-effectiveness. For instance, mug shots are now taken with digital cameras and stored in computers; this allows for photographic images of inmates to be readily available for prison staff at a fraction of the cost that once was required and enhances inmate recognition by staff. Likewise, fingerprints are now

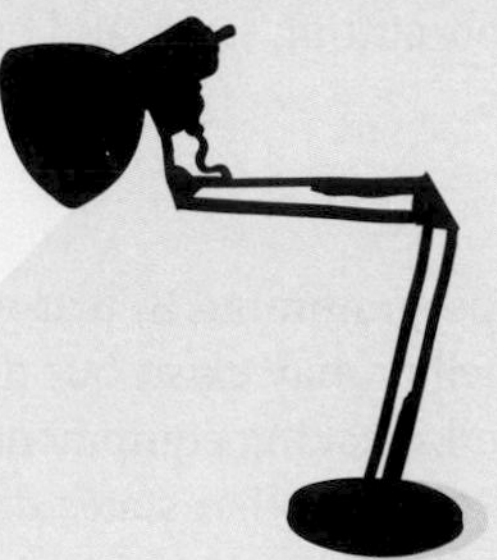

APPLIED THEORY 7.1

Routine Activity Theory, Inmate Traffic Flow, and Institutional Infractions

According to routine activity theory (see Chapter 6), crime will occur at locations where a motivated offender, a suitable target, and a lack of capable guardians come together. Because, at least in theory, a prison consists entirely of motivated offenders, there is a heightened likelihood that some form of criminal activity or victimization will occur. The presumption is that prison security—in terms of both personnel and security mechanisms—will be able to thwart the attempts of such offenders to commit crimes while in prison.

However, we know that trafficking and trading of contraband continue within the walls of prisons. Different forms of victimization also occur, as do illicit activities such as gambling. Thus, it seems that there are indeed suitable targets (victims, or, in victimless crimes, activities), and the guardians of the prison (security staff) may not always be capable of detecting and preventing this behavior.

The prevention of institutional infractions and victimization within prisons consists of many facets. First, security staff members' awareness of blind spots will enhance their ability to detect and prevent infractions. Second, the usefulness of technology can be enhanced when it is utilized within key areas that are vulnerable to inmate exploitation. Third, since the design of the facility itself will naturally impact inmate traffic flow, creating areas where more contact between inmates will occur, special care should be taken in these areas. Lastly, the operational schedule of the institution will affect the ebb and flow of likely violations as inmates are moved from one function to another throughout the daily routine of prison operations, so security staff should be on high alert during these times.

Pod-based dome technology has already been presented in this chapter as an ideal facility design to minimize security problems, both internal and perimeter-based. Likewise, the use of CCTV has been touched upon briefly for its ability to detect crime. However, it is important to further showcase the use of CCTV, both with real cameras and with decoy cameras, since it enhances the deterrence, detection, and prevention of likely violations.

For the most part, many modern facilities already use camera surveillance to monitor and record inmate visitation rooms in order to supervise visits and detect the exchange of drugs or other contraband. Monitoring is conducted from remote areas of the prison, which means that inmates are not aware if they are being watched. Institutions can even place cheap-to-construct decoy cameras that do not actually conduct surveillance throughout some areas of the prison. This can help deter infractions since inmates do not know which cameras work and which do not, and it extends the budget of the institution that cannot afford a great number of cameras.

maintained in online data systems, and retina imaging and iris-scanning equipment have undergone innovations and improvements.

In addition, some facilities have begun to use wristbands with bar codes that are used to track inmates throughout the prison. In this way, prison staff can monitor the movement of individual inmates in real time by using touch-key control systems. Similar tracking technology is being used in Los Angeles, where the tracking of inmates in the nation's largest jail system is now conducted with radio-linked wristbands (Etter, 2005). These devices allow security staff to pinpoint inmates' location within a few feet. Los Angeles County uses these devices at Pitchess Detention Center in Castaic, about 40 miles northwest of downtown Los Angeles, and has plans to expand the program to another 6,000 inmates at the county's central jail and then to other facilities (Etter, 2005).

In addition to tracking inmates around cell blocks, this technology has the potential to allow work-release crews to roam within an electronic fence construction that could be easily moved wherever needed (Etter, 2005). This is an important innovation because it can make work processes more secure for prison farms, minimum-security facilities, and prison camps where inmates work on wilderness and highway construction projects. Further still, with the use of surveillance systems inside the facility, a specific inmate can be tracked by both central security and that in the immediate vicinity of the inmate.

CONCLUSION

This chapter demonstrates that the physical features of a prison require a great deal of forethought prior to the ground being broken at the construction site. Issues related to the location of the prison facility, the types of custody levels and security, the function of the facility, and even logistical support for the facility are all important considerations. The design of the prison should be such that security is not compromised, but there is no true consensus on the best way to design a prison facility to address logistic issues while optimizing security features. In modern times, the use of large penitentiaries with gothic architecture has become antiquated. The formidability of modern security designs is obvious, particularly when one considers the introduction of the supermax facility to the realm of prison structures. Prison complexes have also emerged as a means of addressing the logistics of prison operational costs. Thus, both the design and the location of prison facilities can impact financial, operational, and security issues for correctional systems in the United States.

The various services within a facility and the different functions of the prison are again emphasized. Attention to the design of kitchen and laundry spaces is important, both for security purposes and for institutional living standards. Other services, such as religious services, recreational services, and tool shops where inmates can develop experience in specific trades, are also important for many reasons. These additional services eliminate idle inmate hands and minds and also give administrators some leverage in the control of inmate behavior; failure to comply with institutional rules can lead to restriction from these programs. Thus, the allocation of space and materials for these prison features can be important to future operational considerations. Though the cost to accommodate such features can be high, the likely reductions in prison offenses and misbehavior may offset such financial concerns.

Lastly, technological developments in the field of corrections have led to numerous improvements in security. Improvements in cell block and electric fence construction have made facilities even more secure, in terms of both internal and external security. Progress has also been made with regard to inmate identification and tracking. These advents in technology make the prison facility a part of a broader system that incorporates many other aspects of criminal justice and the surrounding community, enhancing security both inside and outside the prison.

DISCUSSION QUESTIONS

1. What is a panopticon and how is this design used today?
2. What are the various levels of security that classify prison facilities? What are the various levels of security used to classify cell blocks within facilities?
3. What is the supermax or Marion Model of prison facility construction?
4. What were some of the constitutional issues that emerged as a result of *Madrid v. Gomez*?
5. What are the various components of perimeter security of a correctional facility?
6. What are the primary components of internal security within a correctional facility?
7. What are some points to consider when integrating auxiliary programs into the design of a prison facility?
8. How does routine activity theory relate to inmate traffic flow and institutional infractions within a prison facility?

KEY TERMS

Alcatraz, 154
Americans with Disabilities Act (ADA), 157
Bastille, 150
Blind spots, 165
Direct supervision design, 152
Isolation zone, 162
Maximum-security facilities, 153
Medium-security facilities, 153
Minimum-security facilities, 153
Panopticon, 152
Perimeter security system, 159
Pods, 153
Special housing unit syndrome, 157
Supermax facility, 154
USP Florence ADMAX, 155
USP Marion, 155

KEY CASES

Bruscino v. Carlson (1988), 155 *Madrid v. Gomez* (1995), 157

APPLIED EXERCISE 7.1

You are the CEO of a large private prison company that is known for providing excellent correctional services. The time period is sometime between 2010 and 2014, and the current emphasis in the correctional industry is on offender reentry rather than incarceration. During the 1990s and early 2000s, your area experienced a boom in the inmate population and thus in the number of facilities needed. Because of this, you have a number of prisons within your state. However, the beds in your prisons are emptying, and since you are a private company you know that you will need to do something to modify your organizational emphasis to dovetail with the current demands within the correctional industry.

At one of your board meetings, your chief of operations noted that recent emphasis has been placed on prison industries, work release programs, and the need for offenders to have specified job skills in green technology and other forms of modern construction techniques. With that in mind, you have decided to modify your prison facilities to create a variety of products and services that will appeal to various industries throughout the nation. Along the way, inmates participating in these programs will learn valuable job skills.

TO THE STUDENT: For this assignment, explain how you would design a prison facility so that it has both security features and auxiliary services that will both generate income for the prison organization and provide job skill training for inmates scheduled to be released within a year.

In particular, you will need to address issues related to the custody levels of the inmates who would likely be utilized for these programs, the security that would need to be considered with the inmate population, and the potential for financial success of the industrial activities used in your design. Also, be sure to discuss any architectural considerations that may need to be considered when developing this program.

WHAT WOULD YOU DO?

You are the public relations officer for the state department of corrections. Recently, the state system has identified an area for a new prison site, but, once word of this decision was presented to the local community, a number of letters were sent to the governor's office expressing concern and resistance to this idea. You have been assigned the task of addressing these concerns and have been asked to mitigate public reactions to the idea of building a prison in the area. It is very clear that the state intends to build the facility regardless but would like to resolve the public relations issue that has emerged.

The community is midsize; it has a population of approximately 75,000, with some outlying towns also existing in the area. The nearest major metropolitan area is well over 3 hours' driving distance away. The community's economy is somewhat stable but lacks significant industrial development and is mostly agricultural in nature.

The prison is slated to be a minimum- to medium-security facility that will house 1,800 inmates. Many of these inmates will likely be in various industrial and educational programs. Security officers, educational specialists, and other employees within the prison will be needed, which might mean jobs for community members. This additional employment might also draw persons from outside of the area, which will increase the need for various goods and services (e.g., dry cleaning, groceries, restaurant services, home purchases) from business owners in the local area.

The governor's office has tasked you with showcasing the positive impact that this facility can have on the community while also alleviating concerns about the potential pitfalls to having a prison in the area.

What would you do?

PRACTICE AND APPLY WHAT YOU'VE LEARNED

edge.sagepub.com/hanser2e

HEAR IT FROM CORRECTIONAL PRACTITIONERS: PRISON TOUR VIDEOS

Head to the study site, where you'll find:

- Exclusive, **original SAGE video interviews** with wardens, correctional officers, inmates, and more
- Exclusive footage from inside **Angola Prison** and **Richwood Correctional Center**

CLASSIFICATION AND CUSTODY LEVELS

RECLASSIFICATION OF A GANG MEMBER

Cheryl Veracruz went to her office and pulled out the folder that she had on inmate Juan Rodriguez. She sat at her desk and looked up some additional information on his behavior history while in the custody of the state prison system. It seemed like he had done well, and she confirmed, again, that her automated report on his classification status had been updated correctly.

Juan had requested to be transferred to another prison facility so that his family could more easily visit him during the last 18 months of his sentence. His current location in the eastern part of Texas was several hundred miles away from where his family resided. However, his previous custody status had been at a level that did not allow him to transfer to the prison near where his family resided. Now that had changed.

Cheryl looked up to see Juan Rodriguez standing in her doorway.

"Hello Ms. Veracruz. I am here whenever you are ready to see me."

Cheryl waved a hand at him. "C'mon in and have a seat."

Juan slid into the seat across from her and sat with his hands outside of his pockets.

Folding her arms on her desk, Cheryl said, "The reason you are here is for reclassification. I just completed your review and you have been updated to minimum security."

Juan smiled but remained silent, listening closely to what she said.

"As you know, this means that you do qualify for a transfer," Cheryl continued. "Now, Juan, much of this has to do with your completion of the GRAD program about a year and a half ago, and also your completion of your GED and your work history." GRAD stood for the Gang Renouncement and Disassociation program, an important aspect of Juan's success.

Juan asked, "Ms. Veracruz, can I say something?"

"Yes?"

Juan shifted in his seat. "Look, I know you might be concerned that if I'm near home again I may fall back in with the gang life. But I'm out for good and I have to stay out if I'm gonna raise my kids and go to college. They have a work release program over there, also, and I need to get into a job in that area so that I can get some money up. It will keep me from draining my family."

Cheryl sat back in her chair and considered him. "So, what are you going to do when one of your old *familia* asks you about your quitting the gang?"

Juan did not hesitate to respond. "I have no debts and I made sure everything was clean. I have already told them that I'm out, and I did everything that was required to have my name cleared. . . . That is all beyond what I had to do in the GRAD program." He paused for a moment then added, "I know that we are not supposed to make deals with prior gang members, but I had to if I was really going to be done with the gang life, and now I am good to go with no worries."

LEARNING OBJECTIVES:

1. Discuss the history and development of classification processes in corrections.
2. Identify the legal rationale for classifications.
3. State the main goals of classification systems.
4. Identify different custody levels and the methods used for housing assignments and reclassification.
5. Describe the different categories of special housing assignments.
6. Discuss how classification processes are central to prison service operations.

SAGE edge™

Get the edge on your studies: edge.sagepub.com/hanser2e

- Take a quiz to find out what you've learned.
- Review key terms with eFlashcards.
- Watch videos that enhance chapter content.

Cheryl did not tell him that she had received a memo from the prison system's gang intelligence department confirming that Juan had apparently completed some type of assignment from his gang family that allowed him to peacefully resign from membership. This correspondence was found among written communications between other gang leaders who had agreed to let Juan exit the gang without further repercussions.

"Juan, we are going to transfer you," Cheryl said. "When we do, I am going to recommend that you take that fatherhood program that they have there, Malachi Dads. You okay with that?"

Juan grinned. "Yes, definitely, I think that would be great. It will help me to be a better father and hopefully a better husband to Marisol."

Marisol was Juan's wife and the mother of his two children. Though Juan was only 23, he had two children with her. During his past 4 years in prison, Marisol had stayed with Juan and maintained a good relationship with Juan's mother.

Cheryl smiled. "Yeah, actually, I think that Marisol will be your best bet in keeping you on the right track."

Juan leaned forward and spoke earnestly. "When I am out there, I'm not going to forget what you have done for me, Ms. Veracruz . . . and in couple of years, I would like to be in touch with you so that I can show you that you have not wasted your time."

Robert Hanser

■ PHOTO 8.2 The use of automated classification systems is now standard practice in both prisons and community-based correctional agencies. These systems keep track of programming, sentence time served, and other important aspects of the offender who is serving time.

of mentally disturbed inmates within the general population (where they are often victimized), and mitigate them. Solutions might include the separation of predatory inmates from likely victims or separating rival gang members. Prisons that use effective screening and classification and base their security decisions on the outcomes of these processes will likely be effective in providing reasonable protection of inmates in their custody.

Control Inmate Behavior

The control of inmate behavior often occurs by providing rewards or punishments for actions that are committed. Inmates who are repetitive rule violators can be reclassified to a level of custody that provides them with fewer privileges and prosocial activities. Inmates who maintain good behavior can be placed in less restrictive correctional facilities (e.g., minimum security) or may be given a special status, such as an inmate mentor on a given cell block, in which capacity they will assist both staff and fellow inmates. In addition, screening for offenders who have special risks (e.g., suicidal inmates or those with medical or mental health conditions) can help to identify those inmates who will require special security or treatment assignments. Effective security and custody placement can reduce fear, violence, escapes, and potential litigation.

Prison Tour Video Link

External and Internal Security, Inmate Escape Attempts, and Chase Efforts

Provide Planning and Accountability

Classification systems allow correctional agencies allocate their resources where they are most needed while not overspending on inmates who do not need as much supervision or intervention. Thus, these systems can save tax dollars and thereby help prisons to operate more efficiently. As mentioned before, the elimination of overclassification is very important when determining budgetary allocations. If inmates are repeatedly overclassified, they will be placed under restrictions that are more costly than is necessary, or they will be provided services that are not appropriate and are thereby wasted.

Classification systems are extremely important for developing prison budgets, determining the types of units to build in the future, determining staffing levels, and providing services. Classification systems can also provide information on the characteristics of a system's prison population as a means of making security, custody, and staffing projections or even in determining if a new prison may need to be built within a system. This can help administrators avoid the error of overestimating the need for expensive maximum-security cells while underestimating the need for less expensive minimum-security beds. Thus, classification processes are critical to the management of any correctional system, whether it be a prison, a jail, or even a community-based program or facility, since the underlying goal of effective resource allocation applies to all spectrums of the correctional industry.

ELEMENTS OF ALL CLASSIFICATION SYSTEMS

Generally speaking, classification processes are divided into two phases: the initial classification phase and later points of reclassification. This means that classification is a continual process that follows inmates throughout their sentence. This is, in many respects, similar in concept to what Maconochie had implemented where commensurate good behavior led to a reclassification of an inmate's likelihood for release. The same is true today; as inmates exhibit behavior that is desired, their custody level and their overall time in prison can be greatly modified. Likewise, if inmates continue to exhibit

TECHNOLOGY AND EQUIPMENT 8.1

Automated Classification Systems

Information technology (IT) and computational developments have been found to enhance the productivity of prison classification systems in several jurisdictions. Because classification is data dependent, it requires high-quality data and sufficient computational capacity. With this in mind, classification productivity is categorized into two main components—efficiency and effectiveness—each of which has several subcomponents. Each element is important when considering how advances in IT and computer power may enhance productivity.

Brennan, Wells, and Alexander (2004) conducted case studies in seven prisons that had shown innovations in classification, management information systems, and IT. Several important findings emerged from their research. First, criminal justice databases are slowly becoming more integrated, and classification should gain profoundly from the speed, comprehensiveness, and integrity of the data. Second, prison classification is showing a trend toward more comprehensive systems, broader information, and multiple goals. This shift will increase the demands on IT for comprehensive data. Third, the management of change and innovation remains a challenge, but there have been many lessons learned regarding implementation and change management, especially with regard to IT and classification.

Florida is one of the correctional systems that Brennan et al. (2004) examined. Florida's Department of Corrections has an excellent automated classification system known as CARS (the Custody Assessment and Reclassification System). Florida's classification system and related inmate management applications are principally based on its mainframe-driven Offender Based Information System (OBIS), which is accessible by every facility. The two classification applications running under OBIS are CARS and the Risk and Needs System. OBIS is supplemented by mini-mainframe systems in each of the five reception and intake centers. The principal application is the Computer Assisted Reception Process (CARP). All three classification applications are integrated to facilitate data sharing and lookups and to minimize redundant data entry. Future plans call for additional local area network (LAN) and wide area network (WAN) personal computer (PC)–based applications, such as drug testing, enhanced visitation tracking, the implementation of drug interdiction, and the identification of gang activity, to augment and integrate with the current systems. Plans also call for these PC-based applications to incorporate artificial intelligence engines to identify gang, drug, and contraband patterns throughout the entire prison system and overlay color-coded analysis on Global Positioning System (GPS) maps of the system.

With assistance from the Northeast Florida Center for Community Initiatives and the National Institute of Corrections, the Florida Department of Corrections Bureau of Classification and Central Records recently developed and implemented its new Risk and Needs System. This internal classification uses objective assessments (academic, vocational, and substance abuse, along with the inmate's risk factors) to determine internal placement decisions regarding housing and work assignments. Completing the Risk and Needs System requires the collection of information through a face-to-face interview with the inmate and through official data previously entered in OBIS. The information compiled and scored in the Risk and Needs System serves as the basis for the Inmate Management Plan. This plan is the means by which classification decisions are made and documented and by which progress is tracked throughout incarceration. Management plans are reviewed at least every 12 months. The plan comprises primary work or program recommendations, housing recommendations, and goals and objectives to be achieved during incarceration.

While many state classification systems use automated programs (in fact, most all of them do), the state of Florida's is particularly well developed. The technology used in the Florida system allows classification to integrate a number of factors into the decision with mathematical precision and much more quickly than could be done by a human being. This allows for more effective, more efficient, and more objective assessment as well as the development of logical and consistent Inmate Management Plans. Florida's program is a good example of what other correctional agencies might wish to implement in their own systems.

SOURCE: Brennan, T., Wells, D., & Alexander, J. (2004). *Enhancing prison classification systems: The emerging role of management information systems.* Washington, DC: National Institute of Corrections.

antisocial behavior, their custody level can become more restrictive and they will likely stay behind bars for the full duration of their sentence. If they should commit additional criminal acts while behind bars, they can be prosecuted and given additional time for these new crimes. In such cases, the classification process would again modify the inmate's overall standing within the system.

Level of security: The type of physical barriers that are utilized to prevent inmates' escape and are related to public safety concerns.

Custody level: Related to the degree of staff supervision that is needed for a given inmate.

Security and Custody Issues

The **level of security** provided for a particular inmate refers to the type of physical barriers utilized to prevent that inmate's escape and is related to public safety concerns. As long as the inmates are kept within the prison grounds, it is less likely that they can harm persons in the community. On the other hand, the **custody level** is related to the degree of staff supervision needed for a given inmate. This is more related to safety and security within the prison facility itself, though this can also impact the likelihood that the inmate will be able to engage in activities that affect the public.

Initial Security Classification

Audio Link
Judge Offers View From the Bench

The initial point of classification actually tends to occur well before the inmate arrives at the prison facility. Such classification is usually conducted by community supervision staff right after the offender is sentenced. The federal system serves as a good example of how community supervision officers, who are often called pretrial services officers, provide the initial assessment that begins the later classification process in the federal prison system. This process entails the construction of a *presentence investigation (PSI) report*, as students may recall from earlier, which is used to inform the judge of the circumstances associated with the offender prior to sentencing.

Because there are no specific standard forms of classification used by all states but all systems tend to have initial classification processes that are, by necessity, similar, a single system will be used as an example of how initial classification may be conducted. For purposes of this discussion, we will refer to the document titled *Program Statement: Bureau of Prisons Inmate Classification System* (2006), which serves as the basis of initial classification in the Federal Bureau of Prisons (BOP). Within the BOP, institutions are classified into one of five security levels—minimum, low, medium, high, and administrative—based on the level of security and staff supervision the institution is able to provide (see Table 8.1). An institution's level of security and staff supervision is based on the following factors:

1. Mobile patrol
2. Internal security
3. Towers
4. Type of inmate housing
5. Perimeter barriers
6. Inmate-to-staff ratio
7. Detection devices
8. Any special institutional mission

An inmate's security point score is not the only factor used in determining a commensurate security level. The SENTRY system (discussed in more detail below) cannot assign a security level unless prison employees complete an Inmate Load and Security Designation Form. This form serves as a basic data collection tool. BOP inmates are classified based on both security and treatment issues, as noted in earlier parts of this chapter. Specifically, the BOP considers the level of security and supervision the inmate requires and the inmate's program needs (substance abuse treatment, educational/vocational training, individual counseling, group counseling, medical/mental health treatment, etc.).

In summary, just as with most state correctional systems, the initial assignment (designation) of an inmate to a particular institution within the BOP is based primarily upon the following:

1. The level of security and supervision the inmate requires.
2. The level of security and staff supervision the institution is able to provide.
3. The inmate's program needs.

Figure 8.2 provides students with a view of the Inmate Load and Security Designation Form, which helps to clearly demonstrate the information that is tracked when making initial classification

■ Table 8.1: Federal BOP Inmate Classification Scheme

Security level	Custody level	Male	Female
MINIMUM	COMMUNITY and OUT	0–11 points	0–15 points
LOW	OUT and IN	12–15 points	16–30 points
MEDIUM	OUT and IN	16–23 points	*
HIGH	IN and MAXIMUM	24+ points	31+ points
ADMINISTRATIVE	All custody levels	All points totals	All points totals

SOURCE: Federal Bureau of Prisons. (2006). *Program statement: Bureau of Prisons inmate classification system.* Washington, DC: Author.

■ Figure 8.2: Inmate Load and Security Designation Form for the Federal Bureau of Prisons

BP-337 **INMATE LOAD AND SECURITY DESIGNATION FORM**		**FEDERAL BUREAU OF PRISONS**	
INMATE LOAD DATA			
1. REGISTER NUMBER			
2. LAST NAME	3. FIRST NAME	4. MIDDLE	5. SUFFIX
6. RACE / 7. SEX	8. ETHNIC ORIGIN	9. DATE OF BIRTH	
10. OFFENSE/SENTENCE			
11. FBI NUMBER		12. SSN NUMBER	
13. STATE OF BIRTH	14. OR COUNTRY OF BIRTH		15. CITIZENSHIP
16. ADDRESS-STREET			
17. CITY	18. STATE	19. ZIP	20. OR FOREIGN COUNTRY
21. HEIGHT FT ___ IN ___	22. WEIGHT _____ LBS	23. HAIR COLOR	24. EYE COLOR
25. ARS ASSIGNMENT			
SECURITY DESIGNATION DATA			
1. JUDGE	2. REC FACILITY	3. REC PROGRAM	4. USM OFFICE

5. VOLUNTARY SURRENDER STATUS **0** = NO **(-3)** = YES
IF YES, MUST INDICATE: 5a. VOLUNTARY SURRENDER DATE: ________________
5b. VOLUNTARY SURRENDER LOCATION: ____________

6. MONTHS TO RELEASE ________

7. SEVERITY OF CURRENT OFFENSE
0 = LOWEST **3** = MODERATE **7** = GREATEST
1 = LOW MODERATE **5** = HIGH

8. CRIMINAL HISTORY SCORE
0 = 0-1 **4** = 4-6 **8** = 10-12
2 = 2-3 **6** = 7-9 **10** = 13 +

8a. SOURCE OF DOCUMENTED CRIMINAL HISTORY ____ - PRESENTENCE INVESTIGATION REPORT or ____ - NCIC III

9. HISTORY OF VIOLENCE	NONE	>15 YEARS	10-15 YEARS	5-10 YEARS	<5 YEARS
MINOR	0	1	1	3	5
SERIOUS	0	2	4	6	7

10. HISTORY OF ESCAPE OR ATTEMPTS	NONE	>15 YEARS	>10 YEARS	5-10 YEARS	<5 YEARS
MINOR	0	1	1	2	3
SERIOUS	0	3(S)	3(S)	3(S)	3(S)

11. TYPE OF DETAINER
0 = NONE **3** = MODERATE 7 = GREATEST
1 = LOWEST/LOW MODERATE **5** = HIGH

12. AGE
0 = 55 and over **4** = 25 through 35
2 = 36 through 54 **8** = 24 or less

13. EDUCATION LEVEL
0 = Verified High School Degree or GED
1 = Enrolled in and making satisfactory progress in GED Program
2 = No verified High School Degree/GED and not participating in GED Program

13a. HIGHEST GRADE COMPLETED ______________

14. DRUG/ALCOHOL ABUSE **0** = Never/>5 Years **1** = <5 Years

15. SECURITY POINT TOTAL

16. PUBLIC SAFETY FACTORS
A-NONE
B-DISRUPTIVE GROUP (males only)
C-GREATEST SEVERITY OFFENSE (males only)
F-SEX OFFENDER
G-THREAT TO GOVERNMENT OFFICIALS
H-DEPORTABLE ALIEN
I-SENTENCE LENGTH (males only)
K-VIOLENT BEHAVIOR (females only)
L-SERIOUS ESCAPE
M-PRISON DISTURBANCE
N-JUVENILE VIOLENCE
O-SERIOUS TELEPHONE ABUSE

17. REMARKS

18. OMDT REFERRAL (YES/NO) ____

SOURCE: Federal Bureau of Prisons. (2006). *Program statement: Bureau of Prisons inmate classification system.* Washington, DC: Author.

decisions about an inmate. Tables 8.2 and 8.3 illustrate how the point system in the federal classification scheme also incorporates other factors related to public safety to determine the inmate's overall security point total; Table 8.2 pertains to male inmates whereas Table 8.3 pertains to female inmates.

Other factors may be considered, depending on the circumstances. Factors that come into play when designating an inmate to a particular institution include, but are not limited to, the following:

1. The inmate's release residence.
2. The level of overcrowding at an institution.
3. Any security, location, or program recommendation made by the sentencing court.

SENTRY system: A comprehensive database used by the Federal Bureau of Prisons to classify and track inmates within the system.

The **SENTRY system** is a comprehensive database used by the BOP to classify and track inmates within the system. Initial designations to BOP institutions are made in most cases by staff at the Designation and Sentence Computation Center (DSCC) in Grand Prairie, Texas, who assess and enter

Table 8.2: Inmate Security Designation Based on Classification Score and Public Safety Factors—Male Inmates

SECURITY DESIGNATION TABLE (MALES)		
Inmate Security Level Assignments Based on Classification Score and Public Safety Factors		
Security Point Total	Public Safety Factors	Inmate Security Level
0–11	**No Public Safety Factors**	**Minimum**
	Deportable Alien	Low
	Juvenile Violence	Low
	Greatest Severity Offense	Low
	Sex Offender	Low
	Serious Telephone Abuse	Low
	Threat to Government Officials	Low
	Sentence Length	
	Time remaining > 10 Yrs	Low
	Time remaining > 20 Yrs	Medium
	Time remaining > 30 Yrs (Includes non-parolable life and death penalty cases)	High
	Serious Escape	Medium
	Disruptive Group	High
	Prison Disturbance	High
12–15	**No Public Safety Factors**	**Low**
	Serious Escape	Medium
	Sentence Length	
	Time remaining > 20 Yrs	Medium
	Time remaining > 30 Yrs (Includes non-parolable life and death penalty cases)	High
	Disruptive Group	High
	Prison Disturbance	High
16–23	**No Public Safety Factors**	**Medium**
	Disruptive Group	High
	Prison Disturbance	High
	Time remaining > 30 Yrs (Includes non-parolable life and death penalty cases)	High
24+		**High**

SOURCE: Federal Bureau of Prisons. (2006). *Program statement: Bureau of Prisons inmate classification system.* Washington, DC: Author.

■ **Table 8.3: Inmate Security Designation Based on Classification Score and Public Safety Factors—Female Inmates**

SECURITY DESIGNATION TABLE (FEMALES)		
Inmate Security Level Assignments Based on Classification Score and Public Safety Factors		
Security Point Total	Public Safety Factors	Inmate Security Level
0–15	**No Public Safety Factors**	**Minimum**
	Deportable Alien	Low
	Juvenile Violence	Low
	Serious Telephone Abuse	Low
	Sex Offender	Low
	Threat to Government Officials	Low
	Violent Behavior	Low
	Prison Disturbance	High
	Serious Escape	High
16–30	**No Public Safety Factors**	**Low**
	Prison Disturbance	High
	Serious Escape	High
31+		**High**

SOURCE: Federal Bureau of Prisons. (2006). *Program statement: Bureau of Prisons inmate classification system.* Washington, DC: Author.

information from the sentencing court, the U.S. Marshals Service, the U.S. Attorney's Office or other prosecuting authority, and the U.S. Probation Office about the inmate into the computer database known as SENTRY. Once data are entered, SENTRY then calculates a point score for that inmate, which is then matched with a commensurate security-level institution (see Table 8.1 for classification levels).

Inmate Needs, Services, and Housing and the Classification Team

Determining an inmate's programming and housing needs requires that information be considered from a variety of sources. At intake, a medical screening of inmates is conducted in most correctional departments. This screening usually occurs on the first day of reception, and, if medical conditions warrant it, the inmate may be separated from the general population. If the inmate has only slight medical issues or issues that are able to be handled through routine visits to the prison infirmary, he or she will be housed as usual.

The initial screening for services usually includes a review of the PSI report and, in the federal system, a scan of the information in the SENTRY system. Specifically, this screening is a search for a history of sexually aggressive behavior on the part of the inmate and/or to determine if the inmate has been the victim of such behavior. Other characteristics that the inmate may possess are considered to prevent victimization by other inmates. All of these procedures are conducted in the interest of the safety of the inmate and the security of the institution.

Web Link
State of North Carolina, Department of Correction, Division of Prisons, Unit Management

Within the BOP, CFR Title 28, Part 524, Section 524.11(a) and (b) states,

> (a) at a minimum, each classification (unit) team shall include the unit manager, a case manager, and a counselor. An education advisor and a psychology services representative are also ordinarily members of the team. Where the institution does not have unit management, the team shall include a case manager, counselor, and one other staff member.
>
> (b) Each member of the classification team shall individually interview the newly arrived inmate within five working days of the inmate's assignment to that team.

The classification team is headed by a unit manager who supervises the other primary unit team members, who include case managers, correctional counselors, and staff representing education, psychology, and other disciplines contributing to an offender's law-abiding lifestyle. The

Robert Hanser (top and bottom)

■ PHOTO 8.3 The first photo shows a jail control room with the lights on. This area serves as the security center for the facility. Correctional officers coordinate communications and surveillance from this room throughout numerous dormitories. Sgt. Amber Rawls and Warden Brown stand by and observe monitors and security screens. Note that the windows are one-way mirrors that turn opaque when the interior lights are on. The second photo shows a similar control when the lights are turned off. In this case, it is easy to see out into the dormitory and observe inmate movement therein.

unit manager directs the housing unit activities and is responsible for the unit's operation and the quality control of all correspondence and programs. Figure 8.3 illustrates the authority level of the unit manager over the classification team and in relation to other management personnel within the prison facility.

The **case manager** reports directly to the unit manager and has major responsibility for case management matters within the unit. The case manager and other staff will assist with unit inmates and participate in other operations as directed by the unit manager. The case manager's responsibilities include all the traditional duties required to move an individual through a correctional institution. These responsibilities include being aware of policies, possessing the technical expertise to assess correctness of reports, being knowledgeable about parole board procedures and the legalities involved, and so forth. In addition, since caseloads are small, the case manager takes an active role in direct treatment intervention. That is, he or she will also conduct counseling sessions or other treatment modalities that make up the unit's therapeutic approach.

The **correctional counselor** develops and implements programs within the unit to meet the needs of the inmates; this programming includes both individual and group counseling. He or she may be assigned to either a general or a specialized unit, and is usually assigned to one case manager and a specific caseload. The correctional counselor plays a key role in maintaining and enhancing the security of the unit and institution through his or her extensive contacts with the inmates. The correctional counselor's role includes being a direct implementer of the agreed-upon treatment modalities, a fully functioning member of the classification team, an overseer of activities outside the unit (e.g., work assignments) and their implications for the classification process, an organizer and/or monitor of recreation and leisure activities, and so on. In general, the correctional counselor will have the most immediate, prolonged, and intensive relationship with many of the facility's inmates.

The **education adviser** is the unit team's consultant in all education matters, and this person normally will be a permanent member of the unit team. He or she sees that all of the unit inmates are properly tested and informed of available education opportunities. The education adviser may also be responsible for monitoring and evaluating unit inmates in education programs and will provide counseling in education matters as needed. Depending upon the specific needs of the prison population, it is the educator's responsibility to recommend training alternatives in order to help each individual reach goals agreed upon in collaboration with the facility. He or she may also be required to develop special classes that provide inmates with information of relevance to the intent of the prison's program.

Unit manager: Directs the housing unit activities and is responsible for the unit's operation and quality control of all correspondence and programs.

Case manager: Is directly responsible to the unit manager and has major responsibility for case management matters.

The **psychology services representative** (psychiatrist, psychologist, psychiatric nurse) of the classification team has a multifaceted role. This person is expected to be involved in the admission and information-gathering process prior to classification; he or she is a member of the decision-making team. This professional is usually a psychologist and is generally responsible for the performance of diagnostic, therapeutic, research, educational, and evaluative functions relating to psychological services. This individual plans, organizes, participates in, and provides professional expertise for unit counseling programs. This function includes the assessment of inmate needs and the design of corresponding programs to meet those needs. This professional monitors, supervises, and/or conducts therapeutic sessions as needed within the facility.

It is important to point out that the culture of the facility should be one that expedites effective classification of inmates for both security and programming purposes (see Focus Topic 8.1). The use of classification teams with members from a variety of backgrounds can aid in this. Both treatment staff and security staff will need to find common ground in the day-to-day operations of the prison facility if classification processes are to have optimal outcomes.

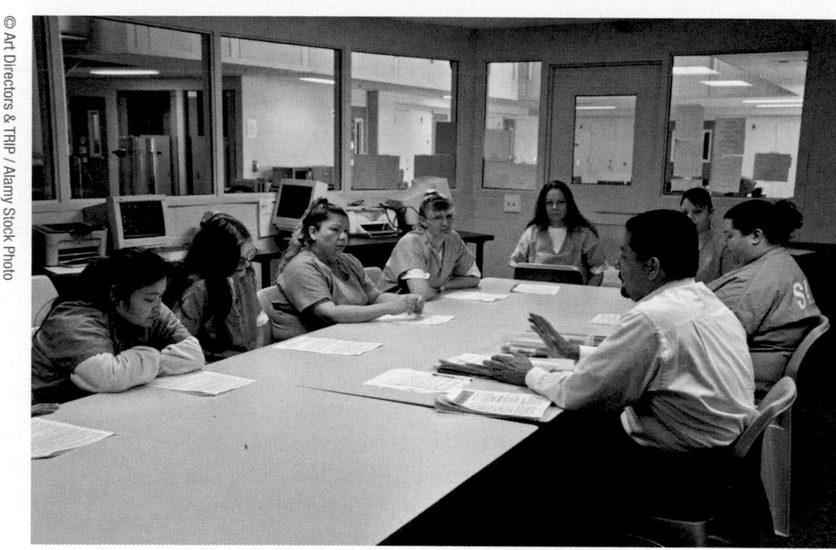

■ PHOTO 8.4 **This clinician is providing substance abuse counseling to female inmates in a prison treatment program.**

Reclassification Processes

At first, an inmate's custody is determined by the custody levels that exist within the facility that he or she is assigned to. The lowest level of custody, called community, is usually reserved for those inmates who meet the criteria for participation in community-based activities. Inmates within this custody level may be allowed to reside in the least secure housing, with some such facilities existing outside of the perimeter of the prison itself. These inmates may be allowed to work outside the prison with very little supervision, and they may participate in community-based programming

Video Link
Prison Garden Helps Inmates Turn Over New Leaf

Correctional counselor: Develops and implements programs within the unit to meet the individual needs of the inmates confined.

Education adviser: The unit team's consultant in all education matters.

Psychology services representative: A member of the decision-making team who is expected to be involved in the admission and information-gathering process prior to classification.

■ Figure 8.3: Administrative Lines of Authority for Classification Teams Among Prison Employees and Management

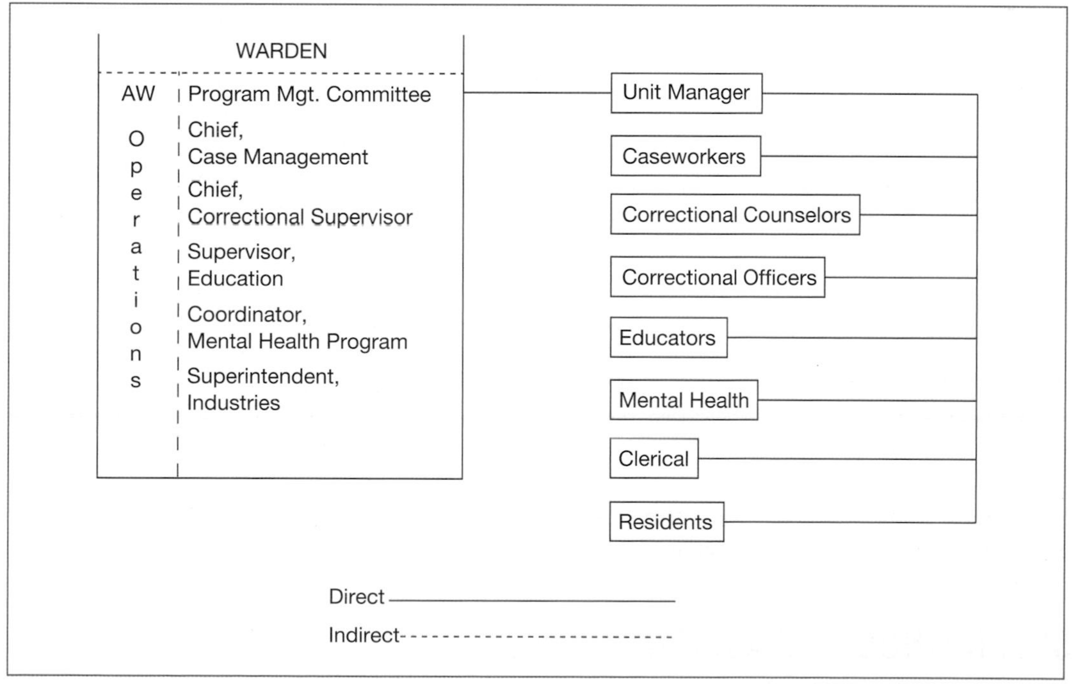

SOURCE: National Institute of Corrections. (1995). *Corrections information series: Unit management.* Washington, DC: Author.

FOCUS TOPIC: 8.1

The Confluence of Assessment, Classification, and Staff Attitudes in Determining Program Effectiveness

In the state of West Virginia, an ingenious study took place in 2006 that examined the use of effective assessment and classification systems implementing the LSI-R (Level of Service Inventory–Revised). The researchers also examined the effects of staff culture and attitudes toward reentry and rehabilitative orientations. The authors determined that research consistently shows correctional staff can have a strong influence on the predicted success or failure of a program that is implemented by a correctional agency. This is an important aspect of the classification process that is rarely (if ever) considered a variable in most assessment and/or classification systems. It may well be that staff attitudes could explain some of the variance that exists between predicted offender outcomes and the actual outcomes.

Some of the results that these researchers found are as follows:

1. Programs or interventions that depart substantially from the principles known to inform effective correctional programming are much less likely to lead to reductions in recidivism.
2. Given that staff members, such as case managers, counselors, and parole officers, interact with prisoners on a daily basis, they can determine the success or failure of any initiative undertaken by a correctional organization.
3. The identification of appropriate service and level of supervision after release should be contingent upon the accurate assessment of offender risk and needs.
4. Research has consistently shown that objective risk and needs assessments based on statistical probabilities more accurately predict the level of risk than personal or staff positions.
5. The success of a program can be significantly hampered by individual attitudes and personal opinions toward a new strategy, and the implementation of that strategy may be responsible for its success or failure.
6. Older organizations with well-embedded institutionalized organizational cultures and larger organizations with more layers of bureaucracy have more difficulty with communication and coordination.
7. Conflict between individual values of the staff and the values of the organization negatively impacts implementation strategies.
8. Detachment between staff attitudes and organizational values translates into role conflict. Role conflict produces stress and job dissatisfaction, contributing to a negative organizational culture.
9. Organizational culture drives staff behavior and knowledge of what is valued in the organization.
10. Staff tended to support the West Virginia initiative when they were advocates of rehabilitation, were more human-service oriented, liked to work with others, liked their job, were empathetic toward inmates, and believed the department was committed to staff training and professional development.
11. A large majority of correctional staff were found to have a punitive orientation toward inmates, did not believe in the efficacy of rehabilitation, and were not oriented toward a human-service career.
12. The initial report concluded that a substantial change in the human orientation of staff and greater support for rehabilitative efforts may be necessary to achieve greater support for reentry initiatives among correctional staff.

This study is important because it illustrates that the predictions of offender behavior can be mitigated and/or aggravated by the actions of supervision and treatment staff within an agency. These factors are important both for the prognosis of individual offenders and for evaluating agency outcomes. These authors, through this research approach, found a link between individual offender treatment planning and agency evaluation outcomes. Because of this, it is perhaps a good recommendation that future classification systems take into account agency staff and organizational culture since these factors are seldom assessed and have direct bearing on the success or failure of offenders who are released to community supervision.

SOURCE: Haas, S. M., Hamilton, C. A., & Hanley, D. (2006, July). *Implementation of the West Virginia Offender Reentry Initiative: An examination of staff attitudes and the application of the LSI-R.* Charleston, WV: Mountain State Criminal Justice Research Services.

activities on some occasions. The distinction between the status of offenders behind the walls and that of offenders on community supervision can become quite blurred in some cases.

SPECIAL HOUSING ASSIGNMENTS

Special housing assignments are provided for a number of reasons, but in this section we focus on those related to security. In earlier parts of this text, inmates in protective custody have been discussed, particularly in Chapter 7, where the design of such facilities was considered. In this

CORRECTIONS AND THE LAW 8.1

Court Cases and Legal Issues With Protective Custody

Throughout this chapter, we have explored a number of sometimes controversial legal issues associated with both classification and the use of protective custody. While protective custody is a costly form of security and protection for inmates, prudent administrators should understand that such a cost is miniscule in comparison to the potential costs if legal damages are incurred due to negligent standards of care. One unsavory aspect of protective custody is that some of the most despicable criminals are those who are afforded these added protections. Indeed, it is often precisely because of the nature of their crime that they are considered for such additional security measures.

Consider, for example, John J. Geoghan, a defrocked Catholic priest who was convicted of molestation in 2002 and was serving time at Souza-Baranowski Correctional Center, a maximum-security facility located in Lancaster, Massachusetts. The Souza-Baranowski facility was thought to be very safe, as it was technologically advanced and utilized modern security features.

Geoghan was 67 years old when he was first incarcerated, and, due to the nature of his offense, he was placed into protective custody. However, the entire Massachusetts DOC had only two facilities with protective custody housing, and at Souza-Baranowski, requests from inmates for this type of protection were constant. As such, protective custody cells were in high demand and administrators would double bunk the cells, placing two inmates in each. It was thought that persons placed in the same cell together would both seek refuge from violence and victimization and would not, therefore, be a threat to one another.

This turned out to be completely untrue for Geoghan. He was placed in cell number 2 of a two-tiered protective custody cell block in Souza-Baranowski. Roughly a month or so later, another inmate, Joseph Druce, was also assigned to the protective custody cellblock. Within a few short weeks, it was clear that Druce had developed a strong dislike of Geoghan and, one day in August 2003, just after lunch, Druce snuck into Geoghan's cell while it was open, jammed the cell door closed, and strangled Geoghan to death. Various sources note that Druce was a self-pronounced white supremacist who was given a life sentence without parole for murdering a man who had, according to Druce, solicited Druce for sex. Because of this, many external officials as well as the media criticized the prison administration for being careless and negligent. Indeed, it was also alleged that prison officials had been warned by various inmates that Druce was planning to harm Geoghan. Thus, many contended that prison officials deliberately turned a blind eye to the risk of injury to Geoghan.

As the matter was investigated, it was found that some inmates in the prison were disgusted with Geoghan because he had been talking with other sex offenders in the facility and bragging about his sexual assaults of young boys while he was a priest. Internal and external investigators gathered testimony that indicated that Druce was one of the inmates who was upset about this and that he had planned the murder of Geoghan for over a month. Indeed, Druce himself later commented that he considered the murder of Geoghan a prize, implying that he had derived honor and respect from others at Souza-Baranowski for this act. Ultimately, Druce was convicted for the first-degree murder of Geoghan and in 2006 was sentenced to another life-without-parole sentence.

Later, in mid 2007, a YouTube video was released on the Internet that clearly showed correctional officers attempting to open Geoghan's prison cell while Druce strangled Geoghan. Druce had managed to block the door from being opened by cramming a thick book in the rail tracks that allowed the door to open and close. It was never officially determined who had released the video to the press and to the public, but Massachusetts DOC officials pointed to Druce, alleging that he was somehow responsible. (The video is, at the time of writing this text, still available on YouTube.)

Given the circumstances associated with this incident, students should take the time to ask themselves if other alternatives were available to the Massachusetts DOC and whether the state acted prudently. Such questions must be considered by federal courts when addressing the use of protective custody and other restrictive assignments and when considering liability in regard to the protection of inmates in a system's custody.

chapter, we look at the rationale and reasons for placing an inmate in special housing, which includes protective custody. The other primary form of unique housing that requires special security considerations is administrative segregation. This type of housing assignment is not punitive but is a designation intended to prevent potential disruption of institutional security. It seeks to ensure the safety of staff and inmates who may be in danger if a given inmate is allowed to freely intermingle within the general population of the prison.

We begin with protective custody and follow with a discussion of administrative segregation. It is perhaps worth mentioning that the author of this text worked for several years in an administrative segregation department with violent and gang-related offenders, with occasional tours of

■ PHOTO 8.5 Individual housing units such as the ones pictured here consist of individual cells that are adjacent to a common dayroom, in a barred section of the jail facility.

duty in the protective custody section of the Texas prison facility where he was employed. When appropriate, information regarding these types of special housing may be derived from professional experience gained during that employment.

Protective Custody

According to the National Institute of Corrections (1986), **protective custody** includes "special provisions to provide for the safety and well-being for inmates who, based on findings of fact, would be in danger in the general population" (p. 41). This general definition, provided by the premiere clearinghouse on correctional research, will serve as the definition of protective custody for this text. The designation of protective custody as an official classification did not emerge until the 1960s, but its usage began to grow in the mid-1980s. During this period, the number of inmates in protective custody nationwide exceeded 25,000; this number declined to around 7,500 by 2001. Figure 8.4 provides an illustration of the trends in protective custody between 1980 and 2001. This trend is consistent with two other important occurrences within the field of corrections during these time periods. First, the 1980s saw a rise in the use of protective custody as a result of a number of federal court rulings and injunctions during the late 1970s and 1980s that required many prison systems to revamp their programs. Second, prisons during the 1980s began to see more gang-related membership; this was followed by an influx of drug offenders in the 1990s, when another small increase (in 1990) was observed among those in protective custody. These trends impacted both protective custody and administrative segregation populations.

The reasons for being placed in protective custody can be many, but some are more common:

1. Sexual harassment and/or pressure for sexual favors from other inmates.
2. Providing information to correctional or law enforcement officials; being an informant.
3. Being in debt to other inmates, usually through gambling of one sort or another.
4. The type of crime that the offender committed prior to incarceration, such as with pedophiles.
5. Having been previously employed in law enforcement or corrections.

Poore (1994) provides a very good overview of these reasons for assigning protective custody, and her work is presented here to highlight the complications of this form of inmate classification and custody. The following are, according to Poore, typical reasons an inmate is assigned to protective custody, along with the attendant concerns and considerations of that reason:

- **Sexual harassment.** Because most inmates know that sexual violation is considered inexcusable, there is a strong suspicion its frequent citation as a reason for protective custody may be more for effect than for cause. Nevertheless, there are certainly cases when inmates have been seriously threatened and/or actually raped. This is a reason often cited by first offenders who want to be in protective custody, even if they have not actually been subjected to such treatment.
- **Assistance/informants.** In the next category are those who may be in danger due to their assistance to law enforcement prior to coming to prison. Additionally, a large number of inmates have assisted prison officials in preventing escapes, curtailing drug traffic, or handling other illegal activity while incarcerated. These inmates often cannot live in the general prison population.

Protective custody: A security-level status given to inmates who are deemed to be at risk of serious violence if not afforded protection.

- **Debts.** Because of the availability of contraband in prison and the prevalence of gambling and other such activities, many inmates get into debt and are unable to pay. If there is no other arrangement to satisfy the debt, the lender is obligated to keep his other customers in line by making examples of those who will not pay. Many inmate arguments, fights, assaults, and even murders have been the end result of bad debts.
- **Type of crime.** Contrary to the belief of many citizens, there are relatively few inmates who must seek protection as a result of having committed an especially repugnant crime. Child molesters and rapists, who once faced great difficulties when living with other inmates, often are protected by rules of confidentiality and are aware that it would be in their best interests to lie about their crimes.
- **Former law enforcement.** Inmates who once worked in law enforcement may be at risk of harm due to the natural animosity that may exist between them and other offenders who are aware of their past line of work.

The classification process should continually reevaluate inmates in such custody with regard to both their level of security and their participation in various types of programming. The courts have made it clear that inmates in protective custody and administrative segregation should be afforded the same types of programming as inmates in the general population whenever possible. If an inmate has engaged in appropriate types of programming, it is feasible that that he or she could be reclassified back to the general population, presuming that safety of that inmate is no longer an issue.

Angelone (1999) notes that protective custody units of state prisons are becoming more difficult to manage due to the variety of backgrounds and behavioral traits of inmates afforded this type of protection. In some of the larger institutions, some form of separation within the protective custody section itself is necessary to safeguard protective custody inmates from each other; this is particularly true if one inmate has victimized another prior to their both entering protective custody or if inmates are rival gang members.

While in protective custody, inmates are entitled to almost all of the privileges and opportunities that they would have in the general population of a prison. Thus, modifications to educational programs, recreational activities, religious activities, legal resources, and so forth are all required.

Figure 8.4: Inmates in Protective Custody Nationwide

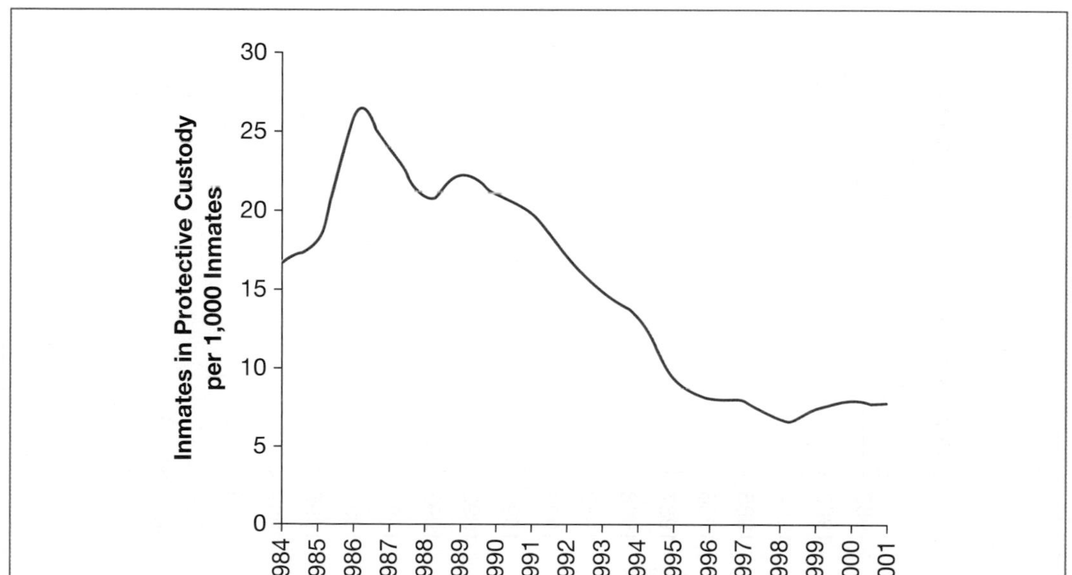

SOURCE: Association of State Correctional Administrators. (2004). *Fact sheet: Corrections safety: What the research says.* New York, NY: Author.

NOTE: Most recent data available

Naturally, this places an additional burden on administrators in terms of both monetary and human resources. For all these reasons, protective custody is a challenging aspect of prison operations that has become more frequently necessary as the prison population becomes more violent. This has been particularly true within the last 3 decades.

Administrative Segregation

Administrative segregation is a type of classification that is nonpunitive in nature but requires the separation of inmates from the general population due to the threat that they may pose to themselves, staff, other inmates, or institutional order (see Figure 8.5 for rates of inmates placed in this custody level). Classification officials may cite a number of reasons for imposing this custody level upon an offender. One of the most common reasons is membership in a prison gang. Thus, many administrative segregation programs consist of a large number of gang members. Focus Topic 8.2 provides an interesting article on prison gang affiliation in Texas and the steps being taken toward easing gang-related inmates from administrative segregation to the general population within Texas prisons.

Inmates in administrative segregation are usually housed in single cells where they receive the basic necessities and services, including food, clothing, showers, medical care, and even visitation privileges. Usually these inmates are provided 1 hour of recreation time daily, on a confined recreation yard that has some type of fencing to prevent inmates from having physical contact with other inmates. Though they may be able to see one another through the fencing (such as with chain-link fencing), they are not allowed to engage in recreational activities on the same yard. Though many of the amenities available for general population inmates are also provided to inmates in administrative segregation, some privileged activities and/or items may be restricted due to an inmate's gang status and the likelihood of dangerousness or because certain items may be used in the manufacture of homemade prison weapons. Indeed, the author of this text has a collection of prison weapons made by inmates while in administrative segregation; the types of deadly creations that can be made are limited only by one's imagination.

Administrative segregation: A nonpunitive classification that requires the separation of inmates from the general population for safety.

Lastly, as with inmates in protective custody, inmates in administrative segregation receive routine reviews of their classification status. They may be eligible for reclassification, depending on the

Figure 8.5: Inmates in Administrative Segregation Nationwide

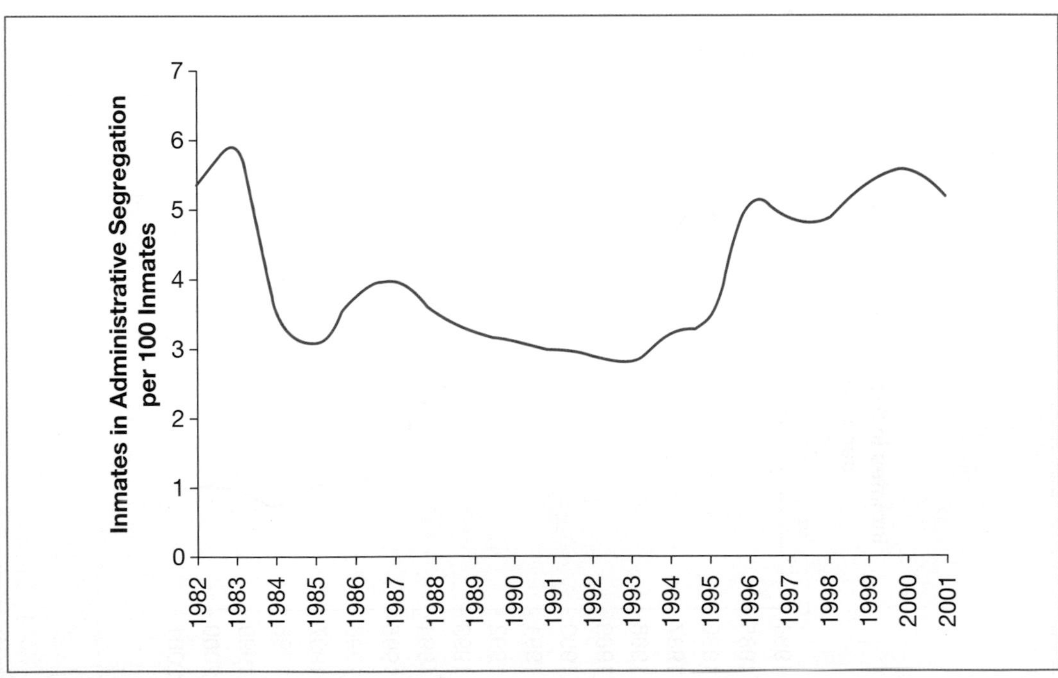

SOURCE: Association of State Correctional Administrators. (2004). *Fact sheet: Corrections safety: What the research says.* New York: Author.

NOTE: Most recent data available

FOCUS TOPIC: 8.2

Leaving Gang Life and Administrative Segregation Behind in Texas

While gang life may have seemed like a good choice for some Texas offenders when they were on the outside, many inmate gang members are starting to rethink that decision during their incarceration. With the Texas Department of Criminal Justice (TDCJ) sending all confirmed members of eight Texas gangs—ranging from the Mexican Mafia to the Aryan Circle—directly into administration segregation, those inmates have nearly 23 hours a day to sit alone in their cells and reevaluate their decision to belong to a gang.

To help inmates who want to break away from that way of life, TDCJ created the Gang Renouncement and Disassociation (GRAD) program to give them a way out.

The GRAD program began four years ago at the Ramsey I Unit in Rosharon, Texas, and targets offenders who belong to one of the eight security threat groups (STG) that TDCJ has identified for automatic placement into administrative segregation. All in all, about 6,000 inmates in the system belong to one of those gangs, which include the Aryan Brotherhood of Texas, Mexican Mafia, Barrio Azteca, Aryan Circle, Texas Mafia, Raza Unida, Texas Syndicate, and Hermanos Pistoleros Latinos.

After conducting research on the best way to channel confirmed gang members out of administrative segregation and back into the general population, TDCJ came up with a nine-month program designed to transition former gang members back into the rest of the inmate population.

Getting Into GRAD

In order to be considered for the program, inmates must first submit a written statement to their STG officer stating their desire to renounce their membership to a particular gang. Afterwards, officers conduct a complete investigation of that inmate on their unit, to ensure that they truly intend to break their gang ties.

Beyond the written letter and the investigation, inmates must meet a variety of other requirements before they are accepted into the program:

- no offender assaults for a period of two years
- no staff assaults for a period of two years
- no major disciplinary cases for at least one year
- no extortion cases for a period of two years
- no weapons possession cases for a period of two years
- no sexual misconduct for a period of two years
- must be level one status for a minimum of one year
- must not have been involved in any STG act for a minimum of two years
- cannot have a security precaution designator of escape, staff assault, or hostage situation

If an inmate is approved for the GRAD program, he is put on a waiting list, which now has 740 people on it. And there are another 1,000 inmates who have submitted, in writing, their intent to renounce their gang memberships and are currently being monitored in their administrative segregation units.

Every month, 16 new offenders are entered into the program and transferred to Ramsey I, where they live apart from the general population for the first two phases of the three-phase program.

Easing Back Into the General Population

During phase one, the inmates live in single cells. It is an adjustment for a lot of the inmates to come out of administrative segregation—where they were handcuffed and shackled at all times when they were out of their cells—to an environment like Ramsey.

After the inmates become accustomed to living at Ramsey and spend two months in phase one, they enter phase two, during which inmates from different STGs live together in double cells for four months. The fact that former rival gang members are sharing a living space has never created any security issues.

Throughout phases one and two, the inmates attend four hours of educational programming each day, including anger management, cognitive intervention, and substance abuse classes.

Once the inmates advance to phase three, they are mixed in with the other inmates at Ramsey, but still monitored by GRAD program officers. At this point, they take classes and work with the general population at the facility.

After phase three, which lasts for three months, the inmates graduate from the GRAD program, their classifications are changed to reflect that they are now ex-gang members, and they are transferred to other facilities, where they are integrated into the general population.

A Win-Win Situation

Although the STG officers in the units the offenders transition to are aware of their ex-gang member statuses and keep a closer eye on them in the general population, so far, they have not had problems with offenders acting up or rejoining gangs after they have completed the GRAD program.

Because of the program's success, a proposal to double it is currently being considered by officials at TDCJ.

SOURCE: Mandeville, M. (2004, September 6). Leaving gang life behind in Texas.

APPLIED THEORY 8.1

Differential Association: Minimizing Further Associations Through Effective Classification Processes

Differential association theory, according to Edwin Sutherland, is based on the premise that the excess of definitions favorable to crime over those unfavorable to crime will increase the likelihood for a person to commit criminal activity. Thus, the association that the person has with other criminals will increase his or her likelihood to engage in further criminal behavior.

Further, Sutherland asserts that criminal behavior is learnable and learned in interaction with other criminally minded persons. Through this association, the inmates learn not only techniques of certain crimes but also specific rationale, motives, and so forth. This would then mean that inmates who interact with other inmates have an increased likelihood of further engaging in criminal behavior.

It is with this in mind that most classification programs will seek to separate low-risk inmates from high-risk inmates as much as is reasonably possible. Indeed, this kind of separation of inmates, as well as overall public safety, is the key reason for using classification systems. Thus, for the most part, it can be said that classification systems in the field of corrections are used for the same basic premises that differential association details.

Such methods of eliminating the association of inmates with one another, or at least minimizing that association, are a perfect example of how theory and application meet one another within the real world of corrections. Given that prison has been found to have a criminalization effect in which longer prison terms can lead to higher recidivism, it seems reasonable to presume that the less time an offender spends around criminal associations, the more likely he or she is to successfully reform. It is with that notion in mind that classification again becomes the important and central organizing aspect to the correctional processing of offenders.

SOURCE: Lilly, J. R., Cullen, F. T., & Ball, R. A. (2007). *Criminological theory: Context and consequences* (4th ed.). Thousand Oaks, CA: Sage.

circumstances and whether they are affiliated with a gang. Typically, regardless of behavior, if an inmate is a known gang member, he or she will remain in administrative segregation due to the danger posed to the institution. But even in these cases, as demonstrated in Focus Topic 8.2, programs may exist to help inmates eventually get out of administrative segregation, if they so desire. We will discuss gang offenders in jails and prisons extensively in Chapter 9 and will demonstrate how the emergence of gangs has impacted both prison operations and the general norms and culture of state prison systems around the nation.

Specialized Offender Categories

Many inmates have a variety of characteristics, issues, or specialized needs that set them apart from the remaining prison population (Hanser, 2007). From a classification standpoint, the various needs that inmates may have can affect the decision to place them within a given facility, and, within that facility, these issues can affect individual housing decisions. It is important to note that each of these categories of the offender population creates the need for effective assessment and classification processes.

Further, one issue is very prevalent within the inmate population and directly relevant to the majority of the offender population: drug use. Because this issue is related to specific offender categories discussed later in this text and because this issue affects a large number of offenders in jail and prison, a section on drug use and the need for screening and classification has been included in this chapter. Thus, we now turn our attention to screening, assessment, and classification issues when faced with placement decisions for substance abuse treatment programs.

Substance Abuse Issues, Assessment, and Classification

Many offenders in state and federal prisons are convicted of violating drug laws. In fact, 22.4% of all federal inmates and 32.6% of all state inmates reported being under the influence of drugs or alcohol at the very time that they committed the offense for which they were incarcerated (Bureau of Justice Statistics, 1998). In addition, more than 83% of all state inmates and more than 73% of all federal inmates reported past drug use, with most of that past drug use occurring during the year prior to their offense (Centers for Disease Control and Prevention, 2003). The problem is compounded by the fact that substance abuse is closely related to recidivism; inmates with prior convictions are significantly more likely than first-time offenders to be regular drug users.

Given the association between injection drug use and HIV/AIDS, detoxification also provides counseling to reduce AIDS-related risk behaviors (McNeece, Springer, & Arnold, 2002). Later, in Chapters 11 and 14, the student will see that drug abuse elevates the risk of contracting HIV/AIDS and other communicable diseases. This largely is associated with drug abusers who use intravenous drugs and those who engage in risky sex behaviors, particularly when prostitution and drug use are combined. In addition, students will learn in Chapter 14 that many cases of mental illness in jails and prisons co-occur with substance abuse disorders. We will expound on these interconnections in Chapter 14 but mention them here to demonstrate the importance of this issue and of having effective screening, assessment, and classification processes with the drug-abusing offender population.

Screening and Placement Criteria

Every form of treatment program involves some sort of screening. According to Myers and Salt (2000), screening serves two major purposes: It attests to the presence of a condition that may go unrecognized if not detected, and it provides data to decide whether a client is appropriate for a specific treatment program, or vice versa

In the first use of screening, social, health, and criminal justice workers determine if there are sufficient grounds for referral of an inmate to a particular drug/alcohol treatment program. This screening is very important because the earlier the intervention takes place, the better the prognosis for the client. Obviously, the odds of reforming a drug experimenter are much better than when treating a compulsive user. The second use of screening is to determine client appropriateness for a given treatment modality. It should be pointed out that the discretion in placement may not only consider the client's individual characteristics; the ability of a given agency to provide these services must also be considered. For example, fiscal constraints can be a factor despite the fact that the treatment program may be ideal for the client. In any case, it is this use of screening that provides the placement criteria for drug offenders in the criminal justice system.

Placement criteria are very important when processing drug offenders. The initial placement is important for both public safety and treatment-oriented concerns. When deciding upon placement criteria, a match must be made between the severity of the addiction and the level of care needed, which can include (from most serious to least serious) medical inpatient care, nonmedical inpatient care, intensive outpatient care, or outpatient care (Hanson, Venturelli, & Fleckenstein, 2011). Further, matching the client's profile to a treatment modality is more likely to achieve lasting success, which can translate to the enhanced evaluation of program effectiveness. For example, a client with attention deficit/hyperactivity disorder might be unsuited for the regimentation of a therapeutic community. Conversely, a person with low self-esteem, insecurities, and a fragile sense of self-worth would not be appropriate for a highly confrontational style of intervention.

Robert Hanser

■ PHOTO 8.6 This group counseling session includes inmates who are in an 84-day intensive treatment program. Upon completion of the program, they will have opportunities to participate in additional recovery service programming, depending on their needs and their own recovery desires.

Goldberg (2003) notes that several questions should be asked before placing

CROSS-NATIONAL PERSPECTIVE 8.1

Electronic Monitoring, Housing, Classification, and Inmate Activity in Australia

As noted throughout this chapter, classification determines housing and programming assignments within prison systems. Once inmates are assigned a custody level and programming regimen, they are subject to periodic review for reclassification. The means by which they are tracked throughout the completion of their sentence has also been an important issue in terms of both public and/or prison safety and programming success. The nation of Australia has partnered technological advances with prison operations in a manner that enhances both prison security and programming options. The following example addresses how such advances can improve classification assignments and outcomes:

Two Australian companies, Alanco Technologies and NEC Australia, have begun the implementation and installation of a special Wi-Fi tracking system that is housed at the Alexander Maconochie Centre Prison, located in Canberra, Australia. These two companies have agreed to integrate their security system technologies as a means of offering state-of-the-art, real-time tracking to the more than 100 prison facilities that are located throughout Australia and New Zealand. Currently, the Maconochie Centre Prison is being used as the prototype implementation; this facility has multiple levels of prisoner classification. This facility includes young adults who are both male and female.

This security system will allow prison staff to monitor the physical location of inmates and will aid in controlling their movement between various segments of the population. It will also detect potential escape attempts and therefore act as an enhanced security mechanism for public safety as well as institutional security.

This system will also optimize staff efficiency and is expected to reduce long-term costs to the facility. The project is valued at over $1 million, but, due to the benefits in staff efficiency, the reduced likelihood of inmate infractions inside the institution, and the enhanced level of public safety, the rewards will outweigh the costs of this program.

Naturally, because these private companies hope to sell this security product to as many buyers as possible, they have engaged in an intense marketing campaign. The use of this system at the Maconochie facility will allow for the public showcasing of this technology and the product that is available. While the system was originally intended for Australia and New Zealand, there is nothing to say that this product could not and/or will not be available to other potential buyers around the world. This is especially true when one considers how globalization impacts the criminal justice field in today's world, including the field of corrections.

QUESTION 1: From what you can tell, how progressive does the nation of Australia seem to be in relation to inmate security? Is this similar to or different from the state of correctional operations in the United States, in your opinion? Provide a brief explanation for your answer.

QUESTION 2: Do you believe that such programs can enhance the outcomes and assignments derived from automated classification systems? Briefly explain why or why not.

SOURCE: GPS News. (2008). *Alanco/TSI PRISM and NEC Australia partner for inmate tracking system.* Scottsdale, AZ: Author.

clients in treatment and that these questions should also be considered before a program begins to go into operation—or, if a program is already being administered, officials should be willing to change the program if necessary. According to Goldberg (2003, p. 297), these questions are:

1. Which treatment produces the best outcome for a specific group or person?
2. Do members of certain ethnic or socioeconomic groups respond similarly to certain types of treatment?
3. Is the effectiveness of a specific program linked to the age of participants?
4. Do females and males differ in their response to treatment?

The matching of treatment to gender, culture, ethnicity, language, and even sexual orientation has been shown to improve the odds of achieving positive outcomes in a variety of treatment settings for a variety of treatment issues (Goldberg, 2003). The utilization of culturally competent programs for various racial/ethnic groups should be particularly addressed given the fact that minorities are highly prevalent within the correctional population. Goldberg (2003) also points out the importance of addressing issues relevant to female drug offenders, among these the need for prenatal care and treatment and the need for contact with their children. As will be seen in Chapter 10, a high proportion of female offenders on community supervision (72%) are the primary caretakers of children under 18 years of age (Bloom, Owen, & Covington, 2003). Many female offenders may initially be motivated by the desire to reduce drug-related harm to their expected babies or to improve their relationship with and ability to attend to their children. This should not be overlooked, as it can be used to encourage these offenders to complete their treatment, thereby improving their chances for long-term recovery.

The main point is that treatment programming must be effectively matched to the specific inmate. Certain groups of inmates may also have needs that are common to that group (e.g., as based on ethnicity, age, or gender), and they may have other, more individualistic factors (e.g., divorce, abuse trauma) that may significantly affect their likelihood of success in treatment. In either event, treatment programs must rely on effective screening, assessment, and classification processes for inmate selection if they are expected to have successful outcomes. However, there is often a widespread tendency to simply place all inmates into drug treatment because substance abuse issues are so prevalent among the inmate population. As mentioned earlier, we will touch upon drug abuse issues with the inmate population in Chapter 11 and Chapter 14, where it will become clear that substance abuse is a primary co-occurring concern when working with female offenders, mentally ill offenders, and offenders who have HIV/AIDS or other communicable diseases.

CONCLUSION

The classification process is very important to institutional corrections. Indeed, it has been likened to the "brain" of the prison facility. Effective classification is essential in determining both security needs and the specific needs of the inmate toward reformation. Without an adequate scheme for these types of decisions, corrections would likely be little more than guesswork. Thus, Alexander Maconochie changed the landscape of corrections with his mark system.

Given the scarcity of resources among most correctional agencies, it is important that they be able to predict how their funds can be most effectively allocated. Classification systems can help with this consideration. The elimination of overprediction of dangerousness is one means by which classification keeps prison facilities from having even larger operational budgets. Couple this with goal of keeping the institution safe, and it becomes clear why classification processes are the cornerstone of any well-run facility.

Offender placement in various security levels within a prison can be important for the safety of staff, other inmates, and the offenders themselves. Thus, the welfare of all hinges on the classification process. Appropriate classification is also important with regard to treatment approaches. The ability of classification and treatment staff to correctly place clients into the appropriate substance abuse intervention program is critical to assisting the offender. As we move into future chapters on prison culture and the processing of specialized offenders, it will become clear that effective assessment and classification are critical to the correctional process. Without effective classification, we are likely wasting the tax dollars obtained from the public. Society counts on the field of corrections to ensure public safety and to maintain security over offenders within its jurisdiction. This is an impossible mission without effective classification processes. Building a program on faulty assessment and classification processes is, arguably, a form of negligence to our obligation to protect society. Ultimately, public safety is *job one*, and it is, therefore, important that corrections fulfill its obligation to treat public safety with the due diligence that it deserves.

DISCUSSION QUESTIONS

1. Provide a brief overview of the key historical figures in the development of modern-day classification systems.
2. Discuss the importance of the Supreme Court case of *Palmigiano v. Garrahy* (1977).
3. What are the four broad goals of classification?
4. What are the different custody levels of inmate housing, and what methods are used to determine the housing assignments of inmates?
5. Who are the various members of a classification team, and what are the functions for each member?
6. Define the term *administrative segregation*. How is it usually used (and with what population it is usually used) within a prison?
7. What are four reasons for inmates being placed in protective custody in a prison facility?
8. How do the classification process and differential association operate along a similar set of premises?

SAGE edge™ **Test your understanding of chapter content. Take the practice quiz.**

KEY TERMS

Administrative segregation, 192
Case manager, 186
Correctional counselor, 186
Custody level, 181
Education adviser, 186
English Penal Servitude Act, 177
Level of security, 181
Mark system, 176
Protective custody, 190
Psychology services representative, 186
SENTRY system, 184
Unit manager, 186

SAGE edge™ **Review key terms with eFlashcards.**

KEY CASES

Morris v. Travisono (1970), 178
Palmigiano v. Garrahy (1977), 178

APPLIED EXERCISE 8.1

Determine whether the following inmates should be given minimum-, medium-, or maximum-level security or if they should be given either administrative segregation or protective custody. Be sure to explain your answer.

Inmate Al is a member of a known street gang that is well represented in your correctional system. He denies being a member of a gang but has been identified by law enforcement as a bona fide member when operating in the community.

Inmate Nancy is a female offender who has two kids and is incarcerated for check fraud. She has served the majority of her sentence and seems to be doing well in educational and vocational programs offered in the prison. She often reflects on getting out, getting a good job, and taking care of her children.

Inmate Butch is a known sexual predator who has sexually assaulted a number of inmates and even one female correctional officer throughout his stint in prison. Butch is not liked by many inmates but is considered very masculine within the prison subculture. He seems to have no guilt or remorse for any of his acts.

Inmate Tom was a priest who was convicted of sexually abusing dozens of young boys within his church. He is slight of build and is a fairly docile-appearing man. He just arrived at your facility a couple of days ago.

Inmate Conway minds his own business and does not talk much with prison staff. He keeps out of trouble, for the most part, but has an independent quality that keeps him a bit at odds with the programming aspects of prison. He has not been identified as dangerous (he was convicted of burglary), but he also does not seem to make great strides toward getting released early.

WHAT WOULD YOU DO?

You are a counselor in a substance abuse treatment program within a state prison facility. You run a group each morning from 8:30 to 10:00, Monday through Friday. The program is intensive, and the inmate participants are required to attend each and every session. As a reward for being selected as a participant and for successfully completing the program, inmates are given an extra 180 days of good time during the yearlong program. Further, these inmate participants are allowed to stay in a dorm specifically set aside for them.

While conducting group, you notice that one of your participants has missed several meetings. When you inquire about this, you learn from the other inmate participants that this individual does not act as if he understands that he is supposed to go to group. Further, security staff had not been notified as to when he would need to attend group; thus, security did not have any reason to require the inmate to leave the dorm.

The inmate participant has missed 8 days of group, and this is your first time meeting him. From your meeting, it is clear to you that this inmate has numerous challenges and that he really has a limited capacity to understand the requirements he must adhere to. You are not sure what to do. On the one hand, you could remove him from group, and he will not gain good time and will likely be given disciplinary action due to his failure to attend. On the other hand, you could ignore this oversight and allow him to continue in the program with the knowledge that he will likely have more mishaps in the future. In addition, you are not sure what the other inmates will think if you should deviate from the rules; they all know that this inmate was supposed to be attending group.

You talk with your group about the situation and find that many of the group members are empathetic to his situation. Likewise, the clinical supervisor has indicated that he is understanding of the circumstances, but he is not sure how classification and/or the prison administration will process this situation.

You have some degree of discretion in resolving this situation and wish to be ethical and fair in your decision. You also want to ensure that you do not leave any loopholes for other offenders who might attempt to manipulate the program. Such inmates might find reasons to not attend therapy, instead using that time to attend to other self-identified priorities. Given the manipulative nature of the inmate population at this prison, this outcome is not an unlikely one.

How do you handle this situation, formally or informally? Who will you consult in resolving this? What do you tell the other members of the group? Do you ask classification about this situation, noting that this inmate may not have been placed into the correct treatment group?

In short, the question is . . .

What would you do?

PRISON SUBCULTURE AND PRISON GANG INFLUENCE

©iStockphoto.com/C_FOR

THE GANG IS MY FAMILY; THE GANG IS MY PURPOSE

I will stand by my brother
My brother will come before all others
My life is forfeit should I fail my brother
I will honor my brother in peace as in war.

Aryan Brotherhood Oath

James Harris, known as "Cornfed" to his family and friends, was a member of "The Brand" (a term for the Aryan Brotherhood, or AB). He was hanging on the recreation yard with "Blinky," another member of The Brand. Blinky was family to Cornfed; they had known each other for years, both inside and outside of prison.

"So, if you keep your nose clean, you get on parole, you're going on a mission, right?" Cornfed asked Blinky.

Blinky nodded. "Yep, that's right. In fact, I am taking the mission, and then I'll be free to conduct *rahowa* all that I want. I know I'll end up back here, but at least I'll have paid my debt and taken a couple of them with me."

Cornfed looked at the ground and thought about what Blinky had said. Blinky had been "down" (doing time) for many years, and he had benefitted from the AB substantially throughout those years. His "mission" would be to operate a meth lab for the AB, as he was known to be a very good "cook"—someone skilled in manufacturing methamphetamine.

Cornfed also understood why Blinky would be going on *rahowa*, the term in the AB for "racial holy war," which would ultimately entail some form of hate crime against African Americans. He knew that Blinky would be highly motivated to engage in *rahowa* because many of the AB members would be expecting it due to his past experiences.

Initially, Blinky had stayed out of the gang life, but then he had been sexually assaulted by two black men while working in the laundry area of the prison. The men had told him from that point on he would be their "punk," a term for someone who has been "turned out" and given the identity of a woman in prison. Blinky fought during the assault, but they had caught him off guard and he was unable to defend himself. The second time they attempted to rape him, he was ready and was able to hold them off until "Big John" unexpectedly entered the shop. Big John did not work in the laundry but had been sent to gather some towels to clean up blood from another assault that had occurred just 10 minutes ago.

Big John saw what was going on and said, "My only regret today has been that I wasn't involved in what La Eme just finished. . . .I hate being the one who has to do the cleanup for somebody else's handiwork." He reached behind his back with one hand and pulled out an 8-inch blade. "I want you to meet my friend here, Aryan Express. Like American Express, I never leave home without it."

Big John carved both of the men up, holding one in the air by the throat while he repeatedly gouged the other in the abdomen. He then reached around the man he was holding and buried the knife into the small of his back. With a satisfied grunt, Big John threw the man down on the ground. Then he glared at Blinky. "You better not say nuthin,' you understand?"

Blinky nodded vigorously as Big John stepped over to the first man and slashed the man's throat. Then he moved to the other man and kicked him repeatedly in the head until he was a bloody, unrecognizable mess.

When he had finished, Big John turned back to Blinky. "You now owe the AB, unless of course you like being a punk, in which case you can be the AB's punk. They're gonna be locking me up in just a bit, but my brothers will come for you. This completes my *rahowa* for now." Kneeling, he wiped the blade across the shirt of the first man he killed and hid it under a spare mattress in the shop.

LEARNING OBJECTIVES:

1. Compare importation theory with exportation theory.
2. Discuss the modern inmate subculture standards.
3. Evaluate the impact of prison culture on corrections staff.
4. Describe the process of prisonization.
5. Identify various aspects of guard subculture, including the unique subculture of female correctional officers.
6. Discuss the impact that prison gangs have had on prisons, including the traditional prison subculture.
7. Explain what prison systems do to control gang problems that occur in their facilities.

SAGE edge™

Get the edge on your studies: edge.sagepub.com/hanser2e

- Take a quiz to find out what you've learned.
- Review key terms with eFlashcards.
- Watch videos that enhance chapter content.

"When they come to talk with you about joining the family, let them know where I put the metal, okay?"

Blinky agreed. Leaning against one of the laundry tables, Big John pulled out a cigarette and handed another to Blinky. They smoked together in silence until the guards came.

Now Cornfed looked at Blinky and said, "My brother, when you're out there, just know that I'm proud of you and I'll honor your name here on the inside."

Blinky smiled and gazed through the chain-link fence at the world beyond. Soon he would be on the outside with his family, the Aryan Brotherhood of Texas.

INTRODUCTION

This chapter examines a very unique aspect of the world of corrections. Students will learn that within the institutional environment, a commonality of experiences arises between those who are involved—both inmates and staff. Many people may not be aware that in fact the mind-set and experiences of inmates often affect the mind-set of security personnel who work with those inmates. In essence, there is an exchange of beliefs and perspectives that produces a fusion between the two groups. This creates a singular subculture that is the product of both inmate norms being brought in from the outside and norms being taken from the prison to the outside community.

It is important for students to understand that prison staff are not immune to the effects of the profound social learning that occurs in prison, and, over time, as they become more enmeshed in the prison social setting, they begin to internalize many of the beliefs and norms held by the prison subculture. While this may seem to be counterproductive and/or even backward from what one might wish within the prison environment, this is an inevitable process as prison staff find themselves interacting with the street mentality on a day-to-day basis. In actuality, this has a maturing effect on correctional workers, as they begin to see a world that is not necessarily black and white but instead has many shades of gray. When staff get to know inmates on a personal level, issues become more complicated than being simple "good guy-bad guy" situations. The nuances and differences between different offenders tend to complicate what initially might seem like obvious, easy decisions.

Because correctional staff interact with offenders on a daily basis, a sense of understanding develops both among correctional staff and between staff and the inmate population. Inmates come to expect certain reactions from correctional staff, and staff come to expect certain reactions from inmates. Informal rules of conduct exist where loyalty to one's own group must be maintained, but individual differences in personality among security staff and inmates will affect the level of respect that an officer will get from the inmate population, or, for inmates, the amount of respect that they gain from others serving time. Correctional staff learn which inmates have influence, power, or control over others, and this may affect the dynamics of interaction. Further still, some inmates may simply wish to do their time, whereas others produce constant problems; to expect security staff to maintain the same reaction to both types of inmates is unrealistic.

The dynamics involved in inmate-inmate, inmate-staff, and staff-staff interactions create circumstances that do not easily fall within the guidelines of prison regulations. In order to maintain control of an inmate population that greatly outnumbers the correctional staff, many security officers will learn the personalities of inmates and will become familiar with the level of respect that they receive from other offenders. Likewise, and even more often, inmates watch and observe officers who work the cell block, the dormitory, or other areas where inmates congregate. They will develop impressions of the officer, and this will determine how they react to him or her. The officer is essentially labeled by the inmate population, over time, as one who deserves respect or one who deserves contempt. In some cases, officers may be identified as being too passive or "weak" in their ability to enforce the rules. In such cases, they are likely to be conned, duped, or exploited by streetwise convicts.

The various officer-inmate interactions impact the daily experiences of those involved. Understanding how a myriad of nuances affect these interactions is critical to understanding how and why prisons operate as they do. In prisons that have little technology, few cameras, and shortages of staff, the gray areas that can emerge in the inmate-staff interactional process can lead to a number of ethical and legal conundrums. It is with this in mind that we now turn our attention to factors that create and complicate the social landscape of American prisons.

THEORIES OF PRISON SUBCULTURE

Importation Theory

The key tenet of **importation theory** is that the subculture within prisons is brought in from outside the walls by offenders who have developed their beliefs and norms while on the streets. In other words, the prison subculture is reflective of the offender subculture on the streets. Thus, behaviors respected behind the walls of a prison are similar to behaviors respected among the criminal population outside of the prison. There is some research that does support this notion (Wright, 1994). Most correctional officers and inmates know that the background of an offender (or of a correctional officer) has a strong impact on how that person behaves, both inside and outside of a prison; this simply makes good intuitive sense.

There are two important opposing points to consider regarding importation theory. First, the socialization process outside of prison has usually occurred for a much longer period of time for many offenders and is, therefore, likely to be a bit more entrenched. Second and conversely, the prison environment is intense and traumatic and is capable of leaving a very deep and lasting influence upon a person in a relatively short period of time. While this second point may be true, most inmates in prison facilities have a history of offending and will tend to have numerous prior offenses, some of which may be unknown to the correctional system. This means that inmates will likely have led a lifestyle of dysfunction that is counter to what the broader culture may support. Thus, these individuals come to the prison with years of street experience and bring their criminogenic view of the world to the prison.

It has been concluded by some scholars (Bernard, McCleary, & Wright, 1999; Wright, 1994) that though correctional institutions may seem closed off from society, their boundaries are psychologically permeable. In other words, when someone is locked up, they still are able to receive cultural messages and influences from outside the walls of the prison. Television, radio, and mail all mitigate the immersion experience in prison. Visitation schedules, work opportunities outside of the prison, and other types of programming also alleviate the impact of the prison environment. Indeed, according to Bernard et al. (1999), "Prison walls, fences, and towers still prevent the inside world from getting outside, [but] they can no longer prevent the outside world—with its diverse attractions, diversions, and problems—from getting inside" (p. 164). This statement serves as a layperson explanation of importation theory that is both accurate and practical.

Indigenous Prison Culture and Exportation Theory

In contrast to the tenets of importation theory is the notion that prison subculture is largely the product of socialization that occurs inside prison. It was the work of Gresham Sykes (1958) that first introduced this idea in a clear and thorough manner. His theory has been referred to as either the deprivation theory of prisonization or the indigenous model of prison culture. Sykes (1958) referred to the pains of imprisonment as the rationale for why and how prison culture develops in the manner that it does. The **pains of imprisonment** is a term that refers to the various inconveniences and deprivations that occur as a result of incarceration. According to Sykes, the pains of imprisonment tended to center on five general areas of deprivation, and it was due to these deprivations that the prison subculture developed, largely as a means of adapting to the circumstances within the prison. Sykes listed the following five issues as being particularly challenging to men and women who do time:

SAGE Journal Article Link
Revisiting the Pains of Imprisonment

1. The loss of liberty.
2. The loss of goods and services readily available in society.
3. The loss of heterosexual relationships, both sexual and nonsexual.
4. The loss of autonomy.
5. The loss of personal security.

Inmates within the prison environment essentially create value systems and engage in behaviors that are designed to ease the pains of deprivation associated with these five areas. Research has examined the effects of prison upon inmates who are forced to cope with the incarceration existence.

For instance, Johnson and Dobrzanska (2005) studied inmates who were serving lengthy sentences. They found that incarceration was a painful but constructive experience for those inmates who coped maturely with prison life. This was particularly true for inmates who were serving life sentences (defined to include offenders serving prison terms of 25 years or more without the benefit

Importation theory: Subculture within prisons is brought in from outside by offenders who have developed their beliefs and norms while on the streets.

Pains of imprisonment: The various inconveniences and deprivations that occur as a result of incarceration.

Andrew Lichtenstein/Corbis/APImages

■ PHOTO 9.1 This inmate proudly displays his gang-affiliated tattoos.

of parole). As a general rule, lifers came to see prison as their home and made the most of the limited resources available there; they established daily routines that allowed them to find meaning and purpose in their prison lives—lives that might otherwise seem empty and pointless. The work of Johnson and Dobrzanska points toward the notion that humans can be highly adaptable regardless of the environment.

Many of the mannerisms and behaviors observed among street offenders have their origins within the prison environment. Indeed, certain forms of rhyming, rap, tattoos, and dress have prison origins. For example, the practice known as "sagging," when adolescent boys allow their pants to sag, exposing their underwear, originates from jail and prison policies denying inmates the use of belts (because they could be used as a weapon or means to commit suicide). This practice is thought to have been exported to the streets during the 1990s as a statement of African American solidarity as well as a way to offend white society.

Another example might be the notion of "**blood in—blood out**," which is the idea that in order for inmates to be accepted within a prison gang, they must draw blood (usually through killing) in an altercation with an identified enemy of the gang. Once in the gang, they may only leave if they draw blood of the enemy sufficient to meet the demands of the gang leadership or by forfeiting their own blood (their life). This same phrase is heard among street gangs, including juvenile street gangs, reflecting the fact that these offenders mimic the traditions of veteran offenders who have served time in prison. Consider also certain attire that has been popular off and on during the past decade, such as when Rhino boots became popular footwear, not due to their stylishness or functionality but because they were standard issue for working inmates in many state prison systems.

THE INMATE SUBCULTURE OF MODERN TIMES

Prison Tour Video Link
An Inmate's Experience, Relationships, and Typical Day

In all likelihood, the inmate subculture is a product of both importation and indigenous factors. Given the complicated facets of human behavior and the fact that inmates tend to cycle in and out of the prison system, this just seems logical. In fact, attempting to separate one from the other is more of an academic argument than a practical one. The work of Hochstellar and DeLisa (2005) represents an academic attempt to negotiate between these two factors. These researchers used a sophisticated statistical technique known as structural equation modeling to analyze the effects of importation and indigenous deprivation theories. They found evidence supporting both perspectives but found that the main factor that determined which perspective was most accountable for inmates' adaptation to prison subculture was their level of participation in the inmate economy (Hochstellar & DeLisa, 2005).

This is an important finding because it corroborates practical elements just as much as it navigates between academic arguments regarding subculture development. The prison economy is one of the key measures of influence that an inmate (and perhaps even some officers) may have within the institution. The more resources an inmate has, the wealthier he or she will be in the eyes of the inmate population. Oftentimes, those inmates who are capable of obtaining such wealth are either stronger, more cunning, or simply smarter (usually through training and literacy, such as with jailhouse lawyers) than most other members of the inmate population. Thus, these inmates are likely to be more adept at negotiating the prison economy, and they are likely to have more influence within the prison subculture. They are also more likely to be successfully adapted to the prison culture (the influence of indigenous prison cultural factors) while being able to procure or solicit external resources (this being a source of exportation outside the prison walls). In short, those who master the economy often have effective and/or powerful contacts both inside and outside of the prison. This is consistent with the findings of Hochstellar and DeLisa (2005).

Blood in—blood out: The idea that for inmates to be accepted within a prison gang they must draw blood from an enemy of the gang.

The Convict Code and Snitching

The prison subculture has numerous characteristics that are often portrayed in film, in academic sources, and among practitioners (see Focus Topic 9.1). Chief among these characteristics is the somewhat fluid code of conduct among inmates. This is sometimes referred to as the **convict code**, and it is a set of standards in behavior attributed to the true convict—the title of *convict* being one of respect given to inmates who have proven themselves worthy of that title. Among academic sources, this inmate code emphasizes oppositional values to conventional society in general and to prison authorities in particular. The most serious infraction against this code of conduct is for an inmate to cooperate with the officials as a snitch. A **snitch** is the label given to an inmate who reveals the activity of another inmate to authorities, usually in exchange for some type of benefit within the prison or legal system. For example, an inmate might be willing to tell prison officials about illicit drug smuggling being conducted by other inmates in the prison in exchange for more favorable parole conditions, transfer to a different prison, or some other type of benefit.

Audio Link
"Stop Snitching" Movement Confounding Criminal Justice

Among all inmates, it is the snitch who is considered the lowest of the low. In traditional "old school" subcultures (i.e., those of the 1940s through the 1970s), snitches were rare and were afforded no respect. Their existence was precarious within the prison system, particularly because protection afforded to snitches was not optimal. During riot situations and other times when chaos reigned, there are recorded incidents where inmates specifically targeted areas where snitches were housed and protected from the general population. In these cases, snitches were singled out and subjected to severely gruesome torture and were usually killed. Perhaps the most notorious of these incidents occurred at the New Mexico Penitentiary in Santa Fe. This prison riot occurred in 1980 and resulted in areas of the prison being controlled by inmates. These inmates eventually broke into Cell Block 4, which housed known snitches in the prison. The media-reported details of how the snitch-informers were tortured and killed shocked the public conscience.

One thing should be noted about snitches in the modern world of corrections; they are much more frequently encountered nowadays. Though there is still a supposed code against snitching, during the 1990s, with the emergence of the War on Drugs, more and more inmates consented to being informants for law enforcement as a means of securing better sentencing deals. Further, the new breed of inmate that was observed during this time did not reflect behavior that was "honor bound" like that of the older inmates in prison. Though there continued to be verbal opposition to inmate snitching, wardens and other prison administrators noted the sharp increase in informants within their institutions during this period. It would appear that among modern-day inmates, the willingness to do one's time with honor is a lower priority. Many veteran prison officials and older inmates (particularly inmates who are serving life sentences) contend that this is reflective of modern society where people are not as accustomed to being inconvenienced—a fast-food and instant coffee generation.

Sex Offenders and Punks

Sex offenders, particularly child molesters, are also afforded no respect in prison. In the early to mid-1900s, child molesters typically had a high mortality rate in prison and were often abused by other inmates. However, these types of offenses are becoming more prevalent and are more often detected by the justice system. Thus, there are higher proportions of these types of offenders in most prison systems. Further still, many prison systems have developed therapeutic programs that separate these offenders from the general population. However, this is not always the case.

Of those inmates who are sex offenders, many are singled out by prison gangs to be "turned out." Turning out occurs when an inmate is forced to become a punk for the prison gang. The term **punk** is common prison vernacular for an inmate who engages in homosexual activity; it is a derogatory term that implies that the inmate is feminine, weak, and subservient to masculine inmates. In other words, the punk is considered a woman in prison and is often forced to engage in sexual acts for the pleasure of one or more inmates. Sex offenders in prison are disproportionately represented within this prison population and are considered to be at high risk for this type of victimization.

Convict code: An inmate-driven set of beliefs that inmates aspired to live by.

Snitch: Term for an inmate who reveals the activity of another inmate to authorities.

Punk: A derogatory term for an inmate who engages in homosexual activity; implies that the inmate is feminine, weak, and subservient to masculine inmates.

The Prison Rape Elimination Act of 2003

The Prison Rape Elimination Act of 2003 (PREA; Public Law 108-79) requires the Bureau of Justice Statistics (BJS) to carry out a comprehensive statistical review and analysis of the incidence and

FOCUS TOPIC 9.1

Focus From the Inside With Jonathan Hilbun, Inmate With Richwood Correctional Center.

Robert Hanser

■ PHOTO 9.2 Jonathan W. Hilbun is an inmate at Richwood Correctional Center who is a dorm mentor in the Successful Treatment and Recovery (STAR) program. He stands here in front of a bookshelf that is part of the inmate library for the STAR program.

Hyenas are inmates who only prey on the weak inmates, and they will back off if the weaker inmate strikes back. But, if the weak one does not fend for himself, then the hyenas will devour him.

An interesting point regarding inmate behavior, particularly hyena behavior, has to do with the inmates' interactions with security. In many cases, hyenas will have no respect for authority but, at the same time, be hesitant to directly challenge authority. Rather, they will tend to use subversive or indirect means of ridiculing the officer. For instance, when the "freeman" (another term for a prison guard) comes on the dorm to count, an inmate may holler something across the dorm that is crude and crass. It is at this point that the officer must make a stand quickly. If he or she does not, then the other hyenas will join along and will taunt and tease the officer to see how much they can get away with. This can actually get pretty bad, as it may even set up an ongoing officer-inmate dynamic that can go on for the remainder of the officer's employment at the facility, if such misbehavior is left unchecked enough times.

In response, the officer will usually react by applying some type of punitive measures to inmates on the dorm. For instance, he will usually restrict the TV privileges and secure the phone lines as well, if the facility allows inmates to make phone calls. Likewise, he may decide to do a "special count" that requires all inmates to sit or lie in their own rack, prohibiting them from getting up and walking about the dorm. It can get pretty frustrating, over time, to sit in the bed for prolonged periods of time, and the officer knows this. It is doubly frustrating for those inmates who did not make the comment and who do not really respect the cowardly actions of the hyena.

Usually, one of the inmates will finally tell the officer the identity of the hyena who made the unruly comments, and, in many cases, this results in a type of understood bond of respect between the officer and the inmate. Though there is nothing necessarily spoken between the two, the officer knows that the inmate is going against the common wisdom of the prison subculture in doing this, and, at the same time, the inmate knows that the officer cannot get compliance until he or she breaks through the veneer of the hyenas who have openly and publicly challenged his or her authority and mocked the officer for all to see. It is a delicate interplay, in this middle-ground area, between officer and inmate, where both groups must learn to coexist with one another within a set of informal and formal parameters.

Naturally, it takes quite a bit of courage to tell on another inmate. Inmates usually will view the act of disclosing the identity of the person who commits an infraction as an act of snitching. This is usually not respected, but, in cases where a hyena has acted in a cowardly manner and where the rest of the dorm is made to pay for his action, respect is lost for the hyena, especially if he does not step forward and take his charge, so to speak. In addition, there is one other aspect that can make this approach actually respectable in the eyes of other inmates. This is when the informing inmate talks to the officer on behalf of the dorm and makes it clear that he cannot and will not take any incentives or benefits for the information. If he also makes it clear that he is not trying to get too cozy with the officer but, instead, is trying to simply live under the conditions of détente that exist within the prison subculture between inmates and officers, this will be considered acceptable. This is especially true if other inmates know, in advance, that this inmate will likely inform on behalf of the dorm.

At this point, the hyena is obviously crossed out among others on the dorm and is held in even lower regard by other inmates as a coward who sidesteps his charge and allows others to "pay his lick," so to speak. In some ways, this process of maintaining some semblance of decency and tangible respect for institutional authority is a means of redemption for the inmate and the dorm. In this regard, it is viewed that these men are capable of reform on at least a base level, contrasting with the typical saying that "there is no honor among thieves." In essence, even the inmate subculture has standards that the hyena has failed to maintain. Thus, the lack of respect goes to the hyena, and, so long as the officer conducts his job in a firm but fair manner, the officer is afforded his due respect.

This information was drawn from an interview with Jonathan Hilbun. It is worth mentioning that Mr. Hilbun has been incarcerated for 18 and a half years in a variety of institutions, including Angola and Richwood Correctional Center.

SOURCE: Jonathan Hilbun. (2011, December 2). Personal interview. Used with permission.

effects of prison rape for each calendar year. The review must include, but is not limited to, the identification of the common characteristics of both victims and perpetrators of prison rape and prisons and prison systems with a high incidence of prison rape. In accomplishing this, the PREA requires the review adhere to the following guidelines:

1. Be based on a random sample, or other scientifically appropriate sample, of not less than 10% of all federal, state, and county prisons, and a representative sample of municipal prisons. The sample must include at least one prison from each state.
2. Use surveys and other statistical studies of current and former inmates from a representative sample of federal, state, county, and municipal prisons and ensure the confidentiality of each survey participant.
3. Provide a list of institutions in the sample, separated into each category and ranked according to the incidence of prison rape in each institution, and provide a list of any prisons in the sample that did not cooperate with the survey

We will cover the impact of the PREA later in Chapter 10, when discussing female offenders. However, in male prisons, the negative aspects of being a punk in prison means that homosexual, transgender, or even just more effeminate males are at great risk for being assaulted behind bars. With this concern in mind, the BJS issued additional tabulations for its PREA work titled *Supplemental Tables: Prevalence of Sexual Victimization Among Transgender Adult Inmates*. This work found the following:

1. An estimated 35% of transgender inmates held in prisons and 34% held in local jails reported experiencing one or more incidents of sexual victimization by another inmate or facility staff in the past 12 months or since admission, if less than 12 months.
2. About a quarter of transgender inmates in prisons (24%) and jails (23%) reported an incident involving another inmate. Nearly three-quarters (74%) said the incidents involved oral or anal penetration, or other nonconsensual sexual acts.
3. When asked about the experiences surrounding their victimization by other inmates, 72% said they experienced force or threat of force and 29% said they were physically injured.
4. Transgender inmates reported high levels of staff sexual misconduct in prisons (17%) and jails (23%). Most transgender inmates who had been victimized reported that the staff sexual misconduct was unwilling on their part (75%) and that they experienced force or threat of force (51%) or were pressured by staff (66%) to engage in the sexual activity.
5. Among those victimized by staff, more than 40% of transgender inmates in prison and jails said they had been physically injured by the staff perpetrator.

Two issues with this data are worth noting. First, the majority of the transgendered population within the custodial environment is male-to-female; the female-to-male transgendered population is miniscule within the correctional population around the nation. Second, the notion of being effeminate, gay, or transgendered has severe and profound negative consequences within the male prison subculture, but this is not so much the case within female facilities. Thus, this is an important area of concern within male prisons, and the results from recent PREA data confirm this.

The Strong, Silent Type and the Use of Slang

Also common within the prison subculture is the belief that inmates should maintain themselves as men who show no emotion and are free from fear, depression, and anxiety. Basically, the "strong, silent type" is the ideal. Today's young offenders may attempt to maintain this exterior image, but the effects of modern society (the prevalence of mental health services, reliance on medications, technological advances, and a fast-changing society) often preclude this stereotypical version of the offender because a reliance on those services and medications is viewed as being "weak" in many prisons. Inmates are also expected to refrain from arguments with other inmates. The general idea is

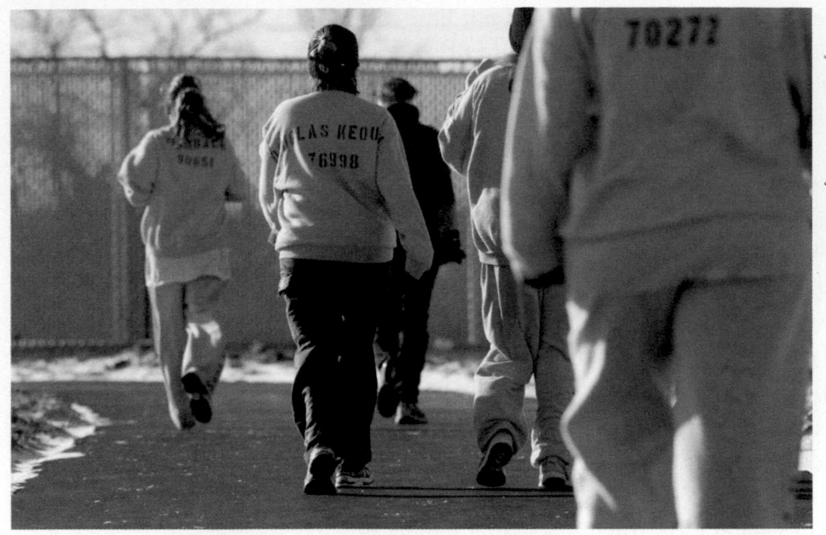

Keith Myers/The Kansas City Star/Newscom

■ PHOTO 9.3 When weather permits, these female inmates are allowed to walk and jog in the recreation yard of a women's prison.

that inmates must do their own time without becoming involved in the personal business of others. Getting involved in other people's business is equated to being a gossip, and this is considered more of a feminine behavior. Thus, to be manly in prison, inmates must mind their own business.

Inmates who stick to these two rules of behavior are generally seen as in control, fairly wise to the prison world, and not easily manipulated. In some cases, these inmates may be referred to as a *true convict* rather than an inmate. In the modern prison culture, the title of **convict** refers to an inmate who is respected for being self-reliant and independent of other inmates or the system. Convicts are considered mature and strong, not weak and dependent on others for their survival. They are considered superior to the typical inmate, and, while not necessarily leaders of other inmates (indeed, most do not care to lead others but simply wish to do their own time), they are often respected by younger inmates becoming acculturated into the prison environment.

Within prison systems, there evolves a peculiar language of slang that often seems out of place in broader society. This slang has some consistency throughout the United States but does vary in specific terminology from state to state. The language often used by inmates, including slang, is affected by their racial and gang lineage. For instance, members of the Crips or the Bloods have certain terms that usually are only used by their group, often as a means of identifying or denigrating the other group. Likewise, Latino gang members in the Mexican Mafia and/or the Texas Syndicate tend to have their own vernacular, much of which is either Spanish phraseology or some type of unique slang. Terms like *punk*, *shank* (a knife), *bug juice* (referring to psychotropic medications), and *green light* (referring to clearance to assault another inmate) are commonly used in most prison systems.

Maintaining Respect

In nearly every prison around the United States, one concept is paramount among inmates: respect. This is perhaps the most important key to understanding the inmate subculture. Prison status revolves around the amount of respect given to an inmate and/or signs of disrespect exhibited toward an inmate. **Respect** is a term that represents an inmate's sense of masculine standing within the prison culture; if inmates are disrespected, they are honor-bound to avenge that disrespect or be considered weak by other inmates. If an inmate fails to preserve his sense of respect, this will lead to the questioning of his manhood and his ability to handle prison and will lead others to think that he is perhaps weak. The fixation on respect (and fixation is an appropriate description in some prisons) is particularly pronounced among African American gang members in prison. This is also glorified in much of the contemporary gangsta music that emerged in the 1990s and continues today. Because inmates have little else, their sense of self-respect and the respect that they are able to garner from others is paramount to their own welfare and survival.

In addition, it is usually considered a sign of weakness to take help or assistance from another inmate, at least when one is new to the prison environment. Indeed, inmates will be tested when new to the prison world; they may be offered some type of item (e.g., coffee or cigarettes) or provided some type of service (e.g., getting access to the kitchen), but this is never for free or due to goodwill. Rather, inmate subculture dictates that a debt is thus owed by the *newbie* (a term for inmates who are new to a prison). New inmates may be required or coerced to do "favors" for the inmate who provided them with the good or service. For example, they might be asked to be a "mule" for the inmate or the inmate's gang. A **mule** is a person who smuggles drugs into prison for another inmate, often using his or her own body cavities to hide the drugs from prison authorities. In other cases, the inmate may be forced to become a punk for that inmate or for an entire prison gang.

Convict: An inmate who is respected for being self-reliant and independent of other inmates or the system.

Respect: An inmate's sense of standing within the prison culture.

Mule: A person who smuggles drugs into prison for another inmate.

APPLIED THEORY 9.1

Labeling Theory as a Paradigm for the Etiology of Prison Rape: Implications for Understanding and Intervention

According to labeling theory, group reactions are the key determinant to events that become considered antisocial in nature. Labeling theory essentially asks why some acts are labeled deviant when others are not (Akers, 2000). This theory asserts that social group reactions serve to make certain behaviors deviant, regardless of the individual context in which they occur (Vold, Bernard, & Snipes, 1998). This begs the question as to who creates the label associated with deviant behavior. The answer to this inquiry lies with those who hold the power within a given social structure.

With the prison population being drawn disproportionately from the less affluent members of society, it should come as no surprise that prison norms may, in various subtle ways, exemplify power status norms held by the lower classes (Miller, 1958; Tucker, 1981). The members of the "prison society" are even less socially powerful than their socioeconomic counterparts who are not incarcerated. In the prison setting, physical prowess and coercion become the primary method of achieving power. Thus, aside from some rare exceptions, such as successful writ writers or inmates who have affluent family members, those who are physically powerful tend to also be the most socially powerful within the prison. Within the male inmate subculture, the expression of physical prowess as power is frequently paired with roles of masculinity, which, in turn, reinforces the subculture of physical prowess within the prison setting (Messerschmidt, 1999).

It is through both the means and the threat of violence that dominance and control are achieved, with the victim ultimately being given the label of "punk." This is true even in cases that prison officials may term "voluntary" or "consensual" sex. This process, referred to as being "turned out" or "punked out," effectively redefines and labels the victim's role in prison as that of a punk, or subjugated homosexual (Tucker, 1981). Thus, the homosexual orientation and label placed upon the deviant is not one of self-choice or personal preference; it is forced upon him by more powerful members of the inmate subculture.

Labeling Theory as a Paradigm for Prison Rape Etiology

According to Lemert (1999), the deviant is a product of gradual, unconscious processes that are part of socialization, especially subcultural socialization. Lemert also asserted that the personality change that occurs from accepting and internalizing a deviant label is not always gradual but can be sudden. As Lemert (1999) states, "It must be taken into consideration that traumatic experiences often speed up changes in personality" (p. 386). This is especially true for inmates who are victims of prison gang rape. For these inmate-victims, entering into a sexual relationship with one man in return for protection can be an adaptive coping mechanism for survival within the prison subculture.

Lemert (1999) further states that "when a person begins to employ his deviant behavior or role . . . as a means of defense, attack, or adjustment to the overt and covert problems created by the consequent societal reaction to him, his deviance is secondary" (p. 388). In the previous example, the initial gang rape can be thought of as the source of primary deviance, whereas the deliberate decision to engage in "consensual" homosexuality with one partner essentially results in a more solidified self-identity. But this process creates a degree of cognitive dissonance within the individual, which, when resolved, tends to leave the victim more willing to engage in future homosexual conduct. Indeed, this dissonance is the crux of this adjustment process, in which the victim's original identity is juxtaposed against his or her newly ascribed identity, resulting in an eventual psychological metamorphosis from the point of primary deviance to that of secondary deviance through future acts of homosexuality (Festinger, 1958; Lemert, 1999). Throughout the process of coping with this dissonance, typical acute symptoms of this trauma, such as intrusive recollections and/or dreams about the assault, intense distress over stimuli that remind the victim of the assault, hypervigilance, difficulties sleeping and eating, and unexplained or exaggerated outbursts of anger, are likely to be experienced. Those who cannot successfully navigate this dissonance present with the previous symptoms on a chronic level, coupled with more serious and self-damaging psychological impairments associated with rape trauma (e.g., self-mutilation and suicide). The fact that these victims must repetitively subject themselves to subsequent victimization naturally exacerbates their likelihood for long-term psychological impairment and emotional injury.

But the victim of male prison rape will find it necessary to adjust to this new role since the sexual values of mainstream society are completely inverted within the prison subculture. The inmate perpetrator who willingly engages in predatory homosexual activity would typically be given the marginalized label of "homosexual" or "bisexual" in the broader society. Ironically, however, within the prison there is exactly the opposite effect, with a corresponding increase in social status and "manhood" for the perpetrator of sexual assault. Within the prison subculture, rapists are considered masculine conquerors of effeminate punks (Weiss & Friar, 1974). The aggressor is not held as homosexual in orientation but is simply assuming a position of power within the subcultural norms of prison life. The victim of the prison sexual assault, however, suffers an injury greater than the sexual assault alone, as the victim's entire social position within the prison is effectively compromised and redefined.

SOURCE: Hanser, R. D. (2003). *Labeling theory as a paradigm for the etiology of prison rape: Implications for understanding and intervention.* Washington, DC: National Institute of Corrections.

The Con and the Never-Ending Hustle

Among inmates, there is the constant push and pull between the need to "con" others and, at the same time, avoid being conned. Naturally, this constant and contradictory set of expectations completely impedes the ability for inmates to develop any sort of true trust; they must always remain vigilant for the potential "hustle" within the prison system. **Hustle** refers to any action that is designed to deceive, manipulate, or take advantage of another person. Further, consider that the very term *convict* includes the word *con*, which implies that the individual cannot and should not be trusted. Thus, convicts are, stereotypically, always on the hustle, so to speak.

Inmates who are able to "get over" on others and or "skate" through work or other obligations in the prison system are considered particularly streetwise and savvy among their peers. In fact, some prison systems, such as the Texas prison system, have a term for this concept: *hogging*. **Hogging** implies that a person is using others for some type of gain or benefit—manipulating others into doing work or fulfilling obligations on his or her behalf. When inmates are able to find some means to manipulate others into doing their dirty work, they are active in the art of the con. The process by which they encourage or manipulate a person to provide such a service is all part of the hustle.

A classic portrayal of this type of logic, though not a prison example, can be found in *The Adventures of Tom Sawyer* by Mark Twain. In this novel, Tom Sawyer convinces other boys in the area that painting a fence (a chore assigned to young Tom) is a fun activity. So fun is it, according to Tom, that he will not allow anyone to help him unless they pay him to do so. Ultimately, other boys pay Tom for the "opportunity" to paint the fence and join in the fun. Once several other boys pay their fee for the privilege of painting the fence, Tom slips off to spend the money that he has procured from those duped into doing his assigned work. This example demonstrates all the fine points of the con, the hustle, and the act of hogging others.

THE IMPACT OF THE INMATE SUBCULTURE ON CORRECTIONS STAFF

SAGE Journal Article Link
Legitimacy and Authority Revisited

Perhaps one of the most interesting dynamics within prison can be found between the inmates and the prison staff. This area of discussion is both complicated and paradoxical in many respects. The paradox involved with this dynamic is that although inmate subculture restricts inmates from "siding" with officers and officer culture restricts officers from befriending inmates, there is a natural give-and-take that emerges between both groups. In fact, a symbiotic relationship usually emerges between prison security staff and the inmate population. This **symbiotic prison relationship** is a means of developing mutually agreeable and informal negotiations in behavior that are acceptable within the bounds of institutional security and also allow inmates to meet many of their basic human needs. This relationship is grounded in the reality of the day-to-day interactions that prison security staff have with inmates.

Because prison is a very intense environment that has a very strong psychological impact on both inmates and staff, it is only natural that this type of relationship often emerges. While the rules of the institution are generally clearly written, these rules are not always pragmatic for the officers who must enforce them. For example, a rule to restrict inmates from having more than one blanket in their cell may, on the face of it, seem easy enough to enforce. However, consider the following scenarios when considering rule enforcement:

Hustle: Any action that is designed to deceive, manipulate, or take advantage of another person.

Hogging: A term used to imply that a person is using others for some type of gain or benefit.

Symbiotic prison relationship: When correctional staff and inmates develop negotiation behavior that is acceptable for institutional security and also meets inmates' basic human needs.

Scenario 1

> *A veteran officer with many years of experience may find that a given inmate, Inmate X, who upholds the convict code and has respect within the institution, has the flu during the winter. The officer has access to additional blankets, and this is known among the inmates. Inmate X tends to mind his own business and usually does as he is expected when the officer is on duty. In this case, the officer may decide to offer Inmate X an additional blanket and would do so with no expectation that the inmate give something in return. Likewise, the inmate (as well as others watching) would know that the officer's kindness should not be taken for weakness or no further empathy will be shown to convicts.*

Scenario 2

This same veteran officer finds that Inmate Y, who does not uphold the convict code and generally has average clout (at best) within the prison culture, also has the flu. Inmate Y sometimes causes problems on the cell block and is sarcastic with officers. The veteran officer, in this case, would likely not give an additional blanket to Inmate Y, even if Inmate Y were to be courteous enough to ask for it. In most cases, Inmate Y would know better than to ask, since he knows that he does not honor the convict code or work within the commonsense bounds of the symbiotic prison relationship. If he were to ask and especially if he were to push the issue, the veteran officer would inform him that "the rules are the rules" and would indicate that he needs to keep quiet and go to sick call when that option is available. Further discourse from Inmate Y would result in comments from the veteran officer that would imply that he is being a troublemaker and that he is not doing his time "like a man," which would result in a loss of respect for Inmate Y among others on the cell block. This would likely shame Inmate Y and cause him to lose status, but the veteran officer would likely gain *status among the inmates for being firm, streetwise, and cognizant of subcultural norms. Because he does not give in to Inmate Y, he would be perceived as strong and capable, not subject to manipulation and not an easy mark.*

Obviously, Inmate X and Inmate Y are being given different standards of treatment. Regardless of whether it is overtly stated or simply presumed, veteran officers will tend to leave convicts and/or trouble-free inmates unbothered and may, in some cases, even extend some degree of preferential treatment, within acceptable boundaries that allow them to maintain respect on the cell block. However, this does not mean that they will do so for all inmates; they reserve the right to use discretion when divvying out the paltry resources available within the prison. In short, these veteran officers become effective resource and power brokers as a means of gaining compliance and creating an informal system of fairness that is understood among the inmates. Essentially, veteran officers and inmates operate with this understanding:

Prison Tour Video Link
Officers' Experience and Reputation, Inmates' Feedback Influence, and Grievances

"I will let you do your time, but you will let me do my time—one shift at a time."

Convict boss/officer: A correctional officer with a keen understanding of convict logic and socialization.

This concept is important because it creates a connection between both groups; they are both in a noxious environment and have a role that they must uphold. Yet, at the same time, some degree of give-and-take is necessary to avoid extremes in rules that do not, ultimately, create just situations. So long as inmates allow the officer to generally do his time, one shift at a time, he will, in turn, leave them to serve their time without problems. On the other hand, if an inmate does not honor this understanding, he should expect no mercy or consideration from the prison security staff; the rules are the rules, and any sense of discretion will simply cease to be acted upon.

Officers who master these types of negotiations tend to gain respect from inmates and even from other officers. They may sometimes be referred to as "convict bosses" by inmates. The term **convict boss** or **convict officer** is applied to a correctional officer who has developed a keen understanding of convict logic and socialization and uses that knowledge to maximize control over his or her assigned post. This term denotes respect gained from inmates and generally comes with time, experience, sound judgment, and

Robert Hanser

■ PHOTO 9.4 Sergeant Tatum talks with inmates regarding the organization of an upcoming function in a meeting hall of the prison. The means by which officers and inmates talk to each other set the tone for respect or disrespect in the prison.

a cunning personality that is not easily deceived or manipulated. The officer is not perceived as weak but is instead thought to possess a good degree of common sense by inmates within the facility.

One important note should be added to this discussion. Students should keep in mind that the examples in the prior scenarios present a veteran officer with several years of experience. The use of this type of discretion by newer officers who do not have sufficient time and experience working with the inmate population will not have the same result. If a newer or younger officer attempted such discretion, he or she would likely be seen as a "sucker" and someone who could be easily marked for future exploitation. This person would not be perceived to understand the fine nuances of discretion with regard to prison rules, norms, and mores. This person would also not likely be trusted by peers who, generally, would expect him or her to stay "by the book" until he or she developed the level of expertise to make fine distinctions in blurry situations. This officer would likely be labeled "weak" among inmates and might even be considered an "inmate lover" by other officers. These labels should be avoided in hard-core institutions because once they are applied, it is very difficult (if not impossible) to be rid of them.

Lastly, the mannerisms that are displayed, both by inmates and officers, often reflect the type of upbringing that one has had and also tend to indicate the value system from which that person operates. Within the prison, this is important because during an inmate or beginning officer's first few weeks of indoctrination to the prison experience, he or she is being "sized up" or appraised by others who observe them. Both the officers and the inmates begin to determine if the person is likely to be easily influenced and/or manipulated. This formative period whereby inmates and staff are socialized into the prison culture is important due to the influences of the prison subculture that include the inmate's subculture, the officer's subculture, and the need to master the symbiotic prison relationship between the two.

PRISONIZATION

Video Link
Prison State

Prisonization is the process of being socialized into the prison culture. This process occurs over time as the inmate or the correctional officer adapts to the informal rules of prison life. Unlike many other textbook authors, the author of this text thinks that it is important to emphasize that correctional officers also experience a form of prisonization that impacts their worldview and the manner in which they operate within the prison institution. In his text on prisonization, Gillespie (2002) makes the following introductory statement:

> Prison is a context that exerts its influence upon the social relations of those who enter its domain. (p. 1)

The reason that this sentence is set off in such a conspicuous manner is because it has profound meaning and truly captures the essence of prisonization. Students should understand that the influence of the prison environment extends to *all* persons who enter its domain, particularly if they do so over a prolonged period of time. Thus, prisonization impacts both inmates and staff within the facility. While the total experience will, of course, not be the same for staff as it is for inmates, it is silly to presume that staff routinely exposed to aberrant human behavior will not be impacted by that behavior.

With respect to inmates, Gillespie (2002) found that both the individual characteristics of inmates and institutional qualities affect prisonization and misconduct. However, he found that individual-level antecedents explained prisonization better than did prison-level variables. This means that the experiences of inmates prior to being imprisoned are central to determining how well they will adapt to the prison experience. For this text, this contention will also be extended to prison guards; their prior experiences and their individual personality development prior to correctional employment will dictate how well they adapt to both the formal and informal exchanges that occur within the prison.

THE GUARD SUBCULTURE

Prisonization: The process of being socialized into the prison culture.

This area of discussion is controversial and has led to a great deal of debate. One reason for developing this text and providing a discussion on this particular topic is to provide students with a realistic and no-nonsense appraisal of the world of corrections, particularly as practiced in the prison environment. In providing a glimpse of the guard subculture (and this text contends that a guard subculture *does* exist), it is important to keep in mind that the specific characteristics of this subculture vary from prison system to prison system and even from prison to prison within the same state system. The reasons for this are manifold but are mostly due to the fact that, unlike inmates, guards are not forced to remain within the prison environment 24/7. Rather, guards have the benefit of time away from the institution, and they can (and sometimes do) transfer from facility to facility, depending on their career path.

Prison Tour Video: Prison Culture. Prisonization affects both inmates and correctional staff. Watch an interview with prisoners about prison culture and behavior.

Further, since guards are routinely exposed to external society (contact with family, friends, the general public, the media, etc.), they are able to mitigate many of the debilitating effects of the prison environment. Likewise, their integration into society mitigates the degree to which prison socialization will impact them, personally and professionally. Thus, there is greater variability in the required adaptations of prison guards when compared to inmates. The type of institution that they find themselves working within can also impact this socialization. A guard who works at a maximum-security institution or one for particularly violent offenders will likely experience a different type of socialization than a guard assigned to a minimum-security dormitory. All of these factors can impact how the prison culture affects individual officers and the degree to which they become enmeshed into the guard subculture.

The discussion that follows is intended to address guard subculture in maximum-security prisons or those institutions that have histories of violence among inmates. Larger facilities that have more challenging circumstances tend to breed the type of subculture that will be presented here. Though modern-day correctional agencies seek to circumvent and eliminate these subcultural dimensions, they nonetheless still exist in various facilities.

The popular Hollywood image of prison guards is that they are brutal and uncaring and that their relationships with inmates are hostile, violent, and abusive. However, this is a very simplistic and inaccurate view of prison guards that makes for good entertainment but does not reflect reality. For many, corrections work is a stable job available to persons in rural areas where few other jobs exist, and it produces a livable wage for the effort. For others, prison work may be a stepping-stone to further their career, particularly if they are interested in criminal justice employment. Indeed, the author of this text worked at Eastham Unit in Texas while attending school at a state university in the area, and this was a common practice among many students of criminal justice or criminology studies. This means that, at least in this case, many of the prison guards employed in the region actually had an above-average education and most likely possessed depth and purpose that exceeded the Hollywood stereotype.

The author of this text would like to acknowledge the work of Kelsey Kauffman (1988) in explaining the overall processes behind prison guard socialization and the development of prison guard subcultures. Like Kauffman, the author of this text encountered a similar transitional experience where, over time, the aloof and distant feeling between himself and his fellow coworkers grew into a feeling of camaraderie and close connection in identity. To this day, this author considers himself, first and foremost, a prison guard at heart. However, it is Kauffman who so eloquently and correctly penned the formation and description of the guard subculture, and it is her work that will be used as the primary reference for this section.

According to Kauffman (1988), the guard subculture does not develop due to any single contextual characteristic, such as prisonization, indigenous forms of influence, or the importation of values. Rather, the culture is a product "of a complex interaction of importation, socialization, deportation, and cultural evolution" (Kauffman, 1988, p. 167). Kauffman notes that prison guards have a distinct and identifiable subculture that separates them from other professionals. The central norms of this subculture dictate how they proceed with the daily performance of their duties, such as with the example scenarios provided earlier when discussing the impact of the inmate subculture on custodial staff. In describing the prison guard subculture, Kauffman produced a list of the basic tenets behind it. These same tenets are presented in this text due to the author's perception that they are reflective of those encountered in most prisons throughout the United States. They include the following:

1. **Always go to the aid of an officer in distress.** This is the foundation for cohesion among custodial staff. This tenet also can, in times of emergency, provide justification for violating norms within the bureaucratic system. This tenet applies to all guards, regardless of how well accepted the officer in distress may or may not be. This norm is key to officer safety and is fundamental. If an officer fails to uphold this norm, he or she will likely be ostracized from the group and will be treated as an outsider.
2. **Do not traffic drugs.** This is also considered fundamental because of the danger that it can create as inmates fight for power over the trade of these substances. In addition, the use of drugs is illegal and does not reflect well on officers, who are supposed to keep drug offenders behind bars. If an officer violates this tenet, it is considered justified within the subculture to inform authorities, but most will not do so due to the reluctance to betray a fellow officer. However, it would not be uncommon for guards to take it upon themselves to put pressure on the officer who violates this norm through threats, intimidation, and coercion. In addition, officers will likely isolate the officer from interactions and will not invite him or her to functions outside of work. The officer will be treated as persona non grata.
3. **Do not be a snitch.** In many respects, this is a carryover from the inmate subculture. This dictate comes in two forms. First, officers should never give information to inmates that could get another officer in trouble. Generally speaking, officers are expected not to discuss other officers, their business, or their personal lives with inmates. The second prohibition applies to investigative authorities of the prison system. Officers are expected to stay silent and not divulge information that will "burn" another officer, particularly when the Internal Affairs Division (IAD) is investigating an incident. While it is expected that officers will not knowingly place their coworkers in legally compromising situations where they must lie for their coworkers, it is still equally expected that coworkers will not snitch on their fellow officer.

   This tenet is perhaps one of the most difficult to follow because, in some cases, it puts officers in a position where they must lie to cover for their coworkers, even when they were not directly involved. This can occur during investigations and even if officers are brought to court in a lawsuit. Officers who comply with institutional rules still cannot be assured that they will be safe from liability if they have covered for a fellow officer. This may be the case regardless of whether the officer initiating the situation was acting responsibly or not.
4. **Never disrespect another officer in front of inmates.** This tenet reflects the importance of respect and the need to maintain "face" within the prison culture. Officers who are ridiculed or made to look weak in front of inmates have their authority subject to question by inmates since the word will get around that the officer is not respected (and therefore not well supported) by his peers. This sets the officer up for potential manipulation in the future.
5. **Always support an officer who is in a dispute with an inmate.** This applies to all types of instances ranging from verbal arguments with inmates to actual physical altercations. Simply put, one's coworker is always right, and the inmate is always wrong. However, behind the scenes, officers may not get along and may disagree on issues related to the management of inmates. Indeed, one officer may write up an inmate for a disciplinary infraction but another may overtly object when in the office out of earshot of the inmate population. The reasons for this may be many, but generally older, more seasoned officers will be adept at informally addressing inmate infractions whereas junior officers will tend to rely on official processes. However, given the threat of employee discipline that exists within the system and the need for control of the inmate population, most officers will ultimately maintain loyalty to each other during the final stages where their official support is necessary.

CORRECTIONS AND THE LAW 9.1

Nonlethal Force and Criminal and/or Civil Liability

Daniel Gordon and Eric Newsome, correctional officers at the Greenville Federal Correctional Institution, were indicted by a federal grand jury for violating the civil rights of an inmate and then lying to cover up the crime, Wan J. Kim, assistant attorney general for the Justice Department's Civil Rights Division, and acting United States attorney Randy Massey for the Southern District of Illinois announced today. The indictment alleges that the two defendants assaulted the inmate in his cell using fists and handcuffs to strike and injure the inmate. The grand jury charged both men with conspiracy to violate the inmate's civil rights and with filing false reports after the incident. Additionally, the grand jury charged Newsome with lying to a special agent of the United States Department of Justice's Office of the Inspector General. A trial date has been set for September 11, 2006.

Each defendant faces a maximum term of 10 years in prison on each of the civil rights counts, 10 years on the conspiracy count, and 20 years on each count of filing a false report. Newsome potentially faces an additional 5 years in prison for lying to the special agent of the Office of the Inspector General.

The indictment resulted from an investigation by Special Agent Kimberly Thomas from the Chicago field office of the Inspector General, Assistant U.S. Attorney Richard H. Lloyd from the United States Attorney's Office, and Trial Attorney Michael Khoury from the Civil Rights Division.

An indictment is an accusation and is not evidence of guilt. The defendants are presumed innocent and are entitled to a fair trial at which the United States has the burden of proving guilt beyond a reasonable doubt.

The Civil Rights Division is committed to the vigorous enforcement of every federal criminal civil rights statute, such as those laws that prohibit the willful use of excessive force or other acts of misconduct by law enforcement officials. The division has compiled a significant record on criminal civil rights prosecutions in the last 5 years. Since FY 2001, the division has increased the conviction rate of defendants by 30%.

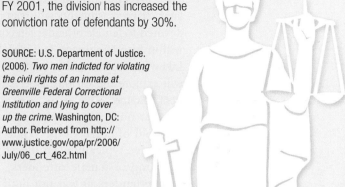

SOURCE: U.S. Department of Justice. (2006). *Two men indicted for violating the civil rights of an inmate at Greenville Federal Correctional Institution and lying to cover up the crime.* Washington, DC: Author. Retrieved from http://www.justice.gov/opa/pr/2006/July/06_crt_462.html

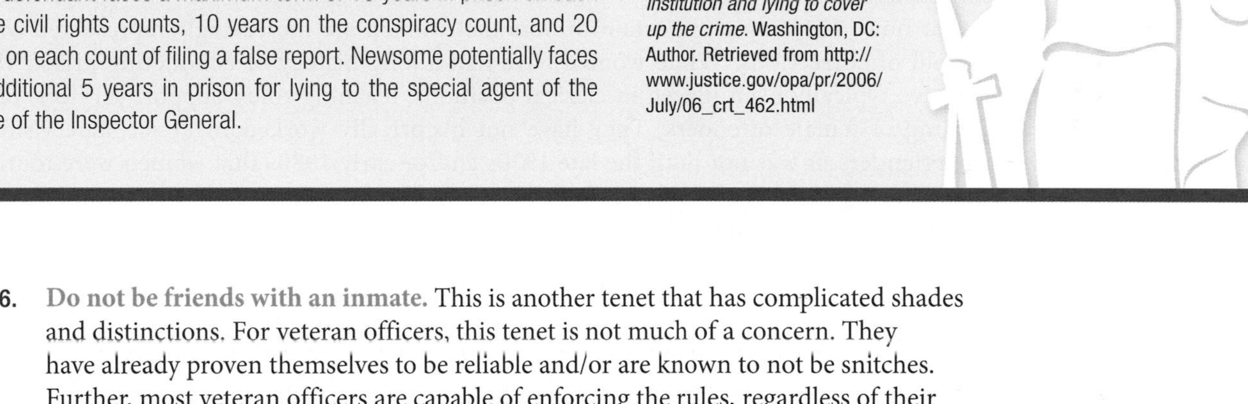

6. **Do not be friends with an inmate.** This is another tenet that has complicated shades and distinctions. For veteran officers, this tenet is not much of a concern. They have already proven themselves to be reliable and/or are known to not be snitches. Further, most veteran officers are capable of enforcing the rules, regardless of their prior conversations with an inmate. However, it is not uncommon for veteran officers (and even supervisors) to have one or two inmates whom they talk with, at least on a topical level. Though they may not consider themselves friends with the inmate, they may allow that inmate some privileges and opportunities that others would not, simply because they have developed a symbiotic prison relationship with that inmate that has existed for a long period of time. In return, these inmates may do the officer small favors, such as reserving higher-quality food from the kitchen for that officer or even, in prisons where the subculture has truly created permeable boundaries, letting the officer know when supervisors or others are watching him or her while on duty. This allows the officer to operate his or her cell block in a more leisurely manner, and, as such, the entire cell block benefits from the officer's laid-back approach.
7. **Maintain cohesion against all outside groups.** In this tenet, *outside groups* applies to members of the supervisory ranks, the outside public, the media, and even one's own family. This tenet is based on the belief that the general public does not understand the pressures placed upon officers and that the media tend to be sympathetic to the plight of the inmate, not the officer. Officers do not wish to implicate their family members and also do not want them to fear for their safety; thus, details are seldom disclosed. Further, the administration is not seen as trustworthy but instead as being politically driven. Administrators care only about their careers and moving up the corporate ladder and are too far removed from the rank-and-file to still understand the complexities of the officer's daily concerns. It is therefore better that officers not talk about what goes on in the institution to persons not within their ranks.

These tenets perhaps most clearly summarize the prison guard subculture. Again, these "guidelines" may not occur exactly as presented in all prisons, but in most larger and older facilities, at least some of them will be familiar to correctional staff.

As we have seen in prior chapters, numerous lawsuits emerged during the 1960s, 1970s, and 1980s, and their aftermath greatly impacted the field of corrections in the 1990s as well as the current millennium. Prison systems had to modify and adjust their operations to be considered constitutional, and this required that these systems institute organizational change among their prison staff. An emphasis on professionalism emerged throughout the nation, and, as the War on Drugs resulted in a swelling inmate population, so too swelled the number of prison guards who were hired. In addition, the elimination of building tender and trusty supervision schemes used in many southern states necessitated the recruiting and hiring of more prison security staff. During the 1990s, the term *prison guard* became outdated and was replaced with the official job classification of correctional officer in many state prison systems.

Female Correctional Officers

The correctional field has traditionally been stereotyped as a male-dominated area of work. In later chapters, students will read more about women in the correctional field; an entire chapter is devoted to female offenders in correctional systems (Chapter 10). A general subculture also exists within women's prison facilities, but it is separate and distinct from the male prison subculture. Likewise, the issues that confront women who work in corrections tend to be different as well. We will explore the various aspects related to both women inmates and correctional workers in the next chapter.

For now, it is simply important to note that women are increasingly represented within the field of corrections. While women have had a long history of conducting prison work, they have typically been placed in clerical positions, teaching roles, support services, or the guarding of female offenders. They have not historically worked in direct supervision of male offenders. It was not until the late 1970s and/or early 1980s that women were routinely assigned to supervise male inmates (Pollock, 1986). The introduction of women into the security ranks has greatly impacted the organizational culture of many prison facilities and the subculture within them.

Women generally do not have the same aggressive social skills that men in prison tend to exhibit. Further, the prison environment tends to emphasize the desire to "be a man" and denigrates women as inferior. This means that women were not widely accepted among correctional officers and/or inmates. Since women have become integrated into the correctional industry, the male-oriented subculture has been weakened. The introduction of women into the security ranks, along with the inclusion of diverse minority groups, the professionalization of corrections, and the proliferation of prison gangs, has eroded the influence of the male-dominated and male-oriented convict code. While the convict code still exists and has its adherents, it is no longer considered a primary standard of behavior in many prison facilities but instead has become more of an ideal.

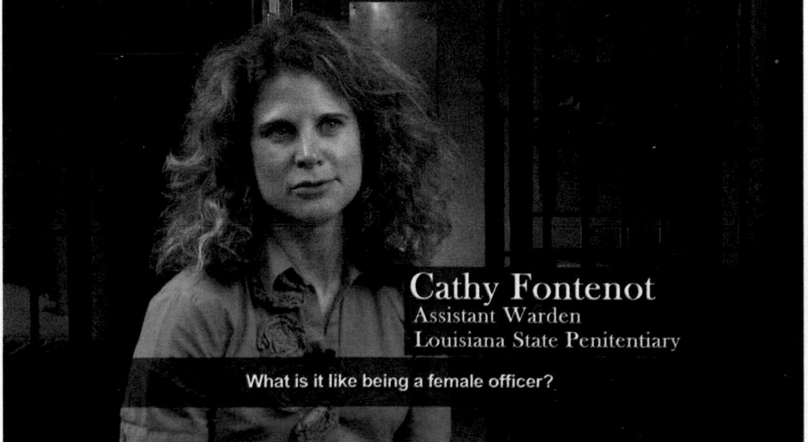
Cathy Fontenot
Assistant Warden
Louisiana State Penitentiary
What is it like being a female officer?

Prison Tour Video: Female Correctional Officers. Women working in corrections bring key strengths to the role. Watch an interview with a female correctional officer.

THE IMPACT OF GANGS UPON PRISON SUBCULTURE

Gang members are another group that tends to not adhere strictly to the tenets of the convict code (Mobley, 2011). This is particularly true among Latino and African American gangs. These gangs, which represent the majority racial lineages among prison gangs, typically view prison stints as just another part of the criminal lifestyle. As such, they have no true use for the convict code since it is their gang family who will protect them, not their reputation according to the code. Their alliances and their allegiances are tied to outside street gangs with members who sometimes get locked up and therefore find themselves operating within prison walls as well (Mobley, 2011). Many young inner-city African American and Latino males who have been incarcerated are able to find homeboys or hombres in nearly every correctional facility within their state (Mobley, 2011). Thus, the young gang member does not need to trouble himself with adapting to the prison subculture (Mobley, 2011).

Gangsters comprise a distinct subculture whether on the street or in prison (Mobley, 2011). They "look out for" one another and protect each other, living in a nearly familial lifestyle. Few African American gang members speak to inmates outside of their gang "set," at least about anything of substance. Though most would claim that they do not snitch to "the man," and most would say that they just wish to do their own time, their true loyalty is to their gang family. Gang members "run with their road dogs" from "the hood" and meet up with each other in prison, forming bonds and making plans for when they reunite in their respective communities, the turf for their street gang activity (Mobley, 2011). This constant cycle, in and out of prison, creates a seamless form of support for many gang members.

The Impact of Cross-Pollination: Reciprocal Relationships Between Street Gangs and Prison Gangs

It is perhaps the emergence of gang life that has been the most significant development within prison subcultures throughout various state systems. In many texts on prisons and/or the world of corrections, there is a section on prison gangs. In most cases, these texts tend to present gang membership as isolated to the prison environment, with little emphasis on the notion that gang membership is permeable, found inside and outside the prison. But members of prison gangs do not simply discard membership once their sentence is served or when they are paroled out into society. Rather, their membership continues, and they will often continue to answer to gang leaders who may still be locked up in prison. In other cases, they may be required to report to other leaders outside of the prison walls and will continue criminal work on behalf of the gang, plying their criminal trade on the streets and in broader society.

Many prison gang members were prior street gang members. An offender may engage in street gang criminal activity for a number of years, with frequent short stints in jail. As noted earlier in this chapter, few inmates in state prison systems are locked up with long-term sentences for their first offense; rather, they have typically committed several "priors" before that point, some of which might not be known to law enforcement. During their activity on the streets, these offenders will develop a reputation, particularly within their gang or their area of operation (if in an urban or a suburban setting) and will develop associations with other gang members. Once they finally do end up with a long-term sentence in a state facility, they have usually already embedded themselves within the gang structure on the outside, which includes members who have been locked up inside the prison system.

In some cases, those doing state time may be the upper leadership of the street gang; these members will tend to direct prison gang activities internally and also "call the shots" for members on the outside. The term *shot caller* refers to those inmates and/or gang members who dictate what members will do within the gang hierarchy. The point to all of this is that a gang's membership does not begin or end with the prison walls. Rather, prison is simply a feature that modern-day gangs must contend with—an obstacle that increases the overhead to conducting criminal enterprise.

Because gang membership is porous in nature, social researchers can only vaguely determine likely gang growth both inside and outside the prison. In 1998, there were an estimated 780,000 gang members across the nation. A large proportion of these gang members had served time behind bars at one point or another throughout their criminal careers. In fact, some prison systems, such as Texas's, were nearly controlled by gangs; the gangs even controlled many of the staff in these systems through various tactics like friendships or occasional intimidation.

As this shows, prison gangs in some state systems can be both persuasive and very powerful. Potential recruits for existing prison gangs enter prison with natural feelings of anxiety and quickly learn the value of having some form of affiliation. Indeed, inmates without the protection of affiliation are likely to be the target of other inmates who *are* members of a gang.

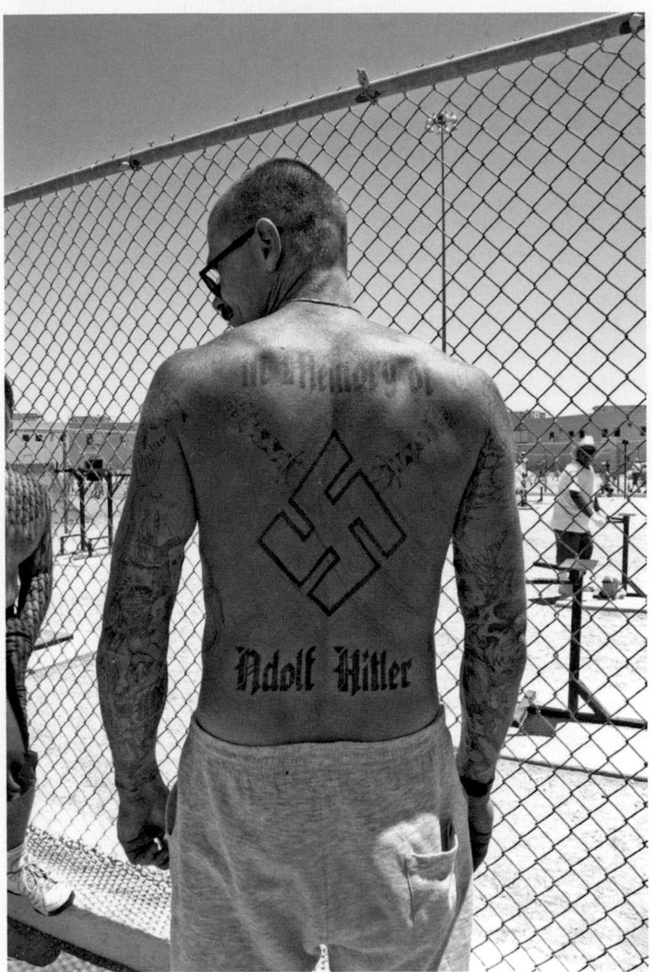

■ PHOTO 9.5 **This member of the Aryan Brotherhood has clear markings of his gang affiliation for all to see. Members with these bold markings usually remain in the gang for life.**

Affiliations tend to be based along racial allegiances—in fact, most prison gang membership is strictly defined by the race of the member.

Historically speaking, the main distinction between prison gangs and street gangs has been the internal structure and the leadership style of the gang (Fleisher & Rison, 1999). However, over time this distinction has become so blurred as to be meaningless in the offender world (Fleisher & Rison, 1999). In the correctional environment of today, prison gangs such as the Mexican Mafia and the Texas Syndicate are just as influential and powerful as classic street gangs like the Gangster Disciples and Latin Kings (Fleisher & Rison, 1999). More telling is the fact that the Mexican Mafia, the Aryan Brotherhood, and even emerging local groups such as the Barrio Aztecas have become just as formidable in their own respective ethnic and/or culturally based neighborhoods or regions as they are in prisons. Indeed, it is sometimes common for leaders of a gang to be incarcerated but still giving orders to members outside the prison operating within the community. For this text, we will refer to **gang cross-pollination**, which means that a gang has developed such power and influence as to be equally effective regardless of whether its leadership is inside or outside of the prison walls.

When discussing gang cross-pollination, the term **security threat group (STG)** will be used to describe a gang that possesses the following high-functioning group and organizational characteristics:

1. Prison and street affiliation is based on race, ethnicity, geography, ideology, or any combination of these or other similar factors (Fleisher, 2008, p. 356).
2. Members seek protection from other gang members inside and outside the prison, as well as insulation from law enforcement detection (use of safe houses when wanted).
3. Members will mutually take care of an incarcerated member's family, at least minimally, while the member is locked up since this is an expected overhead cost in the organization.
4. The group's mission integrates an economic objective and uses some form of illicit industry, such as drug trafficking, to fulfill the economic necessities to carry forward other stated objectives (Fleisher, 2008). The use of violence or the threat of violence is a common tool in meeting these economic objectives.

Gang cross-pollination: Occurs when a gang has developed such power and influence as to be equally effective regardless of whether its leadership is inside or outside of prison walls.

Security threat group (STG): A high-functioning, organized gang that uses an illegal industry to fund their objectives.

Other characteristics common to prison gangs go beyond racial lines of membership. These characteristics are common to most any gang within jail and/or prison, though they are not necessarily common to those gangs based primarily on the street. First, prison gangs tend to have highly formal rules and a written constitution that are adhered to by all members who value their affiliation, and sanctions are taken against those who violate the rules. Second, prison gangs tend to be structured along a semi-military organizational scheme. Thus, authority and responsibility are very clearly defined within these groups. Third, membership in a prison gang is usually for life. This tendency has often been referred to, as noted above, as *blood in—blood out* among the popular subculture. This is one of the root causes of parolees continuing their affiliation beyond the prison walls, and this lifelong membership rule is enforced if someone attempts to exit the prison gang. Thus, when gang members leave the prison environment, they are expected to perform various "favors" for the members who are still incarcerated. Lastly, as members circulate in and out of

CROSS-NATIONAL PERSPECTIVE 9.1

Prison Gang Riots and Warfare in Guatemala and El Salvador

Gang members staged simultaneous riots in at least seven Guatemalan prisons on Monday (August 2005), attacking rivals with grenades, guns, and knives in coordinated chaos that left 31 inmates dead, officials said.

The riots apparently began with attacks by members of the Mara Salvatrucha gang against rivals of the MS-18 gang, said Interior Minister Carlos Vielmann.

He said 31 inmates died before the riots were brought under control shortly after noon.

An Associated Press photographer saw 18 bodies, many riddled with bullet wounds, carried from El Hoyon prison, which was specifically built to hold gang members in Escuintla, 30 miles south of the capital. A guard and 61 inmates were injured at El Hoyon, and tattooed gang members bleeding from knife wounds were carried from the prison on stretchers.

Escuintla Gov. Luis Munoz said the riot began with the explosion of two grenades.

As explosions echoed from inside the small, converted police barracks in downtown Escuintla on Monday morning, nearby storekeepers rattled metal shutters down over the shop windows and crowds of visitors pressed police for information.

The explosions stopped within an hour. Police first began removing the injured, then the dead.

Dozens of relatives, many of them the mothers of young gang members, wept hysterically as stretchers were carried from the prison. The dead were taken to a morgue. So many were injured that they overflowed the capacity of the two local hospitals, forcing officials to take some elsewhere.

"Constant Communication"

Vielmann said visitors had brought guns into the prisons. "Until we have finished the high-security prisons (now under construction), that problem will persist," he said.

Speaking about the apparent coordination of the attacks, Vielmann said, "The gangs maintain constant communication. They have a Web page and not only synchronize in Guatemala, they synchronize with El Salvador, Honduras and with the United States."

He said they also use cellular phones and messages passed by prison visitors.

Human Rights Prosecutor Sergio Morales said there was evidence that police had helped gang members smuggle weapons into El Hoyon.

El Hoyon holds 400 alleged gang members. It was opened at an old police barracks after a December 2002 riot involving gang members at another prison in which 14 inmates died.

In the other riots Monday, three inmates died at the Canada Prison Farm 12 miles further south, and officials said eight died in rioting at Guatemala's top-security Pavon prison, about 15 miles east of the capital.

Two Stabbings

Two others were stabbed to death at a prison in Mazatenango, 85 miles southwest of the capital, according to officials.

Vielmann said smaller disturbances were quashed at three other prisons.

Law enforcement officials say the gangs emerged in Los Angeles and later spread to Central America when criminal migrants were deported back home.

Governments throughout Central America have been waging a campaign against the Mara Salvatrucha and related gangs, tightening laws and throwing thousands of the tattooed gang members into prisons, which have often seen clashes between feuding factions.

In May 2004, a fire swept through a prison in San Pedro Sula, Honduras, killing 107 inmates, most of them Mara Salvatrucha members.

That fire came 13 months after some suspected gang members were locked in their cells, doused with gasoline, and set ablaze during a riot at the El Porvenir prison farm near the Honduran city of La Ceiba. Nearly 70 people, including prisoners, visitors, and guards, were killed.

In El Salvador, riots broke out in February when an alleged gang member was transferred to a top-security facility, and one inmate was killed. In September, 800 gang members rioted at two Salvadoran prisons.

QUESTION 1: Discuss the reach of these gangs throughout their country of origin and even in other countries in the general region.

QUESTION 2: In your opinion, what should these countries do to address the challenges associated with violent prison gangs in their correctional systems? Briefly explain your answer.

SOURCE: Associate Press. (2005, August 15). *At least 31 killed in Guatemala prison gang war*. Used with permission.

prison, they are involved in gang activities both inside and outside of the penal institution. Thus, the criminal enterprise continues to be an active business, and prison simply becomes part of the overhead involved in running that business.

MAJOR PRISON GANGS IN THE UNITED STATES

During the 1950s and 1960s, there was a substantial amount of racial and ethnic bias in prisons. This was true in most all state prison systems, but was particularly pronounced in the southern United States and in the state of California. During the late 1950s, a Chicano gang formed known as the Mexican Mafia (National Gang Intelligence Center, 2009). Its members were drawn from street gangs in various neighborhoods of Los Angeles. While many of its members were in San Quentin, they began to exercise power over the gambling rackets within that prison. Other gangs soon began to form as a means of opposing the Mexican Mafia, including the Black Guerilla Family, the Aryan Brotherhood, La Nuestra Familia, and the Texas Syndicate.

This section provides a brief overview of some of the major prison gangs found throughout the nation. These gangs are presented in a manner that is as accurate and historically correct as possible, with attention paid to the basic feeling of the time and context during each gang's development (see Table 9.1). Much of the information presented has been obtained from a recent document titled the *National Gang Threat Assessment 2009*. The following pages provide an overview of 13 of the most prevalent prison gangs in the United States.

The Mexican Mafia prison gang, also known as La Eme (Spanish for the letter *M*), was formed in the late 1950s within the California Department of Corrections. It is loosely structured and has strict rules that must be followed by its 200 members. Most members are Mexican American males who previously belonged to a southern California street gang. The Mexican Mafia is primarily active in the southwestern and Pacific regions of the United States, and its power base is in California. The gang's main source of income is extorting drug distributors outside prison and distributing methamphetamine, cocaine, heroin, and marijuana within prison systems and on the streets. Some members have direct links to Mexican drug traffickers outside of the prison walls. The Mexican Mafia also is involved in other criminal activities, including gambling and homosexual prostitution in prison.

■ Table 9.1: Timeline History of Prison Gang Development in the United States

Year Formed	Jurisdiction	Name of Gang
1950	Washington	Gypsy Jokers
1957	California	Mexican Mafia
1958	California	Texas Syndicate
1965	California	La Nuestra Familia
1966	California	Black Guerrilla Family
1967	California	Aryan Brotherhood
Mid-1970s	Arizona	Arizona Aryan Brotherhood
1976	Puerto Rico	Ñeta
1977	Arizona	Arizona Old Mexican Mafia
1980	New Mexico	New Mexico Syndicate
Early 1980s	Texas	Aryan Brotherhood of Taxes
Early 1980s	Texas	Texas Mafia
Mid-1980s	California	Bulldogs
1984	Arizona	Arizona's New Mexican Mafia
1984	Texas	Mexikanemi
1984	Texas	Mandingo Warriors
1985	Federal system	Dirty White Boys
1985	California	415s
1986	Texas	Hermanos de Pistoleros Latinos
1988	Texas	Tango Blast
1990	Connecticut	Los Solidos
1993	New York	United Blood Nation

SOURCE: Orlando-Morningstar, D. (1999). *Prison gangs.* Washington, DC: Federal Judicial Center.

The Black Guerrilla Family (BGF), originally called Black Family or Black Vanguard, is a prison gang founded in San Quentin State Prison, California, in 1966. The gang is highly organized along paramilitary lines, with a supreme leader and central committee. The BGF has an established national charter, code of ethics, and oath of allegiance (see Table 9.2). BGF members operate primarily in California and Maryland.

The Aryan Brotherhood (AB; see Figure 9.1) was originally formed in San Quentin in 1967. The AB is highly structured with two factions—one in the California Department of Corrections and the other in the Federal Bureau of Prisons. Most members are Caucasian males, and the gang is active primarily in the southwestern and Pacific regions. Its main source of income is the distribution of cocaine, heroin, marijuana, and methamphetamine within prison systems and on the streets. Some AB members have business relationships with Mexican drug traffickers who smuggle illegal drugs into California for AB distribution. The AB is notoriously violent and is often involved in murder for hire. The AB still maintains a strong presence in the nation's prison systems, albeit a less active one in recent years.

■ Table 9.2: Sample Black Guerrilla Family (BGF) Code

BG Term	Meaning
Annette Brooks	Aryan Brotherhood
Bobby G. Foster	BGF
Central High	mainline
Compton	hole or segregation
D. C.	decision or deciding
Kiss	marked for death
Mary Mitchell	Mexican Mafia
Nelson Franklin	Nuestra Familia
Paula	police officer
Record shop	hospital
Salt	hacksaw
Sammy Davis, Jr.	bootlicking
Supermarket	killed or dead

The Crips are a collection of structured and unstructured gangs that have adopted a common gang culture. The Crips emerged as a major gang presence during the early 1970s. Crips membership is estimated at 30,000 to 35,000; most members are African American males from the Los Angeles metropolitan area. Large, national-level Crips gangs include 107 Hoover Crips, Insane Gangster Crips, and Rolling 60s Crips. The Crips operate in 221 cities in 41 states and can be found in several state prison systems.

The Bloods are an association of structured and unstructured gangs that have adopted a single-gang culture. The original Bloods were formed in the early 1970s to provide protection from the Crips street gang in Los Angeles, California. Large, national-level Bloods gangs include Bounty Hunter Bloods and Crenshaw Mafia Gangsters. Bloods membership is estimated to be 7,000 to 30,000 nationwide; most members are African American males. Bloods gangs are active in 123 cities in 33 states, and they can be found in several state prison systems.

Ñeta is a prison gang that was established in Puerto Rico in the early 1970s and spread to the United States. Ñeta is one of the largest and most violent prison gangs, with about 7,000 members in Puerto Rico and 5,000 in the United States. Ñeta chapters in Puerto Rico exist exclusively inside prisons; once members are released from prison, they are no longer considered part of the gang. In the United States, Ñeta chapters exist inside and outside prisons in 36 cities in nine states, primarily in the Northeast.

The Texas Syndicate (see Figure 9.2) originated in Folsom Prison during the early 1970s. The Texas Syndicate was formed in response to other prison gangs in the California Department of Corrections, such as the Mexican Mafia and Aryan Brotherhood, which were attempting to prey on native Texas inmates. This gang is composed of predominantly Mexican American inmates in the Texas Department of Criminal Justice (TDCJ). Though this gang has a rule to only accept members who are Latino, it does accept Caucasians into its ranks. The Texas Syndicate has a formal organizational structure and a set of written rules for its members. Since the time of its formation, the Texas Syndicate has grown considerably, particularly in Texas.

■ Figure 9.1: Symbol of the Aryan Brotherhood

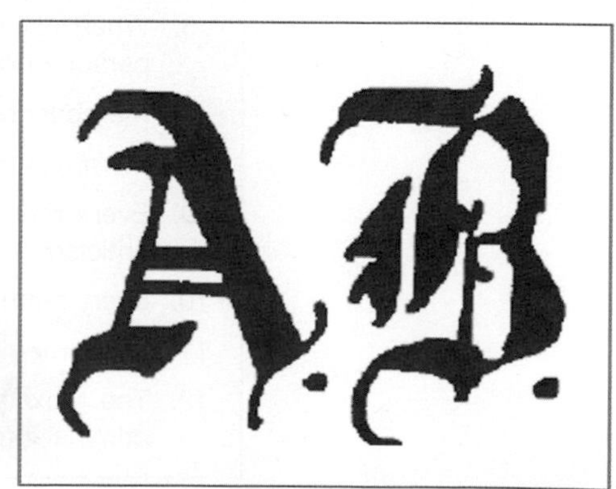

The Mexikanemi prison gang (also known as Texas Mexican Mafia or Emi; see Figure 9.3) was formed in the early 1980s within the TDCJ. The gang is highly structured and is estimated to have 2,000 members, most of whom are Mexican nationals or Mexican American males living in Texas at the time of incarceration. Mexikanemi poses a significant drug trafficking threat to communities in the southwestern United States, particularly in Texas. Gang members reportedly traffic multi-kilogram quantities of powder cocaine, heroin, and methamphetamine; multi-ton quantities of marijuana; and thousand-tablet quantities of MDMA from Mexico into the United States for distribution inside and outside prison.

The Nazi Low Riders (NLR) evolved in the California Youth Authority, the state agency responsible for the incarceration and parole supervision of juvenile and young adult offenders, in the late 1970s or early 1980s as a gang for Caucasian inmates. As prison officials successfully suppressed Aryan Brotherhood activities, the AB appealed to young incarcerated skinheads, the NLR in particular, to act as middlemen for their criminal operations, allowing the AB to keep control of criminal undertakings while adult members were serving time in administrative segregation. The NLR maintains strong ties to the AB and, like the older gang, has become a source of violence and criminal activity in prison. The NLR has become a major force, viewing itself as superior to all other Caucasian gangs and deferring only to the AB. Like the AB, the NLR engages in drug trafficking, extortion, and attacks on inmates and corrections staff.

■ Figure 9.2: Symbol of the Texas Syndicate

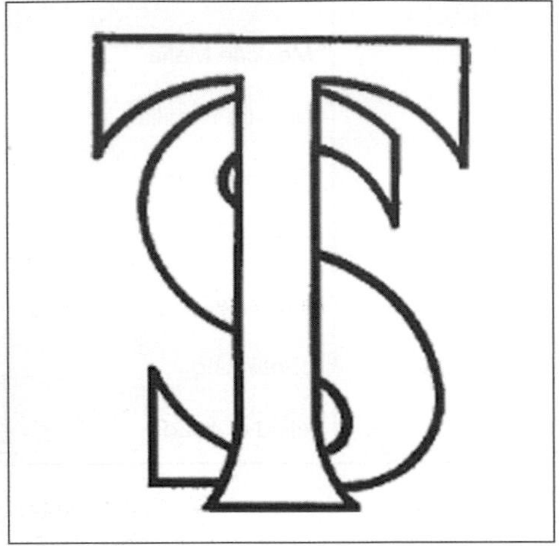

SOURCE: Orlando-Morningstar, D. (1997). *Prison gangs. Special needs offenders bulletin.* Washington, DC: Federal Judicial Center.

Barrio Azteca was organized in 1986 in the Coffield Unit of TDCJ by five street gang members from El Paso, Texas. This gang tends to recruit from prior street gang members and is most active in the southwestern region, primarily in correctional facilities in Texas and on the streets of southwestern Texas and southeastern New Mexico. The gang is highly structured and has an estimated membership of 2,000. Most members are Mexican national or Mexican American males.

Hermanos de Pistoleros Latinos (HPL) is a Hispanic prison gang formed in the TDCJ in the late 1980s. It operates in most prisons and in many communities in Texas, particularly Laredo. HPL is also active in several cities in Mexico, and its largest contingent in that country is in Nuevo Laredo. The gang is structured and is estimated to have 1,000 members. Members maintain close ties to several Mexican drug trafficking organizations and are involved in trafficking quantities of cocaine and marijuana from Mexico into the United States for distribution.

■ Figure 9.3: Constitution of the Mexikanemi

1. Membership is for life ("blood in, blood out").
2. Every member must be prepared to sacrifice his life or take a life at any time.
3. To achieve discipline within the Mexikanemi brotherhood, every member shall strive to overcome his weakness.
4. Members must never let the Mexikanemi down.
5. The sponsoring member is totally responsible for the behavior of a new recruit. If the new recruit turns out to be a traitor, it is the sponsoring member's responsibility to eliminate the recruit.
6. When insulted by a stranger or group, all members of the Mexikanemi will unite to destroy the person or other group completely.
7. Members must always maintain a high level of integrity.
8. Members must never relate Mexikanemi business to others.
9. Every member has the right to express opinions, ideas, contradictions, and constructive criticism.
10. Every member has the right to organize, educate, arm, and defend the Mexikanemi.
11. Every member has the right to wear tattoo of the Mexikanemi symbol.
12. The Mexikanemi is a criminal organization and therefore will participate in all activities of criminal interest for monetary benefits.

SOURCE: Orlando-Morningstar, D. (1997). *Prison gangs. Special needs offenders bulletin.* Washington, DC: Federal Judicial Center.

TECHNOLOGY AND EQUIPMENT 9.1

Using Scanners to Detect Contraband Brought Into and Out of Prison Facilities

This was no ordinary telephone call. A Baltimore man allegedly used a cell phone to arrange a murder, offering to pay $2,500 for the crime, according to Maryland federal prosecutors. Moreover, the man should not have had a cell phone—he was in the Baltimore City Jail on the evening he allegedly placed the fateful call. Indeed, according to the federal indictment, he was being held on a murder charge and made the call to arrange the killing of a witness to the original murder. Cell phones and the electric chargers that power them are just one form of contraband that correctional institutions grapple with daily. Corrections officers also face attempts to smuggle drugs and weapons into the facilities as well as inmates who fashion weapons out of ordinary materials.

Testing Airport Scanners in Prisons

One NIJ-sponsored pilot program that enjoyed success used a millimeter wave imaging system to scan visitors at the Graterford State Correctional Institution in Pennsylvania. The imaging system can look through clothing to detect weapons, cell phones, and nonmetallic objects. Currently used by the Transportation Security Administration (TSA) to scan passengers at an increasing number of airports, the system was tested and evaluated at Graterford, a maximum-security facility that houses about 3,100 inmates outside Philadelphia.

The pilot project at Graterford involved scanning visitors. Thomas Dohman, Graterford's intelligence captain, said the system was used for more than a year, and officials believe it was successful. "It's very effective at discouraging smuggling," he said. To address privacy concerns, prison officials used a privacy screen that cut out the most explicit views but still allowed the system to signal if something was hidden beneath a person's clothing. Graterford officials also set up laptop computers when they introduced the system so visitors could see for themselves how the images looked. "The public accepted it," Dohman said.

The Graterford system completed between 400 and 600 scans in a typical week, and each scan was completed in seconds. "It really didn't slow down the [screening] process," Dohman said. The manufacturer made the system available for free during the testing period, and the NIJ coordinated the pilot project because it provided an opportunity to do an operational evaluation in a correctional environment that involved a commercially available system.

Overall, the millimeter wave system improved the contraband situation at Graterford, Dohman said. On several occasions, the system detected cell phones. Yet Dohman believes the system's greatest success is in its deterrent effect. According to Dohman, people who knew about the system did not even try to smuggle something through it. "It's infrequent that people had anything concealed," he said.

Although this technology detects contraband hidden under clothing, it does not detect contraband secreted in body cavities. To address this need, the NIJ is currently funding the development of a system that can identify contraband hidden in body cavities. The system, which is based on electric field tomography (EFT), is being developed by Quantum Magnetics Inc.

Portable Scanner Spots Improvised Prison Weapons Made by Inmates

Although millimeter wave portals can identify objects hidden under clothing, they are large, fixed, and relatively expensive. Corrections officials have told the NIJ that they would also like to be able to use inexpensive, handheld devices. These would give corrections officials more flexibility by allowing them to screen people at entrances and to perform spot checks anywhere. The NIJ is sponsoring the development of a handheld device that can detect everything from cell phones to Plexiglas. Many correctional institutions have reported that while their metal detection systems work well, the institutions face constant challenges in detecting nonmetallic objects, such as improvised weapons made of wood or hard plastics.

SOURCE: Bulman, P. (2009). *Using technology to make prisons and jails safer.* Washington, DC: National Institute of Justice.

Tango Blast is one of largest prison/street criminal gangs operating in Texas. Tango Blast's criminal activities include drug trafficking, extortion, kidnapping, sexual assault, and murder. In the late 1990s, Hispanic men incarcerated in federal, state, and local prisons founded Tango Blast for personal protection against violence from traditional prison gangs such as the Aryan Brotherhood, Texas Syndicate, and Texas Mexican Mafia. Tango Blast originally had four city-based chapters in Houston, Austin, Dallas, and Fort Worth. These founding four chapters are collectively known as Puro Tango Blast or the Four Horsemen. In addition to the original four chapters, former Texas inmates established new chapters in El Paso, San Antonio, Corpus Christi, and the Rio Grande Valley. In June 2008, the Houston Police Department estimated that more than 14,000 Tango Blast members were incarcerated in Texas. Tango Blast is difficult to monitor. The gang does not conform to either traditional prison/street gang hierarchical organization or gang rules. Tango Blast is laterally organized, and leaders are elected sporadically to represent the gang in prisons and to lead street gang cells. The significance of Tango Blast is exemplified by corrections officials reporting that rival traditional prison gangs are now forming alliances to defend themselves against Tango Blast's growing power.

■ PHOTO 9.6 This collection of prison contraband consists of an array of small weapons that were confiscated during routine "shakedowns" within a prison facility.

United Blood Nation is a universal term that is used to identify both West Coast Bloods and the United Blood Nation (UBN). The UBN started in 1993 in Rikers Island George Mochen Detention Center (GMDC) to form protection from the threat posed by Latin Kings and Ñetas, who dominated the prison. While these groups are traditionally distinct entities, both identify themselves by "Blood," often making it hard for law enforcement to distinguish between them. The UBN is a loose confederation of street gangs, or sets, that once were predominantly African American. Membership is estimated to be between 7,000 and 15,000 along the U.S. eastern corridor.

Gang Management in Corrections

Gang management requires a comprehensive policy that specifies legal precedents, procedures, and guidelines, including the verification of gang members. Over the years, most state systems have developed gang intelligence units and have trained correctional staff on gangs and gang activity. In modern times, state and federal corrections refer to gangs as security threat groups, or STGs, as noted above. Students may notice that most of the 13 gangs listed in the prior subsection have links to outside society where they engage in criminal activities that usually have an economic objective. This means that these gangs are all STGs because they operate inside and outside the prison and possess all the other characteristics discussed in previous subsections of this chapter.

Web Link
Homeboy Industries

The technical aspects of combating STGs in prison, such as the paper classification and procedures needed to investigate gang members, are fairly straightforward. However, the human element is what makes the fight against STGs much more difficult. In correctional facilities that do not emphasize professionalism or do not encourage open communication among security staff, if there is a strong underlying prison subculture (both inmate and correctional officer), STGs are likely to proliferate. When selecting correctional staff to serve on gang task forces, the prison administrator must exercise care and remain vigilant. In some cases, an inmate's sibling, cousin, girlfriend, former wife, or friend may be employed within the facility. This is, of course, a common tactic used by gangs who seek to infiltrate the correctional system.

Gang Control, Management, and Administrative Segregation

In addition to the physical security of the facility, there are many psychological tactics that can be used to control gang activity. For instance, the immediate tendency of corrections officials may be to restrict privileges for gang-related inmates. But, as Fleisher (2008) notes, withdrawing incentives or placing these inmates in long-term states of restricted movement can have financial and social consequences for the prison facility. For instance, in Texas, many gang-related inmates are kept in administrative segregation. Administrative segregation is a security status that is intended to keep the assigned inmate from having contact with the general population. It is not punitive in nature, like solitary confinement. This custody status is intended to protect the general population from the inmate in segregation. However, this form of custody is very expensive.

Further, there is a tendency for prison systems that use administrative segregation to house inmates of the same gang in the same area. This prevents them from coming into contact with enemy gang members and cuts costs that would ensue if they were kept on different cell blocks or dormitories. But doing this replicates the street gang culture, as they are all together but geographically isolated. In other words, on the street it would be one neighborhood, one gang, and here it is one cell block, one gang. This can build solidarity for the group. It can also lead to problematic situations where inmates exercise power (through the gang rank structure) over a cell block or dormitory, encouraging security to work with those in power because the gang leaders can help them maintain authority over the other lower-ranking inmates of that gang. Naturally, this should be avoided because it validates the gang's power and undermines the security staff. Fleisher (2008) notes that other undesirable behaviors can also emerge. For instance, gangs may attempt to run cell blocks, "sell" cells on the cell block, or "own" territory on the recreation yard. These behaviors reinforce their feeling that they have power over the institution and should be avoided.

CONCLUSION

This chapter has provided students with a glimpse of the behind-the-scenes aspects of the prison environment. The notion of a prison subculture, complete with its own norms and standards that are counter to those of the outside world, has been presented to give students an idea of the values and principles that impact the day-to-day operation of many prisons. There has been substantial debate as to whether this informal prison subculture is the product of adjustments and adaptations to prison life or if it is more the product of norms brought in from the outside world—from the street life.

The informal subculture within prisons tends to be largely driven by inmates. The convict code has typically been presented as the "gold standard" of behavior among inmates. This code represents perceptions from older eras, and its guidelines are now out of date and not in sync with the modern era. The effects of professionalism within the correctional officer ranks, the diversity of correctional staff, and the difference in the mind-set of this generation of inmates all have led to the near demise of the honor-bound convict code. Within the informal subculture, correctional staff also have some of their own unwritten standards and expectations. The work of Kauffman (1988) has provided very good insight on the behavior of correctional staff in prisons.

The norms associated with both the subculture of prison staff and the convict code of inmates are in a state of flux and decline. The subculture among correctional staff has been impacted by the emphasis on professionalism and the diversification in staff recruiting. These two factors have changed the face of corrections over time and have also undermined the tenets of the prison subculture. What has resulted is a state of ambiguity where inmates may pay lip service to tenets of respectable behavior (according to prison logic) but often break these rules when put under pressure. Simply put, there is truly no honor among thieves.

Gangs have emerged as a major force in state prison systems. The first recorded prison gangs began to emerge in the late 1950s and the early 1960s, primarily in the California prison system. Since that time, gangs have proliferated around the United States and have exerted substantial influence over the prison subculture and even dynamics in prison operations. In this chapter, we have covered 13 of the larger and more well-known prison gangs in the nation. From the coverage of these gangs, it is clear that they have networks that extend beyond the prison walls, and this, in turn, increases their power and influence within the prison walls. Indeed, when offenders in a street gang enter prison, they do not forfeit their membership in their gang. Likewise, when these inmates leave prison, they again do not leave their gang obligations behind. Rather, gangs exist both inside and outside the prison walls.

The methods used to control gang activity inside prisons have been discussed in this chapter. Prison gang intelligence units must have effective means of investigating potential membership and collecting data on gang members. Utilizing electronic equipment for identification, storage, and retrieval is essential to maintaining an effective antigang strategy. The ability to share data with other agencies enhances the public safety in the region surrounding the prison and also improves security within the facility. Whether we like it or not, the prison has an impact on outside society due to the manner in which the inmate population cycles into and out of prison. Thus, it is clear that prisons impact society, both in terms of keeping dangerous persons locked up and in terms of the learned prison behaviors of those persons once they are released back into society.

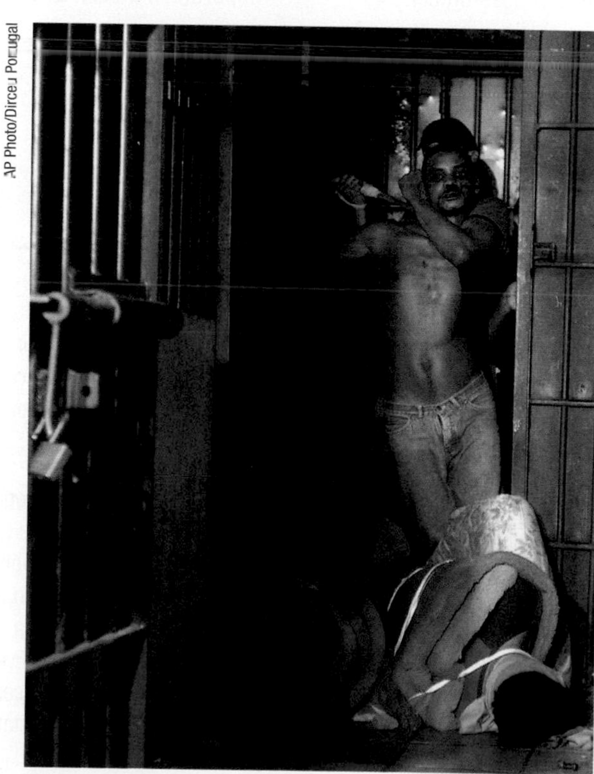

AP Photo/Dirceu Portugal

■ PHOTO 9.7 An inmate holds another inmate hostage with a homemade shank.

Want a better grade?

Get the tools you need to sharpen your study skills. Access practice quizzes, eFlashcards, video, and multimedia at **edge.sagepub.com/hanser2e**

SAGE edge™

DISCUSSION QUESTIONS

1. How are the prison subcultures for inmates and correctional officers often interrelated?
2. Compare importation theory with exportation theory. Which one do you believe is the stronger influence on prison subculture, and why?
3. Explain some of the common outlooks and views of prison subculture. How does this contrast with the conventional logic of outside society?
4. How have professionalization and the diversification of correctional staff impacted the prison subculture?
5. Explain what a "hyena" is. What are some examples of how these inmates affect group behavior in prison facilities?
6. Identify at least three prison gangs, and explain how they have impacted corrections in their respective jurisdictions. Note their allies and adversaries in the prison, and explain how this affects prison operations.
7. Explain what prison systems can or should do to control gang problems that occur in their facilities.
8. Within the prison subculture, how is labeling theory related to prison rape?

SAGE edge™ **Test your understanding of chapter content. Take the practice quiz.**

KEY TERMS

Blood in—blood out, 204

Convict, 208

Convict boss/officer, 211

Convict code, 205

Gang cross-pollination, 218

Hogging, 210

Hustle, 210

Importation theory, 203

Mule, 208

Pains of imprisonment, 203

Prisonization, 212

Punk, 205

Respect, 208

Security threat group (STG), 218

Snitch, 205

Symbiotic prison relationship, 210

SAGE edge™ **Review key terms with eFlashcards.**

APPLIED EXERCISE 9.1

You are the assistant warden of a large, medium-security facility within a state prison system in the southeastern United States. Your facility has a disproportionate number of African American inmates (common in prison systems throughout the United States) and a disproportionate number of Caucasian officers.

In response to concerns from the Grievance Department regarding inmate allegations of racism from officers inside the facility, the warden has asked you to develop a comprehensive diversity training program for the security staff in your facility. Currently, your facility holds an annual 1-day "refresher" course for staff. This course is actually only a 4-hour block of instruction provided at the state training facility. Everyone throughout the system knows that this instruction is not taken seriously and is simply offered as a means of documenting that the state has made the training available.

Your warden desires to change this within your facility for two reasons. First, it is just a good and ethical practice to take diversity seriously. Second, the dollars spent to resolve grievances and other allegations are getting costly enough to make diversity training a fiscally sound alternative to potential litigation.

With this in mind, you are given the following guidelines for the training program that you are to implement:

1. The program should be 1.5 days in length and be given once annually.
2. The program should address numerous areas of concern, including race, gender, age, and religion.

Students should keep in mind that workplace diversity has two components. First, it involves fair treatment and the removal of barriers. Second, it addresses past imbalances through the implementation of special measures to accelerate the achievement of a representative workforce. Further, workplace diversity recognizes and utilizes the diversity available in the workplace and the community it serves.

Workplace diversity should be viewed as a means to attaining the organizational objectives of the correctional facility—not as an end in itself. The link between the agency objectives and the day-to-day processes that occur among staff in the facility is crucial to the success of workplace diversity initiatives.

For this assignment, outline the content that you would recommend for the training session, and explain the rationale behind your recommendation. Also, explain how you will "sell" these ideas to prison staff to ensure that they take the training seriously. Lastly, explain how this training, if successful, can improve security and safety in the institution. Your submission should be between 500 and 1,000 words.

WHAT WOULD YOU DO?

You are a caseworker in a state facility and work closely with the institution's classification department on a routine basis. You have one inmate on your caseload, Jeff, who has presented with a number of challenges. Jeff is a 35-year-old male who is an inmate in your maximum-security facility. He has recently been transferred to your facility from another facility, largely for protective reasons. Jeff has come to you because he is very, very worried. Jeff is a pedophile, and he has been in prison for nearly 8 years on a 15-year sentence. He is expected to gain an early release due to his excellent progress and behavior in prison and due to prison overcrowding problems. He has been in treatment, and, as you look through his case notes, you can see that he has done very well.

But a powerful inmate gang at Jeff's prior prison facility did not want to see him get paroled. Jeff had received "protection" from this gang in exchange for providing sexual favors to a select trio of its members. Jeff discloses that he had to humiliate himself in this way to survive in the prison subculture, particularly since he was a labeled pedophile. The gang knew this, of course, and used it as leverage to ensure that Jeff was compliant. In fact, the gang never even had to use any physical force to gain Jeff's compliance. Jeff notes that this now bothers him, and he doubts his own sense of masculinity. Jeff also discloses that he has had suicidal ideations as a result of his experiences.

Thus, while Jeff has performed well in his treatment for sex offenders, he has also been adversely affected by noxious sexual experiences inside the prison. You are the first person that he has disclosed this to. As you listen to his plight, you begin to wonder if his issues with sexuality are actually now more unstable than they were before he entered prison. Though his treatment notes seem convincing, this is common among pedophiles, and the other therapist did not know that Jeff had engaged in undesired sexual activity while incarcerated. This activity has created a huge rift in Jeff's masculine identity. Will this affect his likelihood for relapse on the outside? Does Jeff need to resolve his issues with consensual versus forced homosexual activity?

As you listen to Jeff, you realize that if you make mention of his experiences in your report, then the classification system is not likely to release him, and this condemns him to more of the same type of exploitation. Putting him in protective custody is not an option because Jeff adamantly refuses this custody level. He fears that the gang would think he was giving evidence against them and would then seek to kill him. However, if you do not mention any of this information and thereby allow a person with a highly questionable prognosis to be released, you run the risk of putting the public's safety at risk.

What would you do?

FEMALE OFFENDERS IN CORRECTIONAL SYSTEMS

Stockbyte/Thinkstock

A MOM BEHIND BARS

Maria flopped down on her bunk and looked around the dormitory. She thought to herself, *I wonder how many of these women are not mothers?* With a sigh she addressed her "neighbor," Chelsea. "Chelz, tell me, why do we get involved with these a-holes again?"

Chelsea grinned. "Because we're fools for love . . . and they think we're a bunch of *putas*!"

"Maybe you're right, but he is the baby's daddy, and it seems like there's no getting around that . . . " Maria trailed off and muttered under her breath, ". . . even though he never really helps out much."

She thought about her daughter, Ariana, who was 3 years old. Ariana stayed with Maria's parents, and they had passed word that she was asking about her mommy. The only contact Maria had with Ariana was by phone and a few infrequent visits when Maria's parents would bring Ariana to the prison visitation building. They lived far from the prison, however, and could only come once a month or so, if that.

Maria felt terrible that her parents were raising her daughter while she did time, but they knew the circumstances. She had fallen in love with the wrong man—Juan, a good-looking young man who had lots of "respect" on the streets. He was *cholo* (Spanish describing lower class and/or street gang culture), but he was a dreamer. When he met Maria, he would talk about wanting to get out of the gang life, wanting to go to school, maybe be a school teacher. But, unfortunately, he was into drugs.

They "dated" for about 3 months or so, going to block parties or all-hours night clubs where his *familia* (gang) were considered exclusive members. He seemed to be popular everywhere he went. Then she found out that she was pregnant. She remembered that day because she was so afraid to tell Juan. To her surprise, Juan was excited and told all of his friends that he was going to be a father. He told her, "We gotta get engaged, and I'll marry you. . . . I hope your father approves."

Eventually, they moved in together. One day when Maria was about 5 months pregnant, Juan had asked her to hold on to some of the black tar heroin that he had recently obtained from contacts in Guadalajara, Mexico. Maria never used heroin—she smoked pot, sure, and drank a little Patron from time-to-time, but she absolutely stayed away from other drugs. Naturally, while pregnant, she did not smoke or drink at all.

Juan needed her to walk to an area on the outskirts of the city and leave the heroin in a trash can outside of a local store. Later, some guy who worked at the store would "empty the trash" and obtain the drugs; no one would contact anyone, and nothing would be exchanged in person. Since they had moved in together, Maria had learned more about Juan. He was very macho, expected her to do all of the house work, and would sometimes yell at her when he was drinking or coming off of his drugs. He was not physically abusive, but did have a mean streak.

LEARNING OBJECTIVES:

1. Discuss some of the characteristics of female offenders, and compare rates of incarceration and terms of sentencing between male and female offenders.
2. Discuss the history of corrections with relation to female offenders.
3. Describe some of the issues associated with modern-day female offenders.
4. Identify some of the considerations associated with effective correctional operations when considering female offenders.
5. Discuss the legal issues involved with female offenders in the correctional facility.
6. Identify various treatment implications related to female offenders.

Maria was hesitant, but Juan said, "Look, one or two more deals like this and I can get out of the street life. I will have the money to quit. Besides, our *familia* is very careful, and we do not use the same location twice in a row. *Nobody ever gets caught*, but I can't do it this time; our rules require that we break it up a bit when doing drop-offs. Come on Maria, *this is our way out*!"

Maria agreed and went through with the drop-off. All seemed well until a few days later. She had been under observation, as Juan and his *familia* were the subject of a large-scale undercover narcotics investigation. When all of the various gang members and their associates were rounded up, numerous people were sent to prison. Even worse, many of those arrested snitched on one another to cut deals with the police. Juan did not sell out Maria, but he did not cop to any of the charges, either. He had enough money to afford a legal defense and got out of jail quickly since no evidence was attached to him. Maria was lucky—she only got a 4-year sentence with the likelihood of making parole in 18 months or so.

Now she had received word from the parole commission that she would be out in approximately 3 months. She had just finished a year in the female correctional center. As her time grew shorter, letters from Juan were arriving more frequently. She was not sure if she really wanted to be with him after she got out because she had heard he was still active in the gang and she knew he was using drugs. She wondered what she would do once she was out again.

INTRODUCTION

This chapter will familiarize the student with the common problems associated with the female offending population. While the majority of this chapter will address issues regarding women in prison, some discussion regarding community-based sanctions will also be included. As will be seen, women offenders have several physiological and psychological characteristics that set them apart from male offenders. Some of these characteristics are common also to the female population in broader society, but others are unique to women who find themselves involved in the criminal process. Of the offending population, only about 7% are women (Carson, 2015). However, female jail, prison, and probation populations grew at a faster rate than the male populations in the years between 2000 and 2010 (Heberman & Bonczar, 2014; Minton & Zeng, 2015). This growth rate ensures that issues regarding the female offending population will be of increasing importance for the police, courts, and corrections system for some time to come.

FEMALE OFFENDERS BEHIND BARS: A DETAILED LOOK AT PERCENTAGES AND RATES

While the total number of female offenders incarcerated increased steadily over the past few decades, recently there has been a slight downturn in this growth. The reasons for this are not clear but may be due to a combination of factors related to a greater emphasis on reentry, treatment, and community-based sanctions.

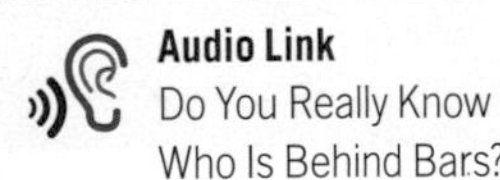

Audio Link Do You Really Know Who Is Behind Bars?

Despite the general increase in the female prison population, women offenders are, as noted above, a small proportion of the overall prison population. To ensure that the numbers are kept in perspective, consider that at the end of 2015, U.S. prisons held 1,402,404 men compared with 106,232 women. The rate of incarceration for men was 890 out of every 100,000, whereas the rate for women was 65 out of 100,000 (Carson, 2015). These numbers reflect lower overall rates of

■ Table 10.1: Female Offenders in Selected States: A Comparison Between 2013 and 2014

State Jurisdiction	2013	2014	Percentage Change 2013–2014
Arizona	3,775	3,964	5.0
California	6,297	6,382	1.3
Florida	7,271	7,303	0.4
Georgia	3,559	3,511	−1.3
Illinois	2,916	2,888	−1.0
Missouri	2,782	3,106	11.6
Ohio	4,150	4,208	1.4
Pennsylvania	2,662	2,758	3.6
Texas	13,830	14,326	3.6
Virginia	2,849	3,015	5.8

SOURCE: Carson, A. E. (2015). *Prisoners, 2014.* Washington, DC: Bureau of Justice Statistics.

prison population growth, largely due to states reducing their prison populations as a means of saving money in a tight economy. Because of the War on Drugs and the extended sentences associated with that era, many women were incarcerated for lengthier sentences, and this helped fuel the growth in the female inmate population. Given the rates of drug use among female offenders, their increased number behind bars is not surprising.

Currently, the United States incarcerates more women than any other country in the world. When considering the female inmate population, it is clear that a sizeable portion of that population is concentrated in three states: (1) Texas, which in 2014 held 14,326 female inmates in its prisons and jails, (2) Florida, which held 7,303, and (3) California, which held 6,382 (Carson, 2015). Students should refer to Table 10.1 for a comparison of female offenders incarcerated in 2013 and 2014 in these three and several other selected states.

RATES OF WOMEN HELD IN STATE PRISONS, IN LOCAL JAILS, OR ON COMMUNITY SUPERVISION

According to Carson (2015), when considering rates of female incarceration in state prisons or jails, the top five states are Oklahoma (136 female offenders per 100,000 state female residents), Idaho (142 per 100,000), Kentucky (108 per 100,000), and Arizona (104 per 100,000). These states are different than those in the top three listed above (Texas, Florida, and California) because although those three states have the most total offenders, they do not have the highest *rate per 100,000* of female offenders. In other words, their *overall populations* are larger but the *rate of imprisonment* for females is not higher, per capita, due to their larger populations.

Conversely, those states with the lowest rates of incarceration were Rhode Island, Maine, Vermont, Minnesota, and New Hampshire (Carson, 2015). It is perhaps interesting that these states are typically considered more progressive and are also more prone to using treatment schemes, restorative justice approaches, and other innovations rather than prison. This is likely to at least partially explain why these states have such low incarceration rates. The opinion of this author is that these states tend to also be more affluent than those with the highest incarceration rates. Affluent regions generally have lower crime rates and, therefore, lower rates of imprisonment. In addition, the duration of prison sentences in these areas is typically shorter. Unfortunately, states that have higher incarceration rates tend not to be economically stable enough to afford this (Texas being the exception).

The five states with the largest number of women on probation in 2010 were Texas (109,639), Florida (59,995), Georgia (46,530), Pennsylvania (44,878), and Ohio (42,872). The states with the least number of women on probation were New Hampshire (1,017), North Dakota (1,080), Maine (1,278), Alaska (1,370), and Wyoming (1,409). The states with the largest number of women on parole were Pennsylvania (19,823), California (11,823), Texas (10,527), New York (3,112), and

Figure 10.1: Number of Female Offenders in the Federal Prison System

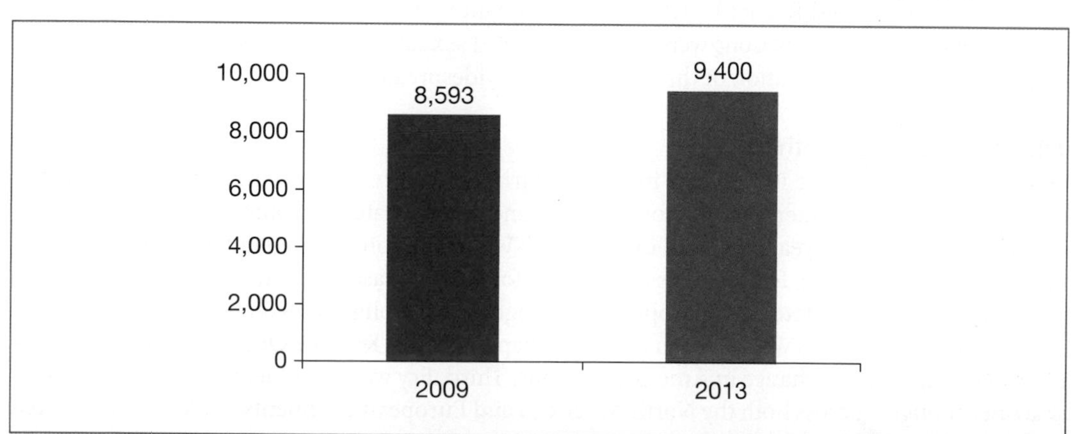

SOURCE: United States Sentencing Commission. (2014). *Quick facts: Women in the federal offender population.* Washington, DC: Author.

■ **Figure 10.2: Most Common Offenses for Female Offenders in 2013**

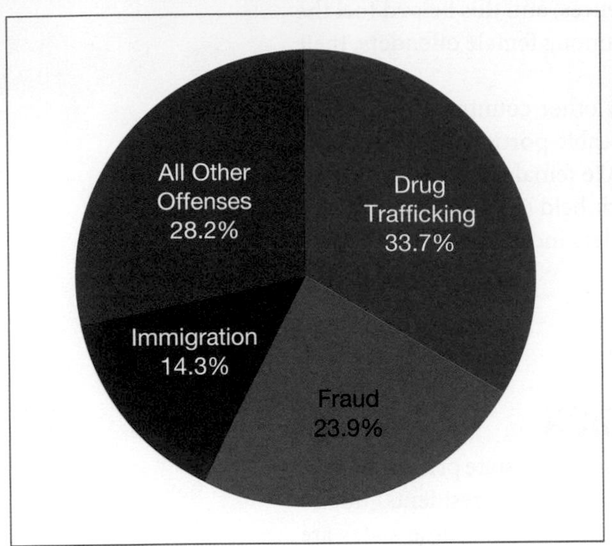

SOURCE: United States Sentencing Commission. (2014). *Quick facts: Women in the federal offender population.* Washington, DC: Author.

Arkansas (3,046). The states with the least number of women on parole were Maine (1; Maine stopped using parole in 1975), Rhode Island (41), Delaware (44), Wyoming (108), and Montana (115). All of these are either small states or states with a fairly sparse population (Glaze & Bonczar, 2011). Of women on community supervision (both probation and parole combined), about 6 in 10 tend to be Caucasian, one-fourth tend to be African American, and roughly 1 in 10 are Latino American (Bloom, Owen, & Covington, 2003). Of those women on community supervision, roughly 40% have no high school diploma or GED, 42% are single, and 72% are the primary caretakers of children under 18 years of age (Bloom et al., 2003).

The federal prison system holds a large share of female prisoners, with a population of 13,999 at the close of 2014 (Carson, 2014). The proportion of female offenders rose slightly from 12.1% in 2009 to 13.3% in 2013, with overall numbers going from 8,593 in 2009 to 9,400 in 2013 (see Figure 10.1). While the rise is slight, it is important to note that as recently as 2013 this proportion was still rising in relation to male offenders. Of the approximately 9,400 female offenders in the federal system, 33.7% were sentenced for drug trafficking, another nearly 24% were sentenced for crimes of fraud, and 14.3% had charges related to immigration issues. (See Figure 10.2 for an illustration of these statistics.) Thus, it can be seen that the vast majority of female offenders are nonviolent. Further, most of these women have usually had little or no prior criminal history, and their average age of sentencing tends to be a bit later in life (38 years of age), which means that the majority have not lead an extensive criminal lifestyle.

HISTORY OF WOMEN BEHIND BARS

Prior to the 1800s, women were generally imprisoned in the same facilities with men. As students may recall, this was true even in England, where women, children, and men were imprisoned together on floating gaols in the Thames. John Howard's work in the late 1770s helped to draw attention to the plight of women, and, with the developments in prisons in Pennsylvania, the issue of women inmates was squarely addressed. Though men and women were separated during this time, the living conditions were equally unhealthy. Like the men, women suffered from filthy conditions, overcrowding, and harsh treatment.

In 1838 in the New York City Jail, for instance, there were 42 one-person cells for 70 women. In the 1920s at Auburn Prison in New York, there were no separate cells for the 25 or so women serving sentences up to 14 years. They were all lodged together in a one-room attic, the windows sealed to prevent communication with men (Rafter, 1985). Further, sexual abuse was reportedly a common occurrence at this time, with male staff raping women in prison. Consider that in 1826, a female inmate named Rachel Welch became pregnant while in solitary confinement. Examples abound where women in prisons were routinely abused sexually, and, in the state of Indiana, there were accounts that prostitution of these women was widespread (Rafter, 1985).

The Work of Elizabeth Fry

One activist who fought for women in prison during the early 1800s stands out. Elizabeth Fry (1780–1845) was a Quaker prison reform activist and an advocate for women who were incarcerated during these early years. Though most of Fry's work was done in England, her beliefs became known around the world. Fry's work is noteworthy for several reasons. First, she was one of the first persons in the United States and Europe to truly highlight the plight of women in prison. Second, she was a Quaker, and, as we have seen in earlier chapters of this text, the Quakers were instrumental in effecting positive change in American prisons. Third, Fry was so influential as to be invited to share her thoughts across both the North American and European continents; seldom were women held in such high regard during this time.

In the early 1800s, Fry visited Old Newgate Prison in England. This prison was notorious for the squalid conditions that it provided for inmates. For female inmates, the circumstances were worse: Approximately 300 women and children were collectively housed in two large cells. Cooking, the elimination of waste, sleeping, and all other activities were conducted in those cells. No fresh linens were provided, nor were nightclothes available. Fry would bring food, clothing, and straw bedding to those unfortunate enough to be at Newgate (Hatton, 2006).

Department of Education, Arts & Libraries London Borough of Barking & Dagenham.

■ PHOTO 10.1 **Elizabeth Fry reads to female inmates at Old Newgate Prison in 1823.**

Eventually, in 1817, Fry organized a group of women activists into the Association for the Improvement of the Female Prisoners in Newgate (Samuel, 2001). These women created a school curriculum for female inmates at Newgate, and provided materials so inmates could sew, knit, and make crafts that could be sold for income. Naturally, there was a religious orientation to these services, and the women at Newgate were given regular Bible studies to help them form a constructive and spiritually therapeutic outlook on their plight. Fry's concern for women in prison, and for the field of corrections in general, culminated in the completion of a book, *Observations on the Visiting, Superintendence, and Government of Female Prisoners* (Samuel, 2001), in which Fry discusses the need for prison reform extensively.

Prior to the 1800s and even during the early 1800s, judges in the United States were hesitant to sentence women for serious crimes unless they were habitual offenders (Feeley & Little, 1991). Indeed, it would appear that the chivalry hypothesis was the guiding notion behind the view of women and criminality. The **chivalry hypothesis** contends that there is a bias in the criminal justice system against giving women harsh punishments. This is true so long as the offenses that they commit are considered "gender appropriate," or consistent with the stereotyped role that women are expected to maintain.

This type of thinking is typical of the **Victorian Era**, during which women were viewed through a lens of inflexible femininity and considered to be pious and naïve of the evils of the world. Because this was how women were seen, the criminal courts were often hesitant to punish women whom norms defined as pure, passive, and childlike in their understanding and primarily driven by emotion rather than reason. Further, Pollak (1950) has noted that during this era, men were expected to act in a fatherly and/or protective manner. Thus, the male-dominated criminal justice system (including police and judges) tended to downplay female crime, making it less likely to be detected, reported, prosecuted, and sentenced.

The stereotypes regarding appropriate conduct for women come from ideas about their "proper" place in society (Brennan & Vandenberg, 2009). Women who fell outside of these expectations were considered abnormal. Those who fell well outside of these expectations, such as female criminals who committed serious crimes, were considered evil or abhorrent. Thus, if a woman committed a crime that fell outside of what seemed understandable based on gendered stereotypes, such as murder or assault, her punishment was actually likely to be much harsher that what might be given to a man. On the other hand, when a woman committed a crime more gender-based, such as prostitution, substance abuse, or theft, she was often given a light sentence or simply avoided official action.

Chivalry hypothesis: Contends that there is a bias in the criminal justice system against giving women harsh punishments.

Victorian Era: Viewed women from a lens of inflexible femininity where women were to be considered pious and naïve of the evils of the world.

Female Criminality From 1850 Onward

Records of criminal convictions and imprisonment for women increased during and after the Civil War. In speculating why this was the case, it may be concluded that the absence of men (who were off to war) and the industrialization that occurred in the North impacted views of women by creating circumstances where women were more visible within society (Kurshan, 1996). Further, an increase in crimes occurred throughout the nation among both men and women. This meant that by midcentury there were enough women inmates to necessitate the emergence of separate women's quarters. The separation of women from men in prison facilities led to other changes in later years.

In 1869, Sarah Smith and Rhoda Coffin, two Quaker activists, were appointed to inspect correctional facilities, both in Indiana (the state in which they lived) and in other areas of the nation. They concluded that the state of morals and integrity among staff in female prisons was deplorable (Rafter, 1985), and they spearheaded a social campaign against the sexual abuse that they had discovered in Indiana prisons. Their work led to the first completely separate female prison in 1874. By 1940, 23 states had separate women's prisons (Kurshan, 1996).

The Evolution of Separate Custodial Prisons for Women and Further Evidence of the Chivalry Hypothesis

Eventually, as central penitentiaries were built or rebuilt, many women were shipped there from prison farms because they were considered "dead hands" as compared with the men. At first the most common form of custodial confinement was attachment to male prisons; eventually independent women's prisons evolved out of these male institutions. These separate women's prisons were established largely for administrative convenience, not reform. Female matrons worked there, but they took their orders from men.

Women in custodial prisons were frequently convicted of felony charges, most commonly for crimes against property, often petty theft. Only about a third of female felons were serving time for violent crimes. The rates for both property crimes and violent crimes were much higher than for the women at the reformatories. On the other hand, relatively fewer women were incarcerated for public order offenses (fornication, adultery, drunkenness, etc.), which were the most common in the reformatories. This was especially true in the South, where these so-called morality offenses by African Americans were generally ignored, and where authorities were reluctant to imprison Caucasian women at all. We will discuss reformatories for women in greater detail later in this chapter.

The reasons of women for committing crime, especially violent crime, tend to be quite different from those usually observed among male offenders. Data from New York's Auburn Prison on homicide between 1909 and 1933 reveal the special nature of the women's "violent" crime (Freedman, 1981, p. 12). Most of the victims of murder by women were adult men. For many feminist researchers, this would not be surprising; the crime would be taken more seriously if it was against the male social order. Further, as we know from more current research today, most homicides committed by women tend to be domestic in nature. In many cases, issues related to long-term spouse abuse are at the heart of what ultimately turns out to be an instance of victim-turned-perpetrator—the female partner killing her abuser in reaction to years of mistreatment. During the 1800s, issues related to spouse abuse were not identified as they are nowadays, and this means in most cases concepts such as battered woman's syndrome—the term for when abused women show identifiable symptoms of trauma associated with domestic battering and psychological abuse—would have been alien in courthouses. Thus, the murders of men, particularly adult men, likely resulted from dynamics that were not acknowledged by courtrooms of that time. In fact, laws often gave husbands the right to use force in their household, including force against their wives. Women, on the other hand, had no such right; they did not even have the right to vote at this time.

Other evidence exists that the chivalry hypothesis and/or stereotyped expectations of women may have been a partial explanation for female criminality. For instance, the Women's Prison Association of New York, which was active in the social purity movement, declared in 1906 that women who committed crimes were often immigrants who were immoral menaces to sons and daughters throughout society, polluting American values with promiscuous behavior (Rafter, 1985).

This demonstrates how, even in the 1900s, social views related to women and criminality were tied to moralistic outlooks regarding their sexuality and identity as mothers. Consider also that during this time, performing an "illegal" abortion was classified as a violent crime that carried a sentence of imprisonment (Freedman, 1981, p. 12). Naturally, these abortions were illegal in every circumstance because there was no such thing as a "legal" abortion. Since abortion was considered murder, women who exercised autonomy over their own body and wished to avoid unwanted pregnancies had no choice but to commit the ultimate crime, regardless of the circumstances that

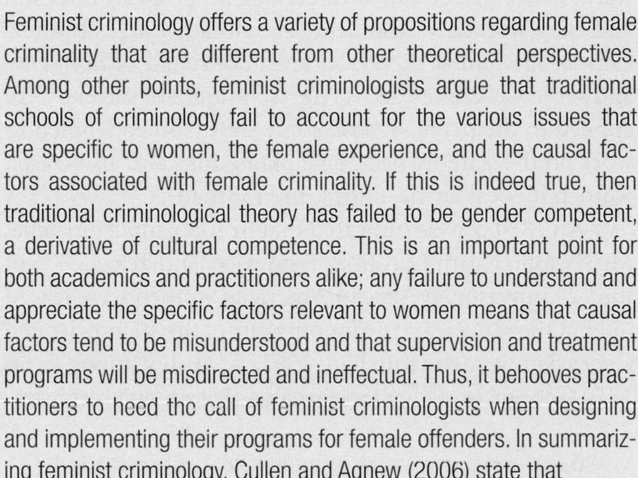

APPLIED THEORY 10.1

Feminist Criminology and the Female Offender

Feminist criminology offers a variety of propositions regarding female criminality that are different from other theoretical perspectives. Among other points, feminist criminologists argue that traditional schools of criminology fail to account for the various issues that are specific to women, the female experience, and the causal factors associated with female criminality. If this is indeed true, then traditional criminological theory has failed to be gender competent, a derivative of cultural competence. This is an important point for both academics and practitioners alike; any failure to understand and appreciate the specific factors relevant to women means that causal factors tend to be misunderstood and that supervision and treatment programs will be misdirected and ineffectual. Thus, it behooves practitioners to heed the call of feminist criminologists when designing and implementing their programs for female offenders. In summarizing feminist criminology, Cullen and Agnew (2006) state that

> crime cannot be understood without considering gender, crime is shaped by the different social experiences of and power exercised by men and women. Patriarchy is a broad structure that shapes gender-related experiences and power. Men may use crime to exert control over women and to demonstrate their masculinity—that is, to show that they are "men" in a way that is consistent with societal ideas of masculinity. (p. 7)

From the reading thus far in this chapter and when considering the description of feminist criminology presented by Cullen and Agnew (2006), it should be clear to the student that there is a great deal of similarity between these two portrayals of female offending. From this chapter, it is evident that much of female crime is shaped by gender-related experiences and power. Participation in the sex industry, a prime area of involvement for female offenders, seems to indicate that much of the activity related to female criminality is indeed rooted in gender-related experiences. Further, when one considers that the overwhelming majority of domestic violence victims are female and that female offenders experience higher rates of domestic violence perpetrated against them, this lends further credence to feminists who contend that men use crime to exert control over women and to demonstrate their power over them. Naturally, acts of sexual abuse directed at young girls also back up this theory, and, as this chapter demonstrates, female offenders generally have higher rates of prior childhood sexual abuse.

Finally, the effects of this abuse and the corresponding ravages associated with being raised in a criminogenic family environment tend to manifest themselves through various mental health symptoms and maladaptive coping mechanisms. It is perhaps for this reason, as well as other factors related to a poor sense of self-efficacy (common among many female offenders), that substance abuse may be so high among these offenders. The use of drugs as well as comorbid problems with depression and anxiety put female offenders at further risk of having difficulties. Nevertheless, women tend to be more verbally communicative than men, and this means that they also tend to do better in treatment regimens that utilize talk therapy. As a result, these offenders often have a better prognosis when in treatment than do their male counterparts. Perhaps, then, treatment programs for female offenders should continue to be intensified, with a continued focus on female-specific factors and theoretical frameworks that are consistent with feminist criminology. To fail to do so essentially puts the female offender, her children (as most female offenders have children), and the rest of society at risk for future criminality. In short, it simply makes good sense to integrate this theoretical perspective into the various supervision and treatment regimens designed for female offenders.

SOURCE: Cullen, F. T., & Agnew, R. (2006). *Criminological theory: Past to present* (3rd ed.). Los Angeles, CA: Roxbury Publishing Company.

led to their pregnancy. Because sexual abuse of women went largely unaddressed, many women (especially young girls) who were victims of rape and/or molestation were expected to endure this experience and to birth the offspring of their victimization. A failure to do so would be seen as contradictory to the nurturing and caring image that women were expected to maintain and would, therefore, be demonized by society and by the criminal justice system.

Minority Female Offenders Compared to Caucasian Female Offenders in American History

Despite our discussion of female offending and incarceration throughout past generations, one key point to understanding how women have been sentenced has not yet been addressed: racial disparities that have existed and continue to exist among the female population, particularly among those who are incarcerated. This is a very important point that deserves elaboration. Kurshan (1996) provides excellent insight into this issue, and much of her work has been adapted

Video Link
Kimberle Crenshaw on Black Girls in the Prison Pipeline

Thinkstock Images

■ PHOTO 10.2 A female inmate carries her property while being escorted to her cell.

in this chapter to elaborate on the inherent racism that existed in the justice system when processing female offenders.

Consider that prison camps emerged in the South after 1870, and the overwhelming majority of women in these camps were African American; the few Caucasian women there were imprisoned for much more serious offenses, yet experienced better conditions of confinement. For instance, at Bowden Farm in Texas, the majority of women were African American, incarcerated for property offenses, and they worked in the field (Freedman, 1981). The few Caucasian women there had been convicted of homicide and served as domestics. As the techniques of slavery were applied to the penal system, some states forced women to work on the state-owned penal plantations and also leased women to local farms, mines, and railroads.

An 1880 census indicated that in Alabama, Louisiana, Mississippi, North Carolina, Tennessee, and Texas, 37% of the 220 imprisoned African American women were leased out but the same was true for only one of the 40 imprisoned Caucasian women (Kurshan, 1991, p. 3). Testimony in an 1870 Georgia investigation revealed that, in one instance,

> there were no white women there. One started there, and I heard Mr. Alexander (the lessee) say he turned her loose. He was talking to the guard; I was working in the cut. He said his wife was a white woman, and he could not stand it to see a white woman worked in such places. (Freedman, 1981, p. 151)

Acknowledgment of the disparity between minority women and Caucasian women is important for two reasons. First, it is seldom addressed in most textbooks on corrections or correctional systems and practices. Second, we continue to see disparity between minority women and Caucasian women in today's society. Whereas in generations past, much of the disparity was residual from the prior slave era, particularly in the South, the reasons for such disparity are perhaps no longer the same, yet they are real and still exist. It can be seen that women who commit crimes have been demonized throughout history, and, for those who were double minorities (particularly African American women), the treatment and type of prison experience received were significantly different. Female offenders were not (and still are not) all cast from one mold—they are diverse, and the experiences for minority women are even more noxious than they tend to be for Caucasian women. This is not to minimize the impact of incarceration upon Caucasian women but is meant to highlight even more the demographics and conditions of confinement for women throughout American correctional history. This provides a more historically correct view of how circumstances have evolved for women in the correctional system and also demonstrates that the disparity that we see today is simply an extension of past dynamics (see Focus Topic 10.2).

WOMEN'S REFORMATORIES IN THE EARLY TWENTIETH CENTURY: A FEMINIST PERSPECTIVE

Reformatories for women: Developed as alternatives to the penitentiary's harsh conditions of enforced silence and hard labor.

Reformatories for women developed alongside custodial prisons. These were parallel, but distinct, developments. **Reformatories for women** developed due to the efforts of an early generation of women reformers who appeared between 1840 and 1900, but their use became more widespread as activists

FOCUS TOPIC 10.1

Disproportionate Sentencing and Incarceration of Minority Women

To further highlight the disparity between minority women inmates and Caucasian women inmates, consider that in 2015 African American females were between 1.6 and 4.1 times more likely to be imprisoned than Caucasian females of any age group (Carson, 2015). Further, research by Carson (2015) also shows that for female inmates ages 30 to 34, the highest imprisonment rate was among African Americans (264 per 100,000), then Caucasians (163 per 100,000), then Latina inmates (174 per 100,000). In addition, African American females ages 18 to 19 (33 inmates per 100,000) were almost 5 times more likely to be imprisoned than Caucasian females (7 inmates per 100,000), according to Carson (2014).

SOURCES: Carson, A. E. (2015). *Prisoners, 2014.* Washington, DC: Bureau of Justice Statistics.

Carson, A. E. (2014). *Prisoners, 2013.* Washington, DC: Bureau of Justice Statistics.

pressed for alternatives to the penitentiary's harsh conditions of enforced silence and hard labor (Kurshan, 1991; Rafter, 1985). The move to housing female offenders in reformatories occurred at the same time that these facilities began to be used for the male population; this was a time that many texts refer to as the reformatory era. The women who advocated reform for the housing conditions of female offenders were working in tandem with other prison reformers who have been discussed in earlier chapters of this text. Their work, though focused on the plight of female offenders, was consistent with the times in which they lived.

In particular, these activists contended that the use of mixed prisons was problematic and provided female inmates with no privacy. This left the women vulnerable to humiliation, physical abuse, and sexual abuse. The reformatories, on the other hand, were more humane, and conditions were better than at the traditional female penitentiaries (Kurshan, 1991). The use of reformatories eliminated much of the risk of abuse at the hands of male inmates and even male prison staff. Reformatories also resulted in more freedom of movement and opened up a variety of opportunities for work that were often reserved for male inmates. Kurshan (1991) notes that

> children of prisoners up to two years old could stay in most institutions. At least some of the reformatories were staffed and administered by women. They usually had cottages, flower gardens, and no fences. They offered discussions on the law, academics and training, and women were often paroled more readily than in custodial institutions. However, a closer look at who the women prisoners were, the nature of their offenses, and the program to which they were subjected reveals the seamier side of these ostensibly noble institutions. (p. 5)

As with most of the inmates in prisons throughout the nation, women in the reformatories were of the working class. Many of them worked outside the home. At New York State's Albion Correctional Facility, for instance, 80% had, in the past, worked for wages. Reformatories were also overwhelmingly institutions for Caucasian women; fewer minority women were placed in these facilities. This is not because they were sentenced less frequently but because African American, Native American, and Latino American women were more likely to be placed in a prison rather than a reformatory. Thus again, the racial discrimination seen among correctional systems of this era emerged in the operation of reformatories. Kurshan (1991), in discussing the racial discrimination among women processed in the criminal justice system, notes the following:

> Record keeping at the Albion Reformatory in New York demonstrates how unusual it was for black women to be incarcerated there. The registries left spaces for entries of a large number of variables, such as family history of insanity and epilepsy. Nowhere was there a space for recording race. When African Americans were admitted, the clerk penciled "colored" at the top of the page. African American women were much less likely to be arrested for such public order offenses. Rafter suggests that black women were not expected to act like "ladies" in the first place and therefore were reportedly not deemed worthy of such rehabilitation. (p. 5)

It is important to emphasize that there were no institutions devoted to correcting men for "moral" offenses. In fact, such activities were not considered crimes when men engaged in them, and therefore men were not as a result imprisoned (Freedman, 1981; Rafter, 1985). A glance at these crimes for women shows the extent to which society was bent on repressing women's sexuality. More than half of women were imprisoned because of "sexual misconduct" (Kurshan, 1991, p. 7). Women were incarcerated in reformatories primarily for various public order offenses or so-called moral offenses: lewd and lascivious carriage, stubbornness, idle and disorderly conduct, drunkenness, vagrancy, fornication, serial premarital pregnancies, keeping bad company, adultery, venereal disease, and vagrancy (Kurshan, 1991). In many cases, when young girls rebelled against abusive behavior (often sexual in nature), they were doubly victimized by the family and/or relatives, who would have them sentenced and placed within a prison or reformatory (Kurshan, 1991). Naturally, these dysfunctional families would lie and concoct stories of inappropriate behavior, and, since belief systems were different and technology was primitive during these times, girls and young women had little ability to defend themselves from these false charges. Thus, this type of system is thought to have basically trapped girls and women in subjugation within a male-dominated society and a male-dominated criminal justice system.

Feminist criminologists have contended that reformatories were institutions of patriarchy and that they were designed to reinforce stereotypes of women (Kurshan, 1991). **Patriarchy** is a term that describes any social system where fathers tend to be considered the head of the family and where men tend to hold economic, political, legal, and social power. At this time in history, it could hardly be argued that men held all the power, including that exercised over penal operations. Due to the types of offenses targeted for sentencing and the manner in which reformatories operated, it would seem the accusations of patriarchy were convincing ones. Though reformatories were not run in the same authoritarian style as penitentiaries, they reinforced norms and expectations of the Victorian Era and attempted to quash nonstereotypical behavior among women.

Further, the type of sentencing used was often open-ended or indeterminate. This meant that the length of time that a woman would have to serve under this type of socialization system depended on her willingness to comply with institutional expectations. In other words, if she became more "ladylike," then she was more likely to be released. The length of time that she served had little to do with the actual offense and/or her likelihood of committing future crimes but more to do with her meeting the expectations of a patriarchal system. However, this was disguised by a veneer of respectability with the official rationale for such undefined terms being the interests of the rehabilitative ideology. Thus, a woman's incarceration was not of fixed length because the notion was that a woman would stay for as long as it took to accomplish the task of reforming her (Kurshan, 1991). Naturally though, her "reform" was determined by how well she obeyed and adhered to the patriarchal standards that had been established for her to follow.

Patriarchy: A male-oriented and male-dominated social structure that defers to men and sees women in a subservient position to men.

■ Figure 10.3: National Profile of Women Offenders

A profile based on national data for women offenders reveals the following characteristics:

- Disproportionately women of color.
- In their early to mid-30s.
- Most likely to have been convicted of a drug-related offense.
- From fragmented families (that include other family members who also have been involved with the criminal justice system).
- Survivors of physical and/or sexual abuse as children and adults.
- Individuals with significant substance abuse problems.
- Unmarried mothers of minor children.
- Individual with a high school or general equivalency diploma (GED) but limited vocational training and sporadic work histories.

ISSUES RELATED TO THE MODERN-DAY FEMALE OFFENDER POPULATION

When discussing female offenders, it becomes clear that most are minority members with few options and limited economic resources. Thus, many of these offenders are excluded in multiple ways from the access to success and stability commonly attributed to broader society. Of those women who are incarcerated, approximately 44% have no high school diploma or GED, and 61% were unemployed at the point of incarceration (Bloom et al., 2003). In addition, roughly 47% were single prior to incarceration while an approximate 65% to 70% were the primary caretakers of minor children at the point that they were incarcerated (Bloom et al., 2003). Lastly, over one-third of those incarcerated can be found within the jurisdictions of the federal prison system or the state prison systems of Texas and California (Harrison & Karberg, 2004).

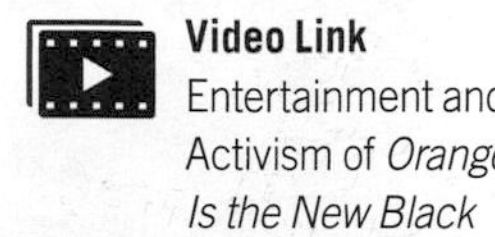

Video Link
Entertainment and Activism of *Orange Is the New Black*

Female offenders are less likely than men to have committed violent offenses and more likely to have been convicted of crimes involving drugs or property. Often, their property offenses are economically driven, motivated by poverty and by the abuse of alcohol and other drugs. Women face life circumstances that tend to be specific to their gender, such as sexual abuse, sexual assault, domestic violence, and the responsibility of being the primary caregiver for dependent children. Approximately 1.3 million minor children have a mother who is under criminal justice supervision, and approximately 65% of women in state prisons and 59% of women in federal prisons have an average of two minor children.

Women involved in the criminal justice system thus represent a population marginalized by race, class, and gender. African American women are overrepresented in correctional populations. While they constitute only 13% of women in the United States, nearly 50% of women in prison are African American. Black women are 8 times more likely than white women to be incarcerated. The age and racial characteristics of women who are incarcerated are summarized in Table 10.2 for students wishing to see a more detailed breakdown.

The Female Inmate Subculture and Coping in Prison

The conditioning of women in the United States regarding the traditional social role of motherhood and the forced separation from their family during incarceration has a considerable effect on women in prison. A significant aspect of the female coping mechanism inside the prisons is their development of family-like environments with the other female prisoners. These fictional family atmospheres or kinship structures enable the women to create a type of caring, nurturing environment inside the prison (Brown, 2003; Engelbert, 2001). Associating with a prison family provides a woman with a feeling of belonging and social identity. Many of these relationships are formed as friendships and develop into the companionship roles of "sister-to-sister" and "mother-to-daughter" bonds. These relationships can become intimate and include touching and hugging without having sexual overtones.

However, sexual relationships in prison do exist and are not uncommon. Some women who are in prison for an extended period of time may become involved with another female inmate in order to fill their need for love and companionship. In many of these cases, one will act in a male role and take on male mannerisms. She may walk and talk like a man, cut or shave her hair, and attempt to dress in a manly fashion. The other partner will typically behave in a traditional feminine manner. Some of these women become involved in these relationships only while in prison, and therefore do not consider themselves to be lesbian in the strictest sense of the word. Similar to male prison settings, sexuality inside the walls is considered separate from sexual identity outside of the walls.

SAGE Journal Article Link
Foodways and Social Networks in a Women's Prison

For these women, involvement in a same-sex relationship is intended to simply fulfill their need to be "loved" and desired just as they would wish when outside the prison. There are additional advantages associated with belonging to a prison family structure. J. W. Brown, author of *The Female Inmate* (2003), explains that "in the female prison, 'family' members provide goods and services to those members of the family who demonstrate need. This 'kinship' network becomes the main conduit of illicit goods and services in the female prison." The functions of the kinship relationships within the prison are many and varied. They provide support and protection, and they may be encouraged by the prison administration due to the social control aspect of keeping the female inmates out of trouble.

Scott Houston/Polaris/Newscom

■ PHOTO 10.3 These female inmates are preparing for work on a chain gang detail outside of the facility. Prior to going outside, they will all be chained together in a manner that provides adequate security but also allows them to work, as well.

Upon release, nearly all female inmates return to traditional heterosexual roles in which they most often play a feminine role. Regardless of whether the kinship relationships are as defined as some believe, there is no doubt studies have revealed interesting information pertaining to the female subculture within the prison system. Women, just like male inmates, are faced with surviving the term of their sentence inside the prison walls, and this requires that they create some type of acceptable social environment in which to cope with the situation.

CONSIDERATIONS FOR FEMALE OFFENDERS

We now will turn our attention to several other characteristics that have been found to be common among the female offending population. The remainder of this chapter will consider key issues associated with female offenders in an effort to demonstrate the multitude of difficult problems that confound effective intervention for many of these offenders. The issues that affect most women who are processed in the justice system tend to be much different from those of men.

Domestic Violence

The research on the prevalence of **domestic violence** and its impact on women in the United States is so abundant that it goes beyond the scope of this chapter to discuss. However, when limiting the discussion to female offenders and their experiences with domestic violence, it appears that they are at greater risk for physical abuse than those in the general population. According to a study by the Women's Prison Association (2003), female offenders who are incarcerated are very likely to have histories of physical abuse; in fact, the association found 57% of adult women were victims of physical or sexual abuse. Furthermore, this study found that this violence is most likely to have been perpetrated by a boyfriend or husband.

Incarcerated women report being subjected to the most violence at ages 15 to 24 (Bloom et al., 2003). This means that this abuse tends to follow female offenders throughout their life span, indicating that these offenders return to a lifestyle that is self-damaging. Women on probation and parole are likely to be socially isolated from common social circles, and their peer network will probably be limited (Bloom et al., 2003). At best it will include other women in a similar situation, or perhaps persons from employment (keep in mind the educational level, unemployment rate, and vocational skills of these women). More likely, these women will continue to associate within their subculture of origin, meaning that many of the friends and family that they return to are likely to be, or have been, criminal offenders themselves. This may be much more common since many women who offend often tend to do so as secondary accomplices with a male primary offender. Thus, these women do not typically have many resources to rely on and may find themselves quite dependent on a man—perhaps even an abusive man.

Physical and Sexual Abuse

A study on self-reported prior abuse conducted by Harlow in 1999 found that female offenders are abused more frequently than male offenders. State prison inmates reported both physical and sexual abuse experiences prior to being sentenced. The results found that 57.2% of females had experienced abusive treatment, compared to 16.1% of males. Of this same group, 36.7% of the female offenders and 14.4% of the male offenders reported that the abuse occurred during their childhood or teenage years. Other findings from this study are as follows:

Domestic violence: Behaviors used by one person in a relationship to control the other.

■ **Table 10.2: Percentage of Female Inmates in State and Federal Facilities by Age and Race in 2014**

Age Group	Average of Female Demographic Groups	Caucasian	African American	Latina	Other
18–19	0.6%	0.4%	0.9%	1.1%	0%
20–24	10.0	8.3	11.5	12.4	8.6
25–29	17.5	17.3	16.8	19.7	18.0
30–34	18.6	18.8	16.8	20.8	18.8
35–39	14.7	14.7	13.7	15.7	14.8
40–44	12.8	13.4	12.8	11.2	13.3
45–49	10.9	11.1	12.4	9.0	10.9
50–54	7.7	8.1	8.4	5.6	7.8
55–59	3.9	4.0	4.4	2.8	3.9
60–64	1.8	2.1	1.8	1.1	1.6
65 & older	1.2	1.5	0.9	0.6	1.6
Total Number of Sentenced Inmates	106,232	53,100	22,600	17,800	12,800

SOURCE: Carson, A. E. (2015). *Prisoners, 2014.* Washington, DC: Bureau of Justice Statistics.

1. Males tend to be mistreated as children, but females are mistreated as both children and adults.
2. Both genders reported much more abuse if they had lived in a foster home or another structured institution.
3. Higher levels of abuse were reported among offenders who had an incarcerated family member.
4. Offenders reporting prior sexual abuse had higher levels of drug and alcohol abuse than those not reporting prior sexual abuse. Further, female offenders who were abused used drugs or alcohol more frequently than did male offenders.

Sex Industry Activity and Sexually Transmitted Diseases

A large body of research shows that female criminals often have some history of prostitution, although the causal factor(s) and the order of causal factors are not very clear. A debate, indeed a schism, exists among researchers as to whether this is the case due to economic necessities or whether prior sexual victimization is at the root of this common form of female offense. Many researchers contend that prior victimization (especially sexual) is at the origin, pointing toward the high rate of incidence of sexual abuse among female criminals and the high rate of female criminals' involvement in prostitution.

The rate of HIV/AIDS infection is higher for female offenders than for male offenders. According to the Women's Prison Association (2003), the percentage of women in state and federal prisons who are infected with HIV/AIDS is 3.6%, which is 12 times the national rate of infection. For men in prison, the percentage is 2.1%, which is a third lower than for women in prison (Women's Prison Association, 2003). In the general public, the rate for HIV/AIDS is twice as high for men as for women. Research indicates that female inmates tend to have higher rates of HIV due to involvement in risky sexual behavior. Interestingly, there is also a connection between this risky behavior and these women having experienced prior sexual abuse (Women's Prison Association, 2003).

Drugs

Drug use is a major contributor to female criminality. Female offenders use drugs more often than male offenders, though differences are not extreme and research focuses primarily on arrested and incarcerated subjects. Consider that between 1985 and 1994 women's drug arrests increased by 100% whereas men's drug arrests increased only by about 50%. The point is when dealing with female offenders, addressing drug use is critical if you are to prevent recidivism. Further, female offenders engage in riskier drug habits than male offenders as they report higher levels of needle usage and needle sharing (Women's Prison Association, 2003). This social problem is further compounded because a high number of female offenders who are intravenous drug users likewise engage in prostitution and sex industry activity to support their habits.

Violent Crime

It is important to note that when it comes to violent crime, there is a huge disparity between male and female offenders. Simply put, female offenders do not commit violent crimes with great frequency. Most of their crimes revolve around larceny, theft, and fraud. Of those women who do commit homicides, the vast majority of these homicides involve the killing of intimates, usually in self-defense or in retaliatory response to long-term abusive relationships (Brown, 2003). Female chronic offenders are similar to male chronic offenders in that they are likely to be a minority group member, single, and a substance abuser, and have a history of spouse abuse. But they differ in that they show differences in years of education (women typically have more), and female offenders tend to paradoxically score lower on IQ tests, are more likely to come from homes of divorce, and are more likely to come from criminogenic families. When both genders are compared, men are likely to be sentenced to prison for violent, property, and drug offenses, while women are likely to be sentenced to prison for drug offenses and property crimes (Brown, 2003).

Given the high rates of abuse that the female offending population experiences (both in childhood and in adulthood), the female offender is commonly referred to as the victim-turned-offender. The prior victimization of female offenders, particularly through domestic violence, is held as a primary causal factor in predicting female criminal behavior. This concept goes hand-in-hand with the tenets of the chivalry hypothesis and with feminist thought on criminality. While some may scoff at these types of concepts and explanations, it is hard to refute three key points. First, most crimes against women are committed by male perpetrators. Second, women tend to only attack men when they have been victimized. Third, women commit far fewer crimes that are about power and control.

Mental Health Issues

The experience of prison can exacerbate the prevalence and/or severity of mental illness. Incarceration can deteriorate existing mental conditions and lead to a breakdown in mental health in an otherwise well-adjusted individual. The mental health issues for female offenders are often tied to stages in their life cycle and development, such as with puberty, adolescence, and phases of reproductive development (Seiden, 1989). However, because a disturbing number of women are sexually and physically abused as girls and as adult women, attention has been focused on the anxiety, depression, and other psychological illnesses resulting from these events (Seiden, 1989). The trauma of early sexual and physical abuse may be manifested through a number of mental health symptoms and diagnoses as well as the more common post-traumatic stress disorders (PTSD) and alcoholism (Seiden, 1989). As with most forms of mental illness, these disorders develop largely in response to stressors that push an already overtaxed psyche. Because of their higher rates of abuse and victimization, coupled with their drug use, female offenders may have numerous "predispositions" that make them prone to mental illness when the stressor of incarceration is added.

Depression is a very common mental illness among the incarcerated and is even more pronounced among the female offending population because this disorder tends to have higher prevalence rates among females in general. Further, depression is a common symptom among drug abusers, so when the numerous problem variables are taken together, female offenders are very susceptible to bouts of depression and to the full array of mood disorders.

A recent study examined mental health issues among inmates in prisons and jails throughout the United States (James & Glaze, 2006). The study found that female inmates had much higher rates of mental health problems than male inmates (see Table 10.3). An estimated 48% of females in state prisons, compared to 22% of male inmates, had a recent history of mental health problems. In local jails, 40% of females compared to 18% of males had a recent history of mental health problems.

■ Table 10.3: Female Inmates Presenting With Mental Health Problems in State Prisons and Local Jails

Mental Problem	Percentage of Inmates in ____			
	State Prison		Local Jail	
	Male	Female	Male	Female
Recent history	22%	48%	18%	40%
Diagnosed	8	23	9	23
Overnight Stay	5	9	4	9
Medication	16	39	12	30
Therapy	14	32	9	23
Symptoms	48%	62%	59%	70%

SOURCE: James, D. J., & Glaze, L. E. (2006). *Mental health problems of prison and jail inmates.* Washington, DC: Bureau of Justice Statistics.

Among female state prison inmates, 23% indicated that they had been diagnosed with some type of mental health disorder during the past 12 months (see Table 10.3). This same percentage was found for women in jail. This was almost 3 times the rate of male inmates (around 8%) who had been told they had a mental health problem. It seems that male offenders tend to mask their depression with anger and aggressive reactions that serve as defensive "fronts" or displays of force. Much of this is due to socialization, but for women socialization tends to ensure that their symptoms of depression are recognized for what they are. Thus, men who are incarcerated may simply be diagnostically labeled as aggressive, and, when in a prison environment, this can go one step further into a classification of being assaultive. Though from the view of institutional security this is accurate, it nonetheless fails to detect the sense of depression that the male inmate may be experiencing.

On the other hand, for female inmates, socialization provides tolerance for acts of depression and the expression of emotional sorrow. Thus, prevalence rates among female and male inmates in prison may be compounded by social expectations and norms to which prison staff are accustomed. Further, as would be expected, prior abuse plays a role in addiction and depression, further cementing these two variables together as correlates among female offenders. Likewise, when it is considered that female victims of battering tend to present with depressive disorders and PTSD, and given the fact that domestic battering is targeted at female victims much more frequently than male victims, it is not surprising that this variable also aggravates rates of depression among the female offending population.

Female Offenders as Mothers

In 1998, female offenders in the criminal justice system were mothers to approximately 1.3 million children. Many female offenders under criminal justice supervision face losing custody of their children. Some female offenders have relatives or friends who will care for their children while they are incarcerated, but many do not. For those who are able to arrange placement with relatives, the likelihood of permanent separation between mother and child is significantly reduced. It has been observed that maternal grandmothers most often care for the children of female prison inmates (Bloom, Brown, & Chesney-Lind, 1996). If a mother is unable to place her children with relatives or friends, the local child welfare agency will most likely put the child in foster care. When children of imprisoned mothers are placed in foster care, caseworkers are expected to make concerted efforts to sustain family ties and to encourage family reunification (Bloom et al., 1996). Most incarcerated mothers, particularly those who are mentally ill, do not have access to the resources they need to meet other reunification requirements imposed by the court, such as parent education, counseling, drug treatment, and job training. Upon release from custody to community corrections, mothers face numerous obstacles in reuniting with their children. They must navigate through a number of complex governmental and social service agencies in order

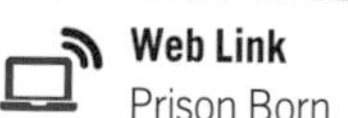
Web Link
Prison Born

Shaul Schwarz/Getty Images

■ PHOTO 10.4 Prison officials hope the connections that take place between mothers and children in the nursery will help keep the inmate mothers from reoffending once they are released. Many facilities with women are designed to address parenting and family issues due to the importance placed on children and family among many female offenders.

to regain custody. Although differences may exist across jurisdictions, in many cases, it is considered beyond the purview of probation and parole agencies to intervene in child custody cases.

When fathers are incarcerated, there is usually a mother left at home to care for the children. However, when mothers are incarcerated, there is not usually a father in the home. This situation is further exacerbated by the fact that there are fewer women's prisons, and because of this these units tend to be great distances from one another and from the likely location where the female offender lived prior to incarceration. Thus, there is a higher risk that female offenders will be incarcerated at a greater distance from their children than males (Bloom et al., 1996). Indeed, the average female inmate is more than 160 miles farther from her family than a male inmate, and at least half the children of imprisoned mothers have either not seen or not visited their mothers since they were incarcerated (Bloom et al., 1996). This low rate of contact between mother and child tends to weaken family bonds, which then causes psychological and emotional damage both to the child and to the incarcerated mother. In addition, recidivism rates tend to go up when inmate mothers have diminished contact with their children (Bloom et al., 1996).

Video Link Relationships Between Incarcerated Mothers and Children

This separation between mother and child causes what has been called **collateral damage** to children and society due to the current incarceration trends of female offenders who typically commit property and/or drug crimes (Crawford, 2003). Though female offenders separated from their children are at an increased risk of later recidivism, the damage done to the children is probably more serious than to the adult when a parent is incarcerated (Bloom et al., 1996; Crawford, 2003). A number of children display symptoms of PTSD, namely depression, feelings of anger and guilt, flashbacks about their mother's crimes or arrests, and the experience of hearing their mother's voice. Children of incarcerated mothers may also display other negative effects, such as school-related difficulties, depression, low self-esteem, aggressive behavior, and general emotional dysfunction (Bloom et al., 1996).

CONDITIONS OF CARE FOR FEMALE OFFENDERS

It is considered general knowledge that female prison institutions do not meet the inmates' needs as effectively as do male prisons. As a testament to the poor services that tend to be delivered to female inmates, consider the case of *Glover v. Johnson* (1988). This case involved the Michigan Department of Corrections and the issue of parity in service programming between female and male offenders. A class action lawsuit was filed on behalf of all female inmates in the state of Michigan, and this suit alleged that the constitutional rights of female inmates throughout the state had been violated because these inmates were being denied educational and vocational rehabilitation opportunities that were being provided to male inmates. Ultimately, the Michigan Department of Corrections was found liable, and a decree was issued for the Department of Corrections to provide the following to female inmates within its jurisdiction:

Collateral damage: Any damage incidental to an activity.

1. Two-year college programming.
2. Paralegal training and access to an attorney to remedy past inadequacies in law library facilities.

CROSS-NATIONAL PERSPECTIVE 10.1

Free to Grow Up: Home for Female Inmates With Children in Europe

The province of Milan opened a home for imprisoned women with children in the Lombardy capital in Viale Piceno, Italy. The home, opened by a ministerial decree, was created in collaboration with the Milanese Penitentiary Administration and other area agencies that wish to end the intergenerational cycle of crime and criminal behavior. This program started life as a pilot institute based on a law passed in 2001, which focused on the issue that women with children under 3 years of age in exceptional cases should not be sentenced to stay in prison.

It is easy to comprehend the difficulties that small children in an institution can encounter in their psychic-physical development. Specifically, this program seeks to alleviate the trauma and sense of abandonment that youth tend to encounter when separated from their mothers. Conversely but just as useful is the fact that women in this program tend to fare better in their treatment programming and also tend to have a better prognosis with various life-skills aspects in their day-to-day functioning. Thus, it is clear that children are, themselves, an important resource in the paths of change and growth of these sentenced women. It was this premise that moved the project experimented in Milan to the Institution of Attenuated Custody for Mothers (ICAM).

The project planning was set forth in the field of the consolidated collaboration with local territorial bodies with particular reference to the Milanese area and started with the sharing by all the bodies involved in pedagogic, juridical reflections, according to which the phenomenon, even if not having vast statistical dimensions, represents a particularly relevant aspect for all society due to the unexpected spin offs on the infantile population of their stay in prison. Consequently society at large is involved in identifying solutions of mediation between the application of the mother's custody in prison and guaranteeing the child a serene infancy.

The child and the mother both require specific intervention. This program addresses the needs of both the child and the mother simultaneously and in a coordinated fashion that mitigates the affective impact on the child and optimizes the opportunities for the mother. In between, both maintain routine contact and are given therapeutic work that enhances the mother-child relationship, changing dysfunctional bonds to those that are likely much more healthy. For instance, issues of child parentification are addressed, and faulty parenting processes are redesigned through parent training and child education regarding the appropriate role of parent and child within the family system. Other dynamics are addressed as well, all with the intent to create a normalized family system that insulates both from the effects of unhealthy living.

This program is particularly suited for mothers who are addicted to drugs and alcohol. The Milan Prison has allocated a new housing building for the program, which is referred to as the Attenuated Custody Institute for Drug-Addicted Mothers (ICAM). The ICAM is located in an urban area so that women can access all of the various services that are necessary. This is a superior location to a rural area where services would be hard to reach and where family and friends might have difficulty visiting. This location also enhances educational opportunities for the children.

The combination of effective programming and enhanced location has created an effective program that addresses the needs of parent and child. Overall, it would seem that the program is a success. The program has been designed to overcome many of the hurdles associated with female offender service delivery that occur in most prison systems. It seems that these modifications and enhancements have worked well; current initial outcomes have proven to be positive. The Milan Prison's ICAM seems to hold promise as a showpiece that other programs around the world may desire to replicate. By all accounts, this might be an optimal approach in many countries that have noted the challenges for female offenders and their children.

QUESTION 1: After reading this article, explain how this type of program addresses specific issues outlined in this chapter with female offenders. In other words, how are the issues between female offenders in Italy similar to those in the United States?

QUESTION 2: How does this type of program improve upon some of the deficiencies noted with many correctional facilities for female offenders?

SOURCE: European Programme for the Prevention of and Fight Against Crime. (2007). *Free to grow up: Home for female inmates with children.* Retrieved from http://praxis-psychosoziale-beratung.de/mcproject.htm

3. A revision of the wage policy for female inmates to ensure parity with male inmate wage compensation policies.
4. Access to programming that had previously only been provided to male inmates.
5. Prison industries that previously existed only at male facilities.

Despite such legal precedents, it appears that practices have not improved substantially in other parts of the nation. Consider, for example, California, which has the largest state correctional

CORRECTIONS AND THE LAW 10.1

Legal Issues Regarding Female Offenders in Jail and Prison

When maintaining custody of female offenders, a number of legal issues arise that are unique to this population. This is particularly true due to the typically male-dominated nature of this industry. Agencies must be proactive in their policy approach, and they must ensure that their staff are knowledgeable on issues related to women in custody.

This insert will address the following three legal issues concerning women offenders: (1) equal protection and access to facilities, programs, and services; (2) staffing and supervision; and (3) sexual misconduct.

Each of these three issues is, in and of itself, an important and somewhat broad point of concern. To the extent possible, these issues will be distilled to specific points that students should keep in mind.

1. Equal Protection and Title IX: Equivalent Access to Programs and Services

Although the goal is to provide parity of treatment for all prisoners, regardless of gender, administrators may not be required to provide the same level of facilities and services to men and women if they can justify the differences. For instance, there is no requirement that the same policies, facilities, programs, and services offered to male offenders be offered to female offenders. The modern trend treats gender as governed by *Turner v. Safley* (1987), unless the gender discrimination is purposeful (see Chapter 3 of this text regarding the standards set by *Turner v. Safley*), in which case regulations must satisfy protocols for exceptions (due to security or safety) that the Supreme Court has ruled on.

Regardless of whether the issue meets *Turner* guidelines or qualifies as an exception that has been given sufficient scrutiny, different policies, facilities, programs, and services can satisfy equal protection even if the populations are similarly situated as long as a valid penological justification exists for the differences. Fairness and rehabilitative concerns dictate that parity should be the goal even when not constitutionally required.

2. Staffing and Litigation Issues

A number of lawsuits involving female offenders have been based on cross-gender supervision. Administrators must balance competing institutional claims with the privacy interests of women offenders. The law on cross-gender supervision and searches is very fact specific. However, challenges brought by female inmates appear to be treated more favorably than those brought by male inmates. Thus, women are more likely than men to be successful in suits that implicate privacy interests. This outcome stems from society's apparent view that women should be afforded more privacy than men. Also, because many female offenders have been victims of sexual and physical assault, cross-gender supervision can cause them additional trauma.

When considering cross-gender strip searches and pat-downs, prison administrators should ensure that all strip searches are conducted between same-sex staff and inmates. In some cases, general practices that allow opposite-gender searches may violate the Eighth Amendment rights of female inmates, such as with a female inmate who is known to suffer from trauma from sexual abuse.

However, as long as there are no egregious circumstances, opposite-gender searches of male inmates by females tend to be upheld, while cross-gender searches of females by male guards have a greater chance of being struck down. This is, to some extent, a double standard that relates to the differing expectations of privacy for male and female inmates. However, this is grounded in the reality that most incidents of custodial sexual abuse occur among male officers and female inmates.

Another key area of consideration is the potential for lawsuits resulting from sexual harassment, sexual misconduct, or cross-gender supervision. The best means for agencies to defend against these lawsuits is to establish clear policies and procedures and ensure that employees follow them.

3. Sexual Misconduct

It is important to understand that there are historical, cultural, and psychological reasons why women may feel more violated and/or intimidated by cross-gender supervision than men. Consider the problematic history that exists with custodial sexual misconduct in several female facilities throughout the nation. During the 1980s and 1990s, roughly 23 correctional departments were involved in class action or individual lawsuits related to staff sexual misconduct with female inmates. One notorious case in particular occurred in Georgia and included staff throughout the entire institution and at all levels of supervision (*Cason v. Seckinger* [1984]).

Much of the **custodial sexual misconduct** included the use or threat of force targeted toward female offenders in multiple state correctional systems. Correctional staff also used their authority and ability to procure goods and services for the female inmates to encourage the inmates to engage in an exchange for sexual favors. Some of the misconduct was "consensual" between inmate and staff, but this is nonetheless abuse on the part of correctional staff. Many of the female offending population were abused prior to incarceration, as children and/or as adults. Because of this, the dysfunctional exchange and confusion between sex and a mature, emotionally intimate relationship is normalized for many of these women. In either event, it is the obligation of staff to ensure that appropriate boundaries are set and that these are not violated.

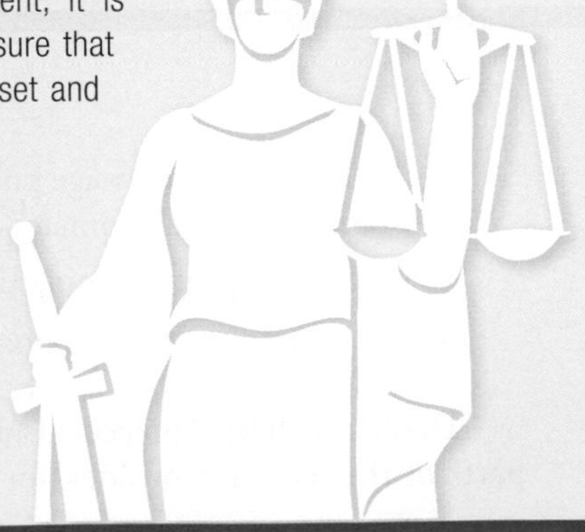

SOURCE: Bloom, B., Owen, B., & Covington, S. (2003). *Gender responsive strategies: Research, practice and guiding principles for women offenders.* Washington, DC: National Institute of Corrections.

system in the United States. An internal watchdog agency known as the **Little Hoover Commission** was tasked with providing recommendations to the state governor and legislature. This commission found that the correctional system was not operating well and that conditions were particularly bleak for female offenders (Vesely, 2004).

Guiding Principles to Improve Services for Female Offenders

The foremost principle in responding appropriately to women is to acknowledge the implications of gender throughout the criminal justice system. The criminal justice field has been dominated by the rule of parity, with equal treatment to be provided to everyone. However, this does not necessarily mean that the exact same treatment is appropriate for both women and men. The data are very clear concerning the distinguishing aspects of female and male offenders. They come into the criminal justice system via different pathways; respond to supervision and custody differently; exhibit differences in terms of substance abuse, trauma, mental illness, parenting responsibilities, and employment histories; and represent different levels of risk within both the institution and the community. To successfully develop and deliver services, supervision, and treatment for women offenders, we must first acknowledge these gender differences.

Research from a range of disciplines (e.g., health, mental health, and substance abuse) has shown that safety, respect, and dignity are fundamental to behavioral change. To improve behavioral outcomes for women, it is critical to provide a safe and supportive setting for supervision. A profile of women in most correctional facilities indicates that many have grown up in less than optimal family and community environments. In their interactions with women offenders, criminal justice professionals must be aware of the significant pattern of emotional, physical, and sexual abuse that many of these women have experienced. Every precaution must be taken to ensure that the criminal justice setting does not reenact female offenders' patterns of earlier life experiences.

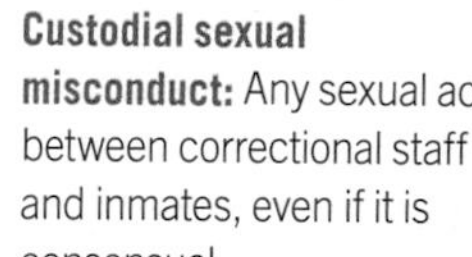

Custodial sexual misconduct: Any sexual act between correctional staff and inmates, even if it is consensual.

Little Hoover Commission: An internal state "watchdog" agency that was tasked with providing recommendations to the state governor and legislature in California.

Because of their lower levels of violent crime and their low risk to public safety, women offenders should, whenever possible, be supervised with the minimal restrictions required to meet public safety interests. Understanding the role of relationships in women's lives is fundamental because the theme of connections and relationships threads throughout the lives of female offenders. When an understanding of the role of relationships is incorporated into policies, practices, and programs, the effectiveness of the system or agency is enhanced. This concept is critical when addressing the following.

1. Reasons why women commit crimes.
2. Impact of interpersonal violence on women's lives.
3. Importance of children in the lives of female offenders.
4. Relationships between women in an institutional setting.
5. Process of women's psychological growth and development.
6. Environmental context needed for programming.
7. Challenges involved in reentering the community.

Attention to the above issues is crucial to the promotion of successful outcomes for women in the criminal justice system. Substance abuse, trauma, and mental health are three critical, interrelated issues in the lives of women offenders. These issues have a major impact on a woman's experience of community correctional supervision, incarceration,

Jim West imageBROKER/Newscom

■ PHOTO 10.5 A correctional officer maintains security over female inmates in a prison chow hall.

SAGE Journal Article Link
The Intersectional Alternative: Explaining Female Criminality

and transition to the community in terms of both programming needs and successful reentry. Although they are therapeutically linked, these issues historically have been treated separately. One of the most important developments in health care over the past several decades is the recognition that a substantial proportion of women have a history of serious traumatic experiences that play a vital and often unrecognized role in the evolution of their physical and mental health problems.

Further, it should be obvious that programs will have to address both the social and material realities of female offenders, just as is true with the male inmate population. This is an important aspect of correctional intervention, particularly at the point of reentry. The female offender's life is shaped by her socioeconomic status, her experience with trauma and substance abuse, and her relationships with partners, children, and family. Most female offenders are disadvantaged economically and socially, and this is compounded by their trauma and substance abuse histories. Improving outcomes for these women requires preparing them through education and training so they can support themselves and their children.

The Prison Rape Elimination Act of 2003 Revisited

Earlier in this text, discussion regarding the PREA was provided, particularly in regard to findings with male institutions. With this noted, it should be added that the PREA applies to all correctional facilities, including prisons, jails, juvenile facilities, military and Native American tribal facilities, and Immigration and Customs Enforcement (ICE) facilities. Due to the sensitive nature of violent victimization and potential reluctance to report sexual assault, estimates of the prevalence of such acts do not rely on a single measure. The act requires the Bureau of Justice Statistics (BJS) to carry out, for each calendar year, a comprehensive statistical review and analysis of the incidence and effects of prison rape. The act further specifies that the review and analysis shall be based on a random sample or other scientifically appropriate sample of not less than 10% of all prisons and a representative sample of municipal prisons. In 2014, more than 7,600 prisons, jails, community-based facilities, and juvenile correctional facilities nationwide were covered by the PREA. Among the findings of the 2014 data collection and analyses were the following:

1. Administrators of adult correctional facilities reported 8,763 allegations of sexual victimization in 2011, a statistically significant increase over the 8,404 allegations reported in 2010 and 7,855 in 2009.
2. The number of allegations has risen since 2005, largely due to increases in prisons, where allegations increased from 4,791 allegations to 6,660 in 2011 (up 39%).

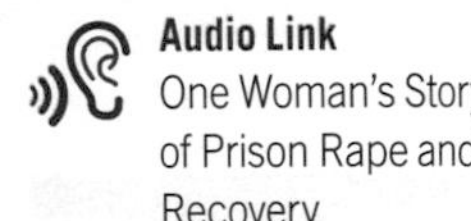

Audio Link
One Woman's Story of Prison Rape and Recovery

3. In 2011, 902 allegations of sexual victimization (10%) were substantiated (i.e., determined to have occurred upon investigation).
4. State prison administrators reported 537 substantiated incidents of sexual victimization in 2011, up 17% from 459 in 2005.
5. About 52% of substantiated incidents of sexual victimization in 2011 involved only inmates, while 48% of substantiated incidents involved staff with inmates.
6. Injuries were reported in about 18% of incidents of inmate-on-inmate sexual victimization and in less than 1% of incidents of staff sexual victimizations.
7. Females committed more than half of all substantiated incidents of staff sexual misconduct and a quarter of all incidents of staff sexual harassment.

Clearly, administrators must be concerned with issues related to sexual assault in prisons and jails. As can be seen from the results of the 2014 data, these assaults are completed by both women and men, and they are also completed by both inmates and staff, in nearly equal numbers. During the 1990s, significant attention was focused on female sexual abuse in custodial environments. Much of the reporting from groups such as Human Rights Watch and the news media, coupled with civil case litigation, led to the enactment of the PREA in 2003.

Since that time, the PREA has shed light on sexual misconduct in jails and prisons and, along the way, the dynamics have been found to be much more diverse than many practitioners may have expected. Much of the sexual assault on women behind bars is at the hands of custodial staff,

TECHNOLOGY AND EQUIPMENT 10.1

Evaluating the Use of Radio Frequency Identification Device Technology to Prevent and Investigate Sexual Assaults in a Correctional Setting

In recent years, the problem of sexual violence in correctional facilities has gained national prominence, largely due to the passage of the Prison Rape Elimination Act (PREA) of 2003 (Public Law 108-79, now codified as 45 U.S.C. 15601 to 15609). As stated in the act, sexual violence may present serious problems in correctional facilities, affecting not just the victims of violence but the correctional population as a whole. In response to the increased attention on this issue, correctional administrators have sought ways to harness new training methods, management tools, and technologies.

A key objective is to explore the use and effectiveness of one such measure: radio frequency identification device (RFID) technology, which enables correctional staff to track inmate locations in an effort to prevent prohibited acts, including sexual assault. The gravity of the consequences associated with custodial sexual abuse of females suggests that RFID technology designed to support prison management efforts to prevent sexual assaults, to effectively investigate them, and to increase inmates' perceptions of safety from sexual victimization would benefit the entire culture of a prison.

In correctional facilities, RFID transmitter chips can communicate the locations and movements of inmates within prison facilities to staff. The technology can be programmed to issue alerts when inmates are out of place, in prohibited locations, or in proximity to individuals with whom they have conflict. In addition, RFID historical records can be used to investigate allegations of inmate misconduct.

RFID technology enables users to authenticate, locate, and track objects or people tagged with a unique identifier (National Law Enforcement and Corrections Technology Center, 2005). In correctional settings, inmates can be fitted with RFID units on their ankles or wrists that enable correctional officers to track their locations and movements, potentially increasing the perceived risks of being detected when engaging in sexual assaults and other prohibited behaviors. RFID technology may deter inmates from committing prohibited acts by increasing their perceived risk of detection, especially when officers confirm inmates' perceptions by responding to RFID alerts and following through with disciplinary action. Similarly, it is feasible that RFID technology increases inmates' perceptions of safety from sexual assault based on the belief that perpetrators are more likely to be apprehended.

Because the system maintains historical data on inmates' locations, RFID technology may be a useful tool for investigating assaults, identifying which inmates were at the location where the assault took place, and aiding in the substantiation of allegations of sexual and other assaults. Thus, from a theoretical perspective, RFID technology should effectively increase an inmate's perceived risk of detection for both the perpetration of sexual assaults and the reporting of false allegations.

In 2006, the Urban Institute completed an assessment of RFID technology funded by the National Institute of Justice. The assessment investigated how RFID technology was being implemented in correctional settings across the country and found that 13 correctional facilities had implemented or were in the process of implementing RFID technology at that time. That study, however, simply identified likely evaluation sites, as evaluating the impact of RFID technology on prison management at these locations was beyond the scope of the contract. From a knowledge-building perspective, no published evaluations currently exist of RFID use as a correctional management tool, much less as a tool to prevent sexual and other violence. Correctional institutions across the country have expressed interest in obtaining RFID systems, but may be hesitant to expend scarce correctional resources in the absence of reliable evidence that the technology works.

SOURCE: La Vigne, N., Halberstadt, R., & Parthasarathy, B. (2009). *Evaluating the use of radio frequency identification device (RFID) technology to prevent and investigate sexual assaults in a correctional setting.* Washington, DC: Urban Institute. Reprinted by permission of the author, Nancy La Vigne.

though not necessarily forcible in nature (i.e., a staff member agreeing to assist a female inmate in obtaining free-world goods in exchange for sex), whereas most of the sexual assaults on men are inmate-on-inmate. However, in some cases, female correctional staff will become involved with male inmates, and there are instances where female staff have sexually exploited female inmates, though this is somewhat rare. Lastly, prisons do have to be alert to the fact that in male institutions, some male inmates are assaulted by male prison staff. Thus, the various circumstances associated with custodial sexual assault can be quite varied, but it is the female offender population that seems to be most targeted by corrupt prison staff.

FEMALE OFFENDERS AND TREATMENT IMPLICATIONS

In a study of 110 programs that deal with female offenders, it was found that programs conducive to treatment success of female offenders used female role models and paid particular attention to gender-specific concerns not common to male offenders (Bloom et al., 2003). Treatment for female offenders requires a heightened need to respond to expression of emotions and the ability to communicate openly with offenders.

Based on the research presented and the specific needs of female offenders, it is obvious treatment considerations for female offenders can be quite complicated. Indeed, it is plausible that a female offender could have the sundry challenges outlined in this chapter as well as numerous others included in other chapters of this text. Thus, many female offenders can be viewed as "special needs plus" when considering the myriad issues that may be present. With this in mind, specific recommendations regarding treatment programs for female offenders are outlined as follows:

1. Treatment plans must be individualized in structure, including:
   a. Clear and measurable goals.
   b. Intensive programming with effective duration.
   c. Appropriate screening and assessment.
2. Female offenders must be able to acquire needed life skills:
   a. Parenting and life skills are taught—these are both *critical.*
   b. Anger management must be addressed.
   c. Marketable job skills are important because female offenders typically have few job skills and, unlike male offenders, have more difficulty obtaining jobs in the manual labor sectors that pay higher (construction, plant work, etc.).
3. Must address victimization issues:
   a. Programs should address self-esteem, which is typically tied into previous abuse issues, which in turn increase likelihood of substance abuse and prostitution, two main segments of female crime.
   b. Programs must address domestic violence issues. These are highly common among female offenders. The violence may have come from the family of origin and/or from previous boyfriends and/or spouses; often this is intergenerationally transmitted.

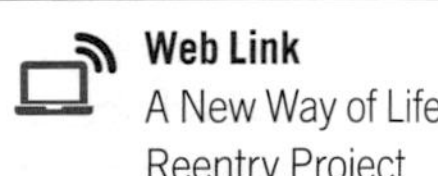

Web Link
A New Way of Life Reentry Project

Dolan, Kolthoff, Schreck, Smilanch, and Todd (2003) discuss the importance of having gender-specific treatment programs for correctional clients with co-occurring disorders. Their insights are important for a couple of key reasons that should be emphasized. First, it is becoming increasingly clear within the treatment literature that therapists and caseworkers and the curriculum that they use must be able to address diverse populations. Many individuals do not consider that women, the elderly, and the disabled should be part of most diversity programs, just like ethnic and racial groups. Correctional programs must deal with this issue. Second, it is important that co-occurring disorders be addressed by correctional systems in order to not only lower recidivism rates but also to improve the mental health and overall functioning of those offenders who return back to the community. Just because they may not commit more crime, they will still have issues with stress, depression, anxiety, trauma, and so forth that can impair their ability to successfully function in society.

In Iowa, the First Judicial District Department of Correctional Services established a community-based treatment program in its correctional facility (incidentally, this demonstrates how both correctional facilities and community supervision programs can successfully interface with one another). This program established a gender-specific female program to provide integration of treatment services designed to focus on dual diagnosis of female offenders. This is important since female offenders may be at heightened risk of having dual diagnoses given their frequent prior abuse trauma, maternal concerns for their children, and high rate of substance abuse.

The program addresses physical and sexual abuse issues, substance abuse, mental disorders, family based counseling, and parenting issues. It is founded on the notion that most of its clients have grown up in dysfunctional families so it is difficult for these clients to even conceive of how a functional family operates on a routine basis. This program specifically strives to include the children in the treatment process since it has been found that this increases likelihood of client program completion and aids in the client's recovery from various other issues. Thus, treatment is optimized because the offender's role as a parent is used as a therapeutic tool to enhance the relevance of the treatment to the client.

Specific issues pertaining to physical health care, adult sexuality, preventative pregnancy education, and education on sexually transmitted diseases are addressed within this program, as are feelings of grief/loss pertaining to the offender's role as a parent. A consortium of individuals and agencies are involved, including staff from the local Planned Parenthood, the local police force, community supervision, private therapists, and so forth. The topics covered by these individual providers are also discussed in the group therapy sessions to reinforce the learning process. Dolan et al. (2003) note that treatment for a woman with a dual diagnosis and a history of violence is optimized when it does the following:

■ PHOTO 10.6 These female deputies work at the Louisiana Transitional Center for Women (LTCW) in Tallulah, Louisiana. LTCW is a reentry facility for female offenders who are leaving prison and will be returning to the community. These officers are shown here at North Delta Regional Training Academy while taking correctional officer training to meet certification standards set by the state.

Robert Hanser

1. Focuses on the woman's strengths.
2. Acknowledges the woman's role as a parent.
3. Improves interactions between the parent and child.
4. Provides comprehensive, coordinated services for the mother and her children.

The Iowa program is an excellent example of how most programs for female offenders should be structured because it is comprehensive and demonstrates how the multitude of issues pertinent to female offenders can be addressed within a single facility while utilizing a wide array of services within the community. This program falls well within the theme of this text, demonstrating how community resources and public and private agencies can combine to address complicated social ills with cost-effective methods. Because of this, it is suggested that other areas of the nation should look to this program when designing treatments for their female offender populations.

CONCLUSION

While female offenders are a small proportion of the offending population, they are a rapidly growing group, and it is increasingly clear that institutional and community intervention programs are inadequately serving these offenders. There is a need to address specific social ills that are fairly unique to female offenders, such as domestic violence, sexual abuse, drug use, prostitution, sexually transmitted diseases, and child custody issues. Many of the problems associated with female offenders have hidden costs that affect the rest of society in a multifaceted manner. Any failure to improve services to this offending population will simply ensure that future generations likewise adopt criminogenic patterns of social coping. This is specifically the case given the "collateral damage" that emanates from the impairment of children whose mothers (and likely sole caretakers) are incarcerated. When thinking long term, it becomes both socially and economically sound practice to work to improve services and ensure that accommodations are made for the special needs of the female offender.

Numerous legal considerations emerge with female inmates. These legal issues can range from the provision of services to pregnancy issues behind bars. The potential for staff misconduct is also a serious problem that resulted in a number of scandals during the 1990s. In addition, liability issues can emerge when employees conduct functions (such as strip searches and pat searches) where cross-gender interactions take place. Agency administrators must be sure to have clear and specific policies in place and see their staff are appropriately trained in supervising female inmates.

In order to prepare female inmates for reentry and to make their time in prison more constructive, agencies should follow several key guiding principles. First, agencies must recognize that gender does indeed matter, and agencies should provide an environment that fosters safety, respect, and dignity for women behind bars. Agencies should also develop policies and practices that are relational in nature and that promote good relationships with children, family, significant others, and the community. Agencies must address substance abuse, trauma, and mental health issues in a manner that is culturally competent. In addition, as with male inmates, agencies should provide female inmates with job and life skills that will allow them to change their socioeconomic circumstances. Lastly, effective and collaborative reentry processes must be utilized if agencies wish to realistically lower the likelihood of recidivism for female offenders.

Want a better grade?

Get the tools you need to sharpen your study skills. Access practice quizzes, eFlashcards, video, and multimedia at **edge.sagepub.com/hanser2e**

SAGE edge™

DISCUSSION QUESTIONS

1. What are some of the demographic and statistical characteristics of the female offender population?
2. Compare and contrast the rates of incarceration and the terms of sentencing for male and female offenders.
3. Who was Elizabeth Fry? What did she do to assist female offenders, and why was this unique during her time in history?
4. What is patriarchy? How might this concept be associated with the dynamics of women who are incarcerated?
5. How does feminist criminology help to explain criminal behavior among women?
6. Which states are the most punitive for female offenders? Why (based on your prior readings) might this be the case?
7. What have been some common legal problems associated with female offenders in the correctional facility? What has been done in corrections to address these issues?
8. Identify and discuss at least three guiding principles associated with effective correctional operations when considering female offenders.
9. Discuss the various treatment considerations related to female offenders.

SAGE edge™ **Test your understanding of chapter content. Take the practice quiz.**

KEY TERMS

Chivalry hypothesis, 233
Collateral damage, 244
Custodial sexual misconduct, 246
Domestic violence, 240
Little Hoover Commission, 247
Patriarchy, 238
Reformatories for women, 236
Victorian Era, 233

SAGE edge™ **Review key terms with eFlashcards.**

APPLIED EXERCISE 10.1

For this exercise, students should consider how professionalism in correctional officer training has gained support during the past couple of decades. This trend was discussed in the previous chapter (Chapter 9), and students were required to develop a training program on workforce diversity in Applied Exercise 9.1. While that training program was to be comprehensive and address multiple facets of diversity, such programs cannot always go into the depth required when facilities are designed to meet the specific needs of a singly identified group, such as female offenders.

Consider your assignment in Applied Exercise 9.1. With that in mind, you are again asked to assume the role of the assistant warden who was tasked with developing the diversity training program. You have done so, as your warden requested, and the program has been highly successful in reducing grievances based on racial differences. In addition, the overall sense of professionalism possessed by officers in your facility has improved. In fact, your warden made a point to praise your work, even letting the regional director know about your program and the positive impact that it has had on your facility.

It appears that you have done very well indeed. The regional director ultimately created a region-wide position, the director of the new Office of Diversity and Specialized Needs. You were given this new job along with a pay raise. In short, you have been promoted. However, with every promotion comes added responsibilities and duties. Your case is no different. The regional director has asked that you go to the state's largest female prison, which is located in a remote area. He would like you to accomplish two tasks.

First, develop a training program for officers that is 1.5 days in length and addresses ***gender-specific*** considerations in security, safety, and human services. You will need to develop an outline of the content as well as an explanation for that content. This training will be implemented within the facility during the next fiscal year, when budgeting allows for additional training.

Second, you are to write a brief memo that outlines the top five issues that you believe are important to meeting the special needs of female offenders in your facility. One of these concerns might be the remote location of the current facility, away from friends and family who can visit.

For this assignment, students should create a brief outline of the training session on gender-specific issues in security, safety, and human services. This aspect of the assignment will require anywhere from 250 to 750 words. In addition, the memo, addressed to the regional director of state prison operations, should be approximately 500 to 750 words in length. A brief listing of the five recommendations and the reasons for those recommendations should be included.

WHAT WOULD YOU DO?

You are a correctional officer in a minimum-security facility that houses female inmates. While on your shift you are required to do a "shakedown" of the various inmates' living quarters throughout the day. You are given a list of inmates whose property you are to search. One of these inmates is Lorianna Marisol Vasquez. Her cubicle is ready to be searched, and she is standing close by in case you need to talk with her while conducting the search.

While searching the cubicle, you find a letter that Vasquez has written, which appears to be addressed to one of the male guards at the facility who works the evening shift (you work the day shift). The letter explains that Vasquez is in need of several hygiene products and also desires some cigarettes and sundry food products. Further, the letter seems to imply that Vasquez will make it well worth the officer's time to obtain these items. However, the letter is written in a vague and comical manner, as if the entire idea were just a game or for sport, rather than being a serious proposition. In addition, you cannot tell from the letter if this has been an ongoing arrangement or if this would be the initial proposition. You look, but find no letters from the officer to Vasquez. However, you have heard rumors that this officer frequently talks with Vasquez for extended periods of time, and you have even detected a degree of jealousy among the other female inmates in the dorm. As it turns out, this officer is a good-looking fellow, and he is fond of being excessively polite to the women on the dorm. It makes you wonder if there is in fact something going on between Vasquez and this officer.

What would you do?

SPECIALIZED INMATE POPULATIONS

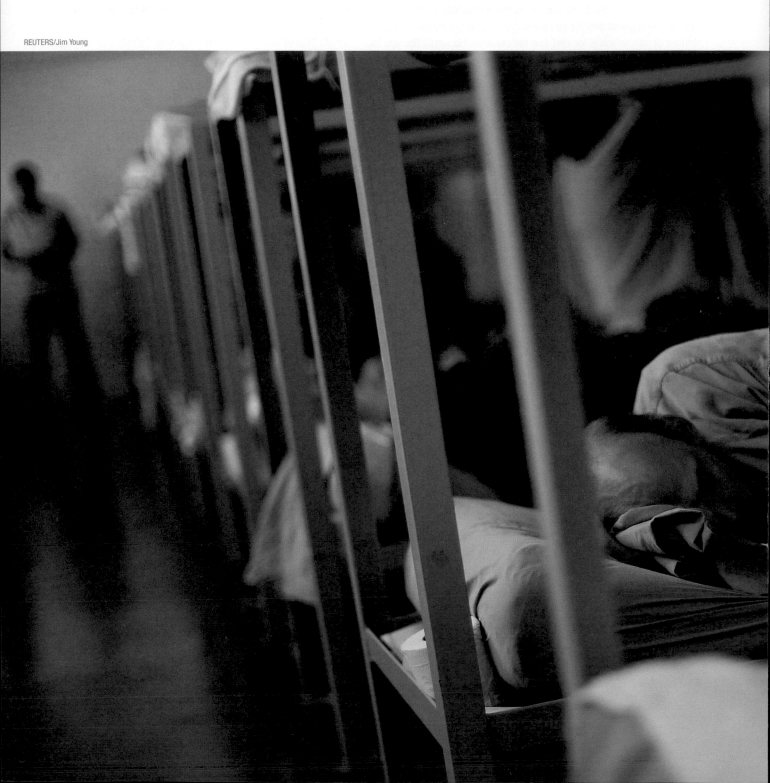

REUTERS/Jim Young

NAE-NAE, A TRANSSEXUAL BEHIND BARS

Nate, known as "Nae-Nae" by the other inmates on the dorm, sat on his bunk and thought about the situation. It was not an easy decision to make, and he was so close to possibly being granted early release.

Nate was a preoperative transsexual, with the secondary characteristics of a female (breasts and cosmetic facial alterations), serving a 4-year sentence on a drug charge. In the "free world," he had been an active advocate for gay, lesbian, and transsexual rights. He was open about his orientation, had a good job in graphic design, and had been in a committed relationship for years. He had taken hormones and completed some cosmetic surgery with the intention of ultimately completely changing his sex.

Nate's job eventually required that he relocate to another state, one that was more socially conservative, but the position was a promotion to management. His partner, Karl, had supported the move. Karl was in grad school and between jobs, so it seemed like a perfect time for them both to move as Karl was expected to complete his degree in less than 3 months. Nate would move to the new location and get settled in, and Karl would wrap up everything at their (then) current residence and follow Nate to the new location with degree in hand.

Nate made the move and all seemed well . . . at first. Then he received word that Karl would not be joining him; Karl had been seeing someone else, and it was for this reason that he had been so supportive of Nate taking the job out of state.

As expected, Nate found his new location was not nearly as progressive as his old one. The new job was okay, but the managerial challenges required that he alter his mind-set. Also, he was emotionally down over losing Karl and being alone. This resulted in his relapse on alcohol and pain killers; the numbing effect helped him to cope with the changes, so he thought.

When Nate was first booked, he had to complete a strip search. He remembered how the jailers treated him during the process. They were degrading—one in particular made issue of a tattoo that Nate had on the small of his back. The jailer said, "Hey everyone, look at the tramp stamp that this queenie has on her back!" He pointed at a four-leaf clover with the words "Get Lucky" in a semi-circle above the shamrock design.

From that point onward, the deputies would tease him, usually within earshot of other inmates, asking him if he would show them his tramp stamp or asking if anyone in the dorm had "got lucky" recently.

Nate had typically gone by the name "Natalie" on the outside when involved with Karl, but he was given the nickname "Nae-Nae" by the other inmates inside the institution.

Now, 3 years after his arrest, he was involved with a man named Reggie who was doing time on the same dorm. Reggie was scheduled to be released in 2 days and, of course, would not be seeing Nae-Nae on a daily basis once released. When news of Reggie's parole spread, another man named Jerome stepped forward and announced to everyone, "I claim Nae-Nae as my punk."

LEARNING OBJECTIVES:

1. Discuss some of the common administrative considerations facing prison systems when housing specialized inmate populations.
2. Explain how the prison subculture impacts, interacts with, and reacts to inmates who are mentally ill, have HIV/AIDS, and/or are elderly.
3. Discuss the prevalence of mental illness within state prison systems and the difficulties of care and treatment.
4. Describe the difficulties with sex offender management in prisons.
5. Summarize the various challenges facing prison systems housing inmates who have HIV/AIDS.
6. Identify the various classifications of elderly inmates within an institution.
7. Identify some of the challenges and issues that correctional agencies face when housing elderly offenders.

SAGE edge™

Get the edge on your studies:
edge.sagepub.com/hanser2e

- Take a quiz to find out what you've learned.
- Review key terms with eFlashcards.
- Watch videos that enhance chapter content.

Jerome was a huge, strong man who had a prior history of sexual assault. He was currently doing time for armed robbery and was not usually questioned on the dorm. Nobody challenged his claim, and Reggie was not on the dorm at the time.

When Nate told Reggie about the situation, Reggie said, "Look, you know I've done what I can to keep you protected, but you know how it is. . . . Once our time is up, we gotta put this behind us. I can talk with him, but really, you are just gonna have to do what you got to do to survive."

Whether Nate, Natalie, or Nae-Nae, one thing was a common denominator: things looked bleak. Jerome would likely be abusive, and there was no way that Nate would be able to fight the man or prevent the upcoming sexual abuse. He contemplated talking to staff. He only had a few more months to do and figured it would be his safest bet. He did not have to worry about losing honor by being a snitch—as a punk, he had no respect on the dorm anyway. However, he did not like the idea of living in a restrictive protective custody cell during the last few months. Plus, there might be retribution if he talked to authorities. He was also concerned as to whether prison staff would seriously consider his concerns and requests. Nate sighed. Time was short, and he had to make a decision of some sort.

INTRODUCTION

As we saw in Chapter 8, any modern correctional program relies on being able to reliably and validly classify and determine the needs of offenders. This classification ensures that a facility is able to match treatments and inmates in a manner that optimizes the outcome of the program. From a legal and historical context, the concept of *needs* has been pivotal in designing responses to different types of offenders (juvenile offenders, mentally challenged offenders, etc.). However, when we use the term *need*, this implies that the issue involves something that is absolutely necessary, not something that is a mere desire or preference. Thus, if the individual does not have this need met, he or she will experience some form of serious social, psychological, physical, or emotional impairment in his or her daily functioning. Because correctional institutions are liable for legally defensible standards of care for inmates in their custody, they must be prepared to address specialized needs that may emerge among their prison populations.

For purposes of this text, the term **offender with special needs** refers to specialized offenders who have some notable physical, mental, and/or emotional challenge. These challenges prevent either a subjective or an objective need from being fulfilled for that individual, and the lack of this need impairs the individual's day-to-day ability to function within the confines of the criminal law.

ADMINISTRATIVE CONSIDERATIONS

During the first few hours of being received, an inmate should be given a medical screening or examination. While a full examination is the most effective approach, this may not always be practical. However, screenings can be easily conducted, even when large groups of inmates are being processed into the system simultaneously. The medical screening process is basically a preliminary triage to sort out serious issues from those that are likely to be more routine among other inmates on a cell block or within a dormitory. Likewise, this process can be used to identify medical issues that require immediate attention, thereby alerting staff to the need for a full examination and for additional medical service. During this process, mental health professionals should be available to assist inmates with issues that, while medical in nature, may impact an offender's state of mind.

Offender with special needs: A specialized offender who has some notable physical, mental, and/or emotional challenge

Prison Tour Video: Specialized Populations. Offenders with special needs provide unique challenges for correctional practitioners. Watch a clip about services provided for specialized populations.

Access to Program Activities and Availability

Access to specific programs, such as education, addiction treatment, and vocational training, can result in increased satisfaction and improved health while in the prison. Further, participation in these programs can increase the offender's likelihood of receiving early discharge through good-time accumulation and can improve the prognosis of the offender's later integration into the community. Because of these factors, implementing the Americans with Disabilities Act (ADA) requirements may be prudent for correctional administrators for reasons beyond just the legal liabilities involved. Such incorporation may also serve to improve the plight of corrections in the future if these problems are addressed in a proactive manner. As Appel (1999) notes, the ADA is the law, and compliance with the ADA is a classic case of "pay me now or pay me even more later." Thus, the long-term benefits for the wise correctional administrator will likely offset any of the short-term costs paid in the meantime.

Separate Care or Inclusion in General Population

Once the agency has identified special needs offenders, the next important step is to determine specifically how these offenders will be addressed. One primary question is whether these offenders should be kept in contact with the mainstream population of inmates or be segregated. This is an important issue because the welfare of the inmate is at stake, and, as we have seen in Chapter 3 and will see in Corrections and the Law 11.1, the agency can be held liable for failing to protect inmates from assault or abuse, even when this occurs at the hands of another inmate. Other reasons often given for separating special needs inmates from the general population are as follows:

1. Cost containment: It is generally more efficient and cost-effective if special needs offenders are kept in the same location (both the same facility and the same housing area in that facility), where they can be treated as a group.
2. Managed care: More effective care can be focused on a specialized unit where specifically trained staff can strategically target their skills to populations most in need.
3. Concentration of resources: Relevant staff and resources can be more concentrated if special needs inmates are housed in one central location.

Mainstreaming, or the integration of an inmate with a disability into the general prison population, is a general expectation of the ADA, and this is because it is expected that disabled inmates will be provided full and complete access to prison programs, activities, and services. However, the ADA does allow correctional administrators to remove an inmate from the general population if his or her health condition is a threat to other inmates or if an inmate is at risk of victimization from other inmates due to his or her impairment. What typically occurs is a mix of both separation and inclusion within prison facilities, where, depending on the pertinent circumstances, some inmates are handled separately and apart from the main population while others remain in the general population.

Special Facilities and Housing Accommodations

Many special needs offenders need housing designed to accommodate their specific circumstances. Inmates who are mentally ill or who have cognitive deficits may need to be placed in specialized facilities. When considering facility and/or housing accommodations, both physical plant conditions and safety should be considered. It is often the physical plant issues that most concern correctional administrators because they have the potential for exceeding the capacity of already tight budgets. Although the overall spending for corrections has risen along with the increase in inmates throughout the nation, even these larger budgets do not cover the specialized facilities and services required by the elderly and/or disabled. The main problems are with costs of renovating existing facilities; often building a new facility with all of the features required by the ADA is cheaper than modifying an older building. The special equipment and physical modifications needed to bring existing facilities into compliance can result in tight operating budgets being stretched beyond their limits.

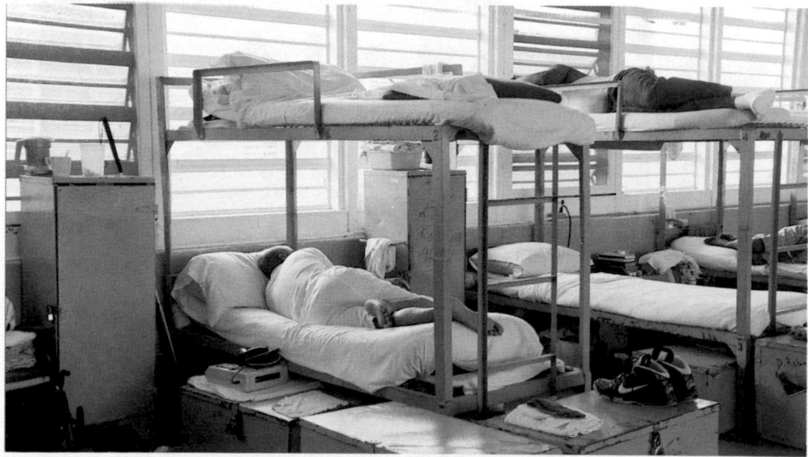

Prison Tour Video: Housing for Specialized Populations. Correctional practitioners have to carefully consider housing for inmates with special needs. Watch a correctional officer discuss housing for specialized populations.

Special Facilities and Support

When considering facilities and physical support for special needs inmates, agencies should use a concept that Anderson (2008) calls universal design. **Universal design** refers to prison construction design that complies with ADA requirements and accommodates all inmate needs in a universal fashion, regardless of how varied the needs may be from inmate to inmate. This type of design is ideal for agencies that wish to ensure that future construction efforts meet ADA and other standards of care.

This approach to prison facility construction and to implementing support services within future buildings will likely be the upcoming trend for prison systems. Examples of universal design features might be wider doors, ramps rather than stairs, and heavier building materials that allow safety bars or railings to be added to the construction in later years, if needed (Anderson, 2008). The key issue is that this type of design planning allows for the accommodation of additional needs among the population housed. "While universal design is initially more expensive, it costs less over time as modifications are easier and not as expensive to implement" (Anderson, 2008, p. 364).

PRISON SUBCULTURE AND SPECIAL NEEDS OFFENDERS

In Chapter 9, extensive discussion was given to the prison subculture. This subculture idealizes certain standards of behavior, but, as noted, these norms are in a state of flux due to the emergence of gang life inside and outside of the prison. There are two major points of concern related to the prison subculture and special needs offenders. The first concern has to do with inmate reactions to the increasing representation of special needs inmates within prison facilities. Second, concerns regarding agency staff and their understanding of the issues associated with special needs offenders are important from the perspective of inmate welfare as well as agency liability.

With regard to the inmate population, serious attention should be given to special needs offenders because they are likely to be very vulnerable to exploitation by other inmates. This is true both for elderly offenders, who physically are weaker and may also not be as mentally adept as they were in younger years, and for inmates with a variety of mental health conditions, such as anxiety-based disorders and affective disorders. These inmates are vulnerable to manipulation and are also likely to be victimized by predatory inmates due to their sense of fear (with anxiety-related disorders) or their sense of self-neglect (with affective disorders). Those with serious psychiatric disorders are likely to be taunted, ridiculed, and generally worked into heightened emotional states by other, more stable inmates who may find their reactions amusing or entertaining. Inmates with cognitive impairments are likely to have their property stolen by other inmates, and they are likely to be duped by wiser cons who act as if they wish to befriend them. Sex offenders and inmates with alternative sex identities and/or preferences are likely to be sexually and physically victimized by other inmates.

Universal design: Prison construction design that complies with ADA requirements and that accommodates all inmate needs in a universal fashion.

Greyhounds: Older inmates who have acquired respect within the offender subculture due to their track record, criminal history, and criminogenic ideals.

As we have seen, respect within the prison subculture is very important. It should be clear to students that special needs inmates would command no respect within the prison environment. In fact, it is likely that regular inmates would be considered weak or soft if they were to associate too closely with special needs inmates, and if those special needs inmates were sex offenders or homosexual offenders, an inmate who associated with them would likely be ostracized completely from the main inmate power structure. Even with the gang culture that has emerged as a primary shaping mechanism for prison culture, these various types of offenders are not likely to gain respect, with one exception: the elderly inmate.

AP Photo/Steve Pope

■ PHOTO 11.1 Inmates participate in a group therapy session as part of a substance abuse program in the Iowa Correctional Institution for Women. Many correction institutions now offer programs to address substance abuse, mental health issues, and even family issues.

The elderly inmate who has lived by the convict code or is a veteran member of a gang is likely to have status among his peers. These inmates, for this text's purposes, will be referred to as greyhounds. **Greyhounds** are older inmates who have acquired respect within the offender subculture due to their track record and criminal history both inside and outside the prison; they are career criminals who have earned status through years of hard-won adherence to prison and criminogenic ideals. These inmates are hardly ever likely to be victims within the inmate subculture, and, if they were burned in the past, they generally were able to "even the score" with those who committed a wrong against them. In short, greyhounds are not seen as weak throughout their life of crime or while serving prison time.

Another concern when dealing with special needs inmates is the training and knowledge of correctional staff. Some staff may not understand mental illness and may be ill equipped to deal with inmates who present with odd or maladaptive behaviors. These inmates may have difficulty following institutional rules and may become a source of frustration for security staff. Thus, training is important for staff who will routinely deal with these types of inmates. In addition, in facilities designed for specialized inmates, security staff should be especially well trained in communication techniques, problem-solving approaches, the identification of many mental health illnesses, the best ways to address problematic or challenging inmate populations, sexual issues, communicable diseases, suicidal inmates, and so forth. As one can tell from this long list of criteria, the staff dealing with these populations should be highly specialized.

Lastly, the officer subculture must definitely be professionalized among those who routinely work with various types of special needs inmates. In many cases, correctional officers see themselves as working in a helping capacity as much as a security capacity. However, this may be quite a stretch in job definition for some security staff, particularly those who see their role as more punitive in nature. These offenders are convicted felons and not likely to elicit the sympathy of many correctional staff. This is particularly true for the sex-offending population. The training of correctional officers and organizational change implemented by leadership within correctional agencies is perhaps the best prescription for addressing staff obligations to special needs offenders.

MENTALLY ILL OFFENDERS

Mentally ill inmates are those who have a diagnosable disorder that meets the specific and exact criteria of the ***Diagnostic and Statistical Manual of Mental Disorders* (DSM-5)**. This reference tome was formed by gatherings of psychiatrists and psychologists from around the world and sets forth the guidelines in applying a specific diagnosis to a person presenting with a mental

***Diagnostic and Statistical Manual of Mental Disorders* (DSM-5):** A reference manual that sets forth the guidelines in applying a diagnosis of a mental disorder.

Table 11.1: Recent Symptoms and History of Mental Health Problems Among Prison and Jail Inmates

	Percentage of Inmates in ____		
Mental Health Problem	State Prison	Federal Prison	Local Jail
Any mental health problem	56.2%	44.8%	64.2%
Recent history of mental health problem[a]	24.3%	13.8%	20.6%
Told had disorder by mental health professional	9.4	5.4	10.9
Had overnight hospital stay	5.4	2.1	4.9
Used prescribed medications	18.0	10.3	14.4
Had professional mental health therapy	15.1	8.3	10.3
Symptoms of mental health disorders[b]	49.2%	39.8%	60.5%
Major depressive disorder	23.5	16.0	29.7
Mania disorder	43.2	35.1	54.5
Psychotic disorder	15.4	10.2	23.9

SOURCE: James, D. J., & Glaze, L. E. (2006). *Mental health problems of prison and jail inmates.* Washington, DC: Bureau of Justice Statistics.

NOTE: Includes inmates who reported an impairment due to a mental problem. Data are based on the Survey of Inmates in States and Federal Correctional Facilities, 2004, and the Survey of Inmates in Local Jails, 2002. See *Methodology* for details on survey sample.

[a]In year before arrest or since admission. [b]In the 11 months prior to the interview.

CORRECTIONS AND THE LAW 11.1

The Case of Ruiz v. Estelle *and Mental Illness in Prison Environments*

In 1972, David Ruiz sued the director of the Texas Department of Criminal Justice (William J. Estelle) over dangerous and inhumane working and living conditions. This was a long, embattled suit that ended in 1982 with a final consent decree that the Texas prison system was required to obey. In this class action suit, it was held that the Texas prison system constituted "cruel and unusual punishment," which is prohibited by the Eighth Amendment to the U.S. Constitution. Some of the specific problems noted in this case are as follows:

1. Overcrowding—the prison system had been placing two or three inmates within a single cell designed for only one inmate.
2. Inadequate security—the prison system utilized a system of security that incorporated selected inmates as guards. This practice led to numerous injustices and civil rights violations.
3. Inadequate health care—the prison system did not have an adequate number of medical personnel and also used the services of nonprofessional personnel (including inmate "surgeons" and "orderlies") to deliver medical care. Likewise, the therapy for psychiatric patients was deficient.
4. Unsafe working conditions—unsafe conditions and procedures were the norm for inmate laborers.

Ultimately, all of these complaints were rectified within the Texas prison system. However, this case made even more stipulations that affected the future of all mentally ill and mentally challenged inmates in Texas and throughout the entire nation. For example, the Court further ruled that it was cruel and unusual punishment to confine mentally ill inmates in solitary confinement. In response to this ruling, the prison administration in Texas developed the Administrative Segregation Maintenance Psychiatric Program. This program provides intensive counseling to inmates with serious mental illness in need of high-security housing and helps them transition back to the general prison population. Correction officials also increased mental health training for security staff and established oversight through regular on-site audits by various outside review bodies.

SOURCE: *Ruiz v. Estelle*, 503 F. Supp. 1165 (SD Tex. 1980), in Out of State Models.

disorder. For the purposes of this chapter, **mental illness** will be defined as any diagnosed disorder contained within the DSM-5, as published by the American Psychiatric Association. Mental illness causes severe disturbances in thought, emotions, and ability to cope with the demands of daily life. Mental illness, like physiological forms of illness, can be acute, chronic, or under control and in remission.

Audio Link
Mentally Ill Are Often Locked Up in Jails That Can't Help

In 2005, nearly 776,000 prison inmates were identified as possessing some type of mental health problem, according to James and Glaze (2006). This number included over 705,000 in state prison systems as well as another 70,000+ inmates in the Federal Bureau of Prisons. When added to another 479,900 inmates in local jails who were also found to have an identified mental health problem, the total count of incarcerated persons in the nation with a mental health issue in 2005 was over 1,255,000. These figures mean that during that year, approximately 56% of state inmates and 45% of federal inmates had some type of mental health issue, along with another 64% of all jail inmates (see Table 11.1 for an illustration of these data). And with the current trend toward increased sentence length, it is clear that this number will continue to rise. In addition, the proportion of inmates needing mental health assistance will also increase as the correctional population continues to age behind bars.

The burden placed on institutional corrections is compounded by the significant number of inmates who have a dual diagnosis of both mental illness and substance abuse. This burden is further exacerbated by the severe financial constraints that states have experienced. Indeed, it is estimated that funding across all 50 states was reduced by at least $3.5 billion between 2009 and 2012. Indeed, four-fifths of all states participating in an annual survey reported budget reductions to program activities despite increasing numbers of inmates presenting with mental health and substance abuse problems (Osher, D'Amora, Plotkin, Jarrett, & Eggleston, 2012).

Mental illness: Any diagnosed disorder contained within the DSM-5.

Further still, numerous inmates have only marginal levels of mental health problems but find these problems worsened by the conditions of incarceration, which causes them to deteriorate to a more severe state of mental illness. Due to this progressive deterioration, inmates with behavioral health needs tend to require additional resources because they are more likely to be involved in circumstances that require extra correctional management assistance (Osher et al., 2012). For example, in the Iowa Department of Corrections, it has been estimated that approximately 76% of all violent acts, suicide attempts, illnesses, and injuries involve inmates with a mental health problem (Osher et al., 2012, p. 8). Because of this, it is absolutely essential that facilities screen for mental health problems at intake, and it is necessary to identify any inmate who may be at risk of suicide. This is important for the welfare of the offender but is also a necessity to evade liability.

Getty Images Photographer Stephen Ferry

■ PHOTO 11.2 Medications are routinely given to offenders who have mental health and cognitive impairments in prison. Sometimes, due to security issues for dangerous inmates, this is done through the cell bars, as pictured here.

Access to Care: The Four Standards of Mental Health Care

Correctional facility administrators are legally required to implement an adequate health care delivery system that ensures inmate access to health care and health care providers (Johnson, 1999). This legal requirement also extends to mental health care (Hanser, 2002). A care delivery system for mental health services in a correctional facility must address a range of specialized needs. In the Supreme Court case of *Ruiz v. Estelle* (1975), the Court set several requirements for meeting minimally adequate standards for mental health care in a correctional environment. The following requirements articulated by the *Ruiz* Court are pertinent to this chapter:

1. Correctional administrators must provide an adequate system to ensure mental health screening for inmates.
2. Correctional facilities must provide access to mental health treatment while inmates are in segregation or special housing units.
3. Correctional facilities must adequately monitor the appropriate use of psychotropic medication.
4. A suicide prevention program must be implemented.

These **four standards of mental health care** are common to all jail and prison systems in the United States. The case of *Ruiz v. Estelle* was instrumental in laying much of the groundwork for correctional responsibilities to provide adequate mental health care. Other cases soon followed that clarified various fine points of law regarding liability issues, involuntary confinement, and so forth, but these four standards are generally considered to have evolved from the decisions in *Ruiz*.

Screening, Treatment, and Medication

Mental health care services begin at the point of screening. As discussed earlier in this chapter, this is a form of triage that is designed to sort out less serious mental health issues from those that require genuine psychiatric care. Given the volume of inmates entering the correctional environment and the fact that the presentation of these individuals is often unplanned, it is important to have a good initial mental health screening system in place. The primary goal of screening is to quickly identify emergency situations and inmates who might require more extensive intervention prior to placement in the prison population (Johnson, 1999). Further, proper mental health intake screening will determine the type and immediacy of mental health needs. The need for appropriate screening and identification of problem issues is important for both mental health and substance abuse issues. In fact, the two are very difficult to separate. When offenders abuse drugs, many of the drugs elicit

Four standards of mental health care: Legal requirement for adequate health care also extends to mental health care.

symptoms of depression, mania, anxiety, and/or other characteristics that become full-blown diagnosable disorders. These mental disorders that occur in tandem with drug use are referred to as co-occurring disorders.

From the data provided in Table 11.2, it can be seen that in 2006 a full 61% of prison inmates who had a current or past violent offense had some sort of mental health problem. In addition, 74% of these same inmates had some sort of substance dependence or abuse in their histories (see Table 11.3). The statistics among jail inmates were similar in that around three-fourths of all jail inmates who had a mental health problem also had a substance abuse problem. These numbers are even more disturbing when one notes that even among prison inmates who did not have a mental health issue, half reported drug use in the month right before arrest, and 42% of jail inmates without a mental disorder also reported the use of substances during the month before arrest.

What these statistics mean is that the vast majority of inmates, whether in prison or in jail, are drug abusers. These statistics also demonstrate that these drug abusers are at an increased likelihood of having mental health problems while in prison. Thus, modern prison and jail systems should all have some sort of effective drug treatment component to mitigate the symptoms of inmates while they serve time behind bars. It behooves correctional agencies to provide these services since this may lower the number of institutional infractions among inmates.

Beyond Screening: Mental Health Assessment

Inmates requiring further assessment should be housed in an area with staff availability and observation appropriate to their needs. The assessment should be assigned to a specific mental health staff member and consist of interviews, a review of prior records and clinical history, a physical examination, observation, and, when necessary, psychological testing. The types of services needed to address these problems are similar throughout each phase of the correctional system's process

■ Table 11.2: Prevalence of Mental Health Issues Among Prison and Jail Inmates in the United States

	Percentage of Inmates in ____			
	State Prison		Local Jail	
Selected Characteristics	With Mental Problem	Without	With Mental Problem	Without
Criminal record				
Current or past violent offense	61%	56%	44%	36%
Three or more prior incarcerations	25	19	26	20
Substance dependence or abuse	74%	56%	76%	53%
Drug use in month before arrest	63%	49%	62%	42%
Family background				
Homelessness in year before arrest	13%	6%	17%	9%
Past physical or sexual abuse	27	10	24	8
Parents abused alcohol or drugs	39	25	37	19
Charged with violating facility rules*	58%	43%	19%	9%
Physical or verbal assault	24	14	8	2
Injured in a fight since admission	20%	10%	9%	3%

SOURCE: James, D. J., & Glaze, L. E. (2006). *Mental health problems of prison and jail inmates.* Washington, DC: Bureau of Justice Statistics.

*Includes items not shown.

■ Table 11.3: Substance Dependence or Abuse Among Prison and Jail Inmates, by Mental Health Status

	Percentage of Inmates in ____					
	State Prison		Federal Prison		Local Jail	
Substance Dependence or Abuse	With Mental Problem	Without	With Mental Problem	Without	With Mental Problem	Without
Any alcohol or drugs	74.1%	55.6%	63.6%	49.5%	76.4%	53.2%
Dependence	53.9	34.5	45.1	27.3	56.3	25.4
Abuse only	20.2	21.1	18.5	22.2	20.1	27.8
Alcohol	50.8%	36.0%	43.7%	30.3%	53.4%	34.6%
Dependence	30.4	17.9	25.1	11.7	29.0	11.8
Abuse only	20.4	18.0	18.6	17.7	24.4	22.8
Drugs	61.9%	42.6%	53.2%	39.2%	63.3%	36.0%
Dependence	43.8	26.1	37.1	22.0	46.0	17.6
Abuse only	18.0	16.5	16.1	17.2	17.3	18.4
No dependence or abuse	25.9%	44.4%	36.4%	50.5%	23.6%	46.8%

SOURCE: James, D. J., & Glaze, L. E. (2006). *Mental health problems of prison and jail inmates.* Washington, DC: Bureau of Justice Statistics.

NOTE: Substance dependence or abuse was based on criteria specified in the *Diagnostic and Statistical Manual of Mental Disorder* (4th ed.) *(DSM-IV)*. For details, see *Substance dependence, abuse and treatment of jail inmates, 2002.*

(e.g., jail detention, imprisonment, community supervision). As noted earlier, offenders may enter the system with a certain degree of mental illness that is further aggravated by imprisonment, or they may present new symptomology once incarcerated (Johnson, 1999).

The stress of being involved in the criminal justice process can itself serve as a causal factor for some mental illness. Stressors might include navigating the legal system, separation from community and/or family support systems, and interactional problems with other offenders within the correctional facility. If mental illness is already present, offenders are often subject to victimization from the remainder of the inmate population (Hanser & Mire, 2010). In fact, those who present with mental illness (particularly along the spectrum of **mood disorders** and/or anxiety disorders) are at an inflated risk of sexual assault within the prison environment (Hanser & Mire, 2010). Further, several documented cases link this victimization with later suicidal ideation and completion among the inmate population (Hanser & Mire, 2010).

Problems with sleeping and eating may be experienced due to limited access to anxiety-reducing activities such as television, exercise, socialization, and smoking (Hanser & Mire, 2010). All of this is compounded by a lack of control over one's environment and the diminished sense of autonomy that is experienced. Thus, inmates arriving at the correctional facility must be closely watched and screened upon initial entry and during their first 90 to 180 days so that their integration into the institution can be appropriately monitored.

The correctional institution has an obligation to maintain security and control over the day-to-day routine for the welfare of staff and inmates involved. This means that inmates who present with psychological problems in coping must be kept in "check" so that they do not create a breach in institutional security. This is important and will likely be the primary (if not only) concern among security staff personnel. When disruptions do occur, it is common practice for security personnel to utilize methods of seclusion and/or restraint that are not necessarily consistent with clinical considerations. This can, to some extent, pit security staff against mental health staff on some occasions. However, these same mechanisms of control may be used as part of the treatment regimen

Mood disorders: Disorders such as major depressive disorder, bipolar disorder, and dysthymic disorder.

when acutely disturbed psychiatric patients are involved (Hanser & Mire, 2010). A closely monitored review system must be implemented to ensure that these special security procedures are only used when necessary. Valid reasons for the use of these procedures are generally restricted to the imminent risk of harm to self or others and/or the imminent likelihood of serious damage to property. Inmates in seclusion require enhanced monitoring, which may mean continuous observation by line staff. This is especially true if self-injury is a potential risk. Inmates kept in restraints must be routinely assessed to ensure that they are not injured as a result of the restraining procedure and to ensure that they are able to maintain hygiene and nutritional requirements.

Malingering

Hanser and Mire (2010) note that malingering may occur within institutions. **Malingering** is when inmates falsely claim and consciously fake symptoms of an illness. Inmates may malinger to avoid being responsible for their behavior because it may allow them to avoid certain consequences. Malingering may result in an inmate being referred for mental health evaluation or treatment. It is important that security staff do not attempt to discern between inmates who are malingering and those with a true mental illness. Security staff may be prone to do this when the inmate in question tends to be manipulative or if a security staff member has had previous disciplinary problems with the inmate. However, failure to assess a mentally ill offender correctly can simply compound the problems for him or her, and this will ultimately lead to further problems for the institution as a whole, including security staff. Thus, this determination should only be made by qualified mental health professionals who have a detached and objective eye during the assessment period.

Legal Requirements, Transfers, and Involuntary Commitment for Psychiatric Treatment

Some offenders may exhibit behaviors that become progressively worse over their term of incarceration. Because of this, some of these offenders will be deemed more suitable for psychiatric hospitalization. Indeed, nearly half of all persons in secure mental hospitals were transferred from a prison system (Hanser & Mire, 2010). Though a substantial number of persons committed to psychiatric hospitals come from prisons, the reverse—that a substantial number of prison inmates actually came from a psychiatric facility—is also true. This means that prisons then have become the essential "catch-all" or "dumping ground" for much of society's mentally ill. In 1980, the Supreme Court held in *Vitek v. Jones* that a transfer of any inmate to a mental health hospital required, at a minimum, an administrative hearing to determine the appropriateness of such confinement. While this is generally not a difficult requirement to comply with, in the current era of budgetary constraints, the reality is that most hospitals no longer have the ability to accept these individuals, as they are now often at maximum capacity, just like prison systems.

Malingering: When inmates falsely claim symptoms of an illness.

Co-occurring disorders: When an offender has two or more disorders.

AP Photo/Mick Groll

■ PHOTO 11.3 Inmates participate in a wellness self-management class at Fishkill Correctional Facility in New York. This facility, like others, is striving to help mentally ill inmates learn more about their conditions.

Broad Array of Pathology

Specific types of disorders have been found to be more problematic than others among the offending population. Among these are mood, schizophrenic, and personality disorders. As we have noted, a high proportion of offenders have addiction or substance abuse disorders that are comorbid with their primary diagnosis (Hanser & Mire, 2010). When an offender has two or more disorders, he or she is said within the treatment community to have **co-occurring disorders**. In most cases, when an offender is said to have co-occurring disorders, the clinician is referring to a substance abuse–related disorder accompanied by some type of

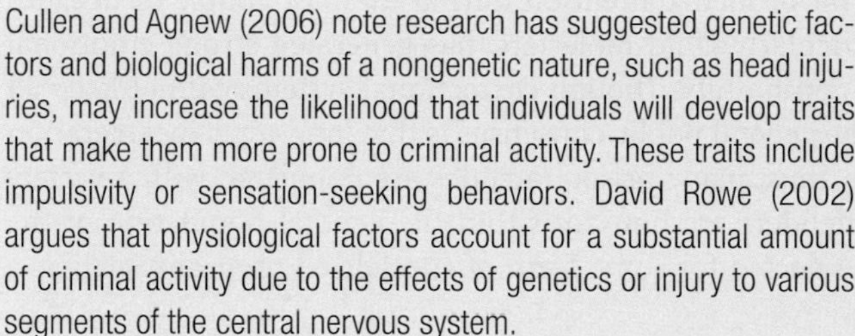

APPLIED THEORY 11.1

Individual Trait Criminological Theories and Criminal Activity

Cullen and Agnew (2006) note research has suggested genetic factors and biological harms of a nongenetic nature, such as head injuries, may increase the likelihood that individuals will develop traits that make them more prone to criminal activity. These traits include impulsivity or sensation-seeking behaviors. David Rowe (2002) argues that physiological factors account for a substantial amount of criminal activity due to the effects of genetics or injury to various segments of the central nervous system.

In particular, Rowe has focused on the chemical messengers, called neurotransmitters, that exist within our nervous system and transmit electronic signals between the billions of neurons in our brain. The neurotransmitters are many, but serotonin and dopamine are particularly important because they affect our mood and emotional stability and because even slight changes in the amount of each in our bloodstream can lead to different levels of emotional response or behavior. Rowe (2002) and others have also examined critical hormones like testosterone that help to regulate various impulses, such as sex drive and reaction to stressors.

This research is not just important from a mental health perspective. It also can be applied to many of the substance abuse issues that are corollary to inmates with mental disorders, to female offenders, to offenders with HIV/AIDS, and to elderly and juvenile offenders. Most illicit drugs impact our serotonin and dopamine release levels, and this release of neurotransmitters gives people their sense of "high" when using a substance. This provides direct reinforcement to the cerebral areas affected. In addition to this physiological effect, many drug users experience additional social reinforcers due to social contact with other drug users and acceptance within that crowd.

Though it may seem far-fetched, substantial research has demonstrated a connection between nervous system functioning and criminal activity (Hanser, 2010; Raine, 2004). This is true for both juvenile and adult offenders as well as for both nonviolent and violent offenders. Numerous cases exist where offenders were found to have various imbalances in their neurochemistry. Andrea Yates, a female offender who drowned her own children during a serious bout of postpartum depression, is one classic example. Others abound throughout the literature, particularly in regard to the study of the classic psychopath, whose central nervous system does not process anxiety-related impulses, making the person less able to feel empathy for his or her victims. Indeed, brain imaging with MRIs and PET scans has pinpointed specific biological deficits involved in criminal dispositions among a variety of offender types; these deficits appear to be in the frontal cortex area of the brain, an area that regulates higher-order functioning.

Given the confluence of these physiological factors—mental illness, substance abuse, and criminal activity—the individual trait theories are important to consider. These theories are grounded in medical science and study specific physiological effects, producing results that are much more valid and reliable than the survey-based research attributed to most social-based theories. In effect, these theories seem to point toward inherent risk factors possessed by the person before any social learning takes place. Naturally, these theories hold serious implications for correctional agencies. Such theories seem to point to the utility of selective incapacitation strategies and to the notion that some offenders may simply not be able to change—at least not without making modifications to their neurochemistry.

SOURCE: Cullen, F. T., & Agnew, R. (2006). *Criminological theory: Past to present* (3rd ed.). Los Angeles, CA: Roxbury Publishing Company.

DSM-5-diagnosed mental health disorder, such as depression, anxiety-based disorders, schizophrenia, or other type of debilitating mental health issues.

Impact of Institutionalization on Mental Illness

Throughout this section, it has been pointed out that the effects of incarceration can aggravate mental health problems affecting inmates. Indeed, schizophrenia tends to be greatly magnified when inmates are placed in solitary confinement or segregation for prolonged periods of time. Other disorders, such as antisocial personality disorder, are particularly impacted by the inmate subculture, including the gang subculture. Because antisocial personality inmates are so criminogenic in orientation, the socialization from the inmate subculture simply entrenches them further into their disordered perceptions and beliefs. Likewise, inmates with this disorder exercise an undue influence on the prison and, in the process, further exacerbate security problems and indoctrinate other inmates into the life of crime encouraged by the inmate subculture.

The prison experience is itself stressful and, as a result, will likely intensify reactions of inmates who are anxiety prone. This can be especially true in institutions where assaults frequently occur and where inmate safety is not a priority. Rates of post-traumatic stress disorder

(PTSD) are high in prisons, and the disorder is particularly aggravated for those who are victimized within the prison environment. This is especially true for victims of prison rape and/or custodial sexual abuse. Lastly, rates of depression are often high among prison inmates due to the negative and restrictive environment (prisons are not cheery places, after all). Events that occur outside the prison (e.g., loss of a loved one, inability to assist family members, news of divorce) can also increase rates of depression and suicide.

SEX OFFENDERS

Sex offenders have been given quite a bit of media attention during the past couple of decades or so. Public fear of sex offenders, particularly child molesters, has generated strong emotional opposition to their being placed in the community. Though correctional systems cannot keep all sex offenders behind bars indefinitely, the general public consensus is that long-term incarceration is the best sentence for these offenders. Thus, many prison facilities are populated with a variety of sex offenders. Typically, most sex offenders are housed within the general population of the correctional institution unless they are selected for some form of specialized program, such as a residential therapeutic community.

Assessment and Classification

The assessment and classification of sex offenders is not always an easy process. This is partly because official records are not always complete and/or may have missing information, especially if the case had extensive legal history, if the charge was pled down, or if offenders were charged for an offense other than the sex offense. Further, sex offenders are seldom forthcoming about their activity. Trained staff who are knowledgeable about typical sex offender profiles are ideal for assessment and classification in these cases. These staff will usually be skilled at developing a rapport with these offenders while ensuring that they do not seem to condone the behavior. In addition, though the sex-offending behavior may be the primary issue of concern, persons conducting assessments should stay attentive regarding the other types of criminal activity that the offender may report. Often, these offenders are willing to discuss their other crimes as a form of psychological bargaining in which they believe that by relating other crimes, they can evade discussing their sex offending. The details of these other crimes can be very helpful in properly classifying a sex offender.

Assessment processes will determine whether the offender is amenable to treatment. Most will be provided treatment if they are willing, and those determined to be most motivated will likely be given a special form of incarceration through a therapeutic community. The **therapeutic community** environment provides necessary behavior modifiers in the form of sanctions and privileges that allow offenders immediate feedback about their behavior and treatment progress. This is important to note because these types of programs occur while offenders are theoretically "behind bars," yet they are utilized to eventually reintegrate the offender into the community.

Basic Sex Offender Management

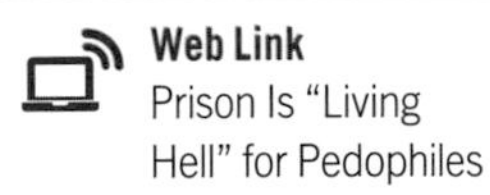
Web Link
Prison Is "Living Hell" for Pedophiles

Institutions must focus on correctly identifying sex offenders as soon as possible after incarceration. For this to realistically occur, assessment and classification (just discussed) must take place. After the classification process, the offender should be separated from the general population of inmates when possible. At a minimum, a separate area for sex offender treatment should exist, and separate housing should be provided if feasible. Much of this has to do with the fact that these inmates are vulnerable to attack from other inmates since, as we have learned, these offenders are not respected within the inmate subculture and are specific targets within that subculture and for gangs active within a facility. Despite the recommendation that sex offenders be given separate housing, this is not often the case, and most are housed in the general population. This is because resources are scarce and because prison facilities are not required to separate sex offenders from the population as long as they are given reasonable protection.

Therapeutic community: An environment that provides necessary behavior modifiers that allow offenders immediate feedback about their behavior and treatment progress.

Staff Issues With the Sex Offender Population in Prison

Ingram and Carlson (2008) perhaps says it best in noting that "the most essential step in developing and running a useful program for sex offenders is having trained staff who have the right attitude toward these inmates" (p. 377). Security staff should not view sex offenders as horrible persons who deserve the worst punishment possible. Nor should they be sympathetic to sex offenders to the point that they entertain excuses for the criminal behavior, such as the unfairness of sex laws regarding consent, issues with a troubled home, and/or misunderstandings regarding appropriate sexual activity (Ingram & Carlson, 2008). Rather, security staff should be realistic and mature. They should view the behavior of the sex offender as inappropriate but should be willing to consider that these offenders can change.

Security staff who will work within sex offender treatment programs should meet high criteria. Most staff who seek to work in this field will already have come to terms with the idea that treatment of sex offenders goes beyond punitive sanctions. However, the reasons that persons may seek these specialized assignments can vary, and some of them may not be healthy. Thus, careful screening and investigation of the person's background should be conducted.

The treatment personnel involved with this type of program should also be well qualified. Typically, a psychologist or psychiatrist is charged with supervising these types of programs, but many treatment providers may be master's-level social workers and/or counselors. These individuals will often have specialized forms of education and/or training that is required to work with sex offenders. In fact, most states will have a registry or roster of mental health professionals who are given the legal authority to work with sex offenders. This demonstrates how important it is to ensure that those who work with this population are appropriately trained and credentialed.

Treatment of Sex Offenders

Sex offender programs today most often use a combination of cognitive-behavioral techniques and relapse prevention strategies (Ingram & Carlson, 2008). These programs usually include individual counseling sessions and group therapy sessions to break through offenders' denial of their activity and help them attempt to build empathy for victims of their crime (Hanser, 2010). When using group therapy, an effective technique to combating denial is to invite offenders who are in an advanced treatment group to challenge offenders in the less experienced group who are in denial. The idea is that more experienced offenders in treatment will be more adept at challenging offenders in denial than others. In other cases, treatment staff may find it more effective to simply create a group of offenders who all exhibit levels of denial. This is called the "deniers group" since it consists of sex offenders who are all in denial. Essentially, this is a "pre-group" that lasts from 11 to 16 weeks as a means of getting the offender in denial primed for the actual group therapy process. According to the Center for Sex Offender Management, treatment providers who employ this method report that the great majority of offenders are able to come out of their denial. This approach targets two major issues:

1. Eliminating cognitive distortions, which, if left intact, allow offenders to continue denying or minimizing.
2. Developing victimization awareness, which can allow offenders to understand the physical and psychological harm they inflict and, thus, render them more reluctant to commit future assaults.

One primary concern of group members is often related to confidentiality, particularly regarding information divulged by other group members. One way to address this concern is to ask the group participants to come to an agreement among themselves about their own confidentiality. In virtually every instance, the agreement they make is that what is discussed in group does not get discussed outside of group. Typically, it is best to have the group members come to this agreement themselves rather than imposing this rule on them for two reasons. First, it is a simple way to get them involved in a discussion they are likely to understand and be interested in without addressing any threatening content, such as sex offending. This provides practice for what will be occurring in the group. Second, it requires that the group build cohesiveness and trust among its members, at least about this issue. Building trust among themselves can be a useful exercise because it leads to group members sensing that they can be helpful to each other.

Prison Subcultural Reactions and Treatment

Chapter 9 included extensive discussion on the prison subculture. In this discussion, it was made clear that sex offenders tend to have no status behind bars, and, depending on the type of sex offender, they are likely to be victimized. This is particularly true for child molesters and other similar types of sex offenders. However, as with the outside community, social forces have changed some of the beliefs within the prison environment. Nowadays, it is fairly common for younger inmates to have committed some type of sex offense, but this is usually some type of rape of an adult female rather than the molestation of a child. While rape of women tended to also carry negative connotations within the older prison culture prior to the 1960s, the stigma of this is not as great in today's modern prison environment.

There are many reasons for the shift in how the prison subculture responds to different types of sex offenders. First, the gangsta movement during the 1990s consisted of rap music and attitudes that overtly denigrated women and referred to them in terms that implied they were to be exploited. This created an air of tolerance for female victimization among many younger offenders, particularly gang offenders. Second, youth now tend to be very sexually active, and boys are committing acts of violence more often than in past years; the shocking aspect of sex crimes has diminished. Thus, a culture has bred where women are considered lowly in status, and younger offenders no longer have incentives to be "gentlemen" but instead gain status points for "sexing" young girls and women into gang membership. Further, many gangs may engage in different types of rape as a preferred choice of criminal behaviors. These types of sex offenders will not be stigmatized in the prison culture but instead will be considered part of their gang family.

However, this is not the case for other sex offenders (again, particularly those who have molested children), inmates with sexual identity issues, or inmates who succumb to pressure for same-sex activity inside the prison. These individuals will be stigmatized and very likely sexually victimized in many of the older facilities and/or systems where the prison subculture predominates. In any event, these inmates will be afforded no respect by other inmates in the facility.

HIV/AIDS-RELATED OFFENDERS

HIV/AIDS: A chronic, potentially life-threatening condition caused by the human immunodeficiency virus.

HIV/AIDS is a chronic, potentially life-threatening condition caused by the human immunodeficiency virus. At year-end 2010, roughly 20,093 inmates in prisons and jails throughout the United States were HIV-positive, and 9,723 of these inmates had full-blown AIDS. This is significant decline in the number of inmates who were HIV-positive since the last edition of this text. As can be seen in Figure 11.1, since 2001, there has been a continuous decline in the number of state inmates who are HIV-positive.

■ Figure 11.1: Rate of HIV/AIDS Cases and AIDS-Related Deaths Among State and Federal Prison Inmates, 2001–2010

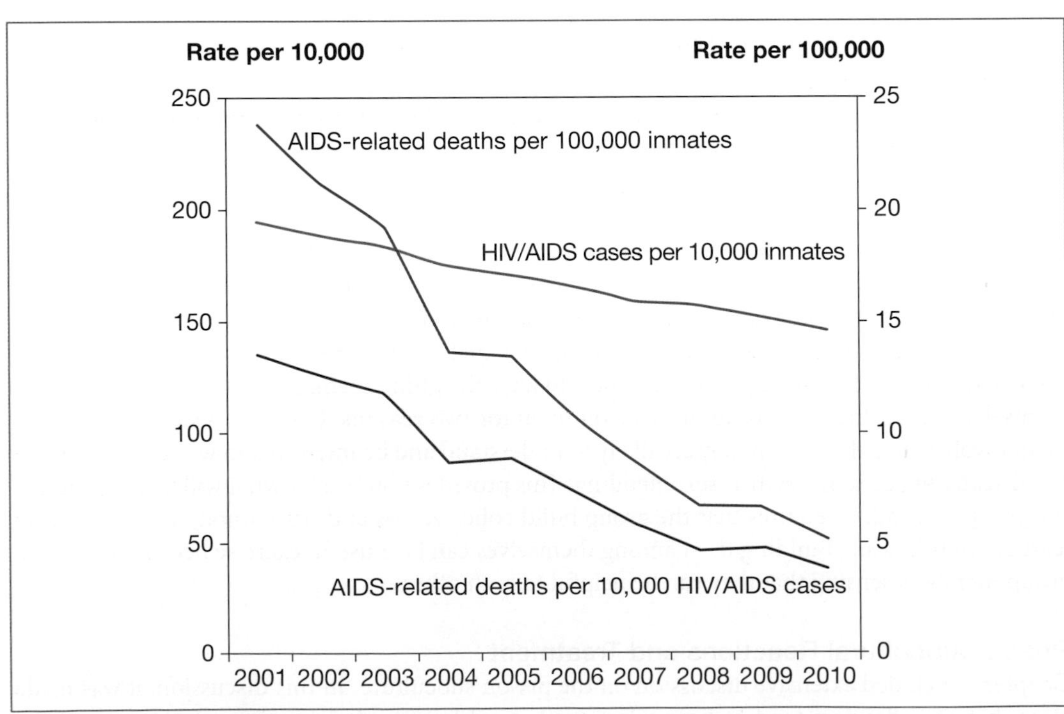

SOURCE: Maruschak, L. (2015). *HIV in prisons, 2001–2010—revised March, 2015.* Washington, DC: Bureau of Justice Statistics.

■ **Figure 11.2: Inmates in Custody of State or Federal Prison Authorities and Reported to be HIV-Positive or Have Confirmed AIDS, by Jurisdiction, Year-End 2010**

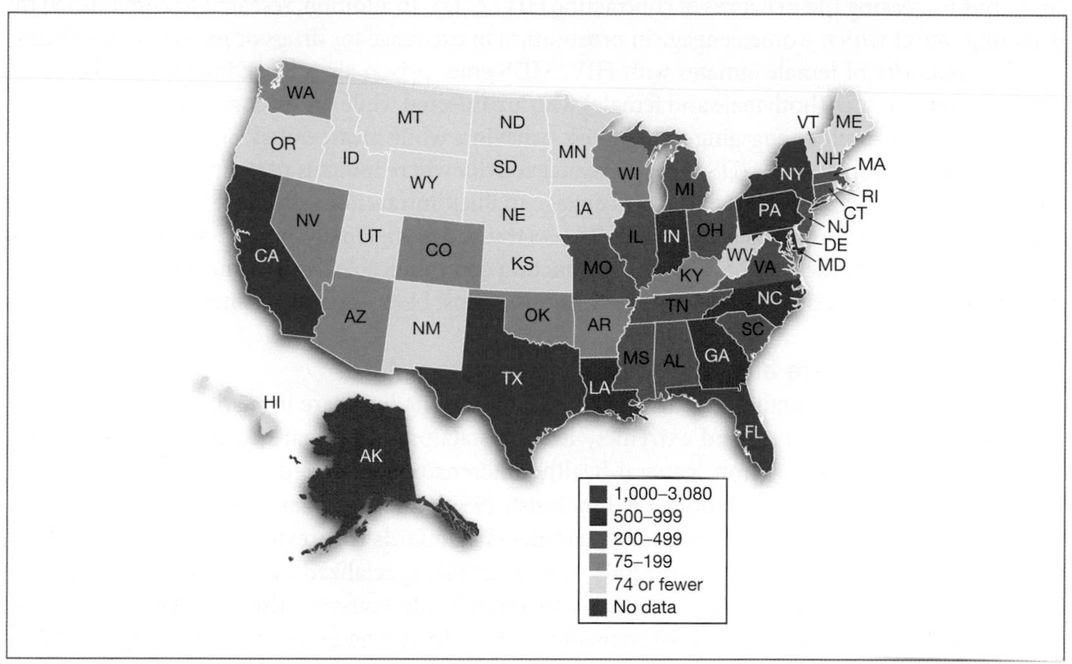

SOURCE: Maruschak, L. (2015). *HIV in prisons, 2001–2010—revised March, 2015.* Washington, DC: Bureau of Justice Statistics.
Note: Excludes inmates held in private facilities. Counts published in previous reports may have been revised.
Excludes data from Alaska due to incomplete reporting. Excludes inmates in jurisdictions that did not report data. *The number of HIV/AIDS cases in Oregon was based on a 3/9/09 count for 2008.

This essentially means that in 2010 about 1.5% of all state prison inmates, 0.9% of federal prison inmates, and 1.6% of all jail inmates were infected with HIV. In each of these categories, an overall decrease in this percentage has continued (see Figure 11.2 for a detailed state-by-state count of HIV/AIDS cases in prison systems within the United States). Despite these decreases, this rate of infection is still much greater than that of the general population.

It should be noted that roughly half (51%) of all the HIV-positive inmates are located within the state prison systems of California, New York, Florida, and Texas. This is not surprising since these four states include the Top Three in corrections, as identified earlier. In 2010, the number of inmates in each of these states who were HIV-positive or had confirmed cases of AIDS was quite different than a decade prior. During this year, the state of New York had 3,080 HIV-positive inmates (2,820 male and 260 female), Florida had 2,920 (2,636 male and 284 female), Texas had 2,394 inmates (2,153 male and 241 female), and California had 1,098 (1,023 male and 75 female). It is important to note that the total number in all four states had decreased substantially, with New York's total number being less than half in 2010 what it had been 11 years prior, in 1999. In fact, the only state to have experienced an increase was Florida, and this is attributed to intravenous drug use (heroin) that has persisted among the drug-using population in that state. For each of these states, their numbers are fairly consistent with the relative prevalence of HIV/AIDS among injection drug users (commonly referred to as IDUs) in each of these states.

While the concentration of HIV/AIDS in prisons poses a serious threat to inmates in general, research indicates that it poses an increasingly serious threat to female inmates specifically. Figure 11.3 compares the rates of male and female inmates infected with HIV/AIDS over a 4-year period. The rate of infected women remains consistently higher than the rate of their male counterparts, with the most current data, 2010, indicating that women are infected at a rate that is approximately 36% higher than males.

The ways in which women are exposed to HIV/AIDS reflect their lack of information and education related to infection as well as their propensity to engage in high-risk behavior. Women are infected through the use of intravenous drug needles and unprotected sex with infected partners. As we have seen in Chapter 10, more women than men suffer from drug addiction, and they tend to use drugs more frequently than men prior to incarceration. This has a direct effect on the likelihood that women will engage in high-risk drug-related behavior (e.g., intravenous drug use and needle sharing), thus increasing their chances of contracting HIV/AIDS. In addition, research has established the alarming rate at which women engage in prostitution in exchange for drugs or money to buy drugs.

The majority of female inmates with HIV/AIDS enter prison already having the disease. There are, however, inmates (both male and female) who are infected while under correctional supervision. This occurs as a result of engaging in high-risk behaviors while incarcerated. Studies have indicated that inmates transmit HIV/AIDS through sexual activity where inmates participate in both consensual and coerced sex. In addition, inmates engage in illicit intravenous drug use, oftentimes sharing needles, further increasing their risk of HIV/AIDS transmission. Finally, inmates who receive tattoos while in prison increase the possibility of contracting communicable diseases, including HIV/AIDS, due to unsterile needles and inadequate protections against blood-borne transmission.

Inmate Medical Care and HIV/AIDS

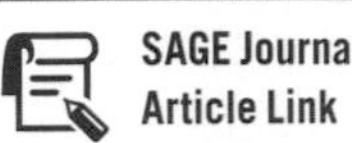

SAGE Journal Article Link
Health Status and Service Needs of Male Inmates Seriously Ill With HIV/AIDS

For the most part, the quality and delivery of health and medical care in institutional corrections are poor. Inmates have reported extremely low satisfaction with regard to the accessibility and quality of medical service, from general health concerns to specialized care. This is particularly the case for female inmates (Lindquist & Lindquist, 1999) as medical care offered in women's prisons has failed to provide constitutionally guaranteed standards (for reviews, see Anderson, 2003; Belknap, 2001; and Young & Reviere, 2001). For example, specialized health care personnel such as gynecologists, obstetricians, and dietitians are often located off-site. This is specifically relevant because women in prison have a host of medical needs, including gynecological concerns such as sexually transmitted diseases, reproductive-related health problems, and high-risk pregnancies, and thus may need access to on-site medical treatment and counseling.

When medical specialists are not available on-site, inmates must be transported to receive care. This often results in transportation and scheduling conflicts (Belknap, 2001) as well as additional expenses and potential safety concerns, which can lead to a delay in health service. In order to increase access to medical specialists, many prisons have experimented with telemedicine, a system whereby specialists provide consultation to prisoners via videoconferencing (see Technology and Equipment 11.1 for more on the use of telemedicine).

Research has indicated that roughly 25% of institutions do not screen or test for HIV/AIDS. This can be seen in Table 11.4, which shows the various screening and testing procedures employed by U.S. correctional facilities. Moreover, most institutions have screening methods that rely on

Figure 11.3: Number of HIV/AIDS-Infected Prison Inmates, by Year and Sex

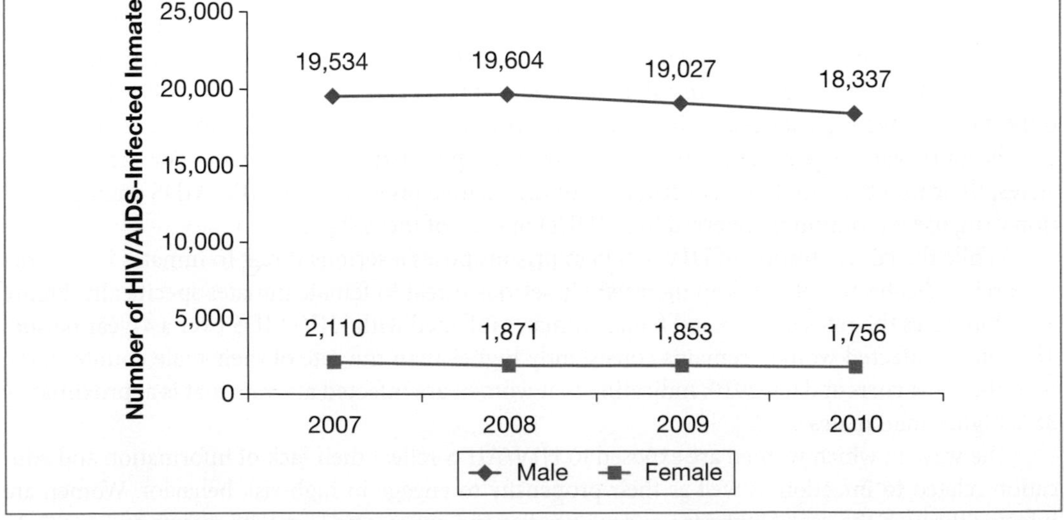

SOURCES: Maruschak, L. (2015). *HIV in prisons, 2001–2010—revised March, 2015.* Washington, DC: Bureau of Justice Statistics.

inmate request before HIV/AIDS testing is done. While some facilities screen inmates based on specific clinical indications, others rely on blind or unlinked studies where blood is tested but there is no identifying information that connects the inmate to the results of the test. This form of testing provides aggregate numbers of infected inmates but does not allow for any type of medical treatment or educational follow-up. Lack of screening has problematic consequences when a host of inmates with the disease or infection are unaware of their HIV-positive status.

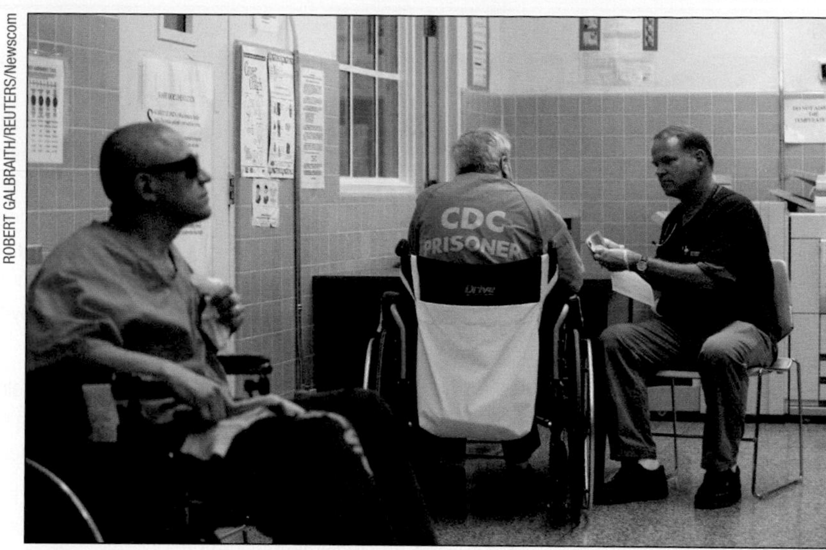

■ PHOTO 11.4 These inmates are receiving medical assistance within the prison infirmary.

Improvements in Medical Services for Inmates With HIV/AIDS

Recent data has shown that inmates with HIV/AIDS are receiving better medical services, as evidenced by mortality rates that have continued to decline the past 15 years or so. Indeed, rates of HIV/AIDS cases and AIDS-related deaths have declined across all sizes of prison populations. To illustrate this trend, consider that in 2009, the AIDS mortality rate among state prison inmates (6 per 100,000) fell below the rate for the U.S. general population (7 per 100,000). This has been true among a number of specific subgroups of the inmate population. For example, AIDS-related deaths in state prisons declined from 89 in 2009 to 69 in 2010 among males, from 70 to 43 among black non-Hispanics, and from 87 to 60 among all state inmates age 35 or older.

Between 2001 and 2010, the estimated number of inmates with HIV/AIDS declined by 16%, and the number of AIDS-related deaths in prison declined by 77%, resulting in declines in the rates of HIV/AIDS-related deaths among all inmates. At year-end 2001, the estimated rate of HIV/AIDS among state and federal prison inmates was 194 HIV/AIDS cases per 10,000 inmates. By year-end 2010, the estimated rate was 146 cases per 10,000. Among the total inmate population, the rate of AIDS-related deaths declined from 24 per 100,000 inmates in 2001 to 5 per 100,000 in 2010. Among the inmate population with HIV/AIDS, the rate declined from 134 AIDS-related deaths per 10,000 inmates in 2001 to 38 per 10,000 in 2010.

Lastly, regardless of the size of the state prison population, as measured by the number of inmates in custody at year-end 2010, trends in the rates of HIV/AIDS cases and AIDS-related deaths in state prisons followed the overall decline of the national rate. In fact, when considering AIDS-related deaths of inmates aged 15–54 in state prisons who were incarcerated between the years of 2001 and 2009, it is clear that the decline among state inmates is much more significant than what has been seen in outside society (see Figure 11.4). As a result, the AIDS-related death rates in state prisons were below the rate of those found in the outside U.S. general population in 2009.

Rights to Privacy and Inmate Subcultural Views

Correctional staff must understand that inmates may have difficulty trusting that staff will treat their health and security as a concern. But for treatment programs to be successful (and this is the only way to improve long-term safety for both inmates and staff), a solid relationship must exist between the inmate client and medical staff or clinicians. Facilities and clinicians must deal with the inmate's mistrust of authority and unfamiliarity with health care providers and services and be clear and open about the limits to, and likely success of, various interventions.

HIV/AIDS counseling and testing includes HIV antibody testing and individual, client-centered risk reduction counseling. These types of programs are designed to assist individuals in deciding if they will get further help. These programs may take place in different forms (e.g., during and following the initial intake medical screening or during or following education and prevention sessions).

The counseling and psychoeducational programs should also be available to noninfected inmates. By counseling noninfected inmates on how to avoid infection, these programs can reduce further infection and can save both correctional agencies and society an enormous amount of

TECHNOLOGY AND EQUIPMENT 11.1

Telemedicine Can Cut Medical Costs for Inmate Populations

The use of telemedicine has been hailed as a technological tool that can save correctional agencies substantial financial resources. Telemedicine is a process whereby physicians at a prison conduct different procedures and/or services with the consultation and guidance of more senior and specialized medical staff who are contacted by either phone, Internet, or both. In the late 1990s, a leased telemedicine network was installed to serve four federal prisons. The purpose of this demonstration was to test the feasibility of remote telemedical consultations in prisons and to estimate the financial impacts of implementing telemedicine in other prison systems. Abt Associates Inc. was contracted to evaluate the demonstration and estimate the costs and savings associated with the use of telemedicine in these selected prisons. As in most federal prisons, medical care was traditionally delivered through a combination of four types of providers:

© F. Carter Smith/Sygma/Corbis

■ **PHOTO 11.5 Specialists at the University of Texas prescribe treatment following video consultations with inmates.**

1. Routine primary care was largely the responsibility of prison employees. Telemedicine was not intended to substitute for any of these encounters.
2. Specialty care was provided in regularly scheduled, in-person clinics for which the prisons entered into annual contracts with local specialists.
3. Inmates requiring less common specialties or hospital care were transported outside the prison to nearby health care facilities (usually hospitals).
4. Some inmates who needed more extensive care were transported to a Bureau of Prisons (BOP) federal medical center, by air charter if necessary.

During the demonstration period, a fifth mode of care—remote encounters with specialists via telemedicine—was added to determine whether the prisons could use telemedicine to overcome local problems in accessing needed specialists and improve security by averting travel outside the prison walls. The demonstration was also designed to supply data on costs and utilization to support a decision about whether and where to implement telemedicine in other prisons. During the period in which telemedicine processes were evaluated by the BOP, the following seven observations were noted:

1. Telemedicine was adopted quickly and used frequently in several medical specialty areas. By the end of the demonstration, 1,321 teleconsultations had been conducted.
2. Physicians reported that telemedical consultations were effective substitutes for direct, in-person consultations in some specialties (e.g., psychiatry and dermatology), but less than adequate in others (e.g., cardiology and orthopedics).
3. The use of telemedicine averted 13-14 transfers by air charter to a federal medical center (FMC). Nearly all of these transfers would have been for psychiatric reasons. The availability and skill levels of prison psychiatrists at FMC Lexington (Kentucky) contributed to better management of psychiatric patients at the demonstration prisons.
4. In an operational telemedicine system with optimal design, the savings generated by approximately 1,544 encounters would equal the purchase cost of the telemedicine equipment. The demonstration produced about 100 encounters per month with monthly savings of about $14,200, ultimately.
5. Telemedicine also improved some indicators of the quality of care available to prisoners. The time between a prisoner's referral to a specialist and an actual consultation with the specialist declined in the demonstration prisons; probably specialists were more frequently available by telemedicine.
6. Prison administrators in the project hypothesized that the prisons were calmer, with fewer incidents of violence because of the improved psychiatric care available through telemedicine. There were fewer assaults at FCI (Federal Correctional Institution) Allenwood and USP (United States Penitentiary) Allenwood after the demonstration began than in the previous year.
7. The evaluation demonstrates convincingly that telemedicine was widely embraced by officials and prisoners once it was established within the prisons. Further, the evaluation establishes that a correctional agency such as the BOP can add telemedicine to its medical program with the expectation that taxpayer dollars will not be wasted, and, if anything, substantial savings associated with the new technology may be realized.

Clearly telemedicine can have some advantages for prisons, particularly for prison facilities designed to house specialized offender populations. For elderly offenders, offenders with HIV/AIDS, and mentally ill inmates, this type of service delivery may be more effective, create fewer security risks, and be less expensive than traditional methods of providing medical services. Thus, the use of telemedicine procedures can and should be seriously considered as a means of offsetting some of the costs associated with the expense of housing a special needs population.

SOURCE: Nacci, P. (2000). *Telemedicine can reduce correctional healthcare costs: An evaluation of a prison telemedicine network.* Washington, DC: National Institute of Justice.

Table 11.4: HIV Testing Practices for State and Federal Inmates by Jurisdiction, 2012

Jurisdiction	All Inmates Offered	Some Inmates Offered	Only on Inmate Request	Other	Do Not Provide
Federal			X		
Alabama[a]				X	
Arizona			X		
Arkansas				X	
California		X			
Colorado			X		
Connecticut					X
Delaware		X			
Florida	X				
Georgia	X				
Hawaii			X		
Idaho					X
Indiana			X		
Iowa					X
Kansas			X		
Kentucky					X
Louisiana			X		
Maine			X		
Maryland[b]				X	
Massachusetts			X		
Michigan			x		
Minnesota					X
Mississippi			X		
Missouri[c]				X	
Nebraska	X				
Nevada[a]				X	
New Hampshire			X		
New Jersey			x		
New Mexico	X				
New York		X			
North Carolina			X		
North Dakota			X		

(Continued)

■ **Table 11.4: (Continued)**

Jurisdiction	All Inmates Offered	Some Inmates Offered	Only on Inmate Request	Other	Do Not Provide
Ohio			X		
Oklahoma			X		
Oregon			x		
Pennsylvania	X				
Rhode Island					X
South Carolina			X		
South Dakota[d]				X	
Tennessee			X		
Texas[a]				X	
Utah[e]				X	
Vermont			X		
Virginia	X				
Washington			X		
West Virginia	X				
Wisconsin			X		
Wyoming			X		

SOURCE: Maruschak, L. M., Berzofsky, M., & Unangst, J. (2015). *Medical problems of state and federal prisoners and jail inmates, 2011-2012.* Washington, DC: Bureau of Justice Statistics.

NOTE: Alaska, Illinois, and Montana did not report data on testing practices during discharge planning.

[a]All inmates tested for HIV on discharge. [b]Inmates were tested for HIV on request and offered HIV testing for upcoming releases.

[c]HIV testing was mandatory for all offenders not already HIV positive. [d]All inmates were offered HIV testing at Mike Durfee State Prison. At South Dakota State Prison and South Dakota Women's Prison, inmates were only tested on inmate request. [e]Utah State Health Department tested all inmates for HIV on day of parole.

money and future grief and misery. It should be noted that the estimated lifetime treatment cost for an inmate with HIV/AIDS varies from $165,000 to $267,000 for correctional agencies that must foot the bill. Thus, HIV/AIDS prevention and psychoeducational interventions can save a great deal of money, even if just a handful of cases are prevented.

Just as with the broader population outside of the prison environment, the confidentiality of HIV/AIDS test results is a crucial concern when providing effective services. The fear is that if an inmate believes others may find out he or she has HIV/AIDS, that inmate might avoid or refuse testing. Confidentiality in the correctional setting can be difficult because privacy is harder to maintain. This is particularly true when one considers that everyone within the prison may know when and where appointments for HIV-positive inmates occur. Information may leak fast through inmate orderlies, and inmates visiting prison infirmaries during the allocated time may quickly be identified by other inmates and/or staff as being positive for HIV/AIDS. This can have serious and damaging consequences for individuals who seek medical services for their infection, and these potential consequences can prevent other inmates from seeking testing. This then simply aggravates the problem with HIV/AIDS in the prison setting since the virus is left unchecked due to social concerns. It should be noted that this places both inmates and staff in potential jeopardy and at risk of being infected in the future.

The potential disclosure of inmates suspected of having HIV/AIDS is very important when one considers the effects of the informal subculture within many state prison systems. Hanser and Moran (2004) discuss at length the effects of the prison subculture on sex and sexuality identification within the prison setting. Inmates who are identified as HIV-positive (even if they have not actually been diagnosed as such) may be targeted by inmate perpetrators who are sexually assaultive (and are also HIV-positive) since the inmate is considered to be already infected. This marks the inmate as "fair game" among HIV-positive sexually assaultive inmates. Inmates who are not HIV-positive are likely to condone this victimization since this prevents spreading of the infection to other inmates who are not HIV-positive and since the subculture will see the inmate as a punk and therefore deserving of further victimization. Thus, whether the inmate is or is not positive becomes a moot point as he or she becomes singled out as a likely target.

The inmate suspected of potentially being HIV-positive will likely be shunned by many other inmates who desire to avoid infection. This inmate will find his or her standard of living and social inclusion to be very limited. Opportunities to recreate and engage in other activities may be substantially impaired due to social pressure from other inmates who seek to block HIV-positive inmates from participating in group functions. In fact, in some prison systems, HIV-positive inmates may be segregated from the remainder of the prison population.

■ Figure 11.4: Rate of AIDS-Related Deaths in State Prisons and in the U.S. General Population Among Persons Ages 15–54, 2001–2009

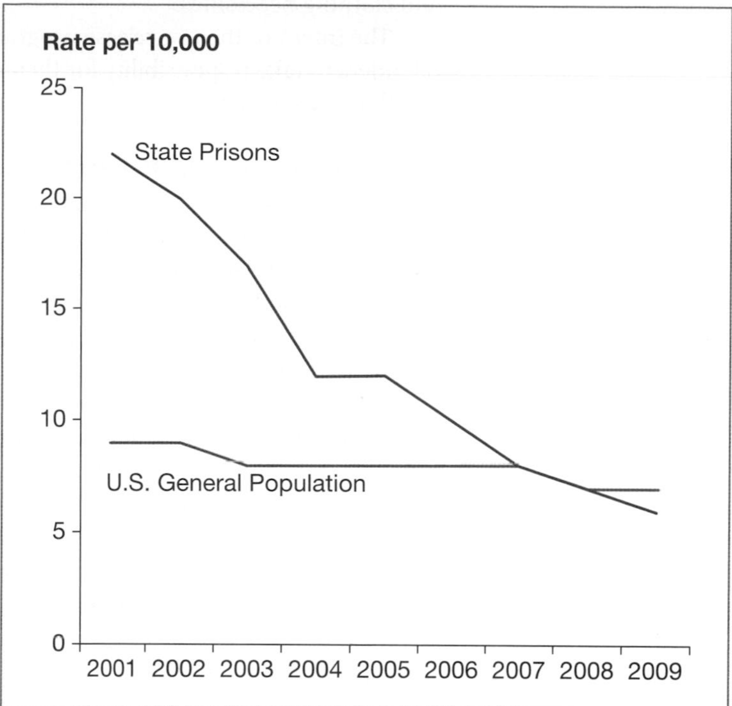

SOURCE: Maruschak, L. (2015). *HIV in prisons, 2001–2010—revised March, 2015.* Washington, DC: Bureau of Justice Statistics.

The segregation of HIV positive inmates has drawn substantial debate in recent years. The state of Alabama is regarded as one of the toughest correctional systems in the nation on HIV-positive inmates. Alabama's prisoners are tested upon entry into the Department of Corrections, and HIV-positive inmates are segregated and placed in separate dormitories. Some correctional experts consider this to be a more practical and effective manner of delivering services to the HIV-positive prison population. This argument for segregation may be very sound regardless of the social penalty that inmates may perceive with this type of intervention. Indeed, it is thought that the use of segregation can allow agencies to extend their resources by identifying gaps in services and filling those gaps during incarceration all the way through reentry into society.

Alabama's Department of Corrections does address prevention and in-house care that continues with effective aftercare while on community release. The state provides pre-release programming to inmates who are within 30 to 90 days of release that includes multiple life enrichment modules that address various issues related to the offender's reentry into society. One of these modules is titled Project H.E.L.P. (Health Education for Proper Living), and it has leveraged the assistance of community-based organizations (including outside health clinics) to provide primary and secondary education about HIV/AIDS and the treatment of the virus. Health education related to a variety of STDs, hepatitis, tuberculosis, tobacco use, body piercing, tattooing, diabetes, cardiovascular disease, breast and cervical cancer, nutrition, and physical fitness is also provided.

The Alabama DOC pre-release program also includes other modules that consist of numerous classes and services offered both inside the prison and during aftercare. One module, Clean and Sober: A New Way of Life, includes classes on addition that provide information on relapse prevention models and techniques, 12-step programming, other peer support programs (both secular and faith-based), and information regarding drug-free halfway houses and other community resources. Another module, Project I.N.V.E.S.T. (Initiating Necessary Vocational/Economic Security Training), provides assistance with job searches and career planning, vocational training, resume writing, and financial management.

Other modules that are part of the pre-release program include Project B.R.I.D.G.E. (Bringing Resources, Information, Direction, Guidance, and Encouragement), which addresses challenges for offenders returning to their families; Project H.E.A.L. (Helping Everyone Acquire Love), which addresses spiritual enrichment and mentoring; and Project R.I.D.E. (Renewing Information/Documentation Effectively), which assists with obtaining needed identification cards and papers for the outside world, necessary background checks, parole papers, transportation arrangements, and clothing necessities.

The intent of the pre-release program and its various life enrichment modules is to empower offenders to take responsibility for themselves upon release so they will be less of a burden and/or health risk to society.

HIV/AIDS and Custodial Staff Safety

From the discussion in the previous section, it should be clear that custodial staff are likely to be concerned about their own personal safety when dealing with inmates who have HIV/AIDS. This is completely understandable. However, it should also be clear that the prison subculture perpetuates fear and builds upon that fear to the point that those offenders who are even suspected of having HIV/AIDS are subject to direct and indirect victimization, and this should be avoided.

As we have discussed, a move toward increased professionalization among correctional personnel is occurring in the United States. This trend has helped to mitigate many of the negative effects of the prison subculture as well as the gang influences within prison facilities. In keeping with this trend, it is suggested that agencies provide ongoing training to their employees regarding HIV/AIDS and safety precautions that will prevent staff from becoming infected with a communicable disease. Employees should be trained to use universal precautions, which refers to a method of infection control in which all human blood and other potentially infectious materials are treated as if known to be infected with HIV/AIDS (Norman, 1991).

Legal Liabilities for Staff

As with any issue of safety and security that must be afforded to inmates, there is the potential for those inmates to file suit if the conditions of care are perceived to be substandard. In most respects, jail or prison staff must only make reasonable efforts to ensure that appropriate medical care is provided to inmates with HIV/AIDS. If suit is filed by an inmate, in most cases it will be under Section 1983 of Title 42 U.S. Code, commonly referred to as a Section 1983 suit. These types of lawsuits were discussed in Chapter 3 of this text. As students may recall, these suits allege that jail or prison staff have violated an inmate's constitutional rights while acting under color of law. This is the most common avenue inmates will take to file suit; they allege that their Eighth Amendment rights against cruel and unusual punishments have been violated due to the use of some type of restriction or regulation that has impeded their ability to obtain adequate medical services.

However, as we have seen, the Supreme Court has provided good guidance to aid decision makers tasked with crafting policies and procedures related to the health and welfare of staff and inmates within their institutions. In *Turner v. Safley* (1987), the Court noted that a regulation or procedure was valid if it could be shown to be "reasonably related to legitimate penological interests" (p. 89). This test continues to be the primary basis in determining the constitutionality of a facility's restrictions.

Despite the fact that such regulations must be minimally restrictive, the real world of prisons requires that some pains of imprisonment may be unavoidable regardless of how practitioners implement protective policies. For instance, as we have seen, an inmate who is suspected of being HIV-positive will likely be shunned by many other inmates who desire to avoid infection. This inmate will find his or her standard of living and social inclusion very limited. However, these concerns, though substantive, are likely to be secondary if the welfare of the institution is optimized.

Safety, Security, and Assistance for LGBTI Inmates

Lesbian, gay, bisexual, transgender, intersex (LGBTI) and gender-nonconforming inmates are a highly vulnerable population within the prison environment. This group has distinct medical, safety, and treatment needs that are no longer able to be overlooked by prison staff and administrators. Though many of the concerns for the different categories in this group are similar, it is important to understand that the transgender and gender-nonconforming population is distinct from the gay, lesbian, and bisexual inmate populations (King & Baker, 2014). Because of this, the risk-based classification that a prison will use with the LGBTI population must take into consideration the unique characteristics that will be associated with potential victimization for differing individuals. Specifically, for transgender inmates, this will require individualized decisions regarding gender placement, meaning that classification will need to determine whether the inmate will ultimately be kept in a male or a female facility.

During the past 10 to 12 years, the Prison Rape Elimination Act (PREA) has become increasingly prominent in prison administration. This law was first enacted in 2003, and its purpose was to provide for the analysis of the incidence and effects of prison rape in federal, state, and local institutions (National PREA Resource Center, 2015). This act also created the National Prison Rape Elimination Commission, which was empowered to generate standards and guidelines for correctional facilities to safeguard against prison rape. For now, our discussion of the PREA will be focused on provisions for the LGBTI population. In later chapters, more information will be provided on other provisions and requirements associated with this groundbreaking law.

Since the act's passage, state correctional systems, local jails, and juvenile facilities have worked to demonstrate that they are in compliance with these federal regulations. As correctional administrators work to be in compliance with the act, they do so amidst changes and additions to these guidelines, which initially were focused more on heterosexual sexual assaults but have increasingly begun to target the heightened risks that the LGBTI population faces (Schuster, 2015).

This is very important because these changes run completely counter to the old-school thinking that has traditionally been part of the prison subculture. As a result, correctional systems have now found that they must go beyond rape prevention and must address homophobic slurs and other forms of verbal harassment (Schuster, 2015). Further, unlike in the past, correctional systems will be required to discipline and relocate the perpetrators of this harassment rather than isolating or relocating victims "for their own protection." Correctional administrators will now also be required to consider input from transgendered inmates as to whether they feel safe and/or more comfortable living within a male or a female facility; in times past, the inmate was not given any type of documented input on this decision. Schuster (2015) provides an excellent synopsis of these changes by stating that the PREA prohibits

> any hard-line rule about housing these inmates based on their assigned sex at birth. Jails, prisons, and juvenile facilities are now required to determine on a case-by-case basis whether a trans-inmate will be safer housed with men or women. They also must give serious consideration to an inmate's own views regarding his or her safety. Importantly, "transgender" is not defined by whether a person has undergone surgery or hormone treatment to change his or her anatomy or appearance. It is defined solely by a person's internal sense of feeling male or female. (p. 3)

This means that a trans-woman (male-to-female) inmate cannot be excluded from being granted protective consideration because she has male genitalia or because prison staff do not believe that she appears to be "female enough" to quality (Schuster, 2015).

The National Prison Rape Elimination Commission, as a fact-finding body of inquiry, has found that trans-women, who often have breasts and a feminine appearance, are disproportionately the target of unnecessary, rough, and sexually oriented frisks and strip searches by male staff within cor-

AP Photo/Pat Sullivan

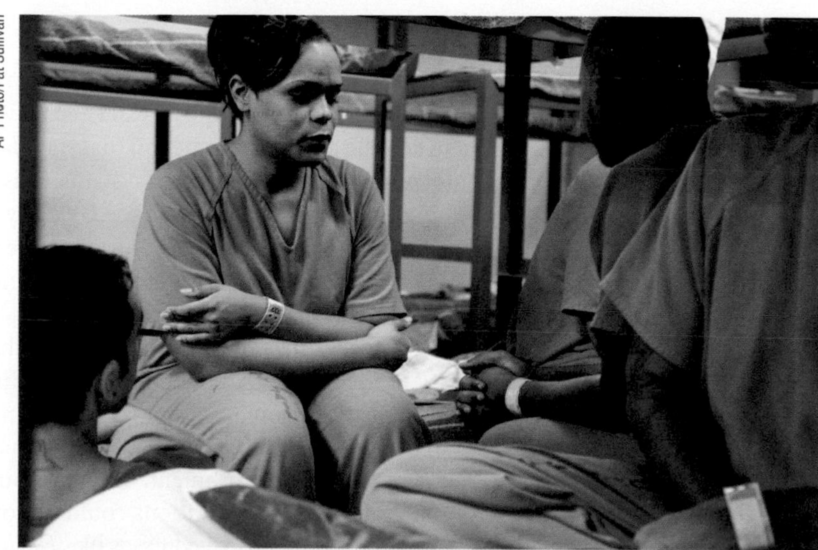

■ PHOTO 11.6 This facility has implemented changes in housing for gay, lesbian, bisexual, and transgender inmates.

rectional facilities. In addition, these inmates are often the focus of unwanted negative and stigmatizing attention by inmates and staff in shower and recreational facilities. Indeed, in many prison subcultures, the belief among both inmates and staff is that the transgendered inmate has invited the derogatory sexual attention by choosing to make these changes in her physical appearance.

The PREA also prohibits the classification of LGBTI inmates as sex offenders based simply on their sexual orientation or identity. While correctional facilities may, of course, prohibit consensual sexual activity between inmates and punish them for engaging in such acts, the PREA requires that this activity be identified as separate from acts of sexual abuse. This is because in times past inmates who engaged in consensual acts of sex would be given punishments that were harsher and more restrictive, such as solitary confinement or even new criminal charges. These practices have been found to disproportionately harm LGBTI inmates.

However, this new requirement has caused difficulties for prison administrators in cases where what appears to be consensual is not. For example, some LGBTI inmates may be the "property" of a prison gang. Due to coercion and out of fear, they may "freely" engage in providing sexual favors in return for protection and/or commissary supplies. Such sexual activity may appear to be consensual to the outside observer, but it is in fact due to pressure from other inmates. To avoid harm, often the LGBTI inmate will deny that such coercion exists and claim that he or she is engaging in the sexual behavior willingly. In such a case it will be the responsibility of prison PREA investigators to conduct a thorough investigation to distinguish between this subversive victimization and actual consensual sexual activity.

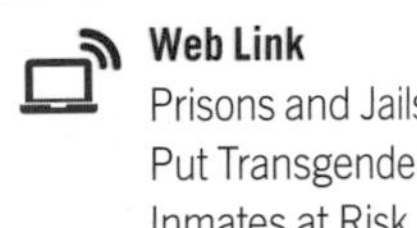
Web Link
Prisons and Jails Put Transgender Inmates at Risk

To further showcase the past treatment of the LGBTI population, consider that many state classification systems had presumed at intake that LGBTI inmates were more likely to be sexual perpetrators and would, therefore, place them in housing usually allocated for sex offenders. This, ironically, put the LGBTI inmate is even worse circumstances, further increasing the likelihood for victimization.

As can be seen, the standards of care for the LGBTI inmate population have been greatly revised in the past decade. These changes are in stark contrast to the old-school prison subculture discussed elsewhere in this text. While these changes are required by administrators, there is still significant resistance among both correctional staff and the inmate population. Just because the laws have been enacted does not mean persons within facilities have changed their own personal views regarding LGBTI offenders. This is, of course, no different than what is seen in outside society in which the population is in conflict regarding views on gay marriages and other issues related to sexual orientation and identity. Nevertheless, just as we have seen significant social change in this area in broader society, similar changes are now permeating the correctional environment as well.

ELDERLY OFFENDERS

The graying of America is a phenomenon that is now fairly common knowledge among most of the public, particularly among those who keep up with recent news and events. However, there is a consequence to the aging phenomenon that stays largely out of view: an elderly inmate population that is burgeoning within state prison systems. This ever-growing and ever-aging population tends to have a multiplicity of problems. Indeed, elderly inmates tend to have physiological symptoms that mimic health conditions that are roughly 10 years in advance of their actual chronological age. Thus, a 50-year-old inmate will, on the average, tend to have the physiological health of a 60-year-old in outside society (Fabelo, 1999).

It is a legal fact, indeed a constitutional fact, that prison systems are responsible for the safety and security of the inmates in their charge. Administrators simply cannot run from this responsibility; standards of decency and human treatment require that appropriate medical attention be provided to inmates within their stead. The Eighth Amendment itself ensures that inmates are free from cruel and unusual punishment. Thus, prison administrators cannot inflict harmful conditions upon inmates if these conditions could be considered cruel, malicious, or unusual. In addition, the Supreme Court has ruled cases like *Estelle v. Gamble* (1976) and *Wilson v. Seiter* (1991) that administrators cannot remain deliberately indifferent to the safety and/or security needs of inmates in their custody. Thus, turning a blind eye to the needs of elderly inmates is not, and will not be, an option for correctional practitioners.

CROSS-NATIONAL PERSPECTIVE 11.1

Japan to Upgrade Care of Elderly Inmates

The swelling number of elderly inmates in Japan's prisons has prompted the government to begin a major revamp of its jails to provide elevators, handrails, and wheelchair ramps for incarcerated seniors.

Renovation plans are set to begin by the end of March [2007] in three of the country's 75 prisons to accommodate seniors who require assistance, the Justice Ministry said this week.

The government will spend $76 million to create senior-friendly facilities for about 1,000 inmates, the first step in a program likely to be expanded in the future, ministry officials said.

The number of inmates 60 or older was 8,700 at the end of 2006, close to a threefold increase from a decade earlier. Older inmates make up about 11 percent of all inmates in Japan, according to the Justice Ministry.

Most elderly convicts are repeat offenders and have been convicted of theft or fraud, according to the National Police Agency. Less than 1 percent committed violent crimes such as murder, the agency said.

Experts believe some elderly inmates deliberately get themselves jailed because they see few options in the outside world.

"The number of elderly repeat offenders is on the rise because it is extremely difficult for them to start their life over again after release," said Maiko Tagusari, a lawyer specializing in prison conditions.

"Some of them even intentionally repeat petty crimes in an attempt to return to prison," she said.

In 2006, the total number of arrests across all age groups fell by 2.3 percent from a year earlier, but the number of arrested senior citizens rose by more than 10 percent, according to the National Police Agency.

About 900 elderly prisoners have trouble walking, feeding themselves, or fulfilling prison duties, according to the ministry. A larger number have significant health problems but are able to take care of themselves well enough to live in prison without substantial assistance, the ministry said.

While those with dementia or serious health problems are kept at prison hospitals, most elderly inmates are in ordinary prisons and are required to provide compulsory labor.

The new prison facilities will be equipped with elevators, ramps, and handrails in hallways and bathrooms, as well as medical staff trained for nursing care. Many prisons do not have full-time doctors.

Hisato Honda, a ministry official in charge of corrections, said the changes will improve living conditions for the inmates and make taking care of them easier for guards and prison officials.

"The idea is to relieve prison officials' burden of attending to the senior inmates," Honda said. "When they're in good health, senior inmates are fine. But once they get weaker, they're a big burden for everyone."

The graying of the prison population reflects a shift in Japan's overall demographics.

People over 60 account for about 27 percent of Japan's population, and that percentage is rising. The aging trend has caused concerns about Japan's fiscal future, as well as the welfare and living conditions of the elderly—including those in prison.

QUESTION 1: After reading this article, how similar do circumstances in Japan regarding elderly offenders seem to be when compared to those in the United States? Provide a brief explanation for your answer.

QUESTION 2: In your opinion, what should prison systems do to address the challenges associated with housing elderly Inmates? Briefly explain your answer.

SOURCE: Yamaguchi, M. (2007, January 9). *Japan to upgrade care of elderly inmates.* Used with permission.

Classification of Elderly Offenders

Perhaps the first step in ensuring that any offender's needs are appropriately met is the process of assessment. This assessment then must classify the elderly offender into categories that will ensure that the right standard of care is given. This accomplishes three goals: The process (1) ensures that the inmate receives adequate care, (2) ensures that precious resources are not wasted on inmates not needing more intensive care, and (3) provides a guide when deciding housing and security levels for these offenders to protect them and others from possible harm.

It is also important to note that any classification system for elderly inmates should include a protocol that distinguishes between inmates who entered the prison system before age 50 and those who reached that age while in prison. In essence, the data should clearly and prominently note if the offender falls within the category of an **elderly first-time offender**, a **habitual elderly offender**, or an **offender-turned-elderly-in-prison**. This is an important security consideration that most correctional administrators will find useful when running their institution. Once the elderly offender

Elderly first-time offenders: Those who commit their first offense later in life.

Habitual elderly offenders: Have a long history of crime and also have a prior record of imprisonment throughout their lifetime.

Offender-turned-elderly-in-prison: Inmates who have grown old in prison who have long histories in the system.

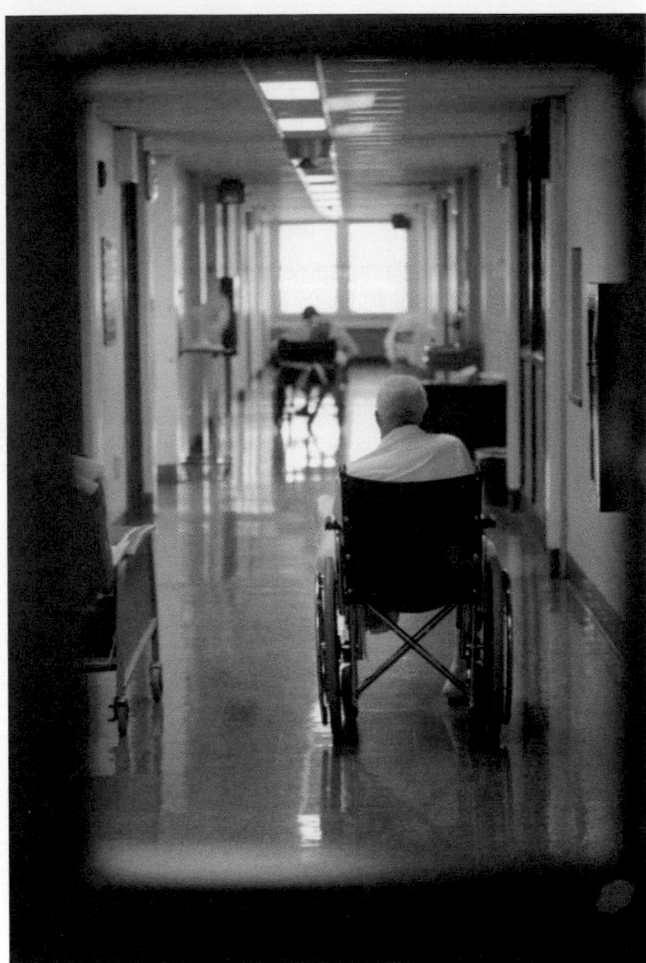

© Mark Peterson/CORBIS

■ PHOTO 11.7 Elderly offenders and offenders with disabilities are very costly to correctional facilities.

has been appropriately classified and once any necessary security precautions are resolved, prison staff will then be able to adequately ensure that the needs of these offenders are met.

The rise in numbers of habitual elderly offenders and offenders-turned-elderly-in-prison has to do largely with the advent of three-strikes felony sentencing in many states (Anno, Graham, Lawrence, & Shansky, 2004). These sentences require that third-time felony offenders serve mandatory sentences of 25 years to life. It should be noted that committing a felony does not necessarily mean that the offender is violent in nature. Also adding to these statistics are the punitive sentencing measures associated with the War on Drugs of the 1980s and 1990s. During this period, drug-using offenders were locked up at an all-time high, regardless of whether the crime involved violence or any form of drug trafficking (Anno et al., 2004).

Thus, habitual elderly offenders and offenders-turned-elderly-in-prison are the result of a confluence of social factors and criminal justice polices. These offenders, for various reasons, have been given enhanced penalties that preclude their release in the community. This greatly distinguishes them from the elderly first-time offender, who does not share a similar criminogenic background. Though they may look the same while in inmate clothes in the prison facility, they are usually quite different from one another, and the public would be well served to keep this squarely in mind. States that have abolished parole and other community outlets may want to consider establishing specialized court interventions for this type of offender. It is at this point that we turn our attention to the three typologies of elderly offenders, with each being briefly discussed in the paragraphs that follow.

Elderly First-Time Offenders

Elderly first-time offenders are those who commit their first offense later in life. It is estimated that approximately 50% of elderly inmates are first-time offenders, incarcerated when they were 60 or older. For these offenders who commit violent crimes, these are usually crimes of passion rather than premeditated crimes. Conflicts in primary relationships appear to increase as social interactions diminish with age. Older first-time offenders often commit their offenses in a spontaneous manner that shows little planning but is instead an emotional reaction to perceived slights or disloyalties. These offenders do not typically view themselves as criminal, per se, but instead see their situation as unique and isolated from their primary identity. First-time offenders are more likely to be sentenced for violent offenses. These offenses will usually be directed at a family member due to proximity, if nothing else. Some experience a crisis of one sort or another due to disparity regarding the aging process, and this is also thought to instill a sense of abandonment and resentfulness that may lead to aberrant forms of coping. Also, sexual offenses involving children are common among the first-time offending elderly. For persons over the age of 65, aggravated assault is the violent offense most often committed, followed by murder (Aday, 1994).

These offenders are also the most likely to be victimized in prison as their irascible behavior and demeanor are likely to draw the attention of younger inmates (Aday, 1994). These offenders are the most likely to have strong community ties and are therefore usually the most appropriate for community supervision because of this.

Habitual Elderly Offenders

Habitual elderly offenders have a long history of crime and also have a prior record of imprisonment throughout their lifetime. These offenders are usually able to adjust well to prison life because they have been in and out of the environment for a substantial portion of their life. They are a good source of support for first-time offenders and, if administrators are wise enough to implement this, are able to act as mentors. These offenders quite often fit the mold of greyhounds within the prison facility and command a degree of respect within the prison subculture. While they may cope well with prison life, these offenders typically have substance abuse problems and other chronic issues that make coping with life on the outside difficult. Some of these inmates are not considered violent but instead serve several shorter sentences for lesser types of property crimes. This is the group most likely to end up as geriatric inmates who die in prison.

Offenders-Turned-Elderly-in-Prison

Offenders-turned-elderly-in-prison have grown old while incarcerated. They have long histories in the system and are the least likely to be discipline problems. Long-term offenders are very difficult to place upon release because they have few ties in the community and a limited vocational background from which to earn a living. These offenders are often afraid to leave the prison and go back to the outside world because they have become so institutionalized to the predictable schedule of the prison. This also means that these individuals might consider suicide, particularly just prior to release, or even within a short time after release. This phenomenon is no different from that noted in the classic movie *The Shawshank Redemption,* which portrays a released inmate who cannot cope with life on the outside so he chooses to end his life by hanging himself.

Video Link
Elderly Prisoners Up by 250 Percent: Should They Be Released to Save Money?

Health Care Services and Costs

It should be clear to students that elderly offenders require substantial medical attention. The provision of this medical attention is very expensive and impairs many state prison systems around the nation. The cost of incarcerating an inmate who is 60 years of age or older is around $70,000 a year—roughly 3 times the cost for the average inmate. These inmates require specialized housing facilities, special programming, and sometimes even hospice and/or palliative care. Further, prison agencies must remain compliant with standards set by the ADA. All of these various requirements create a serious price tag for prisons, and since the population continues to age, it is likely that these expenses will continue to climb. How states and the federal government will afford these costs is a question often on the mind of many prison wardens and correctional administrators, particularly during times of economic challenge. The answer has yet to emerge, and this represents yet another challenge facing correctional agencies of the modern era.

CONCLUSION

This chapter has provided the student with an overview of specialized offenders, sometimes referred to as special needs offenders. These offenders tend to have special physical or mental needs that require extra consideration and action from correctional agencies. These offenders also tend to entail considerable costs for agencies and present challenges to the institution's ability to ensure their safety and/or security. However, correctional agencies are obligated to provide sufficient resources and services for these offenders; this has been established by Supreme Court rulings.

Among the various types of specialized offenders, those who have mental disorders are particularly problematic. These offenders tend to have high rates of institutional infractions and present with more problematic behaviors than do other inmates. Safety of these inmates is a bit more difficult to manage, and security is compromised due to various issues, such as the administration of medications and the supervision of these offenders in the population—a population that may victimize or dupe them when the opportunity presents. Further still, these inmates tend to have substance abuse problems that are comorbid with their mental illness. In many cases, the substance abuse may be their primary disorder, and the presenting mental illness may be co-occurring.

Inmates with HIV/AIDS have also become a major concern in corrections. HIV/AIDS is more prevalent among the offender population due to the offenders' risky lifestyles, which often include unsafe sex or needle sharing. Further, this disease is transmitted between inmates due to unhealthy sexual practices, intravenous drug use, and/or tattooing that occurs in prison. Female inmates have been identified as particularly susceptible to this disease, and it has been shown that they have higher rates of infection than do male inmates. This presents an additional area of concern when providing adequate care for the female population.

Lastly, elderly offenders were presented in this chapter as having distinct classifications that are determined by their prison history. The particular history of an inmate, such as whether that offender has engaged in a life of crime or committed a single crime resulting in a long-term sentence, affects the dynamics of his or her experience and the manner in which he or she is perceived within the prison subculture. Elderly inmates are a costly group to house, and, as we have seen, this cost is only going to continue to rise as we see a continued graying of the prison population.

Want a better grade?

Get the tools you need to sharpen your study skills. Access practice quizzes, eFlashcards, video, and multimedia at **edge.sagepub.com/hanser2e**

SAGE edge™

DISCUSSION QUESTIONS

1. What are some of the common problems encountered with specialized inmate populations in prison?
2. What is the definition of mental illness? How prevalent is it within state prison systems?
3. What are some safety and security concerns associated with the housing of inmates who are infected with HIV/AIDS? Do these inmates have special legal protections that should be considered? If so, what are these rights or protections?
4. Identify and define the various classifications of elderly inmates within an institution.
5. What are some of the specialized requirements/considerations for prisons when housing elderly offenders?
6. How does the prison subculture impact, interact with, and react to inmates who are mentally ill, HIV-positive, and/or elderly?
7. How do individual trait criminological theories explain criminal activity among some specialized criminal populations?

SAGE edge™ **Test your understanding of chapter content. Take the practice quiz.**

KEY TERMS

Co-occurring disorders, 264

Diagnostic and Statistical Manual of Mental Disorders (DSM-5), 259

Elderly first-time offenders, 279

Four standards of mental health care, 261

Greyhounds, 258

Habitual elderly offenders, 279

HIV/AIDS, 268

Malingering, 264

Mental illness, 260

Mood disorders, 263

Offender with special needs, 256

Offender-turned-elderly-in-prison, 279

Therapeutic community, 266

Universal design, 258

SAGE edge™ **Review key terms with eFlashcards.**

APPLIED EXERCISE 11.1

In the case of *Farmer v. Brennan*, 511 U.S. 825 (1994), the Supreme Court of the United States ruled that a prison official's "deliberate indifference" to a substantial risk of serious harm to an inmate violates the cruel and unusual punishment clause of the Eighth Amendment. The case concerned Dee Farmer, a pre-op male-to-female transsexual who had been incarcerated with the general male population after being transferred to USP Terre Haute in Indiana. Farmer was repeatedly raped and beaten by the other inmates and acquired HIV/AIDS as a result. Farmer claimed that the prison administration should have known that she was particularly vulnerable to sexual violence.

Consider this case and what you have learned in prior chapters regarding the legal liability of a prison staff member.

Answer the following questions in a 500- to 1,000-word essay:

1. Do prison personnel have a legal responsibility to safeguard effeminate inmates who have same-sex preferences? Why or why not? Be sure to explain your answer.
2. What measures should be taken to safeguard offenders with alternative sex identities and/or characteristics? How is this relevant to the reduction of HIV/AIDS in a prison facility?
3. What complications and challenges might occur for prison staff who safeguard inmates who engage in behaviors that are counter to the tenets of the prison subculture, which was discussed in Chapter 9 of this text?
4. Are prison staff required to protect inmates from potential exposure to HIV/AIDS?

● WHAT WOULD YOU DO?

You work within the administrative segregation unit of a maximum-security prison as a sergeant. You supervise approximately 25 officers on your shift, each of whom works in a different position throughout the five cell blocks that you supervise. One day, while doing your rounds and signing paperwork maintained by your officers, you notice that a pair of officers are on the second level of the cell block standing in front of a cell. You do not reveal your presence, but you listen closely; they are laughing at and ridiculing an inmate in the cell who is known to take a variety of medications due to symptoms of schizophrenia. Their joking is not violent, but it is demeaning, and it is likely to further aggravate the inmate's future mental condition.

This particular inmate attempted to stab an officer 2 months ago with a homemade blade, and thus he is not liked by many of the officers. However, you suspect (based on information from other inmates) that the officer who was attacked had been taunting this inmate and humiliating him for weeks. As their sergeant, you are expected to identify with the other officers and to not befriend inmates. Nor should you, according to the tenets of correctional officer subculture, take the word of inmates over that of other officers.

This situation creates a bit of a dilemma for you, but, if left unresolved, it can escalate to another potential stabbing incident in your department. You consider the options you have as you listen to the laughter from the officers and from other inmates listening in nearby cells.

What would you do?

12 JUVENILE CORRECTIONAL SYSTEMS

©iStockphoto.com/Windzepher

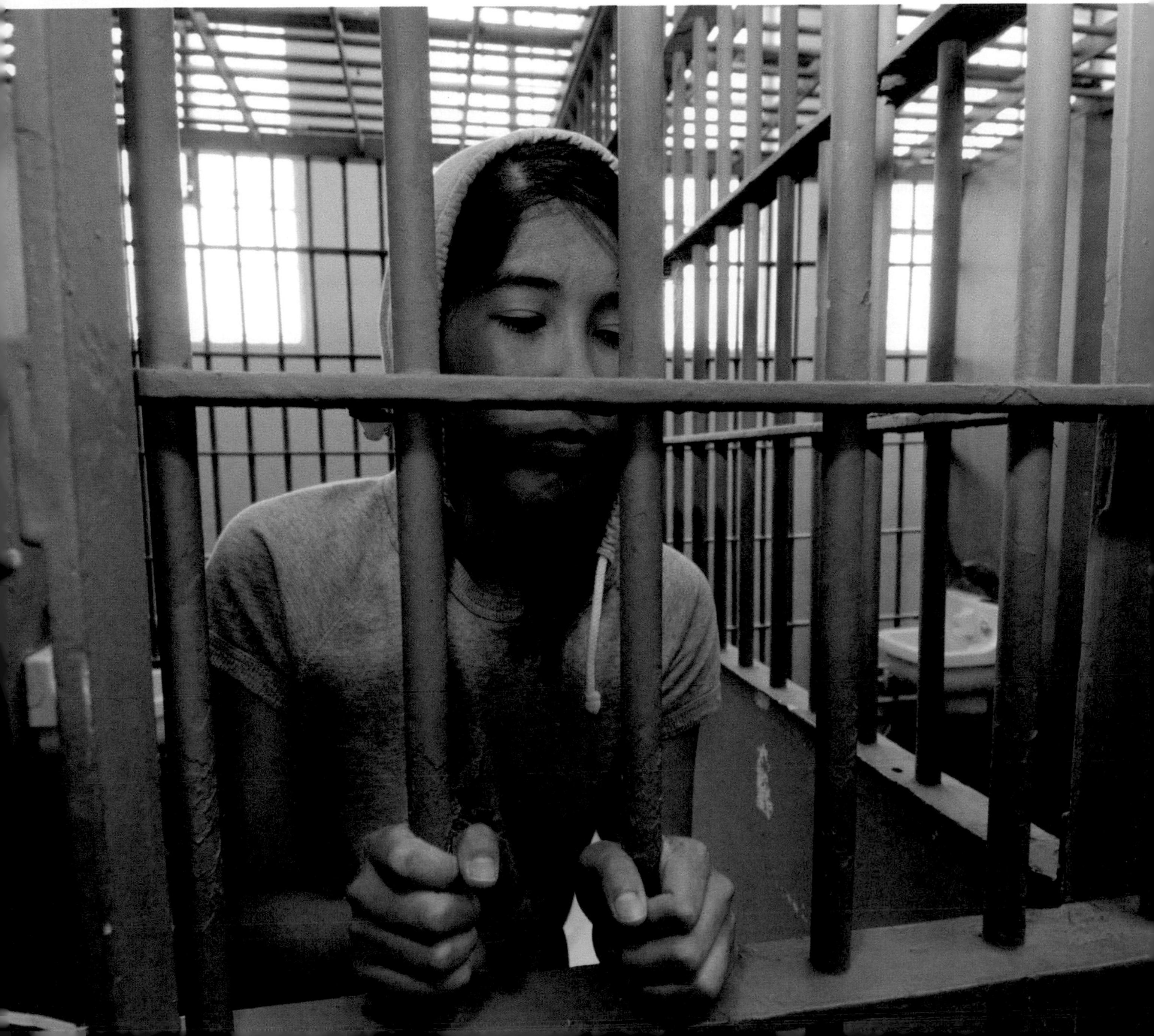

A GAME OF YAHOO GONE BAD

Jimmy Ray listened to the radio as it played a really old song, one that he remembered from when he was 16 years old. He remembered the song well because it was the one that was playing the night that he committed the crime that got him life without parole.

Jimmy, now 48, thought back 32 years ago to that night. He was riding around with his best friend, Tommy Eugene, in an old model Camaro, and the music was blaring. The song "Twilight Zone" by Golden Earring was playing, and the lyrics "*And you will come to know, when the bullet hits the bone*" were in his head.

Tommy Eugene took a long draw on the joint that he was smoking. He glanced over at Jimmy Ray and exclaimed, "Hey man, we're out of beer!"

Jimmy replied, "Well, I'm pretty buzzed with this skunk weed, but I got cotton mouth from smoking . . . so let's go get some beer to wash it down!"

Tommy frowned. "I ain't got no money."

Jimmy considered his own financial situation. He had not been able to cash his paycheck. He had an ATM card but did not want to spend money on Tommy and the two girls that they were planning to meet later that night at a party. Tommy was older than Jimmy and should have had money, but Tommy always seemed to "forget" his money and leave it to Jimmy to pay.

Jimmy said, "Well, looks like it is time for a good game of *Yahoo*!"

Tommy looked at Jimmy with a huge grin. "No way, man, you're kidding, right?"

Jimmy just shrugged. "If you want beer, you're gonna have to work for it."

The plan was to leave the car running, go into the convenience store, and each grab a 12-pack of their preferred beer. This seemed to work well . . . at first. The clerk was not even at the counter when they went into the store. The boys slowly approached the cooler, reached in, and pulled out two 12-packs of beer. As they walked toward the counter, they noticed the clerk still was not back. *What a lucky break!* Jimmy thought to himself. *We will be in the car and on our way before the guy comes back and realizes that we heisted the beer.*

As they walked out of the store, they yelled "Yahoo!" Then they looked behind them and saw the clerk standing next to the front door, smoking a cigarette. He grinned at them and said, "Hey man, I know you guys are in a hurry, but I am on my smoke break—I was out back."

As Jimmy and Tommy kept walking toward the car, they noticed the engine had been shut off.

The clerk laughed. "You guys missing these?" he asked as he held up Tommy's car keys. Tommy yelled several obscenities at the clerk, who just kept smiling and laughing at Tommy.

Jimmy said, "Look, how about we put the beer back and you give us the keys back; we can just act like nothing happened."

LEARNING OBJECTIVES:

1. Discuss the history and development of juvenile corrections.
2. Explain the legal precepts of the juvenile justice system and legal rights for juveniles.
3. Describe how juveniles are screened and classified as offenders.
4. Evaluate the relationship between prior abuse and current offending patterns of juveniles.
5. Summarize the unique characteristics and challenges of female juvenile offenders.
6. Describe the unique characteristics and challenges of having juvenile gang members in custody.
7. Compare and contrast detention versus incarceration for juveniles, and discuss incarceration of juveniles in adult facilities.
8. Discuss the various types of facilities and institutions used to house juvenile offenders.

The clerk shook his head. "Nope, ain't happening," he said, in a very matter of fact tone. Then he just looked at them, taking another drag from his cigarette.

What happened next was a blur to Jimmy. Tommy approached the clerk and hit him in the head with the 12-pack of beer. It made a loud thunking sound when the bottles met the side of the man's skull, and he staggered, dazed by the blow.

Tommy yelled, "Now why don't you give me my keys before I kill you!"

Jimmy tried to wrestle the keys from the clerk but could not pry them from the man's hand. Using their fists and the beer bottles, he and Tommy beat the man to death. Leaving the body twitching on the concrete, they grabbed the keys and peeled away from the convenience store. The clerk must have called the police before he confronted the boys, however, because as they pulled out on the road, a police squad car came barreling up the road and began to pursue them.

Tommy gunned the car as he pulled out a .38 revolver from under his seat. He tried to shoot out the window at the police car behind them but could not do so and drive.

He shoved the gun at Jimmy. "You shoot, I'll drive! I can't go to jail over this!"

The high-speed chase that followed ended when Tommy wrapped the car around a telephone pole. Tommy emerged with the gun in his hand, instigating a shoot-out in which he was killed. Jimmy had sustained a number of broken bones in the crash and was taken into custody.

The end result was an attempted capital murder charge for shooting at the police, a murder charge in the first degree for killing the clerk, and a sundry array of lesser charges, such as resisting arrest, armed robbery, and drug possession. This crime took place during a time when America was in a panic about the juvenile predator, often portrayed in the news media.

Jimmy was tried as an adult and received life with no parole. His life was over, at least as he knew it.

Now, however, he had recently read a newspaper article that noted the Supreme Court would consider making sentences such as his retroactive, thereby allowing him a shot at parole. Jimmy had been a model inmate during his 30 years of doing time. He wondered what it was like out in the free world. When he was 16, cell phones, the Internet, and computer technology had not even existed.

Jimmy did not want to get his hopes up, but he could not help but wonder if he would ever be able to enter the world again. He tried to focus on other stuff as the song by Golden Earring came to a close and faded off the air.

INTRODUCTION

This chapter is unique from all of the other chapters in this text because it addresses an area of corrections that is in most respects separate and distinct from the other segments of the criminal justice system, including the correctional system. The juvenile system has a different orientation, emphasis, and set of terms and concepts that make it unique from adult corrections. For instance, the use of secure facilities is avoided if at all possible. The vast majority of youth who are processed through the juvenile justice system are placed on some form of community supervision. While this is also true in the adult system, this trend is even more salient within the juvenile system. Youth are not considered to be as culpable as adult offenders, and it is presumed that they are more impressionable than adults. Thus, the use of restrictive environments can have negative and counterproductive outcomes. Again, this is true with adult offenders as well, but it is not as pronounced as with juveniles.

The means by which we process juvenile offenders are grounded in historical occurrences and legal precedents that have led to many unique considerations for youth. It is important that students are familiar with this history so that the philosophical underpinnings to our current juvenile correctional system will be better understood. Because of this, we will first focus on the history of juvenile justice, punishment, and corrections, followed with a discussion of the legal precedents that have shaped our modern-day understanding of juvenile justice. In doing so, much of this discussion has been adapted from a historical account of the juvenile system titled *Juvenile Justice*, by Cox, Allen, Hanser, and Conrad (2011). This is because the author of this text is one of the contributors to *Juvenile Justice* and is therefore familiar with its content. Further, this account is well written and succinct when one considers the scope and breadth of the developments that have occurred within the field of juvenile justice throughout the years.

HISTORY OF JUVENILE CORRECTIONS

Age of responsibility: Roman civil law made distinctions between juveniles and adults based on the notion of age of responsibility.

The distinction between youthful and adult offenders coincides with the beginning of recorded history. Some 4,000 years ago, the Code of Hammurabi (2270 B.C.) discussed runaways, children who disowned their parents, and sons who cursed their fathers (see Chapter 1). Approximately 2,000 years ago, Roman civil law made distinctions between juveniles and adults based on the notion of **age of responsibility**. In ancient Jewish law, the Talmud specified conditions under which immaturity was to be considered in imposing punishment. There was no corporal punishment prior to puberty, which was considered to be the age of 12 years for females and 13 years for males. No capital punishment was to be imposed for those under 20 years of age. Similar leniency was found among Muslims, where children under the age of 17 years were typically exempt from the death penalty (Bernard, 1992).

By the fifth century B.C., codification of Roman law resulted in the Twelve Tables, which made it clear that children were criminally responsible for violations of law and were to be dealt with by the criminal justice system (Nyquist, 1960). Punishment for some offenses, however, was less severe for children than for adults. For example, theft of crops by night was a capital offense for adults, but offenders under the age of puberty were only to be flogged. Adults caught in the act of theft were subject to flogging and enslavement to the victims, but children received only corporal punishment at the discretion of a magistrate and were required to make restitution (Ludwig, 1955). Originally, only children who were incapable of speech were spared under Roman law, but eventually immunity was afforded to all children under the age of 7 years as the law came to reflect an increasing recognition of the stages of life. In general, only children who were approaching puberty were considered to know the difference between right and wrong and were held accountable for their crimes.

English Origins

Roman and canon law undoubtedly influenced early Anglo-Saxon **common law** (law based on custom or use), which emerged in England during the eleventh and twelfth centuries. For our purposes, the distinctions made between adult and juvenile offenders in England at this time are most significant. Under common law, children under the age of 7 years were presumed to be incapable of forming criminal intent and, therefore, were not subject to criminal sanctions. Children between the ages of 7 and 14 years were not subject to criminal sanctions unless it could be demonstrated that they had formed criminal intent, understood the consequences of their actions, and could distinguish right from wrong (Blackstone, 1803, pp. 22–24). Children over the age of 14 years were treated much the same as adults.

Another important step in the history of juvenile corrections occurred during the fifteenth century when chancery or equity courts were created by the king of England. **Chancery courts**, under the guidance of the king's chancellor, were created to consider petitions of those who were in need of special aid or intervention, such as women and children left in need of protection and aid by reason of divorce, death of a spouse, or abandonment, and to grant relief to such persons. Through the chancery courts, the king exercised the right of ***parens patriae*** ("parent of the country") by enabling these courts to act ***in loco parentis*** ("in the place of parents") to provide necessary services for the benefit of women and children (Bynam & Thompson, 1992). In other words, the king, as ruler of his country, was to assume responsibility for all of those under his rule, to provide parental care for children who had no parents, and to assist women who required aid for any of the reasons just mentioned. Although chancery courts did not normally deal with youthful offenders, they did deal with dependent or neglected children, as do juvenile courts in the United States today.

Throughout the 1600s and most of the 1700s, juvenile offenders in England were sent to adult prisons, although they were at times kept separate from adult offenders. The Hospital of St. Michael, the first institution for the treatment of juvenile offenders, was established in Rome in 1704 by Pope Clement XI. The stated purpose of the hospital was to correct and instruct unruly juveniles so that they might become useful citizens (Griffin & Griffin, 1978, p. 7). The first private separate institution for youthful offenders in England was established by Robert Young in 1788. The goal of this institution was "to educate and instruct in some useful trade or occupation the children of convicts or such other infant poor as [were] engaged in a vagrant and criminal course of life" (Sanders, 1974, p. 48).

Common law: Law based on custom or use.

Chancery courts: Created to consider petitions for special aid or intervention and to grant relief to such persons.

***Parens patriae*:** "Parent of the country."

***In loco parentis*:** "In the place of parents."

Evolution of Juvenile Corrections in the United States

Meanwhile, in the United States, dissatisfaction with the way young offenders were being handled was increasing. As early as 1825, the Society for the Prevention of Juvenile Delinquency advocated separating juvenile and adult offenders (Snyder & Sickmund, 1999). Up to this point in time, youthful offenders had been generally subjected to the same penalties as adults, and little or no attempt was made to separate juveniles from adults in jails or prisons. This caused a good deal of concern among reformers, who feared that criminal attitudes and knowledge would be passed from the adults to the juveniles. In 1818, a New York City committee on pauperism gave the term *juvenile delinquency* its first public recognition by referring to it as a major cause of pauperism (Drowns & Hess, 1990, p. 9). As a result of this increasing recognition of the problem of delinquency, several institutions for juveniles were established between 1824 and 1828. These institutions were oriented toward education and treatment rather than punishment, although whippings, long periods of silence, and loss of rewards were used to punish the uncooperative. In addition, strict regimentation and a strong work ethic were common.

Under the concept of *in loco parentis,* institutional custodians acted as parental substitutes with far-reaching powers over their charges. For example, the staff members of the New York House of Refuge, established in 1825, were able to bind out wards as apprentices, although the consent of the child involved was required. Whether or not such consent was voluntary is questionable given that the alternatives were likely unpleasant. The New York House of Refuge was soon followed by other such institutions in Boston and Philadelphia (Abadinsky & Winfree, 1992).

According to Simonsen and Gordon (1982), "By the mid-1800s, **houses of refuge** were enthusiastically declared a great success. Managers even advertised their houses in magazines for youth. Managers took great pride in seemingly turning total misfits into productive, hard-working members of society" (p. 23, boldface added). However, these claims of success were not undisputed, and by 1850 it was widely recognized that houses of refuge were largely failures when it came to rehabilitating delinquents and had become much like prisons. As Simonsen and Gordon (1982) stated,

> In 1849 the New York City police chief publicly warned that the numbers of vicious and vagrant youth were increasing and that something must be done. And done it was. America moved from a time of houses of refuge into a time of preventive agencies and reform schools. (p. 23)

Houses of refuge: Institutions that were oriented toward education and treatment for juveniles.

Reform school: An industrial school.

In Illinois, the Chicago Reform School Act was passed in 1855, followed in 1879 by the establishment of industrial schools for dependent children. These schools were not unanimously approved, and contrasting rulings on their constitutionality continued through the late 1800s. Ultimately, despite the well-meaning intentions, the new **reform schools**, which existed in both England and the United States by the 1850s, were not effective in reducing the incidence of delinquency. Despite early enthusiasm among reformers, there was little evidence that rehabilitation was being accomplished.

Library of Congress

■ PHOTO 12.1 Reform schools such as the one pictured above were hailed by reformers but ultimately were not found to be effective in reducing delinquency among youth.

The failures of reform schools increased interest in the legality of the proceedings that allowed juveniles to be placed in such institutions. During the last half of the nineteenth century, there were a number of court challenges concerning the legality of failure to provide due process for youthful offenders. Some indicated that due process was required before incarceration (imprisonment) could occur, and others argued that due process was unnecessary because the intent of the proceedings was not punishment but rather treatment. In other words, juveniles were presumably being processed by the courts in their own "best interests."

During the post–Civil War period, an era of humanitarian concern emerged, focusing on children laboring in sweatshops, coal mines, and factories. These children,

CROSS-NATIONAL PERSPECTIVE 12.1

Overview of Family Court Jurisdiction in Juvenile Cases in Japan

The present Juvenile Act provides that the family court has jurisdiction over juveniles who (1) habitually disobey the proper control of their custodian, (2) repeatedly desert their home without proper reason, (3) associate with persons who have a criminal tendency or are of immoral character, or immoral persons, or frequent places of dubious reputation, and (4) habitually act so as to injure or endanger their own morals or those of others, provided that from their character or environment there is a strong likelihood that the juveniles involved will become offenders.

As provided by the Child Welfare Act, children under 14 years of age are primarily handled by the child guidance center when they have committed acts that would constitute a crime under the penal acts if committed by a person aged 14 or over. These children come under the jurisdiction of the family court only when the prefectural governor or the chief of the child guidance center refers them to the family court. The family court ordinarily has jurisdiction over any juvenile under 20 years of age.

Proceedings for Juvenile Delinquency Cases

Family court proceedings involving juveniles are generally commenced in the following cases:

1. A judicial police officer or public prosecutor sends a juvenile case to the court.
2. A prefectural governor or chief of the child guidance center refers a juvenile case to the court.
3. A family court probation officer who has found a delinquent juvenile reports the case to the court.
4. Someone who is in charge of the protection of a juvenile, a schoolteacher, or any other person informs the court of the case.

When a case is filed in the family court, the judge assigns the case to a family court probation officer and gives directions for the investigation. The officer then undertakes a thorough and precise social inquiry into the personality, personal history, family background, and environment of the juvenile. When the juvenile needs to be taken into protective custody, the judge may detain the juvenile in a juvenile classification home (***shonen-kanbetsu-sho***). The maximum detention period is 4 weeks in general. However, the detention period may be extended up to 8 weeks when the examination of evidence is necessary because the juvenile denies the facts constituting the alleged delinquency.

Upon completion of social inquiry by the family court probation officer, the officer sets down the juvenile's social record and his or her opinion as to the case, together with the recommendations about its disposition, and submits this as a report to the judge. Taking this report into consideration, the judge sets a time and place for a hearing.

The Family Court Judge Renders a Decision

There are several determinations the judge might make. The determination is made on the basis of the family court probation officer's report, the judge's own research and inquiry, and the results of the hearing. The possible decisions are as follows:

1. A decision to refer the case to a child guidance center.
2. A decision to dismiss the case.
3. A decision to refer the case to the public prosecutor.
4. A decision to place the juvenile under one of the following protective measures:
    a. The juvenile is placed under the probation of the probation office.
    b. The juvenile is placed in a support facility for development of self-sustaining capacity (***jidojiritsushien-shisetsu***) or a home for dependent children (***jido-yogo-shisetsu***).
    c. The juvenile is placed in a juvenile training school (***shonen-in***).

QUESTION 1: From what you can tell, how is the juvenile justice process in Japan similar to that in the United States? Provide a brief explanation for your answer.

QUESTION 2: What are the similarities and differences in the use of juvenile confinement in Japan and the United States?

SOURCE: *Supreme Court of Japan: Juvenile delinquency cases.* Retrieved from http://www.courts.go.jp/english/proceedings/juvenile.html

and others who were abandoned, orphaned, or viewed as criminally responsible, were a cause of alarm to reformist "child savers." The child savers movement included philanthropists, middle-class reformers, and professionals who exhibited a genuine concern for the welfare of children. As a result, the 1870s saw several states pass laws providing for separate trials for juveniles, such as Massachusetts in 1874 and New York in 1892. However, the first juvenile or family court did not appear until 1899 in Cook County, Illinois.

LEGAL PRECEPTS AND ORIENTATION OF THE JUVENILE JUSTICE SYSTEM

By incorporating the doctrine of *parens patriae,* the juvenile court was to act in the best interests of children through the use of noncriminal proceedings. The basic philosophy contained in the first juvenile court act reinforced the right of the state to act *in loco parentis* in cases involving children who had violated the law or were neglected, dependent, or otherwise in need of intervention or supervision. This philosophy changed the nature of the relationship between juveniles and the state by recognizing that juveniles were not simply miniature adults but rather children who could perhaps be served best through education and treatment. By 1917, juvenile court legislation had been passed in all but three states, and by 1932 there were more than 600 independent juvenile courts in the United States. By 1945, all states had passed legislation creating separate juvenile courts.

The period between 1899 and 1967 has been referred to as the era of socialized juvenile justice in the United States (Faust & Brantingham, 1974). During this era, children were considered not as miniature adults but rather as persons with less than fully developed morality and cognition (Snyder & Sickmund, 1999). Emphasis on the legal rights of the juvenile declined, and emphasis on determining how and why the juvenile came to the attention of the authorities and how best to treat and rehabilitate the juvenile became primary. Prevention and removal of the juvenile from undesirable social situations were the major concerns of the court.

Clearly, the developers of the juvenile justice system intended legal proceedings to be as informal as possible given that only through suspending the prohibition against hearsay and relying on the preponderance of evidence could the "total picture" of the juvenile be developed. The juvenile court exercised considerable discretion in dealing with the problems of youth and moved further and further from the ideas of legality, corrections, and punishment toward the ideas of prevention, treatment, and rehabilitation. In 1955, the U.S. Supreme Court reaffirmed the desirability of the informal procedures employed in juvenile courts. In deciding not to hear the *Holmes* case, the Court stated that because juvenile courts are not criminal courts, the constitutional rights guaranteed to accused adults do not apply to juveniles (***In re Holmes* [1955]**).

***In re Holmes* (1955):** Held that because juvenile courts are not criminal courts, the constitutional rights guaranteed to accused adults do not apply to juveniles.

Then, in the 1966 case of *Kent v. United States,* 16-year-old Morris Kent Jr. was charged with rape and robbery. Kent confessed, and the judge waived his case to criminal court based on what he verbally described as a "full investigation." Kent was found guilty and sentenced to 30 to 90 years in prison. His lawyer argued that the waiver was invalid, but appellate courts rejected the argument. Kent then appealed to the Supreme Court, arguing that the judge had not made a complete investigation and that he was denied his constitutional rights because he was a juvenile. The Court ruled that the waiver was invalid and that Kent was entitled to a hearing that included the essentials of due process or fair treatment required by the Fourteenth Amendment. In other words, Kent or his counsel should have had access to all records involved in making the decision to waive the case, and the judge should have provided written reasons for the waiver. Although the decision involved only District of Columbia courts, its implications were far-reaching due to its consideration that juveniles might be receiving the worst of both worlds—less legal protection than adults and less treatment and rehabilitation than promised by the juvenile courts (*Kent v. United States,* 1966).

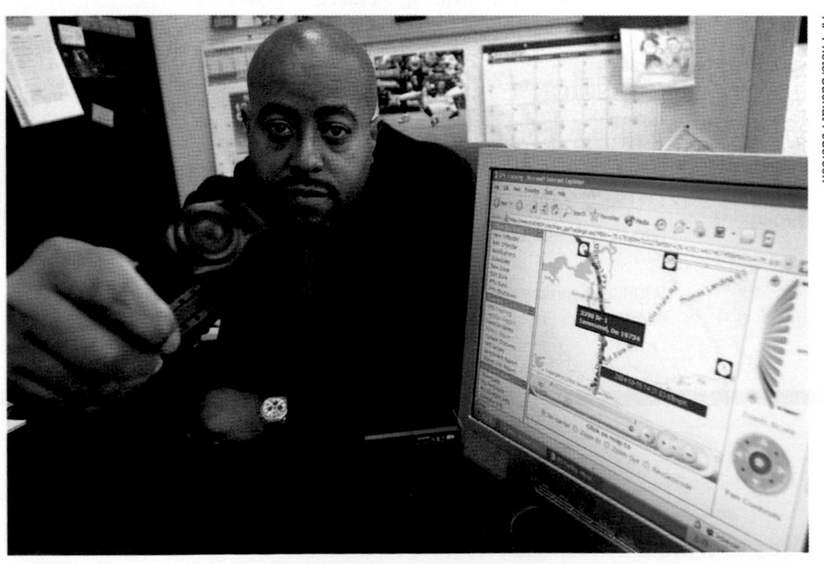

AP Photo/Suchat Pederson

■ PHOTO 12.2 Steven Wesley, regional manager for the state of Delaware's juvenile probation and aftercare program, holds a transmitter that uses GPS to track the movements of juveniles under house arrest. Juvenile probation officers play a key role in the juvenile system.

In 1967, forces opposing the extreme informality of the juvenile court won a major victory when the Supreme Court handed down a decision in the case of Gerald Gault, a juvenile from Arizona. The extreme license taken by members of the juvenile justice network became abundantly clear in the *Gault* case. Gault, while a 15-year-old in 1964, was accused of making an obscene phone call to a neighbor who identified him. The neighbor did not appear at the adjudicatory hearing, and it was never demonstrated that Gault had, in fact, made the obscene comments. Still, Gault was sentenced to spend the remainder of his minority in a training school. Neither Gault nor his parents were notified properly of the charges against him. They were not made aware of their right to counsel, their right to confront and cross-examine witnesses, their right to remain silent, their right to a transcript of the proceedings, or their right to appeal. In ***In re Gault* (1967)**, the Court ruled that juveniles have all of these rights in hearings that may result in institutional commitment. The Court's decision in this case left little doubt that juvenile offenders are as entitled to the same protection of constitutional guarantees as their adult counterparts, with the exception of participation in a public jury trial.

Juvenile Rights

During the years that followed *In re Gault*, the U.S. Supreme Court continued the trend toward requiring due process rights for juveniles. In 1970, in the *Winship* case, the Court decided that in juvenile court proceedings involving delinquency, the standard of proof for conviction should be the same as that for adults in criminal court—proof beyond a reasonable doubt (*In re Winship*, 1970). In the case of ***Breed v. Jones* (1975)**, the Court decided that trying a juvenile who had previously been adjudicated delinquent in juvenile court for the same crime as an adult in criminal court violates the double jeopardy clause of the Fifth Amendment when the adjudication involves violation of a criminal statute. The Court did not, however, go so far as to guarantee juveniles all of the same rights as adults. In the case of ***McKeiver v. Pennsylvania* (1971)**, the Court held that the due process clause of the Fourteenth Amendment did not require jury trials in juvenile court. Nonetheless, some states have extended this right to juveniles through state law.

In the case of ***Roper v. Simmons* (2005)**, the U.S. Supreme Court reversed a 1989 precedent and struck down the death penalty for crimes committed by people under the age of 18 years. The Court held that "evolving standards of decency" govern the prohibition of cruel and unusual punishment. The decision noted there is a scientific consensus that teenagers have "an underdeveloped sense of responsibility," therefore, it is unreasonable to classify them among the most culpable offenders (Bradley, 2006). This was despite the fact that the crime involved in this case was heinous and barbaric in nature.

In ***Graham v. Florida* (2010)**, the Court banned the use of life without parole for juveniles not convicted of homicide. The Court held that the Eighth Amendment's ban on cruel and unusual punishment forbids such sentences. At that time, *Graham* was considered a watershed case that impacted sentencing practices for many states around the nation. Two years later, the case of *Miller v. Alabama* (2012) led to the Supreme Court ruling that mandatory sentences of life without the possibility of parole are unconstitutional for juvenile offenders. This ruling extended the earlier ruling in *Graham v. Florida*. Essentially, *Miller* eliminated murder from being a justification for a life sentence without the possibility of parole for juveniles.

Process Involved With Juveniles in Custody

Initially, youth enter the juvenile justice system through some sort of contact with law enforcement. A juvenile can be taken into custody under the laws of arrest or by law enforcement if there are reasonable grounds to believe that the child is in immediate danger from his or her environment or if the youth has run away from home. In addition, court orders may be executed that require that youth to be taken into custody. The Uniform Juvenile Court Act (UJCA) is a document that provides guidance on how courts should process juveniles. Section 16 of the UJCA states that delinquent youth can be kept in a jail or another type of adult facility when other options are not available. In such a case, the detention space must be a room separate from adults, and the youth can be kept in detention only if it seems warranted as a means to ensure public safety. The purpose of this section is to protect youth from exposure to criminals and the negative effects that jails and other secure adult environments may have upon the youth.

Video Link
A Deeply Troubled Family

***In re Gault* (1967):** Ruled that in hearings that may result in institutional commitment, juveniles have all of the constitutional rights afforded to adults.

***Breed v. Jones* (1975):** Held that trying a juvenile who had previously been adjudicated in juvenile court for the same crime as an adult in criminal court violates the Fifth Amendment double jeopardy clause.

***McKeiver v. Pennsylvania* (1971):** Held that the due process clause of the Fourteenth Amendment did not require jury trials in juvenile court.

***Roper v. Simmons* (2005):** Ruled that the death penalty was unconstitutional when used with persons who were under 18 years of age at the time of their offense.

***Graham v. Florida* (2010):** Ruling that juveniles who commit crimes in which no one is killed may not be sentenced to life in prison without the possibility of parole.

CORRECTIONS AND THE LAW 12.1

Miller v. Alabama *(2012)*

This case was the third of three watershed Supreme Court rulings that addressed juvenile sentencing. Within a 7-year period, the High Court had (1) ruled that it was unconstitutional to give the death penalty to offenders who were juveniles at the time that they committed the crime; (2) prohibited life without parole for all crimes committed by juveniles, except homicide; and (3) ultimately banned the use of life without parole for juvenile offenders for all crimes, including homicide. But while *Miller v. Alabama* made it illegal to sentence youth to life without parole, there was still no guarantee that they would necessarily be given parole once eligible.

The impetus behind these decisions was grounded as much in new findings in social science research as in legal principles. Indeed, during this time, much attention was being given to research that demonstrated the adolescent brain is not fully developed. According to the ruling in *Graham v. Florida*, adolescents are subject to "transient rashness, proclivity for risk, and inability to assess consequences," and this should serve to mitigate juvenile sentencing. The Court further indicated that judges should consider the circumstances and characteristics of youth so that a more appropriate and individualized sentence could be administered.

While these issues were the bedrock upon which all three cases were decided, the *Miller* case was unique in that its ruling held implications that did not just concern future juvenile cases but also presented implications for past cases. Indeed, upon the decision, the question immediately emerged as to what should be done with the approximately 2,500 offenders who were serving life sentences without the possibility of parole for crimes committed while they were teenagers.

Thus, the issue at hand was whether the *Miller* case should be interpreted as retroactive. States have been mixed in their answer to this. Fourteen state Supreme Courts (Arkansas, Connecticut, Florida, Illinois, Iowa, Massachusetts, Mississippi, Nebraska, New Hampshire, New Jersey, Ohio, South Carolina, Texas, and Wyoming) have ruled that *Miller* applies retroactively, while seven other states (Alabama, Colorado, Louisiana, Michigan, Minnesota, Montana, and Pennsylvania) have ruled that *Miller* is not retroactive. Further, six additional states (California, Delaware, Nebraska, Nevada, North Carolina, and Wyoming) proactively passed juvenile sentencing legislation that applied retroactivity to juveniles who had been sentenced to life without parole.

At the time of the writing of this text, the Supreme Court has not yet ruled on whether the outcome of *Miller* must be administered retroactively. However, the Court has agreed to hear the case of 68-year-old Henry Montgomery, who has been sentenced to prison with no chance of parole since 1963.

In *Montgomery v. Louisiana*, Henry Montgomery was convicted for killing a deputy sheriff; Montgomery was 17 years of age at the time that he committed his crime. The killing automatically carried a sentence of life in prison without the possibility of parole, as per Louisiana law. As a result, Montgomery was sentenced without any real consideration for his age, the circumstances in which the crime occurred, or other potential mitigating factors.

After the ruling in *Miller v. Alabama*, Montgomery filed a petition to the Court claiming that his sentence amounts to cruel and unusual punishment in violation of the Eight Amendment and the 2012 ruling in *Miller*. Whether the Court will rule in favor of Montgomery, thereby requiring that all 2,500 youth in similar circumstances be given retroactive consideration, has yet to be seen. Nevertheless, this case has demonstrated how far-reaching a Supreme Court decision can be within our justice system.

SOURCES: Kingsmill, A. B. (2015). Lives hang in limbo: SCOTUS to hear case on whether ruling prohibiting mandatory life sentences for juveniles applies retroactively. *Louisiana Law Review, 75*(4).

The Sentencing Project. (2015). *Juvenile life without parole: An overview.* Washington, DC: Author.

SCREENING AND CLASSIFICATION OF JUVENILE OFFENDERS

Once it has been determined that a juvenile offender will be charged, the need to classify him or her is important. Students may recall mention in Chapter 8 of an instrument used in corrections for supervision and treatment decisions when classifying inmates, the Level of Service Inventory-Revised (LSI-R). This instrument is widely recognized in the field of corrections and comports well with many of the treatment programs for adults and juveniles that are grounded in cognitive-behavioral types of interventions. One instrument that has emerged as particularly useful with juvenile offenders is the Youth Level of Service/Case Management Inventory (YLS/CMI), which was developed and adapted from the LSI and is consistent with the theory and structure of the LSI-R (Flores, Travis, & Latessa, 2003).

This instrument is currently used in a variety of juvenile correctional settings in a number of jurisdictions. This same instrument has been employed to classify youth for judicial disposition decisions, placement into community programs, institutional assignments, and release from institutional custody. Proponents of the YLS/CMI claim that the instrument is a valid risk prediction tool for youth as well as a valid needs assessment tool that provides information relevant to intervention decision making. Juvenile courts, probation offices, and residential programs in a substantial number of states have adopted the YLS/CMI for case classification.

One specific area of importance in screening and assessment for juvenile offenders is substance abuse. As noted in Chapter 8, substance abuse issues are tied to the criminality of many adult offenders in both the state and federal correctional systems. Substance abuse is likewise a very important aspect of juvenile treatment because many young offenders experiment with drugs and alcohol. Further, persons who are under the influence of drugs or alcohol or who have a tendency to use drugs and alcohol typically have a higher rate of suicide when in jails or prisons. As suicide rates tend to be higher than average among teens in general, juvenile offenders are at particular risk for substance abuse–related suicide and/or additional mental health problems (e.g., depression and anxiety) when they are detained and/or placed in a secure environment.

The use of screening tools has become commonplace in many juvenile facilities, but only 50% of juvenile offenders in custody are in places that use standardized assessment tools to identify youth with substance abuse problems (Sedlak & McPherson, 2010). Despite the high rate of substance-related problems, nearly one-fifth (19%) of youth in custody are in facilities that do not screen for substance use problems, and more than one-third (36%) are in facilities that screen some, but not all, youth. Table 12.1 provides additional data regarding the substance abuse screening practices used for youth admitted into detention or residential facilities.

Regardless of the specific instrument used, the decisions regarding juvenile justice treatment for thousands of youth in all types of correctional settings are based on some type of screening, assessment, or classification process. This assessment is particularly important with juvenile offenders because of temporal considerations in the youth's development. At this point, the criminal justice system makes its first determination of a juvenile offender, and this determination is likely to have a very long-range outcome. All types of treatment and intervention given to these offenders will be based entirely upon the results of the assessment(s) given. Thus, at this point the trajectory for future offending or future reformation is initialized. Juveniles may not commit any further offenses, or, if they are inappropriately treated, this may increase the likelihood of their becoming an adult criminal.

■ Table 12.1: Youth in Custody by Their Facility's Practices for Screening Youth to Identify Substance Abuse Problems

Facility Screening Practice	Percentage
Who does the facility screen? When?	
All youth, definitely within 24 hours	27
All youth, at least some in 24 hours	12
All youth, none in 24 hours	24
Some youth, some in 24 hours	7
Some youth, none in 24 hours	10
No youth	19
What screening methods are used? (*all that apply*)	
Staff-administered question/interview	63
Standardized self-report instruments	50
Visual observation, medical exam, drug tests	47
Self-report checklist inventory	41
Records of previous tests, treatments	5

SOURCE: Sedlak, A. J., & McPherson, K. S. (2010). *Youth's needs and services: Findings from the survey of youth in residential placement.* Washington, DC: Office of Juvenile Justice and Delinquency Prevention.

Emphasis on Treatment

As we have seen, the primary purpose within the juvenile justice system is to treat and reform youth rather than to punish them. The system has been specifically designed with the mind-set that youth should be spared the stigma of a conviction and the trauma of full incarceration, when practical. The juvenile justice and mental health fields have increasingly recognized the scope of the mental health needs of youth involved in the juvenile justice system and the inadequacy of services to meet these needs (see Focus Topic 12.1 for more details). As we discussed in the prior subsection, standardized screening instruments have gained more acceptance within most treatment programs.

One reason that this is important is because youth in juvenile facilities tend to present with affective disorders, adjustment difficulties, and issues related to trauma and stress. For instance, symptoms of depression and anxiety were found to be very common among nationally surveyed

FOCUS TOPIC 12.1

Adolescents With Mental Health Needs

In an effort to improve services to this specialized population, the Texas Juvenile Probation Commission (TJPC) was tasked with creating a mental health screening instrument to be used by all departments. The TJPC has developed a comprehensive array of mental health services for this population. The project was named the Special Needs Diversionary Program and consists of juveniles with mental health issues that are supervised by juvenile probation officers who, in turn, work closely with mental health practitioners (eliminating the "organizational cracks" in the intervention process that are discussed in this chapter), guaranteeing the delivery of the necessary mental health services. The goals of the project are to keep the offenders at home within the community, reduce recidivism of those in the project, and have juvenile probation officers work closely with local mental health providers to ensure both proper assessment and interventions for juvenile probationers in the program. Some of the elements contained in this project's package of interventions are listed as follows:

1. Coordinated service delivery and planning between probation and mental health staff.
2. Provision and monitoring of medication.
3. Individual and/or group therapy.
4. Skills training.
5. In-home services such as multisystemic or functional family services.
6. Family focus support services.
7. Co-location of supervision and treatment services.

Youth participation is determined by indicators on the mental health screening instrument and the availability of a caretaker/ guardian willing to work with the mental health and probation departments. At this point, an additional clinical assessment is made to determine the child's ability to function in society. As a side note, it was found that 22% of these youth suffered from depression, 19% qualified for the diagnosis of oppositional defiant disorder, 18% had the diagnosis of conduct disorder (a precursor to antisocial personality disorder), and 9% had attention deficit/ hyperactivity disorder.

The Special Needs Diversionary Program illustrates how important assessment can be to both community supervision and mental health services. This program also demonstrates how public safety and offender needs can be better served when disparate community agencies create partnerships in providing service to special needs populations. Such partnerships, when coupled with accurate assessment instruments and procedures, can provide better interventions that are tailored for the offender. Interventions then will be more likely to have a better "goodness of fit" with the needs of the juvenile offender and will be better able to target those most at risk of recidivating when released on community supervision.

SOURCE: All material for this special insert was adapted from Spriggs, V. (2003). Identifying and providing services to Texas: Juvenile offenders with mental health needs. *Corrections Today, 65*(1), 64–66.

youth in treatment facilities, with 51% of the custody population reporting that nervous or worried feelings have kept them from doing what they want to do over the past few months and 52% indicating that they feel lonely for significant periods of time (Sedlak & McPherson, 2010).

Mental health services in the form of evaluation, ongoing therapy, or counseling are nearly universally available in juvenile facilities, with 97% of youth in places that provide one or more of these services either inside or outside the facility. However, despite the relatively high suicide risk in the placement population, individual screening for suicide risk is not common. More than one-fourth (26%) of juvenile offenders are in facilities that do not screen all youth for suicide risk, 45% are in facilities that fail to screen all youth within 24 hours, and 26% are in facilities that do not screen any youth at intake or during the first 24 hours (Sedlak & McPherson, 2010).

Suicide is the third leading cause of death among adolescents, and a prior suicide attempt is the single most important risk factor to look for (Wintersteen, Diamond, & Fein, 2007). One-fifth of youth in placement admit having two or more recent suicidal feelings. The prevalence of past suicide attempts (22%) of juvenile offenders is more than twice the rate for youth in the general population and nearly quadruple the rate in national samples.

COMMONALITY OF JUVENILE AS VICTIM OF PRIOR ABUSE

When delinquent behavior occurs, it may bring about further abuse, resulting in a vicious cycle that generates behavior that continues to get worse and worse. Children and adolescents who exhibit patterns of delinquency that emanate from the home often imitate the behaviors of parents or other family members. In some extremely dysfunctional homes, children may even be instructed on how to commit crimes. Though this may sound unusual, it is not unheard of, and there have been court cases where such occurrences have specifically been noted. Consider also that the crime of **contributing to the delinquency of a minor** is a form of neglect where an adult specifically facilitates the ability of youth to commit delinquent or criminal acts and encourages these youth to engage in such acts.

Video Link
Alabama 8-Year-Old Charged With Murder in Toddler's Beating Death

Abuse and neglect also foster delinquency in children due to the trauma produced by such experiences. For instance, Ireland, Smith, and Thornberry (2002) examined official records and utilized longitudinal survey data and found a strong relationship between maltreatment and delinquent behaviors. The research by Ireland et al. (2004) is important because it aids in demonstrating where much of the more serious offending among youth and young adults may come from. Though this does not explain all juvenile misbehavior, it does tend to be consistent in explaining etiology within a substantial portion of the more serious youthful offending as well as later adult offending. Consider also the research by English, Spatz Widom, and Brandford (2002), who note that there is strong support for a relationship between child abuse, neglect, delinquency, adult criminality, and future violent criminal behavior. The research by English et al. clearly underscores our contention that prior home life circumstances are interlaced with the youth's offending behavior for the majority of hard-core juvenile offenders. From the research just presented, it should be clear that youth who come from abusive homes indeed have an increased likelihood of engaging in serious delinquency, drug abuse, and later adult criminality. While a large number of youth engage in minor forms of delinquency, most of these offenses (e.g., teenage sex, use of alcohol at an occasional outing, speeding and minor traffic violations, violating minor ordinances) are part and parcel to the development of many teens. Indeed, these activities are often simply considered the process by which youth experience their newly budding sense of adolescent autonomy. However, when delinquency goes beyond these minor types of activity, such as with full-fledged burglaries (as opposed to petty shoplifting), drug use that goes beyond alcohol and marijuana, assaultive behavior, and other actions, such as teen rape, we contend that in many cases prior childhood socialization and exposure to noxious family and peer influences are a common thread in etiology.

Contributing to the delinquency of a minor: A form of neglect where an adult encourages and facilitates the ability of youth to commit delinquent or criminal acts.

Other researchers share similar views on minor delinquent behavior among adolescents, going so far as to say that it is statistically normal among young boys growing up in the United States (Moffitt, 1993). According to Terrie Moffitt (1993), youthful antisocial and risk-prone acts are personal statements of independence. For example, these youth may engage in underage drinking or cigarette smoking, particularly with their peers, as a means of displaying adult-like behaviors. Another common form of delinquency for this group might be minor vandalism that is often perceived more as a "gag" than as an act of victimization, such as the defacing of road signs, the destruction of residential mailboxes, and other petty forms of destruction. Shoplifting may also be encouraged among some members of this group for the occasional "five-finger discount" in chosen music and/or clothing stores that are frequented by the peer group. This allows a youth to display bravado among his or her peers and, incidentally, obtain an item that is valued by the individual and the peer group in the process. Lastly, some of these individuals may engage in occasional truancy from school, particularly if they are able to hide their absence. These adolescents typically commit acts of defiance or nonconformity simply as a means of expressing their developing sense

■ PHOTO 12.3 These youth have pooled all of their drug supply together to engage in a longlasting group drug binge.

of autonomy. However, these adolescents are not likely to continue their activities into late adulthood. Moffitt (1993) refers to these youth as **adolescent-only offenders.**

Adolescent-only offenders: Adolescents who typically commit acts of defiance or nonconformity to express their developing sense of autonomy; they are not likely to continue their activities beyond adolescence.

Life-course-persistent juvenile: Adolescent who lacks many of the necessary social skills and opportunities possessed by the adolescent-limited delinquent.

Child neglect: Occurs when a parent or caretaker does not provide the proper support or care required by a state's law.

Physical neglect: Includes abandonment, the expulsion of a child from the home, a failure to provide medical care, supervision, food, clothing, and shelter.

Emotional neglect: Inadequate nurturing or affection; allowing a child to engage in inappropriate or illegal behavior; and ignoring a child's basic emotional needs.

Educational neglect: Occurs when a parent or teacher permits chronic truancy or ignores the educational and/or special needs of a child.

While youth who might be classified as adolescent-only offenders may occasionally be in need of some sort of counseling for any number of life-course issues, they seldom will need to see a treatment provider who specializes in the offender population. In more instances than not, these youth will age out of their behavior and will have no need for a correctional counselor. Rather, general counseling that addresses teen development, social pressure, peer groups, and other common aspects of development are likely to be more effective for this group. On the other hand, some adolescents continue their delinquent behavior into and throughout adulthood, and these are what Moffitt (1993) referred to as the **life-course-persistent juvenile** delinquents (see Applied Theory 12.1 for more information on Moffitt's work).

Types of Child Abuse and Detection of Abuse

In many cases, juvenile youth are victims of various forms of neglect or abuse. This is a very important aspect of juvenile offending, particularly when trying to provide treatment services for such offenders. In many cases, community supervision officers will find themselves networking with child protection agencies, and these officers will likewise tend to have offenders on their caseloads who are in need of parenting assistance, whether the offender realizes it or not. In addition, one must consider that over 70% of female offenders on community supervision are also the primary caretakers of their children. This is an important observation, especially when one considers that the number of female offenders on community supervision is much higher than the number of those incarcerated. This means that community supervision officers are likely to come across issues related to the welfare of children on a fairly frequent basis. Further, disproportionate rates of abuse and neglect occur among a high number of delinquent youth.

In discussing these issues, we first turn our focus to child neglect since such maltreatment is often a precursor to later forms of abuse and since neglect also often occurs in conjunction with abusive treatment. **Child neglect** occurs when a parent or caretaker of a child does not provide the proper or necessary support, education, medical care, or other remedial care required by a given state's law, including food, shelter, and clothing. Child neglect also occurs when adult caretakers abandon a child that they are legally obligated to support (Cox et al., 2011). Neglect is typically divided into three types: physical, emotional, and educational (Cox et al., 2011). **Physical neglect** includes abandonment, the expulsion of the child from the home (being kicked out of the house), a failure to seek or excessive delay in seeking medical care for the child, inadequate supervision, and inadequate food, clothing, and shelter (Cox et al., 2011). **Emotional neglect** includes inadequate nurturing or affection; allowing the child to engage in inappropriate or illegal behavior, such as drug or alcohol use; and ignoring a child's basic emotional needs (Cox et al., 2011). Lastly, **educational neglect** occurs when a parent or even a teacher permits chronic truancy or simply ignores the educational and/or special needs of a child (Cox et al., 2011).

AP Photo/Mark Hertzberg

■ PHOTO 12.4 A student and his mother attend truancy court at Park High School in Racine, Wisconsin. Also in attendance are the municipal court judge, a social worker, the municipal court clerk, and a bailiff.

Acts of abuse are even more serious forms of maltreatment and include both physical and psychological forms of harm. **Child abuse** occurs when a child (youth under the age of 18 in most states) is maltreated by a parent, an immediate family member, or any person responsible for the child's welfare (Cox et al., 2011). According to Cox et al. (2011), **physical abuse** "can be defined as any physical acts that cause or can cause physical injury to a child" (p. 266). It is not uncommon for physically abusive parents to have been abused themselves as children, resulting in an intergenerational transmission of violence through their behavior. Psychological abuse is another frequently

APPLIED THEORY 12.1

Adolescent-Limited Versus Life-Course-Persistent Juvenile Offenders: The Theoretical Work of Terrie Moffitt

The most well-established developmental taxonomy in the study of youth aggression revolves around the distinction between life-course-persistent and adolescent-limited antisocial behavior (Moffitt, 1993). To understand this concept, it must first be understood that there is a significant difference between adolescent-limited and life-course-persistent offenders. However, during the adolescent period it is very difficult to distinguish between these two offenders because their delinquent behaviors are very similar (Moffitt, 1993).

The majority of individuals who are delinquents during childhood and adolescence stop offending before they reach adulthood. According to Moffitt (1993), those adolescents who desist from delinquency are referred to as adolescent-limited juvenile delinquents. Through antisocial conduct, adolescents reject the ties of childhood and demonstrate that they can act independently. It should be noted that self-report studies indicate that most teenage males engage in some criminal conduct, leading criminologists to conclude that participation in delinquency is a normal part of teen life (Scott & Grisso, 1997). Thus, adolescent-limited delinquents are likely to engage in crimes that are profitable or rewarding, but they also have the ability to abandon these actions when prosocial styles become more rewarding (Bartol & Bartol, 2010). The adolescent-limited youths are relatively free from personality disorders or poor decision making based on life skills deficiencies. Because of this, this group usually has adequate social skills to both compete and cooperate within the strictures of day-to-day society.

Some adolescents, however, continue their delinquent behavior into and throughout adulthood, and these are the life-course-persistent juvenile delinquents. These adolescents lack many of the necessary social skills and opportunities possessed by the adolescent-limited delinquent.

It has been found that many life-course-persistent delinquents are children with inherited or acquired physiological deficiencies that develop either prenatally or in early childhood. To compound this problem, many of these children come from high-risk social environments, reflecting the parental deficiencies thought to be genetically transmitted from parent to child (Moffitt, 1993). This combination of the difficult child and an adverse child-rearing context serves to place the child at risk for future delinquent behavior, setting the initial foundation for a life-course-persistent pattern of antisocial behavior during years when the child is usually most impressionable (Moffitt, 1993). Moffitt also found that early aggressive behavior is an important predictor of later delinquency and could possibly be a marker for the life-course-persistent offender.

The greater prevalence of late-onset youth violence refutes the myth that all serious violent offenders can be identified in early childhood. In fact, the majority of young people who become violent show little or no evidence of childhood behavioral disorders, high levels of aggression, or problem behaviors—all predictors of later violence. However, despite the fact that early predictors may not accurately assess the most *numerous* violent offenders, these factors are more likely to correctly identify the most *dangerous* juvenile offenders (Surgeon General Executive Summary, 2002). It is for this reason alone that appropriate assessment is so critical; it may not necessarily lower overall delinquency rates significantly, but it is likely to reduce violent crimes against members of society. Certainly, this is the category of crime that concerns the public most.

This distinction is important from an assessment point of view. Knowledge of these early indicators can allow the appropriate specialists an advantage in identifying children most at risk for delinquency. This knowledge then translates to an enhanced ability to provide effective interventions during an age when the child is likely to be more receptive. During early childhood, negative behaviors such as aggression have not been as clearly reinforced as they are by the time the child reaches adolescence. Thus, the earlier the intervention, the better the chance of saving the potential life-course-persistent offender from a life of misery and trouble.

SOURCE: Based on Moffitt, T. E. (1993). Adolescence-limited and life-course-persistent antisocial behavior: A developmental taxonomy. *Psychological Review, 100*, 674–701.

reported form of child abuse. **Psychological abuse** is also sometimes referred to as emotional abuse and includes actions or the omission of actions by parents and other caregivers that could cause a child to have serious behavioral, emotional, or mental impairments. Often, there is no clear or evident behavior of the adult caregiver that provides indication of psychological abuse. Rather, the child displays behavior that is impaired and/or has emotional disturbances that result from profound forms of emotional abuse, trauma, distance, or neglect with no direct evidence of the abuse usually existing.

Sexual abuse of youth consists of any sexual contact or attempted sexual contact that occurs between an adult or designated caretaker and a child. It should be noted that it is rare that physical indicators of sexual abuse are found. This means that most sexual abuse is detected due to behavioral indicators and/or when the youth discloses such acts. Possible behavioral indicators include an unwillingness to change clothes or to participate in physical education classes; withdrawal,

Child abuse: Occurs when a child is maltreated by any person responsible for the child's welfare.

Physical abuse: Abuse that consists of some type of physical battery and/or abuse that causes some type of physiological harm.

SAGE Journal Article Link
From Child Welfare to Juvenile Justice: Race, Gender, and System Experiences

fantasy, or infantile behavior not typical of a teen; bizarre sexual behavior; sexual sophistication that is beyond the child's age (which can be a bit hard to gauge with teens); delinquent runaway behavior; and reports of being sexually assaulted.

The behavior of parents also may provide indicators of sexual abuse. Such behaviors may include jealousy and being overprotective of a child. A parent may hesitate to report a spouse who is sexually abusing his or her child for fear of destroying the marriage or for fear of retaliation. In some cases, intrafamilial sex may be considered a better option than extramarital sex. Lastly, sexual abuse of children can have numerous side effects, including guilt, shame, anxiety, fear, depression, anger, low self-esteem, concerns about secrecy, feelings of helplessness, and a strong need for others. In addition, victims of sexual abuse have higher levels of school absenteeism, less participation in extracurricular activities, and lower grades.

FEMALE JUVENILES IN CUSTODY

As with adult female offenders, the needs of female juvenile offenders differ from those of males, as do the services they receive. Female juvenile offenders in placement have more mental health and substance use problems and worse abuse histories (Sedlak & McPherson, 2010). Higher percentages of females report an above-average number of mental or emotional problems and traumatic experiences, compared to male juveniles. The work of Sedlak and McPherson (2010) has been integrated into this section to illustrate some of the differences between male and female juveniles. According to their research, females report nearly twice the rate of past physical abuse (42% versus 22%), more than twice the rate of past suicide attempts (44% versus 19%), and more than 4 times the rate of prior sex abuse (35% versus 8%) as males. As we have seen in earlier sections of this chapter and in Chapter 10, prior childhood abuse (particularly sexual abuse) produces long-term damage to female offenders; often this translates into long-term criminality for the most severely troubled girls and young women who are victimized.

Female juvenile offenders are more commonly placed in residential treatment programs (compared to other types of programs), and nearly all youth in residential treatment programs are in facilities that provide on-site mental health services. Among these young female offenders, more receive individual counseling (85%), while fewer receive group counseling (67%). Females tend to give their counseling less positive ratings (Sedlak & McPherson, 2010). This last point is a bit troubling and points toward the need for correctional programs to improve services for young female offenders, just as is needed for adult female offenders (see Figure 12.1).

Psychological abuse: Includes actions or the omission of actions that could cause a child to have serious behavioral, emotional, or mental impairments.

Lastly, female juvenile offenders report significantly more drug experience than males, with 91% saying they had used at least one of the drugs listed (including marijuana, cocaine/crack, ecstasy, meth, heroin, inhalants, and an "other illegal drug" category), compared to 87% of males. More females than males report using nearly every substance listed, and 47% (compared to 33% of males) report having used four or more of the listed substances. Although males and females use drugs and/or alcohol at the same frequency just before entering custody, more females report recent substance-related problems (71% versus 67%). Despite females' greater substance abuse problems, they are often housed in facilities that provide less access to substance abuse treatment and education than are males (Sedlak & McPherson, 2010).

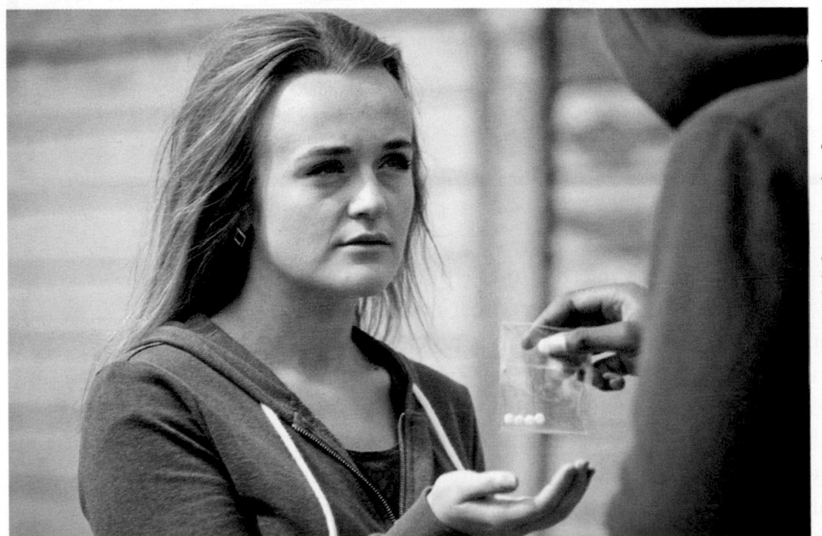

©iStockphoto.com/Highwaystarz-Photography

■ PHOTO 12.5 Although more males than females are arrested for delinquency, the number of female offenders has increased significantly during recent years.

JUVENILE GANG MEMBERS

When working with juveniles in the correctional setting, gang membership will be encountered on a fairly frequent basis. This is particularly true if the community supervision agency referring the youth is in a large or midsize metropolitan area or if the correctional

Figure 12.1: Percentage of Males and Females With Above-Average Numbers of "Yes" Responses to Mental and Emotional Survey Questions

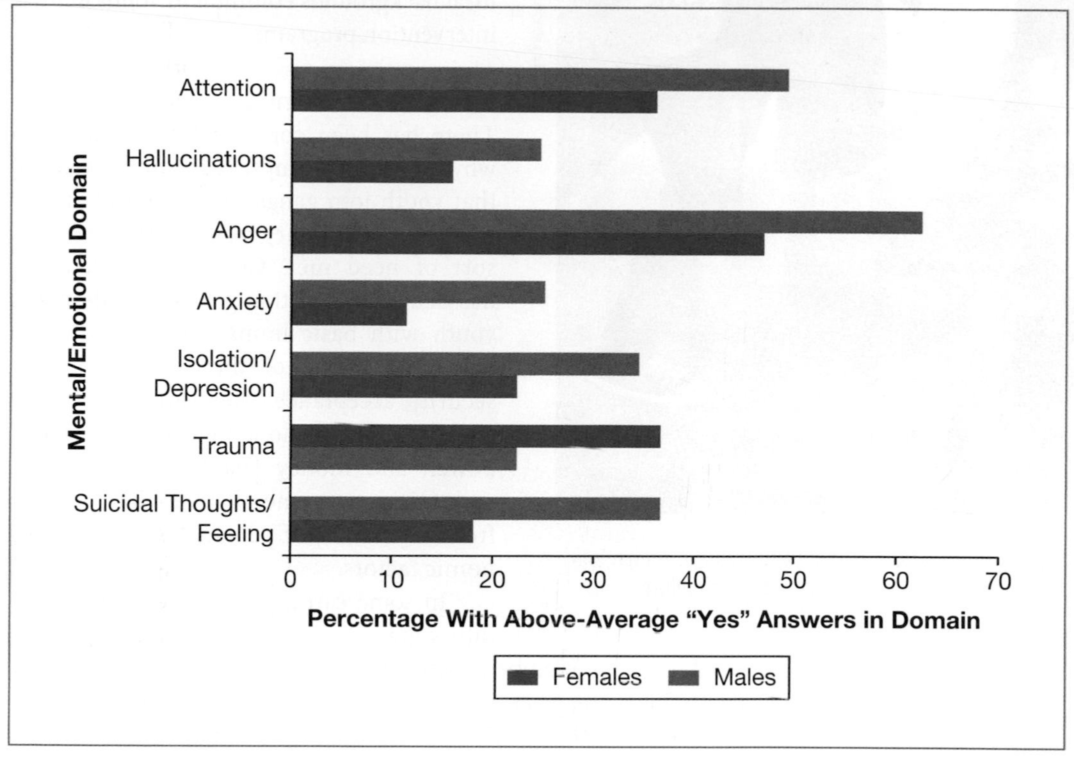

SOURCE: Sedlak, A. J., & McPherson, K. S. (2010). *Youth's needs and services: Findings from the survey of youth in residential placement.* Washington, DC: Office of Juvenile Justice and Delinquency Prevention.

counselor works with youth in a state-operated facility. For correctional staff who work with juveniles, it is advisable that they develop a working knowledge of the different gang groups in their area and among their juvenile population. An understanding of the tenets of a particular gang, how leadership structures operate, and gang alliances can be important in rapport building and can also provide staff with an understanding of the youth's world, which will, undoubtedly, be influenced by the activities of his or her gang. This basic knowledge will provide staff with a better ability to competently provide services to these youth.

Audio Link
Fixing California's Juvenile Justice "Black Hole"

Lifestyle, Peer Groups, and Youth Subculture

Peer groups are important for youth, and the peer group will likely be the primary source of socialization aside from the youth's family. Indeed, if the family is seriously dysfunctional, it is likely that the youth only identifies with his or her peer group. A number of subcultural groupings exist among juvenile offenders that will be important reference points for these youth, and it is helpful for counselors to be familiar with them. In particular, it should be noted that the gangsta movement has had a particularly strong impact on youth culture, particularly among delinquent youth. The "thug" look and/or genre of music is fairly common among youth who are processed throughout the juvenile system. While other subcultural groups exist (goths, alternative, etc.), they are not as well represented among the hard-core juvenile offender population. This is not to say that knowledge of such groups is not relevant to correctional counseling, but these groups are not as prevalent, largely due to the fact that they are not as widespread in popularity among today's youth and the public media.

A disproportionate amount of minority youth are processed through the justice system. Thus, in many juvenile systems, youth will tend to congregate along racial lines just as they might along subcultural lines. African American and Latino American youth are particularly represented, and these youth will likely affiliate with their own racial categories. In many cases, the youth from these minority groups will also come from families who are not affluent, with economic challenges common to their background. These factors will tend to impact the socialization process that has been experienced by these youth, and this is likely to be quite different from the backgrounds

©iStockphoto.com/Yuri

■ PHOTO 12.6 These youth exemplify those who are ready and willing to engage in violence to achieve their means and gain respect in the juvenile gang culture.

of many counselors. Because of this, correctional workers must also understand the cultural backgrounds common to youth in their intervention programs.

Reasons for Joining

There has been considerable debate as to why youth join gangs. It is our contention that youth join gangs for a number of reasons, but the primary reason is to have some sort of need met. Considerable research has demonstrated that gangs provide many youth with basic human needs related to belonging. Some of these needs include security, acceptance, friendship, food, shelter, discipline, belonging, status, respect, power, and money (Valdez, 2009). Thus, gangs and gang membership likely result from any variety of personal, social, or economic factors.

In some cases, youth may be pressured into gangs. This is particularly true where rivalries are rampant and the need to recruit members exists. Peer pressure and intimidation may be the causal factor for some youth. Likewise, protection from victimization at the hands of other gang groups in the community might be another motivator. In addition, there may be expectations from older siblings and/or family members who have also joined a given gang. This is an important consideration because gangs in some areas of Chicago, Los Angeles, and New York have family memberships that span three or more generations. Indeed, some neighborhoods in these metropolitan areas have members throughout who are current members or who were once members before becoming adults and settling down. In such cases, it is not uncommon for that neighborhood to sympathize with the gang and to provide it with support.

In addition to these neighborhood social conditions, the internal influences of the gang membership also work on the youth's development. The youngster may grow up knowing older gang members and may learn to admire these members. Over time, an informal familiarization with the gang may develop. Eventually, the gang psyche is taught via the gang formal indoctrination process. This transformation of a youth into a gang member involves a slow process of assimilation. Once these young people reach an age at which they are able to prove their worth to the gang leadership, they are required to engage in some sort of ritual. In most cases this may consist of getting "jumped in," which is when the gang members beat the youth and the youth is expected to fight until he cannot continue to do so, or it may consist of getting "sexed in," in which some females may be required to have sex with male members to obtain affiliate status.

Consider also that many hard-core juvenile offenders come from abusive and/or neglectful homes. This is one key motivator for these youth to join gangs. This motivation holds true for both male and female juvenile gang members. The family of origin is the primary source for developing the youth's sense of belonging and self-worth. If these youth do not get this support at home, they are likely to seek it elsewhere; gangs provide that source.

DETENTION VERSUS INCARCERATION

Detention facilities are secure residential facilities for youth and are separate from adult prisons, though they still resemble adult prisons in appearance and have locked doors and barred windows. These facilities are, in theory, supposed to be reserved for the most serious juvenile offenders—those who are violent and require secure confinement as a means of protecting society. Nevertheless, it is not uncommon for other youth, such as runaways, homeless youth, and those who are abandoned, to end up in these types of facilities.

These facilities may also hold youth who are scheduled for trial but have not been sentenced or who may be waiting for the imposition of their sentence. This means that youth of differing custody levels may be kept within these facilities. Other youth may be in violation of their probation and being held for revocation or modification proceedings. In recent years, the juvenile justice system has made efforts to remove status offenders and neglected or abused children from these detention facilities, when and where appropriate. But despite the ongoing effort to limit the use of detention, juveniles are still detained in about 20% of all delinquency cases.

Video Link
Insight

The overarching goal of juvenile corrections is to provide treatment services for youth and to avoid traumatizing or stigmatizing them in the belief that such restrictive measures will orient them toward further criminality. The use of juvenile waiver for serious offenders who are sentenced to periods of incarceration is presented in the following section. But for now, this sentencing option is presented to distinguish it from the use of detention. When youth are sent to prison, they are incarcerated with adult offenders. These youth are usually charged for adult offenses, and their sentencing terms are for several years. The types of incarceration that youth may face, whether in a juvenile detention facility or in prison itself, are discussed in the next few sections.

Juvenile Waiver for Serious Juvenile Offenders

For those child and adolescent offenders who are incarcerated for violent crimes, a special form of incarceration may be employed. This occurs when the juvenile case is transferred to adult court and results in what is commonly known as juvenile waiver. Waiver to adult court can theoretically be utilized for any offense, but this process is usually reserved for serious, violent felonies or for property crimes with which juveniles are repeat offenders. Juveniles who are tried in adult criminal court are most often kept in a juvenile facility or separate wing until they are of sufficient age to be transferred to the adult population. Those who are placed in an adult prison are usually separated from the adult population.

The disposition of a juvenile who has been tried and sentenced in an adult court varies from state to state. The usual procedure is that younger offenders who are found guilty are sent to a juvenile detention facility until they are at least 16 to 18 years of age. Their treatment there is basically the same as that of juveniles who were tried under the juvenile justice system. Nevertheless, some youth who are charged as adults may be sent to an adult facility if the crime and circumstances warrant this. The disadvantage to this process is that it sends a message of hopelessness to the youth and society regarding the likelihood of reformation. Further, there is the possibility that this approach will only increase the criminality of juveniles as they are exposed to the adult criminal population. The adult prison system's mission is primarily the punishment of offenders, and this naturally includes those juveniles included within its confines. Perhaps these offenders are best considered to be targeted by a form of legal "selective incapacitation," where the most severe offenders are removed from society for no other reason than to protect society from any further harm from them. However, this automatically translates to an admission from the justice system that it does not have the ability to reform the youth—something that can be disturbing when one considers the sheer number of years left to transpire for a young offender of, say, 14 or 15 years of age.

In 2005, juvenile court judges waived jurisdiction over an estimated 6,900 delinquency cases, sending them to criminal court. This represents less than 0.5% of all delinquency cases handled. The number of cases waived was relatively flat from 1985 to 1988, rose sharply from 1988 to 1994, and then fell back to the levels of the mid-1980s and remained there through 2005.

■ PHOTO 12.7 These juveniles listen to a guest speaker on the negative aspects of incarceration in an adult facility.

For many years, property offense cases accounted for the largest proportion of waived cases. However, since the mid-1990s, person offenses have outnumbered property offenses among waived cases. In 2005, half of waived cases involved person offenses. Table 12.2 provides specific details regarding the number and percentage of cases waived from juvenile court to adult court. As can be seen, the numbers of youth waived to adult court are quite small, and even fewer of these are actually sent to an adult prison by the time that the process is over. Further, it is clear that the use of the waiver process has declined since the 1990s. Though a slight increase occurred from 2001 to 2005, the overall impact since the 1990s has been a reduction of 47% in the use of juvenile waivers (see Figure 12.2).

INCARCERATION OF JUVENILES

Web Link
What Mass Incarceration Looks Like for Juveniles

The most severe dispositional alternative available to the juvenile court judge considering a case of delinquency is commitment to a correctional facility. There are clearly some juveniles whose actions cannot be tolerated by the community. Those who commit predatory offenses or whose illegal behavior becomes progressively more serious might need to be institutionalized for the good of society. For these delinquent juveniles, alternative options may have already been exhausted, and the only remedy available to ensure protection of society may be incarceration. Because juvenile

Table 12.2: Offense Profile of Cases Waived to Criminal Court

	Number of Waived Cases		Percentage of Waived Cases	
Most Serious Offense	2002	2011	2002	2011
Total delinquency	8,200	5,400	100%	100%
Person	3,200	2,500	39	47
Property	3,100	1,600	38	31
Drugs	1,100	700	14	13
Public order	800	500	9	8

SOURCE: Hockenberry, S., & Puzzanchera, C. (2014). *Delinquency cases in juvenile court, 2011*. Washington, DC: Office of Juvenile Justice and Delinquency Prevention.

Figure 12.2: The Use of Juvenile Waiver Continues to Decline

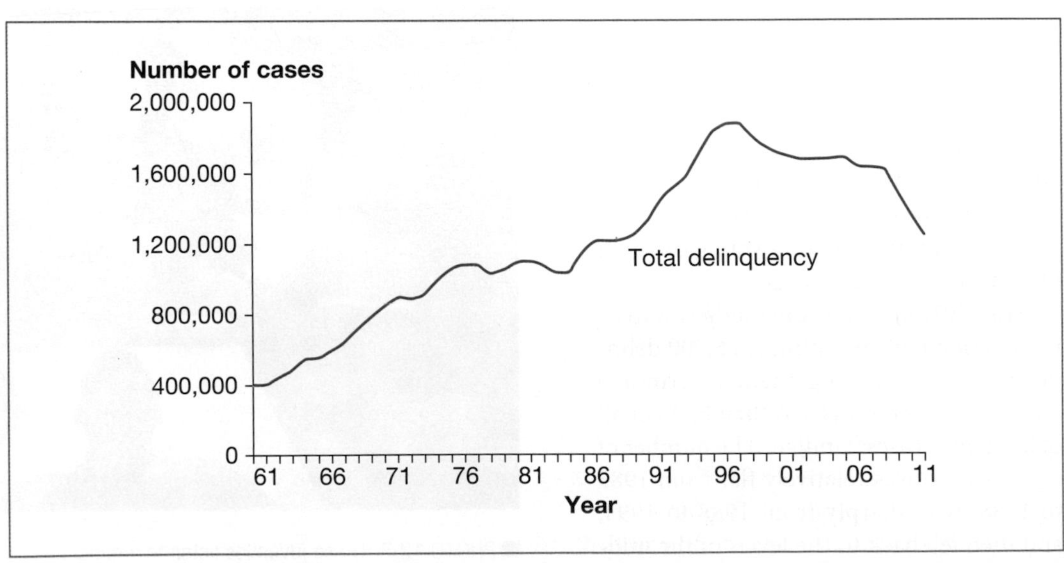

SOURCE: Hockenberry, S., & Puzzanchera, C. (2014). *Delinquency cases in juvenile court, 2011*. Washington, DC: Office of Juvenile Justice and Delinquency Prevention.

institutions are often very similar to adult prison institutions, incarceration is a serious business with a number of negative consequences for both juveniles and society that must be considered prior to placement.

Although incarcerating juveniles for the protection of society is clearly necessary in some cases, correctional institutions frequently serve as a gateway to careers in crime and delinquency. The notion that sending juveniles to correctional facilities will result in rehabilitation has proved to be inaccurate in most cases. Not only do "graduates" from correctional institutions reappear, but also their experiences while incarcerated often seem to solidify delinquent or criminal attitudes and behavior. Most studies of recidivism among institutionalized delinquents lead to the conclusion that although some programs may work for some offenders some of the time, most institutional programs produce no better results than does the simple passage of time.

There are a number of alternative forms of incarceration available. For juveniles whose period of incarceration is to be relatively brief, there are many public and private detention facilities available.

Public detention facilities frequently are located near large urban centers and often house large numbers of delinquents in a cottage- or dormitory-type setting. As a rule, these institutions are used only when all other alternatives have been exhausted or when the offenses involved are quite serious. As a result, most of the more serious delinquents are sent to these facilities. In these institutions, concern with custody frequently outweighs concern with rehabilitation. A number of changes have occurred in juvenile correctional facilities during the past half-century. Cottage-type facilities have been replaced by institutional-type settings, and the number of juveniles incarcerated has increased, as has the severity of their offenses (Gluck, 1997). Typically, we see fences, razor wire, and guards at these facilities more often than we see treatment providers.

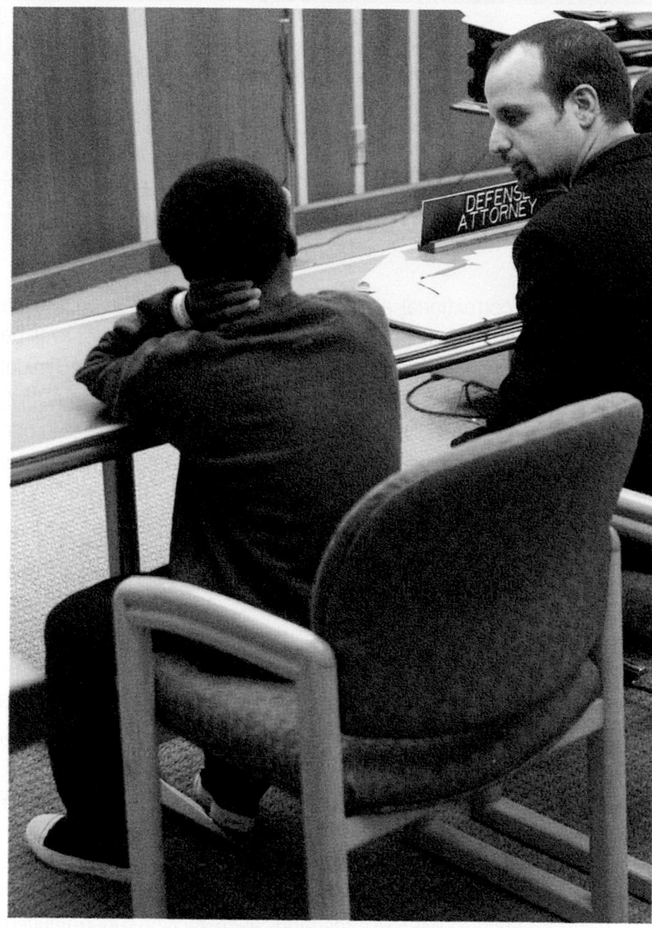

© Reuters/CORBIS

■ PHOTO 12.8 Juvenile court judges must make important decisions regarding both the welfare of the youth who are processed in their court and the interests of public safety.

Secure Correctional Facilities and Youth

Youth may be kept in prisons if they are transferred to adult court. While this can happen, we will separate this aspect of juvenile processing from our discussion because, at the point of waiver, the juvenile is no longer treated as a juvenile; he or she is treated as an adult. However, one interesting point regarding youth and incarceration should be noted. A youth cannot be sentenced to life without the possibility of parole if he or she was a juvenile when the offense was committed. This became true in *Miller v. Alabama* (2012), when, as students may recall, the Supreme Court ruled that mandatory sentences of life without the possibility of parole were unconstitutional for juvenile offenders. In cases where youth are given a life sentence, they will be kept in a secure lockdown detention facility until they are 18, at which time they will be transferred to the state's adult prison system, or, if they are sent immediately to adult prison (a rare likelihood), they are kept separated from the adult population.

As one might guess, secure correctional facilities are not the best places to mold juvenile delinquents into useful, law-abiding citizens. Sending a delinquent to a correctional facility to learn responsible behavior is like sending a person to the desert to learn how to swim. If our specific intent is to demand revenge on youthful offenders through physical and emotional punishment and isolation, current correctional facilities will suffice. If we would rather have those incarcerated juveniles return to society rehabilitated, a number of changes must be made.

It is important to consider the effects of peer group pressure in juvenile correctional facilities. There is little doubt that behavior modification will occur, but it will not necessarily result in the creation of a law-abiding citizen. The learning of delinquent behavior may be enhanced if the

TECHNOLOGY AND EQUIPMENT 12.1

Using COMPSTAT in Juvenile Corrections

Many juvenile correctional agencies across the nation struggle with the challenge of institutional violence. Indeed, "if a male will ever be involved in violence, adolescence is when it will happen." A typical week within the Arizona Department of Juvenile Corrections (ADJC), which houses an average population of 611 males and females in one of four secure care facilities, includes 11 juvenile-on-juvenile assaults and seven juvenile assaults on staff.

Assaults and fights frequently result in injuries to juveniles or staff, and can involve costly medical expenses. Fights disrupt the smooth functioning of a correctional facility and upset the treatment milieu. Unless assaults are handled properly, they can increase juvenile and staff fear, damage the institutional culture, and increase staff turnover. Director Michael D. Branham convenes a biweekly Central Office COMPSTAT review of assaults and other safe environment incidents, which include any crime or behavior that would endanger others. Branham ensures that advice is provided by staff from all of the key ADJC areas including top, mid-level and line facility managers, and representatives from the Education, Clinical, Legal, Inspections and Investigations, and Research and Development departments. During the Central Office COMPSTAT meeting, each facility superintendent presents his or her top problem areas, as well as top successes. A common topic in COMPSTAT meetings is classroom safety. Applause and congratulations are regularly given to unit staff who have reduced violence in the classroom or anywhere else within their respective facilities. Current and proposed intervention strategies to reduce assaults are discussed, and input is provided by all disciplines. Time-bound action plans are presented to address the violence, and they commonly include Individual Behavior Plans for assaultive juveniles, and various management initiatives to promote safe environments.

The ADJC COMPSTAT program was initiated in June 2007, and a comparison of assault rates before and after COMPSTAT was implemented indicates a reduction in violence has occurred. Given all of the other juvenile and institutional factors that affect violence, it is impossible to attribute the decline solely to COMPSTAT, but there is a strong feeling among ADJC staff that COMPSTAT is making a difference. If the heart of the ADJC COMPSTAT program is the proactive and cross-disciplinary approach toward the management of violence, the soul of the program is real-time data. Facility crime maps that identify hot spots of assault activity by location and time are located on the agency Intranet, and all employees have access to them. Incident reports are entered into an automated records system, which all employees also have access to. Icons that represent the number of incident reports by location (called crime data points) are placed on each facility map by the computer. Employees can select from more than 20 incident types, and by pressing a button, the computer will reconfigure the facility map to show where those incidents occurred. Employees can then see the actual incident reports by selecting the location that interests them. Facility maps automatically display the crimes occurring during the last 14 days; however, employees can select the time frame and incident type that interests them. Through the intranet, employees also have access to daily incident summaries, as well as real-time data on such things as type of incident, day of week, and time of day. The maps permit local facility and Central Office analysts to understand which juveniles are involved as suspects and/or victims. They are linked to demographic and delinquency histories of the respective juveniles, allowing for the development of relevant intervention strategies to prevent further violence. The maps, along with the associated links, were created by the tireless efforts of ADJC's Management Information Systems staff.

ADJC has taken the COMPSTAT technique and applied it to juvenile corrections. The resulting violence reduction strategies are using real-time data and cross-disciplinary teams to develop plans that promote institutional safety. A safe correctional environment will allow Deputy Director Kellie Warren and her treatment teams to implement evidence-based programs to address the criminogenic needs of the juvenile offenders committed to the department's care and custody.

SOURCE: Dempsey, J., & Vivian, J. (2009, February 1). COMPSTAT for juvenile corrections. *Corrections Today*. Reprinted with permission of the American Correctional Association, Alexandria, VA.

amount of contact with those holding favorable attitudes toward law violation is increased. Juvenile correctional facilities are typically characterized by the existence of a delinquent subculture that enhances the opportunity for dominance of the strong over the weak and gives impetus to the exploitation of the unsophisticated by the more knowledgeable. We should not then be surprised when juveniles leave these institutions with more problems than they had prior to incarceration.

Disparate Minority Confinement (DMC) and Factors Associated with DMC

During the late 1980s and early 1990s, the disparate minority representation in juvenile lockdowns became a topic of controversy. Most of the data available on this issue emerged during the late 1990s and during the early parts of the new millennium. The reasons for the disparity in juvenile confinement are many. Most published literature on this issue notes that these statistics are not likely to be due to a racist system. While we cannot possibly answer this question within the scope of one discussion within one section of a single textbook, it should have become clear to students that African American men and women have been disproportionately incarcerated throughout the history of corrections in the United States. Given the various historical precedents associated with the civil rights era and other indicators that our society held minorities in a weakened position, and given the institutional racism that officially existed until the 1960s, it is not unreasonable to presume racism may be part of the explanation in some cases.

© Ed Kashi/Corbis

■ PHOTO 12.9 It is clear from statistics in juvenile research that African American youth are represented in the juvenile justice system at a proportion that greatly exceeds that of the broader U.S. population. This photo illustrates a situation where all the youth entering a facility are African American.

Research by Huizinga, Thornberry, Knight, and Lovegrove (2007) investigated the often-stated reason for disparate minority confinement—that it simply reflects the difference in offending rates among different racial/ethnic groups—and found no support for it in their rigorous study examining disparate minority contact with the justice system. Huizinga et al. (2007) note that "although self-reported offending is a significant predictor of which individuals are contacted/referred, levels of delinquent offending have only marginal effects on the level of DMC" (p. i). They found these results in terms of both total offending and more focused data that examined violent offenses and property offenses separately. Thus, it would appear that minority youth are no more delinquent than Caucasian youth.

The work of Hsia (2004) is a compilation of surveys and official investigation into the juvenile correctional systems of all 50 states. She notes the following reasons for why such disparities existed in many state systems:

1. **Racial stereotyping and cultural insensitivity:** Eighteen states identified racial stereotyping and cultural insensitivity—both intentional and unintentional—on the part of the police and others in the juvenile justice system (e.g., juvenile court workers and judges) as important factors contributing to higher arrest rates, higher charging rates, and higher rates of detention and confinement of minority youth. The demeanor and attitude of minority youth can contribute to negative treatment and more severe disposition relative to their offenses.
2. **Lack of alternatives to detention and incarceration:** Eight states identified the lack of alternatives to detention and incarceration as a cause of the frequent use of confinement. In some states, detention centers are located in the state's largest cities, where most minority populations reside. With a lack of alternatives to detention, nearby detention centers become "convenient" placements for urban minority youth.
3. **Misuse of discretionary authority in implementing laws and policies:** Five states observed that laws and policies that increase juvenile justice professionals' discretionary authority over youth contribute to harsher treatment of minority youth. One state notes that "bootstrapping" (the practice of stacking offenses on a single incident) is often practiced by police, probation officers, and school system personnel.
4. **Lack of culturally and linguistically appropriate services:** Five states identified the lack of bicultural and bilingual staff and the use of English-only informational materials for the non-English-speaking population as contributing to minorities' misunderstanding of services and court processes and their inability to navigate the system successfully.

Based on the research by Hsia (2004), it is the general contention of this author that much of the reason for disproportionate confinement among minority youth has to do with a confluence of issues that plague minority members of society who have suffered from historical trauma and, generation after generation, have had restricted access to material, educational, and social resources. Indeed, issues such as poverty, substance abuse, few job opportunities, and high crime rates in predominantly minority neighborhoods are placing minority youth at higher risk for delinquent behaviors. Moreover, concerted law enforcement targeting of high-crime areas yields higher numbers of arrests and formal processing of minority youth. At the same time, these communities have fewer positive role models and fewer service programs that function as alternatives to confinement and/or support positive youth development.

Further, it has been found that a disproportionate number of youth in confinement come from low-income, single-parent households (female-headed households, in particular) and households headed by adults with multiple low-paying jobs or unsteady employment. Family disintegration, diminished traditional family values, parental substance abuse, and insufficient supervision contribute to delinquency development. Poverty reduces minority youths' ability to access alternatives to detention and incarceration as well as competent legal counsel. Thus, all of these factors, associated with historical deprivations over time, have contributed and culminated in the state of affairs that we now witness among minority juveniles in the United States.

Current Status of Disparity in Juvenile Detention and Incarceration

During the past 5 to 10 years, DMC with the juvenile justice system has received widespread attention throughout the nation. Recent data have shown that the likelihood for detention (the act of holding youth prior to adjudication or disposition in a court hearing, or after disposition when awaiting placement elsewhere) was greatest for African American youth when compared with Asian Americans and Native Americans. Indeed, the rate of detention for African American youth is 1.4 times that of Caucasians, 1.2 times that of Asian Americans, and 1.1 times that of Native Americans. These rates are even higher for African Americans in the case of drug-related cases (Sickmund & Puzzanchera, 2014).

SAGE Journal Article Link

Racial Politics of Juvenile Justice Policy Support: Juvenile Court Worker Orientation Toward Disproportionate Minority Confinement

Between 1997 and 2011, the overall number of juvenile offenders placed in residential facilities decreased by nearly 33% (Sickmund & Puzzanchera, 2014). For those youth adjudicated within the juvenile justice system and given sentences that included out-of-home residential placement, options included residential homes, training schools, treatment centers, boot camps, group homes, or drug treatment facilities. From the data available (Table 12.3), it is clear than Caucasian youth are less likely than African American youth to be ordered to residential placement (Sickmund & Puzzanchera, 2014).

The overall use of residential placement has declined during the past decade, however (Sickmund & Puzzanchera, 2014). Much of this decline is due to residential placement reform efforts that have resulted in the movement of many juveniles from secure, large, public facilities to less secure, small, private facilities (Hockenberry, 2013). Likewise, economic factors have resulted in a shift from committing juveniles to high-cost residential facilities to lower cost alternatives, such as probation, day treatment, or other community-based sanctions (Hockenberry, 2013).

Lastly, the use of waiver involves cases where youth are more formally tried in an adult court, the result of which is usually a correctional sentence that is more severe than detention or residential placement. During recent years, the number of juvenile cases waived to adult court have declined, but as can be seen in Table 12.3, more African American youth (59%) are waived into adult court than are Caucasians and other minority groups for which data is available (Sickmund & Puzzanchera, 2014). During the past decade, African American youth are most likely among other racial/ethnic groups to be waived for drug offenses. On the other hand, Native American youth have been found to be the most likely to be waived for offenses against a person (Sickmund & Puzzanchera, 2014).

When considering the overall circumstances for minority youth in custody as compared with Caucasian youth, consider that in every state but Vermont, the custody rate for African American juvenile offenders exceeded the rate for Caucasian youth. Indeed, throughout more than half of the 50 states, the ratio of the minority custody rate to the nonminority custody rate exceeded 3.5 to 1 (see Figure 12.3). Even worse, in four states (Connecticut, New Jersey, Pennsylvania, and Vermont) there are more than eight minority offenders for every one Caucasian offender (Hockenberry, 2013). The custody rate is the number of juvenile offenders in residential placement per 100,000 juveniles, whereas the custody ratio is the number of minority youth per the number of Caucasian

■ **Table 12.3: Percentage of Minority Youth in Secure Detention, Placed in a Residential Facility, or Waived to Adult Court, Compared with Caucasian Youth, 2010**

	Type of Outcome		
Race	Secure Detention	Residential Placement	Waiver to Adult Sentence
Caucasian	19%	24%	50%
African American	25	30	59
Native American	24	27	58
Asian	21	22	57

SOURCE: Sickmund, M., & Puzzanchera, C. (2014). *Juvenile offenders and victims, 2014 national report.* Washington, DC: National Center for Juvenile Justice.

youth who are in custody. For example, in Figure 12.3, states colored in dark blue consist of custody populations that have four minority youth for every one Caucasian youth.

It is worth noting that circumstances are slowly improving for minority juvenile youth. The amount of DMC is disappearing, with rates becoming more similar to those for Caucasian youth. In fact, when examining national data between 1990 and 2010, Sickmund and Puzzanchera (2014) found much more parity in the ratio between African American and Caucasian detentions and waivers to adult court. Further, as seen in Table 12.4, between 1997 and 2010, the population of offenders in residential placement declined for every single racial and ethnic category. Indeed, the total number of youth in custody dropped 33% overall. More specifically, the number of Caucasian youth declined 42%, and the number of minority youth declined 27% (Hockenberry, 2013). The decrease was quite profound for Asian Americans in particular (a decrease of 67%), followed by African Americans (31%). Thus, it would seem that efforts throughout the juvenile system to address DMC have been successful in recent years. Nevertheless, there is still work to be done.

The PREA and Juvenile Facility Standards

As we have seen in prior chapters, the Prison Rape Elimination Act (PREA) has become a major legal requirement for prison administrators. This is also true for administrators of juvenile facilities. Indeed, standards set by the U.S. Department of Justice (2012) call for zero tolerance of sexual abuse and harassment in juvenile facilities and require that an upper-level, agency-wide PREA coordinator develop, implement, and oversee agency efforts to comply with PREA

■ **Figure 12.3: Ratio of Minority Custody Rate to Caucasian Custody Rate, 2010**

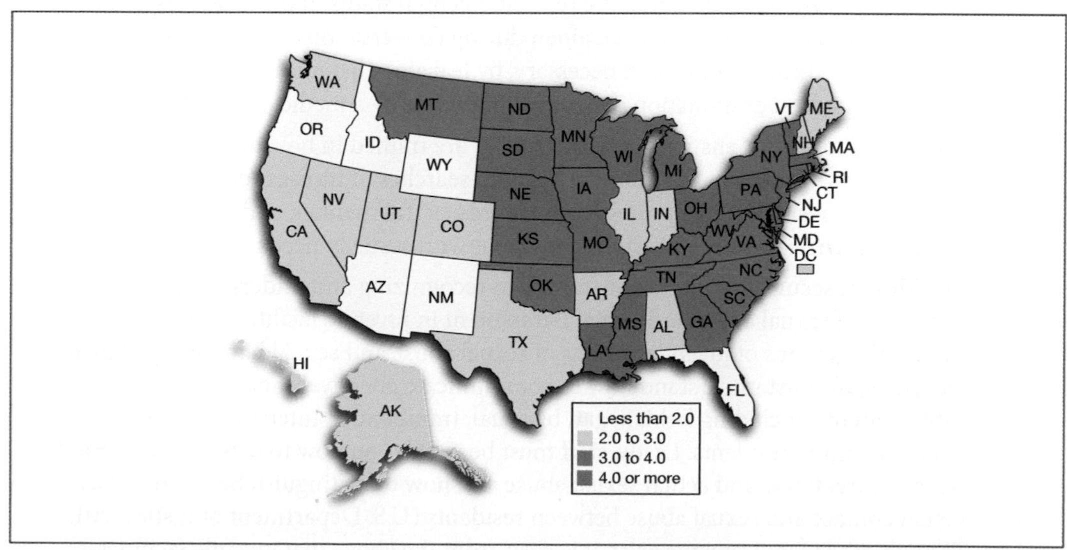

SOURCE: Hockenberry, S. (2013). *Juveniles in residential placement, 2010.* Washington, DC: National Center for Juvenile Justice.

Table 12.4: Minority Juveniles in Custody, 2010

Race/ethinicity	Number	Percent	Percent Change 1997–2010
Total	70,792	100%	–33%
White	22,947	32	–42
Minority	47,845	68	–27
Black	28,976	41	–31
Hispanic	15,590	22	–19
American Indian	1,236	2	–23
Asian	728	1	–67
Other	1,315	2	134

SOURCE: Hockenberry, S. (2013). *Juveniles in residential placement, 2010.* Washington, DC: National Center for Juvenile Justice.

standards in all facilities. More importantly, standards on operations within juvenile facilities were enumerated, as follows:

1. Staff shall not conduct cross-gender strip searches or cross-gender visual body cavity searches (meaning a search of the anal or genital opening) except in exigent circumstances or when performed by medical practitioners.
2. Staff shall not conduct cross-gender pat-down searches except in exigent circumstances.
3. Administrators shall document and justify all cross-gender strip searches, cross-gender visual body cavity searches, and cross-gender pat-down searches.
4. Administrators shall implement policies and procedures that enable residents to shower, perform bodily functions, and change clothing without nonmedical staff of the opposite gender viewing their breasts, buttocks, or genitalia, except in exigent circumstances or when such viewing is incidental to routine cell checks. Such policies and procedures shall require staff of the opposite gender to announce their presence when entering a resident housing unit. In facilities (such as group homes) that do not contain discrete housing units, staff of the opposite gender shall be required to announce their presence when entering an area where residents are likely to be showering, performing bodily functions, or changing clothing.
5. Staff shall not search or physically examine a transgender or intersex resident for the sole purpose of determining the resident's genital status. If the resident's genital status is unknown, it may be determined during conversations with the resident, by reviewing medical records, or, if necessary, by learning that information as part of a broader medical examination conducted in private by a medical practitioner.
6. Administrators must ensure that security staff are trained in how to conduct cross-gender pat-down searches, and searches of transgender and intersex residents, in a professional and respectful manner, and in the least intrusive manner possible, consistent with security needs.

   In addition, security staff must be trained in recognizing and understanding the dynamics of sexual abuse and sexual harassment in juvenile facilities as well as common reactions of juvenile victims of sexual abuse and sexual harassment. Further, security staff must understand how to communicate effectively and professionally with residents, including lesbian, gay, bisexual, transgender, intersex, or gender-nonconforming residents. Lastly, staff must be trained on how to detect and respond to signs of threatened and actual sexual abuse and how to distinguish between consensual sexual contact and sexual abuse between residents (U.S. Department of Justice, 2012). Though other requirements exist, it is clear from the above that juvenile facilities, like adult facilities, must ensure that they are in compliance with PREA standards.

Lastly, as a culture and society, there should be little doubt that the acceptance of same-sex couples is much greater with teens today than in the past. This is particularly true in larger metropolitan areas of the nation, which tend to have greater numbers of homosexual and bisexual youth and where there is less stigma attached to these orientations than in other areas of the United States. Media portrayals and obvious changes in public sentiments toward these sexual orientations reveal that tolerance is much more improved today than even just 20 years ago. Legal decisions and changes in legislative enactments make it all the more clear that these sentiments are becoming codified and serve as official acknowledgment that these individuals are entitled to the rights and privileges extended to any other minority group in the United States.

CONCLUSION

This chapter has introduced the student to some of the differences between juvenile and adult corrections. From early history, the means by which juveniles are processed has been in debate, with the notion of intent and culpability being key concerns. In the past, juveniles were often housed with adult offenders, but it became clear over time that a separate system of detention and confinement was necessary.

In this chapter we have focused on juveniles who are kept in secure environments and/or incarcerated. This is because, for the most part, this text is oriented toward the institutional aspects of corrections. Though most youth do get sentences of probation, a demonstration of the issues they face in detention centers and similar facilities warrants specific and separate consideration. It is clear that numerous issues confront juvenile correctional systems, including disparity issues and the need to attend to the specific needs of different offender groups, such as female juvenile offenders.

We have also discussed the use of waiver to transfer youth to adult court. This is often reserved for the most serious juvenile offenders and is an option that has decreased in popularity in many states. It is clear that the primary objective in processing youth is to reform them and, if possible, refrain from stigmatizing them. This is fundamental to juvenile corrections. The vast majority of youth are treated as if they are salvageable, and, in fact, the entire juvenile system is based on the notion that youth should be given intervention-based as opposed to punitive-based programming.

Many youth have been victims of crime and abuse in their own right. In fact, problems with child abuse and neglect tend to correlate with increased levels of delinquency. Further, these youth report high levels of trauma, substance abuse, and mental illness. This is especially true with female juvenile offenders. Thus, juveniles demonstrate a need for mental health interventions. Current juvenile corrections systems attempt to address these issues to minimize the likelihood that these youth will become further entrenched in crime. As we have seen, some youth engage in delinquency that they age out of after their adolescent years, whereas others tend to progress with this behavior well into adulthood. It is the hope of modern juvenile correctional systems to avoid this latter outcome by providing interventions that can change the trajectory of juvenile offenders and steer them toward a productive life.

DISCUSSION QUESTIONS

1. What is the primary intent in juvenile corrections when processing youthful offenders?
2. Identify, define, and discuss the different categories of abuse and neglect.
3. How do child abuse and neglect connect to delinquency among some youth?
4. How does the juvenile system contrast with the adult system? Does this also include differences specifically related to the

means by which correctional practices are implemented? Explain your answer.

5. Identify and discuss at least two key Supreme Court cases that have impacted the field of juvenile corrections. Explain why you selected these two cases.
6. How can abuse and mental health issues aggravate a juvenile's ability to reform?
7. Identify and discuss how racial disparities exist among youth who are placed in confinement. Why do you think that these disparities exist?
8. Identify and discuss the types of facilities that are used to house juvenile offenders.
9. Discuss the theoretical work of Terrie Moffitt, and explain whether you believe her theory does or does not do well in explaining juvenile delinquency.

SAGE edge™ Test your understanding of chapter content. Take the practice quiz.

KEY TERMS

Adolescent-only offenders, 296
Age of responsibility, 286
Chancery courts, 287
Child abuse, 296
Child neglect, 296
Common law, 287
Contributing to the delinquency of a minor, 295
Educational neglect, 296
Emotional neglect, 296
Houses of refuge, 288
***In loco parentis*, 287**
Life-course-persistent juvenile, 296
***Parens patriae*, 287**
Physical abuse, 296
Physical neglect, 296
Psychological abuse, 297
Reform schools, 288

SAGE edge™ Review key terms with eFlashcards.

KEY CASES

Breed v. Jones (1975), 291
Graham v. Florida (2010), 291
In re Gault (1967), 291
In re Holmes (1955), 290
McKeiver v. Pennsylvania (1971), 291
Roper v. Simmons (2005), 291

APPLIED EXERCISE 12.1

Create an antigang program at a juvenile facility in coordination with the state juvenile justice system.

For this exercise, students will need to read *Report No. 08-56* by the Florida Office of Program Policy Analysis & Government Accountability, which is titled "DJJ Should Use Evidence-Based Practices to Address Juvenile Gang Involvement." This report is available on the student study site or found independently at http://www.oppaga.state.fl.us/MonitorDocs/Reports/pdf/0856rpt.pdf. This document outlines the rise in juvenile gang members that has been found throughout the juvenile justice system of Florida.

Students should read this document and then explain how they would implement an antigang program within a detention facility in Florida. For this assignment, presume that there are currently gang members within the facility and that you are the head administrator for the facility. What means of prevention would you use to keep the gang membership from spreading? Would there be constitutional issues to consider? How would you follow up to demonstrate that the program worked?

Also, keep in mind that gangs tend to cycle in and out of the custodial environment. This is also true with juvenile gangs. Thus, you should explain how you would coordinate with juvenile probation and outside community leaders to identify new gang members who enter your facility and for assistance in providing interventions.

Your exercise should be from 500 to 1,000 words in length and should provide a well-organized plan of approach that incorporates both community and facility resources.

WHAT WOULD YOU DO?

You are a juvenile caseworker and have been working with Tanya, a 15-year-old at your detention facility. You have worked with Tanya for over a year and have noted that she has made considerable progress in treatment and the other aspects of programming. In fact, Tanya is scheduled to be released to aftercare in the near future. During a session, just 2 weeks prior to her release, Tanya discloses to you that her stepfather (who still lives at the domicile) molested her several times when she was young. Neither Tanya nor her mother ever reported this. As Tanya nears release, you must consider how to handle this situation.

What would you do?

13 CORRECTIONAL ADMINISTRATION

AP Photo/ Evan Vucci

SEXUAL HARASSMENT AND PRISON CULTURE

Major Turner read through the allegations made by his employee, Officer Kristy Campbell, regarding her treatment by her supervisor, Sergeant Steinbeck. Turner had requested that an inmate by the name of Butch Buchanan be brought to his office.

When Buchanan arrived, Turner said, "Mr. Buchanan, I have to inquire of you as to whether you have overheard any remarks made by officers in the machine shop that could be construed as being sexual in nature."

Buchanan shrugged. "Not really, but then again, I mind my own business."

"Well, as it happens, I have this report on you that was written yesterday by Officer Kristy Campbell, something about you muttering how you'd like to 'take her for a test drive' and making obscene gestures in her direction." The major leaned forward. "What is that all about?"

Buchanan scowled at him. "I did not say that! She's lying!"

"Sergeant Steinbeck was a witness to this, as were some other inmates in the area . . . and just so you know, Campbell has claimed that she felt very threatened by your comments; they seem to have been pretty graphic, like depicting a rape or something."

"C'mon man, that is bullcrap!" Buchanan protested. He started to speak again, then hesitated for a second before asking, "So Steinbeck is witnessing it, huh?"

The major looked at him and said, "Yep," with no additional explanation. After a few seconds, the major continued. "You know, these ain't the old days and all, with all of this PREA stuff, I cannot ignore this stuff or treat it lightly. I think that this case may be one that is threatening-an-officer, which is a higher charge than what Campbell had put here." He paused to ostensibly consult the report in front of him. "She just charged you with being insubordinate to an officer, but I think it could be seen as a threatening-an-officer case . . . just sayin'." The major grinned and gave a little shrug on the "just sayin".

The major then held up a piece of paper in front of Buchanan's face. It had the signatures of officers on it who worked in the machine shop. "As you can see, Steinbeck is witnessing this, and, if you catch this charge, you are not going to make parole, which is just around the corner for you, isn't it?"

Buchanan held up his hands in surrender. "Okay, look, I did say it, but just because Steinbeck had been egging it on. . . . He's mad at Campbell because she broke up with him. He's setting me up, then siding with her, so that she will be cool with him again. That's what is really going on, and Steinbeck . . . " Buchanan trailed off.

"Yes?"

Buchanan narrowed his eyes at the major. "You gonna' roll me if I explain this, or what?"

LEARNING OBJECTIVES:

1. Discuss the history and organization of the Federal Bureau of Prisons.
2. Discuss common organizational features of state and local prison systems.
3. Describe five common styles of management in prisons.
4. Compare key differences and similarities between managers and leaders.
5. Identify the characteristics of an effective correctional leader.
6. Discuss the benefits and challenges faced by women in correctional management.
7. Describe the importance of racial and cultural diversity and professionalism in the corrections workforce.
8. Identify specific issues involved with emergency management in the corrections system.

SAGE edge™

Get the edge on your studies: edge.sagepub.com/hanser2e

- Take a quiz to find out what you've learned.
- Review key terms with eFlashcards.
- Watch videos that enhance chapter content.

The Major met his gaze and said, very seriously, "You let me know what the hell is going on in that shop, and I will keep it here. . . . This case has not been processed yet nor logged. I will tear it up and make sure that Campbell knows to let it be handled informally. Nobody will know the difference, especially the parole board."

"Alright, this is the deal. Steinbeck is constantly talking about how Campbell is a tease, and he's always telling us to not listen to her in the shop. If we act all funky with her, then he gives us 'extras'—you know, a few smokes and other goodies—and Campbell finds herself having to ask him for help in keeping us under control. Steinbeck is setting her up and grooming her to be dependent on him. . . . I overheard her saying to another female officer that she was reconsidering her feelings about Steinbeck, being that he was such a gentleman and all."

Major Turner gave him a nod and said, "Look, I am going to ask around, but I won't be mentioning you. But too many people have been involved, and I know that something will break loose with this. In the meantime, just go to work, mind your own business, and know that a deal is a deal, okay?"

"Alright," Buchanan muttered.

The major sent Buchanan out, and the officers outside the office escorted the inmate to his dorm. Then Major Turner looked down at the paper with the officers' signatures. It was an attendance sheet with the signatures of officers who had attended a past training on machine shop safety, not a report from Officer Campbell, as Buchanan had thought.

The major then began work on a list of persons he would need to interview regarding the pervasive sexual harassment that he had been hearing about via the rumor mill. He called the prison warden and started by saying, "Warden, this is going to be a bit more complicated than I had thought . . . "

It was just another day in the life of Major Turner, the prison PREA investigator.

INTRODUCTION

Prison Tour Video Link
Release and Educational Background

This chapter introduces the student to some basic issues involved with correctional management, supervision, and leadership. Before providing students with information regarding supervision processes in corrections, we begin with a discussion of the federal and state correctional systems to provide an understanding of their organization and the means by which oversight in operations is maintained. The administrative features of correctional systems are important because this puts a general template to the means by which policies and administrative regulations are promulgated down to individual prisons. Further, students will examine specific traits associated with management and leadership as well as the differences between these terms. Specialized topics within this chapter include the experiences of women in correctional work who are promoted to supervisory positions and management schemes within private prison systems. Lastly, students will gain some insight on issues related to emergency management, including means of response, managerial considerations, and the need to work with agencies external to the prison facility itself.

FEDERAL BUREAU OF PRISONS ADMINISTRATION

Central Office

The head office of the Federal Bureau of Prisons (BOP) is known as the Central Office. The Central Office serves as the BOP headquarters and is overseen and managed by the director of the BOP. This office includes eight divisions that provide oversight of major BOP program areas and operations as well as the National Institute of Corrections. The Central Office is located in Washington, D.C., providing ready access to the U.S. Capitol, federal courts, and the Department of Justice's headquarters building. Each division that is administered from the Central Office oversees its respective functions throughout all six regions of the BOP (see Figure 13.1 for an illustration of each region). From the Central Office, regional offices oversee these same functions that are carried out in prison facilities located in their jurisdiction. The eight service divisions are as follows:

1. The Administration Division is responsible for the BOP's financial and facility management. This division is responsible for budget development and execution, finance, procurement and property, and the inmate trust fund program.
2. The Correctional Programs Division ensures that national policies and procedures are in place that provide a safe, secure institutional environment for inmates and staff and encourages inmate activities and programs designed to eliminate idleness and instill a positive work ethic.
3. The Health Services Division is responsible for medical, dental, and mental health (psychiatric) services provided to federal inmates in BOP facilities, including health care delivery, infectious disease management, and medical designations.
4. The Human Resource Management Division coordinates the BOP's personnel matters, including pay and leave administration, incentive awards, retirement, work-life programs, background investigations, adverse and disciplinary actions, and performance evaluations.

5. The Industries, Education, and Vocational Training (IE&VT) Division is responsible for education and vocational training programs within the BOP. Each federal prison has its own education department that provides educational activities to federal inmates. This division manages literacy and occupational training programs, parenting programs, and adult continuing education activities, which are formal instructional classes designed to increase inmates' general knowledge in a wide variety of subjects, such as writing and math. Lastly, this division also oversees Federal Prison Industries (FPI), one of the most important correctional programs operated by the BOP. Created by federal statute in 1934, it operates as a wholly owned, self-sustaining government corporation under the trade name UNICOR.
6. The Information, Policy, and Public Affairs (IPPA) Division collects, develops, and shares useful, accurate, and timely information to BOP staff, the Department of Justice, Congress, other government agencies, and the public.
7. The Office of General Counsel represents the BOP on a broad range of legal, policy, and management issues. This division includes seven Central Office branches, six regional legal offices, and 24 consolidated legal centers in the field. The primary responsibility of the regional legal offices is to provide litigation support for inmate litigation arising out of the prisons located within the region, and to provide legal advice to regional office and prison administrators.
8. The Program Review Division (PRD) was created in 1988 to establish a self-monitoring system that provides oversight of BOP program performance and compliance. Oversight involves monitoring specific program areas, conducting risk assessments for the purpose of creating review guidelines, and analyzing program performance trends and other data to achieve continuous program improvement. This division conducts reviews of all BOP programs.

Lastly, the **National Institute of Corrections (NIC)** is an agency within the BOP that is headed by a director appointed by the U.S. attorney general. A 16-member advisory board, also appointed by the attorney general, provides policy direction to the institute. The NIC provides training, technical assistance, information services, and policy/program development assistance to federal, state, and local corrections agencies. Through cooperative agreements, the NIC awards funds to support its program initiatives. The NIC also provides guidance with respect to correctional policies, practices, and operations nationwide in areas of emerging interest and concern to correctional executives and practitioners as well as to the makers of public policy.

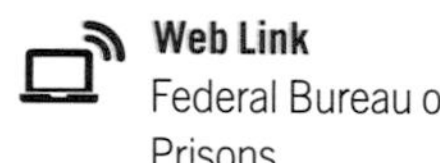

REGIONAL OFFICES AND JURISDICTIONS

Aside from the Central Office in Washington, the BOP has six regional offices that directly oversee the operations of prison facilities within their respective regions of the country. These six regional offices include the Mid-Atlantic Region (MXR), North Central Region (NCR), Northeast Region (NER), South Central Region (SCR), Southeast Region (SER), and Western Region (WXR). Students should see Figure 13.1 for a mapped illustration of these regional jurisdictions.

Regional office staff maintain close contact with staff who work in various prisons and correctional facilities in their jurisdiction. They provide management and technical assistance to facility and community corrections personnel. They also conduct workshops, conferences, and specialized training programs; give technical assistance to state and local criminal justice agencies; and contract to provide offender placement in residential reentry centers.

The Central Office and the regional offices serve as the primary administrative components that coordinate the safety and security of inmates and provide human resources and training for staff within the BOP. At a more local level, each individual prison facility will also have its own human resources office as well as various offices that address specific functions of prison operation, such as security, education, recreation, medical services, and psychological services. These offices each answer to the warden(s) of their facility at the local level as well as the next highest office within the regional chain of command. Then, all reports and records are sent from the regional offices to the Central Office, as deemed appropriate.

National Institute of Corrections (NIC): An agency within the Federal Bureau of Prisons that is headed by a director appointed by the U.S. attorney general.

■ **Figure 13.1: The Regional Jurisdictions of the Federal Bureau of Prisons**

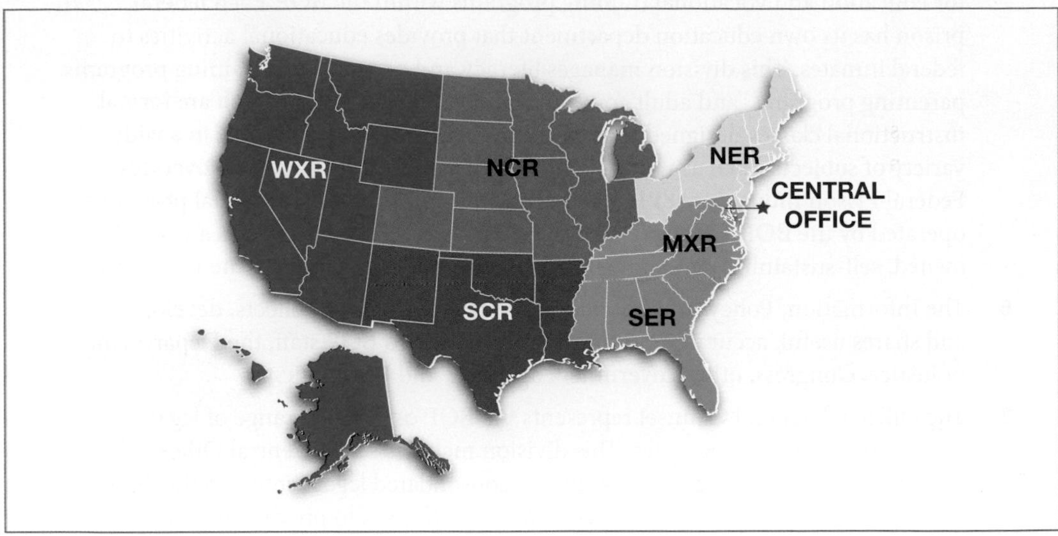

SOURCE: Federal Bureau of Prisons. (2010). *About regional offices.* Washington, DC: Department of Justice.

CORRECTIONAL SYSTEM ADMINISTRATION

At the State Level

Every state is tasked with responsibility for the incarceration, rehabilitation, and street supervision of offenders within its borders. However, states differ by several important aspects, including whether the incarceration, probation, and parole functions are combined into a single agency or placed within separate agencies. In addition, some states merge the probation and parole functions into a single function. Likewise, there is some variation as to whether probation and parole are state or local functions. Because we have covered several state systems throughout this text and because the degree of variability is so great among the different state systems, only a simple and broad overview will be included here regarding the administration of state prison systems.

As we have seen in earlier chapters, each type of state correctional system has developed due to historical and legal occurrences that were more a matter of happenstance than intentional planning. The initial administrative bodies that coordinated and oversaw the operations of these systems often developed in a haphazard manner as well and in many cases were the product of a politicized process where position appointments were grounded in patronage and nepotism. This early history of state correctional administration caused many problems with efficiency and the ability to create an objective and open form of administrative control. However, this was often offset by the paramilitary structure of most prison facilities and the fact that inmate labor served as a source of revenue for many states, particularly in the southern United States.

In today's world of corrections, state agencies are usually organized into a separate department of corrections, and these organizations will usually have a director who is appointed by the governor. In other cases, the prison system may be a division within a larger state department. For example, in Texas, the Texas Department of Criminal Justice—Institutional Division (TDCJ-ID) oversees the prison facilities of the broader TDCJ. Students should examine Figure 13.2 for a schematic on the organizational structure of the Correctional Institutions Division of the TDCJ.

Though this is a common type of organizational arrangement, many correctional administrators consider the separate department to be a more effective means of managing prison systems. One of the key reasons for this is that a separate department is able to control its own use of financial and personnel resources and does not have to compete internally with other divisions for its funding base. In addition, executive directors of departments have more flexibility when establishing policies and procedures.

At the Local Level

Local correctional systems come in the form of county or city jurisdictions, or private institutions. The most common type of local correctional system is the county-based system, which is, most often, run by the sheriff's agency of that county. Most county-level jails house inmates for 1 year or less and are operated by jailers within the sheriff's department. This is typical throughout the nation, and it is not uncommon for jail systems in major metropolitan areas to have populations that parallel some state organizations.

While these types of systems may actually consist of misdemeanant inmates, this is not always the case. For instance, in the state of Louisiana, it is common for many parish-level jails (in Louisiana, the term *parish* is used to denote a county, a product of its unique French cultural heritage), operated by local sheriffs, to house inmates from the state department of corrections. These inmates will have committed felony crimes and have multiple-year sentences. The state-level correctional system contracts out the obligation for security and safety for these inmates, and, for a fee, these jail systems house the inmates. This process is conducted throughout the state because it is less expensive than building newer prisons and because this optimizes jail space throughout

■ Figure 13.2: Organizational Structure of Correctional Institutions in the Texas Department of Criminal Justice

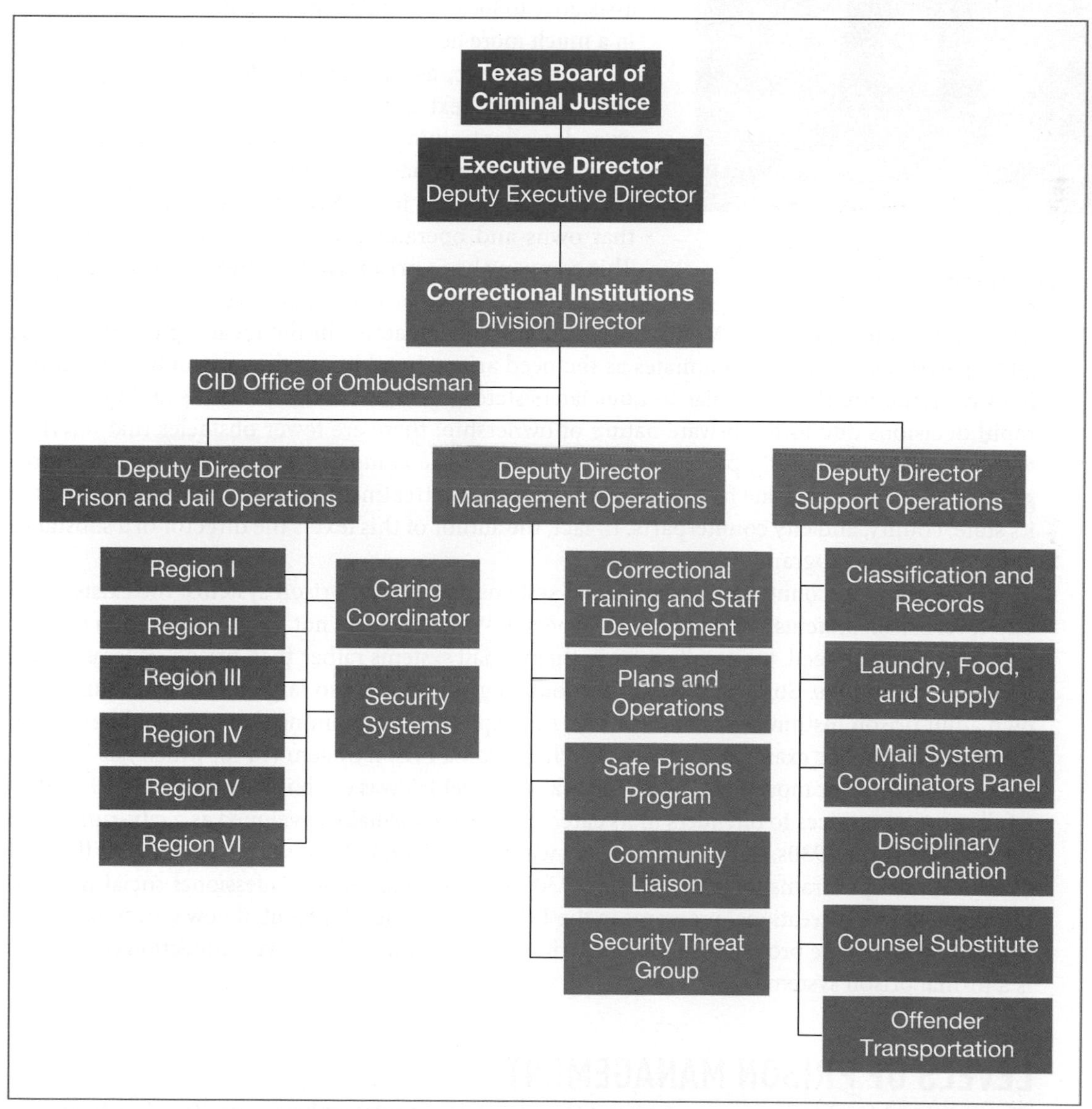

SOURCE: Texas Department of Criminal Justice. (2010). *Organizational charts: Correctional Institutions Division.*

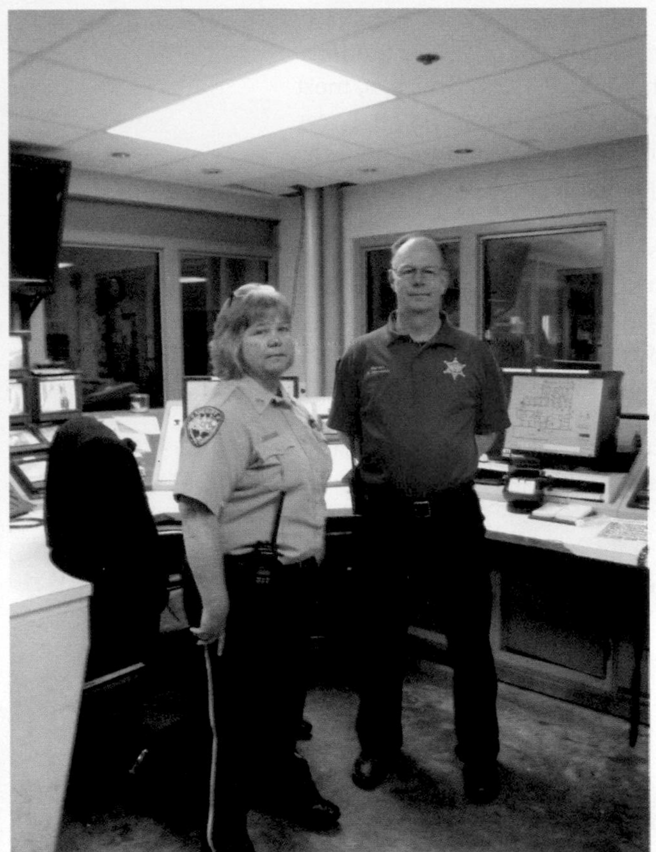
Robert Hanser

■ PHOTO 13.1 Warden Brian Newcomer of Ouachita Correctional Center is pictured here with a fellow staff member.

the state. Further, this system provides more flexibility in housing inmates in various areas of the state that are near to the inmates' families and/or reentry objectives. The author of this text is the administrator of a regional correctional training academy, North Delta Regional Training Academy, which is tasked with training parish-level jailers to ensure that they meet state-level standards of care.

Private prisons can be considered more local in their orientation, though they are, in fact, a unique model of correctional system unto themselves. Private prison systems also contract out with the state prison system to aid in housing the inmate population. These private facilities may also house inmates from within the local area, depending on the circumstances and the agreements made between the company owning the prison and the outlying cities and counties of the region. While private prisons are usually owned by private companies that operate several prison facilities, they are included here because the individual facilities operate under more flexible terms that tend to allow them to be of assistance to local law enforcement and municipal planners in a much more fluid manner than most state facilities.

For example, as mentioned a few moments ago, the author of this text administers a training academy that provides jailer training to parish-level correctional officers. This same academy has provided similar training to private correctional officers for **LaSalle Corrections**, a company that owns and operates prisons in Louisiana and Texas. This company has a prison facility, Richwood Correctional Center, which houses both state-level inmates and city-level inmates for the city of Monroe. Richwood has been active in the local region in housing city-, parish-, and state-level inmates as the need arises. In addition, this prison has an administrative structure that is similar to Louisiana's state system but is flexible in its ability to make rapid decisions due to the private nature of ownership; there are fewer obstacles that interfere with the decision-making process for the owners of the company, unlike with state-run programs. Further, this private facility provides all the same treatment and programming services of its state, county, and city counterparts. In fact, the author of this text is the director of a substance abuse treatment program in Richwood.

In addition to county-level correctional systems and private prison systems, the existence of city-level prison systems should not be overlooked. While these are not the most common types of prison systems (indeed, we usually refer to them as jail systems rather than prison systems), there are some exceptions. Some cities and their outlying suburbs are so large that they require their own adult prison institutions, complete with the requisite programming that one would expect in a prison system. For example, consider the Philadelphia Prison System (PPS), which has its roots in the initial Quaker movements when the Walnut Street Jail was established. Today, the PPS offers a full range of services to offenders in its care. This system formally developed as a city-run prison system during the 1930s, during the same era when the federal BOP was established. With the start of educational programs for adults in the 1930s, the introduction of professional social workers, the expansion of recreational programs in the 1950s, and the development of new vocational training and work-release programs in the 1960s, it is now true that this city-run collection of facilities is a formal prison system.

LaSalle Corrections: A private company that owns and operates prisons in Louisiana and Texas.

System-wide administrators: Managers who are at the executive level and direct the entire system throughout the state.

LEVELS OF PRISON MANAGEMENT

Three general levels of management exist in most state correctional systems. The first level consists of **system-wide administrators**, or managers who are at the executive level and direct the entire system throughout the state. These administrators conduct the broad planning of the agency, which often includes a strategic planning process (see Focus Topic 13.1). The second level of administration includes **regional-level administrators**, or managers who oversee a specific region of a state. Usually, these regions will consist of a northern, southern, eastern, and western area that may be given a name or number for identification. The third level of administration in state agencies comprises the **unit-level administrators**, or personnel who manage the individual prison facility. In most cases, there will be a handful of regions within a state, and each region will have a number of prisons within its borders. We now proceed with a more detailed discussion of the various level administrators in state prison systems.

Regional-level administrators: Managers who oversee a specific region of a state.

Unit-level administrators: The third level of administrator in state agencies; includes personnel who manage the individual prison facility.

Strategic plan: A document that articulates agency goals and objectives and states how they might be realized.

System-Wide Administrators

Within a department of corrections, there is usually a chief executive officer and a set of deputies who implement various policies as determined by agency needs and by state-level politics that impact the agency. This level of administration is also usually responsible for obtaining funds and resources from state budget lines so that the agency can operate effectively, and these administrators will also be responsible for creating strategic plans that guide the spending of allocated money. **Strategic plans** are broad managerial documents that include goals and objectives of the agency, and they state the general direction in which an agency intends to operate. An example of a strategic plan from the state of Texas, along with the mission and philosophy of the agency, is included in Focus Topic 13.1.

This level of management will also coordinate with other state agencies to ensure that services are integrated within the overall state system. For instance, it may be necessary for the department of corrections to work closely with the state police, local and state-level court systems, emergency

FOCUS TOPIC 13.1

Strategic Plan for the Texas Department of Criminal Justice—Institutional Division

Texas Department of Criminal Justice *FY2011–2015 Agency Strategic Plan*

Relevant Statewide Goals and Benchmarks Public Safety and Criminal Justice

Priority Goal: To protect Texans by preventing and reducing terrorism and crime; securing the Texas/Mexico border from all threats; achieving an optimum level of statewide preparedness capable of responding and recovering from all hazards; and confining, supervising, and rehabilitating offenders.

The statewide benchmarks directly applicable to the Texas Department of Criminal Justice are:

- Average rate of adult re-incarceration within three years of initial release
- Number of correctional officer and correctional staff vacancies
- Average annual incarceration cost per offender
- Percent increase in the number of faith-based prison beds
- Percent reduction in felony probation revocations
- Percent reduction in felony probation technical revocations
- Total number of cameras in state correctional facilities
- Number of contraband items seized through the use of correctional security equipment

Texas Department of Criminal Justice Mission	Texas Department of Criminal Justice Philosophy
The mission of the Texas Department of Criminal Justice is to provide public safety, promote positive change in offender behavior, reintegrate offenders into society, and assist victims of crime.	The Texas Department of Criminal Justice will be open, ethical, and accountable to our fellow citizens and work cooperatively with other public and private entries. We will foster a quality working environment free of bias and respectful of each individual. Our programs will provide a continuum of services consistent with contemporary standards to confine, supervise, and treat criminal offenders in an innovative, cost effective, and efficient manner.

SOURCE: Texas Department of Criminal Justice. (2010). *Agency strategic plan for the fiscal years 2011–2015*. Huntsville, TX: Author.

FOCUS TOPIC 13.2

Job Duties of a Warden

- Coordinates activities by scheduling work assignments, setting priorities, and directing the work of subordinate employees.
- Evaluates and verifies employee performance through the review of completed work assignments and work techniques. Assigns, coordinates, and outlines the work methods of subordinate employees.
- Identifies staff development and training needs and ensures that training is obtained.
- Ensures proper labor relations and conditions of employment are maintained.
- Maintains records, prepares reports, and composes correspondence relative to the work.
- Establishes and maintains custody, security, and control measures at a state correctional facility.
- Supervises and controls the inside movement of prisoners, including initial assignment to prison units and transfers within the institution.
- Implements policies and develops procedures in areas of responsibility (housing, treatment, custody, or security).
- Supervises the classification and orientation of new prisoners.
- Reviews written communications from prisoners and interviews them regarding special or personal problems.
- Develops and implements procedures for educational and treatment programs based on department policies.
- Represents the facility to the Department of Corrections' central office, other state departments, local agencies, and the public.
- Reviews job résumés of candidates, prepares and conducts hiring interviews, and selects the most qualified candidate.
- Plans, coordinates, and supervises leisure-time activities of prisoners, such as intramural and varsity sports, music, and library services.

SOURCE: Michigan Civil Service Commission. (2015). *Job specification: Senior executive warden.*

the case, problem inmates provide the spark that sets off a chain of pretrained reactions. In many cases, these types of reactive responses are fashioned in a cookie-cutter style that has been repetitively rehearsed. Naturally, this creates an artificial style of response that is not always suited to the conditions that may exist.

Authoritarian Forms of Management

In authoritarian institutions, all major decisions are made by one person or a very small group of persons. The authoritarian system of management prevailed from the very beginning of prison management in the United States to about the mid-1950s. It was often linked to a system that emphasized punishment and consequences. It is thought that this system was engineered by Elam Lynds, who is considered the innovator behind the Auburn system of prison management (see Focus Topic 13.3).

The key defining feature of the **authoritarian model** of prison management is strict control over staff and inmates with communication that flows in a top-to-bottom process. This model does not consider input from those outside of the system or facility. Thus, this tends to be a closed system of management that does not grow or improve through the processing of additional information from the environment. Generally, authoritarian managers tend to deal with new problems using the same types of responses that they have with previously encountered problems. Obviously, this is not very adaptive and leads to a failure of management to react appropriately to challenges that emerge. These types of managers tend to change, modify, or contort the issue into one that is consistent with their current repertoire of responses, all of which tend to be punitive in nature. Thus, this type of management stymies all sense of creative problem solving and also kills the human spirit.

Authoritarian model: Features strict control over staff and inmates with communication that flows in a top-to-bottom process.

Bureaucratic model: A formal organizational system that is not dependent upon the specific personnel or personalities assigned within it.

Bureaucratic Forms of Management

Bureaucratic methods of running agencies have some advantages over the authoritarian model, but, for the most part, this type of system is not truly superior. The **bureaucratic model** of prison management creates a formal organizational system that is not dependent upon the specific personnel or personalities assigned within it. So long as each person performs his or her basic job functions, this type of system will continue to operate, though not necessarily in the most efficient manner. These types of systems tend to have a hierarchical structure with a formal and defined chain of command. Authority within this system is established along vertical communication patterns that flow from the top of the hierarchy to the bottom with strict channels of communication. Naturally, this type of communication is not the most adaptive because it does not allow for direct feedback from lower-level staff, but it is superior to the authoritarian model because it is not dependent on one sole source of guidance and/or information, making it capable of continued operation even when the highest-ranking administrator is absent.

However, this type of situation tends to produce what we will refer to as holding pattern management within the institution. **Holding pattern management** is where the system continues to operate but in a pattern of stasis where there is no true growth, but neither is there a blockage in the systemic flow. Rather, information and operational procedures continue to show activity and movement, but, over time, no truly appreciable progress toward achieving goals or objectives is realized. Rather, the system continues to simply maintain the status quo throughout the period of operation.

Holding pattern management: Where the system continues to operate but in a pattern of stasis where there is no true growth, nor is there a blockage in the systemic flow.

The Participative Method of Management

This model of management requires that administrators elicit the input and ideas from persons being governed. Thus, the **participative method of management** includes opinions and feedback offered from both inmates and staff when making decisions regarding the operations and governance of the prison facility. This type of management is actually a bit pragmatic in today's world of corrections because most prison facilities are operated with an inmate-to-staff ratio that is quite high. In other words, there are many more inmates than staff, and, even though staff have the upper hand in the long term when inmates become unruly, it is easy for inmates to gain a short-term advantage on a cell block or dormitory due to their sheer numbers compared to prison staff charged with watching them. Thus, in many cases, prison staff will use aspects of the prison subculture to gain leverage and maintain control over inmates as a means of maintaining compliance.

Participative method of management: A form of management that includes opinions and feedback offered from both inmates and staff when making decisions regarding the operations and governance of the prison facility.

FOCUS TOPIC 13.3

Back to the Future in Prison Management

Though authoritarian forms of prison management are not the primary model used in corrections today, this type of management has had a long and influential history. One primary figure who was instrumental in refining this type of approach was Elam Lynds, who was a force behind the Auburn or congregate system of prison management (students may recall that we discussed this type of prison system, developed in New York, in earlier chapters of this text).

As a captain in the Auburn system, Elam Lynds led the development of this system through the use of strict punishment-oriented management. He believed that all inmates should be treated equally and used a highly regimented schedule of activities that included the use of the lockstep marching model of movement. The key was to create uniform and machine-like behavior from inmates. Inmates were all dressed identically in black-and-white striped uniforms and engaged in a regimented routine of work and prayer. Advocates of this type of prison management believed that it had the best chance of reforming inmates into productive citizens. This type of system also ensured that the prison would be at least marginally profitable and did well in maintaining order.

This oppressive type of managerial system was based on an extreme military model that impacted the guards of the facility almost as much as the inmates. Infractions among employees were treated in a punitive manner, and there were few rewards or positive incentives for guards working in the facility. Naturally, since their job entailed the constant enforcement of severe forms of control, the personalities of officers and the climate of the institution were tense, stiff, and uncomfortable. This type of oppressive management (both of inmates and of the staff in employ) built an abusive and calloused culture within the institution. Strict adherence to orders, with no feedback loop to question the orders given, intensified the fear that was the primary source of motivation throughout the institution. Thus, fear was the tool of management in this authoritarian model, and it was used on both inmates and prison staff in the institution.

SOURCE: Excerpted from Carlson, P. M., & Dilulio, J. J. (2008). Organizational management. In P. M. Carlson & J. S. Garrett (Eds.)., *Prison and jail administration: Practice and theory*. Boston, MA: Jones and Bartlett.

Thinkstock/Stockbyte/Thinkstock

■ PHOTO 13.3 The inmate ombudsman asks for input as a means of determining how services can be provided in the most helpful manner possible.

Administrators run into a paradox where too much control and discipline results in a system that is oppressive and plagued with problems but too little control can result in a security risk. Participative methods allow for a third means of management that attempts to balance these extremes. In our earlier discussion regarding proactive correctional management, several examples were given where the warden or other top administrators in the facility might solicit input from inmates during mealtime or other points in the day. This form of management also advocated for these administrators to solicit input from prison staff as well.

Thus, the proactive approach to correctional management works hand-in-hand with the participative method of management because both seek the input of prison staff when identifying problems and formulating solutions. However, the participative method of management emphasizes one additional key feature: It also seeks the input of the inmate population, through both formal and informal venues. Thus, inmates as well as staff are treated as a formal component of the organization and therefore have at least some input on the day-to-day processes that occur within the facility (Silverman, 2001).

In addition, consider that many administrators as well as general prison staff tend to be kept abreast of the happenings within a prison through informal networks, such as the prison grapevine. The **prison grapevine** is grounded in the organization of the prison subculture and is an informal network that consists of information passed through the personal communications of employees to employees, inmates to inmates, employees to inmates, and inmates to employees. When examining the power of the prison grapevine, consider the fact that informal bargaining goes on between inmates and prison staff and that this shows some basis for cooperation among both populations; this then demonstrates that even though both populations are pitted against one another in the prison environment, they can and do work in mutually participative relationships. These relationships tend to be mutually exploitative in many respects but, nevertheless, result in informal deals and negotiation whereby participative approaches emerge. The wise administrator will, at least to some degree, embrace this natural symbiotic relationship between those who govern and those who are governed to create an atmosphere where mediation of the governance process is encouraged.

Prison grapevine: An informal network of information passed through the personal communications of employees and inmates.

Centralized management: Tight forms of control in the communication process that ensure that decision-making power is reserved for only a small group of people.

Decentralized management: The authority and responsibility of management are distributed amongst the supervisory chain, allowing decisions to correspond to the problems confronted by each level of management.

Centralized Versus Decentralized Management

Centralized management consists of tight forms of control in the communication process that ensure that decision-making power is reserved to only a small group of people. This type of managerial style tends to be reflective of bureaucratic models of prison management. The advantage of this type of management system is that decisions tend to be consistent and also reflect the need to operate the facility in a safe and secure manner. On the other hand, disadvantages emerge when mid-level and low-level supervisors do not feel empowered, and, lacking a sense of ownership, they may have little incentive (and authorization) to address issues that emerge but are unnoticed by higher-level management.

Decentralized management occurs when the authority and responsibility of management personnel are divided and distributed amongst various levels of the supervisory chain so that each level of supervision may make decisions that correspond to the problems that confront it at its particular level of management. This approach tends to speed up the decision-making process and allow for the integration of detailed information specific to a particular problem that must be addressed. However, there is less consistency from supervisor to supervisor in how problems are solved, and, without clear policies and guidelines, the entire facility can develop into several subunits that have inconsistent and even confusing forms of operation (Carlson & DiIulio, 2008).

When determining the best form of management between centralized and decentralized approaches, this author's answer is that both are equally useful but depend on the context. In situations of serious emergency when institutional safety and security are under grave threat or danger, the best approach is one that is centralized but directly involves the decision makers in the immediate response that is necessary. In these cases, it is important that the most experienced personnel are vested with concentrated decision-making powers so as to be able to react quickly to the threat while minimizing confusion amidst the ranks; this approach ensures clarity of operations. The use of centralized decision making is also more appropriate to strategic planning than to tactical planning. Strategic planning consists of the determination of long-term goals and objectives for an agency, usually spanning a period of 1 or more years in scope. On the other hand, **tactical planning** consists of ground-level planning that is narrow in focus, usually structured around the resolution of a particular issue or something that confronts the agency on a short-term basis. Higher-level administrators usually set the overall mission of the agency and are therefore best suited to make long-term strategic decisions for the agency. It is appropriate that such decision making is centralized to the upper administration because it is these administrators who are most informed of the macro-level issues that confront the agency as a whole.

Decentralized management is best utilized in situations where routine decision-making takes place and where there is more direct interaction between a particular level of management and the frontline staff who do the work of the agency. While these issues may be routine in nature, it is important to not underestimate the stress involved for employees and inmates who must continually, day in and day out, deal with some seemingly petty nuisance that builds up a continued sense of frustration. These issues can lead to explosive circumstances if not dealt with. Empowering staff so that they can address these types of routine problems can eliminate much of the job stress that they might experience and also provides them with a sense of control (or at least influence) over their environment. The decentralized approach is also the best approach when attempting to maximize input from informal groups as well as the prison subculture (both inmate and staff subculture). Where centralized forms of management will ensure that decision makers are remote from these types of communication networks, decentralized management structures will typically be adept at integrating information that is disseminated through the organizational grapevine.

MANAGEMENT VERSUS LEADERSHIP

In many respects, management differs markedly from leadership. Yet these two characteristics of supervision may exist within the same individual. The term **management** refers to persons who have been vested with an official title by the agency and who tend to be focused on the process of completing functions of operation within the prison facility. These personnel oversee the details of job assignments given to correctional officers and ensure that employees are maintaining behavior that is consistent with the stated policy and procedure of the agency. **Leadership**, on the other hand, entails skills and talents that motivate and influence persons toward a common goal or idea. Persons with leadership talent are often able to elicit commitment from employees that goes beyond mere compliance to the rules and regulations; they are adept at getting people to be inherently committed to a cause, goal, or objective of the agency.

In reality, it may not be easy to separate management from leadership without creating an artificial distinction or category. This artificial distinction is not usually reflective of the "real world" of prison operations but is more a means of distinguishing between the multifaceted roles of various supervisory staff. The key point in discussing these two concepts is that the supervisor's job is hands-on in nature (Carlson & DiIulio, 2008). This means that supervisors should be visible and available to their employees; this is especially true with the upper management of the prison facility. As mentioned earlier in this chapter, wardens should make their rounds throughout the facility and solicit input from employees and inmates to get an informal sense of how the prison is running and to identify concerns of those employees and inmates. In practice, this is done routinely by prison wardens throughout the United States.

Experience, Intelligence, and Emotional Intelligence in Leadership

There has been some debate as to whether experience is more valuable than intelligence in leadership (Robbins, 2005). While it is certain that leaders should have the requisite intelligence to do their job correctly, it is debatable as to whether someone with a genius-level intellect would make a great leader. Indeed, such persons may find it quite difficult to interact with people who are not similarly

Tactical planning: Ground-level planning that is narrow in focus and structured around the short-term resolution of particular issues.

Management: Persons with an official title who tend to be focused on the operational process within the prison facility.

Leadership: Entails skills and talents that motivate and influence persons toward a common goal or idea.

brilliant, and, when considering the behavior of inmates within the facility, they may do a very poor job in working with the correctional population. By the same token, leaders with a great deal of experience may be very familiar with their job, but that does not necessarily mean that they have done that job in the most effective manner possible. In fact, some people may do a job for years and consistently achieve mediocre results; this should not be considered success. Even worse is the case where someone may have done a job for years and done it incorrectly; this is a disastrous outcome.

Within the field of corrections, there are circumstances where one trait is perhaps more important than the other. Naturally, the ideal situation is to have a leader who is both intelligent and experienced, and in most cases leaders will indeed have at least some degree of respectable intellectual ability as well as some degree of experience since many correctional supervisors tend to be promoted from the lower ranks. However, the likelihood of having a perfect balance between both intelligence and experience is very seldom achieved. Thus, it is of importance to know how to assign leaders, based on their levels of experience and intelligence.

In most cases where long-term planning is concerned, leaders who have high levels of intelligence tend to produce superior results. This is particularly true with long-term problem solving and/or strategic planning. The reason for this is that these types of decisions allow for thoughtful and reflective analysis, and, since the various contingencies of these decisions are far-reaching, the level of detailed outcome analysis requires a more thorough examination of the issues decided upon. Persons with high intellects tend to be good at these types of analyses, or they at least tend to be better than persons who are not as intellectually gifted.

On the other hand, in situations where quick, tactical-level decisions must be made, experience tends to be the better arbiter in determining who will lead most effectively. This is especially true in crisis situations where there is less reliance on textbook-like processes and more need for a well-practiced approach. Leaders with years of experience are more likely to have traversed other crises and/or demanding situations and will therefore have more previous and incident-related knowledge to draw from. While they may not necessarily have a high intellect, their prior exposure to similar incidents in their past can give them an edge in how they approach a situation and what they do in response. Obviously, those leaders who are experienced and who also have a high degree of intellect will be the best types of responders and reflect the optimal type of correctional supervisor.

Another factor of effective leadership is very important to consider: emotional intelligence. **Emotional intelligence** describes how adept a person is at noticing and responding to the emotional cues and information exhibited by others with whom he or she interacts. Emotional intelligence is found to be especially useful in jobs that require a high degree of social interaction. Naturally, the field of corrections entails constant interaction between inmates and staff, staff and staff, and staff and the public. Indeed, human interaction lies at the heart of the correctional field of work, and this, therefore, means that emotional intelligence is even more important.

Leadership and the Custodial Staff (What Gets Respect)

Wardens and senior administrators must establish a vision of a successful correctional operation. In developing this vision, administrators must be able to sell their goals to those within the organization so that all persons provide earnest commitment. The best way to do this is through an understanding of the organizational culture that exists within an agency. Supervisory staff play a critical role in shaping and forming organizational culture, and it is through the emphasis on the mid-level and lower-level supervisory staff that upper administrators can best disseminate their vision plan for the future.

It is important that supervisors develop an image of involvement with the rank-and-file staff and that they communicate to all levels of staff the goals of the organization and why they are important. This type of management is based on the idea that the effectiveness of the organization depends on the example that the leaders set for other employees. There is a direct correlation between the expectations of leadership within a facility and the resulting behavior that is observed. When leaders or managers (keep in mind that they can be distinct from one another or in other cases one and the same) tolerate mediocrity, the result will be mediocre at best. On the other hand, when professionalism and excellence are expected, the momentum of the organization increases, and employees perceive the ways they may serve as helpful contributors.

Wright (2008) makes the point that the field of corrections is a "people business" where human relations skills are critical. For correctional supervisors, an understanding of the day-to-day concerns of their staff will allow leaders to more easily develop a rapport with employees and

Emotional intelligence: Describes how adept a person is at noticing and responding to the emotional cues and information exhibited by others.

more effectively motivate them toward agency goals. In addition, agency goals should be set with the agency staff in mind. Administrators must ask themselves, are my goals compatible with my employee population's abilities and interests? If the answer to this question is no, then these administrators must either consider training staff to make them capable of pursuing the identified goals or consider revising the goals that they have set. A failure to choose at least one of these options will lead to bigger organizational problems in the future.

Supervisors must ensure that staff understand that they must follow agency guidelines and be consistent in performing their duties and enforcing rules (Wright, 2008). While this may seem like an obvious point, incidents where employees claim to not be aware of existing guidelines abound, as do circumstances of inconsistent rule enforcement. It is important that supervisors make active efforts to prevent the emergence of "rogues and mavericks" within the facility. **Rogues and mavericks** are employees who tend to act as if they are independent of the broader institution—as if they are the law rather than persons charged with enforcing the laws of the institution. These employees are dangerous to the institution, and they undermine the authority of supervisors and administrators by exerting undue influence through the informal prison subculture. Further, other employees will watch to see if these independent-minded individuals are allowed to run free, and, if this seems to be the case, they will tend to either emulate these behaviors or resent the fact that these employees get away with their behavior; neither outcome is favorable to the institution. Thus, these employees must be dealt with, and, if they refuse to modify their behavior, they must be eliminated from the ranks of the prison staff.

Span of Control and/or Influence

Span of control refers to the number of persons that an administrator supervises. This can vary greatly from as low as one person to several hundred or even thousands of people. In theory, the more people that the supervisor has responsibility for, the wider his or her span of control. However, for this text's purposes, we will modify this traditional understanding because even though, on an organizational chart, the regional administrator may have authority over persons in several prison facilities in his or her region, it is very unlikely that the regional administrator actually exerts any true control over persons who are at the lowest ranks of the agency. Rather it is more likely that the regional administrator exerts influence over those agency employees through the acts and deeds of lower-ranking supervisors, the effects of organizational culture and tradition, and the willingness of the employees to tacitly submit to the authority of someone whom they may have never met (few entry-level correctional officers ever have any true face time with the regional director of their prison system).

Thus, the **span of control** in correctional institutions refers to the sphere of control that supervisors have over employees that they encounter and interact with on a routine basis and whom they are able to consult with to gain observable compliance with their requests, recommendations, and directives. On the other hand, the **span of influence** refers to the extended impact that a supervisor has upon employee behavior that may occur beyond his or her own actual observation but, through the effects of other organizational members, is carried forth as the desired means of operation. This has more to do with the effects of other members of the chain of command repeating and enforcing directives promulgated by the higher-level supervisor and less to do with the upper-level supervisor's own ability to exert control over individual employee behavior.

WOMEN IN CORRECTIONAL MANAGEMENT

With the professionalization of corrections has come the understanding that diversity in the workforce necessitates transparency and ethical behavior behind the walls. In other words, when correctional staff consist of various persons from various groups and backgrounds, there is less likelihood that biases in operations can continue undetected. This is particularly true in cases where the prison subculture, steeped in a staunch male-oriented view, is concerned. The inmate subculture tends to be quite sexist in orientation, with feminine characteristics being considered weak and inferior. Having women in the workforce can counter these biases among inmates, and having female supervisors can be even more effective in developing acceptance of women in the field of corrections. The key issue is whether agencies make a point to facilitate the careers of female security staff; it is very important that they do so in order that subcultural influences can be countered.

Carlson and Garrett (1999) have noted that many women tend to adopt a service-oriented approach that is less confrontational than that used by their male counterparts. This is actually a

Rogues and mavericks: Employees within a facility who tend to act as if they are independent of the broader institution.

Span of control: Refers to the number of persons that an officer supervises.

Span of influence: The extended impact that a supervisor has upon employee behavior.

TECHNOLOGY AND EQUIPMENT 13.1

Strategic Planning Process in Determining the Acquisition of Technology and Equipment for Facility Security Purposes

The flow chart below has been provided to demonstrate to students the various concerns that administrators may have to consider when deciding upon security-related technology. This is particularly true with technology involved in the use of force against inmates or technology that will be used in response to prison disturbances, riots, or escapes.

Strategic Planning Framework

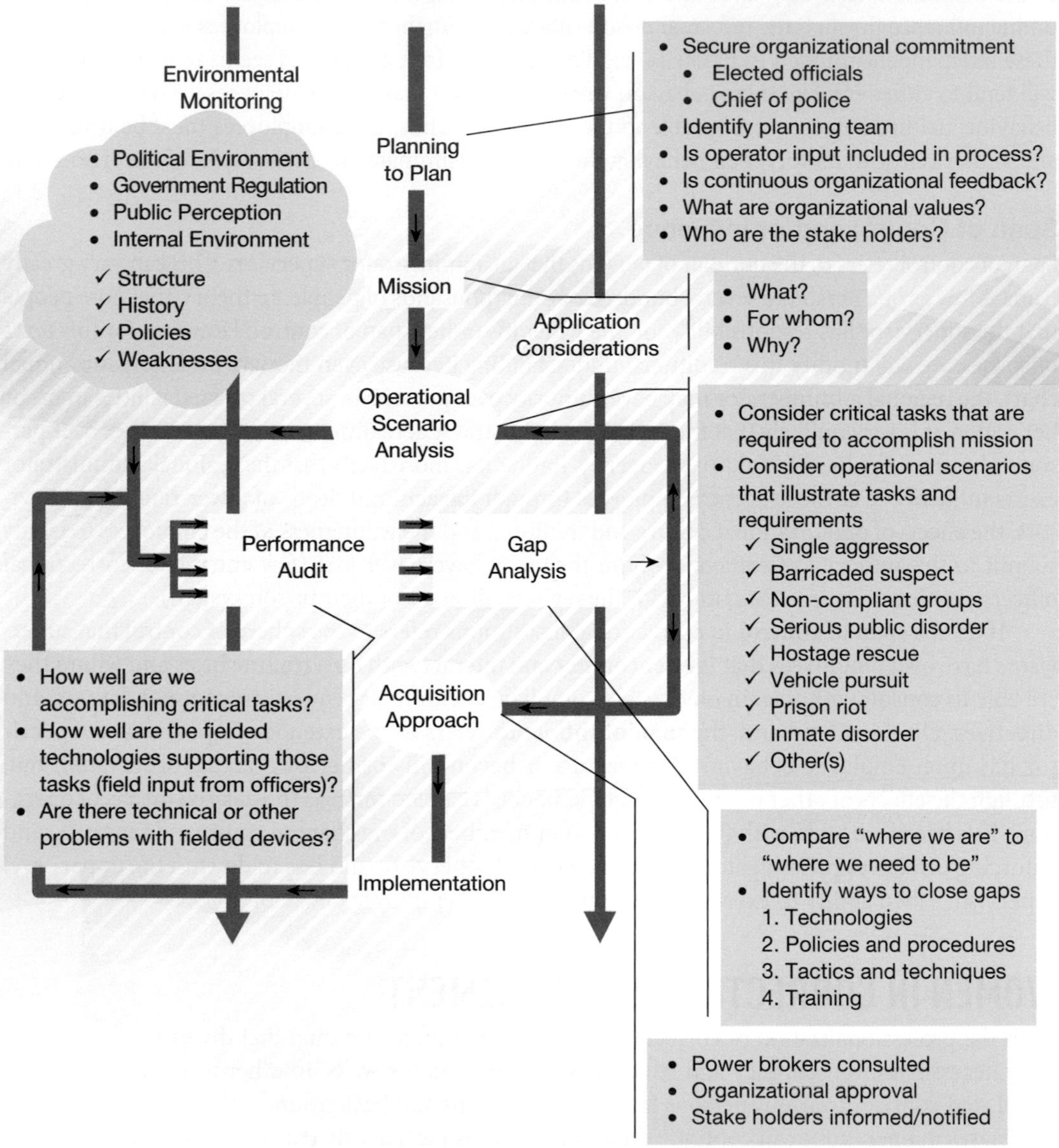

Environmental Monitoring
- Political Environment
- Government Regulation
- Public Perception
- Internal Environment
  - ✓ Structure
  - ✓ History
  - ✓ Policies
  - ✓ Weaknesses

Planning to Plan
- Secure organizational commitment
  - Elected officials
  - Chief of police
- Identify planning team
- Is operator input included in process?
- Is continuous organizational feedback?
- What are organizational values?
- Who are the stake holders?

Mission

Application Considerations
- What?
- For whom?
- Why?

Operational Scenario Analysis
- Consider critical tasks that are required to accomplish mission
- Consider operational scenarios that illustrate tasks and requirements
  - ✓ Single aggressor
  - ✓ Barricaded suspect
  - ✓ Non-compliant groups
  - ✓ Serious public disorder
  - ✓ Hostage rescue
  - ✓ Vehicle pursuit
  - ✓ Prison riot
  - ✓ Inmate disorder
  - ✓ Other(s)

Performance Audit
- How well are we accomplishing critical tasks?
- How well are the fielded technologies supporting those tasks (field input from officers)?
- Are there technical or other problems with fielded devices?

Gap Analysis
- Compare "where we are" to "where we need to be"
- Identify ways to close gaps
  1. Technologies
  2. Policies and procedures
  3. Tactics and techniques
  4. Training

Acquisition Approach
- Power brokers consulted
- Organizational approval
- Stake holders informed/notified

Implementation

SOURCE: *Adapted from: Goodstein, Nolan, and Pfeiffer* (1993).

Administrators at the executive level (i.e., regional directors and above) and even at the facility level (i.e., prison wardens) must consider how well the equipment or technology will meet agency needs, the expense involved, potential legal issues that can emerge, the reliability of the equipment, the training of staff who will use the equipment, and likely perceptions generated by the media if the equipment is used in an incident. In making their decisions, executive administrators often develop strategic plans specifically related to the integration of technology, particularly when considering lethal and/or less lethal devices. Such a plan not only provides the general guidance necessary but also establishes priorities, allocates resources, and assigns responsibilities. This is of particular importance with regard to less lethal devices because there are no universally accepted standards, no commonly accepted taxonomy, no standardized training requirements, and no reliable methods for comparison. Consequently, each agency is left to develop its own protocols and policies. It seems prudent, then, to establish some criteria for devices that promise to fulfill the particular requirements for a given agency and to avoid those that seem promising but are expensive, awkward, publicly unacceptable, or otherwise inappropriate.

A strategic plan is not a static document—it is a dynamic process that anticipates requirements and provides a means by which those requirements might be addressed. It is essential that this process be integrated into the overall strategic planning process for the entire agency. While there are numerous frameworks available, most have common features. Most simply, strategic planning is a thought process that includes three major considerations: *the ends* (the agency goals that support the mission), *the ways* (the methods that the organization uses to achieve those ends), and *the means* (the resources used to accomplish the ways). There are a number of strategic planning frameworks that can be integrated into the correctional agency's processes as a means to "think through" the ends, ways, and means in a more rigorous fashion.

Strategic planning for technological devices, particularly those involved with the use of force, should determine equipment necessary to accomplish tasks that support the agency mission. This part of planning provides the necessary focus and ensures that the efforts of all involved are complementary, not competing or counterproductive. Considering different operational scenarios that illustrate and support required tasks and their relative frequency is one method of identifying potential technology requirements. Most strategic planning involves a review process and feedback loops. Situations change, and assumptions often prove invalid. A review process ensures that the plan is continually "tuned" to adapt to changes in the environment and overcome obstacles. A dynamic strategic planning process enables the exploitation of opportunities and avoids or mitigates emerging threats. Such planning often proves an advantage when opportunities for acquiring new technologies and/or obtaining funding unexpectedly present themselves. The process also ensures both proper consideration of "stakeholder" input (e.g., from the officers in the field and the community) and necessary support of "powerbrokers" (e.g., the governor, the superintendent of corrections, elected officials, the community).

SOURCES: Goodstein, L. D., Nolan, T. M., & Pfeiffer, J. W. (1993). *Applied strategic planning: How to develop a plan that really works.* New York, NY: McGraw-Hill.

Weapons and Protective Systems Technologies Center. (2010). *A guidebook for less-lethal devices: Planning for, selecting, and implementing technology solutions.* Philadelphia, PA: Pennsylvania State University.

very valuable asset to agencies because it minimizes the number of grievances, potential lawsuits, personal injury claims, and other legal pitfalls associated with conflicts in prison. Likewise, the overall climate on cell blocks and in dorms that are handled in a less aggressive manner tends to be calmer; this can add to institutional safety. Though this approach has its benefits, there have been mixed results. In jail settings, research has found that women officers are perceived by male officers to be less effective in breaking up fighting inmates or controlling large and/or aggressive inmates. On the other hand, male officers tend to view women as skilled at calming inmates and working with those who are mentally or emotionally disturbed (Carlson, 1999). Female supervisors tend to have these same skills and abilities, and, even in cases where male inmates are aggressive, women who hold rank seem to be just as adept as men at maintaining control of the cell block or dormitory.

It is advisable that correctional agencies continue to recruit and promote more female representation within the management circles. As we have seen, the role of the supervisor requires effective communication skills and the ability to share the agency's mission and values. If the agency is truly sincere about professionalism, ethical behavior, and a desire to develop a safe institution, then having optimal female representation can add to all of these objectives. This is especially true since the inclusion of women with supervisory power will tend to counter the negative aspects of the prison subculture, which will create an organizational culture that does not promote the sexist views that male inmates tend to hold within the institution.

Challenges to Upward Mobility

There is some debate as to whether the glass ceiling still exists within corrections. The **glass ceiling** is a term for official or unofficial barriers to promotion that exist for women within the workforce. For all practical purposes, it should be considered that some sort of barrier does indeed exist because there are substantially fewer female supervisors than male supervisors within correctional facilities. Further, throughout history, women who worked in corrections tended to do so in facilities for women, and, since the female offender population was proportionally smaller than the male offender population, the need for women to work in corrections was much less than that for men.

In addition, there are social constraints in society that tend to frown upon women working within the prison environment. Historically, this type of employment was not considered ladylike and therefore engendered social aversion. Due to this, and the intensely masculine nature of the

Glass ceiling: Barriers to promotion that exist for women within the workforce.

AP Photo/Houston Chronicle, Mayra Beltran

■ PHOTO 13.4 The warden of this facility answers a question provided by one of her ranking officers regarding inmate rule enforcement.

prison subculture, the hard-nosed population of male guards who already worked in prisons, and the dangerousness of the job, it is not surprising that during the past 100 years women were not often employed in this field. However, the modern era of corrections is seeing a change, and women are more commonly seen within this area of employment.

People placed in situations in which they are powerless and have limited promotional potential tend to lower their goals and develop approaches to work that are defensive and not postured for upward mobility. In many cases, women may not utilize the same set of aggressive social skills that their male counterparts employ and may therefore be at a socialized disadvantage. These skills may need to be learned on the job, and, for women in particular, there may be a need to learn about the prison environment's social cues. This means that women may have to adjust their body language and facial expressions to assert an authoritative image rather than one that is pleasant. In all cases, the stereotyped, subservient image of women must be avoided. Likewise, attempts to make themselves attractive are also problematic within a prison setting. This means that the prison environment is often counterintuitive to the socialization that many women may receive.

Video Link
Female Correctional Officers

Many women in corrections report that they are often still at a disadvantage even when they have the skills and desire to do the job. This is due to the effects of the glass ceiling, which prevents them from being included in informal social circles, gaining appropriate mentoring and on-the-job training from their senior male counterparts, or having access to positions that are more dangerous but more prestigious within the informal guard subculture. Indeed, paternalistic desires to protect female officers may prevent them from working some job assignments, and this places them at a disadvantage in terms of training and experience, resulting in impaired promotional ability.

Prison System Culture

Further still, the problem of sexual harassment affects the prison work site, just as is the case in outside society. However, it is much more pronounced and pervasive in prisons. Harassment can include behaviors such as cursing, intimidation, or inappropriate humor. In the prison or jail setting, male staff as well as inmates may present challenges to women by creating an atmosphere that is demeaning to women. For instance, a male staff member may say to a group of male inmates working in the field, "OK, c'mon ladies, let's get back to work," which implies that women are less accepted and respected than are men. The fact that the guard is referring to the male inmates as "ladies" is meant to be demeaning and reinforces the notion that women have lesser stature within the prison. In cases where inmates "punk one another out" or say "you just got punked out," the implication is that the person holds a sexual role that is passive or subservient; this is typically equated to female behavior and/or a nonaggressive (and therefore weak) person. All of these biases toward women and anything that is effeminate exist in many prison environments and are juxtaposed against an environment of hypermasculinity.

In order that women can be integrated more fully into the world of prison operations, it is necessary that sexist opinions, beliefs, and informal exchanges be minimized by administrators. However, higher-level supervisors must do more than craft a policy and act punitively to enforce the policy; this will likely breed resistance to the idea. Rather, upper administrators should ensure that positive accomplishments of female staff and supervisors are showcased and rewarded within the agency. At the same time, administrators should ensure that these rewards are balanced with those given to male employees. The key is to change the image of the agency by demonstrating support for female officers and supervisors while doing so within the framework of acknowledging, showcasing, and rewarding *all* officers within the agency. This will be particularly effective if women who perform difficult duties in close contact with inmates are specifically noted within the agency.

Further, it is important that female supervisors be present and represented in male facilities, not just female facilities. While this can lead to some complications in certain situations, agencies must be committed to working around and through legal issues related to cross-gender searches, privacy issues for male inmates in shower areas and/or locations where strip searches may occur, and so forth. Ultimately, this acknowledgment of women in corrections is healthy for the sexist subculture that tends to exist among inmates and some correctional officers. Providing training on sexual equality, sexual harassment, and other similar topics is also important and should be mandatory.

THE CORRECTIONS WORKFORCE

Racial and Cultural Diversity

Prior to the 1980s, prisons tended to be in rural regions and to hire staff from within the local area. The demographics of correctional staff in the United States have changed greatly since those times. The change toward a more multicultural setting is reflected in broader society and most all criminal justice agencies. This trend toward multiculturalism and diversity will only continue, both with the staff who are employed and with the inmates who are supervised.

The diversity that has developed in the correctional workforce has followed the move toward professionalization of the correctional system. Prior to this shift, women and minorities were considered a threat to the cohesion of the correctional work group and were often subject to discrimination and harassment. However, the professionalization of corrections has opened the door for more fair and balanced work environments, and correctional staff have become more sensitized to different perspectives in the workplace.

Further, administrators of correctional facilities have made attempts to hire persons from diverse backgrounds since it has become increasingly clear that this is a benefit when contending with a diverse inmate population. This reflects the shift in prison operations away from one in which the primary purpose was to simply respond to problematic behavior with force. The use of effective communication skills as a means of preventing problems and addressing issues in a more professional manner requires a sense of cultural competence among agencies and certainly among staff. One means of improving agency cultural competence is through the hiring of diverse workers who can relate to the inmate population's own diversity. Having officers with proficiency in the various languages that are spoken in the facility and with the same customs and beliefs as inmate groups enhances the ability of the agency to address problematic issues related to racial and/or cultural barriers. Thus, diverse work groups can mitigate many of the negative effects of the prison subculture as well as of gangs that tend to be structured along racial lines.

Professionalization of Corrections

During the 1970s, amidst the increase in hiring that began to take place in corrections, concern arose regarding the training and competency of correctional officers. Indeed, in 1973 the National Advisory Commission on Criminal Justice Standards and Goals encouraged state legislators to take action to improve the education and training of correctional officers. Further, correctional administrators cited the need for security staff to study criminology and other disciplines that could aid in working with difficult populations. The National Advisory Commission on Criminal Justice Standards and Goals (1973) also indicated that "all new staff members should have at least 40 hours of orientation training during their first week on the job, and at least 60 hours additional training during their first year" (p. 494). This represents some of the first national-level attempts to mandate professional training and standards for correctional officers. Though these first steps were certainly headed in the correct direction, progress was slow. In 1978, it was determined that only half of all states were actually meeting the 40-hour entry-level training requirement, and even fewer were meeting the recommended 60 hours of training during the officer's first year.

The educational progress of correctional officers had not improved much during this time. Roughly 13% of the agencies did not even require a high school diploma, and the remaining 77% required only that—college was not even a remote consideration. Given the importance of this type of work, it is clear that more intensive training should be provided to correctional officers and the acquisition of higher education should be encouraged.

Robert Hanser

■ PHOTO 13.5 Brittany Naron is completing her bachelor's degree in criminal justice while employed as a correctional officer. She has also received post-level training in corrections and completed internship experiences while working and attending college.

Throughout the past decade, the American Correctional Association (ACA) has generated a major push for professionalization of the field of corrections. This has resulted in a pattern of steadily increasing entry-level educational requirements consistent with a broader trend toward correctional officer professionalism. However, the term *professionalism* itself has been touted by various correctional systems without much of an attempt to articulate what this specifically means. The ACA advocated for the professionalization of correctional officers, and states began to adopt the standards set by that organization.

Most states have adopted the majority of the ACA standards, and corrections is moving in a progressive direction, but there is still much more work to be done. Further, given the widespread budget cuts common in many states throughout the nation, money and resources for improved training and educational standards may be lacking. Yet this is at a time when these resources are needed the most. How well prison systems fare in the future is yet to be seen, but one thing is clear: A failure to train and educate this workforce will only ensure that the potential corrective efforts of prison systems are minimized, and this will then create a potential risk to the public safety of society as a whole.

Professionalization of Correctional Officers and the Convict Code

Students may recall the impact of the convict code upon prison subculture from Chapter 9. Though this code is still alive, it is not universally found in all modern-day institutions, and newer generations of inmates do not seem to stay as loyal to it as do older generations. The professionalization of the corrections field has also limited the effectiveness of the convict code (Mobley, 2011). Authorities' unwillingness to allow inmates to enforce the convict code and to essentially police themselves (as with the building tender system discussed in prior chapters) has removed an important element of power from inmate groups (Mobley, 2011). The enforcement of rules through violence is no longer tacitly or implicitly permitted like it once was among prison guards (Mobley, 2011). Inmates who seek to enforce this code now get punished in some institutions and/or transferred as a means to disrupt their power.

The growing number of institutions in most state prison systems has enhanced the trend toward professionalization in corrections (Mobley, 2011). This has likewise resulted in more interest in this area of employment, particularly since 2009, when a depressed economy made this area of employment more desirable for many of the working and middle class. Bureaucratic tendencies to centralize expanding prison systems and staff institutions with better-trained personnel stem largely from the same causes that have boosted incidences of snitching among the younger generation of inmates (Mobley, 2011). The criminalization of drug use during the 1990s and the prioritization of law enforcement resources against drugs—known as the War on Drugs—are the primary factors that have influenced prison systems to grow and professionalize and have also aided in the slow but sure decline of the convict code within the inmate subculture (Mobley, 2011).

Emergency preparedness: The planning, training, and budgeting process involved prior to the occurrence of an emergency.

Emergency response: The intervention used, the management of that intervention, the containment of the emergency, and the successful resolution of the emergency.

EMERGENCY MANAGEMENT

This subsection on emergency management issues is not meant to be comprehensive or all-encompassing. It is intended to simply address the fact that administration, management, and leadership must focus on the likelihood that the unexpected can and does occur within prison environments. It is good practice to ensure that administrators have put into place appropriate forms of reaction prior to the emergency event. Further, it should be pointed out that there is a difference between emergency preparedness and emergency response. **Emergency preparedness** consists of the planning, training, and budgeting process that is involved prior to the occurrence of an emergency. **Emergency response** consists of the actual intervention that is used, the management of that intervention, containment of the emergency, and the successful resolution of the emergency event. In planning these two stages, correctional administrators should be informed of their facility's general inmate and staff cultural climate since this will typically provide some advanced notice of developments that can become problematic. Thus, we now turn our attention to the need to gauge the climate within the prison facility in the interest of alleviating problems before an emergency state of affairs develops.

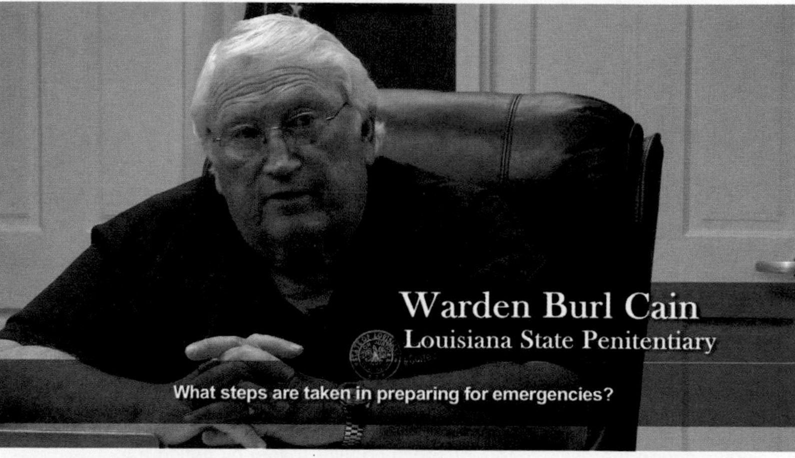

Warden Burl Cain
Louisiana State Penitentiary
What steps are taken in preparing for emergencies?

Prison Tour Video: Emergency Management. Emergency management is a key component of correctional administration. Watch a warden talking about mangaging and preparing for emergencies.

Gauging the Climate

In prior chapters, we have examined the impact of the prison subculture on prison operations, and we have determined that a significant underground economy exists within the prison. Further, we have also noted that it is important that administrators make the rounds throughout their facility to be seen both by inmates and by officers. With this in mind, administrators should conduct routine tours of their facility. Further, correctional supervisors should engage inmates and staff regarding rumor control, which requires that leaders identify rumors that arise (Armstrong, 2008). **Rumor control** is the active process of administrators to circumvent faulty information that is disseminated among staff or inmates and has the potential to cause unrest or disharmony throughout the facility. To be informed of rumors, a rapport with inmates and officers is necessary. Once a rumor is identified, the administrator should bring it up to inmates or staff in a nonconfrontational manner and either confirm or deny the rumor, depending upon whether it is true or false. This will take away the power of the rumor and those who generate the rumor, and it will also eliminate the perception of defensiveness among the upper administration. A willingness to engage in rumor control will prevent and/or reduce many problems that might emerge within a facility (Armstrong, 2008).

Depending upon the type of emergency or crisis that occurs within the facility, different levels of response are required. For each type of response, different teams with incident-specific training should be used (Stepp, 2008). Regardless of the type of incident training, certain characteristics should exist among all response team members. All teams should be composed of volunteers, and they should receive specialized training and skills that ensure that they are experts on their specific area of response. Further, they should be knowledgeable on policy and law regarding their type of response. These personnel should also be required to pass rigorous physical, academic, and psychological screening.

When using teams for emergency management, the most common and the least lethal type of team is the disturbance control team. **Disturbance control teams** are specialized teams trained to respond to, contain, and neutralize inmate disturbances in prisons. These teams are trained in riot control formation and the use of defensive equipment, such as batons, stun guns, and chemical weapons. Disturbance control teams are trained to contain both large and small disruptive groups. These response teams use less lethal technology for circumstances where life-and-death issues are not at stake. It is strongly recommended that some type of certification process be included that requires knowledge of agency policy and emergency plans as well as proficiency in the use of related equipment.

The next level of response includes armed disturbance control teams. **Armed disturbance control teams** deal with disturbances that have escalated to matters with life-and-death outcomes. Training and certification for these teams must be even more intense than for teams armed with nonlethal weaponry. There may be more potential for liability with this type of team. When using armed teams, it is important to not use weapons unless administrators are sure that those weapons can be protected and there is no danger of them being seized by inmates. Administrators should not establish policies where staff may be expected to shoot to disable an offender. It is unlikely these officers will have the continual training necessary to maintain the needed skill level. Further, if they shoot to disable and kill the offender, liability issues may ensue as well.

Lastly, tactical response teams are the most highly trained and skilled emergency response security staff. These teams are often referred to as **Special Operations Response Teams (SORT)**, which are

Rumor control: The active process of administrators to circumvent faulty information that is disseminated among staff or inmates and has the potential to cause unrest or disharmony throughout the facility.

Disturbance control team: Specialized teams trained to respond to, contain, and neutralize inmate disturbances in prisons.

Armed disturbance control team: Deals with disturbances that have escalated to matters of life and death.

Special Operations Response Teams (SORT): Teams designed to respond to serious crises within a prison facility.

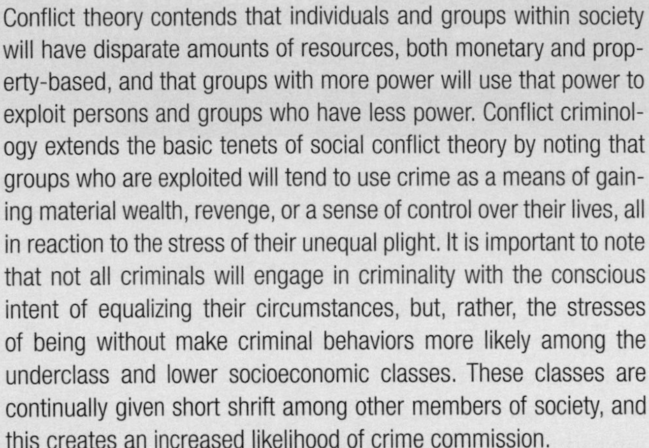

APPLIED THEORY 13.1

Conflict Theory and Prison Management

Conflict theory contends that individuals and groups within society will have disparate amounts of resources, both monetary and property-based, and that groups with more power will use that power to exploit persons and groups who have less power. Conflict criminology extends the basic tenets of social conflict theory by noting that groups who are exploited will tend to use crime as a means of gaining material wealth, revenge, or a sense of control over their lives, all in reaction to the stress of their unequal plight. It is important to note that not all criminals will engage in criminality with the conscious intent of equalizing their circumstances, but, rather, the stresses of being without make criminal behaviors more likely among the underclass and lower socioeconomic classes. These classes are continually given short shrift among other members of society, and this creates an increased likelihood of crime commission.

Further, underprivileged neighborhoods tend to have less social and political clout and are therefore subject to poorer representation in society. This also occurs in the legal system, where those without money are more likely to be prosecuted and much more likely to receive prison sentences. This means that much of the inmate population will be drawn from backgrounds of poverty and/or lower incomes. The means by which this can impact prison operations are many, but beyond anything else, this is likely to lead to challenges in communication between prison staff and inmates as well as a skepticism among inmates towards many of the social ideals that espouse the "work hard to get ahead" ethic that is common in society. For many inmates from this background, their hardworking families have remained poor. The payoff is therefore hard to see.

Many prison administrators understand that the job of correctional officer is not very prestigious. In fact, many of the personnel who work in corrections may come from economic conditions that are not too different from those of the inmates that they supervise. This may impair the overall ability of prison managers to empower prison staff to achieve levels of performance that go beyond minimal expectations. In addition, since exploitation will have been a fact of life for these individuals, they may see their role as exploitative by nature and intent.

Regardless of whether conflict theory adequately explains criminality, it is certain that those who have fewer material resources are more often represented in prisons than are those groups who have substantial monetary resources. It is important for prison administrators to keep this in mind when addressing the inmate population as well as when working with the inmate subculture. Just as importantly, administrators must consider how this can and does impact correctional staff, who may also view the world as one where the rich subjugate the poor.

The question then is whether prisons, as institutions, are simply mechanisms designed to keep poor people—who act out against the stresses of their poverty—contained and separated from persons who have economic power. If so, does this mean that persons who work in corrections are simply slaves to the system who unwittingly contribute to the exploitation by enforcing the will of those who are rich and therefore powerful? Naturally, these questions can only be answered on the basis of opinion. But, it is important that students consider these possibilities. These thoughts and questions open the door for prison leaders to demonstrate to staff that they are able to impact something much broader than their own individual plight. Through motivation and vision, the effective correctional leader can empower prison staff to understand that the ability to break out of an exploitative economic system is increased for every inmate who does reform and for every officer who is not harmed by crime. An understanding of the social dynamics that have, perhaps, brought inmates, officers, and administrators together in the prison environment can thus serve as the catalyst for a positive purpose behind the mission of the prison—that purpose being to eliminate further exploitation of persons without money through the creation of nonviolent environments and the reduction of criminal tendencies.

teams designed to respond to crises within a prison facility where the security of the institution is seriously at risk, posing a threat to public safety. They are similar to the typical special weapons and tactics teams found in many police departments. Within the Federal Bureau of Prisons, a typical SORT has 15 members, including an emergency medical treatment specialist, a firearms instructor, a rappel master, a security/locking systems expert, a blueprint expert, and several firearms and tactical planning/procedures experts. All members must be proficient with weapons used in emergency response situations and, within 90 days of becoming a team member, must become proficient in tactical responses, riot control techniques, and rappelling. Each candidate also undergoes a panel interview with an associate warden, captain, team leader, and staff psychologist before being placed on the team. Lastly, SORT team members receive collateral specialty training that reinforces the special skills of individual team members. To meet both the rigorous mandatory training requirements and the collateral specialty training, most team members participate in a substantial amount of training on their personal time.

Gang Management Data

The modern prison facility has improved surveillance, layout, and intelligence-gathering strategies that have worked well to thwart the activities of gang members. One essential aspect of a comprehensive gang intelligence program is the use of data that is continuously validated. Fleisher (2008) notes that prison administrators should do the following:

AP Photo/Michael Conroy

■ PHOTO 13.6 This team is suited in special protective equipment that allows the officers to safely engage inmates who are violent and dangerous. These types of response teams are critical to institutional security during emergency operations.

1. Develop strong nationwide ties to gang units in police departments.
2. Participate in national correctional conferences on gang intelligence.
3. Maintain good relations with fellow STG management persons in other agencies.
4. Establish strong contact with local police agencies and the state's attorney's office.

It is important to point out that gang data are of no assistance if they are not well organized and carefully analyzed. The modern intelligence team should be well trained on databases and should have the ability to customize databases for various projects.

The first phase in developing an effective program is to initiate an intelligence and communications network that can accurately indicate how many inmates have gang affiliations, which gangs they are affiliated with, and their status within those gangs. The database should also provide information on which facilities gang members are in and their institutional classification. All of this information can provide the department with data on the proliferation or concentration of any group so that it can forecast where or when a buildup could cause problems. Strategic transfers of inmates can assist the agency in controlling the establishment of gang power bases and can ensure that some individuals do not have undue influence over others.

In addition, good gang intelligence programs will have developed a digitized imaging program that offers numerous advantages for identifying gang members and keeping track of their status, behavior, and control. The complete history and personal data of gang members can be recorded, and digitized images (front and side) can be taken. Digitized images should also be made of any tattoos, distinguishing marks, or scars. These images are usually clearer than those obtained by film, and this negates the need for taking additional photographs or for film storage or development. The digitized images can be entered into a computer and downloaded into the database. This process tends to take about 2 minutes per individual and produces a permanent record that can be promptly updated as circumstances require.

Prison staff should, of course, be appropriately trained in the use of these types of tools, and they should also be trained in gang recognition skills. This training also requires a good deal of ethics training since gang populations can be very manipulative. Ensuring that staff are prepared and confident will help the institution run well and will keep security at its peak. This will also curb gangs from growing and/or exerting undue pressure upon others. Staff training will be the prime factor that determines whether policies and/or technical tools are utilized effectively.

Administrative Cooperation With Outside Agencies

During times of crisis, administrators must be sure that emergency response plans include mutually agreed-upon cooperative plans with outside agencies, particularly local law enforcement. The cooperative plans should be signed by the outside agency administrator and the unit warden. This means that preexisting memoranda of understanding that establish the terms and conditions for assistance should be on file. These prewritten documents help to reduce confusion during hectic times of response. Administrators must be able to implement plans and take

CORRECTIONS AND THE LAW 13.1

Conditions of Confinement and Case Law—Implications from Wilson v. Seiter

The following is adapted from the article cited below this insert and is an earlier publication from the National Institute of Corrections. This article examines the primary case law from the U.S. Supreme Court and determines that although some administrators may believe they are largely insulated from concern over conditions of confinement, they are mistaken. Because most liability cases are settled out of court, administrators may find that their facility has suffered a great financial loss due to the conditions of the facility; often the agency has had to settle out of court to avoid even larger losses. Naturally, this does not bode well for the career of a prison warden or another administrator who is responsible for the conditions in the facility.

The author of this article encourages administrators to not become complacent but to instead maintain safe facilities, humane conditions of incarceration, appropriate standards of medical and mental health care, protection of inmates from abuse, and appropriate staff conduct. Those who do are likely to be promoted, and those who do not may miss promotion or, worse yet, may find themselves liable in a legal suit. We now turn our attention to the ruling from *Wilson v. Seiter* (1991), the primary case addressing conditions of confinement, and an excerpt from the article (Wallenstein, 2008) that explains the modern-day importance of this ruling made in 1991 that is still legal and binding today:

Justice Antonin Scalia, writing for the majority in remanding an appeals court decision regarding conditions of confinement, noted that the state of mind of those involved in the conditions was an appropriate area of inquiry. He suggested that the conditions themselves might not rise to an Eighth Amendment violation unless a standard of "deliberate indifference" or wantonness could be shown. The most unusual thought process in the majority opinion may suggest that a broad range of prison and jail conditions might be sustained, even if wholly deficient, in the absence of malicious intent by the administrator or the system.

Some have even suggested that future constitutional challenges to prison and jail conditions may be defended by reference to insufficient funding by state or local government.

I do not concur with this interpretation, nor do I believe that Wilson v. Seiter retreats significantly from twenty years of court-developed doctrine of appropriate jail and prison conditions and administrative responsibility for same. Twenty years of federal court examination of jail and prison conditions, policies, behaviors, and treatment issues have not been swept away.

Let us assume that some major conditions of confinement cases may be made somewhat more difficult to prove under the "deliberate indifference" doctrine. However, this is not likely to inhibit successful challenges to hundreds of jail and prison policies and procedures that are well established in case law and practice as well as in the standards of the field and profession. It is well to remember that the vast majority of federal cases are settled out of court and are not the subject of formal opinions. They are settled out of court because government units recognize that a court will not sustain unconstitutional practices. The hundreds of cases that address injuries to inmates through assaults, self-inflicted injuries or suicide, institutional failure to meet prevailing standards of health care practice, and the like will continue to fall within the area of substandard practice.

Prevailing professional standards accepted throughout our profession require safe facilities, humane conditions of incarceration, appropriate standards of medical and mental health care, protection of inmates from abuse, and appropriate staff conduct. Any administrator who believes that Wilson v. Seiter diminishes the constitutional responsibilities inherent in administration will find little protection in the "deliberate indifference" standard offered by the Court. A thoughtful and conservative jurist, Justice Byron White, reminded all administrators several years ago in Wolff v. McDonnell *418 U.S. 359 (1974) that "There is no iron curtain drawn between the Constitution and the prisons of this country."*

Case law extended these doctrines to jails, and conscientious improvements in jail practices and the responsibility of administrators for same have not been undone. Quality correctional practices will continue to reduce the likelihood of lawsuits.

SOURCE: Wallenstein, A. (2008). *A wholly false sense of security:* Wilson v. Seiter *and jail litigation.* Washington, DC: National Institute of Corrections.

actions to resolve the situation and not debate on the issues involved. As noted earlier in this chapter, leaders operating in this type of situational response will need more centralized management, and this is where experienced leaders will tend to fare better than their more junior counterparts. It is during these times that many of the managerial orientations used in their typical day-to-day schedule will likely be reversed, with less open communication and more directive decision—the leader will become more of a field commander than a person-oriented manager. Understanding this difference in procedure can be the difference between institutional security and pure chaos within the facility.

CONCLUSION

This chapter has provided an overview of the organizational structure of both the federal and state prison systems in the United States. Organization by levels of management and services provided throughout the agency were both addressed, and it is clear that prison agencies are responsible for a disparate array of services and facilities. Students must understand how these systems are organized and how and where rules and regulations originate. It is also important to understand how the lead manager of a facility, the prison warden, must then take these rules and regulations and implement them within his or her own facility. In the process, wardens must emphasize an active form of management, making themselves visible in the facility and communicating routinely with staff and inmates. This informal aspect of prison management is important in dealing with the prison subculture, addressing rumors, and getting a general feel for the climate of the institution.

This chapter stresses that the use of participatory styles of management as well as the delegation of responsibility and authority (when appropriate) can empower staff and allow the institution to better adapt to needs throughout the facility. The importance of effective training and employee development is critical to the overall welfare of the facility and also to developing competent supervisors in the future. The distinction between managers and leaders was also discussed in this chapter, and students will recall that some supervisors may be both good managers and good leaders, but usually they tend to gravitate more in one direction or the other, seldom achieving mastery of both functions.

Issues related to women in corrections have also been discussed, and it has been noted that women historically were restricted to work within specific areas of corrections, such as in facilities that held female inmates. Further, there has been a tendency to not allow women access to specialized areas of correctional work unless it is clerical or office-related. However, this is changing, slowly but surely. Women now work within the security ranks and hold supervisory positions, including wardens and executive-level administrators. Despite this, women are still the minority in these areas of work, and some wonder if the glass ceiling is still holding many women back from attaining career ascension. Perhaps the best means for ensuring that this is not the case is to work to change the culture within prison systems among both staff and inmates.

Topics related to private prison management were covered, and it was noted that such organizations can also operate programs of excellence. Through the use of a unit management system, this type of organization can provide very clear and effective means of governing its employees while also soliciting their input in addressing day-to-day challenges within the organization. Lastly, the reality is that prisons are dangerous institutions, and, as a result, the unexpected can occur and the security and safety of the institution and of the public itself can be jeopardized. Administrators must be ready to deal with these possibilities, and they must be informed of the protocols and guidelines that are in place in the event of an emergency or a disturbance. The use of emergency response teams is necessary during these times of disruption. There are a variety of response teams that exist; all should be rigorously tested, and the selection of members should be restricted to the most qualified personnel. The means by which these teams are managed, including decisions for operational control and partnering with outside agencies to ensure public safety, are all concerns of the correctional administrator.

DISCUSSION QUESTIONS

1. What are some key features of the organizational structure of the Federal Bureau of Prisons?
2. Identify and discuss the different levels of management in state prison systems.
3. What are the differences between centralized and decentralized forms of management?
4. Identify and discuss the various models of managerial motivation and supervision.

5. What is the difference between a manager and a leader?
6. How well are women represented in today's world of corrections? What are some of the challenges that have faced women working in the correctional field?
7. What are some of the primary advantages associated with private prisons? Are there any potential problems that may exist for these types of prisons? Explain your answer.
8. What are some important issues to note when considering emergency management procedures in a prison facility?
9. Refer to Applied Theory 13.1. Explain how conflict theory might be related to dynamics among the prison population and/or the prison subculture.

SAGE edge™ Test your understanding of chapter content. Take the practice quiz.

KEY TERMS

Armed disturbance control team, 333
Authoritarian model, 322
Bureaucratic model, 322
Centralized management, 324
Decentralized management, 324
Disturbance control teams, 333
Emergency preparedness, 332
Emergency response, 332
Emotional intelligence, 326
Glass ceiling, 329
Holding pattern management, 323
LaSalle Corrections, 318
Leadership, 325
Management, 325
National Institute of Corrections (NIC), 315
Participative method of management, 323
Prison grapevine, 324
Proactive style of management, 321
Reactive style of management, 321
Regional-level administrators, 319
Rogues and mavericks, 327
Rumor control, 333
Span of control, 327
Span of influence, 327
Special Operations Response Teams (SORT), 333
Strategic plan, 319
System-wide administrators, 318
Tactical planning, 325
Unit-level administrators, 319

SAGE edge™ Review key terms with eFlashcards.

APPLIED EXERCISE 13.1

Students must conduct either a face-to-face or a phone interview with a correctional supervisor who currently works in a prison facility in their state. The student should use the interview to gain the supervisor's insight and perspective on several key questions related to work in the field of institutional corrections. Students must write the practitioner's responses as well as their own analysis of those responses and submit their write-up by the deadline set by their instructor. The submission should be written in the form of an essay that addresses each point below. The total word count should be 1,200 to 2,000 words.

When completing the interview, students should ask the following questions:

1. What are the most rewarding aspects of your job as a supervisor of other prison staff?
2. What are the most stressful aspects of your job?
3. What are some challenges you find in working with the inmate population?
4. Why did you choose to work in this field?
5. What type of training did you receive for this line of work?
6. What are your future plans for your career in institutional corrections?
7. What would you recommend to someone who was interested in pursuing a similar career?

Students are required to provide the following contact information for the person interviewed. While you will probably not need to contact that person, it may become necessary in order to validate the actual completion of the interview.

Name and title of correctional supervisor: ____________________

Correctional agency: ____________________

Practitioner's phone number: ____________________

Practitioner's e-mail address: ____________________

Name of student: ____________________

WHAT WOULD YOU DO?

You are a warden of a medium-security facility. Lately, as you have made your rounds throughout the prison, you have noticed that there seems to be more tension than usual between African American and Caucasian inmates. Also of concern is the fact that your Internal Affairs Division and your Grievance Office have reported an all-time low in the number of complaints against officers or other inmates during the past 2 months.

While you would like to think that your prison facility is operating more smoothly and that this is the reason for the reduced complaints, you are skeptical. Rates of violence between inmates (some of this gang-related) and justified use-of-force incidents among staff are the same or a bit higher than usual, yet complaints are lower. Generally, when more incidents occur, you have more complaints. It seems as if something is amiss, and you recall from a training conference you attended that prior to major disturbances there tends to be a lull in communication from the inmate population. According to the trainer, "When it comes to prison riots, just remember that it is usually very quiet just before the storm."

Could this be occurring now? You ponder this as you make your way to the visitation area of the prison unit. Upon arrival, you notice that one of the key leaders of the Aryan Brotherhood is in a visitation chair, and sitting across from him is another important leader from the AB who is being monitored by police street gang units. This other leader has always managed to evade arrest but is thought to be active in several incidents of gang-related violence and is also suspected in the burning of an African American church located in the area. There is no law or regulation that prevents him from visiting inmates in the prison since he has no official record and since he has been cleared by the prison agency. However, you know that in order for him to make the visit himself (rather than sending some other member), something important is likely to occur.

As you leave the visitation area and stroll through the prison, you notice that many of your officers do not interact with one another. Indeed, it seems that the Caucasian officers stand with Caucasian officers most of the time, and the African American officers stand with other African American officers; there is little dialogue between officers of different racial groups.

You begin to wonder if racially driven differences among inmates and staff may be leading toward serious problems for the institution. You continue your rounds throughout the prison and stop to glance inside a dayroom where several inmates are watching the TV. Then it becomes clear that something is definitely amiss, both inside and outside of the prison. On the TV a local news reporter is explaining that the influential African American reverend of a local church has been murdered in his own home. Swastikas were spray-painted on the walls, and it is clear that the murder was based on racial hatred.

You are not sure where to begin but realize that these issues in the community are very likely to impact the behavior among your inmates. You fear that you may be facing an upcoming race-related disturbance and wonder how well your officers will address such a situation. In fact, you are now concerned about how well your officers will support one another, given that there seems to be distance (and perhaps tension) between those of differing racial orientations. You decide something proactive must be done.

What would you do?

Write an essay response that addresses, at a minimum, the following:

1. How you would address the racial friction within the inmate population.
2. How you would address staff cohesion and navigate potential employee problems.
3. How you would address the effects of the community and the outside media.

You can be creative in your responses but should refer to this chapter and prior chapters in addressing this issue.

14 PRISON PROGRAMMING

Stockbyte/Thinkstock

RODERICK'S NEW CHAPTER

Roderick listened as Dr. Hanser began to wrap up the session. He glanced around at the rest of the men sitting in the circle and noticed that all of them seemed to also be intent upon the final words that summed up the session.

"In essence, gentlemen, it is up to you to create an entirely new lifestyle. Just quitting the drugs and alcohol is not enough. You have to quit the entire criminal lifestyle," Hanser said, meeting the gaze of each man in the group. "Look, the deal is that you need to make a shift from going around talking about what you are *not* going to do and instead spend more time being concerned about what you *need* to be doing."

Roderick raised his hand, and Hanser nodded at him to speak.

"So you mean that we should make out a schedule of activities that we should be doing and focus more on what things we need to complete than on the people, places, and things that should not be in our lives, right?"

Hanser replied, "Yep, that's exactly right. . . . The more time you spend worrying about what needs to get done, the less time you have to think about relapse."

The group ended, and Hanser began to walk toward his office. As he did so, Roderick followed and said, "Excuse me, Dr. Hanser, but can I speak with you for a minute?"

"Sure, Roderick, come on in."

They sat down in the office, which held a strange mix of items from different areas of the world. A number of volumes on life change and self-improvement were on the bookshelves.

Roderick began. "I'm kind of concerned. As you know, a lot of my family use drugs and stuff, and I am not sure what to do. I mean, New Orleans is all that I know . . . but if I go back, I know it's probably just a matter of time until . . . "

Hanser watched him trail off and then said, "Roderick, you know that we've talked about this before. We both know perfectly well that if you go back to that area, you put all of your hard work at risk."

"Yeah, I know, but you remember that my brothers are not helping my mom out much, right?"

"Yes, I do. But these types of decisions are what make recovery and make life difficult. Roderick, you have to get yourself stable before you can put the welfare of someone else on your plate. You have to get out of the toxic environment. I know that, emotionally, you want to help your mom, but, really, at this point, it is my guess that she would rather you get your life together, first. If you don't, then all you're going to do is go home and, within a few weeks or months, end up back here. If that happens, then you will *not* be able to help your mom at all, and I'm sure it will break her heart as well."

Hanser paused for a moment to let Roderick absorb his last few words, then continued. "If you finish the program, take the job with the reentry house, and extend your therapy in the community program that I suggested, you'll be away from those influences and be able to continue your programming and use the job skills you learned in here. Plus, we can help you get aid at the community college. There is nothing to say that you cannot stay in touch with your mother and even visit her."

Roderick sighed. "Yeah, you're right. So when I finish this program here, the one on the outside is similar?"

"They are designed to augment one another. And your job training here in the joint will be consistent with the job at the factory on the outside."

Roderick considered. "Can I make a call? I want to let my folks know that I've changed my mind and want to make sure that my Ma knows why."

Hanser said, "Sure, just give me the number, and I will dial you out."

Hanser dialed the number and handed Roderick the phone.

Roderick hesitated. "I'm doing the best thing, right?"

"Yeah, man, I think that you're doing the best thing for everyone involved." Hanser heard a distant voice say "Hello."

"Hey, Mom. . . . "

No one said that change was easy, Hanser thought to himself as he watched Roderick lay the groundwork for a new chapter in his life.

LEARNING OBJECTIVES:

1. Explain the medical and food service requirements in prison and how they are typically addressed.
2. Discuss the effects of educational programs on recidivism.
3. Discuss the effects of vocational programs on recidivism.
4. Identify components of substance abuse treatment in prison.
5. Describe some of the concerns for administrators with different types of recreational programming.
6. Identify some of the legal issues associated with religious programming in prisons.

SAGE edge™

Get the edge on your studies:
edge.sagepub.com/hanser2e

- Take a quiz to find out what you've learned.
- Review key terms with eFlashcards.
- Watch videos that enhance chapter content.

INTRODUCTION

This chapter will focus on the various prison programs and services that are typical to any facility, including basic services as well as educational, work, therapeutic, recreational, and religious programming. These types of programming typically go beyond the basics of subsistence and housing. Rather, they tend to be very important in managing offenders' behavior and in improving the outcomes of inmates once they are released from prison. With this noted, it is important to understand that there are two competing views regarding prison programs for inmates. The first view is the **work/education reform view**, which is thought to save society untold millions due to the lack of recidivism of inmates who have obtained employment and/or education through prison programming. The second view is the **minimal services view**, which contends that inmates are entitled to no more than the bare minimum that is required by law. While this second view is certainly true, it is unrealistic and, in all honesty, simply ensures that recidivism will be a continual problem in the United States.

MEDICAL CARE

Outside of prison, citizens must find a way to afford their own health care, and, if they are not able to do so, they will usually have to gain minimal health coverage from public government service. Regardless, free-world persons have at least some say over the types of services that they will receive. For inmates, this is not the case, and because prison health care is not always satisfactory, this has been the basis of many legal actions taken against prison systems.

History of Prison Health Care

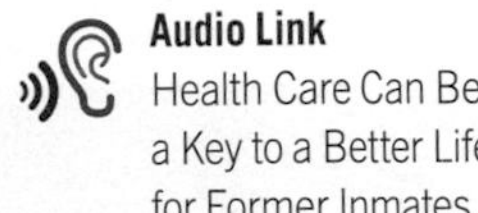

Audio Link
Health Care Can Be a Key to a Better Life for Former Inmates

During the early days of jails and prisons, the public generally did not believe inmates had the right to health care. Indeed, the general consensus was that the lack of health care was perhaps deserved as a result of being sent to prison. This state of affairs lasted for hundreds of years. In the United States, this attitude began to change in 1971 due to a prison riot that took place at the Attica Correctional Facility in the state of New York. Inmates at Attica protested the unsanitary conditions that existed at the prison as well as inhumane practices that prevented them from obtaining appropriate medical services. In many cases, personnel working in the medical sector were unqualified and could not legally practice medicine in outside society.

Deliberate Indifference Revisited

During the 1970s, following the Attica riot, medical care began to draw more attention from correctional officials and the public. This period also saw the Supreme Court hand down decisions in a series of cases regarding health services in prisons. In particular, *Estelle v. Gamble* (1976) ushered in an era where medical services for inmates were normalized and states were required to provide more than just marginal care in prisons.

The *Estelle* decision established a test to determine whether treatment given by prison officials was so insufficient as to constitute cruel and unusual punishment in violation of the Eighth Amendment. According to the Court, it must be proven that prison officials knew of an inmate's serious need of medical services but were deliberately indifferent to that need and denied services to that inmate, almost as an extension of his or her punishment. Some examples of deliberate indifference include denial or delay in providing treatment, providing inadequate treatment, or failing to have qualified medical staff. Incidentally, prison systems cannot evade liability by citing inadequate funding as a reason for failing to provide medical services.

Work/education reform view: Claims that society is saved untold millions due to the lack of recidivism of inmates who have obtained employment and/or education.

Minimal services view: Contends that inmates are entitled to no more than the bare minimum that is required by law.

The Lifestyle of Offenders Inside and Outside

The inmate population tends to cycle in and out of prison. This has been discussed in prior chapters but is again important in the current discussion. When inmates enter prison, they may bring with them conditions and illnesses acquired on the streets due to their unhealthy lifestyles. Likewise, when inmates leave prison and go back to their communities, they bring any illnesses they may have acquired while incarcerated.

The use of drugs and participation in risky life choices deteriorate the health of offenders, and any negative effects from this are exacerbated by the prison environment. Thus, all individuals (including both inmates and correctional staff) within the prison should be educated on communicable diseases and take precautions to avoid contracting germ-based illnesses.

Clinics, Sick Call, and Standards of Care

In many prison facilities, sick call often requires that inmates fill out a form to request a visit to the unit infirmary. Inmates should be appraised of the procedures used to obtain medical services since, unlike in the free world, they cannot simply decide to see a doctor whenever they wish. Perhaps the best time to ensure that inmates are informed of these procedures is during orientation, when written materials are handed out to inmates and they are expected to ask questions.

In order to avoid the abuse of sick call and the likelihood of malingering (faking an illness), many prison facilities have instituted a modest inmate co-pay system. In essence, inmates must pay a small fee to see a medical professional, and this tends to discourage most inmates from taking trips to the prison infirmary unless the request is legitimate. Administrators must be careful that these types of programs are not seen as punitive. The key is for administrators to lend assistance to inmates who are truly ill while holding inmates partially accountable for medical services when the illness is not severe.

Some issues are unique to prisons regarding the standard of care to which inmates are afforded. First, there can sometimes be problems with confidentiality due to the close quarters and constant traffic in and out of spaces, including prison infirmaries. It is important to remember that inmates have a right to medical privacy, which means that medical personnel may not share details about an inmate's health or medical status with other correctional staff. This is particularly true if those persons are not medical staff. However, this does not prevent security staff and other personnel from gaining access to protected medical information in the process of completing work assignments or through conversations with inmates. There are several exceptions to privacy, which are delineated in the **Health Insurance Portability and Accountability Act (HIPAA)**. HIPAA guidelines are well known among medical and mental health personnel, and, for the most part, this act guides professionals on matters regarding the confidentiality of medical information.

Health Insurance Portability and Accountability Act (HIPAA): Guides professionals on matters regarding the confidentiality of medical information.

Medical Services for Female Inmates

Students may recall from Chapter 10 that the needs of female offenders tend to vary from those of male offenders. It would be remiss to discuss medical care of inmates without providing some commentary on the specialized medical issues common to the female inmate population. Ross and Lawrence (2002) note that female offenders as a group are increasingly immersed in the illicit drug culture as alcoholics, drug addicts, or intimate partners of alcoholics or drug addicts. They note that research on syphilis indicates that incidence follows that of cocaine use in such a manner as to suggest the increasing prevalence of a sex-for-drugs lifestyle. Ross and Lawrence (2002) further state that the medical problems of these inmates are associated with those lifestyles prior to arriving in prison.

Common medical issues of female inmates include asthma, diabetes, HIV/AIDS, tuberculosis, hypertension, unintended pregnancy, a variety of sexually transmitted diseases, and other sundry medical problems. While many of these concerns are also common to male inmates, some, such as issues related to pregnancy, are, of course, unique to women offenders. With this in mind, we turn our attention to services for birth control and pregnancy.

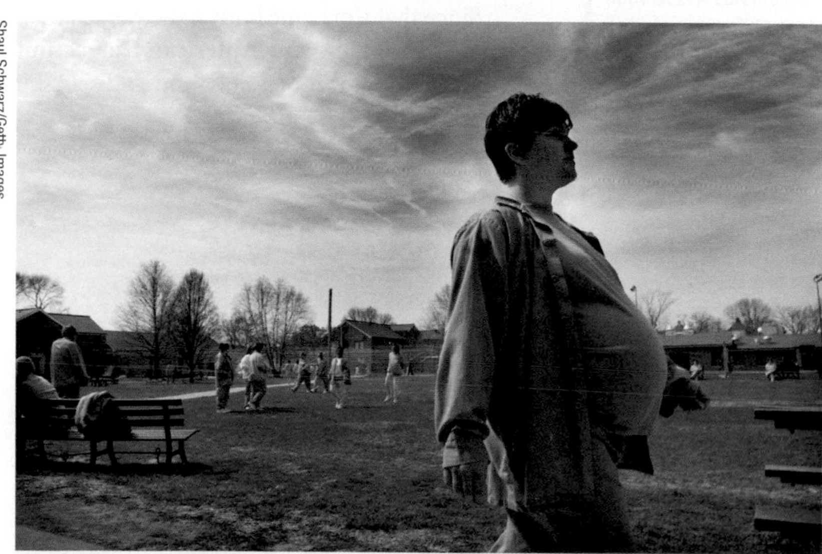

Shaul Schwarz/Getty Images

PHOTO 14.1 This female inmate was pregnant before she was incarcerated. Female prisons are faced with addressing these and other issues for women who have children.

Birth Control and Pregnancy

According to the BOP, female inmates should have access to medical and social services related to pregnancy, birth control, child placement, and abortion. Inmates are medically screened for pregnancy upon admission and are instructed to inform medical staff as soon as they suspect they are pregnant. If necessary, the childbirth takes place at a hospital outside the institution, and arrangements are made with outside social service agencies to aid the inmate in finding an appropriate placement for the child. Newborn children are not permitted to return to the institution with their mothers. Children can visit their mother when under the supervision and care of an adult visitor.

In addition, the BOP provides a community residential program called **Mothers and Infants Nurturing Together (MINT)** for women who are pregnant at the time of commitment. The MINT program is a residential reentry center–based program that promotes bonding and parenting skills for low-risk female inmates who are pregnant. Women are eligible to enter the program if they are in their last 3 months of pregnancy, have less than 5 years remaining to serve on their sentence, and are eligible for furlough. The inmate or a guardian must assume financial responsibility for the child's medical care while residing at MINT. The mother has 3 months to bond with the newborn before returning to an institution to complete her sentence. In select MINT programs, the inmate may stay for an additional period of bonding with the child. The decision to refer an inmate to the MINT program is at the discretion of the inmate's unit team.

Abortion

As per federal law, the BOP is not allowed to use government funds to facilitate the performance of an abortion. Funds are used to pay for abortion services only if the life of the mother would be endangered if the fetus was carried to term or in cases of rape. In all other cases, non-BOP funds must be obtained to pay for an abortion. Inmates receive medical, religious, and social counseling regarding their decision to carry the pregnancy to term or to have an elective abortion. If an inmate decides to have an abortion, arrangements are made for these medical services to be provided in an appropriate clinic outside the institution.

Mothers and Infants Nurturing Together (MINT): A Federal Bureau of Prisons program that promotes bonding and parenting skills for low-risk female inmates who are pregnant.

American Correctional Food Service Association (ACFSA): Represents the correctional food service industry.

FOOD SERVICE

In early prisons, it was not unusual for inmates to be required to pay or work for their own food. Porridge, bread and water, beans, stew, and bitter coffee were typical menu items. This state of affairs continued, for the most part, until the early 1970s when the Attica riot occurred. After the riot, the courts became more involved in determining prison operations, and the federal courts, in particular, were very directive. Nevertheless, there were no clear standards in place as this process unfolded.

Since that time, one body has emerged that sets standards on food service programming in the prison environment: the **American Correctional Food Service Association (ACFSA)**. This organization promotes professionalism and sets standards of performance within this specialized area of correctional operations. It also provides for national certification of professionals working in the corrections food service industry.

Prison Tour Video: Prison Food Service. A lot of preparation and planning goes into delivery of food services in prison. Watch a discussion about prison food service.

Planning the Menu

The menu planning process is usually done on a 28- to 30-day rotation cycle, and the menus are typically prepared by the overall supervisor of food services or the assigned dietitian. Menus are usually planned according to standards set by the National Academy of Sciences. A variety of factors must be considered in food preparation. Connecticut's Department of Correction (2010), in its administrative directive titled *Nutrition and Food Services*, denotes the planning criteria of the master menu as follows:

> Master Menu Planning Criteria. The Correctional Chief of Food Services shall prepare menus considering nutritional adequacy, inmate preferences, costs, physical layout, cost of equipment and staff complement, variety in method of preparation and frequency and other relevant factors to good dietary practice. Preparation shall consider food flavor, texture, temperature, appearance, and palatability. (p. 2)

According to the Connecticut prison system, **common fare** is a diet that meets all nutritional requirements and reasonably accommodates recognized religious dietary restrictions. This demonstrates that the planning of the menu can be somewhat complicated and that general dietary health should be considered at a minimum. Further, the inmate population can be quite diverse both ethnically and due to medical needs, and food service managers may take these issues into consideration as well when preparing their menu cycles.

Training Requirements

Training requirements for prison kitchen staff can vary, but the personnel must have a documented understanding of the planning, preparation, and serving of nutritious meals using sanitary and safe conditions. These individuals usually must have knowledge of kitchen work such that they know how to direct people who must work together in a coordinated fashion. In addition, it is important that the kitchen manager ensures that those working in the kitchen are ethical and appropriate for the job. Because inmates can be unpredictable and spiteful to one another, the kitchen manager will need to ensure that none of the inmate workers (or staff, for that matter) act in an inappropriate or unsanitary manner when serving other inmates. In addition, persons in the kitchen should not give "extra" food during meals to inmates who do not have an authorized basis for such an allocation.

Common fare: A diet that meets all nutritional requirements and reasonably accommodates recognized religious dietary restrictions.

Prison food loaf: A food product that contains all the typical ingredients of a well-balanced meal mixed together and baked as a single loaf-like product that would be served to inmates.

The Quality of Food as Leverage for Social Control

While it is clear that prisons have a legal obligation to ensure that minimal standards for nutrition are met when feeding the inmate population, there is no requirement that they go beyond this. However, there may be incentives for correctional administrators to budget additional funds for their menu list. For instance, on a holiday, most prisons serve some type of meal that is consistent with that holiday. Wardens who are able to allocate additional funds for special meals and events will greatly improve morale among inmates.

Likewise, the type of food is served in prison may be modified due to disciplinary reasons. While it is generally not considered good correctional practice to use food allocation for punishment, prison systems do alter the way it is served to inmates who have some type of special security status or disciplinary consideration. Prison food loaf is sometimes used as a replacement meal for inmates of various disciplinary statuses. In particular, this type of meal alternative may be given to inmates who are hostile and in lockdown (i.e., solitary confinement for assaultive behavior). It is not uncommon for these inmates to throw their food or liquid beverages on correctional officers and/or to use their utensils as weapons. While this may not sound overly problematic, when hot coffee is thrown on an officer or when salt is thrown in the eyes of an officer or another inmate, this can cause injury that lasts for days. The use of products such as the prison food loaf eliminates safety and security concerns when feeding inmates with this type of behavioral history.

Prison food loaf is a food product that contains all the typical ingredients of a well-balanced meal that would be served to inmates with no disciplinary problems; these ingredients are mixed together and baked as a single loaf-like product that, while bland in flavor, meets necessary nutritious requirements. This type of food product is

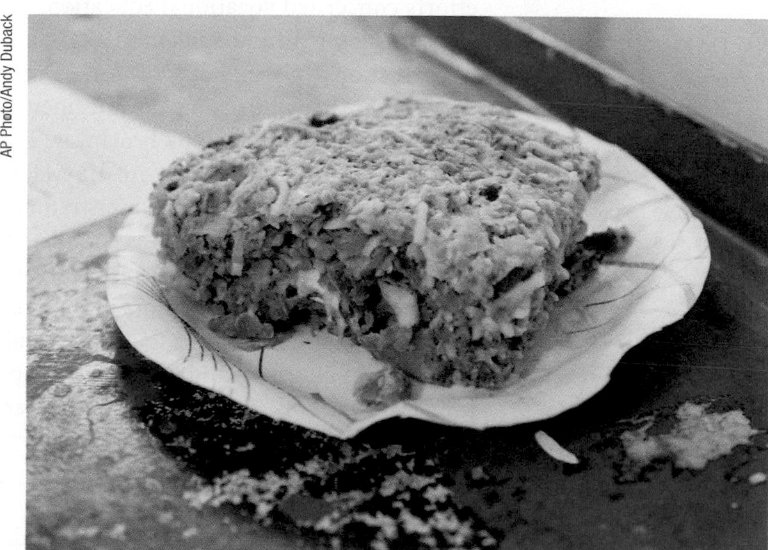
AP Photo/Andy Duback

■ PHOTO 14.2 Prison food loaf, pictured here, is a concoction that mixes the ingredients of a given prison meal into one single baked loaf of food product.

not used for punishment as much as to avoid the possibility of safety problems for inmates and staff, and it is typically served to inmates who are dangerous and unpredictable. Legal issues related to this food product emerged during the 1990s, when inmates contended that being fed prison food loaf was tantamount to cruel and unusual punishment, in violation of their Eighth Amendment rights. One case in particular was ***LeMaire v. Maass* (1993)**. Ultimately, it was determined that the Eighth Amendment only requires that food be provided that is adequate to maintain health, not that it be tasty or appealing.

EDUCATIONAL PROGRAMS

Of all the prison programs available for inmates, education is perhaps the most important. Basic academics are fundamental to functioning in the day-to-day world of work. Without the ability to read, write, and do simple arithmetic, offenders will find it difficult to maintain gainful employment, and many of them have problems with literacy and/or basic mathematics. In this section, we will examine some of the history behind prison education and illustrate how this has been an integral component of the correctional field.

Educational Programs Throughout History

The use of education in the institutional setting can be traced all the way back to America's first penitentiary, the Walnut Street Jail. At this time, education and religious instruction tended to be combined. The Quakers were largely behind the availability of education to inmates, and they were even the first to encourage secular education. However, there was a general fear that criminals would become even craftier if they were educated, and this resulted in minimal education being provided to those who were locked up.

After the Civil War, educational programs were identified as a preferred method for reforming offenders. Indeed, education was at the heart of the reformatory model that prevailed during this period. The origins of this system were largely rooted in the efforts of Zebulon Brockway at the Elmira Reformatory. However, some researchers, such as Schlossman and Spillane (1995), have contended that the credit given to Brockway is perhaps a bit excessive. They note that his programs were largely just replications of programs for adults that were made available to juvenile offenders at Elmira.

Work at Elmira was centered on a contract-driven, factory-based production of goods for the private sector. There tended to prevail a fundamental faith among prison administrators of the late 1800s that hard work was the touchstone of discipline and rehabilitation, regardless of the type of work that it might be. As Brockway (1912) commented in 1888, "There is not any proper education and test of character that does not include training in industry" (p. 268). Most of Brockway's efforts concerned vocational education, which was designed to prepare inmates for the world of work. Schlossman and Spillane (1995) conducted an extensive review of the policies and practices of correctional systems in New York, Ohio, Texas, and Virginia during the 1920s and 1930s, and they found that while some advancements were made in these systems, they lagged well behind the innovations provided by Brockway. There was, however, one other noteworthy emergence in corrections during the 1930s: Austin MacCormick's work *The Education of Adult Prisoners*.

MacCormick, a former administrator at a U.S. Navy prison, was a professor at Bowdoin College when his well-known work was completed. Earlier in his career, he had authorities in New York anonymously commit him to a prison so he could gain firsthand knowledge of the life of an inmate; only a handful of administrators in the prison knew that he was not actually a convicted offender. He had also written his own thesis on penological principles. *The Education of Adult Prisoners* was the result of efforts within the New York prison system to improve educational opportunities for inmates. New York, in tandem with the Carnegie Corporation, hired MacCormick as a consultant to conduct the most comprehensive survey ever undertaken of educational programs for adults in prison in the United States.

During the 1960s and 1970s, correctional education began to become a priority within many state systems. This was true of both academic and vocational programming (Simms, Farley, & Littlefield, 1987). A primary impetus behind this was the passage of the Adult Education Act of 1964, which provided funding for programs that serviced adults who had deficiencies in communication, basic math skills, or social skills that impaired their ability to gain or retain

***LeMaire v. Maass* (1993):** A suit in which the plaintiff considered the conditions of the Oregon prison to be unconstitutional.

employment. The 1980s is perhaps the period when the most fervor and public attention were given to prison-based education. There were several reasons for this, but one key factor was that the prison population had grown considerably during this time. Another was that numerous rulings from the Supreme Court during the 1960s and 1970s on prison conditions and inmate rights tended to cite the need for better educational programs. The climate during this time was more punitive, and less emphasis was placed on correctional treatment programming, but education was an exception since it was not steeped in mental health jargon and was more clearly understood by the general public.

The 1990s saw an intense interest in prison education programs, and these types of programs proliferated throughout the United States. For example, the Windham School District became a major component of prison operations in Texas, which, as students should know by now, has one of the biggest prison systems in the United States. Another noteworthy occurrence during this period was the 1991 creation of the **Office of Correctional Education (OCE)** within the Department of Education. The OCE was created to provide national leadership on issues related to correctional education, and it offers technical assistance to states, local schools, and correctional institutions and shares information on correctional education. The office was authorized by the Carl D. Perkins Vocational and Applied Technology Education Act Amendments of 1990 (Public Law 101-392).

Despite these seeming victories for educational programming, the 1990s are also known for one major policy change that negatively impacted the ability of inmates to obtain higher education while in prison: the elimination of the federal Pell Grant for inmates seeking college education. Prior to this, the federal government had allocated a very small fraction of Pell Grant dollars to those who were incarcerated. **Pell Grants** are need-based federal monies set aside for persons who pursue a college education. The use of the Pell Grant in prisons was the result of legislation in 1965, when Congress passed **Title IV of the Higher Education Act**, which permitted inmates to apply for financial aid in the form of Pell Grants to attend college. Despite abundant research from the BOP and states such as Alabama, Illinois, Ohio, New York, Texas, and Wisconsin that showed college-level education caused a clear and consistent reduction in recidivism rates, this program was ultimately discontinued (Karpowitz & Kenner, 2001).

Office of Correctional Education (OCE): Created to provide national leadership on issues related to correctional education.

Pell Grants: Need-based federal monies set aside for persons who pursue a college education.

Title IV of the Higher Education Act: Permitted inmates to apply for financial aid in the form of Pell Grants to attend college.

During the 1990s, the effects of the War on Drugs were being felt, and there was a mass prison-building boom throughout the nation. Politicians heralded "tough on crime" platforms that included three-strikes initiatives, the elimination of parole, and enhanced penalties against drug offenders. During this time, politicians introduced legislation that resulted in the passage of the Violent Crime Control and Law Enforcement Act, which, as discussed above, eliminated the availability of the Pell Grant for inmates and all but killed the offering of higher education in American corrections.

Since 2008, many state legislatures and even Congress have considered legislation aimed at providing educational benefits for inmates. This demonstrates that even politicians are beginning to see the connection between education and the reduction of future crime rates. This provides a sense of optimism for many correctional educators and prison administrators.

Types of Education Programs in Corrections

The federal system is the premier correctional system and includes a wide range of services that are also common to most state systems. Because many states essentially follow the standards of the federal system, it is perhaps easier to showcase the federal system and/or a handful of examples from among the states. The BOP has long recognized the importance of education both as an opportunity for inmates to improve their knowledge and skills and as a correctional management tool that encourages inmates to use their time in a constructive manner.

Each federal prison has its own education department that provides educational and recreational activities to federal inmates. Of these,

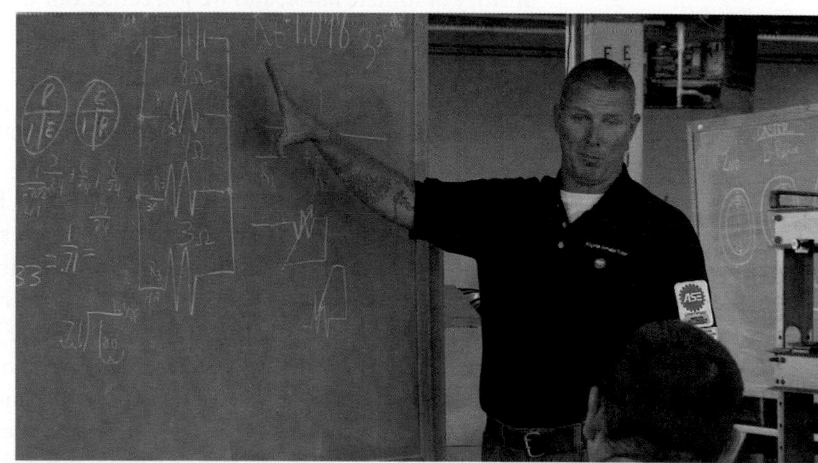

Prison Tour Video: Educational Funding. Educational services for inmates have their benefits and controversies. Watch a clip about educational funding.

literacy education receives the highest priority. With few exceptions, an inmate who does not have a **General Educational Development (GED)** diploma must participate in a literacy program for a minimum of 240 instructional hours or until he or she earns a GED credential. The **English as a Second Language (ESL)** program enables inmates with limited English proficiency to improve their English language skills. Due to legislation passed in 1990, non-English-proficient inmates must participate in an ESL program until they pass competency skills tests at the 8th-grade level.

Web Link
Inside-Out Writers

Celebrating Achievements

One of the most rewarding aspects of educational programs is the sense of empowerment and achievement that is obtained. Inmates who are recognized for their efforts, whether educational, vocational, or treatment-oriented, gain positive esteem and tend to be more motivated as they approach their eventual release into society. For some inmates, this may be one of the few times that they have actually been recognized for an accomplishment. This alone can provide the offender with a new sense of self-worth. Later we will discuss the offering of life skills education and programming as a means of furthering offenders' sense of esteem and ability to effectively cope with stressors that may make them prone to further recidivism. However, for now, students should consider that few offenders have received much—if any—positive attention in their lives. Showcasing their positive outcomes is likely to reinforce that behavior and will serve to instill prosocial norms within their psyches.

PRISON WORK PROGRAMS

Prison work for inmates tends to consist of two types. The first includes those jobs that maintain the functioning of the prison itself. These types of jobs might include the preparation of meals, working in the laundry, and the cleaning of various prison areas. These tasks do not usually provide inmates with a trade or a skill by which they can earn a living in the outside community. The second type of work is industrial or vocational in orientation. These jobs include production, agriculture, craftsmanship, carpentry, construction, and even clerical positions in prison offices where genuine professional skills might be learned.

Inmate Labor Throughout History

The origin of labor in prisons can be traced back to English jails of the eleventh and thirteenth centuries, when inmate labor paid for the costs of imprisonment as well as the salaries of the jailers and the sheriff. During the 1300s, hard labor was considered part of one's payment for keep and was the mainstay activity in workhouses of that time. The emphasis on work continued throughout history, but the types of work usually did not compete with free labor outside of the prison walls. During the mid- to late 1700s, prison reformers such as John Howard and Cesare Beccaria considered inmate labor a key factor in the reformation of offenders.

Unlike discussions on inmate labor in prior chapters, this chapter will focus on a more modern history of inmate labor, and we will center our discussion on the federal system. The primary reason for this is that it has a defined history that is far-reaching and at its base contains all the elements of historical development that are common to most of the state systems. However, the federal system is not given to the peculiarities of history and geography that have defined various state prison systems, such as those in the southern United States that relied largely on agricultural operations.

The History of Inmate Labor in a Model Program: UNICOR

In June 1934, President Franklin D. Roosevelt signed a law that established an organization for federal prison labor called the **Federal Prison Industries Inc. (FPI)**. From this action emerged a full-fledged corporation owned by the U.S. government. This corporation was designed to operate various factories and to ensure that inmates were gainfully employed, when and where appropriate, during the course of their sentence. By the end of World War II, FPI was a producer of more than 70 categories of products at 25 separate shops and factories.

During the World War II era, FPI was a major contributor to the war effort. During this time, inmates worked double and even triple shifts throughout the day and night, with 95% of all products being sold to the military. Among these products were items such as bomb fins and

General Educational Development (GED): The process of earning the equivalent of your high school diploma.

English as a Second Language (ESL): Program enables inmates with limited English proficiency to improve their English language skills.

Federal Prison Industries Inc. (FPI): Organization for federal prison labor.

bomb casings, TNT cases, parachutes, welded products, aircraft sheet metal work, shipbuilding crafts, auto/aviation mechanics, and drafting and electrical products. Many people are not aware that the inmate population, at least at the federal level, has been such a strong contributor to our national defense. During the Korean War of the 1950s, federal inmates again contributed to America's war effort. Indeed, sales by FPI exceeded $29 million, and over 3,800 inmates were employed by the corporation. Following the Korean War, FPI retooled factories and renovated outdated equipment to produce new products in response to changing markets. FPI opened shops that specialized in the refurbishment of furniture, office equipment, tires, and other government property. In addition, FPI introduced new vocational training programs that provided medical benefits for consumers by manufacturing artificial limbs and dentures, and it provided inmate labor for hospital attendant work.

Prison Tour Video Link
Health Services, Medicine in Prisons, Work Trustees, and Inmate Organizations That Give Back to Society

During the Vietnam War, there was another growth in production levels, but this was a short-term occurrence as FPI sought to ease its inmate population out of wartime production and into more mainstream forms of industry. By the late 1960s, military sales had declined significantly and had nearly all but ceased at the close of the Vietnam War. During the late 1970s, FPI changed its name to **UNICOR Inc.** as a means of creating a new civilian and corporate-based identity. In an effort to increase its competitive position, UNICOR introduced new lines in stainless steel products, thermoplastics, printed circuits, modular furniture, ergonomic chairs, Kevlar-reinforced items (such as military helmets), and optics. State-of-the-art production techniques were embraced, including modern printing equipment. Such efforts led to improved product offerings, which, in turn, created new inmate work opportunities to better prepare inmates for post-release employment.

A 7-year study conducted in the 1990s, the **Post-Release Employment Project (PREP)**, conducted by the BOP's Office of Research and Evaluation, validated, conclusively, that UNICOR successfully achieved its mission of preparing inmates for release and therefore provided long-term benefits to society. Further, the PREP study showed that the inmates who participated in UNICOR's industrial or educational programs were less likely to incur misconduct reprimands while incarcerated, less likely to commit crimes following release, and less likely to return to prison than inmates who did not take advantage of such programs.

UNICOR Inc.: An organization for federal prison labor.

Post-Release Employment Project (PREP): A study that demonstrated that UNICOR successfully prepared inmates for release and provided long-term benefits to society.

During the new millennium, UNICOR embarked on a corporate-wide campaign to become a leader in eco-sensitive practices and to set the standard for government. This eco-sensitive industry, commonly known as green technology, became a primary area of industrial growth for UNICOR. To ensure that it fulfilled its commitment to green technology, a senior-level task force was formed to develop a 5-year environmental plan, complete with measurable, corporate-wide objectives. This demonstrates how UNICOR has operated as a forward-thinking operation, providing products and services that are useful to society and that also reform offenders who are subject to release in the community.

Other Prison Work Programs

In many states and especially among three of the largest state correctional systems—Texas, California, and Florida—the employment of inmates in agricultural, forestry, and roadwork services has been a traditional focus of inmate labor (again, students should refer back to Chapters 1 and 2 of this text). These were especially popular forms of labor in the southern prison systems of the United States. Typically, this work included cotton picking, cutting lumber, harvesting crops, road construction, firefighting, and the maintenance of state grounds and property. While this type of work offsets costs of prison system budgets, it does not prepare offenders for work on the outside and therefore does

AURELIA VENTURA/LA OPINION/Newscom

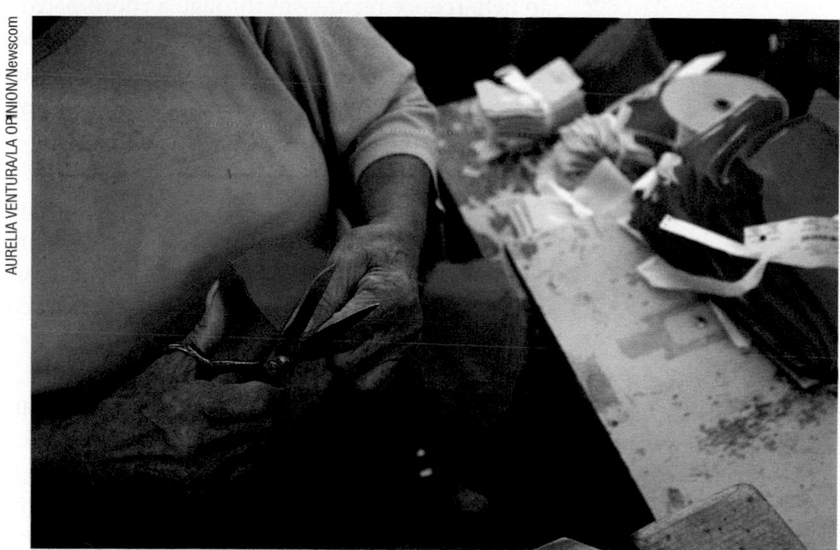

■ PHOTO 14.3 Female inmates, incarcerated at the California Institution for Women, make firefighters' uniforms at the prison's textile factory.

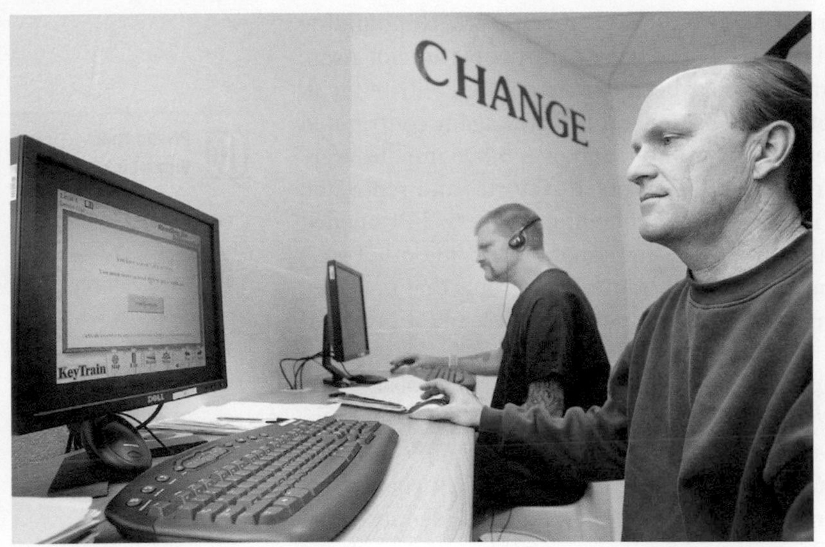

■ PHOTO 14.4 These inmates are working on a computerized education employment program, which allows inmates to work at their own pace; teaches job, employment, and academic skills; and can assist the inmates upon their release.

little to decrease recidivism, particularly when compared with skilled labor experience that allows offenders to support themselves once they are released.

There are examples of state prison systems that operate both agricultural programs and industrial programs; these systems both reduce the costs of prison operations and also prepare inmates for work on the outside. We will examine the Texas industrial system as a means of exploring this point. However, some comments regarding the benefits of agricultural production should be provided.

In Texas, the prison system continues to operate under a directive to be as self-sufficient as fiscally possible while meeting all constitutional requirements. As a result, this prison system's agricultural division grows most of the food consumed by the staff and inmates. The Texas prison agricultural system includes farms that produce millions of pounds of fresh cannery vegetables, substantial dairy products, and poultry products (including eggs). These operations are so successful that they produced surpluses during the 1990s and the early 2000s and kept food costs down to approximately $2 per inmate per day (Benestante, 1996). This is obviously beneficial to the state prison budget but also to Texas taxpayers who are free of the additional fiscal burdens that would be placed upon them if these programs did not exist. However, as noted earlier, agricultural programs do not tend to prepare inmates for work that will provide them opportunities on the outside. Thus, the answer is to allow inmates who are nearing release to train in other job sectors. This is done in Texas, and, as a result, we will briefly showcase this program in the subsections that follow.

Video Link
Obama Bans the Box

The Texas Prison Industry—Texas Correctional Industries

Texas Correctional Industries (TCI) was established in 1963 with the passage of Senate Bill 338, the Prison Made Goods Act of Texas (see Figure 14.1 for organization of prison manufacturing and logistics in Texas). The specific charge of TCI is to provide offenders with marketable job skills to help reduce recidivism through a coordinated program of job skills training, documentation of work history, and access to resources provided by various employment services upon release.

In addition, TCI helps to reduce prison system costs by providing products and services on a for-profit basis to the Texas Department of Criminal Justice (TDCJ) and other eligible entities and to agencies or political subdivisions of the state.

TCI manufactures goods and provides services to state and local government agencies, public educational systems, public hospitals, and political subdivisions. TCI comprises six divisions: Garment, Graphics, Furniture, Metal, Marketing and Distribution, and Offender Work and Training Programs. TCI has 37 facilities that manufacture items such as shirts, pants, coats, shoes, sheets, pillows, mattresses, signs, stickers, printed materials, janitorial supplies, soaps, detergents, license plates, stainless steel goods, park equipment, dump beds, a variety of office and institutional furniture, and modular office systems. All total, sales generated from these activities exceed $95 million annually. The work and training programs offered to offenders help reduce idleness and provide opportunities for offenders to learn marketable job skills and work ethics. On-the-job training and accredited certification programs, along with the Work Against Recidivism (WAR) program (described in more detail in the following pages), are specifically targeted to successfully reintegrate offenders into society.

Texas Correctional Industries (TCI): Provides offenders with marketable job skills to help reduce recidivism.

Windham School District: Secondary education program in Texas prisons.

The division collaborates with the **Windham School District** (a secondary education program in Texas prisons) and other entities to establish work and training programs directed toward the effective rehabilitation of offenders, promoting a seamless integration of training opportunities,

■ **Figure 14.1: Organizational Structure of Manufacturing and Logistics Division of Texas Prison System**

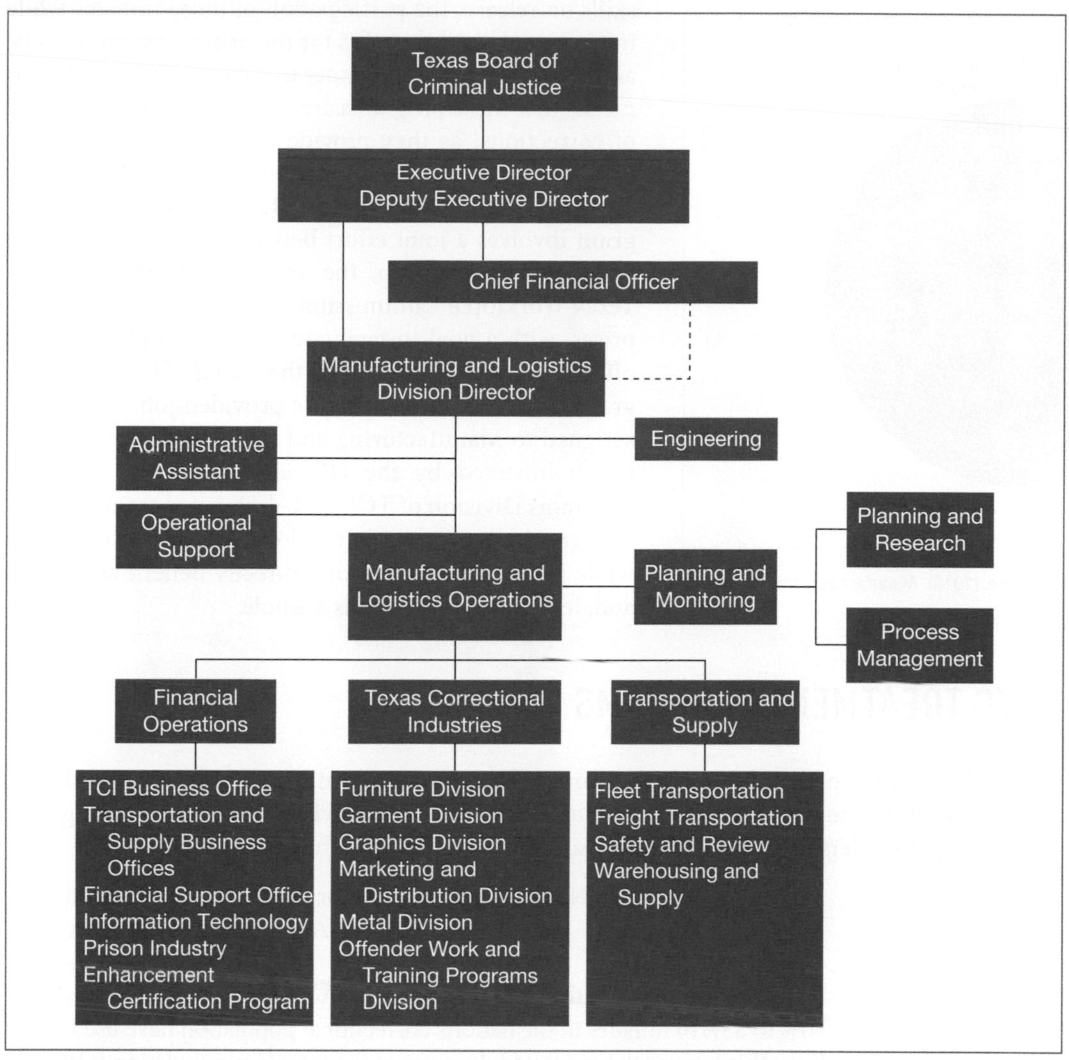

SOURCE: Texas Department of Criminal Justice. (2010). *Manufacturing and logistics annual report fiscal years 2008 and 2009.*

such as apprenticeship programs, diversified career preparation programs, short-course programs, on-the-job programs, and college vocational courses. These programs provide offenders with opportunities to acquire workplace knowledge and skills and help offenders develop a work ethic. The division is composed of Engineering, Operational Support, Financial Operations, Planning and Monitoring, Transportation and Supply, and TCI.

In Texas, the **Prison Industry Enhancement (PIE) Certification Program** is a partnership between the TDCJ and a private company, which allows the company to employ offenders who have volunteered to be a part of the program. The offenders are paid by the private company, and deductions are taken from their wages for their taxes, room and board, dependent support, and restitution, and a contribution is made to a crime victims' fund. This program has successfully offset correctional expenses for inmates who participate. Indeed, more than $17 million of offender earnings (room and board deductions) have been deposited in the state's General Revenue Fund since the program's inception. On average, for each offender employed, $5,071 is deducted for room and board, $1,431 is deducted for family support, $508 is deducted for the state's crime victims' compensation fund, and another $42 is deducted for restitution to victims (see Figure 14.2 for details).

Prison Industry Enhancement (PIE) Certification Program: Partnership between the Texas Department of Criminal Justice and a private company that allows the company to employ offenders.

The PIE Certification Program demonstrates how prison work programs can save taxpayers substantial amounts of money, but, at the same time, these programs are also able to give

■ Figure 14.2: Texas Prison Industry Enhancement Offender Contributions, 1993–2009

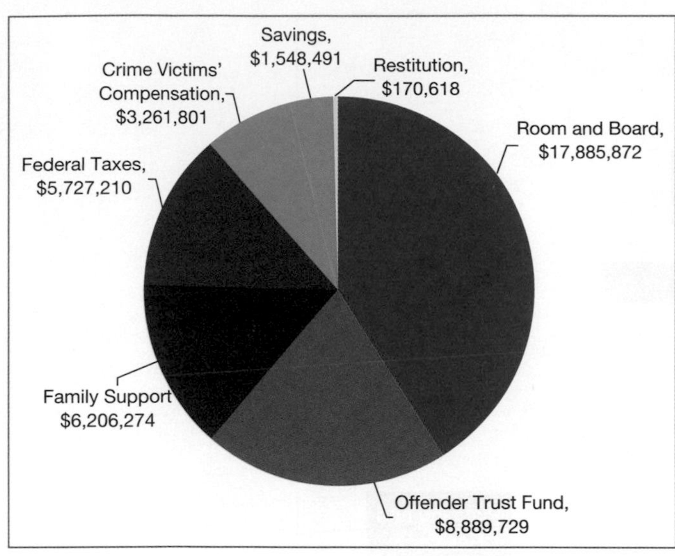

SOURCE: Texas Department of Criminal Justice. (2010). *Manufacturing and logistics annual report fiscal years 2008 and 2009.*

back to victims of crime. Thus, in addition to aiding in recidivism reduction for offenders who have useful job skills on release, the participation of those inmates while incarcerated yields benefits for the prison system, society, and victims in a direct manner that can be measured. This means that these programs are invaluable within the field of corrections, as they provide tangible benefits almost immediately after implementation.

Lastly, the **Work Against Recidivism (WAR) program** involves a joint effort between the Manufacturing and Logistics Division, the Texas Parole Division, the Texas Workforce Commission, and private sector enterprises, with a goal to facilitate the successful reentry of offenders upon release from the TDCJ. The WAR program tracks offenders who are provided job skills while assigned to Manufacturing and Logistics facilities. WAR is administered by the Offender Work and Training Programs Division of TCI. TCI-designated training facilities continue to provide employable skills to offenders while providing services that directly benefit customers and, less directly, society as a whole.

DRUG TREATMENT PROGRAMS

> Studies have consistently shown that comprehensive drug treatment works. It not only reduces drug use but also curtails criminal behavior and recidivism. Moreover, for drug-abusing offenders, treatment facilitates successful reentry into the community.
>
> Dr. Nora D. Volkow, director of the National Institute on Drug Abuse (see Volkow, 2006)

Web Link
Prisoners Face Long Wait for Drug-Rehab Services

The Bureau of Justice Statistics (BJS) and the National Center on Addiction and Substance Abuse (CASA) estimate that 60% to 83% of inmates in the nation's correctional population have used drugs at some point in their lives; this is twice the estimated drug use of the total U.S. population (Office of National Drug Control Policy [ONDCP], 2001). Included in this group are inmates who used an illegal drug at least weekly for a period of at least 1 month, have been imprisoned for selling or possessing drugs, were under the influence of drugs or alcohol when they committed their crime, committed their offense to get money for drugs, or have a history of alcohol abuse. As stated before, drugs are commonly linked with crime, the issue generally being not if but how they are linked.

The primary modality implemented in most jails is simple chemical detoxification. Detoxification is designed for persons dependent on narcotic drugs (e.g., heroin, opium) and is typically found in inpatient settings with programs that last for 7 to 21 days. While many detoxification programs address only the addict's physical dependence, some provide individual or group counseling in an attempt to address the problems associated with drug abuse. Many detoxification programs use medical drugs to ease the process of overcoming the physical symptoms of dependence that make the detoxification process so painful for the addicted substance abuser. For drug offenders in jails and prisons, the mechanism of detoxification varies by the client's major drug of addiction. For opiate users, methadone or clonidine is preferred.

Work Against Recidivism (WAR) program: Specifically targeted to successfully reintegrate offenders into society.

In all detoxification programs, inmate success depends upon following established protocols for drug administration and withdrawal. Regardless, it is important to understand that mere detoxification from a substance is not drug abuse "treatment" and does not help people stay off drugs. This in no way ensures that relapse will not occur, and thus it is important for any program to have much more than a simple detoxification process. This should instead be viewed as nothing more than an initial step of comprehensive treatment.

Peer Support Groups

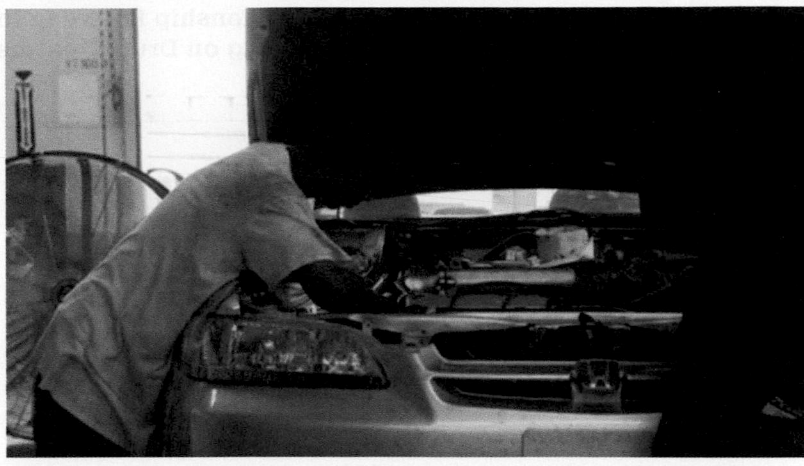

Prison Tour Video: Work Programs. Prison work programs give inmates the opportunity to develop marketable skills. Watch a clip about work programs for prisoners.

Within many prison facilities, peer support programs are integral components of alcohol or drug intervention strategies. These programs are called *peer support* because, in many cases, the facilitators are also prior alcohol or drug abusers. In many prisons, peer support groups are facilitated by other inmates who have progressed to an advanced or senior level of involvement in the program. Perhaps the most widely known peer support group is the 12-step program, in which individuals meet regularly to stabilize and expedite their recovery from substance abuse.

The best known of these programs is Alcoholics Anonymous (AA), in which sobriety is based on fellowship and adhering to the 12 steps of recovery (Hanson, Venturelli, & Fleckenstein, 2006; Myers & Salt, 2000). The 12 steps stress faith, confession of wrongdoing, and passivity in the hands of a "higher power" and forward group members from a statement of powerlessness over drugs and alcohol to a resolution that they will carry the message of help to others and will practice the AA principles in all affairs. In addition to AA, other popular self-help 12-step groups include Narcotics Anonymous and Cocaine Anonymous.

The success of self-help programs in general, and AA in particular, may be explained by the comprehensive network of such a program, which supports abstinence and recovery; frequent attendance at AA meetings where role modeling, confession, sharing, and support take place; and participation in the member network between meetings, which includes obtaining and relying on a senior member or sponsor. Al-Anon, a fellowship for relatives and significant others of alcoholics, was founded in 1951, although it did not take off as a movement until the 1960s. Narcotics Anonymous, the third of the three major 12-step fellowships, was founded in 1953. It was relatively small throughout the 1950s and 1960s but obtained a great deal of popularity during the 1970s and 1980s (Myers & Salt, 2000).

The Therapeutic Community

After the detoxification phase, the residential therapeutic community is the next full-service form of treatment given to substance abusers in jails, prisons, or residential treatment centers. Recovery through this form of treatment depends on positive and negative pressures to change. This pressure is brought about through a self-help process in which relationships of mutual responsibility to every resident in the program are built. In addition to individual and group counseling, this process has a system of explicit rewards that reinforce the value of earned achievement. As such, privileges are earned. In addition, therapeutic communities have their own rules and regulations that guide the behavior of residents and the management of facilities. Their purposes are to maintain the safety and health of the community and to train and teach residents through the use of discipline. There are typically numerous rules and regulations within these facilities (Hanser & Mire, 2010).

The Benefits of Substance Abuse Treatment in Corrections

Aside from education and employment, effective drug treatment is perhaps the most commonly needed form of inmate programming. Every state correctional system offers some variety of drug treatment programming, but it is the means by which these programs are carried out that tend to determine their effectiveness. The best means of reducing recidivism among nonviolent drug offenders is through drug treatment admissions rather than imprisonment.

Further, it has been shown that increased admissions to drug treatment are associated with reduced rates of violent crime (see Figure 14.3). According to the Justice Policy Institute

■ **Figure 14.3: Relationship Between Increase in Drug Treatment Admissions and Federal Spending on Drug Treatment and Decrease in Violent Crime, 1995–2005**

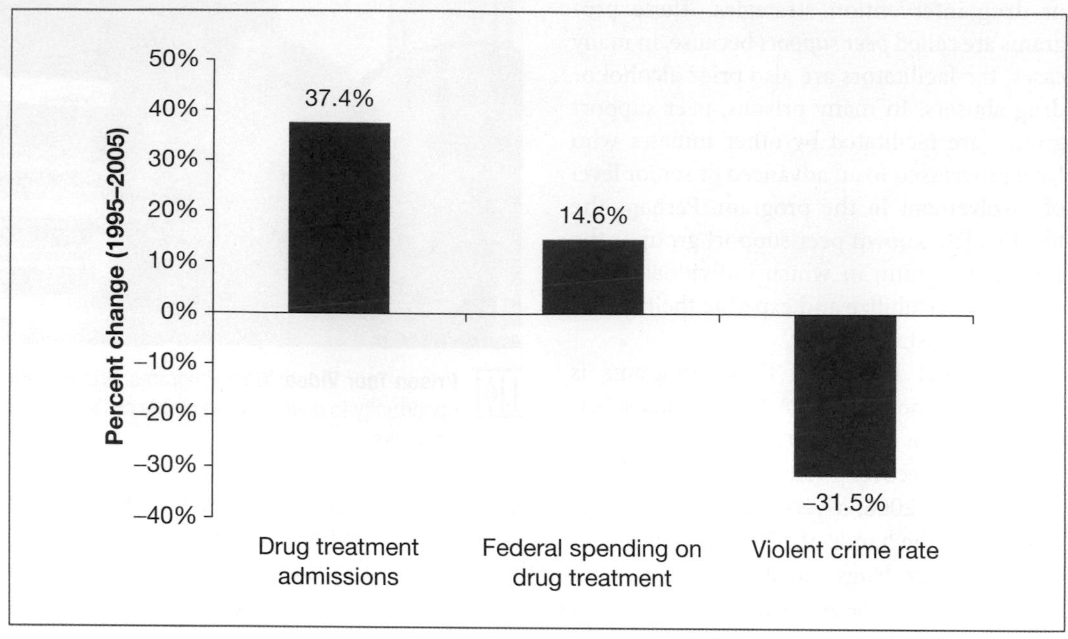

SOURCE: Justice Policy Institute. (2008). *Substance abuse treatment and public safety.* Washington, DC: Author. Copyright © 2008 Justice Policy Institute. Reprinted with permission.

(2008), admissions to drug treatment increased by 37.4%, and federal spending on drug treatment increased by 14.6% from 1995 to 2005. During the same period, violent crime fell by 31.5%.

These reduced rates of violent crime also correspond with lower incarceration rates. Indeed, of the 20 states that admit the most people to treatment per 100,000, 19 had incarceration rates below the national average. Of the 20 states that admitted the fewest people to treatment per 100,000, eight had incarceration rates above the national average (Justice Policy Institute, 2008).

Many offenders with substance abuse problems are sentenced to intensive supervision probation (ISP) if they are not sent to prison. Others, when on parole, will tend to have similarly restrictive programming. In addition, drug offenders on probation or parole may be required to submit to drug screens to ensure compliance with treatment. Court and corrections officials will generally want to know if the offender is complying with treatment and remaining abstinent from drugs. In programs in which access to treatment is limited by available space or funding, those who do not comply may be discharged from treatment. Those who do not successfully complete treatment and continue to have positive drug screens may be sent back to court for further sentencing. While drug testing appears to serve a useful purpose in monitoring offenders with substance abuse problems, this testing alone is not sufficient to keep offenders from using drugs and reoffending. The best approach may be to combine random drug testing with forms of rehabilitative drug treatment to address the addiction and minimize the likelihood that the individual will engage in future criminal behavior.

Drug offenders on probation are usually placed in outpatient treatment programs, which usually include individual and group therapy. Some programs include family therapy and relapse prevention support. Outpatient drug treatment often includes a range of protocols, from highly professional psychotherapies to informal peer discussions (ONDCP, 2001). Counseling services vary considerably and include individual, group, or family counseling; peer group support; vocational therapy; and cognitive therapy. Aftercare, considered necessary to prevent relapse, typically consists of 12-step meetings, periodic group or individual counseling, recovery training or self-help and relapse-prevention strategies, and/or vocational counseling (ONDCP, 2001).

RECREATIONAL PROGRAMS

Recreational activities are an important aspect of prison management and operations. Well-designed recreational programs provide constructive options for inmates to spend idle time and also can serve as incentives for good behavior. Though many people may balk at the notion that inmates are afforded recreational opportunities, it should be pointed out that access to such activities can (and does) keep the inmate population more manageable. Beyond this, many prison systems provide a set of additional rationales for their recreation programs. For example, Washington State's Department of Corrections (2012) provides the following purposes for providing prison recreational programming:

Robert Hanser

■ PHOTO 14.5 Ms. Gail Durban leads a psycho-educational class on gambling addiction with inmates at Richwood Correctional Center. Ms. Durban is a certified compulsive gambling counselor who works for the Office of Behavioral Health (OBH) in Louisiana.

1. Contribute to a safe and secure environment and reduce idleness by allowing offenders an opportunity to participate in supervised and structured physical and prosocial activities.
2. Help offenders take responsibility for their health and wellness by adopting positive lifestyle habits.
3. Reduce the number of disciplinary problems as well as injuries related to stress and strain.
4. Allow offenders to use recreation/wellness activities in conjunction with the offender release plan.

From the four purposes listed above, it can be seen that Washington (like many other prison systems) views effective recreational activities as producing good outcomes for the offender and for the institution.

History

In America's early colonial jails as well as the Pennsylvania and Auburn system prisons, physical exercise was provided to inmates as part of the daily regimen. However, it was Elmira Reformatory, known for its progressive orientation toward inmate supervision and reform, that first offered a diverse array of programming options. At Elmira, inmates could participate in team sports, gymnasium activities, a variety of social clubs to build esteem and social skills, and even acting and artistic pursuits. In addition, inmates could opt to work for the inmate-run newspaper, titled *The Summary*, which first began in 1883. This paper was an eight-page weekly digest of world and local news. Importantly, ***The Summary*** was the first inmate-operated prison newspaper in the entire world (New York Correction History Society [NYCHS], 2008). In today's current prison environment, nearly every prison system (if not every major prison) has an inmate-run newspaper or newsletter.

During the late 1880s, the use of prison labor for profit was banned due to opposition from private corporations and businesses. This led Zebulon Brockway, the historical figure associated with the innovations at Elmira (see Chapter 1), to look for ways to keep the inmates busy with productive activities. As one of many programs, Brockway implemented a military program; when it was in full stride, the inmates were drilling 5 to 8 hours a day. Inmates were organized into companies and regiments, with inmate officers and a brass band. Brockway also took this opportunity to shift the trade school program from evenings to days and to adapt the physical education program to the entire population. A gymnasium with marble floors, a swimming pool, and a drill hall, completed in 1890, allowed military and physical training in all weather (NYCHS, 2008).

The Summary: The first inmate-operated prison newspaper in the world.

TECHNOLOGY AND EQUIPMENT 14.1

Computerized and Web-Enabled Addiction Severity Index

The Addiction Severity Index—Multimedia Version (ASI-MV®) interview is the client self-administered version of the widely used Addiction Severity Index (ASI). Inflexxion, with several grants from the National Institute on Drug Abuse (NIDA), developed and tested the ASI-MV, and studies have shown it to have excellent reliability and validity. Since developing the ASI-MV in the early 1990s, Inflexxion also received NIDA grant support to research and develop the Spanish language ASI-MV and the Comprehensive Health Assessment for Teens (CHAT®).

Clients self-administer these interviews on a computer with audio and video using a mouse. Since these tools do not require staff time to ask the questions or collect data, they save agencies staff time and money, while increasing the consistency of data collection. It has been found that clients are able to easily use these programs, regardless of education level, reading ability, or prior computer experience.

In addition to clinical reports, which are immediately available for treatment planning and level of care placement, the system also includes the Analytics Data Center, which enables providers to

Figure 14.4: ASI-MV Graphic Profiles

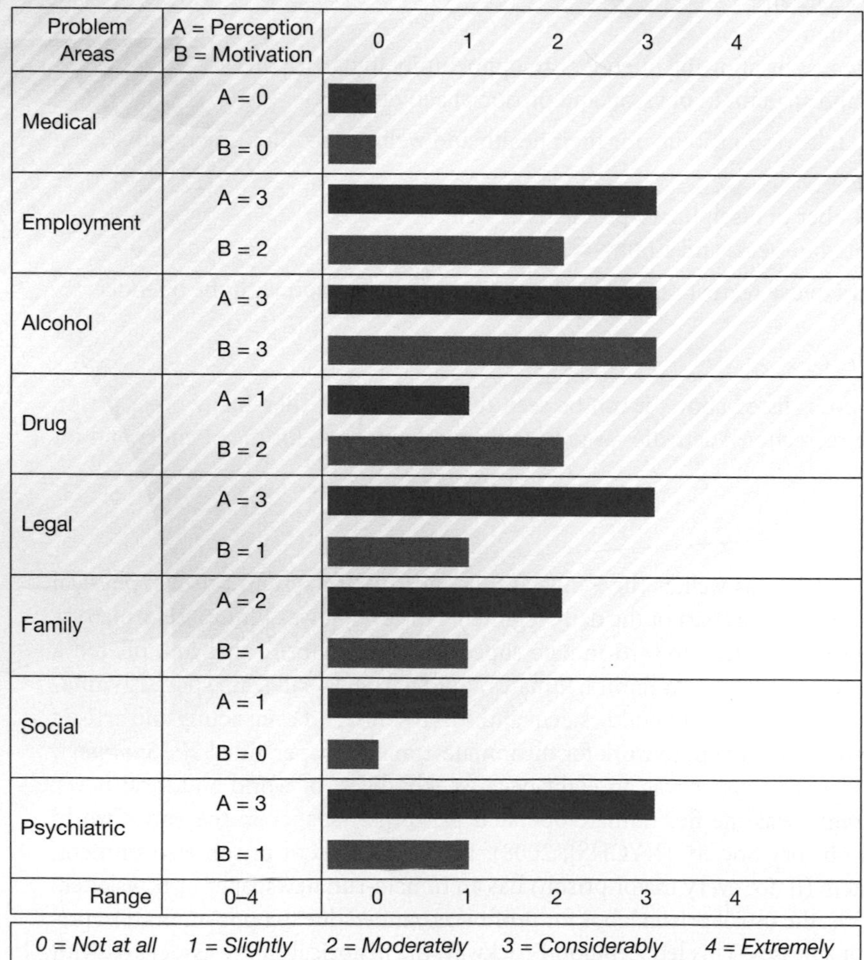

SOURCE: ASI-MV. (2012). Newton, MA: Inflexxion, Inc. Reprinted with permission from Inflexion, Inc./ASI-MV. Retrieved from: https://www.asi-mvconnect.com.

[1]Perception is a how troubled or bothered a client is by problems.

[2]Motivation is how important it is for the client to receive help for problems now.

anonymously track trends, characteristics, and outcomes of their population.

The ASI-MV online system, which includes the ASI-MV and CHAT interviews and analytics, are all part of the Behavioral Health Connect system of tools available only through Inflexxion (www.ASI-MVConnect.com).

ASI-MV Analytics is an online resource for substance abuse and mental health agencies as well as treatment centers that provides easy access to de-identified, aggregate data uploaded from the ASI-MV system through a secure upload process. This enables organizations to easily view assessment, utilization, and outcome data associated with the ASI-MV interview.

The ASI-MV produces, on demand, numerous reports that can be used by treatment staff and administrators. Reports summarize client self-reported data from across all domains, and arrange the data in a useful manner to assist clinicians with treatment planning.

The summary includes problem lists and the following key clusters:

- Client's perception of problems
- Client's motivation to get help for problems
- Possible psychiatric risks
- Potential strengths/supports
- Recovery environment—assets and liabilities

These reports also contain an outcome comparison form, which a clinician can use to track progress; a blank treatment plan form or template; and a sheet listing available client handouts and worksheets. In the world of substance abuse treatment, the optimal integration of assessment and outcome data to maximize client programming makes for a well-designed and comprehensive means of treatment service delivery.

SOURCE: ASI-MV. (2012). Newton, MA: Inflexxion, Inc. Reprinted with permission from Inflexxion, Inc./ASI-MV. Retrieved from https://www.asi-mvconnect.com

FOCUS TOPIC 14.1

Drug Treatment Reduces Violent Crime and Incarceration in the State of California

Case Study: California Proposition 36

The Substance Abuse and Crime Prevention Act of 2000 (SACPA), or Proposition 36, was put into effect in California in order to reduce the use of incarceration for nonviolent offenders, reduce drug-related crime, and increase public health. It requires the use of drug treatment as an alternative to incarceration for nonviolent adult offenders convicted of drug possession for personal use. From its passage in November 2000 to December 2005, the rate of people incarcerated for drug possession in California dropped 34.3%, from 59 to 58 people per 100,000. Implementation of SACPA may not be the sole cause of this rapid decrease; there were, however, no other major public changes during this time.

According to the National Survey of Substance Abuse Treatment Services (NSSATS), this period saw a 25.9% increase in the number of drug treatment facilities in California, but a 2.83% decrease nationally when California is excluded. Along with this increase in treatment facilities, the number of substance abuse clients in California increased 34.1% from 2000 to 2004. Excluding California, the nation as a whole only had a 4% increase in the number of treatment clients during the time. As California's violent crime rate decreased more rapidly than the nation's, the number of California treatment facilities and clients increased.

Those opposing Proposition 36 feared that this decrease in incarceration would lead to an increase in violent crime. In fact, from 2000 to 2004 California's violent crime rate decreased 11.2% while at the same time the national average violent crime rate fell by 8.1%.

Not only did California experience a decrease in violent crime, but the state also saved a substantial amount of money. Using the year 2000 as a baseline for drug possession prison admissions, a Justice Policy Institute (JPI) report estimated that the state saved more than $350 million from 2000 to June 2006 (the end of the initiative's funding) by using drug treatment as an alternative to prison. (Researchers took the cost of the drug treatment programming into account in calculating savings.) Using a similar methodology, JPI found that California saved a total of $412 million on prison and jail operating costs alone over 6 1/2 years.

The University of California's cost analysis of Proposition 36 also saw substantial cost savings. The study showed that California saved a minimum of $2.50 for every dollar spent on the treatment alternative, $4 per person who completed treatment, and a total of $173.3 million in savings to the California government in the first year alone. The cost savings from Proposition 36 are available to be spent on more cost-effective public safety policies for Californians.

SOURCE: Justice Policy Institute. (2008). *Substance abuse and public safety.* Washington, DC: Author.

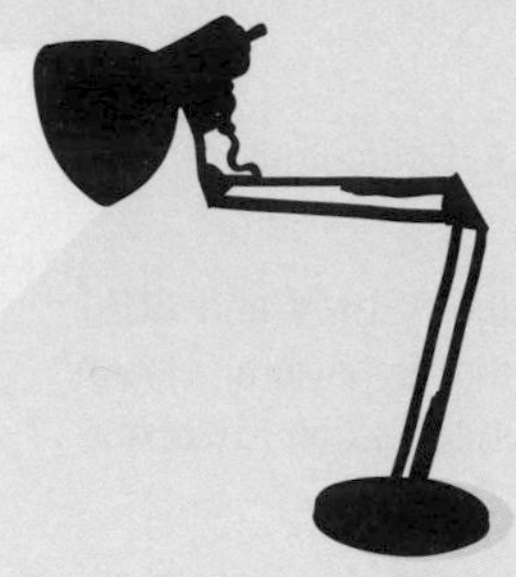

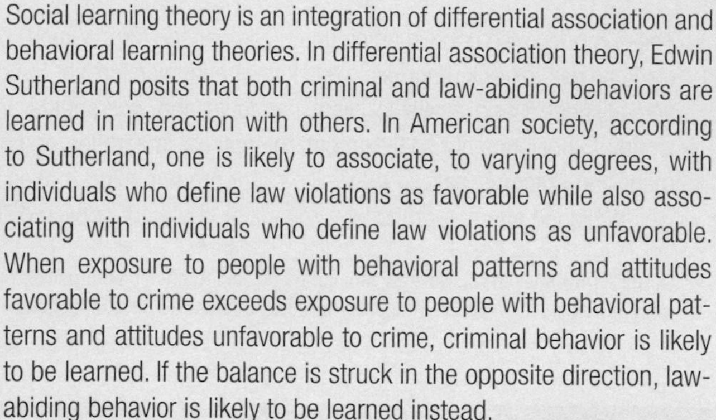

APPLIED THEORY 14.1

Social Learning and Behavior Management

Social learning theory is an integration of differential association and behavioral learning theories. In differential association theory, Edwin Sutherland posits that both criminal and law-abiding behaviors are learned in interaction with others. In American society, according to Sutherland, one is likely to associate, to varying degrees, with individuals who define law violations as favorable while also associating with individuals who define law violations as unfavorable. When exposure to people with behavioral patterns and attitudes favorable to crime exceeds exposure to people with behavioral patterns and attitudes unfavorable to crime, criminal behavior is likely to be learned. If the balance is struck in the opposite direction, law-abiding behavior is likely to be learned instead.

Because of this social learning component that can be both positive and negative, depending on the social circumstances, some treatment programs are separated from the main prison population. For example, the **Successful Treatment of Addiction and Recovery (STAR) program** at Richwood Correctional Center is a drug addiction program that consists of dorms that are separate from the housing units of the main compound. Inmates in this treatment program are kept separate from the general population because it is presumed that they will not be affected by negative associations with persons not in treatment. In addition, inmates in treatment together will likely be positive influences on one another and will, therefore, be likely to give messages and reinforcements conducive to treatment and recovery. Further, like many drug treatment programs, the STAR program emphasizes the people, places, and things that these inmates encounter that can affect likely relapse into drug use and recidivism into criminal activity. These messages demonstrate that associations with healthy people will aid in the offender's recovery from drugs and alcohol while associations with persons who lead unhealthy lifestyles will likely lead to associations that support drug and alcohol use. The same is true with the places in which offenders choose to spend their time as well as the things that they have in their environment. Thus, there is a reinforcing element (operant reinforcers) to this program and an element that also emphasizes the impact of the social setting.

In addition, Richwood Correctional Center places a strong emphasis on religious programming for both Muslim and Christian members. These groups tend to have teachings that are prosocial in orientation, from the perspective of both prison administration and crime prevention upon release into society. Religious programs provide structure and guidance with positive behaviors. The inmate's association with others who are like-minded regarding prosocial activities helps to socially reinforce the individual toward a healthy and positive lifestyle. Naturally, this reduces the pro-criminal and pro-drug messages. Thus, religious programming serves as a very positive adjunct to treatment programming and behavior change among inmates.

Lastly, a social learning mechanism is involved with recreational programs. The use of physical recreation, particularly structured physical recreation, provides additional prosocial behaviors that are physiologically healthy, and this, in and of itself, translates to cognitive rewards: A healthy body leads to a healthy mind. Other recreational programs, such as drawing and painting, music and singing programs, and so forth, provide emotional benefits that are often self-rewarding for the inmate, thereby providing self-reinforcement. When individuals also receive recognition for these accomplishments, this adds an additional layer of reinforcement that can further support their continued activity in these healthy activities. Thus, recreational pursuits can have a therapeutic effect, and they also work hand-in-hand with the premises associated with social learning theory. In the end, any program that provides messages that are prosocial and, at the same time, minimizes those that encourage criminal behavior can be considered consistent with the tenets of social learning theory.

SOURCE: Sellers, C. S., & Winfree, L. T. (2010). *Akers, Ronald L.: Social learning theory.* In F. T. Cullen & P. Wilcox (Eds.), *Encyclopedia of criminological theory.* Thousand Oaks, CA: Sage.

Successful Treatment of Addiction and Recovery (STAR) program: Emphasizes the people, places, and things that inmates encounter that can affect relapse into drug use and criminal activity.

Zimmer Amendment: Restricted the purchase of several types of weight lifting equipment within the Federal Bureau of Prisons.

In 1966, the National Correctional Recreation Association was established. The emergence of this association served as the formal acknowledgment of prison recreational services as a legitimate and central feature in prison operations and management.

During the 1990s, prison systems experienced enormous growth, and the public fervently advocated for a "get tough on crime" approach to incarceration. As a result, many states and even the BOP limited many recreational items and activities in prisons, including in-cell television viewing, R-rated movies, pornographic materials, boxing, wrestling, judo, karate, electronic musical instruments, computers, and in-cell coffee pots and hot plates.

In 1994, weight lifting in particular came under public scrutiny, and, between this time and 1997, several states banned or limited weight lifting in prisons. One particular piece of legislation, passed by Congress in 1996, is known as the **Zimmer Amendment**. This amendment restricted the purchase of several types of weight lifting equipment within the BOP. In recent years, the issue has moved to the back burner, but weight lifting remains banned or limited in approximately a dozen states.

From 2000 onward, a number of states have experienced budgetary problems, and this has in turn severely impacted prison budgets. As a result, cuts in prison system spending have limited the types of recreational activities available. Although recreational opportunities may exist in most prisons, they tend to be funded by the inmates themselves and are restricted to activities such as unstructured physical activity on a recreation yard, singing in prison choirs (especially for religious programming), watching films, and other no-cost programs that do not require anything more than marginal commitment on the part of prison systems.

Recreational Programming

Effective recreational programs require well-trained professionals, adequate equipment and supplies, and space for implementation. In addition, programs should include a variety of indoor and outdoor activities. For an example, we will refer to the Department of Corrections in the state of Montana and its policy document titled *Recreation Programs DOC 5.5.3*. This document lays out in very clear terms the expectations regarding personnel who supervise in recreational services as well as the structure of recreational programming. According to this document, each program will have a full-time recreation program administrator.

This **recreation program administrator** is often responsible for a number of duties, one of which is that this individual is expected to survey the recreational needs and interests of the offender population at least once each year. This is important because it provides inmates with some voice in the matter and, as we have seen from prior history, detracts from the likelihood that inmates will be so disgruntled as to be unruly or, worse yet, resort to a riot. Throughout the year, the recreation program administrator will ensure that recreational facilities are maintained and in good condition.

Recreation program administrators will also oversee recreation programs in locked facilities and be adept at crafting programs for special needs offenders. This is an important aspect of the duties of this administrator. Programming for the elderly must be appropriate for these offenders and is increasingly becoming a requirement in many prison facilities. Often, such programs not only emphasize physical fitness but also integrate wellness programming into the overall service delivery. Programming for women and juveniles also requires additional considerations. This can be true for a number of reasons ranging from the preferences of different groups to potential security or medical concerns.

Recreation program administrator: Responsible for a number of duties, including surveying the recreational needs and interests of the offender population.

Benefits for Inmates and Institutions

One of the key benefits of recreation is the tendency toward a reduction in violence and disciplinary problems. The fact that when inmates are provided constructive activities the institution will

FOCUS TOPIC 14.2

The NCRA Position Statement on Weight Lifting Programs in Correctional Settings

It is the official position of the National Correctional Recreation Association that weight lifting programs are an integral part of rehabilitation services within the spectrum of corrections.

Properly administered weight lifting programs are a vital tool in the daily management of a volatile environment as well as a potentially cost-effective measure. The task of providing a safe environment of positive change is not an easy one, and our tools are few. The elimination of any of these tools would create a void that would be difficult and costly to fill. The reality is that nearly all inmates in our prisons will one day return to society. It is our responsibility to ensure that they have every opportunity to return as more productive citizens than when they came to us. Weight lifting is a vital part of correctional programming, and we strongly encourage its continued presence in America's prisons.

SOURCE: National Correctional Recreation Association. (2010). *About the NCRA*. Retrieved from http://www.strengthtech.com/correct/ncra/ncra.htm#about

likely have fewer discipline problems is simply common sense; boredom can lead to chaos much more quickly than structured activity, particularly activity that is enjoyable. The leverage that prisons can maintain over inmates who desire such activities also helps to maintain compliance that is otherwise difficult to obtain.

Another benefit related to recreational programs is that they can help to elevate the esteem of inmates serving time. Because most programs enable inmates to set their own standard for success, there is a high likelihood that they will be encouraged to participate, and this can add a sense of motivation. It is important that inmates feel motivated since this is a necessary experience if they are to participate in a positive manner in programs such as drug therapy, educational achievement, or job training. Sports such as jogging are intramural in nature and allow the inmates to compete against their own past performance and to gauge improvements in their own activity. Team sports allow inmates to practice group membership, anger control, and the ability to work with authority figures (team captains and such).

Prison Tour Video: Recreational Programs. Recreational programs provide numerous benefits. Watch a clip about the importance of recreational programs.

Recreational Programs as Tools for Rehabilitation

In many respects, recreational programs can be useful as tools for rehabilitation. One term used to describe rehabilitative recreational programs is *therapeutic recreation*. Therapeutic recreation is a type of recreational programming intended to augment treatment planning for clients so that they can achieve optimal physical and mental health. More specifically, **therapeutic recreation (TR)** programs are designed to meet the needs of individuals with a variety of disabilities, impairments, or illnesses by providing specific services such as recreational activities, leisure education, and skills training in the cognitive, physical, behavioral, social, and affective domains (Olson, 2004). The definition provided by Olson (2004) is connected to mental health orientations. It is this perspective that we will take for this subsection, and therefore the definition provided by Olson will be used.

Common activities used in TR programs are arts, crafts, board or card games, music, sports or physical fitness, gardening, and reading activities. Unique activities include relaxation therapy, experiential education, animal-assisted therapy, anger management, parenting groups, diet and wellness groups, martial arts, humor therapy, and current events. The more specialized programs are often conducted in partnership with a mental health professional, such as a professional counselor, social worker, or psychologist. In these cases, there is often a fusion between the therapeutic group and some type of other recreational activity.

For instance, programs related to gardening and therapeutic outcomes have been used in the past and are still used today. In the early 1900s, a prison garden project was implemented by Warden Lewis Lawes of Sing Sing Prison in Ossining, New York. At that time, Charles Chapin, an influential inmate with ties to wealthy community members, had successfully obtained support and materials to create a beautiful and well-maintained garden on prison grounds. This garden, attended by inmates (under the direction of Chapin), grew to be a major project and was purported to have resulted in numerous benefits for inmates. For example, it is likely that naturalistic settings may offer benefits in terms of stress reduction and improved mental states for offenders. In several studies conducted within U.S. correctional facilities, access to outside views and the quality of these views have been shown to have a measurable influence on the behavior and psychological outlook of inmates and staff. Lindemuth (2007) showcases work by Moore (1981) showing that an inmate's view out from the prison cell can have a significant impact on his or her physical well-being. More specifically, Moore found that the view out from a cell (exterior or interior), the cell's relative privacy, and the noise level within the cell are correlated with the number of sick calls to the infirmary.

Therapeutic recreation (TR): Programs designed to meet the needs of individuals with a variety of disabilities, impairments, or illnesses by providing specific services.

Lindemuth (2007) also shows how gardening recreation programs can have therapeutic effects on inmates. One unique gardening program can be found at Rikers Island in the state of New York. In 1997, the Horticultural Society of New York (HSNY) began GreenHouse, a program providing inmates at the Rikers Island jail complex horticulture training and work experience in the design, installation, and maintenance of gardens.

■ PHOTO 14.6 An inmate maintains the garden at the Rikers Island GreenHouse project. GreenHouse operates under the premise that jail can serve as a sustainable resource—one that generates benefits to constituents in jail as well as to entire communities across the city and region.

The garden at Rikers Island features arbors, post and rail fences, birdhouses, a gazebo adjacent to a pond and a waterfall feature, a greenhouse, and a preexisting brick-and-cinder-block building used as an office and a classroom. Walkways are constructed of gravel and brick. Several rabbits are kept near the office, and guinea hens donated from a correctional officer's farm live near the garden. The Rikers Island garden has a strong programming component. Horticulture classes are primarily taught in the winter months when conditions become inhospitable for garden activities. During this time, the greenhouse is transformed into a carpentry shop where inmates construct birdhouses, kestrel and bat boxes, planters, and other wood features for the Rikers garden and citywide schools and parks.

As noted in earlier parts of this chapter, some of the work-related programs offered to inmates provide benefits to others in society, including youth and persons who have disabilities or financial challenges. For example, inmates involved in the GreenHouse program grow plants for schools and other public entities, including libraries in low-income neighborhoods. Vegetables grown on Rikers are donated to cooking classes offered at the Rikers jails and also to area homeless shelters. The Rikers program is a perfect example of how the volunteer work of inmates can help others in the community. For the minimal time and effort required by prison staff, it seems that these types of programs offer huge incentives to everyone involved, and that they are able to improve the prognoses of inmates who also receive mental health services.

Before closing this subsection, one other program, also in New York, should be showcased because of its uniqueness and because it specifically relates to female offenders, making it a genuine rarity that, if replicated in other facilities, could generate enormous benefits. This program is located at Bedford Hills Correctional Facility (BHCF), a maximum-security facility for women. This program includes gardening and also provides grounds for mothers to see visiting children. Like the garden at Sing Sing, the contemporary Children's Center garden and playground at BHCF had strong support from individuals both within and outside the facility. The main goal of the Children's Center is to help women preserve and strengthen relationships with their children while incarcerated.

The gardens at BHCF are maintained by the women who serve time and are created to provide a pleasant area for child visitation. The entire program is quite extensive and includes a nursery, a parenting center, a day care center, a prenatal center, and a child advocacy office. It is important to emphasize that this type of programming affects not only the inmates but their children as well. Thus, it has a direct impact upon persons in the community and, at the same time, helps to maintain the mental health of the female inmates serving time. In addition, this program demonstrates how two different types of programming (gardening and children's visitation programs) can be connected to improve the standards of confinement for inmates, reduce interpersonal problems within the institution, and reduce problems related to child maladjustment that can occur within the broader outside community. Thus, recreational programming can provide numerous benefits, including therapeutic benefits.

RELIGIOUS PROGRAMS

Religion has played a central role in American prisons since the days of the Walnut Street Jail and even before. Students may recall that the Quakers of Pennsylvania were instrumental in achieving jail and prison reform. Indeed, the term *penitentiary* is reflective of the word *penitence,* and the prison was initially meant to be a place where inmates could reflect on their wrongdoings, and where it was hoped that they would come to change their ways. While religious programming today is a key aspect of prison facility operations, the role of hired staff and volunteers who provide religious services has become quite complex. In many cases, religious programming may be infused with treatment programming for addiction recovery, the development of life skills, and even the dietary requirements of various inmates.

History of Religion in Corrections

In earlier chapters, we have discussed the history of corrections and have noted the long and extensive role of religion throughout that history. The work of Dr. Harry Dammer, set out in the *Encyclopedia of Crime and Punishment* (Levinson, 2002), provides a very succinct and interesting historical overview of the role of religion in corrections. Because Dammer's work is so precisely congruent with the goals of several subsections in this chapter that address religion in corrections, it will be used extensively throughout this section. With this noted, we begin with a brief account of the history of religion in corrections, borrowing from the work of Dammer (2002).

Dammer (2002) notes that the influence and practice of religion in the correctional setting is as old as the history of prisons itself. He speculates that the initial entry of religion into prison was probably carried out by religious men who themselves were imprisoned. Indeed, many notable biblical figures were themselves prisoners, such as Joseph and Jeremiah in the Old Testament, and John the Baptist, Peter, John, and Paul in the New Testament. Beginning in the days of Constantine, the early Christian Church granted asylum to criminals who would otherwise have been mutilated or killed. Although this custom was restricted in most countries by the fifteenth century, releasing prisoners during Easter and requests by church authorities to pardon or reduce sentences for offenders were continued practices for centuries.

***Fulwood v. Clemmer* (1962):** Ruled that correctional officials must recognize the Muslim faith as a legitimate religion and allow inmates to hold services.

***Cooper v. Pate* (1964):** Ruling that state prison inmates could sue state officials in federal courts.

***Cruz v. Beto* (1972):** Ruling that inmates must be given reasonable opportunities to exercise their religious beliefs.

***Theriault v. Carlson* (1977):** Ruling that the First Amendment does not protect so-called religions that are obvious shams, that tend to mock established institutions, and whose members lack religious sincerity.

***O'Lone v. Estate of Shabazz* (1987):** Held that depriving an inmate of attending a religious service for "legitimate penological interests" was not a violation of the inmate's First Amendment rights.

In the nineteenth century, when daytime work was initiated by the Auburn system, solitary confinement at night was still the norm in correctional practice. This forced confinement was thought to serve the same repenting purpose as the older penitentiary. Belief in education as a tool for reducing criminal activity also assisted in the growth of religion in prison. Because of the limited budgets of correctional institutions, chaplains were often called upon to be the sole educator in many American prisons.

In the modern world of corrections, religion continues to play a very important part in prison operations. However, as we will see when discussing legal issues in correctional religion, the meaning of the term *religion* has broadened a bit. It now includes groups that were not even in existence during the early colonial history of America and religions that were more prevalent in areas of the world outside of Europe. The religious pluralism in prisons means that inmates will (and often do) raise questions or requests that go beyond the expertise, training, or ecclesiastical endorsement of some clergy member (Van Baalen, 2008). In such cases, these inmates may have to defer to spiritual leaders in the community. In many cases, volunteers may fill that role, or facilities may hire contract chaplains or religious experts to address inmate issues if the need seems to warrant such an expenditure.

Religious Diets and Holy Days

Inmates of various religious groups will request specialized diets that are required for their particular faith. In most instances, prison staff can and do ask inmates to document in advance that such a diet is a required part of their faith. Legitimate requests based on recognized religious tenets must be accommodated (Van Baalen, 2008). Van Baalen (2008) notes that many religious observances for even traditional faiths may require the consumption of particular foods (e.g., Jewish Passover), and some religions may require that food not be consumed at specific times during the day or night (e.g., Muslim Ramadan). Prisons around the United States routinely accommodate these dietary modifications based on religion. There are even some occasions where a religious group may require the setting of a group meal as part of a ceremony; such types of request should

CORRECTIONS AND THE LAW 14.1

Legal Issues and Religious Practices

The First Amendment of the U.S. Constitution protects the freedom of religion as a fundamental right, and this protection extends to inmates. In essence, regardless of whether individuals are locked up, they still have a right to practice the tenets of their religious beliefs without obstruction. The right to religion in prison was not an issue identified as needing court intervention until the 1960s and 1970s. During this time, a handful of cases emerged in federal courts that directly addressed religious practice within the prison setting. Most notable among these cases were *Fulwood v. Clemmer* (1962), *Cooper v. Pate* (1964), and *Cruz v. Beto* (1972). In ***Fulwood v. Clemmer* (1962)**, the U.S. District Court for the District of Columbia ruled that correctional officials must recognize the Muslim faith as a legitimate religion and not restrict those inmates who wish to hold services. During this period, two Supreme Court cases also addressed religion. In ***Cooper v. Pate* (1964)**, the Court ruled that prison officials must make every effort to treat members of all religious groups equally unless they can demonstrate reasonableness to do otherwise. In the case of ***Cruz v. Beto* (1972)**, it was ruled discriminatory and a violation of the Constitution to deny a Buddhist prisoner his right to practice his faith in a comparable way to those who practice the major religious denominations.

Later, the Fifth Circuit Court of Appeals ruled in ***Theriault v. Carlson* (1977)** that the First Amendment does not protect so-called religions that are obvious shams, that tend to mock established institutions, and whose members lack religious sincerity. Further, though inmates have protected rights to exercise their faith, prison staff have the right to regulate religious practices within prisons to ensure that the safety and security of the institution are not compromised. In the case of ***O'Lone v. Estate of Shabazz* (1987)**, it was ruled that depriving an inmate of attending a religious service for "legitimate penological interests" was not a violation of an inmate's First Amendment rights. This fully affirms the fact that, ultimately, the safety and security of the institution is the paramount priority in prisons.

Thirteen years later, a significant piece of legislation emerged that has weathered the tests of litigation: the Religious Land Use and Institutionalized Persons Act of 2000 (RLUIPA). The RLUIPA has helped to refine and clarify inmates' religious rights under the First Amendment. The primary intent of this law is to further safeguard (not restrict) the rights of inmates to practice their religious tenets in state and federal facilities. The Supreme Court issued a ruling in ***Cutter v. Wilkinson* (2005)** addressing the constitutionality of the RLUIPA and its application to nontraditional religions. In this case, the inmates asserted that they were adherents of "nonmainstream" religions, namely the Satanist (typically the Church of Satan, which opposes Christian churches), Wicca (nature worship that includes witchcraft), and Asatru (the name for a Nordic-based religion that reveres Odin) religions. In addition, some of the plaintiffs in this lawsuit included members of the Church of Jesus Christ Christian (CJCC), which has ties to an extremist group and criminal gang, the Aryan Nation. These inmates complained that Ohio prison officials, in violation of the RLUIPA, failed to accommodate their religious exercise in a variety of different ways, including retaliating and discriminating against them for exercising their nontraditional faiths, denying them access to religious literature, denying them the same opportunities for group worship granted to adherents of mainstream religions, forbidding them to adhere to the dress and appearance mandates of their religions, withholding religious ceremonial items substantially identical to those that the adherents of mainstream religions are permitted, and failing to provide a chaplain trained in their faith (*Cutter v. Wilkinson,* 2005, p. 713).

The Court unanimously decided in favor of the inmates and found that the state of Ohio had violated the rights of the inmates.

The Court concluded that the RLUIPA neither established nor promoted any specific religion nor interfered with religious observance, including the right to *not* observe a religion or belief system. Thus, the Court reasoned, the RLUIPA did not violate the Establishment or Free Exercise Clause.

SOURCES: See References section for all court cases and referencing of the Religious Land Use and Institutionalized Persons Act of 2000 (RLUIPA).

be accommodated so long as appropriate notice is given to prison administrators (Van Baalen, 2008). In these cases, the chaplain or another religious expert will aid security staff in providing the accommodations to ensure that misunderstandings are minimized.

Chaplain Functions and the ACCA

According to the American Correctional Chaplains Association, correctional chaplains are professionals who provide pastoral care to those who are imprisoned as well as to correctional facility staff and their families when requested. In early U.S. prison history, chaplains held positions of relative importance, which is not surprising considering they were part of a system created by religious groups. They were responsible for visiting inmates and providing services and sermons, and they also served as teachers, librarians, and record keepers. At times the chaplain would also act

***Cutter v. Wilkinson* (2005):** Held religious inmates do not have more legal rights than nonreligious inmates.

FOCUS TOPIC 14.3

Focus From the Inside With Ronald "Raúl" Drummer; Criminal Charge: Aggravated Battery and Attempted Armed Robbery

My quest for self-identification started when I realized my own failure to make rational decisions. I was constantly driven by either my environment, emotions, or a desire rooted in unrealistic expectations. As the result of years of pondering and searching, I developed the Triangular Approach to Complete Liberation in Prison (TACLP). The basic tenet to this is that we function best when we have persistent stimulation in all three realms of existence, consisting of the spiritual, mental, and physical.

During this time, I had a choice to give credence to a higher power in accordance with Alcoholics Anonymous and the 12 steps. I also tried to rely on self-education and Islam, and I even studied under a cult leader named Dr. Malachiz York. I was introduced to Christianity with emphasis on the death, burial, and resurrection of Jesus the Christ. I noticed that this belief system challenged me more than anything else in my life, thus far. After being in the faith for about 2 years and practicing for over 11 years, I observed two types of Christians. One used the notion that faith is all that is needed of a person (thereby remaining on the surface level of their spiritual development), whereas the other consisted of those brave souls who plunged into their commitment to the word with no reservations (there was no point of return). I wanted that sort of dedication, and it went so deep that it pierced my very heart.

However, I soon learned that the principles of the Bible would continually keep me at a crossroads. At every checkpoint I had to leave a piece of myself behind in order to advance to the next. This has made all the difference in my incarceration—total abandonment of my old way of thinking that would be inconsistent with what I now believed to be the truth. This process showed through my conduct in the prison. My disciplinary reports went down to none at all. I was once unapproachable—now people can hardly believe this is the same person they had known. In addition, prison officials liked to have me around and eventually trusted me with responsibilities. Most important of all, I had no "good time" incentives to influence my behavior based on early release. I simply was making these changes for my own good . . . and all the while I was serving "flat time" on my sentence.

With the spiritual aspect of development on the go, I eventually focused more on the mental aspects of functioning. With this, I focused on information dealing with addiction and drug rehabilitation. Although my faith was the rock, awareness of my addiction was the undergrowth. Taking classes in a therapeutic environment opened my mind to the threat of drug use to my body and mind. During this time, I delved into various philosophical readings and a series of thought-provoking tomes. Ultimately, my development of both spiritual and information-based areas gave me stability in mind and spirit, but I was still lacking in my physical development.

Robert Hanser

■ PHOTO 14.7 **Ronald Drummer, an inmate at Richwood Correctional Center, served as a dorm mentor in the Successful Treatment and Recovery (STAR) program. He stands here in front of a bookshelf that is part of the inmate library for the STAR program.**

While my introduction to exercise was a much needed step in the right direction, I lacked motivation to maintain my regimen. I applied the same technique to physical fitness as I did to discovering God and comprehending available information about drug addiction. I started out jogging around the prison. I pushed myself until I went from 245 pounds to 178 pounds. Through access to the prison facilities, I took advantage of weight lifting. It turned out that I was well suited for this form of exercise, and, once results started coming, I felt a sense of motivation and gratification that was unparalleled in the physical world.

For the first time in my life I had found my point and purpose in the most unlikely of places. Now, I am completely liberated in every area of my life, which is the ultimate goal of the TACLP. If I did not have access to these resources, I would still be mentally, spiritually, and physically impaired and unfit. Now I am able to smile without effort, laugh and not hurt, and love without restraint. My life started when I was locked up. My family is my fellow prisoners and the staff. We give each other hope. I am connected openly with my prison brothers and discreetly with the staff. Coming to prison was the best thing that happened to me. I am only sorry that the incident that led to my incarceration hurt the victim of the crime. At this point in my life, I thank my mom, dad, and family for the support throughout the years. Most of all, I thank God for giving me a willingness to change.

Mr. Drummer was incarcerated for over 19 years before being released on parole. He is now a house manager with Freed Men, Inc., a non-profit faith-based reentry organization. He also has recently become a certified fitness instructor and has worked for over a year as a fitness trainer.

SOURCE: Ronald Drummer. (2011, December 1). Personal interview. Used with permission.

CROSS-NATIONAL PERSPECTIVE 14.1

The Prison System of France and the Muslim Inmate Population

Home to Europe's biggest Muslim population and a robust counter-terrorism system, France has long kept a keen watch on Islamic radicalism. In recent years it has been spared big bombings of the kind seen in London and Madrid. But France is no stranger to attack by jihadists, and officials fear it is just a matter of time before they strike again.

The authorities are particularly worried about recruitment to militant Islam in France's overcrowded prisons. "French prisons are a preferred recruiting ground for radical Islamists," Michèle Alliot-Marie, the interior minister, told *Le Figaro* newspaper. She and her EU counterparts have been working on a joint handbook on how to counter the phenomenon, which touches many European countries, notably Britain. At the end of September, Ms. Alliot-Marie will host an EU seminar, in the heavily Muslim Paris *banlieue* of Saint-Denis, to discuss what to do.

Fiercely secular, France does not collect official statistics based on religion. But Farhad Khosrokhavar, a French specialist on the subject, estimates that Muslims make up well over half France's prison population—far higher than their 8% or so share of the total population. Among these there are currently some 1,100 people behind bars in France for terrorist-related activities, according to Alain Bauer, a criminologist. Ms. Alliot-Marie said that another 55 have been detained this year.

Proselytizing among inmates is common. Security officials are worried that many radicals jailed around the time of the 1998 football World Cup, hosted by France, are starting to be released. "Radicalised Islamists become more influential in prison," says Mr. Khosrokhavar. He reckons there are a few hundred Islamists actively recruiting behind bars in France.

It is hard to know how to counter this. Concentrating jihadists in one or two penitentiaries, as many countries do, may help them plot attacks from prison. Yet dispersing them, or regularly moving them between high-security prisons in order to disrupt networks, may spread radical ideology and increase recruitment.

Less crowded cells might help. France, whose jail population has grown by 30% since 2001, is building three new prisons to this end. Another idea is to provide more Muslim chaplains to offer a moderate spiritual outlet for Muslim inmates.

Azzedine Gaci, head of the Regional Council of the Muslim Faith in Lyon, makes such visits to the prison in Villefranche-sur-Saône, where he reckons 70% of its 700-odd inmates are Muslim. "They need a different interlocutor," he says. In the absence of competent chaplains, extremists fill the vacuum. France currently has 1,100 chaplains accredited to visit its 63,000 inmates across 195 prisons—yet only 117 of them are Muslim.

QUESTION 1: How might it aid security within French jails and prisons to add more Muslim chaplains to their overall count?

QUESTION 2: In your opinion, how appropriate is it for French administrators to have only 117 of their 1,100 accredited chaplains be of Muslim orientation when approximately half of all the country's inmates are Muslims by faith?

SOURCE: From "Jailhouse jihad: Fears that terrorism is breeding in French prisons" in *The Economist*, September 18, 2008.

as an ombudsman for the inmates when issues of maltreatment would arise. During the 1800s and early 1900s, chaplains were often viewed as naïve and easily duped by inmates. Almost in response to this perception, the clinical pastoral education movement emerged during the 1920s and 1930s and promoted the serious study of chaplaincy. This field of study applied the principles, resources, and methods of organized religion to the correctional setting in a structured, disciplined, and professionalized manner. This resulted in the development of competent professional chaplains who were able to meld with the rehabilitation ideas that surfaced from the 1930s through the 1960s.

Correctional chaplains are now recognized as integral professionals in the field of corrections. The **American Correctional Chaplains Association (ACCA)** is a national organization that provides representation and networking opportunities for chaplains who work in various correctional environments. The organization also provides members with research on best practices in the field of correctional chaplaincy. This organization also provides training and certification for correctional chaplains as a means of furthering the standards of service that these professionals provide.

American Correctional Chaplains Association (ACCA): Provides representation and networking for chaplains who work in correctional environments.

The specific types of religious groups vary from prison to prison and state to state. Nearly all state and federal correctional institutions provide support for at least some of the four traditional faith groups—Catholic, Protestant, Muslim, and Jewish. However, in recent years a

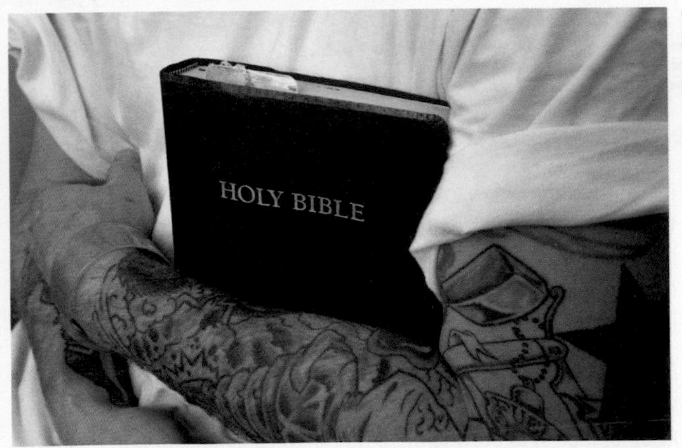

© Robin Nelson/ ZUMA/CORBIS

■ PHOTO 14.8 **Religious programming is an important element of the daily schedule in many correctional facilities.**

number of nontraditional religious groups have been established in prison environments. These include, but are not limited to, Hinduism, Mormonism, Native American religions, Buddhism, Rastafarianism, Hispanic religions (Curanderism, Santeria, Espiritismo), Jehovah's Witnesses, Christian Scientists, and two of the newest faith groups to enter correctional facilities, Witchcraft and Satanism. The religious programs and practices conducted by the different faith groups differ according to the beliefs of the group, inmate interest, amount of time and space available in the prison, competence of the religious staff, and the support of the correctional authorities. It is not uncommon for a large prison to have numerous religious services on a daily basis. As one can see, the role of the chaplain in modern corrections can be quite complicated, and this is, in part, what has led to the various legal challenges noted in this chapter.

Prison Tour Video Link
Religion Accomodations

Religious Volunteers

Religious volunteers are commonplace in most prison systems. In most cases, faith-based volunteers will desire to minister to their own religious groups, and they are likely to be part of a larger church membership outside the prison within the community. The availability of volunteers to assist religious staff is a boon, but it does have its limits. Most volunteers are not necessarily trained in clinical skills to provide professional counseling, and they are usually oblivious to many of the security practices necessary to operate a prison. Volunteers should be given very specific instructions regarding security at the very beginning of their involvement within a program. The volunteer, according to ACAA standards, should be provided some type of orientation, a tour of the prison, and materials that include a handbook and/or guidelines for the prison. The list of rules and regulations for inmates should also be provided to ensure that inmates cannot manipulate the volunteer into assisting them with something that is unauthorized.

Are Inmates Really Motivated by Religion?

There is perhaps a good deal of dissent among practitioners in the field of corrections when addressing the question of whether or not inmates are truly motivated by religion. According to Dammer (2002), there is a belief among many who work in prison environments that inmates "find religion" for manipulative reasons (p. 1375). However, though this may sometimes occur, there is evidence that inmates have received positive benefits resulting from their incarceration and religious practice (Dammer, 2002). Research by Johnson, Larson, and Pitts (1997) found that participants in religious programming had significantly fewer infractions while in prison than did inmates who did not participate in such programs. Even more convincing is the finding that inmates who participated frequently in religious programming services were less likely to be arrested when examined a year after their release. Thus, it would appear that prison religious programs have both short-term and long-term positive effects.

SAGE Journal Article Link
Religious Engagement in the Lives of Life-Sentenced Women

More recent research provides continued empirical evidence indicating that religious programming reduces crime and recidivism among adult offenders (Hercik, 2007). For instance, Johnson and Larson (2003) conducted a preliminary evaluation of the InnerChange Freedom Initiative, a faith-based prisoner reform program. Results show that program graduates were 50% less likely to be rearrested and 60% less likely to be reincarcerated during a 2-year follow-up period.

Contrary to dour views held by skeptics, numerous studies seem to demonstrate the efficacy of faith-based programs, both within the prison facility itself and later when offenders are released into the community. Thus, it appears that most inmates really are motivated by religious programming. With empirical quantitative evidence of positive outcomes, it should be concluded that religious programs in corrections are just as important as other forms of programming.

CONCLUSION

This chapter has provided an extensive overview of many of the typical programs offered to inmates within the prison environment. We have discussed basic services, such as food and medical services, and various types of programming, including educational, vocational, drug treatment, recreational, and religious. Though other types of programs are available to inmates, these types tend to be universal in their implementation, and they all tend to be used by nearly every inmate who serves time in the United States. This conclusion will not address each of these programs individually but will instead point toward one key theme that has been consistently mentioned throughout this chapter.

Students have learned that each of these programs works to improve inmate conditions within the prison and that each reduces observed infractions among inmates as well as the likelihood of lawsuits and/or prison riots. Further, most of these programs have legal requirements that make them at least marginally necessary within the prison environment. Regardless of whether each program is constitutionally required, it is clear that each provides benefits to both the inmates and the prison staff. This is an important observation because it can therefore be said that these programs reduce problems in prison facilities, and, even more encouraging, they reduce recidivism when inmates are released into the community. Thus, prison programming is a smart investment that saves taxpayers more money in the long term than it costs them and enhances public safety in future years when inmates are released from prison. To overlook the importance of prison programming is to be negligent in safeguarding our community's safety.

Want a better grade?

Get the tools you need to sharpen your study skills. Access practice quizzes, eFlashcards, video, and multimedia at **edge.sagepub.com/hanser2e**

SAGE edge™

DISCUSSION QUESTIONS

1. Provide an overview of one of the prison work programs presented in this chapter.
2. What are some distinct forms of programming that exist for female offenders?
3. What are some of the important legal issues associated with food services in corrections?
4. What are therapeutic communities? How are they utilized in prison facilities?
5. How do substance abuse treatment programs affect potential recidivism?
6. Discuss some of the concerns for administrators with different types of recreational programming (e.g., weight lifting).
7. Discuss at least two Supreme Court cases associated with religious programming in prisons. Be sure to explain why you selected those two cases for your discussion.
8. How can social learning mechanisms be both positive and negative within a prison environment? Provide an example of a treatment program that attempts to capitalize on the positive aspects and minimize the negative aspects.

SAGE edge™ **Test your understanding of chapter content. Take the practice quiz.**

KEY TERMS

American Correctional Chaplains Association (ACCA), 365

American Correctional Food Service Association (ACFSA), 344

Common fare, 345

English as a Second Language (ESL), 348

Federal Prison Industries Inc. (FPI), 348

General Educational Development (GED), 348

Health Insurance Portability and Accountability Act (HIPAA), 343

Minimal services view, 342

Mothers and Infants Nurturing Together (MINT), 344

Office of Correctional Education (OCE), 347

Pell Grants, 347

Post-Release Employment Project (PREP), 349

Prison food loaf, 345

Prison Industry Enhancement (PIE) Certification Program, 351

Recreation program administrator, 359

Successful Treatment of Addiction and Recovery (STAR) program, 358

Texas Correctional Industries (TCI), 350

The Summary, 355

Therapeutic recreation (TR), 360

Title IV of the Higher Education Act, 347

UNICOR Inc., 349

Windham School District, 350

Work Against Recidivism (WAR) program, 352

Work/education reform view, 342

Zimmer Amendment, 358

KEY CASES

Cooper v. Pate (1964), 363

Cruz v. Beto (1972), 363

Cutter v. Wilkinson (2005), 363

Fulwood v. Clemmer (1962), 363

LeMaire v. Maass (1993), 346

O'Lone v. Estate of Shabazz (1987), 363

Theriault v. Carlson (1977), 363

APPLIED EXERCISE 14.1

Students must conduct either a face-to-face or a phone interview with a staff person in a prison facility who works in one of the following fields: (1) inmate education, (2) job training, (3) recreational supervision, (4) substance abuse treatment, or (5) religious programming. The student should use the interview to gain the practitioner's insight and perspective on several key questions related to work in his or her field. Students must write the practitioner's responses, analyze those responses, and submit their draft by the deadline set by their instructor. Students should complete this application exercise as an essay that addresses each point below. The total word count should be 1,400 to 2,100 words.

When completing the interview, students should ask the following questions:

1. What are the most rewarding aspects of your job?
2. What are the most stressful aspects of your job?
3. How does your work help offenders to eventually reintegrate into society?
4. What are some challenges that you have in helping inmates?
5. Why did you choose to work in this field?
6. What type of training have you received for this line of work?
7. What would you recommend to someone who was interested in pursuing a similar career?

Students are required to provide contact information for the auxiliary staff member. While instructors will probably not need to contact him or her, it may become necessary so that they can validate the actual completion of an interview.

Name and title of correctional supervisor: ______________________

Correctional agency: ______________________

Practitioner's phone number: ______________________

Practitioner's e-mail address: ______________________

Name of student: ______________________

WHAT WOULD YOU DO?

You are a correctional officer assigned to the agricultural section of a minimum-security facility. Your facility is large, with over 2,800 inmates who live on the property, most of them in dorm-like structures. The classification of most of these inmates is either trustee or minimum security. None of them is known to be violent.

You have recently been assigned to a field squad run by several "field bosses," who are correctional officers with experience supervising inmates who work in agricultural settings. Each field boss has his or her own horse, field radio, revolver, and rifle to ensure that security is maintained during the day. The work is hot, and the inmates work very hard.

On your fourth day of work, you notice that the ranking officer, Sergeant Gunderson, allows two inmates, Dooley and Craft, to go off into a wooded section at the edge of the clearing. They emerge a little later and talk with the sergeant and then go back to work.

You watch this same routine continue during much of the month of July. You finally ask one of the other officers about what you've noticed, and he says, "You know, Mack, I just tend to watch over my assigned inmates and don't worry about too much else. So long as they ain't escaping and as long as the sarge is happy, I just stay out of it. Maybe they gotta use the restroom or something . . . like, maybe they got bladder control problems or something."

You ponder this, and after 2 more days, you decide to speak to Sergeant Gunderson himself about the situation.

Sergeant Gunderson eyes you for a moment, pushing his straw-rimmed Stetson hat back a bit on his forehead before speaking. "I wouldn't be worried about them. They're old trustees who never hurt nobody and will likely be here forever. They just wanna ride their time out, and I really don't see the need to rock the boat. Besides, you need to know that they have a long history with one of the assistant wardens here. Believe it or not, those two like to work this detail, but anytime that they want they can pick another detail at the dorm or elsewhere, and they'll get the job switch within 48 hours. They have their reasons, and I have mine, for why things work as they do. You understand?"

You nod. "Yeah, I get it," you say, and leave the issue alone.

However, later that day, you happen to observe the two inmates load a couple of watermelons into the back of a wagon holding work tools and sundry items. They also have several potatoes stacked on the wagon. They cover the produce with a tarp as you ride up and shoot each other worried looks. You ask them what they are doing.

Dooley responds, "We were just gonna see if there were any more work hoes available, but there aren't. Why? What's wrong, boss?"

You stare at him for a beat. "Nuthin'. Just thought I would see what was going on—you guys get back to work." You watch them turn and go toward the main group.

The next day, you wait until Sergeant Gunderson is preoccupied explaining the details of some work assignment to another officer. You quickly guide your horse to the edge of the woods where you have spotted Dooley and Craft disappear so often. You see a faint trail, and when your crane your neck, you spy at its end a small clearing containing a watermelon patch and several potato plants.

Knowing what you know about inmates and the prison subculture, you recognize these two items as being prime ingredients for making homemade alcohol. In fact, some officers who work the dorms have noted that some inmates have appeared drunk on recent occasions.

You look around for Sergeant Gunderson and see that Dooley and Craft have their backs to you, nearly 50 yards away. You gently pull the reins on your grey gelding so as not to turn him too quickly or too obviously. You ride slowly back to a post that provides a full field of vision over the inmates you are supervising. You count them and find that all are accounted for.

You turn over what you have just discovered in your mind. You think, *Those two inmates are growing products to make alcohol, and Gunderson is allowing it.* You wonder how long this has been going on and who else might know about it.

Squinting up at the hot sun, you mutter to yourself, ***What would you do?***

15 PAROLE AND REINTEGRATION

MAKING PAROLE

Rob Hanser drove down the winding, seemingly endless country road, making his way to David Wade Correctional Center for a parole hearing. He arrived at the prison and parked in the visitor's section. As he pulled the keys from his ignition, he glanced over and saw a car parked two spaces away from him. Some people were in the car but did not get out. He thought they looked similar to some photos he had seen before.

Hanser got out of his car, walked over to the other car, and waved through the windshield. Sure enough, it was Ronald's mother and sister.

Hanser leaned down and spoke through the open driver's window. "Ms. Drummer?"

The lady in the car said, "Yes, are you Dr. Hanser?"

"Yes ma'am, I am; it is nice to finally meet!"

The two women, Linda Drummer (Ronald's mother) and Laquitter—pronounced Laquitta—Drummer (Ronald's sister), got out of the car and exchanged introductions and small talk. After these formalities, all three walked toward the entrance to the prison. At the gate, they provided their IDs to the guard and waited.

They were escorted into the building, went through security, and were patted down to ensure that they were not bringing contraband into the prison. Once inside the waiting room, Linda beamed as she saw her son, Ronald "Raúl" Drummer, enter the room. The four sat together at a table.

"How you doing?" Hanser asked Ronald.

"I'm good, just a little nervous, but that's normal, right?"

After about 30 minutes of waiting, Ronald, his family members, and Hanser were in the parole interview room. It was not a large room and, as it turned out, the parole board was in Baton Rouge doing the interview remotely. The board members asked questions of Ronald regarding his job prospects and his place of residence, and they commented on how many courses and programs that he had finished. Then they asked about a letter that had been written.

One of the members said, "I see this letter from the director of your program. . . . Looks like it is from Dr. Hanser; is he here?"

Hanser spoke up. "Yes, sir, I am here."

The board asked Hanser if he wanted to add any comments, noting that the letter very clearly supported granting Ronald parole and that it had provided some very convincing narrative to that end.

Hanser stated, "Well, first I would like to say that I don't do this very often. I get a lot of guys ask me to write them letters and such, but I usually don't do it. I only write a letter if I am completely convinced of my appraisal. I certainly don't travel and speak on their behalf unless I'm certain of them. I can say with 100% certainty that Mr. Drummer exceeds all expectations as a mentor in our program. He is intelligent, motivated, and sincere in his efforts. Further, I and several of my colleagues with Freedmen Inc. will keep our eye on him. He will be staying at one of our reentry homes and will be employed with us there. He will also continue his peer support meetings, Bible studies, and other forms of programming in the community. I can ensure that."

After this, the board deliberated a bit and had Ronald, his family, and Hanser step out for a few moments.

When they were summoned back in, the board made its announcement. The head of the panel said, "Mr. Drummer, we are impressed with your record and the fact that you have gone well beyond what you needed to do, minimally, to qualify. You also really seem to have everything in place in the community to help you succeed." The board member paused for a moment, and all that could be heard was the shuffling of some papers. Then he spoke again. "So

LEARNING OBJECTIVES:

1. Define *parole* and basic parolee characteristics.
2. Discuss the historical development of parole.
3. Know and understand the basics regarding state parole, its organization, and its administration.
4. Evaluate the use of parole as a correctional release valve for prisons.
5. Describe the role of parole officers.
6. Explain the common conditions of parole and how parole effectiveness can be refined and adjusted to better meet supervision requirements that are based on the offender's behavior.
7. Be able to discuss the parole selection process, factors influencing parole decisions, and factors considered when granting and denying parole.
8. Describe the process for violations of parole, parole warrants, and parole revocation proceedings.

SAGE edge™

Get the edge on your studies: edge.sagepub.com/hanser2e

- Take a quiz to find out what you've learned.
- Review key terms with eFlashcards.
- Watch videos that enhance chapter content.

Mr. Drummer, what I am saying is that we have unanimously decided to award parole. Congratulations."

Linda Drummer let out a shout of excitement, Laquitter clapped her hands in amazement, and Ronald gave the board a wide grin in response.

"Now, Mr. Drummer, you will have some fees, some community service to perform, and, in addition, we're going to require that you commit to volunteering some of your time to speaking to kids at schools or social events on the hazards of drug use and a criminal lifestyle."

"Yes, sir, I understand," said Ronald.

The board allowed for the family to celebrate for a moment, congratulated Ronald again, and then noted that they had a long docket for the day.

Since that time, Ronald Drummer has been the house manager of his reentry home for Freedmen Inc. for over a year. He has also held a full-time job at Planet Fitness for over a year and has received two pay raises. He is studying to become a certified fitness trainer. He has served a leadership role in several community-based intervention programs and has spoken to numerous middle and high school students on the vagaries of the criminal lifestyle. By all accounts, he has been successful and productive while on parole.

INTRODUCTION

This chapter addresses a type of offender outcome that represents a successful end to his or her incarceration experience: the release from prison on parole. This response to offender behavior falls within the field of corrections but comes at the end of the institutional process. This early release from prison reflects the fact that the offender has been well behaved in prison and represents a new beginning for that offender; basically, it is a reward for his or her prosocial behavior in prison. It should be pointed out that the parolee population tends to be quite small within the community-based correctional population when compared with the probation population. Further, the parolee population exists within only a select number of states. This chapter is provided primarily to ensure that this text is complete in its presentation of the correctional system, but it should not be viewed as a fully comprehensive authority on the use of parole.

PAROLE AND PAROLEE CHARACTERISTICS

Parole: The early release of an offender from a secure facility upon completion of a certain portion of his or her sentence.

Parole is a mechanism that has been nearly as controversial as the death penalty (for more on this topic, students should refer to Chapter 16). Parole has had a tortured history, resulting in a slow and ongoing effort to eliminate and/or restrict its use in the federal system, and it has also been eliminated in many states throughout the nation. Nevertheless, a substantial number of inmates are on parole throughout the nation, with some of them still serving the remainder of their sentences under the outdated federal system. **Parole** can be defined as the early release of an offender from a secure facility upon completion of a certain portion of their sentence; the remainder of their sentence is served in the community. As of 2013, the nation's parole population had grown slightly to 853,200 offenders. Mandatory releases from prison due to good time provisions accounted for nearly 50% of those offenders who were released on parole (Herberman & Bonczar, 2013). Figure 15.1 shows that the number of individuals on parole has remained fairly stable from 2010 through 2013.

Robert Hanser

■ PHOTO 15.1 Parole means that offenders will have many more options than might be encountered in a dayroom such as the one shown in this photo.

Among those on parole, roughly 1 out of every 8 is a female offender. During the past decade, the proportion of female parolees has increased from 10% to 12%, a number that remained stable through 2013. The percentage of parolees who are

■ **Figure 15.1: Adults on Parole at Year-End, 2000–2013**

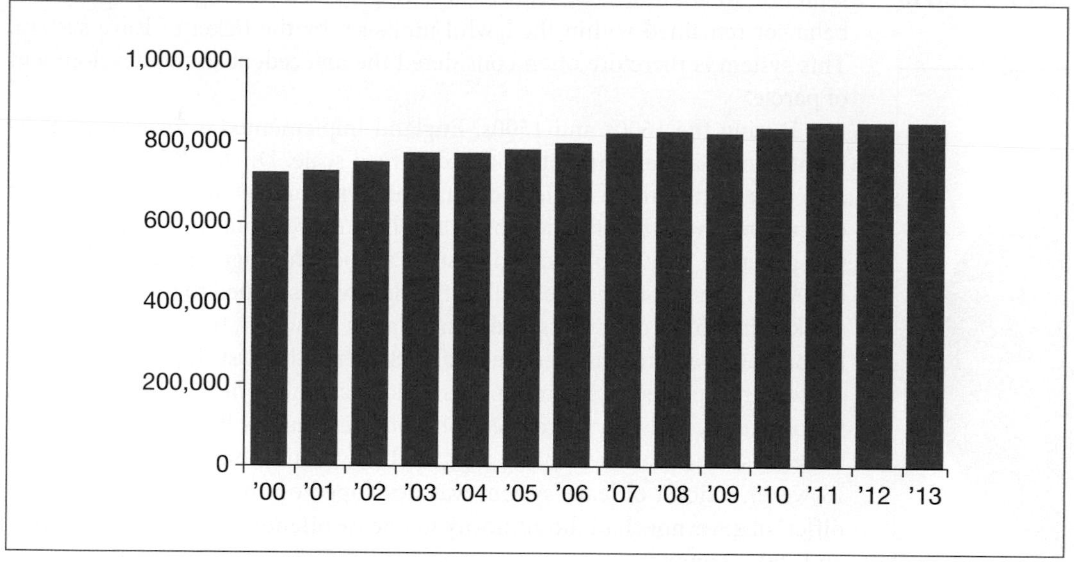

SOURCE: Herberman, E. J., & Bonczar, T. P. (2015). *Probation and parole in the United States, 2013.* Washington, DC: Bureau of Justice Statistics.

African American tends to be around 38%. The proportion of Caucasian parolees has increased during the past several years, comprising 43% of the overall parole population in 2013. Roughly 17% of all parolees nationwide are Latino American, and another 2% come from other racial categories. Lastly, the majority of parolees were convicted of drug offenses, with 32% of the total parolee population having some drug-related conviction. Another 29% had convictions for violent offenses, and another 22% for property offenses. Figure 15.2 provides an examination of the U.S. parole population by offense.

Lastly, when considering outcomes for parolees around the nation, it has been found that about 9.3% of all parolees were reincarcerated in 2013, which is approximately the same as in 2012 (see Figure 15.3). The 2013 data shows that the rate of parolees going back to prison for violating the terms of their parole was 5.4%, whereas those who went to prison due to committing a new, separate, criminal violation resulting in a new sentence was about 3% (Herberman & Bonczcar, 2015). As can be seen in Figure 15.3, revocations of parole have gone down substantially from about 2011 to 2013, and the percentage of parolees who commit new criminal violations (thereby getting a new sentence) is already low and appears on track to further decline. Thus, one might conclude that, overall, parole is proving to be a viable option for offender supervision.

Ticket of leave: A permit given to a convict in exchange for a certain period of good conduct.

THE BEGINNING HISTORY OF PAROLE

The development of parole is attributed to two primary figures: Alexander Maconochie and Sir Walter Crofton. Alexander Maconochie was in charge of the penal colony at Norfolk Island during the 1840s, and Sir Walter Crofton directed the prison system of Ireland in the 1850s. While Maconochie first developed a general scheme for parole, it was Crofton who later refined the idea and created what was referred to as the **ticket of leave**. The ticket of leave was basically a permit that was given to an offender in exchange for a certain period of good conduct. Through this process, the prisoner could

Prison Tour Video: Parole Decisions. There are many factors to consider when evaluating an inmate for parole. Watch a warden discuss the role correctional officers play in parole decisions.

Figure 15.2: Parolee Characteristics by Type of Offense in 2013

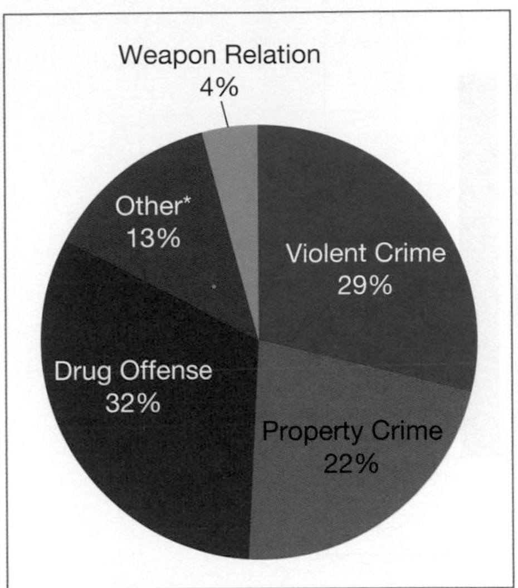

SOURCE: Herberman, E. J., & Bonczar, T. P. (2015). *Probation and parole in the United States, 2013.* Washington, DC: Bureau of Justice Statistics.

*Includes public order offenses

instead earn his own wage through his own labor prior to the expiration of his sentence. In addition, other liberties were provided so long as the prisoner's behavior remained within the lawful limits set by the ticket of leave system. This system is therefore often considered the antecedent to the development of parole.

During the 1600s and 1500s, England implemented a form of punishment known as banishment on a widespread scale. During this time, criminals were sent to the American colonies under reprieve and through stays of execution. Thus, the offenders had their lives spared, but this form of mercy was generally only implemented to solve a labor shortage that existed within the American colonies. Essentially, offenders were shipped to the Americas to work as indentured servants under hard labor. However, the American Revolution put an end to this practice until 1788 when the first shipload of prisoners was transported to Australia. Australia became the new dumping ground for offenders, and they were used for labor here just as they had been in the Americas. The labor was hard, and the living conditions were challenging. However, a ticket of leave system was developed on this continent in which different governors had the authority to release offenders who displayed good and stable conduct.

In 1840, Alexander Maconochie, a captain in the Royal Navy, was placed in command over the English penal colony in New South Wales at Norfolk Island, which was nearly 1,000 miles off the eastern coast of Australia. The prisoners at Norfolk Island were the worst of the worst; they had already been shipped to Australia for criminal acts committed in England only to be later shipped to Norfolk Island due to additional criminal acts or forms of misconduct committed while serving time in Australia. The conditions on Norfolk Island were deplorable—so much so that many convicts preferred to be given the death penalty rather than serve time upon the island (Latessa & Allen, 1999).

Figure 15.3: Estimated Percentage of the Parole Population Returned to Incarceration, 2000–2013

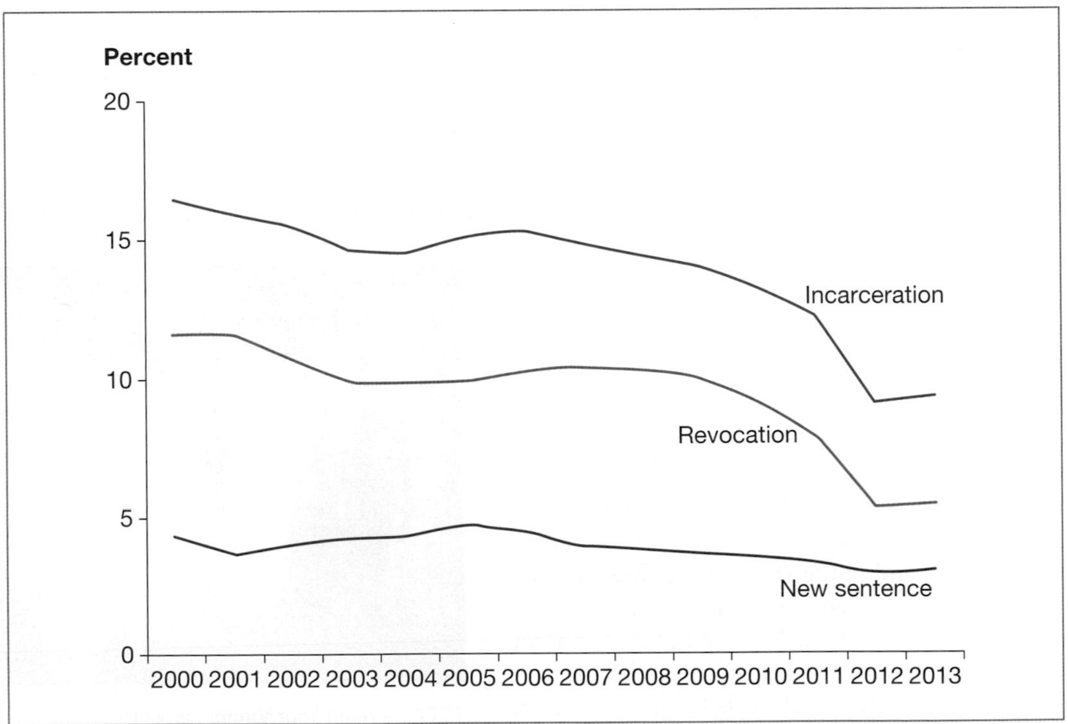

SOURCE: Herberman, E. J., & Bonczar, T. P. (2015). *Probation and parole in the United States, 2013.* Washington, DC: Bureau of Justice Statistics.

While serving in this command, Maconochie proposed a system where the duration of the sentence was determined by the inmate's work habits and righteous conduct. Though this was already in use in a crude manner through the ticket of leave process in Australia, Maconochie created a **mark system** in which "marks" were provided to the offender for each day of successful toil. This system was quite well organized and thought out. It was based on five main tenets, as described by Barnes and Teeters (1959, p. 419):

1. Release should be based not on the completing of a sentence for a set period of time but on completion of a determined and specified quantity of labor. In brief, time sentences should be abolished and task sentences substantiated.
2. The quantity of labor a prisoner must perform should be expressed in a number of "marks" that he must earn, by improvement of conduct, frugality of living, and habits of industry, before he can be released.
3. While in prison he should earn everything he receives. All sustenance and indulgences should be added to his debt of marks.
4. When qualified by discipline to do so, he should work in association with a small number of other prisoners, forming a group of six or seven, and the whole group should be answerable for the conduct of labor of each member.
5. In the final stage, a prisoner, while still obliged to earn his daily tally of marks, should be given a proprietary interest in his own labor and be subject to a less rigorous discipline, to prepare him for release into society.

Under this plan, as first described in Chapter 1, offenders were given marks and moved through phases of supervision until they finally earned full release. Because of this, Maconochie's system is considered indeterminate in nature, with offenders progressing through his five specific phases of classification: (1) strict incarceration, (2) intense labor in forced work group or chain gang, (3) limited freedom within a prescribed area, (4) a ticket of leave, and (5) full freedom. This system was based on the premise that inmates should be gradually prepared for full release. Due to the use of primitive versions of indeterminate and intermediate sanctioning utilized, Maconochie's mark system is perhaps best thought of as a precursor to both parole and the use of classification systems for offenders. Maconochie's system provided a guide to predicting the likelihood of success with an offender, making his process well ahead of its time.

However, Maconochie's system appears to have been *too* far ahead of its time; many government officials, influential persons, and even ordinary citizens in both Australia and England believed this approach was too soft on criminals. (This is not much different from today, when prisons and punitive sanctions are the preferred forms of punishment in the opinion of most Americans.) For his part, Maconochie was fond of criticizing prison operations in England; he believed that confinement ought to be rehabilitative in nature rather than punitive (note that this is consistent with the insights of John Augustus and his views on the use of probation). Due to the unpopularity of his ideas, Maconochie was ultimately dismissed from his post on Norfolk Island for being too lenient with offenders. Nevertheless, Maconochie was persistent, and in 1853 he successfully lobbied for the **English Penal Servitude Act**, which established several rehabilitation programs for offenders.

The English Penal Servitude Act of 1853 applied to prisons in both England and Ireland. Though Maconochie had spearheaded this act to solidify, legalize, and make permanent the use of ticket of leave systems, the primary reason for this act's success had more to do with the fact that free Australians were becoming ever more resistant to the use of Australia as the location for banished English prisoners. Though this act did not necessarily eliminate the use of banishment in England, it did provide incentive and suggestions for more extensive use of prisons. This law provided guidelines for the length of time that inmates should serve behind bars before being granted a ticket of leave and served as the basis for a general form of parole. The conditions mentioned in the English Penal Servitude Act of 1853 are also common to today's use of parole in the United States, though, of course, there are now many more technical aspects involved. However, the guidelines clearly stated that the offender's early release was contingent on his or her continued good behavior and avoidance of crime and criminogenic influences. Because of

Mark system: A system where the duration of the sentence was determined by the inmate's work habits and righteous conduct.

English Penal Servitude Act: Established several rehabilitation programs for convicts.

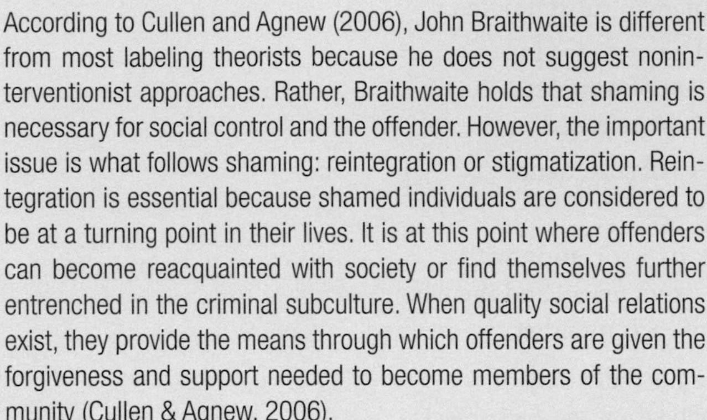

APPLIED THEORY 15.1

Braithwaite's Crime, Shame, and Reintegration as Related to Parole

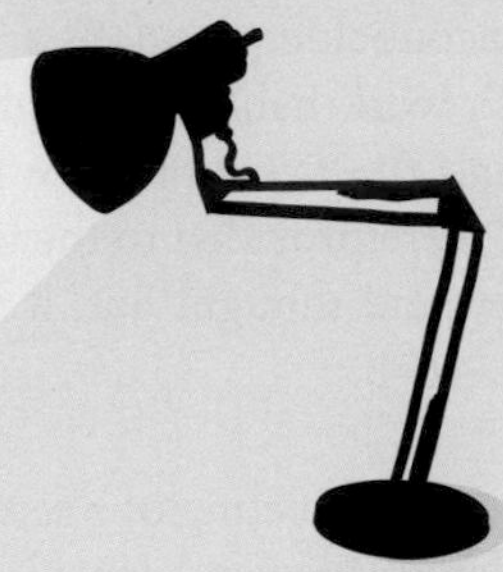

According to Cullen and Agnew (2006), John Braithwaite is different from most labeling theorists because he does not suggest noninterventionist approaches. Rather, Braithwaite holds that shaming is necessary for social control and the offender. However, the important issue is what follows shaming: reintegration or stigmatization. Reintegration is essential because shamed individuals are considered to be at a turning point in their lives. It is at this point where offenders can become reacquainted with society or find themselves further entrenched in the criminal subculture. When quality social relations exist, they provide the means through which offenders are given the forgiveness and support needed to become members of the community (Cullen & Agnew, 2006).

According to Cullen and Agnew (2006), "Restorative justice programs most closely mirror Braithwaite's admonition to meld shaming with reintegration" (p. 277). Restorative justice programs seek to restore and heal the victim, repair the damage to the community, and reintegrate offenders after they have made their commitment to the victim. From this point, "repentant offenders potentially are granted a measure of forgiveness by victims and are reaccepted by their family and community" (p. 277). These attempts at shaming and further reintegration provide much more effective alternatives to stigmatizing sanctions used in the criminal justice system.

In this chapter, the mention of reintegration is particularly important since these offenders will be reentering the community after serving years in prison. In addition, the "measure of forgiveness" that Cullen and Agnew (2006) refer to is important since this will be a necessary ingredient if offenders are to have a chance at reintegrating into the community. Thus, Braithwaite's work specifically applies to the reintegration of paroled offenders and explains that, although reconnection with the community is the primary end goal, there is a shaming element that is both proper and necessary. In other words, there must be a genuine consequence to aberrant and/or illegal behavior if the learning mechanisms are to take place. However, once those consequences have been meted out and once the offender has experienced the full impact of those consequences, society has an ethical obligation to cease and desist from applying additional consequences to the offender; to do so is unethical, disproportional, and unproductive. In fact, excessive consequences that go beyond the norm are likely to produce more crime.

Given that there are serious labeling implications for ex-cons well after they have served their term in prison, it is clear that the consequences continue to follow them long after they have completed the duration of their sentence. This is true even after they finish their parole or early release obligations. Further, these additional consequences affect the prior offender's ability to obtain jobs and necessary resources to function in society. Because of these consequences, the punishments are perhaps excessive, and high recidivism rates are therefore to be expected.

The primary point to Braithwaite's work is that a shaming process is indeed necessary and should be public and hold the offender accountable. However, once that process of accountability has been fulfilled, society must then assume the burden of reintegrating the offender back within the community. Otherwise, we should not be at all surprised when individuals turn back to criminal behavior. In fact, when we fail to offer the chance for reintegration, we essentially have contributed to the recidivism. As a society, it could be argued that if we continue to add consequences beyond the original sentence, and if we do this with the knowledge that it is likely to increase recidivism, then we essentially encourage further criminality among those in need of our support and guidance.

SOURCE: Cullen, F. T., & Agnew, R. (2006). *Criminological theory: Past to present* (3rd ed.). Los Angeles, CA: Roxbury Publishing Company.

his work spearheading this act, his advocacy for other significant improvements in penal policies in England, and his contributions to early release provisions in England, Maconochie has been dubbed the **Father of Parole**.

During the 1850s, as first described in Chapter 8, Sir Walter Crofton was the director of the Irish penal system. Crofton was familiar with Maconochie's ideas, which he drew upon to create a classification system for the Irish prison system. In this system, an inmate's classification level was measured by the number of marks that he had earned for good conduct, work output, and educational achievement. This idea was, quite obviously, borrowed from Maconochie's system on Norfolk Island. It is important to point out that the Irish system developed by Crofton was much more detailed. It provided specific written instructions and guidelines that provided for close supervision and control of the offender and the use of police personnel to supervise released offenders in rural areas. It also called for an inspector of released prisoners in the city of Dublin (Cromwell et al., 2002).

Father of Parole: Alexander Maconochie, so named due to his creation of the mark system, a precursor to modern-day parole.

Release was contingent upon certain conditions—for example, offenders had to submit monthly reports to either a police officer or another designated person and curtail their social involvements. Violations of these conditions could lead to reincarceration. This obviously is similar to modern-day parole programs. In fact, it could be said that contemporary uses of parole in the United States mimic the conditions set forth by Sir Walter Crofton in Ireland.

Parole From 1960 Onward

From 1930 through the 1950s, correctional thought reflected the medical model, which centered on the use of rehabilitation and treatment of offenders (see Chapter 2). The medical model presumed that criminal behavior was caused by social, psychological, or biological deficiencies that were correctable through treatment interventions. The 1950s were particularly given to the ideology of the medical model, with influential states such as Illinois, New York, and California turning to this type of treatment. In general, support for the medical model of corrections began to dissipate during the late 1960s and had all but disappeared by the 1970s.

The reintegration era, which lasted until the late 1970s, advocated for very limited use of incarceration; only a small proportion of offenders were imprisoned, and short periods of incarceration were most commonly recommended. Probation was the preferred sentence, particularly for nonviolent offenders. Indeterminate sentences were utilized, and deinstitutionalization was the theme for this period of corrections. However, this era in corrections was short-lived and received a great deal of criticism. Indeed, the prior medical model of corrections had hardly come to its full conclusion before the reintegration model was also being seriously questioned by skeptics.

Prison Tour Video Link
Counseling as a Profession

The mid- to late 1970s saw a slowly emerging shift in corrections thought due to high crime rates that were primarily perceived as the result of high recidivism among offenders. Skepticism of rehabilitation was brought to its pinnacle by practitioners who cited (often in an inaccurate manner) the work of Robert Martinson. As students may remember from Chapter 2, Martinson conducted a thorough analysis of research programs on behalf of the New York State Governor's Special Committee on Criminal Offenders. Martinson (1974) examined a number of various programs that included educational and vocational assistance, mental health treatment, medical treatment, early release, and so forth. In his report, often referred to as the Martinson Report, he noted that "with few and isolated exceptions, the rehabilitative efforts that have been reported so far have had no appreciable effect on recidivism" (Martinson, 1974, p. 22).

From this point forward, there was a clear shift from a community model of corrections to what has been referred to as a crime control model of corrections (see Chapter 1). During the late 1970s and throughout the 1980s, crime was a hotly debated topic that often became intertwined with political agendas and legislative action. The sour view of rehabilitation led many states to abolish the use of parole. Indeed, from 1976 onward, more than 14 states and the federal government abolished the use of parole. The state of Maine abolished parole in 1976, followed by California's elimination of discretionary parole in 1978, and then the full elimination of parole in Arizona, Delaware, Illinois, Indiana, Kansas, Minnesota, Mississippi, New Mexico, North Carolina, Ohio, Oregon, Virginia, and Washington (Sieh, 2006). In addition, the federal system of parole was also phased out over time. Under the Comprehensive Crime Control Act of 1984, the U.S. Parole Commission only retained jurisdiction over offenders who had committed their offense prior to November 1, 1987. The act also provided for the abolition of the Parole Commission over the years that followed, with this phasing-out period extended by the **Parole Commission Phaseout Act of 1996**. This act extended the life of the Parole Commission until November 1, 2002, but only in regard to supervising offenders who were still on parole from previous years. Thus, though the Parole Commission continued to exist, continued use of parole was eliminated, and federal parole offices across the nation were slowly shut down over time (see Figure 15.4 for further information on various developments in parole).

Parole Commission Phaseout Act of 1996: Extended the life of the Parole Commission until November 1, 2002, but only in regard to supervising offenders who were still on parole from previous years.

In addition to eliminating parole, many states implemented determinate sentencing laws, truth-in-sentencing laws, and other such innovations that were designed to keep offenders behind bars for longer periods of time. The obvious flavor of corrections in the 1980s was toward crime control through a correctional ideology of incapacitation. This same crime control orientation continued through the 1990s and even through the beginning of the new millennium, with an emphasis on drug offenders and habitual offenders during the 1990s. Also of note were developments in intensive supervision probation (ISP), more stringent bail requirements, and the use of

■ Figure 15.4: Historical Developments in Parole

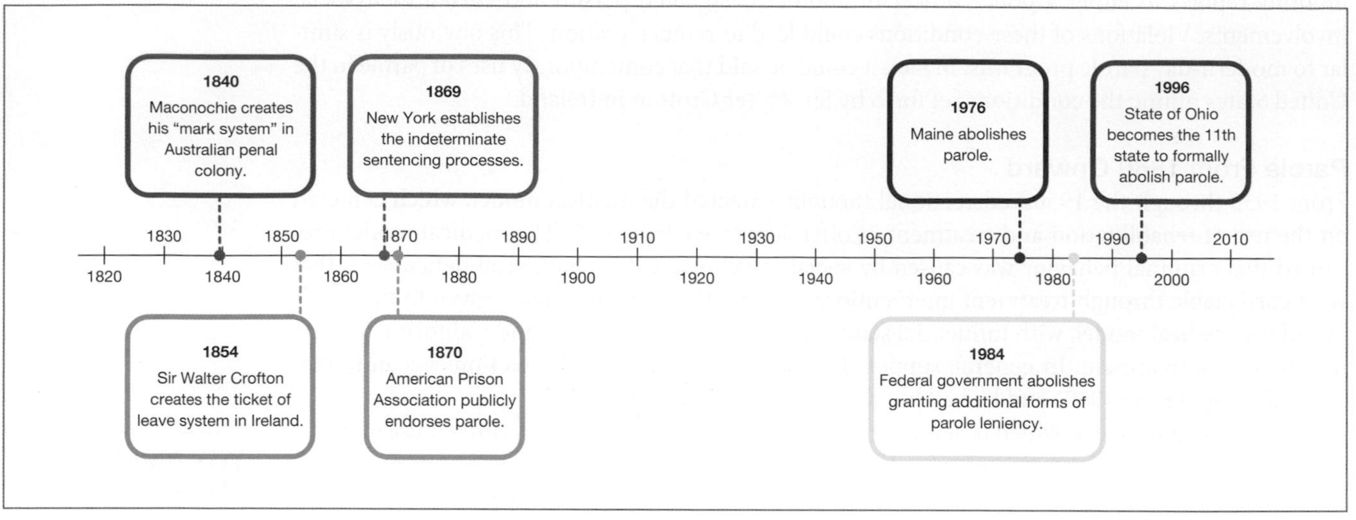

SOURCE: Adapted from the Association of Paroling Authorities International (2001). *Parole Board Survey.*

three-strikes penalties. The period during the last half of the 1990s and beyond the year 2000 had a decidedly punitive approach. The costs (both economic and social) have received a great deal of scrutiny even though crime rates lowered during the new millennium. Though there was a dip in crime during this time, it was not necessarily made clear if this was, in actuality, due to the higher rate of imprisonment or due to other demographic factors that impacted the nation. Further, as we have seen during recent years, this led to correctional systems having to implement mass forms of early release of inmate populations that had swollen during the 1990s and early 2000s. This has very serious potential implications for meeting public safety objectives in corrections.

History of Federal Parole and Supervised Release

Parole of federal inmates began after enactment of legislation on June 25, 1910. At that time, there were three federal penitentiaries, and parole was granted by a parole board at each institution, with the membership of each parole board consisting of the warden of the institution, the physician of the institution, and the superintendent of prisons. By 1930, a single Board of Parole in Washington, D.C., was established. This board consisted of three full-time members appointed by the attorney general. The Federal Bureau of Prisons performed the administrative functions of the board. In August 1945, the attorney general ordered that the board report directly to him for administrative purposes. In August 1948, due to a postwar increase in prison population, the attorney general appointed two additional members to the board, increasing it to five members (Hoffman, 2003).

Legislation in 1950 saw the board increase to eight members who served 6-year terms. The board was placed in the Department of Justice for administrative purposes. Three of the eight members were designated by the attorney general to serve as the Youth Corrections Division pursuant to the Youth Corrections Act. In October 1972, the board began a pilot reorganization project that eventually included the establishment of five regions, the creation of explicit guidelines for parole release decision making, the provision of written reasons for parole decisions, and an administrative appeal process (Hoffman, 2003).

Parole Commission and Reorganization Act: Established the U.S. Parole Commission as an independent agency within the Department of Justice.

Comprehensive Crime Control Act of 1984: Created a U.S. Sentencing Commission to establish federal sentencing guidelines favoring determinate sentences.

In May 1976, the **Parole Commission and Reorganization Act** took effect. This act retitled the Board of Parole as the U.S. Parole Commission and established it as an independent agency within the Department of Justice (Hoffman, 2003). The act provided for nine commissioners appointed by the president, with the advice and consent of the Senate, for 6-year terms. These members included a chair, five regional commissioners, and a three-member National Appeals Board. In addition, the act incorporated the major features of the Board of Parole's pilot reorganization project that were listed above.

Eight years later, the **Comprehensive Crime Control Act of 1984** created the U.S. Sentencing Commission to establish sentencing guidelines for the federal courts and established a regimen of determinate sentences (Hoffman, 2003). The chair of the Parole Commission is an ex-officio, nonvoting member of the Sentencing Commission. The decision to establish sentencing guidelines was based in large part on the success of the Parole Commission in developing and implementing its parole guidelines. In 1987, the Sentencing Commission submitted to Congress its initial set of sentencing guidelines, which took effect that year. As set forth by the Crime Control Act, offenders whose acts were committed on or after November 1, 1987, serve determinate terms under the sentencing guidelines and are not eligible for parole consideration (Hoffman, 2003).

■ PHOTO 15.2 This inmate stands before the parole board, answering questions regarding his eligibility for early release.

As per the Sentencing Commission's guidelines, parole for federal inmates was essentially abolished, but the use of supervised release from federal prisons was not entirely eliminated. While official parole and the use of parole boards no longer exist within the federal justice system, the modified version of early release is afforded some federal inmates based on requisites related to sentence completion. This post-release supervision is termed **supervised release** and is provided as a separate part of the sentence under the jurisdiction of the court. This type of early release is administered by the sentencing court for a given inmate, similar to community supervision under probation. In the federal system, the court, not the parole board, has the authority to impose sanctions on released inmates if they violate the terms or conditions of their supervision.

The Comprehensive Crime Control Act of 1984 provided for the official abolition of the Parole Commission on November 1, 1992, 5 years after the sentencing guidelines took effect. This phase-out provision did not adequately provide for persons sentenced under the law in effect prior to November 1, 1987, who had not yet completed their sentences. Elimination of, or reduction in, parole eligibility for such cases raised a serious ex post facto issue. To address this problem, the **Judicial Improvements Act of 1990** extended the life of the Parole Commission until November 1, 1997 (Hoffman, 2003). However, this extension still did not sufficiently address the complexities related to the residual paroled population, and this resulted in yet another act, the Parole Commission Phaseout Act of 1996, which again extended the life of the Parole Commission, this time until 2002. In addition, it required the attorney general to report to Congress annually beginning in 1998 on whether it was more cost-effective for the Parole Commission to continue as a separate agency or for its remaining functions to be transferred elsewhere. It is important to note the U.S. attorney general has reported each year that it is more cost-effective for the Parole Commission to continue as a separate agency. After the Phaseout Act's date expired, the 21st Century Department of Justice Appropriations Authorization Act of 2002 extended the life of the Parole Commission until November 1, 2005.

Currently, the U.S. Sentencing Commission oversees the supervision of offenders who leave federal confinement early due to credit for good behavior. According to the *2007 Federal Guidelines Manual*, the court:

> is required to impose a term of supervised release to follow imprisonment if a sentence of imprisonment of more than one year is imposed or if a term of supervised release is required by a specific statute. The court may depart from this guideline and not impose a term of supervised release if it determines that supervised release is neither required by statute nor required for any of the following reasons: (1) to protect the public welfare; (2) to enforce a financial condition; (3) to provide drug or alcohol treatment or testing; (4) to assist the reintegration of the defendant into the community; or (5) to accomplish any other sentencing purpose authorized by statute.

Supervised release: Postrelease supervision.

Judicial Improvements Act of 1990: Extended the life of the Parole Commission until November 1, 1997.

Though the Sentencing Commission oversees the majority of federal offenders released from prison, there is apparent support for the continued use of the Parole Commission. On July 21,

2008, during the meeting of the 110th session of Congress, the **United States Parole Commission Extension Act of 2008** was passed to provide for the continued performance of the Parole Commission (U.S. Congress, 2008). It became Public Law No. 110-312. So strong was support for this act that the initial bill passed in the Senate by unanimous consent and was ultimately signed by then-president George Bush (GovTrack.us, 2010).

From this brief discussion of federal parole, it should be clear that this mechanism is a vestige from the past, but it continues to reemerge as an operational organization. Although it is unknown if federal parole will ever return to its previous prominence, it is clear that the federal system, like the state systems, will continue to need to supervise offenders released from prison, regardless of the agency mechanism that is ultimately used.

PAROLE AT THE STATE LEVEL

Video Link
New York's Broken Parole System

With respect to the administration and organization of parole boards, it is clear that there is a great deal of variation in their structure and implementation. Table 15.1 shows that state parole board systems select members through a variety of means (most typically including selection by the state's governor). Factors such as the term of service for parole board members, the number of persons serving on parole boards, and the use of either part-time or full-time members vary greatly from state to state. The types of activities that each board may perform and/or the sources of information that each board may use also vary greatly. This demonstrates that there is a great deal of disparity throughout the United States among the top organizationally ranked decision-making bodies that decide on issues related to parole.

The variation in state implementation of the day-to-day supervision of parolees (for example, either as a separate function or combined with probation caseloads) and the variation that exists among parole boards themselves make it clear that the entire organizational structure can be quite complicated. However, there is a great deal of similarity in the types of laws, forms of supervision, and regulations that are required throughout the nation. While each state has the right and ability to administer community supervision functions in a manner that is most suitable for that state, there are as many similarities between probation and parole programs around the nation as there are differences.

United States Parole Commission Extension Act of 2008: Provided for the continued performance of the U.S. Parole Commission.

Table 15.1: State Parole Board Appointments, Structure, Terms, and Functions From Selected States

	Governor Appoint	Leg. Confirm.	Term Years	Number on the Board	F (Full) or P (Part) Time	Use of Parole Analysis
California	X	X	7	6	F	YES
Florida	X	X	6	3	F	YES(1)(2)
Louisiana	X	X	11	7	F	NO
New Jersey	X	X	6	15	F	YES(1)
Ohio	Dir. of Corr.		Life	9	F	YES(2)(4)
Texas	X	X	6	18	F	YES(3)
Wisconsin	X	X	2(5)	7	F	NO

SOURCE: Adapted from the Association of Paroling Authorities, International. (2001). *Parole board survey.*

(1) Case reports writing and interviews.

(2) Hold probable cause hearings

(3) Hold revocation hearings

(4) Hold parole consideration hearings

(5) The chair 2 years, others on merit

The Granting of Parole in State Systems

In most states, offender cases are assigned to various individual parole board members who are tasked with reviewing the case so that they can formulate their initial recommendations. The recommendations that they provide are typically honored and accepted as written. Most states that follow this process hold a formal hearing where parole board members may share their views. When the parole hearing is conducted with the offender seeking parole, all members involved with the decision may be present (as is often the case in television or movie portrayals), but it is also possible that just one member is present. Lastly, when parole hearings are conducted, the board may convene at the facility where the inmate is located (requiring the board to travel), or the inmate may be brought to the board, wherever the board is located (in many cases, the state capital).

The process and guidelines for parole selection vary considerably from state to state. Some states have a minimum amount of time that must be served. Others have stipulations on the types of crimes that the offenders have committed. Some states use both of these criteria as well as others. However, the actual decision by any parole review body is often made by members who have a great deal of discretion. Indeed, it appears that parole boards are influenced by a wide variety of criteria, many of which are not necessarily noted by statute or official agency guidelines. Institutional infractions, the age of the offender, marital status, level of education, and other factors may all weigh into the parole board's decision. Students should refer to Table 15.2 for specific details of parole populations within each state correctional system.

Naturally, one of the key concerns with granting parole is the probability of recidivism. To a large extent, the prediction process has been little better than guesswork. For decades, the development of prediction tools has continued in an attempt to standardize risk factors. Psychometric tools and statistical analyses have ultimately rested upon actuarial forms of risk prediction. In most cases, it is the objective use of statistical risk prediction that turns out to be more accurate than that which allows for individual subjectivity. There are, of course, some exceptions since the context surrounding the statistical data may be important and may provide alternative explanations as to why a certain set of numbers and/or statistical outcomes may have been obtained. However, this often simply results in the overprediction of likely reoffending. Overprediction of offending is costly to prison systems because they will continue to incarcerate persons who are, in reality, at no risk of reoffending. In some states, there may be a need to reduce prison system overcrowding and such overprediction can further exacerbate problems with this overcrowding.

Prison Tour Video Link
Drug Testing and Parole Issues

Indeed, parole mechanisms can serve as release valves for prison systems that become overstuffed with offenders. When this occurs, there may be a need for a certain amount of offender releases, and parole boards may have to make tough decisions that do not necessarily comport with the formal risk assessment based on a standardized instrument. This is where the difficulty tends to occur, and this demonstrates why, on the one hand, it is counterproductive for standardized risk assessment instruments to overpredict (as with the Wisconsin Risk Assessment scale), yet, on the other hand, subjective decision making is a necessary evil that is fraught with peril, resulting in incorrect predictions that ultimately lead to serious mistakes in determining an offender's likelihood to recidivate.

Other factors also affect the decision to grant parole. For instance, an inmate may (according to a standardized instrument) have a high likelihood of reoffending. But the type of reoffending may be of a petty nature. In such instances, parole boards may decide to grant parole despite the fact that the offender is not considered a good risk based on a pure analysis of whether he or she will or will not reoffend. Thus, it is clear that the specific type of reoffending is also an important consideration among parole board personnel. As just noted, this may be an especially important consideration when parole boards are aware that the state's prison system is overcrowded and that a certain number of releases will assist prison administrators in maintaining their prison population levels. Therefore, it is better to release a person likely of relapsing on drugs and/or alcohol or who may commit some form of shoplifting than it is to release someone likely of committing some form of violent crime. It is using this next-best-solution approach that parole boards may be compelled (though not legally required) to make their releasing decisions.

It is important for students to appreciate the problems associated with prison overcrowding. As discussed in past chapters, federal court rulings during the 1970s and 1980s penalized many state prison systems and essentially forced them to honor a variety of civil rights standards when incarcerating inmates. Thus, the issue of overcrowding cannot be taken lightly by prison administrators, and state systems resort to a number of alternatives to alleviate this issue. In states that still utilize parole, this is one method state prison systems use to resolve their overcrowding problems, which means community correctional systems are used to augment and support the states' institutional correctional systems. Thus, parole boards may play a key role in bridging these two components in an effort to ameliorate challenges facing a state correctional system.

Video Link
Parole Hearing Stirs up Controversy for City Council Members

The fact that parole boards can play such a role should not be underestimated. They may, in fact, be under some pressure to assist the overall state system. Further, consider that these boards are often constructed by the governor of a given state. In some cases, state politics and state priorities may come into play, affecting the decisions in some parole board cases. This is particularly true when the parole board's administration is consolidated rather than independent in nature (as discussed earlier in this chapter). The point in this discussion is to demonstrate that parole boards do not operate in a complete vacuum. The influences of the surrounding contextual reality are inevitable, and these influences come from a number of directions. Indeed, prison wardens, state offices, victims, the parolee's family, and the public media may all have an impact upon the discretion employed by parole board members, individually and collectively. Students should refer to Table 15.2 for details of parole populations throughout the nation, including the federal system; all states combined; the Top Three in corrections (California, Florida, and Texas); and a few other select states. It should be noted that three states (California, New York, and Texas) had reductions in their overall parole populations (Table 15.2). California, in particular, had a very significant reduction that reflects the major changes that state has made in its correctional system, as has been discussed in prior chapters of this text.

PAROLE AS THE CORRECTIONAL RELEASE VALVE FOR PRISONS

The intent behind parole, at least initially, was to provide an incentive to inmates for exhibiting prosocial behavior while also providing for a gradual process of reintegration into society. This process was intended to be based upon the behavior of the inmates and their progress in work assignments and programming while serving their sentence. The use of parole was not intended to be a mechanism to assist prisons in maintaining their population overflow. In fact, the soundest decisions for parole do not consider prison populations at all but instead are based entirely upon the factors relevant to the inmates and their behavior.

Nevertheless, states around the nation find themselves considering the increased use of parole or early release due to problems with prison overcrowding (see Figure 15.5). State correctional systems may find it difficult to house the influx of offenders when their budgets are not increased to accommodate this continual flow of new inmates. Whenever correctional systems use parole with the intent to reduce correctional populations rather than facilitate reintegration of offenders, they are using parole as a **release valve mechanism** for their prison population.

The state of Arkansas is a very good example of how prison overcrowding has become a basis for the increased use of parole options. In 2001, the Arkansas Board of Correction and Community Punishment implemented an accelerated parole scheme to release over 500 inmates, citing the need to free prison and jail space due to the state's record-breaking incarcerated population. The state's system was so backlogged that over 1,000 state inmates were being held in county jails due to a lack of prison space ("Arkansas Speeds Parole to Ease Jam," 2001). In addition, the state had a shortage of correctional officers. To deal with the overcrowding issue, Arkansas lowered the security level of many cell blocks and facilities from maximum to medium security and from medium to minimum security; these changes meant fewer correctional officers were required to guard the inmates. Further, inmates who were classified at lower security levels were eligible for parole at a much quicker rate and therefore were released from confinement more quickly. The paroling of more inmates also reduced the number of correctional officers needed. It is clear that policies such as these—in particular, artificially lowering inmate security levels—were dangerous and based not on the security of the institution or society but on economic concerns.

Release valve mechanism: When correctional systems use parole to reduce correctional populations.

The use of parole as a release valve is becoming increasingly more common due to the recent economic challenges that have faced state governments. While reentry efforts such as parole can be useful in reforming offenders and thereby reducing their likelihood of recidivism, such practices should operate regardless of prison population levels. If prison population levels determine the likelihood of release, then release decisions are made due to monetary, not public

■ Figure 15.5: Adults on Parole in the Federal System and Select State Systems, 2013

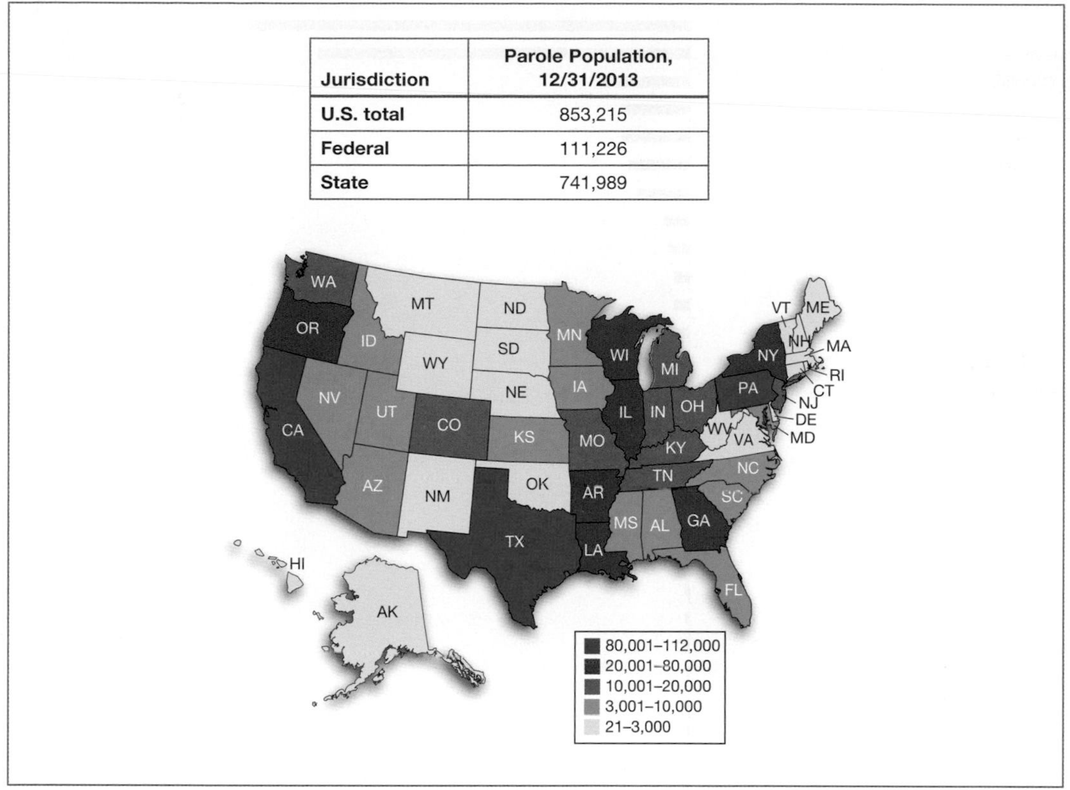

Jurisdiction	Parole Population, 12/31/2013
U.S. total	853,215
Federal	111,226
State	741,989

SOURCE: Herberman, E. J., & Bonczar, T. P. (2015). *Probation and parole in the United States, 2013*. Washington, DC: Bureau of Justice Statistics.

safety, considerations. This is a dangerous game to play in corrections and puts the public at risk for future criminal victimization.

Video Link
California Budget Woes Squeeze Overcrowded Prisons

THE ROLE OF INSTITUTIONAL PAROLE OFFICERS

Institutional parole officers, often referred to as case managers or caseworkers, will work with the offender and a number of institutional personnel to aid the offender in making the transition from prison life to community supervision while on parole. This professional serves both a security function (assessing suitability for parole) and a reintegration function (providing casework services inside the prison and networks that extend beyond the prison). Much of the information presented in this section regarding prerelease planning and the role of the institutional parole officer draws on information from the state of Oklahoma's Pre-Release Planning and Reentry Process guidelines (Jones, 2007).

During prerelease planning, prison staff work together to provide a bridge of services that connect the offender to the outside world. A great deal of work can go into the planning and preparation process of an inmate's exit from prison. This section will shed some light on the institutional parole officer's function, since these professionals provide a link between the prison world and the outside community.

Upon determining that an inmate is suitable for parole, the institutional parole officer will begin the prerelease planning process that attends to the offender's transition from prison to the community. This process typically begins about 6 months prior to release and involves a shift from institutional case planning to individual community preparedness. The goal of a good reintegration program should be to ensure that the offender has the support, information, and contacts necessary to begin anew prior to exiting the prison. Even small details must be attended to, such as providing offenders with essentials like clothing and shoes that

Institutional parole officer: Works to aid the offender in making the transition from prison life to community supervision.

■ **Figure 15.6: Parole Population Increases and Decreases by State**

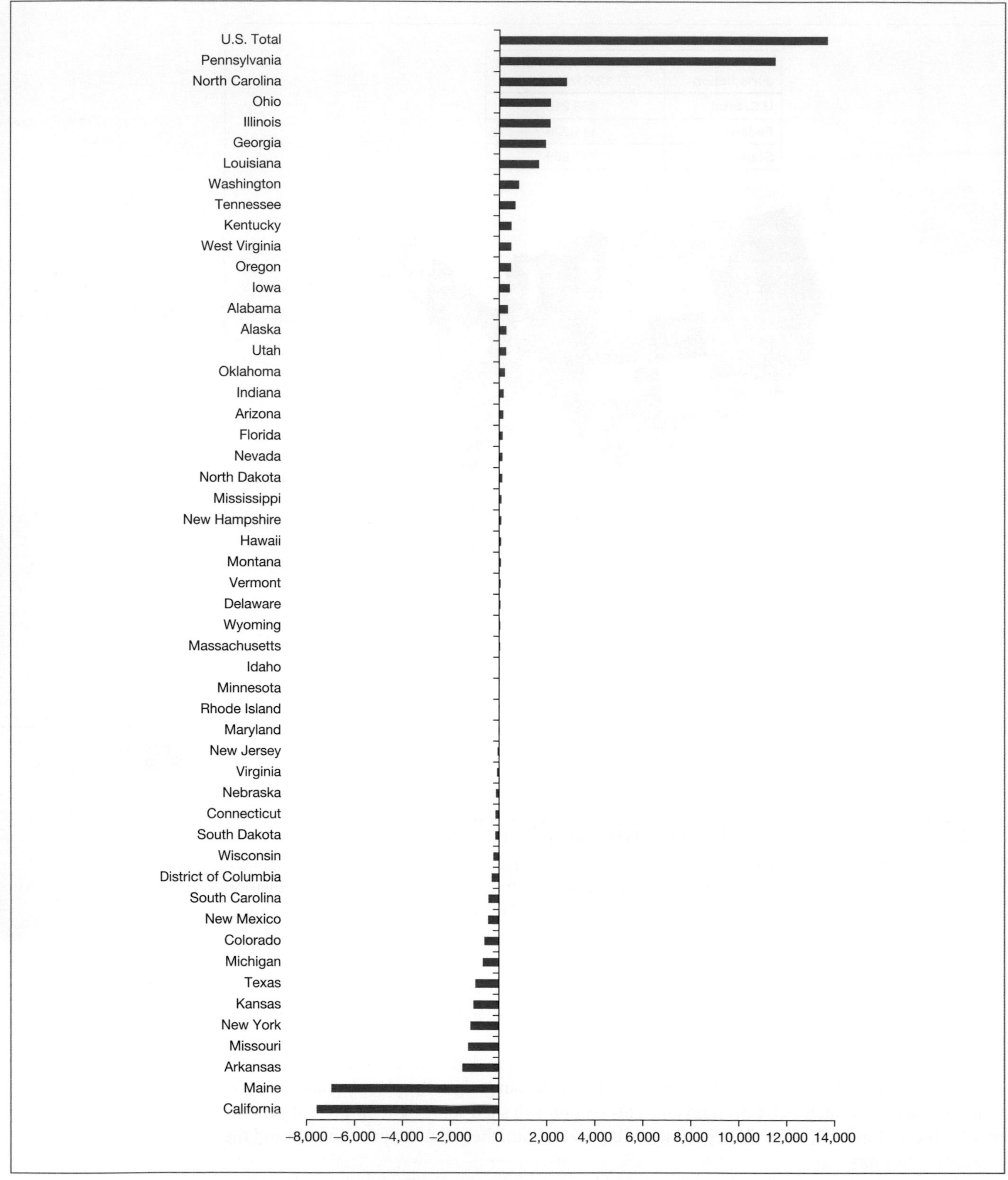

SOURCE: Glaze, L. E., & Bonczar, T. P. (2009). *Probation and parole in the United States, 2008*. Washington, DC: U.S. Department of Justice.

are appropriate for the season, proper identification, and appropriate referrals to community agencies that can assist with other services.

Throughout the process, agency administration will tend to track the offender's progress, keeping a careful eye on the 6 months prior to release. At this point, the offender may experience

CORRECTIONS AND THE LAW 15.1

Liability of Parole Board Members for Violation of Substantive or Procedural Rights

For the most part, it is clear that parole boards are not typically liable for violations of substantive or procedural rights when determining initial parole decisions. This should not be confused with decisions during parole revocation hearings. In terms of revocation hearings, the Supreme Court case of *Morrissey v. Brewer* (1972) clearly established a number of rights related to due process through a prompt informal inquiry before some form of impartial hearing officer. However, initial decisions to grant parole are simply a privilege to which an inmate has not constitutionally secured the right. Though inmates do not have a right to parole, they do have a right not to be discriminated against on the bases of race, religion, sex, creed, and so forth when such determinations are being made. One case, *United States v. Irving* (1982), was filed under Section 1983 of 42 U.S. Code in the Seventh Circuit. In this case, the offender alleged systematic racial discrimination against African American inmates with respect to parole board decisions for release. Interestingly, the circuit court did hold that the parole board members themselves had absolute immunity when faced with such suit. However, the circuit court noted that the offender could still sue for declaratory relief (essentially requesting an injunction that the parole board change its practices) due to the fact that the court found evidence that tended to demonstrate discrimination on the part of the parole board.

Thus, it may be that individual parole board members are immune from liability when performing their functions. But offenders still retain certain civil rights under the Fourteenth Amendment that must be honored by parole boards just as they must be honored by custodial corrections officials. This is a reasonable point since, after all, the desire to eliminate bias and discrimination among government officials was the reason that Section 1983 forms of redress were created. Just as prison officials must provide constitutional treatment of prisoners, so should parole-granting bodies.

One additional point of interest regarding parole board liability revolves around the rights of offenders who are released on parole only later to find out that the release was a mistake on the part of the parole board. While such instances are not common, they have occurred frequently enough to be ruled on by more than one federal court. Indeed, two lower courts have held that the protections in *Morrissey* also confer some substantive protections for inmates who are mistakenly released. In both *Ellard v. Alabama Board of Pardons and Paroles* (1987) and *Kelch v. Director, Nevada Department of Prisons* (1993), it was determined that once a state confers a right to be released, the inmate's due process rights go beyond the contours set by *Morrissey*.

Indeed, it was determined that the grant of freedom places substantive limits on a state's power to reincarcerate an inmate who has been mistakenly released. In the *Ellard* case it was held that a mistakenly released inmate could not be reincarcerated unless the release violated some sort of state law and that this departure from state law substantially undermined a state's penological interests (see the 1987 U.S. Supreme Court case, *Turner v. Safley*, for a discussion on legitimate penological interests). A similar ruling was found in the *Kelch* case as well, demonstrating a consistency among circuit court rulings and thereby lending support for the point that parolees do not have a right to parole prior to the parole-granting decision. However, this changes when they are actually released on parole, with *Morrissey* protections affecting revocation proceedings for those legitimately on parole and a subsequent expectation of parole surfacing when offenders are mistakenly and prematurely released from the prison environment by parole board officials.

SOURCE: Barton, B., & Hanser, R. D. (2011). *Community-based corrections: A text/reader.* Thousand Oaks, CA: Sage.

problems with anxiety due to nervousness over his or her expected freedom, the responsibilities of the outside world, and the effects of prisonization inside the facility. A good prerelease program will address these issues, preparing the inmate psychologically for release. As with their initial entry into prison, this period is often one of the most stressful for offenders since so much of their future is uncertain and they will be held to expectations that they have not had to meet in years.

Interviews, forms, and checklists will be completed during this time as part of the review case plan that documents the offender's approach toward release. These interviews will seek to identify various needs that the offender might have upon release. Needs-based assessment instruments perform this function. Identified needs can be many and varied but often include some program that the offender did not complete while in prison, such as an educational plan or substance abuse program. Other needs may be related to the payment of restitution, transportation, or making provisions for child support.

In addition to these concerns, correctional staff should note any unique circumstances in the prerelease plan that might provide a challenge to the successful reintegration of the offender.

CROSS-NATIONAL PERSPECTIVE 15.1

Parole Officers in Canada

Driving up to the warehouse at 8 p.m. on a Thursday, the parole officer hopes his client will be hard at work inside. So far, every meeting with the client has gone well, as have the meetings with the parolee's employer. But this is an unscheduled meeting, and the probation officer knows a good start by someone on parole doesn't always mean the virtuous behavior will continue.

"I don't like it when the guys return to jail," explains Rob Christensen. "It can be a very (defeating) feeling. When you do see someone come out and succeed, it's very good." In his 9 years on the job, the Calgary parole officer has seen his share of successes and failures. Regardless of what happens from case to case, though, his main goal remains to help offenders released from prison do well in the community while protecting the public at the same time.

It's a busy and demanding job. And, like other careers within law enforcement, it comes with its good and its bad, especially because parole officers must maintain constant contact with all aspects of the parolees' lives. "You see some really terrible stuff in the files, and you have to deal with these people professionally," Christensen says. "You're always looked at as the bad guy when all you're trying to do is help the guy. And it can be confrontational at times. But, for me, there are many pluses as well. I like the interaction with all the different characteristics of people. I like helping when I can and the law enforcement side of things."

Working for Correctional Service Canada as a parole officer in the community, Christensen's duties see him travel throughout the city meeting those on parole in their homes and at their jobs. Parole officers must also try and meet employers, family, friends, and others in regular contact with the parolee to ensure everything is on the straight and narrow, or to find a way to get more help to the parolee. This could include enrolling the parolee in a substance abuse program. As all these matters are legal issues, parole officers spend plenty of time taking notes and completing paperwork in the office as well.

The law always held an attraction for Christensen, who originally contemplated applying for the Royal Canadian Mounted Police while he was in college. "I was looking at law enforcement of some sort," he says. But the thought of moving all over the country held little appeal. In discussing his future with others, someone suggested applying at the Bowden penitentiary. He did, was accepted, and began work as a federal corrections officer in 1989 and worked his way up the ladder. (Provincial corrections officers deal with those who receive sentences of less than 2 years.) He spent 6 years as a parole officer in the institution before moving to Calgary.

He now puts in a regular workweek of 40 hours, but the days and times of his shifts may vary. Parole officers are paid on a sliding scale up to about $63,000 a year. Knowing the ins and outs of parole, however, is but a small part of what's required of a parole officer. Christensen says a parole officer needs solid communication skills, patience, and strong interpersonal skills. "You need to be able to interact on a professional level and a personal level. You have to be able to read people in a hurry."

Parole officers have been around for decades, and that's likely to continue, Christensen says. And he offers this advice to those considering this line of work: "Don't feel like you can change the world, and don't feel like you can change everybody. Take the satisfaction from the ones who do [change]."

Question 1: In what ways do the functions of parole officers in Canada seem similar to those in the United States?

Question 2: From the information in the article, does it appear that parole considerations in Canada follow a punitive model or a reintegrative model?

SOURCE: Sproxton, M. (2002). *Parole officers constantly deal with the good and bad.* Nextsteps.org.

This will typically be included in the adjustment review and also in what is often referred to as the Offender Accountability Plan. The **Offender Accountability Plan** addresses needs for restitution, the need to respect the rights and privacy of prior victims, and any particular arrangements that have been made with the victim as well as any necessary provisions to ensure the offender's responsibility to the community at large.

Offender Accountability Plan: Addresses needs for restitution, any particular arrangements that have been made with the victim, and provisions to ensure the offender's responsibility to the community at large.

The actual day of release is an important milestone for the offender and is actually critical to his or her successful reintegration. This should be treated as more than a nostalgic moment, and the seriousness of the new challenge ahead should be kept in focus. (This is illustrated in this chapter's opening vignette when the Louisiana Parole Board made note of additional requirements for the parolee, Ronald Drummer. Note that this vignette is based on true events during a hearing that the author actually attended to provide recommendations for the offender's release to the parole board.) Activities should focus on the last few tasks required for a seamless transition to the community. In addition, the offender should be provided a portfolio of the various services available, requirements of parole, and so forth, allowing him or her to keep the information and requirements organized. Organizational skills may be somewhat impaired given the newness of the release experience and the likely excitement that will be experienced.

Lastly, Torres (2005) points out that although release from the prison facility can be a euphoric experience, it can also result in unexpected disappointment and frustration for the offender. Torres (2005) provides an insightful description of the psychological challenges associated with offenders' reintegration as they navigate between their life prior to incarceration and the life that they now face:

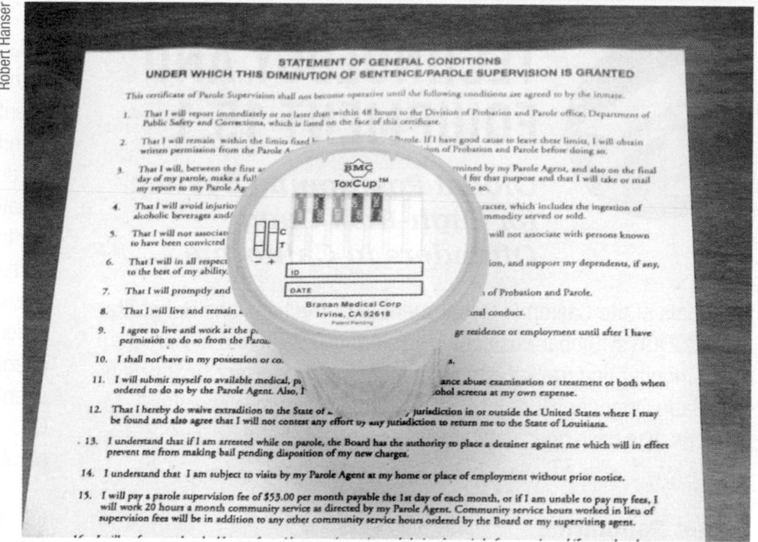

Robert Hanser

■ PHOTO 15.3 The sheet of paper underneath this urinalysis cup clearly identifies the conditions of an offender's parole. In this case, the parole officer is making it clear that the offender is expected to remain drug free by placing the urinalysis cup directly on top of the list of parole conditions.

> The parolee's memories of family, friends, and loved ones represent snapshots frozen in time, but in reality, everyone has changed, moved away, taken a new job, grown up, or perhaps most disappointingly become almost strangers. The attempts to restore old relationships can be very threatening and eventually disappointing. In addition, the presence of almost complete freedom after years of living in a structured, confined prison setting can also add tremendous stress to adjusting to the open community where the offender must now assume major responsibilities of transportation, obtaining a driver's license, finding a job, reporting for drug testing, and so on. If married, with children, the spouse may unrealistically expect the offender to immediately begin providing financial relief to the family that perhaps has endured financial hardships while the breadwinner was away. Other barriers to success include civil disabilities that prohibit the felon from voting . . . and most importantly, from being employed in certain occupations. (p. 1125)

Audio Link The Role of Institutional Parole Officers

Institutional parole officers are cognizant of the situation that faces upcoming parolees. They must ensure that the offender has the full range of support necessary to face the potentially traumatic adjustment to the outside world. The offender will need to come to grips with issues that most people do not consider, making the experience of release sometimes a bit bittersweet. Offenders may (or may not) themselves realize the full range of emotional experiences that they will have upon release, and it is one job of the institutional parole officer to ensure that appropriate support for coping is provided to the offender who may be disappointed and/or overwhelmed by the experience.

COMMON CONDITIONS OF PAROLE

The terms and conditions for parolees, in most cases, are identical to many of those for offenders on probation. For instance, the state of Oklahoma requires parole fees of $40 at a minimum and clearly outlines the potential outcomes if an offender violates the terms of his or her parole. These outcomes include additional levels of supervision, reintegration training, the addition of day reporting centers, weekend incarceration, nighttime incarceration, intensive parole, jail time, and incarceration. This is similar to what happens if offenders on probation violate the terms and conditions of their supervision. If possible, the parolee will be kept on supervision (depending on the nature of the violation) but will experience a graduated set of increasingly restrictive sanctions and requirements that will become additional conditions to his or her parole requirements. Figure 15.6 provides an example of some of

TECHNOLOGY AND EQUIPMENT 15.1

Global Positioning System for High-Risk Gang Offenders in California

The goals of the California Department of Corrections and Rehabilitation's (CDCR's) Global Positioning System (GPS) monitoring program are to monitor and track the movement of parolees. The CDCR's High-Risk Gang Offender (HRGO) GPS monitoring program is specifically for parolees who have been categorized as high risk for gang involvement or activity.

Target Population

Parolees are categorized as high risk for gang involvement or activity by the CDCR's GPS Monitoring Gang Eligibility Assessment Criteria before receiving their parole supervision assignment. Parolees are categorized as high risk if they meet at least one of the mandatory criteria of the assessment. These criteria include being validated as a prison gang member or associate, being assigned a special condition of parole to not associate with any prison or street gang member, and previous involvement in gang activity. If a parolee meets any of the eligibility criteria, the parole agent of record and the parole unit supervisor hold a conference to determine whether the GPS monitoring program is appropriate based on additional criteria such as prior offenses and current compliance with parole conditions.

Program Components

GPS Monitoring. The GPS monitoring portion of the HRGO program uses cellular and GPS technology to track parolees in real time. The unit takes a data point every minute and transmits location data every 10 minutes to the monitoring center. The monitoring center then provides the parole agent with location information in two formats. The first format is a daily summary report, which details all activity recorded by the GPS unit, such as device charging activity, zone violations, strap tampers, and other violations. Parole agents are also able to review the movement patterns, or "tracks," of the parolee on a Web mapping application. This information allows parole agents to investigate any unusual or suspicious movements. The second format is the immediate alert (IA) notifications, which are automatically generated text messages sent to the parole agent of record for specific types of high-priority violations. If a parole agent needs to get in contact with a parolee the agent can signal the GPS device worn on the offender to beep or vibrate, signaling to the parolee the need to contact his parole agent.

Intensive Supervision. The intensive supervision portion of the HRGO program includes frequent contact between the parole agents and parolees. Soon after release from prison, parole agents must meet face-to-face with the parolee and conduct an initial interview. During this first meeting, parole agents are required to inform the parolee of the GPS monitoring as a special condition of parole, and to explain that participation is mandatory and refusal will result in return to prison. As part of the intensive supervision, parole agents must meet at the parolee's residence soon after release, conduct a minimum number of face-to-face contacts monthly, conduct a minimum number of collateral contacts monthly (i.e., acquaintances and family members of the parolee), conduct a minimum number of random drug tests monthly, meet with law enforcement to update parole information a minimum number of times each year, and conduct a case review a minimum number of times each year.

SOURCE: Crime Solutions.gov. (2013). *Global positioning system for high-risk gang offenders (California).* Washington, DC: National Institute of Justice.

the terms and conditions of parole in the state of Connecticut. The terms and conditions, for the most part, tend to be very similar from state to state. Conditions (such as noted in #14 of Figure 15.6) unique to the offender are not as frequently used (aside from additional fines and/or community service) unless the offender happens to be in a specialized category of population typologies (such as with sex offenders), but even in these cases restrictions tend to be similar to those required of other sex offenders.

Video Link
Parole and Reentry

Offender reentry: Includes all activities and programming conducted to prepare ex-convicts to return safely to the community and to live as law-abiding citizens.

REENTRY INITIATIVES

Before we can discuss offender reentry programs, we must understand what constitutes offender reentry. Some observers note that offender reentry is the natural byproduct of incarceration because all prisoners who are not sentenced to life in prison and who do not die in prison will reenter the community at some point. According to this school of thought, reentry is not a program or some kind of legal status but rather a process that almost all offenders will undergo. A variant on this approach to reentry is the concept that **offender reentry**, simply defined, includes all activities and programming conducted to prepare ex-offenders to return safely to the community and to live as law-abiding citizens (Nunez-Neto, 2008).

FOCUS TOPIC 15.1

Freedmen Inc. Halfway House for Offenders Released From Prison

Freedmen Inc. is a faith-based organization that works with a variety of organizations in the community to provide offenders with housing, transportation, employment, job skills, spiritual guidance, mental health, and substance abuse assistance. This organization's board of directors includes numerous people who are active in reentry efforts in their community. The House of Healing, as it is called, is the primary home in which offenders are housed, but there are other homes as well.

It is important to understand that most of the efforts of this organization are funded through donations and church-based collaborations. Naturally, this means that there is a strong biblical basis to much of the programming. While this may be problematic to some people, this program is designed for offenders who desire this type of reentry experience.

Though this program was originally designed for men, there is now a sister program that aids female offenders in reentry. This points toward the growing reentry needs of the community. These women engage in programming that is similar to the programs in which their male counterparts engage; however, they do not stay in the same facility as the male participants.

This organization is one example of how grassroots efforts in communities can provide services that aid persons trying to rebuild their life after incarceration while, at the same time, making the community safer by offering participants alternatives to crime.

SOURCE: Louisiana Department of Public Safety and Corrections. (2010). *Reentry in Louisiana*. Baton Rouge, LA: Author.

To demonstrate how the reentry effort has become a nationwide priority, consider the Second Chance Act, which was signed into law on April 9, 2008, and designed to improve outcomes for people returning to communities from prisons and jails. This first-of-its-kind legislation authorizes federal grants to government agencies and nonprofit organizations to provide employment assistance, substance abuse treatment, housing, family programming, mentoring, victim support, and other services that can help reduce recidivism.

VIOLATIONS OF PAROLE, PAROLE WARRANTS, AND PAROLE REVOCATION PROCEEDINGS

SAGE Journal Article Link
Putting Parolees Back in Prison: Discretion and the Parole Revocation Process

No discussion pertaining to parole (and particularly an entire chapter on the subject) would be complete without at least noting some of the issues associated with the revocation of that sentencing option. The revocation process is often a two-stage one that was initially set forth in the Supreme Court ruling of *Morrissey v. Brewer* (1972). The first hearing is held at the time of arrest or detention and is one where the parole board or other decision-making authority will determine if probable cause does, in fact, exist in relation to the allegations against the parolee that are made by the parole officer. The second hearing then is tasked with establishing the guilt or innocence of the parolee. During this hearing, the parolee possesses a modified version of due process; he or she is provided with written notice of the alleged violations, is entitled to the disclosure of evidence to be used against him or her (similar to discovery), has the right to be present during the hearing and to provide his or her own evidence, has the right to confront and cross-examine witnesses, has the right to a neutral and detached decision-making body, and has the right to a written explanation of the rationale for revocation.

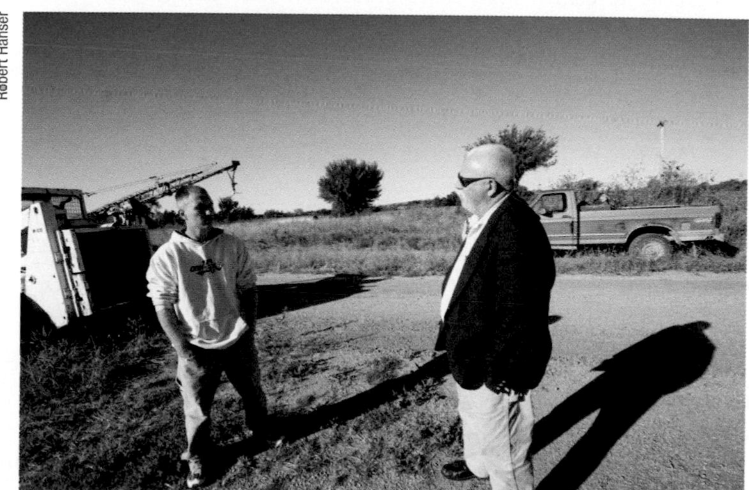

Robert Hanser

■ PHOTO 15.4 This parole officer is checking on one of his parolees who is at work.

■ **Figure 15.7: Example of Terms and Conditions of Parole in the State of Connecticut**

State of Connecticut
Board of Pardons and Paroles

Statement of Understanding and Agreement

CONDITIONS OF PAROLE

NAME ____________________ CJIS NO. ____________ RELEASE ON OR AFTER ____________

1. **RELEASE DIRECTION**. UPON RELEASE YOU WILL REPORT TO YOUR ASSIGNED PAROLE OFFICER AS DIRECTED AND FOLLOW THE PAROLE OFFICER'S INSTRUCTIONS. YOU WILL REPORT TO YOUR PAROLE OFFICER IN PERSON, BY TELEPHONE AND IN WRITING WHENEVER AND WHEREVER THE PAROLE OFFICER DIRECTS.
2. **LEVELS OF SUPERVISION**. YOUR PAROLE OFFICER WILL ASSIGN YOU TO ONE OF SEVERAL LEVELS OF COMMUNITY SUPERVISION, DEPENDING UPON YOUR CIRCUMSTANCE. THESE LEVELS OF COMMUNITY SUPERVISION MAY INCREASE DEPENDING UPON CHANGES IN CIRCUMSTANCES, AT THE DISCRETION OF THE PAROLE OFFICER, AND MAY INCLUDE RESIDENTIAL PLACEMENT, ELECTRONIC MONITORING, CURFEW, AVOIDANCE OF SPECIFIC GEOGRAPHICAL AREAS AND AVOIDANCE OF SPECIFIC SOCIAL CIRCUMSTANCES OR INDIVIDUALS.
3. **RESIDENCE**. YOU WILL LIVE IN A RESIDENCE APPROVED BY YOUR PAROLE OFFICER AND YOU WILL COORDINATE ANY CHANGES IN YOUR PLACE OF RESIDENCE THROUGH YOUR PAROLE OFFICER BEFORE MOVING. YOUR PAROLE OFFICER HAS THE RIGHT TO VISIT YOUR RESIDENCE AT ANY REASONABLE TIME.
4. **EMPLOYMENT**. YOU WILL SEEK, OBTAIN AND MAINTAIN EMPLOYMENT THROUGHOUT YOUR PAROLE TERM, OR PERFORM COMMUNITY SERVICE AS DIRECTED BY YOUR PAROLE OFFICER. YOUR PAROLE OFFICER HAS THE RIGHT TO VISIT YOUR PLACE OF EMPLOYMENT OR COMMUNITY SERVICE AT ANY REASONABLE TIME.
5. **MARITAL/DOMESTIC STATUS**. YOU WILL KEEP YOUR PAROLE OFFICER INFORMED OF ANY CHANGES IN YOUR MARITAL OR DOMESTIC STATUS.
6. **FIREARMS PROHIBITED**. YOU WILL NOT USE OR HAVE IN YOUR POSSESSION OR CONTROL FIREARMS, AMMUNITION, OR ANY OTHER WEAPON OR OBJECT THAT CAN BE USED AS A WEAPON.
7. **SUBSTANCE ABUSE TREATMENT**. YOU WILL PARTICIPATE IN AN ADDICTION SERVICES EVALUATION AND TREATMENT AS DEEMED APPROPRIATE. YOU WILL FOLLOW THE INSTRUCTIONS OF THE PROGRAM STAFF AND YOUR PAROLE OFFICER AND WILL NOT MAKE ANY CHANGES WITHOUT THE EXPRESS PERMISSION OF THE PROGRAM STAFF AND YOUR PAROLE OFFICER. YOU WILL ALSO SUBMIT TO RANDOM URINALYSIS FOR THE BALANCE OF YOUR PAROLE TERM.
8. **MENTAL HEALTH TREATMENT**. YOU MAY BE REQUIRED TO PARTICIPATE IN A MENTAL HEALTH SERVICES EVALUATION AND TREATMENT AS DEEMED APPROPRIATE. YOU WILL FOLLOW THE INSTRUCTIONS OF THE PROGRAM STAFF AND YOUR PAROLE OFFICER AND WILL NOT MAKE ANY CHANGES WITHOUT THE EXPRESS PERMISSION OF THE PROGRAM STAFF AND YOUR PAROLE OFFICER.
9. **DRUGS PROHIBITED**. YOU WILL NOT USE, OR HAVE IN YOUR POSSESSION OR CONTROL, ANY ILLEGAL DRUG, NARCOTIC OR DRUG PARAPHERNALIA.
10. **TRAVEL**. YOU WILL NOT LEAVE THE STATE OF CONNECTICUT WITHOUT PRIOR PERMISSION OF YOUR PAROLE OFFICER.
11. **OBEY ALL LAWS, REPORT ANY ARREST**. YOU WILL OBEY ALL LAWS, AND TO THE BEST OF YOUR ABILITY, FULFILL ALL YOUR LEGAL OBLIGATIONS, INCLUDNG PAYMENT OF ALL APPLICABLE CHILD SUPPORT AND ALIMONY ORDERS. YOU WILL NOTIFY YOUR PAROLE OFFICER WITHIN 48 HOURS OF YOUR ARREST FOR ANY OFFENSE.
12. **GANG AFFILIATION**. YOU WILL NOT ASSOCIATE OR AFFILIATE WITH ANY STREET GANG, CRIMINAL ORGANIZATION OR WITH ANY INDIVIDUAL MEMBERS THEREOF.
13. **STATUTORY RELEASE CRITERIA**. YOUR RELEASE ON PAROLE IS BASED UPON THE PREMISE THAT THERE IS A REASONABLE PROBABILITY THAT YOU WILL LIVE AND REMAIN AT LIBERTY WITHOUT VIOLATING THE LAW AND THAT YOUR RELEASE IS NOT INCOMPATIBLE WITH THE WELFARE OF SOCIETY. IN THE EVENT THAT YOU ENGAGE IN CONDUCT IN THE FUTURE WHICH RENDERS THIS PREMISE NO LONGER VALID, THEN YOUR PAROLE WILL BE REVOKED OR MODIFIED ACCORDINGLY.
14. **ADDITIONAL CONDITIONS**. YOU ALSO MUST ABIDE BY THE FOLLOWING INDIVIDUAL CONDITIONS:

FAILURE TO COMPLY WITH THESE CONDITIONS MAY RESULT IN THE REVOCATION OF PAROLE, AND, IF APPLICABLE, THE LOSS OF GOOD CONDUCT CREDITS EARNED WHILE IN PRISON.

I HAVE READ OR HAVE HAD READ TO ME, IN MY PRIMARY LANGUAGE, THE CONDITIONS OF PAROLE RELEASE. I FULLY UNDERSTAND MY OBLIGATIONS AND AGREE TO COMPLY WITH THESE CONDITIONS OF RELEASE ON PAROLE. IN ADDITION, I UNDERSTAND THAT THESE CONDITIONS SHALL APPLY TO ANY TERM OF SPECIAL PAROLE FOR WHICH I MAY HAVE BEEN SENTENCED TO SERVE.

Parolee	Date	Witness	Date
For the Board of Parole	Date	Hearing Location	Date

SOURCE: State of Connecticut Board of Pardons and Parole. (2008).

Parole revocations officer: Primarily tasked with the routine holding of preliminary parole revocation hearings by reviewing allegations made by parole officers against parolees.

In some states, such as South Carolina, a person known as the **parole revocations officer** is primarily tasked with the routine holding of preliminary parole revocation hearings. This officer reviews the allegations made by parole officers against parolees. These hearings are administrative and not nearly as formal as those held by a judge in a true court of law. Typically, these courts are routine in nature, but some rulings and findings of fact may vary. Though most hearings are not complicated, a degree of discretion is required on occasion when determining if the evidence has been presented well and/or to determine if the violation requires a true revocation of parole or just more restrictive sanctions. The position of parole revocations officer does not require formal legal training but instead simply requires that the officer know the laws and regulations involved with that state's parole system.

Regardless of whether the decision-making body consists of the parole board itself or a parole revocations officer, there are some situations where the offender may be entitled to some form of legal counsel. In ***Gagnon v. Scarpelli* (1971)**, it was held that parolees do have a limited right to counsel during revocation proceedings, as determined by the decision-making person or body and to be determined on a case-by-case basis. This is, of course, relevant only to those circumstances where the parolee contests the allegations of the parole officer, and the retaining of counsel is done at the parolee's own expense; there is no obligation on the part of the state to provide such representation.

Robert Hanser

■ PHOTO 15.5 Parole officer and supervisor Pearl Wise (middle) is pictured here with officers David Jackson (left) and Chris Miley (right) in tactical gear. As parole officers, they are required to complete in-service tactical training that includes nonlethal and lethal weapons proficiency. Ms. Wise is well known throughout her community as an active supporter of reentry efforts in Louisiana.

CONCLUSION

This chapter has provided students with a view of parole, the process by which offenders are allowed to leave prison before serving the entirety of their sentence. Parole has often been criticized due to the concern for public safety when inmates are released. Citizens around the nation read news reports of offenders who are released early from prison and commit heinous acts shortly after reentering society. This obviously makes it seem as if our justice system is being soft on criminals and prison authorities are indifferent to the safety of surrounding communities. However, prison authorities largely have their hands tied and must rely on the direction of the central state administrations that generate parole decisions. Prison overcrowding can and has led to legal complications as it can pose a violation of Constitutional rights held by inmates in confinement. Thus, the only options are to build more prisons, house inmates in some other type of facility, or let them out on early release. Parole is one of the early release mechanisms used by some prison systems and thus has been likened to a release valve that opens when prisons are overstuffed with inmates. These types of "numbers game" release decisions are not safe for society and result in continued crime problems.

***Gagnon v. Scarpelli* (1971):** Held that a probationer's sentence can only be revoked after a preliminary and final revocation hearing have been provided.

The correctional process must often contend with public concern and controversy. It is almost as if the correctional system can never meet the competing demands placed upon it by society. On one extreme is the desire to punish; on the other is the desire to reform. Amidst this is the concern for the victim, which has become increasingly more important to the field of corrections. What may be in store for the correctional system and its practitioners is a matter of debate, but it is certain that the challenges will never disappear.

Prison Tour Video: Reentry Programs. Reintegrating inmates into society is an enormous challenge for correctional practitioners. Watch a clip about parole and reentry programs.

FOCUS TOPIC 15.2

Reentry in Louisiana

Approximately 15,000 state offenders are released each year from Louisiana prisons to Louisiana communities—usually the communities where they were living when they committed their crimes. Many offenders are released with only a bus ticket and $10. Once in the community, they are expected to get a job, earn a living, contribute to the well-being of a family, follow the law, and generally get along with their law-abiding neighbors. Within 5 years, half will be back in prison, either for violating conditions of their release or for committing new crimes. That translates into more dollars, more victims, more frustration, and diminished success when the offender is released the next time.

People are spending years, sometimes decades, cycling in and out of probation and parole offices and prisons, seemingly unable to disengage from the criminal justice system. In Louisiana, the recidivism rate is approximately 50% after 5 years. Reducing this rate by even 10% would result in significant dollar savings for the state and its citizens and, hopefully, an enhanced quality of life in communities across the state. The question of what happens to men and women when they leave prison has never been as urgent as it is today.

Louisiana's Response

In 2002, the Louisiana Department of Public Safety and Corrections organized and standardized programs and services to deal with these issues and to better prepare offenders for a successful reintegration into their communities. Offenders are provided the opportunity to participate in a variety of educational, vocational, faith-based, and therapeutic programs to aid their reentry efforts. Louisiana's response will improve public safety, reduce recidivism, decrease victimization, and reduce the financial burden of its correctional system.

Two unique forms of programming offered for offenders reentering the community include substance abuse and religious programming. While these types of interventions are common to most correctional systems, Louisiana has implemented two unique programs that merit specific mention and consideration.

Substance Abuse

Of the offenders in the state correctional system, 80% have substance abuse problems that contribute to their criminality. It is imperative that the department continue to provide substance abuse treatment and education for incarcerated offenders and subsequently link them with services in the community upon release. The department continues to develop and expand community partnerships with local government and community organizations through parish sheriffs, community volunteers, and private companies to improve substance abuse education and treatment to offenders.

One example is the Blue Walters Substance Abuse Treatment Program, which is a comprehensive program designed to rehabilitate eligible offenders with a history of alcohol and drug abuse who are nearing release. The program goal is to provide substance abuse treatment and prevention education, to develop a collaborative relationship between outside treatment service providers and jail-based treatment programs, and to assist offenders in developing a recovery base and making a safe and successful transition into society. The transition occurs through a combination of halfway house placement, aftercare, and/or work release. The author of this text is the program director of the Blue Walters Substance Abuse Treatment Program at Richwood Correctional Center in Louisiana.

Values Development

Most offenders have a values base that is inconsistent with what it takes to adjust in society. It is imperative that we continue to provide faith-based and character-based programs to offset these deficits. Faith-based programs can help an offender prepare for successful reentry into the community by establishing a spiritual foundation from which he can make sound, moral decisions. Developing partnerships with faith-based institutions that can help ex-offenders maintain their good intentions and positive efforts is crucial to the success of reentry.

Unique in the nation is the New Orleans Baptist Theological Seminary's "Angola Campus" at the Louisiana State Penitentiary. The seminary, established in 1995, offers two college-level degree programs for the offender population, a 2-year associate degree in pastoral ministries, and a 4-year bachelor's degree in theology. As many of Angola's offenders are serving life sentences, the department sees their role in the reentry process as mentors—helping other offenders transition back into the community. Some offenders who have earned their bachelor's degree are being transferred to other institutions, where they work under the supervision of the chaplain to strengthen religious programming. Approximately 90 offenders are consistently enrolled in the seminary, which offers one of the most unique educational opportunities for state offenders and has proven to be a life-changing experience.

SOURCE: Louisiana Department of Public Safety and Corrections. (2010). *Reentry in Louisiana*. Baton Rouge, LA: Author.

Want a better grade?

Get the tools you need to sharpen your study skills. Access practice quizzes, eFlashcards, video, and multimedia at edge.sagepub.com/hanser2e

SAGE edge™

DISCUSSION QUESTIONS

1. Identify and discuss the contributions of Alexander Maconochie to the development of parole.
2. Identify and discuss the contributions of Sir Walter Crofton to the development of parole.
3. What are some basic concepts regarding state parole, its organization, and its administration?
4. How does the parole selection process work, and what are the various factors that influence parole decisions?
5. What is meant by the "release valve" function of parole?
6. How is an effective reentry program a component of any effective crime prevention model through the reduction of recidivism?
7. Discuss Braithwaite's theory on crime, shame, and reintegration, and explain how it is related to the effectiveness of parole.

SAGE edge™ **Test your understanding of chapter content. Take the practice quiz.**

KEY TERMS

Comprehensive Crime Control Act of 1984, 378

English Penal Servitude Act, 375

Father of Parole, 376

Institutional parole officer, 383

Judicial Improvements Act of 1990, 379

Mark system, 375

Offender Accountability Plan, 386

Offender reentry, 388

Parole, 372

Parole Commission and Reorganization Act, 378

Parole Commission Phaseout Act of 1996, 377

Parole revocations officer, 390

Release valve mechanism, 382

Supervised release, 379

Ticket of leave, 373

United States Parole Commission Extension Act of 2008, 380

SAGE edge™ **Review key terms with eFlashcards.**

KEY CASE

Gagnon v. Scarpelli (1971), 391

APPLIED EXERCISE 15.1

Students must conduct either a face-to-face or a phone interview with a parole officer or other parole specialist who currently works in a community corrections setting. The student should use the interview to gain the practitioner's insight and perspective on several key questions related to work in his or her field. Students must write the practitioner's responses, provide their own analysis of those responses, and submit their draft by the deadline set by their instructor. Students should complete this application exercise as an essay that addresses each point below. The total word count should be 1,400 to 2,100 words.

When completing the interview, students should ask the following questions:

1. What are the most rewarding aspects of your job in parole?
2. What are the most stressful aspects of your job in parole?
3. What is your view on treatment and/or reintegration efforts with offenders?
4. What are some challenges that you have in keeping track of your caseload?
5. Why did you choose to work in this field?
6. What type of training have you received for this line of work?
7. What would you recommend to someone who was interested in pursuing a similar career?

Students are required to provide contact information for the parole practitioner. While instructors will probably not need to contact this person, it may become necessary so that they can validate the actual completion of an interview.

Name and title of correctional supervisor: ______________________

Correctional agency: ______________________

Practitioner's phone number: ______________________

Practitioner's e-mail address: ______________________

Name of student: ______________________

WHAT WOULD YOU DO?

You are a state parole officer who has been active in various aspects of offender reentry. You currently work and live in a medium-sized community. On occasion, your supervisor asks you to serve on community committees and advisory boards in order to increase partnerships in your area and extend the sources and abilities of your own agency. Recently, you have been asked to serve with a group of agencies, some state level, some county level, and many of them private or nonprofit in nature. This group is known as the Community Reentry Initiative (CRI). It has had very good success in creating employment opportunities for parolees in the community, and this has been a great help in reducing recidivism. This group has also had some success in obtaining affordable housing for offenders who do not have a place to stay.

The CRI has decided to add a restorative justice component to its efforts. This will require contact with prior victims of crime and will require their consent in participating in the process. This is likely to provide a challenging aspect to the project. However, all victims must be allowed to provide their input in the process as offenders are paroled into the community and integrated into the restorative justice process.

While at the meeting, it becomes clear that many people look to you as an expert on reentry issues. In fact, several members suggest that a subcommittee be created to begin the development of the restorative justice program, and they would like you to lead this subcommittee. However, there has been a recent backlash in the community against offender reentry initiatives. Some citizens have even gone to city hall to protest the implementation of these initiatives. Due to this, you are a bit uneasy with this responsibility, but you know that your supervisor would be disappointed if you did not agree to help with this task. Your supervisor is very progressive and is fond of saying, "Change is good, so let's have more good by making more change!" So, with no real time to consider the implications, you hesitantly agree to accept the position as head of the subcommittee.

At this point, you want to help but do not know exactly what you should do. Your subcommittee consists of two local religious leaders, a police officer assigned to the neighborhood stabilization team, a victim's rights advocate from a local domestic violence facility, a low-ranking person from a local television station, a social services supervisor, a classification specialist who is employed by the regional prison, and a counselor from a local substance abuse treatment facility. Your parole agency supervisor encourages you to help this group and even offers to give you a half day off each week so that you can spend time supporting this initiative.

What would you do?

PRACTICE AND APPLY WHAT YOU'VE LEARNED

▶ edge.sagepub.com/hanser2e

REVIEW. PRACTICE. IMPROVE.

Head to the study site, where you'll find:

- An **online action plan** that includes tips and feedback on progress through the course and materials
- **Learning objectives** that reinforce the key concepts in each chapter

16 THE DEATH PENALTY

California Department of Corrections and Rehabilitation

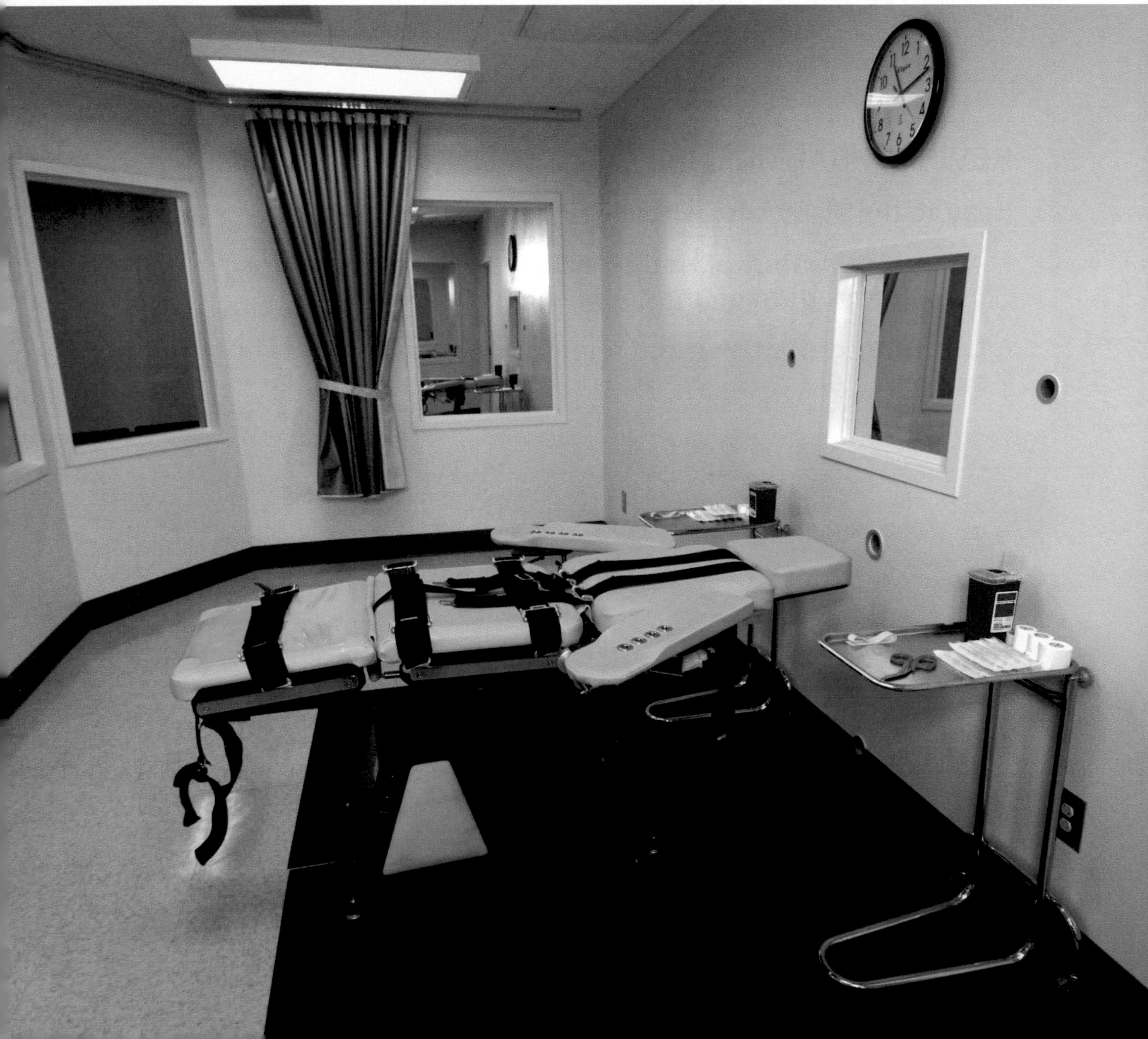

THE DEATH PENALTY SONG

Duane waited in his cell as he listened to the country music station on his very primitive FM radio. The song playing—an old Merle Haggard song titled *Sing Me Back Home*—was almost foreshadowing. Duane remembered listening to this song as a youngster, never thinking it would be applicable to him.

The warden led a prisoner down the hallway to his doom
And I stood up to say goodbye like all the rest
And I heard him tell the warden just before he reached my cell
"Let my guitar playing friend do my request"

Let him sing me back home with a song I used to hear
And make my old memories come alive
And take me away and turn back the years
Sing me back home before I die

I recall last Sunday morning a choir from off the streets
Came in to sing a few old gospel songs
And I heard him tell the singers, "There's a song my mama sang
Could I hear it once before you move along?"

Won't cha sing me back home, with the song I used to hear
Make my old memories come alive
Take me away and turn back the years
Sing me back home before I die
*Sing me back home before I die**

As Duane listened to the song, Warden Johnson and Chaplain Stevens were examining the death chamber where they would soon be leading Duane for execution. Warden Johnson looked around the room, confident that everything was in its place. Even though could not see through the windows facing inside the chamber, he knew that behind one was a room containing the family of the victim and behind the other was Duane's family.

Duane had been on death row for several years, and during that time Warden Johnson had become familiar with him and the circumstances of his case. Duane was guilty of killing two men, that was for sure, but the warden knew Duane's background and knew that this outcome was not surprising. And besides, the two men he killed were not saints themselves—they were drug traffickers who had tried to screw Duane over in a botched drug deal. To some extent, Duane never really had a fair shake at things, but Warden Johnson knew, of course, that this was no excuse for murder. Still, things were complicated sometimes.

Within a few minutes, Warden Johnson and a couple of officers escorted Duane to the chamber. The officers ensured that Duane was secured in the gurney. He engaged in his last rites with the chaplain and waited as the needle entered his arm, injecting the quick-acting poison that would end his existence. After a few seconds, Duane began to struggle to remain conscious. In those moments he was heard very faintly singing to himself: "*There's a song my momma sang, could I hear it. . .once. . .before I move along. . . .*" Then he expired.

Behind the window for the offender's family, tears were shed as Duane's mother, at 61 years of age, watched her son die.

In the other room where the victim's family sat, there was nothing but silence until the victim's sister spoke up. "This really wasn't what I thought it would be. It's pretty much anticlimactic." There was a hollow sound to her voice.

Warden Johnson looked at the clock. It was 12:06 a.m. Sighing inwardly, he thought to himself, *I'm glad I don't have another one of these scheduled for this year.* Then he motioned to the correctional officers to begin removal of the body.

LEARNING OBJECTIVES:

1. Discuss constitutional aspects and case law rulings on the death penalty.
2. Analyze the various statistics associated with the death penalty and those who have received this sentence.
3. List the various methods of execution used in the United States.
4. Discuss the various controversial issues associated with the death penalty.
5. Identify the common philosophies related to the use of the death penalty.
6. Evaluate some of the correctional challenges associated with death row inmates.

SAGE edge™

Get the edge on your studies: edge.sagepub.com/hanser2e

- Take a quiz to find out what you've learned.
- Review key terms with eFlashcards.
- Watch videos that enhance chapter content.

INTRODUCTION

This chapter addresses the most extreme outcome when offenders are at the end of the correctional process: the death penalty, which is also referred to as **capital punishment**. Obviously, the death penalty results in the end of the offender's journey through the correctional process and entails no true rehabilitative efforts on the part of the correctional facility. Thus, this chapter covers the death penalty, but it should be noted that extensive focus is not given to the issue because it is, comparatively speaking, not a major area of focus in the day-to-day operation of correctional systems.

CONSTITUTIONALITY OF THE DEATH PENALTY

The death penalty has always been the source of substantive debate in the United States, but it was most hotly deliberated within the courts during the civil rights movement of the 1960s. Prior to this time, most proponents of the death penalty interpreted it as conforming to the Fifth, Eighth, and Fourteenth Amendments of the Constitution. However, the notion that this sanction was perhaps a violation of the "cruel and unusual" punishment clause of the Eighth Amendment led some of these proponents to reconsider their stance, and numerous cases began to appear that challenged the legality of the death penalty

Web Link
Justice Breyer Resurrects an Old Debate: Is the Death Penalty Constitutional?

In 1958, the Supreme Court made a ruling in the case ***Trop v. Dulles*** that was seemingly unrelated to concerns with the death penalty. In *Trop*, the Court developed a phrase that would be cited in future cases because it fit so well with many compelling arguments in favor of reform within the correctional system. According to the Court, there existed "evolving standards of decency that marked the progress of a maturing society" (*Trop v. Dulles,* 1958, p. 86). This statement has been used by opponents of the death penalty to justify why the death penalty should be eliminated from the range of sentencing options.

Capital punishment: Putting the offender to death.

***Trop v. Dulles* (1958):** Developed a phrase that would be cited in future cases because it fit with many compelling arguments in favor of correctional reform.

***Witherspoon v. Illinois* (1968):** Held that it was not constitutional to strike a potential juror from serving if the juror had doubts or reservations about the use of the death penalty.

***Furman v. Georgia* (1972):** Ruling that the death penalty was arbitrary and capricious and violated the prohibition against cruel and unusual punishment.

***Coker v. Georgia* (1977):** Ruling that the death penalty was unconstitutional for the rape of an adult woman if she had not been killed during the offense.

In 1968, the Supreme Court made an important decision regarding the jury selection process in cases where the death penalty might be given. The Court held that it was not sufficient to strike a potential juror from serving if he or she had doubts or reservations about the use of the death penalty (***Witherspoon v. Illinois,* 1968**). Rather, it was determined that jurors could only be disqualified if it could be shown that they were incapable of being impartial in their decision making while on the jury.

Perhaps one of the most important cases, at least from a historical standpoint, was ***Furman v. Georgia* (1972)**. In *Furman*, it was determined that the death penalty had been administered in an arbitrary and capricious manner. The Court, in ruling on Georgia's death penalty statute, noted the wide discretion given to juries, who were largely unguided in the application of death penalty decisions. This was considered arbitrary in nature and a violation of the Eighth Amendment prohibition against cruel and unusual punishments. This decision resulted in the commutation of hundreds of death row sentences to life imprisonment.

In discussing the *Furman* decision, it is important to emphasize that the Supreme Court did not rule that the use of the death penalty, in and of itself, was unconstitutional. Rather, the Court simply ruled that the manner in which the death penalty was applied was unconstitutional.

Once states were clear on the point made in *Furman*, many quickly acted to revise their laws so that their own use of the death penalty would not be stricken down. According to the Death Penalty Information Center (2004), Florida was the first state to rewrite its death penalty statute, just 5 months after the *Furman* ruling. Shortly after this, another 34 states proceeded to enact new death penalty statutes. Nevertheless, as we will see in the next subsection, the ability to apply the death penalty has been eroding over time due to increasingly more challenging restrictions on its use. We now turn to several U.S. Supreme Court decisions that have shaped and tempered the use of the death penalty since the ruling in *Gregg v. Georgia* (1976) (see Chapter 3).

Constitutional Limits on the Death Penalty

Numerous Supreme Court decisions followed the ruling in *Gregg v. Georgia* that have greatly limited the use of the death penalty. For instance, in 1977, just 1 year after the *Gregg* decision, the Supreme Court ruled in ***Coker v. Georgia*** that the death penalty was unconstitutional when used for the rape of an adult woman if she had not been killed during the offense. In other words, the commission of a rape alone was found to not be sufficient grounds for the death penalty. Later, in 1986, the Court further restricted the use of the death penalty for those who were insane in ***Ford v. Wainwright* (1986)**. Thus, defendants who could successfully use the insanity defense could avoid the death penalty. Much later still, in ***Atkins v. Virginia* (2002)**, the Court ruled that the execution of the mentally retarded was also unconstitutional. This issue had a controversial one with earlier Court rulings allowing mental retardation to be used as a mitigating factor to reduce sentence severity of offenders eligible for the death penalty. With the rulings in *Ford* and *Atkins*, it was clear that the death penalty was not likely to be considered legal if the offender suffered from some serious mental defect that impacted his or her knowing intent to commit the crime.

AP Photo/Rapid City Journal, Steve McEnroe

■ Photo 16.1 This death row inmate is being escorted by two officers down a prison hallway.

Later, the issue of juveniles and the death penalty was finally resolved after years of continued Supreme Court rulings that had slowly minimized the application of the death penalty to this offender population. In the 2005 case of ***Roper v. Simmons*** (see Chapter 12), the Supreme Court ruled that the death penalty was unconstitutional when used with persons who were under 16 years of age at the time of their offense. The reason for this was simply that juveniles are not considered culpable in the same manner that adults are and therefore cannot have the intent necessary to qualify for a death penalty charge.

Prior to this, in ***Thompson v. Oklahoma* (1988)**, the Supreme Court found that the Eighth and Fourteenth Amendments prohibited the execution of a person who was under 16 years of age at the time of his or her offense, though only four of the justices fully concurred with this ruling. In *Stanford v. Kentucky* (1989) and *Wilkins v. Missouri* (1989), the Supreme Court sanctioned the imposition of the death penalty on offenders who were at least 16 years of age at the time of the crime. The decision in *Roper* overturned these prior judgments.

Key U.S. Supreme Court Decisions

One area of concern with the death penalty has been the potential for racial disparity, both in how the case is treated and in the outcome of the case. Two key cases come to mind when considering racial factors and the death penalty. The first case is *Batson v. Kentucky* (1986), in which the Court addressed the manner by which juries are formed in death penalty cases. In *Batson*, the Court ruled that prosecutors had to provide nonracial reasons for eliminating potential jurors from serving on the jury. Essentially, race is not allowed to be a factor in the jury selection process, and, when prosecutors remove a disproportionate number of citizens with the same racial identity of the defendant (the person facing the death penalty), they may be required to explain their actions.

Another important case regarding racial issues and the death penalty was *McClesky v. Kemp* (1987). In *McClesky*, the Court held that statistical data used to demonstrate disparities in the use of the death penalty were not sufficient evidence to invalidate its use. In other words, if it is shown that a higher-than-expected number of minority offenders are put to death when compared with Caucasians, this is not grounds against the use of the death penalty. In this case, the Court contended that Georgia's application of the death penalty was discriminatory, and statistical analyses were used to show a pattern of racial disparity determined by the race of the victim. In particular, when the victim was Caucasian and the defendant was African American, the death penalty was much more likely to be given. However, the Court held that racial disparities would not be recognized as a constitutional violation of "equal protection of the law" unless deliberate racial discrimination against the defendant could be shown.

Aside from racial disparities, other questions and concerns have arisen with regard to the death penalty. One of these is whether judges should be allowed to determine if the death penalty will be given with no input from a jury. In *Ring v. Arizona* (2002), the Court held that juries, rather

***Ford v. Wainwright* (1986):** Ruling that defendants who could successfully invoke the insanity defense could avoid the death penalty.

***Atkins v. Virginia* (2002):** Held that the execution of the mentally retarded is unconstitutional.

***Roper v. Simmons* (2005):** Ruled that the death penalty was unconstitutional when used with persons who were under 18 years of age at the time of their offense.

***Thompson v. Oklahoma* (1988):** Held that the Eighth and Fourteenth Amendments prohibited the execution of a person who is under 16 years of age at the time of his or her offense.

than judges, are to be the body that determines if the death penalty will be given to a convicted murderer. This ruling overturned the death penalty processes of several states that had previously allowed judges to make this determination on their own. Another stipulation of the *Ring* decision is that any and all aggravating factors that would increase the likelihood of a defendant incurring the death penalty must be included in the initial indictment. Due to this requirement, the federal government itself had to revise some of its death penalty laws.

Two cases that address legal representation and/or procedural issues during death penalty proceedings are also worthy of mention. In *Strickland v. Washington* (1984), the Supreme Court ruled that defendants in capital cases have a right to representation that is objectively reasonable. To demonstrate that their representation was not sufficient, defendants must show that the ruling against them would be appreciably different if they had not used the specific legal counsel that had been afforded them; this is a very difficult standard to meet. In *Uttecht v. Brown* (2007), the Court made a ruling that seemed to undermine its earlier ruling in *Witherspoon v. Illinois* (1968). In the *Uttecht* ruling, the Court held that it was, in fact, acceptable to remove potential jurors from service if they expressed mere doubts about the use of the death penalty. In this case, the trial court had removed a potential juror who had expressed doubts about, but not absolute opposition to, the death penalty.

Lastly, there is one case that is most unusual because it cited trends and legal rulings in other countries and also addressed the consequences when a defendant who is a citizen of another country is put to death in the United States. In *Medellin v. Texas* (2008), a Mexican citizen who raped two young girls in Texas had been given a death sentence. The nation of Mexico sued the United States because the Mexican national consulate had not been notified about Medellin's case, a requirement of the Vienna Convention on Consular Relations. The state of Texas rejected this notion and continued to pursue the death penalty for Medellin. What is most interesting about this case is that the Bush administration sought to influence the Supreme Court, entering the case on behalf of Medellin in an attempt to get the Supreme Court to overturn the Texas court's ruling.

The concern of the Bush administration was that the Texas ruling and the carrying out of the death sentence would place the United States in breach of its obligation to comply with the oversight of the World Court (Murphy, 2008). Despite the persistence of federal government officials, Texas maintained its stance on the death penalty and its own authority to implement judicial decisions within its jurisdiction. Ultimately, this led to the U.S. government withdrawing from the Vienna Convention's optional protocol that gave the International Court of Justice jurisdiction over disputes related to the treaty between the United States and Mexico. Despite this, in July 2008 the International Court of Justice asked for a stay of execution for Medellin on the grounds of unfair trial practices. The state of Texas did not heed this request and executed Medellin in August 2008.

Mona Reeder/MCT/Newscom

■ PHOTO 16.2 These two women are happy because they have received word that their relative in the prison behind them (known as the "Walls Unit" in Texas) will not receive the death penalty.

DEATH ROW STATISTICS

The statistics related to the death penalty are, like the sanction itself, somewhat controversial but demonstrate that offenders who receive death sentences are a small minority when compared with the entire correctional population of the United States. The data in Figure 16.1 help to illustrate this point. From these data, it can be seen that the total number of death sentences throughout the nation in any given year does not typically exceed 300. While this is not to say that the death penalty should not be taken seriously, it does demonstrate that the number of death sentences is actually quite low in relation to the overall population of offenders who are sentenced. Further still, in Figure 16.2, it can be seen that from 1976 to 2015, a total of only 1,416 persons were put to death in the United States. Again, while this is not to minimize the severity of this sanction or the importance of examining it, it is clear that 1,416 offenders is a very small number, particularly when one considers that this is the total number of offenders executed over the span of 39 years. In fact, if one took this total number of executions and compared it to the entire prison population currently housed (there are over 1.2 million inmates in the United States), the number of executed offenders represents no more than 1% of this year's current prison population. When one adds the offender population on community supervision, the percentage of offenders who have been put to death is even lower. Indeed, the total number of offenders put to death in any given year (again, see Figure 16.2) is less than .05% of the prison population of that corresponding year. Simply put, the number of those put to death is very small compared to the overall correctional population.

All of the aforementioned is simply to point out that the controversy associated with this penalty perhaps outweighs the actual level of impact that it has on state correctional systems. Aside from the costs associated with the lengthy appeal process, this sanction has little effect on the criminal justice system. This is particularly true when one considers that the effectiveness of deterrence objectives is quite questionable. In essence, the death penalty is a minor aspect of the correctional process, especially at a systemic level, but, because of its unique permanence and severity, it receives a considerable amount of attention.

Figure 16.1: Number of Death Sentences per Year

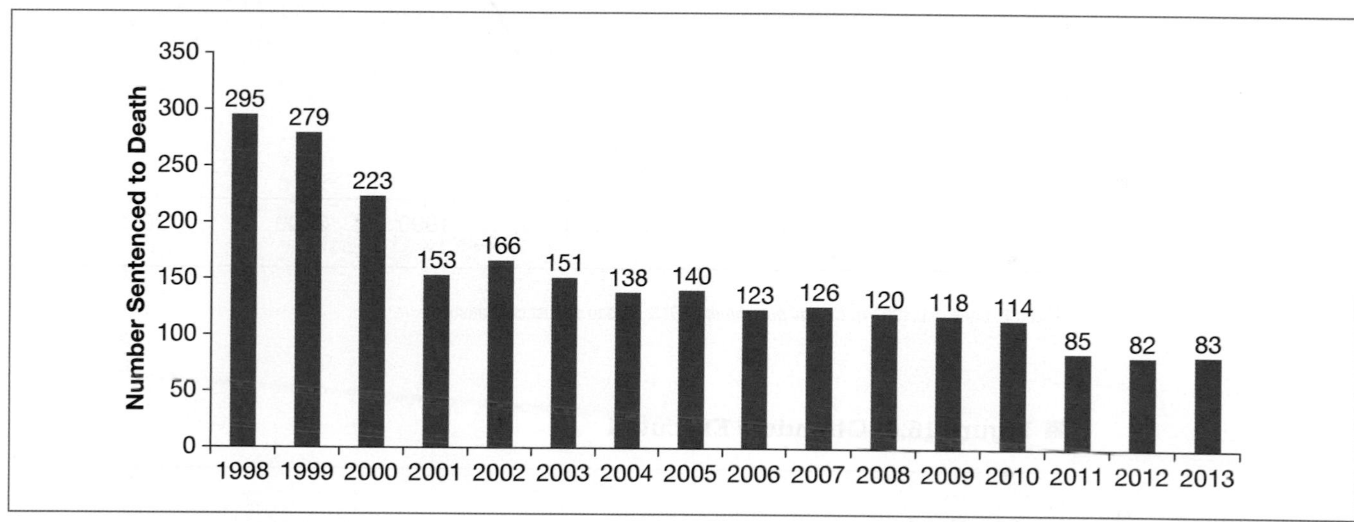

SOURCE: Snell, T. L. (2014). *Capital punishment 2013.* Bureau of Justice Statistics.

*Estimate based on DPIC's research.

Figure 16.2: Number of Executions per Year

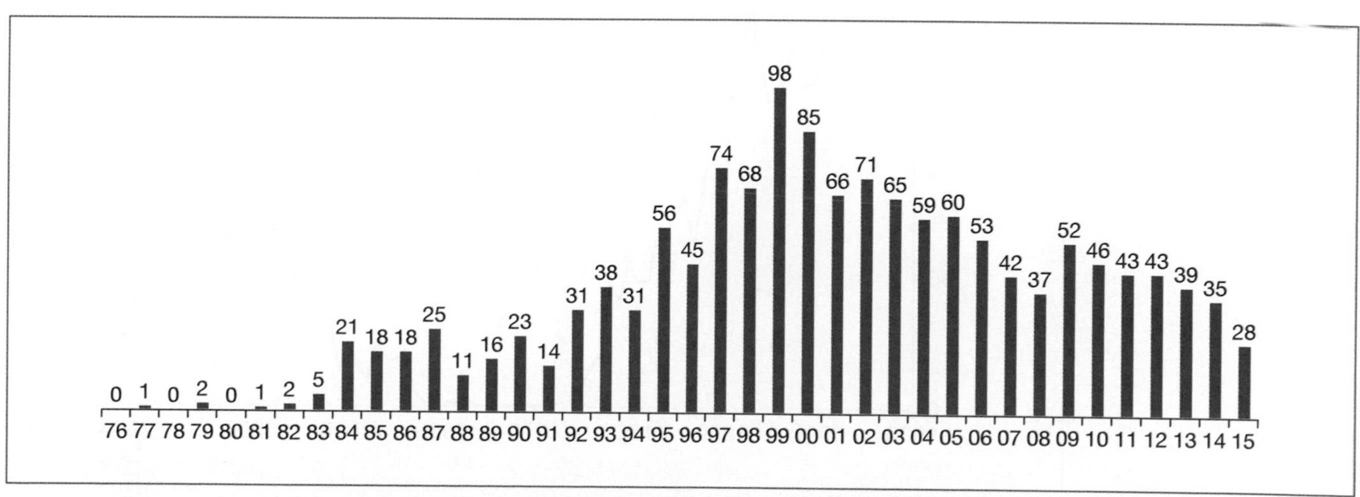

SOURCE: Death Penalty Information Center. (2015, December 15). *Executions by year.* Washington, DC: Author.

Looking at Figures 16.3 and 16.4, students can see that the number of offenders on death row rose sharply from 1954 to about 2002 but has decreased slightly since that time. Indeed, the number of prisoners under sentence of death decreased for the 8th consecutive year in 2008, according to the BJS. The number of actual executions hit a sharp peak in 1999 then mostly decreased until 2009, when a total of 52 inmates were executed; this was 15 more than in 2008. These figures

■ **Figure 16.3: Offenders on Death Row**

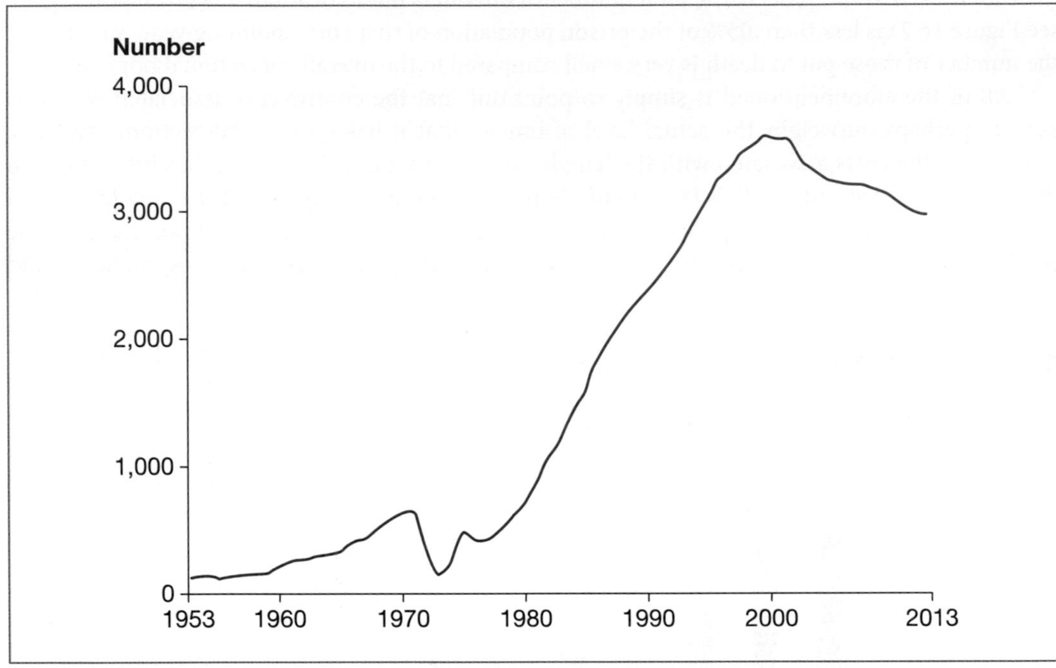

SOURCE: Snell, T. L. (2014). *Capital punishment 2013*. Bureau of Justice Statistics.

■ **Figure 16.4: Offenders Executed**

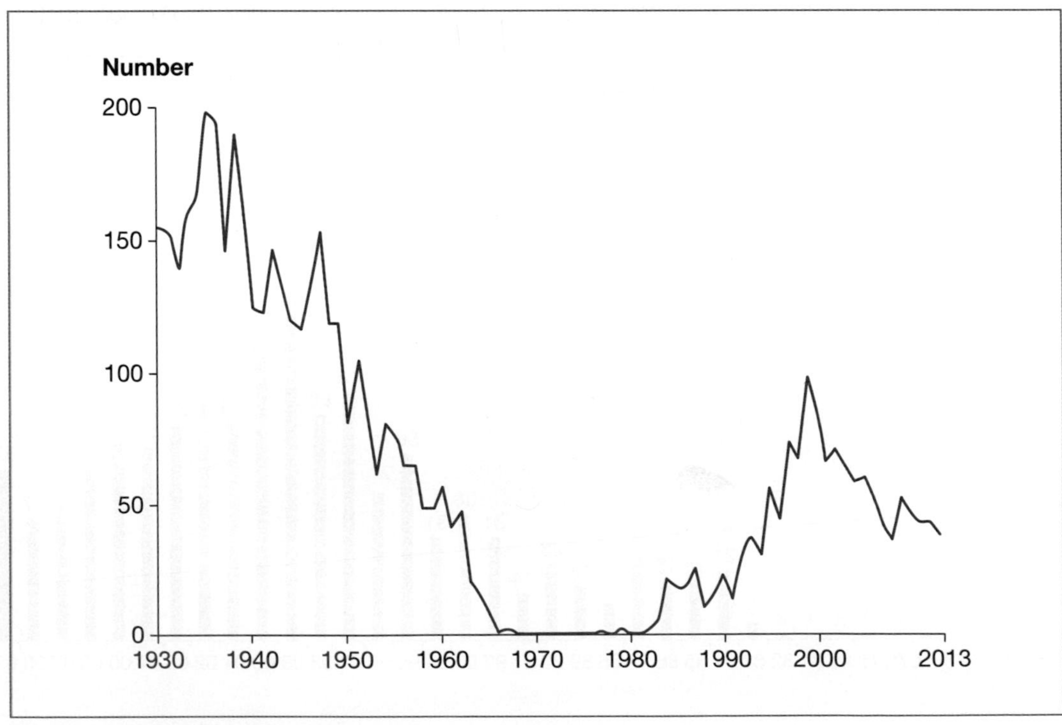

SOURCE: Snell, T. L. (2014). *Capital punishment 2013*. Bureau of Justice Statistics.

provide a visual depiction of the up-and-down nature of the death penalty as it is given during sentencing and actually used against offenders.

Table 16.1 shows that as of 2014, the three states with the largest death row populations were California, Florida, and Texas. This is an interesting point because we have referred to these states as being the Top Three in corrections due to the size of their correctional populations and the various characteristics of each state. Figure 16.5 examines these same data from a regional perspective, and, as we have noted in earlier chapters regarding prison operations, it appears that the southern region of the United States is particularly punitive in nature, as it has the highest number of executions when compared with other regions of the country.

While the impact of the death penalty may be relatively minimal in regard to the day-to-day operations of the criminal justice system, one thing is for certain—it is a very costly sanction to maintain. The costs associated with the death penalty tend to largely be due to the legal fees associated

Table 16.1: Number of Death Row Inmates by State as of 2014

NUMBER OF DEATH ROW INMATES BY STATE AS OF 2014					
California	745	*U.S. Gov't*	63	Utah	9
Florida	404	Mississippi	49	Washington	9
Texas	267	S. Carolina	47	Virginia	8
Alabama	198	Missouri	39	*U.S. Military*	6
Pennsylvania	188	Oregon	36	Maryland	4
N. Carolina	160	Kentucky	35	S. Dakota	3
Ohio	144	Arkansas	33	Colorado	3
Arizona	123	Delaware	18	Montana	2
Georgia	90	Indiana	14	New Mexico	2
Louisiana	85	Connecticut	12	N. Hampshire	1
Nevada	78	Idaho	11	Wyoming	1
Tennessee	75	Nebraska	11		
Oklahoma	49	Kansas	10	**TOTAL**	3,035

Figure 16.5: Executions by Region From 1976 to 2015

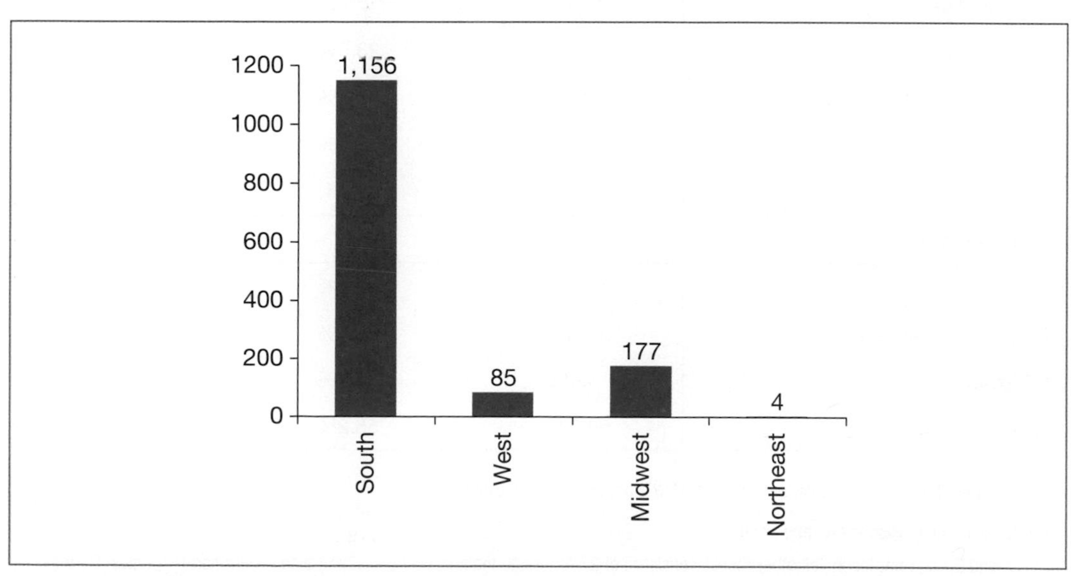

SOURCE: Death Penalty Information Center. (2015, December 9). *Number of executions by state and region since 1976*. Washington, DC: Author

with the appeals process in death penalty cases as well as the cost for long-term and secure housing. Indeed, the death penalty is much more expensive than the use of a simple life sentence without parole. This truly calls to question the utility of the death penalty since it affects such a small group of offenders yet costs so much to implement. Since research on the deterrent effect of the death penalty is mixed, this makes it even more questionable as to whether the death penalty is truly a logical sentence to implement. Given that state budgets are strapped for income and that this penalty does not necessarily improve public safety, it may be that the use of life sentences is a superior means of punishment for heinous crimes.

An Analysis of Persons on Death Row

Death row: Persons who have been sentenced to be executed but are awaiting their execution.

When we refer to persons on death row, it is important to explain what we mean by "death row" and to get a good idea of the characteristics of those who fall within this category. The term **death row** refers to persons who have been convicted and sentenced to be executed but are waiting for their execution to take place. As we can see in Table 16.2, during 2013, just under 3,200 inmates

Table 16.2: Demographic Characteristics of Prisoners Under Sentence of Death, 2013

Characteristic	Prisoners Under Sentence of Death, 2013		
	Year-end	Admissions	Removals
Total inmates	2979	83	115
Gender			
Male	98.1%	100%	96.5%
Female	1.9%	0%	3.5%
Race[a]			
Caucasian	55.8%	59%	60.9%
African American	41.9%	39.8%	37.4%
All other races[b]	2.3%	1.2%	1.7%
Hispanic/Latino origin			
Hispanic/Latino	14.4%	18.3%	12.1%
Non-Hispanic/Latino	85.6%	81.7%	87.9%
Education			
8th grade or less	13.1%	15.7%	22%
9th–11th grade	34.8%	23.5%	32%
High school graduate/GED	42.8%	47.1%	40%
Any college	9.4%	13.7%	6%
Median	12th	12th	11th
Marital status			
Married	21.53%	22.4%	26.5%
Divorced/separated	20%	20.9%	27.5%
Widowed	3.6%	1.5%	4.9%
Never married	54.8%	55.2%	41.2%

SOURCE: Snell, T. L. (2014). *Capital punishment 2013*. Bureau of Justice Statistics.

[a]Includes persons of Hispanic/Latino origin.

[b]At year-end 2008, inmates in "all other races" consisted of 27 American Indians, 35 Asians, and 9 self-identified Hispanics. During 2008, 1 Native American and 1 Asian were admitted, and 1 Asian and 1 self-identified Hispanic were removed.

NOTE: Calculations are based on those cases for which data were reported. Detail may not add to total due to rounding.

were on death row at the close of the year. Of these, the overwhelming majority of inmates were male offenders (98.1%), which means that very few women were serving time on death row. It is also clear that most offenders on death row in 2013 were either Caucasian (55.8%) or African American (41.9%), with only about 2% being of some other race. This means that there were very few Latino Americans or Asian Americans on death row.

Video Link
Witness to Innocence: Pains of Imprisonment

Nearly half of all offenders on death row in 2013 did not have a high school education. This is a common problem among the offender population and points toward the need for educational services for those inmates who are not on death row. Conversely, only about 9% of all offenders on death row had attained any type of college or university course work. Thus, it is most likely that offenders who end up on death row are in the lower socioeconomic categories of society, particularly when one considers that educational levels and income levels tend to correlate. Lastly, most offenders on death row were not married at the time of their offense. The information in Table 16.2 shows that over 50% were never married, indicating that these offenders reported as not having spouses.

In regard to age, Table 16.3 shows that only 18% of all offenders on death row committed their offense prior to the age of 30 years old (see Admissions column), meaning that crimes for which the death penalty is given tend to be committed later in life. According to the Bureau of Justice Statistics (2015), the average age of persons serving a death sentence is 47 years old (the mean age of these offenders is 47; the median age is 46). Approximately 12.2% are 60 years and older, but only 2.4% are older than 65 years of age. This means that most offenders on death row had committed the crime for which they received a death sentence in later years of their life but that very few commit their crimes in their later elder years.

Only 60 women were on death row in 2013. The majority of these women came from two states: California and Texas. Students should consult Table 16.4 for a state-by-state breakdown of the number of women on death row. As can be seen, no state has more than six women on death row, aside from California and Texas. Naturally, this is a very small number of offenders on death

■ Table 16.3: Age at Time of Arrest for Capital Offense and Age of Prisoners Under Sentence of Death at Year-End 2013

	Prisoners Under Sentence of Death		
Age	**Total Year-End**	**Admissions**	**Removals**
19 or younger	0%	0%	0%
20–24	0.7	6	0.9
25–29	3.4	12	3.5
30–34	9.2	20.5	4.3
35–39	13.2	18.1	10.4
40–44	18.3	16.9	17.4
45–49	16.1	7.2	17.4
50–54	16.3	8.4	15.7
55–59	10.6	6	10.4
60–64	6.4	2.4	8.7
65 or older	5.8	2.4	11.3
Mean age	47 yrs.	39 yrs.	49 yrs.
Median age	46 yrs.	38 yrs.	49 yrs.

SOURCE: Snell, T. L. (2014). *Capital punishment 2013.* Bureau of Justice Statistics.

NOTE: The youngest person under sentence of death was a black male in Texas, born in June 1988 and sentenced to death in June 2007. The oldest person under sentence of death was a white male in Arizona, born in September 1915 and sentenced to death in June 1983.

■ Table 16.4: Women Under Sentence of Death, by Race and Jurisdiction, December 31, 2013

Jurisdiction	All Races[a]	White[b]	Black[b]
Total	60	41	15
California	20	14	2
Texas	9	5	4
Florida	5	2	3
Alabama	4	3	1
North Carolina	3	2	1
Pennsylvania	3	1	2
Arizona	3	3	0
Mississippi	2	2	0
Louisiana	2	1	1
Federal	1	1	0
Indiana	1	0	1
Ohio	1	1	0
Georgia	1	1	0
Kentucky	1	1	0
Oklahoma	1	1	0
Tennessee	1	1	0
Idaho	1	1	0
Oregon	1	1	0

SOURCE: Snell, T. L. (2014). *Capital punishment 2013.* Bureau of Justice Statistics.

[a]Includes America Indians, Alaska Natives, Asians, Native Hawaiians, and other Pacific Islanders.

[b]Excludes persons of Hispanic/Latino origin.

row, particularly when compared to the broader correctional population throughout the United States. In fact, only 11 women have actually been put to death since the moratorium on the death penalty was lifted in 1976. All of these women committed murders of one kind or another.

Among those women who have been put to death, Karla Faye Tucker stands out due to the violent and unique characteristics of her crime. Tucker and some male accomplices killed a man and a woman in their domicile because they owed her money. What was most unique about Tucker is that she murdered the couple with a pickax, a bloody and savage means of killing individuals. Even more unusual for a female offender was that she claimed to have experienced sexual gratification when committing both murders. These types of traits are usually only observed among male murderers, in terms of both the violence used and the sexual gratification associated with that violence. Tucker's execution drew national attention that included nightly reports from various major TV newscasters as well as live nationwide coverage from the prison where she was executed. Tucker was the second woman to be executed in the United States since the death penalty was reinstated in 1976 by the U.S. Supreme Court.

Another well-known female who was executed was an infamous serial killer named Aileen Wuornos, who, while prostituting herself, lured multiple men to locations where she could kill them. During 1989 and 1990, several male bodies were found along the highways of central Florida, all murders perpetrated by Wuornos. So rare is the female serial killer as a crime phenomenon that within 2 weeks of her arrest Wuornos had sold the movie rights to her story. This case ultimately resulted in several books and movies. Wuornos represents a classic case that feminist criminologists point to when advocating for the victim-turned-offender hypothesis. Her father was a child molester who was killed in prison when Wuornos was 13. By age 14, Wuornos was pregnant, had dropped out of school, and eventually became a prostitute who hitchhiked along roadways and at truck stops. Wuornos was the 10th woman to be executed in the United States after the death penalty moratorium was lifted in 1976.

Students should see Focus Topic 16.1 for details on women who have been executed and the crimes that they committed. The types of murders committed vary between these offenders but demonstrate how unusual these women are when compared to most female offenders. It is arguable that these women were put to death due to the fact that they broke the social mold and expectations of our patriarchal society, as feminist scholars might contend (students should refer back to Chapter 10 for more on these points). One thing is certain: Because of their rarity, these offenders tend to generate substantial public attention.

Audio Link
Supreme Court Takes on Racial Discrimination in Jury Selection

Race of Offender and Victim in Death Penalty Cases

A primary source of controversy related to the death penalty relates to perceptions of racial bias in its application. Statistics such as those from Figure 16.6 show that approximately 55% of all persons who are executed are Caucasian and 35% are African American. While the argument can be made (particularly among those who are not familiar with demographics in the United States and/or are neophytes in research) that most persons executed are Caucasian, this still reveals disparity in the application of execution. When one considers that African Americans account for only around 13% of the population, it seems that the percentage who are on death row and executed is disproportionately high. Conversely, when one considers that Caucasians account for around 70% to 75% of the population (depending on classifications of Hispanic Americans), it seems that the percentage of those given the death penalty and executed is disproportionately low (U.S. Census Bureau, 2000).

Because of these and other observations, some contend that the death penalty is administered in a racially and class-biased manner. Although it was true that outright racism existed in

CORRECTIONS AND THE LAW 16.1

Racism and the Death Penalty: The Supreme Court Case of Miller-El v. Cockrell *(2003)*

In the 2003 Supreme Court case of *Miller-El v. Cockrell*, the Supreme Court ruled by a vote of 6-3 in favor of Miller-El that he should have the opportunity to prove that his death sentence was the result of discriminatory jury practices. In choosing a jury to try Miller-El, an African American defendant, prosecutors struck 10 of the 11 qualified African American panelists. The Supreme Court said the prosecutors' race-neutral reasons given for the strikes were suspicious and concluded that the selection process was replete with evidence that prosecutors were selecting and rejecting potential jurors because of race.

Justice Souter, writing for the majority, set out the evidence that race governed who was allowed on the jury. This evidence included disparate questioning of Caucasian and African American jurors, the so-called Texas shuffle to limit or eliminate African American jurors, a culture of bias within the prosecutor's office, and a training memo instructing prosecutors on ways to skew juries based on race.

In considering the merit of the plaintiff's claims of racial discrimination, the Court noted that Miller-El's criticism of the prosecution's use of jury shuffling had merit. This practice permitted parties to rearrange the order in which potential jurors were examined so as to increase the likelihood that visually preferable candidates would be selected. Using no information about the prospective jurors other than their appearance, the party requesting the procedure would literally shuffle the juror cards, and the members were then reseated in the new order. This shuffling process affected jury composition because any prospective jurors not questioned were dismissed, and a new panel of jurors appeared the following week. Thus, jurors who were shuffled to the back of the panel were less likely to be questioned and then less likely to serve on the jury.

On at least two occasions the prosecution requested shuffles when a predominant number of African Americans were in the front of the panel. On yet another occasion the prosecutors complained about the purported inadequacy of the card shuffle by a defense lawyer but lodged a formal objection only after the new panel composition revealed that African American prospective jurors had been moved forward.

In *Miller-El*, the Court seemingly contradicted its own prior ruling in *McClesky v. Kemp* (1987) by pointing toward statistical data to support its concern with the practices of prosecutors in the Texas court system. The Court said that

> in this case, the statistical evidence alone raises some debate as to whether the prosecution acted with a race-based reason when striking prospective jurors. The prosecutors used their peremptory strikes to exclude 91% of the eligible African-American venire members, and only one served on petitioner's jury. In total, 10 of the prosecutors' 14 peremptory strikes were used against African-Americans. Happenstance is unlikely to produce this disparity.

The Court stated that the Texas court's finding of no discrimination smacked of racism and was both unreasonable and erroneous. The facts and circumstances of the case determined that the Texas court was indeed racially biased, resulting in a reversal of that court's rulings. Miller-El was granted legal relief and a new trial.

SOURCE: *Miller-El v. Cockrell.* (01-7662) 537 U.S. 322 (2003). Cornell University Law School.

the system during the early to mid-1900s, oversight by the Supreme Court has helped to mitigate this a bit. Now, the issue of discriminatory application has shifted to the race of the victim who is killed. Students can see in Figure 16.6 that over 75% of murder victims in cases resulting in the execution of the offender were Caucasian. Conversely, only 15% of those crimes where African Americans were victimized resulted in the offender getting the death penalty. Simply put, if you murder a Caucasian, you are more likely to be executed, but if you murder an African American, you have lower odds of being executed.

This is an important observation because it does perhaps point to some bias in the justice system regarding the value of persons who are victimized. Where the race of the defendant may be relevant to some extent due to socioeconomics and the inability to obtain effective legal counsel, this should not matter in regard to victims. The prosecutor is the body responsible for seeking a death sentence, and, after this, it is the appeals process that generally determines how quickly the execution will follow. Because the resources available to district attorneys are often plentiful and because the same is true for the state (at least in comparison to the resources available to most offenders and their legal counsel), it would be expected that executions would not be influenced by the race of the defendant. All of this is mentioned because as an overall general economic demographic, Caucasians tend to have more affluence and property ownership in the United States than do most minority groups. The question is, then, what makes persons who kill Caucasians more likely to be executed than those who kill African Americans?

■ **Figure 16.6: Race of Defendants and Race of Victims in Death Penalty Cases**

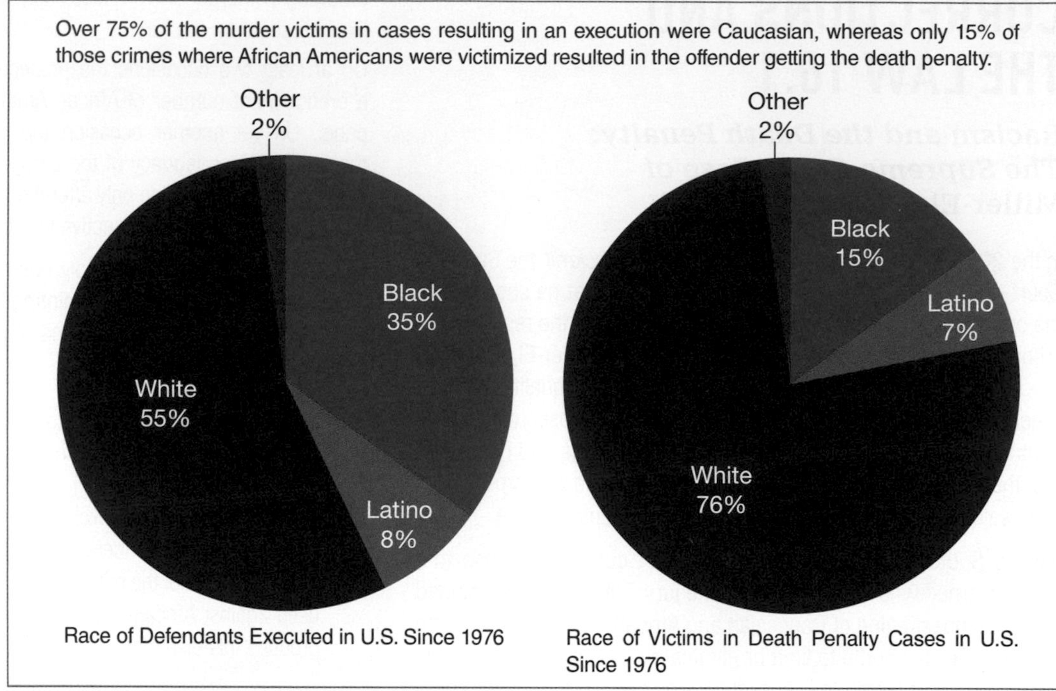

SOURCE: Death Penalty Information Center. (2015). *Facts about the death penalty.* Washington, DC: Author.

FOCUS TOPIC 16.1

Women Who Have Been Executed Since Gregg v. Georgia *(1976)*

Velma Barfield	Executed in 1984 for poisoning multiple people with arsenic. Murders were committed to gain money for life insurance claims.
Karla Faye Tucker	Executed in 1998 for violently stabbing a man and a woman to death with a pickax.
Judy Buenoano	Executed in 1998 for poisoning her husband to death and also killed one of her children in a staged canoeing accident. Attempted to kill a boyfriend with a car bomb. Collected $240,000 in fraudulent life insurance benefits for the murders.
Betty Lou Beets	Executed in 2000. Killed two husbands with a handgun and hid bodies for years before being caught.
Christina Riggs	Executed in 2000 for smothering to death her two young children with a pillow. She was a licensed nurse and used lethal drugs to attempt suicide but failed. Suffered from depression and asked for no defense at her jury trial.
Wanda Jean Allen	Executed in 2001 for killing her same-sex partner outside of a police station. Her partner was in the process of filing a domestic complaint against Allen, and Allen shot her before she could do so. They had met in prison as lovers when Allen was serving time for manslaughter of another prior intimate partner.
Marilyn Plantz	Executed in 2001. Hired two teenagers to kill her husband and assisted them in disposing of husband's body.
Lois Smith	Executed in 2001 for stabbing and shooting her son's girlfriend. Smith believed that the woman had conspired to kill her son and transported the woman to the crime scene, psychologically tortured her, and shot her nine times.
Lynda Block	Executed in 2002 for fatally shooting a police officer. She shot the officer in partnership with her common-law husband in a Walmart parking lot.
Aileen Wuornos	Executed in 2002 for shooting seven men to death. In each case, Wuornos had hitchhiked and prostituted herself to lure the men to their death.
Frances Newton	Executed in 2005 for shooting her husband and her two children. Contended that the crime was committed by an unknown drug dealer who was collecting money from her husband.

Before answering this question, let us further consider research that supports the notion that persons who kill Caucasians are more likely to get the death penalty than those who kill African Americans. One study by the General Accounting Office (1990) of the federal government evaluated 28 other studies that covered homicide cases for different time periods throughout several states in various regions that had the death penalty. These studies found a pattern of evidence that indicated racial disparities in death penalty processing after the *Furman* decision. In fact, in 82% of those studies, the race of the victim was found to influence the likelihood of the offender being charged with capital murder or receiving the death penalty—that is, those who murdered Caucasians were more likely to be sentenced to death than those who murdered African Americans. What was amazing is that these findings were remarkably consistent across data sets, states, data collection methods, and analytic techniques. The findings held for high-, medium-, and low-quality studies that the General Accounting Office analyzed (1990).

To discover why persons who kill Caucasians are more likely to be executed than those who kill African Americans, we can turn to the research just presented. That answer has to do partly with prosecutorial discretion in early stages of the criminal justice process. But is the issue truly this simple, or is there perhaps something else at play? In this chapter, the contention will be that there is indeed another set of factors to explain this phenomenon. But before explaining, we will name this phenomenon the *prosecutorial death discretion outcome*. The **prosecutorial death discretion outcome** basically observes that prosecutors are overwhelmingly Caucasian and when they are determining whether to seek the death penalty, they tend to do so disproportionately more often when the victim is also Caucasian than when the victim is African American. The reasons for this, however, are more likely to be due to politics than racism.

Most district attorneys (prosecutors) achieve their positions by public election. This means that they are voted into office, and, as such, their communities must generally be happy with their performance. In many cases, it is the affluent within a community who tend to have more political power in that community, and they also tend to vote more. Prosecutors may be tempted to ensure that the affluent members of their community remain satisfied with decisions that are made, or, at the very least, they may try to ensure that they do not upset this strata of citizens too greatly. In addition, when members of this group are close to someone who is killed, their families tend to have more influence and likely will more effectively ensure that their case is prosecuted with vigor to the maximum extent of the law.

On the other hand, minority communities (particularly African American communities) tend to have fewer resources and less political clout. This does not mean that crimes against members of this community will not be prosecuted, but it does mean that there will be a stronger likelihood for plea bargains and life sentences without parole to be given. This is even truer when one considers that most crimes are intraracial, with African American offenders tending to kill African American victims. In addition, the voting potential of minority communities tends to be lessened due to lower numbers in most jurisdictions and other factors. In inner-city jurisdictions that are largely African American, crime rates may be higher, including violent crime. Given this observation, the fact that most crime is intraracial, and that drugs and gangs may be associated with these areas of the United States, the desire for a long and drawn-out legal prosecution may not be as strong, particularly if the crime involves offender-on-offender violence, such as with rival gang members or drug dealers.

All of these factors—more affluence (on the average) among families of Caucasian victims, the lack of socioeconomic power among much of the African American community, and crime dynamics in many African American urban communities—tend to impact courthouse dynamics. Discretionary decisions made at the time of plea bargaining tend to favor those with more social or political clout. If the victim's family has substantive influence, this too affects whether or not an offender is prosecuted to the fullest degree, up to and including the death penalty.

Prosecutorial death discretion outcome: Observes that prosecutors are overwhelmingly Caucasian and seek the death penalty disproportionately more often when the victim is also Caucasian.

Federal Death Penalty and Death Row

In 1790, the first Congress established the death penalty for several offenses that today would not be considered constitutional. At that time, crimes of treason, forgery, piracy, counterfeiting, and crimes on the high seas were death penalty–eligible offenses. Today, only treason and crimes affiliated with some type of murder are eligible for the death penalty.

CROSS-NATIONAL PERSPECTIVE 16.1

Nations That Impose the Death Penalty for Drug Offenses

Results from a survey conducted in 2011 of nations that utilize the death penalty for drug offenses show that in most of these nations, the majority of offenders who face execution are not from the country in which they are sentenced. A follow-up survey by Harm Reduction International demonstrated that in most of the 32 countries or regions with drug laws carrying a capital sentence, the offenders are of other nationalities. Indeed, it would appear that there are thousands of non-nationals who are awaiting the death penalty for drug violations, including citizens of Australia, France, Israel, Liberia, Mexico, Mongolia, the Netherlands, Nepal, Nigeria, Peru, the Philippines, Sweden, Turkey, the United Kingdom, the United States, and Zambia. Harm Reduction International also found that the number of individuals put to death for drug offenses is over a thousand, particularly if one includes data from nations that typically do not divulge their death penalty statistics to international oversight bodies.

Because of this, governments should consider their counter-narcotics assistance to those nations that continue to sentence drug offenders to death, as this does not comport with standards accepted by the international community. International law through the World Court places limits on the legal application of the death penalty, and nations who implement the death penalty against drug offenders are in violation of that law. This has attracted the attention of the United Nations, and human rights workers have expressed concern about the number of foreign citizens given the death penalty in countries in which they are not a citizen. Those nations that persist in giving the death penalty for drug offenses claim that this is done as a deterrent to drug trafficking and drug use, which they claim is rampant in their countries. However, there is no statistical evidence that these penalties actually do have any deterrent effect. In fact, given that drug trafficking and drug use persists despite the application of these penalties, these laws probably have little, if any, deterrent effect.

In completing the survey and analyzing the data obtained, Harm Reduction International has provided the following highlights:

1. Indonesia has approximately 100 persons on death row who are drug offenders. Of these, about 80 are foreign to Indonesia, being citizens of Australia, the Netherlands, and the United States.
2. In Saudi Arabia, it is estimated that about 85% of executions for drug offenses were administered to foreign nationals.
3. The national of Singapore has executed at least five people for drug offenses since 2008.
4. In Iran during the year 2010, approximately 590 out of 650 persons executed were put to death for drug offenses.
5. In the People's Republic of China, numbers are not exact because China does not publish them to the international community. Despite this, experts acknowledge that executions for drug offenders occur more often in the PRC than in any other country.

In closing, it should be noted that many countries have the death penalty as a potential sanction for drug traffickers, but, in most cases, these countries do not actually impose this sentence. Rather, the death penalty is routinely administered to drug offenders in six countries, including China, Iran, Saudi Arabia, Vietnam, Malaysia, and Singapore. Naturally, this does not comport with international standards on rehabilitation, particularly in nontrafficking circumstances. Over time, it is likely that these nations will find it necessary to adjust this use of the death penalty. For now, illicit drug offenders should be warned that if they are caught in these nations, they will not be given consideration for rehabilitation but will instead be eligible for the most punitive sanction available, with little recourse available to them, making death a likely outcome.

SOURCE: *The Economist.* (2015, April 28). *Which countries have the death penalty for drug smuggling?*

Within the federal court system, defendants who are found guilty have a second hearing to determine whether a death sentence is justified (U.S. Department of Justice [USDOJ], 2001a). This hearing is held before a jury of 12 members (USDOJ, 2001a). At the hearing, the prosecutor presents evidence in support of the aggravating factors for which notice has previously been provided, and the defense is free to present evidence concerning any mitigating factors. The government must prove the existence of aggravating factors beyond a reasonable doubt, and the jury must unanimously agree that this has been established (USDOJ, 2001a). The defendant need only establish the existence of mitigating factors by a preponderance of the evidence, and each juror is free to conclude that such factors have been established, regardless of whether other members of the jury agree. To recommend a sentence of death, the jury must determine that the defendant had the requisite culpability with respect to the victim's death and must unanimously agree that the aggravating factor or factors presented sufficiently outweigh any mitigating factors to justify a capital sentence (USDOJ, 2001a).

As of November 2009, there were a total of 48 inmates on death row in the federal correctional system. Of these, 21 were Caucasian, 26 were African American, and one was Latino. There were also three female inmates on death row in the federal system; all were Caucasian. Ages for inmates on death row ranged from 25 to 59 years old. As noted earlier, the overall population of death row inmates is quite small, and this is true in the Federal Bureau of Prisons as well. Regardless, this system, including its death penalty sentencing, has undergone extensive research and evaluation.

In 2001, an evaluation of the federal death penalty system was conducted. When released, the report prompted then attorney general Janet Reno to note that the information in the report showed racial/ethnic disparities in the federal death penalty system when compared to the general population. Specifically, in the 682 cases submitted to the Department of Justice's death penalty review procedure between 1995 and July 2000, 20% involved Caucasian defendants, 48% involved African American defendants, and 29% involved Hispanic defendants (USDOJ, 2001a).

Despite this report, up until 1995 federal executions were not a major concern to the U.S. justice system. Indeed, between 1963 and 1995, there were no executions conducted by the federal government. In 1995, the execution of David Ronald Chandler was set. Chandler had been convicted for his involvement in a 1990 drug-related murder of a police informant. Ultimately, Chandler's death sentence was commuted, and he now serves life in prison at Fort Leavenworth in Kansas. Others have been executed since then, however, including the infamous Timothy McVeigh, who committed the Oklahoma City bombing of the Alfred P. Murrah building. Two others also executed since this time are Juan Raul Garza (executed in 2001) and Louis Jones (executed in 2003). In comparison to state systems, the federal system does not execute offenders on a frequent basis.

When the ruling in *Furman v. Georgia* (1972) invalidated the death penalty in the United States, the federal branch of the justice system did not follow suit with the various state justice systems by revising its own statutes. Rather, the potential use of the death penalty lay dormant until 1988, when the president signed the **Anti-Drug Abuse Act of 1988.** A part of this law made the death penalty available as a possible punishment for certain drug-related offenses. The option of capital punishment in federal criminal cases expanded significantly further on September 13, 1994, when the president signed into law the Violent Crime Control and Law Enforcement Act, which included the **Federal Death Penalty Act of 1994.** This act established constitutional procedures for imposition of the death penalty for 60 offenses under 13 existing and 28 newly created federal capital statutes, which fall into three broad categories: (1) homicide offenses, (2) espionage and treason, and (3) nonhomicidal narcotics offenses. Two years after the Federal Death Penalty Act was passed, the federal government established the **Antiterrorism and Effective Death Penalty Act of 1996**, which added another four federal offenses to the list of capital crimes.

From this discussion, it is clear that the death penalty process has gone through substantial revision in the federal justice system. As the laws related to the death penalty have changed, so too have the internal decision-making processes in federal death penalty cases (USDOJ, 2001b). In 1995, the federal government adopted the policy—commonly known as the death penalty "protocol"—under which U.S. attorneys are required to submit for review all cases in which a defendant is charged with a death penalty–eligible offense, regardless of whether they actually desire to seek the death penalty in the defendant's case. The submissions are initially considered by a committee of senior federal attorneys in Washington, D.C., known as the **Attorney General's Review Committee on Capital Cases** (Review Committee), which makes an independent recommendation to the attorney general. From January 27, 1995, to July 20, 2000, U.S. attorneys submitted a total of 682 cases for review, and the attorney general ultimately authorized seeking the death penalty for 159 of those defendants (USDOJ, 2001b).

While a case progresses through the Department of Justice review process, it simultaneously continues in the U.S. Attorney's Office and in the court system. Some cases submitted for review are subsequently withdrawn due to events outside the review process (USDOJ, 2001b). For example, the defendant and the attorney general may enter into a plea agreement that disposes of the case and results in the imposition of a prison term. In other cases, a judicial decision may result in the dismissal of either the entire case or the specific charges that are punishable by death. As a result, the total number of cases considered by the Review Committee is smaller than the total number submitted, and the total number of defendants considered for the death penalty by the attorney

Anti-Drug Abuse Act of 1988: Made the death penalty available as a possible punishment for certain drug-related offenses.

Federal Death Penalty Act of 1994: Established constitutional procedures for imposition of the death penalty.

Antiterrorism and Effective Death Penalty Act of 1996: Required inmate to provide clear and convincing evidence of a constitutional violation before granting a certificate of appeal.

Attorney General's Review Committee on Capital Cases: Makes an independent recommendation to the attorney general regarding death penalty cases.

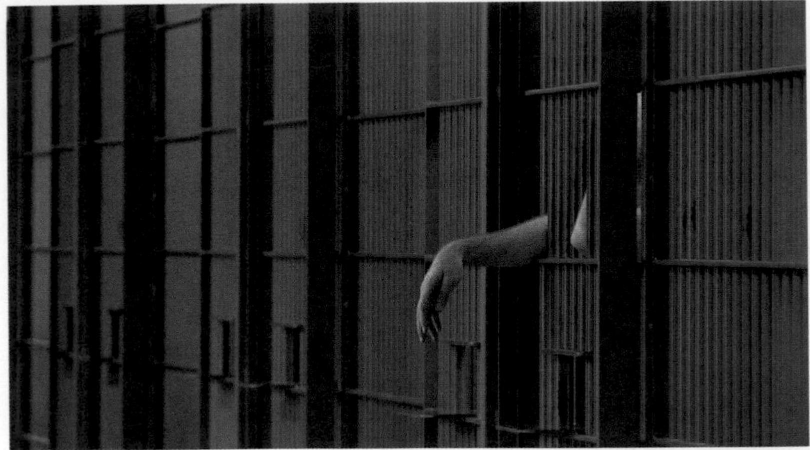

Prison Tour Video: Death Row Housing. Inmates on death row may be separated from the general prison population. Watch a warden discuss death row housing.

general is smaller still. Furthermore, not all defendants who proceed to trial ultimately receive the death penalty (USDOJ, 2001b).

Due to this process of culling out offenders who may receive the death penalty, the federal government plays a miniscule role in administering the death penalty in this country. Indeed, since the reinstatement of the death penalty within the federal system, only 75 individuals have been given a death sentence and, of those, only three have been executed (Death Penalty Information Center, 2015) Lastly, and simply as a point of interest, the federal government has designated **United States Penitentiary (USP) Terre Haute** as the physical location for the federal death row (see Focus Topic 16.2). In 1995 and 1996, USP Terre Haute was modified to accommodate death row inmates and provide functions necessary for this population. On July 13, 1999, the Special Confinement Unit at USP Terre Haute opened, and the Bureau of Prisons transferred male federal death row inmates from other federal prisons and from state prisons to USP Terre Haute. The federal government chose Terre Haute as the location of the men's death row due to its central location within the United States.

METHODS OF EXECUTION

United States Penitentiary (USP) Terre Haute: The physical location for federal death row.

In Figure 16.7, students will see that there are generally three primary means of executing offenders on death row—lethal injection, electrocution, and lethal gas—all of which will be discussed briefly. Death by firing squad is only used in two states: Oklahoma and Utah. Hanging is likewise very rare, and, again, only three states authorize its use: Delaware, New

Figure 16.7: Method of Execution by State, 2015

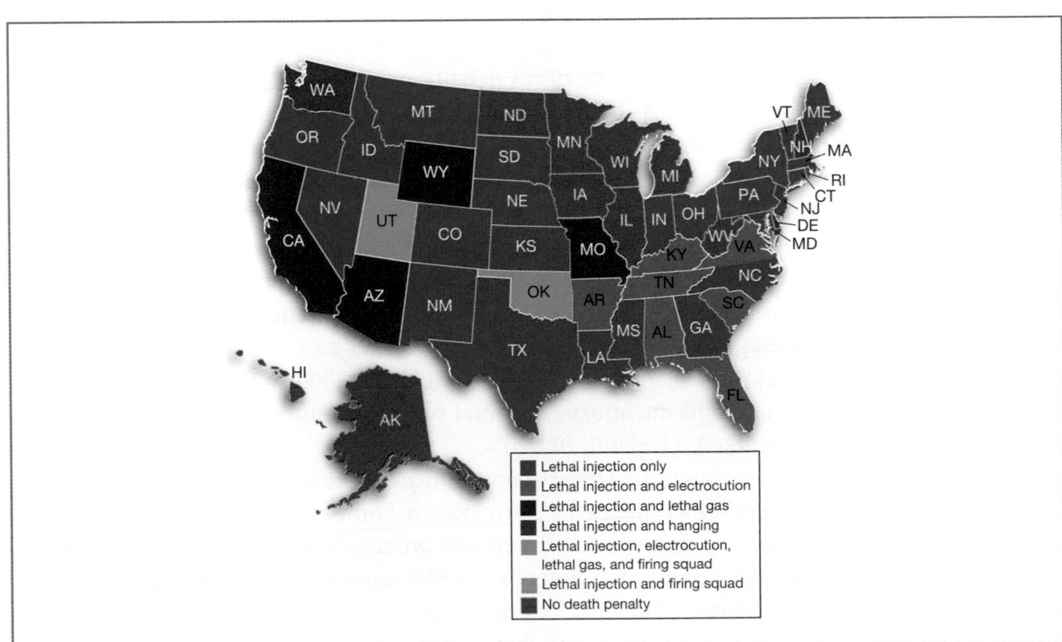

SOURCE: Snell, T. L. (2014). *Capital punishment 2013*. Bureau of Justice Statistics.

FOCUS TOPIC 16.2

Special Confinement Unit Opens at USP Terre Haute

On July 13 [1999], the United States Penitentiary (USP) Terre Haute, Indiana, opened a Special Confinement Unit to provide humane, safe, and secure confinement of male offenders who have been sentenced to death by the federal courts. As a result of this action, this week, inmates with federal death sentences have been transferred from other federal and state correctional facilities to USP Terre Haute for placement in this Special Confinement Unit.

© Reuters/CORBIS

■ PHOTO 16.3 **Aerial view of the U.S. federal prison in Terre Haute, Indiana. As can be seen, USP Terre Haute is a large and sprawling facility. This is where the federal death penalty is administered.**

Based on the increasing number of federal death penalty cases throughout the country, opening the Special Confinement Unit at USP Terre Haute has become necessary to implement federal death sentences under applicable federal statutes and regulations. This unit will be managed in a manner consistent with Bureau of Prisons' policies and procedures. The staff who work in this unit have received specialized training for managing this type of special offender.

The physical design of this two-story renovated housing unit includes 50 single-cells, upper tier and lower tier corridors, an industrial work shop, indoor and outdoor recreation areas, a property room, a food preparation area, attorney and family visiting rooms, and a video-teleconferencing area that is used to facilitate inmate access to the courts and their attorneys.

The Special Confinement Unit operations ensure inmates are afforded routine institution services and programs such as work programs, visitation, commissary privileges, telephone access, and law library services.

On July 19, 1993, USP Terre Haute was designated as the site by the Bureau of Prisons where implementation of the federal death penalty would occur, including the establishment of a Special Confinement Unit for federal death penalty cases. In 1995–1996, the facility was modified to accommodate this responsibility. Prior to housing special confinement cases, this unit was used to house Cuban detainees.

USP Terre Haute was constructed in 1940. The grounds of USP Terre Haute cover 33 acres enclosed by a secure perimeter double fence. Today, USP Terre Haute is one of nine federal high-security prisons that confine the bureau's most dangerous offenders. Adjacent to the USP Terre Haute is a minimum-security camp for male offenders. USP Terre Haute's inmate population is currently 1,070; it has a rated capacity of 741. The minimum-security facility inmate population is 307; it has a rated capacity of 340.

SOURCE: Dunne, D. (1999). *Special Confinement Unit opens at USP Terre Haute.* Washington, DC: Office of Public Affairs Press Releases.

Hampshire, and Washington. Thus, this discussion will remain restricted to the more common forms of execution used in the United States.

Execution by Lethal Injection

The execution protocol for most jurisdictions authorizes the use of a combination of three drugs. The first, sodium thiopental or Sodium Pentothal, is a barbiturate that renders the prisoner unconscious. The second, pancuronium bromide, is a muscle relaxant that paralyzes the diaphragm and lungs. The third, potassium chloride, causes cardiac arrest. Each chemical is lethal in the amounts administered.

The inmate is escorted into the execution chamber and is strapped onto a gurney with ankle and wrist restraints. The inmate is connected to a cardiac monitor, which is connected to a printer outside the execution chamber. IVs are started in two usable veins, one in each arm, and a flow of normal saline solution is administered at a slow rate. At the warden's signal, the injection of intravenous chemicals occurs. The most common problem encountered is collapsing veins causing an inability to properly insert the IV.

Currently, 20 states and the federal government authorize lethal injection as the sole method of execution (see Figure 16.7). Other states provide for lethal injection as the primary method of

■ PHOTO 16.4 This is an older-model electric chair. Electric chairs are less frequently used today as a means of execution.

execution but provide alternative methods depending upon the choice of the inmate, the date of the execution or sentence, or the possibility of the method being held unconstitutional.

Execution by Electrocution

The execution protocol for most jurisdictions authorizes the use of a wooden chair with restraints and connections to an electric current. The offender enters the execution chamber and is placed in the electric chair. The chair is constructed of oak and is set on a rubber matting and bolted to a concrete floor. Lap, chest, arm, and forearm straps are secured. A leg piece (anklet) is laced to the offender's right calf, and a sponge and electrode are attached. The headgear consists of a metal headpiece covered with a leather hood, which conceals the offender's face. The metal part of the headpiece consists of a copper wire mesh screen to which the electrode is brazened. A wet sponge is placed between the electrode and the offender's scalp. The safety switch is closed, the circuit breaker is engaged, and the execution control panel is activated. The most common problems encountered include burning of varying degrees to parts of the body and a failure of the procedure to cause death without repeated shocks. Witness accounts of many botched executions over the years have caused electrocution to be replaced with lethal injection as the most common method of execution.

Currently, only Nebraska currently uses electrocution as the sole method of execution. Nine other states provide for electrocution as an alternative method, depending upon the choice of the inmate, the date of the execution or sentence, or the possibility of the method being held unconstitutional. Interestingly, in 2008, the Nebraska Supreme Court ruled that the use of the electric chair as a method of execution violates the Nebraska Constitution. With no alternative methods of execution on the books, Nebraska is practically without a death penalty.

Execution by Lethal Gas

The execution protocol for most jurisdictions authorizes the use of an airtight steel execution chamber equipped with a chair and attached restraints. The inmate is restrained at his chest, waist, arms, and ankles, and wears a mask during the execution. The chair is equipped with a metal container beneath the seat. Cyanide pellets are placed in this container. A metal canister is on the floor under the container and filled with a sulfuric acid solution. There are three executioners, and each executioner turns one key. When the three keys are turned, an electric switch causes the bottom of the cyanide container to open, allowing the cyanide to fall into the sulfuric acid solution, producing a lethal gas. Unconsciousness can occur within a few seconds if the inmate takes a deep breath. However, if the inmate holds his or her breath, death can take much longer, and the inmate usually goes into wild convulsions. A heart monitor attached to the inmate is read in the control room, and after the warden pronounces the inmate dead, ammonia is pumped into the execution chamber to neutralize the gas. Exhaust fans then remove the inert fumes from the chamber into two scrubbers that contain water and serve as a neutralizing agent. Death is estimated to usually occur within 6 to 16 minutes of the lethal gas emissions.

The most common problems encountered are the obvious agony suffered by the inmate and the length of time to cause death. Currently, only four states—Arizona, California, Missouri, and Wyoming—authorize lethal gas as a method of execution, all as an alternative to lethal injection, depending upon the choice of the inmate, the date of the execution or sentence, or the possibility of lethal injection being held unconstitutional.

ARGUMENTS FOR AND AGAINST THE DEATH PENALTY

The debate over the death penalty has been active in the United States for generations. Generally, it is not difficult to find people who have strong views regarding this sanction, both pro and con. These arguments generally focus on one of three common themes: deterrence, retribution, and arbitrariness. Each of these themes will be discussed separately to allow for a more clear presentation of the arguments associated with it.

Deterrence

Students may recall that we discussed the notions of general and specific deterrence earlier in this text. We again use these terms to explain the pros and cons of the death penalty as a potential method of deterrence. Supporters of the death penalty contend that when murderers are sentenced to death and executed, other would-be murderers will reconsider their acts due to the fear of also being executed. This is an argument for the death penalty having a general deterrence effect. This naturally presupposes that offenders contemplate their actions to such an extent before committing those actions. Other supporters argue in favor of more specific deterrence rather than general deterrence. Specific deterrence is achieved in such cases because that specific offender who is put to death will not be able to commit another crime again because, simply put, he or she is dead. This is perhaps the most effective and most guaranteed means of preventing recidivism that is known.

Video Link
Witness to Innocence: Spreading Awareness

Opponents of the death penalty who argue against deterrence as a rationale for using the death penalty note that while numerous statistical studies have been conducted, there is no conclusive evidence that the death penalty lowers crime. In fact, there may even be some indication that its use can increase crime (this will be discussed in more detail later in the brutalization hypothesis section of this chapter). Support for this can be seen when comparing states that do not employ the death penalty with those that do; generally crime rates and murder rates are lower in states that do not have the death penalty. Interestingly, the United States, an ardent proponent of the death penalty, has a higher murder rate than do countries in Europe and Canada, which do not have the death penalty.

Further, most people who commit murders do not usually plan on being caught, and most commit their crimes due to fits of anger when in impaired states, such as when they are drunk or high on drugs. These types of circumstances do not allow for an offender to contemplate the outcome of his or her actions, and, depending on the offender's emotional framework at the time of the crime commission, it may be doubtful that the knowledge of this sanction would be a deterrent. Since these factors—the unpremeditated nature of the crime, the offender's altered state of mind due to the substance abuse—are often cited as reasons to mitigate the punishment an offender may receive, it is clear that such circumstances may not truly justify the death penalty, at least not on a logical basis.

Lastly, life sentences without the possibility of parole are just as effective as death sentences. Both can arguably deter crime in a general and specific manner. However, the life sentence allows for remediation in cases where it may later be found that an offender was, in fact, innocent. In addition, life sentences tend to be less expensive for prison administrators (and taxpayers) than death sentences. It is also worth noting that most murderers on death row are very well mannered and do not represent an institutional hazard.

Shelka04

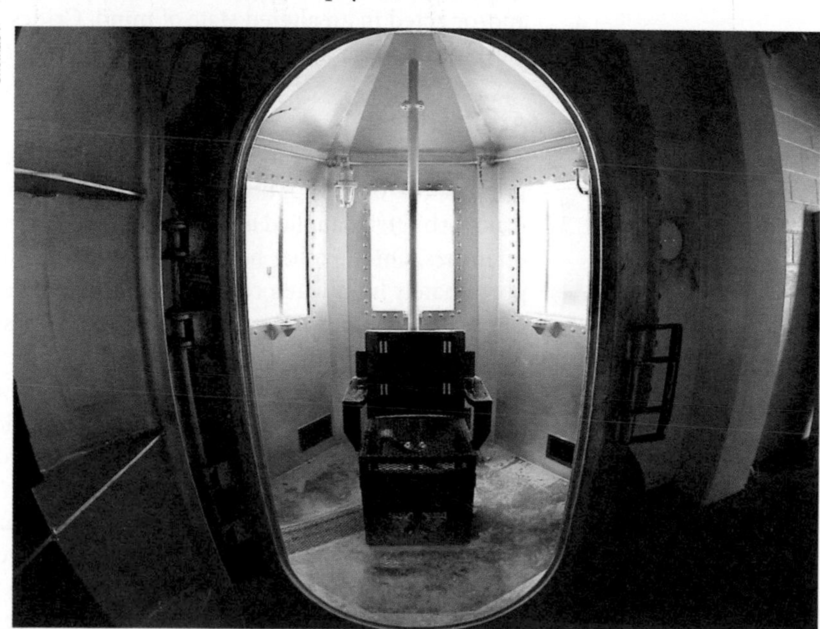

■ PHOTO 16.5 Gas chambers are airtight execution chambers equipped with a chair and attached restraints. Cyanide pellets are introduced to sulfuric acid solution to create a lethal gas.

Retribution

The second theme around which arguments for and against the death penalty tend to revolve is the desire for retribution. Students may recall that we discussed the concept of retribution in Chapter 2 of this text. The concept of retribution is sometimes given biblical reference with the saying "an eye for an eye," which implies an offender committing a crime should be punished in a manner that is commensurate with the severity of the crime that he or she has committed. This is also referred to as the "just desserts" model, which demands that punishments match the degree of harm that criminals have inflicted on their victims (Stohr, Walsh, & Hemmens, 2009).

While many people tend to confuse retribution with simple revenge, it is not the same thing. Rather, retribution is based on a logical premise that if a person commits an infraction the logical consequence is a penalty calibrated to the severity of that infraction—as much as is humanly possible, of course. It is recognized by most proponents of retribution that this approach cannot restore the victim and/or the victim's family members to their state of existence before the murder was committed, but it is thought that the execution of the offender will bring closure to the criminal activity and to the ordeal of the victim(s). This symbolic closure has a logical connotation and outcome.

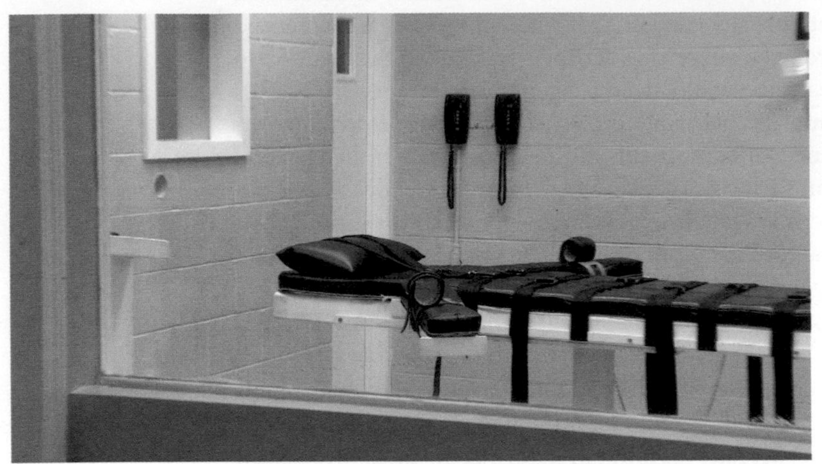

Prison Tour Video: Preparing for Execution. This lethal injection table is used in a state prison. Watch a clip about preparing an inmate for execution.

While retribution has been couched as a logical approach, there is an emotional component that is also addressed: Families of the victim can see that, if nothing else, there is some connection between the action and the consequences received. In addition, the death penalty can help to facilitate the grieving process Angola as some families may desire reciprocation commensurate to the loss that they have incurred. To ask for a payment of anything less than the offender's life would seem to indicate that the life of the victim was somehow less valuable. Thus, there may indeed be an emotional sense of justice that is fulfilled. While many critiques of retribution might not find this adequate as a rationale, supporters may contend that families of murder victims have a right to feel as they do and, correspondingly, are entitled to seek relief as they are allowed within the law.

Opponents of retribution may hold that at its base, retribution is simply a form of revenge. The contention is that retribution simply provides a reason and rationale behind the pursuit of unbridled revenge. In fact, opponents of retribution tend to believe that the use of the death penalty itself contradicts the "evolving standards of decency" espoused by the Supreme Court. The mark of a civilization is how it aids those who are troubled, which many believe should not be through the eradication of their existence. This is even truer when the offender has a diminished capacity and/or acted in an altered state of mind. Critics often claim the use of the death penalty is simply barbaric and that justifications based on retribution do not make this penalty more civilized.

Arbitrariness

The last theme that many arguments involving the death penalty tend to adhere to is the arbitrary nature of the application of the death penalty. Supporters of the death penalty argue that it is not arbitrarily applied and even note that more Caucasian offenders are executed than minority offenders. On the other hand, the number of African Americans on death row tends to be disproportionately high when compared to their overall population numbers. Thus, this racial disparity can seem to point to some degree of arbitrariness in the use of this sanction.

Consider also that one study found that nearly half of a total of 1,936 capital punishment cases ended with a plea bargain. This included cases where there were two or even three victims. From this, we can conclude that there is a degree of variability in determining exactly who is actually put to death. In fact, most plea bargains are made according to the evidence that exists in a case and/or the representation that the offender is able to obtain. This means that determining whether the offender gets the death penalty has little to do with the ultimate outcome of justice but instead is reliant on other factors associated with the case. Obviously, this creates disparate and potentially arbitrary outcomes.

Regardless of whether racial disparities do indicate arbitrariness, there is general consensus that no matter how much we try, we can never perfectly calibrate a sanction to be exactly commensurate with the crime that is committed. The inability to ensure proportionality, therefore, undermines the argument for retribution and instead further illustrates how we, as a society, are at risk of enabling arbitrary practices.

TECHNOLOGY AND EQUIPMENT 16.1

The Use of DNA Technology Frees Death Row Inmates, Brings Others to Justice

In 2015, the Washington, D.C.–based Death Penalty Information Center (DPIC) reported that as of that year, 20 death row inmates had been exonerated with the help of DNA evidence.

While many death row inmates await only their execution, others hope for new tests that could spur their release.

In 2004, the U.S. Congress passed legislation that encourages all states to enable post-trial DNA tests. The legislation also provides funding for such tests.

Texas Department of Public Safety (DPS) spokesperson Tela Mange notes that her agency's crime lab has handled 49 such inmate requests (not all of them death penalty cases) for DNA retesting. A significant percentage of the inmates have been exonerated.

Such post-trial exonerations are likely to become a thing of the past because modern, accurate, affordable DNA testing has become a common pretrial practice.

"We have an increasing number of between 2,500 [and] 3,000 DNA cases each year," Mange said. "Juries are coming to expect it, especially because they are being trained by TV. But there is a disconnect between *CSI* and the things that we can do, and that's a concern. We can't get returns on DNA cases in an hour."

DNA evidence is also subject to human error. Confidence in many testing labs has been shaken by confirmed cases of botched, falsified, and otherwise erroneous procedures, most infamously at the Houston Police Department crime laboratory, where a 17-year-old boy was convicted for rape based on improperly processed DNA samples.

Reform Needed?

Rob Warden, director of the Center on Wrongful Conviction at the Northwestern University School of Law in Chicago, said the United States' many labs and controlling agencies are in need of fundamental reform.

"The most fundamental reform would be to establish reliable scientific procedures in crime labs," he said. "They should be independent of law enforcement agencies. Scientists should not know what the desired outcome of the test is. Instead, it sometimes happens [that officials say], 'Here's a semen sample from the victim, and here's the suspect's sample—can you match them?' That shouldn't be the question."

Even when DNA evidence is accurately managed, using it to prove innocence or guilt is not always straightforward.

"People confuse the presence of biological material and DNA with its ultimate use," said John Bradley, the district attorney of Williamson County, Texas.

"DNA means that a biological material is present, but there is still a lot of work to be done to draw truthful inferences from it, from the prosecutors' or defendants' viewpoint. You can go into any room anywhere and likely find some DNA, but it doesn't resolve the question of what does that DNA mean?"

Bradley explained that not only are juries becoming more DNA savvy but defendants are as well.

"In a few interesting cases defendants have come close to manipulating DNA in ways that led the case away from themselves," he explained.

For instance, a serial rapist paid prostitutes for semen-filled condoms and used the fluid to confound DNA testing. Also, several Texas prisoners switched identity armbands prior to blood sampling, fooling a nurse who did not know the inmates.

Despite the challenges, DNA is helping law enforcement to close the books on many cases that had been unresolved for years.

The United States' Combined DNA Index System (CODIS) compares DNA profiles of convicted sex offenders and other violent criminals with evidence from unsolved cases.

"We had a serial rapist who raped two little girls, and the detectives had decided that there was no way to solve the case," Mange, the Texas Department of Public Safety spokesperson, said. "But 5 years later we submitted the evidence [to CODIS], and we got a match. We never would have solved this case in a million years without CODIS, and these girls were living in fear because they thought that this person was out there."

The booming use of DNA testing has led to enormous backlogs in many labs, and lack of public funding for the tests has frustrated prosecutors and defenders alike.

With DNA's importance likely to grow, both groups hope that increased funding will help the wheels of justice turn fairly and quickly.

SOURCE: Handwerk, B. (2005, April 8). *The use of DNA technology frees death-row inmates, brings others to justice.* National Geographic News.

BRUTALIZATION HYPOTHESIS

There is some evidence that the death penalty may not only be a failure at deterring crime but may actually increase homicide levels in areas where executions occur. This observation is often based on the notion that violence begets violence and is referred to as the brutalization hypothesis. The **brutalization hypothesis**, first introduced in Chapter 1, contends that the death penalty may actually cause an increase in murders because it reinforces the use of violence. Because of this,

brutalization hypothesis: The contention that the use of harsh punishments sensitizes people to violence and teaches them to use it.

APPLIED THEORY 16.1

Death Penalty and Rational Choice Theory

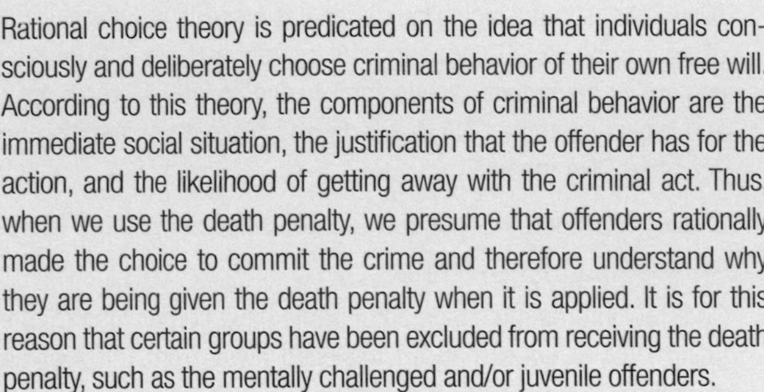

Rational choice theory is predicated on the idea that individuals consciously and deliberately choose criminal behavior of their own free will. According to this theory, the components of criminal behavior are the immediate social situation, the justification that the offender has for the action, and the likelihood of getting away with the criminal act. Thus, when we use the death penalty, we presume that offenders rationally made the choice to commit the crime and therefore understand why they are being given the death penalty when it is applied. It is for this reason that certain groups have been excluded from receiving the death penalty, such as the mentally challenged and/or juvenile offenders.

According to Keel (2005), the concepts associated with rational choice theory are rooted in the analysis of human behavior developed by the early classical theorists Cesare Beccaria and Jeremy Bentham. Keel (2005) notes the central points of this theory:

1. The human being is a rational actor.
2. Rationality involves an end-means calculation.
3. People (freely) choose *all* behavior, both conforming and deviant, based on their rational calculations.
4. The central element of calculation involves a cost-benefit analysis: *pleasure* versus *pain*.
5. Choice, with all other conditions equal, will be directed toward the maximization of *individual* pleasure.
6. Choice can be controlled through the perception and understanding of the potential pain or punishment that will follow an act judged to be in violation of the social good, the *social contract*.
7. The state is responsible for maintaining order and preserving the common good through a system of laws (this system is the embodiment of the social contract).
8. The *swiftness, severity, and certainty* of punishment are the key elements in understanding a law's ability to control human behavior.

The key issue is that rational choice is a highly subjective concept. When determining whether an offender exercised rational choice, numerous conditions may have to be considered. Rather than consider these points, rational choice theory simply focuses on the act that was committed and those variables that may make the act less desirable in the future. However, it is clear from our readings that it is questionable if the death penalty actually has a deterrent effect at all. Advocates of rational choice theory tend to ignore many of the mitigating factors that might be associated with an outcome and tend to presume that offenders are fully aware of their actions and the potential outcomes of those actions. This leaves substantial room for error.

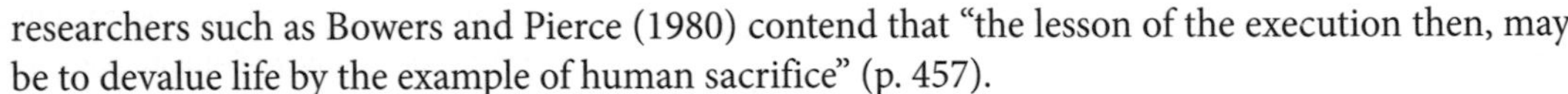

researchers such as Bowers and Pierce (1980) contend that "the lesson of the execution then, may be to devalue life by the example of human sacrifice" (p. 457).

Other researchers, such as Cochran, Chamlin, and Seth (1994), examined the reinstatement of the death penalty in Oklahoma. They found "no evidence that Oklahoma's reintroduction of the execution produced a significant decrease in the level of criminal homicides during the period under investigation" (Cochran et al., 1994, p. 129). Even further, they noted that the death penalty seemed to produce a brutalizing effect that further encouraged offenders to commit murders if they had feelings that their own life or circumstances were fundamentally unfair.

Video Link
Anthony Ray Hinton, Exonerated Alabama Death Row Inmate, Freed From Prison

Regardless of the argument that one believes, the research is clearly quite mixed on the utility of the death penalty. In short, no one can seem to prove whether "it works" at doing anything in the manner that is intended, and both advocates and opponents are able to generate evidence for their views. This makes the entire issue difficult to resolve. Work by Kohen and Jolly (2006) demonstrates the mixed state of affairs in researching the efficacy of the death penalty. When looking at Table 16.5, it can be seen that there are numerous studies that have had different results. Some studies find support for deterrence, and some do not; others occasionally find support for the brutalization effect. While Kohen and Jolly (2006) were making a case against the death penalty in their review of the research, it is our point now to simply understand that it seems that there is no airtight case for *or* against the death penalty despite years of debate.

We will close our discussion of the death penalty with these final thoughts. It has clearly not been proven that the death penalty works as deterrent to crime. And, if we do not know for a fact that this sanction deters crime, then the most logical response is to not use this sanction when others are available until it can be proven that it does indeed have a deterrent effect—*if* that day ever comes. If we do otherwise, we must then admit that deterrence is not our rationale for using the death penalty. This would mean that the death penalty would be a sanction steeped in retribution, and our government would be ethically obligated to uphold its social contract to take a life when another was taken. To fail to do so would mean that the government is fraudulently or negligently failing to uphold its end of the social contract. On the other hand, when the government executes an innocent individual due to some sort of error in the justice system, it also fails in meeting its social contract by infringing on the liberty of the innocent and subjecting a person to the terrifying experience of being on death row, knowing all the while that he or she did not commit the crime. Let us close by noting that as long as humans are in charge of determining guilt or innocence, the use of the death penalty will lead to an innocent person's death from time to time. This is the price of doing business in the justice system.

CORRECTIONAL ASPECTS OF THE DEATH PENALTY

As can be seen from our discussion on the death penalty thus far, it is questionable how well the death penalty impacts future criminal behavior. Thus, it is open to debate whether the death penalty truly fulfills any particular correctional agenda with any degree of success. However, there are some additional considerations regarding the impact that death row can and does have upon inmates and staff who are subjected to the experience.

Harrison and Tamony (2010) have provided some interesting research on how death row is managed, specifically focusing on the use of solitary confinement with death row inmates. They provide two terms, *death row phenomenon* and *death row syndrome,* to describe psychological reactions that offenders present when in solitary confinement for excessive periods of time. According to Harrison and Tamony (2010), **death row phenomenon** describes the harmful effects of death row conditions, including exposure to extended periods of solitary confinement and mental anxiety that is experienced while waiting for one's ultimate demise. **Death row syndrome** describes the states of mental illness that can develop over time as a result of the death row phenomenon. The

Death row phenomenon: The harmful effects of death row conditions that are experienced while waiting for one's demise.

Death row syndrome: The states of mental illness that can develop over time as a result of the death row phenomenon.

Table 16.5: Selected Studies of the Deterrent Effect of the Death Penalty

Study	Unit of Analysis	Period	Result
Sellin, 1959	Matched state comparison	1920–1962	No deterrent
Ehrlich, 1975b	U.S. (aggregate)	1933–1969	7–8 fewer murders per execution (C.I. 0–24)
Bowers and Pierce, 1980	New York state	1907–1963	2 more homicides per month after an execution
Mocan and Gittings, 2003	State-level	1977–1997	5 fewer homicides per execution
Katz, Levitt, Shepherd, 2003	State-level	1950–1990	No systematic evidence of a deferent (+3.1 to -5.6)
Dezhbakhsh, Rubin, and Shepherd, 2003	Country-level	1977–1996	16 fewer homicides per execution
Shepherd, 2004	State-level	1977–1999	3 fewer murder per execution
Zimmerman, 2004	State-level	1978–1997	14 fewer murders per execution
Shepherd, 2005	Country-level	1977–1996	21 states have brutalization effect 6 states have deterrent effect 23 states have no effect Overall, 4.5 fewer murders per execution
Donohue and Wolfers, 2005	Canada v. U.S.	1950–2003	No deterrent

SOURCE: Kohen, A., & Jolly, S. J. (2006). *Deterrence reconsidered: A theoretical and empirical case against the death penalty.* Paper presented at the annual meeting of the Midwest Political Science Association, Palmer House Hilton, Chicago.

implication, according to Harrison and Tamony (2010), is that such a prolonged period of waiting for death may not be constitutionally sound due to the likelihood of death row offenders developing mental illnesses.

Harrison and Tamony (2010) are not alone in their assertions. Indeed, Butler (2014) wrote in her nationally recognized *Lyman Report* about the debilitative effects of this type of system of housing death row inmates in the state of Texas. In her report, she notes the effects that this has on inmates serving time on death row, and also notes that these circumstances invite security risks for correctional staff because inmates who present with psychiatric problems and aberrant behaviors tend to be more dangerous and more problematic. Lastly, Butler notes that this was not always the means by which the TDCJ-ID processed death row inmates. Indeed, prior to a security breach in the 1990s, inmates on death row were allowed to work and engage in programming while waiting for their execution date. These types of activities, according to Butler (2014), kept inmates more mentally stable and also made them less likely to commit assaults or other institutional violations.

SAGE Journal Article Link
Lackey Claims, Excessive Delay, and Evolving Standards of Decency

In her research, Partyka (2004) showed how the prison environment on death row can take a toll on both inmates and staff alike. Partyka (2004) found that primary stressors for correctional officers who work on death row included hostility and manipulation from inmates, difficult relationships with other officers, lack of support from administration, and difficulty fulfilling job/role expectations. When considering inmates on death row, Partyka (2004) found that deprivation, isolation, intrusion, helplessness, and self-reflections that generated painful memories were common. The research by Partyka (2004) is unique and shows that the correctional experience for both staff and inmates on death row is one of hardship where both languish until the final day when the offender is put to death. Whether this does or does not warrant revamping of the procedures used to house death row inmates is yet to be seen. But for now, it would seem that these additional complications and negative effects simply add to the list of problems that have been identified in regard to the United States' tenacious embrace of the death penalty as a correctional sanction.

CONCLUSION

Video Link
Witness to Innocence: A Word to Students Entering the Field

This chapter has provided students with a view of the most final sanction of all: the death penalty. The application of the death penalty is a confession that we cannot or do not wish to correct the behavior of certain offenders. This sanction is considered cruel and inhumane by a number of people in society and many wish to see it abolished. When considering the types of crimes associated with the death penalty, for the most part only offenders who have been convicted of murder will be found on death row. Most of these offenders have committed prior offenses, and most have also served prior jail or prison sentences. This is important because it demonstrates that most have led a life of crime that goes beyond the single crime for which they are sentenced. Though their civil liberties must still be protected and though they are entitled to the full range of appeals guaranteed by law, this small group of offenders (remember, only a tiny minority of offenders are sentenced to death) does tend to have a long history of offending.

There is a noticeable disparity in racial representation on death row, with African Americans being disproportionately represented. This disparity has been observed among various state systems and even specifically noted within the federal system's use of the death penalty. While this may occur for any number of reasons, it is worth noting that offenders are more likely to be given the death penalty if the victim was Caucasian. Different researchers emphasize this point for a variety of reasons. For our purposes, we conclude that much of this has to do with partisanship issues, where the more affluent members of society tend to be Caucasian (on the average this is true throughout the nation) and these persons have a strong influence on outcomes within the justice system.

Want a better grade?

Get the tools you need to sharpen your study skills. Access practice quizzes, eFlashcards, video, and multimedia at **edge.sagepub.com/hanser2e**

SAGE edge™

DISCUSSION QUESTIONS

1. What are some arguments in favor of the death penalty?
2. What are some arguments against the death penalty?
3. Select two Supreme Court cases that you believe are important regarding the death penalty. Explain why you believe that they are important.
4. What is the victim-turned-offender hypothesis, and how does it comport with the tenets of feminist criminology introduced in Chapter 10?
5. What are the different means of execution used in administering the death penalty?
6. How does racial disparity come into play regarding the death penalty?
7. In your own words, why do you believe that deterrence theory is or is not a good justification for the use of the death penalty?

SAGE edge™ **Test your understanding of chapter content. Take the practice quiz.**

KEY TERMS

Anti-Drug Abuse Act of 1988, 411

Antiterrorism and Effective Death Penalty Act of 1996, 411

Attorney General's Review Committee on Capital Cases, 411

Capital punishment, 398

Brutalization hypothesis, 417

Death row, 404

Death row phenomenon, 419

Death row syndrome, 419

Federal Death Penalty Act of 1994, 411

Prosecutorial death discretion outcome, 408

United States Penitentiary (USP) Terre Haute, 412

SAGE edge™ **Review key terms with eFlashcards.**

KEY CASES

Atkins v. Virginia (2002), 399

Coker v. Georgia (1977), 398

Ford v. Wainwright (1986), 399

Furman v. Georgia (1972), 398

Roper v. Simmons (2005), 399

Thompson v. Oklahoma (1988), 399

Trop v. Dulles (1958), 398

Witherspoon v. Illinois (1968), 398

APPLIED EXERCISE 16.1

Students must conduct either a face-to-face or a phone interview with either an inmate on death row or a correctional officer who has worked in a death row setting. The student should use the interview to gain the practitioner's or inmate's insight and perspective on several key questions related to the death penalty. Students must write the responses of the inmate or practitioner, provide their own analysis of those responses, and submit their draft by the deadline set by their instructor. Students should complete this application exercise as an essay that addresses each point below. The total word count should be 800 to 1,100 words.

When completing the interview, students should ask the following questions:

1. What is the most unique aspect of death row in the typical prison facility?
2. What are some common things that you think about when on death row?
3. What do you think that the public needs to understand about death row?

Students are required to provide contact information for the practitioner or inmate. While instructors will probably not need to contact this person, it may become necessary so that they can validate the actual completion of an interview.

Name and title of interviewee: ______________________________

Correctional agency: ______________________________

Correctional officer's phone number (if applicable): ______________

Correctional officer's e-mail address (if applicable): ______________

Name of student: ______________________________

WHAT WOULD YOU DO?

You are a religious services officer who works at Louisiana State Penitentiary Angola, and you often work with the inmates on death row. One inmate in particular, nicknamed "Greyhound" because of his advanced years in age, is scheduled for execution in 48 hours. You are aware that he will not be given a stay on his execution and that he will, in fact, be put to death at that time. Over the years of working on death row, you have gotten to know many of the men who do their time until their execution date, and Greyhound is one of them.

You are also aware of one other detail that he recently divulged to you. He did not commit the crime for which he will soon die. The crime was one in which the daughter of a small-town mayor was raped and strangled to death back in 2004; her body was found hidden in the woods near the town. Greyhound was seen near the area and ultimately confessed to the killing.

However, Greyhound has disclosed to you that it was his own son, James, who committed the murder. Greyhound loved his son, who was expected to leave on a football scholarship to Notre Dame after the summer that the crime was committed. According to James, the incident was accidental. It appeared that James and the murdered girl, Cheryl, had a long history of experimentation with sexual activity. In fact, the two had had sex together in which they experimented with different types of autoerotic asphyxiation. They had been seeing each other for over a year and had learned of this type of sexual activity on the Internet. They had experimented with this multiple times, and all was well, but on the last occasion, the situation went wrong.

James would usually hold Cheryl and, with some degree of force, would squeeze her neck around her carotid arteries while penetrating her sexually. This particular evening, they had been drinking, and Cheryl was quite drunk. He thought that she had passed out while they had sex and did not realize he had in fact choked her at first. Due to the tension on her neck and her drunken state, she was dead, but it had been an accident. The two were in the woods, late at night, on a blanket, near the shore of Lake Livingston. James, who was terrified, contacted his father rather than the police.

His father arrived at the lake, but any plan they might have come up with was circumvented when Cheryl's parents noticed her gone. Cheryl's little brother, Timmy, knew of the location where Cheryl would meet James for their sexual trysts. Timmy told his parents, who went to catch the teens in the act. James and his father were forced to leave the scene prematurely, and Cheryl's body was found by her parents. The entire situation was heartbreaking and shocked the citizens of the town.

Greyhound had told his son to keep quiet. He concocted a story and took the blame for the crime. James went on to Notre Dame amidst his father's court involvement and ultimate sentencing to death. James has often wanted to come forward, but given the cover-up of the murder and the circumstances, his father has been adamant that he say nothing. Greyhound is telling you all this because he is a very religious man, and he wants to cleanse his soul. He does not want you to mention this, ever—he notes that you are required to keep this confidential and that he is expecting you to do so.

You know that if you say nothing, the wrong person will be put to death for a crime that he did not do, all to protect the welfare of his son. On the other hand, if you do say something, it is likely that both Greyhound and his son will be in legal trouble, and this will also ruin James's life. James is now an electrical engineer with a wife and two kids. You struggle with the dilemma in which you are caught.

What would you do?

PRACTICE AND APPLY WHAT YOU'VE LEARNED

► edge.sagepub.com/hanser2e

HEAR IT FROM CORRECTIONAL PRACTITIONERS: PRISON TOUR VIDEOS

Head to the study site, where you'll find:

- Exclusive, **original SAGE video interviews** with wardens, correctional officers, inmates, and more
- Exclusive footage from inside **Angola Prison** and **Richwood Correctional Center**

17 PROGRAM EVALUATION, EVIDENCE-BASED PRACTICES, AND FUTURE TRENDS IN CORRECTIONS

©iStockphoto.com/mediaphotos

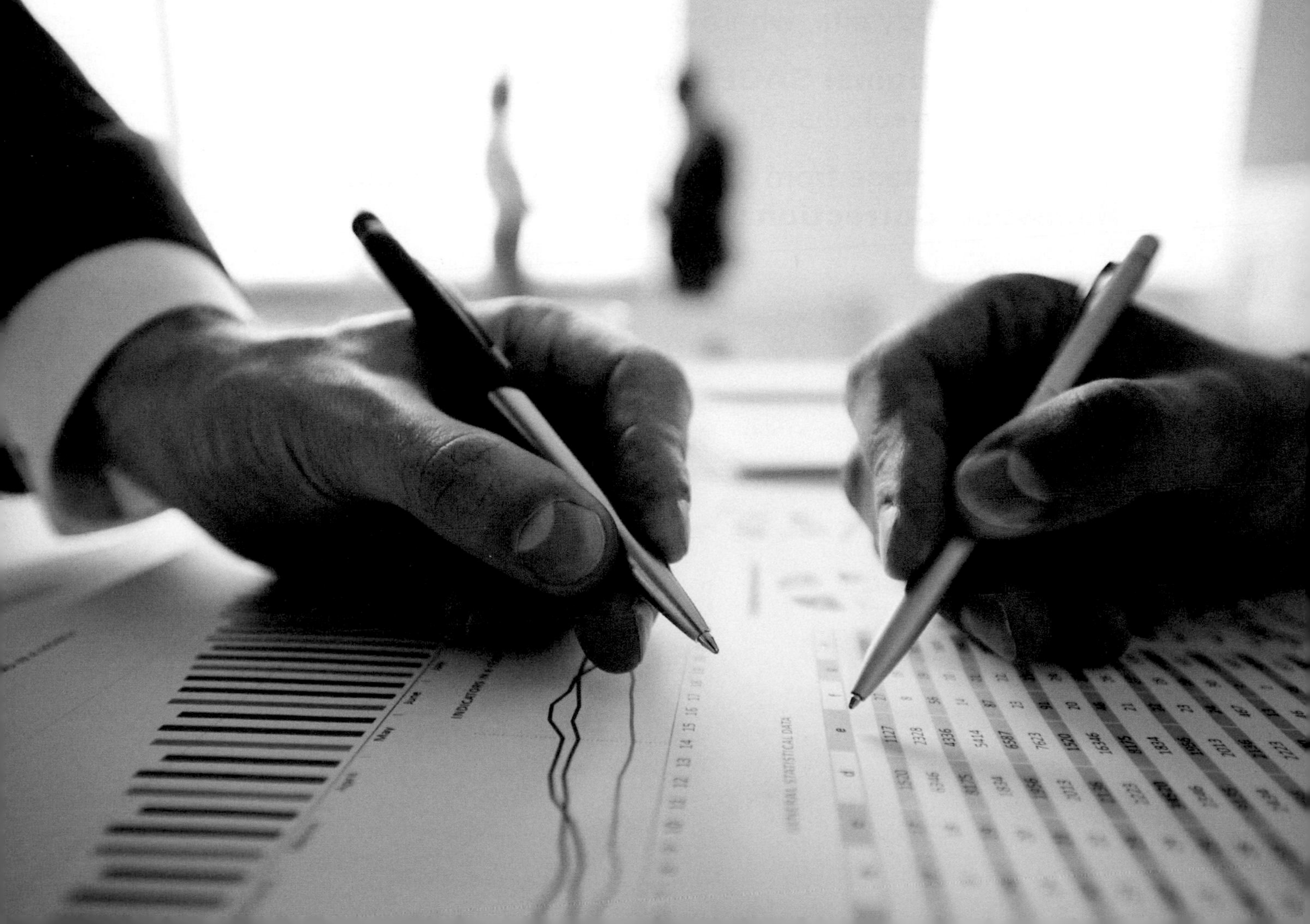

RESEARCH-BASED FUNDING DECISIONS FOR REHABILITATION IN THAILAND

The date was Monday, August 3, 2015, and Rob Hanser sat on the panel that had been gathered at the Grand Mercure Bangkok Fortune Hotel. Like the other correctional experts surrounding him, he had been invited to lend his expertise on correctional rehabilitation to about 80 professionals within the Kingdom of Thailand's national corrections service.

Thailand was in the process of revamping and restructuring its correctional system to accommodate and emphasize a rehabilitative orientation rather than one that was focused solely on security. Thus, the International Meeting on Offender Rehabilitation had been coordinated to bring experts from other parts of the world together with Thai correctional administrators to exchange ideas and to discuss matters related to rehabilitation.

The project under which this process was implemented had been named Through Care: A Model for Thailand's Coherent Rehabilitation by its two key researchers, Dr. Srisombat Chokprajakchat and Dr. Attapol Kuanliang. The two professors had been awarded a government grant to begin setting the groundwork for developing a rehabilitation model in the country.

The various administrators listened with interest to the panel members, who were from Japan, Singapore, the United Kingdom, and the United States. During his presentation, Hanser noted his involvement with various facets of correctional treatment but, in particular, showcased his work with Freedmen Inc., an organization that operated reentry homes for ex-offenders. After his presentation, the panel broke for coffee.

During the break, Hanser was approached by two people from a regional nongovernmental organization (NGO) that aided offenders in their reentry efforts. The director of the program presented some focused questions to Hanser.

"So, when you do reentry, does the government pay you to do this, or do they just give you permission to engage in the activity?" asked the director.

"Well, really they just partner with us in providing logistical support and access to facilities. We do work in collaboration with our probation and parole office, but, in the end, we are a self-funded program."

The director nodded. "It is the same with us here. It is important that if we are going to discuss rehabilitation, the government must make it a priority. . . . If they are not willing to give any money to this assistance, then I wonder if it is really a priority."

"Yes," Hanser replied, "I have said the very same thing in the United States. As you know, it is difficult to get the community to understand that if the offender is reformed, we all save trauma and expense by not having crimes in the future. The government understands this but will not act on it unless the public pressures them to do so. And the public will not pressure them unless it is educated on the importance of reentry programming and the need to fund such programs."

Both men shook their heads regretfully. The director then invited Hanser to come to his facilities to visit and to share ideas on reentry programming. Hanser thanked him, and both exchanged business cards, agreeing that Hanser would visit later that week.

Once the break ended, the Q & A portion of the panel began. The NGO director who had talked with Hanser during the break posed a question to one of the other members of the panel. He noted that his organization received marginal government funding but that it seemed as if programs from other countries that were being showcased often received government funding. He also pointed out that some of the countries represented at the meeting had correctional populations that were substantially smaller than Thailand's. He asked the panel member to comment on this and whether this was an important factor to consider when writing a reform bill for rehabilitation in Thailand.

The panel expert responded by acknowledging that her country's correctional population was indeed smaller than Thailand's. She noted that this did make the program much more manageable.

Then, a high-ranking administrator from the Thai correctional system rose and stated, "I know that it is true that we do not fund most of our reentry homes, and that is unfortunate. But currently money is not always available, and there are many pushes and pulls on the system."

The NGO reentry director shook his head and acknowledged that matters were complicated. He nonetheless reminded the administrator that NGOs and other partners were a critical component to reducing recidivism among released offenders in Thai society.

LEARNING OBJECTIVES:

1. Identify the process of evaluative research and distinguish between process and outcome measures.
2. Identify and discuss the use of evidence-based practices in corrections.
3. Be aware of likely future trends in correctional agencies.

Hanser listened intently to the discussion and realized that most all of the challenges that he faced in the United States were being faced by correctional administrators in Thailand as well. This was, of course, the point to the conference—to compare practices, research, and outcomes of various programs so that the Thai could determine the best course of action for rehabilitation with their own correctional population.

As Hanser pondered this, he thought to himself, *It's a small world after all.*

INTRODUCTION

Effective research and evaluation of correctional programs is critical if we are to begin to understand what is likely to produce lasting change in offenders. If correctional systems do not take these important steps, they are resigning their efforts to chance. Mere chance is not acceptable, however, when huge amounts of money and human lives are at stake. Therefore, the question becomes, how do we effectively evaluate correctional programs, and how do we know that those programs are working? In response to this, we begin this chapter with an explanation of the specific function of evaluation research, which can be described as a form of explanatory research. We conclude the chapter with a discussion of trends likely to impact corrections in the future. This last aspect is based on prior research as well as observations of policy and decision making that have been touted among numerous correctional agencies around the nation.

EVALUATION RESEARCH

In the past several years a massive effort on behalf of the U.S. government has been aimed at enhancing evaluation practices and services of the correctional system. Various documents have been published and placed in the public domain to help the administrators of community corrections programs better understand the impact of various treatment services. Much of the following information is borrowed from the Center for Substance Abuse Treatment (2005), a government agency responsible for implementing and evaluating many treatment programs that attempt to better serve offenders suffering from mental illness and co-occurring disorders.

SAGE Journal Article Link
A Census of Prison-Based Drug Treatment Programs

Research and evaluation is a critical dimension of correctional programs. Evaluations are needed for program monitoring and for decision making by program staff, criminal justice administrators, and policymakers. Evaluations provide accountability, identify strengths and weaknesses, and provide a basis for program revision. In addition, evaluation reports are useful learning tools for others who are interested in developing effective programs. Many treatment programs in the criminal justice system have operated without evaluations for many years only to find out later that essential outcome data were needed to justify program continuation.

Conducting an adequate evaluation requires one to clearly formulate the treatment model, reasonable program goals, and specific objectives related to client needs. General goals must be translated into measurable outcomes. The evaluator generally works closely with program administrators to translate the evaluation guidelines into operational components. In essence, scientific principles for conducting research should be carefully adhered to in order to enhance the viability of findings.

There are three basic types of evaluation: implementation, process, and outcome. An important note before we discuss these components is that although implementation and process evaluations can begin when the program is initiated, outcome evaluation should not begin until the program has been fully implemented. Outcome evaluations are generally more costly than other types of evaluation and are warranted for programs of longer duration that are aimed at modifying lifestyles (such as therapeutic communities), rather than drug education interventions that are less intensive and less likely to produce long-term effects.

Robert Hanser

■ PHOTO 17.1 The government-sponsored International Symposium on Offender Rehabilitation was held in Bangkok, Thailand. At this conference, Robert Hanser provided input on rehabilitation programming in the United States.

Implementation Evaluation

While programs often look promising in the proposal stage, many do not succeed as planned in the security-oriented correctional environment. Sometimes programs are too rigidly implemented and adjustments are not made for the realities of community corrections; this often renders these programs less effective. **Implementation evaluation** is aimed at identifying both complications and accomplishments during the early phases of program development in order to provide helpful feedback to clinical and administrative staff. Such evaluations involve informal and formal interviews with correctional administrators, staff, and offenders to ascertain their degree of satisfaction with the program and their perceptions of any problems.

Process Evaluation

Traditionally, **process evaluation** refers to the assessment of the effects of a program on clients while they are in the program; this makes it possible to assess the institution's intermediary goals. Process evaluation involves analyzing records related to the following:

1. Type and amount of services provided.
2. Attendance and participation in group meetings.
3. Number of offenders who are screened, admitted, reviewed, and discharged.
4. Percentage of offenders who favorably complete treatment each month.
5. Percentage of offenders who have infractions or rule violations.
6. Number of offenders who test positive for substances (this can be compared to urinalysis results for the general prison population).

Effective programs produce positive client changes. These changes initially occur during participation in the program and ideally continue upon release into the community. The areas of potential client change that should be assessed include the following:

1. Cognitive understanding (e.g., mastery of program curriculum).
2. Emotional functioning (e.g., anxiety and depression).
3. Attitudes/values (e.g., honesty, responsibility, and concern for others).
4. Education and vocational training progress (e.g., achievement tests).
5. Behavior (e.g., rule infractions and urinalyses results).

Within institutional corrections, it is also important to evaluate program impact on the host prison facility itself. Well-run treatment programs often generate an array of positive developments affecting the morale and functioning of the entire inmate population. Areas to examine include the following:

1. *Offender behavior.* Review the number of rule infractions, the cost of hearings, court litigation expenses, and inmate cooperation in general prison operations.
2. *Staff functioning.* Assess stress levels, which may become manifest in the number of sick days taken and the rate of staff turnover. Generally, the better the program, the lower the stress and the better the attendance, the involvement, and the commitment of staff.
3. *Physical plant.* Examine the physical properties of the program. Assess general vandalism apparent in terms of damage to furniture or windows as well as the presence of graffiti. Assess structural damage to walls and plumbing, for example.

Implementation evaluation: Identifying problems and accomplishments during the early phases of program development for feedback to clinical and administrative staff.

Process evaluation: Traditionally refers to assessment of the effects of the program on clients while they are in the program, making it possible to assess the institution's intermediary goals.

Outcome evaluation: Involves quantitative research aimed at assessing the impact of the program on long-term treatment outcomes.

Outcome Evaluation

Outcome evaluations are more ambitious and expensive than implementation or process evaluations. An **outcome evaluation** involves quantitative research aimed at assessing the impact of a program on long-term treatment outcomes. Such evaluations are usually carefully designed studies that compare outcomes for a treatment group with outcomes for other, less intensive treatments or a no-treatment control group (i.e., a sample of offenders who meet the program admission

FOCUS TOPIC 17.1

Commonly Used Measures of Reentry Program Performance

Process Measures

Substance abuse treatment services received

Employment services received

Housing assistance received

Family intervention and parent training received

Health and mental health services received

Outcome Measures

Rearrest rates

Reincarceration rates

Proportion employed

Rates of drug relapse

Frequency and severity of offenses

Proportion self-sufficient

Participation in self-improvement programs

SOURCE: Bureau of Justice Assistance, Center for Program Evaluation. (2007). *Reporting and using evaluation results.* Washington, DC: Author.

Prison Tour Video Link

Getting Out and Performance Grid

criteria but who do not receive treatment). These evaluations involve complex statistical analyses and sophisticated report preparation.

Follow-up data (e.g., drug relapse, recidivism, employment status) are the heart of outcome evaluation. Follow-up data can be collected from criminal justice records and face-to-face interviews with individuals who participated in certain programs. Studies that use agency records are less expensive than those that involve locating participants and conducting follow-up interviews. Outcome evaluations can include cost-effectiveness and cost-benefit information that is important to policymakers. Because outcome research usually involves a relatively large investment of time and money as well as the cooperation of a variety of people and agencies, it must be carefully planned. A research design may be very simple and easy to implement, or it may be more complex. In the case of more complex studies, it is usually advisable to enlist the assistance of an experienced researcher.

Program Quality and Staffing Quality

In addition to outcome and process measures, there are a number of other areas that agencies may wish to evaluate. These other areas may or may not require the input of the offender, and they may or may not be dependent upon the offender population's outcome results. One example of this is when agencies wish to assess the quality of their program, their staff, or their curricula. Each of these three components is very important and may require more than simple outcome evaluation measures. In some cases, such as with program curricula, it may be necessary to examine the general process measures of a program as a whole. It is important when agencies evaluate curricula that they keep this aspect of a program separate and distinct from the effects that staff may have upon the process. Staff members may modify the general process through their own therapeutic slant and/or means of implementing aspects of a job requirement. In other words, the individual preferences of different persons employed in the agency may not be what you hope to observe in a curricular assessment; rather, it is the uniform and written procedures that are of interest.

Evaluative transparency: When an agency's evaluative process allows an outside person to have full view of the agency's operations, budgeting, policies, procedures, and outcomes.

Therefore, it is clear that evaluations can be quite complex and detailed, depending on the approach taken by the agency. The key to an effective and ethical evaluation is evaluative transparency. **Evaluative transparency** is when an agency's evaluative process allows for an outside person (whether an auditor, an evaluator, or the public at large) to have full view of the agency's operations, budgeting, policies, procedures, and outcomes. In transparent agencies there are no secrets, and confidential information is only authorized when ethical or legal requirements mandate that the information not be transparent. In some cases, information should *not* be available to the general public; such information may include a client's treatment files and/or a victim's

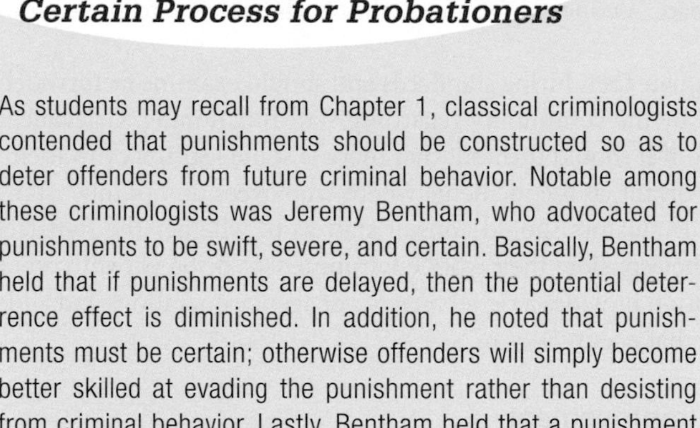

APPLIED THEORY 17.1

The Tenets of Classical Criminology and the HOPE Program: A Swift and Certain Process for Probationers

As students may recall from Chapter 1, classical criminologists contended that punishments should be constructed so as to deter offenders from future criminal behavior. Notable among these criminologists was Jeremy Bentham, who advocated for punishments to be swift, severe, and certain. Basically, Bentham held that if punishments are delayed, then the potential deterrence effect is diminished. In addition, he noted that punishments must be certain; otherwise offenders will simply become better skilled at evading the punishment rather than desisting from criminal behavior. Lastly, Bentham held that a punishment should carry enough consequence to leave an impact on the offender if it is to reduce future offending. However, according to Cesare Beccaria, a punishment should be proportionate to the severity of the crime.

The goals of **H**awaii's **O**pportunity **P**robation with **E**nforcement (HOPE) program are completely aligned with classical criminology's emphasis on rational choice and deterrence. By addressing probation violations in a *swift, certain,* and *proportionate* manner, HOPE has reduced both violations and revocations of probation, encouraging probationers to break the cycle of recidivism.

HOPE begins with a direct, formal warning delivered by a judge in court to offenders enrolled in the program. The warning explicitly states that any future probation violations will result in an immediate, brief jail stay. Probationers with drug issues are assigned a color code at the warning hearing and are required to call the HOPE hotline each weekday morning to find out which color has been chosen for that day. Probationers whose color is selected must appear at the probation office before 2 p.m. the same day for a drug test. Offenders not involved with drugs must comply with their conditions of probation and may be required to attend treatment. When probationers violate the conditions of probation, they are arrested or an arrest warrant is issued. As soon as a probation officer detects a violation, he or she completes a motion to modify probation form and sends it to the judge, who promptly holds a violation hearing.

A probationer found to have violated the terms of probation is sentenced to a short jail stay. Upon release, the probationer reports to his or her probation officer and resumes participation in HOPE. Each successive violation is met with an escalated response (i.e., a longer stay in jail).

A National Institute of Justice–funded evaluation of HOPE found that when compared with probationers in a control group, after 1 year the HOPE probationers were:

1. Fifty-five percent less likely to be arrested for a new crime
2. Seventy-two percent less likely to use drugs
3. Sixty-one percent less likely to skip appointments with their supervisory officer
4. Fifty-three percent less likely to have their probation revoked

As a result, HOPE probationers served 48% fewer days in prison, on average, than the control group members. Thus, it is thought that this program's swift, certain, and proportionate application of sanctions has been successful in reducing recidivism. This lends support to the tenets of classical criminology and demonstrates that sometimes we can go back and successfully apply historical criminological theories to current modern-day issues. The fact that we are going back to Chapter 1 in this text as a basis for a research study in the last chapter further reinforces the idea that the past, present, and future of corrections can be conceptually interconnected, both in the world of the researcher and in the world of the practitioner.

SOURCE: McEvoy, K. (2012). HOPE: A swift and certain process for probationers. Washington, DC: National Institute of Justice.

personal identity. In such cases, the intent is a benevolent safeguarding of the client's welfare, not the agency's own welfare.

If one is to evaluate the quality of a program, it stands to reason that the program must be transparent to the evaluator who is tasked with observing that program. Agencies that seek to meet high ethical standards must be transparent. This is a core requisite to ensuring the quality of the program that is implemented. Further, programs of quality are accountable to the public, which is, in part, an element of transparency. Public accountability is a matter of good ethical standing, and this is consistent with the reason that ethical safeguards are put into place—to protect the public consumer. In the case of corrections agencies, the product that is "sold" to the public is community safety, and it is the obligation of the agency to be accountable and transparent to the public when

Prison Tour Video Link
Return Rate and Rules

providing this product to its jurisdiction. Thus, the quality of the program should be measured by its ability to deliver ethical, open, and honest services that hold community safety as paramount.

In regard to staffing quality, agencies should also make a point to evaluate the support that they provide to their staff. Naturally, recruitment and hiring standards should be evaluated routinely, and it is also important that agencies examine their own support services for staff. Some examples of necessary support for staff include the existence of an effective human resources division, sufficient budgeting for equipment to effectively do one's job, and the nature of the job design, particularly in regard to caseload. As one might guess, this is also related to the overall quality of the program.

Quite naturally, agencies should evaluate their hiring standards and should examine factors such as the number of complaints generated by the community regarding staff functioning. Grievances made by offenders can also be examined if it should turn out that there is some legitimacy to them. Employee standards of conduct are important, as are incidents where employees do not meet standards that are expected by the agency. Evaluators should consult staff as to whether the staff feel prepared for their jobs and/or whether they consider their work environment to be on par with other agencies. All of this staff-related information provides a richer analysis of agency operations and adds transparency to the day-to-day routines that occur.

Feedback Loops and Continual Improvement

In evaluating correctional agencies, it is important that the information obtained from the evaluation serve some useful purpose. The Bureau of Justice Assistance Center for Program Evaluation (2007) elaborates on the need for evaluations to be constructed in a manner that is useful to the stakeholders of the evaluation. **Stakeholders** in corrections evaluations include the agency personnel, the community in which the agency is located, and even the offender population that is being supervised. According to the Bureau of Justice Assistance (BJA), it is important for evaluators to be clear on what agency administrators wish to evaluate, and it is also important that evaluators ensure that administrators understand that evaluative efforts are to remain objective and unbiased in nature.

It is also important that evaluators provide recommendations for agencies based on the outcome of the evaluation (BJA, 2007). It is through the use of these recommendations that agencies can improve their overall services and enhance goal-setting strategies in the future. Indeed, evaluation information can be a powerful tool for a variety of stakeholders (BJA, 2007). Program managers can use the information to make changes in their programs that will enhance their effectiveness (BJA, 2007). Decision makers can ensure that they are funding effective programs. Other authorities can ensure that programs are developed as intended and have sufficient resources to implement activities and meet their goals and objectives (BJA, 2007).

Agencies that are adept at implementing evaluative information and recommendations are sometimes referred to as learning organizations. **Learning organizations** have the inherent ability to adapt and change, improving performance through continual revision of goals, objectives, policies, and procedures. Throughout this process, learning organizations respond to the various pushes and pulls that are placed upon them by utilizing a continual process of data-driven, cyclical, and responsive decision making that results in heightened adaptability of the organization. The ideal community corrections agency is a learning organization—one that can adjust to outside community needs and challenges as well as internal personnel and resource challenges.

Lastly, in its ideal state, evaluation is an essential component in the process of program planning, goal setting, and modification and improvement. The BJA (2007) notes that evaluation findings can be used to revise policies, activities, goals, and objectives (see Focus Topic 17.2) so that community supervision agencies can provide the best possible services to the community to which they are accountable.

This is to demonstrate the importance of policymaking as well as the setting of goals and objectives that guide a community supervision agency into the future. This cyclic pattern of going from assessment to implementation to evaluation demonstrates a continual circle of development that uses past data to better face future challenges. This is the most effective means of utilizing real-world research to tailor programs that can meet the challenges within a jurisdiction. With this in mind, we once again look to the work of Van Keulen (1988), who roughly 20 years ago noted that

Stakeholders: Agency personnel, the surrounding community, and the offender population.

Learning organizations: Have the inherent ability to adapt and change, improving performance through continual revision of goals, objectives, policies, and procedures.

goals and objectives also play a critical role in evaluation by providing a standard against which to measure the program's success. If the purpose of the program is to serve as an alternative to jail, the number of jail-bound offenders the program serves would be analyzed. If the program's focus is to provide labor to community agencies, the number of hours worked by offenders would be examined. Last, having a statement of goals and objectives will enhance your program's credibility by showing that careful thought has been given to what you are doing. (p. 1)

Van Keulen (1988) demonstrates the reasons why clarity in the definition and purpose behind a community corrections program is important. Clearly articulated goals not only help to crystallize the agency's philosophical orientation on the supervision process but also provide for more measurable constructs that lend themselves to effective evaluation. Clarity in program goals and objectives allows the agency to perform evaluative research to determine if its efforts are actually successful or if they are in need of improvement. Such clarity then facilitates the ability of the agency to come "full circle" as the planning, implementation, evaluation, and refinement phases of agency operations unfold.

Community Harm With Ineffective Programs, Separating Politics From Science in the Evaluative Process

As we near the close of this text, it is important to reflect on the potential consequences that might be incurred if agencies are allowed to operate ineffectively. Public and institutional safety and security constitute the top priority for correctional agencies. However, one of the best long-term approaches to improving public safety is the use of effective reintegration efforts. Thus, programs that fail to adequately oversee offenders on community supervision run the risk of allowing the community to be harmed. Likewise, programs that fail to implement effective treatment approaches also put the community at risk.

Multiple methods of supervising offenders have been provided throughout this text. All of these supervision interventions—jails and prisons, residential treatment facilities, probation, intermediate sanctions, parole, and even the death penalty—should be implemented so that the intervention chosen best fits the offender and his or her likely level of risk. This comes back to one of the most critical aspects of corrections, the assessment and classification process. As noted in Chapter 8, it is this process that sets the stage for determining how an offender is housed and supervised. It is also at this point where correctional resources can be optimized by ensuring the best fit between resources and offender risk as well as offender treatment and needs.

The evaluation of correctional agencies is directly tied to the assessment component that occurs as the offender is first processed. Indeed, the assessment of the offender typically serves as the baseline measure when examining evaluation processes. Both process and outcome evaluations

FOCUS TOPIC 17.2

What Are Policies, Activities, Goals, and Objectives?

Policy: A governing principle pertaining to goals, objectives, and/or activities. It is a decision on an issue not resolved on the basis of facts and logic only. For example, the policy of expediting drug cases in the courts might be adopted as a basis for reducing the average number of days from arraignment to disposition.

Activities: Services or functions carried out by a program (i.e., what the program does). For example, treatment programs may screen clients at intake, complete placement assessments, provide counseling to clients, and so on.

Goals: A desired state of affairs that outlines the ultimate purpose of a program. This is the end toward which program efforts are directed. For example, the goal of many criminal justice programs is a reduction in criminal activity.

Objectives: Specific results or effects of a program's activities that must be achieved in pursuing the program's ultimate goals. For example, a treatment program may expect to change offender attitudes (objective) in order to ultimately reduce recidivism (goal).

SOURCE: Bureau of Justice Assistance Center for Program Evaluation. (2007). *Reporting and using evaluation results.* Washington, DC: Author.

CROSS-NATIONAL PERSPECTIVE 17.1

Research Project to Formulate the Offender Rehabilitation Act of Thailand

In the Kingdom of Thailand, the correctional system is in a state of transition as the nation considers adopting a more rehabilitative approach to processing inmates. With this in mind, officials in Thailand have set out to examine rehabilitation models around the world, the idea being that the nation will need to decide whether to adopt a system that is currently used, create a new model that is ideally suited to its own needs, or develop some type of hybrid program that combines existing approaches with aspects of its own design.

The current funded research project has been developed to examine philosophies toward the treatment of offenders, the classification of offenders, punishment schemes utilized, and public attitudes toward corrections and rehabilitation, as well as budgetary considerations.

Once researchers have completed their comparison of different aspects of rehabilitation implementation, they will then propose a comprehensive approach (referred to as through-care) that will be grounded in Thai social and cultural contexts. Upon proposing the design, it is expected that an Offender Rehabilitation Bill will be drafted that will provide standards and guidance for a unified approach to treatment programming of offenders.

It is hoped that the results of this study will lead to a harmonization of rehabilitation work and enhance the efficiency of the Thai justice system. These goals are in response to the Thai minister of justice's desire to raise public confidence in offender treatment and reform.

Research Questions

Being that this project is both an actual study and a process whereby legal decrees will be developed, Dr. Srisombat Chokprajakchat and Dr. Attapol Kuanliang decided upon some key research questions that would allow them to directly address the inquiries of the Thai Ministry of Justice as well as concerns of many correctional administrators. The questions are as follows:

1. Why are current rehabilitative efforts ineffective and inefficient (particularly in reducing recidivism and creating public confidence that ex-offenders are not threats to society)?
2. Would comprehensive through-care models that have been adopted by other countries help address the problems or fill in the gaps of the current system?
3. What is the most appropriate through-care model for Thailand?
4. What strategy should be adopted to allow for fast and effective adoption of a through-care model in Thailand?

From this point, it was determined that the project would need to consist of two phases. Phase 1 would consist of the conceptualization of a through-care rehabilitation model that is suitable for Thailand by undertaking documentary analysis and interviewing experts and academics in the fields of rehabilitation and economics in order to evaluate obstacles and challenges in rehabilitation and capacity. In addition, international meetings, such as the one discussed in the Chapter 17 vignette, were organized to collate knowledge on through-care rehabilitation.

After this, Phase 2 of the project would entail the formulation of the actual legislation of the Offender Rehabilitation Bill. It was anticipated that an initial draft would need to be reviewed by all the stakeholders in the Thai correctional community and that it would need to be revised before officially proposed as a law.

Concluding Comments

From this project, it should be clear that these are exciting and daring times for the correctional field in Thailand. In fact, students should understand that these are historically significant occurrences in that country. These changes will be a source of curious observation as they unfold, not only in Thailand but also among other nations in the Asian community. What is also significant to point out is that the Thai are making a serious effort to provide careful thought and planning in crafting legislation on correctional policy. Indeed, the government has decided to adopt accepted methods of social science research and inquiry as a means of determining the best practices that should be implemented. Further, this project will ultimately entail an evaluation component where the Thai will assess and evaluate their rehabilitation outcomes. This is a perfect example of what is discussed in Focus Topic 17.2: Policies, Activities, Goals, and Objectives. The Thai are using research methodologies as an inquiry process to determine the best course of action in the future with the idea that they will ultimately use the scientific research process to then measure the programs that they have implemented. Such precision, organization, and clarity when setting goals and objectives in correctional policy is not often encountered, demonstrating a progressive orientation in policymaking in the Kingdom of Thailand.

SOURCE: Chokprajakchat, S., & Kuanliang, A. (2015). Research project to formulate the Offender Rehabilitation Act of Thailand. Bangkok, Thailand.

tend to examine data from the initial assessment against the data received when the offender exits a particular program or sentencing scheme. It is in this manner that the evaluation of correctional supervision programs serves to reinforce the initial assessment process. The initial assessment and classification process will be considered effective if at the end of the offender's involvement in a given supervision program, the evaluation of the program demonstrates that the offender is indeed less likely to recidivate, particularly if this likelihood falls below that experienced at other agencies in the area and throughout the country. Thus, the evaluation process is a feedback loop into the initial assessment process, demonstrating to agencies that their programs are (or are not) working. If a program is found to be in need of improvement, evaluators can then determine if this is due to the initial assessment or to some process issue further within the program's service delivery. Checking the initial assessment and ensuring that this process is adequate follows a "garbage in, garbage out" philosophy.

This process in which an agency is constantly assessing and evaluating itself is known as the **assessment-evaluation cycle**. This is the process whereby assessment data and evaluation data are compared to determine the effectiveness of programs and to find areas where improvement of agency services is required. Agencies that successfully implement the assessment-evaluation cycle tend to use public resources more effectively and are also less prone to placing the community at risk of future criminal activity. On the other hand, agencies that do not successfully implement the assessment-evaluation cycle will be more likely to waste agency resources and place the community at a level of risk that otherwise would be preventable.

EVIDENCE-BASED PRACTICE

Evidence-based practice is a significant trend throughout all human services that emphasizes outcomes. Interventions within community corrections are considered effective when they reduce offender risk and subsequent recidivism and therefore make a positive long-term contribution to public safety. In this section of the chapter, students are presented with a model or framework based on a set of principles for effective offender interventions within state, local, or private correctional systems. **Evidence-based practice (EBP)** implies that (1) one outcome is desired over others, (2) the outcome is measurable, and (3) the outcome is defined according to practical realities (e.g., public safety) rather than immeasurable moral or value-oriented standards (Colorado Division of Criminal Justice, 2007). Thus, EBP is appropriate for scientific exploration within any human service discipline, including the discipline of corrections.

Research Evaluation for Effectiveness of Evidence-Based Practice

Too often programs or practices are promoted as having research support without any regard for the quality of the research support or the research methods that were employed. Consequently, a research support pyramid (see Figure 17.1) has been included that shows how research support for evidence-based practices might be conducted and/or implemented.

The highest-quality research support depicted in this schema (gold level) reflects interventions and practices that have been evaluated with experimental/control design and with multiple site replications that concluded significant sustained reductions in recidivism were associated with the intervention. The criteria for the next levels of support progressively decrease in terms of research rigor requirements (silver and bronze), but all the top three levels require that a preponderance of the evidence supports a program's effectiveness. The next rung lower in support (iron) is reserved for programs that have inconclusive support regarding their efficacy. Finally, the lowest designation (dirt) is reserved for those programs that have been subjected to research (utilizing methods and criteria associated with gold and silver levels) but the findings were negative and the programs were determined to be not effective (National Institute of Justice, 2005).

SAGE Journal Article Link
If "Something Works" Is the Answer, What Is the Question?

THE FUTURE OF CORRECTIONS

It is fitting that this chapter concludes with a section on future trends since it is through the use of the evaluative research discussed so far that we predict future trends in correctional agencies throughout the nation. It is on this note, and with much trepidation, that some speculative predictions regarding future trends in community corrections will be provided. Before doing so, it should be noted that many psychologists, particularly behavioral psychologists, claim that the best predictor of future human behavior is past human behavior. In fact, empirical research has shown this to be generally true. Keeping this in mind, we will also look at prior research from the field of corrections and make some general observations and predictions.

Assessment-evaluation cycle: Comparing assessment and evaluation data to determine the effectiveness of programs and to find areas for improvement.

Evidence-based practice (EBP): A significant trend throughout all human services that emphasizes outcomes.

CORRECTIONS AND THE LAW 17.1

Challenges of Conducting Research in Prisons

Prison is a self-contained environment in which everyone's activity is tightly regulated and monitored. Simply getting access to a prison can be difficult for researchers. Furthermore, prisoners are regarded as a vulnerable population for research study purposes. The Department of Health and Human Services regulations on human subjects protection designate prisoners, along with other groups such as children and pregnant women, as especially vulnerable. The regulations require additional protections for prisoners. It is critical that the consent form state that a prisoner's participation in research is voluntary and will not affect parole or correctional programming decisions.

Indeed, some experts believe that prisoners can never give true informed consent because they live in an environment in which they have little or no freedom to make an informed decision.

Research subjects must be told of the potential risks and benefits of their participation, and they must receive enough understandable information to make a voluntary decision. Informed consent and voluntary participation are fundamental ingredients of ethical research. Consequently, researchers who want to conduct prison research face heightened scrutiny from institutional review boards.

In addition, in correctional settings, it is difficult to implement rigorous evaluation designs that could isolate the effects of one factor and provide completely comparable groups of inmates for a study, such as randomized trials. As a result, researchers must often rely on weaker, quasi-experimental designs with comparison groups that may not completely rule out competing hypotheses to explain apparent differences and outcomes.

Despite the challenges involved, researchers have completed a variety of studies of prison life, using everything from mailed surveys to personal interviews to obtain information. Having outsiders arrive in a closed environment may in itself affect the perceptions of prisoners about the institutions they live in, and the effects may be larger still for those in solitary confinement. Researchers arriving to interview inmates is a major event in the monotonous routine of prison life, especially for an inmate who is in isolation 23 hours a day. Researchers have examined a variety of factors that could affect their subjects and the research.

One such factor is the **Hawthorne effect,** in which social and behavioral researchers' interactions with and observation of subjects being studied affect the subjects' behavior. The name stems from a study of factory workers at Western Electric's Hawthorne plant in Illinois in the late 1920s and early 1930s. Researchers set out to see what effect, if any, changes in lighting would have on the workers' productivity. They found that regardless of the changes made, productivity increased. They decided that the productivity increased because the workers saw themselves as special participants in an experiment.

Recent examinations of Hawthorne data question the original conclusions and suggest there was either no effect or a placebo effect. Perhaps the Hawthorne effect was present in the Colorado study of administrative segregation. If such an effect were present, the prisoners might be expected to have a more positive view of their situation by virtue of being study participants.

Additionally, people in isolation might be more inclined to participate in a study simply because it would involve receiving attention from an interviewer.

On the other hand, inmates may be wary of researchers. Establishing trust in order to collect accurate information is a prime concern for researchers, who know that inmates may withhold information or tell researchers only what they think the researchers want to hear.

SOURCE: National Institute of Justice. (2012). Challenges of conducting research in prisons. Washington, DC: Author.

First, it should be noted that this text has been addressing three key trends in corrections that are likely to continue in the future. These trends are (1) the tendency for technology to have more impact on correctional agency operations, (2) the need for continued training of correctional staff, and (3) an increased emphasis on the reentry process for offenders. These trends are likely to continue for a variety of practical rather than theoretical reasons. Evidence of this already exists throughout the correctional literature, and, as this text clearly demonstrates, agencies around the nation have already been incorporating these themes into their future operations.

The use of technology is already commonplace within the correctional industry. However, it is the effectiveness of technology that will determine its usefulness and if it is worth the cost. Technology is becoming increasingly reliable and also more affordable for state agencies. Technology can also save on the amount spent on human resources. Thus, technology will continue to be a driving force that will shape the landscape of correctional services in the future.

Hawthorne effect: When inmates see themselves as special participants in an experiment.

Regardless of the role that technology will play in corrections, there will still be a need for trained and educated staff. In fact, the proliferation of technology will require that persons who work in corrections be competent enough to utilize high-tech tools of the trade. No longer will it be sufficient for staff to act as mere turnkeys; rather, they will be required to use sophisticated equipment and tools. In addition, correctional populations are becoming more complex in terms of mental and medical issues as well as cultural factors that must be considered. Due to legal requirements and concerns with liability, staff cannot be negligent and/or careless. Rather, they must act competently as trained professionals when working with the inmate population—a population that can be deceptive and dangerous.

Lastly, the correctional population will continue to grow, and our nation's prisons are full. Continuing with a "stuff 'em and cuff 'em" mentality will simply not work for a system that is already over capacity. If something cannot be done to alleviate the continued overcrowding of prisons and the already overloaded case management approaches that exist, then either correctional systems will need much larger budgets or offenders will have to simply be set free without any form of supervision. Obviously, the latter possibility is too dangerous to consider, and the former will

Video Link
10 Ways to Reduce Prison Overcrowding and Save Taxpayers Millions

Figure 17.1: Research Support Pyramid for Evidence-Based Practice Implementation

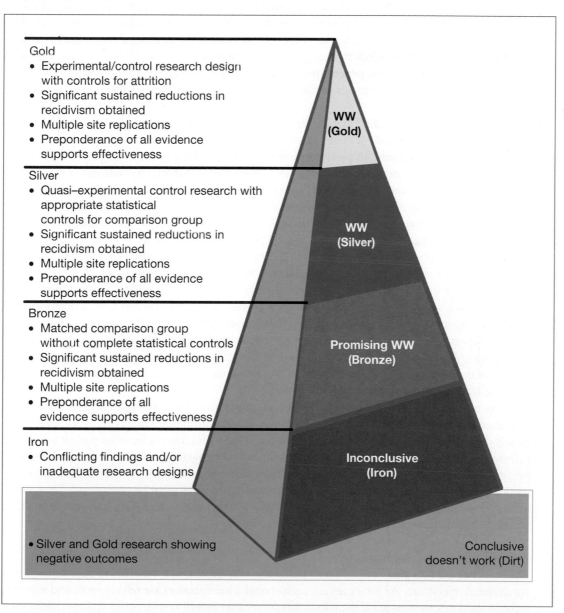

SOURCE: National Institute of Justice. (2005). *Implementing evidence based practice in corrections.* Washington, DC: U.S. Department of Justice.

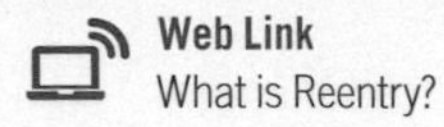
Web Link
What is Reentry?

just result in more of the same problems that already face the criminal justice system. Thus, reentry initiatives will be used with much greater frequency in the future, due both to practicality and economic concerns. With this in mind, a discussion of the likely trends in community supervision programs will follow.

Privatization in Corrections

The use of privatized operations in corrections carries some degree of controversy. This is largely because some people have a moralistic opposition to the idea that money might be made off the misery of others. In other words, some people may take exception to the idea that in order for one person to fulfill his or her sentence, the pockets of a private corporation must be lined. However, it is probably a more realistic view to understand that inmates must be housed *somewhere* when serving a stint of incarceration, and, so long as their constitutionally protected rights are upheld, the specific ownership of the physical facility is irrelevant. In fact, if the private prison company can maintain security with less overhead to the taxpayers, then this is a good thing for everyone concerned.

The simple reality is that, like it or not, private corrections is here to stay, and the use of private facilities is growing steadily each year. Private companies must ensure that they stay within budget and operate in an efficient and productive manner; to do otherwise results in a loss of revenue. For many business-minded administrators, this is superior to many state systems that are full of inherent waste, red tape, and civil service regulations that paralyze agencies from moving in an adaptive fashion. Private correctional systems, however, adhere to all of the same legal requirements as state institutions but are able to adapt to changes much more quickly and with little need for excessive staggering of new policies and procedures. For the most part, executive-level decision makers can generate a memo or set of protocols and disseminate it in a day, if they so desire; state systems do not have this flexibility.

Also, one must keep in mind that it is the state correctional systems that have had legal problems related to the constitutionality of their operations, not the private systems. It appears then that state systems are not superior and, in some cases, may be more lacking in legal integrity than privately run operations. Thus, state systems may provide worse services than private systems (in some cases) while still being more costly to taxpayers. Also consider that in Texas and the Federal Bureau of Prisons, the vocational and/or industry operations of these prison systems that produce revenue do so through private corporations (PEI in Texas, UNICOR for the Bureau of Prisons). The point in mentioning this is that it may well be that these types of operations are most appropriate for profit-generating endeavors, and such programs are generally viewed as successful in operation.

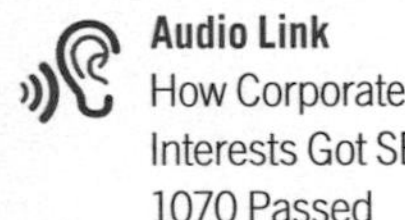
Audio Link
How Corporate Interests Got SB 1070 Passed

In situations where states may be reluctant to resort to complete privatization of industrial or security operations, hybrid versions of privatization may be utilized. The author of this text works as a substance abuse counselor in a private prison (Richwood Correctional Center, owned and operated by LaSalle Corrections) that houses inmates from the Louisiana Department of Corrections. Counselors in the treatment program are hired by either the state or by LaSalle Corrections, depending on budgetary constraints and offender-client population levels. This integration of state and private service delivery allows for services to continue at optimal levels beyond what the state could afford to provide on its own.

The use of private correctional facilities has grown more in some states than in others, but regardless of how common privatization becomes, it is doubtful that state systems will ever completely disappear. States will likely always maintain at least a fraction of facilities since it is unlikely private systems will be appropriate for housing the most dangerous of inmates. But with budgets being reduced throughout the nation, it is unlikely that many states will be able to fund their correctional systems to the level that is necessary; other alternatives must be considered. Thus, while private prisons will probably never completely replace state prisons, it is likely that private facilities will become much more common than they currently are.

Increased Use of Technology

The world as a whole has become more technologically driven, and this has, of course, impacted correctional operations. As time goes on, correctional administrators are relying more and more on technological innovations to aid them in matters of security as well as with peripheral operations such as visitation, food service, and/or telemedicine services. As this technology continues to develop, there will be a need to assess and evaluate the effectiveness of these innovations (see Technology and Equipment 17.1). This points to a continued need for future research in corrections as well.

While it is not clear in most cases whether there are likely drawbacks to relying so heavily on technology, it is clear that facilities are becoming more sophisticated in their operations. This means that many people working in the correctional field will need to develop some degree of technical savvy lest they be unable to utilize basic equipment and/or security system innovations. Throughout this text, it has been shown that technology can assist in aiding security, improving living standards, enabling safe working conditions, and safeguarding against liability. For all of these reasons and more, the world of corrections will become more technologically driven.

Standards and Accreditation

From our readings in Chapter 13, we have seen that an abundance of professional organizations and associations represent a wide variety of professions in the field of corrections. This is a positive trend in corrections that will likely continue with increased enthusiasm. The desire to professionalize the workforce is strong since this can add legitimacy to a facility's operations. In addition, when employees adhere to the requirements of various governing bodies, it is presumed that they are at least meeting the nationally accepted standards of competence within these associations.

In addition, when employees meet the standards of external governing bodies, agencies are unlikely to be open to lawsuits for failing to properly train their staff or other types of negligence. This is an effective incentive for most agencies, including private ones. Further, many individual practitioners will seek to obtain credentials that may help them to receive promotions and/or higher levels of pay. Thus, the incentives for systems and facilities to improve standards and credentials are strong, and this translates to a desire among agencies to obtain accreditation. When agencies seek accreditation, they are making strides to enhance their reputation and to make a public statement that demonstrates their integrity.

Accreditation speaks volumes to the agency's professionalism and sense of ethical responsibility. The transparency of management necessary to obtain and maintain accreditation means that administrators have nothing to hide. This is of benefit when one considers the closed nature of corrections from the broader community. A correctional agency's image within the community is likely to be enhanced when it is accredited, and this is likely to generate community support for correctional personnel. As we have seen in prior chapters, this can benefit the administrators and staff who are the "face" of the agency for which they work. It can be a morale booster for employees and generate a culture of pride in the mission and work of the agency.

An Emphasis on Cultural Competence Will Continue to Be Important

Earlier chapters of this text addressed cultural competence and the increasing representation of minority offenders in the criminal justice system. It is clear that the United States is becoming more racially and culturally diverse. Thus, multilingual skills and knowledge of different religious beliefs, lifestyle orientations, and other matters of diversity will become mandatory for future corrections employees. The continued diversity of inmates, along with other challenges they present (such as mental health needs), means that offender populations are likely to become much more complicated to manage in the future. Naturally, this can add to the already stressful conditions under which correctional staff work, so agencies will need to mitigate these challenges and the stress associated with them.

Robert Hanser

■ PHOTO 17.2 This treatment group participates in a discussion of a controversial issue.

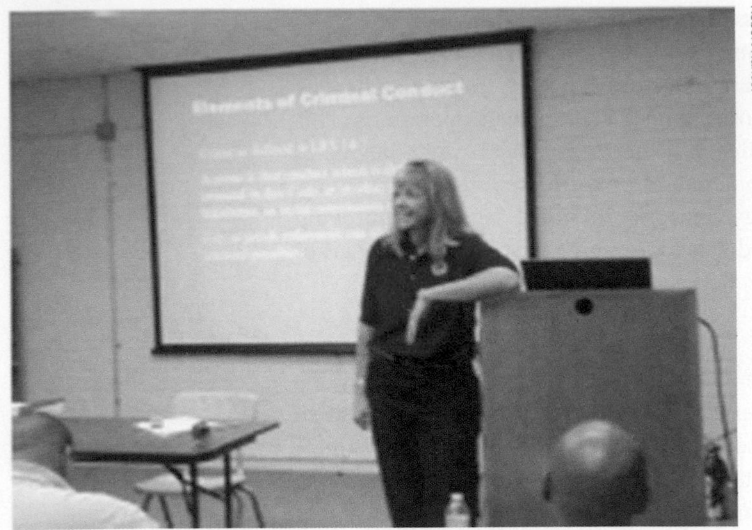

Robert Hanser

■ PHOTO 17.3 Dr. Bonner trains correctional staff on diversity and cultural competence at North Delta Regional Training Academy.

An Emphasis Will Be Placed on Employment Programs

Research has shown that offenders need jobs if they are to be able to make ends meet while paying restitution, fines, and other obligations to society. Chapter 14 of this text has provided sufficient evidence to demonstrate that recidivism among offenders will decline if they are given the minimal educational and vocational skills necessary to function. Programs such as Project RIO in Texas are proving vocational programs that aid in job placement are quite effective in reducing recidivism. Also, since employers are able to secure tax incentives for hiring offenders, these programs benefit society as a whole. These programs ensure that society is compensated for property crimes and can often repair damage resulting from nonviolent crimes when used within a restorative justice or victim compensation framework. This is important because the victim, society, and the offender all benefit from such programs. Thus, vocational training will be critical, and the use of work-release and restitution programs will continue to be necessary.

Processing of Geriatric Offenders Will Be Shifted to Community Supervision Schemes

The entire population is graying in the United States, and the nation's prison population is graying at a faster rate than is the general society. This issue has been given considerable attention in recent years, with Texas, California, Florida, New York, and Louisiana all experiencing a rise in per-capita elderly inmates who are incarcerated. As noted previously, the states just mentioned have either one of the largest prison populations or one of the highest rates of incarceration in the country. The costs associated with the elderly inmate are exponentially higher than those associated with the average inmate. This leads administrators to look for possible solutions to this problem, such as the possibility of early release of inmates who are expected to die or the implementation of human caregiver programs like hospice. However, accountability to the public places prison administrators in a dilemma since public safety is the primary concern for all custodial programs. The sobering reality is that society will, one way or another, pay for the expense of keeping elderly inmates.

ROBERT GALBRAITH/REUTERS/Newscom

■ PHOTO 17.4 This elderly inmate has equipment for breathing assistance in his cell. Such accommodations are becoming increasingly necessary with the greying of the prison population.

It is with this point in mind that state-level correctional systems will need to increase their use of community supervision programs with elderly offenders, including those who are chronically ill. This may seem to be an oversimplified recommendation, but it is one that has not truly been implemented by many states. Most states do have programs designed for the early release of elderly inmates, but these programs are not used extensively. The recommendation here is that community supervision be *automatically implemented* when an inmate reaches the age of 60 years old, unless he or she is a pedophile. In the case of pedophiles, the typical risk assessment methods should remain intact since these offenders have such poor prognoses for reform. However, all other

TECHNOLOGY AND EQUIPMENT 17.1

Evaluating Video Visitation Technology for Prisons

In 2012, the NIJ awarded the Vera Institute of Justice a multiyear grant to conduct the first-ever system-wide evaluation of video visitation technology for prisons. The study is using a mixed-methods design to better understand how to create policies about family-inmate contact, inform investment decisions and policies related to video visitation technology, and understand video visitation's role in reducing recidivism.

The Washington State Department of Corrections started rolling out its video visitation program in January 2013 with the goal of setting up operational systems at every state facility. At the same time, the Vera Institute began conducting its system-wide analysis of the video visitation program by initiating interviews with offenders, visitors, and correctional staff.

The Vera Institute is combining administrative data, surveys, and information from focus groups and interviews to determine whether access to video visitation improves the nature and frequency of inmates' contact with their families and others who support them. The study is also exploring whether these contacts improve inmates' compliance with custodial rules and outcomes after their release from prison.

If the data analysis shows that the program has a positive impact, the Vera Institute also will assess the program's effect on corrections culture, operations, and budgets. This information will help determine whether and how the program could be replicated in other jurisdictions. Vera will also assess the cost effectiveness of the technology.

The final report is expected in 2015. Students should take note of two key points related to this upcoming report. First, this is yet another example of how data, surveys, and interviews are used in corrections to test and evaluate whether new ideas are a success or a failure. Second, it is significant that the Vera Institute will examine whether video visitation has impacted the correctional culture of facilities within their study. As we have seen in prior chapters, the culture of a prison facility can have a significant bearing on how well the facility is run and the order of priority that is given to differing demands within the institution. Whether video visitation can help ameliorate some of the pains of imprisonment by providing a beneficial behavior-management component should be of future interest to administrators of custodial facilities and correctional researchers alike.

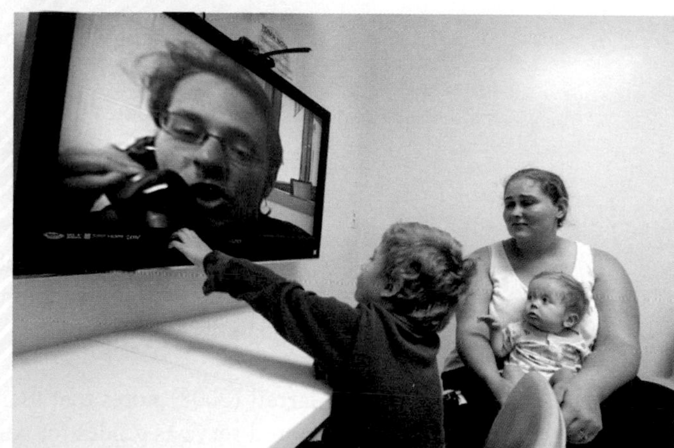

AP Photo/David J. Phillip

■ PHOTO 17.5 The use of video equipment to facilitate visitation between inmates and their family has become more common in prison facilities.

SOURCE: National Institute of Justice. (2012). *Evaluating video visitation technology for prisons*. Washington, DC: Author.

elderly inmates should be automatically placed on community supervision since this would reduce costs of upkeep significantly.

Those inmates being automatically released should be given intensive supervision that uses the latest and greatest forms of human supervision and electronic gadgetry. Though this adds to the cost, the outcome is much cheaper than prison alternatives. Through routine weekly contact by probation/parole officials, frequent electronic phone monitoring, the use of GPS tracking devices, house arrest, and other such innovations, the risk to public safety can be greatly minimized. Further, it is a simple fact that recidivism for elderly offenders is very low, and the crimes committed are seldom assaultive in nature. Thus public safety is not compromised. In fact, this is the safest population to place on community supervision, as long as one excludes using such a policy for pedophiles.

Media and Political Interest in Correctional Operations

Prison facilities need to establish community-based partnerships to ensure community support. The local population can be very helpful to the prison since many local merchants may deal with the prison or staff employed at the prison and since the community sometimes acts as a source of volunteers. Further, it is just "good business" to have an amicable relationship with persons who live in the vicinity. The media can also make the prison more visible so that community members will be apprised of developments within the facility. Indeed, the media can prove pivotal in the success and/or the failure of any prison's interface with the community.

Certain groups of offenders, such as sex offenders, have drawn a great deal of public attention and concern. This is understandable, but the public may make erroneous conclusions regarding the offender population if they are not given correct information. This can completely undermine a prison's ability to implement an effective reentry program and cast negative views on the prison if the public perceives that it is just letting offenders out so they can commit crime again. **Media effects** are an important consideration in corrections and refer to the effects that the media have upon the public perception of prison or community supervision programs. How the media report on specific incidents can affect this. When programs are successful and/or innovative, the media can provide effective coverage of these as well to ensure that the public is getting the most accurate information possible.

Garrett (2008) notes certain points to consider when deciding upon the involvement of the media in corrections:

1. To what extent will the media representatives disrupt the day-to-day operations of the prison? Will schedules and routine activities be hindered?
2. How are inmates likely to react to the media coverage, and how is this likely to impact their future behavior in the prison?
3. How are people in the community likely to react to the coverage? Will this impair the operation of the prison?
4. To what extent will any pictures that are taken provide the public or inmates with information that could help to form an escape plan or plan disruptive activities within the prison, such as a riot?

Garrett (2008) notes that there are no right or wrong answers to the previous questions, but they should serve as guides for administrators who must balance the pros and cons when dealing with the media. However, prison administrators who are attempting to build collaborative partnerships must foster good relations with the media and must always be aware that the media can be a double-edged sword when presenting coverage on prison operations.

CONCLUSION

Research and assessment of correctional programs are vital in this day and age. Through this process, we are able to identify program strengths and weaknesses that serve to inform the literature. The ultimate question that should guide research and assessment projects is, so what? In other words, if we choose to conduct a research project, will the results provide a meaningful contribution to what is known about some phenomena? Or, if we did *not* conduct the research project, would there continue to be a significant gap in the literature, hindering our ability to make optimal decisions regarding community corrections programs?

It is important to keep in mind that the assessment process is an integral component of the evaluation of any agency. This means that what agencies put into their program will be reflected in its final output. Thus, assessment can be seen as a measure of what goes into a program, and evaluation can be seen as a measure of what comes out of the program. The two work hand-in-hand. Because of this, students should be familiar with the assessment-evaluation cycle, since this is the primary means by which community supervision agencies measure their performance and since this is what ultimately determines if an agency is meeting its goals and objectives. For agencies with unfavorable evaluations, an examination of the policies and activities of that agency may be in order, or, in some cases, a reassessment of the goals and objectives may take place.

Lastly, this chapter reflected on some of the themes that have emerged throughout this text. These themes are important to contemporary correctional practices and will also be a focus for corrections agencies in the future. A number of likely trends were noted, and recommendations were given for agencies that will face challenges that loom on the horizon. The field of corrections is both dynamic and demanding; practitioners who work in this field have their work cut out for

Media effects: The effect that the media has upon the public perception of prison or community supervision programs.

them. However, the work of correctional personnel is critical and warrants support from the various funding sources as well as the public at large. Without this support, the entire public is likely to pay dearly for such negligence.

Want a better grade?

Get the tools you need to sharpen your study skills. Access practice quizzes, eFlashcards, video, and multimedia at edge.sagepub.com/hanser2e

SAGE edge™

DISCUSSION QUESTIONS

1. How is evaluative research conducted, and why is it important?
2. Compare process and outcome measures. Why is each important to evaluation projects?
3. Explain, in your own words, how the assessment-evaluative cycle works in correctional research.
4. What is meant by the term *evidence-based practice*? Provide at least two examples of how such a practice might be used in a correctional agency.
5. Why does the author note that more emphasis on diversity and multiculturalism will be important in the field of corrections?

SAGE edge™ **Test your understanding of chapter content. Take the practice quiz.**

KEY TERMS

Assessment-evaluation cycle, 433

Evaluative transparency, 428

Evidence-based practice (EBP), 433

Hawthorne effect, 434

Implementation evaluation, 427

Learning organizations, 430

Media effects, 440

Outcome evaluation, 427

Process evaluation, 427

Stakeholders, 430

SAGE edge™ **Review key terms with eFlashcards.**

APPLIED EXERCISE 17.1

For this exercise, you will need to consider what you have learned in this chapter as it applies to the information in Chapter 14 on prison programming, and in particular life skills programs for offenders. Your assignment is as follows:

You are a researcher recently hired by the prison system of your state, and you have been asked to design and evaluate a prison life skills program. Specifically, you are asked to determine if the completion of the life skills program actually reduces recidivism among the offenders who take it. You will need to provide a clear methodology for testing and evaluating your proposed program, taking into account such factors as the validity and reliability of your study, the validity and reliability of your instruments (if any), the use of control and experimental groups, distinctions between process and outcome measures, and any ethical issues that might be involved with conducting your research.

Your response to each of the questions below must consist of 300 to 700 words. You should complete this application exercise as an essay that explains the program that you develop and then addresses each question. The total word count should be 900 to 2,100 words.

1. Identify the specific aspects of the life skills program that you would evaluate, and explain why each would be important to your evaluation. Further, identify and distinguish between the process and the outcome measures within your study.
2. Identify and discuss the various research methods considerations that you might wish to employ. Be sure to discuss the likely validity and reliability of your study as well as the validity and reliability of the instruments that you might use. Also, determine if you will be able to use a control group and/or a comparison group within your study.
3. Be sure and explain how you would use your evaluative study to determine the effects of a life skills program. (Note that the student has a wide degree of latitude with this aspect of the assignment.)
4. Spelling, grammar, and writing style will be considered. In addition, the paper *must* be within the prescribed range in word count. Lastly, students *must* cite and reference their work, in APA format, or no credit will be given for this question.

● WHAT WOULD YOU DO?

You are a correctional officer working the graveyard shift at a maximum-security prison. One night, during turnout, the lieutenant explains to you and the other staff on your shift (there are about 50 of you) that there will be a researcher who will be coming to each officer and giving you a survey. This will be done intermittently throughout the week, and the lieutenant makes it clear that while you are not required to fill out the survey, the study is quite beneficial, and he and the other "rank" officers appreciate any participation that you would be willing to give. He introduces to the group two persons dressed in semiformal attire, Dr. Smith and Dr. Wilson, both criminologists from the university located about 35 miles from your prison facility.

Once they are introduced, Dr. Smith explains, "Our study examines inmate sexual assault in prisons. Basically, there is a tendency for inmates around the nation to underreport incidents, and this naturally makes it impossible to truly know how prevalent it may be."

As the pair beings to pass out the surveys, Dr. Wilson adds, "So, we've decided to ask the custodial staff about their perceptions regarding this issue since you're the ones who spend the most time in proximity to the inmates who are involved in this behavior, when and if it occurs on your shift."

Once everyone has a survey, Dr. Wilson continues. "While on your shift and when you have time, we are asking that you complete this survey. Later we will follow up and interview some of you, as time permits throughout the night. We know that you're busy and that you may not wish to participate. If you wish to decline participation, we will naturally honor your wishes without comment."

After the doctor finishes speaking, the lieutenant lets the shift personnel know that he will not be keeping track of whoever participates. Rather, he and the sergeants will be staying out of sight as much as possible throughout the night to ensure that they do not obstruct the data collection efforts of the researchers. At that point, work details are assigned to all staff members and you are dismissed to relieve the prior shift and assume their duty posts.

As luck would have it, you are assigned to the escort crew, which means that your assignment is to patrol the prison on foot, going from one cell block to another to relieve officers for their mealtime and/or scheduled breaks, taking inmates to the infirmary or other areas of the prison as required, and conducting security checks throughout the night. You will also escort inmates to early morning breakfast later in your shift. This is considered a good detail because the mobility keeps the shift from becoming monotonous, and you get to talk and visit with numerous people throughout the night. There are about seven of you assigned to the escort crew. At one point in the evening, you go to relieve an officer on one of the cell blocks so that he can go have dinner.

While you are on the cell block, three other members of the escort crew join you. One of them says, "Hey, we're gonna hang out in the dayroom and fill out our surveys, watch some TV, and wait until the break relief is over. After that, Sarge says we gotta go to the laundry room and let some inmates get some supplies—we just wanted you to know."

You tell them okay and go to make your rounds. While making your rounds, you hear the other officers laughing. You approach the dayroom and hear one of them say, "Man, this survey is whacked—those brainiacs are crazy if they think that I am gonna tell them about what goes on with those convicts."

Another responds, "Yeah, man, like I give a damn if some convict gets his booty stolen—serves 'em right. The assholes will stay out of here if they don't like it."

All the officers laugh, and one says, "Look, I got an idea—let's just fill them out real fast and put that nothing ever happens. Maybe we could put that they are all lying and making false allegations against inmates that they owe money to! That would really mess up the study and give them something to scratch their heads about, huh?"

"Hell, yeah, great idea, we can make this fun! After all, the surveys are anonymous, right?"

You finish your security rounds while thinking about what you have just heard. You have not yet filled out your survey and have not even looked at it, but you begin to feel a little sorry for the researchers. You think to yourself, *Maybe this is why things never get better. No matter how much research they do, everybody is always lying to them. I wonder if they know how much of this probably takes place.*

You enter the dayroom just in time to see the last of the officers place his survey in the envelope that each officer was given and seal it. At this time, the officer you were relieving returns from dinner, and as you are walking off the cell block, you see the researchers walking toward the dayroom. They offer to collect the sealed envelopes from the other officers, who hand the doctors their envelopes and head off to the laundry room.

Dr. Smith looks at you and says, "If possible, we would like to interview you since you are next on our list. It will not affect your survey results, and we've told the sergeant that you might need to follow about 10 minutes behind everyone. Is that okay?"

Since the interview is really not optional (you know your supervisors would think it rude to decline the polite request of the researchers) and since you really are not in a hurry to go to the laundry room, you say, "Okay, sure." However, you know that they have no idea about the surveys that they just received, and you are a bit undecided as to what you think about all of this "research stuff," anyway. You contemplate what you may or may not say to them in the interview.

What would you do?

Absolute immunity: Protection for persons who work in positions that require unimpaired decision-making functions.

Administrative segregation: A nonpunitive classification that requires the separation of inmates from the general population for safety.

Administrator: An individual in an agency who operates in a managerial or leadership role beyond immediate supervisory capacity.

Adolescent-only offenders: Adolescents who typically commit acts of defiance or nonconformity to express their developing sense of autonomy; they are not likely to continue their activities beyond adolescence.

Age of responsibility: Roman civil law made distinctions between juveniles and adults based on the notion of age of responsibility.

Aggravating circumstances: Magnify the offensive nature of a crime and tend to result in longer sentences.

Albert W. Florence v. Board of Chosen Freeholders of the County of Burlington, et al. *(2012):* Prison staff may strip search minor offenders and detainees within a jail or detention facility.

Alcatraz: A prison built on Alcatraz Island, California. First opened in 1934, it is considered to be the first U.S. supermax facility.

American Correctional Chaplains Association (ACCA): Provides representation and networking for chaplains who work in correctional environments.

American Correctional Food Service Association (ACFSA): Represents the correctional food service industry.

Americans with Disabilities Act (ADA): Requires correctional agencies to make reasonable modifications to ensure accessibility for individuals with disabilities.

Anti-Drug Abuse Act of 1988: Made the death penalty available as a possible punishment for certain drug-related offenses.

Antiterrorism and Effective Death Penalty Act of 1996: Required inmate to provide clear and convincing evidence of a constitutional violation before granting a certificate of appeal.

Armed disturbance control team: Deals with disturbances that have escalated to matters of life and death.

Assessment-evaluation cycle: Comparing assessment and evaluation data to determine the effectiveness of programs and to find areas for improvement.

Atkins v. Virginia *(2002):* Held that the execution of the mentally retarded is unconstitutional.

Attorney General's Review Committee on Capital Cases: Makes an independent recommendation to the attorney general regarding death penalty cases.

Auburn system: An alternative prison system located in New York.

Authoritarian model: Features strict control over staff and inmates with communication that flows in a top-to-bottom process.

Banishment: Exile from society.

Bastille: A fortification in Paris, France that was a symbol of tyranny and injustice for commoners and political prisoners.

Baxter v. Palmigiano *(1976):* Determined that inmates do not have the right to counsel for disciplinary hearings that are not part of a criminal prosecution.

Bell v. Wolfish *(1979):* Determined that body cavity searches of inmates after contact visits is permissible, as are searches of inmates' quarters in their absence. Double bunking does not deprive inmates of their liberty without due process of law.

Big House prisons: Typically large stone structures with brick walls, guard towers, and checkpoints throughout the facility.

Black Codes: Separate laws were required for slaves and free men who turned criminal.

Blind spots: In correctional facilities, these occur when areas of the prison are not easily viewed by security staff and/or surveillance equipment.

Blood in—blood out: The idea that for inmates to be accepted within a prison gang they must draw blood from an enemy of the gang.

Blood testing: Using blood samples to determine if an offender has been using drugs.

Bounds v. Smith *(1977):* Determined that prison systems must provide inmates with law libraries or professional legal assistance.

Branding: Usually on thumb with a letter denoting the offense.

Breed v. Jones *(1975):* Held that trying a juvenile who had previously been adjudicated in juvenile court for the same crime as an adult in criminal court violates the Fifth Amendment double jeopardy clause.

Bruscino v. Carlson *(1988):* Ruling that the high-security practices of USP Marion were constitutional.

Brutalization hypothesis: The contention that the use of harsh punishments sensitizes people to violence and *teaches* them to use it.

Bureaucratic model: A formal organizational system that is not dependent upon the specific personnel or personalities assigned within it.

Capital punishment: Putting the offender to death.

Case manager: Is directly responsible to the unit manager and has major responsibility for case management matters.

Centralized management: Tight forms of control in the communication process that ensure that decision-making power is reserved for only a small group of people.

Chancery courts: Created to consider petitions for special aid or intervention and to grant relief to such persons.

Child abuse: Occurs when a child is maltreated by any person responsible for the child's welfare.

Child neglect: Occurs when a parent or caretaker does not provide the proper support or care required by a state's law.

Chivalry hypothesis: Contends that there is a bias in the criminal justice system against giving women harsh punishments.

Classical criminology: Emphasized that punishments must be useful, purposeful, and reasonable.

Code of Hammurabi: The earliest known written code of punishment.

Coker v. Georgia *(1977):* Ruling that the death penalty was unconstitutional for the rape of an adult woman if she had not been killed during the offense.

Collateral damage: Any damage incidental to an activity.

Common fare: A diet that meets all nutritional requirements and reasonably accommodates recognized religious dietary restrictions.

Common law: Law based on custom or use.

Compensatory damages: Payments for the actual losses suffered by a plaintiff.

Comprehensive Crime Control Act of 1984: Created a U.S. Sentencing Commission to establish federal sentencing guidelines favoring determinate sentences.

Conflict theory: Maintains that concepts of inequality and power are the central issues underlying crime and its control.

Consent decree: An injunction against both individual defendants and their agency.

Contract labor system: Utilized inmate labor through state-negotiated contracts with private manufacturers.

Contributing to the delinquency of a minor: A form of neglect where an adult encourages and facilitates the ability of youth to commit delinquent or criminal acts.

Convict: An inmate who is respected for being self-reliant and independent of other inmates or the system.

Convict boss/officer: A correctional officer with a keen understanding of convict logic and socialization.

Convict code: An inmate-driven set of beliefs that inmates aspired to live by.

Co-occurring disorders: When an offender has two or more disorders.

Cooper v. Pate *(1964):* Ruling that state prison inmates could sue state officials in federal courts.

Correctional counselor: Develops and implements programs within the unit to meet the individual needs of the inmates confined.

Corrections: A process whereby practitioners engage in organized security and treatment functions to correct criminal tendencies among the offender population.

Crime control model: An approach to crime that increased the use of longer sentences, the death penalty, and intensive supervision probation.

Cruz v. Beto *(1972):* Ruling that inmates must be given reasonable opportunities to exercise their religious beliefs.

Custodial sexual misconduct: Any sexual act between correctional staff and inmates, even if it is consensual.

Custody level: Related to the degree of staff supervision that is needed for a given inmate.

Cutter v. Wilkinson *(2005):*Held religious inmates do not have more legal rights than nonreligious inmates.

Day reporting centers: Treatment facilities to which offenders are required to report, usually on a daily basis.

Death row: Persons who have been sentenced to be executed but are awaiting their execution.

Death row phenomenon: The harmful effects of death row conditions that are experienced while waiting for one's demise.

Death row syndrome: The states of mental illness that can develop over time as result of the death row phenomenon.

Decentralized management: The authority and responsibility of management are distributed amongst the supervisory chain, allowing decisions to correspond to the problems confronted by each level of management.

Declaratory judgment: A judicial determination of the legal rights of the person bringing suit.

Defamation: Some form of slander or libel that damages a person's reputation.

Detention: Secure confinement of juvenile offenders.

Determinate discretionary sentence: Type of sentence with a range of time to be served; the specific sentence to be served within that range is decided by the judge.

Determinate presumptive sentence: This type of sentence specifies the exact length of the sentence to be served by the inmate.

Determinate sentences: Consist of fixed periods of incarceration with no later flexibility in the term that is served.

Detoxification: The use of medical drugs to ease the process of overcoming the physical symptoms of dependence.

Diagnostic and Statistical Manual of Mental Disorders (DSM-V): A reference manual that sets forth the guidelines in applying a diagnosis of a mental disorder.

Direct supervision design: Cells are organized on the outside of the square space, with shower facilities and recreation cells interspersed among the typical inmate living quarters.

Discrimination: A differential response toward a group without providing any legally legitimate reasons for that response.

Disparity: Inconsistencies in sentencing and/or sanctions that result from the decision-making process.

Disturbance control team: Specialized teams trained to respond to, contain, and neutralize inmate disturbances in prisons.

Domestic violence: Behaviors used by one person in a relationship to control the other.

Eastern State Penitentiary: Part of the Pennsylvania system located near Philadelphia.

Education adviser: The unit team's consultant in all education matters.

Educational neglect: Occurs when a parent or teacher permits chronic truancy or ignores the educational and/or special needs of a child.

Elderly first-time offenders: Those who commit their first offense later in life.

Electronic monitoring: The use of any mechanism worn by the offender for the means of tracking his or her whereabouts through electronic detection.

Elmira Reformatory: The first reformatory prison.

Emergency preparedness: The planning, training, and budgeting process involved prior to the occurrence of an emergency.

Emergency response: The intervention used, the management of that intervention, the containment of the emergency, and the successful resolution of the emergency.

Emotional distress: Refers to acts that lead to emotional distress of the client.

Emotional intelligence: Describes how adept a person is at noticing and responding to the emotional cues and information exhibited by others.

Emotional neglect: Inadequate nurturing or affection; allowing a child to engage in inappropriate or illegal behavior; and ignoring a child's basic emotional needs.

English as a Second Language (ESL): Program enables inmates with limited English proficiency to improve their English language skills.

English Penal Servitude Act: Established several rehabilitation programs for convicts.

Estelle v. Gamble *(1976):* Ruled that deliberate indifference to inmate medical needs constitutes cruel and unusual punishment and is unconstitutional.

Evaluative transparency: When an agency's evaluative process allows an outside person to have full view of the agency's operations, budgeting, policies, procedures, and outcomes.

Evidence-based practice (EBP): A significant trend throughout all human services that emphasizes outcomes.

Ex parte Hull *(1941):* Ruling that marked the beginning of the end for the hands-off doctrine.

Farmer v. Brennan *(1994):* Held that a prison official is not liable injury inflicted on an inmate by another inmate unless he/she knew of the excessive risk of harm and disregarded it.

Father of Parole: Alexander Maconochie, so named due to his creation of the mark system, a precursor to modern-day parole.

Federal Death Penalty Act of 1994: Established constitutional procedures for imposition of the death penalty.

Federal Prison Industries Inc. (FPI): Organization for federal prison labor.

Fine: A monetary penalty imposed as a punishment for having committed an offense.

Ford v. Wainwright *(1986):* Ruling that defendants who could successfully invoke the insanity defense could avoid the death penalty.

Four standards of mental health care: Legal requirement for adequate health care also extends to mental health care.

Fulwood v. Clemmer *(1962):* Ruled that correctional officials must recognize the Muslim faith as a legitimate religion and allow inmates to hold services.

Furman v. Georgia *(1972):* Ruling that the death penalty was arbitrary and capricious and violated the prohibition against cruel and unusual punishment.

Gagnon v. Scarpelli *(1971):* Held that a probationer's sentence can only be revoked after a preliminary and final revocation hearing have been provided.

Gang cross-pollination: Occurs when a gang has developed such power and influence as to be equally effective regardless of whether its leadership is inside or outside of prison walls.

Gaol: A term used in England during the Middle Ages that was synonymous with today's jail.

Gates v. Collier *(1972):* One of a series of federal cases that declared a state prison system unconstitutional.

General deterrence: Punishing an offender in public so other observers will refrain from criminal behavior.

General Educational Development (GED): The process of earning the equivalent of your high school diploma.

Generalized anxiety disorder: Characterized by excessive anxiety and worry that occurs more days than not for at least 6 months.

Glass ceiling: Barriers to promotion that exist for women within the workforce.

Global Positioning System (GPS): Allows offenders to be tracked to their exact location through the use of satellite monitoring and remote tracking.

Good faith defense: The person acted in the honest belief that the action taken was appropriate under the circumstances.

Graham v. Florida *(2010):* Ruling that juveniles who commit crimes in which no one is killed may not be sentenced to life in prison without the possibility of parole.

Great Law: Correctional thinking and reform in Pennsylvania that occurred due to the work of William Penn and the Quakers.

Gregg v. Georgia *(1976):* Held that death penalty statutes that contain sufficient safeguards against arbitrary and capricious imposition are constitutional.

Greyhounds: Older inmates who have acquired respect within the offender subculture due to their track record, criminal history, and criminogenic ideals.

Habitual elderly offenders: Have a long history of crime and also have a prior record of imprisonment throughout their lifetime.

Hair testing: Using hair samples to determine if an offender has been using drugs.

Hands-off doctrine: The policy of the courts of avoiding intervention in prison operations.

Hawes-Cooper Act: Required that prison products be subject to the laws of the states to which those products are shipped.

Hawthorne effect: When inmates see themselves as special participants in an experiment.

Health Insurance Portability and Accountability Act (HIPAA): Guides professionals on matters regarding the confidentiality of medical information.

Hearing stage: Stage of a revocation proceeding that allows the probation agency to present evidence of the violation, which the offender is given the opportunity to refute.

Hedonistic calculus: A term describing how humans seem to weigh pleasure and pain outcomes when deciding to engage in criminal behavior.

HIV/AIDS: A chronic, potentially life-threatening condition caused by the human immunodeficiency virus.

Hogging: A term used to imply that a person is using others for some type of gain or benefit.

Holding pattern management: Where the system continues to operate but in a pattern of stasis where there is no true growth, nor is there a blockage in the systemic flow.

Holt v. Hobbs *(2015):* In cases of legitimate religious actions, the government must show that substantially burdening the religious exercise of an individual is "the least restrictive means of furthering that compelling governmental interest."

Holt v. Sarver I *(1969):* Ruled that prison farms in the state of Arkansas were operated in a manner that violated the prohibition against cruel and unusual punishments.

Holt v. Sarver II *(1970):* Second part of the initial federal ruling on prison farm operations in the state of Arkansas.

Home detention: The mandated action that forces an offender to stay within the confines of his or her home for a specified time.

Houses of refuge: Institutions that were oriented toward education and treatment for juveniles.

Hudson v. Palmer *(1984):* Held that prison cells may be searched without the need of a warrant and without probable cause.

Hustle: Any action that is designed to deceive, manipulate, or take advantage of another person.

Hutto v. Finney *(1978):* Held that courts can set time limits on prison use of solitary confinement.

Implementation evaluation: Identifying problems and accomplishments during the early phases of program development for feedback to clinical and administrative staff.

Importation theory: Subculture within prisons is brought in from outside by offenders who have developed their beliefs and norms while on the streets.

In loco parentis: "In the place of parents."

In re Gault *(1967):* Ruled that in hearings that may result in institutional commitment, juveniles have all of the constitutional rights afforded to adults.

In re Holmes *(1955):* Held that because juvenile courts are not criminal courts, the constitutional rights guaranteed to accused adults do not apply to juveniles.

Incapacitation: Deprives offenders of their liberty and removes them from society, ensuring that they cannot further victimize society for a time.

Indeterminate sentences: Sentences that include a range of years that will be potentially served by the offender.

Individual personality traits: Traits associated with criminal behavior.

Injunction: A court order that requires an agency to take some form of action(s) or to refrain from a particular action(s).

Institutional parole officer: Works to aid the offender in making the transition from prison life to community supervision.

Intensive supervision probation (ISP): The extensive supervision of offenders who are deemed the greatest risk to society or are in need of the greatest amount of governmental services.

Intentional tort: The actor, whether expressed or implied, was judged to have possessed intent or purpose to cause an injury.

Intermediate sanctions: A range of sentencing options that fall between incarceration and probation.

Isolation zone: Designed to prevent undetected access to the outer fencing of the prison facility.

Jail: A confinement facility, usually operated and controlled by county-level law enforcement, designed to hold persons who are awaiting adjudication or serving a short sentence of 1 year or less.

Jail reentry programs: Programs usually interlaced with probation and parole agencies as a means of integrating the supervisory functions of both the jail and community supervision agencies.

Johnson v. Avery *(1969):* Held that prison authorities cannot prohibit inmates from aiding other inmates in preparing legal documents.

Judicial Improvements Act of 1990: Extended the life of the Parole Commission until November 1, 1997.

Juvenile waiver: Occurs when the juvenile case is transferred to adult court.

Kingsley v. Hendrickson *(2015):* For claims of excessive force brought by pretrial detainees, it is only necessary to show that the force used was objectively unreasonable.

Labeling theory: Contends that individuals become stabilized in criminal roles when they are labeled as criminals.

LaSalle Corrections: A private company that owns and operates prisons in Louisiana and Texas.

Leadership: Entails skills and talents that motivate and influence persons toward a common goal or idea.

Learning organizations: Have the inherent ability to adapt and change, improving performance through continual revision of goals, objectives, policies, and procedures.

LeMaire v. Maass *(1993):* A suit in which the plaintiff considered the conditions of the Oregon prison to be unconstitutional.

Level of security: The type of physical barriers that are utilized to prevent inmates' escape and are related to public safety concerns.

Lex talionis: Refers to the Babylonian law of equal retaliation.

Libel: Written communication intended to lower the reputation of a person where such facts would actually be damaging to a reputation.

Life-course-persistent juvenile: Adolescent who lacks many of the necessary social skills and opportunities possessed by the adolescent-limited delinquent.

Life development intervention: A comprehensive approach to linking sport and recreation to counseling psychology that emphasizes continuous growth and positive change.

Life Skills for State and Local Prisoners Program: Provides financial assistance for establishing and operating programs designed to reduce recidivism through the development and improvement of life skills.

Little Hoover Commission: An internal state "watchdog" agency that was tasked with providing recommendations to the state governor and legislature in California.

Madrid v. Gomez *(1995):* Case where the constitutionality of supermax facilities was questioned.

Major depressive disorder: Characterized by one or more major depressive episodes.

Malicious prosecution: Occurs when a criminal accusation is made without probable cause and for improper reasons.

Malingering: When inmates falsely claim symptoms of an illness.

Management: Persons with an official title who tend to be focused on the operational process within the prison facility.

Mandatory minimum: A minimum amount of time or a minimum percentage of a sentence must be served with no good time or early-release modifications.

Mark system: A system where the duration of the sentence was determined by the inmate's work habits and righteous conduct.

Martinson Report: An examination of a number of various prison treatment programs.

Maximum-security facilities: These high-security facilities use corrugated chain-link fence. These fences will be lit by floodlights at night and may even be electrified and eliminate "blind spots" in security where inmates can hide.

McKeiver v. Pennsylvania *(1971)*: Held that the due process clause of the Fourteenth Amendment did not require jury trials in juvenile court.

Media effects: The effect that the media has upon the public perception of prison or community supervision programs.

Medical model: An approach to correctional treatment that utilizes a type of mental health approach incorporating fields such as psychology and biology.

Medium-security facilities: Consist of dormitories that have bunk beds with lockers for inmates to store their possessions and communal showers and toilets. Dormitories are locked at night with one or more security officers holding watch.

Megan's laws: Term for legislation that mandates a public notification process when sex offenders are released into the community.

Mental illness: Any diagnosed disorder contained within the *DSM*-5.

Minimal services view: Contends that inmates are entitled to no more than the bare minimum that is required by law.

Minimum-security facilities:.

Mitigating factors: Circumstances that make a crime more understandable and help to reduce the level of culpability that an offender might have.

Mood disorders: Disorders such as major depressive disorder, bipolar disorder, and dysthymic disorder.

Morris v. Travisono *(1970)*: Resulted in a detailed set of procedures for classifying inmates that was overseen by the federal court system.

Mothers and Infants Nurturing Together (MINT): A Federal Bureau of Prisons program that promotes bonding and parenting skills for low-risk female inmates who are pregnant.

Mule: A person who smuggles drugs into prison for another inmate.

National Commission on Correctional Health Care (NCCHC): Sets the tone for standards of care in correctional settings.

National Institute of Corrections (NIC): An agency within the Federal Bureau of Prisons that is headed by a director appointed by the U.S. attorney general.

Negative punishment: The removal of a valued stimulus when the offender commits an undesired behavior.

Negative reinforcers: Unpleasant stimuli that are removed when a desired behavior occurs.

Negligence: Doing what a reasonably prudent person would not do in similar circumstances or failing to do what a reasonably prudent person would do in similar circumstances.

O'Lone v. Estate of Shabazz *(1987)*: Held that depriving an inmate of attending a religious service for "legitimate penological interests" was not a violation of the inmate's First Amendment rights.

Offender Accountability Plan: Addresses needs for restitution, any particular arrangements that have been made with the victim, and provisions to ensure the offender's responsibility to the community at large.

Offender reentry: Includes all activities and programming conducted to prepare ex-convicts to return safely to the community and to live as law-abiding citizens.

Offender with special needs: A specialized offender who has some notable physical, mental, and/or emotional challenge.

Offender-turned-elderly-in-prison: Inmates who have grown old in prison who have long histories in the system.

Office of Correctional Education (OCE): Created to provide national leadership on issues related to correctional education.

Old Newgate Prison: First prison structure in America.

One hand on, one hand off doctrine: More conservative rulings are being handed down from the Court, reflecting an eclipse of the hands-off doctrine.

Outcome evaluation: Involves quantitative research aimed at assessing the impact of the program on long-term treatment outcomes.

Pains of imprisonment: The various inconveniences and deprivations that occur as a result of incarceration.

Palmigiano v. Garrahy *(1977)*: Ruling that attested to the importance of effective and appropriate classification systems.

Panopticon: Designed to allow security personnel to clearly observe all inmates without the inmates themselves being able to tell whether they are being watched.

Parens patriae: "Parent of the country."

Parole: The early release of an offender from a secure facility upon completion of a certain portion of his or her sentence.

Parole Commission and Reorganization Act: Established the U.S. Parole Commission as an independent agency within the Department of Justice.

Parole Commission Phaseout Act of 1996: Extended the life of the Parole Commission until November 1, 2002, but only in regard to supervising offenders who were still on parole from previous years.

Parole revocations officer: Primarily tasked with the routine holding of preliminary parole revocation hearings by reviewing allegations made by parole officers against parolees.

Participative method of management: A form of management that includes opinions and feedback offered from both inmates and staff when making decisions regarding the operations and governance of the prison facility.

Passive agent: Views his or her job dispassionately as just a job and tends to do as little as possibles.

Paternal officer: Uses a great degree of both control and assistance techniques in supervising offenders.

Patriarchy: A male-oriented and male-dominated social structure that defers to men and sees women in a subservient position to men. .

Pell Grants: Need-based federal monies set aside for persons who pursue a college education.

Perimeter security system: A collection of components or elements that, when assembled in a carefully formulated plan, achieve the objective of confinement with a high degree of confidence.

Physical abuse: Abuse that consists of some type of physical battery and/or abuse that causes some type of physiological harm.

Physical neglect: Includes abandonment, the expulsion of a child from the home, a failure to provide medical care, supervision, food, clothing, and shelter.

Pods: Prefabricated sections in most modern prisons. Inmates will usually have individual cells with doors controlled from a secure remote control station.

Podular jail: Includes rounded architecture for living units and allows for direct supervision of inmates by security staff.

Positive punishment: Punishment where a stimulus is applied to the offender when the offender commits an undesired behavior.

Positive reinforcers: Rewards for a desired behavior.

Post-Release Employment Project (PREP): A study that demonstrated that UNICOR successfully prepared inmates for release and provided long-term benefits to society.

Preliminary hearing: Initial examination of the facts of the arrest to determine if probable cause does exist for a violation.

Presentence investigation report: A thorough file that includes a wide range of background information on the offender.

Prison food loaf: A food product that contains all the typical ingredients of a well-balanced meal mixed together and baked as a single loaf-like product that would be served to inmates.

Prison grapevine: An informal network of information passed through the personal communications of employees and inmates.

Prison Industry Enhancement (PIE) Certification Program: Partnership between the Texas Department of Criminal Justice and a private company that allows the company to employ offenders.

Prison Litigation Reform Act (PLRA): Limits an inmate's ability to file lawsuits and the compensation that he or she can receive.

Prisonization: The process of being socialized into the prison culture.

Private wrongs: Crimes against an individual that could include physical injury, damage to a person's property, or theft.

Proactive styles of management: Seek to anticipate and correct problems before they develop.

Probation: A control valve mechanism that mitigates the flow of inmates sent directly to the jailhouse.

Process evaluation: Traditionally refers to assessment of the effects of the program on clients while they are in the program, making it possible to assess the institution's intermediary goals.

Procunier v. Martinez *(1974):* Prison officials may censor inmate mail only to the extent necessary to ensure security of the institution.

Progressive Era: A period of extraordinary urban and industrial growth and unprecedented social problems.

Prosecutorial death discretion outcome: Observes that prosecutors are overwhelmingly Caucasian and seek the death penalty disproportionately more often when the victim is also Caucasian.

Protective custody: A security-level status given to inmates who are deemed to be at risk of serious violence if not afforded protection.

Psychological abuse: Includes actions or the omission of actions that could cause a child to have serious behavioral, emotional, or mental impairments.

Psychology services representative: A member of the decision-making team who is expected to be involved in the admission and information-gathering process prior to classification.

Public Safety Realignment (PSR): A California state policy designed to reduce the number of offenders in that state's prison system to 110,000.

Public wrongs: Crimes against society or a social group.

Punitive damages: Monetary awards reserved for the person harmed in a malicious or willful manner by the guilty party.

Punitive officer: Sees himself or herself as needing to use threats and punishment in order to get compliance from the offender.

Punk: A derogatory term for an inmate who engages in homosexual activity; implies that the inmate is feminine, weak, and subservient to masculine inmates.

Qualified immunity: Legal immunity that shields correctional officers from lawsuits, but first requires them to demonstrate the grounds for their possession of immunity.

Rational basis test: Sets guidelines for the rights of inmates that still allow correctional agencies to maintain security.

Reactive styles of management: When a supervisor waits until a problem develops and then responds to remedy the situation.

Recreation program administrator: Responsible for a number of duties, including surveying the recreational needs and interests of the offender population.

Reform school: An industrial school.

Reformatories for women: Developed as alternatives to the penitentiary's harsh conditions of enforced silence and hard labor.

Regional-level administrators: Managers who oversee a specific region of a state.

Rehabilitation: Offenders will be deterred from reoffending due to their having worthwhile stakes in legitimate society.

Reintegration: Focused on the reentry of the offender into society by connecting offenders to legitimate areas of society that are gainful and productive.

Reintegration model: Used to identify programs that looked to the external environment for causes of crime and the means to reduce criminality.

Release valve mechanism: When correctional systems use parole to reduce correctional populations.

Religious Land Use and Institutionalized Persons Act of 2000: Prohibits the government from substantially burdening an inmate's religious exercise.

Respect: An inmate's sense of standing within the prison culture.

Restorative justice: Interventions that focus on restoring the community and the victim with involvement from the offender.

Retribution: Offenders committing a crime should be punished in a way that is equal to the severity of the crime they committed.

Rogues and mavericks: Employees within a facility who tend to act as if they are independent of the broader institution.

Roper v. Simmons *(2005):* Ruled that the death penalty was unconstitutional when used with persons who were under 18 years of age at the time of their offense.

Ruiz v. Estelle *(1980):* Ruled that the Texas prison system was in violation of the prohibition against cruel and unusual punishments.

Rumor control: The active process of administrators to circumvent faulty information that is disseminated among staff or inmates and has the potential to cause unrest or disharmony throughout the facility.

Rural jail: Usually small jails in rural county jurisdictions that are often challenged by tight budgets and limited training for staff.

Saliva testing: Using samples of saliva to determine if an offender has been using drugs.

Sally port: Entry design that allows security staff to bring vehicles close to the admissions area in a secure fashion.

Sanctuary: A place of refuge or asylum.

Security threat group (STG): A high-functioning, organized gang that uses an illegal industry to fund their objectives.

Selective incapacitation: Identifying inmates who are of particular concern to public safety and providing them with much longer sentences.

Sentencing stage: When a judge determines if the offender will be incarcerated or continue his or her probation sentence under more restrictive terms.

SENTRY system: A comprehensive database used by the Federal Bureau of Prisons to classify and track inmates within the system.

Shock incarceration: A short period of incarceration followed by a specified term of community supervision.

Short-term jail: A facility that holds sentenced inmates for no more than 1 year.

Slander: Verbal communication intended to lower the reputation of a person where such facts would actually be damaging to a reputation.

Smarter Sentencing Act of 2014: A bill that adjusts federal mandatory sentencing guidelines in an effort to reduce the size of the U.S. prison population.

Snitch: Term for an inmate who reveals the activity of another inmate to authorities.

Social learning theory: Contends that offenders learn to engage in crime through exposure to and adoption of definitions that are favorable to the commission of crime.

Span of control: Refers to the number of persons that an officer supervises.

Span of influence: The extended impact that a supervisor has upon employee behavior.

Special housing unit syndrome: The negative mental health effects of extended isolation.

Special Operations Response Teams (SORT): Teams designed to respond to serious crises within a prison facility.

Specific deterrence: The infliction of a punishment upon a specific offender in the hope that he/she will be discouraged from committing future crimes.

Stakeholders: Agency personnel, the surrounding community, and the offender population.

Strain theory/institutional anomie: Denotes that when individuals cannot obtain success goals they will tend to experience a sense of pressure often called *strain*.

Strategic plan: A document that articulates agency goals and objectives and states how they might be realized.

Strategic planning: Consists of the determination of long-term goals and objectives for an agency, usually spanning a period of one or more years in scope.

Successful Treatment of Addiction and Recovery (STAR) program: Emphasizes the people, places, and things that inmates encounter that can affect relapse into drug use and criminal activity.

Supermax facility: A highly restrictive, high-custody housing unit within a secure facility, or an entire secure facility, that isolates inmates from the general population and from each other.

Supervised release: Postrelease supervision.

Sweat testing: Using samples of sweat excretion to determine if an offender has been using drugs.

Symbiotic prison relationship: When correctional staff and inmates develop negotiation behavior that is acceptable for institutional security and also meets inmates' basic human needs.

System-wide administrators: Managers who are at the executive level and direct the entire system throughout the state.

Tactical planning: Ground-level planning that is narrow in focus and structured around the short-term resolution of particular issues.

Technical violations: Actions that do not comply with the conditions and requirements of a probationer's sentence.

Texas Correctional Industries (TCI): Provides offenders with marketable job skills to help reduce recidivism.

The Summary: The first inmate-operated prison newspaper in the world.

Theory of disablement: The offender is isolated or maimed as a means of preventing a type of crime in the future.

Therapeutic community: An environment that provides necessary behavior modifiers that allow offenders immediate feedback about their behavior and treatment progress.

Therapeutic recreation (TR): Programs designed to meet the needs of individuals with a variety of disabilities, impairments, or illnesses by providing specific services.

Theriault v. Carlson *(1977):* Ruling that the First Amendment does not protect so-called religions that are obvious shams, that tend to mock established institutions, and whose members lack religious sincerity.

Thompson v. Oklahoma *(1988):* Held that the Eighth and Fourteenth Amendments prohibited the execution of a person who is under 16 years of age at the time of his or her offense.

Ticket of leave: A permit given to a convict in exchange for a certain period of good conduct.

Title IV of the Higher Education Act: Permitted inmates to apply for financial aid in the form of Pell Grants to attend college.

Top Three in corrections: Texas, California, and Florida are the largest prison systems in terms of inmate count.

Tort: A legal injury in which a person causes injury as the result of a violation of one's duty as established by law.

Totality of the conditions: A standard used to determine if conditions in an institution are in violation of the Eighth Amendment.

Tower of London: One of the earliest examples of a jail used for confinement purposes.

Trial by ordeal: Very dangerous and/or impossible tests to prove the guilt or innocence of the accused.

Trop v. Dulles *(1958):* Developed a phrase that would be cited in future cases because it fit with many compelling arguments in favor of correctional reform.

Turnkeys: Inmates who are tasked with opening and closing interior locked gates and doors of the prison.

Turner v. Safley *(1987):* A prison regulation that impinges on inmates' constitutional rights is valid if it is reasonably related to legitimate penological interests.

UNICOR Inc.: An organization for federal prison labor.

Unit-level administrators: The third level of administrator in state agencies; includes personnel who manage the individual prison facility.

Unit manager: Directs the housing unit activities and is responsible for the unit's operation and quality control of all correspondence and programs.

United States Parole Commission Extension Act of 2008: Provided for the continued performance of the U.S. Parole Commission.

United States Penitentiary (USP) Terre Haute: The physical location for federal death row.

United States v. Booker *(2005):* Determined judges no longer had to follow the sentencing guidelines that had been in place since 1987.

Universal design: Prison construction design that complies with ADA requirements and that accommodates all inmate needs in a universal fashion.

Urine testing: Using urine samples to determine if an offender has been using drugs.

USP Florence ADMAX: A federal prison with a design that is nearly indestructible on the inside. Essentially, these offenders have no contact with humans.

USP Marion: A special closed-custody unit designed to house the Federal Bureau of Prisons' worst inmates.

Victorian Era: Viewed women from a lens of inflexible femininity where women were to be considered pious and naïve of the evils of the world.

Vitek v. Jones (1980): Inmates are entitled to due process in involuntary transfers from prison to a mental hospital.

Walnut Street Jail: America's first attempt to incarcerate inmates with the purpose of reforming them.

Weekend confinement: Confinement that is restricted to the weekends or other times when the person in custody is off from work.

Welfare worker: Views the offender more as a client rather than a supervisee on his or her caseload.

Western State Penitentiary: Part of the Pennsylvania system located outside of Pittsburgh.

Wilson v. Seiter *(1991):* Deliberate indifference is required for liability to be attached for condition of confinement cases.

Windham School District: Secondary education program in Texas prisons.

Witherspoon v. Illinois *(1968):* Held that it was not constitutional to strike a potential juror from serving if the juror had doubts or reservations about the use of the death penalty.

Wolff v. McDonnell *(1974):* Inmates are entitled to due process in prison disciplinary proceedings that can result in the loss of good time credits or in punitive segregation.

Work Against Recidivism (WAR) program: Specifically targeted to successfully reintegrate offenders into society.

Work/education reform view: Claims that society is saved untold millions due to the lack of recidivism of inmates who have obtained employment and/or education.

Writ writer: An inmate who becomes skilled at generating legal complaints and grievances within the prison system.

Zebulon Brockway: The warden of Elmira Reformatory.

Zimmer Amendment: Restricted the purchase of several types of weight lifting equipment within the Federal Bureau of Prisons.

Abadinsky, H., & Winfree, L. T., Jr. (1992). *Crime and justice* (2nd ed.). Chicago, IL: Nelson-Hall.

ABC Primetime. (2004, November 4). *Inside a maximum security women's prison.* Retrieved from http://abc news.go.com/Primetime/story?id=227295&p age=1

Aday, R. H. (1994). Aging in prison: A case study of new elderly offenders. *International Journal of Offender Therapy and Comparative Criminology, 38*(1), 121.

Agnew, R. (1992). Foundation for a general strain theory of crime and delinquency. *Criminology, 30*(1), 47–87.

Akers, R. A. (2000). *Criminological theories: Introduction, evaluation, and application*. Los Angeles, CA: Roxbury.

Allen, H. E., Simonsen, C. E., & Latessa, E. J. (2004). *Corrections in America* (10th ed.). Upper Saddle River, NJ: Prentice Hall.

Allen, J. M., & Sawhney, R. (2010). *Administration and management in criminal justice*. Thousand Oaks, CA: Sage.

Allen, R. L. (1974). *Reluctant reformers: Racism and social reform movements in the United States*. Washington, DC: Howard University Press.

American Correctional Association. (1998). *Causes, preventive measures, and methods of controlling riots and disturbances in correctional institutes*. Upper Marlboro, MD: Graphic Communications.

American Correctional Association. (2001). A short history of direct-supervision facility design. *Corrections Today*. Alexandria, VA: Author.

American Jail Association. (1993). *American Jail Association code of ethics.* Retrieved January 28, 2003, from http://www.corrections.com/aja/resolutions/index.html

American Probation and Parole Association. (1991). *Issue paper on caseload standards.* Washington, DC: Author.

American Probation and Parole Association. (2011). *Probation and parole FAQs*. Washington, DC: Author.

American Psychiatric Association. (2000). *Diagnostic and statistical manual of mental disorders* (4th ed., text rev.). Washington, DC: Author.

Anderson, J. C. (2008). Special needs offenders. In P. M. Carlson & J. S. Garrett (Eds.), *Prison and jail administration: Practice and theory* (2nd ed.) (pp. 361–372). Sudbury, MA: Jones and Bartlett.

Anderson, J. F., Mangels, N. J., & Dyson, L. (2010). *Significant prisoner rights cases*. Durham, NC: Carolina Academic Press.

Anderson, T. (2003). Issues in the availability of health care for women prisoners. In S. F. Sharp (Ed.), *The incarcerated woman: Rehabilitative programming in women's prisons* (pp. 49–60). Englewood Cliffs, NJ: Prentice Hall.

Angelone, R. (1999). Protective custody inmates. In P. M. Carlson & J. S. Garrett (Eds.), *Prison and jail administration: Practice and theory* (pp. 236–231). Gaithersberg, MD: Aspen.

Anno, B. J., Graham, C., Lawrence, J. E., & Shansky, R. (2004). *Correctional health care: Addressing the needs of elderly, chronically ill, and terminally ill inmates.* Washington, DC: National Institute of Corrections.

Appel, A. (1999). Accommodating inmates with disabilities. In P. M. Carlson & J. S. Garrett (Ed.), *Prison and jail administration* (pp. 346–352). Gaithersburg, MD: Aspen.

Applegate, B. K., & Sitren, A. H. (2008). The jail and the community: Comparing jails in rural and urban contexts. *The Prison Journal, 88*, 252–269.

Arkansas speeds parole to ease jam. (2001, November 30). *Corrections Digest*.

Armstrong, J. J. (2008). Causes of institutional unrest. In P. M. Carlson & J. S. Garrett (Eds.), *Prison and jail administration: Practice and theory* (2nd ed.) (pp. 461–468). Sudbury, MA: Jones and Bartlett.

Ashford, J. B., Sales, B. D., & Reid, W. H. (2002). *Treating adult and juvenile offenders with special needs*. Washington, DC: American Psychological Association.

Associated Press. (2001). *Prison escape probe to focus on lax security.* Retrieved January 28, 2003, from http://www.clickonsa.com/ant/news/stories/news-20010108-085202.html

Atkins v. Virginia, 536 U.S. 304 (2002).

Augustus, J. (1972). *John Augustus' original report of his labors*. Montclair, NJ: Patterson Smith. (Original work published in 1852)

Ayers, E. L. (1984). *Vengeance and justice: Crime and punishment in the nineteenth century American South*. New York, NY: Oxford University Press.

Baird, S. C., & Austin, J. (1985). *Current state of the art in prison classification models: A literature review for the California Department of Corrections*. Sacramento, CA: Carter Center.

Barnes, H. E. (1968). *The evolution of penology in Pennsylvania.* Montclair, NJ: Patterson Smith. (Original work published in 1927)

Barnes, H. E., & Teeters, N. K. (1959). *New horizons in criminology* (3rd ed.). Upper Saddle River, NJ: Prentice Hall.

Bartol, C. R., & Bartol, A. M. (2010). *Criminal behavior: A psychosocial approach* (9th ed.). Upper Saddle River, NJ: Prentice Hall.

Baxter v. Palmigiano, 425 U.S. 308 (1976).

Bazos, A., & Hausman, J. (2004). *Correctional education as a crime control program.* Los Angeles, CA: UCLA School of Public Policy and Social Research. Retrieved June 28, 2010, from http://www.ceanational.net/PDFs/ed-as-crime-control.pdf

BBC News. (1999). *Many elderly offenders "are mentally ill."* Retrieved from http://news.bbc.co.uk/1/hi/health/294252.stm

Beck, A. J. (2015). *PREA data collection activities, 2015*. Washington, DC: Bureau of Justice Statistics.

Becker, H. S. (1963). *Outsiders: Studies in the sociology of deviance.* New York: Free Press.

Becker, H. S. (1999). Career deviance. In S. H. Traub & C. B. Little (Eds.),

Theories of deviance (pp. 390–397). Itasca, IL: Peacock.

Belenko, S. (2001). *Research on drug courts: A critical review. 2001 update*. New York, NY: National Center on Addiction and Substance Abuse. Retrieved from www.drug policy.org/docUploads/2001drugcourts.pdf

Belknap, J. (2001). *The invisible woman: Gender, crime, and justice*. Belmont, CA: Wadsworth.

Bell v. Wolfish, 441 U.S. 520 (1979).

Bellamy, J. (1973). *Crime and public order in England in the later Middle Ages.* London: Routledge & Kegan Paul.

Benestante, J. (1996, April 19). Presentation before the Texas Board of Criminal Justice Special Committee on Prison Industries. Austin, TX: Texas Department of Criminal Justice.

Bernard, T. J. (1992). *The cycle of juvenile justice*. New York, NY: Oxford University Press.

Bernard, T. J., McCleary, R., & Wright, R. A. (1999). *Life without parole: Living in prison today* (2nd ed.). Los Angeles, CA: Roxbury.

Berzofsky, M., Maruschak, L. M., & Unangst, J. (2015). *Medical problems of state and federal prisoners and jail inmates, 2011–12*. Washington, DC: Bureau of Justice Statistics.

Blackstone, W. (1803). *Commentaries on the laws of England* (12th ed., Vol. 4). London: Strahan.

Bloom, B., Brown, M., & Chesney-Lind, M. (1996). Women on probation and parole. In A. J. Lurigio (Ed.), *Community corrections in America: New directions and sounder investments for persons with mental illness and co-disorders* (pp. 51–76). Washington, DC: National Institute of Corrections.

Bloom, B., Owen, B., & Covington, S. (2003). *Gender responsive strategies: Research, practice, and guiding principles for women offenders.* Washington, DC: National Institute of Corrections. Retrieved from http://www.nicic.org/Library/018017

Bohm, R. (1999). *Deathquest: An introduction to the theory and practice of capital punishment in the United States*. Cincinnati, OH: Anderson Publishing.

Bosworth, M. (2010). *Explaining U.S. imprisonment*. Thousand Oaks, CA: Sage.

Bounds v. Smith, 430 U.S. 817 (1977).

Bowers, W. J., & Pierce, G. L. (1980). Deterrence or brutalization: What is the effect of executions? *Crime & Delinquency, 26*(4), 453–484.

Bowker, L. H. (1980). *Prison victimization.* New York, NY: Elsevier.

Bradley, C. M. (2006, March/April). The right decision on the juvenile death penalty. *Judicature, 89*, 302–305.

Braithwaite, J. (1989). *Crime, shame, and reintegration*. Cambridge, UK: Cambridge University Press.

Branch-Johnson, W. (1957). *The English prison hulks*. Publisher unknown.

Branham, L. S., & Hamden, M. S. (2009). *Cases and materials on the law and policy of sentencing and corrections* (8th ed.). St. Paul, MN: West.

Breed v. Jones, 421 U.S. 519 (1975).

Brennan, P. K., & Vandenberg, A. L. (2009). Depictions of female offenders in front-page newspaper stories: The importance of race/ethnicity. *International Journal of Social Inquiry, 2*(2), 141–175.

Brennan, T. (1987a). Classification: An overview of selected methodological issues. In D. M. Gottfredson & M. Tonry (Eds.), *Prediction and classification: Criminal justice decision making.* Chicago, IL: University of Chicago Press.

Brennan, T. (1987b). Classification for control in jails and prisons. In D. M. Gottfredson & M. Tonry (Eds.), *Prediction and classification: Criminal justice decision making.* Chicago, IL: University of Chicago Press.

Brennan, T., Wells, D., & Alexander, J. (2004). *Enhancing prison classification systems: The emerging role of management information systems.* Washington, DC: National Institute of Corrections.

Brockway, Z. R. (1912). *Fifty years of prison service: An autobiography*. New York State Reformatory at Elmira. Annual report reprinted, Montclair, NJ: Patterson Smith, 1969.

Brown, J. W. (2003). The female inmate. *International Encyclopedia of Justice Studies.* Retrieved from http://www.eijs.com/Corrections/female_inmate.htm

Browne, J. (2010). Rooted in slavery: Prison labor exploitation. *Race, Poverty, & the Environment, 14*(2), 78–81.

Bruscino v. Carlson, 854 F. 2d 162 (7th Cir. 1988).

Bureau of Justice Assistance Center for Program Evaluation. (2007). *Reporting and using evaluation results*. Washington, DC: Author. Retrieved from http://www.ojp.usdoj.gov/BJA/evaluation/sitemap.htm

Bureau of Justice Statistics. (1998). *Substance abuse and treatment, state and federal prisoners, 1997*. Washington, DC: U.S Department of Justice.

Bureau of Justice Statistics. (2008). *Capital punishment statistical tables.* Retrieved from http://bjs.ojp.usdoj.gov/index.cfm?ty=tp&tid=181

Bureau of Justice Statistics. (2010). *Prisoners in 2009.* Washington, DC: U.S. Department of Justice.

Bureau of Labor Statistics. (2011). *Occupational outlook handbook 2010–2011: Probation officers and correctional treatment specialists*. Washington, DC: U.S. Department of Labor.

Bureau of Labor Statistics. (2012). *Occupational outlook handbook* (2012–13 edition). Retrieved from http://www.bls.gov/ooh

Burger, W. E. (1983). Commencement address: Warren E. Burger. *Pace Law Review, 4*(1), 1–9.

Burke, P. B. (1997). *Policy-driven responses to probation and parole violations*. Washington, DC: National Institute of Corrections.

Burrell, B. (2006). *Caseload standards for probation and parole*. Washington, DC: National Institute of Corrections.

Butler, B. (2014). *Liman report: Solitary confinement on Texas's death row*. Yale Law School. Retrieved from http://www.law.yale.edu/intellectuallife/19074.htm

Butterfield, F. (2003). *Prison policy put priest in unit with his killer, experts say*. Retrieved from http://www.nytimes.com/2003/08/29/us/pri son-policy-put-priest-in-unit-with-his-killer-experts-say.html?pagewanted=1

Bynam, J. E., & Thompson, W. E. (1992). *Juvenile delinquency* (2nd ed.). Boston, MA: Allyn & Bacon.

Cahill, A. J. (2001). *Rethinking rape.* Ithaca, NY: Cornell University Press.

Camp, C., & Camp, G. (2003). *The 2002 corrections yearbook: Adult corrections*. Middletown, CT: Criminal Justice Institute.

Campbell, D. T., & Stanley, J. C. (1963). *Experimental and quasi-experimental designs for research.* Boston, MA: Houghton Mifflin.

Carlson, P. M., & DiIulio, J. J. (2008). Organizational management. In P. M. Carlson & J. S. Garrett (Eds.), *Prison and jail administration: Practice and theory* (2nd ed.) (pp. 193–212). Sudbury, MA: Jones and Bartlett.

Carlson, P. M., & Garrett, J. S. (Eds.). (1999). *Prison and jail administration: Practice and theory*. Gaithersburg, MD: Aspen.

Carlson, P. M., & Garrett, J. S. (Eds.). (2008). *Prison and jail administration: Practice and Theory* (2nd ed.). Sudbury, MA: Jones and Bartlett.

Carlson, P. M., Roth, T., & Travisono, A. P. (2008). History of corrections. In P. M. Carlson & J. S. Garrett (Eds.), *Prison and jail administration: Practice and theory* (2nd ed.) (pp. 3–18). Sudbury, MA: Jones and Bartlett.

Carp, R., & Stidham, R. (1990). *Judicial process in America.* Washington, DC: Congressional Quarterly Press.

Carroll, L. (1996). Lease system. In M. D. McShane & F. P. Williams (Eds.), *Encyclopedia of American prisons* (pp. 446–452). London: Taylor & Francis.

Carson, A. E. (2014). *Prisoners, 2013*. Washington, DC: Bureau of Justice Statistics.

Carson, A. E. (2015). *Prisoners, 2014*. Washington, DC: Bureau of Justice Statistics.

Carter, R. (1996). Determinate sentences. In M. D. McShane & F. P. Williams (Eds.), *Encyclopedia of American prisons* (pp. 237–240). London: Taylor & Francis.

Cavan, R. S. (1969). *Juvenile delinquency: Development, treatment, control* (2nd ed.). Philadelphia, PA: J. B. Lippincott.

Center for Sex Offender Management. (2008). *An overview of sex offender treatment for a non-clinical audience*. Washington, DC: Office of Justice Programs, U.S. Department of Justice.

Center for Substance Abuse Treatment. (2005). *Substance abuse treatment for adults in the criminal justice system.* Treatment Improvement Protocol (TIP) Series 44. DHHS Publication No. (SMA) 05-4056. Rockville, MD: Substance Abuse and Mental Health Services Administration.

Center on Addiction and Substance Abuse. (2010). *Substance abuse and America's prison population*. New York, NY: Columbia University.

Centers for Disease Control and Prevention. (2003). *Prevention and control of infections with hepatitis viruses in correctional settings*. Atlanta, GA: U.S. Department of Health and Human Services.

Centers for Disease Control and Prevention. (2006). *Prevention and control of tuberculosis in correctional and detention facilities: Recommendations from CDC*. Washington, DC: Author. Retrieved from http://www.cdc.gov/mmwr/preview/mmwrhtml/rr5509a1.htm

Centers for Disease Control and Prevention. (2011). *Evaluation of large jail STD screening programs, 2008–2009*. Washington, DC: Author. Retrieved from http://www.cdc.gov/std/publications/jailscreening2011.pdf

Champion, D. (2002). *Probation, parole and community corrections* (4th ed.). Upper Saddle River, NJ: Prentice Hall.

Chen, M. K., & Shapiro, J. M. (2002). *Does prison harden inmates? A discontinuity-based approach.* Retrieved from http://129.3.20.41/eps/le/papers/0304/0304003.pdf

Chokprajakchat, S., & Kuanliang, A. (2015). *Research project to formulate the Offender Rehabilitation Act of Thailand*. Bangkok, Thailand.

Clear, T. R., & Cole, G. F. (2002). *American corrections* (6th ed.). Belmont, CA: Wadsworth.

Clear, T. R., Cole, G. F., & Reisig, M. D. (2005). *American corrections* (7th ed.). Belmont, CA: Wadsworth.

Clear, T. R., Cole, G. F., & Reisig, M. D. (2008). *American corrections* (8th ed.). Belmont, CA: Wadsworth.

Cochran, J. K., Chamlin, M. B., & Seth, M. (1994). Deterrence or brutalization: An impact assessment of Oklahoma's return to capital punishment. *Criminology, 32,* 107–133.

Cohen, L., & Felson, M. (1979). Social change and crime rate trends: A routine activity approach. *American Sociological Review, 44*(4), 588–608.

Coker v. Georgia, 433 U.S. 584 (1977).

Coley, R. J., & Barton, P. E. (2006). *Locked up and locked out: An educational perspective on the U.S. prison population.* Princeton, NJ: Educational Testing Service. Retrieved June 28, 2010, from http://www.ets.org/Media/Research/pdf/PICLOCKEDUP.pdf

Collins, W. C. (2004). *Supermax prisons and the Constitution: Liability concerns in the extended control unit.* Washington, DC: National Institute of Corrections.

Colorado Division of Criminal Justice. (2007). *Evidence based correctional practices*. Denver, CO: Office of Research and Statistics.

Connecticut Department of Correction. (2010). *Administrative directive 10.18: Nutrition and food services*. Wethersfield, CT: Author.

Contardo, J., & Tolbert, M. (2010). *Prison postsecondary education: Bridging learning from incarceration to the community.* Retrieved June 19, 2012, from http://www.urban.org/projects/reentry-roundtable/upload/Contardo.pdf

Cooper v. Pate, 378 U.S. 546 (1964).

Cox, S. D. (2009). *The big house: Image and reality of the American prison.* New Haven, CT: Yale University Press.

REFERENCES

Cox, S., Allen, J., Hanser, R., & Conrad, C. (2011). *Juvenile justice: A guide to theory, policy, and practice* (8th ed.). Thousand Oaks, CA: Sage.

Crawford, J. (2003). Alternative sentencing necessary for female inmates with children. *Corrections Today.* Retrieved from http://www.aca.org/publications/ctarchivespdf/june03/commentary_june.pdf

Cressey, D. R., & Irwin, J. (1962). Thieves, convicts and the inmate culture. *Social Problems, 10*(3), 142–155.

Crist, D., & Spencer, D. (1991). *Perimeter security for Minnesota correctional facilities*. St. Paul, MN: Minnesota Department of Corrections.

Cromwell, P., del Carmen, R., & Alarid, L. (2002). *Community-based corrections* (5th ed.). Belmont, CA: Wadsworth.

Crouch, B. M., & Marquart, J. W. (1989). *An appeal to justice: Litigated reform of Texas prisons.* Austin, TX: University of Texas Press.

Cruz, T. (2015, February 12). *Senator Cruz: Smarter Sentencing Act is common sense: Joins bipartisan group in support of legislation to reduce mandatory minimums*. Retrieved from http://www.cruz.senate.gov/?p=press_release&id=2184

Cruz v. Beto, 405 U.S. 319 (1972).

Cullen, F. T., & Agnew, R. (2006). *Criminological theory: Past to present* (3rd ed.). Los Angeles, CA: Roxbury.

Cutter v. Wilkinson, 544 U.S. 709 (2005).

Dammer, H. R. (2002). Religion in corrections. In D. Levinson (Ed.), *The encyclopedia of crime and punishment* (Vol. 3) (p. 1375). Thousand Oaks, CA: Sage. Retrieved from http://academic.scranton.edu/faculty/DAMMERH2/ency-religion.html

Davis, A. J. (1982). Sexual assaults in the Philadelphia prison system and sheriff's vans. In A. M. Scacco Jr. (Ed.), *Male rape: A casebook of sexual aggressions.* New York, NY: AMS Press.

Davis, S. F., & Palladino, J. J. (2002). *Psychology* (3rd ed.). Upper Saddle River, NJ: Prentice Hall.

Death Penalty Information Center. (2004). *Constitutionality of the death penalty in America.* Retrieved from http://deathpenaltycurriculum.org/student/c/about/history/history-5.htm

Death Penalty Information Center. (2010). *Facts about the death penalty*. Washington, DC: Author.

Death Penalty Information Center. (2015, June 26). *Federal death row prisoners*. Washington, DC: Author. Retrieved October 2015 from http://www.deathpenaltyinfo.org/federal-death-row-prisoners

Debro, J. (2008). The future of sentencing. In P. M. Carlson & J. S. Garrett (Eds.), *Prison and jail administration: Practice and theory* (2nd ed.) (pp. 503–510). Sudbury, MA: Jones & Bartlett.

DeJong, C., & Jackson, K. (1998). Putting race into context: Race, juvenile justice processing and urbanization. *Justice Quarterly*, *15*, 487–504.

del Carmen, R. V., Barnhill, M. B., Bonham, G., Hignite, L., & Jermstad, T. (2001). *Civil liabilities and other legal issues for probation/parole officers and supervisors*. Washington, DC: National Institute of Corrections.

del Carmen, R. V., Ritter, S. E., & Witt, B. A. (2005). *Briefs of leading cases in corrections* (4th ed.). Cincinnati, OH: Anderson Publishing.

Department of Education. (1995). *Pell grants for prisoners.* Washington, DC: Author.

Dezhbakhsh, H., Rubin, P. H., & Shepherd, J. M. (2003). Does capital punishment have a deterrent effect? New evidence from post-moratorium panel data. *American Law & Economics Review, 5*(2), 344–376.

Dinitz, S. (2008). *The transformation of corrections: 50 years of silent revolutions.* Washington, DC: National Institute of Corrections.

Directorium Inquisitorum, edition of 1578, book 3, page 137, column 1. Online in the Cornell University Collection. Retrieved May 16, 2008.

Dolan, L., Kolthoff, K., Schreck, M., Smilanch, P., & Todd, R. (2003). Gender-specific treatment for clients with co-occurring disorders. *Corrections Today, 65*(6), 100–107.

Donohue, J. J., & Wolfers, J. (2006). Uses and abuse of empirical evidence in the death penalty debate. *Stanford Law Review, 58*(1), 791–846.

Dorne, C., & Gewerth, K. (1998). *American juvenile justice: Cases, legislation, and comments*. San Francisco, CA: Austin & Winfield.

Dressler, D. (1962). *Practice and theory of probation and parole*. New York, NY: Columbia University Press.

Drowns, R., & Hess, K. M. (1990). *Juvenile justice*. St. Paul, MN: West.

Duncan, M. G. (1999). *Romantic outlaws, beloved prisons: The unconscious meanings of crime and punishment*. New York. NY: New York University Press.

Ecenbarger, W. (1994, January 23). Perfecting death: When the state kills it must do so humanely: Is that possible? *The Philadelphia Inquirer*.

Ehrlich, I. (1975). The deterrent effect of capital punishment: A question of life and death. *The American Economic Review, 65*(3), 397–417.

Engelbert, P. (2001, July/August). Women in prison. *Agenda.* Retrieved from http://www-personal.umich.edu/~lormand/agenda/0107/womenprison.htm

English, D. J., Spatz Widom, C., & Brandford, C. (2002). *Childhood victimization and delinquency, adult criminality, and violent criminal behavior: A replication and extension.* Final report presented to the National Institute of Justice, Grant No. 97-IJ-CX-0017.

Estelle v. Gamble, 429 U.S. 97 (1976).

Etter, S. (2005). *Technology redefined: 2005 in review.* Quincy, MA: Corrections.com. Retrieved from http://www.corrections.com/news/article/6274

Fabelo, T. (1999). *Elderly offenders in Texas prisons*. Austin: Texas Department of Criminal Justice.

Farmer v. Brennan, 511 U.S. 825 (1994).

Farragher, T. (2003, December 2). Behind walls, trouble built into a brutal end. *The Boston Globe*. Retrieved from http://www.boston.com/news/local/massachusetts/articles/2003/12/02/behind_walls_trouble_built_to_a_brutal_end/

Faust, F. L., & Brantingham, P. J. (1974). *Juvenile justice philosophy*. St. Paul, MN: West.

Federal Bureau of Investigation. (2006). *Uniform crime reporting program data: Arrests by age, sex, and race, 2004* [Computer file] (ICPSR04460-v2). Washington, DC: Author.

Federal Bureau of Investigation. (2013). *Crime in the United States: Table 74: Full-time law enforcement employees*. Washington, DC: Author. Retrieved from https://www.fbi.gov/about-us/cjis/ucr/crime-in-the-u.s/2012/crime-in-the-u.s.-2012/tables/74tabledatadecoverviewpdfs/table_74_full_time_law_enforcement_employees_by_population_group_percent_male_and_female_2012.xls

Federal Bureau of Prisons. (2001). *CFR Title 28, Part 524.* Washington, DC: Author. Retrieved from http://www.access.gpo.gov/nara/cfr/waisidx_01/28cfr524_01.html

Federal Bureau of Prisons. (2006). *Program statement: Bureau of Prisons inmate classification system.* Washington, DC: Author.

Federal Bureau of Prisons. (2010a). *The Bureau celebrates 80th anniversary.* Washington, DC: U.S. Department of Justice. Retrieved from http://www.bop.gov/about/history/first_years.jsp

Federal Bureau of Prisons. (2010b). *Quick facts about the Bureau of Prisons.* Washington, DC: U.S. Department of Justice.

Feeley, M. M., & Little, D. L. (1991). The vanishing female: The decline of women in the criminal process, 1687–1912. *Law & Society Review*, *24*, 719–757.

Festinger, L. (1958). The motivating effect of cognitive dissonance. In L. Gardner (Ed.), *Assessment of human motives* (pp. 69–85). New York, NY: Holt.

Fleisher, M. S. (2008). Gang management. In P. M. Carlson & J. S. Garrett (Eds.), *Prison and jail administration: Practice and theory* (2nd ed.) (pp. 355–360). Sudbury, MA: Jones and Bartlett.

Fleisher, M. S., & Rison, R. H. (1999). Inmate work and consensual management in the Federal Bureau of Prisons. In D. van Zyl Smit & F. Dunkel, (Eds.), *Prison labour—Salvation or slavery?* Aldershot, UK: Ashgate.

Fletcher, M. A. (1999, July 22). Putting more people in prison can increase crime: Study says communities suffer when too many men gone. *Washington Post.* Retrieved from http://www.sfgate.com/cgi-bin/article.cgi?f=/c/a/1999/07/22/MN90235.DTL&ao=all

Flores, A. W., Travis, L. F., & Latessa, E. J. (2003). *Case classification for juvenile corrections: An assessment of the Youth Level of Service/Case Management Inventory (YLS/CMI).* Cincinnati, OH: Center for Criminal Justice Research.

Ford v. Wainwright, 477 U.S. 399 (1986).

Franklin, C. A., Fearn, N. E., & Franklin, T. W. (2005). HIV/AIDS among female prison inmates in correctional institutions: A public health concern. *Californian Journal of Health Promotion, 3*(2), 99–112.

Freedman, E. B. (1981). *Their sisters' keepers: Women's prison reform in America, 1830–1930*. Ann Arbor, MI: University of Michigan Press.

Friel, C. M. (2008). *Advanced research design.* Retrieved from www.shsu.edu/~icc_cmf

Fulwood v. Clemmer, 206 F. Supp. 370—Dist. Court, Dist. of Columbia (1962).

Furman v. Georgia, 408 U.S. 238 (1972).

Gacono, C. B., Nieberding, R. J., Owen, A., Rubel, J., & Bodholdt, R. (2001). Treating conduct disorder, antisocial, and psychopathic personalities. In J. B. Ashford, B. D. Sales, & W. H. Reid (Eds.), *Treating adults and juvenile offenders with special needs*. Washington, DC: American Psychological Association.

Gagnon v. Scarpelli 411 U.S. 778 (1973).

Garrett, J. S. (2008). Working with the media. In P. M. Carlson & J. S. Garrett (Eds.), *Prison and jail administration: Practice and theory* (2nd ed.) (pp. 171–178). Sudbury, MA: Jones & Bartlett.

Gates v. Collier, 501 F.2d 1291 (5th cir. 1974).

General Accounting Office. (1990). *Death penalty sentencing: Research indicates pattern of racial disparities*. Washington, DC: Author.

George, R. S. (2008). Prison architecture. In P. M. Carlson & J. S. Garrett (Ed.), *Prison and jail administration: Practice and theory* (2nd ed.) (pp. 39–50). Sudbury, MA: Jones and Bartlett.

Giever, D. (2006). Jails. In J. M. Pollock (Ed.), *Prisons today and tomorrow* (2nd ed.). Sudbury, MA: Jones & Bartlett.

Gillespie, W. (2002). *Prisonization: Individual and institutional factors affecting inmate conduct*. El Paso, TX: LFB Scholarly Publishing.

Glaser, D. (1964). *The effectiveness of a prison and parole system*. New York, NY: Macmillan.

Glaze, L. E., & Bonczar, T. P. (2006). *Probation and parole in the United States, 2005*. Washington, DC: U.S. Department of Justice.

Glaze, L. E., & Bonczar, T. P. (2009). *Probation and Parole in the United States, 2008*. Washington, DC: U.S. Department of Justice.

Glaze, L. E., & Bonczar, T. P. (2011). *Probation and parole in the United States, 2010*. Washington, DC: U.S. Department of Justice.

Glaze, L. E., & Palla, S. (2005). *Probation and parole in the United States, 2004.* Washington, DC: U.S. Department of Justice, Bureau of Justice Statistics.

Gluck, S. (1997, June). Wayward youth, super predator: An evolutionary tale of juvenile delinquency from the 1950s to the present. *Corrections Today, 59*, 62–64.

Goldberg, R. (2003). *Drugs across the spectrum* (4th ed.). Belmont, CA: Wadsworth.

Golub, A. (1990). *The termination rate of adult criminal careers.* Pittsburgh, PA: Carnegie Mellon University Press.

Gordon, M., & Glaser, D. (1991). The use and effects of financial penalties in municipal courts. *Criminology, 29*, 651–676.

Government Accounting Office. (1990). *Intermediate sanctions*. Washington, DC: Author.

GovTrack.us. (2010). *110th Congress 2007–2008*. Washington, DC: Author. Retrieved from http://www.govtrack.us/congress/bill.xpd?bill=s110-3294

GovTrack.us. (2015). *S. 1410 (3rd Congress): Smarter Sentencing Act of 2014*. Washington, DC: Author.

REFERENCES

Retrieved from https://www.govtrack.us/congress/bills/113/s1410

Graham v. Florida, 08-7412, 560 U. S. 48 (2010).

Gramsci, A. (1996). *Prison notebooks* (J. Buttigieg, trans.). New York, NY: Columbia University Press.

Greek, C. (2002). The cutting edge: Tracking probationers in space and time: The convergence of GIS and GPS systems. *Federal Probation, 66,* 51–53.

Greenblatt, A. (2014, July 18). *Drug sentencing guidelines reduced for current prisoners*. National Public Radio. Retrieved from http://www.npr.org/blogs/thetwo-way/2014/07/18/332619083/drug-sentencing-guidelines-reduced-for-current-prisoners

Greenwood, A. (2008). Taste-testing Nutraloaf: The prison food that just might be unconstitutionally bad. *Slate.* Retrieved from http://www.slate.com/id/2193538/

Gregg v. Georgia. 428 U.S. 153 (1976).

Griffin, B. S., & Griffin, C. T. (1978). *Juvenile delinquency in perspective*. New York, NY: Harper & Row.

Guccione, J. (2002, April 15). Doing their time in the working world: Restitution center is for women who stole. They pay their debts, avoid prison. *Los Angeles Times.* Retrieved from http://articles.latimes.com/2002/apr/15/local/me-debt15

Haas, S. M., Hamilton, C. A., & Hanley, D. (2006, July). Implementation of the West Virginia Offender Reentry Initiative: An examination of staff attitudes and the application of the LSI-R. Charleston, WV: Mountain State Criminal Justice Research Services.

Hagan, F. (2000). *Research methods in criminal justice and criminology* (5th ed.). Needham Heights, MA: Allyn & Bacon.

Hanser, R. D. (2002). Inmate suicide in prisons: An analysis of legal liability under Section 1983. *The Prison Journal, 82*(4), 459–477.

Hanser, R. D. (2007). *Special needs offenders in the community*. Upper Saddle River, NJ: Prentice Hall.

Hanser, R. D. (2010a). Adrian Raine: Crime as a disorder. In F. T. Cullen & P. Wilcox (Eds.), *Encyclopedia of criminological theory.* Thousand Oaks, CA: Sage.

Hanser, R. D. (2010b). *Community corrections.* Thousand Oaks, CA: Sage.

Hanser, R. D. (2015). Using local law enforcement to enhance immigration law in the United States: A legal and social analysis. *Police Practice and Research, 16*(4), 17–33.

Hanser, R. D., & Mire, S. (2010). *Correctional counseling*. Upper Saddle River, NJ: Pearson/Prentice Hall.

Hanser, R. D., & Moran, N. R. (2004). Labeling theory as an etiological paradigm for prison rape. In F. P. Reddington & B. W. Kreisel (Eds.), *Sexual assault: The victims, the perpetrators and the criminal justice system.* Durham, NC: Carolina Academic Press.

Hanson, G. R., Venturelli, P. J., & Fleckenstein, A. E. (2006). *Drugs and society* (9th ed.). Burlington, MA: Jones & Bartlett.

Hanson, G. R., Venturelli, P. J., & Fleckenstein, A. E. (2011). *Drugs and society* (11th ed.). Burlington, MA: Jones & Bartlett.

Harer, M. D. (1995, May). *Prison education program participation and recidivism: A test of the normalization hypothesis*. Washington, DC: Federal Bureau of Prisons.

Harer, M. D., & Steffensmeier, D. J. (1996). Rates of prison violence. *Criminology, 34*(3), 323–351.

Harlow, C. W. (1999). *Prior abuse reported by inmates and probationers*. Washington, DC: Bureau of Justice Statistics.

Harrison, K., & Tamony, A. (2010). Death row phenomenon, death row syndrome, and their effect on capital cases in the U.S. *Internet Journal of Criminology*. Retrieved from www.internetjournalofcriminology.com

Harrison, P. M., & Beck, A. J. (2003). *Prisoners in 2002.* Washington, DC: Bureau of Justice Statistics.

Harrison, P. M., & Beck, A. J. (2005). *Prisoners in 2004*. Washington, DC: Bureau of Justice Statistics.

Harrison, P. M., & Beck, A. J. (2006a, May). *Prison and jail inmates at midyear 2005* (NCJ 213133). Washington, DC: U.S. Department of Justice, Office of Justice Programs, Bureau of Justice Statistics. Retrieved May 7, 2007, from http://www.ojp.usdoj.gov/bjs/abstract/pjim05.htm

Harrison, P. M., & Beck, A. J. (2006b, November). *Prisoners in 2005* (NCJ 215092). Washington, DC: U.S. Department of Justice, Office of Justice Programs, Bureau of Justice Statistics. Retrieved May 7, 2007, from http://www.ojp.usdoj.gov/bjs/abstract/p05.htm

Harrison, P. M., & Karberg, J. C. (2004). *Prison and jail inmates at midyear 2003.* Washington, DC: Bureau of Justice Statistics.

Hartney, C. (2007). *The nation's most punitive states for women.* Oakland, CA: National Council on Crime and Delinquency.

Hatton, J. (2006). *Betsy: The dramatic biography of prison reformer Elizabeth Fry*. Grand Rapids, MI: Kregel.

Hayes, L. M. (2010). *National study of jail suicide, 20 years later*. Washington, DC: National Institute of Corrections.

Heberman, E. J., & Bonczar, T. P. (2015). *Probation and parole in the United States, 2013*. Washington, DC: Bureau of Justice Statistics.

Hercik, J. M. (2007). *Prisoner reentry, religion, and research*. Washington, DC: U.S. Department of Health and Human Services.

Hochstellar, A., & DeLisa, M. (2005). Importation, deprivation, and varieties of serving time: An integrated-lifestyle-exposure model of prison offending. *Journal of Criminal Justice, 33*(3), 257–266.

Hockenberry, S. (2013). *Juveniles in residential placement, 2010*. Washington, DC: National Center for Juvenile Justice.

Hoffman, P. B. (2003). *History of the federal parole system*. Washington, DC: U.S. Parole Commission.

Holsinger, A. M., Lowenkamp, C. T., & Latessa, E. J. (2004). Validating the LSI-R on a sample of jail inmates. *Journal of Offender Monitoring,* Winter/Spring, 8–9.

Holt v. Sarver I, 300 F. Supp. 825 (1969).

Holt v. Sarver II, 309 F. Supp. 362 (1970).

Hsia, H. M. (2004). *Disproportionate minority confinement 2002 update*. Washington, DC: Office of Juvenile Justice and Delinquency Prevention.

Hudson v. Palmer, 468 U.S. 517 (1984).

Hughes, E. C. (1945). Dilemmas and contradictions of status. *American Journal of Sociology,* March, 353–359.

Huizinga, D., Thornberry, T., Knight, K., & Lovegrove, P. (2007). *Disproportionate minority contact in the juvenile justice system: A study of differential minority arrest/referral to court in three cities*. Washington, DC: U.S. Department of Justice.

Human Rights Watch. (1996). *All too familiar, sexual abuse of women in U.S. state prisons.* New Haven, CT: Yale University Press.

Human Rights Watch. (1999). *Nowhere to hide: Retaliation against women in Michigan state prisons.* Retrieved from http://www.hrw.org/reports98/women/Mich.htm

Human Rights Watch. (2001). *No escape: Male rape in U.S. prisons.* Retrieved April 10, 2002, from http://www.hrw.org/reports/2001/prison/report.html

Hutto v. Finney, 437 U.S. 678 (1978).

Immigration and Customs Enforcement. (2011). *2009 Immigration detention reforms*. Washington, DC: Department of Homeland Security. Retrieved from http://www.ice.gov/factsheets/2009detention-reform

In re Gault, 387 U.S. 1 (1967).

Inciardi, J. A., Rivers, J. E., & McBride, D. C. (2008). *Drug treatment*. In P. M. Carslon & J. S. Garrett (Eds.), *Prison and jail administration: Practice and theory* (2nd ed.) (pp. 403–412). Sudbury, MA: Jones and Bartlett.

Ingram, G. L., & Carlson, P. M. (2008). Sex offenders. In P. M. Carlson & J. S. Garrett (Eds.), *Prison and jail administration* (2nd ed.) (pp. 373–382). Gaithersburg, MD: Aspen.

International Association for Chiefs of Police. (2008). *Tracking sex offenders with modern technology: Implications and practical uses with law enforcement*. Alexandria, VA: Author.

Ireland, T. O., Smith, C. A., & Thornberry, T. P. (2002). Developmental issues in the impact of child maltreatment on later delinquency and drug use. *Criminology, 40*(2), 359–399.

Jail Equipment World. (2010). *Security convection ovens.* Orlando, FL: Author. Retrieved from http://www.jailequipmentworld.com/

James, D. J., & Glaze, L. E. (2001). *Mental health problems of prison and jail inmates*. Washington, DC: Bureau of Justice Statistics.

James, D. J., & Glaze, L. E. (2006). *Mental health problems of prison and jail inmates*. Washington, DC: Bureau of Justice Statistics.

Johnson, B. R., & Larson, D. B. (2003). *The InnerChange Freedom Initiative: A preliminary evaluation of America's first faith-based prison*. Retrieved from http://www.baylor.edu/content/services/document.php/25903.pdf

Johnson, B. R., Larson, D. B., & Pitts, T. C. (1997). Religious programs, institutional adjustment, and recidivism among former inmates in prison fellowship programs. *Justice Quarterly, 14*(1), 10–24.

Johnson, H. A., Wolfe, N., & Jones, M. (2008). *History of criminal justice* (4th ed.). Southington, CT: Anderson.

Johnson, L. B. (2008). Food service. In P. M. Carlson & J. S. Garrett (Eds.), *Prison and jail administration: Practice and theory* (2nd ed.) (pp. 149–158). Sudbury, MA: Jones and Bartlett.

Johnson, R., & Dobrzanska, A. (2005). *Life with the possibility of life: Mature coping among life-sentence prisoners.* Paper presented at the annual meeting of the American Society of Criminology, Royal York, Toronto, Canada. Retrieved October 26, 2009, from http://www.allacademic.com/meta/p31858_index.html

Johnson, S. C. (1999). Mental health services in a correctional setting. In P. M. Carlson & J. S. Garrett (Eds.), *Prison and jail administration: Practice and theory* (2nd ed.) (pp. 107–116). Sudbury, MA: Jones and Bartlett.

Johnson v. Avery, 393 U.S. 483 (1969).

Johnston, N. (2009). *Prison reform in Pennsylvania.* Philadelphia, PA: Pennsylvania Prison Society. Retrieved from http://www.prisonsociety.org/about/history.shtml

Jones, J. (2007). *Pre-release planning and re-entry process: Addendum 02.* Tulsa, OK: Oklahoma Department of Corrections.

Joseph Druce #1. (2007). YouTube. Retrieved October 2015 from https://www.youtube.com/watch?v=IjkHXDtoXAo

Josi, D. A., & Sechrest, D. K. (1998). *The changing career of the correctional officer: Policy implications for the 21st century*. Boston, MA: Butterworth-Heinemann.

Justice Policy Institute. (2008). *Substance abuse treatment and public safety*. Washington, DC: Author.

Kaftan, S. D. (2007). Management is not leadership. In P. K. Withrow (Ed.), *A view from the trenches: A manual for wardens by wardens* (2nd ed.) (pp. 1–7). Alexandria, VA: American Correctional Association.

Karberg, J. C., & James, D. J. (2005). *Substance dependence, abuse, and treatment of jail inmates, 2002*. Washington, DC: U.S. Department of Justice.

Karpowitz, D., & Kenner, M. (2001). *Education as crime prevention: The case for reinstating Pell Grant eligibility for the incarcerated*. Annandale-on-Hudson, NY: Bard College.

Katz, L., Levitt, S. D., & Shustorovich, E. (2003). Prison condition, capital punishment, and deterrence. *American Law & Economics Review, 5*(2), 318–343.

Kauffman, K. (1988). *Prison officers and their world.* Cambridge, MA: Harvard University Press.

Keel, R. O. (2005). *Rational choice and deterrence theory*. Retrieved May 14, 2012, from http://www.umsl.edu/~keelr/200/ratchoc.html

Kent v. United States, 383 U.S. 541 (1966).

Kerle, K. (1982). Rural jail: Its people, problems and solutions. In D. Shanler (Ed.), *Criminal justice in rural America* (pp. 189–204). Washington, DC: National Institute of Justice.

REFERENCES

Kerle, K. (1999). Short term institutions at the local level. In P. M. Carlson & J. S. Garrett (Eds.), *Prison and jail administration: Practice and theory.* Gaithersburg, MD: Aspen.

King, E., & Baker, M. (2014). *Respectful classification practices with LGBTI inmates: Trainer's manual*. New York, NA: New York State Department of Corrections and Community Supervision.

Knowles, G. J. (1999). Male prison rape: A search for causation and prevention. *Howard Journal of Criminal Justice, 38*(3), 267–283.

Kohen, A., & Jolly, S. K. (2006). *Deterrence reconsidered: A theoretical and empirical case against the death penalty.* Paper presented at the annual meeting of the Midwest Political Science Association, Palmer House Hilton, Chicago, Illinois. Retrieved from http://www.allacademic.com/meta/p140213_index.html

Kupers, T. (1999). *Prison madness: The mental health crisis behind bars and what we must do about it*. San Francisco, CA: Jossey-Bass.

Kurshan, N. (1996). *Women and imprisonment in the U.S. history and current reality.* Retrieved from http://www.freedomarchives.org/Documents/Finder/DOC3_scans/3.kurshan.women.imprisonment.pdf

Labecki, L. S. (1994). Monitoring hostility: Avoiding prison disturbances through environmental scanning. *Corrections Today, 56*(5), 104, 106, 108–111.

Latessa, E. J., & Allen, H. E. (1999). *Corrections in the community* (2nd ed.). Cincinnati, OH: Anderson.

LeMaire v. Maass, 12 F. 3d 1444—9th Circuit (1993).

Lemert, E. M. (1999). Primary and secondary deviance. In S. H. Traub & C. B. Little (Eds.), *Theories of deviance* (pp. 385–390). Itasca, IL: Peacock.

Lempert, R. O., & Visher, C. A. (Eds.). (1987). *Randomized field experiments in criminal justice agencies: Workshop proceedings.* Washington, DC: National Research Council.

Levinson, D. (Ed.). (2002). *The encyclopedia of crime and punishment* (Vol. 3). Thousand Oaks, CA: Sage.

Lilly, J. R., Cullen, F. T., & Ball, R. A. (2007). *Criminological theory: Context and consequences* (4th ed.). Thousand Oaks, CA: Sage.

Lindemuth, A. L. (2007). Designing therapeutic environments for inmates and prison staff in the United States: Precedents and contemporary applications. *Journal of Mediterranean Ecology, 8*, 87–97.

Linder, D. (2005). *A history of witchcraft persecutions before Salem.* Retrieved from http://law2.umkc.edu/faculty/projects/Ftrials/salem/witchhistory.html

Lindner, C. (2006). John Augustus, father of probation, and the anonymous letter. *Federal Probation, 70*(1), 150–165.

Lindquist, C. H., & Lindquist, C. A. (1999). Health behind bars: Utilization and evaluation of medical care among jail inmates. *Journal of Community Health, 24,* 285–303.

Liptak, A. (2011, May 31). Justices, 5-4, tell California to cut prison population. *New York Times.* Retrieved from http://www.nytimes.com/2011/05/24/us/24scotus.html

Little Hoover Commission. (2004). *Breaking the barriers for women on parole.* Sacramento, CA. Retrieved from http://www.lhc.ca.gov/lhcdir/177/execsum177.pdf

Ludwig, F. J. (1955). *Youth and the law: Handbook on laws affecting youth*. Brooklyn, NY: Foundation Press.

MacCormick, A. (1931). *The education of adult prisoners: A survey and a program* [Reprint 1976]. New York, NY: AMS Press.

Madrid v. Gomez, 889 F. Supp. 1146 (1995).

Males, M., & Macallair, D. (2000). *The color of justice: An analysis of juvenile adult court transfer in California*. Washington, DC: Youth Law Center.

Martinson, R. (1974). What works? Questions and answers about prison reform. *Public Interest, 35.*

Maruschak, L. M. (2006). *Medical problems of jail inmates*. Washington, DC: U.S. Department of Justice, Office of Justice Programs.

Mays, G. L., & Winfree, L. T., Jr. (2002). *Contemporary corrections* (2nd ed.). Belmont, CA: Wadsworth/Thomson Learning.

McCollister, K. E., & French, M. T. (2001). *The economic cost of substance abuse treatment in criminal justice settings*. Miami, FL: University of Miami.

McEvoy, K. (2012). *Hope: A swift and certain process for probationers*. Washington, DC: National Institute of Justice. Retrieved from http://www.nij.gov/journals/269/Pages/hope.aspx

McGarry, P. (1990). *NIC focus: Intermediate sanctions*. Washington, DC: National Institute of Corrections.

McGraw-Hill. (2010). *Test of Adult Basic Education TABE*. Columbus, OH: CTB Research.

McKeiver v. Pennsylvania, 403 U.S. 528 (1971).

McNeece, C. A., Springer, D. W., & Arnold, E. M. (2002). Treating substance abuse disorders. In J. B. Ashford, B. D. Sales, & W. H. Reid (Eds.), *Treating adult and juvenile offenders with special needs* (pp. 131–170). Washington, DC: American Psychological Association.

McNeil, D. E., Binder, R. L., & Robinson, J. C. (2005). Incarceration associated with homelessness, mental disorder, and co-occurring substance abuse. *Psychiatric Services, 56*, 840–846.

McShane, M. D. (1996a). Chain gangs. In M. D. McShane & F. P. Williams (Eds.), *Encyclopedia of American prisons* (pp. 144–117). London: Taylor & Francis.

McShane, M. D. (1996b). Historical background. In M. D. McShane & F. P. Williams (Eds.), *Encyclopedia of American prisons* (pp. 455–457). London: Taylor & Francis.

Mears, B. (2003). *Supreme Court upholds sex offender registration laws.* Retrieved from http://www.cnn.com/2003/LAW/03/05/scotus.sex.offenders/index.html

Meko, J. A. (2008). A day in the life of a warden. In P. M. Carlson & J. S. Garrett (Eds.), *Prison and jail administration: Practice and theory* (2nd ed.) (pp. 235–242). Sudbury, MA: Jones and Bartlett.

Merton, R. K. (1938). Social structure and anomie. *American Sociological Review, 3*, 672–682.

Messerschmidt, J. A. (1999). Masculinities and crime. In F. T. Cullen & R. Agnew (Eds.), *Criminological theory: Past to present.* Los Angeles, CA: Roxbury.

Messner, S. F., & Rosenfeld, R. (2001). *Crime and the American dream* (3rd ed.). Belmont, CA: Wadsworth.

Michigan Department of Corrections. (2003). *Michigan presentence investigation*. Lansing, MI: Author. Retrieved from http://courts.michigan.gov/scao/resources/publications/manuals/prbofc/prb_sec4.pdf

Middle Tennessee State University. (2007). *Monitoring Tennessee's sex offenders using global positioning systems: A project evaluation*. Nashville, TN: Author.

Miller, B. A., Nochajski, T. H., Leonard, K. E., Blane, H. T., Gondoli, D. M., & Bowers, P. M. (1990). Spousal violence and alcohol/drug problems among parolees and their spouses. *Women and Criminal Justice, 2,* 55–72.

Miller, W. (1958). Lower class culture as a generating milieu of gang delinquency. *Journal of Social Issues, 14*, 5–19.

Minton, T. D. (2011). *Jail inmates at midyear 2010*. Washington, DC: Bureau of Justice Statistics.

Minton, T. D., & Golinelli, D. (2014). *Jail inmates at midyear 2013—statistical tables*. Washington, DC: Bureau of Justice Statistics.

Minton, T. D., & Zeng, Z. (2015). *Jail inmates at midyear 2014—statistical tables*. Washington, DC: Bureau of Justice Statistics.

Mire, S. M., Forsyth, C., & Hanser, R. D. (2007). Jail diversion: Addressing the needs of offenders with mental illness and co-occurring disorders. *Journal of Offender Rehabilitation, 45*(1/2), 19–31.

Mitchell, M. (2011). Texas prison boom going bust. *Star-Telegram.* Retrieved from http://www.star-telegram.com/2011/09/03/3335901/texas-prison-boom-going-bust.html

Mobley, A. (2011). Garbage in, garbage out? Convict criminology, the convict code, and participatory prison reform. In M. Maguire & D. Okada (Eds.), *Critical issues in crime and justice: Thought, policy, and practice* (pp. 333–349). Los Angeles, CA: Sage.

Mocan, H. N., & Gittings, R. K. (2003). Getting off death row: Commuted sentences and the deterrent effect of capital punishment. *Journal of Law and Economics, 46*(2), 283–322.

Moffitt, T. E. (1990). The neuropsychology of juvenile delinquency: A critical review. In M. Tonry & N. Morris (Eds.), *Crime and justice: A review of research* (pp. 99–170). Chicago, IL: University of Chicago Press.

Moffitt, T. E. (1993). Adolescence-limited and life-course persistent antisocial behavior: A developmental taxonomy. *Psychological Review, 100*, 674–701.

Montana Department of Corrections. (2010). *Recreation Programs DOC 5.5.3.* Helena, MT: Author.

Moore, E. O. (1981). A prison environment's effect on health care service demands. *Environmental Systems, 11*, 17–34.

Morgan, D. W. (2004). *Whips and whipmaking*. Centreville, MD: Cornell Maritime Press.

Morris, N., & Rothman, D. J. (2000). *The Oxford history of prison.* New York, NY: Oxford University Press.

Morris v. Travisono, 310 F.Supp. 857 (1970).

Morrissey v. Brewer 408 U.S. 471 (1972).

Morton, J. B. (1992). *An administrative overview of the older inmate*. Washington, DC: National Institute of Corrections.

Morton, J. B. (2005, October 1). *ACA and women working in corrections*. Washington, DC: Corrections Today.

Mumola, C. J. (2000, August). *Incarcerated parents and their children* (NCJ 182335). Washington, DC: U.S. Department of Justice, Office of Justice Programs, Bureau of Justice Statistics. Retrieved May 8, 2007, from http://www.ojp.usdoj.gov/bjs/abstract/iptc.htm

Murphy, J. F. (2008). *Medellin v. Texas*: Implications of the Supreme Court's decision for the United States and the rule of law in international affairs. Suffolk University: *Suffolk Transnational Law Review, 31*, 247–663.

Myers, P. L., & Salt, N. R. (2000). *Becoming an addictions counselor: A comprehensive text*. Burlington, MA: Jones & Bartlett.

Nacci, P. (2000). *Telemedicine can reduce correctional healthcare costs: An evaluation of a prison telemedicine network*. Washington, DC: National Institute of Justice.

Nacci, P. L., Turner, C. A., Waldron, R. J., & Broyles, E. (2002). *Implementing telemedicine in correctional facilities.* Washington, DC: U.S. Department of Justice.

National Advisory Commission on Criminal Justice Standards and Goals. (1973). *Corrections.* Washington, DC: Government Printing Office.

National Center for Women and Policing. (2003). *Hiring and retaining more women: The advantages to law enforcement agencies*. Beverly Hills, CA: Author.

National Commission on Correctional Health Care (NCCHC). (2002). *The health status of soon-to-be-released inmates: A report to Congress*. Chicago, IL: Author

National Gang Intelligence Center. (2009). *National gang threat assessment 2009: Prison gangs.* Washington, DC: Author. Retrieved January 22, 2010, from http://www.justice.gov/ndic/pubs32/32146/appc.htm#start

National Institute of Corrections. (1986). *Protective custody: Data update and intervention considerations.* Washington, DC: Author.

National Institute of Corrections. (1993). *The intermediate sanctions handbook: Experiences and tools for policymakers*. Washington, DC: Author.

National Institute of Corrections. (1995). *Corrections information series: Unit management.* Washington, DC: Author. Retrieved from http://www.nicic.org/pubs/pre/000159.pdf

National Institute of Corrections. (2001). *NIC research on small jail issues: Summary findings*. Washington, DC: U.S. Department of Justice.

National Institute of Justice. (1992). *Evaluating drug control and system improvement projects: Guidelines for projects supported by the Bureau of Justice Assistance*. Washington, DC: U.S. Department of Justice.

National Institute of Justice. (1998). *Restorative justice: An interview with visiting fellow Thomas Quinn.* Washington, DC: U.S. Department of Justice.

National Institute of Justice. (2005). *Implementing evidence based practice in corrections*. Washington, DC: U.S. Department of Justice.

National Institute of Justice. (2012). *Challenges of conducting research in prisons*. Washington, DC: Author. Retrieved from http://www.nij.gov/journals/269/pages/research-in-prisons.aspx

National Institute of Justice. (2012). *Evaluating video visitation technology for prisons*. Washington, DC: Author. Retrieved from http://www.nij.gov/topics/corrections/institutional/pages/video- visitation.aspx

National Law Enforcement and Corrections Technology Center. (2005). *Technology primer: Radio frequency identification*. Washington, DC: National Institute of Justice.

National PREA Resource Center. (2015). *Prison Rape Elimination Act*. Washington, DC: Bureau of Justice Assistance.

Nelson, K. E., Ohmart, H., & Harlow, N. (1978). *Promising strategies in probation and parole*. Washington, DC: U.S. Government Printing Office.

Neubauer, D. W. (2002). *Courts and the criminal justice system* (8th ed.). Belmont, CA: Wadsworth.

Neubauer, D. W. (2007). *America's courts and the criminal justice system* (9th ed.). Belmont, CA: Wadsworth/Thomson Learning.

New York Correction History Society. (2008). *The nation's first reformatory: Elmira*. Retrieved from http://www.correctionhistory.org/index.html.

Nink, C., Olding, R., Jorgenson, J., & Gilbert, M. (2009). Expanding distance learning access in prisons: A growing need. *Corrections Today, 71*(4), 40–43.

Noonan, M. E., & Ginder, S. (2014). *Mortality in local jails and state prisons, 2000–2012*. Washington, DC: Bureau of Justice Statistics.

Norman, B. (1991). *Health and safety in the prison environment*. Washington, DC: National Institute of Corrections, National Academy of Corrections, Health Services Division.

Nunez-Neto, B. (2008). *Offender reentry: Correctional statistics, reintegration into the community, and recidivism*. Washington, DC: Congressional Research Service.

Nyquist, O. (1960). *Juvenile justice: A comparative study with special reference to the Swedish Welfare Board and the California juvenile court system*. London: Macmillan.

Office of Justice Programs Drug Court Clearinghouse. (2003). *Drug testing in a drug court environment: Common issues to address*. Washington, DC: U.S. Department of Justice.

Office of National Drug Control Policy. (2001). *Fact sheet: Drug treatment in the criminal justice system*. Washington, DC: Author.

Office of Program Policy Analysis and Governmental Accountability. (2010). *Intermediate sanctions for non-violent offenders could produce savings.* Tallahassee, FL: Author.

O'Lone v. Estate of Shabazz, 482 U.S. 342 (1987).

Olson, L. (2004). An exploration of therapeutic recreation in adult federal medical centers and Wisconsin correctional facilities. *UW-L Journal of Undergraduate Research, VII*, 1–3.

Palmigiano v. Garrahy, 443 F.Supp. 956 (1977).

Partyka, R. (2004). *Coping on death row: The perspectives of inmates and correctional officers*. Toledo, OH: University of Toledo.

Patterson, O. (1982). *Slavery and social death: A comparative study*. Cambridge, MA: Harvard University Press.

Peak, K. J. (1995). *Justice administration: Police, courts, and corrections management*. Upper Saddle River, NJ: Prentice Hall.

Philadelphia Prison System. (2010). *About PPS: History of the Philadelphia Prison System*. Retrieved from http://www.phila.gov/prisons/history.htm

Philips, D. E. (2001). *Legendary Connecticut.* Willimantic, CT: Curbstone Press. Retrieved from http://www.curbstone.org/index.cfm?webpage=91

Poe-Yamagata, E., & Jones, M. (2000). *And justice for some: Differential treatment of minority youth in the justice system*. Washington, DC: Youth Law Center.

Pollak, O. (1950). *The criminality of women.* Philadelphia, PA: University of Pennsylvania Press.

Pollock, J. (1986). *Sex and supervision: Guarding male and female inmates*. New York, NA: Greenwood Press.

Pollock, J. (2006). *Prisons today and tomorrow* (2nd ed.). Boston, MA: Jones & Bartlett.

Poore, D. (1994). *Understanding protective management.* Wewahitchka, FL: Florida Department of Corrections. Retrieved from http://www.fdle.state.fl.us/Content/getdoc/52ffc7a7-6d0f-4340-9419-e9c200c377be/Poore.aspx

Pope, C. E., Lovell, R., & Hsia, H. M. (2003). *Disproportionate minority confinement: A review of the research literature from 1989 through 2001*. Washington, DC: Office of Juvenile Justice and Delinquency Prevention.

PRIDE Enterprises. (2009). *Pride in our mission: 2008 annual report*. St. Petersburg, FL: Prison Rehabilitative Industries and Diversified Enterprises, Inc.

Prison kill scene gets on YouTube. (2007). *New York Daily News*. Retrieved October 7, 2015, from http://web.archive.org/web/20080918102451/www.nydailynews.com/news/ny_crime/2007/07/08/2007-07-08_prison_kill_scene_gets_on_youtube.html

Procunier v. Martinez, 416 U.S. 396 (1974).

Quinney, R. (1991). *Criminology as peacemaking*. Bloomington, IN: Indiana University Press.

Rafter, N. H. (1985). *Partial justice: Women in state prisons 1800–1935.* Boston, MA: New England University Press.

Raine, A. (2004). Biological key to unlocking crime. *BBC News.* Retrieved from http://news.bbc.co.uk/2/hi/programmes/if/4102371.stm

Redding, H. (2004). *The components of prison security.* Naples, FL: International Foundation for Protection Officers. Retrieved from http://www.ifpo.org/article bank/components_prison_security.html

Reiman, J. (2007). *The rich get richer and the poor get prison* (8th ed.). Boston, MA: Allyn & Bacon.

Rice, J. S. (1993). *Self-development and horticultural therapy in a jail setting*. (Dissertation). San Francisco, CA: The Professional School of Psychology.

Rideau, W., & Wikberg, R. (1992). *Life sentences: Rage and survival behind bars.* New York, NY: Time Books, Random House.

Riveland, C. (1999). *Supermax prisons: Overview and general considerations*. Washington, DC: National Institute of Corrections.

Robbins, S. P. (2005). *Organizational behavior* (12th ed.). Upper Saddle River, NJ: Prentice Hall.

Robinson, J. J., & Jones, J. W. (2000). *Drug testing in a drug court environment: Common issues to address*. Washington, DC: Office of Justice Programs, Drug Courts Program Office. Retrieved from http://www.ncjrs.gov/pdf.files1/ojp/181103.pdf

Roper v. Simmons. 543 U.S. 551 (2005).

Ross, P. H., & Lawrence, J. E. (2002). Healthcare for women offenders: Challenge for the new century. In R. L. Gido & T. Alleman (Eds.), *Turnstile justice: Issues in American corrections* (pp. 73–88). Englewood Cliffs, NJ: Prentice Hall.

Roth, M. P. (2006). Chain gangs. In M. P. Roth, *Prisons and prison systems: A global encyclopedia* (pp. 56–57). Westport, CT: Greenwood Press.

Roth, M. P. (2011). *Crime and punishment: A history of the criminal justice system*. Belmont, CA: Cengage Learning.

Rowe, D. (2002). *Biology and crime*. Los Angeles, CA: Roxbury.

Ruddell, R., & Mays, G. L. (2007). Rural jails: Problematic inmates, overcrowded cells, and cash-strapped counties. *Journal of Criminal Justice, 35*, 251–260.

Ruiz v. Estelle, 503 F. Supp. 1265 (S.D. Tex. 1980).

Sabol, W. J., & Minton, T. D. (2008). *Jail inmates at midyear 2007*. Washington, DC: Bureau of Justice Statistics.

Sabol, W. J., Minton, T. D., & Harrison, P. M. (2008). *Prison and jail inmates at midyear 2006*. Washington, DC: Bureau of Justice Statistics.

Sacks, S., Sacks, J. Y., & Stommel, J. (2003). Modified therapeutic community programs: For inmates with mental illness and chemical abuse disorders. *Corrections Today, 65*(6), 90–100.

Sahagun, L. (2007, June 2). A mother's plight revives sanctuary movement. *Los Angeles Times.* Retrieved from http://articles.latimes.com/2007/jun/02/local/me-beliefs2

Samuel, B. (2001). *Elizabeth Gurney Fry (1780–1845): Quaker prison reformer*. Quakerinfo.com. Retrieved from http://www.quakerinfo.com/fry.shtml

Sanders, W. B. (1974). Some early beginnings of the children's court movement in England. In F. L. Faust & P. J. Brantingham (Eds.), *Juvenile justice philosophy* (pp. 46–51). St. Paul, MN: West.

Scacco, A. M., Jr. (1975). *Rape in prison.* Springfield, IL: Charles C. Thomas.

Scacco, A. M., Jr. (1982). *Male rape: A casebook of sexual aggressions*. New York, NY: AMS Press.

Schlossman, S., & Spillane, J. (1995). *Bright hopes, dim realities: Vocational innovation in American correctional education*. Berkeley, CA: National Center for Research in Vocational Education.

Schur, E. M. (1973). *Radical nonintervention: Rethinking the delinquency problem*. Englewood Cliffs, NJ: Prentice Hall.

Schuster, T. (2015). *PREA and LGBTI rights*. Hagerstown, MD: American Jail Association.

Schutt, R. K. (2006). *Investigating the social world: The process and practice of research* (5th ed.). Thousand Oaks, CA: Pine Forge Press.

Scillia, A. (1994). *Electronic monitoring: A new approach to work release.* Washington, DC: National Institute of Corrections.

Scott, E., & Grisso, T. (1997). The evolution of adolescence: A developmental perspective on juvenile justice reform. *Journal of Criminal Law and Criminology, 88,* 137–189.

Sedlak, A. J., & McPherson, K. S. (2010). *Youth's needs and services: Findings from the survey of youth in residential placement*. Washington, DC: Office of Juvenile Justice and Delinquency Prevention.

Seiden, A. M. (1989). Psychological issues affecting women throughout the life cycle. In B. L. Parry (Ed.), *The psychiatric clinics of North America* (pp. 1–24). Philadelphia, PA: W. B. Saunders.

Sellin, T. (1953). Philadelphia prisons of the eighteenth century. *Transactions of the American Philosophical Society, New Series, 43*(Part I), 326–330.

Sellin, T. (1959). *The death penalty: A report for the model penal code project of the American Law Institute*. Philadelphia, PA: American Law Institute.

Sellin, T. (1970). The origin of the Pennsylvania system of prison discipline. *Prison Journal, 50*(Spring–Summer), 15–17.

Shepherd, J. M. (2004). Murders of passion, execution delays, and the deterrence of capital punishment. *Journal of Legal Studies, 33*(2), 283–322.

Shepherd, J. M. (2005). Deterrence versus brutalization: Capital punishment's differing impacts among States. *Michigan Law Review, 104*(2), 203–256.

Shusta, R. M., Levine, D. R., Wong, H. Z., & Harris, P. R. (2005). *Multicultural law enforcement: Strategies for peacekeeping in a diverse society* (3rd ed.). Upper Saddle River, NJ: Prentice Hall.

Sickmund, M., & Puzzanchera, C. (2014). *Juvenile offenders and victims, 2014 national report*. Washington, DC: National Center for Juvenile Justice.

Sieh, E. W. (2006). *Community corrections and human dignity.* Sudbury, MA: Jones & Bartlett.

REFERENCES

Silverman, I. J. (2001). *Corrections: A comprehensive view* (2nd ed.). Belmont, CA: Wadsworth.

Simms, B. E., Farley, J., & Littlefield, J. F. (1987). *Colleges with fences: A handbook for improving corrections education programs*. Columbus, OH: National Center for Research in Vocational Education.

Simonsen, C. E., & Gordon, M. S. (1982). *Juvenile justice in America* (2nd ed.). New York, NY: Macmillan.

Singh, D., & White, C. (2000). *Rapua te huarahi tika: Searching for solutions: A review of research about effective interventions for reducing offending by indigenous and ethnic minority youth*. New Zealand: Ministry of Youth Affairs.

Smith, P., Goggin, C., & Gendreau, P. (2002). *The effects of prison sentences on recidivism: General effects and individual differences*. Saint John, Canada: Centre for Criminal Justice Studies, University of New Brunswick.

Smith v. Doe 538 U.S. 84 (2003).

Snyder, H. N., & Sickmund, M. (1999, November). *Juvenile offenders and victims: 1999 national report*. Washington, DC: U.S. Department of Justice.

Solomon, L., & Baird, S. C. (1982). Classification: Past failures, future potential. In L. Fowler (Ed.), *Classification as a management tool: Theories and model for decision-makers*. College Park, MD: American Correctional Association.

Spriggs, V. (2003). Identifying and providing services to Texas: Juvenile offenders with mental health needs. *Corrections Today, 65*(1), 64–66.

Stanko, S., Gillespie, W., & Crews, G. (2004). *Living in prison: A history of the correctional system with an insider's view*. Westport, CT: Greenwood Press.

Steadman, H. J. (1987). Mental health law and the criminal offender: Research directions for the 1990s. *Rutgers Law Review, 39*, 323–337.

Stephan, J. J. (2008). *Census of state and federal correctional facilities, 2005*. Washington, DC: Bureau of Justice Statistics.

Stepp, E. A. (2008). Emergency management. In P. M. Carlson & J. S. Garrett (Eds.), *Prison and jail administration: Practice and theory* (2nd ed.) (pp. 469–478). Sudbury, MA: Jones and Bartlett.

Steurer, S., Smith, L., & Tracy, A. (2001). *Three state recidivism study.* Washington, DC: Office of Correctional Education, U.S. Department of Education.

Stohr, M., Walsh, A., & Hemmens, C. (Eds.). (2009). *Corrections: A text/reader.* Thousand Oaks, CA: Sage.

Stojkovic, S. (1996). Subculture: Historical background. In M. D. McShane & F. P. Williams (Eds.), *Encyclopedia of American prisons* (pp. 455–457). London: Taylor & Francis.

Surgeon General Executive Summary. (2002). *Youth violence: A report of the surgeon general.* Washington, DC: Office of the Surgeon General.

Sykes, G. M. (1958). *The pain of imprisonment*. Princeton, NJ: Princeton University Press.

Tannenbaum, F. (1938). *Crime and the community.* Boston, MA: Ginn.

Tartaro, C., & Ruddell, R. (2006). Trouble in Mayberry: A national analysis of suicides and attempts in small jails. *American Journal of Criminal Justice, 31*(1), 81–101.

Tekagi, P. (n.d.). *The Walnut Street Jail: A penal reform to centralize the powers of the state.* Retrieved from http://www.socialjusticejournal.org/pdf_free/Takagi-Walnut_Street_Jail.pdf

Tennessee Board of Probation and Parole. (2007). *Monitoring Tennessee's sex offenders using Global Positioning Systems: An evaluative report*. Nashville, TN: Author.

Theriault v. Carlson, 495 F. 2d 390—Court of Appeals, 5th Circuit (1974).

Thompson v. Oklahoma, 487 U.S. 815 (1988).

Torres, S. (2005). Parole. In R. A. Wright & J. M. Mitchell (Eds.), *Encyclopedia of criminology*. New York, NY: Routledge.

Townsend, C. K. (2003). Juvenile justice practitioners add value to communities. *Corrections Today, 65*(1), 40–43.

Trop v. Dulles, 356 U.S. 86 (1958).

Tucker, D. (1981). *A punk's song: View from the inside.* Fort Bragg, CA: AMS Press Inc.

Turner v. Safley, 482 U.S. 78 (1987).

United States v. Booker, 543 U.S. 220 (2005).

U.S. Census Bureau. (2000). Census 2000 redistricting data (P.L. 94-171). *Summary file for states, Tables PL1, PL2, PL3, and PL4*. Washington, DC: Author.

U.S. Census Bureau. (2006). *State population estimates by demographic characteristics with 5 race groups (race alone or in combination groups): April 1, 2000 to July 1, 2005.* Population Division. Retrieved May 8, 2007, from http://www.census.gov/popest/datasets.html

U.S. Congress. (2008). *United States Parole Commission Extension Act of 2008.* Washington, DC: Author. Retrieved from http://frwebgate.access.gpo.gov/cgi- bin/getdoc.cgi?dbname=110_cong_bills&docid= f:s3294enr.txt.pdf

U.S. Department of Justice. (1994). *Topics in community corrections: Mentally ill offenders in the community.* Washington, DC: National Institute of Corrections.

U.S. Department of Justice. (2001a). *Attorney general's remarks regarding the federal death penalty study*. Press conference with Attorney General Reno and Deputy Attorney General Holder, Topic: The Death Penalty (September 12).

U.S. Department of Justice. (2001b). *The federal death penalty system: Supplementary data, analysis and revised protocols for capital case review*. Washington, DC: Author.

U.S. Department of Justice. (2001c). *Survey of the federal death penalty system* (1988–2000). Washington, DC: Author.

U.S. Department of Justice. (2006). *Commonly asked questions about the Americans with Disabilities Act and law enforcement*. Washington, DC: Disability Rights Section. Retrieved from http://www.ada.gov/q&a_law.htm

U.S. Department of Justice. (2012). *Prison Rape Elimination Act: Juvenile facility standards* (28 C.F.R Part 115). Washington, DC: Author.

U.S. Department of Justice, Bureau of Justice Statistics. (1994). *Special report: Women in prison.* Washington, DC: Author.

U.S. Department of Justice, Civil Rights Division, Disability Rights Section.

(2010). *Justice Department's 2010 ADA standards for accessible design go into effect*. Washington, DC: Author.

U.S. Sentencing Commission. (2007). *2007 federal guidelines manual.* Washington, DC: Author. Retrieved from http://www.ussc.gov/2007guid/CHAP5.html

U.S. Sentencing Commission. (2014a, April 12). *News release: U.S. Sentencing Commission votes to reduce drug trafficking sentences*. Washington, DC: Author.

U.S. Sentencing Commission. (2014b). *Quick facts: Women in the federal offender population*. Washington, DC: Author.

Uzoaba, J. H. E. (1998). *Managing older offenders, where do we stand?* Montreal: Research Branch of Correctional Service of Canada.

Valdez, A. (2009). *Gangs: A guide to understanding street gangs* (5th ed.). San Clemente, CA: LawTech.

Van Baalen, S. M. (2008). Religious programming. In P. M. Carlson & J. S. Garrett (Eds.), *Prison and jail administration: Practice and theory* (2nd ed.) (pp. 127–138). Sudbury, MA: Jones and Bartlett.

Van Keulen, C. (1988). *Colorado alternative sentencing programs: Program guidelines.* Washington, DC: National Institute of Corrections. Retrieved from http://www.nicic.org/pubs/pre/007064.pdf

Vesely, R. (2004). *California rebuked on female inmates*. Women's E-News. Retrieved from http://www.womensenews.org/article.cfm/dyn/aid/2122/context/archive

Vitek v. Jones, 445 U.S. 480 (1980).

Vito, G. F., & Allen, H. E. (1981). Shock probation in Ohio: A comparison of outcomes. *International Journal of Offender Therapy and Comparative Criminology, 25*, 70–76.

Vold, G. B., Bernard, T. J., & Snipes, J. B. (1998). *Theoretical criminology* (4th ed.). New York, NY: Oxford University Press.

Volkow, N. D. (2006, August 19). Treat the addict, cut the crime rate [Editorial]. *Washington Post*, p. A17.

Wallenstein, A. (1999). Intake and release in evolving jail practice. In P. M. Carlson & J. S. Garrett (Eds.), *Prison and jail administration: Practice and theory*. Gaithersburg, MD: Aspen.

Wallenstein, A. (2014). American jails: Dramatic changes in public policy. In P. M. Carlson, *Prison and jail administration: Practice and theory* (3rd ed.) (pp. 11–26). Burlington, MA: Jones and Bartlett.

Wallenstein, A., & Kerle, K. (2008). American jails. In P. M. Carlson & J. S. Garrett (Eds.), *Prison and jail administration: Practice and Theory* (2nd ed.) (pp. 19–38). Sudbury, MA: Jones and Bartlett.

Ward, D. A. (1994). Alcatraz and Marion: Confinement in super-maximum custody. In J. W. Roberts (Ed.), *Escaping prison myths: Selected topics in the history of federal corrections* (pp. 81–94). Washington, DC: American University Press.

Washington Department of Corrections. (2012). *Recreation program for offenders* (DOC 540.105). Olympia, WA: Author.

Weisberg, J. (1991, July 1). This is your death. *The New Republic.*

Weisburd, D., & Chayet, E. F. (1996). Good time credit. In M. D. McShane & F. P. Williams (Eds.), *Encyclopedia of American prisons* (pp. 358–363). London: Taylor & Francis.

Weiss, C., & Friar, D. J. (1974). *Terror in prisons: Homosexual rape and why society condones it.* Indianapolis, IN: Bobbs-Merril, Inc.

West, H. C. (2010). *Prison inmates at midyear 2009—statistical tables.* Washington, DC: Bureau of Justice Statistics.

Williams, D. J. (2003). The inclusion of strength training to offender substance abuse treatment: A pilot experiment conducted at a day reporting centre. *Empirical and Applied Criminal Justice Research Journal, 3*, 1–11.

Williams, D. J., & Strean, W. B. (2004). Physical activity as a helpful adjunct to substance abuse treatment. *Journal of Social Work Practice in the Addictions, 4*, 83–100.

Williams, D. J., Strean, W. B., & Bengoechea, E. G. (2002). Understanding recreation and sport as a rehabilitative tool within juvenile justice programs. *Juvenile and Family Court Journal, 53*(2), 31–41.

Wilson, D. B., & MacKenzie, D. L. (2006). Boot camps. In B. C. Welsh & D. P. Farrington (Eds.), *Preventing crime: What works for children, offenders, victims and places* (pp. 73–86). Dordrecht, Netherlands: Springer.

Wilson, S. J., & Lipsey, M. W. (2000). Wilderness challenge programs for delinquent youth: A meta-analysis of outcome evaluations. *Evaluation and Program Planning, 23,* 1–12.

Wilson v. Seiter, 501 U.S. 294 (1991).

Winter, M. M. (2003). County jail suicides in a Midwestern state: Moving beyond the use of profiles. *The Prison Journal, 83*, 130–148.

Wintersteen, M. B., Diamond, G. S., & Fein, J. A. (2007). Screening for suicide risk in the pediatric emergency and acute care setting. *Current Opinion in Pediatrics, 19*(4), 398–404.

Witherspoon v. Illinois, 391 U.S. 510 (1968).

Wolff v. McDonnell, 418 U.S. 539 (1974).

Wolfgang, M. E. & Ferracuti, F. (1967). *The subculture of violence: Towards an integrated theory in criminology*. London: Tavistock.

Women's Prison Association. (2003). *A portrait of women in prison.* New York, NY: Author.

Wooldredge, J. (1996). American Correctional Association. In M. D. McShane & F. P. Williams (Eds.), *Encyclopedia of American prisons* (pp. 45–52). London: Taylor & Francis.

Wright, R. A. (1994). *In defense of prisons.* Westport, CT: Greenwood Press.

Wright, R. L. (2008). Governing: Personnel management. In P. M. Carlson & J. S. Garrett (Eds.), *Prison and jail administration: Practice and theory* (2nd ed.) (pp. 225–234). Boston, MA: Jones & Bartlett.

Young, V. D., & Reviere, R. (2001). Meeting the health care needs of the new woman inmate: A national survey of prison practices. *Journal of Offender Rehabilitation, 34,* 31–48.

Zimmerman, P. R. (2004). State executions, deterrence and the incidence of murder. *Journal of Applied Economics, 7*(2), 163–193.

Zupan, L. (1991). *Jails: Reform and the new generation philosophy*. Cincinnati, OH: Anderson.

INDEX